Essay
Exam Writing
for the
California Bar Exam

Essay
Exam Writing
for the
California Bar Exam

THIRD EDITION

MARY BASICK

TINA SCHINDLER

ASPEN PUBLISHING

To contact Customer Service, e-mail customer.service@aspenpublishing.com, call 1-800-950-5259, or mail correspondence to:

Aspen Publishing
Attn: Order Department
1 Wall Street
Burlington, MA 01803

Printed in the United States of America.

1 2 3 4 5 6 7 8 9 0

ISBN 978-1-5438-5838-9

ABOUT ASPEN PUBLISHING

Aspen Publishing is a leading provider of legal education content and digital learning solutions in the United States and globally. Our innovative products and platforms—designed based on best practices in learning science—engage students and enhance outcomes. From textbooks and audiobooks authored by renowned experts to digital platforms and products like LEAF, Connected eBooks, Connected Quizzing, PracticePerfect, and JD-Next, we empower the next generation of legal professionals with innovative, trusted, and accessible resources.

The Aspen Casebook Series, affectionately known as the "red and black" casebooks among law faculty and students, includes hundreds of highly regarded textbooks across more than 80 disciplines. These range from foundational courses like Torts and Contracts to emerging electives such as Sustainability and the Law of Policing. Our study aids, including the popular *Examples & Explanations* series, help law students master complex topics with clarity and confidence.

Aspen's expertise extends to undergraduate education with our Paralegal, Criminal Justice, and Business Law series, offering the same hallmark quality to a broader audience. JD-Next, our groundbreaking online law school prep course and admissions test, provides a realistic preview of law school, equips students with essential skills for academic success, and evaluates their readiness for legal studies.

Aspen Publishing Is Proud to Be a UWorld Company

Since 2003, UWorld has been a global leader in developing high-quality learning tools for students preparing for high-stakes exams. With a commitment to excellence, UWorld has helped millions of students in undergraduate, graduate, and professional programs in fields such as medicine, nursing, finance, and law achieve their academic and career goals.

Founded by Chandra S. Pemmasani, M.D., during his medical residency, UWorld began focusing on medical education and has since expanded into various academic fields, including law. In 2020, UWorld launched its Legal vertical, starting with its comprehensive Multistate Bar Exam (MBE®) Question Bank, followed by the acquisition of Themis Bar Review, which integrated resources to provide a complete bar exam preparation experience. In 2024, UWorld expanded its offerings by acquiring Aspen Publishing, enhancing its suite of legal education products.

Today, UWorld offers an unparalleled range of study materials that blend active learning methods with expert content, ensuring students and educators can access the most effective resources. From bar preparation to law school success, UWorld is committed to supporting the next generation of legal professionals. Learn more at uworld.com.

Summary of Contents

Contents

Preface

Dear Bar Exam Taker,

This book includes everything you need to know to write a passing essay answer for the California bar exam. After much experience working with potential bar takers and extensive analysis of past California bar exams, we have created this book to be a condensed, yet thorough, review of all subjects covered on the exam, including instruction in the skill of essay writing.

The introduction covers the skills involved in successfully writing a passing California bar essay. In particular, this section includes valuable information on how to successfully organize and write a passing answer within the allotted time frame.

The substantive law is presented in several ways to assist you in understanding the law and then using it to solve the problem posed by an essay question. Each chapter includes the law in a checklist format for use in issue spotting, a memorization attack sheet to aid in memorizing the rules and their elements, and an efficient rule outline annotated throughout with exam, issue spotting, and memorization tips.

Practice essay questions and sample passing answers are included for each subject, and all crossover questions are identified as such. We also include our assessment of each question to point out additional subject-specific tips and essay-taking strategies. In addition, each question has a corresponding grid identifying the issues, rules, analysis, and conclusions that were required of a passing answer to aid you in assessing your own performance.

We wish you the best of luck on the upcoming bar exam!

Mary Basick and Tina Schindler

March 2025

Acknowledgments

Many people made this book possible, and we are grateful for the support of everyone who has helped us along the way. We must thank our wonderful families for their love, support, and most importantly, their patience, since writing a book is an all-consuming endeavor. Tina has the encouragement of Jim, Madilyn, and J. C. Schindler. Mary has the support of Mark, Zachary, Annie, Kori, Abby, Tara, and Blake Ribisi, and Valerie Fletcher. We are both lucky enough to teach law students, which we love doing, and want to thank our students who inspire us every day. We are also grateful for the support of the Aspen team.

Essay
Exam Writing
for the
California Bar Exam

INTRODUCTION

THE BASICS OF ESSAY EXAM WRITING

The essay portion of the California bar exam essentially tests two different things simultaneously: (1) a large quantity of substantive material and rules, and (2) essay exam writing skills under extreme time pressure. Success on the essay portion of the exam requires mastery of both. This introduction condenses into one handy reference section everything you need to know to succeed on the essay portion of the bar exam. As you study for the exam, return to these introductory pages frequently to reinforce your mastery of the most effective essay exam-taking approach and skills. This introduction covers techniques for mastering the substantive material tested on the essay exam, a review of the key exam-taking skills that are also tested on the exam, an approach for successfully combining the substantive mastery with the exam-taking skills, remote testing strategy, and a section on exam-day strategy.

I. MASTERING THE ESSAY SUBJECTS — MEMORIZATION

There is a vast quantity of substantive material that you are responsible for knowing and may potentially be tested on for the essay portion of the California bar exam. Depending on how you combine the subjects, there are at least 12 substantive areas of law eligible for testing on the essay portion of the exam. The first step in successfully preparing for the essay exam is creating a study schedule that will allow you to master the material so that you can fully understand and memorize the material. For each substantive area of law, this book contains an *issues checklist* to aid in issue spotting, a *memorization attack sheet* for easy memorization, and a *subject outline* that is tailored to focus on the issues that are essay tested within that subject. Our goal is to keep the rules compact here, so we have not included the more detailed or nuanced rules that are exclusively tested on the multiple-choice questions (MCQs).

Create a Study Schedule: It is important to map out day by day what you plan to accomplish to successfully prepare for the bar exam. A large amount of work must be done, and a schedule is an essential tool for staying on track and ensuring that you are adequately prepared for all the subjects and skills you must master. If you are not using a commercial bar preparation program that provides a study schedule, you must create your own schedule. Plan to spend two to four days studying each subject eligible for testing, with the time varying depending on the relative depth of the subject and your own facility with the subject. For each subject, you will need to study and understand the substantive material, memorize the rules, practice issue spotting and roadmapping essay exams, and practice writing essay exams under exam-type conditions. It is also important to spend time assessing your progress and reviewing your essays to ensure that you successfully spotted all the issues, properly identified and stated the applicable rules, and included all pertinent facts and arguments in the analysis. Of course, your study schedule should also include time dedicated to studying and practicing for the MCQ and performance test portions of the exam.

Memorization: Since the essay covers such a large quantity of substantive material, it is important to have a plan for accurately memorizing all this material. You will notice that each subject is presented here in various formats, with an increasing amount of detail to assist in both your understanding of the subject and to aid memorization. First, each subject is presented in the broad *issues checklist* format, which basically lists the main issues that can arise in that subject. This is followed by the more detailed *memorization attack sheet,* which includes the rule elements. Lastly, there is a detailed *rule outline* for each subject, which explains the rules and presents them in sentence format, as they would be written in an exam.

To memorize, take each subject one at a time. Start by reviewing the subject outline. First, be sure to understand the meaning of each rule element. The key to both effective issue spotting and factual analysis is having an understanding of how and when a rule applies. Rote rule memorization without understanding the meaning of the rules will not lead to success. To illustrate, one of the rule elements required for a permanent injunction is "feasibility." Without understanding what it means for a permanent injunction to be "feasible," it is likely the corresponding analysis would be unsatisfactory. Simply memorizing the element "feasible" would not identify what is meant by the term and thus what facts would make feasibility at issue in an essay question. This would lead either to a missed issue or poor analysis. Make every effort to have an understanding of the meaning of the rules, as well as memorizing the rules themselves. A good way to see if you have sufficient understanding of a rule is to try to explain it step by step, using examples and non-examples, to someone with no legal knowledge. If you can come up with examples and non-examples to illustrate a concept, you know it well enough to issue spot it, and how to properly analyze it.

Generally, whatever memorization strategies worked in law school should be the main strategies you employ now. However, you may want to try some new ones as well. Start with memorizing individual rules. To memorize rules you can use flashcards, flowcharts, or outlines. You can say the rules aloud or use a recording device or artificial intelligence application to record your own recitation of the rules and replay them later in the car or at the gym. Go through the issues checklist and try to state or write a rule for each issue listed, which reinforces both the rules and the overall structure of a subject. The memorization attack sheets are also a handy way to quiz yourself on the rule elements. Another effective memorization strategy is to practice writing out full rules in sentence format, which gives you an opportunity to practice writing and crafting rule statements that you will use later on the essay exams.

Once you have many of the individual rules memorized, move on to reviewing the entire subject. To review an entire subject, try to recreate your entire subject outline (or flowchart) from memory. Start with the macrostructure of the big concepts, then add the subtopics, then add the rules that fall under the subtopics, then add the rule elements for each rule, then add the explanations and exceptions for each rule element using examples. This approach reinforces rule memorization, the overall structure of the subject, and how the legal concepts relate to one another, which aids in issue spotting. You can do this on paper, or on a whiteboard, or orally. Each time you use this technique, start building out the subject outline in a different part of the checklist so you don't fall into the trap of knowing the first half of a subject much better than the second half. This method will help you identify the rules you know and the rules you don't know, so your studying can be more efficient as you target your energy on understanding and memorizing the rules you don't already know well. This study method also assists in issue spotting since the rules in the checklist are presented in the order that they logically arise in an essay question. Reviewing a subject this way also will reinforce how the concepts are interconnected and relate to one another.

Another approach is to try to explain an entire subject, including all issues and how they interrelate, to a willing friend or family member. Challenge yourself to adequately explain the rules in a manner that is logical, correct, and understandable. Use examples to illustrate the concepts. Have your listener ask questions so you must further explain or rephrase a concept whenever they get confused. This method also ensures that you know the rules well and how they relate to one another. The added bonus is you can spend some time with a loved one without feeling guilty about missing study time.

Once you have worked on a subject, plan to review it weekly. This method ensures that you don't forget a subject you already studied while you've moved on to mastering new subjects. There are two methods that work well. Depending on how far along you are in your studies, you can review a memorization attack sheet, or part of one, every night before bed. Read the attack sheet like it's a boring story before bed. Studies show that working on memorization right before sleeping improves retention, too. Another approach is to pick a day a week, like Sunday, and review all the previous subjects you have studied or divide the subjects over seven days so you study each subject (or portions of them) every week once you've covered the subject initially. The point of the review is to remind yourself about the rules you already learned so they stick in your memory while you continue to acquire more and more subjects.

II. MASTERING THE ESSAY SKILLS

In addition to the vast substantive material covered on the essay exam, the exam also tests essential lawyering skills. The most important of these skills are issue spotting, fact application and analysis, effective time management, and the ability to discern what is more important from what is less important and spend your limited time accordingly.

Issue Spotting

Issue spotting is an essential skill for any lawyer and is also essential for success on the bar exam. In this book the substantive material is presented in the order that the issues logically arise in an essay exam to make issue spotting easier. Checklists are great tools to use for issue spotting. A checklist should include the essential issues and be concise enough to be jotted down in less than one minute. We've provided generic checklists for each subject, but each subject checklist should be personalized to be most effective for you. The purpose of a checklist is to help you spot the issues on an exam, so don't include issues that you would never miss spotting because they're so obvious it simply isn't necessary to take time to write them down. Likewise, do include issues that you have a hard time remembering or have a tendency to miss. It may also be helpful to have mini-checklists for subcategories. For example, on your main constitutional law issues checklist, you might just have First Amendment free speech listed as an issue. If after reading the essay you realize that the majority of the question involves free speech, you can use a mini-issues checklist that includes all possible issues that can arise regarding free speech. You should have these checklists memorized for each subject tested on the bar exam. When doing an essay question, you can jot down your issue spotting checklist for the corresponding subject on your whiteboard or virtual scratch paper as soon as you recognize the subject being tested, unless the call is very specific and tells you exactly what issues they want you to address. We used full words on the issues checklists for your convenience, but you should create your own short-hand abbreviations for the issues when you memorize them to save time when writing them out. Another approach is to write the key terms from your checklist at the top of your answer, and then delete it before you finish. As you issue spot the exam, you can consult your checklist to ensure you don't miss any issues because missing issues can be fatal on the bar exam. However, be certain to discuss only the issues actually raised by the fact pattern. Discussion of a nonissue is worth no points and wastes valuable time.

The issues checklist also acts as a final check for issue spotting. Remember there are typically no "red herrings" or "homeless" facts on the essay portion of the bar exam. So, if you have facts remaining unused after you have organized the entire question, you should double-check your issues checklist to ensure that the "homeless" facts don't correspond to one of the issues you forgot to address. Although the points on the essay exam are mainly earned in the analysis of an issue, you will never get to the analysis if you don't spot the issue in the first place, which is why issue spotting is crucial to your success on the essay exam.

Fact Application and Analysis

The key to effective analysis is explaining how or why the applicable fact proves or disproves the rule element in question. A good answer will include so many facts that someone can recreate the fact pattern just from reading the answer. Just as you should double-check your issues checklist for any issues corresponding to "homeless" facts, you should also use your issues checklist to ensure that you aren't missing a key argument within your analysis or that the facts don't establish a rule element that you are omitting.

The most important aspect of analysis is being able to explain the legal significance of the facts rather than just reciting them in the appropriate place. Thus, when comparing your organized or written essay answer to the corresponding sample answer or grid, you should spend ample time comparing which facts were used and how they were used in your answer compared to the sample. Make sure that you are explaining how and why each applicable fact either proves or disproves the rule element that you are analyzing. Use the word "because" or "since" in your analysis because doing so forces you to explain how or why the fact is important. For example, consider the following analytical sentence: "Tom spit on Bob and being spat on would offend a reasonable person's sense of dignity *since* spitting is generally known in society as a sign of extreme disrespect and thus is offensive." Notice that the key *fact* (Tom spit on Bob) is tied to the *rule element* (offensive) with an explanation of *why* the conduct is offensive (offends a reasonable person's sense of dignity **since** it is a sign of extreme disrespect by societal standards). Compare the analytical sentence above to this one, "On the element of offensive, here the facts state that Tom spit on Bob and spitting offends a reasonable person's sense of dignity, therefore it is offensive." Notice that the key *fact* (Tom spit on Bob) is still tied to the *rule element* (offensive) but there is no explanation of *why* spitting is offensive. The facts are merely recited, and this is followed by the conclusion. This is not proper analysis, but rather a "fact sandwich," because the facts are sandwiched between the rule element and the conclusion with no explanation of why or how the fact (spitting) establishes the rule element (offensive). Always explain how and why the facts prove or disprove the rule or rule element in issue. Good analysis = fact + how/why that fact proves or disproves the rule element + rule/element. If you can write analysis using this format, they will be passing essays.

Sometimes it is necessary to make logical inferences or assumptions from the facts given to properly analyze a question. This skill arises most often on torts and constitutional law essays and is discussed in more depth within the introduction to those subjects. Sometimes an example is the best way to make a point and should be included in the analysis. Overall, remember that issue spotting enables you to identify the rules at issue, and it is expected that you know the rules, but it is the use of the facts in the analysis that results in points being earned on an essay.

Time Management

The skill of time management is a large part of what is being assessed with essay questions. If they gave examinees 90 minutes per essay question, everyone could write a passing answer. The extreme time pressure puts a premium on planning and organizational skills. Plan to spend 10-15 minutes organizing your answer and the remaining time writing your answer. Many students will jump to writing their answer because they feel stress from the time pressure, but the funny thing is, doing this actually leads to shorter answers because the student has to go back and forth to reread the facts over and over. A more efficient approach is to think through the question and create a skeletal outline in your answer as you go through the question line by line. As you issue spot, note the key terms from the rules and corresponding facts where they go, and then compose an answer by turning your notes into full sentences.

Some questions are harder than others, but each question is designed to be answered in one hour. To help answer each question well in one hour, it is imperative that you focus your energy on answering only the question asked. Pay attention to the call of the question. Don't rush through reading the fact pattern and misread what the question is asking; any time spent addressing a nonissue is time wasted. There is no extra credit on the bar exam, so thoroughly answer the question asked, but only the question asked.

Pay careful attention to the facts. For example, if the fact pattern is about a contract dispute but the facts state there is a valid contract, do not waste time discussing contract formation issues except in the briefest of terms.

Discerning What Is Important

This concept is related to time management but more accurately addresses the concept of deciding the relative importance of all the issues raised by an essay question and spending your time accordingly. Never lose sight that the goal of the essay answer is to solve the problem presented by the fact pattern. First, focus on the call of the question. Pretend that you are a lawyer and a client walked into your office and told you this story. What issues are raised? What facts pose a problem for the client? Do not shy away from identifying problem areas in the question or identifying areas of ambiguity that need to be resolved. This is what a lawyer would do and that is your task. Your essay answer needs to focus on solving the problem. Spend your time wisely so that you spend the majority of your time on the bigger, more complex issues, and less time on the issues that are more straightforward.

Generally, you can determine which facts are worth the most points and weighted the most heavily by seeing how many facts are available to use with each issue. The more facts that correspond to a particular issue, or the more ambiguity raised by the facts, the more points it is likely worth. Issues that have colorable arguments on both sides are also worth comparatively more points. To determine if there is a counterargument, ask yourself if the opposing party would concede, or if they would make an argument in response. A good strategy is to put yourself in the shoes of the client when you ask this question. This approach will help you to see more counterarguments because while a client will make a weak argument, when you look at it from the point of view of an attorney, you might dismiss making the counterargument because it won't prevail. However, a better answer will include it to gain maximum points. Be sure to organize the issues you spot around answering the call of the question. When outlining your answer, once you have matched up the facts to the issues, you need only glance at your outline to easily see where most of the points are, because they will be the issues with the most facts matched up.

It is essential to plan out your answer before you start writing so you can be strategic and proportionately spend your time where the most points are. It is not as important *how much* you write, but what you choose to write about in your answer. Based on what you plan to write about, your answer is either set up to pass or fail before you even write the first word. Students often make the mistake of treating each issue raised as if they are equally important. They are not. Spend your time where the points are and expand and contract the depth of your analysis accordingly to maximize your essay scores.

III. PUTTING IT ALL TOGETHER

An Approach to Taking Practice Exams

It is essential to write practice essay exams, and the more, the better. It is also imperative that you plan out your answer and create a roadmap of what you plan to cover before you start writing. When you study a subject, for the first few practice exams you may want to double-check your issue spotting against a sample answer or grid so that you can add any missed issues *before* writing out the complete answer. Allow yourself 15 minutes to roadmap the answer from memory, then check your roadmap against a rule source or the sample or grid and add any missing issues. Then allow yourself 45 minutes to write out the essay from your roadmap notes. With this approach you are still working under timed conditions, but you are allowing yourself some support as you become more familiar with the topic. Another benefit is that you will still get practice writing on all the issues contained in the essay, even if you didn't spot them all at first. Some students prefer to work under exam conditions from the very first essay, organize their answer and immediately write their essay under timed conditions, and only complete the assessment after they've finished. If this is your preferred approach, it is a good idea to go back and write out the answer to address any missed issues for practice after self-assessing your original essay. Writing out all issues also aids in memorization, because the more you write out the rules, the easier they become to recall.

Bar exams are different from the law school exams you are used to. It is essential to practice for the bar exam in replicated bar exam conditions to maximize your effectiveness. You must practice writing the essay exams within the one-hour time limit (subject to initial learning as explained above) for two important reasons. First, you need to know exactly what you are capable of completing within one hour so you can properly manage your time during the exam. Second, you want to have already practiced and become comfortable writing on a wide variety of legal issues so during the exam the writing flows quickly and smoothly. For this reason, it is also good to write out more than one essay at a time to simulate real exam conditions. So, if you plan to write two to three essays in a day, do them at the same time just as you would on the real bar exam, rather than one in the morning and another one later in the day. The bar is a marathon, and you have to train for it. Work on building your stamina because you are going to need it for the first day of the exam. Most law school exams are three hours and cover a single subject, whereas the first day of the bar exam consists of six and a half hours of writing in one day and covers many subjects.

Create a Roadmap to Organize a Passing Essay Answer

The goal is to write a passing essay, and the key to writing a good essay is solving the problem presented. Identify all the issues, use all the relevant facts, make it easy for the reader to score your essay by using issue headings, identify any problematic areas or ambiguities for the reader, spend your time wisely, and finish within one hour. If you are not used to organizing your answer before you write, you need to learn this essential skill. Be patient with yourself. It may take you longer to organize your answers until you get the hang of it. Use the following approach:

1. **Read the call of the question first.** This will provide some context as you read the fact pattern. Usually, the call of the question will identify the subject, and sometimes a specific call will even identify and limit the legal issues.

2. **Read the fact pattern through once** before you make notes or start typing on your virtual scratch paper. Sit on your hands if you must, but it is important to get a good grasp of the overall story of the fact pattern before you do anything else.

3. **Once you've read the fact pattern, carefully consider the call of the question.** If the call is very specific and, for example, asks, "Can plaintiff get specific performance?" then the bar examiners have issue spotted the exam for you. If the call of the question is more general, write down on your virtual scratch paper, whiteboard, or on your exam answer your memorized checklist for the subject (or subjects) being tested. Read the facts carefully and slowly and issue spot as you go. Use your checklist to assist you in identifying additional issues.

4. **Roadmap your answer *before* you begin writing.** You should spend 10-15 minutes thinking and organizing your answer before you begin writing your answer. A passing essay starts with good organization. Even though you may feel compelled to start writing because of the time pressure, it is not possible to write a passing answer if you don't spot all the issues and use all the available facts, so it is imperative that you slow down and get it right at the organizational stage. Writing an answer without proper planning is like running a race in the wrong direction. Don't waste time making your notes look good; they only need to be functional. Liberally use abbreviations, initials, and symbols. You can roadmap on virtual scratch paper, whiteboard, or in your answer document (but delete the notes when you are done), or a combination of both. Try several methods until you find one that works well for you.

5. **Organize by the call of the question and include all issues, rule elements, and facts.** Use the question call to create your macro-organization. Note the legal issues you spot for each question call. Identify the rule elements that correspond to each issue. Next, identify the pertinent facts you will use to analyze each rule or element. Be certain to use all the facts from the fact pattern in your analysis. You should be able to highlight the facts as you use them. Do not rely on your memory of the facts; make sure they are accurate by typing them out. Unlike law school exams, there are rarely "red herrings" in bar fact patterns. If there is a "homeless" fact in the fact pattern that you haven't figured out how to use, take a moment while outlining to consider what you can do with it. Go through your issues checklist and see if it raises a new issue you didn't catch. Also, look at the issues you have already identified and see if you can use the facts to add weight to the analysis. However, be aware that some facts can be used to analyze more than one issue. Finally, be cognizant of crossover questions as they are popular with the bar examiners.

6. **Consider if there are two sides to each issue in the question.** Issues with contrasting arguments are always worth a lot of points, and you don't want to miss these points. Also, it helps to remember that there are always two parties and two sides in a real legal dispute, so always consider what the opposing side would argue when you are arguing one side. Consider if the *client* would make an argument in response, and if so, include it. This technique helps you to capture more issues since, when you are wearing your lawyer hat, students can more easily dismiss arguments because they won't be successful. There will not always be a colorable argument for the other side, but often there is, and students can miss it because they are looking at the issue from only one perspective. Another pitfall is that students can get personally swept up in the facts. The questions are not about real people. Don't feel sorry for the girl who was kidnapped or the man whose car was stolen to the extent that you automatically write yourself out of points by concluding on their side because you want them to win. Even if the facts are horrible or gruesome, you must follow the law and not your feelings.

7. **Be strategic. Decide which issues are major and which are minor and plan to apportion your time.** Before you begin to write, look at the roadmap you've organized and assess where the points are. Issues with a lot of facts to use and those with two-sided arguments are always worth a lot of points, so apportion your writing time appropriately. If an essay has five key issues, you can do more in-depth analysis than if an essay has 15 key issues to address. Organize your answer first so you know what is being asked of you before you start to write because it is essential that you finish the essay.

Writing a Passing Essay Answer

After you've organized your answer, the next step is to turn your notes into a composed essay answer. A good essay answer should include the following:

Format: Your answer should look organized and sound lawyerly. Write clearly and use proper grammar, spelling and punctuation. The answer should be organized as an IRAC with an issue heading for each legal issue, followed by a rule statement, and then a separate paragraph for the corresponding analysis for that issue, followed by a conclusion. If there are multiple rule elements for the issue, each rule element can be separated and analyzed in its own paragraph. The rule elements should be analyzed in the same order that they are presented in the rule. If the elements have their own sub-rules or definitions, depending on time considerations, you may opt to have subheadings for these subrules/elements (essentially you will then have mini-IRACs for each element). Issue statements are not necessary on the California essay and are not worth any points so you can skip them. Don't waste time on introductions, restating the facts as a warmup, random musings, or nonissues. Use whitespace by skipping lines between paragraphs and issues to make it easy for the grader to read.

Issues: Identify each issue raised by the fact pattern. Analyze one issue at a time and use issue headings to separate each issue. Each issue should have its own IRAC structure. Preferably, each IRAC will also have its own issue heading, which is nothing more than the issue—for example, "Specific Performance." The heading doesn't have to be fancy or long but makes it easy for the grader to find the issues and give you points. You don't want to bury a great issue spot or key factual analysis where the reader (grader) can easily miss it. While there are examples of passing answers without headings, you risk the grader missing your issues if you don't use headings. It's not a hard and fast rule, but generally, if a rule element has its own rule, consider including a heading for the sub-rule. At a minimum, set off the analysis for each element in its own paragraph. Using headings and separate paragraphs also forces you to IRAC one issue at a time rather than combining multiple issues and rules into one paragraph, which often results in lost points because it is easier to omit some elements or analysis when you are combining multiple elements and issues together.

Rules: Have an accurate and grammatically correct rule statement for each rule. The rules should be precise and concise and contain all key elements and commonly used buzz words. Remember, this is a problem-solving exercise, not a dissertation, so you only need to use as much of the rule as you need to solve the problem posed. It is most effective to memorize a general statement for each rule, rather than to tailor it to include facts from the fact pattern.

Analysis: Analysis is the "A" in our IRAC formula. Analyze each rule element separately, and in the order given in the rule. Each piece of analysis must include the legally significant **fact**, the rule or rule element, and an explanation of **how or why** that fact proves or disproves the rule or **rule element** at issue. Think of this as the sub-formula: Analysis = fact + how/why + rule element. Be sure to include all components of the analysis in your answer. The order of these three components is interchangeable (for example, you can have the rule first followed by the facts and explanation of why/how the fact proves or disproves the rule, or you can have the facts first followed by rule and explanation). The key to success is that your analysis contains all three components. Analyze each rule element in the order given in the rule and analyze each rule element separately in its own paragraph. Another consideration when crafting analysis is if an issue is major or minor. An issue is major where it requires (1) an analysis of a pivotal issue, (2) analysis of an issue where there is an abundance of facts available to use in the analysis, or (3) where the available facts can be used to argue both sides of the issue. When you have an issue that has colorable arguments on both sides, be sure to explain which side has the strongest argument prior to concluding. A good approach is to start with the weaker argument, then write the stronger argument, and roll right into the conclusion. Though it is important to identify all issues that are raised by the facts, major issues are worth more points than minor issues and are thus worth more time and more real estate in your answer. An issue is minor where it is a "slam dunk" and few students are likely to miss it. For minor issues, you still need to properly address them, but you can typically do so in a more cursory way. Weave the rule and analysis into one sentence where possible. Efficiently identify how the fact establishes the rule or element and move on. If you consider an issue, but aren't sure whether or not to include it, err on the side of inclusion, but know that it is likely a minor issue, so spend little time on it.

Conclusion: The conclusion can often go either way. The important thing is to have a conclusion that is consistent with your analysis. Never become so focused on the conclusion on an issue that you write yourself out of the question by failing to see alternative issues that may arise if an issue were to conclude the other way. Also, do not recap the analysis in your conclusion. Be brief and move on.

Self-Assessment

As part of a successful bar preparation strategy, it is essential that you develop the skill of assessing your own performance. You need to be able to assess your own practice essays with a critical eye so you can identify any problem areas in your essay writing or substantive knowledge and work to correct them. We have provided an Essay Exam Self-Assessment form at the end of the introduction, which you may want to use in your self-assessments. Many students find that it is difficult to accurately assess their own written work, and you may need to get some help with this if you are having difficulty.

After writing a practice essay, first consider how you did on the key skills of time management, organization and writing. Next, consider how you did substantively by comparing your answer to a sample answer or an answer grid and assess your performance on the following criteria:

Issue Spotting: Issue spotting is key because you can't analyze an issue if you don't spot it first.

Did you spot and identify the same issues?
Did you spot issues that weren't there?

Headings: It is not essential to use the same headings as the sample answer or grid, but the important point is that someone reading your paper should be able to easily find all the key analysis. Be brief. Use a key word, not an entire sentence, for the heading. Don't bury important analysis in a place where a grader can't easily locate it.

Did you use the same or similar headings?

Rules: It is important that you accurately state the rules in your essay answer since the rules provide the basis for the analysis that follows.

The language can be different, but is the rule correctly stated, including all essential elements?
Is your rule significantly shorter, or longer, than the one in the sample answer?
Did you use the "buzz words" associated with the rule?
Is the rule in sentence format?

Analysis or Fact Application: The analysis is the most important part of an essay answer and is also the most difficult part to self-assess. This is because there are many ways to adequately analyze an issue. Consequently, you aren't looking for an exact comparison between your answer and the sample, but more of a general similarity of the analysis and the use of the available facts in the analysis.

Compare your answer to the sample answer (or a grid) issue by issue. Start with the first issue. Locate the first fact used in the analysis of that issue in the sample answer. Now, look for that fact in your analysis of that issue. Highlight your answer where you used the same fact in approximately the same way. If the sample answer used the fact in a more thorough or different way than you did, make a note of it. If the sample answer used a fact that you ignored, make a note of it. If you used a fact that the sample answer did not use for that issue, make a note of it. Continue the process looking at all the facts in the first issue, then move on to the subsequent issues and repeat the process. Also, pay close attention to what other components the sample answer linked with the facts. Often the analysis will contain three components, as explained above: the facts, the rule element, and the why or how the facts prove or disprove the rule. A good assessment mechanism is to highlight the facts in yellow, the rule element in blue, and the why and how in pink. This way you can easily see which components of your analysis are missing, if any, remembering that each sentence should be structured to combine these three pieces to make your analysis complete. It is not analysis if each of the above are on their own and not linked together. If you have ever been told your analysis is conclusory, you are missing the how/why part of the analysis. Now, take a critical look at your analysis:

Did you analyze each legal concept separately?
Did you analyze each rule element separately?
Did the sample answer use facts from the fact pattern that you ignored?

Did you identify the appropriate facts but leave it to the reader to determine how the existence of that fact established the legal element?

Did you present a one-sided argument when there were two sides to the analysis of that issue or rule element?

Was your analysis of an issue more cursory than the sample answer?

Was your analysis of an issue deeper than the sample answer?

Did your answer summarize and condense the facts?

Did your answer contain all three parts required for proper analysis (do you see all three highlighted colors linked together in your analysis: fact + rule/element + how/why)?

Conclusion: Sometimes the conclusion reached isn't important, and sometimes there is only one logical conclusion or correct answer (especially in Professional Responsibility), but even in that case the points will be missed in the analysis section, so the conclusion isn't the focus. The important thing about a conclusion is to have one, and to make sure that it is consistent with your analysis.

Troubleshooting Tips to Improve Exam Performance

Process: If you are struggling with the process, try these tips:

Problem	Solution
Roadmapping takes too long	• If outlining before writing is new to you, you won't be working within time limits at first. • Bifurcate the process and take longer outlining while you learn the outlining skill, but always write your answer in 45 minutes. As you get more practice, your outlining time will lessen. • Try different organizing methods until you find one that works for you.
Can't finish an essay in one hour	• Outline so you know what you're going to write before you start writing. • Be strategic and expand and contract your analysis depending on if an issue is major or minor.
Answer is too short so analysis is too thin	• A typical student can write approximately 1400-1500 words in 45 minutes. If you are significantly below that, you need to increase your typing speed. • Short essays can result from poor planning up front, so roadmap first to prevent jumping back and forth from question to answer.

Issues: If you missed an issue, or spotted an issue that wasn't there, ask yourself why.

Problem	Solution
Missed issue because did not know the rule	• Study and memorize the rule. • Use a checklist to issue spot. • Add the rule to your checklist.
Did know the rule, but not well enough to identify how the facts would raise it as an issue	• Understand the meaning of the rule elements, rather than rote memorization. • Practice issue spotting exams that raise the issue to identify how facts will be used (see Issues Tested Matrix to locate). • Review fact patterns testing the issue to identify which facts tend to trigger the issue and create fact triggers for these issues by listing facts from the various essays you organize that test this issue (some fact triggers are already included in the outlines).
Saw the issue, but dismissed it as a nonissue	• Your job is to use the facts to prove and **disprove** legal issues. Any issue that requires thought to dismiss should be included in the answer. I.e., "This rule is not established because. . ."
The issue seemed too minor to include	• Minor issues should be included, but with truncated analysis.

Problem	Solution
Did not use all the facts in the fact pattern	• Check off facts or highlight them as they are used to ensure that all are used.
Addressed a nonissue	• Don't write about issues where there are **no facts** available from the fact pattern to use.

Headings: Were the headings sufficient?

Problem	Solution
Did not use a heading where needed	• Every legal concept should be set off with its own heading so it is easy to locate, including elements that have their own rules.

Rules: Were the rules accurate and adequate?

Problem	Solution
Did not remember the rule	• Memorize the rules and review all subjects weekly to reinforce.
Rule is shorter than sample	• Make sure the rule you memorize includes all essential elements.
Rule is longer than sample	• Review the rule to determine if it includes elements that are unnecessary or duplicative and remove them. • Carefully craft rule so that it is stated as concisely as possible. • Only use as much rule as needed to solve the problem.
Rule is missing important "buzz words"	• Craft the rule to include key "buzz words" that are associated with the rule; do not use synonyms.
Rule is not in sentence format	• Draft a grammatically correct sentence that includes all rule elements; memorize it.

Fact Application: Was the analysis logically organized, sufficient, and thorough?

Problem	Solution
Legal issues are merged together	• Analyze each legal issue separately by IRACing each issue separately with headings.
Analysis is jumbled or hard to follow	• Analyze each element of a rule in the same sequential order given in your rule statement.
Missing analysis on some of the rule elements	• Be methodical to ensure that you analyze each element of the rule and don't skip any rule elements.
Missing key facts in the analysis	• When organizing the answer, strike each fact or highlight it as it is used to ensure all are used. • Identify a fact to correspond to each rule element.
Analysis did not explain how or why a fact established the issue or rule element	• Listing the facts is not enough; the analysis must explain how or why the fact establishes the rule element. • Use the words "since" or "because" to force yourself to explain the how or why. • **Analysis = fact + how/why** that fact proves or disproves rule **+ rule element**. • Review your practice answers and highlight the three components of analysis (fact, how/why, rule element) in different colors to ensure you include the how and why every time.

Problem	Solution
Analysis did not link your fact and how/why explanation to the rule element it proves or disproves	• **Analysis = fact + how/why** that fact proves or disproves rule + **rule element.** • Review your practice answers and highlight the three components of analysis (fact, how/why, rule element) in different colors to ensure you link to your rule element every time.
One-sided argument instead of two-sided	• Decide if there is a plausible contrary argument for each issue/rule element. • Role-play and pretend to represent each side of the dispute to see both sides.
Analysis is deep when it should be cursory, or analysis is cursory when it should be deep	• At the organization step, decide whether an issue is major or minor and treat each accordingly. • For minor issues, practice writing cursory or truncated analyses by weaving the rule and facts together into one sentence. • For major issues, be certain to use all available facts to analyze each element. • For each issue/rule element, always consider if there is a plausible contrary argument, and if so, argue it.
Facts are summarized and less effective	• Use the facts exactly as they appear in the fact pattern, including using quotes. • Expand on the facts where appropriate by making logical factual inferences.

IV. REMOTE TESTING STRATEGY

> As of this writing, the administration format of the California bar exam is in flux. The State Bar attempted a fully remote administration in February 2025, which was infamously unsuccessful. The July 2025 administration will be held in person with paper questions, but the State Bar plans to revisit implementing a remote administration in the future. The February administration did not allow applicants to use scratch paper, but did allow a small whiteboard. For this reason, throughout this edition we refer to organizing and note taking during the exam on a whiteboard or virtual scratch paper, but we are referring to the note taking process available to use during the exam.

There are advantages and disadvantages to taking the bar exam remotely. This testing format is new in 2025, but remote testing was utilized during 2020 as a response to the COVID-19 pandemic, so we have an idea of what to expect. Applicants will either be taking the exam from their own homes (or other private testing location) or may opt to go to a testing center. Note that applicants with some disabilities may have to use a testing center, depending on the specific testing accommodation required.

One advantage to remote testing is that applicants can tackle the essays and performance test one question at a time. This is a huge advantage compared to taking three questions in a three-hour block. This will help substantially with fatigue and focus since you will be able to take a moment to collect yourself and reset between questions. Another advantage is being able to take the exam from the comfort of your own home. The old format of testing at huge convention centers was both expensive and stressful. Most applicants had to stay in a nearby hotel, which added significant cost. Sleeping in your bed, eating your preferred food, being surrounded by loved ones (or alone if you prefer), and eliminating travel time are big benefits that will make the experience comparatively less stressful. Further, it would be hard to overstate the added psychological impact of being in a huge room filled with stressed-out bar takers. The anxiety in the testing room was palpable. There was also a lot of wasted downtime while the proctors checked everyone in and out.

While remote testing is mostly a positive development, there are a few disadvantages, too. Working exclusively off a single computer screen is more difficult than having a paper copy of the question that you can mark up and annotate. This is especially true for the performance test, which typically runs about 20 pages long. Applicants can also worry about the remote proctoring, being unintentionally interrupted during the exam, or having an unexpected difficulty with their Wi-Fi connection. While we can't alleviate all of your concerns, most of the things that applicants worry about never occur. If you don't have a good place at home to take the exam, source out a suitable location in advance, or you can always opt to take the exam at one of the in-person testing centers.

Below are some helpful strategies pertaining to remote testing and exam day that you should implement to maximize your potential exam score and minimize your stress.

- **Practice using digital/virtual scratch paper (a notes box) and a whiteboard:** While it was nice to be able to mark up right on the question, now there may be some form of scratch paper, digital scratch paper, and/or a 8.5 × 11 whiteboard to serve that function. Practice using them in advance. As an alternative, you may want to practice writing notes directly into your answer that you delete before you are done. If you do this, be sure to also implement a plan that ensures you delete any notes to yourself before time is up and practice that, too.
- **Organize before you write:** It is more important than ever to organize your answer before you start writing. You want to be able to have thought the question all the way through and jotted down the significant notes you need to craft a good answer within about 10-15 minutes, and then spend 45 minutes writing your answer from your notes. Practice this approach so it becomes second nature. This approach will make your answer both better and longer because you won't waste precious time flipping back and forth between the question and your answer.
- **Practice like exam day:** When doing practice essays, pull the question up on one side of your laptop and write the answer on the other half to simulate working from a digital question. Use the tools that will be available on exam day, like digital scratch paper and a whiteboard. It makes sense to do your practice essays in the same method you will be using on exam day. If your bar company does not have the questions available in a digital format, you can probably find them on the California state bar website filed in the "past exams" section, and search using the exam administration date.
- **Exam day tips:** As of this writing, the current test features support using the following tips for maximum organization and strategy during the exam.
  - **Multiple Choice (MCQ):** There may be no strike through feature to eliminate wrong answers on the MCQs. Instead, write A, B, C, and D down the side of your whiteboard, then write an X next to the answers you want to eliminate. Erase the X's between questions.
  - **Essay:** When you issue spot, also jot down a few notes to yourself about the facts you will use in the analysis and if there is two sided analysis. Skip two lines between issues to identify minor issues, and three or four lines between issues to indicate major issues as a visual cue to yourself. Currently, the essay prompt will appear at the top of your answer field. If possible, copy/paste the essay prompt into your digital notes field so you can easily reference the facts while you are writing your answer.
  - **Performance Test:** It is more important than ever to be well organized. Methodically pull the necessary information out of the file and library and place the information where you can use it to strategically build your answer. Be selective and strategic in using the copy/paste function, if available.
- **Utilize the mock exam:** You will be required to take a mock exam a few weeks before the exam. Instead of rushing through, take advantage of the opportunity to use the exam software and become familiar with the features that will be available on exam day. Then, replicate those features in your practice leading up to the exam so exam day feels like just another study day.
- **Take the day before the exam off.** Marathon runners don't run a marathon the day before the race, and neither should you. Relax and get some rest.
- **Write one question at a time, and when it's over, forget it.** Do not spend a single brain cell worrying about what you wrote on question number two while you are working on question number three. First, these are graded on a curve, so you have no way of knowing how you did. If you found a question hard, so did everyone else, probably. Second, it is completely unhelpful. Let it go because you need to focus on the question in front of you. Even if it's true that you did a terrible job on a question

(which as we just said, is impossible to know), so what? It is only one question. You can do badly on one question (or more) and pass this exam. Shake it off and do your best on the next one.

- **Don't panic if you have no idea what to do with an essay question.** There is usually one unusual question on every bar exam. Take a deep breath. The bar exam is graded on a curve. If you have properly studied for the exam, you can be certain that if you are befuddled by the question, so is everyone else taking the exam. Figure out what the underlying subject is and write down your checklist. Take the fact pattern sentence by sentence and look for issues. Shake it off and don't think about it again once it's over. One way to help with these unusual exam questions is to ensure that you use the facts in a logical manner, even if you aren't sure of the rule. Imagine yourself in front of a judge with new facts that you are surprised by and you need to make a plausible argument. Think on your feet and do your best. The key is to show the examiners that you can solve a problem and express yourself in a lawyerlike manner.

- **Do not talk about the essay questions on the exam.** Just as in law school, the people who talk the most and loudest (and on Reddit) often have the least idea of what they are talking about. No good can come from listening to self-appointed experts theorize about what issues were on the essay questions, and it can be harmful if it rattles your confidence or makes you doubt yourself. It is best not to do a post-mortem on this exam, but if you must, wait until the entire exam is over for all applicants and then only discuss it with someone whose judgment you trust.

ESSAY EXAM SELF-ASSESSMENT

ESSAY SKILLS:

- **TIME MANAGEMENT**
  - _____ Proper time prioritization/allocation and finished exam

- **ORGANIZATION**
  - _____ Logical and responsive to call
  - _____ Headings used for each legal issue (one or two words only)
  - _____ Uses white space between issues to assist grader
  - _____ IRAC used in analysis consistently

- **WRITING**
  - _____ Proper grammar, capitalization, punctuation and few typos
  - _____ Clarity of writing and expression

CONTENT:

- **ISSUE SPOTTING**
  - _____ All major issues identified, most minor issues
  - Areas **to improve — issue spotting:**
  - _____ Missed major issues
  - _____ Missed minor issues
  - _____ Included nonissues

- **RULES**
  - _____ Accurate and complete rule statements were used
  - Areas **to improve — rules:**
  - _____ Rule included unnecessary elements (too much rule)
  - _____ Rule failed to include necessary elements (too little rule)
  - _____ Rule missed important "buzz words"

- **ANALYSIS**
  - _____ Analysis explained how and why the facts established the rules
  - Areas **to improve — analysis:**
  - _____ Failed to analyze each legal issue separately
  - _____ Analysis did not explain "how or why" facts prove or disprove
  - _____ Important facts were missing from the analysis
  - _____ Facts were summarized instead of using key, specific facts
  - _____ Analysis was cursory where it should have been deep
  - _____ Analysis was deep where it should have been cursory
  - _____ Missed a two-sided argument
  - _____ Analysis didn't link the three analysis components together (fact + rule + how/why)

- **CONCLUSION**
  - _____ Conclusion logically flowed from analysis

PART I *BUSINESS ASSOCIATIONS*

BUSINESS ASSOCIATIONS TABLE OF CONTENTS

INTRODUCTION TO BUSINESS ASSOCIATIONS

The topic of business associations encompasses the subjects of corporations, agencies, and partnerships. There are a lot of substantive rules eligible for testing, so preparing for business associations essays can be quite the challenge. The key is to organize as many essays as you can so you can expose yourself to as many areas of testing as possible. The agency issues involving agent authority and general partnership issues are the most tested within those subjects. For corporations, the questions vary quite a bit. Some test very nuanced rules such as specific duties of officers inside the corporation versus outside directors. Other essays test specific information regarding shareholder agreements and rights. Others test, albeit not as frequently, securities laws and insider trading violations. Common areas of testing still include the duties of care and loyalty owed by officers and directors. But anything is fair game, so you need to be prepared for any topic.

In business association questions it is important to analyze the conduct of each person presented in the fact pattern separately. There will frequently be a fact pattern that identifies two or more corporate officers or directors, and/or shareholders, and the directors or officers will usually take a corporate action leading to shareholders losing money and thus initiating a shareholder suit, which also gives rise to breaches of a fiduciary duty. Usually, each party is privy to different information and thus won't have equal responsibility. Be certain to analyze the facts pertaining to each party under the rule separately to avoid missing key analysis. Other essays will have multiple parties who are partners or members and one of them will enter a contract or do something that may or may not bind the partnership or others, which will require you to analyze authority rules within the agency.

Regardless of what area of law is being tested, be certain to thoroughly go through the issues checklist looking for issues pertaining to each party identified in the fact pattern to successfully issue spot a business associations essay. Business association issues tend to cluster in predictable ways. A party who is in violation of 16(b) is almost always also in violation of 10b-5 (though not necessarily the other way around), and they may have also breached the duty of loyalty. With few exceptions, when the duty of care is at issue, the duty of loyalty is also at issue. The facts that raise issues relating to pre-incorporation liability, piercing the corporate veil, and ultra vires acts also typically raise the issues of duty of care and/or duty of loyalty. The duty of care and duty of loyalty is almost always tested on business associations questions, so be sure to know those rules very well.

Business association essay questions typically provide a lot of factual detail to analyze, and many of the issues can, and should, be argued both ways to receive maximum points. Business association essays are frequently crossover questions. The business association topics may cross over with each other. For example, an essay may cover corporations and the agency relationship of a corporate promoter or a director who exceeds authority. It is also common to see business associations cross over with professional responsibility where one of the parties is either a lawyer or seeks the advice of a lawyer. Recently, the examiners have crossed over business associations with torts and remedies as well, so anything is possible. We recommend you review many crossover questions by viewing the issues tested matrix to see which questions are crossovers and issues, especially the professional responsibility/business associations crossover questions.

ISSUES CHECKLIST

CORPORATIONS

Formation
De facto and de jure corp.
Close corp.
Piercing the corp. veil
Ultra vires acts
Promoter liability

Corp. Management, Directors & Officers
Duty of care (BJR)
Duty of loyalty

Shareholders
Rights
    Meetings and elections
    Voting
    Inspection
    Dividend distribution
Shareholder agreements
Shareholder derivative suits

Federal Securities Laws
16(b)
10b-5
    Fraudulent statements
    Insider trading
Sarbanes-Oxley

Fundamental Changes
Dissolution

AGENCY

Formation
Principal's duties and remedies
Agent's duties and remedies
P's liability for A's k's (authority)
P's liability for A's torts (scope)

PARTNERSHIP

General Partnerships
Formation
Partnership assets
Partner rights & duties
Relations of partner to 3rd parties
Partner liability
Dissociation/Dissolution/Winding up

Limited Partnerships
Formation
Ltd. partner rights & duties
Ltd. partner liability
Dissociation/dissolution/winding up

LLP

Formation
LL Partner rights & duties
LL Partner liability
Dissociation/Dissolution/Winding up

LLC

Formation
LLC member rights & duties
LLC member liability
Dissociation/Dissolution/Winding up

MEMORIZATION ATTACK SHEET

CORPORATION—FORMATION

- ◆ **Formation**
  - De jure corporation—file articles of incorporation:
    - ◆ **P**urpose of corporation
    - ◆ **A**uthorized # of shares
    - ◆ **N**ame/address of incorporators
    - ◆ **I**nitial agent's name and address
    - ◆ **C**orporation name
    - ◆ **S**treet address—office
  - De facto corporation
  - Corporation by estoppel
  - Close corp. (< 35 SH; not publicly traded)

- ◆ **Pierce corporate veil**
  - Alter ego
  - Undercapitalization
  - Fraud
  - Estoppel

- ◆ **Deep Rock Doctrine**

- ◆ **Ultra vires**
  - Act outside business purpose

- ◆ **Shares of stock issued**
  - Subscription agreement
  - Types of shares issued
  - Consideration required
  - No preemptive right for existing shareholder

- ◆ **Pre-incorporation liability**
  - Promoter: personal liability
  - Corp: not liable unless
    - ◆ Adopt contract, or
    - ◆ Accept benefit

CORPORATE DIRECTORS & OFFICERS

- ◆ **Meetings**
  - Quorum required
  - No voting agreements/proxies
  - Presence by any means
  - Withdraw can break quorum
  - Dissent/abstention

- ◆ **Duty of care**
  - Reasonable prudent person
  - Business judgment rule
    - ◆ Good faith
    - ◆ Corp's best interests

- ◆ **Duty of loyalty—no conflicts of interest**
  - **No self-dealing**
    - ◆ Presumed unfair, but
    - ◆ Conflict can be cured if authorized/ approved & fair
  - **No usurp corp. opportunity**
    - ◆ Ok if good faith rejection &
    - ◆ Full disclosure
    - ◆ Remedy: disgorge profits
  - **No unfair competition**

- ◆ **Duty to disclose material info**

- ◆ **Rights of directors & officers**
  - Compensation
  - Indemnification
  - Inspection

- ◆ **Liability of directors & officers**
  - No personal liability generally

CORPORATE SHAREHOLDERS

- ◆ **Rights of shareholders**
  - Meetings
  - Voting
    - ◆ Right to vote by stock type
    - ◆ Voting by proxy allowed
    - ◆ Quorum required
  - Inspection
  - Dividends

- ◆ **Shareholder agreements**
  - Voting trust (transfer shares to trustee)
  - Voting agreement (SH vote as agreed)
  - Management agreement
  - Restrictions on stock transfer

- ◆ **Shareholder suits**
  - Direct suit ($ to SH)
  - Derivative suit on corp. behalf ($ to corp.)

- ◆ **Shareholder duties**
  - General rule: no fiduciary duty
  - Modern trend: controlling shareholders owe a duty care & loyalty

- ◆ **Shareholder liability**
  - General rule: no personal liability
  - Except: professional corps.
  - Except: pierce corp. veil

FEDERAL SECURITIES LAW

- ◆ 16(b) — no short-swing profits
  - Corporation
    - ◆ On national exchange, OR
    - ◆ 10 million assets &
    - ◆ 2000 shareholders
  - Corporate insiders
    - ◆ Officers & directors
    - ◆ Over 10% shareholders
  - Trading within 6 months
  - Damages/Remedy: disgorge profits

- ◆ 10b-5 — no insider trading
  - Fraud/Misrepresentation requires
    - ◆ Intent
    - ◆ Material misrepresentation
    - ◆ Reliance
    - ◆ Buy or sell securities
    - ◆ Interstate commerce
    - ◆ Remedy: disgorge profits
  - 10b-5 insiders — 4 ways
    - ◆ Insider direct trading
    - ◆ Tipper: giving information
    - ◆ Tippee: receiving information
    - ◆ Misappropriator

- ◆ Sarbanes-Oxley
  - Enhanced corporate reporting requirements
  - Increased criminal penalties

CORPORATE FUNDAMENTAL CHANGES

- ◆ **Typical procedure**
  - Board adopts resolution
  - Written notice to shareholders
  - Shareholders approve
  - Update articles/file with state

- ◆ **Types of changes**
  - Merger
  - Share exchange
  - Asset sale
  - Conversion of corporate form
  - Amend bylaws or articles
  - Dissolution & winding up

- ◆ **Dissenter appraisal rights**

AGENCY

- ◆ **Formation**
  - Agreement
  - Benefit of principal
  - Control of agent
  - All contract formalities not required

- ◆ **Principal duties: as required in the contract**

- ◆ **Agent duties**
  - **Duty of care (BJR)**
  - **Duty of loyalty — no conflicts**
    - ◆ No self-dealing
    - ◆ No usurp principal opportunity
    - ◆ No secret profits
    - ◆ No commingling funds
  - **Duty of obedience**
  - **Duty of communicate**
  - **Express contractual duties**

- ◆ **Agent is personally liable for third-party contracts only if**
  - Agent acts with no authority
  - Principal's identity not revealed
  - Principal's existence and identity undisclosed
  - All parties intend so

- ◆ **Principal is liable for agent contracts if**
  - **Actual express authority**
  - **Actual implied authority**
  - **Can be terminated by:**
    - ◆ Breach of agent's duty
    - ◆ Lapse of stated, or reasonable time
    - ◆ Operation law
    - ◆ Changed circumstances
    - ◆ Happening of specified event
    - ◆ Unilateral termination by either party
  - **Apparent authority**
    - ◆ Notice to third party required if actual authority terminated
    - ◆ Written "lingering" authority
    - ◆ Agent exceeds authority
  - **Ratification**
  - **If no authority: agent personally liable**

- ◆ **Principal liability for agent torts**
  - **Normal tort:** Liable if tort is within scope of relationship
    - ◆ Except frolic, but mere detour ok
  - **Employees (presumed unless independent contractor)**
  - **Independent contractors:** Not liable (no control of methods)
    - ◆ Except:
      - Ultrahazardous activities
      - Nondelegable duties
      - Negligent selection
      - Estoppel (hold out as agent)
  - **Intentional torts:** Not liable
    - ◆ Except:
      - Specifically authorized
      - Natural result
      - Motivated by desire to serve

PARTNERSHIP — GENERAL

◆ **Formation**
  - No formalities required
  - Intent to be co-owners required
  - Agency-like relationship

◆ **Partnership assets**
  - **Titled property (RUPA)**
    - Titled as partner
    - Partnership funds
  - **Untitled property**
    - Partnership funds
    - Close relationship/use of property
    - Listed as an asset in books

◆ **Partnership rights**
  - Ownership of property
  - Equal control, can't transfer
  - No right to salary (except for winding up)
  - Equal right to profits & losses (unless agreement otherwise)
  - Indemnification

◆ **Partner duties**
  - **Duty of care** (BJR)
  - **Duty of loyalty** — no conflicts (no self-dealing, usurping opportunity, secret profits, competition)
  - **Duty to disclose** material info
  - **Duty to account**
  - **Duty of obedience**
  - **Duty of good faith/fair dealing**

◆ **Partner relations w/3rd parties**
  - Personal liability for debts
  - Contract authority
    - Actual authority
    - Apparent authority
    - Estoppel
  - Torts: joint & several liability

◆ **Partnership liability**
  - Civil liability extends to:
    - Contracts within the scope
    - Tort within the scope
    - Liability is joint & several
  - Incoming partners
  - Outgoing partners

◆ **Dissociation** — partner leaves

◆ **Dissolution** — partnership ceases

◆ **Winding up**
  - Compensation allowed

  - Priority of distribution
    - Creditors
    - Partner loans
    - Capital contributions
    - Profits & surplus

PARTNERSHIP — LIMITED

◆ **Formation:** file certificate

◆ **Partner rights and duties**
  - General: same as general
  - Limited: no right to act on behalf & owe no duties

◆ **Partner liabilities**
  - General: same as general
  - Limited: not liable beyond capital contribution

◆ **Dissolution** — can be prompted by:
  - Time specified in certificate
  - Written consent of all
  - Dissociation of general partner
  - 90 days after dissociation of last limited partner
  - Judicial decree

◆ **Winding up activities**
  - Priority of distribution
    - Creditors
    - Partners & former partners previous distribution
    - Capital contributions
    - Partners

LLP

  - Formed by filing statement
  - LL partners have no personal liability
  - Duty of care & loyalty owed
  - Dissociation/dissolution similar to regular partnership

LLC

  - Formed by filing articles of organization
  - LLCs have no personal liability
  - Management interest not freely transferable (limited liquidity)
  - Duty of care & loyalty owed
  - Dissolution-jx split

BUSINESS ASSOCIATIONS RULE OUTLINE

I. CORPORATIONS

A. **Corporation formation and structure:** A corporation is a legal entity that exists separate from its owners, thus **shielding the owners and managers from personal liability** for the actions of the corporation.

1. **Corporate formation:**

a. A **de jure corporation** meets all of the mandatory statutory requirements including that the incorporators/directors (need at least one) **sign** and **file an articles of incorporation** with the Secretary of State that includes:

1. **P**urpose/profession of the corporation that is lawful
2. **A**uthorized number of shares *(maximum allowed)*
3. **N**ame and address *of each* incorporator/director named
4. **I**nitial agent's name and street address *for the corporation for service of process*
5. **C**orporation's name (must contain "corporation" or "incorporated" or similar words)
6. **S**treet address for corporation's initial principal office

> **Memorization tip:** Remember "**PANICS**" to include all of the information required on the **articles of incorporation.**

b. A **de facto corporation** exists where there is **actual use of corporate power** and a **good faith**, but unsuccessful, **attempt to incorporate** under a valid incorporation statute.

1. **Limited liability:** The law will treat the defectively formed corporation as an actual corporation, and the **shareholders will not be personally liable** for corporate obligations.
2. **Determination:** The state may **deny corporate entity status** in a quo warranto proceeding, but third parties may not attack the corporate status.

c. **Corporation by estoppel:** A person who deals with a business entity **believing it is a corporation**, or one who **incorrectly holds the business out as a corporation**, may be estopped from denying corporation status. This applies on a case-by-case basis and only in contract (reliance on corporate status), not to tort cases.

d. **Piercing the corporate veil:** Generally, a corporate shareholder is not liable for the debts of a corporation, except when the court pierces the corporate veil and disregards the corporate entity, thus **holding shareholders personally liable** to **avoid an injustice or inequitable result**. It is easier to find liability in closely held corporations (those with few shareholders that make the decisions).

1. **The veil can be pierced for the following reasons:**

a. **Alter ego:** Where the shareholders fail to treat the corporation as a separate entity, but more like an alter ego where **corporate formalities are ignored** and/or **personal funds** are **commingled,** resulting in an injustice or **inequitable result**.
b. **Undercapitalization:** Where the shareholders' **monetary investment** at the time of formation is **insufficient** to cover **foreseeable** liabilities.
c. **Fraud:** Where a corporation is formed to commit fraud or as a mechanism for the shareholders **to hide behind to avoid existing obligations.**
d. **Estoppel:** Where a shareholder **represents that they will be personally liable** for corporate debts.

2. **Effect of piercing the corporate veil:** Active shareholders will have personal joint and several liability.
3. *Deep Rock* **Doctrine:** When a corporation is insolvent, third-party creditors may be paid off before shareholder creditors, thus subordinating the shareholder claims.

e. **Close corporation:** A close corporation is a small corporation with limited shareholders (35 max) who manage and control the corporation. The articles of incorporation must identify the entity as a "close corporation," and they cannot be publicly traded. They don't have to comply with all corporate formalities (such as notice for annual meetings, etc.). These are often used for small family businesses.

> **Issue spotting tip:** Where piercing the corporate veil is at issue, the facts often will also raise the issue of promoter liability for pre-incorporation contracts and breaches of fiduciary duties by directors. This issue often arises in situations where there are few shareholders and courts are more likely to pierce the corporate veil for tortious acts and not for contract issues. Look for facts that would result in an injustice or inequitable result if the shareholders weren't found liable.

2. **Corporate powers**
   a. **Purpose:** It is presumed that all corporations are formed for **any lawful business purpose** unless the articles define a limited, specific purpose.
   b. **Ultra vires acts:** *If* a corporation has a limited stated purpose and it **acts outside its stated business purpose,** it is acting "ultra vires."
      1. Modernly, ultra vires acts are **generally enforceable.**
      2. **Ultra vires acts may be raised when**: (1) the ultra vires act causes the state to seek dissolution, (2) the corporation sues an officer, or (3) a shareholder sues to enjoin the proposed act.

> **Issue spotting tip:** Any time an essay identifies the purpose of the corporation, or places a restriction on corporate activities, consider whether ultra vires is an issue. While ultra vires is usually not an effective defense, on an exam it is important to spot the issue and complete the analysis if the facts give rise to it.

   c. **Acquire debt:** Corporations may borrow funds from outside sources to pursue the corporate purpose. Lenders do not acquire an ownership interest in the corporation. Debts may be secured (a bond) or unsecured (a debenture).
   d. **Issue shares of stock in the corporation**
      1. A **stock subscription agreement** is a contract where a **subscriber** makes a written promise **agreeing to buy a specified number of shares** of stock.
         a. A **post-incorporation subscription** creates a contract between the subscriber and the corporation once the corporation accepts the subscription (revocable until then).
         b. A **pre-incorporation subscription** is **irrevocable for six months** unless otherwise stated in the agreement or all subscribers agree to revocation (under the RMCBA — not adopted in CA).
      2. **Shares of stock** are equity securities that give the shareholder an ownership interest in the corporation.
         a. **Quantity of shares available:** The articles of incorporation authorize the number of shares available to be sold. Shares that are sold are issued and outstanding. Shares that have yet to be sold are authorized but unissued.
         b. **Types of shares:** The articles of incorporation can provide that different classes of stock shares are available (common or preferred). **Preferred** shares must state:
            i. The **number** of shares in each class,
            ii. A **distinguishing name/classification** for each class, and
            iii. The **rights, preferences, limitations, etc.,** of each class (all shares within the same series must have the same voting rights, privileges, etc.).
         c. **Consideration is required** in exchange for stock shares and can include any tangible or intangible property or benefit to the corporation, such as cash, an exchange for services rendered, or cancellation of a debt owed, etc. Jurisdictions are split as to

whether to include the exchange for future services or an unsecured debt (e.g., the RMBCA does allow these; CA does not).

    i. **Traditional par value approach**: Price is the stated minimum issuance price and stock may not be sold for less than par value.

    ii. **Board's good faith**: **No par** means there is no minimum issuance price for the stock; generally the board of directors' good faith determination of the price is conclusive.

    iii. **Treasury stock** is stock that was previously issued and had been reacquired by the corporation. It can be re-sold for less than par value and is treated like no par stock.

  3. **Preemptive rights** refer to the right of an existing shareholder to **maintain their percentage of ownership** in a corporation when there is a new issuance of stock for cash. **Modernly**, unless the articles provide otherwise, a **shareholder does not have preemptive rights**.

  3. **Pre-incorporation actions by a promoter:** Promoters are persons **acting on behalf** of a corporation that is **not yet formed.** Prior to incorporation it is common for a promoter to raise capital and contract for a location, business materials, equipment, etc.

    a. **Liability for promoter contracts:**

      1. **Promoters are personally liable** for pre-incorporation contracts **until** there has been a **novation** replacing the promoter's liability with that of the corporation or there is an **agreement** between the parties that expressly states that the promoter is not liable.

        a. **Right of reimbursement:** The promoter may have a right to reimbursement based on a quasi-contract for the value of the benefit received by the corporation, or on the implied adoption of the contract.

      2. A **corporation is not generally liable** for, or bound to, pre-incorporation contracts.

        a. **Except** that a corporation will be liable where the corporation expressly **adopts the contract** or **accepts the benefits** of the contract (note that the promoter is also still liable unless there has been a novation—where there is an express agreement that the promoter's liability is released).

    b. **Promoter duties:** A promoter has a fiduciary relationship with the proposed corporation requiring **good faith.** Promoters cannot make a secret profit on their dealings with the corporation.

Promoter liability (pre-incorporation) fact triggers:
- Rent contract entered into before incorporation
- Equipment contract entered into before incorporation
- De facto company because of failure to properly incorporate
- Piercing the corporate veil

B. Corporation management, directors, and officers

  1. **Corporate management structure:**

    a. **Director required:** All corporations must have at least one director, though they may have as many directors as they wish (including variable numbers); any named directors included in the articles of incorporation must also sign the articles of incorporation when filing them.

      1. Directors can be **inside directors** (employees of the company) or **outside directors** (non-employees of the company). Both have **full authority** to vote and object.

Essay tip: California law requires that all **publicly held** corporate **boards** have **at least one female and one underrepresented director** (numbers increase depending on the total number of board members). However, this law is currently being challenged and one lower court found it to be unconstitutional. Regardless, the examiners continue to test these nuanced areas recently, so it is important for you to know, if they do test directors, that is an area of uncertainty for the foreseeable future with no definitive laws on the make-up required of a board in California.

---

b. **Articles of incorporation** are filed with the state to establish the corporation, and any provisions contained in the articles will govern the corporation.

c. **Bylaws:** Management of the corporation is conducted in accordance with the articles of incorporation and any corporate bylaws adopted by the board, which typically contain management provisions.

d. **Election of the board of directors:** The initial board is elected at the first annual meeting and each year thereafter unless terms are staggered as established in the articles.

e. **Officers and committees are appointed** by the board of directors to implement the board decisions and carry out operations.

f. **Officer authority:** Officers have authority to act on behalf of the corporation based on agency law principles. An officer's authority to bind the corporation may be express, implied, or apparent. (See Agency, section II.C.)

g. **Removal:**

1. **Director:** A director can be removed with or without cause by a majority shareholder vote, unless the articles state removal only with cause permitted or in other limited circumstances (i.e., votes cast against the director removal would be sufficient to elect them at a cumulative voting election).

2. **Officer:** The board may remove an officer with or without cause.

h. **Resignation** of an officer or director is allowed at any time with notice.

2. **Actions of the board of directors**

a. **Meetings:** The board of directors must hold meetings, which can be **regular meetings** in accordance with the bylaws without notice, **or special meetings** requiring at least two days' notice if personal or by telephone, or four days' notice if by mail.

1. **Quorum requirement:** A quorum, which is a **majority of the board** of directors, **must be present** at the time a vote is taken for board action to be valid, unless the bylaws or articles allow otherwise (but can be no fewer than one-third of the board members).

   a. **Presence:** Presence can be by **any means of communication** so long as all members can hear each other, and the means is not prohibited by the articles or bylaws (but members with conflicts don't count toward the quorum).

   b. **Withdrawal allowed:** Unlike shareholders, a director may break quorum by withdrawing from a meeting before the vote is taken.

   c. **Dissenting members**: A member is deemed to assent to an action unless they object at the beginning of the meeting (or when they arrive), their dissent or abstention is recorded in the minutes, or they deliver a written notice of such before the meeting is adjourned.

2. **Voting:** Directors cannot vote by proxy or enter into voting agreements (like shareholders). Doing so is a breach of their fiduciary duties of care and/or loyalty.

b. **Actions without meetings:** An action may be taken without a meeting if **all directors sign a written consent** describing the action taken and include that in the minutes or file it with corporate records.

c. **Delegation:** The board may delegate authority to a committee, or an officer.

3. **Duties of directors and officers:** A director or officer owes the duty of **care**, duty of **loyalty**, and duty of **disclosure** to the corporation.

a. **Duty of care:** A director or officer owes the corporation a duty of care, including **reasonable inquiry**, to act in **good faith** as a **reasonably prudent person** in a manner they **reasonably believe** is in the best interest of the corporation.

1. The **business judgment rule (BJR)** applies the **reasonable standard of care** imposed for business judgments and provides the **presumption** that the directors or officers made a decision in **good faith** and in the **best interests of the corporation** and its shareholders. The BJR is violated when a director's or officer's conduct is **unreasonable**.

   a. **Reliance on others**: It is not unreasonable for a director to rely on information from officers, employees, legal counsel, independent accountants, committees, etc., whom the director reasonably believes to be reliable and competent.

Duty of care fact triggers:

- Corporation changes to less profitable line of business
- Large expenditure when a merger is pending
- Officer misrepresents financials to induce contracting
- Subsidiary corp. sells items at cost to corporate owner
- Failure to investigate business opportunity/sale of company
- Issuing stock as a gift or refusing to issue dividends
- Officer makes business decision on personal bias
- Director takes inventory without paying
- Board member starts a competing company
- President makes several costly changes to shift purpose of corporation
- Making a large donation to a university that a board member attended

---

b. **Duty of loyalty:** A director or officer owes a duty of loyalty to the corporation. A director must put the **interests of the corporation above their own interests.** The duty of loyalty arises in three ways:

1. **Conflict of interest (self-dealing):** A director or officer has a conflict of interest when they (or a corporation they own or have a relationship with, or their family member) enter into a **contract** with the corporation or have a **beneficial financial interest** in a contract.
   a. **Self-dealing contracts are presumed unfair** and voidable.
   b. **Conflict can be cured** if:
      i. **Authorized** by disinterested board members after material disclosure; or
      ii. **Approved** by majority of disinterested shareholders after material disclosure; and
      iii. The transaction is **fair to the corporation**.

Duty of loyalty (conflict of interest) fact triggers:

- Directors vote to sell company or give a profitable contract to a director's or owner's company or relative
- Directors change business model to benefit corporate owner
- Director or officer buys stock based on insider info
- No proper investigation or inquiry to reveal self-dealing
- Director or relatives benefit from a corp. acquisition
- Any time a director has any personal interest in a transaction
- Directors vote to make a large donation to a university that a board member attended
- Board member starts a competing company

---

2. **Usurping a corporate opportunity:** A director or officer may not personally act on a business opportunity without **first offering it to the corporation** where the corporation would expect to be presented the opportunity.
   a. The director or officer may take the opportunity only after **good faith rejection** of the opportunity by the corporation if there was **full disclosure** of all material facts to a **disinterested board majority**.
   b. **Remedy:** If the director or officer usurps a corporate opportunity, then the corporation may compel the director/officer to turn over the opportunity or **disgorge profits (constructive trust/equitable restitution theory).**

Duty of loyalty (usurp corp. opportunity) fact triggers:

- Officer takes a business opportunity as a side job
- Officer takes opportunity to make a windfall on a deal themselves
- Any time a director learns of a business opportunity
- Director or family member is on other side of a deal from corporation

---

   3. **Unfair competition:** A director or officer **may not unfairly compete** with the corporation.

  c. **Duty to disclose:** Directors and officers have a duty to disclose **material information** relevant to the corporation to board members.

> **Exam tip:** When the duty of care is implicated, the duty of loyalty is usually also an issue. Similar facts give rise to both issues which is why some of the fact triggers are the same. When analyzing the duties owed by a director or officer, always analyze the conduct of each party separately.

  4. **Rights of directors and officers**
   a. **Compensation:** A director or officer is entitled to **fair compensation**, the rate of which the board of directors determines (it is not a conflict for the board to set reasonable director compensation unless the articles or bylaws state otherwise).
   b. **Indemnification:**
    1. **Mandatory:** A director or officer is entitled to indemnification for expenses incurred on behalf of the corporation, and for expenses incurred if they **prevail in a proceeding brought against them** by the corporation.
    2. **Discretionary:** The corporation *may* indemnify directors or officers for unsuccessful proceedings against them if the directors or officers acted in **good faith** and they believed their actions were in the best interest of the corporation, unless the directors or officers are liable due to an improper financial benefit.
   c. **Inspection:** A director or officer has a right to a reasonable inspection of corporate records or facilities.
  5. **Liability of directors and officers:** An officer or director can be personally liable for negligent or intentional acts, unless the articles of incorporation **provide for indemnification.**
   a. **No indemnification allowed** if the director or officer received an **unfair financial benefit** or **committed intentional wrongful acts or crimes.**
   b. **No participation exception:** Officers and directors are not liable if they dissented or abstained from a decision, in writing, or were absent from a meeting when a decision was made.
 C. **Shareholders** (person or entity who own at least one share of a company)
  1. **Rights of shareholders**
   a. **Meetings** are typically where shareholders convene and vote on corporate management issues. There are two types of meetings:
    1. **General meetings** or annual meetings occur **once a year** and are where most shareholder voting occurs (10-60 days' notice required).
    2. **Special meetings** can be held upon reasonable notice of the date, time, place, and business to be discussed (10-60 days' notice required and purpose).
   b. **Voting:** Shareholders have only **indirect corporate power** through the right to vote to elect or remove members of the board and approve fundamental changes in the corporate structure, such as mergers, dissolutions, etc.
    1. **Right to vote:** The **right to vote attaches to the type of stock held** by the shareholder. A corporation can have two types of stock: common and preferred. If the articles do not specify voting rights, both classes of stock may vote. Each outstanding share is entitled to one vote, unless the articles provide otherwise.
    2. **Voting by proxy:** A shareholder may vote in person or by proxy. A proxy is a **signed writing (can be electronic) authorizing another to cast a vote** on behalf of the shareholder. It is valid for 11 months, unless it states otherwise.
     a. A **revocable proxy** is an agency relationship between the shareholder and the proxy.
     b. An **irrevocable proxy** occurs when the **proxy is coupled with interest**. The irrevocable proxy must be so **labeled**. The interest can relate to an interest in the shares (e.g., creditor or prospective purchaser) or an interest in the corporation (e.g., performance of services or granting credit in exchange for proxy rights).

3. **Quorum:** For an action to pass there must be a quorum, which is a **majority of outstanding shares represented** (in person or by proxy) at the meeting. Quorum is based on the number of shares, not shareholders.
    a. **Majority vote:** If a quorum is present, a majority of **votes cast** validates the proposed shareholder action.
    b. **Except** votes regarding a **fundamental change** require a **majority vote of all outstanding shares** to validate the proposed action. (A higher standard.)
4. **Vote calculation:** Two methods are employed:
    a. **Straight voting:** Each shareholder casts one vote per share held. Therefore, a shareholder with more than 50% of the shares controls the vote.
    b. **Cumulative voting for directors** allows a shareholder to multiply the number of shares held by the number of directors to be elected and then cast all votes for one or more directors.
5. **Unanimous written consent:** Shareholders may also take action with unanimous written consent of all shareholders.
c. **Inspection:** A **shareholder has a right to inspect** the corporate books (articles, resolutions, shareholder meeting minutes, etc.) upon a showing of a **proper purpose** with **five days' written notice.** As to accounting or shareholder records or board minutes, the demand must be made in **good faith** and describe with reasonable particularity the purpose for the inspection, and the records must be directly connected to the stated purpose.
d. **Dividends** are payments of cash, property, or stock that a shareholder may receive from the corporation.
    1. **Discretionary:** Dividends are given at the board's discretion. But a distribution is not permitted if it would lead to insolvency or is not allowed in the articles.
    2. **Types of dividend distribution:**
        a. **Preferred with dividend preference:** Paid first to preferred with dividend preference as to stated amount, then remaining amount is paid to common stock.
        b. **Preferred and participating:** Paid first to preferred and participating as indicated in preferred amount, then remaining amount is paid to common stock. (Preferred and participating stockholders also get a share of the dividends paid to common stockholders, if any.)
        c. **Preferred and cumulative:** Paid first to preferred and cumulative as indicated for number of years not paid in the past, then remaining amount is paid to common stock.
        d. **Cumulative if earned:** Dividends cumulate only if the corporation's total earnings for the year are more than the total amount of preferred dividends that would need to be paid out for the year.
        e. **Common stock (nonpreferred):** Paid last and all shares are paid in equal amount.

2. **Shareholder agreements**
    a. A **voting trust** occurs when shareholders agree in writing to transfer their shares to a trustee who votes and distributes dividends in accordance with the voting trust. Often seen in closely held corporations. (Duration valid as specified in the agreement, for up to 10 years in California.)
    b. A **voting agreement** is a written agreement where the parties agree to vote their shares as agreed. Often seen in closely held corporations. Contract principles apply (offer, acceptance, consideration, and no valid defenses).
    c. A **management agreement** occurs where the shareholders agree to manage the corporation in an agreed-upon way as set forth in the articles or bylaws. (Duration valid as specified in the agreement, for up to 10 years in California.)
    d. **Restrictions on share transfers** are generally **upheld if reasonable**—for example a right of first refusal, or subject to a voting agreement. Absolute restraints are usually not reasonable. A third party will only be bound if the restriction is **conspicuously** noted on the **face of the certificate** such that the other party had **actual knowledge** of its existence.

3. **Shareholder suits**
   a. **Direct suit:** A shareholder may bring a suit for **breach of fiduciary duty owed to the shareholder** (not the corporation itself but the shareholder).
   b. **Derivative suit:** A shareholder may bring a derivative suit **on behalf of the corporation** for harm done to the corporation. The corporation receives the recovery, if any, and the shareholder is entitled to reimbursement for the expenses of litigation. The shareholder bringing the suit must:
      1. **Own stock** at the time the claim arose.
      2. **Adequately represent** the corporation.
      3. **Make a written demand** on directors to bring suit or redress the injury and the demand is rejected (corporation has 90 days to respond unless waiting that long would cause irreparable injury). The demand requirement used to be excused if doing so would be futile, but it is required modernly.
      4. **Post a bond** if the court requires.

> **Issue spotting tip:** When a shareholder derivative suit is at issue, also look for the issues of breach of loyalty, breach of care, or disgorging of profits under 16(b).

4. **Shareholder duties**
   a. **General rule:** A **shareholder owes no fiduciary duty** to the corporation or other shareholders.
   b. **Modern trend: Controlling shareholders owe a fiduciary duty** to the corporation and minority shareholders of the duty of **care** and duty of **loyalty. A controlling shareholder is one with enough voting strength to have a substantial impact on the corporation (not always 50% or more).**
      1. **Sale of controlling shares to a looter:** Controlling shareholders cannot sell control of the corporation to a looter if they know, or have reason to know, that the buyer intends to harm the company.
      2. **Sale of controlling shares at a premium** may be allowed where the transaction is made in good faith and is fair. However, a controlling shareholder may not sell their controlling shares and receive a personal benefit for the sale of a corporate asset or corporate office.

> **Issue spotting tip:** Whenever a controlling shareholder sells shares, consider whether these issues are raised. The analysis is very fact-dependent and many facts will be available to use in the analysis. For example, consider how high a premium is paid over trading value for the controlling shares, and if there are any side deals regarding the transaction. Analyze overall fairness.

5. **Shareholder liability:** Shareholders are **not personally liable** for the actions of the corporation.
   a. **Except professional corporations:** Typically, licensed professionals may incorporate but remain personally liable for malpractice (e.g., lawyers, doctors).
   b. **Except when they pierce the corporate veil** (see section I.A.1.d above).
D. **Federal securities laws**
   1. **Section 16(b) short-swing profits:** Any short-swing trading profits received within a **six-month period** by a **corporate insider** must be **disgorged** to the corporation. Requirements of 16(b):
      a. **Corporation** must:
         1. **Be listed on a national exchange**, or
         2. Have **$10 million** or more in assets **and** at least **2,000 shareholders** (or at least **500** if the shareholders **are not accredited investors**). Accredited investors include high income or net worth individuals and officers and directors of the issuer.
      b. **Corporate insiders** are officers, directors, and shareholders who own more than 10% equity stock in the corporation.

1. **Officers and directors** must be in their positions at the time of *either* the **purchase or the sale** of shares.
        2. **Over 10% of shareholders** must be in that position at the time of *both* the **purchase and the sale** of the shares.
    c. **Trading** is making a **profitable** purchase and sale (or sale and purchase) of company equity stock within a **six-month period.**
    d. **Remedy:** The insider must **disgorge the profit** back to the corporation.

> **Issue spotting tip:** 16(b) may be at issue any time a director, officer, or shareholder buys or sells company stock. Section 10b-5 may also be at issue.

2. **Section 10b-5** disallows **insider trading** and provides liability for any person who employs **fraud or deception** in connection with the **purchase or sale** of any **security** by means of any **instrumentality of interstate commerce.** In other words, **trading securities based on nonpublic corporate information** is not permitted.
    a. **Fraud (misrepresentation) prima facie case requirements;**
        1. **Intent (can be recklessness)** to defraud, deceive, or manipulate.
        2. **Material misrepresentation:** Information is material where there is a **substantial likelihood that a reasonable investor would consider it important** in making an investment decision.
        3. **Reliance:** There must be **actual reliance** on the misrepresentation. (Typically a failure to disclose is relied upon anytime one buys or sells securities as a result of a material omission.)
        4. **Purchase or sale** of securities (in connection with).
        5. **Interstate commerce:** The trade must involve the use of some means of interstate commerce, such as a telephone, mail, email, national securities exchange, etc.
        6. **Damages/Remedy:** Damages are calculated as the difference between actual proceeds and what should have transpired based on the real value of the stock. These profits must be **disgorged** to the company.
    b. **10b-5 may be violated in the following four ways:**
        1. **Direct trading by an insider**
            a. An **insider** is a director, officer, shareholder, employee, or any other **holder of material, nonpublic corporate information.** Insiders can include temporary holders of information such as underwriters, accountants, lawyers, etc., but an individual hired for an independent purpose, such as a person hired to print announcements, will not qualify as an insider.
        2. **Tippers** (those providing insider information) are liable if **the information was shared for the improper purpose** of personal gain.
            a. **Personal gain** can include money, a gift, or an increase in reputation.
            b. The tipper does not have to trade in securities themself to be liable, so long as the insider information is used by another to trade.
        3. **Tippees** (those receiving insider information) are liable only if the **tipper breached a fiduciary duty, the tippee knew (scienter)** the duty had been breached, and the **tipper personally benefitted** (note there is uncertainty in lower federal courts as to this personal benefit element).
        4. **Misappropriators** (those obtaining corporate private information through other means) may be in breach of a duty owed to the source of the information. (E.g., an eavesdropper or lawyer who received information for a proper purpose but then traded.)

> **10b-5 fact triggers:**
> - Officer gives a misleading press conference/statement
> - Remark overheard in public, intentionally or not intentionally
> - Officer gives inside info to lawyer who then trades or tips (look for a professional responsibility crossover)

> **Exam tip:** 10b-5 may be at issue whenever there is a stock transaction. There is a two-step analysis: 1) Determine if the party is in a position to be liable under 10b-5 as a direct insider, tipper, tippee, or misappropriator. 2) Establish the prima facie case. A party may be subject to 10b-5 liability in more than one way — for example, as both a tippee and a tipper, or as a direct violator and a tipper. It is important to analyze each potential violation separately. Also, look for multiple parties in the question to violate 10b-5. Section 16(b) may also be at issue. Although this is no longer a heavily tested topic, when it is tested, these rules comprise most of the essay, so make sure you understand them well.

3. The **Sarbanes-Oxley Act sets standards** for publicly traded companies by creating a board that **oversees public accounting firms** that perform audits and create rules pertaining to corporate financial reporting.
   a. There are **enhanced reporting requirements**, including:
      1. An **audit committee, consisting of board members,** must be established by each corporation to oversee work performed by the registered public accounting firm.
      2. A **senior executive** (i.e., CFO, CEO, etc.) must sign financial reports verifying that they contain true statements.
      3. If a **filing is inaccurate** and the corporation has to restate financial reports, the CEO and CFO must **reimburse** the corporation for any incentive-based compensation received during the 12 months after the inaccurate reports were filed.
   b. **Criminal penalties:** The act provides criminal penalties for:
      1. **Destroying or altering** corporate documents and/or audit records is punishable by a $5 million fine and up to 20 years in prison.
      2. **Securities fraud** is punishable up to 25 years in prison.
      3. **Statute of limitations** is the later of 2 years after discovery or 5 years after the action accrued.
      4. **Whistleblowers** are afforded protection.
E. **Corporate fundamental changes**
   1. **Fundamental changes to the corporate business** or structure must be approved by a **majority shareholder vote. Typical procedure** to make a fundamental change:
      a. Board **adopts a resolution.**
      b. **Written notice** is given to shareholders (10-60 days before next shareholder meeting where vote will occur).
      c. **Shareholders approve** the change by majority vote (some jurisdictions require the vote to be by a majority from all votes entitled to be cast, which is a higher standard than the typical quorum rule).
      d. The change is **updated in the articles,** which are **filed with the Secretary of State.**
   2. **Types of fundamental changes**
      a. **Merger** occurs when one corporation acquires another corporation. Shareholder approval is required (majority vote of outstanding shares, unless articles require more).
         1. **Exception for shareholder approval:** Shareholder approval of the surviving corporation is not needed where the **change is not significant** (this occurs when the articles will remain the same, shareholders hold the same number of shares, and the voting power of the shares issued will not be more than 20%).
         2. **Short-form merger** allowed where a 90%-owned subsidiary is merged into the corporate owner (no approval needed by subsidiary).
      b. **Share exchange** occurs where **one corporation purchases all shares** of one or more classes of another corporation in exchange for other securities (only a fundamental change for the corporation with shares purchased; purchasing company doesn't need shareholder approval).
      c. **Asset sale** occurs where a company **sells all or substantially all of its assets** (75%) to another corporation (only a fundamental change for the corporation being sold; purchasing company doesn't need shareholder approval).

d. **Conversion** occurs when one entity **changes corporate form**—for example, from a corporation to a LLC.

e. **Amendment** of articles or bylaws after shares have been issued **requires approval** of the directors and shareholders and the amendment must be filed with the state (no shareholder approval needed to delete names of directors or agents, change company name or corporate abbreviations (e.g., Inc. to Corp.), or to change the number of shares in share split if only one class); if more than one class of shares, then each class can vote as a group.

f. **Dissolution and winding up:** The last phase of a corporation is the period from the dissolution, which occurs when the corporation ceases to exist, and through the winding up period where remaining corporate affairs are settled.

   1. **Voluntary dissolution** occurs when a corporation chooses to take the action to dissolve. This requires a **majority vote** by the directors and shareholders. Fundamental change procedures must be followed.

   2. **Administrative dissolution** occurs when the **state forces** a corporation to dissolve because of administrative failures, such as the failure to pay fees or penalties, declare annual statement, maintain an agent for service, etc.

   3. **Judicial dissolution** occurs on grounds of fraud, ultra vires action, or a defective corporation; or in an action brought by shareholders where there is misconduct; or by creditors for an unsatisfied judgment.

3. **Dissenter appraisal rights**: Shareholders who dissent from a proposed fundamental change *may* have the right to have the **corporation purchase their shares**.

   a. **Exceptions:** Appraisal rights are **not available to holders of shares of public companies** (those listed on a national securities exchange) or large companies with at least **2,000 shareholders** and a market value of **$20 million**.

   b. **Requirement:** Shareholder must give **written notice** of objection and **intent to demand payment** before a vote is taken, **cannot vote in favor** of proposed action, and must **demand payment in writing** after the vote.

   c. **Appraisal:** Shareholder receives **fair market value** and **interest**.

II. **AGENCY:** An agency relationship exists when a **principal authorizes an agent** to act on their behalf and **represent the principal** in dealings with third parties.

   A. **Formation of principal-agent relationship** requires:

   1. **Agreement** between both parties that the agent's conduct must be for the **principal's benefit**, and the principal has the **right to control** the agent.

   > **Memorization tip:** Remember ABC: Agreement-Benefit-Control.

   a. **Distinguish from an independent contractor:** A principal has the right to control the method and manner in which an agent performs, but does not control this with an independent contractor.

   b. **Subagents and borrowed agents** must meet the same agency requirements of agreement, benefit, and control.

   c. **Estoppel:** An agreement can be created by estoppel if a **third-party relies** on the principal's communication (similar to apparent authority below in section II.C.4).

   > **Exam tip:** On an essay question, look for one of the required elements to be missing since that is typically the case.

   2. Capacity

   a. **Principal** must have **capacity to contract** (i.e., not be a minor) and must be mentally competent.

   b. **Agent** must have minimal capacity, so an agent must be mentally competent but can be a minor.

3. **All contract formalities not required:** An agency relationship does not require consideration or a writing, unless the Statute of Frauds requires a writing (e.g., a contract regarding real property).

B. **Duties of principal and agent and remedies for breach**

1. **Principal duties**

   a. **The principal owes the agent all duties imposed by their contract**, such as compensation, cooperation, indemnity, and reimbursement, and any other contractual duties imposed.

   b. **Remedy for breach:** Where the principal is in breach, the agent may do any of the following:

      1. **Terminate the agency** and refuse to perform further.
      2. **Seek contract damages** and/or an accounting (but must mitigate damages).
      3. **Seek a possessory lien** for money due.

2. **Agent duties**

   a. **The agent owes the principal** the fiduciary duties of:

      1. **Duty of care** to act as a **reasonably prudent person** would act under similar circumstances (local community standards).

         a. The **business judgment rule (BJR)** applies in some jurisdictions where the agent's duties are in a business setting and provides the presumption that the agent will act in **good faith** and in the **best interests of the principal.**

      2. **Duty of loyalty:** An agent owes a duty of loyalty to the principal. An agent must put the **interests of the principal above their own interests.**

         a. **No conflicts of interest**
            i. No **self-dealing.**
            ii. No **usurping the principal's business opportunity.**
            iii. No making **secret profits.**

         b. **No commingling of funds.**

      3. **Duty of obedience** to follow all reasonable instructions given by the principal.
      4. **Duty to communicate** relevant information that would affect the principal.
      5. Any other **express contractual** duties.

   b. **Remedy for breach:** Where the agent is in breach, a principal may do any of the following:

      1. **Discharge** the agent.
      2. **Withhold compensation** from the agent.
      3. **Seek an accounting** or **contract remedies**, such as an action to disgorge profits, rescission, constructive trust, etc. (must mitigate damages).
      4. **Seek tort damages for intentional or negligent performance.**
      5. **Seek indemnity** for liability to third parties occasioned by the agent's **wrongful actions beyond the agency scope.**

   c. **Subagent duties**

      1. **Subagent duties** depend on whether or not the subagent is acting with authority.

         a. **Acting with authority** (principal authorized the agent to appoint the subagent): The subagent **owes the principal the same duties** owed by an agent.

         b. **Acting without authority:** The subagent **only owes duties to the agent.**

      2. The **agent is liable** to the principal for the subagent's breach.

   d. The **agent is personally liable for contracts** with third parties in the following cases:

      1. The agent is acting with **no authority** from the principal (acts with implied warranty of authority when none exists).
      2. Principal's **identity is not revealed** (partial disclosure because principal's existence is known or should reasonably be known).
      3. Principal's **existence and identity are undisclosed/unknown.**
      4. All of the **parties intend** that the agent be treated as a party to the contract.

C. **Principal's liability for agent's contracts:** The **agent's actions will bind** the principal if the agent was **acting under the actual or apparent authority** to act for the principal. **Types of authority:**

1. **Actual express authority is specifically granted** to the agent by the principal. It may be oral, but a writing is required if the Statute of Frauds applies.

2. **Actual implied authority:** The agent **reasonably believes** the principal gave them authority because of **necessity** (task reasonably necessary to accomplish agency goals), **custom**, or **prior dealings**.
3. **Termination of actual authority:** Actual express or implied authority may be terminated by any of the following:
   a. **Breach** of agent's fiduciary duty.
   b. **Lapse** of a stated period, or a reasonable time if none is stated.
   c. **Operation of law:** By the **death or incapacity** of either party (unless durable power of attorney exists), or **bankruptcy** of the principal.
   d. **Changed circumstances** where it is clear the agent's services are no longer needed, such as a **significant change** in the market, law, or subject matter.
   e. **Happening** of a specified event.
   f. **Unilateral termination** by either party since agency is usually terminable **at will with notice** (but can't terminate if agent has an interest in the subject matter or a power is given for security — i.e., consideration provided).

   > **Memorization tip:** Use the mnemonic BLO–CHU to memorize the six ways an agency can terminate. Blow bubble–chew gum.

4. **Apparent authority:** The agent's actions will bind the principal when the principal has provided the agent with the **appearance of authority**, on which a third party reasonably relies. The analysis centers on what occurred between the **principal and the third party**.
   a. **Notice requirement:** Where an agent's actual authority has terminated (unless by death or incapacity), they **continue to have apparent authority** to transact with known third parties with whom they previously transacted on the principal's behalf **until the third parties receive** actual or constructive **notice** of the termination.
   b. **Written authority:** An agent may have **"lingering authority"** where an agent's actual authority has been terminated, but if a **third party relies** on **written authority** of the agent, the agent's apparent authority is not terminated.
      1. **Death of principal:** Traditionally, death or incapacity of the principal terminated all authorities; **modernly, authority is NOT terminated**.
   c. **Agent exceeds actual authority** (also called inherent authority): The principal **may still be bound** if the agent is in a position that would normally allow the agent to take such action (e.g., corporate officer), or if the principal previously allowed the agent a similar excess of authority.

   > **Apparent authority fact triggers:**
   > - Secret instruction to agent
   > - "Lingering authority" where third party not notified that agent no longer has authority
   > - Action taken by a corporate officer
   > - Action taken by partner without permission
   > - Sr. attorney at a firm agrees to give a prospective client a discount despite a firm policy against discounts without approval from the partners

5. **Ratification occurs** when an agent takes action without proper authority, and the **principal subsequently** engages in conduct that **approves** (through words or conduct) **the agent's action**. The principal will be bound where they have capacity, knowledge of all material facts, and accept the agent's transaction. Agent no longer liable if this occurs.
6. **No authority:** Where the agent acts without actual or apparent authority, the **principal is not liable** on the contract, and the agent is personally liable.
D. **Principal's liability for agent's torts:** A principal is liable for an agent's torts that are committed **within the scope** of the principal-agent relationship.

1. **Scope of principal-agent relationship:** An act is within the scope of the relationship if the conduct was of the **kind the agent was hired to perform**, the **tort occurred on the job**, and/or the **agent intended their action to benefit** the principal.
   a. **Except frolic or mere detour:** A **principal is not liable** for torts committed by an agent while the agent is **substantially deviating** from the planned conduct such that they are acting for their **own purposes** (frolic). However, a **small deviation** from the planned conduct (mere detour) **is permissible**, and the agent will still be within the scope of the agency relationship.

   > **Exam tip:** When the issue of frolic or mere detour occurs on an essay question, be prepared to argue the issue both ways since it will be a close call.

2. **Independent contractors: A principal is not generally liable** for the torts of an independent contractor.
   a. **Independent contractor definition:** A principal **does not control the manner and method** by which an independent contractor performs, but does have the right to control the manner and method by which an agent performs.
   b. **Exceptions:** A **principal is liable** for the torts of an independent contractor when the conduct involves:
      1. **Ultrahazardous** activity,
      2. **Nondelegable duties,**
      3. **Negligent selection** of the independent contractor, or
      4. If **estoppel** applies where the principal held the independent contractor out as an agent.
3. **Employees:** An individual hired to work **for pay** for another is **presumed to be an employee** and not an independent contractor **unless** the hiring company can prove the worker is free from control and direction of the hiring entity, performs work outside the usual course of the business, and is customarily engaged in an independently established trade or occupation.
4. **Intentional torts:** A **principal is not liable** for the agent's intentional torts, **except** where the conduct was:
   a. **Specifically authorized** by the principal (e.g., force is authorized),
   b. **Natural result** from the nature of the employment (e.g., a bouncer), or
   c. The tortious act was **motivated by a desire to serve** the principal.

   > **Issue spotting tip:** Agency issues usually arise where one person is acting on behalf of another person or business entity in a contract transaction.

III. PARTNERSHIP: There are two types of partnership, general and limited.
A. General partnership
1. **Definition:** A partnership is an association of **two or more persons** who are carrying on as **co-owners of a business for profit**, whether or not the parties intend to form a partnership. A **partner** is a person who intends to carry on a business for profit as a co-owner.

   > **Exam tip:** On the bar exam, determining if the parties are partners is often a close call. Argue both ways.

2. **Formation**
   a. **No formalities required:** There are no formalities required to form a general partnership (based on contract and/or agency laws) so a partnership is found based on the **intent of the parties** to carry on a business as co-owners. **Intent of the parties can be established by:**
      1. **Contribution in exchange for profit:** The contribution of **money or services in exchange for a share of profits** creates a **presumption** that a general partnership exists. The exchange for profit is the key factor here, so an exchange for payment of a debt, rent, etc., will not create the presumption.

      2. **Common ownership:** Other indications (but not presumptions) that a partnership exists include title to property held as joint tenants or tenants in common, the parties designate their relationship as a partnership, or the venture undertaken requires extensive activity by the partners.

      3. **Sharing of gross revenue** does *not* necessarily indicate the parties are partners.

      4. The **absence of an agreement to share losses** is evidence that the parties did not intend to form a partnership.

  b. **California** has adopted its own version of the Revised Uniform Partnership Act (RUPA), but partners may still agree in their partnership agreement to rules not governed by RUPA, and then RUPA only governs those rules not provided for in the agreement. However, certain RUPA provisions cannot be waived, such as the duty of loyalty.

  c. **Partners have a fiduciary, agency-like relationship:** Partners are bound by **contracts** entered into with authority by their co-partners and are liable for **torts** committed by their co-partners within the scope of the partnership.

3. **Partnership assets**

  a. **Titled property** (under RUPA)

      1. **Property is deemed a partnership asset if:**

        a. **Titled** in partnership name, or

        b. It is titled in a partner's name, and the instrument transferring title identifies the person's **capacity as a partner, or the existence of the partnership.**

      2. **Property is presumed (rebuttable) a partnership asset if purchased with partnership funds,** cash or credit, regardless of how title is held.

      3. **Property is not a partnership asset and is presumed (rebuttable) separate property if:** Property held in the name of a partner does not indicate the person's capacity as a partner or mention the partnership and was not purchased with partnership funds, even if it is used for partnership purposes (e.g., car).

  b. **Untitled property** (ownership follows common law principles)

      1. **Property is partnership property** based on the parties' **intent.** Courts are more likely to find that the parties intended the property to belong to the partnership if:

        a. **Partnership funds** were used to acquire, improve, or maintain the property.

        b. There is a **close relationship** between the property and the partnership business operations or **property used** by partnership business.

        c. The partnership **lists it as an asset** in its books.

4. **Partnership rights and duties**

  a. **Partnership rights**

      1. **Ownership:** Property acquired by the partnership is **property of the partnership itself** and not of the partners individually.

      2. **Transferability:** A partner is not a co-owner of partnership property and has **no transferable interest** in it.

        a. **Except** a partner's own share of partnership profits and surplus is transferable since they are their own personal property.

      3. **Use of property:** A partner can only use the partnership property for the **benefit of the partnership**.

      4. **Control:** Each partner is entitled to **equal control** (vote) **and management** of the partnership and receives no salary for services performed (except compensation to wind up the partnership is allowed). Ordinary business decisions are controlled by majority vote; extraordinary decisions (including matters outside the ordinary course of business) require consent of all partners.

      5. **Profits and losses:** The default rule is that profits are **shared equally and losses are shared in the same proportion as profits**. For example, if the partners agree to share profits 60/40, then both profits and losses are calculated at this rate; if the partners agree only to share losses 60/40 then profits are still shared equally.

      6. **Indemnity:** A partner **may be indemnified** for liabilities and expenses incurred on behalf of the partnership.

   b. **Partnership duties: Partners have a fiduciary relationship** and are fiduciaries of **each other** and the **partnership**. Partners have the following fiduciary duties:
      1. **Duty of care** to use reasonable care.
         a. The **business judgment rule** applies where the partner's duties are in a business setting (in most jurisdictions).
      2. **Duty of loyalty** to further the **partnership interests over their own** interests.
         a. **No conflicts of interest:**
            i. No **self-dealing,**
            ii. No **usurping a partnership business opportunity,**
            iii. No making **secret profits (implies a duty to account), and**
            iv. No **competing** with the partnership.
      3. **Duty to disclose:** Partners must disclose any **material fact** regarding partnership business (all partners can also inspect and copy the books).
      4. **Duty to account:** Partners can bring actions against other partners for losses caused by breach and may disgorge a breaching partner of profits.
      5. **Duty of obedience**: Partners are agents of the partnership and must act in accordance with their authority as partners.
      6. **Duty of good faith and fair dealing**: implied (as in contracts).
5. **Partnership relations with third parties**
   a. **Debts: General partners are personally liable** for the debts of the partnership. (Although limited partners are not; see Limited Partnerships, below.)
   b. **Contracts:** Each **partner is an agent of the partnership** for the purpose of conducting its business. The partners' authority to bind the partnership when dealing with third parties follows agency law principles:
      1. **Actual Authority:** Where the partner **reasonably believes** they have **authority to act** based on the partnership agreement or a vote by the partners, the **partnership will be bound**.
      2. **Apparent Authority:** Any partner may act to carry out ordinary partnership business and doing so will bind the partnership.
         a. **Except** if the partner had **no authority to act** for the partnership in the matter and the **third party actually knew or** received **proper notice** that the partner lacked such authority.
      3. **Estoppel:** If a person represents to a third party that a general partnership exists, they will be liable as if it does exist.
   c. **Torts:** The partnership members are **joint and severally liable for torts** committed by a partner in the **scope of the partnership**.
6. **Partnership liability**
   a. **Civil liability**
      1. **Contracts:** The partners are **liable for all contracts** entered into by a partner that are within the **scope of partnership** business and/or are made with **authority** of the partnership.
      2. **Torts:** The partners are **liable for all torts** committed by any partner or partnership employee that occur within the **course of partnership** business or are made with **authority** of the partnership.
      3. **Joint and several:** Partnership liability is joint and several for all obligations. **Each partner is personally liable** for the entire amount of partnership obligations. However, a partner paying more than their share may **seek contribution or indemnity** from the other partners.
   b. **Liability of incoming partners:** Incoming partners are **not personally liable for debts incurred prior** to joining the partnership, but any money paid into the partnership by an incoming partner can be used by the partnership to satisfy prior debts.
   c. **Liability of outgoing (dissociated) partners**
      1. **A dissociating (outgoing) partner remains liable** for partnership debts incurred prior to dissociation unless there has been a **novation or release of liability**.

      2. **A partnership can be bound** by an act of a dissociated partner (and the dissociated partner **may be liable** for acts) undertaken within two years after dissociation if:
        a. The act **would have bound** the partnership before dissociation,
        b. The other party **reasonably believed** the dissociated partner was still a partner, and
        c. The other party **did not have notice** of dissociation.
           i. If a notice of dissociation is **filed with the state**, all parties are deemed to have received notice within **90 days** of the filing.

  7. **Dissociation, dissolution, and winding up**
    a. **Dissociation** occurs when a **partner ceases to be a partner** in the partnership.
      1. **Dissociation does not necessarily terminate the partnership** (unless there are only two partners).
      2. **Dissociation** may be **voluntary or involuntary**, where the other partners expel a partner.
      3. **The partnership must purchase** a dissociated partner's interest in the partnership.
      4. **A dissociated partner may still bind** the partnership and may **remain liable** for partnership (see section III.A.6.c.2, above).
    b. **Dissolution** occurs when the **partnership stops being active** and the partnership business is wound up. A partnership may dissolve for several reasons:
      1. **Voluntary dissolution** occurs when a partnership is formed for a specific purpose and the objective is achieved, or the agreement specified an end date, or when all partners agree, or in an at-will partnership when one party notifies the other.
      2. **Involuntary dissolution** can occur when the partnership is engaged in an unlawful activity, or by court decree at the request of a partner.
    c. **Winding up** is the **period between the dissolution and termination of the partnership** in which the remaining partners liquidate the partnership's assets to satisfy creditors, an accounting is made, and the remaining assets are distributed to the partners.
      1. **Compensation:** Partners receive compensation for winding-up activities.
      2. **Old business:** The partnership and general partners **remain liable** for all transactions entered into to **wind up old business with existing creditors**.
      3. **New business:** The partnership and general partners **remain liable** on **new business** transactions **until notice** of dissolution is given to creditors or until 90 days after filing a statement of dissolution with the state.
    d. **Priority of distribution.** Assets are distributed in the following order, with each level fully satisfied before distributing to the next level:
      1. **Creditors**, including partners who are creditors.
      2. **Partners who** are entitled to compensation for winding-up activities.
      3. **Capital contributions** by partners.
      4. **Profits and surplus**, if any remain, are shared equally amongst the partners unless there is an agreement otherwise.

> **Note:** If the partnership does not have enough assets to repay a partner's capital contribution, the other partners will need to put in an equal share to satisfy that debt. Further, a partner who pays more than their share of partnership debts is entitled to contribution from the partners.

B. Limited partnership
  1. **Definition:** A **limited partnership** is a partnership that has **at least one general partner** and at least **one limited partner**, which creates a two-tiered partnership structure with differing rights, duties, and liabilities for general and limited partners. The main difference is that a **limited partner** is **liable for the obligations of the partnership only to the extent of their capital contribution** and is **not entitled to manage** or control the partnership business.
  2. **Formation:** To form a limited partnership the partners must:
    a. **File a limited partnership certificate of formation, signed by all general partners,** with the Secretary of State;

b. **Identify the name** of the partnership, which includes the words "limited partnership";
c. **Identify the street address** of the initial principal office;
d. **Provide the names and addresses** of the agent for service of process and of each general partner; and
e. **Maintain records:** In the state of organization, the limited partnership must have an office containing records of the certificate, any partnership agreements, the partnership's tax returns for the three most current years, etc. There must also be a record of the amount and description of each partner's contribution, any special distribution rights of each partner, etc.

> **Exam tip:** A limited partnership that is not properly formed (for example, if the certificate is not filed) will be deemed a general partnership.

3. **Partnership rights and duties**
   a. **General partners in a limited partnership** have the **same rights and duties** as noted above in the general partnership (see section III.A.4, above).
      1. **Indemnity:** A general partner is **not entitled to a salary** for services performed for the partnership, but the partnership must **indemnify a general partner for liabilities** incurred as a result of partnership activities.
   b. **Limited partners generally have no right to act on behalf of the partnership and owe no fiduciary duties** to the partnership and are free to compete with the partnership and have interests adverse to those of the partnership unless an agreement provides otherwise. Limited partners have a right to a full accounting and to inspect the partnership books.
   c. **Both general and limited partners** have the following rights:
      1. **Distribution:** Distributions are made on the basis of the partner's contribution. However, a contribution can be in the form of any benefit bestowed on the partnership including money, property, services, etc.
      2. **Consent:** A partner's contribution obligation is only excused by the consent of all partners, and is not excused by death or disability.
      3. **Transferability:** A partner's right to distributions is personal property that may be transferred.
      4. **Dissolve:** Right to apply for dissolution of the limited partnership.
4. **Partner liabilities**
   a. **General partners in a limited partnership** are subject to the **same liabilities** as a regular general partner (see section III.A.6, above).
   b. **Limited partners** are **not liable for the obligations of the partnership itself beyond their capital contributions** and generally have **no right to manage** the business, though they may. However, a limited partner may be found liable as a general partner if a third party has reason to believe the limited partner is actually a general partner.
5. **Dissolution**
   a. **A limited partnership will dissolve:**
      1. At the **time specified** in the limited partnership certificate.
      2. Upon **written consent** of all general partners and of limited partners holding a majority interest (i.e., they received distributions).
      3. Upon **dissociation of a general partner**, unless the agreement provides otherwise, or the partners appoint a new general partner within 90 days.
      4. After 90 days upon **dissociation of the last limited partner**.
      5. Upon **judicial decree** of dissolution.
   b. **Winding up:** The limited partnership will continue to exist for the purpose of the winding-up activities.
   c. **Priority of distribution:** Assets are distributed in the following order:
      1. **Creditors,** including outside creditors and partner loans.
      2. **Partners and former partners** in satisfaction of **distribution previously required** under the limited partnership agreement.
      3. **Capital contributions** by partners must be paid.

4. **Partners** for the **amount due under the partnership agreement**, or if not specified then in proportion to their distribution share.

IV. **LLP—LIMITED LIABILITY PARTNERSHIPS**
   A. **Definition:** An LLP is a form of partnership where the **partners are not personally liable** for the obligations of the partnership.
   B. **Formation:** To form an LLP a partnership must:
      1. **File a statement** of qualification with the Secretary of State executed by one or more partners authorized to execute a registration,
      2. Identify the **name and street address of an agent for service of process**,
      3. **Identify the name and address** of the partnership,
      4. Have a **partnership name ending in "LLP"** or "RLLP",
      5. Provide a brief **statement of the business** in which the partnership engages,
      6. Address any **other matters** that the partnership determines to include.
   C. **Liability of limited liability partners**
      1. **LL partners have no personal liability for the partnership:** All partners are not personally liable for the debts and obligations of the partnership, whether contract, tort, or otherwise.

   > **Note:** This is different than a limited partnership where only the limited partners are not personally liable, but the general partner is liable.

      2. An **LL partner** will still have **personal liability for their own wrongful acts.**
   D. **Fiduciary obligations:** Partners owe LLP duties similar to those a director owes to a corporation, including a **duty of care** and **duty of loyalty**.
   E. **Dissociation and dissolution** operate similarly to a limited partnership.

V. **LLC—LIMITED LIABILITY COMPANIES**
   A. **Definition:** An LLC is a business entity that has the **limited liability of a corporation** combined with the **tax advantages of a partnership**. A member is an owner of an LLC.
   B. **Formation:** To form an LLC the members must:
      1. **File an "articles of organization" with the Secretary of State** (which is similar to an article of incorporation),
      2. **Identify the name** of the LLC and the **address** of the principal office,
      3. Provide a statement that the purpose of the LLC is to engage in a lawful activity,
      4. Identify the name and street address of the initial agent for service of process, and
      5. Provide a statement identifying how the LLC is to be managed. In the absence of an agreement, the members will have an equal right to manage and control.
   C. **Rights and duties of LLC members**
      1. **LLC member rights**
         a. **Profits and losses:** Sharing of profits and losses are **based on contributions** unless an operating agreement provides otherwise.
         b. **Management and control: Members typically control** the LLC, but the articles may provide for another type of management.
         c. **Transferability: Management interests are not freely transferable** and members can only transfer their right to receive profits and losses, so an LLC has **limited liquidity**.
      2. **LLC member fiduciary duties:** Members owe the LLC and other LLC members the **duty of care** and **duty of loyalty**.
   D. **Liability of LLC members:** LLC members are **not personally liable** for the obligations of the company itself beyond their own capital contributions; however, **courts may pierce the LLC veil of limited liability** (as they do in corporations for alter ego, inadequate capitalization, or fraud—but not for lack of formalities).
   E. **Dissolution:** There is a split of authority on what terminates an LLC.
      1. **Traditional rule:** Dissociation of any LLC member, such as by death, retirement, resignation, bankruptcy, etc., generally causes dissolution; or
      2. **Modern trend (including California):** Dissolution is only caused by one of the following:

a. An **event specified** in the operating agreement,
b. **A vote by 50% of members,** unless articles say otherwise,
c. **90 days with no members,**
d. **Judicial decree** (unlawful actions, fraud, etc.), or
e. **Administrative decree** (failure to submit annual fee or report).

Essay tip: The examiners often test agency, partnerships, and/or corporations in one essay. Be careful to know the differences in language among the various entities as well as the owners of the entities. For example, if a call asked about whether various attorneys were employees, partners, members, or shareholders, you would need to know what each of these means. An **employee** is a person hired to work for a company and paid to do so but isn't necessarily a partner, etc. A **partner** is a partner as described in partnerships (but could be either limited or general partner). **Members** are owners of LLCs. And **shareholders** are owners of shares of stock in a company. So, you would need to have all of your entity hats on, so to speak, to go through all of these as they pertain to each different entity.

BUSINESS ASSOCIATIONS ISSUES TESTED MATRIX

Continued >

Date	Fact Pattern	Crossover	Corp. De Facto De Jure Pierce Corp. Veil Ultra Vires	Corp. Promoter Pre-incorporation Liability	Corp. Officers & Directors Duties Duty of Care BJR Duty of Loyalty	Corp. Shareholder Rights Agreements Derivative Suits	Corps. Federal Securities Law 10b5 16b	Corps. Fundamental Change Dissolution	Agency	Partnerships General & Limited	LLP	LLC
July '24 Q1	PickWinners Inc. markets to wealthy investors & Dir. Cate starts E-Save Inc.				X	X						
July '23 Q1	Amy from ABC law firm caused a car accident with Priya	Torts (neg.) but not identified as c/o by bar								X		
July '22 Q4	Alijah & Bowen voted for Palmer as president of Corp. who made changes		X		X	X						
February '22 Q5	Arnold & Betty launch a business to sell durable paint that A patented	Remedies	X	X					X	X		
October '20 Q2	Acme Inc. w/board members Brown & Chase & 10 outside directors				X	X						
February '20 Q5	A, B, & C formed a law firm; share profits; titled sr. attys as nonequity partners		X		X	X			X	X	X	X
February '17 Q4	Retail, Inc. buys some of XYZ Co. and ceases business							X				
July '15 Q5	Online, Inc. internet provider enters joint venture with LargeCo.	Prof Resp			X	X		X				

Date	Description	Crossover	Corp. De Facto / De Jure / Pierce Corp. Veil / Ultra Vires	Corp. Promoter Pre-incorporation Liability	Corp. Officers & Directors Duties / Duty of Care / BJR / Duty of Loyalty	Corp. Shareholder Rights / Agreements / Derivative Suits	Corps. Federal Securities Law 10b5 / 16b	Corps. Fundamental Change Dissolution	Agency	Partnerships General & Limited	LLP	LLC
February '15 Q5	Andy, Ruth, and Molly start The Batting Average (TBA)		X						X	X		
July '14 Q3	AB Law represents Sid who sues Renco	Prof Resp					X				X	
February '13 Q6	Molly and Lenny computer software business hired atty Lenny	Prof Resp	X						X	X		
February '12 Q4	Testco/Amy sign contract with Examco		X		X				X			
February '11 Q5	Bob & Cate own Corp.; Bob wants to sell to sister Sally	Prof Resp			X	X		X				
July '10 Q4	ABC Computers start-up with Alfred, Beth & Charles									X		
February '10 Q2	ABC LLP leases offices to other lawyers								X		X	
February '09 Q6	Stage Inc. is a closely held Corp. operating comedy clubs	Prof Resp	X		X							
February '08 Q6	Albert & Barry, a librarian, provide law services	Prof Resp	X	X								
February '07 Q2	Fred & Rita own Rita's Kitchen and have 75 investors	Prof Resp		X	X	X				X		
July '06 Q4	B, C & D are directors of Web; Web creates Adco's website on credit		X		X							
July '05 Q3	Sportco & Carole on board; Carole sells land to another	Prof Resp			X				X			

Continued >

	Crossover	Corp. De Facto / De Jure / Pierce Corp. Veil / Ultra Vires	Corp. Promoter / Pre-incorporation / Liability	Corp. Officers & Directors / Duties / Duty of Care / BJR / Duty of Loyalty	Corp. Shareholder / Rights / Agreements / Derivative Suits	Corp. Federal / Securities Law / 10b5 / 16b	Corps. Fundamental / Change / Dissolution	Agency	Partnerships / General & Limited	LLP	LLC
February '05 Q3	Molly & Ruth form Dryco, which is insolvent & dissolves	X	X		X		X				
July '03 Q1	Officer tells Lawyer corp. info for tax advice; Lawyer buys stock	Prof Resp					X					
February '02 Q3	Acme merges with Bigco, but President Paul buys stock first				X		X	X				
February '01 Q2	Adam owns Sellco; Sellco owns Buildco., which sells houses at cost				X	X						

BUSINESS ASSOCIATIONS PRACTICE ESSAYS, ANSWER GRIDS, AND SAMPLE ANSWERS

Business Associations Question 1
July 2022, Question 4

The Articles of Incorporation for Corp Inc. (Corp) provide that it is a closely-held corporation formed for the purpose of manufacturing televisions. Corp has been highly profitable in this business for twenty years. The Articles also provide that, for the purpose of electing directors, each shareholder shall have one vote per share that they own multiplied by the number of open director positions, i.e., cumulative voting.

Aliyah and Bowen each owned sufficient shares to elect, through cumulative voting, one of the three directors of Corp. Aliyah and Bowen entered into a signed written agreement stating that they will vote to elect themselves to the board of Corp and agree on the election of any successor board members and, if they cannot agree on a particular successor, will abstain from voting in that election. They also agreed that, once they became directors, they would select Palmer as the new president of Corp. The agreement stipulated that it is binding on all subsequent owners of the shares. Aliyah and Bowen stamped "Subject to Agreement" on the backs of all of their share certificates.

Aliyah and Bowen were subsequently elected to Corp's board of directors, along with Chantal. At the next board meeting, Aliyah and Bowen voted to select Palmer as the new president of Corp, Chantal abstained, and Palmer was named as president.

Palmer immediately instituted several costly changes intended to shift Corp solely into the manufacturing of bicycles. Palmer reasoned that, by the time the directors heard anything about the changes, Corp would be so profitable that no one would complain. Bowen discovered almost immediately what Palmer had done.

Bowen then informed Daya of all of these facts, sold his shares to her, and resigned from the board.

Esgar, a shareholder of Corp since its inception, wishes to seek legal relief regarding Palmer's actions and Corp's change to solely manufacturing bicycles.

1. Is the agreement between Aliyah and Bowen valid? Discuss.

2. Is Daya bound by Aliyah and Bowen's voting agreement with respect to the election of successor directors? Discuss.

3. On what theory or theories, if any, might Esgar bring an action to enjoin Corp from moving solely into manufacturing bicycles, and what is the likely outcome? Discuss.

4. On what theory or theories, if any, might Esgar bring an action for damages against Palmer related to Corp moving solely into manufacturing bicycles, and what is the likely outcome? Discuss.

Business Associations Question 1 Assessment
July 2022, Question 4

This was an easy question *if* you knew the rules, but because they tested very specific questions that included some extremely nuanced issues and rules that had never been tested before, a simple reading of the calls, let alone the facts, likely landed you in the midst of having a mini panic attack. But not to worry, as you were not alone. When you find yourself in a bind with specific questions, just think big picture about what issue they are getting at and make up a rule that you think makes sense from a commonsense stand-point. Many of the business associations questions in recent years have been shockingly, dare we say, crazy. But at the end of the day, you have to answer the questions, so do your best and make up reasonable rules if you don't know the specifics.

The first call in particular asked about voting agreements. While most outlines and students know the basics about shareholder agreements, most didn't likely dive into the deep ocean in regard to directors who are also shareholders making an agreement to limit them as directors while simultaneously being shareholders in a close corporation. So here you are — put on your thinking cap. You know that shareholders can have voting agreements, but knowing that directors owe fiduciary duties and have a higher standard to uphold, you should come up with some rule that distinguishes and points out that you notice the distinction between an agreement between shareholders and one between directors. Even if you couldn't remember the specific rule (or didn't know it), this will be enough to get you by because it shows you read the facts carefully, noticed the differences, and are able to think critically and coherently.

The second question also tests a very nuanced issue of restricting share transfers. Again, if you didn't know the specific rule, go with something that is "reasonable" as that is always a good fallback rule when dealing with director and shareholder duties and it will get you some points (and it just so happens that it is part of the actual rule!), so do your best and just show the graders that you are capable of thinking critically.

The third and fourth call are very similar. The third call asks about what theories Esgar can seek to "enjoin" Corp from making the change from selling televisions to bicycles whereas the fourth call asks about what theories Esgar can seek for "damages" for the same issue. You can see how drastically different the state-released answers are here. However, both answers address ultra vires in call three. The fact that one of the remedies in ultra vires acts is to "enjoin" the action is likely why that is the main issue there. Since the call is broad, technically you could have also thrown in other issues there such as injunctions or, as one answer did, shareholder suits. However, the shareholder suits were better in call four because the remedy is usually damages for those suits, which are either given back to the shareholder in a direct suit or to the corporation in a derivation action. But as you can see, there was a lot of flexibility with these two calls. The key was seeing somewhere how the President was engaging in ultra vires acts and that Esgar as a shareholder could seek both a direct and a derivative shareholder action.

Again, this question was a doozy, but you survived, and looking at passing answers, they are all over the place with some commonalties as discussed above. So, use your smarts and show the graders that you can tackle any questions thrown your way.

Note the areas highlighted in **bold** on the corresponding grid. The bold areas highlight the issues, analysis, and conclusions that are likely **required** to receive a passing score on this question. In general, the essay grids are provided to assist you in analyzing the essays, and are much more detailed than what a student should create during the exam to organize their own response to a question.

Issue	Rule	Fact Application	Conclusion
Agreement between Aliyah and Bowen			
Shareholder Voting Agreement	A voting agreement is a written agreement where the parties agree to vote their shares as agreed. This is often seen in closely held corporations. **Contract principles apply.** Cumulative voting is permissible.	Here, **Aliyah and Bowen were SH b/c they each owned sufficient shares to elect, through cumulative voting, one of the three directors of Corp.** Here, there was likely an offer and acceptance when Aliyah and Bowen entered into a signed written agreement stating that they will (1) vote to elect **themselves to the board of Corp and agree on the election of any successor board members, and (2) that if they cannot agree on a particular successor, will abstain from voting in that election.** There would be consideration b/c both were giving up their ability to vote as they wanted, and they even stipulated that it is binding on all subsequent owners of the shares and they stamped "Subject to Agreement" on the backs of all of their share certificates. There is no SOF defense as their agreement was in writing. **And cumulative voting is allowed so it isn't against public policy or anything, and it was allowed per the Articles.** Since contract principles apply, the agreement to elect themselves and other board members or abstain is likely valid b/c all elements of a valid contract are met and this is a closely-held corp. where these types of agreements are common.	The agreement between Aliyah and Bowen is valid as it pertains to their ability to vote for themselves and other directors or abstain.
Director Agreements	**Directors cannot enter into voting agreements like shareholders. Such agreements violate their fiduciary duty of care.**	Although they also attempted to enter a valid contract with an offer and acceptance when they agreed that **once they became directors, they would select Palmer as the new president of Corp, this would not be allowed as it is against public policy and violates their fiduciary duties since they are directors now, not just shareholders, and are expected to vote using their independent judgment.**	Agreement to select the new President would not be valid.

Continued>

Issue	Rule	Fact Application	Conclusion
Alijah and Bowen's voting agreement binding on Daya?			
Restrictions on share transfers	**Restrictions on share transfers are upheld if reasonable and the restriction is conspicuously stated on the face of the certificate such that the third party had actual knowledge of the restriction.**	**Here, Bowen sold his shares to Daya when he resigned. While the certificate itself was stamped that the shares were "Subject to Agreement," it was on the back of the certificate and not the face and didn't state what the agreement was, and arguably might be an absolute restraint since Daya could not vote as she wanted. However, it was likely acceptable as it did notify Daya that it was limited by some agreement so she had knowledge and could have inquired further.**	**Restriction likely valid.**
Theories Esgar can use to enjoin Corp			
Close Corporation	**Closely held corporations are those that have few shareholders (35 max) and have to labeled as a "close corporation" and cannot be publicly traded.**	**Here, the articles of incorporation provided that Corp was a closely held corporation formed for the purposes of manufacturing televisions.**	**Corp is a closely held corporation with a specific stated purpose.**
Ultra Vires	**If a corporation has a limited stated purpose in its Articles of Incorporation and acts outside its stated business purpose, it is acting "ultra vires."** Modernly, ultra vires acts are enforceable and may be raised when the ultra vires act causes the state to seek dissolution, the corporation sues an officer, or a shareholder sues to enjoin the proposed act.	**Here, Corp had a limited purpose to manufacture televisions and has been highly profitable doing so successfully for 20 years.** So, when Palmer instituted several costly changes intended to shift Corp solely into manufacturing bicycles, he was acting ultra vires since bicycles have nothing to do with televisions. Esgar, as a SH, can seek to enjoin this proposed act.	Edgar can seek an injunction to enjoin the proposed act and would likely succeed.
Theories Esgar can bring for damages against Palmer			
Direct Suit	**A shareholder may bring a suit for breach of fiduciary duty owed to the shareholder (not the corporation itself but the shareholder). Any recovery goes directly to the SH.**	**Here, Esgar can seek a direct suit against Palmer's new changes because Palmer is breaching a fiduciary duty by changing what has been a very profitable business with no input or vote from shareholders (see below).**	**Esgar can seek a direct suit against Palmer** and would likely succeed.

Continued>

Issue	Rule	Fact Application	Conclusion
Shareholder derivative suit [Note one state-released answer addressed these under call 3 instead of 4 but both addressed these somewhere. Since call 3 asks about "enjoining" and that language is directly in the rule for ultra vires, that is the issue they were looking for there, whereas these suits usually deal with damages.]	**A shareholder may bring a derivative suit on behalf of the corporation for harm done to the corporation. The shareholder bringing the suit must own stock, adequately represent the corp., and first make a demand of the directors to redress the injury** (and wait 90 days for response); used to **excuse if demand would be futile** (no longer excused under modern law); and post a bond if required. **Recovery goes back to the corporation not the SH directly.**	Here, Esgar has been a SH since Corp's inception and continues to be a SH, his suit would adequately represent Corp b/c Palmer's actions will impact the entire Corp and change how it operates and has operated for the last 20 years in violation of the Articles, but it doesn't appear that he made a demand on the board so he needs to make a demand prior to filing a suit. **However, it is possible his demand will be futile since the board only contains two members, Aliyah and Chantal. And Aliyah voted for Palmer, but Chantal abstained so she might respond to Palmer's changes. Bowen resigned so he is no longer a board member.**	**Esgar needs to file a written demand with the board before he can commence a derivative suit** but would likely succeed.
Duty of care/BJR	An officer owes the corporation a duty of care to act as a reasonably prudent person would act under similar circumstances. The business judgment rule protects officers who manage the corporation in good faith and in the best interests of the corporation and its shareholders.	As the President, Palmer is an officer and owes the Corp a duty to act as a reasonable officer in similar circumstances. A reasonable President would not likely entirely change the purpose and manufacturing of a company that had been highly profitable for 20 years. Further, they would not make any substantial changes without getting input and approval from the directors and shareholders, especially since the changes were costly and made immediately. Although Palmer thought these changes would be profitable so that nobody would complain and might claim he was thus acting in good faith, he still needed to seek approval from shareholders and directors since a reasonable president new to a position would not instantly change an otherwise successful 20-year company.	Palmer likely breached his duty of care.

Business Associations Question 1 Sample Answer
July 2022, Question 4

1. Agreement between Aliyah and Bowen

Shareholder Voting Agreement

A voting agreement is a written agreement where the parties agree to vote their shares as agreed. This is often seen in closely held corporations. Contract principles apply to shareholder voting agreements. Cumulative voting is an acceptable form of voting for corporations and can be included in the Articles of Incorporation.

Here, Aliyah and Bowen were shareholders because they each owned sufficient shares to elect, through cumulative voting, one of the three directors of Corp. There was likely an offer and acceptance when Aliyah and Bowen entered into a signed written agreement stating that they will (1) vote to elect themselves to the board of Corp and agree on the election of any successor board members, and (2) that if they cannot agree on a particular successor, will abstain from voting in that election. There would be consideration because both were giving up their ability to vote as they wanted, and they even stipulated that it is binding on all subsequent owners of the shares, and they stamped "Subject to Agreement" on the backs of all of their share certificates. There is no statute of frauds defense as their agreement was in writing. Finally, cumulative voting is allowed and isn't against public policy or anything, and it was allowed per the Articles as well. Since contract principles apply, the agreement to elect themselves and other board members or abstain is likely valid because all elements of a valid contract are met, and this is a closely-held corp. where these types of agreements are common.

Thus, the agreement between Aliyah and Bowen is valid as it pertains to their ability to vote for themselves and other directors or abstain.

Director Agreements

Directors cannot enter into voting agreements like shareholders. Such agreements violate their fiduciary duty of care.

Although Aliyah and Bowen also attempted to enter a valid contract with an offer and acceptance when they agreed that once they became directors they would select Palmer as the new president of Corp, this would not be allowed as it is against public policy and violates their fiduciary duties since they are directors now and not just shareholders and are expected to vote using their independent judgment.

Thus, the agreement to select the new President would not be valid.

2. Whether Aliyah and Bowen's voting agreement is binding on Daya

Restrictions on share transfers

Restrictions on share transfers are upheld if reasonable and the restriction is conspicuously stated on the face of the certificate such that the third party had actual knowledge of the restriction.

Here, Bowen sold his shares to Daya when he resigned. While the certificate itself was stamped that the shares were "Subject to Agreement," it was on the back of the certificate and not the face and didn't state what the agreement was, and arguably might be an absolute restraint since Daya could not vote as she wanted. However, it was likely acceptable as it did notify Daya that it was limited by some agreement, so she had knowledge and could have inquired further. Thus, the restriction is likely valid.

3. Theories Esgar can use to enjoin Corp

Close Corporation

Closely held corporations are those that have few shareholders (35 max), have to be labeled as a "close corporation," and cannot be publicly traded. Here, the articles of incorporation provided that Corp was a closely held corporation formed for the purposes of manufacturing televisions. Thus, Corp is a closely held corporation with a specific stated purpose.

Ultra Vires

If a corporation has a limited stated purpose in its Articles of Incorporation and acts outside its stated business purpose, it is acting "ultra vires." Modernly, ultra vires acts are enforceable and may be raised when the ultra vires act causes the state to seek dissolution, the corporation sues an officer, or a shareholder sues to enjoin the proposed act.

Here, Corp had a limited purpose to manufacture televisions and has been highly profitable, doing so successfully for 20 years. So, when Palmer instituted several costly changes intended to shift Corp solely into manufacturing bicycles, he was acting ultra vires since bicycles have nothing to do with televisions. Thus, Esgar, as a shareholder, can seek to enjoin this proposed act and would likely be successful in doing so.

4. Theories Esgar can bring for damages against Palmer

Direct Suit

A shareholder may bring a suit for breach of fiduciary duty owed to the shareholder (not the corporation itself but the shareholder). Any recovery goes directly to the shareholder and not the corporation.

Here, Esgar can seek a direct suit against Palmer's new changes because Palmer is breaching a fiduciary duty by changing what has been a very profitable business for 20 years with no input or vote from directors or shareholders (see below for breach of duty of care). Thus, Esgar can seek a direct suit against Palmer and would likely succeed. Any recovery would go directly to Esgar and not the corporation.

Shareholder derivative suit

A shareholder may bring a derivative suit on behalf of the corporation for harm done to the corporation. The shareholder bringing the suit must own stock, adequately represent the corporation, and first make a demand of the directors to redress the injury and wait 90 days for a response. Common law would excuse the demand if it would be futile. However, modernly a demand is made. Further, some courts require the shareholder to post a bond. Recovery goes back to the corporation, not the shareholder directly.

Here, since Esgar has been a shareholder since Corp's inception and continues to be a shareholder, his suit would adequately represent Corp because Palmer's actions will impact the entire Corp and change how it operates and has operated for the last 20 years in violation of the Articles. However, it doesn't appear that he made a demand on the board, so he needs to make a demand prior to filing a suit. It is possible his demand will be futile since the board only contains two members, Aliyah and Chantal, and Aliyah voted for Palmer. Chantal might respond to challenges regarding Palmer's changes because she abstained when voting for him, so she wasn't necessarily in support of him. Bowen resigned so he is no longer a board member. Regardless, Esgar needs to file a written demand with the board before he can commence a derivative suit, but he would likely succeed.

Duty of care/BJR

An officer owes the corporation a duty of care to act as a reasonably prudent person would act under similar circumstances. The business judgment rule protects officers who manage the corporation in good faith and in the best interests of the corporation and its shareholders.

As the President, Palmer is an officer and owes the Corp a duty to act as a reasonable officer in similar circumstances. A reasonable President would not likely entirely change the purpose and manufacturing of a company that had been highly profitable for 20 years. Further, they would not make any substantial changes without getting input and approval from the directors and shareholders, especially since the changes were costly and made immediately. Although Palmer thought these changes would be profitable so that nobody would complain and might claim he was thus acting in good faith, he still needed to seek approval from shareholders and directors since a reasonable president new to a position would not instantly change an otherwise successful 20-year company.

Thus, Palmer likely breached his duty of care giving rise to Esgar's ability to see a direct and derivative action against him.

Business Associations Question 2
February 2017, Question 4

Years ago, Art incorporated Retail, Inc. He paid $100 for its stock and lent it $50,000. He elected himself and two family members to the Board of Directors, which in turn elected him as President and approved a ten-year lease for a store. He managed the store and was paid 10% of Retail's gross revenues as compensation.

Subsequently, Barbara bought 20% of Retail's stock from Art.

Retail's board approved a contract to buy 30% of the inventory of XYZ Co., a company owned by Art.

Subsequently, Art began taking home some of Retail's inventory without paying for it.

Retail had net profits in some years and net losses in others. It paid dividends in some years, but not in others. In some years, Retail's board met three times a year; in others, it never met.

Recently, Retail ceased business. Its assets were limited to $5,000 in cash. Among the claims against Retail was one by Supplier, who was owed $10,000 for computer equipment. Another claim was Art's, for the $50,000 that he had lent and had just become due. Supplier and Barbara, individually, filed lawsuits against Retail and Art.

1. On what legal theory, if any, can Supplier reasonably seek to recover against Art on its claim against Retail? Discuss.

2. Does Barbara have a cause of action against Art, either derivatively or personally? Discuss.

3. If Retail is forced into bankruptcy court, will Art be able to collect from Retail any portion of his $50,000 loan? Discuss.

Business Associations Question 2 Assessment
February 2017, Question 4

This question focuses on the business association of a corporation, and in particular on the role of a controlling corporate shareholder and the duties they owe to the corporation and minority shareholders. To adequately answer this essay question, there are many factual inferences that need to be used in the analysis as the facts are sparse.

This question is organized by specific calls, which seems to be a modern trend in California bar exam questions as they are testing subjects more specifically as opposed to overall "discuss" type questions, especially in business associations essays. This makes issue spotting easier than it used to be. However, with some of the calls, it is still necessary to write out an issues checklist (e.g., duties owed by a director/majority shareholder) to ensure you don't miss any issues.

There are a lot of missing facts that would be helpful in your analysis such as what each of the corporations do (this would help with determining whether taking inventory could have been to benefit the other company, which would raise duty of loyalty issues); also missing are facts that would indicate whether buying 30 percent of XYZ's inventory was fair (this would help with your analysis of the BJR to shield Art from liability); also missing is what the articles state they can do and what formalities are required since it could be a close corporation (so formalities aren't all necessary — this would result in a different conclusion for whether not having annual meetings was a problem or if it was allowed). Where there are missing facts, you need to use logical inferences and see both sides. This is why the examiners provide you with two state-released answers that come to opposite conclusions (one said the court will pierce the corporate veil and the other answer said it would not). This indicates the conclusion is irrelevant, but what matters is that you see both sides and explain why you think one side has the better argument.

There is a fine line between making logical inferences and making up facts. For example, one could state that Art took inventory without paying but likely intended to pay it back later. This is a made-up fact. There are no facts to indicate that Art had any intention of paying back the company for the inventory he took. Instead the facts tell you he took it without paying. They want you to see that perhaps this is a breach of his duty of care and/or loyalty. So, a better answer would use a logical inference. For example, you could state that Art took the inventory without paying and even though he may have had an unknown reason for doing so, it would still imply that he was commingling his assets with company assets since he was taking company assets for his own use without any further indication as to why he was taking them. The fact that he didn't pay implies that they were still company assets (property) that he took and mixed with his own assets or treated as his own assets. Review the difference and see how the latter inference makes better analysis by inferring logical explanations for why a rule is met (breached duty of loyalty and care here) rather than making up new facts that don't really prove or disprove the actual rules.

Note the areas highlighted in **bold** on the corresponding grid. The bold areas highlight the issues, analysis, and conclusions that are likely **required** to receive a passing score on this question. In general, the essay grids are provided to assist you in analyzing the essays and are much more detailed than what a student should create during the exam to organize their own response to a question.

Issue	Rule	Fact Application	Conclusion
Supplier v. Art			
Corporate Formation	A corporation is a legal entity that exists separate from its owners, thus shielding the owners and managers from personal liability.	**Here, the facts state that A "incorporated" Retail, Inc., which indicates Retail, Inc., is a corporation that met all necessary requirements and has "Inc." in its name, signifying it is a corporation.**	Retail is a corporation
	A corporation requires that the incorporators sign and file an articles of incorporation with the Secretary of State that includes names and addresses of incorporators, authorized numbers of shares, purpose, agent for service of process, street address, and the corp. name.		
Corporate Type	**Closely held corporations are those that have few shareholders** (35 max) and have to be labeled as a "close corporation" and cannot be publicly traded.	Here, A owned all of the stock that he purchased for $100; later Barbara bought 20% of the stock, so the number of shareholders were one and then two — which is a small number and likely qualifies as a close corp. if they indicated in the articles that it was a "close corporation."	**Retail is a closely held corporation**
Piercing the Corporate Veil	**Courts will hold shareholders liable and pierce the corporate veil when:** • **SH treats corp. as alter ego (e.g., doesn't follow corporate formalities, commingles funds, etc.)** • **Undercapitalization (SH invests insufficient money at formation to foreseeably sustain company)** • **Fraud** • Estoppel (if SH says they will be personally liable)	**Here, A failed to follow corporate formalities by not having regular meetings;** although they had 3 meetings some years it was not reasonable to have 0 meetings other years. Since it was a close corp. they did not need to follow all corporate formalities, but they should follow what rules they have in their articles. **A also took inventory without paying, which could also be considered commingling corporate and personal goods.** A also only had himself and two family members direct the company, which could be to use the company to his advantage, but that itself is not an alter ego unless he fails to act in the best interest of the corporation like when he took inventory and did not hold meetings. **Also buying 30% of XYZ inventory could be to serve his alter ego and not in the best interest of the corporation;** it isn't clear what XYZ or Retail do, but since he took inventory it could be for the other company, which implies they compete, but if not then he still commingled property.	Could have concluded either way (state released answers different here); if veil pierced Supplier can recover against A; if not then he can't

Continued>

Issue	Rule	Fact Application	Conclusion
		Not clear if company was undercapitalized since it did have $5K left and only owed creditors $10K, but he did only invest $100 in stock initially and did lend $50K which is still outstanding (both released answers came to different conclusions here).	
Barbara v. Art			
Shareholder derivative suit	A shareholder may bring a derivative suit **on behalf of the corporation for harm done to the corporation. The shareholder bringing the suit must own stock, adequately represent the corp., and first make a demand of the directors to redress the injury** (and wait 90 days for response); used to excuse if demand would be futile (no longer excused under modern law); and post a bond if required. **Recovery goes back to the corporation not the SH directly.**	**Here, B did own stock at the time and adequately represents the corp. since she is the only non-director SH and 1 of 2 SH; but it isn't clear that she ever made a demand;** under old law her demand may have been futile since A and his two family members are on the board but modernly, she still needed to make the demand and have them reject it.	B needs to file a written demand with the board before she can commence a derivative suit
Direct Suit	**A shareholder may bring a suit for breach of fiduciary duty** owed to the shareholder (not the corporation itself but the shareholder). Any recovery goes directly to the SH.	**Here, B can sue A directly for breach of fiduciary duties** (as discussed below).	**B can sue A directly**
Director's duty of care	A director owes the corporation a duty of care to act as a reasonably prudent person would act under similar circumstances. The business judgment rule protects directors who manage the corporation in good faith and in the best interests of the corporation and its shareholders.	**A is a director of Retail; while he elected to pay himself 10% of Retail's gross revenues, this by itself is not unreasonable; nor is having profits and losses in given years; nor is paying dividends in some years and not others as many companies operate like this and sales vary year to year.** However, not meeting regularly in some years is likely not reasonable as any director should ensure that the board informs the other SH of their meetings via minutes (if this is a close corp.; if not then they need annual meetings too). **Also, taking inventory without paying is not reasonable as it commingles personal assets with corporate assets and treats the latter as his own; this action is not in the best interest of Retail and is not in good faith. Thus, A won't be shielded by the BJR.**	A likely breached the duty of care

Continued>

Issue	Rule	Fact Application	Conclusion
Director's duty of loyalty	**Director owes a duty of loyalty to the corporation.** **Directors cannot self-deal/have conflicts of interest,** usurp a corporate opportunity, or unfairly compete with the corporation.	Here, A approved to buy 30% of XYZ inventory and he owns XYZ; thus he has an interest on both sides of the deal and should have refrained from engaging or voting on this deal as he is an interested director; if the terms were fair to Retail and SH like B then it would be fine but facts aren't clear; and the fact that A took inventory without paying for it shows he is personally benefiting by taking unpaid property or benefitting XYZ if the inventory is the same (again facts not clear); this could be competing with Retail and would be a violation of the duty of loyalty.	A likely breached the duty of loyalty
Controlling shareholder duties	**A controlling shareholder can't use their position to gain a personal benefit at the expense of the other shareholders.**	Here, A was a controlling SH as he owned 80% of the stock of Retail and B only owned 20%. He also agreed to purchase 30% of XYZ inventory and he owns XYZ but it isn't clear if he did so to benefit XYZ or himself and not Retail; since he took inventory without paying for it, one could infer he personally used the inventory or used it for his other company, either of which would be a violation of his position as a majority SH to B as a minority SH; since Retail is now ceasing to exist it is possible that buying 30% of XYZ was not in Retail's best interest (or B as a minority SH) but facts unclear here as to whether these harmed B or Retail.	Unlikely A violated his duty as a majority SH to B
Can Art Collect from Retail?			
Deep Rock Doctrine	When a corporation is insolvent, third-party creditors may be paid off before shareholder creditors, thus subordinating the shareholder claims.	Here, A lent Retail $50,000 initially and is owed his money back but Retail only has $5,000 and owes Supplier $10,000 too; Supplier is a third-party creditor and A is a SH who violated various duties; thus the remaining $5,000 would go to Supplier and A would get nothing.	A will not be able to collect any of his $50,000 from Retail

Business Associations Question 2 Sample Answer
February 2017, Question 4

1. Supplier v. Art

Corporate Formation

A corporation is a legal entity that exists separate from its owners, thus shielding the owners and managers from personal liability. A corporation requires that the incorporators sign and file an articles of incorporation with the Secretary of State that includes the purpose of the corporation, the name and address for the agent for service of process, the corporation name and street address, the authorized numbers of shares, and the name and address of each incorporator.

Here, the facts state that A "incorporated" Retail, Inc., which indicates Retail, Inc. is a corporation that must have met all necessary requirements to be able to incorporate. Further, Retail has Inc. in its name signifying it is a corporation. Thus, Retail is a corporation.

Corporation Type

Closely held corporations are those that have few shareholders, no more than 35, identify themselves as a "close corporation" when filing with the State, and are not publicly traded. Here, A initially owned all of the stock that he purchased for $100. Later, Barbara bought 20% of the stock so the number of shareholders were only two, which is a small number. Thus, Retail is likely a closely held corporation if it identified itself as such when filing. If they are a close corporation, then they can avoid some of the formalities of general corporations as provided in its articles.

Piercing the Corporate Veil

Courts will hold shareholders liable and pierce the corporate veil in four situations: (1) when shareholders treat the corporation as their alter ego (for example if they fail to follow corporate formalities or commingles funds); (2) undercapitalization such that shareholders initially invest an insufficient amount of money at formation to foreseeably sustain the company; (3) when they create the corporation to perpetuate fraud; and (4) through estoppel if the shareholders state they will be personally liable.

Here, A may have failed to follow corporate formalities by not having regular meetings since they failed to meet at all some years. Although they had three meetings some years, it was not reasonable to have zero meetings other years since boards are supposed to meet regularly during any given year. However, if they were a close corporation, it is possible they were not required to have formal meetings as they could adjust the articles to provide for fewer formalities. Further, A also took inventory from Retail without paying for it, which could also be considered commingling corporate and personal goods since he treated Retail assets as his own, given that he didn't pay for the inventory. A also only had himself and two family members direct the company which could be to use the company to his advantage. However, this by itself is not likely an alter ego unless he fails to act in the best interest of the corporation. Finally, A buying 30% of XYZ inventory could be to serve his alter ego rather than to best serve the interests of Retail, especially since A owned XYZ. However, it isn't clear what XYZ or Retail corporations do as businesses, but since A took inventory from Retail, it could be for XYZ, which implies they compete. Even if not for the other company, then it would be for himself, and he still commingled property. Thus, a court would likely pierce the corporate veil.

As to undercapitalization, it is not clear if the company started with sufficient funds since it did have $5,000 left and only owed creditors $10K. But A did only invest $100 in stock initially and did lend $50,000, which is still outstanding. Given the lack of financial information and that Retail did incorporate years ago indicating it survived for several years, it is unlikely that a court will find it was undercapitalized initially.

Overall, the court will likely pierce the corporate veil based on A treating Retail as his alter ego.

2. Barbara v. Art

Shareholder Derivative Suit

A shareholder may bring a derivative suit on behalf of the corporation for harm done to the corporation. The shareholder bringing the suit must own stock, adequately represent the corporation's interests, make a demand of the directors to redress the injury giving them 90 days to respond before the shareholder can commence the suit, and if required post a bond. Under the common law, a demand was excused if it would be futile. However, the RMBCA does not provide for this excuse. In a derivative action, recovery goes back to the corporation and not to the shareholder directly.

Here, B did own stock at the time and adequately represents the corporation as she is the only shareholder other than A. Based on the facts it isn't clear that she ever made a demand on the board. Under the common law, her demand may have been futile since A and his two family members are on the board but modernly, she still needed to make the demand and have them reject it in order to file a derivative suit. Thus, B needs to file a written demand with the board before she can commence a derivative suit.

Direct Suit

A shareholder may bring a suit for breach of fiduciary duty owed to the shareholder (not the corporation itself but the shareholder). Here, B can sue A directly for breach of fiduciary duties (as discussed below).

Director's Duty of Care

A director owes the corporation a duty of care to act as a reasonably prudent person would act under similar circumstances. The business judgment rule protects directors that manage the corporation in good faith and in the best interests of the corporation and its shareholders.

Here, A is a director of Retail along with his two family members. While he elected to pay himself 10% of Retail's gross revenues, this by itself is not unreasonable because it is a small percent for compensation and likely reasonable compared to other companies. Further, having profits and losses in given years as well as paying dividends in some years and not others also appear to be reasonable as many companies operate similarly and sales and resulting dividends often vary year to year with numerous companies.

However, not meeting regularly in some years is likely not reasonable as any director should ensure that the board follows corporate formalities and informs the other shareholders of their meetings via minutes even if it is just to state that the company has remained steady and constant. If it were a close corporation and they are exempt from some of the corporate formalities such as annual meetings, then it is possible this was reasonable. Further, A taking inventory without paying is not reasonable as it commingles personal assets with corporate assets and treats the latter as his own. Since these actions would not be in the best interest of Retail and are not likely made in good faith, A will not be shielded by the business judgment rule. Thus, A breached his duty of care.

Director's Duty of Loyalty

Director owes a duty of loyalty to the corporation. Directors cannot self-deal or have conflicts of interest, usurp a corporate opportunity, or unfairly compete with the corporation.

Here, A approved for Retail to buy 30% of XYZ inventory while he owned XYZ. Thus, he has an interest on both sides of the deal and should have refrained from engaging or voting on this deal as he is an interested director. If the terms were fair to Retail then it is possible that B would be fine with it as it would not prejudice her interest in the corporation and it wouldn't be a breach. Even if that purchase was fair, the fact that A took inventory without paying for it shows he is personally benefiting by taking unpaid property or benefitting XYZ if the inventory is the same. Thus, he is either personally benefiting by taking unpaid inventory or using Retail inventory for XYZ which would imply the companies are similar and likely competitors both owned by A. Regardless of the reason, taking inventory without paying likely breaches the duty of loyalty.

Controlling Shareholder Duties

A controlling shareholder must refrain from using their position to gain a personal benefit at the expense of the other shareholders.

Here, A was a controlling SH as he owned 80% of the stock of Retail and B only owned 20%. He also agreed to purchase 30% of XYZ inventory, and he owns XYZ, but it isn't clear if he did so to benefit XYZ or himself and not Retail. Since he took inventory without paying for it, one could infer he personally used the inventory or used it for his other company, either of which would be a violation of his position as a majority SH to B as a minority shareholder. Further, since Retail is now ceasing to exist it is possible that buying 30% of XYZ was not in Retail's best interest, which would negatively affect B the only other shareholder. However, the facts are unclear as to whether these actions harmed B or Retail. Thus, there are insufficient facts to show that A violated his duty as a majority shareholder.

3. Can Art Collect from Retail?

Deep Rock Doctrine

When a corporation is insolvent, third-party creditors may be paid off before shareholder creditors, thus subordinating the shareholder claims.

Here, A lent Retail $50,000 initially and is owed his money back, but Retail only has $5,000 and owes Supplier $10,000. Since Supplier is a third-party creditor and A is a controlling shareholder, who violated various duties, the courts will pay Supplier before A. Thus, the remaining $5,000 would go to Supplier and A would get nothing if there is only $5,000 remaining and Retail files bankruptcy. Therefore, A will not be able to collect any of his $50,000 from Retail.

Business Associations Question 3
February 2022, Question 5

Arnold and Betty agreed to launch a business selling a durable paint that Arnold had developed and patented. They agreed to share all profits and to act as equal owners. Betty agreed to contribute $100,000 to the business venture. Arnold agreed to contribute his patent for durable paint. Arnold told Betty that he thought the patent was worth $100,000. He did not tell Betty that he had previously tried to sell the patent to several reputable paint companies but was never offered more than $50,000. Arnold and Betty agreed that Betty would be responsible for market research and marketing and Arnold would be responsible for incorporating the business and taking care of any other steps needed to start the enterprise.

Arnold first located a building within which to operate the business, owned by Landlord Co., and entered into a one-year lease in the name of Durable Paint, Inc. Subsequently, after Arnold took the necessary steps, Durable Paint, Inc. was incorporated. At the corporation's first board of directors meeting, Arnold and Betty were named as sole directors and officers. During that meeting, Arnold and Betty voted for the corporation to assume all rights and liabilities for the lease and to accept assignment of Arnold's patent rights.

Over the next six months, Durable Paint, Inc. faced unforeseen and costly manufacturing and supply problems. At the end of the first six months, the corporation had exhausted all its capital and was two months behind on rent. To make matters worse, a competitor developed a far superior product, making Durable Paint, Inc.'s patent effectively worthless. Durable Paint, Inc. had no other assets.

Landlord Co. sued Arnold and Betty personally for damages for breach of the lease.

Betty sued Arnold.

1. On what theory or theories might Arnold be found personally liable for damages to Landlord Co.? Discuss.

2. On what theory or theories might Betty be found personally liable for damages to Landlord Co.? Discuss.

3. On what theory or theories might Arnold be found personally liable for damages to Betty? Discuss.

Business Associations Question 3 Assessment
February 2022, Question 5

This is yet another business association question that tests some of the more convoluted areas, but it also tests some common authority issues that are fairly easy to address. The difficulty with this question stems from the dual entity analysis needed. At first, A and B form a partnership since they are not yet incorporated. Thus, the initial analysis needs to focus on the partnership and what the rights and liabilities are for partners. Then, one partner enters into a contract for a lease prior to incorporation, triggering pre-incorporation promoter liability. Of course, the calls of the question ask about not only that partner's liability, but also the other partner. Hence, the authority analysis. Then there is the issue about the initial agreement when A didn't fully disclose to B that the patent wasn't worth as much as he indicated. This not only triggers a possible undercapitalization argument for piercing the corporate veil, but is the essence of call three.

The problem here is one issue triggers another. They all relate in some form or another. And the timeline and sequence of events are those that would be normal in the real world. The key here is to see how each event and sequence triggers various issues that then lead to other issues. The best way to approach these questions is to map out the events and issue spot within each event. So for the first "event" when the parties agree to start a business, think about all issues triggered—partnership—and then from there think about what duties, rights, and liabilities partners have as it relates to their various actions.

From there, the next "event" is when A signs a lease. The key issue here is whether A will be personally liable for the lease (based on call one) and whether B will be personally liable for the lease (based on call two). This triggers the rights and liabilities as mentioned before that should be addressed the minute you realize that there is a partnership.

From there, the next "event" is the incorporation, so quickly discuss that it is now a corporation. The corporation assumes all liabilities for the lease. This "event" triggers a discussion of novation or a corporation taking responsibility for the partnership liabilities, which affects both calls one and two because if the corporation is liable, then A and B may not be personally liable. Of course, this triggers exceptions, such as when the corporate veil is pierced, which would still hold A and B liable.

As you can see, each event triggers various issues, but all issues relate to one another. This is why it is important for subjects like business associations to understand the big picture. There are a lot of rules, so the best way to understand how they apply is to understand how they all relate to each other.

In terms of organization, there is not one way to approach these essays, as is seen in numerous business associations sample answers released by the state bar. For example, for this essay, one answer discussed the partnership upfront and corporation assuming the liabilities whereas the other answer discussed all in call two. The key was that they both discussed the issues, and the state bar didn't seem to care where they addressed them. Business associations essays are like a puzzle. If you have all the pieces of a puzzle and eventually put the puzzle together, the end result is the same regardless of whether you started with the edges or center. Both approaches get to the same result with the same pieces. The key is to make sure you weren't missing any pieces. If you were, go back to your issues checklist and see what issues you might need to add to it.

Note the areas highlighted in **bold** on the corresponding grid. The bold areas highlight the issues, analysis, and conclusions that are likely **required** to receive a passing score on this question. In general, the essay grids are provided to assist you in analyzing the essays and are much more detailed than what a student should create during the exam to organize their own response to a question.

Continued>

Issue	Rule	Fact Application	Conclusion
Theories for Arnold's damages to Landlord			
General Partnership [note that one state-released answer discussed all partnership and authority issues in call 2 instead of call 1]	A partnership is an association of two or more persons who are carrying on as co-owners of a business for profit, whether or not the parties intend to form a partnership. No formalities are required.	Here, Arnold (A) and Betty (B) agreed to launch a business selling durable paint. They agreed to share profits and to act as equal owners indicating they intended to form a partnership, until they later incorporated. The fact that they agreed that B would be responsible for research and marketing and that A would be responsible for incorporating the business and taking care of any other steps as needed does not change the partnership. Similarly, B contributing $100,000 and A contributing his patent does not change the partnership since they both intended to carry on together as co-owners of the business regardless of their different initial contributions and responsibilities.	A and B formed a partnership initially.
Partner Rights and Liabilities	Each partner has equal rights to control and manage the partnership. General partners are liable for the debts of the partnership. Each partner is an agent of the partnership for the purpose of conducting business and can bind the partnership and other partners if they acted with actual or apparent authority.	Since A was a partner and was an equal owner, he was able to locate the building to operate the lease and enter into the one-year lease. However, he entered the lease in the name of Durable Paint, Inc., and it was not yet incorporated, so the lease would be a lease entered into under the partnership and each partner would be liable if A had authority to enter the contract.	A is liable for the lease if he had authority to act.
Actual Authority	Actual authority exists where the partner reasonably believes they have authority to act based on the partnership agreement or a vote by the partners. The partnership will then be bound.	Here, A had actual authority to enter the lease because A and B agreed that A would take care of the steps needed to start the enterprise, which would include finding a building to sell the paint.	A would be liable for the lease.
Apparent Authority	Any partner may act to carry out ordinary business and doing so will bind the partnership unless the partner had no authority to act and the third party actually knew or received proper notice that the partner lacked authority.	Here, A had authority b/c leasing a building is an act carried out in an ordinary business that is just starting. Also, Landlord had no reason to believe that he didn't have authority nor was Landlord given any notice. Landlord could have inquired into the corporate status since A entered the lease on behalf of the corporation that was not incorporated yet, but it would still bind the partnership including A.	A would be liable for the lease.

Issue	Rule	Fact Application	Conclusion
Pre-incorporation actions by a promoter Adoption/Novation	Promoters are persons acting on behalf of a corporation that is not yet formed. Common tasks include entering into a contract for a location. Promoters are personally liable for pre-incorporation contracts until there has been a novation replacing the promoter's liability with that of the corporation or there is an agreement between the parties that expressly states that the promoter is not liable. When a corporation adopts a contract, both the corporation and promoter remain liable.	Here, A was acting as a promoter for Durable Paints because they were not incorporated. However, after Durable Paints was incorporated, A and B were named as the sole directors, and at the corporation's first board of directors meeting they voted for the corporation to assume all rights and liabilities for the lease, so the corporation would now be liable for the lease, but since the agreement was an adoption and not a full novation, A would still be liable too.	Corporation assumed the lease but no novation so A still liable as is the corporation.
Corporate Formation	A de jure corporation is formed when all of the statutory requirements are met.	Here, A took the necessary steps and Durable Paint, Inc. was incorporated.	A valid corporation exists.
Shareholder liability/piercing the corporate veil	Generally, a corporate shareholder is not liable for the debts of a corporation, except when the court pierces the corporate veil and disregards the corporate entity, thus holding shareholders personally liable as justice requires. It is easier to find liability in closely held corporations. Courts will hold shareholders liable and pierce the corporate veil when: • **SH treats corp. as alter ego** (e.g., doesn't follow corporate formalities, commingles funds, etc.) • **Undercapitalization** (SH invests insufficient money at formation to foreseeably sustain company) • **Fraud** • **Estoppel** (if SH says they will be personally liable) Courts are hesitant to pierce the corporate veil for contracts.	Assuming that A and B are also SH, Landlord will argue that the corporation was undercapitalized because it could not make payments on a one-year lease. However, $100,000 is not a small amount and the facts indicate that over six months, Durable Paint faced unforeseen and costly manufacturing and supply problems, so the $100,000 likely was foreseeable at the time of formation since the later issues were unforeseen.	Court unlikely to pierce the corporate veil.

Continued>

Issue	Rule	Fact Application	Conclusion
Theories for Betty's damages to Landlord			
Partner Liability	Partners are bound by contracts entered into with authority by their co-partners. General partners are liable for the debts of the partnership. Each partner is an agent of the partnership for the purpose of conducting business and can bind the partnership and other partners if they acted with actual or apparent authority.	Since B was a partner with A, B would be liable to the same extent A was above since B did not enter the lease outside of his authority as a partner.	B liable for the lease the same as A.
SH/pierce corp. veil	See above.	See above.	B liable for the lease the same as A.
Theories for Arnold's damages to Betty			
Partner duty to disclose/ misrepresentation	Partners have a duty to disclose any material fact regarding partnership business. **Partners should not misrepresent facts to other partners.**	**Here, A did not disclose to B that the patent was really not worth $100,000, as several reputable companies** never offered him more than $50,000. This would be a material fact and a **misrepresentation because she may not have contributed more capital than the patent would be worth** and might have decided against going into the business with him. Also, she likely contributed $100,000 because she thought that was the worth of his patent so she likely wouldn't have donated more than $50,000 if she knew that was the only amount he was essentially donating.	A violated his duty to disclose to B and made a misrepresentation **so B can recover damages from A.**
Partner duty of care	Partners have a duty to use reasonable care and the business judgment rule applies.	When A misrepresented the value of his patent as discussed above, he likely didn't act as a reasonable partner would under the circumstances, since partnerships need to be based on transparency and accuracy. BJR would not apply because he didn't act reasonably when he lied.	B may be able recover damages from A.

Business Associations Question 3 Sample Answer
February 2022, Question 5

1. Theories for Arnold's damages to Landlord

General Partnership

A partnership is an association of two or more persons who are carrying on as co-owners of a business for profit, whether or not the parties intend to form a partnership. No formalities are required.

Here, Arnold (A) and Betty (B) agreed to launch a business selling durable paint. They agreed to share profits and to act as equal owners, indicating they intended to form a partnership, until they later incorporated. The fact that they agreed that B would be responsible for research and marketing and that A would be responsible for incorporating the business and taking care of any other steps as needed does not change the partnership. Similarly, B contributing $100,000 and A contributing his patent does not change the partnership since they both intended to carry on together as co-owners of the business regardless of their different initial contributions and responsibilities.

Thus, A and B formed a partnership initially.

Partner Rights and Liabilities

Each partner has equal rights to control and manage the partnership. General partners are liable for the debts of the partnership. Each partner is an agent of the partnership for the purpose of conducting business and can bind the partnership and other partners if they acted with actual or apparent authority.

Since A was a partner and was an equal owner, he was able to locate the building to operate the lease and enter into the one-year lease. However, he entered the lease in the name of Durable Paint, Inc. and it was not yet incorporated, so the lease would be a lease entered into under the partnership and each partner would be liable if A had authority to enter the contract.

A is liable for the lease if he had authority to act.

Actual Authority

Actual authority exists where the partner reasonably believes they have authority to act based on the partnership agreement or a vote by the partners. The partnership will then be bound. Here, A had actual authority to enter the lease because A and B agreed that A would take care of the steps needed to start the enterprise, which would include finding a building to sell the paint. Thus, A would be liable for the lease.

Apparent Authority

Any partner may act to carry out ordinary business, and doing so will bind the partnership unless the partner had no authority to act and the third party actually knew or received proper notice that the partner lacked authority.

Here, A had authority because leasing a building is an act carried out in an ordinary business that is just starting. Also, Landlord had no reason to believe that A didn't have authority, nor was Landlord given any notice. Landlord could have inquired into the corporate status since A entered the lease on behalf of the corporation that was not incorporated yet, but it would still bind the partnership including A.

Thus, A would be liable for the lease.

Pre-incorporation actions by a promoter/Adoption/Novation

Promoters are persons acting on behalf of a corporation that is not yet formed. Common tasks include entering into a contract for a location. Promoters are personally liable for pre-incorporation contracts until there has been a novation replacing the promoter's liability with that of the corporation, or there is an agreement between the parties that expressly states that the promoter is not liable. When a corporation adopts a contract, both the corporation and promoter remain liable.

Here, A was acting as a promoter for Durable Paints because they were not incorporated. However, after Durable Paints was incorporated, A and B were named as the sole directors, and at the corporation's first board of directors meeting, they voted for the corporation to assume all rights and liabilities for the lease, so the corporation would now be liable for the lease; but since the agreement was an adoption and not a full novation, A would still be liable too. Thus, although the corporation assumed the lease, there was no novation, so A is still liable.

Corporate Formation

A de jure corporation is formed when all of the statutory requirements are met. Here, A took the necessary steps, and Durable Paint, Inc. was incorporated. A valid corporation exists.

Shareholder liability/piercing the corporate veil

Generally, a corporate shareholder is not liable for the debts of a corporation, except when the court pierces the corporate veil and disregards the corporate entity, thus holding shareholders personally liable as justice requires. It is easier to find liability in closely held corporations. Courts will hold shareholders liable and pierce the corporate veil when a shareholder treats the corporation as its alter ego, starts the corporation and it is undercapitalized, engages in fraud, or through estoppel. Courts are hesitant to pierce the corporate veil for contracts.

Assuming that A and B are also shareholders, Landlord will argue that the corporation was undercapitalized because it could not make payments on a one-year lease. However, $100,000 is not a small amount, and the facts indicate that over six months, Durable Paint faced unforeseen and costly manufacturing and supply problems, so the $100,000 likely was foreseeable at the time of formation since the later issues were unforeseen. Thus, the court is unlikely to pierce the corporate veil.

2. Theories for Betty's damages to Landlord

Partner Liability

Partners are bound by contracts entered into with authority by their co-partners. General partners are liable for the debts of the partnership. Each partner is an agent of the partnership for the purpose of conducting business and can bind the partnership and other partners if they acted with actual or apparent authority.

Since B was a partner with A, B would be liable to the same extent A was above since B did not enter the lease outside of his authority as a partner. Thus, B is liable for the lease the same as A.

Shareholder/pierce corp. veil

The same rules and analysis that applied to A also apply to B. Thus, B is still liable for the lease the same as A.

3. Theories for Arnold's damages to Betty

Partner duty to disclose/misrepresentation

Partners have a duty to disclose any material fact regarding partnership business. Partners should not misrepresent facts to other partners.

Here, A did not disclose to B that the patent was really not worth $100,000, as several reputable companies never offered him more than $50,000. This would be a material fact and a misrepresentation because she may not have contributed more capital than the patent would be worth and might have decided against going into the business with him. Also, she likely contributed $100,000 because she thought that was the worth of his patent, so she likely wouldn't have donated more than $50,000 if she knew that was the only amount he was essentially donating.

Thus, A violated his duty to disclose to B and made a misrepresentation, so B can recover damages from A.

Partner duty of care/BJR

Partners have a duty to use reasonable care, and the business judgment rule applies. When A misrepresented the value of his patent as discussed above, he likely didn't act as a reasonable partner would under the circumstances since partnerships need to be based on transparency and accuracy. BJR would not apply because he didn't act reasonably when he lied. Thus, B may be able to recover damages from A.

Business Associations Question 4
February 2020, Question 5

Andrew, Bob, and Christine are attorneys who formed a law firm. They filed no documents with the Secretary of State or any other state office. They equally share the firm's profits after paying all expenses and make all business and management decisions. Associate attorneys are paid a fixed salary, plus 25% of gross billings for any clients they bring to the firm. Senior attorneys are paid based upon the number of hours they bill plus an annual bonus if they bill more than 2,000 hours in a year. The senior attorney bonus pool is equal to 5% of firm profits, which is split equally by the number of qualifying senior attorneys each year. Andrew, Bob, and Christine agreed to bestow the title "non-equity partner" on senior attorneys even though senior attorneys have no management authority. The firm website and business cards for senior attorneys list their title as "partner."

Martha, a senior attorney, met Nancy at a social function. Nancy told Martha about her business's legal problems. Martha gave Nancy her business card. After looking at the card, Nancy asked Martha if as a "partner" she can agree to the firm handling her legal problems at a reduced hourly rate in return for a promise of future business. Martha was aware that the firm has a strict policy of not reducing hourly rates, but signed a written agreement for it to handle Nancy's legal matters at a reduced hourly rate.

1. What type of business entity is the firm using to conduct business? Discuss.

2. Are the associate attorneys employees, partners, members, or shareholders of the firm? Discuss.

3. Are the senior attorneys employees, partners, members, or shareholders of the firm? Discuss.

4. Is the firm bound by the agreement that Martha signed with Nancy? Discuss.

Business Associations Question 4 Assessment
February 2020, Question 5

As is common with business associations essays, the calls are very specific, which makes issue spotting a lot easier. However, as is also modernly common with business association essays some of the calls are odd and require you to know non-traditional rules. The first call is fairly straightforward as you need to know the various types of entities involved in business transactions and you need to be able to identify which type was established. While general partnerships are the most commonly tested type of partnership, this essay also requires you to analyze the less frequently tested issues of a limited partnership, limited liability partnership, as well as LLC (and corporation formation, but that is heavily tested). This shows the graders that you understand the difference between the various entities. Since the call is broad as to entities, it is best to go through all the various types of entities. This also helps you in call two where you are asked about the type of job description the various attorneys hold. For example, you can't analyze whether the attorneys are members (for an LLC) or shareholders (for a corporation) if you didn't already establish that those entities weren't created here.

When getting to the second and third calls, that is where things get a bit tricky. The call is specific when it asks about the difference between associate and senior attorneys. As soon-to-be lawyers, you probably think of the difference as an associate being an attorney working crazy hours while trying to prove themselves so they can one day become a partner and the partner being the one who makes all the money. While that is somewhat true, that answer won't cut it here. The key here was understanding the difference in all of these "labels" the examiners use. Because they specifically spell out employee, partner, member, and shareholder, you should know and understand what each of these labels means and to which fact patterns each applies. Because this is the first time they have asked about these labels with such specificity, we thought it was a good essay to expose you to. Part of our goal is to select a variety of essays to expose you to as much testable material as possible. That being said, you need to organize far more essays than this book contains to fully prepare for this exam.

As to this essay in particular, it helps to keep the big picture in mind. Common sense can guide you on many of these labels. What do you think an employee is? You've likely been one at some point in life. Common sense tells you that an employee is generally viewed as a person who works for another person or company, collects a paycheck, and probably doesn't run the show. Whereas a partner usually is one who has some managerial control and authority. A member might be one that stumped you. It is not heavily tested, but if you know the different types of entities then you will recall that LLCs use the term "member," so a member would be one involved in an LLC. Finally, a shareholder is one who has invested in a corporation through share ownership. So, each of these labels aligns with a particular type of entity. This is another reason why understanding the big picture and how the pieces fit together is helpful.

Call four is a more typical question that is often tested and requires you to analyze whether Martha had authority to act and bind the firm. There are only so many ways they can test agency principles, so agency questions should lean on the easy side once you've organized a few of them. The key is practice. And remember you don't have to be perfect. So keep practicing, because practice makes progress!

Note the areas highlighted in **bold** on the corresponding grid. The bold areas highlight the issues, analysis, and conclusions that are likely **required** to receive a passing score on this question. In general, the essay grids are provided to assist you in analyzing the essays and are much more detailed than what a student should create during the exam to organize their own response to a question.

Issue	Rule	Fact Application	Conclusion
1. Type of Business entity			
General Partnership	A partnership is an association of two or more persons who are carrying on as co-owners of a business for profit, whether or not the parties intend to form a partnership. **No formalities are required.**	Here, A, B, and C are all attorneys who formed a law firm and equally share the firm's profits and make all business and management decisions which shows they are carrying on as co-owners to make a profit.	A, B, and C formed a general partnership.
Limited Partnership	A limited partnership is a partnership that has at least one general partner and at least one limited partner, which creates a two-tiered partnership structure with differing rights, duties, and liabilities. To form a limited partnership, they must file a limited partnership certificate of formation, signed by all general partners, with the Secretary of State, identify the name of the partnership with the words "limited partnership," identify the name and address of the agent for service of process and each general partner, and the street address of the initial principal office.	While the structure does appear to have a tiered structure because there senior and associate attorneys, **there were no certificates of formation filed with the Secretary of State to create a limited partnership.**	No limited partnership formed.
Limited Liability Partnership (LLP)	An LLP is a form of partnership where the partners are **not personally liable** for the obligations of the partnership. To form an LLP, they must file a statement of qualification with the Secretary of State executed by one or more partners authorized to execute the registration, identify the name and address of an agent for service of process, the name and address of the partnership, have a name ending with LLP or the like, a brief statement of the business purpose, and any other matters they want to include.	Here, there were no documents filed with the Secretary of State or any other state office, so no LLP was formed because filing with the Secretary of State is required to form an LLP.	No LLP was formed.

Continued>

Issue	Rule	Fact Application	Conclusion
Corporation	A corporation is a legal entity that exists separate from its owners thus shielding the owners and managers from personal liability for the actions of the corporation. **A de jure corporation is formed when at least one incorporator/director sign and file an articles of incorporation with the Secretary of State. The articles must include the purpose of the company,** the authorized number of shares, the name and address of the agent for service of process and each director, the corporation's name with "incorporate" or similar words, and the principal office street office. A de facto corporation exists if there is a good faith effort to form a corporation but an unsuccessful attempt to incorporate.	**Here, there were no documents filed with the Secretary of State, so no corporation was formed.** Here, there was no attempt to incorporate, so no de facto corporation either.	No corporation.
Limited Liability Corporation (LLC)	An LLC is a business entity that has the **limited liability of a corporation** combined with the tax advantages of a partnership. **To form an LLC the members must file an articles of incorporation with the Secretary of State,** identify the name of the LLC and the address of the principal office, a statement of the purpose, the name and address of the initial agent for service of process, and a statement identifying how the LLC is to be managed.	**As indicated above, there was nothing filed with the Secretary of State so there was no LLC formed.**	No LLC.
2. Associate attorneys – employees, partners, members, or shareholders			
Employee	**An individual hired to work for pay for another is presumed to be an employee** and not an independent contractor unless the hiring company can prove the worker is free from control and direction of the hiring entity, performs work outside the usual course of the business, and is customarily engaged in an independently established trade or occupation.	**Here, given that the associate attorneys are paid a fixed salary,** plus 25% of gross billings for any clients they bring to the firm, **they are likely employees b/c they work for the firm and are paid.**	Associate attorneys are employees of the firm.

Continued>

Continued>

Issue	Rule	Fact Application	Conclusion
Partner	**A partner is a person who intends to carry on a business for profit as a co-owner.**	**Here, the associate attorneys are paid a fixed salary, so they are not sharing in the profits** like A, B, and C do. Although they do earn 25% of gross billings for clients they bring in, **they do not get a share of the net profits from all clients,** like A, B, and C do. They are also not given the label of partner like senior attorneys **and do not appear to make any management decisions.**	Associate attorneys are not partners.
Member	**A member is an owner of an LLC.**	**Here there is no LLC so the associate attorneys cannot be members.**	Associate attorneys are not members.
Shareholder	**A person or entity who own at least one share of a company.**	**Here there is no corporation so the associate attorneys cannot be shareholders.**	Associate attorneys are not shareholders.
3. Senior attorneys – employees, partners, members, or shareholders			
Employee	**See above.**	The senior associates are paid by the firm b/c they get paid based on the number of hours they bill and then a bonus if they bill more than 2,000 hours in a year. **They do not have management control, so they are just employees.**	Senior associates are employees of firm.
Partner	**See above.**	**The senior associates do not share in the net profits** like A, B, and C do. Instead they are paid based on the number of hours they bill plus an **annual bonus if they bill more than 2,000 hours in a year. This bonus pool is equal to 5% of firm profits, which is split equally by the number of qualifying senior attorneys each year. While they are earning some of the firm profits, it is not all profits and it is only if they earn it** so it is not automatic like the profits shared among true partners regardless of how many hours they bill. **Further, although the actual partners, A, B, and C agreed to bestow the title "non-equity partner" on senior attorneys and are listed as partners on the website and business cards, they have no management authority and the label alone without actual control and power is not conclusive.** And the fact that A, B, and C "agreed to bestow" this title on them shows that they don't have the same control as A, B, and C.	Senior associates are not partners.

Issue	Rule	Fact Application	Conclusion
Member	See above.	Here there is no LLC so the senior attorneys cannot be members.	Senior associates are not members.
Shareholder	See above.	Here there is no corporation so the senior attorneys cannot be shareholders.	Senior associates are not shareholders.
4. Is the firm bound by Martha's agreement			
Partnership liabilities	Partners are agents of the partnership and will bind the partnership if they acted with authority.	Martha is an employee of the firm and has the label of partner but is an employee and is still an agent of the firm.	Martha is an agent of the firm.
Actual Express Authority	Authority expressly granted to the agent by the principal (may be oral unless SOF requires a writing).	The firm did not give Martha power or authority to enter any contracts, and it is against the firm's policies to offer reduced rates, so there was no actual express authority.	No actual express authority.
Actual Implied Authority	Authority when the agent reasonably believes the principal gave them authority because of necessity, custom, or prior dealings.	For the same reason above, Martha did not reasonably believe she had authority to offer a reduced rate b/c she knew of the firm's policy against that.	No actual implied authority.
Apparent Authority	The agent's actions will bind the principal when the principal has provided the agent with the appearance of authority, on which a third party reasonably relies.	It is possible that Martha provided Nancy with the appearance of authority b/c she was listed as a partner on the website and the business card which she gave to Nancy, which a third party could rely on to believe she had the ability to make decisions on behalf of the firm, especially since Nancy even asked her if she could agree to making the reduced hourly rate promise. And people often talk business at social functions and Martha did have her business cards with her. Further, if Martha sent a signed written agreement, it likely was on firm letterhead and she would have signed it as a partner presumably.	The firm will be bound by Martha's agreement with Nancy b/c of Martha's apparent authority.

Business Associations Question 5

February 2002, Question 3

Acme Corporation was a publicly traded corporation that operated shopping malls. Because of an economic slowdown, many of Acme's malls contained unrented commercial space. Additionally, the existence of surplus retail space located near many of Acme's malls prevented Acme from raising rents despite increasing costs incurred by Acme.

In June 2001, Sally, president and sole owner of Bigco, approached Paul, Acme's president. She proposed a cash-out merger, in which Bigco would purchase for cash all shares of Acme, and Acme would merge into Bigco. Sally offered $100 for each outstanding share of Acme's stock even though Acme's stock was then currently trading at $50 per share and historically had never traded higher than $60 per share.

Paul, concerned about Acme's future, decided in good faith to pursue the merger. In July 2001, before discussing the deal with anyone, Paul telephoned his broker and purchased 5000 shares of Acme at $50 per share. Paul then presented the proposed merger to Acme's board of directors and urged them to approve it. The board met, discussed the difference between the current market share price and the offered price, and, without commissioning a corporate valuation study, voted to submit the proposed deal to a shareholder vote. The shareholders overwhelmingly approved the deal because of the immediate profit they would realize on their shares. Based solely on shareholder approval, the board unanimously approved the merger, and all shareholders received cash for their shares.

In December 2001, shortly after completing the merger, Bigco closed most of the Acme malls and sold the properties at a substantial profit to a developer who intended to develop it for light industrial use.

1. Did Paul violate any federal securities laws? Discuss.

2. Did Paul breach any duties to Acme and/or its shareholders? Discuss.

3. Did the board breach any duties to Acme and/or its shareholders? Discuss.

Business Associations Question 5 Assessment
February 2002, Question 3

This business associations question covers the common corporations topics of the federal securities laws and the duties of care and loyalty. This is an older question, but we opted to leave it in as it does a good job of going through the securities laws issues, and the rules apply the same way. This used to be one of the most heavily tested topics. In the last 20 years or so, they have only tested it about once every 10 years. However, if and when they do test it, you need to know the rules well and they are actually quite easy to run through if you know them since they are very elemental (similar to torts). It is important to note that the rule has been slightly altered (since 2024) as the Supreme Court removed the pure "omission" part from the material omission. While it was argued on this exam that the failure of Paul to disclose the difference in stock price breached the duty of loyalty and care, in addition to insider trading, it could also be argued as a misrepresentation. The idea is to see how these rules play out overall. The most recent question testing the federal securities rules as of the writing of this book was back in 2014 and that was a crossover with Professional Responsibility. Since this question was a full-blown business associations question, we opted to leave it in here for you to practice with these rules.

The first two calls of the question deal with Acme's president, Paul, and his liabilities under the securities laws, 16(b) and 10b-5, and the breach of his fiduciary duties of due care and loyalty. The first call does not pose much difficulty since the facts relating to the securities violations are straightforward. Paul clearly received short-swing profits, and engaged in insider trading, so analyzing these issues is simply a matter of identifying the proper rules and the applicable facts to establish each element.

The second call deals with Paul's breach of fiduciary duties. The factual analysis is more nuanced here because while Paul acted in good faith, and the proposed merger was beneficial to the corporation, he still is likely in breach of the duty of due care because he encouraged the board to jump at what looked like a good deal without fact checking or making a reasonable investigation. The merger deal was good for Acme, but a reasonable investigation would have revealed a much better deal. Paul is also liable for the breach of the duty of loyalty because of his own considerable interest in the outcome of the merger deal because of the insider trading in which he had engaged. These two issues often arise in an essay question as an issues cluster so be on the lookout, since insider trading often leads to a breach of the duty of loyalty.

The third call requires an analysis of the same facts and fiduciary duties, but on behalf of the board that went along with Paul's recommendation and approved the merger. Again, while the board can rely on some representations of the president, they are required to do what is in the best interests of the corporation and as such should have also investigated further. The facts indicate that the shareholders approved the board action, but approval by the shareholders will never absolve the board from a breach of their fiduciary duty. The shareholders have every right to rely on the board's recommendation.

Note the areas highlighted in **bold** on the corresponding grid. The bold areas highlight the issues, analysis, and conclusions that are likely **required** to receive a passing score on this question. In general, the essay grids are provided to assist you in analyzing the essays and are much more detailed than what a student should create during the exam to organize their own response to a question.

Issue	Rule	Fact Application	Conclusion
Call #1: Paul			
16(b)	**Any short-swing trading profits received within a six-month period by a corporate insider must be disgorged to the corporation.** Corporate insiders are officers, directors and shareholders owning 10% or more equity stock in the corporation. Trading is making a profitable purchase and sale (or sale and purchase) of company equity stock within a six-month period.	**Paul is the president of Acme, which is a publicly traded company, and is thus a corporate officer and insider.** **Paul bought 5,000 shares in July 2001 at $50 per share.** At some point Bigco purchased all of the outstanding shares of Acme stock for $100 per share, which means that Paul would have sold his shares to Acme. **It is unclear when Bigco purchased all of the Acme shares, but all of the malls Acme owned were closed down in December 2001, which occurred after the merger** (thus, when Paul would have sold all his shares). Paul made a profit by engaging in buying and selling stock within a six-month period and is thus liable for insider trading. **Paul had a short swing profit of $250,000 and this must be disgorged to the corporation.**	**Paul is in violation of 16(b)**
10b-5	**Section 10b-5 provides liability for any person who employs fraud or deception in connection with the purchase or sale of any security by means of any instrumentality of interstate commerce.** An insider is a director, officer, shareholder, or any other holder of material nonpublic corporate information. Establishing fraud requires a showing of: • **Intent to defraud** • **Material misrepresentation (one that a reasonable investor would consider important)** • **Reliance on the representation** • **Purchase or sale of securities** • **Use of interstate commerce** • **Damages**	As Acme's president, Paul held material corporate nonpublic information. Paul made use of insider information regarding the proposed buyout for his own benefit. **Paul purchased 5,000 shares of Acme stock at $50 each at a time when he knew that Bigco had offered $100 per share in a proposed cash-out merger. Paul intended to deceive since he wanted to retain the profits for himself.** **Paul arguably misrepresented the amount that the stock was worth since he knew it was offered at $100 but acted as though it was only $50** — that is information that any investor would consider **important** when he purchased shares at a reduced price for his own benefit, which is a material misrepresentation. Paul's misrepresentation was relied on by the seller of the securities, since, had Paul disclosed the insider information as he was required to do, it is very unlikely the seller would have sold to Paul at $50 per share.	**Paul is in violation of 10b-5**

Continued>

Issue	Rule	Fact Application	Conclusion
10b-5 (continued)		The stock is traded on the national exchange and Paul made the trade by placing a telephone call to his broker, both of which are sufficient for a finding the use of interstate commerce as required under section 10b-5. Paul is in violation of 10b-5 and must disgorge the profits back to the corporation.	
Call #2: Paul			
Duty of care	A director or officer owes the corporation a duty of care to act as a reasonably prudent person would act under similar circumstances. The business judgment rule provides that the directors must manage the corporation in good faith and in the best interests of the corporation and its shareholders.	Paul is an officer and director of the corporation by virtue of his position of president and as such owes a duty of care. Paul must manage the corporation in good faith and in the best interests of the corporation as he pursues a potential merger with Bigco. At first blush it appears that the merger would be beneficial to Acme, a company undergoing difficult times because of the economic slowdown, which prevents Acme from leasing all of their space or increasing rents. Further, Paul pursued the merger in good faith. However, it does not appear that Paul did any fact checking or investigating of alternatives, which is what a reasonable person would do, before taking the proposed merger to the board and urging them to approve it. In addition, the unusually high offer price should have alerted Paul that something was suspicious and he should have investigated further. Had Paul investigated he may have found that there was a developer interested in the properties and Acme could have sold the properties themselves and realized a much greater profit than the sale to Bigco generated. Paul breached his duty of care.	Paul breached the duty of care

Continued>

Issue	Rule	Fact Application	Conclusion
Duty of loyalty	**A director or officer owes a duty of loyalty to the corporation.** **A director or officer has a conflict of interest when they (or a corporation they own or has a relationship with, or their family member) enters into a contract with the corporation or has a beneficial financial interest in a contract.**	**Paul is required to put the needs and best interests of Acme ahead of his own interests.** Once Paul engaged in improper insider trading (above) he had a conflict of interest with the corporation. He no longer had the ability to be objective and impartial about the proposed merger since he had invested $250,000 of his own money and had a personal interest in the outcome. **Paul is in breach of the duty of loyalty.**	Paul breached the duty of loyalty
Call #3: Board			
Duty of care	See above	**The board has the same fiduciary duties to the corporation and shareholders that an individual director or officer has. A reasonably prudent person would have investigated the proposed merger opportunity before signing off on it based solely on Paul's representations and urgings.** There are no facts to suggest that Paul is an expert in this area. **The board failed to commission a corporate valuation study or consider any alternatives, even after noticing the discrepancy between the offered price of $100 per share and the current value of $50 per share, which at the least should have made them suspicious.** **The shareholders approved the corporate action of the merger, but this does not relieve the directors of their duty of care.** The shareholders are permitted to rely on the recommendation of the board, which they did here. **The board breached its duty of care.**	The board breached the duty of care
Duty of loyalty	See above	The board may have a conflict of interest and be engaged in self-dealing if the board members were also shareholders, though the facts do not indicate they were. **Unless they had a personal interest in the transaction, the board members are not in breach of the duty of loyalty.**	The board may have breached the duty of loyalty

Business Associations Question 6
February 2015, Question 5

Andy, Ruth, and Molly decided to launch a business called The Batting Average (TBA), which would publish a monthly newsletter with stories about major league baseball players. Andy, a freelance journalist, was responsible for writing the stories. Andy conducted all of his business activities via a close corporation called Baseball Stories, Inc., of which he was the only employee. Ruth was responsible for maintaining TBA's computerized subscriber lists, mailing the newsletter every month, and billing TBA subscribers. Molly provided all equipment necessary for TBA. Andy, Ruth, and Molly expressly agreed to the following: Molly would have exclusive authority to buy all equipment necessary for TBA; and TBA's net profits, if any, would be equally divided among Andy, Ruth, and Molly.

Andy subsequently wrote a story in the newsletter stating that Sam, a major league baseball player, had been taking illegal performance-enhancing drugs. Andy knew that the story was not true, but wrote it because he disliked Sam. As a result of the story, Sam's major league contract was terminated. While writing the story, Andy's computer failed. He bought a new one for TBA for $300 from The Computer Store. The Computer Store sent a bill to Molly, but she refused to pay it.

Sam has sued Andy, Ruth, Molly, TBA, and Baseball Stories, Inc. for libel.

The Computer Store has sued Andy, Ruth, Molly, and TBA for breach of contract.

1. How is Sam's suit likely to fare? Discuss.

2. How is The Computer Store's suit likely to fare? Discuss.

Business Associations Question 6 Assessment
February 2015, Question 5

This business associations question focuses on partnership issues as well as agency issues coupled with a slight Torts/Con Law crossover by bringing in defamation. Note that the bar examiners only classified this essay as a Business Associations essay but both state-released answers addressed libel as was necessary to determine whether libel actually occurred for liability purposes. The reason it was necessary to first address whether in fact libel occurred is because without libel, nobody would have liability. The only way the various partnerships and partners would be liable is if the elements of libel can be established. This style of testing is common with other recent essays testing negligence as the underlying issue, but again the examiners are not identifying those questions as crossover questions because the focus and bulk of the question is on testing business associations.

Similar to the format of many business associations questions, here you are tasked with identifying what type of business was created. As is common, here the type of partnership that is being tested is a general partnership (this is the most common type of partnership tested). And as is common with agency, here they are testing whether there was authority for Andy to act. The difference is that here they are testing the authority of a partner within a partnership. Note that they often test authority, but what varies is the person with whom authority has been vested (or not). The person can be a partner in a partnership, an officer or director in a corporation, an agent who is not a part of a partnership or corporation but simply an employee, and so forth. But regardless of who the person is, the rules for the types of authority are still the same and need to be analyzed the same. Thus, you can easily have an approach prepared in advance for how you need to organize and approach agency authority type questions as the format and approach will be the same for everyone.

As explained above, it is also becoming more common for the bar examiners to give slight crossover questions that they are not even identifying as a crossover question. Don't panic about seeing multiple topics or subjects. It is actually often easier to have more than one subject because then the issue spotting is easier and the calls are often more straightforward than the older, one question "discuss" in general style of essay call (which is still very common in Professional Responsibility essays).

Finally, what has become increasingly common in bar exam essays are significant organizational variations among the state-released answers (as noted in the first essay for July 2022 in this chapter). For example, here state released Answer A discussed libel first and didn't go through the partnership rules until much later, whereas Answer B discussed the partnership rules upfront and then did libel later. So, keep in mind that what you begin with can vary so long as you ultimately discuss all necessary issues. Always use headings to make it easy for the grader to follow your organization. Note that some topics (such as how you approach authority) can be prewritten and organized in advance, which saves time. But other unrelated topics (like libel and partnership on this essay) can be organized in different orders.

Note the areas highlighted in **bold** on the corresponding grid. The bold areas highlight the issues, analysis, and conclusions that are likely **required** to receive a passing score on this question. In general, the essay grids are provided to assist you in analyzing the essays, and are much more detailed than what a student should create during the exam to organize their own response to a question.

Issue	Rule	Fact Application	Conclusion
Sam v. Andy, Ruth, Molly, TBA, and Baseball Stories, Inc.			
For Sam v. Andy Directly Defamation (Libel)	Libel is written or printed publication of a defamatory statement of or concerning the plaintiff that causes damage to the plaintiff. Fault also must be proven and if the person is a public figure, malice must be proven. Falsity must also be proven.	Here, the publication was printed and published to subscribers in a monthly newsletter. It was defamatory as it harmed S's reputation by stating he had been taking illegal performance-enhancing drugs. It concerned S as it identified him and he was in fact terminated after the article arose, which caused damages as well although they are presumed for libel. S as a major league baseball player was a public figure and the publication was done with malice by A since he knew it was false and did it because he didn't like S.	A is directly liable to S for libel
General Partnership	A partnership is an association of two or more persons who are carrying on as co-owners of a business for profit, whether or not the parties intend to form a partnership. No formalities are required.	Here, A, R, and M all agreed to launch TBA to publish monthly newsletters about baseball players; likely for a profit too since they had subscribers and agreed to share equally the net profits.	GP formed for TBA by A, R, and M and thus TBA will be liable for A's actions on behalf of TBA
Sam v. TBA Partnership Liability	All partners are considered agents of a partnership and are generally authorized to act on behalf of the partnership unless there is an agreement to the contrary. A principal is liable for an agent's torts that are committed within the scope of the principal-agent relationship. An act is within the scope of the relationship if the conduct was of the kind the agent was hired to perform, the tort occurred on the job, and/or the agent intended his action to benefit the principal.	Here, A, R, and M are all partners and thus agents of TBA. Arguably writing the article was within the scope of the agreement since that is what A was responsible for, but it is possible that he exceeded his scope since he knew the article was false and he only did it since he didn't like S. Here, arguably A substantially deviated from the plan because he wrote the article for his own benefit because he disliked S and thus he likely acted outside the scope permitted to him.	TBA may be liable (could conclude either way depending on whether it was within scope)

Continued>

Issue	Rule	Fact Application	Conclusion
Partnership Liability (continued)	A principal is not liable for torts committed by an agent while the agent is substantially deviating from the planned conduct such that she is acting for her own purposes (frolic). However, a small deviation from the planned conduct (mere detour) is permissible, and the agent will still be within the scope of the agency relationship.		
Sam v. Molly and Ruth Partner Liability	The partnership members are joint and severally liable for torts committed by a partner in the scope of the partnership or done with authority. Partners can seek indemnification from other partners if they are paying more than their share.	Here, A is liable personally for the tort of libel and TBA may be liable too if the libel is considered within the scope of the partnership. Since the purpose is to write baseball articles and that is what A did, it is likely that the partnership will be liable. Arguably, writing known false information is not within the scope since it is more likely they intended to provide accurate and honest stories. Here, since A is the one who wrote the story, R and M may seek indemnification from A for the tort he committed arguing it was outside the scope and thus he should be more liable than TBA and them personally.	TBA may be liable for A's torts and in the event TBA has insufficient funds, A, M, and R will all be personally liable but R and M can seek indemnification from A
Sam v. Baseball Stories, Inc. Respondeat Superior	Companies are liable for the acts of their employees if they occur within the scope of their employment.	Here, A was the only employee of BSI and conducted all of his business via this close corporation as a freelance writer. If A's article was within the scope of his freelance writing, then BSI would be liable too as his employer.	BSI likely liable if within scope
Overall conclusion	A liable first, and then TBA and BSI vicariously liable unless they can prove article was not within scope of employment; M and R liable as partners of TBA but can seek indemnification from A.		M and
Computer Store v. Andy, Ruth, Molly, and TBA			
General Partnership	All partners are considered agents of a partnership and are generally authorized to act on behalf of the partnership unless there is an agreement to the contrary.	Here, as discussed above, TBA is a GP and thus all partners have authority to act with most matters (except with agreement as discussed below).	GP and partners are agents

Continued>

Issue	Rule	Fact Application	Conclusion
Actual authority	**Actual express authority is specifically granted to the agent by the principal.** It may be oral, but a writing is required if the Statute of Frauds applies. **Actual implied authority: The agent reasonably believes the principal gave them authority because of necessity** (task reasonably necessary to accomplish agency goals), custom, or prior dealings.	**Here there was an express agreement about purchasing all equipment that only M had the exclusive authority to buy equipment.** **A did not reasonably believe he had authority because they all expressly agreed that M had exclusive authority to buy all equipment necessary.**	A did not have actual authority to buy computer
Apparent authority	**The agent's actions will bind the principal when the principal has provided the agent with the appearance of authority, on which a third party reasonably relies.**	**Here, it is possible that Computer Store believed that A had authority to buy the computer as he was the writer and responsible for writing stories for TBA and needed a computer to do so.** However, since Computer Store sent the bill to M they arguably knew that A didn't have funds to pay and thus should have inquired about his ability to buy it if he didn't have funds to actually make the purchase. But many employees and partners charge companies and don't pay themselves.	Apparent authority possible (could have concluded either way)
Ratification	Ratification occurs when an agent takes action without proper authority, and the principal subsequently engages in conduct that approves the agent's action. The principal will be bound where they have capacity, knowledge of all material facts, and accepts the agent's transaction. Agent no longer liable if this occurs.	**Here, the partners and principal did not ratify the purchase because they all expressly agreed that M would have exclusive authority to buy all equipment necessary for TBA.**	Purchase not ratified
No authority	Where the agent acts without actual or apparent authority, the principal is not liable on the contract and the agent is personally liable.	Here, A acted without authority and thus only A should be personally liable.	A should be personally liable

PART 2 *CIVIL PROCEDURE*

CIVIL PROCEDURE TABLE OF CONTENTS

INTRODUCTION TO CIVIL PROCEDURE

Civil procedure is a straightforward, rule-based subject that shouldn't be particularly difficult on the essay portion of the bar exam. However, one potential for difficulty is that both the federal rules and the California rules are eligible for testing. Oftentimes, a legal principle operates the same and is simply called by a different name in the federal system and the California system, which is something the bar examiners seem less concerned with testing. However, the bar examiners do seem interested in testing the areas where there is a substantive difference between the federal rule and California rule. We have identified the areas where the rules differ between the federal rule and the California rule; you should be sure to know those areas well. This is true especially in an area where the application of the facts to the two different rules would lead to a different result—for example, a fact pattern where application of the federal transactional rule or the California primary rights theory in res judicata would lead to different outcomes. However, the bar exam tends to favor testing federal law over California law—California law has been testable since 2007 but has only been tested twice in over 30 bar exams. We have included one of those essays for you to practice.

Civil procedure is similar to contracts in that the events transpire in a predictable way. It is easiest to issue spot an exam question if you think about the civil procedure issues within the context of the life cycle of actual litigation. First, there are preliminary issues dealing with the proper court in which the action should be brought. Then there are issues that arise pretrial; the potential for a disposition of the case without a trial; issues pertaining to the trial itself; issues that arise post-trial; issues pertaining to an appeal; and, lastly, the appropriate use of a prior judgment in subsequent litigation. The issue spotting checklist provided lists the issues in that order. However, issue spotting is typically not a challenge in civil procedure essays if you know the rules well, and the recent trend of the bar examiners has been to identify the issues for you in the call of the question or by reference using a motion to dismiss in the call that you can refer to in the facts for the specific issue.

The issues that often require in-depth factual analysis on an essay include personal jurisdiction, subject matter jurisdiction, collateral estoppel, and res judicata. Supplemental jurisdiction, removal, venue, and joinder of parties and claims are also frequently tested companion topics. Make sure you are very comfortable with those concepts and can issue spot and analyze an essay dealing with those issues too. Testing these issues makes logical sense because the State Bar indicates that the purpose of the essays is to "test legal analysis under a given fact situation" in which answers "demonstrate the applicant's ability to analyze the facts in the question, to tell the difference between material facts and immaterial facts, and to discern the points of law and fact upon which the case turns." Thus, the goal of the State Bar can only be accomplished by testing issues that require factual analysis.

That being said, recent civil procedure essays have heavily focused on discovery, such that entire essays test only discovery, so make sure you know the discovery rules (which you need to know to practice law anyway). Some students prefer the discovery rules because they don't require in-depth factual analysis but rather involve straight rule memorization. This doesn't accomplish what the State Bar claims the goal of the essays is, but given recent essays, you must be prepared for both ways of testing—in-depth analysis or straight rule memorization. There are also many detailed rules in civil procedure that pertain to dates and other requirements for pleadings, and rules of that type could certainly appear on an exam, but don't get hung up on them; they are typically not a fertile area for essay testing, and consequently, they wouldn't be worth many points even if they were on the exam. To maximize your results, spend your limited study time practicing essays dealing with the frequently and recently tested topics.

ISSUES CHECKLIST

PROPER COURT PRELIMINARY ISSUES

Personal jurisdiction (PJ)
Subject matter jurisdiction (SMJ)
Supplemental jurisdiction
Removal and remand
Venue
Notice
Choice of law

PRETRIAL PROCEDURES

Pleadings
Joinder of parties
Joinder of claims
Class action
Discovery

DISPOSITION WITHOUT TRIAL

Dismissal/default
Motion for summary judgment (MSJ)

TRIAL

Right to a jury
Judgment as a matter of law (JMOL)/directed verdict in Cal.

POST-TRIAL

Renewed JMOL/JNOV in Cal.
New trial
Motion to set aside judgment
Remittitur/additur

APPEAL

FINAL JUDGMENT RULE (FJR) & EXCEPTIONS

USE OF FINAL JUDGMENT

Res judicata (claim preclusion)
Collateral estoppel (issue preclusion)

MEMORIZATION ATTACK SHEET

PROPER COURT ISSUES

◆ **Personal jurisdiction (PJ)**
- Traditional bases
  - ◆ Consent
  - ◆ Domiciled in forum
  - ◆ Present & served
- Modern: minimum contacts
  - ◆ Long-arm statute AND
    - **Cal.**: to constitutional limits
    - Specific statute: as limited
  - ◆ Const. requirements
    - Relatedness
    - Minimum contacts
      - Purposeful availment
      - Foreseeability
  - ◆ Fairness factors
    - Burden on D
    - P's interest
    - State's interest
    - Interstate/shared states

◆ **Subject matter jurisdiction (SMJ)**
- Federal question
- Diversity of citizenship
  - ◆ Complete diversity required
    - Person: domicile
    - Corporation: may have 2
      - Incorporation state &
      - PPB state (nerve ctr.)
    - Unincorporated Assoc.: domicile of members
    - Alienage: foreign citizen and U.S. citizen
  - ◆ AND Exceeds $75k

◆ **Cal. subject matter jurisdiction**
- Unlimited case: exceeds $35k
- Limited case: $35k or less
- Small claims: person $12.5k, business $6.25k

◆ **Supplemental jurisdiction**
- Common nucleus of operative fact
- Same transaction or occurrence

◆ **Removal jurisdiction**
- Defendants only may remove
- 30 days–1 year max.

◆ **Remand**
- To state court if removal improper

◆ **Venue**
- Claim arose
- Defendant resides
  - ◆ **Fed.**: any Ds reside, all in same state
  - ◆ **Cal.**: any D resides
- Reside venue definition:
  - ◆ Person: domicile
  - ◆ Corp.
    - **Fed.**: where subject to PJ
    - **Cal.**: PPB, or contract entered into, performed, or breached
- Fallback—any D subject to PJ

◆ **Transfer of venue**
- Original venue proper
  - ◆ **Fed.**—could have been filed or all consent
  - ◆ **Cal.**—impartial jury, conven.
- Original venue improper
  - ◆ **Fed.**—dismiss or transfer
  - ◆ **Cal.**—may transfer proper county
  - ◆ Forum non conveniens
    - Public factors
    - Private factors

◆ **Notice**
- Service of process
- Method of service
  - ◆ Personal service
  - ◆ Substituted service
    - **Cal.**: must mail too only if personal service can't be made
  - ◆ Constructive service
- Service in foreign country

◆ **Choice of law**
- *Erie*
  - ◆ State substantive law
  - ◆ Fed. procedural law
  - ◆ If unclear:
    - State int.
    - Fed. int.
    - Outcome determinative
- **Cal.** conflict of law
  - ◆ Tort: comparative impairment test
  - ◆ Contract: depends on choice of law clause
    - No clause: comparative impairment test
    - Yes clause: okay if reasonable basis & no Cal. conflict

PRETRIAL PROCEDURES

- ◆ **Pleadings**
  - **Fed.:** notice pleading + plausible
  - **Cal.:** fact pleading
- ◆ **Complaint**
  - Identify parties
  - Statement of claim & SMJ
  - Demand for relief
  - Signature
- ◆ **Response**
  - Pre-answer motions
    - ◆ Motion for a more definite statement
      - **Cal.:** demurrer
    - ◆ Motion to strike
      - **Cal.:** Anti-SLAPP/SLAPPback
  - **Fed.:** 12b(6) motions
    - ◆ Lack of SMJ
    - ◆ Lack of PJ — 1st response
    - ◆ Improper venue — 1st response
    - ◆ Insufficient process — 1st response
    - ◆ Insufficient service of process — 1st response
    - ◆ Failure to state a claim
    - ◆ Failure to join an indispensable party
  - **Cal.:** General Demurrer
    - ◆ Fail to state COA
    - ◆ Lack of SMJ
  - **Cal.:** Special Demurrer (unlimited cases)
    - ◆ Uncertain pleading
    - ◆ Liability theory unclear
    - ◆ Lack of legal capacity
    - ◆ Another case exists
    - ◆ Misjoinder of parties
    - ◆ Contract pleadings not okay
    - ◆ Certificate if required
  - **Cal.:** Add'l motions
    - ◆ Lack of PJ
    - ◆ Insufficient process
    - ◆ Insufficient service of process
    - ◆ Inconvenient forum
  - Answer
    - ◆ Respond
    - ◆ Assert affirmative defenses
- ◆ **Amended Pleadings**
  - Right to amend
  - Fed. relation back doctrine
    - ◆ Claims: Same conduct, transaction, or occurrence
    - ◆ Defendants
      - Same conduct, transaction, or occurrence
      - New party knew of action
      - Would have been named

- **Cal.:** "Doe" amendments:
  - ◆ Timely filed
  - ◆ Genuine ignorance of:
    - Identity of party
    - Facts giving rise to action
    - Law allows cause of action
  - ◆ Ignorance pled
  - ◆ 3 yrs. to substitute
- ◆ **Joinder of parties**
  - Permissive joinder
  - Necessary party is:
    - ◆ No complete relief
    - ◆ Interest harmed
    - ◆ Multiple inconsistent obligations
  - Join necessary party if
    - ◆ Personal jurisdiction, and
    - ◆ Diversity not destroyed
  - If can't join, court may
    - ◆ Dismiss because indispensable, or
    - ◆ Proceed without
  - Impleader: D can add a 3rd party D
  - Intervention: nonparty wants to join
  - Interpleader: property holder wants single lawsuit
- ◆ **Joinder of claims**
  - Counterclaim
    - ◆ Compulsory
      - Same transaction or occurrence
      - Supplemental jurisdiction will extend
    - ◆ Permissive
      - Not same transaction or occurrence
      - Supplemental jurisdiction will not extend
  - Cross claim: against co-party
    - ◆ Not compulsory
    - ◆ Same transaction or occurrence
    - ◆ Supplemental jurisdiction will extend
    - ◆ **Cal.:** called a "cross complaint"
- ◆ **Class Action**
  - Fed. Requirements
    - ◆ Numerosity
    - ◆ Commonality
    - ◆ Typicality
    - ◆ Adequacy
  - **Fed.:** type of class
    - ◆ Prejudice
    - ◆ Injunctive relief sought
    - ◆ Damages — Qs of law/fact common
  - **Fed.:** citizenship issues
    - ◆ Diversity — named rep
    - ◆ Class Action Fairness Act
      - Any class member diverse
      - Aggregate exceeds $5 million
      - 100 + class members

- **Cal.:** class action—no types
  - Ascertainable class
  - Member community interest
    - Common questions of law or fact
    - Adequate representative
    - Class substantial benefit
- **Discovery**
  - **Fed.:** Rule 26 mandatory disclosures
    - Initial disclosures
    - Expert information
    - Pretrial witnesses & documents
- **Discovery tools**
  - Depositions
  - Interrogatories
  - Request for admissions
  - Request to inspect & produce
  - Electronically stored data
  - Physical or mental exam
  - **Cal.:** limited cases, less discovery
- **Scope of discovery**
  - Need not be admissible
  - No privileged material
  - No attorney work product
  - Disputes/sanctions

DISPOSITION WITHOUT TRIAL

- **Dismissal**
  - Voluntary
  - Involuntary
  - Failure to state a claim
- **Default judgment**
- **Motion summary judgment**
  - No genuine dispute of material fact & entitled to judgment as matter of law

TRIAL

- **Right to jury trial**
  - **Fed.:** legal, then equity
  - **Cal.:** equity, then legal
- **Judgment as a matter of law**
  - Reasonable people could not disagree
  - **Cal.:** directed verdict

POST-TRIAL ISSUES

- **Renewed JMOL**
  - Only allowed if JMOL first
  - **Cal.:** called JNOV & not required to file DV first
- **Motion for new trial**
- **Motion to set aside judgment**
- **Conditional new trial on damages**
  - Remittitur: damages too high
  - Additur: damages too low (not allowed in fed. ct.)

APPEAL

- **Final Judgment Rule (FJR)**
- **FJR exceptions**
  - Injunctions
  - Collateral issues
  - Multiple claims/parties
  - Extraordinary writ
  - Certification of class action
- **Standards of review**

USE OF FINAL JUDGMENT

- **Res judicata (claim)**
  - Valid final judgment on the merits
    - **Fed.:** final when rendered
    - **Cal.:** final when appeals done
  - Same P & same D
  - Same claim
    - **Fed.:** same transaction or occurrence
    - **Cal.:** primary rights theory
- **Collateral estoppel (issue)**
  - Valid final judgment on the merits
    - **Fed.:** final when rendered
    - **Cal.:** final when appeals done
  - Same issue actually litigated & determined
  - Issue was necessary (essential to judgment)
  - Use against party/privity only
  - Use by:
    - **Fed.:** party or privy only
    - **Cal.:** stranger allowed if fair
      - Defensive use—fair opportunity to be heard
      - Offensive use—if fair and equitable & could not join

CIVIL PROCEDURE RULE OUTLINE

I. **PROPER COURT—PRELIMINARY ISSUES:** The first inquiry in civil procedure always centers on whether it is proper for the court selected to resolve the case at hand. To hear a case, the court must have jurisdiction over the persons involved and the subject matter of the suit, the case must be held in the proper venue, the defendant must have notice of the suit, and the proper law must be used to resolve the issues.

    A. **Personal jurisdiction** means the court must have proper **jurisdiction over the parties** to an action. Personal jurisdiction will be proper where there is a sufficiently close relationship between the forum state and the defendant. Personal jurisdiction can be found through a traditional basis or where there is a long-arm statute and constitutional requirements are met.

        1. **Traditional basis for personal jurisdiction** exists where the defendant:

            a. **Consents** to jurisdiction in the forum state (i.e., forum selection clause or appointing an agent for service of process in a state).

            b. Is **domiciled** in the forum state. A person's domicile is the state in which they have a **physical presence** and the **subjective intent to remain**. A corporation's domicile is its principal place of business **and** its state of incorporation.

            c. Is **present** in the forum state **when served** with process ("tag" jurisdiction).

        2. **Modernly,** the **minimum contacts standard** allows personal jurisdiction over nonresidents of the forum state provided there is a **long-arm statute, and** the exercise of **jurisdiction meets the constitutional requirements.**

            a. A **long-arm statute** is the mechanism that gives a state the power to **reach beyond its own borders** and assert jurisdiction over a nonresident. There are two types of long-arm statutes:

                1. **California's long-arm statute** gives its state courts power over any person or property **up to the limits of the Constitution,** thus the minimum contacts standard is applied. California's long-arm statute permits the exercise of jurisdiction as broadly as is allowed by the U.S. Constitution, so it is co-extensive with the Constitution, and many other states have adopted similar statutes.

> **Exam tip:** In an essay exam, a broad long-arm statute similar to California's is typified by language such as, "State X may exercise jurisdiction on any basis not inconsistent with the Constitution of the United States."

                2. **Specific long-arm statutes:** Some states have specific long-arm statutes that give its courts power over nonresidents **only under certain specified situations**—for example, the commission of a tort while in the state. Where a specific long-arm statute applies, the exercise of jurisdiction must satisfy that statute and also meet the constitutional requirements of the minimum contacts standard.

> **Exam tip:** Where personal jurisdiction is not based on a traditional basis of jurisdiction, both the underlying long-arm statute and minimum contacts must be analyzed. If the long-arm statute is specific, do the analysis of the specifics of that statute and then do the minimum contacts analysis. If the state long-arm statute is co-extensive with constitutional limits, such as California's, simply identify that fact and do the analysis under the minimum contacts portion of the answer. If there is no long-arm statute in the facts, explain the two types and analyze the facts as if the CA long-arm statute applies, since most states have adopted similar ones.

            b. **Constitutional requirements:** A defendant must have **sufficient minimum contacts with the forum state** such that asserting jurisdiction over them **does not offend traditional notions of fair play and substantial justice.**

1. **Relatedness of claim to contact with forum:** The court will consider the relatedness between the claim at issue and the defendant's contacts in the forum state.
   a. **Specific jurisdiction** arises when **the claim** is directly **related to or arises from** the defendant's contact with the forum state.
   b. **General jurisdiction** arises when one is **essentially at home in the state by meeting one of the traditional bases** even though the claim is unrelated to the defendant's contacts with the forum state.
2. **Minimum contacts:** First, assess the defendant's minimum contacts with the forum state to determine if the defendant has **purposefully availed** themself of the **benefits and protections of the state** such that it is **reasonably foreseeable that their activities in the forum state subject them to being haled into court** there.
   a. Entering a **contract** alone in a state is insufficient to show purposeful availment.
   b. **Economic activity** or **distributing a product** alone in a state does not establish minimum contacts; the contact needs to be continuous and targeted, not random or isolated.

Minimum contacts fact triggers:
- Advertise or solicit business in a state
- Distributor or salesperson for a product in a state
- Small retail store near state border
- Awareness that a product is being used in a state
- Driving through a state on the way to another state
- Housing state X prisoners in state Y

---

3. **Fairness factors** (address only if specific jurisdiction is at issue): Next, the exercise of jurisdiction must be fair. To analyze fairness, assess the following factors:
   a. The **burden of the defendant** (most important factor).
   b. The **plaintiff's interest in obtaining convenient relief**, including the location of **witnesses and evidence**.
   c. The forum **state's interest** in **regulating activity** within its borders and **protecting its citizens**.
   d. The **interstate judicial system's interest** and the **shared interest of the several states** to further social policies.

Exam tip: Personal jurisdiction is frequently tested. If time permits, analyze the traditional basis of jurisdiction, but typically these bases will not be satisfied, and a full-fact intensive minimum contacts analysis will be required. Minimum contacts and fairness factors only need to be addressed when specific jurisdiction is at issue (if general jurisdiction is met through one of the traditional bases, then there is no need to get into the minimum contacts or fairness analysis).

Memorization tip: Use the mnemonic "Rolling Stones Grow Moss Partially For Frogs During Pond Slippery Invasions" to remember the key buzz words in the minimum contacts analysis: Relatedness, Specific Jx, General Jx, Minimum contacts, Purposeful availment, Foreseeability of being haled into court, Fairness factors, burden on Defendant, Plaintiff's interest, State's Interest, and Interstate judicial interests.

B. **Subject matter jurisdiction** means the court must have proper **jurisdiction over the subject matter of** an action. Federal courts have limited subject matter jurisdiction and may only hear cases involving **federal questions or diversity of citizenship**.

1. **Federal question:** Federal district courts have subject matter jurisdiction over civil actions **arising under federal law** (e.g., U.S. Constitution, federal statutes, treaties, etc.).
   a. **Well-pleaded complaint:** Plaintiff's complaint must reference the federal question or issue raised; a federal issue cannot arise in an anticipated defense.
2. **Diversity of citizenship:** Federal district courts have subject matter jurisdiction over actions **between citizens of different states where the amount in controversy exceeds $75,000.**
   a. **Complete diversity is required.** No plaintiff may be a citizen of the same state as any defendant **at the time the action is commenced**.
      1. A **natural person's citizenship is determined by their domicile.** A person's domicile is the state where they are **physically present** and have the **subjective intent** to make it their permanent home. Each person can only have one domicile at a time.
      2. A **corporation is a citizen** of
         a. The **state where the business is incorporated; and**
         b. The **one state where the corporation has its principal place of business** (PPB). A corporation may be the citizen of more than one state.
            i. The **PPB** is determined by the **"nerve center" test** and refers to the place where a corporation's **officers direct, control, and coordinate the corporation's activities.** Typically, this is where the corporation maintains its headquarters.
      3. **Citizenship of unincorporated associations** is determined by the citizenship of all members, including limited and general partners (e.g., Partnerships, LLCs, etc.).
      4. **Citizenship of minors, decedents, and incompetents** is determined by their own citizenship, not the citizenship of their representative.
      5. **Alienage jurisdiction** will permit subject matter jurisdiction when there is a case between a U.S. citizen and a foreign subject or citizen for establishing diversity.
         a. **Alienage restriction:** There is no federal jurisdiction for an action by an alien against another alien, unless there are also **U.S. citizens on both sides** of the controversy.
   b. **The amount in controversy must exceed $75,000**, excluding attorney fees and interest.
      1. **At the time of filing:** The amount in controversy is determined at the time the action is filed from the plaintiff's **good faith evaluation**.
      2. **Aggregation:** Claims can be aggregated to meet the amount if there is **one plaintiff** and **one defendant**, or if there are joint tortfeasor defendants, or if there are two plaintiffs with a common undivided interest.
         a. If the plaintiff recovers less than $75,000, they may have to pay the defendant's litigation costs (usually when the estimate was not made in good faith).
         b. The value of any counterclaim cannot be aggregated to meet the exceeding $75,000 requirement.

Note: The amount in controversy must exceed $75,000, not equal $75,000.

---

   c. **Exceptions to federal subject matter jurisdiction:** Federal courts will not hear actions involving issuance of divorce, alimony, or child support, or to probate an estate.
3. **California state court subject matter jurisdiction:** California courts have general subject matter jurisdiction and can hear any case not within the exclusive jurisdiction of another court. **Civil cases are classified** as unlimited, limited, or small claims. If a case is misclassified, either party or the court may seek reclassification.
   a. **Unlimited civil cases** are heard in Superior Court and require an amount in controversy exceeding $35,000. There are no limitations on pleadings, discovery, or relief available, and a claimant can recover any amount.
   b. **Limited civil cases** are heard in Superior Court and require an amount in controversy of $35,000 or less. There are limitations placed on the use of process and the equitable relief available, and a claimant cannot recover more than $35,000.

c. **Small claims cases** are heard in Small Claims Court and require that, if the plaintiff is an individual, the claim is $12,500 or less; or if the plaintiff is a business entity, the claim is $6,250 or less.

4. **Supplemental jurisdiction** allows the extension of subject matter jurisdiction when an additional claim does not itself invoke **federal** subject matter jurisdiction, but **the additional claim shares a common nucleus of operative fact** with a claim that does properly invoke federal subject matter jurisdiction (federal question or diversity). A common nucleus of operative fact means that the claim arises from the **same transaction or occurrence.**

> **Issue spotting tip:** Where supplemental jurisdiction is at issue, look for subject matter jurisdiction to be at issue. In a **diversity case** a plaintiff cannot use supplemental jurisdiction to circumvent **diversity** requirements (the numerous rules that bar a plaintiff from using supplemental jurisdiction in a diversity case are mainly tested on the MCQs, but pay close attention on essays, too, because recent CA bar exam essays have tested more nuanced issues).

5. **Removal jurisdiction** allows the **defendant** to have a case originally filed in state court **removed to federal court** where the case could have properly been brought in either state or federal court in the first place.
   a. **Only defendants are eligible to remove** cases, and **all defendants must agree** to remove.
   b. **Diversity case:** In **diversity** cases, once the defendant **has been served**, they **may not remove** to federal court if they are a **citizen of the forum state**.
   c. **Venue:** The case can be removed to the federal district court embracing the state court where the case was originally filed.
   d. **Timing:** The defendant must remove no later than **30 days** after service of the first "removable" document (typically service of the initial pleading), but **in diversity cases**, it can never be later than **one year** after the initial filing.

6. **Remand:** When a defendant attempts to remove a case to federal court and the **removal is improper, the federal court can remand the case back to state court.**
   a. **Timing:** The plaintiff must move to remand the case within **30 days** of the removal (the court can also remand on its own), but there is no time limit if the federal court lacks subject matter jurisdiction over the case since that may be raised at any time.

> **Issue spotting tip:** Where removal and/or remand are at issue, look for subject matter jurisdiction (SMJ) to be at issue as well. A case can only be removed to federal court if there is proper SMJ, and the facts often won't tell you that SMJ is proper, so you will need to analyze SMJ to see if removal was proper.

C. **Venue** concerns which **geographic district is the proper place** for a particular case to be heard. (There still must be jurisdiction over the subject matter of the claim (SMJ) and personal jurisdiction over the parties (PJ).)
   1. **Venue is proper where** the **claim arose or the defendant resides**, or if neither work, then use **fallback venue.**
      a. **Claim arose (transactional venue)**
         1. **Federal:** Venue is always proper in the **district** where a substantial part of the **claim arose** (injury occurred or contract entered into or breached) or where the **land in dispute** is located (local actions). This can be more than one district (i.e., where contract was entered into and breached if in two different districts).
         2. **California:** Venue is proper in the **county** where the **claim arose** (injury occurred or contract entered into) or where the **land in dispute** is located (local actions).
      b. **Defendant resides (residential venue)**

1. **Federal:** For transitory actions (not local actions), venue is proper in any district where **any defendants reside** if all defendants are residents of the **same state**.
2. **California:** Venue is proper in a county where **any defendant resides** at the time the case is filed. If no defendants reside in California, then any county is acceptable.
3. **Definition of "reside" for venue purposes**
   a. **Natural persons reside** at their **domicile** of their judicial district (Fed.) or county (California). A person's domicile is where they are **physically present** and have the **subjective intent to remain.**
   b. **Corporations and other business entities reside**
      i. **Federal:** For **plaintiffs**, they reside only in the judicial district of its **PPB**; for **defendants**, they reside in all districts where they are subject to **personal jurisdiction** if the district were a state. This is assessed at the time the case is filed.
      ii. **California:** In the county where they have their **PPB**, or where a contract was entered into or performed, or where contract breach occurred, or where liability arises.

> **Note:** A corporation's residence for venue purposes is not defined the same way as a corporation's citizenship for SMJ diversity purposes. Also, for venue the residence rules apply the same for corporations and other entities (unlike SMJ).

   c. **Fallback venue: If no district satisfies** the venue requirements in (a) or (b) above, venue is proper in any district where **any defendant is subject to the court's personal jurisdiction.**
2. **Transfer of venue**
   a. **Original venue proper:**
      1. **Federal:** Venue *may* be transferred to another federal court where the **case could have been filed or all parties consent** and there is proper personal jurisdiction, subject matter jurisdiction, and venue.
         a. The court has discretion and **may consider** the convenience of the parties, witnesses, and the interests of justice.
      2. **California:** The venue can be changed at the judge's discretion where an **impartial trial** cannot be had, **convenience of the parties and ends of justice** would be served by such a transfer, there is **no qualified judge**, or the court is **not the proper court.**
   b. **Original venue improper:**
      1. **Federal:** The court *must* **dismiss** or **in the interests of justice, transfer** to a proper venue where the case could have been brought and there is personal jurisdiction, subject matter jurisdiction, and venue.
      2. **California:** Allows for the **transfer of venue to a proper county** when the **court** designated in the complaint is not the proper court (for real property, venue is the county where the land is located).
      3. **Improper venue can be waived** (both Fed. and Cal.) by the parties and will be deemed waived in the absence of a timely objection.
   c. **Forum selection clauses** in contracts are generally upheld.
3. **Forum non conveniens**
   a. **Federal:** A court may dismiss or stay a case if there is a **far more appropriate forum elsewhere**, such as another state or country.
   b. **California:** A court may dismiss or stay a case if another forum in another state or country is more suitable by looking at the **interests of justice**.
   c. When looking at other forums, courts consider public and private interest factors.
      1. **Public factors**: What law applies, which community should be burdened with jury service, court congestion, local interests, and conflicts of laws; and
      2. **Private factors**: Convenience, location of witnesses, access to evidence, etc.

D. **Notice:** A defendant must be **properly notified** of a pending action by a reasonable method and must be given an **opportunity to be heard**.
   1. **Service of process** means to provide a defendant with notice of a pending action by delivery by a non-party to defendant of a **summons** (formal court notice of suit and time for response) and a copy of the **complaint** within 90 days of the filing of the case.
   2. **Method of service:** Service can be made by **anyone who is at least 18** years old and **not a party** to the action.
      a. **Personal service** is always adequate and occurs when the notice is personally delivered to a defendant.
      b. **Substituted service** is usually adequate:
         1. **Federal court:** Service of process can be left at **defendant's usual abode** and served upon **someone of suitable age and discretion** who **resides there**; or served to **defendant's authorized agent**; or served by methods permitted by state law.
         2. **California: Allows substituted service if personal service cannot be accomplished** with reasonable diligence. The service of process must be left at defendant's **usual abode or place of business** with a competent member of the household or person in charge at the business, who is **at least 18 years old**, and that person must be informed of the contents. The server **must then mail a copy of the papers** to the other party at the address the papers were left using **first-class mail**.
            a. **California corporation:** Service of process may be made on defendant's agent or one apparently in charge at the office during usual office hours.
      c. **Constructive service:** Defendants can be **served by registered mail**, but only **if the defendant agrees to waive service** of process.
         1. **California** allows **service by publication** only if nothing else works. Plaintiff's attorney must provide an affidavit that defendant cannot be served after reasonable diligence.
   3. **Service on parties in a foreign country:** Service can be done as the court directs, or in accordance with the laws of the foreign jurisdiction, or in accordance with the rules of an international treaty such as the Hague Service Convention.
   4. **Due Process:** Defendant must be given an **opportunity to be heard** (in addition to notice). Courts will consider whether a state's procedure for service violates due process by considering the **private interest** affected, the **risk of erroneous deprivation** of an interest through the procedures used and the probable value of additional safeguards, and the **government's interest,** including fiscal and administrative burdens.
E. **Choice of law in diversity actions**
   1. *Erie* **doctrine:** A federal court **sitting in diversity** must apply **state substantive law,** including statutes of limitations and the state's conflict of law rules, **and federal procedural law** (federal law can't abridge or modify state substantive rights, but incidental effects are fine). The goal is to prevent forum shopping and unfair administration of laws. If it is unclear whether a law is substantive or procedural, the judge will balance the following factors:
      a. The **state's interest,**
      b. The **federal government's interest,** and
      c. **How the outcome will be affected** depending on which law applies (if the issue substantially affects the outcome, it is likely substantive).
   2. **California conflict of laws rules** are deemed substantive law under *Erie*. The following rules determine the appropriate substantive law for a federal court sitting in diversity to apply.
      a. **Tort actions:** Where two state laws are in conflict, the court evaluates the **comparative impairment to each state's interest** in having its own law applied.
      b. **Contract actions** depend on whether there is a choice of law provision in the contract.
         1. **Contracts without a choice of law provision:** The court evaluates the **comparative impairment** to each state's interest in having its own law applied.
         2. **Contracts with a choice of law provision**
            a. **No conflict:** The provision will be applied so long as it has a **reasonable basis and does not conflict** with California policies.

       b. **Conflict:** If the choice of law provision conflicts with California policies, the California law will apply *if* California has a **materially greater interest** in having its law applied than the chosen state.

      c. **Real property actions:** The court will use the law of the state in which the property is located.

II. PRETRIAL PROCEDURES

A. **Pleadings** are the documents that set forth the claims and defenses to a case (i.e., complaint, answer, etc.).

  1. **Purpose of pleadings:** The purpose of pleadings is to communicate with the opposing party and the court.

    a. **Federal courts use notice pleading,** the goal of which is to provide the opposing party with reasonable notice of the **nature and scope** of the claims being asserted and facts showing a **plausible claim.**

      1. Certain claims must plead **specific facts** including those for **fraud or mistake** or special damages.

    b. **California courts use fact pleading,** which is also called *code pleading* and is more specific than notice pleading. Parties must plead ultimate facts to support each element of the cause of action.

  2. **Pleading requirements: Rule 11** requires all attorneys or a party representing themselves to **sign** all pleadings, written motions, and papers filed, certifying that the paper is **made in good faith, the legal contentions are warranted by law, and the factual contentions have evidentiary support.**

    a. **Sanctions** may be imposed for violations of this rule, but they are **subject to a 21-day safe harbor rule.** If a motion for sanctions is served, the served party has 21 days to withdraw or correct the pleadings giving rise to the sanctions motion.

    b. **Note:** Rule 11 does not apply to discovery documents.

    c. **Sanctions** can be **imposed on the parties and their attorney** such as reasonable expenses incurred, attorney fees, non-monetary sanctions such as ethics classes, dismissal, etc.

  3. **Types of pleadings**

    a. **Complaint:** A complaint is used by a plaintiff to raise issues.

      1. **Federal:** A federal complaint must include:

        a. **Identification of the parties.**

        b. A statement of **proper subject matter jurisdiction.**

        c. A **statement of the claim** showing the factual basis on which plaintiff is entitled to relief using notice pleading (see supra II.A.1.a).

        d. A **demand for the relief sought.**

        e. The **signature** of the plaintiff, or their attorney.

      2. **California:** A complaint in California must include:

        a. **Identification of the parties:** However, California allows plaintiffs to sue fictitious "Doe" defendants where the identity of a defendant is unknown.

        b. A **statement of the claim,** using fact pleading (see supra II.A.1.b).

        c. A **demand for judgment,** including the amount of damages sought, unless the damages sought are for actual or punitive damages for a personal injury or wrongful death action.

        d. The **signature** of the plaintiff, or their attorney.

    b. **Response: Federal Rule 12** requires a defendant to **respond by either a motion or by an answer** within **21 days** after service of process (or within 60 days in the U.S. if service is waived). **California** allows **30 days** to respond.

      1. **Pre-answer motions**

        a. **Motion for a more definite statement** is used where the complaint is too vague.

          i. **California:** This would be done by a **special demurrer** on the grounds the pleading is uncertain.

b. **Motion to strike** aimed at pleadings containing immaterial or redundant issues (e.g., demand for a jury trial when there is no right to one).

    i. **California also has an Anti-SLAPP** (Anti-Strategic Lawsuits Against Public Participation) **motion to strike** targeting suits brought to chill the valid exercise of free speech and petition (exemptions for commercial speech, public interest lawsuits, and illegal conduct). A defendant can make an Anti-SLAPP motion to strike, which shifts the burden to the plaintiff to show a probability of winning on the merits.

    ii. **California also has a SLAPPback** action used for malicious prosecution or abuse of process from the filing of a prior action that was dismissed because of an Anti-SLAPP motion (so a defendant that won an Anti-SLAPP motion can "SLAPPback" at the plaintiff).

c. **Federal Rule 12(b) motion to dismiss defenses** (these can be raised by a pre-answer motion or in the answer).

    i. **Lack of subject matter jurisdiction:** This can be raised **anytime before all appeals are exhausted.**

    ii. **Lack of personal jurisdiction:** This must be raised in the **first Rule 12 response** or is deemed waived.

    iii. **Improper venue:** This must be raised in the **first Rule 12 response** or is deemed waived.

    iv. **Insufficient process** (something is wrong with papers): This must be raised in the **first Rule 12 response** or is deemed waived.

    v. **Insufficient service of process:** This must be raised in the **first Rule 12 response** or is deemed waived.

    vi. **Failure to state a claim** on which relief can be granted: This can be raised **anytime until the trial is concluded.**

    vii. **Failure to join an indispensable party:** This can be raised **anytime until the trial is concluded.**

Rule understanding tip: For defenses that are waivable if not raised in the first Rule 12 response, make sure the first response is **under Rule 12. Ex:** If lack of PJ is raised alone in a motion to dismiss, then the right to later raise venue is waived. But if a motion to request a time extension is the first response, that would not be a first response under Rule 12 so the right to later contest venue, etc. would not be waived.

---

d. **California demurrer** (general or special) is typically used to respond to the complaint. These issues can also be raised in the answer.

    i. **General demurrer** (available in both unlimited and limited civil cases)

        (A) **Pleadings failed to state facts sufficient to constitute a cause of action.**

        (B) **Court lacks subject matter jurisdiction.**

    ii. **Special demurrer** is only allowed in **unlimited civil cases** for limited reasons (these must be raised as affirmative defenses in the answer). A special demurrer may be based on

        (A) **Uncertain or ambiguous pleading** (similar to a federal motion for a more definite statement).

        (B) Complaint is unclear about **which theories of liability** are asserted against each of the defendants.

        (C) **Lack of legal capacity to sue.**

        (D) **Existence of another case** between plaintiff and defendant on the same cause of action.

        (E) **Defect or misjoinder of parties.**

        (F) Failure to plead whether a **contract** is oral, written, or implied by conduct.

        (G) Failure to file a **required certificate** (e.g., for professional negligence claim).

        iii. **Meet and confer:** Before filing a demurrer, the demurring party must **meet and confer** with the party that filed the challenged pleading to try to resolve the issues raised in the demurrer.

     e. **California Additional Motions:** This is done by means of a special appearance and must be made separately from the answer. This motion must be made either **before or concurrently** with the filing of the demurrer or motion to strike or the answer, or the following defenses are deemed waived:

        i. **Quash service of summons for lack of personal jurisdiction:** A defendant must raise personal jurisdiction on or before the last day of their time to plead or it is waived.

        ii. **Dismiss for insufficient process** (something is wrong with the papers).

        iii. **Dismiss for insufficient service of process.**

        iv. **To stay or dismiss** the action on the ground of **inconvenient forum**.

  c. **Answer:** An answer is the defendant's response to the complaint. A defendant must respond within **21 days** after service of process (or within 60 days in the U.S. if service is waived). **California** allows **30 days** to respond.

     1. **The defendant must respond to the allegations** by denying them, admitting them, or stating they lack sufficient information to do either (failure to deny can operate as an admission).

     2. **The defendant must also assert any affirmative defenses** and compulsory counterclaims in the answer and include a signature of the defendant or their attorney.

       a. **California: Fact pleading** requires factual detail regarding each legal element when asserting affirmative defenses.

4. **Amended pleadings**

  a. **Right to Amend**

     1. **Federal:** A plaintiff has a right to **amend once within 21 days of service,** or 21 days after service of a responsive pleading or pre-answer motion. A defendant has a right to amend once within 21 days of serving their answer. Otherwise, a party must get written consent from the opposing party to amend or seek leave of court to amend, which the court will grant freely if justice so requires.

     2. **California:** A plaintiff has a right to **amend once** before the answer, or motion to strike, to the complaint is filed, or after the demurrer is filed but before the hearing on the demurrer. Otherwise, a party can amend upon stipulation by the parties or through leave of court, which the court will typically grant liberally.

  b. **Federal relation back doctrine:** Amends the pleading back to the date of the original filing for purposes of the statute of limitations.

     1. **Amended claims "relate back"** (after the statute of limitations has run) if they concern the same **conduct, transaction, or occurrence** as the original pleading.

     2. **Amended defendants "relate back"** if:

       a. They concern the **same conduct, transaction, or occurrence** as the original complaint,

       b. The **new party knew** of the original action within 90 days of its filing and is not prejudiced in maintaining a defense, and

       c. The new party knew that, but for a mistake, they **would have been named** as a defendant in the original complaint.

  c. **California relation back "Doe" Amendments:** California permits suing a defendant using a fictitious "Doe" designation.

     1. The "Doe" amendment will be permitted if:

       a. The original complaint was timely filed and includes allegations against the "Doe" defendants,

       b. The plaintiff was **genuinely ignorant** of the **identity** of the fictitiously named "Doe" defendant, the **facts giving rise to the cause of action** against that defendant, or the fact that the **law provides a cause of action**, and

       c. Plaintiff's **ignorance is pled with specificity** in the complaint.

2. **The plaintiff must substitute a named defendant** for a "Doe" defendant within **three years** of the filing, and it will "relate back" to the filing date of the original complaint.

> **Exam tip:** Pleadings are not typically tested outright, but Federal Rule 12, motions to strike and dismiss, the sufficiency of notice pleadings, and amendments have been tested in conjunction with other issues. They are not usually the most heavily weighted issues, but you should still practice essays testing these nuanced issues.

B. **Joinder of parties and claims**
  1. **Joinder of parties:**
     a. **Permissive joinder:** Plaintiffs and/or defendants may be joined to an existing case if the claims arise from the **same transaction or occurrence** and raise at least **one common question of fact or law**. However, there still must be **subject matter jurisdiction.**
     b. **Required joinder**
        1. **Definition:** A party is a **necessary party** if:
           a. The court **cannot provide complete relief** without the necessary party; or
           b. The absent party's **interest will be harmed** if they are not joined; or
           c. Existing parties may be **subject to multiple or inconsistent obligations**.
        2. **Join:** A necessary party **must be joined if:**
           a. The court has **personal jurisdiction** over them; and
           b. Joining them **doesn't destroy diversity**, where diversity is the basis of federal subject matter jurisdiction.
        3. **Unable to join:** If a necessary party cannot be joined because of one of the reasons noted above, the court will consider whether the party is indispensable by assessing factors including:
           a. The **prejudice to the parties or absent party**,
           b. Whether the **court can shape relief to lessen the prejudice,**
           c. Whether **judgment would be adequate** without the absent party, and
           d. Whether **plaintiff would have an adequate remedy** if the case was dismissed.
        4. After assessing the factors, the **court may either:**
           a. **Dismiss** the case because the **party is indispensable**; or
           b. **Proceed** with the case without the necessary party.
     c. **Impleader** is a mechanism a **defending party** can use to **add a third-party defendant** in order to seek indemnity, subrogation, or contribution.
        1. **Supplemental jurisdiction will apply** because the claim will meet the "common nucleus of operative fact" requirement and no independent basis for subject matter jurisdiction is required.
        2. **California calls this a cross complaint.**
        3. **Venue need not be proper** for the third-party defendant.
     d. **Intervention** applies when a **nonparty claims an interest** in the property or transaction that is the subject of the pending lawsuit and is **mandatory** (of right) if disposition in their absence will **impair their rights**, or **permissive** if the claim or defense shares a **common question of law or fact** with the main action.
        1. **California** allows intervention if the potential intervener's interest is **direct and immediate** and does not allow intervention if the interest is indirect and consequential.
     e. **Interpleader** is an action where **one holding property** (the stakeholder) forces all potential claimants (people who claim the property) into a **single lawsuit** to avoid multiple and inconsistent litigation. There are two types of interpleader:
        1. **Statutory (Federal):** Requires only that **one claimant must be diverse** from **one other claimant**, the amount in controversy must be **$500** or more, and plaintiff must deposit a bond with the court.
        2. **Federal Rule 22 interpleader:** Requires that the **stakeholder** must be **diverse from every claimant** and the amount in controversy must **exceed $75,000.**

      3. **California:** The stakeholder files a cross complaint and posts a bond in the amount claimed on the contract or property at issue.

  2. **Joinder of claims**

    a. **Counterclaim** is an offensive claim **against an opposing party**.

      1. **There are two types:**

        a. **Compulsory counterclaims** arise from the **same transaction or occurrence** as the plaintiff's claim and **must be raised** in the pending case or the claim is waived.

          i. **Supplemental jurisdiction:** An independent basis for subject matter jurisdiction is not required since supplemental jurisdiction will extend to a compulsory counterclaim.

        b. **Permissive counterclaims** do not arise from the same transaction or occurrence and may be raised in the pending case or in a separate case.

          i. **No supplemental jurisdiction:** A permissive counterclaim must have an independent source of subject matter jurisdiction.

      2. **California uses the term cross complaint** for all third-party actions, such as counterclaims, cross claims, impleader, etc.

    b. **Cross claim** is an offensive claim against a **co-party** and must arise from the **same transaction or occurrence.** Cross claims are never compulsory. (This is called a *cross complaint* in California.)

      1. **Supplemental jurisdiction:** An independent basis for subject matter jurisdiction is not required since supplemental jurisdiction will extend to a cross claim.

    c. **Number of claims: A party** asserting a claim, counterclaim, crossclaim, or third-party claim may join **as many claims as it has** against **an opposing party** (but each claim needs SMJ or Supplemental Jurisdiction).

> **Issue spotting tip:** Where joinder of parties or claims is at issue, also look for issues of personal jurisdiction, subject matter jurisdiction, and/or supplemental jurisdiction.

  C. **Class action** is a case where a **named representative sues on behalf** of a group.

    1. **Federal court class actions**

      a. **Requirements:** A federal class action is proper if the class meets the following requirements:

        1. **Numerosity:** There are too many class members for joinder to be practical;

        2. **Commonality:** The questions of law or fact are common to the class;

        3. **Typicality:** The representative's claims or defenses are typical of those in the class; and

        4. **Adequacy of representation** such that it will fairly represent the class.

      b. **Type of class:** The class must also fit within one of the following types of classes:

        1. **Prejudice:** Class treatment is necessary to avoid inconsistent results or member interests will be prejudiced (impaired or impeded); or

        2. **Injunctive or declaratory relief is sought** (e.g., employment discrimination); or

        3. **Damages are sought** but **questions of law/fact common to the class predominate** over questions affecting individuals, and a class action is a **superior method** to resolve the issues (e.g., damages for a mass tort). One can opt out of a damages class (unlike other classes).

      c. **Federal class action citizenship issues**

        1. **Diversity action:** To determine citizenship for class actions based on diversity, only the **citizenship of the named representative(s)** is taken into account, and the over-$75,000 **amount in controversy requirement can be satisfied by any named class representative.**

        2. **Class Action Fairness Act** (2005) relaxes the federal jurisdiction requirements for some class actions. It applies where there isn't complete diversity and allows a federal court to hear a class action if the following requirements are met:

          a. **Diversity: Any class member** is diverse from **any defendant; and**

          b. **Aggregation:** The class claims aggregate to exceed **$5 million; and** *c.* **100 members:** There are at least 100 proposed class members.

  2. **California class actions**

    a. A **California class action** is allowed if there is

      1. An **ascertainable class**; and

      2. A **well-defined community of interest** among class members. To analyze this interest the court looks at whether:

        a. **Common questions of law or fact** predominate;

        b. The **representative** will **adequately represent the class interests**; and

        c. The class will result in **substantial benefit** to the parties and the court (superiority).

    b. **Type of class:** In California there is only **one type of class** and distinctions are not made based on the purpose the class serves as in federal court.

    c. **Notice:** Individual notice is not required and publication is an acceptable method of notice.

D. Discovery

  1. **Discovery disclosure** requirements

    a. **Federal Rule 26 requires the mandatory disclosure** of information about the pending case to the opposing party. There are three types of mandatory disclosures:

      1. **Initial disclosures** that supply information about disputed facts, including:

        a. Identifying **those likely to have discoverable information** that the disclosing party may use to support their claim or defense;

        b. Copies or description of **tangible evidence** such as documents that the disclosing party may use to support their claim or defense;

        c. A **damages computation** and supporting documentation; and

        d. Copies of applicable **insurance documents.**

      2. **Expert testimony** information for experts who will be used at trial, including:

        a. **Identity** of the expert,

        b. The expert's **qualifications,** and

        c. The expert's **final written report** (which includes opinions, facts, exhibits, cases testified in, compensation, list of publications).

      3. **Pretrial disclosures,** including a list of all nonexpert **witnesses, witness testimony** (i.e., depositions), and a list of **documents** or exhibits.

    b. **California requires disclosure** of the same initial disclosures as the federal rules within 60 days of a demand by any party to the action (for all cases filed after 1/1/24).

  2. **Discovery tools**

    a. **Depositions:** An **examination of a witness** that occurs under oath and is recorded by sound, video, or stenography. Questions can be oral or written but the answers are oral.

      1. **Parties** can be deposed and **nonparties** can be deposed by means of a subpoena.

      2. **Once only:** A person may not be deposed twice without court approval.

      3. **Limits**

        a. **Federal** rules permit only **ten depositions** per side and the deposition cannot exceed one 7-hour day unless the court orders otherwise.

        b. **California** has no limits as to the number of depositions in unlimited cases.

        c. **Experts employed only for trial preparation** that are not expected to be called at trial **may not be deposed,** unless there are exceptional circumstances.

    b. **Interrogatories:** Questions propounded **in writing** to another **party**, which must be answered in writing under oath and the responding party must respond within 30 days. Interrogatories **may not be asked of nonparties.**

      1. **Limits**

        a. **Federal** rules permit no more than **25 questions**, including subparts, unless the court orders otherwise.

        b. **California** allows an **unlimited number of form interrogatories** and a maximum of **35 specific interrogatories in unlimited cases**, unless a court permits additional ones.

        c. Interrogatories cannot be used to obtain **facts or opinions held by experts** employed **only for trial preparation** that are not expected to be called at trial, unless there are exceptional circumstances.

2. **Objections:** Grounds for objecting must be stated with **specificity** and signed by the attorney. Any ground not stated timely is **waived** unless the court, for good cause, excuses it.

c. **Requests for admissions** request another **party** to admit the truth of any discoverable matter. The purpose is to identify areas that are not in controversy. Requests for admission may not be asked of nonparties.

   1. **California** allows a **maximum of 35** requests for admission in unlimited cases, unless a court permits additional requests.

d. **Requests to inspect and produce**

   1. **Federal:** Any party may request another **party**, or a **nonparty** with subpoena, to make available for review and copying documents, electronic copies, or other tangible items, or permit entry onto property.

   2. **California allows for a party** to make requests to inspect and produce on another party, but **not for a nonparty.** However, the same result could be accomplished by taking the nonparty's deposition and serving a subpoena duces tecum.

e. **Electronically stored data:** Parties must **meet to discuss** the discovery and preservation of electronically stored data and report back to the court. If such data is not **reasonably accessible** because of burden and cost, the court may still order production and impose **cost-sharing measures**.

   1. **Preservation:** Parties must take **reasonable steps** to preserve electronically stored information when litigation is reasonably foreseeable or be **sanctioned**.

f. **Request for physical or mental examination** of a **party** may be sought by an opposing party. A party requesting such an independent exam must obtain a **court order** upon a showing that the **physical or mental condition of the party is at issue,** and there is **good cause for an examination.**

   1. **California** allows the defendant to have **one physical exam** of the plaintiff as a right when the plaintiff's physical condition is at issue. Other physical or mental examinations require **leave of the court**. The attorney for the party being examined can attend the physical exam.

g. **California limited cases have limited discovery** and only allow each party a 35 maximum total for all interrogatories, inspection demands, and requests combined.

h. **Timing:** Parties cannot seek discovery until **after the Federal Rule 26 discovery conference** (except for requests to produce documents). **California** requires parties to meet and confer before they have a case management conference.

3. **Scope of discovery**

a. **Need not be admissible: Relevant** materials can be discovered even if not admissible so long as the item is **reasonably calculated to lead to the discovery of admissible evidence**.

   1. Must be **proportional** to the needs of the case and not unduly cumulative or burdensome.

b. **Privileged material is not discoverable** (see Evidence chapter for common privileges).

   1. A party must **expressly claim** the material is privileged **and describe** the nature of the documents, communications, or tangible things not produced or disclosed.

    a. **Privilege log:** Parties must also provide the court with a privilege log with all necessary communications and documents with dates, names, subject matter, etc.

c. **Attorney work product is not generally discoverable.**

   1. **General rule:** Work product is material **prepared in anticipation of litigation** and is generally not discoverable **unless** there is **substantial need** and the **inability to obtain** the information through other means or it was a **previous written statement** previously adopted by the person.

   2. **Absolute privilege** applies to **mental impressions**, opinions, conclusions, and legal theories.

    a. **Federal:** Applies if generated by a **party** or **attorney** or **representative** of a party.

    b. **California:** Applies only if generated by an **attorney** or their **agent**.

d. **California Constitution recognizes a right of privacy**, which is balanced against the need for discovery.

4. **Discovery disputes:** Where there are disputes, the parties must **first meet and confer** before seeking a **motion to compel** or protective order. Noncompliance can result in sanctions.

5. **Sanctions:** For violations of discovery, sanctions may be imposed including holding a noncomplying party in **contempt, striking pleadings, imposing fees, and ordering default judgment.**

> **Exam tip:** Essays testing discovery rules can be quite complicated because they test nuanced rules that require memorization. These types of essays tend to test your ability to issue spot and recall the rules rather than your ability to analyze rules.

III. **DISPOSITION OF A CASE WITHOUT A TRIAL:** Sometimes a case will be resolved prior to the end of the trial.

A. **Dismissal**
   1. **Voluntary dismissal:** A plaintiff may obtain **one** voluntary dismissal without prejudice (so it may be relitigated) before defendant files their answer or motion for summary judgment (MSJ), or if all parties agree. The trial court has discretion to grant a dismissal after an answer or MSJ is filed, unless substantial prejudice to the defendant would occur.
   2. **Involuntary dismissal:** The court may do this at the defendant's request, or at the court's own discretion. Such a dismissal is usually with prejudice, so it may not be relitigated.
   3. **Dismissal for failure to state a claim** occurs in a situation where if the court assumes all allegations are true, the plaintiff still cannot win based on the face of the complaint.
      a. **California:** This is a general demurrer.
   4. **California mandatory dismissal** occurs if the case is not brought to trial within five years of filing the complaint.
   5. **California permissive dismissal** occurs if service is not made within two years after the action is commenced or the action is not brought within three years after commencement.

B. **Default judgment** can occur if the defendant fails to respond within **21 days** after service federally (60 days if service waived in the U.S.), or **30 days** of service in California. Plaintiff must request the **court clerk** to enter default before requesting the **court** to enter default **judgment**.

C. **Motion for summary judgment** (MSJ) will be ordered where the moving party can establish there is **no genuine dispute of material fact and that they are entitled to judgment as a matter of law.**
   1. Evidence must be capable of presentation in **admissible form.**
   2. Evidence viewed in **light most favorable to the nonmoving party.**
   3. Evidence must be comprised of **firsthand knowledge** and **credibility is not weighed.**
   4. A **court can grant a partial** summary judgment as to one of several causes of action and can raise a MSJ on its own.

> **Exam tip:** Civil procedure essay exams will often phrase a call by asking if a party is entitled to a MSJ, or if a party's motion to dismiss (MTD) should be granted. This is almost always a method employed to ask about the underlying procedural issues present in the question, such as jurisdiction or res judicata. Keep in mind that a MTD only looks at the complaint (well-pleaded facts) whereas a MSJ looks at all admissible evidence in the record.

IV. **TRIAL**
   A. **Right to a jury trial**
      1. **Federal Seventh Amendment:** In federal court, the Seventh Amendment preserves the **right to a jury in civil actions at law**; however, a **judge decides issues of equity.**
         a. **Legal issues first, then equitable:** If a case has both legal and equitable claims, the jury decides the factual legal issues first, then the judge determines the equity claim.
         b. **Demand for jury:** Plaintiff must **demand in writing no later than 14 days** after service of the last pleading that they are raising a jury triable issue and demands a jury trial, or it is waived.

c. **Jury composition**
1. **Each side** (not party, as in California) has **unlimited** challenges on voir dire for **cause** (bias, prejudice, related to a party), and **three peremptory** challenges (still must be used in a gender and race-neutral way).
2. A jury may contain **6-12 jurors** with no alternates; and a **unanimous vote** is required.

2. **California:** The California Constitution grants a right to a jury trial. The demand for a jury must be made at the time the case is set for trial, or within five days after notice of setting.
   a. **Equity issues first, then legal:** *Unlike in federal court*, if a case has both legal and equitable claims, the judge decides the equitable issues first, then the jury decides the legal issues.
   b. **Equitable clean-up doctrine:** Where the main purpose of a case is equitable, and the only legal issue concerns damages that are merely incidental, then the judge may hear the whole case, and a jury is not required.
   c. **Jury composition**
      1. **Each party** (not each side, as in federal court) is entitled to **unlimited** challenges for **cause** (bias, prejudice, related to a party) and **six peremptory** challenges (cannot be based on race, ethnicity, gender, gender identity, sexual orientation, national origin, religious affiliation, etc.—CA has broad protection). If there are more than two parties, then each side will have eight peremptory challenges.
      2. A jury contains **12 jurors** and alternates; and only a **three-quarters juror vote** is required (civil cases only; for criminal cases a unanimous verdict is required).

B. **Judgment as a matter of law (JMOL)** occurs when one party files a motion after the other side has been heard at trial (so a defendant can usually move twice), contending that **reasonable people could not disagree on the result,** and asks for a judgment as a matter of law. Essentially this serves to take the case away from the jury.
   1. **California-directed verdict:** This is called a motion for a **directed verdict** or a **demurrer** to the evidence in California court.

> **Exam tip:** Civil procedure essays may ask if a party is entitled to a JMOL as a mechanism to ask about the underlying substantive claim, such as a tort.

V. POST-TRIAL ISSUES

A. **Renewed judgment as a matter of law (RJMOL)** occurs after the jury has reached a verdict, contending that **reasonable people could not disagree on the result,** and asks for a judgment as a matter of law. **The losing party must have originally filed a JMOL** or they cannot later file a RJMOL since it is a *renewal* of the earlier motion.
   1. **Timing**
      a. **Federal:** The motion must be made within **28 days** after entry of judgment.
      b. **California:** The motion must be made within **15 days** after mailing or service of notice of entry of judgment, or 180 days after the entry of the judgment, whichever is earliest.
   2. **California — Motion for judgment notwithstanding the verdict (JNOV):** This is called a *motion for judgment notwithstanding the verdict* (JNOV), and unlike in federal court, the losing party is **not required to make a directed verdict motion first** in order to make the JNOV motion.

B. **Motion for a new trial:** After judgment has been entered, the losing party requests a new trial based on errors made at trial. This can also be filed with a RJMOL as an alternative.
   1. **Timing**
      a. **Federal:** The motion must be made within **28 days** after entry of judgment.
      b. **California:** The motion must be made within **15 days** after mailing or service of notice of entry of judgment, or 180 days after the entry of the judgment.
   2. **Grounds for a new trial include the following:**
      a. **Prejudicial/plain error** at trial that makes the judgment unfair.
      b. **New evidence** that could not have been obtained for the original trial through due diligence.
      c. **Prejudicial misconduct** of a party, attorney, third-party, or juror.

    d. Judgment is **against the weight of the evidence.**

    e. **Excessive damages or inadequate damages**.

C. **Motion to set aside (seek relief from) the judgment** can be based on:

    1. **Clerical errors;**

    2. **Neglectful mistakes;**

    3. **Newly discovered evidence** that could not reasonably be discovered for the original trial;

    4. **Fraud,** misrepresentation, or other misconduct of a party;

    5. **Judgment is void or has been satisfied**; or

    6. **Any other reason that justifies relief**.

    7. **Timing:** A motion to set aside a judgment based on fraud, neglectful mistakes, or newly discovered evidence may not be brought **more than one year** after the judgment. Other reasons must be brought within a reasonable time.

D. **Conditional new trial on damages only: remittitur and additur**

    1. **Remittitur** occurs when a judge orders that a new trial for the defendant will take place unless the **plaintiff agrees to a reduced award** of damages because the judge finds that the damages awarded by the jury were **so excessive as to shock the conscience.**

    2. **Additur** occurs when a judge orders that the plaintiff will get a new trial unless the **defendant agrees to an increased award** of damages because the judge finds the damages awarded by the jury were insufficient.

        a. **Federal:** Additur is **not permitted in federal** court.

        b. **California:** Additur is **permitted in California** courts.

VI. APPEAL

A. **Final judgment rule**

    1. **Final judgment rule:** Only final judgments may be appealed. A final judgment is an ultimate decision made by the trial court on the merits of an entire case such that there is a final judgment as to all parties and all causes of action.

        a. **Motion to remand:** An order remanding a case to State court is **not reviewable on appeal** with limited exceptions for cases against federal officers or agencies and civil rights cases.

    2. **Exceptions to the final judgment rule:** Despite the rule, the following orders may be appealed before a final judgment:

        a. **Injunctions and some interlocutory orders.**

        b. **Trial court certifies** an interlocutory order for appeal.

        c. **Collateral orders**, such as those regarding procedural issues.

        d. **Multiple claims or parties** are involved in the case and some issues are pending, but the issue is resolved as to one claim or party and the judge expressly determines that the order as to that party is final.

            1. **California:** A judgment as to **one of several parties is considered a final judgment** and can be appealed. *Unlike the federal rule,* an express determination is not required.

        e. **Extraordinary writ:** If an order is not otherwise appealable and the circumstances are exceptional, the aggrieved party may seek a writ of mandate to compel the lower court to act, or refrain from acting.

        f. **Certification of class actions.**

B. **Time limits for appeals**

    1. **Federal:** Must file notice of appeal within **30 days** after entry of final judgment or an appealable order.

    2. **California:** Must file notice of appeal within **60 days** after service of notice of entry of judgment; **or 180 days** after entry of the judgment if no notice is served.

C. **Standards of Review**

    1. **Matters of law are reviewed de novo**, which means the appellate court can substitute its judgment for that of the trial judge.

    2. **Questions of fact determined by a judge** are reviewed using a **clearly erroneous** standard. **Questions of fact determined by a jury** are reviewed using the even more deferential standard

of viewing the finding of fact in a **light most favorable to affirming the jury's verdict**, and determining whether a reasonable jury could have **reached the same conclusion**.

3. **Mixed questions of fact and law are often reviewed de novo,** which means the appellate court can substitute its judgment for that of the trial judge.
4. **Matters discretionary to the judge** are reviewed using an **abuse of discretion** standard, which means such matters will only be overturned if clearly wrong.
5. **Harmless error** will be found when a trial court's erroneous admission of evidence did not affect any party's substantial rights.

VII. **USE OF FINAL JUDGMENT:** Where a claim or issue has already been resolved by litigation the matter may be barred from being relitigated.

  A. **Res judicata (claim preclusion) precludes relitigation** of a **claim** that has **already been decided in prior litigation** between the same parties. A subsequent suit based on the same claim will be barred where the first claim meets the following requirements:

    1. There is a **valid final judgment on the merits**.
      a. **Federal:** A judgment is **final** when the judgment is **rendered.**
      b. **California:** A judgment is **final** when the **appeals have concluded.**
      c. **Valid** occurs when all **jurisdictional** requirements are met.
      d. **On the merits** is when the judgment was entered in favor of the claimant (i.e., jury verdict, summary judgment, default judgment, etc.).

> **Issue spotting tip:** Look for facts such as a prior judgment that was not based on the merits, but based on failure to join a party, jurisdiction, default judgment, consent, etc.

    2. The **same plaintiff and same defendant** were parties (or privies) in the prior case and subsequent case in the same order (i.e., P v. D in the first case and second case).
      a. A **privy** is a successor in interest to the property or claim, or is a representative (e.g., trustee) of the party.
      b. **"Strangers"** to the prior litigation cannot be bound under res judicata.
    3. The **same claim** (cause of action) is asserted in the prior case and the subsequent case.
      a. **Federal:** All legal theories arising from the **same transaction or occurrence are the same claim.**
      b. **California follows the primary rights theory,** which allows a **separate cause of action** for the invasion of each primary right. Thus, a plaintiff may sue separately for personal injury and property damage, even if both occurred from the same transaction or occurrence, since under the primary rights theory they are not considered the "same claim." (E.g., a single car accident causing both property damage and personal injury would implicate two different primary rights.)

  B. **Collateral estoppel (issue preclusion) precludes relitigation** of a particular **issue** that has **already been decided in prior litigation**. A subsequent suit based on the same issue will be barred where the first claim meets the following requirements:

    1. There is a **valid final judgment on the merits**.
      a. **Federal:** A judgment is final when the judgment is **rendered.**
      b. **California:** A judgment is final when the **appeals have concluded.**
      c. **Valid** occurs when all **jurisdictional** requirements are met.
      d. **On the merits** is when the judgment was entered in favor of the claimant (i.e., jury verdict, summary judgment, default judgment, etc.).
    2. The **same issue** was **actually litigated and determined.**

> **Issue spotting tip:** Look for facts such as that the underlying court heard "extensive evidence."

3. The **issue was necessary (essential to the judgment)** in the first case.

> <u>**Necessary/essential to the judgment fact triggers (this can be tricky to spot):**</u>
>
> - Underlying court finds plaintiff didn't own the property in dispute, but finds defendant was not negligent anyways.
> - Underlying court finds doctor is not an agent of the hospital being sued, but finds on negligence issue anyway.
> - Look for facts that seem peripheral to a judgment.
> - Look for specific findings for the underlying judgment.

4. **Collateral estoppel can be used only** *against* someone who was a **party (or in privity with a party) in the prior suit** in the interest of fairness (so they have an opportunity to defend the action).
5. **Collateral estoppel can only be used** *by*:
    1. **Traditionally the rule of mutuality applied** and a party asserting collateral estoppel had to be a party (or a privy) in the prior case to assert collateral estoppel in the subsequent case. Thus, a "stranger" to the first case could not use a prior judgment.
    2. **California** (and other jurisdictions where the mutuality rule is not employed) **allows a "stranger" to the prior case to rely** on a prior judgment if doing so is "fair."
        a. **Defensive use** of prior litigation *to avoid liability* in a subsequent suit will be allowed where the party against whom collateral estoppel is being asserted had a **fair opportunity to be heard on the critical issue** in the prior case.
        b. **Offensive use** of prior litigation *to establish an issue* in a subsequent suit is disfavored and will be allowed only when it **is fair and equitable**, and the **new party could not have easily joined** in the first case (courts have broad discretion).

> **<u>Issue spotting tip:</u>** If a fact pattern includes a prior judgment or lawsuit, look for res judicata and/or collateral estoppel.

> **<u>Exam tip:</u>** Understand res judicata and collateral estoppel since both are very frequently tested on the essay exam. Some questions will test both principles at once, while others will test one or the other. Some questions will test the principles as they apply to different parties involved in the litigation. Be sure to apply the facts to the general rule and to the California rule distinctions (which is also a minority rule in other jurisdictions, so address this minority rule even if CA law is not specifically asked about), which will often lead to a different result.

CIVIL PROCEDURE ISSUES TESTED MATRIX

Date	Cal or Fed		Crossover	Personal Jx / Service of Process	Subject Matter Jx	Supplemental Jx	Removal & Remand	Venue	Choice of Law (Erie & Cal.)	Pleadings	Joinder of Parties	Joinder of Claims	Class Action	Discovery	Without Trial (Default, MSJ, Dismissal)	Trial (Jury/JMOL)	Post-Trial (New Trial/FJR/Appeal)	Res Judicata	Collateral Estoppel
July '24 Q4	Cal	Palma sues Motor and some jurors have connections to Motor														X	X		
February '23 Q1	Fed	Pam crashed after DuraTires installed by M						X			X			X					
July '21 Q1	Fed	Jiff (CA), Shearer (NV); Jiff breaks vase cleaning																X	X
July '19 Q1	Fed	Priscilla injured at Grocery; interrogatories & discovery												X					
February '19 Q4	Fed	Dave in CA; Petra in NV; water tank leak dispute	Evidence		X														
July '17 Q4	Fed	Buyer NY; seller CA; contract for Rothko painting and CA property			X	X			X	X		X				X			
July '16 Q1	Cal	Paul, from Mexico, sues snack Co. in Germany		X	X		X	X											
July '15 Q1	Fed	Patient sues Dr. and Valvco for defective heart valve		X	X		X											X	X
February '15 Q3	Fed	Diana hit Phil, court orders mental/physical exams							X	X				X		X		X	X
February '14 Q3	Fed	Paul sues hotel for wrongful termination			X		X										X		
February '13 Q5	Fed	Pat sues Devon Co. for releasing toxic chemicals								X				X					

Continued>

	Cal or Fed	Crossover	Personal Jx / Service of Process	Subject Matter Jx	Supplemental Jx	Removal & Remand	Venue	Choice of Law (Erie & Cal.)	Pleadings	Joinder of Parties	Joinder of Claims	Class Action	Discovery	Without Trial (Default, MSJ, Dismissal)	Trial (Jury/JMOL)	Post-Trial (New Trial/FJR/Appeal)	Res Judicata	Collateral Estoppel
July '12 Q1 — Pam and Pat hit by truck owned by Canadian Co.	Fed		X	X	X													
July '11 Q2 — Dr. performs spine surgery with metal rod on Perry	Fed	Evidence												X			X	X
July '09 Q5 — Diane builds dam for camp for disadvantaged kids	Fed	Remedies Prof. Resp.															X	
July '09 Q1 — Patty transports human organs, David blocks bridge	Fed	Torts							X									
February '09 Q2 — Copyco. in state A, Sally in state B injures her hand	Fed		X	X			X		X				X					
February '06 Q4 — Pat & Ed v. Busco, tour bus trip of State C	Fed		X														X	X
February '04 Q6 — Paul v. Tom, Danco employee & car accident	Fed		X	X	X					X	X							
February '03 Q1 — Petra v. Dave & Kola over patented bottle cap	Fed		X	X		X										X		
February '02 Q1 — Pam v. Danco, breach of k for paper goods	Fed			X		X	X								X			
July '01 Q1 — Pam v. Don's Market & Rita for car accident	Fed			X												X	X	
July '00 Q5 — Paul v. Bigcorp & Amcorp power saw accident	Fed		X	X						X							X	

CIVIL PROCEDURE PRACTICE ESSAYS, ANSWER GRIDS, AND SAMPLE ANSWERS

Civil Procedure Question 1
February 2023, Question 1

DuraTires manufactures and installs specially coated tires. DuraTires advertised that a scientific report declared that its tires will not go flat for the first 7,000 miles of use if driven properly. DuraTires' scientific report was created at the direction of its legal counsel and contained research on flat tire incidents involving DuraTires.

Pam purchased four new tires from DuraTires and had them installed by Maurice, a mechanic. Pam drove 100 miles and one tire went flat, causing Pam to swerve and crash into another car. Pam was not physically injured in the accident. Pam gathered a written statement from the other driver, Wynne, who suffered a minor injury. Wynne's statement was favorable to Pam's case.

Pam filed and properly served a complaint in federal court against DuraTires for breach of warranty and negligent installation and manufacture of the tires. The federal court had proper jurisdiction over Pam's complaint. Pam alleged that she suffered property damage and emotional distress as a result of the accident.

DuraTires filed a motion to dismiss for failure to join Maurice as a defendant. The court denied DuraTires' motion. DuraTires filed and properly served an answer to Pam's complaint.

Pam served her initial disclosures on DuraTires, but did not produce Wynne's statement. DuraTires filed and served motions to compel Pam to produce Wynne's statement and for Pam to submit to a physical examination. The court granted both of DuraTires' motions.

DuraTires served its initial disclosures, but did not include the advertised scientific report. Pam met and conferred with DuraTires, which refused to produce its scientific report. Pam filed a motion to compel DuraTires to produce its scientific report. The court granted Pam's motion and ordered DuraTires to produce its scientific report.

1. Did the court properly deny DuraTires' motion to dismiss? Discuss.

2. Did the court properly grant DuraTires' motions:

   A. To compel production of the statement from Wynne? Discuss.

   B. To compel a physical examination of Pam? Discuss.

3. Did the court properly order DuraTires to produce its scientific report? Discuss.

Civil Procedure Question 1 Assessment
February 2023, Question 1

The first call of this essay is typical of how many civil procedure questions test issues that are not readily identifiable in the call of the question. The bar examiners use motions to dismiss or motions for summary judgment to test other issues. When there is a call that asks whether a court should grant or deny (or if the court was correct in its decision) involving a motion to dismiss, the first thing you should do is look at the facts to see what the motion to dismiss was based on. Here, a quick glance shows you that the motion to dismiss was based on the "failure to join Maurice as a defendant." This tells you the issue is about required joinder since you know that failure to join a required party is one of the mechanisms to dismiss a case under Rule 12.

The other calls are all very specific — compel production of a statement (discovery), compel a physical examination (discovery), and produce a scientific report (discovery). The good news is all issues are specific, so you don't need to issue spot. The not as good news is that essays with very specific calls often require you to regurgitate very specific and often nuanced rules. So, passing essays like this one that focus on nuanced discovery rules is going to focus more on your rule memorization as opposed to issue spotting or in-depth analysis. Recent bar exams, especially in Civil Procedure, have more frequently been asking very specific calls in nuanced areas that were previously not as heavily tested.

In particular, discovery was rarely tested on older bar exam essays. Recently, the examiners have tested discovery several times and at a micro level in terms of knowing the rules. However, you need to know all these nuanced rules for the multiple-choice portion of the bar exam anyway, so you should be able to recall the rules being tested. And in terms of your score and weighting of issues, it is likely that the joinder issue is worth more than each individual discovery issue since required joinder has a multi-step rule and requires more factual analysis than the discovery rules they tested.

If you can't remember the specifics of some nuanced discovery rules, use your common sense and think about the big picture. The point of discovery is to ensure both sides have access to evidence to enable the efficient exchange of information to better understand the opponent's claims and defenses. This process helps expedite cases and often leads parties to attempt to negotiate and settle without going to a full trial, which is costly for all parties. Thus, if you could not remember what the exact rule for producing a statement or report or what was required for a party to request a physical examination, come up with a fair logical rule about what you think it should be and run with it. We can all agree that it is likely more difficult to have a person submit to a physical examination as opposed to turning over a statement. It is this type of critical thinking that will make you a good lawyer and what the bar examiners are often looking for. And remember, if you adequately studied and organized (not necessarily wrote out) numerous practice essays, then most essays you will encounter on the actual bar exam should contain some issues that are not new to you. And if there is an issue that entirely new to you, it is likely it is entirely new to most others in the room as well. So be confident, think logically, and answer the call of the question. Don't let your mind get the best of you — you know this!

Make note of the areas highlighted in **bold** on the corresponding grid. The bold areas highlight the issues, analysis, and conclusions that are likely **required** to receive a passing score on this question.

Issue	Rule	Fact Application	Conclusion
1. Did the court properly deny DuraTires' motion to dismiss (for failure to join Maurice as a defendant)?			
Required Joinder	A party is **necessary** if: • The court **cannot provide complete relief** w/o them • **Absent party's interest will be harmed** if not joined • **Existing parties may be subject to multiple or inconsistent obligations** **Joint tortfeasors are not necessary parties.** A necessary party must be joined if: • The court has PJ over the person • Joining them doesn't destroy diversity (if no fed. question) Unable to join — **see if party is indispensable**, the court will consider: • **Prejudice to all involved** • **Ability to lessen prejudice** • If judgment would be adequate w/o person • If P would have an adequate remedy if case dismissed Court then will dismiss the case if party is indispensable or proceed without the necessary party if not indispensable.	Although M installed the tires and P's complaint alleged negligent installation as one of the claims, DT is also liable as they manufactured the tires and if M worked for them as a mechanic, then joint and several liability exists. DT manufactured the tires so even if M improperly installed them, it can still be held liable and provide P relief with or without M, as it can sue M later and DT is liable for the warranty that the tires would last 7,000 miles. **M's interest won't be harmed as he can defend himself against DT later if they seek indemnification.** DT will not be subject to multiple or inconsistent obligations as it is a single suit involving one incident. Jx proper per facts; not clear where M is from so not clear if he would destroy diversity, but he isn't necessary anyway. None of the parties will be prejudiced if M not joined as discussed above so no need for the court to lessen the prejudice. Judgment adequate w/o M b/c P can fully recover from DT, but even if the case is dismissed P could sue in state court.	**Maurice is not a required party, so the court properly denied DuraTires' motion to dismiss.**
2a. Did the court properly grant DuraTires' motion to compel production of the statement from Wynne?			
Scope of Discoverable Evidence	**Must be relevant, not privileged, not work product, and proportional to the needs of the case.** **Need not be admissible but reasonably calculated to lead to the discovery of admissible material.**	**W's statement was favorable to P's case, so it supported her claim, which indicates it would be relevant to her claim.** **W was also injured, so her statement is likely relevant to her possible claims and defenses that could arise as well** since she was the other driver in the accident with P and may seek recovery from P. **There is no undue burden or cumulative effect** of producing a single statement that P already obtained, **so it would be proportional to the needs of a personal injury case.**	**Wynne's statement is relevant and proportional,** not privileged and not work product.

Continued>

Issue	Rule	Fact Application	Conclusion
Scope of Discoverable Evidence (continued)		W's statement is also likely admissible as W could take the stand or it could be present sense impression or prior statement. W's statement is not privileged and not work product as there were no attorneys involved and it appears to be a statement that P gathered at the accident.	
Mandatory Initial Disclosures	Parties must disclose: • Identities of those likely to have discoverable info that may support their claim/defense; • Copies or descriptions of tangible evidence that may support their claim/defense; • Damages computation and supporting documentation; • Applicable insurance documents. Parties must meet and confer when there are discovery disputes prior to seeking a motion to compel.	Since W was the other driver in the car accident with P and W was injured, and her statement was favorable to P's case, P should have disclosed it initially. DT did not meet and confer with P before seeking a motion to compel as required so the court should not grant their motion.	The court erred by compelling Pam to produce Wynne's statement because DuraTires did not meet and confer first (but Pam should have disclosed it initially under the mandatory disclosures and courts do have a lot of latitude in discovery).

2b. Did the court properly grant DuraTires' motion to compel a physical examination of Pam?

Issue	Rule	Fact Application	Conclusion
Physical Examination of a Party	A party requesting a physical examination of another party must obtain a court order upon a showing that the physical condition of the party is at issue, and there is good cause for an examination.	Here, P was not physically injured in the accident and is not seeking damages for any physical injury, so her physical condition is not at issue. Rather, P is seeking property damage and emotional distress damages, so there is no good cause for a physical examination. While P's mental health is at issue since she is seeking emotional distress damages, that would require a mental examination, not a physical examination.	The court erred in granting DuraTires' motion to compel Pam to submit to a physical examination.

Continued>

Issue	Rule	Fact Application	Conclusion
3. Did the court properly order DuraTires to produce its scientific report?			
Scope of Discoverable Evidence	**See above for rule.** **Attorney client privilege protects communications between an attorney and client made for the purpose of obtaining legal advice.** **Work product is material prepared in anticipation of litigation and is generally not discoverable unless there is substantial need and the inability to obtain the info otherwise. Mental impressions and opinions are never discoverable.**	DT scientific report is relevant to P's case because her tire went flat after 100 miles when the report indicated the tires would not go flat the first 7,000 miles, which helps prove her breach of warranty claim. It is also proportional to the case as it is only one report and does not cause an undue burden to disclose it. It is not privileged as it is not a communication between a lawyer and client even though legal counsel directed the report to be created. Also, they advertised the results of the report so arguably they would have waived the privilege if it did apply. DT may try to argue that the report was work product as legal counsel had it prepared in anticipation of a possible future accident. However, it does not appear that the report was created in anticipation of litigation, as there were no pending lawsuits at the time and DT disclosed the contents of the report in an effort to advertise and gain customers, so it seems it was used more for marketing purposes. Also, the report information about flat tire accidents is likely info that P would have a substantial need for due to her accident and it is unlikely she can obtain it elsewhere as it would be unreasonably burdensome for her to do independent research on flat tires.	The court properly ordered DuraTires to produce its scientific report.
Mandatory Disclosures	**See above for rule for initial disclosures.** **Expert testimony disclosure is mandatory if the expert will testify at trial and only their final reports must be turned over to the other side. Final reports must contain the expert's opinions and facts that it used to reach its conclusions.**	DT scientific report will not likely be used to support its defenses because it doesn't support their case as P's tire went flat after 100 miles when the report indicated the tires would not go flat the first 7,000 miles. However, P could argue that it will be used to support DT defense as they could claim that P wasn't driving properly as is required under the report. Also, P did meet and confer with DT first before filing her motion to compel. Here the report itself is at issue and it is not clear that DT will call the expert who generated the report to testify, but if they do then they will have to provide a final report which would contain the data it used to make its determinations, so P would get the information that way too.	The court properly ordered DuraTires to produce its scientific report.

Civil Procedure Question 1 Sample Answer
February 2023, Question 1

1. DuraTires' motion to dismiss for failure to join Maurice

A party can file a motion to dismiss for failure to join a required party. To determine if the court will dismiss the case, it must determine whether the party is necessary, jurisdiction is proper, and if the party is indispensable if the court is unable to join them.

Necessary

A party is necessary if the court cannot provide complete relief without them, the absent party's interest will be harmed if not joined, or existing parties may be subject to multiple or inconsistent obligations if the absent party is not joined. Joint tortfeasors who are jointly and severally liable are not considered necessary parties.

Here, although Maurice installed the tires and Pam's complaint alleged negligent installation as one of the claims, DuraTires is also liable as they manufactured the tires and issued the warranty for the tires, which are also claims asserted by Pam, so joint and several liability likely exists. And if Maurice worked for DuraTires as a mechanic for that company, then joint and several liability exists in that capacity as well. Further, since DuraTires manufactured the tires, even if Maurice improperly installed them, it can still be held liable and provide Pam relief with or without Maurice as it can sue Maurice later and DuraTires is liable for the warranty that the tires would last 7,000 miles.

Next, Maurice's interest will not be harmed if he is not joined because he can defend himself against DuraTires later if they seek indemnification or contribution in a separate lawsuit.

Finally, DuraTires will not be subject to multiple or inconsistent obligations as Pam filed a single suit involving one incident.

Thus, it is unlikely that Maurice is a necessary party.

Jurisdictional Requirements

A necessary party must be joined if the court has personal jurisdiction over the person and joining them does not destroy diversity if subject matter jurisdiction is based on diversity.

In the event there is not joint and several liability and Maurice is necessary, then Maurice would need to be from a different state from Pam since the claim is not based on federal law. The facts aren't clear as to which jurisdictions the parties are from.

Indispensable

If a party is unable to join due to jurisdictional issues, the court will determine if the party is indispensable by considering the prejudice to existing parties or the absent party, whether the court can shape relief to lessen the prejudice, whether the judgment would be adequate without the absent person, and whether plaintiff would have an adequate remedy if the case was dismissed. Based on these factors, the court will then either dismiss the case if the party is indispensable or proceed without the necessary party if not indispensable.

While it is likely that Maurice is not necessary, if he was, then none of the parties involved will be prejudiced if Maurice is not joined as discussed above so there would be no need for the court to shape alternative relief to lessen the prejudice. Further, judgment would be adequate without Maurice because Pam can fully recover from DuraTires alone and it can seek indemnification or contribution from Maurice in a separate lawsuit. And even if the case is dismissed Pam could sue in state court.

Overall, Maurice is not a required party, so the court properly denied DuraTires' motion to dismiss.

2(a). Motion to Compel Wynne's Statement

Scope of Discoverable Evidence

For discovery purposes, evidence must be relevant, not privileged, not work product, and proportional to the needs of the case. The evidence does not need to be admissible as long as it is reasonably calculated to lead to the discovery of admissible material.

Here, Wynne's statement was favorable to Pam's case so it supported her claims which indicates it would be relevant to her claims as it would help prove the tires were defective. Wynne was also injured so her statement is likely relevant to her possible claims and defenses that could arise as well, since she was the other driver in the accident with Pam and may seek recovery from Pam.

Further, there is no undue burden or cumulative effect of producing a single statement that Pam already obtained so it would be proportional to the needs of a personal injury case. Wynne's statement is also likely admissible because Wynne could take the stand or it could be a present sense impression or a prior statement as hearsay exceptions if she did not testify.

Lastly, Wynne's statement is not privileged and not work product as there were no attorneys involved at the time and it appears to be a statement that Pam gathered at the accident.

Overall, the statement is discoverable.

Mandatory Initial Disclosures

Without request, within 14 days of the discovery planning conference, parties must disclose to the other parties the identity of those likely to have discoverable information that may support the disclosing party's claim or defense, copies or descriptions of tangible evidence that may support the disclosing party's claim or defense, damages computation and supporting documentation, and applicable insurance documents. Parties must also meet and confer when there are discovery disputes prior to seeking a motion to compel.

Here, Wynne was the other driver in the car accident with Pam and was injured, and her statement was favorable to Pam's case indicating it would likely help support Pam's claims. Thus, Pam should have disclosed Wynne's statement initially. However, it does not appear that DuraTires attempted to meet and confer with Pam before seeking a motion to compel as required.

Thus, the court should not grant DuraTires' motion to compel production of the statement until it meets and confers with Pam.

2(b). Motion to Compel a Physical Examination

A party requesting a physical examination of another party must obtain a court order upon a showing that the physical condition of the party is at issue, and there is good cause for an examination.

Here, Pam was not physically injured in the accident and is not seeking damages for any physical injury so her physical condition is not at issue. Pam is seeking property damage and emotional distress damages so there is no good cause for a physical examination. While Pam's mental health is at issue since she is seeking emotional distress damages, that would require a mental examination not a physical examination.

Thus, the court erred in granting DuraTires' motion to compel Pam to submit to a physical examination.

3. Production of Scientific Report

Scope of Discoverable Evidence

See above for general rule.

DuraTires' scientific report is relevant to Pam's case because her tire went flat after 100 miles when the report indicated the tires would not go flat the first 7,000 miles, which helps prove her breach of warranty claim. It is also proportional to the case as it is only one report and does not cause an undue burden to disclose it.

Assuming the report is not privileged or work product, it should be discoverable.

Attorney-Client Privilege

Attorney-client privilege protects communications between an attorney and client made for the purpose of obtaining legal advice.

Here, the report is not privileged as it is not a communication between a lawyer and client even though legal counsel directed the report to be created. Also, DuraTires advertised the results of the report so arguably they would have waived the privilege if it did apply as they did not keep the contents of the report confidential. Thus, the report is not privileged.

Attorney Work Product

Work product is material prepared in anticipation of litigation and is generally not discoverable unless there is substantial need and the inability to obtain the info otherwise. Mental impressions and opinions are never discoverable.

Here, DuraTires may try to argue that the report was work product as legal counsel had it prepared in anticipation of a possible future accident. However, it does not appear that the report was created in anticipation of litigation as Pam had yet to have her accident, there were no pending lawsuits at the time, and DuraTires disclosed the contents of the report in an effort to advertise and gain customers, so it seems the report was used more for marketing purposes and not in anticipation of litigation.

Also, the report information about flat tire accidents is likely information that Pam would have a substantial need for due to her accident and it is unlikely she can obtain it elsewhere as it would be unreasonably burdensome for her to do independent research on flat tires to gather the same information.

Thus, the report is not work product and is discoverable.

Initial/Expert disclosures

See above for initial mandatory disclosure rules. Expert testimony disclosure is mandatory if the expert will testify at trial and only their final reports must be turned over to the other side. Final reports must contain the expert's opinions and facts that it used to reach its conclusions.

Here, DuraTires' scientific report will not likely be used to support its defenses because it doesn't support their case as Pam's tire went flat after 100 miles when the report indicated the tires would not go flat the first 7,000 miles.

However, Pam could argue that it will be used to support DuraTires defense as they could claim that Pam wasn't driving properly as is required under the report.

Also, Pam did meet and confer with DuraTires first before filing her motion to compel.

Here, the report itself is at issue and it is not clear that DuraTires will call the expert who generated the report to testify, but if they do then they will have to provide a final report which would contain the data it used to make its determinations so Pam would get the information that way too.

Overall, the court properly ordered DuraTires to produce its scientific report.

Civil Procedure Question 2
July 2016, Question 1

Paul, a citizen of Mexico, was attending college in San Diego on a student visa. He drove to San Francisco to attend a music festival. While there, he bought and ate a bag of snacks from Valerie, a resident of San Francisco. The snacks had been manufactured in Germany by Meyer Corp., a German company with its sole place of business in Germany. The snacks contained a toxic substance and sickened Paul, who incurred medical expenses in the amount of $50,000.

Paul filed an action pro se against Valerie and Meyer Corp. in the Superior Court of California in San Diego. In his complaint, he alleged that Valerie and Meyer Corp. should have known the snacks were contaminated and demanded $50,000 in compensatory damages.

Paul drove to San Francisco where he personally handed Valerie a summons and copy of the complaint. He sent a summons and copy of the complaint to Meyer Corp. by ordinary mail to the company in Germany.

1. Did Paul validly serve the summons on:

   a. Valerie? Discuss.

   b. Meyer Corp.? Discuss.

2. Does the Superior Court of California in San Diego have personal jurisdiction over:

   a. Valerie? Discuss.

   b. Meyer Corp.? Discuss.

3. Does venue properly lie in the Superior Court of California in San Diego? Discuss.

4. Is Paul's action properly removable to federal court? Discuss.

Civil Procedure Question 2 Assessment
July 2016, Question 1

This question is the first question in which the bar examiners tested California law (and they have only tested California Civil Procedure one other time, which was in July 2024). Nonetheless, the question still focuses on some of the favorite testing areas of personal jurisdiction, venue, and subject matter jurisdiction. The twist is that the action was originally filed in California in order to test on some of the California-specific rules.

Many students were thrown off by this question because it was the first question of the day, and the first call asks about service of process in a foreign country. Further, since it was the first time California Civil Procedure was tested, students had not had the opportunity to practice any California Civil Procedure questions. Put it all together, and it was a very stressful start to the bar exam for many students. Since service of any kind is a more unusual rule to test, under the stress of exam day many students couldn't recall the specifics of the rule, especially as it pertains to service in a foreign jurisdiction. If that situation happens to you, don't panic! Take a deep breath, do your best, keep going and quickly move on to the material you do know how to analyze. Essentially, don't waste a lot of time on a rule that is eluding you. Realistically, the service of process call could not have been worth many points compared to the rest of the issues on this essay, which called for much more fact-rich analyses; it just loomed large as the first issue.

When you can't quite remember a rule, this is what you want to do: Remember as much of the rule or parts of the rule that you can, and make a logical inference on what is missing based on what you do know about the common types of rules used in that subject and the purpose for the rules. For example, the purpose of civil procedure is providing a fair playing field and maintaining order. More specifically, the purpose of service of process is providing fair notice to the opposing party that they are being sued. We also know that the preferred method of service is personal service. If you focused your analysis on that premise, you would have likely seized on the concept that serving a foreign company by use of "ordinary mail" was insufficient. In fact, the bar examiners were probably trying to give you a hint by using the term "ordinary mail." Logically, that can't be correct, so even if you weren't exactly sure what Paul should have done, you could have still earned most of the points by doing some decent factual analysis on the inadequacy of "ordinary mail" for providing notice of an event as serious as being sued.

The rest of this question covers the familiar areas of personal jurisdiction, venue, and subject matter jurisdiction. In the final call, the question asks if removal is proper, but the query about removal is a common method used to ask about the underlying issue of subject matter jurisdiction. The wrinkle in the subject matter jurisdiction analysis is the more unusual factual situation where there are two foreign aliens involved in the suit, which raises an alienage diversity subrule that is uncommonly tested on the essay. Other than that, this question is a classic civil procedure California bar essay question and a good one to practice.

Make note of the areas highlighted in **bold** on the corresponding grid. The bold areas highlight the issues, analysis, and conclusions that are likely **required** to receive a passing score on this question.

Issue	Rule	Fact Application	Conclusion
1. Did Paul validly serve summons?			
Proper Summons/ Service of Process	• **Service of the summons and complaint can be made by anyone at least 18 years old who is not a party.** • **Personal service is adequate.** • **Substituted service is allowed if personal service cannot be accomplished with reasonable diligence.** • **The process must be mailed by first class mail.** • Service on parties in a foreign country can also be done as the court directs, or in accordance with the laws of the foreign jurisdiction, or in accordance with the rules of an international treaty.	**Valerie:** Since P is a college student, he is likely over 18, and he handed the summons and complaint to V, which would typically provide sufficient actual service. **However, as a party to the action, P may not effectuate service.** **Meyer Corp.:** Cal. allows substituted service, so service may be done by mail, since there are no representatives of Meyer Corp. in California. **However, P mailed the summons by ordinary mail, not first-class mail, so this will not provide sufficient service.**	**Summons was improperly served on Valerie and Meyer Corp.**
2. Does San Diego Superior Court in San Diego have personal jurisdiction?			
Personal Jurisdiction Valerie	**Traditional basis of jurisdiction are consent, domiciled in forum state, or present when served in forum state.**	**V is a resident of San Francisco, Cal., so she is domiciled in Cal. and subject to personal jurisdiction.** In addition, V was personally served in the forum.	**Personal jurisdiction is proper over Valerie.**
Personal Jurisdiction Meyer Corp.	**Traditional Basis (see above for rule)** **Long Arm Statute** **Relatedness** • **Specific jx** (claim arises out of or relates to contact w with the forum) • **General jx** "Essentially at Home"	**There is no traditional basis since Meyer did not consent, as a German company it is not domiciled in Cal., and it was not present when served in Cal.** Cal.'s long arm statute is coextensive with the constitution, so the **minimum contacts analysis will be employed.** Facts do not indicate any actions by Meyer targeting Cal. If the action arises out of Meyer's contacts with the forum, such as targeting business there, **there would be specific jurisdiction since the injury was caused by snacks eaten by P in Cal.** **However, as a German company with its sole place of business in Germany, Meyer is not essentially at home in Cal., so no general jurisdiction.**	Personal jurisdiction is likely improper. [Could conclude either way.]

Continued>

Issue	Rule	Fact Application	Conclusion
Personal Jurisdiction (continued)	Min. Contacts/Constitutional Analysis • Purposeful availment/Foreseeability Fairness Factors (if specific jx met) • Burden on defendant • Plaintiff's interest • State's interest • Interstate judicial system's interest and shared interest of the several states	Meyer corps' snacks were eaten in Cal., but P purchased them from V, not Meyer. Meyer corp. manufactured the snacks in Germany and is solely a German company. Meyer would need to have taken some action, such as marketing to the Cal. snack market, to have purposely availed itself of benefits of Cal. and thus make it foreseeable that they could be haled into court there. If instead, V bought the snacks in Germany and sold them in Cal., there would be no purposeful availment. Burden on Meyer: very burdensome because there is no indication Meyer has any contacts with Cal., but they are a corp. All witnesses who made the snacks are in Germany. P is in Cal. and has a strong interest in obtaining redress. All witnesses about the snack purchase and injury from the snacks are in Cal., as is the codefendant. And Cal. has an interest in injuries occurring from contaminated snacks in its jurisdiction, but P is a Mexican citizen on a student visa. Since Cal. and a foreign country are involved and not another state, there are no interstate or shared state interests to balance, but could argue Meyer should be sued in Germany where snacks were made, not Cal.	
3. Is venue proper in San Diego Superior Court?			
Venue	Venue is proper in any county where the claim arose (injury occurred) or the defendant resides.	The cause of action arose in San Francisco since P was attending a musical festival there when he was injured after he purchased and consumed the contaminated snacks from V. V is a resident of San Francisco county and Meyer Corp is a resident of Germany. Venue is improper in San Diego, and proper in San Francisco county.	Venue is proper in San Francisco.

Continued>

Issue	Rule	Fact Application	Conclusion
4. Removable to federal court?			
Removal	• **Defendant may remove to federal court if the case could properly have been brought in federal court.** • All defendants must agree to the removal. • In diversity cases, the defendant may not remove to federal court if they are a citizen of the forum state. • Defendant must remove no later than 30 days after service of the first removable document, but never later than one year after the initial filing in diversity cases.	To have been brought in federal court in the first place, the court must have proper subject matter jurisdiction.	**The action is not removable because there is not sufficient SMJ** (below).
Subject Matter Jurisdiction	Federal question or **complete diversity between the parties and more than $75,000 amount in controversy.** **Domicile determines a person's citizenship.** • A person's domicile is where they are physically present with a subjective intent to remain. • A corporation is a citizen of its state of incorporation and the state of its PPB. • There is SMJ over an alien. An alien is a citizen of the country of citizenship. • However, **diverse U.S. citizens must be on both sides of the controversy for alienage jurisdiction.**	There is no federal question basis to P's claim. **V is domiciled in San Francisco, Cal., and Meyer Corp. is an alien domiciled in Germany since it is a German company doing business solely in Germany. Since P is in Cal. on a student visa and is a citizen of Mexico, he is a domiciliary of Mexico and an alien for diversity purposes** since a student on a student visa is not a permanent resident. However, in diversity cases, the defendant may not remove to federal court if she is a citizen of the forum state and V is a citizen of Cal. **Additionally, since there are aliens on both sides of the action, diversity of citizenship is not met** since there must be diverse citizens of the U.S. on each side. Also, P is alleging $50,000 in damages, which is insufficient for diversity jurisdiction.	**There is no SMJ.**

Civil Procedure Question 2 Sample Answer
July 2016, Question 1

1. Did Paul validly serve?

Proper Summons/Service of Process

To have a proper service of process, the summons and complaint must be served on the defendant. There are several ways to effectuate proper service. The service can be made by anyone at least 18 years old who is not a party to the lawsuit. Service can be made by personal delivery to the defendant. In California, substituted service is allowed if personal service cannot be accomplished with reasonable diligence, which requires the process must be mailed by first-class mail. Service on parties in a foreign country can be effectuated as the court directs, or in accordance with the laws of the foreign jurisdiction, or in accordance with the rules of an international treaty.

a. Valerie

Paul served Valerie by driving to San Francisco and personally handing her the summons and complaint. Since Paul is a college student he is likely over the age of 18, and he handed the summons and complaint to Valerie, which would typically provide sufficient actual service. However, as a party to the action, Paul may not personally effectuate service to Valerie. Since a third party did not serve Valerie, the service of process is improper.

b. Meyer Corp.

Meyer Corp. is a German company with all their business operations in Germany, so they do not have a presence in California. California allows substituted service in this type of situation where personal service is impractical because there are no representatives of Meyer Corp. in California, so service may be done by mail. However, Paul mailed the summons and complaint by ordinary mail, not first-class mail, so this will not provide sufficient service to Meyer Corp. The service was improper.

2. Does Superior Court of California in San Diego have personal jurisdiction?

a. Valerie

Personal Jurisdiction

The court must have proper jurisdiction over the parties to an action and it is proper where there is a sufficiently close relationship between the defendant and the forum state.

Traditional Basis

A traditional basis for personal jurisdiction exists where a defendant consents to the forum, is domiciled in the forum state, or is present when served with process in the forum state.

Valerie is a resident of San Francisco, California, so she is domiciled in California and subject to personal jurisdiction in California. In addition, Valerie was personally served in the forum. Personal jurisdiction for Valerie in the Superior Court of San Diego is proper.

b. Meyer Corp

Personal Jurisdiction

The court must have proper jurisdiction over the parties to an action and it is proper where there is a sufficiently close relationship between the defendant and the forum state.

Traditional Basis

A traditional basis for personal jurisdiction exists where a defendant consents to the forum, is domiciled in the forum state, or is present when served with process in the forum state.

There is no traditional basis for jurisdiction over Meyer Corp. since Meyer Corp. has not consented to jurisdiction. As a German company they are not a domiciliary of California, and Meyer Corp. was not present when served in California.

Long-Arm Statute

A long-arm statute is the mechanism that gives a state power to reach beyond its borders and assert jurisdiction over a nonresident.

California's long-arm statute is coextensive with the limits of the constitution, so the minimum contacts analysis will be employed to determine if there is personal jurisdiction over Meyer Corp.

Minimum Contacts

Due process requires that minimum contacts must exist between the defendant and the forum state, so the suit does not offend traditional notions of fair play and substantial justice.

Relatedness

There is specific jurisdiction if the claim arises out of or relates to the contact with the forum state. General jurisdiction exists if the defendant is essentially at home in the forum state, which is generally only met if one of the traditional bases are met.

Specific Jurisdiction

The facts do not indicate that Meyer Corp. took any actions targeting California. If the action here arose out of Meyer's contacts with the forum, such as targeting business there, there would be specific jurisdiction since the injury was caused by the tainted snacks eaten by Paul in California.

General Jurisdiction

As a German company with its sole place of business in Germany, Meyer Corp. is not essentially at home in California, so there would be no basis for general jurisdiction.

Purposeful Availment/Foreseeability

The defendant's contacts with the forum state must be assessed to determine if the defendant purposefully availed themself of the benefits and protections of the forum state, such that it is reasonably foreseeable that their activities in the forum subject them to being haled into court there.

Paul ate a bag of snacks in California that were manufactured by Meyer Corp., which manufactured the snacks in Germany and is solely a German company. Paul purchased the snacks from Valerie while in San Francisco, not from Meyer Corp. It is unclear how Valerie obtained the snacks from Meyer Corp. Meyer would need to have taken some action, such as direct marketing efforts to the California snack market, in order to have purposely availed itself of the benefits and protections of California, thus making it foreseeable they could be haled into a California court. If instead Valerie bought the snacks while in Germany and unilaterally sold them in California, there would be no purposeful availment on the part of Meyer Corp.

Fairness Factors

The exercise of jurisdiction must be fair and reasonable, so the court will assess a number of factors, including: the burden on the defendant, which is the most heavily weighted factor, the plaintiff's interest in convenient relief, the location of witnesses and evidence, the forum state's interest in regulating activities and protecting its citizens, and interstate efficiency interests and the interests of the shared several states.

Paul is presently in California and has a strong interest in obtaining redress for his injuries from the tainted snacks. California as a forum may be unfair because all witnesses regarding the manufacture of the snacks are in Germany, so even though they are a corporation, it would be very financially burdensome to defend a suit in California since Meyer has no contacts in California. However, all witnesses about the snack purchase and the injury resulting from the snacks are in California, as is the co-defendant Valerie. Further, California has a strong interest in redressing injuries occurring from contaminated snacks consumed in its jurisdiction, but since Paul is a Mexican citizen on a student visa, the state's interest is slightly less. Overall, it would not be unfair or unreasonable, assuming Meyer Corp. had directed some activities towards the California market.

Personal jurisdiction is likely improper unless Meyer Corp. had directed snack-marketing activities towards the California market.

3. Does venue properly lie in California Superior Court in San Diego?

Venue

Venue is proper in any county where the claim arose (injury occurred) or the defendant resides.

The cause of action arose in San Francisco, since Paul was attending a musical festival there when he was injured after he consumed the contaminated snacks he had purchased from Valerie. Valerie is a resident of San Francisco County and Meyer Corp. is a resident of Germany. Thus, there is no basis for venue in San Diego, but venue is proper in San Francisco County.

4. Is Paul's action removable?

Removal

A defendant may remove a case to federal court if a case is brought in state court but could have properly been brought in federal court. However, when the basis for subject matter jurisdiction is diversity and one of the defendants is a citizen of the forum state, the action is not removable. All defendants must agree to the removal and must remove no later than 30 days after service of the first removable document, but never later than one year after the initial filing in diversity cases.

To have been brought in federal court in the first place, the first inquiry is if the federal court has proper subject matter jurisdiction.

Subject Matter Jurisdiction

Federal subject matter jurisdiction means the court has proper jurisdiction over the subject matter of an action. Federal courts have limited subject matter jurisdiction and may only hear cases involving federal questions or diversity of citizenship (or alienage jurisdiction), which requires complete diversity and where the claim exceeds $75,000. Domicile determines a person's citizenship.

There is no federal question to Paul's claim so that will not provide a basis for subject matter jurisdiction. For diversity purposes, Valerie is domiciled in San Francisco, and Meyer Corp. is an alien since it is domiciled in Germany and solely conducts business in Germany. Since Paul is in California on a student visa and is a Mexican citizen, he only temporarily has a California domicile because while he is physically present, he does not have a subjective intent to remain, making him an alien for diversity purposes. While the parties are fully diverse from one another, this will not satisfy the diversity requirement because there are aliens on both sides of the action, and there also must be diverse citizens of the U.S. on each side of the controversy, and here there are not. Further, in diversity cases the defendant may not remove to federal court if she is a citizen of the forum state, and Valerie is a citizen of California.

Lastly, Paul is alleging $50,000 in damages, which is insufficient for diversity jurisdiction.

Paul's action is not removable for lack of subject matter jurisdiction.

Civil Procedure Question 3

July 2015, Question 1

Doctor implanted a valve in Patient's heart in State A, where both Doctor and Patient lived. The valve was designed in State B by Valvco. Valvco was incorporated in State C, but had its headquarters in State D.

Patient was visiting State B when he collapsed due to his heart problems. Patient decided to remain in State B for the indefinite future for medical treatment.

Patient sued Doctor and Valvco in state court in State B for $100,000, alleging that Valvco defectively designed the valve and Doctor negligently implanted it. Another patient had recently sued Valvco alleging that it defectively designed the valve, and had obtained a final judgment in her favor after trial on that issue.

Doctor and Valvco each moved the state court to dismiss the case on the ground of lack of personal jurisdiction. The state court granted Doctor's motion and denied Valvco's.

Valvco then filed a notice in federal court in State B to remove the case. Patient immediately filed a motion in federal court to remand the case to state court. The federal court denied Patient's motion.

Relying solely on the judgment in the other patient's action, Patient then filed a motion in federal court for summary adjudication of the issue that Valvco defectively designed the valve. The federal court granted the motion.

1. Did the state court properly grant Doctor's motion to dismiss? Discuss.

2. Did the state court properly deny Valvco's motion to dismiss? Discuss.

3. Did the federal court properly deny Patient's motion for remand? Discuss.

4. Did the federal court properly grant Patient's motion for summary adjudication? Discuss.

Civil Procedure Question 3 Assessment
July 2015, Question 1

This question is a more challenging Civil Procedure question because it is more of a racehorse style covering many issues, but it also has much deep factual analysis. It covers the highly tested concepts of personal jurisdiction, subject matter jurisdiction, and res judicata and collateral estoppel. This question is fairly typical in that it tests the same concepts more than once, but with a slight change of facts. In one call, you are asked about personal jurisdiction regarding one defendant, and in the second call, you are asked to assess the personal jurisdiction of the second defendant. Not surprisingly, the facts are slightly altered so you can demonstrate your facility with the concepts.

While the concepts noted above are tested by the bar examiners frequently, the removal and remand issues covered in the third call are less frequently tested and would be challenging if you didn't know the rules. As you can see from the grid, to fully analyze removal and remand, though there was no specific call for it, you must first analyze subject matter jurisdiction since that rule is embedded in the remand and removal rules. This is the type of issue where you can demonstrate that you not only understand each concept, but that you also understand how the various rules work together when solving a factual problem. It would be especially challenging to analyze this call if you did not organize your answer before writing, since you needed to figure out that the Doctor's motion to dismiss was proper, so the Doctor did not need to agree to the removal since the Doctor was properly dismissed. On a normal day this is easy to see; during a stressful exam day, this is the type of wrinkle that can cause confusion. Stay calm and methodical, and always organize before you write to avoid going off on ineffective tangents.

The fourth call, pertaining to Patient's motion for summary judgment, had some of the more complicated analysis. The res judicata issue was a slam-dunk since the two cases did not involve the same parties. It would have been perfectly fine to jump right to the point to solve that issue. If you thought about your answer first in the outlining phase, you would have noticed that while the res judicata issue was easy, the collateral estoppel issue was much more complicated. There were good facts to use for each of the elements. The bar examiners were looking for a good discussion on the more sophisticated issues to analyze of actually litigated, determined, and necessary. The facts weren't given; rather, you needed to make a logical inference based on your understanding of a product defect type case. The mutuality issue also required you to make some logical factual inferences in order to do a good job on the analysis. That important analysis includes a discussion of collateral estoppel and, in particular, the concept of the traditional rule of mutuality and the minority rule that California follows not requiring mutuality since a "stranger" is trying to take advantage of the prior judgment. A thorough analysis of all of the mutuality elements is required to receive a passing score on this question.

Make note of the areas highlighted in **bold** on the corresponding grid. The bold areas highlight the issues, analysis, and conclusions that are likely **required** to receive a passing score on this question.

Issue	Rule	Fact Application	Conclusion
1. Doctor's motion to dismiss for lack of PJ			
Personal Jurisdiction	• **Traditional Basis** (domicile, consent, present while served) • **Long-Arm Statute** • **Constitutional Analysis** • Relatedness (Specific jx – relates to or arises from/General jx – at home; traditional basis met) • **Purposeful availment/Foreseeability of being haled into court** • Fairness Factors (only need if specific jx) — can list if time (but not really needed here because no specific jx) *OK to include domicile rules for person here or woven into analysis	• No consent, not served in forum and **Dr. is resident of State A** so no traditional basis. • **No LAS identified in facts, but presumed met so long as there are minimum contacts and does not offend traditional notions of fair play and substantial justice.** Dr.'s actions (negligently implanting the valve) all took place in State A, with no connection to State B, so no specific jurisdiction. • Dr. is not essentially at home in State B since he lives and is domiciled in State A, so no general jurisdiction. • **Dr. has never been to forum State B nor does any business there, so no purposeful availment of benefits and protections of forum State B.** P collapsed in State B, but it is not foreseeable for Dr. to be subject to jurisdiction anywhere P could travel. • No specific jx, but State B is interested in benefitting its citizens (P is currently domiciled in State B and intends to remain there indefinitely to seek further medical treatment). Witnesses regarding the valve are in State B. But all witnesses regarding surgery are in State A. It would be unfair to make all witnesses travel to State B.	No PJ, Ct properly granted Dr.'s motion to dismiss
Q2: Valvco's motion to dismiss for lack of PJ			
Personal Jurisdiction	• **Traditional Basis** • **Long-Arm Statute** • **Constitutional Analysis** • Relatedness (Specific jx – relates to or arises from/General jx – at home; traditional basis met) • **Purposeful availment/Foreseeability of being haled into court** • **Fairness Factors** • **Burden on defendant** • **Plaintiff's interest** • **Forum state's interest** • Interstate judicial system's interest • Shared interest of the several states *OK to include domicile rules for corporation here or woven into analysis	• V is incorporated in State C and HQ in State D, making it domiciliaries of States C and D, no consent, not served in State B, so no traditional bases. • No LAS, but presumed met so long as there are minimum contacts and does not offend traditional notions of fair play and substantial justice. • **The lawsuit is about valve design, which occurred in State D, so specific jurisdiction.** • V is not essentially at home in State B since it is incorporated in State C and HQ in State D, so no general jurisdiction. • Purposefully availed itself of benefits and protections of State B by using labor force in B to design valve and operating part of business there. Foreseeable to be haled into court from business operations in State B; labor or heart valve design happening in State B.	PJ exists, Ct properly denied Valvco's motion to dismiss

Continued>

Issue	Rule	Fact Application	Conclusion
Personal Jurisdiction (continued)		• P domiciled in State B, and State B has an interest in providing redress for its citizens. All witnesses regarding valve design are in State B, so fair to hear in State B, even if potentially financially burdensome to V because companies can afford to travel more than individuals, especially when their products are used in numerous states and V made the valve in State B, so they already have some employees there. State B conflicts of laws would apply, so likely in the interstate and shared states' interests to have case heard in State B.	
Q3: Patient's motion for remand			
Subject Matter Jurisdiction	Federal question or complete diversity between the parties and more than $75,000	• The lawsuit against V is about design defect, which is a state law tort claim, so no federal question. • Parties are completely diverse because P is domiciled in State B (physically present and intends to remain for treatment) and V is domiciled in States C and D (Inc. in State C and PPB in State D). Dr. is no longer a party since motion to dismiss properly granted for lack of PJ; only parties remaining are diverse. • P's lawsuit was for $100,000 from Dr. and V as codefendants and joint tortfeasors. Since Dr. dismissed, V is the only defendant and could be liable for $100,000. There is diversity SMJ.	SMJ valid
Removal	• D may remove to federal court if brought in state court but could have been properly brought in fed. court. • If diversity SMJ and one D is citizen of forum state, action is not removable. • All Ds must agree to the removal. • D must remove no later than 30 days after service of the first removable document, but never later than one year after the initial filing in diversity cases.	• Case could have been brought in federal court under diversity jx (see above). • V is not a citizen of State B because it is incorporated in State C and HQ in State D, so action is removable to State B federal court. • V is the only D left in the lawsuit because Dr. was dismissed for lack of PJ, so no need for all Ds to agree. • Timing is unclear; so long as V filed notice to remove within 30 days of service of first removable document (which would likely be the pleadings here), then removal is valid.	Valid removal

Continued>

Issue	Rule	Fact Application	Conclusion
Remand	A plaintiff can file for remand back to state court where removal to federal court is improper.	• Removal to federal court is not improper because the court would have been able to hear it initially (valid SMJ) and, assuming the timing of the removal request is within 30 days, all requirements for removal are met.	**Remand properly denied**
Q4: Patient's MSJ re: design defect			
Motion for Summary Judgment	No genuine dispute of material fact, and the moving party is entitled to judgment as a matter of law		
Res Judicata	• Prior judgment valid, final, and on merits • **Same parties/privies in same order** • Same claim Fed.: same transaction and occurrence Cal. (and min. jx): primary rights	• Final judgment obtained by a different previous plaintiff in the plaintiff's favor against V. • **P was not a party in the previous lawsuit nor in privity with the parties in the previous lawsuit.** • Same claim regarding defective design of valve by V, but different transaction and occurrence because different heart surgeries for different patients.	**No res judicata**
Collateral Estoppel	• **Prior proceeding resulted in a valid final judgment on merits** • **Same issue actually litigated and determined** • **Necessary (essential)** • **Mutuality of parties** • **Traditional: party/privy** • **Modern/Cal: nonparty ok if** • Defensive: fair opportunity to be heard in prior case • **Offensive: fair and equitable** and new party could not have easily joined first case	• Final judgment obtained against V on heart valve's defectiveness. • **Issue of design defect needed to be litigated fully and determined in order for plaintiff in previous case to receive a judgment in her favor, and would be necessary (essential to the judgment) because plaintiff could not have prevailed without proving all the design defect elements.** • **No traditional mutuality because P is not a party or in privity with plaintiff in previous lawsuit.** • Modernly, P would be able to rely on the previous decision regarding design defect issue because he is using offensive nonmutual collateral estoppel, and it just needs to be fair to apply the previous decision regarding the issue. V likely had a full opportunity to defend on the design defect issue because if not, others could use the decision against them in future lawsuits. P would not have been able to easily join the prior lawsuit as he was injured after that lawsuit.	**Collateral Estoppel exists as to design defect issue.** **Court properly granted motion for summary judgment**

Civil Procedure Question 3 Sample Answer
July 2015, Question 1

1. Doctor's motion to dismiss for lack of personal jurisdiction

Personal Jurisdiction

The court must have proper jurisdiction over the parties to an action, and it is proper where there is a sufficiently close relationship between the defendant and the forum state.

Traditional Basis

A traditional basis for personal jurisdiction exists where a defendant consents to the forum, is domiciled in the forum state, or is present when served with process in the forum state.

Doctor did not consent and was not served in State B and is domiciled in State A. There is no traditional basis for jurisdiction.

Long-Arm Statute

A long-arm statute is the mechanism that gives a state power to reach beyond its borders and assert jurisdiction over a nonresident.

There is no long-arm statute identified in the facts, but presuming it is similar to California's and that of many jurisdictions, it will be met so long as there are minimum contacts and the exercise of jurisdiction does not offend traditional notions of fair play and substantial justice.

Minimum Contacts

Due process requires that minimum contacts exist between the defendant and the forum state such that the suit does not offend traditional notions of fair play and substantial justice.

Relatedness

Courts will consider the relatedness between the claim at issue and the defendant's contacts with the forum state. There must be either general or specific jurisdiction.

Essentially at Home — General Jurisdiction

The modern rule for general jurisdiction requires that the defendant be "essentially at home" in the forum state such that one of the traditional bases is met. Here, Doctor lives and is domiciled in State A, so he is not essentially at home in State B, so there is no basis for general jurisdiction.

Specific Jurisdiction

If the plaintiff's claim is directly related to or arises from the defendant's contacts with the forum state, then there will be specific personal jurisdiction for that claim only. Here, Doctor's actions of negligently implanting the valve all took place in State A, and nothing is connected to State B, so there is no specific jurisdiction.

Minimum Contacts — Purposeful Availment/Foreseeability

The defendant's contacts with the forum state must be assessed to determine if the defendant purposefully availed themselves of the benefits and protections of the forum state, such that it is reasonably foreseeable that their activities in the forum subject them to being haled into court there.

Doctor has never been to forum State B, nor does he do any business in State B, so he has not purposely availed himself of the benefits and protections of the state. Further, while his former patient collapsed in State B, it is not reasonably foreseeable for Doctor to be haled into court there since Doctor had no activity in State B. Otherwise, since all former patients can travel unimpeded, this would subject Doctor to jurisdiction everywhere.

Fairness Factors

The exercise of jurisdiction must be fair and reasonable, so the court will assess a number of factors if specific jurisdiction is met, including: the burden on the defendant, the plaintiff's interest in convenient relief including the location of witnesses and evidence, the forum state's interest in regulating activities and protecting its citizens, and interstate and shared states' efficiency interests.

Although specific jurisdiction is not met, if the court still considered the fairness factors, State B is interested in benefitting its citizens like Patient, who is currently domiciled there and intends to remain there indefinitely seeking further medical treatment. The witnesses regarding the heart valve design are also in State B. However, all witnesses regarding the surgery itself and any negligence stemming from it are in State A where the surgery occurred, so it would be unfair and impractical for all witnesses to travel to State B, thus it would be unfair to exercise jurisdiction over Doctor.

The court does not have personal jurisdiction over Doctor, and the court properly granted Doctor's motion to dismiss on those grounds.

2. Valvco's motion to dismiss for lack of personal jurisdiction

Personal Jurisdiction

Rule supra.

Traditional Basis

Rule supra.

Valvco has not consented to the forum and was not served in the forum. Valvco is not domiciled in State B because it is incorporated in State C with its corporate headquarters in State D, making Valvco a domiciliary of States C and D, so there is no traditional basis for jurisdiction.

Long-Arm Statute

Rule and analysis supra.

Minimum Contacts

Rule supra.

Relatedness

Rule supra.

Essentially at Home — General Jurisdiction

Rule supra.

Here, since Valvco is incorporated in State C and their corporate headquarters are in State D, they are not essentially at home in State B, so there is no general jurisdiction.

Specific Jurisdiction

Rule supra.

The lawsuit is about the design of the valve, all of which occurred in State B, so the claim directly relates to and arises out of Valvco's contacts in State B. So specific jurisdiction exists for a suit about the heart valve in State B.

Minimum Contacts — Purposeful Availment/Foreseeability

Rule supra.

Here, Valvco has purposefully availed itself of the benefits and protections of State B since the heart valve was designed in State B with a State B labor force, thus they've operated at least a part of their business in

State B. Doing so makes it foreseeable that they could be haled into court in State B resulting from issues arising from their business operations or any labor-related issues.

Fairness Factors

Rule supra.

Patient is domiciled in State B, and State B has an interest in providing redress for its citizens. All witnesses regarding the design of the valve are also in State B since that is where it is designed, so it is fair to hear the case in State B, even though it could potentially be financially burdensome for Valvco to travel for the suit. Also, Valvco is already present in State B to some extent since the valve was designed there with its employees and support. And since State B conflicts of laws would likely apply using State B law, it is in the shared states' and interstate interest for courts in State B to hear the case.

Thus, personal jurisdiction exists over Valvco and the court properly denied Valvco's motion to dismiss on that ground.

3. Patient's motion for remand

Subject Matter Jurisdiction

Federal subject matter jurisdiction means the court has proper jurisdiction over the subject matter of an action. Federal courts have limited subject matter jurisdiction and may only hear cases involving federal questions or diversity of citizenship, which requires complete diversity and where the claim exceeds $75,000.

The lawsuit against Valvco is about a defectively designed heart valve, which is a state law tort claim, so there is no federal question here. Patient is domiciled in State B since he is currently physically present and intends to remain there indefinitely for medical treatment. Valvco is domiciled in State C, which is its state of incorporation and State D, where it has its headquarters and which is its principal place of business. Since Doctor's motion to dismiss for lack of personal jurisdiction was properly granted, he is no longer party to this lawsuit. Thus, the only remaining parties are Valvco and Patient, and they are completely diverse from one another.

Patient's initial lawsuit was for $100,000 against Doctor and Valvco as codefendants and most likely, joint tortfeasors. Since Valvco is the only remaining defendant, Valvco could be found liable for $100,000, which exceeds the $75,000 required.

Therefore, there is federal subject matter jurisdiction here based on diversity.

Removal

A defendant may remove to federal court if a case is brought in state court but could have properly been brought in federal court. However, when the basis for subject matter jurisdiction is diversity and one of the defendants is a citizen of the forum state, the action is not removable. All defendants must agree to the removal and must remove no later than 30 days after service of the first removable document, but never later than one year after the initial filing in diversity cases.

Here, the case could have been brought in federal court based on diversity jurisdiction as discussed above. As noted above, since Valvco is not a citizen of State B, the action is removable to State B federal court. Further, since the court granted the Doctor's motion to dismiss for lack of personal jurisdiction, no other party needs to agree to the removal. The timing of the motion is unclear, but as long as Valvco filed notice to remove the case within 30 days of service of first removable document (which would likely be the pleadings here), the removal is valid.

Remand

A plaintiff can file for remand back to state court where removal to federal court is improper. Since the removal to federal court is not improper as noted above, the request for remand was properly denied.

4. Patient's motion for summary judgment on design defect

Summary judgment is proper where the moving party can establish there is no genuine dispute of material fact and they are entitled to judgment as a matter of law.

Res Judicata

Res judicata precludes a claim from being relitigated where there is a valid final judgment on the merits, the same parties were involved in both cases in the same order, and the case involves the same claim. Traditionally, the same claim means the claims derive from the same transaction or occurrence. Some states, including California, apply the primary rights doctrine, which permits separate claims for each primary right invaded.

Here, a final judgment was obtained by a different plaintiff in the plaintiff's favor in a suit against Valvco for a defective heart valve. Patient was not a party in the previous lawsuit or in privity with the parties in the previous lawsuit. Patient is now litigating the same type of claim regarding the defective design of Valvco's heart valve, but this is a different transaction and occurrence because these cases involve different heart surgeries for different patients.

Thus, res judicata does not apply, and the court should not grant Patient's motion as to summary adjudication based on res judicata.

Collateral Estoppel

Collateral estoppel precludes relitigation of a particular issue that has already been decided where there is a prior valid judgment on the merits, and the same issue was actually litigated and determined, and necessary (essential) to the judgment. Traditionally, the mutuality principle required privity between the parties. Modernly, some states, including California, allow a nonparty to assert collateral estoppel offensively where it would be fair and equitable and the party was not able to easily join in the prior lawsuit.

Here, there was a final judgment on the merits against Valvco on the issue of their heart valve's defectiveness. The issue of defective design would have been litigated fully and determined in order for the other plaintiff in the previous case to receive a judgment in her favor. The issue of the valve's defectiveness would have been necessary and essential to the judgment because without proving each element needed to establish the design defect, the plaintiff could not have prevailed.

Patient is not a party nor in privity with the plaintiff in the previous lawsuit so there is no traditional mutuality of parties. However, modernly and in California, Patient would be able to rely on the previous decision regarding the issue of design defect because he is using offensive non-mutual collateral estoppel, and it would be fair to assert collateral estoppel against Valvco because it likely provided a vigorous defense on the design defect issue as a sound business decision because if not, they would expose themselves to greater liability since third parties could try and use the decision against them in future lawsuits, as is being done here. Further, Patient could not have easily joined the first lawsuit as he was injured yet.

Thus, it would be fair to apply collateral estoppel against Valvco, and the court properly granted Patient's motion as to summary adjudication on the issue of the valve's defectiveness.

Civil Procedure Question 4
February 2002, Question 1

Pam, a resident of State X, brought suit in state court in State X against Danco, a corporation with its principal place of business in State Y. The suit was for damages of $90,000 alleging that Danco breached a contract to supply Pam with paper goods for which she paid $90,000 in advance. In her complaint, Pam requested a jury trial. State X law provides that contract disputes for less than $200,000 must be tried to a judge.

Danco removed the case to federal court in State X. Danco moved to strike the request for a jury trial. The federal court denied the motion.

A few days before trial, Pam learned for the first time that Danco was incorporated in State X. She moved to have the case remanded to state court on this ground. The federal court denied the motion.

At trial, Pam testified that she paid for the goods but never received them. Danco admitted receiving Pam's payment and then presented evidence from its dispatcher that it had sent a truck to Pam's office with the paper goods. Danco also called as a witness Rafe, who works in a building next to Pam's office. Rafe testified he saw a truck stop at Pam's office on the day Danco claimed it delivered the goods. Rafe also testified he saw the truck driver take boxes marked "paper goods" into Pam's office that same day.

At the close of all the evidence, Pam moved for judgment as a matter of law. Danco opposed the motion, and the court denied the motion. The jury returned a verdict in favor of Pam.

Danco then moved for judgment as a matter of law, which Pam opposed. The court denied Danco's motion.

Did the court rule correctly on:

1. Danco's motion to strike the request for a jury trial? Discuss.

2. Pam's motion to have the case remanded to state court? Discuss.

3. Pam's and Danco's motions for judgment as a matter of law? Discuss.

Civil Procedure Question 4 Assessment
February 2002, Question 1

This civil procedure question is included as a practice question because it provides an example of a less typical civil procedure question covering more unusual topics. This question is difficult only because it tests some less common issues, including the right to a trial by jury, removal and remand, and the right to a judgment as a matter of law (JMOL). This question also includes the frequently tested topic of subject matter jurisdiction. The only difficulty posed by the question may be because a student may not remember the infrequently tested rules covered on the exam, or the student has not practiced trying to write such a question so it feels unfamiliar.

Since the question does not test many issues, it is important to flesh out the factual analysis using all of the facts provided in the question. This is especially true in the factual analysis of the jury trial issue, subject matter jurisdiction, and particularly the JMOL motion, which is entirely fact-dependent.

This question was administered before the California rules of civil procedure were specifically tested on the California bar exam. The California rule distinctions are included on the grid so you can see how they should have been addressed in the event they do test these issues applying California law.

Make note of the areas highlighted in **bold** on the corresponding grid. The bold areas highlight the issues, analysis, and conclusions that are likely **required** to receive a passing score on this question.

Issue	Rule	Fact Application	Conclusion
1. D's Motion to Strike			
Jury Trial	7th Amend. preserves right to jury in civil actions at law in federal court.	Here, P's claim is for damages based on breach of contract, which is a civil action at law and not equity.	The court properly denied D's motion to strike
	Plaintiff must demand in writing, no later than 14 days after service of the last pleading, that they want a jury trial, or it is waived.	Although it is in federal court because D removed the case to federal court, if the court remands it back to state court, then it would follow state laws and State X law would apply, barring a jury trial since it is only for $90,000 in damages, less than the $200,000 required by State X law.	
		Since this is a civil action at law and is in federal court, P is entitled to a jury trial. And P requested a jury trial in her complaint, so it was timely and in writing.	
2. P's Motion for Remand			
Remand	A federal court can remand a case back to state court if removal was improper.	Here, the federal court can remand the case back to state court if the removal was improper.	Need to analyze removal
Removal	D can remove a case from state court to federal court if the court has subject matter jurisdiction and personal jurisdiction.	Need to analyze subject matter jurisdiction and personal jurisdiction to determine if removal was proper.	Removal improper b/c no SMJ (see below)
Subject Matter Jurisdiction	Need a federal question or diversity of citizenship.	No federal question here since it is a breach of contract claim for damages.	The court does not have subject matter jurisdiction, so removal improper — court should grant P's motion to remand, so the court erred
	For complete diversity, amount must exceed $75,000 & D and P must be citizens of different states.	Here, P is suing D for damages of $90,000, which exceeds the $75,000 requirement.	
	Citizenship of natural persons is determined by place of domicile.	P is a resident of State X.	
	Citizenship of corporations can be dual: principal place of business and state where incorporated.	D is a resident of State Y since its principal place of business is located in State Y; however, D is also a resident of State X since it is incorporated in State X.	
		Since D and P are both citizens of State X, there is not complete diversity.	

Continued>

Issue	Rule	Fact Application	Conclusion
3. P & D Motion for JMOL			
JMOL—P's motion	After the close of evidence for the other side, the moving party must show that based on the evidence before the court, no reasonable jury could find in favor of the opposing party. (Cal.: called *directed verdict* or *demurrer to the evidence*)	Here, P brought her JMOL after the close of all evidence, so it was acceptable from a timing perspective. P claims that she paid for and did not receive the paper goods she ordered from D and if the jury finds her to be credible could believe her. On the other hand, D presented evidence from the dispatcher that it sent a truck to P's office with the paper goods as well as witness testimony from Rafe that he saw the truck driver take boxes marked "paper goods" into P's office that same day, both of whom a jury could also believe rather than P if they decide to. Since a jury could reasonably believe either P or D, JMOL is improper and should not be allowed.	The court properly denied P's motion
JMOL—D's motion	After the jury reaches its verdict, the losing party can file a renewed JMOL only if it filed a JMOL during the trial. (Cal.: called a *JNOV* and the losing party is not required to make a previous directed verdict motion to file a *JNOV*)	Here, D never filed a JMOL during the trial after the close of either P or D's case, so he cannot now file one after the jury's verdict for the first time. However, even if the JMOL had been filed timely, a jury could have reasonably believed P because they found her more credible, even if it was only her testimony against D's dispatcher and witness testimony, so D is not entitled to a JMOL. Note: In Cal., the motion would be allowed, but D would likely still lose because a reasonable person could still believe P instead of D.	The court properly denied D's motion

Civil Procedure Question 5
July 2021, Question 1

Jiff, a California citizen who resides in Truckee, California, just west of Reno, Nevada, provides cleaning services. At Jiff's request, customers submit written evaluations of his services so he can monitor their satisfaction.

Jiff entered into a contract with Shearer, a Nevada citizen who operates a beauty salon in Reno, Nevada. The contract, signed in Reno, obligated Jiff to use due care in cleaning. One night while cleaning, Jiff accidentally broke an antique vase, which Shearer claimed was worth $100,000.

Shearer sued Jiff for negligence in the United States District Court for the Eastern District of California, which includes Truckee. The complaint alleged that Jiff's lack of due care caused breakage of the vase. Shearer moved to compel production of evaluations completed by Jiff's customers in the past year. The court denied the motion.

Following a trial, the jury returned a general verdict in favor of Jiff and the court entered judgment on the verdict. Shearer did not appeal.

Six months later, Shearer sued Jiff again in the same court for breach of contract. The complaint alleged that Jiff's lack of due care caused breakage of the vase.

1. Was venue properly laid in the Eastern District of California? Discuss.

2. Did the court err in denying Shearer's motion to compel? Discuss.

3. May Jiff take advantage of the judgment in the first suit in defending against the second suit? Discuss.

Civil Procedure Question 5 Assessment
July 2021, Question 1

This question is a rather straightforward Civil Procedure question. The calls are specific, so issue spotting is not a challenge. But some of the rules tested are in areas less heavily tested, making the essay more difficult if you cannot recall the specific rules. At first glance some students think this essay is testing California law because Jiff is from California and is suing in California. However, after a close read of the facts, you should see that Shearer filed suit in a United States District Court. This tells you it is in federal court. If the case were occurring in California state courts it would say Superior Court or California state court.

The first call is testing venue as clearly stated in the call. The difficulty with venue rules is that sometimes you are required to know other issues such as personal jurisdiction if you have to analyze the fallback venue rule and possible *Erie* or choice of law rules to determine the proper venue if you apply federal or state venue rules. However, here the issue is straightforward. You may see that some student answers discuss "preliminary issues" such as subject matter jurisdiction, personal jurisdiction, or venue. This is not necessary. Follow the call of the question. It asked about venue. If the examiners wanted to test your knowledge about subject matter jurisdiction, they would have asked. There are several sample passing answers to this question that did not discuss any preliminary issues that the examiners did not ask about. You could easily pass this call by focusing on the venue issue alone and following the very specific call of the question. There is no need to make the bar exam more complicated than it already is.

The second call is less specific in that it asks about a motion to compel, so you need to see what they are trying to compel. Always look at the facts to see what exactly the party tried to compel. You can easily see that Shearer moved to compel production of evaluations completed by Jiff's customers in the past year. This leads you to the discovery rules, which can be nuanced and tricky. This is a rather specific discovery tool, but it still requires you to know what a party needs to do to compel discovery, the scope of discovery, and the requirements before a party can file a motion to compel discovery. This does not require deep analysis or fact usage but rather straight rule memorization similar to what multiple-choice test questions require. The good news is that this essay tests federal law and you need to know these rules for the multiple choice portion of the test, so dig deep and recall these rules.

The third call doesn't specifically state the issue by using the terms res judicata or collateral estoppel (or claim or issue preclusion). However, it does ask about "taking advantage of the judgment in the first suit" in the second suit, and the facts give rise to two claims. The first clue they are testing preclusion is that there are two cases. And since a judgment can be used to preclude a second claim or issue, it is best to analyze both res judicata and collateral estoppel when the facts could give rise to either, such as here. Further, the facts indicate the second complaint is for "Jiff's lack of due care," which gives rise to the issue (not claim) of due care as opposed to a claim such as negligence and breach of contract. So, you needed to discuss both preclusion doctrines. The collateral estoppel issue was a great opportunity to see if you really understood how the various elements applied or if you just memorized the words and didn't really understand how they applied. A true understanding would have made your analysis turn on whether the issue was necessary, which was not clear. This is exactly what is required of lawyers—they must understand the rules, not just memorize them.

Overall, this was an essay that covered one straightforward issue, one complex issue that required you to fully understand how the elements apply rather than just memorize the rule, and a touch of discovery with random nuanced rules, but it has been tested frequently in recent years.

Make note of the areas highlighted in **bold** on the corresponding grid. The bold areas highlight the issues, analysis, and conclusions that are likely **required** to receive a passing score on this question.

Issue	Rule	Fact Application	Conclusion
1. Was the venue properly laid in the Eastern District of California?			
Venue	**Proper district if:** • **Claim arose** • **Defendant resides** • **If neither of the above apply, any district where any defendant is subject to personal jurisdiction** Some answers include a brief *Erie* discussion that this case is in federal court so federal procedural rules apply and venue is a federal procedural issue. Time permitted you could include this, but it was not necessary.	**District is in the Eastern District of California based on negligence for breaking a vase while cleaning; later claim for breach of contract over same incident.** **Contract to clean arose in Reno, NV, not E.D. of CA.** **The accident where the vase broke and alleged negligence occurred was also in NV while cleaning for S, a NV corporation with its beauty salon in Reno, NV.** **Defendant J resides in Truckee, CA which is in the E.D. of CA so venue ok.**	Venue was proper in the E.D. of CA.
2. Did the court err in denying Shearer's motion to compel?			
Mandatory Initial Disclosures	**Parties must disclose:** • **Identities of those likely to have discoverable info that may support their claim/defense;** • **Copies or descriptions of tangible evidence that may support their claim/defense;** • Damages computation and supporting documentation; • Applicable insurance documents.	Here, if the documents in question, the customer reviews, support J's defense that he was not negligent, then he would have been required to turn those over initially in the initial disclosures as they could be used to support his defense.	Jiff may have been required to turn over the reviews initially (a court could consider this when ruling on the motion to compel).
Production of Documents	**Any party may request another party, or a nonparty with subpoena, to make available for review and copying documents,** electronic copies, or other tangible items. **Parties must meet and confer when there are discovery disputes prior to seeking a motion to compel.**	**Requesting the documents or electronic copies of written reviews would be an appropriate and proper request as J is a party and is in possession of the documents. Provided they are** relevant and within the scope of discovery, S **could request for J to produce the documents.** **But S cannot file a motion to compel production from the court until after they have attempted to meet and confer with J and the facts don't indicate this occurred.**	Court properly denied the motion to compel if Shearer did not meet and confer first.

Continued>

Issue	Rule	Fact Application	Conclusion
Scope of Discoverable Evidence	**Must be relevant, not privileged, not work product, and proportional to the needs of the case.** **Need not be admissible** but reasonably calculated to lead to the discovery of admissible material.	**Reviews could be relevant** as they often contain good and bad reviews and could show other incidences of when personal items were damaged or broken or whether other clients thought J used reasonable care when cleaning since this claim was based on negligence. J may argue the reviews are not relevant as he requests the reviews for his own use to monitor customer satisfaction, but the reason he requests the reviews does not make them irrelevant for other purposes. Reviews would be proportional as S only requested the last year of reviews, not all reviews, so the request was limited and sharing reviews for one year for a $100,000 case is not too burdensome. **May not be admissible** as hearsay but can still lead to other discoverable evidence such as contacting the names of others who left reviews.	**If Jiff did meet and confer, then the requested documents would be discoverable.**

3. May Jiff take advantage of the judgment in the first suit in defending against the second suit?

Issue	Rule	Fact Application	Conclusion

Res Judicata	• **Prior judgment valid, final, and on merits**
	  • In federal court the judgment is final once rendered.
	  • In California, the judgment is final once all appeals are concluded.
	• **Same parties/privies in same order**
	• **Same claim**
	
	Fed: same transaction and occurrence
	Cal. (and min. jx): primary rights
		There was a valid final judgment on the merits because there was a jury trial and the jury returned a general verdict in favor of J and the court entered judgment on the verdict. And the appeals would not matter in federal court, but S did not appeal anyway.
		
		S and J are the same parties in first case and second case and in the same order.
		
		In federal court, the claim was the same transaction and occurrence even though the first claim was negligence and the second claim was breach of contract because both involved the same cleaning contract and incident where J broke the vase cleaning.
			Shearer's second breach of contract claim is likely barred by res judicata so Jiff could take advantage of the judgment in the first suit.

Continued>

Issue	Rule	Fact Application	Conclusion
Res Judicata (continued)		S might argue in Cal., which follows the **primary rights theory that the negligence (tort) and breach of contract (contract) claims are different rights. However, both involve damage to the same property** as opposed to property and personal injuries so the same property right is being litigated in and in particular the due care regarding that vase.	
Collateral Estoppel	• **Prior proceeding resulted in a valid final judgment on merits** • **Same issue actually litigated and determined** • **Necessary (essential)** • **Mutuality of parties** • **Traditional: party/privy** • Modern/Cal: nonparty ok if • Defensive: fair opportunity to be heard in prior case • Offensive: fair and equitable and new party could not have easily joined first case	See above for final judgment on the merits and the parties. **It is possible that the issue of lack of due care would have been actually litigated and determined in the prior negligence case since duty and breach must be analyzed** to determine whether a party has been negligent. It is likely that the jury would have considered these elements and that both parties presented evidence regarding those elements. However, the verdict was a general verdict **so it isn't clear if the issue was necessary/essential because they could have found that J didn't breach a duty, or if perhaps he did (and thus lacked due care), they could have found there was no causation** such that it wasn't foreseeable that the vase would break. It is also possible that S was negligent too and their own negligence barred recovery. It isn't clear from a general verdict why the jury found for J as to which element because J would win if only one element was not met so all elements were not essential because one missing element negates the entire claim.	The issue of due care is not likely barred by collateral estoppel, so Jiff could not take advantage of the judgment in the first suit on that particular issue, but the overall claims would likely be barred under res judicata.

Civil Procedure Question 6
July 2017, Question 4

Buyer, who was living in New York, and Seller, who was living in California, entered into a valid contract, agreeing to buy and sell a painting claimed to be an original Rothko, supposedly worth $1 million, for that amount. In a separate valid contract, Buyer agreed to buy from Seller a parcel of California real property worth $5 million, for that amount. Buyer and Seller completed the purchase of the painting on June 1; they were to complete the purchase of the real property on June 30.

On June 15, Buyer resold the painting, but obtained only $200, because the painting turned out to be a fake. Buyer promptly notified Seller of his intent to sue Seller for damages of $1 million. Seller then informed Buyer that Seller would not go through with the purchase of the real property.

Buyer filed suit against Seller in federal court in California. Buyer claimed fraud as to the painting, alleging only that Seller committed "fraud in the supposed value," and sought $1 million in damages. Buyer also claimed breach of contract as to the real property, and sought specific performance. Buyer demanded trial by jury on all issues.

1. May Buyer join claims for fraud and breach of contract in the same suit against Seller? Discuss.

2. Is Buyer's allegation sufficient to state a claim for fraud involving the painting? Discuss.

3. Does the federal court have subject matter jurisdiction over the suit? Discuss.

4. May the federal court apply California law to decide the breach of contract claim involving the real property? Discuss.

5. On what issues, if any, would Buyer be entitled to a jury trial? Discuss.

Civil Procedure Question 6 Assessment
July 2017, Question 4

At first glance when you see five calls in an essay, you might have a moment of panic. That is fine. Inhale. Exhale. And pull yourself together. Usually when there are numerous calls the issues tend to be more specific, making issue spotting easier. And the depth required on the issues is usually only surface level, meaning that if you know your rules you can usually fare well on these types of essays.

Call one specifically asks about joinder of claims. While this is not a heavily tested topic, you can quickly run through a checklist of the types of joinder and have those ready when you read the facts to see what type(s) of joinder you are dealing with. This is a very easy concept involving basic joinder of claims. There is no need to answer more than is asked. There is one plaintiff and one defendant, so joinder is permissible. There is no need to discuss aggregation or other issues that aren't necessary given the facts. Stick to the call of the question.

The second call is specifically asking about pleading a fraud claim. Hopefully you know your rules well enough to know that fraud must be plead with specificity. Again, this is not an issue heavily tested on essays, but it is straightforward and only requires rule memorization with little factual analysis. Know the rule and you are good to go here.

The third call is specific also and asks about subject matter jurisdiction, which usually requires you to analyze diversity and is not difficult. In fact, this issue is easy with only individual citizens at issue. And the dollar amount is easily met. Get in and get out. Again, there is no need to go into depth about supplemental jurisdiction or aggregation when they are not needed. Only analyze what is asked of you and what the facts give rise to.

The fourth call is where things can get tricky, as it raises the issue of choice of law, which often requires some *Erie* discussion. However, most bar exam essays that test *Erie* and choice of law are much more straightforward and simpler compared to the level of depth you learned in your law school classes. The key usually turns on whether the issue is substantive or procedural as to which law to apply. Here, you did need to mention the California laws that California uses to assess breach of contract claims and real property. But otherwise, it was also a straightforward call.

The final call is also specific, as it deals with the right to a jury trial. When they test this issue, they often test it in terms of knowing whether the claim is equitable or legal to determine if the parties are entitled to a jury trial. You likely learned this in both Civil Procedure and Remedies so you can quickly address this issue too.

Timing is a huge consideration when there are several calls. This is why organizing your essay prior to writing it out is helpful. You can quickly gain insight as to which issues will be straightforward and which issues may require a bit more analysis (like call 4). On exams like these, if you know your rules you can get in and get out. Remember on the bar exam it is like you are snorkeling—one hour essay with several issues, so little time to spend on each call—get in and get out. Law school was equivalent to scuba diving—often you had three-hour finals for a subject (and sometimes six hours of finals if it was a year-long course), so the level of depth required on law school exams was much more, hence the scuba diving analogy. This is why bar exam practice is key. You need to know how the examiners test the issues and the level of depth in analysis required depending on what issues they are testing.

Make note of the areas highlighted in **bold** on the corresponding grid. The bold areas highlight the issues, analysis, and conclusions that are likely **required** to receive a passing score on this question.

Issue	Rule	Fact Application	Conclusion
1. May Buyer join claims for fraud and breach of contract in the same suit against Seller?			
Joinder of Claims	A party asserting a claim, counterclaim, crossclaim, or third-party claim may join as many claims as it has against an opposing party. Each claim needs SMJ or Supplemental Jurisdiction.	Both the fraud claim for the Rothko painting and the breach of contract claim for real property are brought by the same plaintiff, B, against the same defendant, S. Since the same individual parties, B can join both claims against S if there is SMJ or supp. jx. As discussed in call three, the court has SMJ so the claims may be joined.	Yes, B may join the claims.
2. Is Buyer's allegation sufficient to state a claim for fraud involving the painting?			
Pleadings	Federal courts use notice pleading which provides the opposing party with reasonable notice of the nature and scope of the claims and facts showing a plausible claim. A complaint must plead specific facts to prove certain claims including fraud. If a complaint does plead fraud with specificity, the defendant can move to dismiss the claim for failure to state a claim on which relief can be granted.	B's pleading arguably put S on notice of plausible claims for fraud relating to the Rothko painting and breach of contract for the real property by stating the claims. However, it does not have facts to show that a fraud claim is actually plausible as there are no facts the court can take as true to make the claim plausible. Here, B's fraud claim alleged that S committed "fraud in the supposed value" as to the painting which is not specific because it does not specifically plead each element of fraud clearly such as the intentional misrepresentation, reliance, etc. or the facts surrounding the fraud or misrepresentation. Rather B just asked for $1 million in damages. So, S can move to dismiss the claim.	B's allegation was not sufficient to state a claim for fraud.
3. Does the federal court have subject matter jurisdiction over the suit?			
Subject Matter Jurisdiction	Federal question or complete diversity between the parties and more than $75,000 amount in controversy. Domicile at the time of the filing determines a person's citizenship. A person's domicile is where they are physically present with a subjective intent to remain.	Neither fraud nor breach of contract are federal question claims as they are both common law claims. For diversity, B lives in NY and S lives in CA so both parties are diverse. While B might have intended to move to CA after buying the real property, he was domiciled in NY at the time the suit was filed. As to the amount, both claims exceed $75,000 because the painting claim is for $1 million and the property breach of contract claim was valued at $5 million.	SMJ exists over the claims.

Continued>

Issue	Rule	Fact Application	Conclusion
4. May the federal court apply California law to decide the breach of contract claim involving the real property?			
Erie/Choice of Law	A federal court sitting in diversity applies **federal procedural law and state substantive law.**	Here there is no federal law at issue and a breach of contract claim is a substantive issue not a procedural issue so state law would apply.	Yes, the federal court may apply California law.
	California conflicts of laws rules are deemed substantive under *Erie*.	Since the claims were filed in California, the federal court would apply California state law for substantive issues including California's choice of law rules should there be a dispute.	
	For contract actions without a choice of law provision, California uses the comparative impairment test to each state's interest in having its own law applied.	**The property is located in California and the breach of contract claim is for the real property so it is likely the court would apply California law.**	
	For real property, California uses the law of the state in which the property is located.	If the court balanced NY v. CA interests based on the contract, it is likely a court would find CA has a higher interest than NY in ensuring contracts are fairly executed in its state involving real property located in its state. Also, B did file suit in CA not NY even though B is from NY.	
5. On what issues, if any, would Buyer be entitled to a jury trial?			
7th Amendment Right to Jury Trial	**In federal court, there is a right to a jury trial in all civil actions at law. There is no right to a jury trial for equitable actions.**	Here, the fraud issue is an action at law as it seeks $1 million in damages, which is a legal remedy. **However, the breach of contract issue seeks specific performance which is an equitable remedy.**	B is entitled to a jury trial on the fraud claim seeking damages.
	Plaintiff must demand in writing, no later than 14 days after service of the last pleading that they want a jury trial, or it is waived.	B demanded a jury trial on all issues, which likely was in the complaint, so it is likely the timing and writing requirements were satisfied.	
	The court determines equitable issues and the jury determines legal issues. If both legal and equitable issues are involved, the jury decides the legal issues first and the court decides the equitable issues second.	The jury would determine the legal damages for the fraud first and then the court would determine the specific performance equitable issue for the real property second.	

PART 3 <u>COMMUNITY PROPERTY</u>

<u>COMMUNITY PROPERTY TABLE OF CONTENTS</u>

INTRODUCTION TO COMMUNITY PROPERTY

Community property is generally tested in only one of two formats and the rules are fairly simple, so it is a subject that is comparatively easy to handle so long as you follow a specific approach with every question. Using the approach is especially important for those students who have not taken community property as a course in law school.

The first type of fact pattern involves a couple acquiring a variety of assets, either before marriage, during marriage, and/or after separation or divorce. Some assets, such as retirement pensions, may be earned before or during marriage, but not vest until later. Subsequently, the couple either divorces or one spouse dies, perhaps leaving a will devising all of their property to a third party. Consequently, wills and trusts is a frequent crossover question with community property. In these types of fact patterns, the calls are often specifically asking about a particular asset in regard to a number of parties, including the other spouse, children, a subsequent spouse, or third parties. The key is to ensure you properly address all parties when going through each asset.

The second type of fact pattern will present a couple or one spouse who has incurred debt and the creditor is seeking repayment. The debt may be incurred before marriage, during marriage, or after separation or divorce, and may have been incurred for the benefit of the community or not. The rules and outcome will vary based on when the debt was incurred and for what purpose the debt was incurred. Usually, they like to frame these essays in conjunction with when couples separate but don't actually divorce.

Regardless of which format the question is in, community property questions are very fact driven and the chronology of events is critical to successful issue spotting and analysis. For this reason, it is useful to draw a timeline on your scratch paper, or at the top of your answer (remember to delete it before you submit), listing each event disclosed in the fact pattern. The first inquiry is always whether the couple is married or not, and if so when they were married. Pay special attention to all events that have occurred and when they occurred, such as when a marriage, separation, or divorce occurred; when an asset was acquired or debt incurred; or when any other significant event took place, such as one person agreeing to add the other spouse on title to their separate property. Include all significant events on the timeline. You'll find the facts are often vague enough that you may need to do competing analyses. For example, if the premarital agreement is valid, X happens, if the premarital agreement is invalid, Y happens.

Finally, once you have created the timeline, follow the call of the question and analyze each asset or debt using the following approach: Take each asset or debt separately (usually they are already separated by each call) and use your entire checklist to issue spot. First, identify the *source and timing* of the asset or debt (separate property (SP), community property (CP), quasi-marital property (QMP), or quasi-community property (QCP)), and identify any original *presumption* that applies. (For example, an inheritance is presumptively separate property.) Second, identify any *actions* the parties may have taken that would alter the original presumption and change the characterization. (For example, the parties can agree to transmute SP to CP.) Third, identify if any *special classification* rules apply that affect the original presumption. (For example, retirement pay is special and is apportioned using the time rule.) Finally, be sure to actually answer the call of the question and explain the disposition of each asset or debt. This seems obvious, but if the call asks what H and W's rights are regarding each asset, do the simple math and determine the answer; don't stop analyzing once you've characterized the asset or debt as community or separate property. You must go all the way!

Lastly, keep in mind that when there are no dates in the fact pattern for a divorce or separation or death but they use words like "now," you need to refer to the date of that particular bar exam since they assume the date "now" is the date the students took that bar essay. For this reason, we include the date administered on each of our essays.

ISSUES CHECKLIST AND ESSAY APPROACH

Preliminary Issues
    Relationship status
    Premarital agreement
Characterize Property
    Original general presumptions (CP, SP, QCP, QMP)
        Source of funds at time of acquisition
    Does anything change the characterization?
        Title presumptions
        Tracing
        Transmutations
        Management and control
        Contributions/improvements
            CP to SP business (Pereira/Van Camp)
            CP to SP (other spouse or own)
            CP to SP real property
            SP to SP
            SP to CP
        Special rules
            Personal injury
            Pension/retirement/stock options
            Disability/workers' compensation
            Severance pay
            Bonuses
            Education/training
            Life insurance
            Business goodwill
            Federal preemption
        Creditor rights/debts
        Order of debt satisfaction
Distribution at death/divorce

MEMORIZATION ATTACK SHEET

RELATIONSHIP STATUS

◆ **Married**
- Valid in Cal.
- Okay if valid in another state

◆ **Domestic partnership**
- Cal. same rights as married couples
- Okay if valid in another state

◆ **Permanent separation**
- Intent to end marriage communicated, and
- Conduct consistent

◆ **Nonmarried couples**
- Putative spouse, treat as married
  - ◆ Good faith belief
  - ◆ Void/voidable marriage
  - ◆ Estoppel may apply if knew
  - ◆ QMP is property classification
- Unmarried—Contracts law applies

◆ **Premarital agreements—valid**
- Not promote divorce
- In writing/signed by both
- Deemed involuntary unless
  - ◆ Independent counsel or waived in writing
  - ◆ 7 days before signing
  - ◆ Terms/rights in writing in proficient language
  - ◆ No duress, fraud, undue influence
  - ◆ Any other factors court deems relevant
- Not unconscionable
  - ◆ Not unconscionable at execution, and
  - ◆ No knowledge of property, and
  - ◆ No fair full disclosure of property, and
  - ◆ Did not waive disclosure
- Can't waive child support
- Can waive spousal support w/ ind. counsel
- Laches and estoppel are available defenses

GENERAL PRESUMPTIONS

◆ Source of funds and timing
◆ CP = during marriage by labor
◆ SP = before or after marriage, or by devise or inheritance or gift
◆ QCP = domiciled elsewhere but would be CP if in Cal.
◆ QMP = putative spouses

PRESUMPTIONS INFERRED BY TITLE

◆ **Form of title used to rebut presumption**
◆ **Jointly titled prop benefitted by SP**
- *Lucas*: at death jointly held title is presumed CP
  - ◆ No reimbursement
- Anti-*Lucas*: at divorce jointly held title is presumed CP
  - ◆ DIP reimbursement
    - Down payment
    - Improvements
    - Principal
◆ **MWSP** = W's name alone prior to 1975 is her SP

SOURCE OF FUNDS, TRACING, & COMMINGLED FUNDS

◆ Initial characterization
- Source of funds and timing
◆ Tracing **commingled funds**
- Can trace SP to source
- Burden of proof on SP proponent
- Tracing cannot overcome joint title presumption
  - ◆ Exception: bank accounts
- Two tracing methods
  - ◆ Exhaustion method: all CP funds exhausted when property purchased
  - ◆ Direct tracing:
    - Sufficient SP funds at time of purchase, and
    - Intent to use SP funds
  - ◆ If SP cannot be traced, property is CP

TRANSMUTATIONS

◆ **Transmutations**
- Writing required
  - ◆ Real or personal property
  - ◆ Describe change in ownership
  - ◆ Consent of adversely affected spouse
- Exception
  - ◆ Personal gifts of insubstantial nature
  - ◆ No other exceptions to writing requirement
- Pre-1985: oral and inferred from conduct okay

MANAGEMENT AND CONTROL

- ◆ **Fiduciary duties**
  - Full disclosure of material facts
  - Good faith and fair dealing
- ◆ **Community personal property**
  - Equal power to manage CP
  - One spouse can't gift or dispose for less than fair value
  - One spouse can't sell or convey family furnishings without written consent
- ◆ **Community businesses**
  - Managing spouse can make all decisions, but must give written notice to sell
- ◆ **Community real property**
  - Both need to sign to sell or lease for more than 1 yr.
  - Can't convey to 3rd party without other spouse consent
    - ◆ Presumed valid to BFP
      - If done, spouse has 1 yr. to void sale
    - ◆ Non BFP can be voided any time

CONTRIBUTIONS/IMPROVEMENTS

- ◆ **CP to SP**
  - **CP to SP Businesses**
    - ◆ *Pereira*: favors CP
      - Use if spouse skills is reason for growth
      - **SP = initial SP + RRR**
      - **RRR = 10% of SP contributed per yr. during marriage**
      - **CP = value of biz - SP**
    - ◆ *Van Camp*: favors SP
      - Use if character of business reason for growth
      - **CP = fmv salary - family expenses - salary taken**
      - **SP = value of biz - CP**
  - **CP to other spouse's SP**: gift presumed in some jurisdictions
  - **CP to spouse's own SP**: CP reimbursed greater of amount spent on improvement or increase in value
  - **CP to SP real property**
    - ◆ CP % = amount CP contributed to principal/total amount of loan
    - ◆ Then, multiply CP% by capital appreciation
    - ◆ Payments for interest, tax, and insurance are excluded
- ◆ **SP to other spouse's SP**
  - Reimbursed without interest for DIP

- ◆ **SP to CP property or business**
  - Reimbursement DIP
  - Business — Reverse *Pereira* and *Van Camp*

SPECIAL RULES FOR SPECIAL ASSETS

- ◆ **Personal injury by third party**
  - During marriage = CP
    - ◆ Death = CP
    - ◆ Divorce awarded to injured spouse
  - After separation/divorce = SP
  - Can get reimbursement
- ◆ **Personal injury caused by other spouse**
  - Exhaust tortfeasor spouse SP first
- ◆ **Pension**
  - Earned during marriage = CP, regardless of when fully vested
  - Time Rule to apportion
  - Two approaches to divide
    - ◆ <u>Reservation of jurisdiction</u> until spouse retires
      - Other spouse can elect their share when spouse is eligible to retire
    - ◆ <u>Cash out</u>: pension to employed spouse & other assets of = value to other spouse
- ◆ **Stock options**
  - Vests during marriage = CP
  - If for past services = Time rule
  - If for future service = SP
- ◆ **Disability/worker's comp.**
  - SP or CP depends on what it replaces
- ◆ **Severance Pay**
  - If replace retirement benefits earned when married = CP
  - If replace future post-divorce earnings = SP
- ◆ **Bonuses**
  - If earned during marriage = CP
  - If earned after marriage/personal gift = SP
  - Doesn't matter when paid
- ◆ **Education/training**
  - Not community asset
  - CP reimbursed if
    - ◆ It paid for education, and
    - ◆ Earning capacity substantially enhanced
  - Defenses to reimbursement
    - ◆ Community substantially benefited (presumed if > 10 years)
    - ◆ Other spouse received education
    - ◆ Reduced need for spousal support in educated spouse

- ◆ **Life insurance**
  - Whole: lifetime coverage & accumulates cash value
    - ◆ Each estate gets % cash value for % premiums paid
  - Term: coverage for specified term and no cash value
    - ◆ SP or CP based on latest estate to pay premium
  - Decedent can only devise ½ to beneficiary not their spouse, unless written consent
- ◆ **Business goodwill**
  - Expectation of continued public patronage
  - Market value approach
  - Excess earnings approach
    - ◆ Deduct fair return on business
    - ◆ Take professional's annual net earnings
    - ◆ Deduct comparable professional's earnings
    - ◆ Capitalize excess earnings over marriage
- ◆ **Federal preemption**
  - Federal law preempts state law

DEBT AND CREDITOR RIGHTS

- ◆ **Credit acquisitions**
  - **During marriage** = CP debt
  - **Intent of lender** = rebut CP by showing lender relied on SP
  - **Earning capacity**
- ◆ **Timing of debts:** at time of k, tort, etc.

- ◆ **Creditor's rights follow management rights**
  - CP liable for all debts before and during
  - Except earnings shielded in separate account for premarital debts
- ◆ **Order of debt satisfaction**
  - Community interest: CP first
  - Separate interest: SP first
  - SP debts before marriage—all CP and debtor's SP only, but nondebtor can shield CP earnings if separate account
  - SP debts during marriage—all CP and debtor's SP, not nondebtor SP
  - Except for necessaries of life (even post-separation)
  - Injury caused by spouse
    - ◆ If for benefit to comm., CP first
    - ◆ Injury caused by spouse if not for benefit to comm., SP first

DIVISION AND DISTRIBUTION

- ◆ **Divorce:**
  - CP/QCP split equally, each keeps SP
  - Real property out of Cal.—if jurisdiction problem, give equivalent value
- ◆ **Death:**
  - Will: can devise all SP & ½ of CP/QCP
    - ◆ Except not QCP titled in survivor's name
  - No will: all CP to spouse, ⅓, ½ or all SP to spouse, depending on survivors
  - Real property out of Cal.—will probate in jurisdiction

COMMUNITY PROPERTY RULE OUTLINE

I. INTRODUCTION
A. Community property system
1. **California is a community property state**. The premise of the community property system is that earnings from the labors of each spouse during the marriage contribute equally to the accumulation of wealth and debt, which are owned equally by both spouses.
   a. **Community property system will apply automatically** to married couples and domestic partners domiciled in California, unless the couple makes a valid agreement to the contrary.
   b. **California Family Code** governs the community property as a system.
   c. **Not all states follow** the community property system (only nine currently do).

> **Exam tip:** In a community property essay there will be a couple and you will be asked to distribute various pieces of property they've accumulated in the event of death or divorce. For every essay, use the following approach: (1) Start your essay with an introduction providing **rule definitions** for CP, SP (and QCP/QMP if at issue); (2) Address any issues pertaining to the validity of marriage, putative spouse issues, and/ or a premarital agreement; and (3) Take **each piece of property/debt separately** and determine how it should be distributed at death or divorce (as indicated in the question). To do so, first, identify the original **source and timing** of the funds used to acquire the property for the initial characterization. Next, determine if the parties took any **actions** that could potentially change the characterization (the way they took title, a transmutation, tracing, management and control, contributions, etc.) Then, consider if there are any **special rules** that guide the characterization of a special asset (retirement, disability, etc.). Lastly, after considering all of the issues, **answer the call of the question** as to each piece of property and the respective parties.

B. Relationship status
1. **Marriage**
   a. **California:** A marriage is valid in California where there is a consensual **civil contract** between two people followed by the performance of certain legal procedures. The **marital economic community** begins at the date of marriage and ends at permanent separation, dissolution, divorce, or the death of one spouse, whichever occurs first.
   b. **Other jurisdictions:** California recognizes marriages from other jurisdictions if the marriage would be valid by the laws of that jurisdiction.
2. **Domestic partnership**
   a. **California: Registered domestic partners** are legally afforded the **same rights and responsibilities** as married persons (though there are some legal and tax differences). This status is available to all partners over the age of 18 (partners under the age 18 require written consent from a parent or guardian and a court order granting permission). The **domestic partnership economic community** begins at the date of partnership registration and ends at permanent separation, dissolution, or the death of one domestic partner, whichever occurs first.

> **Note:** For purposes of this outline, all references to spouses include domestic partners and all references to divorce include dissolution of a domestic partnership. Spouses refers to both same-sex and opposite-sex couples.

   b. **Other jurisdictions:** California recognizes domestic partnerships from other jurisdictions if the domestic partnership would be valid by the laws of that jurisdiction.

3. **Permanent separation** occurs when there is a **complete and final break** in the marital relationship where one spouse has expressed to the other spouse their **intent to end the marriage**, and the spouse's **conduct is consistent** with their intent to end the marriage.
   a. **Property classification: After the date of permanent separation**, the earnings and accumulations of each party are treated as **separate property** (SP).
4. **Nonmarried couples:**
   a. **Putative spouse/domestic partner:** A putative spouse is **not legally married** because the marriage is void or voidable, but the party must have a **good faith belief** (based on a subjective standard) that they were legally married (or registered domestic partners).
      1. **Void or Voidable marriage:** Since a lawful marriage requires capacity, a marriage can be found void or voidable for the following reasons:
         a. **Void:** A marriage will be found void for reasons such as bigamy or incest.
         b. **Voidable:** A marriage will be found voidable at the election of the interested party for reasons such as fraud, force, incapacity, or a party was a minor.
      2. **Estoppel:** One may be **estopped to assert putative spouse status** if the party making the assertion **knew** that the marriage was **not valid** or knew that it was invalid but acted as though it was valid.
         a. **Jurisdictional split:** Jurisdictions are split on how to treat a party to a void or voidable marriage where that party did not have a good faith belief the marriage was valid. **Some will treat both parties as putative spouses**, while **others will treat only the innocent party as a putative spouse**.
      3. **Quasi-marital property:** The property acquired by a putative spouse will be classified as quasi-marital property (see II.E below)
   b. **Unmarried cohabitants** (meretricious relationships): Courts follow general **contract principles** and use resulting or constructive trusts and quasi-contract principles to allocate property for unmarried cohabitants.
5. **Premarital agreement:** A premarital agreement is one made before marriage that is to become effective upon marriage, in which parties **agree to the characterization of their property** and may limit support obligations. A premarital agreement is typically used to avoid the community property system and **must meet stringent requirements to be valid.**
   a. **Requirements for an enforceable premarital agreement:**
      1. **It must not promote divorce:** Any terms that create a positive incentive for a party to seek a divorce will not be enforced.
      2. **Writing required:** Premarital agreements must be in writing and **signed by both parties**, and **consideration is not required.**
      3. **Must be made voluntarily: Premarital agreements are deemed involuntary unless** the court finds that the party against whom enforcement is sought was:
         a. **Represented by independent counsel** at the time the agreement was signed **or advised** to seek independent counsel **and waived it in a separate writing**;
         b. **Presented** with the final agreement and **advised to seek independent counsel** at least **seven calendar days before signing it** (for agreements between 1/1/2002 and 1/1/2020), *OR* **presented** with the final agreement at least **seven calendar days before signing it, regardless of representation by counsel** (for agreements on or after 1/1/2020);
         c. **If unrepresented** by counsel, the party against whom enforcement is sought must be **fully informed in writing** of the terms and rights the party is giving up (property/ wealth), in a **language in which they are proficient** and **declare in writing** that they received such information and **from whom** they received it;
         d. **Not under duress**, fraud, undue influence, and did not lack capacity; and
         e. **Any other factors** the court deems relevant.
      4. Must **not be unconscionable** (determined by the court as a matter of law):
         a. Occurs when the agreement is **unconscionable at the time of execution; or**
         b. The party against whom enforcement is sought was **not provided a fair, reasonable, and full disclosure** of the property or financial obligations, **did not have adequate**

    knowledge of the property or financial obligations of the other party, and **did not waive the right to the disclosure** in writing.

  b. **Child support and spousal support**

    1. **Child support cannot be waived** by a premarital agreement.

    2. **Spousal support** can be waived by a premarital agreement if **independent counsel** represented the spouse against whom enforcement is sought **at the time the agreement was signed,** or if the provision is **not unconscionable at the time of enforcement**.

  c. **Defenses to enforcement:** Equitable defenses limiting the time for enforcement, including **laches** (unreasonable delay and prejudicial effect) and **estoppel** (detrimental reliance) are available to either party.

> **Exam tip:** Most exams indicate that *H* and *W* are married and relationship status is not at issue. Occasionally a question will include a putative spouse or contractual relationship. If the facts don't establish the existence of the marriage, address the relationship status issues before analyzing any other issues.

II. GENERAL PRESUMPTIONS

 A. **Characterization of property:** All property acquired by married persons while domiciled in California is characterized as **community property** or **separate property**. The original characterization is based on the **source of funds** and the **timing** of the acquisition.

 B. **Community property (CP): The earnings of each spouse and all property, wherever situated, acquired during marriage by the labor of either spouse while domiciled in California is presumptively community property.**

 C. **Separate property (SP):** All property acquired **before marriage or after permanent separation or after divorce is presumptively separate property**. In addition, separate property includes all property acquired, at any time, by **gift, bequest, devise,** or **descent**; and the **rents, issues,** and **profits** derived from that property; and **property acquired with separate property funds** is also **presumptively separate property**.

  1. **Earnings and accumulations** are deemed SP where:

    a. **Separation:** For a spouse **and** the minor children living with that spouse **while separated** from the other spouse, the **earnings** and accumulations are SP; or

    b. **Legal separation:** After a **legal separation** the earnings and accumulations are SP.

    c. **Note:** These **special rules apply to earnings and accumulations**, but not other sources of money/property.

  2. **Permanent separation:** After permanent separation, property of each party is treated as SP.

 D. **Quasi-community property (QCP):** QCP is all property, real or personal, wherever situated, acquired by either spouse while domiciled in a non-CP state, which **would have been classified as CP** had the parties been domiciled in California at the time of acquisition.

 E. **Quasi-marital property (QMP):** QMP is property acquired during a **void or voidable marriage**, which would have been CP or QCP if the marriage had not been void or voidable. The property of a **putative spouse** is classified as QMP. **QMP is treated the same as community property (CP) or quasi-community property (QCP).**

> **Exam tip:** Once the relationship is established (if not already established in the facts), address all applicable general presumptions before moving on to analyze the assets/ debts in question. Only address the general presumptions that apply to the facts. For example, if all events occurred in California, do not discuss QCP.

III. PRESUMPTIONS INFERRED BY TITLE

 A. **Form of title can be used to rebut presumption:** The form of title for a piece of property may rebut the original presumption as CP or SP **when title is inconsistent** with the original presumption.

1. **Source of funds SP, but title is CP:** When the source of funds for a property is SP, but title is taken jointly, it is **presumed to be a gift to the community** and characterized as CP, unless there is a contrary written intent, subject to reimbursement at divorce (see Anti-*Lucas* rule below in section III.B.2).

2. **Source of funds CP, but title is SP:** When the source of funds for a property is CP, but title is taken by one spouse only, the **property will retain its characterization as CP**, unless there is a written transmutation (see transmutation rules below in section V.A).

   a. **Exception where title is evidence of a gift:** Where a spouse intends to give the other spouse a **gift and title is taken in a way to evidence that gift,** the property will be the **SP of the gifted spouse**. There is **no writing requirement**. For example: A husband buys his wife a car for their anniversary and titles it in her name only.

   b. **Exception four-year rule:** The **presumption** that all property acquired during marriage is CP **does not apply** when the **title is held by a person at death** and the **marriage ended** more than **four years** earlier.

B. **Jointly titled property benefitted by expenditures of SP. The following rules only apply to jointly titled property where there is a SP contribution, and the rules differ depending on if the marriage ends in death or divorce.**

   1. *Lucas*: At **death,** all **jointly titled** property of either spouse is **presumed to be CP** at the death of either spouse, **unless** there is an **express agreement to the contrary.**

      a. **No right to reimbursement** for SP contributions. In other words, a gift from the SP to the CP is presumed.

   2. **Anti-*Lucas*: At divorce or legal separation** all **jointly titled** property of the spouses is **presumed to be CP, unless** there is an **express agreement to the contrary.**

      a. **Right to reimbursement** for SP contributions, without interest.

   3. **Reimbursements:** SP reimbursements (whether applicable through an agreement or anti-*Lucas*) are only allowed for expenditures made for **down payments**, **improvements**, and payments that reduce the **principal** of a loan. There is no right to reimbursement for SP that paid interest, taxes, insurance, or maintenance.

   > **Memorization tip:** Use the mnemonic "**DIP**" to remember reimbursements apply to **D**own payments, **I**mprovements, and **P**rincipal.

   > **Exam tip:** Always address title issues in your essay any time a party has taken title in a way that is at odds with the original general presumption applicable to that property. Before addressing *Lucas* and anti-*Lucas* make sure that title is involved and that the title is for property, not bank accounts. In addition, these rules for jointly titled property only apply to situations involving death and divorce, so if the question involves a creditor seeking payment and there has been no death or divorce, these rules do not apply.

C. **Married women's special presumption (MWSP):** Property acquired by a married woman in a **writing**, prior to **1975**, is **presumed to be her SP**.

   1. **Married woman and third person:** Property acquired by a married woman and any other person (including her husband) is a **tenancy in common** unless the instrument indicates otherwise.

   2. **Married woman and her spouse:** Property acquired by a married woman and her spouse is **presumed CP** if the instrument identifies them as **husband and wife**, otherwise it is a tenancy in common.

IV. **SOURCE OF FUNDS, TRACING, AND COMMINGLED FUNDS**

   A. **Source of funds for initial characterization:** To determine if a piece of property is SP or CP, first determine the **source of funds used** to acquire the property and the **timing of the acquisition** (using the definitions for the presumptions contained in section II.).

1. **Community property:** If the property was acquired using **funds from the labor** of either spouse during the marriage, its **initial characterization is CP.**
2. **Separate property:** If the property was acquired **before marriage, after permanent separation or after divorce; or** by **gift, bequest, devise,** or **descent**; or with the **rents, issues,** and **profits derived from SP**; or was acquired **using SP funds**, its **initial characterization is SP.**

B. **Joint title: Joint title trumps tracing for real and personal property,** but tracing is **always allowed for jointly held bank accounts.** Tracing cannot be used to overcome the presumption where title to property was taken jointly, **except** that tracing can be used to overcome the presumption for jointly titled **bank accounts** since bank accounts are governed by the Probate Code.

C. **Tracing:** A mere **change in form of an asset does not change its characterization** as CP or SP, thus **tracing is permitted** to establish the **source of funds** used to acquire an asset.
1. **Commingled funds:** Commingling of SP funds with CP funds does not necessarily transform or transmute property from SP to CP if the spouse advocating that a piece of property is SP can **trace the source of funds** used to acquire property to SP funds. The new property will then be characterized as the source of funds dictate.
   a. **Burden of proof:** The burden of proof is on the **spouse claiming SP** to show that each asset was acquired with SP funds.
   b. **Family expenses presumption**: When tracing funds, there is a presumption that expenditures for **family expenses were made with CP funds** even if SP funds were also available.

D. **Tracing methods** are used by courts to trace the SP:
1. **Exhaustion method:** Requires showing that at the time the property was purchased, all CP funds in a commingled account had been exhausted by community expenses, and thus **only SP funds were available** to purchase the property.
2. **Direct tracing method:** Requires showing a **direct link** from SP funds to the purchase such that sufficient **SP funds in the account were available** at the time of the purchase and the **SP owner intended to use SP funds** to make the purchase.
3. **Unable to trace to SP:** If it is impossible to trace the source of the property or funds in a commingled account to SP, the **property will be considered CP.**

> **Exam tip:** When characterizing the assets/debts, first look to the initial source of funds at acquisition and then apply any general presumptions or presumptions inferred by title. Commingling and tracing are at issue if there was a subsequent purchase and the funds used can be traced back to the original SP source to establish that the particular asset/debt in question is still SP.

V. **TRANSMUTATIONS**
A. **Transmutation:** A transmutation is an **agreement** between spouses **made during marriage to alter the ownership characterization** of property. (For example, changing property from CP to SP, SP to CP, or one spouse's SP to the other spouse's SP.)
1. **Writing required (since 1/1/1985):** A valid transmutation of **real or personal** property requires a **writing**, clearly describing the **change in ownership**, and **consent** of the adversely affected spouse.
   a. **Exception for gifts between spouses of insubstantial value:** Where a spouse intends to give the other spouse a **personal gift of relatively insubstantial value** (i.e., jewelry, clothes, etc.), taking into account the marital assets, the property will be the SP of the gifted spouse. No writing is required.
   b. **No other exceptions or extrinsic evidence allowed:** There are otherwise no exceptions to the writing requirement allowing for extrinsic evidence to prove the transmutation. For example, a statement in a will is not admissible to prove the transmutation. Detrimental reliance will not be taken into account.
2. **Before 1/1/1985 writing not required:** Transmutations could be **oral, written, or inferred** from the conduct of the parties.

> **Exam tip:** After going through the relationship status (if necessary) and the presumptions and tracing issues, determine if the parties did anything to alter the characterization of the asset/debt, such as a transmutation.

VI. MANAGEMENT AND CONTROL

A. Fiduciary duties

1. **Full disclosure:** Each spouse has a **fiduciary duty** to the other spouse to **fully disclose all material facts** about community **assets and debts** and to provide **equal access** to all information upon request.

2. **Good faith and fair dealing:** Each spouse has a **fiduciary duty to use the highest good faith** and fair dealing with the other spouse and never to take unfair advantage of the other. This includes an **accounting to the other spouse** about any transaction by one spouse without the consent of the other spouse that concerns CP, as well as providing access to all transaction books. The court can alter the distribution of property when necessary to compensate for a spouse's bad faith actions.

> ### *Fiduciary duty fact triggers:*
>
> - Anytime one spouse is acting alone, consider fiduciary duty issues.
> - One spouse sells property without the other spouse's consent.
> - One spouse lies or fails to disclose information to the other spouse.

B. Community personal property

1. **Management and control** of the community personal property belongs to **either spouse** with **absolute power of disposition**, other than testamentary, as they have with their SP estate.
   a. **Except gifts:** A spouse may not make a gift or dispose of community personal property for less than fair and reasonable value without the **written consent of the other spouse**.
   b. **Testamentary limitation:** Each spouse can only dispose of **one-half of their CP** through a testamentary disposition (will or trust), since the other spouse owns the other one-half of the CP, though a spouse may dispose of all of their SP.

2. **Personal property in the family dwelling:** A spouse **may not sell, convey, or encumber** community personal property used in the family dwelling, furnishings, clothing of children or the other spouse without **written consent of the other spouse.**

C. Community business

1. **Management and control:** A spouse who is in charge of managing and controlling a community business can make **all business decisions alone** but must provide the other spouse **with written notice of a sale** or disposition of all or substantially all of the personal property used in the business operations.

D. Community real property

1. **Sale or lease: Both spouses must execute** an instrument to convey or **sell** community real property or for **leases** greater than **one year**.

2. **Conveyance to a third person:**
   a. **Conveyance to a BFP:** Conveyance of community real property by one spouse to a **bona fide purchaser** (third-person purchaser who took for value without notice of the other spouse's interest) is **presumed valid**, but a conveyance to a third person **can be voided** by the other spouse **within one year** of filing of the instrument.
   b. **Conveyance to a non-BFP:** Conveyance of community real property by one spouse to a **non bona fide purchaser** (third person who did not take for value or who had notice of the other spouse's interest) **can be voided** by the other spouse **at any time.**

E. Quasi community property
is generally treated like separate property during the marriage for purpose of management and control.

VII. CONTRIBUTIONS AND IMPROVEMENTS (FROM ONE SOURCE OF FUNDS TO ANOTHER)

A. CP contributions to SP

1. **CP contributions to SP businesses:** California courts use two approaches where CP funds or labor enhance the value of a SP business:
   a. The *Pereira* approach **favors the CP estate** and is used by courts when the **spouse's personal labor and management skills** are the primary reason for the business growth.
      1. **SP interest** = SP contribution + reasonable rate of return
         CP interest = *value of business - SP interest (from above)*
         a. **SP contribution** = Value of SP business at the time of marriage or the SP funds used to capitalize the business during marriage.
         b. **Reasonable rate of return** = **10% of** SP contribution **for each year** family had SP business during marriage.
   b. The *Van Camp* approach **favors the SP estate** and is used by courts when the **character of the business** is the primary reason for the business growth
      1. **CP interest** = Fair market value salary - family expenses - salary taken (over the number of years of the business while married)
         SP interest = *value of business - CP interest (from above)*
         a. **Fair market value salary = Fair market value of spouse's managerial services for each year the family had the SP business during marriage.**
         b. **Family expenses =** Actual family expenses paid with business earnings **for each year** the family had SP business during marriage.
         c. **Salary taken = Actual salary taken, if any, by the managing spouse for each year family** had SP business during marriage.

Exam tip: Anytime a separate property business is involved, start by establishing why it is a SP business (i.e., acquired before marriage or capitalized during marriage with SP funds). Remember, just because a business is acquired during marriage doesn't mean it is necessarily CP. (For example, it could be an inheritance.) After establishing that the business is SP, always address <u>both</u> *Pereira* and *Van Camp* and go through each separately, unless the call directs otherwise. Identify which approach favors each estate and explain why, and then go through the equations. If numbers are available to plug into the equations, do the calculations; if not, simply identify the appropriate equation and define all parts of the equation. Finish by explaining which approach the court will likely use and why.

Memorization tip: Use *Pereira* for **P**ersonal labor and *Van Camp* for **C**haracter of business

---

Pereira/Van Camp fact triggers:

- Business started before marriage
- Business inherited during marriage
- Business started with SP funds during marriage
- Business started during marriage with CP labor — explain why *Pereira/Van Camp* don't apply

---

2. **CP used to improve the *other spouse's* SP. There is a jurisdictional split on how to assess. In some jurisdictions,** a gift is presumed, unless there is an agreement to reimburse. In other jurisdictions, a gift is not presumed and reimbursement is granted. For an exam, apply both rules.

CP improving other spouse's SP fact triggers:

- Any purchase that goes with the other spouse's SP
- Any purchase that compliments the other spouse's SP
- Any purchase that improves the look or display of the other spouse's SP

---

3. **CP used to improve *spouse's own SP*:** When a spouse uses CP to improve that spouse's own SP, the **CP is reimbursed** for the cost of the improvement or the increase in the value to the SP, whichever is greater.
4. **CP contributions to *SP real property* (*Marriage of Moore*):** The community gets a **proportional ownership interest** to the extent CP payments **reduce the principal debt**. Appreciation is allocated in proportion to each estate's ownership interest.
   a. **CP interest** = the amount CP contributed to the **principal reduction** ÷ total **original amount of loan**/balance.
   b. **CP share** = the CP interest (see above) is **multiplied** by the amount of **capital appreciation**.
   c. **Excluded costs:** Payments for **interest, taxes, and insurance** are excluded in the calculations.

> **Exam tip:** When determining the percentage or portion of CP and SP contained in a piece of property, remember to multiply that percentage or portion by the appreciation. This step is often omitted but is necessary to identify the total amount of the property that is CP and SP, which then allows for the determination of what the spouses' rights are in the property. Also be careful not to confuse the rules—pay close attention to whether you have SP contributing to CP (triggers *Lucas* if jointly titled property) or CP contributing to SP (triggers *Pereira, Van Camp, Moore* and other issues).

B. **SP contributions to the** *other spouse's SP*
   1. **Reimbursement:** A party will be reimbursed, without interest or appreciation, for contributions/improvements that can be traced from their SP to the other spouse's SP and that is used for **down payments, improvements**, and reducing the **principal** of a loan, **unless there is a written waiver** of the right to reimbursement or a **written transmutation**.
C. **SP contributions to** *CP property or business*
   1. **Reimbursement:** A party will be reimbursed, without interest, for contributions/improvements that can be traced from their SP to CP and that is used for **down payments, improvements**, and reducing the **principal** of a loan, **unless there is a written waiver** of the right to reimbursement. (Remember: "DIP.")
   2. **Businesses :** **Reverse *Pereira* and *Van Camp*** will apply when SP contributes to a CP business after separation/dissolution.
      a. **Reverse *Pereira*: The community receives a fair rate of return, and the remainder is SP.**
         1. **CP interest** = CP contribution (at time of separation) + reasonable rate of return
         2. **SP interest** = value of business - CP interest (from above)
      b. **Reverse *Van Camp*: The separate estate receives a fair salary, less expenses, and the remainder is CP.**
         1. **SP Interest** = fair market value salary - family expenses - salary taken since separation
         2. **CP interest** = the value of the business - SP interest (from above)

VIII. **SPECIAL RULES FOR SPECIAL ASSETS**
   A. **Personal injury recovery**
      1. **Personal injury caused by a third party:** The classification of a personal injury recovery from a third-party tortfeasor as CP or SP **depends on the timing** of the cause of action, which arises upon infliction of the injury.
         a. **During marriage:** If the spouse was injured during marriage, any money received as a result of the injury is treated as **CP.**
            1. **Upon death** of the injured spouse: The personal injury recovery is **CP.**
            2. **Upon divorce**: The personal injury recovery is **awarded entirely to the injured spouse,** unless the interests of justice require otherwise (economic need), but the injured spouse must get at least half.
         b. **Living separate:** If the spouse was **injured while living separate** from the other spouse, the personal injury recovery is **SP** of the injured spouse.
         c. **After permanent separation or divorce:** If the spouse was injured post-permanent separation, the personal injury recovery is the **SP** of the injured spouse.

    d. **Reimbursement allowed:** The **CP or SP of the non-injured spouse** is entitled to **reimbursement** from the **SP money received by the injured spouse** for any **expenses incurred on behalf** of the injured spouse (e.g., medical expenses).

  2. **Personal injury caused by other spouse:** The **SP of the tortfeasor spouse must be exhausted** before CP may be used to discharge the liability for a personal injury recovery against the tortfeasor spouse.

B. **Pension plans and stock options**

  1. **Pension plans** (and other forms of retirement) **earned during marriage are CP** regardless of when the pension is fully vested or exercisable. For pensions **earned both before and during the marriage,** use the **Time Rule** for apportionment.

    a. **Time Rule:** The Time Rule is used to **apportion pensions, retirement,** and **stock options** earned both before and during the marriage. CP interest is calculated by dividing the number of years when the spouses were married while the pension was earned by the total number of years that the employed spouse earned the pension, times the total pension.

$$CP = \text{Total pension/stock} \times \frac{\text{\# years married while pension earned}}{\text{total \# years pension earned}}$$

    b. **Two approaches to divide pensions** are used by the courts:

      1. The **"reservation of jurisdiction"** approach is used where the court reserves jurisdiction over the case **until the employed spouse retires** and then apportions the retirement between each spouse.

        a. **Election: The non-employed spouse** can elect to receive their share of the pension at the **earliest time** that the employed spouse could retire.

      2. The **"cash-out"** approach is where the court **assigns the entire pension to the employed spouse** and **awards other community assets,** equal in value to the community interest in the retirement benefits, to the **non-employed spouse.**

        a. **Present value calculation: An actuary** is used to determine the proper amount to award to the non-employed spouse by estimating the present value of the pension.

  2. **Stock options:** The CP valuation of a stock option can depend on a variety of factors.

    a. **Vests during marriage:** If the stock options **vest during the marriage,** it is **CP.**

    b. **Exercisable after marriage ends:** If the stock option is **awarded during marriage** but is not exercisable until after the marriage has ended, the following guidelines apply depending on the **purpose** of the stock option:

      1. **CP if compensation for past services (i.e., deferred compensation):** The portion earned during the marriage is CP and the CP interest will be calculated using the **Time Rule** (see above).

      2. **SP if compensation for future services (i.e., as an incentive to stay with the company after separation):** The stock option will be SP when awarded to compensate for services performed **after the divorce.**

C. **Disability pay/workers' compensation:** The **classification** of disability pay or workers' compensation as SP or CP depends on what it was **intended to replace,** regardless of when it is actually paid.

  1. **CP if used to replace *marital earnings*:** If the disability pay is intended to replace marital earnings, it is CP.

  2. **SP if used to replace *post-divorce earnings*:** If the disability pay is intended to replace the **spouse's income after separation** or dissolution, it is SP.

  3. **If intended to replace a *pension* use the Time Rule:** To the extent disability benefits are taken in lieu of retirement benefits, disability benefits will be treated like retirement benefits. Use the Time Rule to calculate the CP portion.

D. **Severance pay** is treated similarly to disability pay and a court will look at when the severance **pay accrued and what it is intended to replace** to calculate the CP portion.

1. **CP if used to replace earned *retirement benefits or income*:** If the severance pay replaces **earned retirement benefits or income** from when the couple was married, **or enhances retirement** earned during marriage, **it is CP**.
2. **SP if used to replace *post-divorce earnings*:** If the severance pay is intended to **compensate lost future earnings after separation** or dissolution, **it is SP**. Even if the severance pay is based on the number of years worked while married, courts will still consider it SP if the right to the benefit accrued after separation or dissolution.

E. **Bonuses** are classified based on **when they were earned** and what they are **intended to reward**, rather than when they are paid.
   1. **CP if reward for *good work performed during marriage*:** If an employer provides a bonus for good work performed during marriage, **it is CP**.
   2. **SP if reward for *good work performed after separation* or divorce:** If an employer provides a bonus for good work performed after separation or dissolution, **it is SP**.
   3. **SP if a personal gift:** If the bonus is more like a personal gift, **it is SP**.

F. **Education/training acquired during marriage** is not a community asset/debt, even when the community pays for it, unless there is a **written agreement** to the contrary.
   1. **Right to reimbursement:** At **divorce**, the community is entitled to reimbursement for **CP contributions** to education/training that **substantially enhanced the earning capacity** of the party, with interest, accruing from the end of the calendar year in which the contributions were made.
   2. **Defenses to reimbursement: Reimbursement may be reduced or denied if:**
      a. The community **already substantially benefited** from the education, which is **presumed after ten years**;
      b. The education is **offset by the CP funded education received** by the other spouse; or
      c. The education **reduced the need for spousal support** for the educated spouse.

> **Exam tip:** When education is tested, start the analysis by stating the full general rule and then analyze the reimbursement rule. Next, state the full rule for when reimbursements may be reduced or denied and analyze those that are applicable under the facts.

G. **Life insurance**
   1. **Whole life insurance** provides lifetime **death benefit** coverage and has an investment component that allows it to accumulate a **cash value** for the policy if it were to be forfeited.
      a. **Estate paying premium controls:** Each estate **(CP and SP)** has an **interest** in the cash value of the policy **to the extent that they paid the premiums**.
         1. **CP interest** = amount CP contributed ÷ total amount contributed (CP + SP)
         2. **SP interest** = amount SP contributed ÷ total amount contributed (CP + SP)
         3. Multiply the SP and CP percentage interest by **total cash value** of insurance to determine their respective amounts.
   2. **Term life insurance** provides **death benefit coverage** for a specified term of time in exchange for the payment of a specific sum of money (the premiums) and **does not accumulate cash value**.
      a. **Estate paying premium on latest term controls:** The term policy is CP or SP depending on which estate paid the premium for the **latest term**.
   3. **Devise of CP life insurance:** To the extent the life insurance policy is CP, the decedent can only devise **one-half** to a beneficiary other than their spouse, unless receiving **written consent** from the spouse to do otherwise.

> **Exam tip:** Generally, when life insurance is tested, it is unclear from the facts whether the policy is term or whole. In that situation, analyze both and explain why it is more likely to be one or the other. For example, if the policy is paid annually, it may be more likely term insurance.

H. **Business goodwill** is the value derived from the expectation of continued public patronage that stems from **intangible qualities that generate a business income** beyond that derived from a professional's labor, the reasonable return on capital and physical assets. To the extent that the **goodwill is earned during the marriage, it is CP**. Two common approaches to measure goodwill include:

1. **Market value approach:** Analysis of what a willing **buyer would pay** for the community business if it were sold at the time of separation or divorce.

2. **Capitalization of past excess earnings:** Analysis of the net income of a professional practice for one year minus the reasonable salary for a person with comparable experience after deducting a fair return on tangible assets, multiplied by a fixed capitalization rate (usually determined by an expert forensic accountant).

I. **Federal preemption:** Under the Supremacy Clause, **federal law preempts inconsistent state law** when specific types of income or liabilities are designated as the **sole property of one spouse under federal law**, but they otherwise would be community property under state law.

> **Issue spotting tip:** Whenever there is any type of federal asset such as a federal pension, military life insurance, social security benefits, or U.S. savings bonds, always address preemption. Usually a simple one- to two-line answer is sufficient. If you aren't certain whether the federal asset at issue would be preempted, mention in your response that because it is a federal asset it is possible and identify what the result would be if federal preemption applied and if it didn't.

> **Issue spotting tip:** To aid in issue spotting, you should have all special issues on your issues checklist to cross-reference when reading the facts. When one of the special rules applies, address it after establishing the original source/presumptions since the special rules often alter the original presumption.

IX. **DEBTS AND CREDITORS' RIGHTS**

A. **Credit acquisitions:** There is a **rebuttable presumption** that property **purchased with borrowed funds** (on credit) during marriage is **CP debt**.

1. **Can rebut with the "intent of the lender" test:** A showing that the lender **relied exclusively on SP** when extending credit may rebut the presumption.

2. **Earning capacity:** If the credit is **based on earning capacity, it is a CP debt** because earning capacity is a community asset.

B. **Timing of debts:** Creditor's rights are determined by the time a debt was incurred.

1. **Contract debt** is incurred at the time the **contract is made**.

2. **Tort debt** is incurred at the time the **tort occurs**.

3. **Child or spousal support debt** that doesn't arise out of the marriage is treated as a **debt incurred before marriage** regardless of when the court order is made or modified.

4. **Other debts:** All other debts are incurred at the time the obligation arises.

C. **Creditor's rights follow management rights.** To **satisfy a debt**, a creditor may reach any property over which a debtor has the legal right of **management and control**.

1. **Community property is liable** for all debts incurred **before and during marriage** by either spouse, regardless of which spouse has the management and control of the property and which spouse incurred the debt.

a. **Exception:** The **earnings** of the **non-debtor spouse** are not liable for **premarital debts** of the other spouse if these earnings are held in a **separate deposit account** over which the debtor spouse has no right to withdraw, and the funds are not commingled with other community funds (except an insignificant amount). (This exception allows the non-debtor spouse to shield their earnings, but not other sources of money, subject to the exception for debts for necessaries of life noted in section 2 (d) immediately below.)

2. **Order of debt satisfaction**
   a. If debt is for the **community interest: CP first**, then SP of either spouse.
   b. If debt is for the **separate interest: SP of debtor spouse first**, then CP.
   c. **SP debts incurred** *before* **marriage: All CP and all debtor spouse's SP**, but not the SP of the non-debtor spouse or the earnings of the non-debtor spouse *if* they are held in a separate deposit account.
   d. **SP debt** (by one spouse) **incurred** *during* **marriage: All CP and all debtor spouse's SP, but not the SP of the non-debtor spouse**, subject to exception for necessaries of life. An example of SP debt during marriage would be a debt incurred to hire a criminal defense lawyer.
      1. **Exception for necessaries of life:** A non-debtor **spouse's SP is liable** for debts of the other spouse if it was incurred **during marriage** and was for **necessaries of life** for the **spouse or a child**. Necessaries of life are those appropriate to a person's station in life given their resources, such as food, shelter, and medical care.
      2. **Exception for** *post-separation* **common necessaries:** A non-debtor **spouse's SP is liable** for debts of the other spouse, even if it was **incurred post separation but before divorce** if it was for common necessaries, which are basic necessities of life appropriate to a person's station in life.

3. **Injury/damage caused by a spouse:** A married person is **not personally liable** for injury or damage caused by the other spouse, unless the married spouse would be liable if not married.
   a. **Benefit of the community:** If the act or omission leading to injury or damage **occurred during marriage** for the **benefit of the community**, the liability should be satisfied from the **CP first** and the **SP of the debtor spouse second**.
   b. **Not for benefit of the community:** If the act or omission leading to injury or damage **occurred during marriage** but was **not for the benefit of the community**, then liability should be satisfied from the **debtor's SP first** and the **CP second**.

4. **Reimbursements** are available to either estate (CP, or either spouse's SP) if the debt is one that **should have been first satisfied by another estate,** unless there is an express written waiver. The right to reimbursement shall be **exercised within three years** after the spouse knew the property was used to satisfy the debt, **or at divorce or death, whichever comes first.**

> **Exam tip:** When debts are involved and the entire call of the question focuses on which assets a creditor can use to satisfy a debt, it is best to address the general creditor and debt rules up front. Use the following approach: (1) Assess the type of debt, (2) when it accrued, (3) what estates are liable to pay it, and (4) in what order the property should be used to satisfy the debt. For example, address when the debts are incurred and what estates are liable and in what order first, then go through all the specific debts from the fact pattern.

X. DIVISION AND DISTRIBUTION OF PROPERTY

A. **Divorce:** At divorce all **community assets** and debts are **divided evenly,** and each spouse retains their SP debt and assets.
   1. **Community property:** At divorce, the community assets and debts will be **divided evenly, unless some special rule mandates deviation** from the requirement of equal distribution (e.g., tort liability, federal preemption).
   2. **Separate property:** At divorce, each spouse will **retain their SP** assets and debts.
   3. **Quasi-community property:** QCP is treated exactly the **same as CP** all will be **divided evenly**.
   4. **Quasi-marital property:** At annulment, a putative spouse is entitled to an **equal division** of the QMP (unless the court finds a bad faith spouse should receive less than half).
   5. **Two marriages maintained:** If a spouse is maintaining two marriages, courts will **divide assets equally** between participants **or divide equally between nonguilty participants.** Courts are jurisdictionally split regarding allowing the guilty party to benefit from their wrongdoing.

6. **Real property outside California: At divorce, the court can distribute CP and QCP out-of-state realty**, but there may be a jurisdictional problem. If it is not possible for the court to divide real property located outside the state, the court can require the parties to convey the real property or award to the party that would have benefited from the conveyance the equivalent money value they would have received had the property been conveyed.

B. **Death:** At death, the decedent can **devise** all of their SP and half of the CP. If the decedent dies **intestate**, the surviving spouse is automatically entitled to the decedent's share of the CP and one-third share to a full share of the decedent's SP, depending on whether the decedent left issue or surviving parents.

1. **Devise (will):** The decedent can devise **all of their SP** and their **one-half of the CP** and QCP.

    a. **QCP exception:** At death, the surviving spouse has a one-half interest in the QCP titled in the decedent's name. However, the **decedent does not have an interest in the QCP titled in the survivor's name**, thus QCP only protects the non-acquiring spouse before they die.

2. **Election by surviving spouse:** If the decedent died with a will and tried to dispose of more than their half of the CP, the surviving spouse will need to make an election between their **CP rights without the will** or **take under the will** in lieu of their CP rights.

3. **Intestacy:** If the decedent dies intestate, the surviving spouse is **automatically** entitled to all of the decedent's share of the CP and QCP so the **surviving spouse will receive 100% of the CP and QCP.** For the SP, the surviving spouse will receive all or one-half or one-third of the decedent's **SP**, depending on whether the decedent has surviving issue or parents.

    a. **SP passes all to surviving spouse** when decedent leaves no issue, parent, siblings, or issue of deceased sibling.

    b. **SP passes half to surviving spouse** when decedent leaves only one child or issue of a deceased child, or no issue, but a parent(s) or their issue.

    c. **SP passes one-third to surviving spouse** when decedent leaves more than one living child, or one living child and the issue of at least one deceased child, or the issue of two or more deceased children.

4. **Putative spouse:** Upon death the putative spouse is entitled to a half interest in all QMP, and the same intestacy rights to QMP as apply to CP and QCP, and the same intestacy rights in the decedent putative spouse's SP.

5. **Two marriages maintained:** If a spouse is maintaining two marriages, courts will divide assets equally between participants or divide equally between nonguilty participants. Courts are jurisdictionally split regarding allowing the guilty party to benefit from their wrongdoing.

6. **Real property outside California:** Out-of-state real property will be probated in the state where the property is located.

> **Exam tip:** Always remember to answer the specific question call. For example, if the call asks about H and W's rights, don't simply figure out whether each of the listed assets is CP or SP or QCP, and so forth. Rather, after you have classified the types of property, proceed to distribute the property in accordance with those determinations and properly identify exactly what H and W will receive and why. Likewise, if debts are involved, identify what property H and W own in particular to determine which property the creditor should reach first to satisfy the debt, and explain why.

COMMUNITY PROPERTY ISSUES TESTED MATRIX

	Crossover	QCP	Putative Spouse/QMP	Premarital Agreement	Separation	Title	Lucas/Anti-Lucas	Tracing/Commingled Funds	Transmutation/Gift	Mgmt./Control/fiduciary duty/Gift or Sale to 3rd Party	Pereira/VanCamp (CP to SP business) or in reverse	Moore (CP to SP property)	Improvements	Special Classification	Time Rule	Creditor Rights/Intent of Lender	Debts/Order of Satisfaction
February '24 Q1 — W inherits house & adds H on title; H buys auto garage & forges W name					X	JT w/ H & W			X	X						X	X
July '22 Q5 — H & W in State X for 15 yrs. then CA for 5 yrs; H died with 2 wills	Wills	X				JT with H and daughter			X	X							
February '22 Q2 — H premarital savings; marries W; Acme stock; W disability insurance					X	Stock & investment acct in H's name		X	X	X				Disability payments			X
July '21 Q5 — H & W in State X; had baby; moved to CA; H died first day at work	Wills	X				Land in H's name			X								
February '21 Q3 — W works on antique biz w/ dad; marries H; W inherits biz; H/W separate					X						X						
February '19 Q1 — H & W married in State X and moved to CA; H dies	Wills & Trusts	X			X	Condo & house in H's name		X	X								
July '18 Q4 — W bought house in her name alone; then married H; H paid mortgage						House & motorboat in W's name		X	X	X		X		Pension/personal injury	X		
February '18 Q5 — Ted died leaving START co., 2nd wife Nell and kids A, B, & C	Wills (almost all wills)													Mainly a wills Q—only tests SP & CP presumption			
July '17 Q1 — H inherits condo, buys motorcycle, W buys H camper van						JT condo			X	X						X	

<Continued>

	Facts	Crossover	QCP	Putative Spouse/QMP	Premarital Agreement	Separation	Title	Lucas/Anti-Lucas	Tracing/Commingled Funds	Transmutation/Gift	Mgmt./Control/fiduciary duty/ Gift or Sale to 3rd Party	Pereira/VanCamp (CP to SP business) or in reverse	Moore (CP to SP property)	Improvements	Special Classification	Time Rule	Creditor Rights/ Intent of Lender	Debts/Order of Satisfaction
July '16 Q5	H&W prenup; each buys props; joint savings acct; W has surgery				X	X	H name condo/ W name rental prop		X	X	X							X
July '15 Q4	H pays child support from prior; W gets stock options from work					X				X					Stock options/ personal injury			X
July '14 Q5	H&W marry in non-CP state, move to CA	Trusts	X							X								
February '14 Q2	H&W own home; W buys bldg. for accounting biz						JT home/ W name building	X		X	X	X		X				
July '13 Q3	W uses inheritance to buy stock; H inherits lot; H&W get loan								X	X	X	X	X	X	Stock		X	X
July '12 Q2	H drives drunk, hits ped, W wants divorce, hires Hal	Prof Resp									X				Tort judgment			X
July '11 Q6	H & W engaged and wait to marry for 3 yrs. to use trust						Joint title in car (not married)				X						X	X
July '10 Q6	H & W in Cal., H wealthy family with trust						JT condo/H name cabin	X	X	X	X				Stock		X	X
February '10 Q6	H & W in Cal. with prenup, rare coins				X	X			X	X	X	X						X
July '08 Q6	H & W in NY, XYZ stock	Wills/ trusts	X				W name alone/JT			X	X				Stock			
February '08 Q5	H, F in State X; H lies and moves to Cal. with W		X	X	X		H/W joint & separate			X					PI			
July '07 Q6	H & W in Cal., H goes to law school						H name alone			X					Education/ goodwill			X
February '07 Q4	Tom, from Cal., executed a will	Wills/ trusts								X								

Continued>

Date	Facts	Crossover	QCP	Putative Spouse/QMP	Premarital Agreement	Separation	Title	Lucas/Anti-Lucas	Tracing/Commingled Funds	Transmutation/Gift	Mgmt./Control/fiduciary duty/ Gift or Sale to 3rd Party	Pereira/VanCamp (CP to SP business) or in reverse	Moore (CP to SP property)	Improvements	Special Classification	Time Rule	Creditor Rights/ Intent of Lender	Debts/Order of Satisfaction
February '06 Q2	Tim & Anna try to reconcile	Wills/ trusts			X													
July '05 Q1	H & W, Tech Co. stock					X	H name alone		X						PI/bonus/ stock	X		X
July '04 Q3	Hank, avid skier, daughter Ann	Wills/ trusts	X															
February '04 Q2	H & W in Mont., move to Cal.; H affair with A		X	X		X	TIC/H & A				X						X	X
February '03 Q6	H & W, students at X University		X				JT/H name alone	X		X		X			Education			
July '02 Q6	H & W domiciled in Ill., H lied about CL marriage			X			MWSP/ W's name alone			X				X			X	X
July '02 Q1	Theresa and Henry, child Craig	Wills/ trusts													Life insurance	X		
February '01 Q1	H & W; H owned home before marriage						JT/W's name alone	X	X	X			X	X				
February '00 Q1	H & W married in Franklin, H engineer for Texco		X				JT	X	X						Bonus/stock	X	X	X

COMMUNITY PROPERTY PRACTICE ESSAYS, ANSWER GRIDS, AND SAMPLE ANSWERS

Community Property Question 1
February 2022, Question 2

Harry had premarital savings of $10,000 in a bank account when he married Winona in California in 2015. After the wedding, Harry started working at a new job and deposited his $3,000 salary check into the account. Shortly afterward, he paid $2,000 for rent and $2,000 for living expenses with checks drawn on the account. He then bought $1,000 in Acme stock in his own name with another check drawn on the account. The Acme stock increased in value over time.

During the marriage, Winona purchased disability insurance out of her salary. She later became disabled and could no longer work. As a result, she became entitled to monthly disability insurance payments, which will continue until she reaches the age of 65.

Thereafter, Harry and Winona decided to live separately, but to go to counseling with the hope of reconciling. After Harry moved out of the family home, he used his earnings to gamble at a local casino, winning a large amount of money with which he opened an investment account in his own name. Harry did not tell Winona about his winnings or investment account because she did not approve of gambling.

Subsequently, after a period of counseling, Harry and Winona concluded that they would not reconcile and Harry filed for dissolution. A few days later, Harry took out a loan to pay for a sailboat, hoping that sailing would relieve the stress of the divorce.

What are Harry's and Winona's rights and liabilities regarding:

1. The Acme stock? Discuss.

2. Winona's post-separation disability insurance payments? Discuss.

3. The investment account? Discuss.

4. The loan for the sailboat? Discuss.

Answer according to California law.

Community Property Question 1 Assessment
February 2022, Question 2

This is a very straightforward question since H and W were married and domiciled in California. There is one issue regarding their separation that you needed to address but that is a fairly straightforward rule, and the facts make it clear when the separation occurred if you know your rules. As in contracts, the chronology of events is very important in community property questions. Sketch out a brief timeline of events to keep all the details straight. As is common in community property essays, each call corresponds to an asset or debt. The facts then address each asset and debt in chronological order, so it is fairly easy to follow with each paragraph essentially corresponding to each call.

Once you've organized your answer, you will notice there is actually a manageable amount of assets and issues to consider. When this happens and you notice there aren't quite so many issues to address, take a moment and run the fact pattern back through the issues checklist to see if you missed any issues. Also, look to see if there are any "homeless" facts from the fact pattern that are left unused that may raise an issue, or be used to bulk up some of the analysis. More often than not you probably missed something important. This question presents the more unusual case—where you find that you indeed had identified all of the issues and can proceed to writing out your answer (while thanking your lucky stars that you received at least one manageable question on the bar exam—unless of course you foolishly banked on a particular subject not being tested, which we never recommend).

When drafting the answer, begin with the general presumptions for CP and SP and then address the preliminary issue of when the parties permanently separated. They try to trick you by giving you facts about the parties living separately, but that fact alone is not dispositive for permanent separation as their intent and conduct also dictate whether they are permanently separated. After that you can move immediately to the assets.

On the first asset, the stock, it is fairly simple as you start with your general presumptions and then look to see if anything changed the presumption that it is CP since acquired during marriage. You should have addressed transmutation since H would likely want to claim that it is his SP now. The key was to notice the title was in H's name alone, which is not dispositive. But then, since it is a commingled account, you can use tracing to determine that the funds came from H's SP. If you knew your tracing rules you were perfectly fine here. Also note that one state-released answer only gave H his initial SP contribution back which is not correct as the entire stock would be SP, but their analysis was on point up until the distribution part. This is just yet another piece of proof that you don't need to be perfect to pass this exam!

On the second asset, the disability payments, the time of separation became the deciding factor. The key was to see that the disability payments would be CP up until permanent separation, which was not when H moved out, but rather when he filed for dissolution. Otherwise, this is also a fairly simple asset to address.

The third asset involving the investment fund required you to analyze many of the same rules you already analyzed in the first asset, including transmutation and title in one spouse's name alone. So, you could reference your rules above which saves you time. The difference with this call was noticing the breach of fiduciary duties.

The last call was about a debt not an asset, but like the other calls, the issues were straightforward. You simply need to know that it was a SP debt since it was incurred post-separation. And with that you needed to see that the CP would not be liable for it unless it was for necessaries, which it wasn't. Overall, this essay was easy-peasy!

Finally, make note of the areas highlighted in **bold** on the corresponding grid. The bold areas highlight the issues, analysis, and conclusions that are likely **required** to receive a passing score on this question. In general, the essay grids are provided to assist you in analyzing the essays and are much more detailed than what a student should create during the exam to organize their response to a question.

Issue	Rule	Fact Application	Conclusion
General Presumptions/Preliminary Issues			
Community Property	California is a community property state. CP is property, other than separate property, acquired by either spouse during marriage. All assets acquired during marriage are presumptively CP.		
Separate Property	All property acquired before or after marriage or after permanent separation, or by gift, devise, or bequest is presumed to be SP.		
Permanent Separation	Occurs when there is a complete and final break in the marital relationship where one spouse has expressed to the other spouse their intent to end the marriage and the spouse's conduct is consistent with their intent to end the marriage.	At the point when H and W decided to live separately, they were not permanently separated as they went to counseling with the hope of reconciling, so there was no intent to end the marriage expressed by either spouse at that point. However, when H filed for dissolution after a period of counseling when both of them concluded they would not reconcile, that become the point of permanent separation.	H and W permanently separated when H filed for dissolution.
1. The Acme Stock			
CP presumption	See above	Since H purchased the stock during marriage, it is presumed to be CP, unless H can rebut this presumption.	Presumed CP
Title	Form of title can rebut the original presumption when title is inconsistent with the original presumption. **When the source of funds is CP but title is taken by one spouse only, the property will retain its characterization as CP unless there is a written transmutation.**	Here, the title is in H's name alone which is inconsistent with the presumption it is CP. **Source of funds is an account with commingled funds so need to see if there was a transmutation or the funds can be traced to H's SP.**	Still CP until rebutted
Transmutation	Transmutations are agreements between spouses to change the character of an asset. Before 1/1/1985: transmutations could be oral, written, or inferred from conduct of parties. Post 1/1/1985: need a signed declaration, in writing, by spouse adversely affected expressly stating that a change in ownership is being made OR the gift must be insubstantial in nature.	Here it is after 1985 since they married in 2015. Also, there was no writing signed by W and the stock was not insubstantial as it has increased in value over time.	No transmutation (so still CP unless can be traced)

(Continued>)

Issue	Rule	Fact Application	Conclusion
Commingled Account/Tracing	Courts use two approaches to trace funds in a commingled account: • **Direct tracing: Requires showing a direct link from SP funds to the purchase such that sufficient SP funds in the account were available at the time of the purchase and the** SP owner intended to use SP funds to make the purchase. • **Exhaustion method: Requires showing that at the time the property was purchased, all CP funds in a commingled account had been exhausted by community expenses, and thus only SP funds were available to purchase the property.** BOP on spouse claiming SP. When tracing funds, there is a presumption that expenditures for family expenses were made with CP funds even if SP funds were available.	The source of funds used to buy the stock came from H's premarital bank account which would be SP. But he commingled CP funds to that account when he deposited $3,000 of his earnings into the account that contained $10,000 of his SP funds. He then paid rent for $2,000 which would come from CP funds and then $2,000 living expenses which would also come from CP funds so $1,000 of H's SP funds were used to pay part of the living expenses leaving $9,000 of SP in the account. Without an accounting record, a court might not directly follow and trace the money. However, each transaction appears to be easy to trace and which asset contributed to each deposit or withdrawal can also be directly traced. Also, H exhausted all CP funds and spent $1,000 of SP funds leaving only SP funds left to purchase the stock.	**Stock is H's SP** and will be assigned to H at divorce, including the increase in value.
2. W's post-separation disability insurance payments			
CP	See above	Since W purchased disability insurance out of her salary during marriage and was receiving disability insurance during marriage, it is presumed those payments are CP.	CP unless rebutted
Disability payments	The classification of disability pay as SP or CP depends on what it was intended to replace, regardless of when it is actually paid. • If intended to replace earnings, then it is CP. • If intended to replace post-divorce earnings, then it is SP.	While W received the disability payments during marriage, they were replacing her earnings since she became disabled and could no longer work, so they were CP. However, since they will continue until she reaches the age of 65, they will be used to replace her earnings post-separation so all payments post-separation will be her own SP. As indicated above, the time when H filed for dissolution would be the point at which the disability pay would become W's SP.	All of W's disability payments received prior to their permanent separation are CP and all payments post-separation are W's SP.

Continued>

Issue	Rule	Fact Application	Conclusion
3. The investment account			
CP	See above	Since H opened the investment account during marriage it is presumed CP.	CP unless rebutted
Title/Transmutation	See above	Although title was in H's name alone, this doesn't change the characterization of the property b/c there was no transmutation as there was no writing by W and she even disapproved of his gambling so H didn't even tell her about it.	Still CP
Tracing	See above	Here, the investment account can be traced back to CP funds b/c he used his earnings to gamble at the casino and won a large amount of money from CP funds since earnings are CP funds. So the account was opened with CP funds and there was no transmutation as indicated above. Also, as indicated above, H and W were not permanently separated at this point even though he moved out, so his earnings were still CP at this point.	Investment account is CP and will be distributed equally between H and W at divorce.
Breach of fiduciary duty	Each spouse has a fiduciary duty to fully disclose all material facts about community assets and debts to the other spouse and use the highest good faith and fair dealing and never take advantage of the other.	H may have breached his duty to W when he gambled with community funds because she did not approve of gambling. He also declined to tell her about the winnings because she didn't approve of gambling and opened up the investment account in his name alone, which shows he didn't fully disclose all material facts about assets to her.	The court could give W a larger share of the account since H breached his fiduciary duty.
4. The loan for the sailboat			
Debts	A contract debt is incurred at the time the contract is made. Debts incurred during marriage are presumed to be CP debts. Debts incurred post-separation are presumed to be SP debts, with the exception for debts for necessaries. SP is liable for SP debt; CP can be liable for SP debt if for necessaries.	Here, H took out the sailboat loan a few days after filing for dissolution so it was a SP debt and a sailboat to relieve the stress of the divorce would not be a necessary.	The sailboat loan is H's SP debt and only H's SP debt and his half of the CP can be liable for the debt.

Community Property Question 1 Sample Answer
February 2022, Question 2

General Presumptions

Community Property (CP)

California is a community property state. CP is property, other than separate property, acquired by either spouse during marriage. All assets acquired during marriage are presumptively CP.

Separate Property (SP)

All property acquired before or after marriage or after permanent separation, or by gift, devise, or bequest is presumed to be SP.

Permanent Separation

Permanent separation occurs when there is a complete and final break in the marital relationship where one spouse has expressed to the other spouse their intent to end the marriage and the spouse's conduct is consistent with their intent to end the marriage.

Here, when Harry (H) and Winona (W) decided to live separately, they were not permanently separated as they went to counseling with the hope of reconciling so there was no intent to end the marriage expressed by either spouse at that point.

However, when H filed for dissolution after a period of counseling, when both of them concluded they would not reconcile, that become the point of permanent separation.

Thus, H and W permanently separated when H filed for dissolution.

1. The Acme Stock

CP presumption

See above for rule. Here, since H purchased the stock during marriage, it is presumed to be CP, unless H can rebut this presumption.

Title

Form of title can rebut the original presumption when title is inconsistent with the original presumption. When the source of funds is CP, but title is taken by one spouse only, the property will retain its characterization as CP unless there is a written transmutation.

Here, the title is in H's name alone which is inconsistent with the presumption it is CP. Here, the source of funds is an account with commingled funds, so the characterization of the funds will depend on whether there was a transmutation or whether the funds can be traced to H's SP.

Transmutation

Transmutations are agreements between spouses to change the character of an asset.

Before 1/1/1985, transmutations could be oral, written, or inferred from conduct of parties.

After 1/1/1985, a valid transmutation of property from one form to another requires a signed declaration, in writing, by the spouse adversely affected expressly stating that a change in ownership is being made, or the gift must be insubstantial in nature.

Here, it is after 1985 since they married in 2015. Also, there was no writing signed by W and the stock was not insubstantial as it has increased in value over time. Thus, there was no valid transmutation, so the property is still CP unless it can be traced to H's SP.

Commingled Account/Tracing

Courts use two approaches to trace funds in a commingled account. The first approach is direct tracing which requires showing a direct link from SP funds to the purchase such that sufficient SP funds in the account were available at the time of the purchase and the SP owner intended to use SP funds to make the purchase. The second approach is the exhaustion method which requires showing that at the time the property was purchased, all CP funds in a commingled account had been exhausted by community expenses, and thus only SP funds were available to purchase the property. The burden of proof is on the spouse claiming the property is SP. When tracing funds, there is a presumption that expenditures for family expenses were made with CP funds even if SP funds were available.

Here, the source of funds used to buy the stock came from H's premarital bank account which would be SP. But he commingled CP funds to that account when he deposited $3,000 of his earnings into the account that contained $10,000 of his SP funds because earnings during marriage are presumed CP. He then paid rent for $2,000 which would come from CP funds and then $2,000 living expenses which would also come from CP funds because both are community expenses, so $1,000 of H's SP funds were used to pay part of the living expenses leaving $9,000 of SP in the account.

As to direct tracing, arguably without an accounting record, a court might not directly follow and trace the money. Further, it is not clear that H intended for the stock to be purchased with SP funds. However, each transaction appears to be easy to trace and which asset contributed to each deposit or withdrawal can also be directly traced. So it is possible the court can use direct tracing to trace the funds to H's SP.

Also, H exhausted all CP funds and spent $1,000 of SP funds leaving only SP funds left to purchase the stock, so the stock is H's SP.

Overall, the stock is H's SP and will be assigned to H at divorce, including the increase in value. W will not be entitled to any portion of the stock.

2. W's post-separation disability insurance payments

CP Presumption

See above for rule.

Since W purchased disability insurance out of her salary during marriage and was receiving disability insurance during marriage, it is presumed those payments are CP, unless a special classification changes its characterization.

Disability payments

The classification of disability pay as SP or CP depends on what it was intended to replace, regardless of when it is actually paid. If the payments are intended to replace earnings, then they are classified as CP. If the payments are intended to replace post-divorce earnings, then they are SP.

While W received the disability payments during marriage, they were replacing her earnings since she became disabled and could no longer work, so they were CP. However, since they will continue until she reaches the age of 65, they will be used to replace her earnings post-separation so all payments post-separation will be her own SP. As indicated above, the time when H filed for dissolution would be the point at which the disability pay would become W's SP since that is the date for their permanent separation.

Thus, all of W's disability payments received prior to their permanent separation are CP and all payments post separation are W's SP.

3. The investment account

CP Presumption

See above for rule.

Here, since H opened the investment account during marriage it is presumed CP, unless the presumption is rebutted.

Title/Transmutation

See above for rules.

Although title was in H's name alone, this doesn't change the characterization of the property because there was no transmutation as there was no writing by W and she disapproved of his gambling, so H didn't even tell her about it. Thus, the property is still CP.

Tracing

See above for rules.

Here, the investment account can be traced back to CP funds because H used his earnings to gamble at the casino and won a large amount of money from CP funds since earnings are CP funds. So, the account was opened with CP funds and there was no transmutation as indicated above. Also, as indicated above, H and W were not permanently separated at this point even though he moved out, so his earnings were still CP at this point.

Thus, the investment account is CP and will be distributed equally between H and W at divorce.

Breach of fiduciary duty

Each spouse has a fiduciary duty to fully disclose all material facts about community assets and debts to the other spouse and use the highest good faith and fair dealing and never take advantage of the other.

Here, H may have breached his duty to W when he gambled with community funds because she did not approve of gambling. He also declined to tell her about the winnings because she didn't approve of gambling and opened up the investment account in his name alone, which shows he didn't fully disclose all material facts about assets to her. The court could give W a larger share of the account since H breached his fiduciary duty, but since it didn't affect her half of the community property, she will likely just take her half and H will take his half.

4. The loan for the sailboat

Debts

A contract debt is incurred at the time the contract is made. Debts incurred during marriage are presumed to be CP debts. Debts incurred post-separation are presumed to be SP debts, with the exception for debts for necessaries. SP is liable for SP debt. CP can be liable for SP debt if the debt was incurred for necessaries.

Here, H took out the sailboat loan a few days after filing for dissolution so it was a SP debt and a sailboat to relieve the stress of the divorce would not be a necessary expense.

Thus, the sailboat loan is H's SP debt and only H's SP debt and his half of the CP can be liable for the debt.

Community Property Question 2

February 2021, Question 3

Prior to her 1990 marriage to Hal in California, Wendy helped operate an antiques and rare book business owned by her father.

During the marriage, Wendy continued to work with her father in operating the business. Over the years, Wendy and her father jointly operated the business and in 1995, they signed an agreement whereby Wendy became the owner of a ½ interest in the business. Wendy had developed an exceptional talent for buying antiques and took over that part of the business in 1995. The business doubled in value from 1995 to 2000. In late 1999, Wendy's father died and by his will left his interest in the business to Wendy, including all of the business's real property and inventory.

Wendy and Hal separated early in 2014. They have lived separate and apart since then and are now involved in divorce proceedings.

How should the court allocate the value of the business between Hal and Wendy? Discuss.

Answer according to California law.

Community Property Question 2 Assessment
February 2021, Question 3

At first glance, this seems to be a very straightforward question, and very unusual, since it only asks about one asset — the business. However, you might realize after reading the facts that the allocation of the business value is anything but straightforward. The business appears to go through some transitions. First, it does not appear to be W's SP business because her father owns it. Then a few years later, she owns ½ of the business during marriage, so arguably this would be CP since it was acquired during marriage. However, that isn't clear because the facts are (likely purposefully) ambiguous in regard to whether she paid for her ½ of the business or if it was a SP gift from her father. This is a huge ambiguity because without this information, you don't know whether she owns ½ of a CP or SP business. Thus, you need to analyze it under both options.

Then there are facts that speak to the reason the business doubled in value, which you could argue was in part due to her "exceptional talent," but even that was not clear because a close reading of the facts tells you that she took over the antiques part, but it isn't clear which part of the business, the antiques part which she took over, or the rare book part which her father ran, were the reason for the increase in value. Also, it wasn't clear whether it was their work or the business itself. So, you were left with discussing more ambiguities here which led you to discuss both *Pereira* and *Van Camp*.

Then, W's father died in late 1999, and she inherited his ½ of the business, which would be a SP inheritance. At this point, your *Pereira/Van Camp* bells should be ringing loudly and you are already over it! This might cause you to have some grief and panic, especially if you are one of those students that claimed you went to law school specifically to avoid math and equations. So, take a deep breath, calm down, and know that you can do this because you memorized your rules and did practice exams testing these issues. If you didn't memorize these rules, then here's your chance so take advantage of this learning opportunity. And remember that practice makes progress!

Then, it appears she kept operating the business while married until she separated from H in 2014. This raises another issue as to whether they permanently separated since there are no facts as to their intent. This was an issue you could have addressed upfront to determine the date of separation. This was yet another ambiguous fact because the facts say they lived apart and separated but not that they "permanently separated." And since they didn't divorce for another 7 years, you could infer either way since it isn't clear as to whether they intended to remain separated in 2014 or not.

Note that they are "now" involved in divorce proceedings. It is important to note the dates of the exams (which we include on all of our essays) because the bar examiners will often use dates such as "now" which refer to the date of the actual exam. In this essay, "now" for divorce proceedings would mean February 2021. So, note that they "separated" in 2014 but were not in divorce proceedings until now in 2021.

Although this essay didn't test many issues and only asked about one asset, it required a lot of in-depth knowledge about when a business is a CP business versus a SP business and the rules relating to contributions to the business including goodwill. Needless to say, you might have aged a bit while organizing this essay, especially since it was essay three and the last thing between you and a break with some lunch, at which you can call your family and friends and tell them how much you think the bar examiners hate you! But remember, if you are feeling overwhelmed and you adequately studied, then everyone in the exam is feeling the same way. Just do your best and trust that you know enough to write a coherent essay.

Finally, make note of the areas highlighted in **bold** on the corresponding grid. The bold areas highlight the issues, analysis, and conclusions that are likely **required** to receive a passing score on this question. In general, the essay grids are provided to assist you in analyzing the essays and are much more detailed than what a student should create during the exam to organize their response to a question.

Issue	Rule	Fact Application	Conclusion
General Presumptions/Preliminary Issues			
Community Property	**California is a community property state. CP is property, other than separate property, acquired by either spouse during marriage. All assets acquired during marriage are presumptively CP.**		
Separate Property	**All property acquired before or after marriage or after permanent separation, or by gift, devise, or bequest is presumed to be SP.**		
Permanent Separation	**Occurs when there is a complete and final break in the marital relationship where one spouse has expressed to the other spouse their intent to end the marriage and the spouse's conduct is consistent with their intent to end the marriage.**	At the point when H and W decided to live separately and separate in 2014, it is not clear whether they were permanently separated because there are no facts as to their intent to end the marriage. In fact, they didn't proceed with divorce proceedings until 2021, so it is possible that initially they might have temporarily separated with an intent to possible reconcile, but it isn't clear either way. **However, for purposes of this exam it will be assumed that they permanently separated when the facts said they separated in 2014.**	Date of permanent separation likely 2014
The business value (1990-1995)			
CP presumption	See above.	Between the years of 1990 and 1995 (when W jointly owned the business with her father), Wendy simply worked for her father's business so any income she accrued during this time would be CP. The business was not owned by W at this time.	Any income from the business during this time would be CP & business itself was not W's.
The business value (1995-1999)			
Presumptions	See above.	In 1995, W became the owner of a ½ interest in the business which would arguably be CP since it was a business acquired during marriage. However, it isn't clear if W purchased ½ of the business or if her father gave it to her as a gift, in which case it would be classified as SP. If the business was CP, then any profits from the business earned during these years would be CP and it wouldn't matter the reason the business succeeded, which it appears was mainly from W's exceptional talent for buying antiques but it isn't clear which part of the business was responsible for the increase in value. If the business was a SP business, then the courts would use *Pereira/Van Camp* to analyze the value and how much each party should receive.	

Continued>

Issue	Rule	Fact Application	Conclusion
Pereira/Van Camp	A court may invoke *Pereira* and/or *Van Camp* to value the community share where SP is possibly enhanced by community labor. *Pereira* — tends to favor the community; use when the spouse's personal managment skills are the primary reason for the growth • SP interest = SP contribution + reasonable rate of return • CP interest = value of business - SP interest • SP contribution = Value of SP business at the time of marriage • Reasonable rate of return = 10% of SP contribution for each year family had SP business during marriage *Van Camp* — tends to favor SP estate; use when the character of the business is the primary reason for growth • CP interest = Fair market value salary - family expenses - salary taken (over the # years of marriage with the business) • SP interest = value of business - CP interest	Here, it seems that the court would likely use the *Pereira* formula because the business doubled in value between 1995 and 2000, during which time W became a ½ owner and it was likely due to her exceptional talent for buying antiques if that is the part of the business that was responsible for its increase, but that's not clear either as it could have been the rare books portion that her father oversaw, or the community, the fact that her father got the business up and running initially, or other reasons. There aren't numbers to indicate how much SP contributed, if any, to the business when she first became a part owner, but that amount would be used plus a reasonable rate of return to determine the SP interest and the CP interest would be ½ the value of the business at 1999 (since she only owned half during those years) less the SP interest. If the court applied *Van Camp* because it isn't clear that her exceptional talent was the reason the business value doubled and antiques and rare books naturally increase in value over time, then they would look at the value of the fair market salary less her salary and family expenses for her ½ of the business and that would be the CP interest.	If the business was a gift, then the court would apply one of these formulas to determine the SP and CP interests. If W paid for her ½ interest in the business then it would be CP and the value during these years would be split between H and W as CP.
Goodwill of the business	Business goodwill is the value derived from the expectation of continued public patronage that stems from intangible qualities that generate a business income beyond that derived from a professional's labor, the reasonable return on capital, and physical assets. To the extent that the goodwill is earned during the marriage, it is CP. Courts use two approaches to determine goodwill:	Between 1990 to 1995 and possibly thereafter if the court finds that W's first ½ of the business ownership was CP, it is possible that goodwill derived from W's exceptional talent and labor; the court could add the value of her goodwill to the CP share based on the value someone would offer for the business or her capitalization of past excess earnings.	Business goodwill could also factor into the court's evaluation of the business value for the entire duration of the business during marriage.

Continued>

Issue	Rule	Fact Application	Conclusion
Goodwill of the business (continued)	• Market value approach (value another is willing to pay), or • Capitalization of past excess earnings (income of professional less comparable income deducting a fair return on intangible assets, multiplied by a fixed rate of capitalization).		
The business value (1999-2014)			
Presumptions	See above.	In 1999, W's father died and left his ½ of the business to W, which presumably was the rare book part of the business since in 1995 she became a part owner and took over the antiques part of the business. Since she inherited this ½ of the business it would be her SP. If the first ½ of the business was CP, then any profits from the business earned during these years would be CP as discussed above. If the first ½ and now second ½ of the business was a SP business, then the courts would use *Pereira/Van Camp* to analyze the value and how much each party should receive.	
Pereira/Van Camp	See above for rules.	The same analysis would apply for these years as above, but certainly ½ of the business that W just inherited would be SP, so *Pereira/Van Camp* would apply to at least ½ of the business between 1999 and 2014 and possibly all of the business if her original share was a SP gift. If her original ½ was not a gift and was CP, then ½ the business between these years would be CP and ½ would be SP and analyzed under *Pereira* and *Van Camp* as above.	The court would use these formulas to determine the SP and CP shares for at least ½ of the business. The other ½ would be the same as the analysis above.

Continued>

Issue	Rule	Fact Application	Conclusion
The business value (2014-now at dissolution)			
Presumptions	See above.	At this point, H and W are separated and all property acquired after their separation would be SP. So, any earnings from the business would be entirely SP for her father's ½ that she inherited. The original ½ would be either CP or SP depending on whether she paid for it or it was gifted and it would have retained its CP or SP characterization post separation. However, W's earnings and work would be her SP post-separation so it is possible that her contributions to the business for her original ½ she owned might require contributions from the CP as that was her SP work, so the courts would need to possibly apply reverse *Pereira/Van Camp* for her first ½ of the business for the years from 2014 until their divorce.	
Reverse *Pereira/ Van Camp*	*Reverse Pereira and Van Camp* will apply when SP contributes to a CP business after separation/dissolution. *Reverse Pereira:* The community receives a fair rate of return, and the remainder is SP. • CP interest = CP contribution (at time of separation) + reasonable rate of return • SP interest = value of business - CP interest (from above) *Reverse Van Camp:* The separate estate receives a fair salary, less expenses, and the remainder is CP. • SP interest = fair market value salary - family expenses - salary taken since separation • CP interest = the value of the business - SP interest (from above)	If the efforts of W contributed to the increase in the business from the time of separation in 2014 for the same reasons discussed above, then the court would consider these equations to determine the values of the CP and SP estates; there are no numbers to input here, but it would be from 2014 (separation) to 2021 (when presumably the divorce will be finalized).	The court will determine how much the CP and SP estates receive.

Disposition: The book side of the business is W's SP and will remain her SP at divorce. The antique part of the business might also be W's SP if she received it as a SP gift during marriage, in which case the court will allocate a portion of the value to the CP contributions made during marriage and a portion of the CP that contributed to its success due to her SP services post-separation. If the first ½ of the business was CP, then it will remain CP, but it is likely that W will want to buy H out of his share of the CP part at divorce.

Community Property Question 2 Sample Answer

February 2021, Question 3

General Presumptions

Community Property (CP)

California is a community property state. CP is property, other than separate property, acquired by either spouse during marriage. All assets acquired during marriage are presumptively CP.

Separate Property (SP)

All property acquired before or after marriage or after permanent separation, or by gift, devise, or bequest is presumed to be SP.

Permanent Separation

Permanent separation occurs when there is a complete and final break in the marital relationship where one spouse has expressed to the other spouse their intent to end the marriage and the spouse's conduct is consistent with their intent to end the marriage.

At the point when Hal (H) and Wendy (W) decided to live separately and separate in 2014, it is not clear whether they were permanently separated because there are no facts as to their intent to end the marriage. In fact, they didn't proceed with divorce proceedings until 2021, so it is possible that initially they might have temporarily separated with an intent to possible reconcile, since many people won't wait 7 years to actually file for a divorce, but it isn't clear either way. However, for purposes of this exam it will be assumed that they permanently separated when the facts said they separated in 2014.

The business value (1990-1995)

CP presumption

See above for rule.

Between the years of 1990 at the time of the marriage and 1995, when W jointly owned the business with her father, Wendy simply worked for her father's business so any income she accrued during this time would be CP. The business was not owned by W at this time. Any income from the business during this time would be CP and the business itself was not W's.

The business value (1995-1999)

CP and SP Presumptions

See above for rules.

In 1995, W became the owner of a ½ interest in the business which would arguably be CP since it was a business acquired during marriage. However, it isn't clear if W purchased ½ of the business or if her father gave it to her as a SP gift, in which case it would be classified as SP.

If the business was CP, then any profits from the business earned during these years would be CP and it wouldn't matter the reason the business succeeded, which it appears was mainly from W's exceptional talent for buying antiques, but it isn't clear which part of the business was responsible for the increase in value. If the business was a SP business, then the courts would use *Pereira/Van Camp* to analyze the value and how much each party should receive.

Pereira/Van Camp

A court may invoke *Pereira* and/or *Van Camp* to value the community share where a SP business is possibly enhanced by community labor.

Pereira Application

Courts use *Pereira* when the spouse's personal management skills are the primary reason for the growth because this formula tends to favor the community. The SP interest is calculated by looking at the value of the SP business at the time of the marriage times a reasonable rate of return (often 10%) on that value for each year the family had the SP business during marriage. The CP interest is then calculated by taking the overall value of the business and subtracting the SP interest.

Here, it seems that the court would likely use *Pereira* because the business doubled in value between 1995 and 2000, during which time W became a ½ owner, and it was likely due to her exceptional talent for buying antiques. However, this assumes that the antique part of the business is the part of the business that was responsible for its increase, which is not clear because it could have been the rare books portion that her father oversaw, or the community, the fact that her father got the business up and running initially, or other reasons that contributed to the doubled value.

If the court applies *Pereira*, there aren't numbers to indicate how much SP contributed, if any, to the business when she first became a part owner but that amount would be used plus a reasonable rate of return to determine the SP interest and the CP interest would be ½ the value of the business at 1999 (since she only owned half during those years) less the SP interest.

Van Camp Application

Courts use *Van Camp* when the character of the business is the primary reason for growth because it tends to favor the SP estate. The CP interest is calculated by taking the fair market value of the salary minus family expenses minus the actual salary taken over the number of years of marriage with the business. The SP interest is then calculated by taking the overall value of business minus the CP interest.

If the court applied *Van Camp* because it isn't clear that her exceptional talent was the reason the business value doubled and antiques and rare books naturally increase in value over time, then they would look at the value of the fair market salary less her salary and family expenses for her ½ of the business and that would be the CP interest. If the business was a gift, then the court would apply one of these formulas to determine the SP and CP interests.

If W paid for her ½ interest in the business, then it would be CP and the value during these years would be split between H and W as CP.

Goodwill of the business

Business goodwill is the value derived from the expectation of continued public patronage that stems from intangible qualities that generate a business income beyond that derived from a professional's labor, the reasonable return on capital and physical assets. To the extent that the goodwill is earned during the marriage, it is CP. Courts use two approaches to determine goodwill. The first is the market value approach, which looks at the value another is willing to pay for the business. The second approach is the capitalization of past excess earnings, which looks at the income of the professional less a comparable income, deducting a fair return on intangible assets, multiplied by a fixed rate of capitalization.

For the years between 1990 to 1995 and possibly thereafter if the court finds that W's first ½ of the business ownership was CP, it is possible that goodwill derived from W's exceptional talent and labor. If the court finds this, then it could add the value of her goodwill to the CP share based on the value someone would offer for the business or her capitalization of past excess earnings. Business goodwill could also factor into the court's evaluation of the business value for the entire duration of the business during marriage (through separation in 2014).

The business value (1999-2014)

Presumptions

See above for rules.

In 1999, W's father died and left his ½ of the business to W, which presumably was the rare book part of the business since in 1995 she became a part owner and took over the antiques part of the business. Since she inherited this half of the business, it would be considered SP.

If the first ½ of the business was CP, then any profits from this part of the business earned during these years would be CP as discussed above. If the first ½ of the business was a SP business and now this ½ is a SP business, then the courts would use *Pereira/Van Camp* to analyze the value and how much each party should receive.

Pereira/Van Camp

See above for rules.

The same analysis would apply for these years as above but for certain ½ of the business that W just inherited would be SP so *Pereira/Van Camp* would apply to at least ½ of the business between 1999 and 2014 and possibly all of the business if her original share was a SP gift.

If her original ½ was not a gift and was CP, then ½ the business between these years would be CP and ½ would be SP and analyzed under *Pereira* and *Van Camp* as above. The court would use these formulas to determine the SP and CP shares for at least ½ of the business, and possibly all of the business during these years. The analysis would be the same as the analysis above.

The business value (2014-now at dissolution)

Presumptions

See above for rules.

At this point, H and W are separated and all property acquired after their separation would be SP. So, any earnings from the business would be entirely SP for her father's ½ that she inherited. The original ½ would be either CP or SP depending on whether she paid for it with CP funds, or it was gifted as SP. The property would retain its CP or SP characterization post separation.

However, W's earnings and work would be her SP post separation, so it is possible that her contributions to the business for her original ½ she owned might require contributions from the CP as that was her SP work, so the courts would need to possible apply reverse *Pereira/Van Camp* for her first ½ of the business for the years from 2014 until their divorce because her SP labor would have continued to improve the CP business (for the first ½ if it was CP).

Reverse *Pereira/Van Camp*

Reverse *Pereira* and *Van Camp* will apply when SP contributes to a CP business after separation or dissolution.

Reverse *Pereira*

The community receives a fair rate of return on the CP contribution at the time of separation, and the remainder is SP.

Reverse *Van Camp*

The separate estate receives a fair salary, less expenses, less the salary taken since the separation, and the remainder is CP.

If the efforts of W contributed to the increase in the business from the time of separation in 2014 for the same reasons discussed above, then the court would consider these equations to determine the values of the CP and SP estates; there are no numbers to input here, but it would be from 2014 (separation) to 2021 (when presumably the divorce will be finalized). The court will determine how much the CP and SP estates receive.

Overall Disposition

The book side of the business is W's SP and will remain her SP at divorce. The antique part of the business might also be W's SP if she received it as a SP gift during marriage, in which case the court will allocate a portion of the value to the CP contributions made during marriage and a portion of the CP that contributed to its success due to her SP services post-separation. If the first ½ of the business was CP, then it will remain CP, but it is likely that W will want to buy H out of his share of the CP part at divorce so the court could award H other property that is of a similar value and give the entire business to W.

Community Property Question 3
February 2008, Question 5

Harvey and Fiona, both residents of State X, married in 1995. Harvey abandoned Fiona after two months. Harvey then met Wendy, who was also a State X resident. He told her that he was single, and they married in State X in 1997. They orally agreed that they would live on Harvey's salary and that Wendy's salary would be saved for emergencies. They opened a checking account in both their names, into which Harvey's salary checks were deposited. Wendy opened a savings account in her name alone, into which she deposited her salary.

Harvey and Wendy moved to California in 1998. Other than closing out their State X checking account and opening a new checking account in both their names in a California bank, they maintained their original financial arrangement. In February 1999, Harvey inherited $25,000 and deposited the money into a California savings account in his name alone.

In 2004, Wendy was struck and injured by an automobile driven by Dan. Harvey and Wendy had no medical insurance. Wendy's medical bills totaled $15,000, which Harvey paid from the savings account containing his inheritance. In 2005, Wendy settled with Dan's insurance carrier for $50,000, which she deposited into the savings account that she still maintained in State X.

Very recently, Harvey learned that Fiona had died in 2006. He then told Wendy that he and Fiona had never been divorced. Wendy immediately left Harvey and moved back to State X. The savings account in State X currently contains $100,000. Under the laws of both State X and California, the marriage of Harvey and Wendy was and remained void.

1. What are Harvey's and Wendy's respective rights in:

   a) The State X savings account? Discuss.

   b) The California checking account? Discuss.

   c) The California savings account? Discuss.

2. Is Harvey entitled to reimbursement for the $15,000 that he paid for Wendy's medical expenses? Discuss.

Answer according to California law.

Community Property Question 3 Assessment
February 2008, Question 5

In community property questions, the issues usually arise in the same order they appear on the issues checklist, which is also the same order they should be addressed in an exam response, unless directed otherwise by the call of the question. First, determine if there is any issue regarding the status of the relationship between the parties or if they have a premarital agreement. If there is — such as in this question where there is a putative spouse issue — address it first since it will impact the rest of the answer.

You'll notice community property answers look slightly different than other subjects because it is most efficient to first identify all applicable general presumptions with no companion analysis, then reference the rules throughout your answer. In this particular question there are four general presumptions that need to be addressed before going through the specific assets. This essay also addressed a premarital agreement, but only one state-released answer did a decent job on this issue (which shows you don't need to be perfect to pass).

As with other exams you've organized, once the applicable presumptions are out of the way, proceed with your typical community property essay approach. Address each asset (or debt) individually. First, classify the asset (State X savings account here) based on the original presumption, then go through the checklist issues to determine if anything changes the original classification. To begin, applying the general presumptions to the savings account, it would be QMP because H and W are putative spouses, thus the account is treated as CP unless the parties did something to change this, or a special classification applies. Next, look to see if the parties did anything to alter the general presumption. First, W took title in her name alone (MWSP issue). Since events occurred post-1975, this does not actually alter the presumption, but it is an issue that you should address since the facts trigger it. Second, the parties made an oral agreement, which gives rise to a transmutation. However, it would not actually alter the presumption since there was no writing here. Next, consider if there are any special classifications. Since there was a deposit of personal injury settlement money, apply the personal injury rule to reach the result that, upon dissolution, the $50,000 from W's injury would go to her as her SP for her injuries, subject to reimbursement from the CP for her medical expenses. The other $50,000 in the account would be treated as CP since the funds derived from earnings. Don't stop there; answer the question call. Go through the distribution issues and determine H and W's respective rights and answer accordingly with specificity. Apply this approach to all assets in community property essay questions. Also, review the grid for how to approach the debt (liability) portion of the question, which will be addressed more thoroughly in another question assessment.

Note the areas highlighted in **bold** on the corresponding grid, which highlight the issues, analysis, and conclusions that are likely **required** to receive a passing score on this question. In general, the essay grids are provided to assist you in analyzing the essays and are much more detailed than what a student should create during the exam to organize their response to a question.

Issue	Rule	Fact Application	Conclusion
Preliminary Issues			
Putative Spouse	**One or both parties believes in good faith that the parties are legally married; some unknown mistake makes it illegal.** One may be estopped to assert the validity or invalidity of a marriage if they knew that the marriage was not valid or knew that it was invalid but acted as though it was valid.	Here, W in good faith believed she was married to H as he told her he was single, and they appeared to get married in 1997. Thus, until she found out the truth in 2006, she and H were putative spouses.	H and W putative spouses—QMP implicated
General Presumptions			
CP	**California is a community property state. CP is property, other than separate property, acquired by either spouse during marriage. All assets acquired during marriage are presumptively CP.**		
SP	**All property acquired before or after marriage or after permanent separation, or by gift, devise, or bequest is presumed to be SP.**		
QCP	**QCP is property acquired while the couple was domiciled in a non-CP state, which would have been classified as CP had it been acquired under the same circumstances in California.** QCP will be treated like CP.		
QMP	**QMP is property acquired during a void or voidable marriage, which would have been CP or QCP if the marriage had not been void or voidable.** QMP will be treated like CP.		
Prenuptial Agreement or **Transmutation**	Must be in writing signed by both parties (but can use estoppel or reliance to get around) Deemed involuntary unless: • Represented by independent counsel at time agreement was signed or advised to seek independent counsel and waived in a separate writing • Presented with final agreement 7 days before signing and told to seek independent counsel (post 1/1/20 need 7 days between presentation and signing even if no independent counsel) • If unrepresented, one must be fully informed in writing of the terms and rights they are giving up, in a language in which the party is proficient, and declare in writing that they received the info and from whom • No duress, fraud, undue influence, or lack of capacity • Anything else the court deems relevant	None of these elements appear to be met here as there is no writing or independent representation by H and W that they would live on H's salary and save W's salary for emergencies (**if oral agreement before marriage**). **Also: No transmutation at all because no writing and after 1985 (if oral agreement after marriage).**	No prenuptial agreement and no transmutation

Continued>

Issue	Rule	Fact Application	Conclusion
1a. State X Savings Account			
QMP/CP	See above	Earnings during marriage are CP; QMP here.	
Title/MWSP	Prior to 1975, title in W's name alone indicated her SP	Here, after 1975, so no MWSP; title in W's name **alone will not change QMP to SP.**	No MWSP
Transmutation	Transmutations are agreements between spouses to change the character of an asset. Before 1/1/1985: transmutations could be oral, written, or inferred from conduct of parties **Post 1/1/1985: need a signed declaration, in writing**, by spouse adversely affected expressly stating that a change in ownership is being made OR the gift must be insubstantial in nature — of a personal nature	Here, arguably since H knew W opened the State X savings acct. in her name alone, he agreed to a transmutation to her SP, but since they agreed that it would be used for emergencies for presumably both of them and **there is no writing, there is no transmutation.**	**No transmutation**
Personal Injury	**If COA arose during marriage: CP** If COA arose before or after marriage: SP (community entitled to reimbursement if medical bills were paid out of community funds) **On divorce: injured spouse's SP** unless the interests of justice require otherwise, but **community entitled to reimbursement**	**Here, the $50,000 deposit into the State X account was QMP since W was injured during their putative spouse marriage, but at separation in 2006 it will become her SP since she was the injured spouse. The remaining $50,000 is QMP because it was W's earnings.** The community (H's SP here) will be entitled to reimbursement for medical expenses, as discussed below in Q2.	**W gets $50k from her personal injury, and W and H each get $25k from other $50k in account**
1b. Cal. Checking Account			
QMP/CP/QCP	See above	**Since H's earnings were to be deposited into this new checking account and it was in both H and W's names, it is QMP, treated as CP. Any State X earnings that may be transferred to this account would be QCP/QMP.**	**H and W each get 1/2**
Transmutation	See above	Since in both names, no indication that there was a change in the character of the account as QMP.	H and W each get ½

Continued>

Issue	Rule	Fact Application	Conclusion
1c. Cal Savings Account			
SP	See above	**H inherited the money in the savings account, so it is presumed to be his SP; the account was in his name alone and no appearance that funds were commingled, so still his SP.**	H's SP
2. Medical Expenses			
Debts	The CP and debtor's SP are liable for debts incurred during marriage, and non-debtor's SP if for necessaries.	Here, the medical expenses were incurred during the putative marriage, so the community is liable and W's SP. If medical treatment was necessary for W's life, then H's SP would be liable too.	CP and W's SP liable
Order of Satisfaction	If to benefit the community, take from CP first, otherwise debtor's SP.	**Here, the court should take from H's SP last since there were sufficient community funds to draw from and some community funds were specifically reserved for "emergencies."**	CP first, then H's SP
Personal Injury	At divorce, the injured spouse receives the money from personal injuries, but the community may be entitled to reimbursement.	Here, since W will get her personal injury settlement, the community will be **entitled to reimbursement for her $15,000 expenses.** But since H's SP paid, H should be reimbursed. This is true even if the debt was for necessaries because the community or W's SP should pay for those medical expenses first before taking from H's SP since it was a debt that benefited W more than H. Further, **they maintained W's savings account for "emergencies," which had sufficient funds to pay this expense before taking from H's SP.**	**H reimbursed**

Community Property Question 3 Sample Answer
February 2008, Question 5

Presumptions

Community Property (CP)

All property, real or personal, wherever situated, acquired by a married person during marriage while domiciled in California that is not classified as separate property, is presumed to be community property (CP).

Separate Property (SP)

Property owned by either spouse before marriage, or after permanent separation, or by gift, devise, or bequest, is presumed to be separate property (SP).

Quasi-community Property (QCP)

Quasi-community property (QCP) is property acquired while a couple are domiciled in a noncommunity property state, which would have been classified as CP had it been acquired in the same circumstances in California.

Quasi-marital Property (QMP)

Quasi-marital property (QMP) is property acquired during a void or voidable marriage, which would have been CP or QCP if the marriage had been valid.

1. H and W's Respective Rights

Putative Spouse

Before determining Harvey (H) and Wendy's (W) respective rights in the assets and liabilities of the parties it is necessary to characterize the nature of their relationship. Where one or both parties to a relationship believes in good faith that the parties are legally married and some unknown mistake makes the marriage illegal, they are considered putative spouses. The property of putative spouses is treated as if it is CP or QCP. While H knew he wasn't actually divorced from Fiona, W believed in good faith that she and H were married since H told her he was single, and H and W had a wedding in 1997. Until such time as W found out the truth in 2006, she and H are considered putative spouses. Therefore, the property acquired during the putative marriage is QMP and will be treated like CP.

Prenuptial Agreement

Parties may orally agree about many things, but a prenuptial agreement that changes the classification of property, or where one spouse gives up rights to property must meet several requirements. The agreement must be in writing and signed by both parties. Such an agreement will be deemed involuntary unless the impacted party is represented by independent counsel at the time the agreement is signed, or waived it in a separate writing, is presented with the agreement seven days before signing it, if unrepresented, fully informed in writing of the terms and rights that are being given up, in a language in which the impacted party is proficient, and declares in writing that they've received the info and from whom, and there may not be fraud, duress, or incapacity. The court can also consider any other factors it deems relevant.

Since the agreement that H and W would live on H's salary and save W's earnings for emergencies was oral and did not meet any of these requirements, it will not be enforceable. Even if it were in writing, it is unclear that deciding to use W's earnings for emergencies designates it as her SP since having an emergency fund would benefit both spouses. All of the property from the putative marriage will be deemed QMP.

1a. State X Savings Account

The money in the State X savings account is composed of W's salary and a $50,000 settlement from a 2004 car accident that injured W. W's earnings during the putative marriage are QMP, so they will be treated as

CP. The funds deposited from the car accident settlement would also be considered QMP and treated as CP because the cause of action arose during the putative marriage. However, at the time of the separation in 2006, the personal injury award will become the SP of W, since she was the injured party.

MWSP

W took title to the savings account in her name alone; however, taking title in a woman's name alone will not change the classification from QMP to SP. Prior to 1975 taking title in a woman's name alone created a presumption the property was SP, but that rule does not apply here since these events occurred in 1995 and later.

Transmutation

A transmutation is an agreement between spouses to change the character of an asset. Oral transmutations were valid prior to 1985, but after January 1, 1985, a valid transmutation required a declaration signed by the adversely affected spouse, unless the gift was insubstantial in nature. W's earnings are not insubstantial, so a written transmutation is required, and there is not one here so the State X savings account is QMP.

W will receive the $50,000 traceable to the personal injury settlement (subject to reimbursement discussed below), and the other $50,000 in the State X savings account is QMP and will be treated like CP; H and W are each entitled to a one-half share of $25,000 each.

1b. California Checking Account

H's earnings from his job that were earned during the putative marriage were deposited into the California checking account. Earnings are presumed to be QMP. Any earnings that were transferred from the State X account are likewise considered QMP. Further, the checking account was titled in both H and W's names, which further supports the classification as QMP. This is QMP and treated like CP for purposes of disposition. Consequently, H and W are each entitled to one-half of the balance.

1c. California Savings Account

H inherited $25,000 and deposited it in the California savings account during the putative marriage. However, an inheritance is presumed to be SP unless it appears the funds were commingled with the community funds (or QMP). Here, H kept the inheritance in a separate savings account titled in his own name, so it retains its classification of SP, and H is entitled to 100% of the money in the California savings account.

2. Medical Expenses

The community—in this case, the QMP—is liable for debts incurred during the marriage, and the non-debtor's SP may even be liable when the debt was incurred for necessaries. Here, the medical expenses and ensuing debt were incurred during the putative marriage, so the community is liable, and W's SP is liable. If the medical treatment W received was necessary for the maintenance of life, it would be considered necessary, and H's SP would also be liable for the debt.

If the debt was incurred for the benefit of the community, payment first comes from the community, then the debtor spouse's SP and then the other spouse's SP (so long as it was for a necessary item). Here, H paid for W's debt with his SP funds from the California savings account when there were sufficient community funds available to pay the $15,000 debt. For example, the State X savings account had $100,000 available for "emergencies" so the debt could have been paid with those QMP funds. Further, W received a $50,000 settlement for the accident, which should have been able to cover the $15,000 in direct medical expenses attributable to the personal injury suffered in the car accident. Assuming there were sufficient community funds available to pay for the medical debt, as it appears there were, H should be reimbursed for the $15,000 he paid in W's medical bills.

Community Property Question 4
July 2016, Question 5

In 2003, while planning their wedding, Harry and Wanda, a California couple, spent weeks discussing how they could each own and control their respective salaries. Sometime before their wedding, they prepared a document in which they stated, "After we marry, Wanda's salary is her property and Harry's salary is his property." At the same time, they prepared a separate document in which they stated, "We agree we do not need legal advice." They signed and dated each document. They subsequently married.

In 2004, Harry used his salary to buy a condominium and took title in his name alone. Harry and Wanda moved into the condominium.

In 2005, Harry and Wanda opened a joint savings account at their local bank. Each year thereafter, they each deposited $5,000 from their salaries into the account.

In 2015, Harry discovered that Wanda used money from their joint account to buy rental property and take title in her name alone.

In 2016, Harry and Wanda permanently separated and Wanda moved out of the condominium. Wanda thereafter required emergency surgery for a medical condition, resulting in a hospital bill of $50,000. Harry later filed a petition for dissolution of marriage.

What are Harry's and Wanda's rights and liabilities, if any, regarding:

1. The condominium? Discuss.

2. The joint savings account? Discuss.

3. The rental property? Discuss.

4. The hospital bill? Discuss.

Answer according to California law.

Community Property Question 4 Assessment
July 2016, Question 1

This question tests a premarital agreement and the distribution of many different assets at marriage dissolution. At first glance, it is apparent there is a lot of material to cover in just one hour, so time management is key to a successful answer. As always, organize your answer on your computer, or on scratch paper, before you start composing your answer since this will help you manage your time. As you write the answer, be careful to allocate your time appropriately to ensure you are able to answer all of the question calls.

The analysis of the premarital agreement is robust and includes many facts that can be utilized in various places throughout your analysis. Since it is difficult to meet the requirements of a valid premarital agreement, it is usually a safe bet that the agreement in question will not be deemed satisfactory. However, a thorough analysis of each key element of a premarital agreement is essential to passing this essay and is where most of the points are congregated.

The analysis of each of the four pieces of property is fairly simple and implicates the frequently tested topics of tracing, form of title, and transmutation. One of the less frequently tested topics on this essay is the breach of fiduciary duty to a spouse. Whenever one spouse is behaving suspiciously and hiding information from their spouse, this is an important issue to analyze. Here, the wife bought real property and kept it secret from her husband. This is exactly the type of situation where you would discuss the spouses' fiduciary duty to each other. Another less frequently tested topic is the wife's hospital bill, which was incurred post-separation. The rule for "necessaries of life" provides an exception to the general rule and allows the creditor to seek payment from the husband's separate property in addition to the wife's separate property and their community property even though the debt was incurred post-separation.

Finally, make note of the areas highlighted in **bold** on the corresponding grid. The bold areas highlight the issues, analysis, and conclusions that are likely **required** to receive a passing score on this question. In general, the essay grids are provided to assist you in analyzing the essays and are much more detailed than what a student should create during the exam to organize their response to a question.

Issue	Rule	Fact Application	Conclusion
General Presumptions			
Community Property	**California is a community property state.** • **All property acquired during marriage by the labor of either spouse while domiciled in California is presumptively community property.** • Upon divorce, community property is divided evenly.		
Separate Property	• **All property acquired before marriage or after permanent separation or after divorce is presumptively separate property.** In addition, property acquired by gift, bequest, devise, or descent and property acquired with separate property funds are also presumptively separate property. • Upon divorce, each party retains their own separate property.		
Premarital Agreement	A premarital agreement is one made before marriage that is to become effective upon marriage, in which parties agree to the characterization of their property and may limit support obligations. • **A prenuptial agreement must be in writing and signed by both parties.** • Prenuptial agreements are not enforceable if they were made involuntarily and they are deemed involuntary unless the court finds that the party against whom enforcement is sought was: 1) represented by independent counsel at the time the agreement was signed or advised to seek independent counsel and waived it in a separate writing; 2) presented with the agreement and advised to seek independent counsel 7 calendar days before signing it (after 1/1/2020 need 7 days regardless of independent counsel); 3) fully informed in writing of the terms and rights the party is giving up, in a language in which he is proficient (if unrepresented) and declared in writing that they received such information and from whom they received it; 4) not under duress, fraud, undue influence, and did not lack capacity; and 5) any other factors the court deems relevant.	H and W attempted to make a premarital agreement and discussed it for weeks before their wedding and prepared the document, which states, "After we marry W's salary is her property and H's salary is his property." It was signed before the marriage and will take effect if it meets the requirements for a valid premarital agreement. • **The document was in writing and signed by both H and W.** Consideration is not required. 1) Neither H or W were represented by or advised to seek independent counsel. Rather, they each signed and dated a document that said, **"We agree we do not need legal advice." This document may be enough to serve as a waiver of counsel, as it was made in a separate document.** 2) H and W prepared the agreement "some time before their wedding." If the draft was signed less than 7 days after it was prepared, the court will deem the agreement involuntary because there was not enough time to review it. Though H and W spent "weeks discussing" the agreement and attempted to waive the need for counsel, the agreement is still presumed involuntary because **neither H nor W were advised to seek independent counsel 7 days before signing,** since *at the same time* they signed the waiver agreeing "they do not need legal advice."	The **premarital agreement is likely not enforceable** because it was not entered into voluntarily.

(Continued>)

Issue	Rule	Fact Application	Conclusion
Premarital Agreement (continued)	• **Prenuptial agreements are not enforceable if they are unconscionable,** which can occur at the time of the execution or when the party against whom enforcement is sought was not provided a full and fair reasonable disclosure of the property or financial obligations, did not have adequate knowledge, and did not waive disclosure.	3) Though they discussed it for "weeks," **it is not clear that both parties were fully informed and knew what rights they were giving up,** so it will be deemed involuntary on this basis as well. • Here, **each party assigned their salaries as their own separate property, which seems fair** as each party is keeping as their own the financial product of his/her own work, but there is still a problem with voluntariness.	
1. Rights to the condominium			
Presumption	**Property obtained during marriage by the labor of either spouse is presumptively CP.**	H used his salary to purchase the condominium in 2004, one year after he and Wanda were married. **Since the condominium was purchased during marriage with H's earnings, it is presumptively CP.**	Condo is CP
Form of Title	**Taking title to CP in one spouse's name alone does not defeat the CP presumption.**	**H taking title in his name alone will not defeat the CP presumption.**	Form of title cannot defeat Condo is CP
Source of Funds/ Tracing	• **One may rebut the CP presumption by tracing the source of funds used to purchase the property to SP funds.** • **The burden of proof is on the spouse claiming SP.**	**H used his salary to purchase the condominium.** **In the absence of a valid premarital agreement, H's salary earned during marriage is CP.**	Source of funds is CP Condo is CP
Transmutation	• A transmutation is an **agreement** between spouses made during marriage to alter the ownership characterization of property. • A valid transmutation of real or personal property requires a **writing,** clearly describing the change in ownership, and consent of the adversely affected spouse.	H took title in his name alone, but that is inadequate for a valid transmutation because there is **no evidence that W,** the spouse adversely affected, knew of the purchase or **agreed in writing that the condo is H's SP,** as would have been necessary since the condominium is real property.	No transmutation Condo is CP
Conclusion: The condominium is CP and will be divided equally between H and W upon divorce.			

Continued>

Issue	Rule	Fact Application	Conclusion
2. Joint savings account			
Presumption/ Joint Title	• **The earnings of each spouse during marriage are presumptively CP.** • **Funds held in a joint savings account are presumptively CP.**	Here, **the savings account was a joint savings account,** where they each deposited $5,000 from their salaries earned during marriage into the account, so the savings account is presumptively CP.	Savings is CP
Source/Tracing	• **The CP presumption can be overcome if the funds in a joint account can be traced to a SP source.**	**The source of funds in the savings account is derived from H and W's salaries earned during marriage, which is CP,** since the prenuptial agreement is invalid, so the source of funds was CP and will not overcome the presumption.	Savings is CP
Conclusion: The funds in the joint savings account are CP, and any remaining funds will be divided equally between H and W upon divorce.			
3. The rental property			
Presumption	Property obtained during marriage by the labor of either spouse is presumptively CP.	While married in 2015, W purchased the rental property. **Since the condominium was purchased during marriage, it is presumed CP.**	Rental is CP
Form of Title	Taking title to CP in one spouse's name alone does not defeat the CP presumption.	W taking title in her name alone will not defeat the CP presumption.	Form of title cannot defeat Rental is CP
Source/Tracing	• **One may rebut the CP presumption by tracing the source of funds used to purchase the property to SP funds.** • Courts use the direct tracing or exhaustion method. • **The burden of proof is on the spouse claiming SP.**	**W used funds from the joint savings account (which, as established above, is CP) to purchase the rental property.** There is no evidence here, but if W were able to show through the exhaustion method or direct tracing that CP funds were exhausted and that only SP funds were used towards the purchase of the rental property, W could establish the rental property was SP. Absent additional information regarding the funds used to purchase the property, it is presumed that W used CP funds from the joint savings account to purchase the rental property.	Source of funds is CP Rental is CP

Continued>

Issue	Rule	Fact Application	Conclusion
Breach of Fiduciary Duty	• Each spouse has a **fiduciary duty of good faith and fair dealing** and to use the highest good faith and fair dealing with each other and never take unfair advantage of the other. • Each spouse has a fiduciary duty of full disclosure of all material facts about community assets and debts, and to provide equal access to all information upon request. • A breach of fiduciary duty towards a spouse may result in the harmed spouse receiving more than half of the CP upon divorce.	In 2015 H discovered W used money from their **joint savings and secretly purchased a rental property in her name only.** As co-owners of the joint savings account used to fund the purchase, **W and H both had right to** total management and control of the funds in **the savings account,** as well as absolute power of disposition. **W did not need H's permission to use the funds** from the account to purchase the rental property, but **W did have a duty to fully disclose the purchase of the rental property to H,** since purchasing property is a material fact about the **community assets.** She altered the nature of the CP assets by changing it from funds in the joint savings account to rental property.	Failure to disclose the purchase to H is a breach of W's fiduciary duty.

Conclusion: **The rental property is CP.** The value of the rental property and any rental income would normally be divided in half between W and H upon divorce. However, **if the court finds that W breached her fiduciary duty towards H, H may receive more than half of the value of the rental property and** rental income.

4. Hospital bill

Issue	Rule	Fact Application	Conclusion
Permanent Separation	**Debts are incurred at the time the obligation arises. Debts incurred after permanent separation are the SP debt of the incurring debtor spouse.** Permanent separation arises when there is a complete and final break in the marital relationship where one spouse has expressed to the other spouse their intent to end the marriage, and the spouse's conduct is consistent with their intent to end the marriage.	**H and W permanently separated in 2016, and W moved out of the house,** ending the marital economic community. **Subsequently, W incurred a debt in the form of the hospital bill of $50,000 after they separated,** thereby making the debt **her own SP debt.**	W's SP debt
Debt for Necessaries of Life	**A spouse's SP is liable for their own debts, but not for debts of the other spouse, unless the debt was incurred during permanent separation prior to divorce, and the debt was incurred for necessaries of life. These can be paid from the debtor spouse's SP first, then CP, and then non-debtor spouse's SP.**	**W's hospital bill will be considered a necessary of life because she required emergency surgery for a medical condition.** **Ordinarily, H's SP would not be responsible for W's hospital bill since it was incurred after permanent separation and prior to divorce, but since the debt was for a necessary of life, his SP may be used to cover the debt.**	Debt is for necessary of life, both will be responsible.

Conclusion: Both spouses will be responsible for the medical bill. **W's SP will be used to pay the bill first, then the CP, and if any remaining debt is owed, H's SP will be used.**

Community Property Question 5
February 2024, Question 1

Henry and Wendy married in California in 2012. Henry got a job as an auto mechanic. Wendy's aunt, who owned a house free and clear of any mortgage, gave it to Wendy. Wendy then added Henry on the title document to the house. Wendy and Henry lived in the house. Wendy then began singing with a local band. Some years later, Wendy and the band began traveling and performing across the state. The band was profitable, and Wendy sent money home to Henry and stayed with him periodically.

Henry decided to purchase an auto repair garage and applied for a loan from a bank for that purpose. Because Wendy was on the road with her band, Henry forged Wendy's signature on the loan documents without her knowledge. The bank approved the loan, using the house as collateral. Henry purchased the auto repair garage with the loan funds. Title to the auto repair garage was taken in Henry's and Wendy's names in joint tenancy.

After a while, Wendy told Henry that the marriage was over. She stopped returning home and also stopped sending money to Henry. She began making independent investments with her earnings. Henry was unable to make the loan payments and the bank demanded payment of the loan in full. Shortly thereafter, Wendy filed for dissolution of marriage.

What are Henry's and Wendy's respective rights and liabilities, if any, regarding:

1. The house? Discuss.

2. The bank loan? Discuss.

3. The auto repair garage? Discuss.

4. Wendy's investments? Discuss.

Answer according to California law.

Community Property Question 5 Assessment
February 2024, Question 1

This is a very straightforward question since H and W were married and domiciled in California. There is one issue regarding their separation that you needed to address but that is a fairly straightforward rule. This is a classic community property essay that addresses the various assets and debts in chronological order, and they mirror the calls of the question.

This question didn't test any special classifications or difficult issues but tested concepts that have been tested quite frequently in the past few years including transmutations, how title is held, breach of fiduciary duties, and debts. This question should be organized just as you've been doing. First, start with the general presumptions of CP and SP. Then, address the separation upfront since it affects some of the assets and debts.

The first asset, the house, starts with a SP presumption since it was inherited, but the property was altered through changing title to both names and effecting a transmutation. It was a very straightforward asset that tested common rules you should know well. The second call asked about a debt, the bank loan. Here, you needed to know about debts and the order of satisfaction for the debts. But what makes this call a bit trickier is the breach of fiduciary duties when H forged W's signature. This also ties into the ability of each spouse to manage and control the property and what one spouse can do if another spouse tries to convey property without consent. This call was likely weighted heavier than the other calls so when allocating your time, make sure you don't treat each call as equal, but rather allocate your time as needed based on the issues being tested.

The third call asked about the garage, which was in both of their names even though W didn't know about it. Again, as it relates to the loan H obtained by forging W's signature, the court could treat this as CP or order H to sell it and pay back the loan since he can't make his loan payments. The last call was the most straightforward as it simply required you to recognize the general presumptions and that her earnings would be CP if she used earnings from during the marriage, or SP if earnings were used after they separated.

Overall, this is a very typical community property essay. If you know your rules, community property can be a very friendly essay to get. However, if you decided to play the subject lottery or rely on some predictions that might not be accurate and skip community property since it is only a possible testing subject, you could set yourself up for failure on an otherwise seemingly easy essay. So make sure you study all subjects and be prepared for any essay you might get.

Finally, make note of the areas highlighted in **bold** on the corresponding grid. The bold areas highlight the issues, analysis, and conclusions that are likely **required** to receive a passing score on this question. In general, the essay grids are provided to assist you in analyzing the essays and are much more detailed than what a student should create during the exam to organize their response to a question.

Issue	Rule	Fact Application	Conclusion
General Presumptions/Preliminary Issues			
Community Property	**California is a community property state. CP is property, other than separate property, acquired by either spouse during marriage. All assets acquired during marriage are presumptively CP.**		
Separate Property	**All property acquired before or after marriage or after permanent separation, or by gift, devise, or bequest is presumed to be SP.**		
Permanent Separation	**Occurs when there is a complete and final break in the marital relationship where one spouse has expressed to the other spouse their intent to end the marriage and the spouse's conduct is consistent with their intent to end the marriage.**	**The point when W told H that the marriage was over and stopped returning home was likely the point of permanent separation since she expressed to him her desire to end the marriage, and her conduct was consistent with this since she stopped coming home and stopped sending him money.**	**H and W permanently separated when W told H the marriage was over.**
1. The House			
Presumptions	See above.	**The house was acquired during marriage so it presumed CP but it was given to W by her aunt so it could be considered a SP gift or inheritance and W's SP.**	House presumed SP
Title	Form of title can rebut the original presumption when title is inconsistent with the original presumption. When the source of funds is SP but title is taken jointly, it is presumed to be a gift to the community and CP unless there is a contrary written intent, subject to reimbursement.	Although the house was W's SP, W added H's name to the title of the house, which would be presumed that she gifted the SP house to the community.	House treated as CP
Transmutation	Transmutations are agreements between spouses to change the character of an asset. Before 1/1/1985: transmutations could be oral, written, or inferred from conduct of parties. Post 1/1/1985: **need a signed declaration, in writing, by spouse adversely affected expressly stating that a change in ownership is being made** OR the gift must be insubstantial in nature.	Here it is after 1985 since they married in 2015. **The deed to the house on which H was added is likely in writing and signed by both parties, but the facts aren't clear. But based on title as discussed above, the presumption can be rebutted.**	**House is CP so H and W each get ½**

Continued>

Issue	Rule	Fact Application	Conclusion
2. The bank loan			
Debts	A contract debt is incurred at the time the contract is made. There is a rebuttable presumption that property purchased with borrowed funds during marriage is CP debt. • **Can rebut with the "intent of the lender" test: A showing that the lender relied exclusively on SP when extending credit may rebut the presumption.** • Earning capacity: **If the credit is based on earning** capacity, **it is a CP debt** because earning capacity is a community asset.	Here, H took out the loan during the marriage, so it is presumed to be a CP debt. Since H forged W's signature and used the house as collateral, it seems as though the bank used CP assets as the reason it loaned the money to H, not H's SP. H may try to argue that he only forged her signature b/c W was on the road a lot with her band and not home very often and that since she did send money home, she likely would have consented. And the loan has both names as the debtors which also implies based on title that the debt is community debt.	The loan is a CP debt
Breach of fiduciary duty	Each spouse has a fiduciary duty to fully disclose all material facts about community assets and debts to the other spouse and **use the highest good faith and fair dealing and never take advantage of the other.**	Here, H breached his fiduciary duty to W by forging her signature on a loan document and using the marital home as collateral for the loan. His actions impacted the community assets and W's liabilities without her knowledge or consent. He also breached his duty by not allowing W to have equal management and control of the community assets.	The court could allocate the loan to H due to his breach of fiduciary duties.
Management and control	Management and control of the personal CP belongs to either spouse but a **spouse cannot convey real property** to a BFP without the consent of the other spouse or the other spouse can void it within 1 year (and void any time if conveyed to a non BFP).	Here, W could possibly void the collateral on the house b/c she did not consent.	W could void the house being conveyed as collateral.

Continued>

Issue	Rule	Fact Application	Conclusion
Order of Satisfaction for Debts	To satisfy a debt, CP is liable for all debts incurred during marriage, as well as the SP of the debtor spouse and the SP of non-debtor spouse if more necessaries.	Ordinarily, the community would be liable for the loan as it is CP debt. Also, it is arguably for the benefit of the community since H used the loan to purchase the garage which was in both H and W's names.	**The debt could be reclassified as H's debt or remain CP but the court can reallocate assets/debts as needed.**
	If the debt is for the community, take from CP first.	**However, since H acted in bad faith by forging W's signature and using their house as collateral, it is possible that the court can allocate the loan debt entirely to H as his SP debt.**	W's SP would not be liable.
	The court can alter the distribution of the property when necessary to compensate for a bad faith action by a spouse.	W's SP would not be liable.	
3. The auto repair garage			
CP	See above	The garage was acquired during marriage in both H and W's name so it is presumed CP.	**CP unless rebutted**
Joint title	Joint title is treated like CP upon divorce.	Title was taken in H and W's name in joint tenancy so at divorce, they can each take their ½.	**Still CP** — the court could order H to sell the garage to pay back the loan since he can't make the payments & this will protect their house used as collateral.
4. Wendy's investments			
Presumptions	See above.	Since W began making investments with her earnings after separation, those earnings would be her SP and thus the investments would be her SP. However, if she made the investments after separation but they were from earnings made during the marriage, then they would be CP as they could be traced to the earnings during marriage.	**Most likely the investments are the SP of W** so H would not be entitled to any of them.

Community Property Question 6
February 2003, Question 6

Henry and Wanda married in 1980 when both were students at State X University. State X is a non-community property state. Shortly after the marriage, Henry graduated and obtained employment with a State X engineering firm. Wanda gave birth to the couple's only child, and Henry and Wanda agreed that Wanda would quit her job and remain home to care for the child. They bought a house in State X using their savings for the down payment and obtained a loan secured by a twenty-year mortgage for the balance of the purchase price. Mortgage payments were subsequently paid from Henry's earnings. The title to the State X house was in Henry's name alone.

In 1990, Henry accepted a job offer from a California engineering firm. The couple moved to California with their child and rented out the State X house.

In 1992, Wanda's uncle died and left her an oil painting with an appraised value of $5,000 and a small cabin located on a lake in California. Wanda took the painting to the cabin and hung it over the fireplace.

In 1993, after reading a book entitled "How to Avoid Probate," Henry persuaded Wanda to execute and record a deed conveying the lake cabin to "Henry and Wanda, as joint tenants with right of survivorship." Wanda did so, believing that the only effect of the conveyance would be to avoid probate.

In 1995, after three years of study paid for out of Henry's earnings, Wanda obtained a degree in podiatry and opened her own podiatry practice. Her practice became quite successful because of her enthusiasm, skill, and willingness to work long hours. Henry continued to work for the engineering firm.

In 2002, Henry and Wanda separated and filed for dissolution of marriage. Wanda had the painting reappraised. The artist, now deceased, has become immensely popular, and the painting is now worth $50,000.

Upon dissolution, what are Henry's and Wanda's respective rights in:

1. The lake cabin? Discuss.

2. The painting? Discuss.

3. The State X house? Discuss.

4. Wanda's professional education and podiatry practice? Discuss.

Answer according to California law.

Community Property Question 6 Assessment
February 2003, Question 6

This is a very typical community property question and requires you to demonstrate mastery of the QCP rules since the parties start their marriage in the noncommunity property state of X, and then move to the community property state of California. While this is an older question, recent questions have constantly tested QCP, but in conjunction with wills and trusts. For this reason, you should review all crossover questions and look at more crossover questions outside of this book to adequately prepare for all possible crossover questions. This question is particularly detailed with many facts to use, all of which go to specific issues, but the analysis is fairly simple once you identify the pertinent rules.

The first call of this question poses a typical transmutation issue. It tries to confuse the issue a bit by adding in facts that H persuaded W to change the title to her SP lake cabin (which she received as an inheritance) as a measure to avoid probate and that W thought avoiding probate was the only effect of the title change. However, W's subjective belief is not relevant to the analysis and the general rule applies that when SP is titled jointly, it is presumed that a gift is made to the community, so the cabin is CP despite W's intent.

Calls 2 and 3 are straightforward. The call regarding the painting requires a simple application of the SP rules. For the call about the home in State X, students must analyze the QCP rules and identify the result when H took title to the home in his name alone, but used QCP funds to pay for the down payment and mortgage.

The final call has two parts and calls for a more robust analysis. First, it asks about the education W received during the marriage. There were many facts available to use to do a full application of the rules regarding when the community can be reimbursed for the cost of one spouse pursuing an education, and the defenses to that reimbursement. Secondly, the question asks about her resulting successful podiatry practice. Both published passing answers provided a full description of the *Pereira/Van Camp* rules, before ultimately coming to the conclusion that the rules did not apply since the podiatry practice was a purely CP enterprise since it originated after the marriage and W's CP labors grew the business. Since the facts provided language about how W's "enthusiasm, skill, and willingness to work long hours" grew the business and that language mirrors the reasoning of when the *Pereira* test applies, it makes good sense to explain the rules, even though you conclude they don't apply here. Remember, your job is to prove or disprove the rules using the facts and the only reason for the bar examiners to include those facts was so you would use them to explain why *Pereira* doesn't apply.

Finally, make note of the areas highlighted in **bold** on the corresponding grid. The bold areas highlight the issues, analysis, and conclusions that are likely **required** to receive a passing score on this question. In general, the essay grids are provided to assist you in analyzing the essays and are much more detailed than what a student should create during the exam to organize their response to a question.

Issue	Rule	Fact Application	Conclusion
General Presumptions			
Community property	**California is a community property state.** • **All property acquired during marriage by the labor of either spouse while domiciled in California is presumptively community property.** • Upon divorce, community property is divided evenly.		California is a community property state while domiciled in California is presumptively community property
Separate property	• **All property acquired before marriage or after permanent separation or after divorce is presumptively separate property.** In addition, property acquired by gift, bequest, devise, or descent and property acquired with separate property funds are also **presumptively separate property.** • Upon divorce, each party retains their own separate property.		
Quasi-community property	**QCP is property acquired while the couple was domiciled in a non-CP state, which would have been classified as CP had it been acquired under the same circumstances in California.** QCP is treated like CP.		
1. Lake Cabin			
Presumption	**Property obtained from an inheritance is presumptively SP.**	Since W received the small lake cabin in 1992 as an inheritance from her dead uncle it was **originally W's separate property.**	Originally SP
Transmutation	Transmutations are agreements between spouses to change the character of an asset. Transmutation after 1985 requires a writing.	**H will assert W made a gift of the cabin and that a transmutation occurred when W executed and recorded a deed naming herself and H as "joint tenants with right of survivorship" since this is sufficient to satisfy the writing requirement.** The fact that W changed the title since H persuaded her it was necessary to avoid probate will not change this determination.	**Transmuted to CP with title change**
Title	**JT title presumed to be CP.**	**Property that is held in joint title, as the lake cabin is, is presumed to be CP in California** for purposes of **distribution at divorce.** This presumption can only be overcome by a collateral written agreement, which H and W do not have here.	Cabin is CP
Reimbursement	Where SP is deeded into CP a spouse may get reimbursement.	W may be able to receive reimbursement for the fair market value of the lake cabin at the time she deeded into a joint tenancy.	**H entitled to ½ value** from time of deeding

Continued>

Issue	Rule	Fact Application	Conclusion
2. Painting			
SP	See above.	**W inherited the painting from her uncle in 1992,** so it was originally SP. **Community funds were not used to enhance the value of the painting and while W kept it at the cabin,** there is no indication she intended to change it from characterization as her SP.	W's SP
3. State X house			
QCP	See above.	**The home was purchased in State X with community funds (H's earnings, a loan, and savings) during the marriage and as such it is QCP and will be treated as CP for division at divorce.**	Each spouse receives ½
Title: H name alone/ Transmutation	At divorce, post-1984, jointly held title presumed to be CP, unless there is an agreement to the contrary (Anti-*Lucas*) Transmutation post-1985 requires a writing	**Though the house was titled only in H's name, not jointly, all contributions to the house were community contributions.** Here, no writing states otherwise so still treated like CP not H's SP since W never agreed in writing to make it H's SP. Further, this was the family home. Taking title in H's name alone can't overcome the presumption of CP and a transmutation requires a writing.	**Each spouse receives ½ home value**
4. Wife education and podiatry practice			
Education	**Education is never CP. The Community is entitled to reimbursement if it paid for the education and the education substantially enhanced the earning capacity of the educated spouse** **Defenses to reimbursement** (could be denied or simply reduced) • **Community already substantially benefited from the education (presumed if > 10 years since education obtained)** • Other spouse also received a community funded education/training, or • Education reduced the need for spousal support for the educated spouse	H will seek reimbursement for the education costs associated with W's pursuit of her podiatry degree, which were paid by the community. H will assert the degree has substantially enhanced W's earning capacity since she was previously a stay-at-home mom, and the community paid for the education so it should be reimbursed. **W will assert the community should not be reimbursed the cost of her education since the community has already received a substantial benefit from her education since she has contributed her earnings from her successful practice to the community for seven years. Though it is not the 10 years required for the presumption to apply,** it is still a substantial contribution to the community. Further, W's education has reduced the need for her support since for many years prior to that she was a nonworking mom and not financially contributing to the family, where she now has a thriving podiatry practice.	Community may be entitled to reimbursement

Continued>

Issue	Rule	Fact Application	Conclusion
Podiatry practice	A court may invoke *Pereira* and/or *Van Camp* to value the community share where SP is possibly enhanced by community labor.	A court may invoke *Pereira* and/or *Van Camp* if SP is possibly enhanced by community labor, **but the podiatry practice was acquired exclusively with community funds (H's earnings and W's enthusiasm, skill, and labor) so *Pereira* and *Van Camp* are inapplicable.** Since all of the podiatry practice was CP both spouses get ½ share.	Each spouse receives ½
	Pereira—tends to favor the community; use when the spouse's personal management skills are the primary reason for the growth		
	Van Camp—tends to favor SP estate; use when the character of the business is the primary reason for growth		

PART 4 *CONSTITUTIONAL LAW*

CONSTITUTIONAL LAW TABLE OF CONTENTS

INTRODUCTION TO CONSTITUTIONAL LAW

Constitutional law essays are similar to torts essays in that they are typically very fact-intensive and require the full use of all applicable facts and factual inferences with comparatively fewer issues to analyze. Although a "racehorse" question with many issues can arise, as shown in our first practice question, it is much less common. Rather, current testing trends indicate that the examiners are looking for in-depth analysis and are less concerned with assessing the skill of issue spotting on constitutional law questions.

Constitutional law essays tend to focus heavily on the issues pertaining to individual rights (equal protection, due process, freedom of speech, etc.). Many of the rules contained in the "Constitutional Law Rule Outline" are rarely essay tested—though they certainly could be—but they are heavily tested on the MCQ portion of the bar exam.

Sometimes a constitutional law essay will have open-ended question calls and not indicate the specific issues to be addressed. This type of question will often ask what claims arising under the Constitution a party may bring, or what constitutional challenges a party can assert under the First and Fourteenth Amendments. To organize your answer, use your issues checklist to aid you in spotting all the issues and avoid missing easily overlooked minor issues such as "state action."

Some constitutional law questions will only ask about one issue. When the call is limited to one issue, the key points stem from the in-depth analysis of each rule element. Consequently, a very detailed understanding of the elements of each rule is necessary. Studying the fact triggers provided in the outline can aid your understanding of how a rule arises and how it functions in various factual situations. When the call is specific there is no need to write out your issues checklist. Rather, write out the rule elements for the identified issue and align the corresponding facts to the elements as you read through the fact pattern line by line.

Constitutional law essays usually require the use of logical inferences when analyzing the elements. For example, a fact pattern will not usually identify the government's interest applicable to a scrutiny level for equal protection, or any issue requiring analysis of the governmental interest. You must infer from the facts what a reasonable governmental interest would be when analyzing this prong of the scrutiny test. The same use of logical inferences also applies to analyzing whether the relation portion of the test is met, such as whether there are reasonable alternatives. Give a few examples for maximum points.

Finally, it is useful to have a predetermined approach to apply to each of the constitutional law issues. If you know in advance how to approach each issue, it will enable you to wisely spend your valuable exam time analyzing the issues. Constitutional law doesn't lend itself to being tested as a crossover with other subjects, with the exception of criminal procedure or real property. The Rules Outline presents the issues in the order they are best approached on an exam, unless directed otherwise by the question call.

ISSUES CHECKLIST

JUSTICIABILITY

Case or controversy
Standing
Ripe
Moot
11th Amendment

STATE ACTION

STATE POWER

FEDERAL POWERS

Congress
Judiciary
Executive

LIMITATIONS ON STATE POWER

Supremacy/Preemption
DCC
Privileges and Immunities Clause
Contracts Clause

LIMITATIONS ON FEDERAL POWER

10th Amendment
Improper delegation of legislative power

**STATE AND FEDERAL POWER LIMITATIONS/
INDIVIDUAL RIGHTS**

1st Amend. — religion
1st Amend. — speech
Freedom of association
Due Process Clause
    Substantive
    Procedural

Equal Protection Clause
Takings

MEMORIZATION ATTACK SHEET

JUSTICIABILITY

◆ **Case/controversy**
  - Actual dispute
  - No political questions
◆ **Standing**
  - Individual
    - ◆ Injury
    - ◆ Causation
    - ◆ Redressability
  - 3rd party
  - Organizational
    - ◆ Elements above, and
    - ◆ Members standing
    - ◆ Organizational purpose
    - ◆ Parties not required
  - Taxpayer
◆ **Timeliness**
  - Ripe (not too early)
  - Moot (not too late)
◆ **11th Amendment**
  - Cannot sue state
  - Bars actions for damages
  - Cities and counties okay

STATE ACTION

◆ **Traditional public function, or**
◆ **Govt. entanglement**

STATES POWER
◆ **10th Amendment**
  - Powers not delegated to fed. govt. saved for states

FEDERAL POWERS

◆ **Congress**
  - Can regulate **commerce** if:
    - ◆ Interstate
      - Channels
      - Instrumentalities
      - Persons & things moving
      - Activities with substantial effect
    - ◆ Intrastate (purely local)
      - Economic
        - Rational belief
        - Substantial economic effect
      - Noneconomic
        - Direct & substantial effect

  - Tax and spend
  - War
  - Naturalization/bankrupt.
  - Necessary and proper—if rationally related
◆ **Judiciary**
  - Cases under Constitution
  - Admiralty/2 states/citizens of diff. states/ foreign
  - Not if independent and adequate state grounds
◆ **Executive**
  - Carry out laws
  - Executive order
  - Treaties
  - Appointments
  - Foreign affairs
  - Pardon federal offenses
  - Veto bills—but no line item
  - Executive privilege is qualified: weigh govt. interest

LIMITATIONS ON STATE POWER

◆ **Supremacy Clause**
  - State law conflicts with fed. law—preempted
◆ **Dormant Commerce Clause**
  - Discriminatory, or Undue burden
  - If discriminatory on its face, must be:
    - ◆ Necessary to
    - ◆ Legitimate noneconomic govt. interest
    - ◆ No reasonable alternative
  - If not discriminatory on its face, then:
    - ◆ Rational basis applied
    - ◆ Balance burden v. benefit
  - Exceptions
    - ◆ Market participant
    - ◆ Congress's consent
◆ **Privileges/Immunities Clause**
  - State cannot discriminate against noncitizens
  - Unless substantially related and no less discriminatory alternatives
  - Rights fundamental to national unity
  - Corps/aliens are not citizens
◆ **Contracts Clause**
  - Private: substantial impairment; reasonable/ appropriate to significant/legitimate public interest

- Public: necessary to important public purpose (stricter application)

LIMITATIONS ON FED. POWER

- ◆ **10th AMENDMENT**
  - Fed. can't commandeer states

LIMITATIONS ON STATE AND FED. POWER

- ◆ **1st Amend. religion**
  - **Free Exercise Clause**
    - ◆ Can't burden religion
    - ◆ Unless compelling govt. interest
    - ◆ Generally applicable laws are okay
      - Except: Rel. Freedom Restoration Act
  - **Establishment Clause**
    - ◆ No coercion
    - ◆ Historical practices & understanding
- ◆ **1st Amend. free speech**
  - **Content-based:** strict scrutiny
  - **Less protected speech**
    - ◆ Obscenity
      - Prurient interest
      - Patently offensive
      - Lacks L.A.P.S.
  - **Misrepresentation/defamation**
    - ◆ Imminent lawless action
    - ◆ Fighting words
  - **Content-neutral**
    - ◆ Substantial govt. interest
    - ◆ Narrowly tailored
    - ◆ Open alternative channels
  - **Time, place, manner**
    - ◆ Public/designated public:
      - Content neutral and viewpoint neutral
      - Substantial govt. interest
      - Narrowly tailored
      - Open alternative channels
    - ◆ Limited public/nonpublic
      - Viewpoint neutral
      - Legitimate govt. interest
      - Reasonably related
  - **Commercial speech**
    - ◆ Substantial govt. interest
    - ◆ Directly advances it
    - ◆ Narrowly tailored (reasonable fit)
  - **Symbolic speech**
    - ◆ Within constitutional power
    - ◆ Important govt. interest
    - ◆ Unrelated to speech
    - ◆ Prohibits no more speech than necessary
  - **Limitations on free speech**
    - ◆ Vague: not clearly defined

- ◆ Overbroad: punishes both protected & unprotected speech
- ◆ Unfettered discretion: no defined standards
- **Prior restraints**
  - ◆ Stop speech before it occurs; unconstitutional unless:
    - Serious public harm
    - Narrowly drawn
    - Final determination
- ◆ **Freedom of association**
  - Freedoms protected by 1st Am. and not social
  - Compelling govt. interest
  - Least restrictive means
- ◆ **Substantive due process**
  - Deprive life, liberty, property interest
  - Fundamental right = strict scrutiny
  - No fundamental right = rational basis
- ◆ **Procedural due process**
  - Fair process prior to deprivation of life, liberty, or property
  - Judicial: hearing, counsel, call witnesses, trial, appeal
  - Nonjudicial: balance private int, procedural safeguards, and govt. interest
- ◆ **Involuntary Servitude**
- ◆ **Equal Protection Clause**
  - Different treatment
    - ◆ On its face
    - ◆ As applied
  - **Levels of review**
    - ◆ Strict scrutiny
      - Necessary to
      - Compelling govt. interest
    - ◆ Intermediate scrutiny
      - Substantially related
      - Important govt. interest
    - ◆ Rational basis
      - Rationally related
      - Legitimate govt. interest
  - **Classifications**
    - ◆ Suspect: race, national origin, state alienage
    - ◆ Quasi-suspect: gender and illegitimacy
    - ◆ Nonsuspect: social; economic; other
    - ◆ EPC—fundamental rights
  - **Level of review required**
    - ◆ Suspect = strict scrutiny
    - ◆ Quasi-suspect = intermediate scrutiny
    - ◆ Nonsuspect = rational basis test
    - ◆ EPC fund. right = strict scrutiny

◆ **Takings Clause**
  - Cannot take private property
  - For public use (rationally related ok)
  - Without just compensation (mkt. value)
  - Total taking if:
    - Permanent physical invasion (per se taking)
    - Use restriction no economic value left
  - Temporary taking: court considers:
    - Economic impact
    - Reasonable expectation of owner
    - Length of delay
    - Good faith
  - Regulatory taking: court considers:
    - Character of invasion
    - Economic impact
    - Interference with investment backed expectation

CONSTITUTIONAL LAW RULE OUTLINE

I. **JUSTICIABILITY IN FEDERAL COURT:** THE FOLLOWING JUSTICIABILITY ISSUES MAY ARISE
   A. **Case or controversy:** There must be an actual case or controversy in dispute.
      1. **Declaratory judgments** are permitted. Declaratory judgments are those that state the legal effect of a regulation or the conduct of parties in regard to a controversy.
      2. **Advisory opinions** are not permitted.
   B. **Political questions** may not be heard by federal courts. If the issue is committed to another branch of the federal government (president or Congress) or if there are no manageable standards by which the court can resolve the issue, the federal court won't hear the issue.
   C. **Standing**
      1. **Individual standing** requires a plaintiff to prove:
         a. An actual or imminent **injury,**
         b. The injury is **caused** by the conduct complained of, and
         c. It is likely that the injury will be **redressed** by a favorable decision.
      2. **Third-party standing** requires the plaintiff to prove they have:
         a. **Individual standing,** and
         b. A **special relationship** between the plaintiff and the third party, **or**
         c. That it is **difficult for the third party** to assert their own rights.
      3. **Organizational standing** requires:
         a. The **members have standing** in their own right,
         b. The interests asserted are **related to the organization's purpose,** and
         c. The case **does not require participation** of individual members (to make individual determinations).
      4. **A federal taxpayer has the limited standing** to sue over a federal tax or spending program that violates the Establishment Clause.

> **Exam tip:** Standing is almost always at issue when an individual or group challenges a statute or regulation. A plaintiff must establish standing prior to having the case heard, so logically it is one of the first issues that should be discussed. However, whether it is a major issue or minor issue depends on the quantity of facts available to use in the analysis and whether the issue was specifically asked about in the call.

   D. **Timeliness: ripeness and mootness**
      1. **Ripeness:** A case will not be heard if there is not yet a live controversy or immediate threat of harm (brought too early).
      2. **Mootness:** A case will not be heard if a live controversy existed at the time the complaint was filed but has since been eliminated (brought too late).
         a. **Except** the case will not be found moot if:
            1. The controversy is **capable of repetition, yet evading review** — e.g., abortion litigation — or
            2. **Voluntary cessation** of the activity by the defendant.

> **Exam tip:** Timeliness is rarely an exam issue, and if it is, it is usually a minor issue so be brief. Ripeness tends to be an issue when the claimant is seeking declaratory relief or when a statute has been enacted but not yet enforced. Otherwise, these are minor issues that need only minimal attention.

   E. The **Eleventh Amendment** provides **immunity to the states** from any federal suit against any one of the states by citizens of another state or a foreign state.
      1. **Actions that have been barred** include actions for damages by citizens of the same state.

2. **Actions that are not barred** include suits by states or the federal government against other states, suits against subdivisions of the state (such as cities or counties), and suits seeking injunctions against state officials.

3. **States have sovereign immunity** from private damage suits brought under federal law against the state in the state's own courts.

II. STATE ACTION: FOR AN ACTION TO VIOLATE THE CONSTITUTION, THERE MUST BE GOVERNMENT INVOLVEMENT WITH THE CHALLENGED ACTION.

A. **Private actor:** The action of a private actor can qualify as state action if:

1. **Public function:** The private actor performs functions that are **traditionally and exclusively public functions** (e.g., parks, prisons, elections); or

2. **Heavy involvement:** The **state is heavily involved** in the activity, such as by **commanding, encouraging,** or being **entangled,** with the activity.

> **Exam tip:** State action is an often-overlooked issue that is worth valuable points and can usually be adequately addressed in one or two sentences. Addressing this issue informs the grader that you understand the claimant must establish that "state action" is present before such action can violate any constitutional rights.

III. POWER RESERVED TO THE STATES

A. **Federalism:** The federal government and state governments coexist.

B. The **Tenth Amendment** provides that the **powers not delegated to the federal** government or prohibited by the Constitution are **reserved to the states.** Therefore, Congress can't compel a city or state to pass a law. (See Section VI for detailed rules.)

IV. FEDERAL POWERS: THERE ARE THREE BRANCHES COMPRISING THE FEDERAL GOVERNMENT—THE LEGISLATIVE BRANCH (CONGRESS), THE JUDICIAL BRANCH, AND THE EXECUTIVE BRANCH (PRESIDENT).

A. **Congress has limited, enumerated powers** granted by the Constitution. Consequently, there must be a **source of power** for any congressional action. Congress has the following enumerated powers:

1. **Regulate commerce:** This includes interstate commerce, intrastate commerce, commerce with foreign nations, and commerce with the Indian tribes. This is a very broad source of power that encompasses many activities.

   a. **Interstate activity regulations:** Congress may regulate activities **between states,** including the:

   1. **Channels** of interstate commerce (e.g., roads, rivers, etc.);

   2. **Instrumentalities** of interstate commerce (e.g., trucks, boats, wires, internet, etc.);

   3. **Persons and things** moving in interstate commerce; and

   4. **Activities that substantially affect** interstate commerce.

   b. **Intrastate activity regulations: Congress may regulate activities that are purely local** in the following situations:

   1. **Commercial or economic activity** may be regulated if there is a **rational basis** to believe that the activity will cause a **substantial economic effect** on **interstate commerce,** or if there is a **substantial cumulative economic effect** (e.g., growing wheat or marijuana).

   2. **Noncommercial or noneconomic activity** may be regulated if the activity has a **direct and substantial effect** on **interstate commerce.** Less deference is given to Congress's power to regulate noncommercial activity.

2. The **Taxing and Spending Clause** gives Congress the broad right to tax and spend for the general welfare of the United States. The allocation of conditional funding must be done unambiguously, in a related area, and cannot be excessively coercive.

3. The **war powers grant** Congress the power to declare war and to raise and support the armed forces.

4. **Naturalization and bankruptcy:** Congress has the power to establish uniform laws of naturalization and bankruptcy.
5. **Post-Civil War Amendments:** Congress has the power to enforce the post-Civil War Amendments such as the **Thirteenth** Amendment's **abolition of slavery**, the **Fourteenth** Amendment's establishment of **equal rights** for all natural citizens, and the **Fifteenth** Amendment's right to **vote** irrespective of race or color.
6. The **Necessary and Proper Clause** grants Congress broad authority to enact laws that shall be **necessary and proper to execute** any of their enumerated powers. The law need only be **rationally related** to the implementation of a constitutionally enumerated power.

> **Exam tip:** Most essays involve actions by state governments and not the federal government. However, should you receive an essay that involves congressional action, quickly write a mini-issues checklist of Congress's powers. Then, also consider all possible limitations on power applicable to the federal government, and remember the Tenth Amendment powers that are reserved to the states, which also serve to limit the federal government's power.

B. **Judiciary**
   1. **Federal judicial power** allows federal courts to review cases:
      a. **Arising under the Constitution** or the laws of the United States,
      b. **Admiralty**,
      c. Between **two or more states**,
      d. Between **citizens of different states**, and
      e. Between a state or its citizens and a **foreign country or foreign citizen**.
   2. **Exception: independent and adequate state grounds.** The Supreme Court will not review a case where there are independent and adequate state law grounds for the state court's decision, even if there is a federal question involved.
C. **Executive branch: powers of the president**
   1. **Execution of laws** made by Congress.
   2. **Supervise the executive branch**, including federal agencies, by issuing an executive order.
      a. **Executive orders** are valid unless they are inconsistent with a congressional statute or some specific provision of the Constitution itself.
   3. **Make treaties** with **foreign nations,** subject to two-thirds Senate approval.
   4. **Speak for the United States in foreign policy** and negotiate executive agreements with foreign countries.
   5. **Appoint ambassadors**.
   6. **Appoint top-level federal officers** subject to 50% Senate approval (e.g., federal judges and cabinet members).
   7. **Issue pardons** for federal criminal offenses, except cases of impeachment.
   8. **Veto a bill passed by Congress** in its entirety (a line-item veto is unconstitutional) by sending it back to Congress unsigned with a message stating the reasons for rejection.
   9. Under **executive privilege**, the president has a **qualified right** to refuse to disclose **confidential information** relating to the performance of their duties. It is qualified to the extent that other compelling governmental interests may outweigh the president's right to refuse to disclose information.

> **Exam tip:** It is rare to have an essay that focuses on executive branch actions. However, it is useful to memorize a mini-issues checklist of all executive powers, just as you do for congressional powers, in the event that you receive an essay question involving an action by the executive branch.

V. LIMITATIONS ON STATE POWER

A. The **Supremacy Clause** states that the Constitution is the supreme law of the land. Any state law that **directly conflicts** with federal law, **impedes the objectives** of federal law, or regulates an **area traditionally occupied** by Congress, will be **preempted** by federal law.

1. **Conflict preemption:** Where a state law is inconsistent with a valid federal law covering the same subject matter, the state law is invalid.

2. **Field preemption:** Where the federal government intends to **"occupy the entire field"** the states cannot regulate in that field.

B. The **Dormant Commerce Clause** (DCC), also known as the Negative Implications of the Commerce Clause, **restricts the states** and local governments from regulating activity that **affects interstate commerce** if the regulation is (1) **discriminatory**, or (2) **unduly burdensome**.

1. **Discriminatory:** A regulation that is **facially discriminatory** against out-of-towners (protectionist to local interests) will be permitted only if it is **necessary** to achieve a **legitimate noneconomic governmental interest** such that there are **no reasonable alternatives**. Facially discriminatory regulations are virtually **per se violations** of the DCC.

    a. The term **"out-of-towners"** refers to a favoring of **local interests** over nonlocal interests and need not apply literally to favoring one state over another but can apply to favoring towns and localities as well.

2. **Undue burden:** A regulation that does not discriminate, but **unduly burdens** interstate commerce will be permitted if it is **rationally related** to a **legitimate government interest**, and the **burden imposed on interstate commerce must be outweighed by the local benefits** to the state. This is essentially a rational basis test plus balancing.

3. **Exceptions**

    a. **Market participant:** When the state is not acting as a regulator, but rather **owns or operates a business**, it may favor local interests over nonlocal interests.

    b. **Congressional consent** to the regulation.

> **Exam tip:** Remember, there must be "state action." If federal governmental action is involved, the *Commerce Clause* is at issue, if state government action is involved, the *Dormant Commerce Clause* is at issue. The call of the question may ask generally about the Commerce Clause and not make this distinction.

> **Issue spotting tip:** Where a state regulation discriminates against out-of-towners, an equal protection issue is raised in addition to DCC because potentially similarly situated people are being treated differently.

> <u>Dormant Commerce Clause fact triggers:</u>
>
> • State legislation requiring all individuals/companies to do something
> • State legislation requirements for some companies and not others
> • State legislation giving discounts to some companies and not others
> • City banning or limiting out-of-towner use/access to state facilities

C. The **Privileges and Immunities Clause of Article IV** prevents a state or city from intentionally discriminating against **noncitizens** regarding rights **fundamental to national unity.**

1. **Rights fundamental to national unity** focus on **commercial** activities, such as one's **right to support oneself**, the right to be employed, engage in business, practice one's profession, or civil liberties.

2. **Corporations and aliens are not considered citizens** for this rule so they will not be afforded protection. Partnerships are treated like corporations.
3. **Test is rigorous scrutiny:** Discrimination against noncitizens will only be allowed if the noncitizens are a **peculiar source of evil** and the discrimination is **substantially related** to this evil and there are **no less discriminatory alternative** means available.

> **Issue spotting tip:** Look for the Privilege and Immunities Clause of Article IV to be at issue when you have a dormant commerce clause issue. They apply different standards, but concern the same issue, so facts triggering one will trigger the other.

> **Exam tip:** Typically, when this issue arises, a corporation is involved, so the Article IV Privileges and Immunities Clause does not apply. After recitation of the rule, one line of analysis indicating that a company was involved, thus making the clause inapplicable, is sufficient.

D. The **Contracts Clause** prevents state governments from passing laws that **retroactively** and **substantially** impair **existing contracts.**
   1. **Private contracts:** If the state is **substantially impairing** private contracts, the law must be **reasonable and appropriate** (for social and economic regulations it must also be **necessary**) to serve a **significant and legitimate public purpose.**
   2. **Public contracts:** Similar to the test above but the court will interpret it more strictly, focusing on the law being **necessary** to serve an **important public purpose.**

> **Exam tip:** Whenever you have an essay with a state acting through a city, government official, or any such mechanism that would constitute state action for the purpose of raising a constitutional issue, always double check the action pursuant to the four limitations on state power above.

VI. **LIMITATIONS ON FEDERAL POWER**
   A. The **Tenth Amendment** reserves to the states all powers not delegated to the federal government by the Constitution.
      1. The federal government **cannot commandeer the states** by imposing targeted or coercive duties on state legislators or officials (such as ordering the passage of a law), but it **can impose regulatory statutes of generally applicable laws** that apply to both private and state actors.
   B. **Improper delegation of legislative power**
      1. **Legislative authority:** Congress **cannot delegate** its legislative authority to make law.
      2. **Regulatory authority:** Congress **can delegate** regulatory powers to other branches of the government if there are **intelligible principles** that govern the exercise of the delegated authority.

VII. **LIMITATIONS ON FEDERAL AND STATE POWER — INDIVIDUAL RIGHTS: THE FOLLOWING CONSTITUTIONAL PROTECTIONS APPLY TO ALL FEDERAL AND STATE GOVERNMENTAL ACTIONS AND PROVIDE INDIVIDUAL RIGHTS FOR THE PEOPLE.**
   A. **Freedom of Religion** is a First Amendment limitation on Congress's actions and is also applicable to the states through the Fourteenth Amendment. There are two clauses.
      1. The **Free Exercise Clause** bars any law that prohibits or seriously **burdens the free exercise** of religion, unless it is **narrowly tailored** to acheive a **compelling government interest.**
         a. **Time, place, manner** regulations of religiously motivated conduct must be **neutral** and serve an **important government interest.**
         b. **Except:** A **neutral law of general applicability** that does **not intentionally burden** religious beliefs and **meets the rational basis test** is allowable.

1. **Except:** The **Religious Freedom Restoration Act** allows a person to challenge a *federal law* of general applicability if there is a **substantial burden** of religious free exercise and the government must meet **strict scrutiny** (narrowly tailored to achieve a compelling government interest) (e.g., law cannot require small company to provide contraceptive coverage to employees since it violates the company's religious beliefs—*Hobby Lobby*).

2. The **Establishment Clause** prohibits the government from aiding or establishing a religion. When the government prefers one sect or religion over another, the law is subject to strict scrutiny. To determine a violation, courts can use **an analysis focused on original meaning and history.** An action is likely allowed if it:

a. **Does not coerce** participation, and

b. Is consistent with **historical practices and understandings.**

> **Exam tip:** Every time religion has been tested, it has been necessary to discuss both the Establishment Clause and the Free Exercise Clause.

B. **Freedom of Speech:** The First Amendment protects an individual's right to free speech and is applicable to the states through the Fourteenth Amendment.

1. **Two classes of speech:** Speech prohibitions can be content based or content neutral, and the rules vary depending on this distinction.

a. **Content-based** speech regulations are those that **forbid the communicative impact** of the expression.

1. **Strict scrutiny** applies to content-based restrictions, and they are rarely allowed. The regulation must be **necessary** (narrowly tailored) to achieve a **compelling governmental interest**.

> **Content-based fact triggers:**
>
> - Banning events promoting particular views
> - Banning specific content or types of content
> - Banning a specific action or conduct
> - Banning the sale of specific items

2. **Unprotected categories** of speech include obscenity, fraudulent misrepresentation and defamation, advocacy of imminent lawless action, and fighting words. For the unprotected categories of speech the only requirement is that the government must **regulate in a content-neutral way** (intermediate scrutiny as discussed below in VII, B, 1, b).

a. **Obscenity:** Speech is considered obscene if it describes or depicts sexual conduct that, taken as a whole, by the average person:

i. Appeals to **prurient interest** in sex (under a community standard);

ii. Is **patently offensive** (under a community standard); and

iii. **Lacks serious Literary, Artistic, Political, or Scientific** value (under a national reasonable person standard). [Think **LAPS**.]

b. **Misrepresentation and defamation** are torts and are covered in detail in the Torts Rules Outline.

c. **Imminent lawless action:** The government can ban speech advocating imminent lawless action if it is **intended to incite** or produce imminent lawless action and is **likely** to produce such action.

d. **Fighting words** are words that are likely to cause the listener to commit an act of violence. However, causing another to be angry alone is insufficient.

b. **Content-neutral** speech (**or communicative conduct**) regulations are those where the regulation is aimed at something other than the communicative impact of the expression.

1. Content neutral regulations are allowed if they:
   a. Serve a **substantial/important government interest**,
   b. Are **narrowly tailored** to serve that interest, and
   c. Leave open **alternative channels** of communication.

Content-neutral fact triggers:

- Denying activities at certain times or days
- Limiting activities in certain places
- Limiting activities to use certain methods (e.g., sound equipment)
- Excluding people from visiting or attending events
- Requiring activities to take place in designated areas
- Banning activities or conduct in specific locations

---

c. **Time, place, and manner** restrictions seek to regulate speech (or communicative conduct) based on the external factors of the time, place and manner in which the speech may be communicated. The rules differ depending on the **type of forum** in which the speech or conduct occurs. All **must be viewpoint neutral**. (Or they are content based and subject to strict scrutiny.)

   1. **Public and designated public forums: Public forums** are forums that are **generally open to the public. Designated public forums** (unlimited public forums) are forums that are not traditionally open to the public but are **opened up to the public at large for a specific purpose**. Speech restrictions in public and limited public forums must:
      a. Be **content neutral (subject matter neutral) and viewpoint neutral**,
      b. Serve a **substantial/important government interest**,
      c. Be **narrowly tailored** to serve that interest, and
      d. Leave open **alternative channels** of communication.

   2. **Limited and nonpublic forums: Limited public forums** are forums that are opened for **limited use by certain groups** or discussion of certain subjects. **Nonpublic forums** are forums that are **closed to the public**. Speech restrictions in limited and nonpublic public forums must:
      a. **Be viewpoint neutral**,
      b. Serve a **legitimate government interest**, and
      c. Be **reasonably related** to serve that interest.

Exam tip: Note that while nonpublic and limited public forum speech restrictions must be viewpoint neutral, they do not need to be subject matter neutral too like the public and designated public forums (e.g., some limited public forums are opened up for a particular discussion or a certain subject, so it wouldn't be subject matter neutral).

---

2. **Commercial Speech:** The government may restrict commercial speech (advertising) only if the regulation:
   a. Serves a **substantial government interest**,
   b. **Directly advances** that interest, and is
   c. **Narrowly tailored** such that there is a **reasonable fit** (need not be least restrictive means) to serve that interest.

3. **Symbolic Speech** is the freedom not to speak or the freedom to **communicate an idea by use of a symbol or communicative conduct**. The government may restrict symbolic speech if the regulation:
   a. Is within the **constitutional power** of the government to enact,

b. Furthers an **important governmental interest** unrelated to the suppression of speech (content neutral), and

c. **Prohibits no more speech** than necessary.

4. **Limitations on free speech regulations**

a. **Vagueness:** A speech regulation is unconstitutionally vague if it is so unclearly defined that a **reasonable person would have to guess** at its meaning.

b. **Overbreadth:** A speech regulation is unconstitutionally overbroad if it bans **both protected speech and unprotected speech**.

c. **Unfettered discretion:** A regulation, licensing scheme, or permit regulation is unconstitutional if it leaves unfettered discretion to the decisionmaker by not setting forth **narrow and specific grounds** for denying a permit, or where the permit mechanism is **not closely tailored to the regulation's objective**. Further, the regulation must be a **reasonable means** of maintaining public order.

5. **Prior restraints** prevent speech from being heard **before it even occurs**. These are rarely allowed and carry a heavy presumption of unconstitutionality. A prior restraint is only allowed where the *government can show* that some **irreparable or serious harm** to the public will occur and there must be **narrowly drawn standards** and a **final determination** of the validity of the restraint (restraining body must seek an injunction to prevent dissemination).

a. **Collateral bar rule:** Under the collateral bar rule, if a prior restraint is issued, one cannot violate it first and then defend oneself by asserting that the action is unconstitutional, even if this is correct.

Prior restraint fact triggers:

- Discretion to allow or deny the use of facilities
- Banning the release, display, or sale of things before review
- Denying permits for various activities
- Preventing the publication or disclosure of information

Exam tip: When free speech is at issue, write out a mini-issues checklist including all possible speech issues. First, identify the state action. Next, look at whether the regulation is content based or content neutral or T, P, M, and then apply the appropriate test. If it is arguably either, then analyze both. For example, if the regulation limits the viewing of specific content, but only at certain times of the day, apply both tests. Lastly, consider all other potential speech issues, such as obscenity, overbreadth, prior restraint, commercial speech, etc.

C. **Freedom of Association:** First Amendment case law recognizes an individual's **right to freely associate** with other individuals in groups.

1. **Public job or benefit:** Freedom of association prevents the government from denying a public benefit or job based on a person's association.

2. Freedom of association applies only to freedoms protected by the **First Amendment** and is not for social purposes.

3. The **government can only prevent freedom of association** or require individuals to associate in regard to First Amendment freedoms if there is a **compelling governmental interest** that cannot be achieved by **less restrictive means (narrowly tailored)**.

D. **Due Process** binds the states through the Fourteenth Amendment, and the federal government through the Fifth Amendment. There are two types: substantive due process and procedural due process.

1. **Substantive Due Process (SDP)** limits the government's ability to regulate certain areas of human life, such as the substantive interests in life, liberty, or property. (Regulation of one's **personal autonomy and privacy**.)

a. **Rights subject to SDP** are either fundamental or nonfundamental, and different rules apply to each.
   1. **Fundamental rights:** Under SDP this refers to rights relating to marriage, contraception, living with one's family, childbearing, child rearing, domestic travel, voting, and other First Amendment rights.
      a. **Strict scrutiny** applies to fundamental rights under SDP. The government action must be **necessary** to achieve a **compelling** government objective.
   2. **Nonfundamental rights:** Under SDP this applies to everything else, but typically social and economic regulations (e.g., education, employment).
      a. **Rational basis test** applies to nonfundamental rights under SDP. The government action need only be **rationally related** to achieve a **legitimate** government objective. The burden of proof attaches to the challenger of the government action.
      b. **Abortion:** There is no SDP right to an abortion. States may regulate and rational basis applies.

Substantive Due Process fact triggers:

- Bills requiring specific individuals to do something in violation of their fundamental rights (e.g., mandatory sterilization)
- Denying benefits or permits to individuals or groups
- Penalizing companies or individuals financially
- Preventing individuals from their right to take part in activities

---

2. **Procedural Due Process (PDP)** requires the government to use **fair process** before **intentionally** depriving a person of **life, liberty, or property**.
   a. **Life, liberty, or property interests**
      1. **Liberty interest:** Includes physical liberty as well as intangible liberties, such as the right to drive, raise a family, etc.
      2. **Property interest:** Includes real property, personal property, public education, government employment, government licenses, and government benefits that one is *already* receiving.
   b. **Process due**
      1. **For judicial proceedings** this includes the right to a hearing, counsel, call witnesses, a fair trial, and appeal.
      2. **For nonjudicial proceedings** this involves a **balancing test** by the court to weigh:
         a. The **individual's interest** in the right that will be affected by the government action,
         b. The added value of the **procedural safeguards** used and the possibility of substitute procedural safeguards, and
         c. The **government's interest** in fiscal and administrative **efficiency.**

E. **Involuntary servitude** under the Thirteenth Amendment is unique in that it is applicable to both **state action** (governmental) and **private action.**
   1. The Thirteenth Amendment provides that neither **slavery nor involuntary servitude** (forcing someone to perform work by threatening physical injury or restraint or legal sanction) shall exist within the United States.

F. The **Equal Protection Clause (EPC)** of the Fourteenth Amendment (applicable to the federal government through the Fifth Amendment DPC) prohibits the government from **treating similarly situated persons differently**.
   1. **Different treatment for similarly situated people**
      a. **Violation on its face:** The government treats people differently in a statute or regulation.
      b. **Violation as applied (discriminatory intent and impact):** The government treats people differently through the administration of a statute.

   c. **Intentionally different treatment** is required for heightened review (strict scrutiny and intermediate scrutiny) under EPC, and not just the incidental burdening effect (intent can be found by facial discrimination, discriminatory impact, or discriminatory motive).

2. **Three levels of review can apply to EPC**
   a. **Strict scrutiny** requires the government to prove that the classification is **necessary** to achieve a **compelling** government interest.
      1. *The burden of proof is on the government.*
   b. **Intermediate scrutiny** requires the government to prove that the classification is **substantially related** to achieve an **important** government interest.
      1. *The burden of proof is on the government.*
   c. **Rational basis (low-level scrutiny)** requires the classification to be **rationally related** to a **legitimate** government interest.
      1. *The burden of proof is on the challenger of the classification.*

3. **Classification scheme:** EPC is at issue when people are treated differently based on classifications. (The EPC challenge is to the classification scheme itself, not which category a person belongs in.)
   a. **Suspect classifications** include only those based on **race, national origin,** and state **alienage** (not a U.S. citizen) and are subject to **strict scrutiny.**
   b. **Quasi-suspect classifications** include only those based on **gender** and **illegitimacy** and are subject to **intermediate scrutiny.**
   c. **Nonsuspect classifications** include everything else, including those based on nonsuspect and nonfundamental rights, such as economic and social welfare and are subject to **rational basis** review.
   d. **EPC fundamental rights:** The fundamental rights under the EPC are subject to **strict scrutiny. The most common rights at issue involve:**
      1. **Voting** in state and local elections, except special purpose districts.
      2. Being a **political candidate**.
      3. Having **access to the courts**.
      4. **Migrating from state to state (travel)**.
      5. **First Amendment rights**.
      6. <u>Note:</u> The fundamental rights subject to strict scrutiny under EPC are not exactly the same as the fundamental rights subject to strict scrutiny under SDP.

4. **Level of review required**
   a. **Suspect classifications** and **EPC fundamental rights** receive **strict scrutiny** and thus require **intent** on the part of the government to treat individuals differently. **Strict scrutiny** requires the government to prove that the classification is **necessary** to achieve a **compelling** government interest.
   b. **Quasi-suspect** classifications receive **intermediate scrutiny** and require **intent** on the part of the government to treat individuals differently. **Intermediate scrutiny** requires the government to prove that the classification is **substantially related** to achieve an **important** government interest.
   c. **Nonsuspect** classifications receive **rational basis review.** The burden of proof is on the challenger of the classification. **Rational basis (low-level scrutiny)** requires the classification to be **rationally related** to a **legitimate** government interest.

Exam tip: When analyzing EPC, after finding "state action" determine who is being treated differently and why (classification scheme). Determine the level of review that applies to that type of classification scheme. Then, analyze the level of review under the facts and using factual inferences (particularly to determine the government objective). Be aware that it is possible for more than one type of classification to apply, requiring analysis of each applicable level of review (e.g., gender and age, or an EPC fundamental right and an economic reason). Lastly, analyze the government's intent to discriminate if strict or intermediate scrutiny applies.

> **Equal Protection Clause fact triggers:**
>
> - Treating individuals differently for any reason
> - Denying benefits or funds to select individuals
> - Charging more money to certain people for anything
> - Prohibiting access to events to certain individuals
> - Only allowing select companies to conduct business

G. The **Takings Clause** of the Fifth Amendment provides that **private property** may not be **taken for public use** without **just compensation**.
   1. **Public use** is liberally construed and satisfied if the state's use of the property is **rationally related** to a **conceivable public purpose** and can include public benefit rather than actual public usage.
   2. **Just compensation** is measured by the **market value of the property** at the time of the taking.
   3. Taking or mere regulation:
      a. **Total takings: Regulatory actions** are total takings if there is a:
         1. Permanent **physical invasion** or confiscation of property (this is a "per se" taking), or
         2. **Regulatory use restriction** that denies **all economically beneficial use** of property. (For test, see c. below.)
      b. **Temporary taking:** To determine if a regulation, which denies all economic use temporarily, is a taking requiring just compensation the court will consider all relevant circumstances including the **economic impact** on the owner, the **length of the delay,** the **reasonable expectation** of the owners, and the **good faith** of the government planners.
      c. **Regulatory taking:** Regulations, such as zoning ordinances, that **decrease the economic value** of the property by prohibiting most beneficial use are not considered takings if there is still an **economically viable use** for the property. To make a determination, the court will employ a **balancing test** and consider:
         1. The **character** of the invasion (value to the community of the social goal being advanced),
         2. The **economic impact** on the claimant, and
         3. The extent of interference with the **investment backed expectation** of the owner.
   4. **Zoning variance:** Some jurisdictions allow non-conforming use variances, while others provide for termination of these uses by reasonable **amortization** provisions (which provides a time frame for the owners to comply with the new zoning regulations). (See section V.H.4 in the Real Property Rule Outline.)
      a. **Pre-existing use variance:** An owner may obtain a **non-conforming-use variance** to continue using their land as it was used before the new zoning ordinance which no longer permits the use was adopted if it is **not contrary to public welfare.**
      b. **Post-ordinance variance:** A post-ordinance owner may obtain a non-conforming use variance upon a showing of **undue hardship** and that it is **not contrary to public welfare.**

CONSTITUTIONAL LAW ISSUES TESTED MATRIX

	Crossovers	Ripe/Moot	Standing	11th Amend.	State Action	Federal Powers/Govt. Branches	Federal Preemption	DCC	P&I Clause	K's Clause	1st Amend. Religion	1st Amend. Speech Content-Based v. Neutral	Speech—Vague/Overbroad/Unfettered Discretion	Prior Restraint	Symbolic and/or Commercial Speech	SDP	PDP	EP	Freedom of Association	Takings Clause
February '24 Q2 — State X enacts Organic Farming Act, impacts Chemco and A&L Berries in state Y								X	X									X		
February '23 Q2 — Childhood Physical Education Act requires 50% fruit & vegetables in school lunch		X	X			Congress												X		
July '22 Q2 — Paloma has a tattoo, but school prohibits gang related activities/symbols, etc.		X	X		X							X	X	X	X	X	X	X	X	
July '18 Q5 — State X buys railroad								X	X								X	X		
February '18 Q3 — Len has a wandering dog and a backyard smokehouse	Real Property Torts																			X
February '18 Q2 — County Jail displays 3 of Ten Command-ments											X							X		
July '16 Q4 — State X withholds 10% teacher salary if school standards fall			X	X													X			
July '15 Q6 — City rezoned commercial to residential within 3 months	Real Property																			X

(Continued)

	Crossovers	Ripe/Moot	Standing	11th Amend.	State Action	Federal Powers/ Govt. Branches	Federal Preemption	DCC	P&I Clause	K's Clause	1st Amend. Religion	1st Amend. Speech Content-Based v. Neutral	Speech—Vague/ Overbroad/ Unfettered Discretion	Prior Restraint	Symbolic and/or Commercial Speech	SDP	PDP	EP	Freedom of Association	Takings Clause
February '14 Q5 — Old Ways denied sun symbol display by City			X		X						X	X	X	X	X					
July '13 Q2 — State X drafts high school boy dropouts age 15-18			X		X											X	X	X		
February '12 Q2 — City won't allow AAO to post bulletin at bus station			X		X							X	X	X	X					
February '11 Q2 — Charles enlisted in the U.S. Army and changes religion											X								X	
February '10 Q4 — Paula wants to develop 100 acres of protected wetlands																				X
July '09 Q4 — Statute, Congress, U.S. Sec. Transp. want safe highways			X			Congress												X		
July '08 Q2 — Antiterrorism acts, the president & Homeland Security						Executive	X			X										
July '07 Q4 — Dan stood on capital steps, lights a fire & kills a pedestrian	Criminal Procedure				X							X			X					
February '07 Q5 — City ordinance bans tobacco ads to prevent smoking			X		X							X	X		X					

Continued>

Exam	Crossovers	Ripe/Moot	Standing	11th Amend.	State Action	Federal Powers/ Govt. Branches	Federal Preemption	DCC	P&I Clause	K's Clause	1st Amend. Religion	1st Amend. Speech, Content-Based v. Neutral	Speech — Vague/ Overbroad/ Unfettered Discretion	Prior Restraint	Symbolic and/or Commercial Speech	SDP	PDP	EP	Freedom of Association	Takings Clause
July '06 Q2 Columbia County has porn ordinance; Videorama sues		X	X		X							X	X	X						
February '06 Q3 Mike has 30-yr. master lease and subleases to others	Real Property				X													X		X
February '05 Q1 State X statute requires gasahol			X		X			X	X							X	X	X		
July '04 Q2 State X passes an antiloitering statute			X		X							X	X							
February '04 Q5 NHTSA restricts radar detectors on big trucks			X		X		X	X												
February '03 Q5 Paul wants to be a cheerleader; sues Rural Univ.		X	X		X												X	X		
February '02 Q5 Assembly of Future Life has unpopular beliefs			X	X	X											X	X	X		X
July '01 Q4 Ada denied jail chaplain job because woman and religion			X	X	X						X	X						X		
July '00 Q4 Ruth the reporter observes illegal dog fight	Criminal Procedure		X		X													X		

CONSTITUTIONAL LAW PRACTICE ESSAYS, ANSWER GRIDS, AND SAMPLE ANSWERS

Constitutional Law Question 1
July 2022, Question 2

Public School District (District) in State X is attempting to reduce gang violence in District's high schools. After consulting with local law enforcement, District has determined that most violence results from confrontations between two gangs, the Westsiders and the Eastsiders. As a result, District has adopted the following rule for all high school students: "No student shall wear any label, insignia, words, colors, signs or symbols that reflect gang-related activities. Students violating the policy will be immediately suspended or expelled from school."

For several years, Paloma, a high school senior, has had a small tattoo of a dove on one wrist, her "self-expression" as a peaceful person. Paloma has never been associated with any gang, including the Westsiders and Eastsiders. After learning of Paloma's tattoo, District officials described it to local law enforcement officials who said that it sounded like a Westsider gang symbol, which includes birds. Paloma was suspended for the last ten days of school after she refused District's request that she either wear long sleeves to cover her tattoo or have it removed.

Paloma, now graduated, and attending the college of her choice, has brought a declaratory relief action challenging the validity of District's policy under the First and Fourteenth Amendments to the United States Constitution. District has moved to dismiss Paloma's lawsuit as moot on two grounds: (A) because she is no longer a high school student, and (B) District has now redefined "gang-related activities" in its rule in a manner consistent with State X's criminal code.

1. What arguments can Paloma make in support of her First and Fourteenth Amendment claims? Discuss.

2. Will either or both of District's arguments in support of its motion to dismiss Paloma's lawsuit be successful? Discuss.

Constitutional Law Question 1 Assessment
July 2022, Question 2

The bar examiners like to test free speech, and this question is a good example since it covers many free speech issues. While the favorite free speech testing area is time, place, manner (TPM) restrictions, this question manages to ask about everything else speech-related with very little TPM focus. In addition to asking about the First Amendment speech issues, the first call asks about arguments under the Fourteenth Amendment, and there is a second call of the question asking about District's arguments in response. With one glance at the call of the question, you should suspect this essay is going to cover a lot of issues. A preliminary reading of the facts, with your checklist and fact triggers in mind, should help with the issue spotting and you will quickly discover there are many issues to discuss. While Con Law questions typically cover fewer issues but go into greater depth, this essay is an outlier in that it covers comparatively a lot of issues. You want to quickly realize this and adjust accordingly. Plan from the start that your analysis will need to be targeted and crisp to finish within one hour.

This is the type of question where you need to utilize your mini-issues checklist that you memorized specifically for free speech questions. In this checklist, you should have all possible issues relating to speech, including those that are required to make a claim under the First Amendment at all, such as standing and state action. This more detailed speech checklist will help you avoid missing easily overlooked issues, such as overbreadth and vagueness, which can lead to missing a lot of points.

Once you have spotted all the issues and noted the corresponding rules, you will need to analyze the issues, as you do with many constitutional law questions, by using logical inferences and giving examples to support your arguments. Normally you would give a few examples to support your arguments, but since this essay covers so many topics, you will need to be more cursory. Once you've spotted the issues, hopefully you realized that many of the tests implicated and associated analyses are duplicative. When that happens, you can refer to your prior analysis as demonstrated in this sample answer. There is no need to be duplicative on the rules or analysis.

Since so many issues are included in this question, at the outset you should make a determination on which are the most important to fully analyze since you will be pinched for time. Here, we determined that the analysis on overbreadth, vagueness, content-based speech, symbolic speech, and mootness were the most critical issues since they had the most facts available to use to craft the corresponding analysis. The content neutral and equal protection issues were much less important, since they were comparatively weaker arguments, and thus given less focus. Having given this some thought in advance of writing allows you to spend your time accordingly so you don't run out of time on the last call, which was important on this question.

Finally, make note of the areas highlighted in **bold** on the corresponding grid. The bold areas highlight the issues, analysis, and conclusions that are likely **required** to receive a passing score on this question. In general, the essay grids are provided to assist you in analyzing the essays and are much more detailed than what a student should create during the exam to organize their response to a question.

Issue	Rule	Fact Application	Conclusion
1. Paloma's Arguments: 1st and 14th			
1st & 14th Amendments	**1st Amendment of the U.S. Constitution protects free speech** and is incorporated to the states through the 14th Amendment Due Process Clause.	• Speech is broadly defined to include expressive conduct, like Paloma's tattoo.	
Standing	**Individual standing:** • **Injury,** • **Causation,** • **Redressability**	• District (D) will argue despite the suspension, P was able to graduate and attends the college of her choice, so she was not injured. However, **Paloma (P) did suffer an injury because she was suspended for the last ten days of school.** • **D's new gang policy is the reason P was suspended.** • A favorable ruling could get the suspension removed from P's record.	**P has standing**
State Action	**Government involvement with the challenged action.**	• **The policy came from the public high school district, which is a government state actor.**	**State action**
Vagueness	A speech regulation is unconstitutionally vague if it is so unclearly defined that a reasonable person would have to guess at its meaning.	• **The policy here prohibits "labels, words, colors, signs or symbols that reflect gang-related activities," but there is no further explanation of what colors and symbols are included or what "gang-related activities" are.** • D will argue since the two gangs are well known in the area, the gang-related symbols and activities are obvious to the locals in the community. • P will argue any **student who is not involved in gang activity would not know what is included so the rule fails to put a reasonable person on notice.** Further, a bird is a common animal that is not exclusively known to indicate gang activity. In fact, the dove is a common symbol of peace, and that is the tattoo P had.	**Vague**
Overbroad	A speech regulation is **unconstitutionally overbroad if it bans both protected speech and unprotected speech.**	• D will argue the rule was drawn narrowly to only include "gang-related" activity and symbols, which is unprotected. • However, while the rule attempts to prohibit gang-related symbols of violence, **here it is so broadly drawn it could include anything,** like here where it included a common symbol of peace, the dove. Communication of the symbol of a dove to promote peace should be protected speech. • The rule prohibits both protected and unprotected speech.	**Overbroad**

Continued>

Issue	Rule	Fact Application	Conclusion
Symbolic Speech	To communicate an idea by symbol. Gov. can regulate symbolic speech if: • It is within its constitutional power, • **Serves an important government interest unrelated to the suppression of speech, and** • **Prohibits no more speech than necessary.**	• **Here, P is communicating the idea of "peace" with her small dove tattoo, so it is symbolic speech.** • The district has the power to create rules for the public school students. • **The important government interest here is to control violent gang activity in the town, and keep children safe at school, which is an important government interest unrelated to the suppression of speech.** D will argue that the rule is limited to gang-related activities, so it is already narrowly drawn and prohibits no more speech than necessary. • P will assert that while the government interest of curtailing violence is important, **the regulation protects more speech than necessary since the rule is not limited to gang violence. The rule broadly prohibits virtually all forms of expression that could relate to a gang and could be more narrowly drawn to be more specific. Here,** the rule prohibited a symbol as basic as a bird, which can have many meanings in a variety of contexts, even if the Westsider gang also has a symbol that includes birds. P's small dove tattoo, which represents her "self-expression" as a peaceful person, was included as violating the new rule, **so the rule prohibits more speech than necessary.** That the rule is deemed violated by P's peaceful dove symbol when she has never been associated with any gang is evidence that it prohibits more speech than necessary.	Rule likely prohibits more speech than necessary
Content Based	If content based, strict scrutiny: • **Necessary to achieve** • **Compelling government interest**	• **The regulation here is content based since it prohibits gang-related expressive conduct.** • **While reducing gang violence and protecting students from gang violence is a compelling government interest,** this rule is not necessary to achieve that goal since there are less restrictive ways the government could achieve that goal. For example, as described above, the rule could more clearly define gang-related activity to limit its scope.	Fails strict scrutiny

Continued>

Issue	Rule	Fact Application	Conclusion
Content Neutral Forum	**If content neutral, look to time, place, and manner restrictions. Public or designated public:** • Content neutral and viewpoint neutral, • Serves a substantial government interest, • Narrowly tailored to serve, • Leaves open alternative channels of communication. Nonpublic forum: • Viewpoint neutral • Legitimate government interest • Reasonably related	• P can argue traditional or designated public forum. Public school students do have a right to free speech. • Analysis above for government interest and narrowly tailored. • Leave open alternative channels, which it does since the rule only applies while students are in school. • If nonpublic, it is not viewpoint neutral since targets gangs.	Also fails
Procedural Due Process	**Procedural Due Process requires notice and a hearing prior to taking away the life, liberty, or property of an individual.**	• **P would assert her free speech rights of expression are a liberty interest, and her right to attend public school** is a property interest, which is being denied without any fair process. • Here, **P was suspended for the last 10 days of school** after she refused to cover her tattoo. There is a notice question since she had the tattoo for years without incident. • She did not have the opportunity to be heard first to explain that her dove tattoo is a symbol of peace and that she has never been associated with gang-related activity. • It would not have been burdensome for the school to hold a hearing prior to the suspension.	Likely violates PDP
Substantive Due Process	**Limits the government's ability to regulate life, liberty, or property.** • **If based on a fundamental right, strict scrutiny** (necessary to achieve a compelling gov. interest) • **If based on a non-fundamental right, rational basis** (rationally related to a legitimate gov. interest)	• D will argue it is not a fundamental right to attend public school, thus rational basis should apply. The rule can likely pass rational basis since the gang-related ban is rationally related to the **legitimate government interest in decreasing gang violence and limited gang expression is rationally related to that goal** since it would be harder for rival gang members to identify each other. • **P will argue the rule infringes on her self-expression and free speech rights, which is a fundamental right.** If strict scrutiny applies, the rule will fail (analysis above in content based speech.)	Likely violates SDP

Continued>

Issue	Rule	Fact Application	Conclusion
Equal Protection	**Requires that similarly situated persons be treated similarly** • Suspect class: 1st Am. Fundamental Right, Strict scrutiny (necessary to achieve a compelling gov. interest and uses least restrictive means) and govt intent • **Non suspect: Rational basis (rationally related to a legitimate gov. interest)**	• P may argue that the rule treats public school students who wear gang-related symbols differently than those who do not, but wearing clothes of one's choosing **or gang membership is not a protected class**, nor is participating in gang-related activity. Consequently, rational basis would apply, and as described above in SDP, the rule would pass rational basis review. • EPC is not the best argument.	EPC claim not successful
2. Motion to dismiss for mootness			
1. No longer high school student	A case will not be heard if a live controversy existed at the time of filing, but it has since been eliminated. • **Except, capable of repetition but evading review.**	• **D argues P's suit is moot since she is no longer a high school student.** • However, **P will argue this rule qualifies for review because it is capable of repetition, but evading review. The injury occurred the last 10 days of her senior year and the court process takes a lot of time**, and any student subject to the rule will likely be graduated by the time the case is heard, **which allows the rule to be repeated, but never have review.**	Likely not moot
2. Gang related	A case will not be heard if a live controversy existed at the time of filing, but it has since been eliminated. • **Except voluntary cessation**	• **D argues P's suit is moot since they have voluntarily changed the rule to redefine "gang-related activities" in a manner consistent with State X's criminal code.** • However, **P will correctly note that D's voluntary choice to change the policy should not control** because the district could always change the policy again, which would allow D to never have their policy reviewed.	Likely not moot

Constitutional Law Question 1 Sample Answer
July 2022, Question 2

1. Paloma's Arguments: 1st and 14th Amendment

The 1st Amendment of the U.S. Constitution protects free speech and is incorporated to the states through the 14th Amendment Due Process Clause. Speech is broadly defined to include expressive conduct, like Paloma's tattoo.

Standing

Individual standing requires establishing an injury, causation, and redressability.

First Paloma (P) must establish she has standing to sue. District (D) will argue that despite the school suspension, P was able to graduate and now attends the college of her choice, so she was not injured. However, P did suffer an injury because she was suspended for the last ten days of school. D's new gang policy is the reason P was suspended, and a favorable ruling could get the suspension removed from P's record, redressing the injury, thus P has standing to sue.

State Action

There must be government involvement with the challenged action. Here, the policy was implemented by a public high school district, which is a government state actor, so there is state action.

Vagueness

A speech regulation is unconstitutionally vague if it is so unclearly defined that a reasonable person would have to guess at its meaning.

D will argue since the two gangs are well known in the area, making the gang-related symbols and activities obvious to the locals in the community.

Here, P has a strong argument the new rule is vague. The policy here prohibits "labels, words, colors, signs or symbols that reflect gang-related activities," but there is no further explanation of what colors and symbols are included or what the "gang-related activities" are. P will argue any student who is not involved in gang activity would not know what is included so the rule fails to put a reasonable person on notice. Further, a bird is a common animal that is not exclusively known to indicate gang activity. In fact, the dove is a common symbol of peace, and that is the tattoo P had, but there is no indication a dove is a gang symbol.

Likely the policy is unconstitutionally vague.

Overbroad

A speech regulation is unconstitutionally overbroad if it bans both protected speech and unprotected speech.

D will argue the rule was drawn narrowly to only include "gang-related" activity and symbols, which is unprotected speech.

However, while the rule attempts to prohibit gang-related symbols of violence, here it is so broadly drawn it could include anything, like here where it included a common symbol of peace, the dove. Communication of the symbol of a dove to promote peace should be protected speech. But this rule prohibits both protected and unprotected speech so it is overbroad.

Symbolic Speech

Symbolic speech is protected and occurs when one communicates an idea by use of a symbol. Symbolic speech can be regulated if it is within its constitutional power, serves an important government interest unrelated to the suppression of speech, and prohibits no more speech than necessary.

Here, P is communicating the idea of "peace" with her small dove tattoo, so it is symbolic speech and D was within their constitutional authority to create rules for the public school students.

The government interest here is to control violent gang activity in the town and keep children safe at school, which is an important government interest unrelated to the suppression of speech. Citizen safety, and especially that of children in school, is important and D will argue that the rule is limited to gang-related activities, so it is already narrowly drawn and prohibits no more speech than necessary.

P will assert that while the government interest of curtailing violence is important, this regulation protects more speech than necessary since the rule is not limited to gang violence. The rule broadly prohibits virtually all forms of expression that could conceivably relate to a gang. This rule could be more narrowly drawn to be more specific. Here, the rule prohibited a symbol as basic as a bird, which can have many meanings in a variety of contexts, even if the Westsider gang also has a symbol that includes birds. P's small dove tattoo, which represents her "self-expression" as a peaceful person, was determined to violate the new rule, so the rule prohibits more speech than necessary. That the rule was deemed violated by P's peaceful dove symbol when she has never been associated with any gang is evidence that the rule prohibits more speech than necessary.

P can successfully assert the rule violates her symbolic speech rights.

Content Based

Strict scrutiny applies to a content based speech regulation. The rule must be necessary to achieve a compelling government interest.

The regulation here is content based since it specifically prohibits gang-related expressive conduct. While reducing gang violence and protecting students from gang violence is a compelling government interest, this rule is not necessary to achieve that goal since there are less restrictive ways the government could achieve that goal. For example, as described above, the rule could more clearly define gang-related activity to limit its scope.

The rule will also fail strict scrutiny.

Content Neutral/Forum

If a rule is content neutral, the forum is relevant to a time, place, manner evaluation. A public or designated public forum rule must be content neutral, serve a substantial government interest, be narrowly tailored, and leave open alternative channels of communication. A nonpublic forum rule must be viewpoint neutral and rationally related to a legitimate government interest.

The forum here is a public school and students do have a right to free speech. If the school was found to be a public/designated public forum the analysis is above for the government interest and narrowly tailored prongs.

The rule does leave open alternative channels since the rule only applies while students are in school. If the forum were found to be nonpublic, it is not viewpoint neutral since it targets gangs.

A content neutral analysis is not as helpful to P since the rule in content based.

Procedural Due Process (PDP)

PDP requires notice and a hearing prior to taking away the life, liberty, or property of an individual.

P would assert her free speech rights of expression are a liberty interest, and her right to attend public school is a property interest, both of which are being denied here without notice of any fair process.

Here, P was suspended for the last 10 days of school after she refused to cover her tattoo, but she did not have notice since she had the tattoo for years without incident. P did not have the opportunity to be heard first to explain that her dove tattoo is a symbol of peace, or that she has never been associated with gang-related activity. It would not have been burdensome for the school to hold a hearing prior to P's suspension, so it likely violates her PDP rights.

Substantive Due Process (SDP)

SDP limits the government's ability to regulate life, liberty, or property. For fundamental rights, strict scrutiny applies (necessary to achieve a compelling gov. interest), but for non-fundamental rights, rational basis (rationally related to a legitimate gov. interest) applies.

D will argue it is not a fundamental right to attend public school, thus rational basis should apply. The rule can likely pass rational basis since the gang-related ban is rationally related to the legitimate government interest in decreasing gang violence and limited gang expression is rationally related to that goal since it would be harder for rival gang members to identify each other.

P will argue the rule infringes on her self-expression and free speech rights, which is a fundamental right. If strict scrutiny applies, the rule will fail (see analysis above in content based speech).

The rule likely violates SDP.

Equal Protection (EPC)

The EPC requires that similarly situated persons be treated similarly. Strict scrutiny applies to suspect classes, which includes 1st Am. fundamental rights. For nonsuspect classes, rational basis applies.

P may argue that the rule treats public school students who wear gang-related symbols differently than those who do not, but wearing clothes of one's choosing or gang membership is not a protected class, nor is participating in gang-related activity. Consequently, rational basis would apply, and as described above in SDP, the rule would pass rational basis review. An EPC is not the best argument and would not succeed.

2. Motion to dismiss for mootness

A case will not be heard if a live controversy existed at the time of filing, but it has since been eliminated — except when the controversy is capable of repetition but evading review, or there is voluntary cessation of the activity.

A. P is no longer a high school student

D argues P's suit is moot since she is no longer a high school student. However, P will argue this rule qualifies for review because it is capable of repetition, but evading review. The injury occurred the last 10 days of her senior year and since the court process takes a lot of time, any student subject to the rule will likely be graduated by the time the case is heard. This allows the rule to be repeated, but evade review, likely the case is not moot.

B. Gang related definition

D also argues P's suit is moot since D has voluntarily changed the rule to redefine "gang-related activities" in a manner consistent with State X's criminal code. However, P will correctly note that D's voluntary choice to change the policy should not control because the district could always change the policy again, which would allow D to never have their policy reviewed.

Constitutional Law Question 2
February 2024, Question 2

State X has many small farms selling organic produce, which is grown without the use of any chemical fertilizers or pesticides. Instead of using chemical fertilizers or pesticides, these farms organically enrich their soil with animal manure products from State X's large livestock industry.

Recently, State X enacted the Organic Farming Act (Organic Act). Section 1 of the Organic Act bans the sale and use of chemical fertilizers and pesticides in State X and also bans the sale of any produce grown with, or treated by, chemical fertilizers and pesticides. Section 2 of the Organic Act requires that all publicly funded State X institutions only buy organic produce grown in State X.

In the absence of any federal law, the State X legislature passed the Organic Act after concluding that the use of chemical fertilizers and pesticides contributed to measurable environmental harm. It further found an increased threat to the health of farmers using chemical fertilizers and pesticides, as well as to the health of consumers of the farmers' produce. The State X legislature also declared that it wanted to preserve the existence of small farms and to "protect" those farmers' "way of life."

State X has no significant chemical fertilizer or pesticide industry. Chemco, Inc., in nearby State Y, is a chemical fertilizer and pesticide manufacturer that has always had a significant portion of its revenue come from sales in State X.

A&L Berries is a partnership that grows and sells organic strawberries in State Y. A&L Berries sells some of their strawberries directly to consumers in State X. However, most of their sales are to Organic Produce, Inc., a State Y wholesaler. Both A&L Berries and Organic Produce, Inc. have publicly-funded State X customers who now refuse to do business with them because of the Organic Act.

Chemco, Inc., A&L Berries, and Organic Produce, Inc. have now filed lawsuits in Federal Court in State X.

1. What claims can Chemco, Inc. make under the United States Constitution and how should the court rule? Discuss.

2. What claims can A&L Berries make under the United States Constitution and how should the court rule? Discuss.

3. What claims can Organic Produce, Inc. make under the United States Constitution and how should the Court rule? Discuss.

Constitutional Law Question 2 Assessment
February 2024, Question 2

This question tests dormant commerce clause (DCC), which is a less popular testing topic than First Amendment issues. For that reason, many students are not as comfortable with the subject matter and might feel less confident when faced with a DCC question. We can assure you that you are in good company if you feel that way. On our grids we bold the rules and analysis that both state released students' answers contained. A glance at the bold areas on the grid shows how few areas of commonality there were between the two answers on this question. The two state released answers on this question were not very well done, either organizationally or substantively, which is a good indication that most applicants struggled with this question. When that happens, it lowers the bar for receiving a passing score, so though it might make you nervous at the time you answer the question, it isn't all bad in the end.

This question is also very useful to illustrate the importance of organizing your answers entirely prior to writing out the essay. It is generally necessary to spend 15 minutes organizing the essay and 45 minutes writing the essay. Once you have organized your answer, but before you have started writing, you always want to take a minute to visualize your answer and determine which issues are worth the most points and spend your time accordingly. The interesting thing about this question is that it would appear there are three major issues raised in each of the three calls of the question, but in practice, much of the rules and their corresponding substantive analysis was exactly the same in calls two and three as what was covered in call one. Once an applicant figured that out, it gave them some time to think through how to best handle the major DCC analysis.

This question also posed an organizational challenge because there were three challengers coming from different positions, three major potential legal challenges to the Act (DCC, P&I, and EPC). Further, the Act in question had two different provisions, Sec. 1 and Sec. 2, and the analysis for each was different. Sec. 2 was facially discriminatory, while Sec. 1 was not. This required using two different DCC rules to complete the analysis. You could have analyzed both sections in the first call when analyzing DCC for Chemco, or we opted to analyze the Sec. 1 challenge in Chemco's section, and the Sec. 2 challenge in the A&L Berries section. Again, use headings to guide the grader and they will find the analysis. It is worth noting that neither of the two released state answers were as clear about their analysis of the two separate sections of the Act under the DCC as we have modeled in the grid and answer, so do not worry if your answer is muddier than ours.

The Privileges and Immunities analysis was interesting and provides an example of what to do when you aren't sure about a rule. We all know that the P&I clause does not apply to corporations, but here A&L Berries is a partnership. Now what? A partnership is treated like a corporation for this analysis, but this rule had never been tested before, so in our answer, we modeled a good approach to use when you are not sure about a rule. Indicate that if a partnership is treated like a citizen, one thing happens, and if it is treated like a corporation, another thing happens. This is a safe way to handle it. Again, everyone is studying with the same rules, so if the examiners ask something unusual, like does the P&I apply to a partnership, you can safely bet that most other students don't know the answer either. The only logical options are that it is treated like a corporation, and you can supra your earlier analysis for that possibility, or they are treated like a citizen, and you can add in that analysis. Either way, you're covered.

It is common for issues with more rules and/or rule elements to be worth more points because there are more facts available to analyze with the elements. You can easily see from glancing at the grid below which issues are likely worth more points on this question because the facts are voluminous. We recommend identifying the big issues to help pace yourself as you are writing so you can easily identify where to "go big" with the analysis on a major issue and where to truncate the IRAC on a minor issue.

Note the areas highlighted in **bold** on the corresponding grid. The bold areas highlight the issues, analysis, and conclusions that are likely **required** to receive a passing score on this question.

Issue	Rule	Fact Application	Conclusion
1. Chemco's claims			
Standing	Individual standing — Injury, Causation, Redressability	• Chemco has suffered an injury since they cannot sell their chemical fertilizer and pesticides in State X since passage of the Organic Act. • Chemco's loss of sales and profit is caused by the Organic Act banning the sale of chemical fertilizers and pesticides in State X. • Chemco's injury can be redressed if the Act is stricken as unconstitutional.	Chemco has standing
Preemption	Any state law that directly conflicts with federal law will be preempted.	Chemco cannot argue preemption since there is no federal law on point.	No preemption
Dormant Commerce Clause(DCC)	**Under the Dormant Commerce Clause, the state cannot regulate interstate commerce if (1) it is discriminatory or (2) unduly burdensome.** • If the regulation is facially discriminatory, **it must be necessary to an legitimate, non-economic gov. interest** with no reasonable non-discriminatory alternatives. • For **undue burden**, it must be **rationally related** to legitimate govt. purpose, and **the benefit must outweigh burden.** • **Exceptions:** Market participant, Congress consents	• **The Act is not facially discriminatory** in Sec. 1 since it bans "the sale and use of chemical fertilizers and pesticides in State X" and the sale of any "produce grown with, or treated by, chemical fertilizers and pesticides." The Act **bans the use of all chemical fertilizers and pesticides.** • As a producer of chemicals and pesticides, Chemco would be challenging Sec. 1 of the Act. Chemco would assert the Act is protectionist since State X has many farms selling organic produce and does not have a chemical fertilizer industry. • To determine if there is an undue burden the ban must be rationally related to a legitimate government purpose and the benefit must outweigh the burden. **Here, the government interest is legitimate because it relates to the environment and health of the farmers since the chemical fertilizers/pesticides are contributing to measurable environmental harm and are shown to be a health threat to farmers and consumers using the banned products. Banning the chemicals is rationally related to that purpose.** The fact that the Act burdens fertilizer producers while also benefitting some local farmers, without more is insufficient to show the burden outweighs the benefit. The burden of banning the chemicals does not outweigh the burden of the ban, so it will not be unduly burdensome.	Sec. 1 does not violate DCC
Privileges and Immunities	**The city or state cannot discriminate against non-citizens** regarding rights fundamental to national unity (commercial activities) unless the state has a substantial justification and there are no less discriminatory alternative means available. **Does not apply to Corporations.**	• As a corporation, Chemco is not protected by the Privileges and Immunities Clause.	Chemco cannot assert P&I

Continued>

Issue	Rule	Fact Application	Conclusion
Equal Protection Clause	**Requires that similarly situated persons be treated similarly** • **Suspect class: 1st Am. Fundamental Right → Strict scrutiny** (necessary to achieve a compelling gov. interest and uses least restrictive means) • **Quasi-suspect: Gender → Intermediate scrutiny** (substantially related to an important gov. interest) • **Nonsuspect: All other → Rational basis** (rationally related to a legitimate gov. interest) • For strict and intermediate scrutiny, need to prove intent	• Since State X institutions can only buy organic produce grown in State X, the state is treating out of state producers differently than in state producers, so EPC is implicated. The Act does not implicate a suspect or quasi-suspect class, so rational basis applies. • As noted above, State X can assert a legitimate government interest. They can also establish that banning the chemicals and their use on produce is rationally related to the goal of protecting the environment and the health of the farmers and consumers. • The Act will survive rational basis review.	Act does not violate EPC
2. A&L Berries' claims			
Standing	Rule above	• A&L has an injury since they cannot sell to consumers in State X or through Organic Produce. Their injury is caused by the new act and is redressable if the act is stricken.	A&L has standing
Dormant Commerce Clause	Rule above	• A&L is a partnership from State Y and they will challenge Sec. 2 of the Act. • **Sec. 2 requires all publicly funded institutions only buy organic produce grown in State X, which is facially discriminatory.** Discriminatory schemes are typically a per se violation, but will be permitted if necessary to a legitimate non-economic interest. Here, as described above the government interest is important. However, the discrimination against out of state grown produce is not necessary to promote this interest. The produce could be grown chemical free out of state and State X would still receive the benefits to the environment and the health of produce consumers, so there is a reasonable non-discriminatory alternative and Sec. 2 will violate the DCC. • If a court did not find that the Act was an undue burden, State X could likely successfully argue that they qualify under the **market participant exception since Sec. 2 applies to the state X institutions operations as a purchaser of produce and not all private purchasers of produce.**	Sec. 2 likely violates DCC

Continued>

Issue	Rule	Fact Application	Conclusion
Privileges and Immunities	Rule above	• **If A&L partnership is considered like a corporation, they will be in the same position as Chemco. If a partnership is not considered a corporation for the purpose of a P&I inquiry, A&L may be successful.** • The state will assert they have a **substantial justification** here because of the serious environmental and health concerns. They will assert **there are no less discriminatory alternative means available,** however there is no need to discriminate against out of state producers to achieve their goals. [A partnership is treated like a corporation. However, since this rule had never been tested at the time of this question, we have modeled here a good approach to use when you are uncertain about a rule, as most of the bar takers were when answering this question.]	A&L may be able to assert P&I
Equal Protection Clause	Rule above	• Same analysis as for Chemco.	No EPC violation
3. Organic Produce's claims			
Standing	Rule above	• Organic Produce has an injury because they are unable to sell produce to publicly funded buyers in State X. Their injury is caused by the new act and is redressable if the act is stricken.	Organic Produce has standing
Dormant Commerce Clause	Rule above	• Same analysis as A&L Berries since they are impacted in the same way.	No DCC violation
Privileges and Immunities	Rule above	• Same analysis as Chemco since Organic Produce is also a corporation.	No P&I violation
Equal Protection Clause	Rule above	• Same analysis as outlined above in Chemco.	No EPC violation

Constitutional Law Question 2 Sample Answer
February 2024, Question 2

1. Chemco's claims

Standing

To establish standing there must be an injury, causation, and redressability.

Chemco has suffered an injury since they cannot sell their chemical fertilizer and pesticides in State X since passage of the new Organic Act (Act). That is their business, so they are injured by the new rule. Chemco's loss of sales and profit is caused by the Organic Act, which bans the sale of chemical fertilizers and pesticides in State X. Chemco's injury can be redressed if the Act is stricken as unconstitutional because they can continue to do business in State X as they have been. Chemco has standing to challenge the Act.

Preemption

Any state law that directly conflicts with federal law will be preempted and unenforceable. Chemco cannot argue the Act is preempted since there is no federal law on point.

Dormant Commerce Clause (DCC)

Under the DCC, also known as the negative implications of the commerce clause, the state cannot regulate interstate commerce if (1) it is discriminatory or (2) unduly burdensome. If the regulation is facially discriminatory, it is often a per se violation of the DCC and to be valid it must be necessary to a legitimate, non-economic government interest with no reasonable non-discriminatory alternatives. For a rule that is not discriminatory, but poses an undue burden on interstate commerce, the rule must be rationally related to legitimate government purpose, and the benefit to the state must outweigh the burden. However, there is an exception and the DCC will not pose a barrier where the state is acting as a market participant.

Here, the Act is not facially discriminatory in Sec. 1 since it bans "the sale and use of chemical fertilizers and pesticides in State X" and the sale of any "produce grown with, or treated by, chemical fertilizers and pesticides." The Act bans the use of *all* chemical fertilizers and pesticides, so there is no discrimination against non-locals.

As a producer of chemicals and pesticides, Chemco would primarily be challenging Sec. 1 of the Act. Chemco would assert the Act is locally protectionist since State X has many farms selling organic produce and does not have a chemical fertilizer industry. To determine if there is an undue burden the ban must be rationally related to a legitimate government purpose and the benefit must outweigh the burden.

Here, the government interest is legitimate because it relates to the safety of the environment and the health of the farmers and consumers since the chemical fertilizers/pesticides are contributing to measurable environmental harm and are also shown to be a health threat to farmers and consumers using the now banned products. Banning the chemicals and fertilizers is rationally related to that purpose since it will lessen the exposure of the environment and inhabitants to the chemicals. The fact that the Act happens to burden fertilizer producers while also benefitting some local farmers, without more, is insufficient to show the burden here outweighs the benefit. The burden of banning the chemicals does not outweigh the burden of the ban, so it will not be unduly burdensome.

Sec. 1 does not violate the DCC. (Sec. 2 is analyzed infra.)

Privileges and Immunities Clause

The city or state cannot discriminate against non-citizens regarding rights that are fundamental to national unity, which implicates primarily commercial activities, unless the state has a substantial justification and there are no less discriminatory alternative means available. The Privileges and Immunities Clause protects citizens and does not apply to corporations.

As a corporation, Chemco is not protected by the Privileges and Immunities clause.

Equal Protection Clause (EPC)

The EPC requires that similarly situated persons be treated similarly by our government. The standard of review is determined by the type of classification scheme. Strict scrutiny (necessary to achieve a compelling governmental interest and uses least restrictive means) applies to a suspect class of race or a fundamental right. Intermediate scrutiny (substantially related to an important governmental interest) applies to quasi-suspect classes of gender and illegitimacy. All other classifications are subject to rational basis (rationally related to a legitimate government interest). For strict and intermediate scrutiny, intent must be established.

Here, in Sec. 2 of the Act the state is treating out of state produce producers differently than the in-state producers since State X institutions can only buy organic produce grown in State X, so EPC is implicated. The Act does not implicate a suspect or quasi-suspect class, so rational basis applies.

As noted above, State X can assert a legitimate government interest. They can also establish that banning the chemicals and their use on produce is rationally related to the goal of protecting the environment and the health of the farmers and consumers. The Act will survive rational basis review and does not violate EPC.

2. A&L Berries' claims

Standing

Rule above.

A&L Berries has an injury since they cannot sell to consumers in State X or through Organic Produce to consumers in State X. Their injury is caused by the new act and is redressable because if the act is stricken they can go back to selling in State X. A&L Berries has standing.

Dormant Commerce Clause

Rule above.

A&L is a partnership from State Y and they will primarily challenge Sec. 2 of the Act.

Sec. 2 requires that all publicly funded institutions can only buy organic produce grown in State X, which is facially discriminatory to all organic produce growers from out of state. Discriminatory schemes are typically a per se violation, but they will be permitted if necessary to an important non-economic interest. Here, as described above the government interest is important. However, the discrimination against out of state grown produce is not necessary to promote this interest. The produce could be grown chemical free out of state X and State X would still receive the benefits to the environment and the health of produce consumers, so there is a reasonable non-discriminatory alternative to this Act, and Sec. 2 will violate the DCC.

However, if a court did not find that the Act was an undue burden, State X could likely successfully argue that they qualify under the market participant exception since Sec. 2 applies only to the operations of state X institutions as purchasers of produce and not to all private purchasers of produce.

Sec. 2 likely violates DCC.

Privileges and Immunities

Rule above.

A&L Berries is a partnership. If a partnership is considered similar to a corporation, they will be in the same position as Chemco, analyzed above, and the Privileges and Immunities Clause cannot be used to make a claim.

If a partnership is not considered a corporation for the purpose of a P&I inquiry, and treated like a citizen, then A&L Berries can likely assert a successful claim under the Privileges and Immunities Clause. The state will assert they have a substantial justification for the Act here because of their serious environmental and health concerns. The state will also assert there are no less discriminatory alternative means available, however there is no need to discriminate against all out of state producers to achieve their goals. They could simply require state institutions to buy organic produce from any producer and achieve the same result.

A&L Berries may be able to assert a claim under the Privileges and Immunities Clause.

Equal Protection Clause

Same rule and analysis as for Chemco above.

3. Organic Produce's claims

Standing

Rule above.

Organic Produce has an injury because they are unable to sell produce to publicly funded buyers in State X. Their injury is caused by the new act and is redressable if the act is stricken because they could continue selling to State X institutions. Organic Produce has standing.

Dormant Commerce Clause

Same rule and analysis as A&L Berries since they are impacted in the same way.

Privileges and Immunities

Same rule and analysis as Chemco since Organic Produce is also a corporation.

Equal Protection Clause

Same rule and analysis as outlined above in Chemco section.

Constitutional Law Question 3
February 2014, Question 5

For many years, the Old Ways Fellowship, a neopagan religious organization, received permission from the City's Building Authority to display a five-foot diameter symbol of the sun in the lobby of City's Municipal Government Building during the week surrounding the Winter Solstice. The display was accompanied by a sign stating "Old Ways Fellowship wishes you a happy Winter Solstice."

Last year the Building Authority adopted a new "Policy on Seasonal Displays," which states:

> Religious displays and symbols are not permitted in any government building. Such displays and symbols impermissibly convey the appearance of government endorsement of religion.

Previously, the Building Authority had allowed access to a wide variety of public and private speakers and displays in the lobby of the Municipal Government Building. Based on the new policy, however, it denied the Old Ways Fellowship a permit for the sun display.

After it was informed by counsel that courts treat Christmas trees as secular symbols, rather than religious symbols, the Building Authority decided to erect a Christmas tree in the lobby of the Municipal Government Building, while continuing to prohibit the Old Ways Fellowship sun display.

The Old Ways Fellowship contests the Building Authority's policy and its decision regarding the Christmas tree. It has offered to put up a disclaimer sign explaining that the Winter Solstice greeting is not endorsed by City. The Building Authority has turned down this offer.

The Old Ways Fellowship has filed suit claiming violation of the First Amendment to the United States Constitution.

What arguments may the Old Ways Fellowship reasonably raise in support of its claim and how are they likely to fare? Discuss.

Constitutional Law Question 3 Assessment
February 2014, Question 5

This is a typical free speech constitutional law essay. However, after a quick read of the call you wouldn't know what subject it was, let alone the topic. But after reading the preceding sentence you see that Old Ways filed suit claiming its First Amendment rights were violated, so you know you are in constitutional law, with a focus on the First Amendment. To start, it is only necessary to write out a quick First Amendment issues checklist. After reading the facts, you can quickly see that free speech and religion are at issue.

Since this practice question implicates the freedom of religion, it is important to know that since this question was asked there has been a major change in the freedom of religion laws. There are two main rules in freedom of religion. The Free Exercise Clause protects an *individual's* right to practice their religion. The Establishment Clause prohibits the government from establishing a religion. As noted on the grid, in 2022 the Supreme Court abandoned the longstanding Lemon test, which was the law in place since 1971. *Kennedy v. Bremerton School District*. However, the court did not articulate a clear new test in *Kennedy*. Rather, in *Kennedy*, the court embraced "an analysis focused on original meaning and history." Going forward, look for questions that include facts about the historical origins or length of a practice (such as a city has a longstanding tradition of erecting a holiday display at the historical state building) to analyze and argue both sides.

For free speech questions, you will find using a more detailed checklist helpful. This ensures you don't miss any of the issues. Most students correctly address content-based v. content-neutral restrictions, but many forget other speech issues like prior restraint or overbreadth type issues. By using a checklist, you will avoid missing any issues and have your essay order mapped out in advance of writing. This allows you to spend more time on analysis, which is crucial for constitutional law essays.

As with all essays, you need to be strategic with how you spend your time. For example, any time you have to analyze a level of scrutiny, that analysis often takes longer to write out than an analysis of issues that have straightforward elements, like standing. Analyzing the levels of scrutiny requires more inferences, examples, and reasoning than simple elemental rules like standing. Consequently, those issues are often worth more points on a question, and the more organized you are before you begin to write by having an approach for free speech, the more time you will have for writing analysis where it counts.

You will also save time writing by knowing in advance how you plan to set up your analysis. For the various levels of scrutiny, you should have your first paragraph establish the government interest and make sure you explain why it is compelling, or important, etc. Don't just identify the interest, rather explain why it meets or does not meet the standard for that interest. Then, your second paragraph should analyze whether the regulation is narrowly tailored, or rationally related, etc. using logical inferences, so you explain why the regulation at issue does, or does not, meet the second part of the scrutiny test (which varies depending on the level of scrutiny). If you find on a strict scrutiny analysis that less restrictive means are available, then you should give an example or two of what would be less restrictive. Further, to save time you can supra the analysis later if needed. For example, if you have to analyze strict scrutiny in two different free speech issues then you can supra for the second issue that requires the same test. Being organized in advance allows you to plan for this and do it easily.

Make note of the areas highlighted in **bold** on the corresponding grid. The bold areas highlight the issues, analysis, and conclusions that are likely **required** to receive a passing score on this question.

Issue	Rule	Fact Application	Conclusion
Standing	• Injury • Causation • Redressable Organizational standing requires the above and that the interests are related to the org. purpose and no participation of members is required	Old Ways suffered an injury since they could not display their sun symbol as they always do for Winter Solstice, caused by the new Policy on Seasonal Displays; and injury would be redressed if they could display their symbol as they always do. Interest to display the sun symbol is related to their organization as it is a neopagan religious organization that wants to wish others a happy winter solstice and no members need to participate.	Old Ways has standing
State Action	Need to bring claim under Constitution; traditional public function or heavy gov. entanglement required.	City's Building Authority implementing policy, so part of state/govt. entanglement as City is part of the State.	State action exists
Free Speech **Content Based v.** **Content Neutral**	Content-based regulations must meet strict scrutiny, which requires the regula-tion be necessary to achieve a compelling government interest. Content neutral require: • Serve a significant/important government interest, • Narrowly tailored, & • Open alternative channels of communication.	Policy here regulates seasonal displays but it limits only "religious" displays and symbols so it is about the religious content. Government would argue it isn't content as it is all religions and doesn't distinguish but still religion as a whole would likely be content. Gov. interest in not endorsing religion likely compelling since gov. should not be entangled with religion in a municipal govt. building. Not likely necessary and narrowly tailored because Old Ways can put up a disclaimer as they offered stating that City does not endorse the Winter Solstice greeting/sun symbol; they could also pass out pamphlets or have other ways to show that City doesn't endorse the display. If content neutral, then still not narrowly tailored as discussed above and need to look to see what type of forum it is.	Policy violates free speech

Continued>

Issue	Rule	Fact Application	Conclusion
Free Speech **Time, Place, Manner** **Public Forum** **or** **Designated Public Forum**	Public—open to public or designated public—open to public for a specific purpose Public and designated public forums re-quire: • **Content neutral (subject matter and viewpoint),** • **Serve a significant/important government interest,** • **Narrowly tailored, &** • **Open alternative channels of communication.**	Here, the municipal government buildings are open to the public and arguably are a public forum but since everyone can't use them all of the time and they need permission or permits to display various displays the forum is likely a designated public forum like public libraries. (Both state-released answers came to different conclusions—one said it is a public forum and one said it was a designated public forum—either way the same test applies). Here arguably It is not content neutral as discussed above and even if it is it is not narrowly tailored as discussed above.	Free speech violated
Prior Restraint	Prevents speech from being heard before it even occurs. Only allowed where the government can show: • Irreparable/serious harm to the public will occur, • Narrowly drawn standards, and • A final determination of the validity of the restraint.	Here, City denied Old Ways permit before they could display their sun symbol so Old Ways was prevented from displaying it before the speech occurred. Gov. might be able to show that the harm would be the gov. would appear as though they were endorsing religious views which is harmful to the public as not everyone shares the same religious views. Seems as though there were not narrowly drawn standards as Building Authority did not allow the sun symbol without any clear criteria and they allowed a Christmas tree but they did that only after counsel told them courts consider Christmas trees as secular symbols. Not clear if a restraining order was sought either.	Likely a prior restraint violation.
Symbolic Speech	Freedom not to speak or the freedom to communicate an idea by use of a symbol or communicative conduct, if the regulation is: • Within constitutional power, • Furthers an important governmental interest unrelated to the suppression of speech, and • Prohibits no more speech than necessary.	Old Ways would argue the denial of their permit to display their sun symbol was a violation of symbolic speech; not clear though what the 5-foot diameter of the sun is supposed to symbolize except perhaps something related to winter solstice since it corresponds to that. Regulation to only allow certain displays within a govt. building is likely within the constitutional power of the govt. Important gov. interest is so govt. doesn't appear to endorse religion, but this is related to the speech as the policy only pertains to religious displays and symbols. Also prohibits more speech than necessary as discussed above (can add disclaimer).	Violation under symbolic speech

Continued>

Issue	Rule	Fact Application	Conclusion
	Note that neither prior restraint or symbolic speech are bolded because one state-released answer discussed prior restraint and not symbolic speech, while the other state-released answer discussed symbolic speech and not prior restraint; while both issues are worthy of discussion you likely needed to at least address one of them in your essay to obtain a passing score.		
Overbroad	Overbroad if it bans both protected speech and unprotected speech.	**Arguably it isn't overbroad as it only limits "religious" symbols and displays.**	Policy is not overbroad.
Vague	Vague if it is so unclearly defined that a reasonable person would have to guess at its meaning.	Not clear what constitutes "religious" since Christmas trees allowed and Christmas is religious but since counsel said courts said secular it isn't clear to people what would be religious and what wouldn't be.	Policy is vague.
First Amendment Free Exercise Clause	(Incorporated in states through 14th Amend.) Govt. cannot prohibit or seriously burden the exercise of religion but may regulate if law of general applicability, which does not intentionally burden, and advances important public interests. If substantial burden, RFRA requires strict scrutiny.	Arguably the law doesn't single out any particular religion so it doesn't burden particular religions and is of general applicability. On the other hand, it does burden all religions due to banning all religious displays and symbols and the gov. does not meet strict scrutiny as discussed above.	Could conclude either way here (state-released answers came to opposite conclusions).
First Amendment Establishment Clause	[Note: This Supreme Court abandoned the Establishment Clause Lemon test in 2022 (since this question was asked), but did not clearly articulate a new test. The rule below represents the current state of the law.] Prohibits the government from aiding or establishing a religion. To determine, use "an analysis focused on original meaning and history." An action is likely allowed if it: • Does not coerce participation • Is consistent with historical practices and understandings	Here the Building Authority policy does not coerce participation. Rather, it bans all religious displays and symbols. While Old Ways will argue they are an old neopagan religion, they will have a hard time arguing that a sun Winter Solstice display is in keeping with historical practices and understandings, going back to the time of the founding fathers, who were primarily Christians. It is unclear if the country founders even knew what a winter solstice was, but it certainly would not have been a common practice for there to be an observance by our Christian founders.	Likely a violation of the Establishment Clause. Old Ways will not succeed in an Establishment clause claim.

Constitutional Law 3 Sample Answer
February 2014, Question 5

Standing

To bring a claim, a person must have standing. Standing requires injury, causation, and redressability. Organizational standing requires that the individual members have standing, that the interests asserted are related to the organization's purpose, and that individual members are not required to participate.

Here, Old Ways suffered an injury since they could not display their sun symbol as they always do every year for Winter Solstice. This injury was caused by the City Building Authority's new policy, which bans religious displays and symbols. Finally, the injury would be redressed if the policy is found to be unconstitutional since then Old Ways could display their symbol as they have in past years. Further, the display is related to their organization's purpose as it is to wish others a Happy Winter Solstice, which their neopagan religious organization believes in, and individual members would not be required to participate. Thus, Old Ways has standing.

State Action

Since the Constitution only prohibits governmental infringement of constitutional rights, the plaintiff must prove that there was state action. This occurs when the action performed is one that is a traditional public function or the government is heavily entangled in the action.

Here, City's Building Authority implemented policy. Since City and its agencies are a part of the state there is government entanglement and thus government state action.

Free Speech

Content based v. content neutral

Content-based speech regulations must meet strict scrutiny, which requires that the regulation be necessary to achieve a compelling government interest. Content-neutral regulations require that the regulation serve a significant/important government interest, that it is narrowly tailored, and that it leaves open alternative channels of communication.

Here, the policy regulates seasonal displays, but it limits only "religious" displays and symbols, so it is about the religious content. While City might argue it isn't content as it equally applies to all religions and doesn't distinguish, it is still specific to content as it only limits "religious" displays and symbols and not all displays and symbols.

Under strict scrutiny, City must show it has a compelling government interest to limit the religious displays and symbols. Here, City has an interest in not having the appearance of government endorsement of religion. This is likely a compelling interest since the government should not be entangled with religion in a municipal government building so as to keep church and state separate.

However, the policy is not likely to meet the second part of the strict scrutiny test. The policy is not necessary or narrowly tailored because Old Ways can put up a disclaimer as they offered stating that City does not endorse the Winter Solstice greeting sun symbol. Further, they could also pass out pamphlets or have other ways to show that City doesn't endorse the display while still allowing Old Ways to display it and wish others a Happy Winter Solstice. Thus, the policy is not narrowly tailored since it fails to meet strict scrutiny.

Thus, the policy violates Old Ways First Amendment freedom of speech.

Even if a court found it was content neutral, the policy is still not narrowly tailored as discussed above and would still fail.

Time, Place, Manner Restrictions

Public or designated public forum

Public forums are those open to public, such as parks and streets. Designated public forums are those not traditionally open to the public but are opened up to the public for a specific purpose. Regulations that limit speech in public and designated public forums must be content neutral, both subject matter and viewpoint, serve a significant/important government interest, be narrowly tailored, and leave open alternative channels of communication.

Here, the municipal government buildings are open to the public and arguably are a public forum, but since everyone can't use them all of the time and they need permission or permits to display various displays the forum is likely a designated public forum like public libraries.

As discussed above, the policy is not likely content neutral nor is it narrowly tailored. Thus, the policy would violate the time, place, and manner restriction rules, and Old Ways would have a viable claim for violation of their right to free speech.

Prior Restraint

A prior restraint prevents speech from being heard before it even occurs. These are rarely permitted and carry a heavy presumption of unconstitutionality. A prior restraint is only allowed where the government can show that irreparable/serious harm to the public will occur if the speech isn't prevented, that the determination was made with narrowly drawn standards, and that a final determination of the validity of the restraint was sought.

Here, City denied Old Ways a permit before they could display their sun symbol so Old Ways was prevented from displaying it before the speech occurred.

City might be able to show that the harm would be that allowing the symbol gives the appearance of government endorsement of various religions, which is harmful to the public as not everyone shares the same religious views and government is not supposed to commingle church and state. However, it does not appear that City used narrowly drawn standards to deny the permit as Building Authority did not allow the sun symbol without any clear criteria but they allowed a Christmas tree. Although they only allowed the Christmas tree after counsel told them courts consider Christmas trees to be secular symbols, it doesn't appear that they sought outside counsel advice for whether a sun symbol would be considered secular. Further, using counsel and their opinion as the only source to determine whether a display or symbol is secular or religious does not amount to narrowly drawn standards. Finally, it is not clear if a restraining order was sought by City.

Overall, the policy is likely a prior restraint violation.

Symbolic Speech

Symbolic speech involves the freedom not to speak or the freedom to communicate an idea by use of a symbol or communicative conduct. Regulation of symbolic speech is allowed if the regulation is within the constitutional power of the government to enact, furthers an important governmental interest unrelated to the suppression of speech, and prohibits no more speech than necessary.

Old Ways would argue that the denial of their permit to display their sun symbol was a violation of symbolic speech because it prevents their freedom to communicate an idea to wish others a Happy Winter Solstice through the use of their five-foot-diameter sun symbol. While it is not clear exactly what the 5-foot diameter of the sun is supposed to symbolize except perhaps something related to the winter solstice, it is still a symbol that the City finds to be "religious" as they banned it.

Here, the policy to only allow certain displays within a government municipal building is likely within the constitutional power of the government as there is a Building Authority that City established to control these types of things. Further, there is likely an important government interest so the government doesn't appear to endorse religion. However, the government interest is directly related to the speech as the policy only pertains to religious displays and symbols and it is to avoid religious endorsements. Also, the policy prohibits more speech than necessary as discussed above under strict scrutiny since City can do other things such as allow Old Ways to post a disclaimer.

Therefore, the policy violates Old Ways's First Amendment rights under symbolic speech.

Overbroad

A regulation is overbroad if it bans both protected speech and unprotected speech. Arguably the policy here isn't overbroad as it only limits "religious" symbols and displays rather than all symbols and displays. Thus, the policy is not overbroad.

Vague

A regulation is vague if it is so unclearly defined that a reasonable person would have to guess at its meaning. Here, it is not clear what constitutes "religious" since Christmas trees are allowed and "Christmas" is religious and often those who celebrate Christmas have Christmas trees. However, City would argue that counsel indicated that courts said Christmas trees are secular. But it still would not be clear to people then what constitutes religious and what is secular since there are various views on Christmas being religious and those symbols and displays associated with it such as Christmas trees. Thus, the policy is vague.

First Amendment Religion

Free Exercise Clause

The Free Exercise Clause is incorporated into the states through the Fourteenth Amendment. The government cannot prohibit or seriously burden the exercise of religion, but may regulate under a law of general applicability if it does not intentionally burden and advances important public interests. If there is a substantial burden, the Religious Freedom Restoration Act requires the regulation to meet strict scrutiny.

Arguably the law doesn't single out any particular religion, so it doesn't burden particular religions and is instead a law of general applicability. On the other hand, it does burden all religions by banning all religious displays and symbols and the government does not meet strict scrutiny as discussed above. Thus, it is likely that the regulation also violates Old Ways's First Amendment rights to practice their religion.

Establishment Clause

The Establishment Clause prohibits the government from aiding or establishing a religion. To determine a violation of the Establishment Clause, consider "an analysis focused on original meaning and history." A government action is likely allowed if it does not coerce participation in a religious activity and is consistent with historical practices and understandings.

Here, the Old Ways Fellowship wants to display a sun symbol with a Happy Winter Solstice greeting. However, the new Building Authority policy does not coerce participation. Rather, it bans all religious displays and symbols, so it does not violate the establishment clause by being coercive. While Old Ways will argue they are an old neopagan religion with deep historical roots, they will have a hard time arguing that a sun Winter Solstice display is in keeping with historical practices and understandings going back to the time of the American founding fathers, who were primarily Christians. It is unclear if the founders of our country even knew what a winter solstice was, but it certainly would not have been a common practice for there to be an observance by our Christian founders, and such a display would not be in keeping with the "original meaning and history" of our country.

It is unlikely that Old Ways has a viable claim that its First Amendment rights are being violated under the Establishment Clause.

Constitutional Law Question 4
July 2015, Question 6

City Council (City) amended its zoning ordinance to rezone a single block from "commercial" to "residential." City acted after some parents complained about traffic hazards to children walking along the block. The amended ordinance prohibits new commercial uses and requires that existing commercial uses cease within three months.

Several property owners on the block brought an action to challenge the amended ordinance.

In the action, the court ruled:

1. Property Owner A, who owned a large and popular restaurant, had no right to continue that use, and had time to move in an orderly fashion during the three-month grace period.

2. Property Owner B, who had spent $1 million on engineering and marketing studies on his undeveloped lot in good faith prior to the amendment, was not entitled to any relief.

3. Property Owner C, whose lot dropped in value by 65% as a result of the amended ordinance, did not suffer a regulatory taking.

Was each ruling correct? Discuss.

Constitutional Law Question 4 Assessment
July 2015, Question 6

Many applicants struggled with this question, which is why we have included it here for you to practice. This question provides a good example of how to write a passing answer even when you don't feel on solid ground with your rule knowledge on a topic. This question represents the first, and only, time a question was entirely about the takings clause. Most applicants went into this question knowing only the basics about takings since it was not a commonly tested concept. Even so, an applicant could have easily written a passing answer to this question.

When you get a question that feels like a curve ball, the first thing to do is breathe. Then, remind yourself that the essays are graded on a curve. It is important to know that the bar examiners are not specific about what rules they expect students to know for the exam. Therefore, all of the bar preparation materials are created by the bar prep companies (and professors like us) analyzing all of the previously asked questions and deducing from that which rules the bar examiners expect the applicants to know. Everyone is studying based on the rules that have been asked previously. However, the bar examiners sometimes will ask a question of first impression. When that happens, the rules are either not contained in the bar prep materials, or even if they are, they were not emphasized because there were no corresponding practice questions. It would be practically impossible for the bar prep companies to include every rule that could ever conceivably be tested in their rule books, and even if they did, it would be impossible to memorize everything, so you are wise to focus most of your energy on the most heavily tested topics.

Which leaves you in the situation the applicants found themselves in on this essay — you probably do not know the rules implicated in this essay well, and that will feel very uncomfortable. However, since virtually everyone is using the same materials to study for the bar (which is all based on prior bar questions), take comfort in knowing that no one else taking the exam knows the rules well either (except that one gunner in class who always knew everything) and the essays are graded on a curve. Exhale. It will be fine. Answer in an IRAC format since it is a dead giveaway that an applicant is unsure when they abandon good IRAC format. Just like any good lawyer, never let the graders see you sweat.

First, you need to find a rule to tether your factual analysis to. For example, here, we used the 10th Amendment to ground the discussion of a local zoning ordinance. When in doubt, use a rule that you do know, or start with the parts of the rule you can remember and make a reasonable guess at the rest. For this question you would know the issue is takings, and even if you didn't remember the three prongs of the takings rule, you could make a reasonable guess that at least one prong would have something to do with the government interest since that is thematic in constitutional law, and you would have been right. You could also make a reasonable guess that the government interest would be balanced against the property owners' interest. You might not have all the buzz words right, but you would have been on the right track. Now write that into a rule, and you have the "R" for your IRAC.

Then, spend most of your energy on crafting some good factual analysis. Analyze the heck out of the facts. Argue both sides. Make lots of logical factual inferences. This is where the points are and if you can do a good job here, you have an excellent chance of writing a passing answer even without the perfect rules.

Make note of the areas highlighted in **bold** on the corresponding grid. The bold areas highlight the issues, analysis, and conclusions that are likely **required** to receive a passing score on this question.

Issue	Rule	Fact Application	Conclusion
State Action	State action exists where a state or local government is involved with the challenged action.	• Here, the City Council amended the zoning ordinance, which is state action.	State action
Takings	**The 5th Amendment, applied to the states via the 14th Amendment, provides that the government may not take private property for public use without just compensation.**	• Here, the City Council amended the zoning ordinance to change a block from commercial to residential. • To determine if there was a taking from each property owner, each property owner will be analyzed below.	
1. Did the court rule correctly on the challenge to the ordinance by Property Owner A?			
Zoning	• The 10th Amendment reserves to the states all powers not relegated to the federal government by the Constitution.	• Here, City is a political subdivision of a state and has authority under the 10th Amendment to amend the zoning ordinance for the purpose of safety with respect to the traffic hazards posed to children on the block. • However, Owner A will argue the new zoning ordinance is a violation of the Takings Clause.	Zoning ordinance

Regulatory Takings	• Regulatory takings are total takings if there is a permanent physical invasion, or a use restriction that denies all economically beneficial use of the property.
	• **To determine the economic benefit left to the property, the court will balance**
	  • **The character of the invasion (social goals sought to be promoted),**
	  • **Economic impact on the owner, and**
	  • **The extent of interference with investment backed expectations of the owner.**
		• Here, there was not a total taking since the property was not physically invaded or denied all economic beneficial use.
		
		Character of Invasion/Social Goals Promoted
		
		• **City** will argue they have a strong government interest in promoting the social goal of ensuring safety for the children walking along the block.
		• **However, Owner A** will argue it is unclear how rezoning only a single block reduces traffic and increases safety for children in City, and since it only affects owners on this block, it does not increase safety in the surrounding areas, making Property Owner A largely bear this burden rather than the greater community.
		
		Economic Impact on Property Owner
		
		• **Here,** Owner A operated a popular restaurant on the premises and the impact of the regulation is severe since a good location is important to the success of a restaurant.
		• The economic impact of the ordinance on the property value is unclear, but since the land value is likely less for residential use compared to land used for the economic enterprise of a popular restaurant there is **likely a diminution in property value.**
			On balance, there may not be a regulatory taking.

Continued>

Issue	Rule	Fact Application	Conclusion
Regulatory Takings (continued)		• **Further, since the restaurant is popular and viable, moving it to another location would cost the owner money** and likely customers. **Investment Backed Expectations** • Restaurants require a capital investment, and **it takes time to recoup** the capital **costs** associated with installing restaurant and cooking equipment. • If the large and popular restaurant has **been there for a long period of time, then the economic return expected out of the property may have already occurred** and the court decision is supported. • **However, if the restaurant is newly opened and popular for this reason, the owner has likely not achieved the expected return on their capital investment and this change would interfere substantially with their expectations.**	
Non-conforming-use/Variances	**An owner may obtain a non-conforming-use variance to continue using their land** *as it was used before the new zoning ordinance was adopted if it is not contrary to public welfare.*	• The restaurant, which is not contrary to the public welfare, had been operating lawfully according to City's original zoning law and **became non-conforming only upon City's amendment of the zoning law.** • Given that this restaurant is an established business, three months is likely insufficient time for it to move in order to meet the new zoning ordinance. A more equitable approach would have been to allow the non-conforming use to continue as a variance or allow an extended time period to meet the new zoning ordinance requirements. • Although the regulation likely does not consist of a taking for Property Owner A, the court should allow the restaurant to continue operating in its current capacity by granting a variance to Owner A.	A should be granted a variance
2. Did the court rule correctly on the challenge to the ordinance by Property Owner B?			
Zoning*	A zoning ordinance change is not a taking even when it changes the permissible use of the land and the land itself loses value unless it is a physical appropriation, all economic use is denied, or it interferes with **investment based expectations.**	• Here, Owner B has invested **$1 million on engineering and marketing studies to develop his lot prior to the zoning ordinance change, and now his property has lost value since he can no longer complete his project on the lot.** • **Owner B may argue that he should be entitled to complete the project because of his large financial investment so far, even though the intended use is now impermissible.** • Therefore, the court correctly ruled that Owner B is not entitled to relief.	Owner B is not entitled to relief

Continued>

Issue	Rule	Fact Application	Conclusion
Regulatory Taking*	Full rule above. A taking may be found when there is a **significant investment backed expectation** from the original intended use of the land.	**Character of Invasion/Social Goals Promoted** • The social goal of public safety is a valid social goal, but the nature of the government action is targeted and intrusive because it only applies to a single block. **Economic Impact on Property Owner** • Here, the property owner has an undeveloped lot, and though he would lose the money spent on the engineering and marketing studies, the land itself still has value. A zoning ordinance is still valid even if it changes the permissible uses and devalues a property significantly. **Investment Backed Expectations** • **Owner B has invested $1 million in assessing the lot in "good faith" based on the previous zoning prior to the amendment.** This large investment backed expectation gives **serious weight to a finding of a taking.** • **However, despite the investment, Owner B can still likely see some positive returns on the lot if it is sold, or they may be successful in** establishing the undue hardship necessary to **obtain a post-ordinance variance,** though that would be difficult to get. • Therefore, the court correctly ruled that the amended ordinance is not a taking and Property Owner B is not entitled to relief.	Owner B is not entitled to relief

* A discussion of investment backed expectations was necessary and could have occurred within a discussion of Zoning or Takings.

Call #3: Did the court rule correctly on the challenge to the ordinance by Property Owner C?

| Takings | Rule above | **Character of Invasion/Social Goals Promoted**

• The social goal of public safety is a valid social goal, but the nature of the government action is targeted and intrusive because it only applies to a single block.

Economic Impact on Property Owner

• Here, although there is a **very significant 65% drop in value, the property still retains some economic value** at 35% and it can still be developed residentially.

Investment Backed Expectations

• There are no facts provided about Owner C's use of the property, or their investment backed expectations, but it is likely Owner **C did not expect the property value to drop by 65% due to a change in the ordinance, and such a massive drop is indicative of a large degree of interference with Owner C's investment expectations.**
• Therefore, the court incorrectly ruled that Owner C did not suffer a regulatory taking and Owner C is entitled to relief. [Could conclude either way.] | On balance, there is a regulatory taking |

Constitutional Law Question 5
July 2009, Question 4

In a recent statute, Congress authorized the United States Secretary of Transportation "to do everything necessary and appropriate to ensure safe streets and highways." Subsequently, the Secretary issued the following regulations:

> Regulation A, which requires all instructors of persons seeking commercial driving licenses to be certified by federal examiners. The regulation details the criteria for certification, which require a minimum number of years of experience as a commercial driver and a minimum score on a test of basic communication skills.
>
> Regulation B, which requires that every bus in commercial service be equipped with seatbelts for every seat.
>
> Regulation C, which provides that states failing to implement adequate measures to ensure that bus seatbelts are actually used will forfeit 10 percent of previously appropriated federal funds that assist states with highway construction.

The State Driving Academy, which is a state agency that offers driving instruction to persons seeking commercial driving licenses, is considering challenging the validity of Regulation A under the United States Constitution. The Capitol City Transit Company, which is a private corporation that operates buses within the city limits of Capitol City, is considering challenging the validity of Regulation B under the United States Constitution. The State Highway Department, another state agency, is considering challenging the validity of Regulation C under the United States Constitution.

1. What constitutional challenge may the State Driving Academy bring against Regulation A, and is it likely to succeed? Discuss.

2. What constitutional challenge may the Capitol City Transport Company bring against Regulation B, and is it likely to succeed? Discuss.

3. What constitutional challenge may the State Highway Department bring against Regulation C, and is it likely to succeed? Discuss.

Constitutional Law Question 5 Assessment
July 2009, Question 4

This is one of those rare constitutional law questions that tests congressional (federal) action rather than state action. When you approach this question and begin to consider your issues checklist, there is no need to note all of the limitations on the state because they are totally inapplicable. However, since Congress is acting, you will need your mini-issues checklist for Congress's powers. Then, you need to specifically focus on the limitations that only apply to the federal government as well as those limitations that apply to both the federal and state governments.

Without having some knowledge of Congress's enumerated powers, you would not be able to properly issue spot this question or adequately analyze the issues. The Commerce Clause issue requires a full analysis of the *federal* Commerce Clause and knowledge of the specific rules that apply to commercial or economic regulations, as opposed to noneconomic regulations. Further, standing needs to be addressed with each call and each party since without standing they would not be able to challenge any of the regulations.

This constitutional law question is noticeably different from the typical question that tests the constitutional law concepts through the prism of a state actor. Seeing a question like this puts you on notice of the level of detail and sheer breadth of knowledge you are required to know in order to pass the California Bar Exam. You not only need to know 19 individual subjects (if you break down each subject into its own category), but you also need to know all of the issues included in the checklists provided and in the rules outlines. Further, you need to not only understand the rules with depth, but also be able to write out each of the rules in sentence format. This is why it is so important to not only memorize the rules from the Memorization Attack Sheets, but also to truly understand their meaning and practice writing the rules out in sentence format to have handy and ready for use on the essays.

In another unusual question that was somewhat similar to this one, the state bar examiners tested the executive branch acting to impose a regulation, as opposed to a state or Congress. That question (and questions covering any other constitutional law issues not covered in these questions) can be found in the crossover questions section. To fully prepare for the bar exam, you should be writing out every one of these essays in timed sessions rather than just outlining and issue spotting them. You should also write out the practice essays in the crossover section to see how the various subjects can relate to one another and combine in a question. If timing is an issue at first, that is normal and to be expected since you often don't have all your rules memorized and understood at the beginning of your bar studies. Focus on the writing aspect of exam taking, including spotting all the issues, organization, and using all of the facts. Your timing will improve as you practice writing out more essays and become familiar with how each issue applies to a given set of facts.

As with the other essays, make note of the areas highlighted in **bold** on the corresponding grid. The bold areas highlight the issues, analysis, and conclusions that are likely **required** to receive a passing score on this question.

Issue	Rule	Fact Application	Conclusion
Call #1: State Driving Academy			
Standing	Injury Causation Redressability	Injured because will need to have all instructors certified, which will cost money and they cannot continue to use instructors that aren't certified until they become certified. Caused by Regulation A as before they didn't need to be certified. Redressable because if Regulation A was unconstitutional, they wouldn't need to have all instructors certified.	Yes, standing.
Commerce Clause	Congress can regulate the (1) use of channels of interstate commerce, (2) instrumentalities of interstate commerce, and (3) persons/things in interstate commerce, and activities that substantially affect interstate commerce. For commercial or economic activity, Congress can regulate if it has a rational basis to believe the activity will have a substantial effect on interstate commerce or if there is a substantial cumulative economic effect.	Here, Congress is regulating commercial driving instruction, which involves the instrumentalities and persons in interstate commerce. It is rational to believe that if you have set criteria for licenses and certifying instructors that train commercial drivers, the certified drivers will then be more careful and drive more safely since they will have been trained by drivers with a set number of years of experience who met a minimum score and thus can effectively communicate how to drive to others they are instructing. Also, the safety of highways has a substantial effect on interstate commerce since it involves all parts of interstate commerce.	No violation of Commerce Clause.
Delegation of Powers	Congress can delegate regulatory powers to other branches if there are intelligible principles to govern.	Here, Congress delegated the power to ensure safe streets and highways to the U.S. Secy. of Transportation, another branch of government; although the authority seems broad, the regulation has specific standards and principles to use in governing.	Delegation proper.

Continued>

Issue	Rule	Fact Application	Conclusion
10th Amend.	The federal government cannot commandeer the states by imposing targeted or coercive duties on state legislators or officials, but it can impose regulatory statutes that are of general applicable law that applies to both private and state actors.	Here, the Regulation does impose a duty on state officials since it is a state agency that instructs the drivers, but it applies to both private and state actors and is of general applicability to all commercial drivers in training seeking a license.	No 10th Amend. violation.
Conclusion: State Driving unlikely to succeed.			
Call #2: Capital City Transport			
Standing	See above.	Injured because Capital City Transport will need to expend money installing seat belts in all of its buses; caused by Regulation B and would not need to install them if Regulation was unconstitutional.	Yes, standing.
Commerce Clause	See above.	Since the buses are instrumentalities of interstate commerce, Congress can regulate them. It is rational that if seat belts are installed in buses, there will be fewer injuries in accidents with buses, and thus safety on highways will be improved. It will also substantially affect, in the aggregate, interstate commerce since buses carry thousands of people over time on the highways.	No Commerce Clause violation.
Delegation of Powers	See above.	Similar to above and likely allowed.	Delegation proper.
State Action	Need to bring constitutional claim; traditional public function or heavy entanglement.	Here, federal regulation is involved, which was authorized by Congress, a branch of the government.	Yes, state action.
Equal Protection	Prohibits the government from treating similarly situated persons differently. For nonsuspect classifications, the regulation must be rationally related to a legitimate govt. interest.	Here, the Regulation is treating commercial buses differently from noncommercial buses by only requiring seat belts in commercial buses. Nonsuspect class because not based on race, ethnicity, gender, or legitimacy. Ensuring safety on streets and highways is a legitimate govt. interest because it should be protecting citizens. It is also rationally related because by using seat belts, fewer injuries are likely to occur when accidents happen on streets and highways.	No Equal Protection violation.
Conclusion: Capital City unlikely to succeed.			

Continued>

Issue	Rule	Fact Application	Conclusion
Call #3: State Highway Department			
Standing	See above.	Injured because they have to implement measures or they lose money; caused by Regulation C and wouldn't be an issue if Regulation C was unconstitutional.	Yes, standing.
Tax and Spending Clause	**Congress can tax and spend for the general welfare of the U.S. and can allocate conditional funding** if done unambiguously and **not excessively coercive.**	**Here, Congress is conditioning funding,** but not unambiguously since the Regulations specifically detail what states must do, in that they must see that seat belts in buses are used. **Also, the condition will only take away 10% of funding, which is not excessively coercive since it is such a small amount.**	**No Tax and Spend violation by Congress.**
Delegation of Power	See above.	**Same as above.**	Delegation proper
Conclusion: State Hwy. Dept. unlikely to succeed.			

Constitutional Law Question 6
February 2012, Question 2

City recently opened a new central bus station.

Within the central bus station, City has provided a large bulletin board that is available for free posting of documents. City requires that all free-posted documents be in both English and Spanish because City's population is about equally divided between English- and Spanish-speaking people.

City refused to allow the America for Americans Organization (AAO) to use the bulletin board because AAO sought to post a flyer describing itself in English only. The flyer stated that AAO's primary goal is the restriction of immigration. The flyer also advised of the time and place of meetings and solicited memberships at $10 each.

Does City's refusal to allow AAO to use the bulletin board violate the rights of AAO's members under the First Amendment to the U.S. Constitution? Discuss.

Constitutional Law Question 6 Assessment
February 2012, Question 2

This constitutional law question depicts how to approach a typical First Amendment question. And the call clearly states that you need to focus on First Amendment issues only. While sometimes they test both religion and speech with First Amendment questions, this question focuses only on speech.

Constitutional law questions are similar to torts in that they are usually full of facts to use in the analysis and have many two-sided arguments, and you often have to make logical inferences to fully analyze the government's interest when analyzing many of the tests and levels of scrutiny. In this question, there are very few facts, but you should still elaborate further by making logical inferences. For example, you can explain why having signs in both Spanish and English will serve an important governmental interest by logically inferring that the Spanish-speaking people also read in Spanish and since half of the population is Spanish-speaking and half is English-speaking, it would be beneficial to have signs in both languages to ensure that most of the population rather than just half of them can read pertinent flyers. This is one example of a logical inference that strengthens your analysis and earns you maximum points.

While not necessary to pass, a good answer should also quickly point out some issues that are related to First Amendment violations but are clearly not viable issues for AAO to raise. A few of these issues include freedom of association, overbroad, vague, etc. While these issues are not met, the facts still give rise to them slightly. Think about what issues you would raise if you were the attorney on each side of the case. Here, for AAO none of their arguments will likely win in court, but that doesn't mean that you can just tell the examiners that no rights are violated. Rather, they expect you to go through all the issues that the facts give rise to and explain why they are not violated.

Also, to save time, always remember to follow the call of the question specifically. This question asks only about First Amendment issues. Follow the directions! Going through issues such as Equal Protection and other non-First Amendment issues wastes time and does not gain you any points. Also, it's important to demonstrate that you fully understand how the laws operate by first addressing the standing and state action issues, because without those two preliminary issues being satisfied, AAO can't even get to the First Amendment issues.

Finally, make note of the areas highlighted in **bold** on the corresponding grid. The bold areas highlight the issues, analysis, and conclusions that are likely **required** to receive a passing score on this question.

Issue	Rule	Fact Application	Conclusion
Standing	Individual • Injury • Causation • Redressability Organizational requires • Individual standing (above) • Individual interests asserted are related to the org.'s purpose • Participation of individual members not required	Injury because AAO can't post their immigration poster in English only; caused by City policy that all documents be in English and Spanish; would be redressable if allowed to post only in English. Interests to post in English only are related to organization's purpose of restricting immigration which likely limits Spanish-speaking people. Participation not required since AAO can bring their own suit without member involvement.	AAO has standing.
State Action	Need state govt. action to bring a claim under the U.S. Constitution.	Here, City is a governmental state entity and thus is an extension of the state.	State action exists.
1st Amendment	1st Amend. of the U.S. Constitution applicable to the states through the 14th Amend.		
1st Amend.—Free Speech	Content based v. content neutral If content based, strict scrutiny applies. If content neutral, look to time, place, and manner restrictions.	Here, while AAO will argue the content of Spanish v. English is at issue, the content itself is not at issue as all posted documents regardless of content must meet the language requirements; thus it is about how the content is displayed, not what the content is.	Content neutral speech at issue.
Time, Place, Manner Restrictions Types of Forums	Public forum—open to public (parks, streets, etc.). Designated public—traditionally not open to public but govt. can open up to public. Both public and designated public forums can be regulated if the regulation: • Is content neutral (subject matter neutral) in addition to viewpoint neutral, • Serves a substantial/important government interest, • Is narrowly tailored to serve that interest, and • Leaves open alternative channels of communication.	Bus stations might be considered public forums as anyone can usually go there. Bulletin boards are more likely designated public forums that are not traditionally open to the public, but here City provided a large bulletin board for the public to post documents for free. Viewpoint neutral as it doesn't restrict on a particular viewpoint as discussed above. Govt. interest is to communicate with its residents which is substantial/important and they need to communicate in an effective manner, especially when half the residents speak Spanish and half English. Narrowly tailored as it is only 2 languages and not all languages and it is specific to this population; AAO will argue they could restrict it to heavily populated Spanish areas but bus stations likely to have residents speaking both languages. Open channels available as only requires "free-posted" documents, thus they could use a paid bulletin board or pass out flyers to communicate message.	No T, P, M violation

Continued>

Issue	Rule	Fact Application	Conclusion
TPM Restrictions (continued)	**Limited/nonpublic forum: govt. may regulate if viewpoint neutral and reasonably related to a legitimate govt. purpose.**	**Could be nonpublic also like courts have found for ads on the inside of buses; would be reasonably related to legitimate interest** as that is a lower standard and easier for gov. to meet than above standards.	
Commercial Speech	The government may restrict commercial speech only if the regulation serves a substantial government interest, directly advances that interest, and is narrowly tailored such that there is a reasonable fit (need not be least restrictive means).	AAO will argue gov. is restricting commercial speech since they sought to charge $10 membership making it appear flyer is an advertisement but not likely advertising for a commercial product since it is a political membership and not a product. Even if it was considered commercial speech, the gov. interest is substantial to communicate with residents when half of them speak Spanish (discussed above), and making signs in both English and Spanish directly advances the interest to ensure most of population is informed and narrowly tailored as discussed above.	No commercial speech violation.
Overbroad	A speech regulation is unconstitutionally overbroad if it bans both protected speech and unprotected speech.	Here, the regulation only limits posted signs at a bus station and only requires 2 languages.	Not overbroad.
Vague	A speech regulation is unconstitutionally vague if it is so unclearly defined that a reasonable person would have to guess at its meaning.	Here it is not vague and it clearly states that signs must be in Spanish and English which is clear.	Not vague.
Freedom of Association	Freedom of association prevents the government from denying a public benefit or job based on a person's association. The government can prevent freedom of association or require individuals to associate in regard to First Amendment freedoms only if there is a compelling governmental interest that cannot be achieved by less restrictive means (narrowly tailored).	AAO will argue they are being forced to associate with Spanish-speaking people, which goes against their purpose to restrict immigration. But the City is not telling them they must associate with anyone, rather just how they display their message. Even if it was limiting their right to associate the gov. has a compelling interest in making sure most of the population can read signs that might have pertinent information, and it is narrowly tailored as discussed above.	No Freedom of Association violation.

PART 5 *CONTRACTS*

CONTRACTS TABLE OF CONTENTS

INTRODUCTION TO CONTRACTS

There is a life cycle to any contract and events unfold chronologically on a timeline in a predictable way. This makes issue spotting contracts exams easier than other subjects because certain issues will be raised at certain points in the contracting process. If you know to look for them at that point, you will not miss spotting the issues raised by an essay question. After reading a contracts essay question, it may be helpful to sketch out a brief timeline of events in chronological order with the dates of the communications and what transpired on each date to assist you in issue spotting the exam (on virtual scratch paper, or the dry erase board, or at the top of your answer-but remember to erase your notes). Consider each communication or event in order since chronology of events is particularly important in analyzing contracts.

A well-organized issue spotting checklist is an essential tool to aid in spotting all the issues that can arise in a contracts essay question. The Contracts Issues Checklist follows the lifecycle of a contract and presents the issues in the likely logical order they would arise and be spotted on an essay question. Memorize this checklist and use it to assist you in spotting the issues.

First is the contract formation stage, and the potential issues arising consist of issues related to the applicable law governing the agreement, offer, acceptance, contract terms, adequacy of consideration, and/or promissory estoppel. Other issues that will be identifiable at the contracting stage of the essay are Statute of Frauds problems, parol evidence, misrepresentation, unconscionability, or mistake.

Typically, in a contracts fact pattern, communications or conduct will occur after the contract is entered into. Any communication that occurs *after* the contract is established must either pertain to a new contract, a potential modification of the contract at hand, or an issue related to breach. The issues that can be raised by these communications are the waiver of conditions, the parol evidence rule, contract modification, any issues relating to third parties to the contract, and/or breach.

There are also issues that arise at the point of the breach. The materiality of the breach is often at issue and should be analyzed. Anticipatory repudiation, violation of warranty, and accord and satisfaction will also be identifiable at this point, if present at all.

Facts that raise potential defenses to a contract's enforcement can arise at any time in the contracting process, so look for them as you go through the fact pattern. Sometimes an essay question will ask you to frame your response in the context of the defenses available to one of the contracting parties, rather than in the context of affirmatively proving up the contract. Remember, any failure of the underlying contract can operate as a defense to the contract's enforcement. In addition, consider the traditional contract defenses of impossibility, impracticability, and frustration of purpose.

After the breach has been established, an essay answer often requires a full discussion of remedies, including damages, and perhaps restitution and/or specific performance. Contracts questions are often crossover questions, particularly with remedies.

ISSUES CHECKLIST

APPLICABLE LAW

CONTRACT FORMATION

Offer/termination of offer
Acceptance
Contract terms
Consideration/promissory estoppel

DEFENSES TO CONTRACT FORMATION (ARISING AT TIME OF CONTRACTING)

SOF (Statute of Frauds)
Misrepresentation/fraud
Unconscionability
Mistake

CONTRACT TERMS & OTHER PERFORMANCE ISSUES

Conditions/waiver of conditions
PER (Parol Evidence Rule)
Modification
Third-party issues (TPB/assignment/delegation/novation)

BREACH

Anticipatory repudiation
Material v. minor
Warranties
Accord & satisfaction

DEFENSES TO CONTRACT ENFORCEMENT (ARISING LATER)

Any issue with contract validity
Condition precedent not met
Impossibility/impracticability/frustration of purpose

REMEDIES

Damages
Limitations—foreseeable, mitigation, certainty, causation
Restitution
Rescission/Reformation
Specific performance

MEMORIZATION ATTACK SHEET

APPLICABLE LAW

- ◆ **UCC**
  - • Goods (movable)
  - • Merchant
- ◆ **Common law (C/L)**
- ◆ **Predominance test**

CONTRACT FORMATION

- ◆ **Offer (C/L)**
  - • Intent
  - • Definite terms (QTIPS)
  - • Communicated to offeree
- ◆ **Termination of offer**
  - • Rejection
  - • Counteroffer
  - • Revocation
  - • Lapse of time
  - • Death or incapacity
- ◆ **Irrevocable offers**
  - • UCC firm offers
    - ◆ By a merchant
    - ◆ Signed writing
    - ◆ 3-month max.
  - • Option contract
  - • Detrimental reliance
- ◆ **Acceptance**
  - • Bilateral v. unilateral
  - • Within reasonable time
  - • Only in response
  - • C/L mirror image rule
- ◆ **Mailbox rule (dispatch)**
- ◆ **Mailbox rule *exceptions*:**
  - • Offer says otherwise
  - • Option k: upon receipt
  - • Both acceptance & rejection
    - ◆ Rejection 1st: acceptance if received 1st
    - ◆ Acceptance 1st: on dispatch
- ◆ **Acceptance varies (UCC)**
  - • Added terms
    - ◆ 1 not a merchant: then proposal only
    - ◆ Both merchants: then add the term, unless
      - • Offer limited to its terms expressly
      - • Material alteration
      - • Objection within reasonable time
  - • Different (Conflicting) terms
    - ◆ Knock-out rule

- ◆ UCC gap fillers
- ◆ Min. 1—treat as add'l terms
- ◆ Min. 2—fall out rule
- • Common law—agreed to terms
- ◆ **Acceptance by shipping (UCC)**
  - • Conforming goods acceptance
  - • Nonconform w/o accomm. acceptance and breach
  - • Nonconform w/ accomm. no acceptance—but counteroffer
- ◆ **Consideration**
  - • Illusory promise
  - • Requirements contract
  - • Output contract
  - • Past/preexisting duty
  - • Promissory estoppel

DEFENSES TO FORMATION

- ◆ **SOF (Mr. Dog)**
  - • Marriage
  - • Real property
  - • Debt of another
  - • One year
  - • Goods $500 or more
  - • Exceptions for all
- ◆ **SOF writing requirement**
  - • Essential terms
  - • Signed by party to be charged
  - • **Exception:** merchant's confirming memo
    - ◆ 2 merchants
    - ◆ 1 receives written confirmation
    - ◆ Both are bound
    - ◆ Unless objection within 10 days
  - • **Exception:** admission
  - • **Exception:** promissory estoppel
- ◆ **Misrepresentation**
- ◆ **Fraud**
- ◆ **Unconscionability**
- ◆ **Mistake**
  - • Basic assumption
  - • Material effect
  - • Risk not assumed by party affected
- ◆ **Illegality**

K TERMS/PERFORMANCE

- ◆ **Conditions**
  - Express: strict compliance
  - Constructive: substantial compliance
- ◆ **Waiver of conditions**
  - Keeping the benefit
  - Failure to insist on compliance
  - Can retract waiver unless reliance
- ◆ **PER**
  - Partial integration
    - ◆ PE not to contradict
    - ◆ PE okay to supplement
  - Total Integration
    - ◆ PE not to contradict
    - ◆ PE not to supplement
- ◆ **PER exceptions (PER does not apply)**
  - Subsequent communications
  - K formation defect evidence
  - Condition precedent to k effectiveness
  - Interpret ambiguous terms
    - ◆ Course of performance
    - ◆ Course of dealing
    - ◆ Usage of trade
- ◆ **Risk of loss to buyer**
  - Shipment: to 3P carrier
  - Destination: delivery to buyer
  - FOB: named location
- ◆ **Contract modification**
  - C/L
    - ◆ Mutual assent
    - ◆ Consideration
  - UCC
    - ◆ Mutual assent
    - ◆ Good faith
    - ◆ No consideration required
- ◆ **3rd-party beneficiary**
  - Intended (can sue)
  - Incidental (can't sue)
- ◆ **Assignment: transfers rights**
  - No consideration required
  - Gratuitous assignment okay
  - Assignee stands in shoes
  - Can't if material change
- ◆ **Delegation: transfers duties**
  - Delegator remains liable
  - Can't delegate if duty of skill
- ◆ **Novation**
  - Obligee accepts new performance—and releases delegator
  - Terminates delegator liability

BREACH

- ◆ **Anticipatory repudiation**
  - Unequivocal expression
  - Won't perform
  - Before performance due
  - Non-repudiating party can
    - ◆ Sue immediately
    - ◆ Suspend performance
    - ◆ Treat K as discharged
    - ◆ Urge performance
  - Non-repudiating: mitigate
  - Repudiating: can retract
  - Right to demand adequate assurances
    - ◆ Reasonable grounds for insecurity
    - ◆ In writing
    - ◆ Okay to suspend performance pending assurances
    - ◆ No response = repudiation
- ◆ **Material v. Minor (CL)**
  - Receive substantial benefit?
  - Extent of part performance
  - Willfulness of breach
  - Time not of essence unless contracted for
  - Divisible contract (separate Ks)
- ◆ **UCC: Perfect tender rule**
  - Reject the whole
  - Accept the whole
  - Accept a commercial unit
  - **Except:** does not apply to installment Ks (substantial conformity)
- ◆ **Seller's right to cure (UCC)**
  - Notice
  - Timely new tender
- ◆ **Warranties**
  - Express
  - Implied warranty of merchantability
  - Fitness for particular purpose
  - Implied good faith & fair dealing
- ◆ **Accord**
  - Agree to substitute performance
  - Doesn't discharge original k
- ◆ **Satisfaction**
  - Performance of the accord
  - Discharges both Ks

DEFENSES

- ◆ **Contract defenses**
  - No mutual assent
  - Lack of consideration
  - No writing & writing was required
  - Misrepresentation/fraud/duress/undue influence
  - Unconscionability
  - Lack of capacity
  - Illegality of contract
  - Condition precedent not met
- ◆ **Impossibility**
- ◆ **Impracticability**
- ◆ **Frustration of purpose**

REMEDIES

- ◆ **Damages limitations**
  - Foreseeability
  - Duty to mitigate
  - Certainty
  - Causation
- ◆ **Expectation damages**
  - As if k performed
- ◆ **Consequential damages**
  - Direct foreseeable consequences
  - Unique to plaintiff
- ◆ **Incidental damages**
  - Expenses reasonably incurred

- ◆ **Reliance damages**
  - As if k was never made
- ◆ **Liquidated damages**
  - Difficult to calculate
  - Reasonable approximation of damages
  - Only measure used if okay
- ◆ **Nominal damages**
- ◆ **No punitive damages in k**
- ◆ **Quasi-contract**
  - D derived a benefit
  - Unfair to allow D to keep
- ◆ **Replevin (personal prop)**
- ◆ **Ejectment (real prop)**
- ◆ **Reformation (rewrites k)**
- ◆ **Rescission (undo k)**
- ◆ **Specific performance**
  - Contract is valid
  - K conditions satisfied
  - Inadequate legal remedy
    - ◆ Damages too speculative
    - ◆ Insolvent D
    - ◆ Multiplicity of suits
    - ◆ Property is unique
  - Mutuality of performance
  - Feasibility of enforcement
  - No defenses
    - ◆ Laches
    - ◆ Unclean hands
    - ◆ Other k defenses

CONTRACTS RULE OUTLINE

I. **APPLICABLE LAW TO GOVERN THE CONTRACT**
   A. **Applicable law:** The applicable law governing a contract depends upon the subject matter of the contract.
      1. **UCC:** The Uniform Commercial Code (UCC) governs contracts for the **sale of goods**.
      2. **Common law:** The common law governs **all other contracts** except those for the sale of goods.
   B. **Uniform Commercial Code (UCC):** Article 2 of the UCC governs contracts for the **sale of goods.** Special UCC provisions apply when one or more parties are merchants. As a general principle, the UCC interprets more liberally than common law and endeavors to find that a contract exists where possible.
      1. **Goods** are defined as movable, **tangible property**.
      2. **Merchant:** A merchant is one who **deals in goods of the kind**, or one holding oneself out as having **special knowledge or skills** regarding the practices or goods involved in the contract. Merchant is construed broadly but does not include casual sellers.
   C. **Common law** applies to all contracts that do not involve the sale of goods. Typically, this involves contracts for the provision of **services** or relating to **real property**. Some courts use UCC provisions by analogy to assess common law contracts.
   D. **Predominance test:** Where a contract includes **both goods and the provision of services,** the predominance test determines if the UCC or common law governs the contract. Determine the **predominant purpose** for the contract as a whole and the law governing that area provides the **applicable law for the entire contract**.

   > **Exam tip:** The application of the predominance test will likely have lots of factual analysis and a two-sided argument without a clear answer. If so, throughout your analysis of the rest of the issues, be sure to analyze the facts using both the UCC and the common law where the two rules differ.

II. **CONTRACT FORMATION:** A valid contract requires **mutual assent, which consists of an offer and acceptance, and consideration.**
   A. **Offer (common law):** An offer is a **manifestation of willingness to enter into a bargain.** An offer requires a demonstration of **intent** to enter into a contract, **definite and certain terms**, and **communication to the offeree.**
      1. **Intent:** The words or conduct of the offeror (the person making the offer) must demonstrate a present intent to enter into a contract.
         a. **Language:** The language used by the offeror can help establish the offeror's intent. While precise language, such as "I offer," clearly establishes an offer, it is not required. The **objective standard** of how a reasonable person would interpret the language is used to determine intent.
         b. **Context:** The context in which an offer is made can help establish intent.
            1. **Offers in jest:** An offer made in jest is **not a valid offer**.
            2. **Preliminary negotiations:** A party's language may invite preliminary negotiations but lack present willingness to contract (e.g., "I'm thinking of selling my car." or "I'd consider taking $5,000 for my car.")
               a. **Solicitation of bids** is likely preliminary negotiations.
               b. **Advertisements** are typically invitations to deal and not offers to sell.
                  i. **Exception:** Ads containing **words of commitment** and where the **offeree can be identified** with specificity can be sufficiently definite to be an offer.
               c. **Catalogs** with specified goods and prices are typically an invitation to deal, not an offer.
            3. **Rewards and auction bids:** Can be offers if it is **clear who can accept/win.**

2. **Definite and certain terms:** The offer must contain definite and certain terms such that the **content of the bargain can be determined** and enforced. (The parties can communicate back and forth, which as a whole provides the essential terms, and the court may supply some missing terms.)
   a. **Quantity:** The quantity term must be stated or ascertainable.
   b. **Time of performance** can be a missing term supplied by the court as a "reasonable" time.
   c. **Identity of the parties:** The parties must be identified.
   d. **Price:** Price must be stated for real estate contracts. However, the UCC provides "reasonable price at the time of delivery" if missing.
   e. **Subject matter** must be identified clearly.

> **Memorization tip:** Use **QTIPS** to memorize the essential terms of a valid contract: **Q**uantity, **T**ime of performance, **I**dentity of the parties, **P**rice, and **S**ubject matter.

3. **Communicated to the offeree:** An offer must be communicated to the offeree, such that the **offeree has knowledge** of the offer.

B. **Offer (UCC):** Inviting acceptance in **any manner** and by **any medium reasonable** in the circumstances (the UCC allows for a more liberal interpretation and finds offers easily; a purchase order for example is typically an offer under the UCC). The UCC will use gap fillers for missing terms except for subject matter and quantity.

C. **Termination of the offer**
   1. **Rejection:** An outright rejection of the offer by the offeree.
   2. **Counteroffer:** A counteroffer is an offer made by the offeree to the offeror regarding the same subject matter as the original offer but containing different terms. It is a **rejection** and a **new offer**.
      a. **Distinguish counteroffer from inquiry:** Inquiring about the possibility of another deal will not serve as a counteroffer and rejection. Analyze the language used (e.g., "Would you take less. . .?" is an inquiry, not a counteroffer.)
   3. **Revocation:** An offeror can **revoke an ordinary offer at any time before acceptance,** which terminates the power of acceptance. A revocation can be:
      a. **Direct or indirect (can be from third parties who are reliable).**
      b. **Unambiguous words or conduct** that is inconsistent with the intention to contract (e.g., selling the good that is the subject of the contract to another party.)
      c. **Of which the offeree is aware:** The offeree need only be made aware of words or conduct of the offeror that indicates the offer was revoked.
      d. **Exceptions: Some offers are irrevocable offers, including:**
         1. UCC "firm offers" are irrevocable even without consideration. "Firm offers" require the following:
            a. **Made by a merchant** (one dealing in goods of the kind).
            b. **Signed writing:** In writing and signed (electronic acceptable).
            c. **Gives assurance it will be held open** for a specified time, during which it's irrevocable.
            d. **Three-month limit on irrevocability:** No offer can be irrevocable for longer than three months without consideration. Even if a "firm offer" states it will remain open for longer than three months, it will only be irrevocable for three months. But the offer is *not automatically revoked after three months*. So, for the first three months the offeror cannot revoke the offer, but after three months the offeror *can* revoke their offer. If the offeror *does not revoke* their offer *it will remain open* and can still be accepted.
         2. **Option contract:** An option contract is one where the offeror grants the offeree an "option" to enter into a contract for a specified period of time and promises the offer will

be held open during that time. **Consideration is required** for an option contract. The offer will be **irrevocable for the stated option period**.

   3. **Detrimental reliance and partial performance:** An offer will be temporarily irrevocable if the offeree has **made preparations to perform** in reasonable detrimental reliance on the offer or **has performed** in part.

      a. **Unilateral contract:** Once performance has begun, the offer is temporarily irrevocable.

      b. **Bilateral contract:** Making preparations to perform may make the offer irrevocable if justice requires (e.g., subcontractor bids.)

   4. **Lapse of time:** The offeror can set a **time limit** for acceptance, **or** if none is stated, it remains open only for a **"reasonable" time**. Once the time has passed, the offer lapses and may not be accepted. An oral offer typically lapses at the end of the conversation.

   5. **Death or incapacity of either party:** If either the offeror or offeree dies or loses the legal capacity to enter into a contract, the power to accept an outstanding offer is **terminated automatically**, unless the offer was an option with paid consideration.

D. Acceptance: An acceptance is the **manifestation of assent to the terms of the offer.** This can be by **words** (oral or written) creating an express contract, or by **conduct** creating an implied-in-fact contract.

   1. **Two methods of acceptance:** The offeror is the master of the offer and thus proscribes the method by which the offer can be accepted.

      a. **Bilateral:** A bilateral contract is where **both parties make promises** to perform.

      b. **Unilateral:** A unilateral contract exchanges the **offeror's promise** for the **offeree's actual performance** of the requested act.

   2. **Power of acceptance:** The power of acceptance is subject to some limitations:

      a. **Timing:** Acceptance must be within a **"reasonable time."**

      b. **Only by offeree:** Only a person to **whom the offer is directed** may accept.

      c. **Only in response to an offer:** The offeree must **know of the offer** before accepting. (E.g.: Where a reward has been offered, a person performing the requested act without knowing about the reward cannot "accept" by performance.)

      d. **Manner of acceptance:** An offer must be accepted in the **manner required by the offer.** But, if no method is specified, acceptance can be by **any "reasonable" means.**

      e. **Objective standard:** Acceptance by performance is judged by an objective standard.

   3. **When an acceptance is effective**

      a. **Mailbox rule:** The mailbox rule provides an **acceptance is effective** upon **proper dispatch**.

         1. **Proper dispatch** requires that the offeree **no longer has control** or possession of the acceptance, such as with a properly mailed letter.

      b. **Mailbox rule exceptions:**

         1. Where the **offer itself provides otherwise,** the terms of the offer control.

         2. **Option contract is effective upon receipt.**

         3. **If both an acceptance and a rejection are sent,** the rule depends on which was dispatched first.

            a. **Rejection dispatched first**, the acceptance will only become **effective if it is received first**.

            b. **Acceptance dispatched first** is **effective on dispatch** in accordance with the normal rule.

   4. **Acceptance varying from offer: The rule** depends on if common law or the UCC applies.

      a. **Common law "mirror image" rule:** An acceptance must be a precise mirror image of the offer. If the response conflicts at all with the terms of the offer, or adds new terms, the purported acceptance is a **rejection and counteroffer.**

      b. **UCC 2-207:** Any "expression of acceptance" or "written confirmation" will act as an **acceptance even if terms are "additional to or different from"** those contained in the offer, unless acceptance is expressly made conditional on assent to additional or different terms. The outcome here depends on if the terms are additional or different from those in the offer.

1. **Additional terms in the acceptance:** The **"battle of the forms"** rule determines the outcome and depends on if one or both parties are merchants.
  a. **If one party or more is not a merchant**, any additional term is a **proposal** and will not become a part of the contract unless the other party assents.
  b. **If both parties are merchants,** the additional term **automatically becomes a part of the contract** *unless*:
    i. **Offer expressly limits acceptance to its terms.**
    ii. **Material alteration** with added term (e.g., warranty disclaimer).
    iii. **Objection:** If the offeror objects to the additional term within a **reasonable time.**
2. **Different (conflicting) terms** are treated in three ways depending on the jurisdiction:
  a. **Knock-out rule (majority rule):** Conflicting terms cancel each other out and **neither enters the contract.** The contract then consists of the agreed-to terms, and the court will supply missing terms if needed.
    i. **UCC:** The contract then consists of the **agreed-to terms** and **UCC gap fillers** will supply the missing terms as follows:
      (A). **Price is the "reasonable price"** at the time of delivery.
      (B). **Place of delivery:** buyer **picks up the goods** from the seller.
      (C). **Time for shipment** is a "reasonable time."
      (D). **Time for payment:** Payment is **due upon receipt** of goods.
  b. **Treat as additional terms (minority rule)***:* apply test above in additional terms.
  c. **Fall out rule (another minority rule):** offeror's terms control.
  d. **Common law:** The contract then consists of the **agreed-to terms** and the **court may supply missing terms** on a "reasonable basis" if necessary. The courts can apply the UCC rules through analogy.

5. **Acceptance by shipping goods:** Unless the offer specifies otherwise, an offer to buy goods may be **accepted by shipping the goods** (e.g., a "purchase order" sent to the seller and the seller fills the order). The offer is accepted by promptly shipping **conforming or nonconforming** goods.
  a. **Shipping conforming goods is an acceptance.**
  b. **Shipping nonconforming goods:** The effect of shipping nonconforming goods depends upon whether the seller acknowledges the nonconformity of the shipment.
    1. **Shipment without acknowledging nonconformity:** The offer has been **accepted and breached** simultaneously.
    2. **Shipment with acknowledging nonconformity:** This is an "accommodation" to the buyer and **will not serve as an acceptance.** Rather, the seller is making a **counteroffer** that the buyer is then free to accept or reject.

Exam tip: **Mutual assent** is frequently tested on the bar exam. Some questions will state that the parties have a valid contract so mutual assent is not at issue. If so, do not waste time establishing the contract, just identify the parties and terms of the contract and move on to the issues raised in the question. Where mutual assent is an issue requiring depth of analysis, there will typically be a series of communications (oral or written) between the parties. It is helpful to sketch out a brief **timeline** in chronological order, noting the dates of each communication and what transpired on each date. Analyze each communication in order to determine if a contract has formed. First, **look for an offer**. Determine if the first communication is an offer. If it's not, consider if the next communication is an offer (because it can't be an acceptance). If the first communication is an offer, look to the next communication to determine if it's an **acceptance** or **a rejection and counteroffer**. Continue looking at each communication until you find an offer and acceptance. Any communication that occurs **after** the valid acceptance must pertain either to a new contract, a potential modification of the contract at hand, or an issue related to breach.

E. **Consideration** is a **bargained-for exchange** of legal detriment and can be a promise to do an act, or forbearance from doing an act one is otherwise entitled to do.

1. **Illusory promise:** An illusory promise is one **not supported by consideration** and is thus not enforceable. The promisor appears to promise something, but in fact does not commit to do anything at all. (E.g.: *A*'s promise to buy as many widgets as they want is illusory because *A* can say they don't want any widgets and thus wouldn't have to perform.)

2. **Requirements and output contracts** can appear illusory but are not because the **implied obligation of good faith** requires both parties to use their best efforts to supply the goods and promote their sale.

   a. **Requirements contracts:** In requirements contracts, the parties agree that the seller will be the **exclusive source of all of the buyer's requirements** for a particular item for a specified period of time.

   b. **Output contracts:** In an output contract, the buyer agrees to buy **all of the seller's output** of a particular item for a specified period of time.

   > **Exam tip:** Should a requirements or output contract be at issue on an essay question, analyze the facts under the rules and explain **why** the contract is not illusory.

3. **Inadequate consideration examples:** A court will not inquire into the adequacy of consideration, but some types of promises do not provide adequate consideration.

   a. **Gifts:** A promise to make a gift is unenforceable.

   b. **Sham or nominal consideration** is insufficient, but it must be very obvious because the court is reluctant to inquire into the adequacy of consideration.

   c. **Past consideration:** A promise to pay for a benefit received in the past will **not provide current consideration** on a new bargain subject to **two exceptions:**

      1. **New promise to pay a past debt that is now barred (i.e., statute of limitations has run)** can provide valid consideration if it is made in writing or partially performed.

      2. **New promise to pay for benefits previously received** at the promisor's request or in an emergency can be binding without consideration.

   d. **Preexisting duty rule:** The preexisting duty rule provides that a promise to do something that one is already legally obligated to do will **not provide consideration** for a new bargain unless the duty is owed to a third person.

F. **Promissory estoppel:** A promise that **foreseeably** (to the promisor) **induces reliance**, and is actually relied upon, may be enforceable to prevent injustice, even without consideration.

1. **Substitute for consideration:** Promissory estoppel serves as a substitute for consideration.

2. **Recovery is limited to reliance damages**, so the plaintiff will not get the benefit of the bargain, but rather will be put in the position they would have been in if the promise was never made.

   > **Exam tip:** If a contract is lacking consideration, consider if promissory estoppel could make the promise enforceable. The recovery is higher with a valid contract, but promissory estoppel is a good alternative where consideration is lacking.

III. **DEFENSES TO CONTRACT FORMATION:** These issues can be spotted at the time of contracting.

A. The **Statute of Frauds (SOF)** provides that certain types of contracts are unenforceable unless they are in **writing**.

1. **Five categories** of contracts "fall within" the SOF.

   a. **Marriage:** A contract made upon consideration of marriage, such as a promise to do or not do something if we marry (e.g., prenuptial agreements).

b. **Real property:** The sale of an interest in land (e.g., sale, mortgage, leases, or easements of at least one-year duration).

c. Promise to pay the **debt of another** (suretyship).

d. **One year:** A contract incapable of being fully performed within one year of the making. Time starts to run the day after the contract is made, not how long it takes to perform under the contract. Performance must be **literally impossible** to perform in one year (e.g., contract to perform a concert on a date over one year after the date of contracting).

e. **Sale of Goods of $500 or more.**

> **Memorization tip:** Use **Mr. Dog** to memorize the five categories of contracts to which the SOF applies: **M**arriage, **R**eal Property, **D**ebt of another, **O**ne-year, **G**oods.

2. **SOF Exceptions** apply to each of the five categories of contracts covered by the SOF and an oral contract would be enforceable if:

a. Made **in consideration of marriage** consisting of *mutual promises to marry* (e.g., promises between each other that are not the consideration for the marriage such as agreeing to sign a prenuptial agreement in consideration for marriage).

b. Made for an interest in **real estate** where the *conveyance* has been made, or *performed in part* (payment, improvements, or possession—think PIP) will be enforceable. Most jurisdictions require two out of the three for PIP to work.

c. To pay the **debt of another** where the *"main purpose"* of the agreement is the *promisor's own economic interest or an indemnity contract.*

d. **The contract can't be performed in one year, but full performance has occurred.** If only part performance has occurred, restitution may still be available.

e. **Sale of goods $500 or more where:**
   1. **Goods are accepted or paid for**, or
   2. **Admission** in a pleading or court testimony, or
   3. **Specially manufactured goods** are not suitable for sale to others.

> **Memorization tip:** Following Mr. Dog for the categories that raise the SOF, continue with **Mr. Dog Can Pay Money For A Puppy And Some Milkbones.** That will enable you to memorize all exceptions too (**Can**—consideration for marriage; **Pay**—part performance PIP for real property; **Money**—main purpose or maker's benefit for debt; **For**—full performance for one year rule; **A**—accepted goods; **Puppy**—paid for goods; **And**—admission for goods; **Some Milkbones** for specially manufactured goods).

3. **SOF writing requirement:** There must be one or more writings that combined include the **essential terms** of the contract (including the subject matter) and that is **signed by the party to be charged.** The writing need not be addressed to or sent to the other party. Also, the writing need not be made at the time the promise is made. The writing requirement is subject to three exceptions.

a. **Exception:** The **merchant's confirming memo** allows a writing to be enforced against both the *signer and recipient* where it is:
   1. **Between two merchants.**
   2. **One party receives signed confirmation (can be letterhead, fax, etc.) and has reason to know its contents.**
   3. **Except if the recipient objects within ten days of receipt.**

b. **Exception: Judicial admission** in pleadings or testimony that there was an agreement will allow the agreement to be enforced without a writing.

c. **Exception:** A **promissory estoppel** theory where a party detrimentally relied on the agreement. (This allows a plaintiff to recover only to the extent necessary to prevent injustice.)

Exam tip: The SOF operates as a defense to enforcement of an oral contract. When analyzing the SOF use the following approach: (1) Does the contract **fall within the SOF** (Mr. Dog)? (2) Do any of the Mr. Dog SOF **exceptions** apply? (Mr. Dog Can Pay Money For A Puppy And Some Milkbones.) (3) Does the **writing satisfy the SOF?** (Consider whether the writing includes the essential terms and is signed by the party to be charged or if there is a proper merchant's confirming memo or a judicial admission.) (4) Can the doctrine of promissory estoppel be applied to enforce the oral contract?

B. **Misrepresentation:** The tort of **misrepresentation** may serve as a defense where one party makes a **misrepresentation prior to** the other signing the contract.
   1. The **state of mind** of the party making the misrepresentation **need not be intentional** (if it is intentional it is fraudulent misrepresentation, see below); it can be done negligently or even innocently (nonfraudulent misrepresentation).
   2. **False statement of material fact:** The misrepresentation must pertain to a material fact to the contract, not an opinion.
   3. **Justifiable and actual reliance:** It must be justifiable to rely on the misrepresentation, and the party must in fact rely on the misrepresentation.
   4. **Damages:** Plaintiff must suffer a pecuniary loss.
C. **Fraud:** The tort of **fraud** (intentional misrepresentation) may serve as a contract defense where one party makes an **intentional misrepresentation prior to** the signing of the contract. Prima facie case:
   1. **False statement of material fact:** The misrepresentation must pertain to a material fact to the contract, not an opinion;
   2. **Knowledge of the statement's falsity** or **reckless disregard** of the truth (scienter);
   3. **Intent to induce reliance** so other party will enter into the contract;
   4. **Justifiable and actual reliance:** It must be justifiable to rely on the misrepresentation, and the party must in fact rely on the misrepresentation; and
   5. **Damages:** Plaintiff must suffer a pecuniary loss. Plaintiff may also be eligible to receive punitive damages.
D. **Unconscionability:** If the court finds a contract term so unfavorable to one party that no reasonable person would have agreed to it, the court may decline to enforce the contract or any unconscionable part of the contract. Unconscionability is assessed at the time of contract formation.
E. A **mistake** is a belief not in accord with the facts and can be mutual or unilateral.
   1. A **mutual mistake** is one made by **both parties** to the contract. A contract can be voidable for mutual mistake if:
      a. **Basic assumption:** The mistake is as to a basic assumption that existed at the time the contract was formed; and
      b. **Material effect:** The mistake has a material effect on the deal; and
      c. **Risk:** The adversely affected party did not assume the risk of the mistake.
   2. A **unilateral mistake** is one made by only one party to the deal. The mistaken party must show the three factors for mutual mistake and that the **other party knew, or should have known** of the mistake.
F. **Illegality** of the contract's subject matter.

> **Memorization tip:** Think **DIMSUM** as a quick issues checklist for the defenses to contract formation. **D**efenses, **I**llegality, **M**isrepresentation, **S**tatute of Frauds, **U**nconscionability, and **M**istake.

IV. **CONTRACT TERMS AND OTHER PERFORMANCE ISSUES:** Contract terms are given their **plain meaning.**

A. **Conditions:** A condition is an **event that must occur before performance of the other party is due**. If it does not occur, performance of the second party is excused. Conditions can be express or constructive (implied). Compare this to a promise (if a party does not fulfill a promise the party is in breach and it does not affect the other party's promise to perform.) When unclear, courts tend to favor finding promises over conditions.

1. **Express:** An express condition is created by the language of the parties demonstrating the **intent to have a condition** (e.g., "upon condition that").

2. **Constructive:** A constructive condition is one **supplied by the court** for fairness. Each parties' performance is generally a constructive condition to the subsequent performance required by the other party.

3. **Compliance with conditions**
   a. **Express conditions** require strict compliance.
   b. **Constructive conditions** only require substantial performance.

4. **Waiver of conditions:** The party the condition is intended to benefit always has the power to waive it. Waiver can occur by:
   a. **Benefit:** Receiving and keeping a benefit, **or**
   b. **Failure to insist on compliance** can operate as a waiver.
   c. A **waiver can be retracted** unless the other party detrimentally relied.

B. **Parol Evidence Rule (PER):** The PER limits the extent to which evidence of discussions or writings made **prior to, or contemporaneous with**, the signed written contract can be admitted and **considered as part of the agreement**. It depends on whether the writing is a total integration or partial integration.

1. **Partial integration** is one intended to be the **final expression** of the agreement, but *not* **intended to include all details** of the parties' agreement.
   a. PER is *not* allowed to **contradict** a term in the partial integration.
   b. PER *is* allowed to **supplement** a term in the partial integration.

2. **Total integration** is one that not only is the **final expression** of the agreement but is also **intended to include all details** of the parties' agreement. A **merger clause** states the agreement is complete. Modernly, a merger clause is a factor used to establish a total integration.
   a. PER is *not* allowed to **contradict** or **supplement** a term in the total integration.

3. **PER exceptions:** The PER will not apply to bar certain types of evidence.
   a. **Contract formation or enforcement defects:** The PER does not bar evidence of contract defects (e.g., allegations of fraud, duress, mistake, lack of consideration, illegality, or anything that would make the contract void).
   b. **Conditions precedent to the contract's effectiveness:** The PER does not bar evidence of conditions precedent to the contract's effectiveness. This exception applies to a situation where the parties agree that the **contract itself will not take force** until some stated condition is met. (E.g.: A contract is negotiated between *A* and *B*, but the parties orally agree that the contract will not be in effect until *B*'s board of trustees votes to approve the contract. PER will not bar the introduction of evidence regarding the condition that the board of trustees must approve the contract, because that is a condition precedent to the contract's effectiveness.)
   c. **Ambiguous terms:** The PER does not bar evidence regarding the interpretation of ambiguous contract terms. The UCC provides the following rules to aid in contract interpretation:

1. **Course of performance** refers to evidence of the conduct of **these parties** regarding the **contract at hand**. (This is the best evidence to use if available.)

2. **Course of dealing** refers to evidence of the conduct of **these parties** regarding **past contracts** between them. (Second best.)

3. **Usage of trade** refers to evidence of the meaning **others** in the same **industry and/or locality** would attach to a term. (Least persuasive so only use as evidence if previous two unavailable.)

> **Exam tip:** Whether an agreement is a total or partial integration can be a tricky call. Since there will rarely be a clear answer as to what the contracting parties intended, be prepared on an essay to analyze the PER both ways. Chronology is very important in contracts questions and is critical in analyzing the PER. If communication occurs **after** the writing, analyze it under the PER, explain that the PER does not bar such evidence, and also consider if there is a contract modification or an anticipatory repudiation at issue under the facts since these issues may also arise.

C. **Risk of loss:** Contracts are often silent about which party bears the risk of loss when **goods are damaged** *before* the buyer receives them. If goods are destroyed before the risk of loss passes, the contract is avoided (as if there was no contract).

1. **Goods shipped by third-party carrier:** The risk of loss depends on if the contract is a shipment or destination contract.

   a. **Shipment contract (presumed if not stated):** The **risk of loss passes to the buyer** when the **seller delivers** the goods **to the third-party carrier** *and* **makes a reasonable contract for their carriage** (transport) *and* **notifies the buyer** of the shipment.

   b. **Destination contract:** Delivery is required at a specific location. The **risk of loss passes to the buyer** upon **delivery** of the goods.

   c. **FOB (free on board)** is a contract term followed by a location and means the **risk of loss passes to the buyer at the named location**. FOB contracts can be shipment or destination contracts.

2. **Goods not shipped by third-party carrier** (goods are delivered by the seller or picked up by the buyer): **The risk of loss passes to the buyer** upon **taking possession** of the goods.

D. **Contract modification**

1. **Oral contract modifications:** Oral contract modifications are generally allowed.

   a. **Except Statute of Frauds (SOF):** With an oral contract modification, if the **contract as modified** falls within the **SOF**, the **modification must be in writing.** Where the modification must be in writing and isn't, the modification is unenforceable, and the original contract stands and is enforceable. However, the ineffective oral modification may operate as a waiver.

2. **Contract modification requirements** differ depending on whether the contract is subject to the common law or the UCC.

   a. **Common law: Mutual assent** and **consideration is required.**

      1. **Common law:** "No oral modifications" clauses are **not enforced** at common law, so despite the clause the parties can orally modify the contract.

   b. **UCC: Mutual assent** and **good faith** is required, but **consideration is *not* required.**

> **Issue spotting tip:** If the modification must be in writing and isn't, the original contract stands and the modification is not enforceable. However, consider whether any facts give rise to an analysis of **detrimental reliance** as a way to enforce the modified contract. In addition, whenever there are communications that occur subsequent to contracting, briefly address why the PER does not apply in addition to the potential contract modification.

E. **Contracts of two or more parties**
   1. **Third-party beneficiary** is a person whom the **promisor intends to benefit** by the contract but who is **not already a party** to the contract.
      a. **Intended beneficiary:** An intended beneficiary is one **intended by the promisor to benefit** from the contract. An intended third-party beneficiary **can sue** to enforce the contract. There are two types of intended beneficiaries.
         1. **Creditor beneficiary:** This is a third party whom the promisor intends to benefit because the promisor **owes them money**.
         2. **Donee beneficiary:** This is a third-party beneficiary to whom the promisor intends to give a **gift**.
      b. **Incidental beneficiary:** An incidental beneficiary is one who **indirectly benefits** from the contract, but that result is **not the intent** of the promisor. An incidental third-party beneficiary **cannot sue** to enforce a contract (e.g., an adjacent property owner to a large planned development is an incidental beneficiary).
   2. **Assignment and/or delegation** concern a **transfer** of rights or duties already owed under the contract **to a third person**.
      a. **Assignment:** An assignment is when a party to an existing contract **transfers their rights** under the contract to a **third party**. The **assignor** (party receiving performance) assigns to the **assignee** (third party) the performance due under the contract from the **obligor** (party performing). The general rule is that **all rights are assignable**.
         1. **No consideration** is required.
         2. A **gratuitous assignment** (gift) is allowed.
         3. The **assignee "stands in the shoes"** of the assignor and takes subject to all defenses, set-offs, and counterclaims the assignor has.
         4. **Exception: Can't assign if material change** in duty/risk.

> **Exam tip:** Even if the **contract prohibits assignments,** often the assignment itself will **still be enforceable,** BUT the party who assigned the rights will **be in breach.** Be careful to distinguish the assignment being still valid despite the breach.

      b. **Delegation** is when a party to an existing contract **appoints to a third party** the **duties owed** under the contract. The **delegator** (party owing performance) appoints to the **delegatee** (third party now performing) the performance due under the contract to the **obligee** (party receiving performance). The general rule is that **most duties can be delegated.**
         1. **Delegator** (party owing performance) **remains liable.**
         2. **Exception: Can't delegate duties of special skill** or judgment.
   3. **Novation:** A novation occurs when the obligee (party receiving performance) **expressly agrees to accept** the performance of the delegatee (the new third party performer) instead of the delegator (the original party owing performance) and **releases the delegator from liability.** A **novation terminates the liability of the delegator.**

V. **BREACH OF CONTRACT ISSUES**
   A. **Anticipatory repudiation:** An anticipatory repudiation is an **unequivocal** expression by a party, occurring **before the time for performance** is due, that they **will not perform** under the contract.
      1. **Non-repudiating party response:** Once a party has anticipatorily repudiated, the non-repudiating party can take four courses of action:
         a. **Sue immediately** for breach even though the time to perform under the contract has not yet passed (**cannot do** this if the only part of the performance left is payment), **or**
         b. **Suspend performance** and wait until performance is due to sue, **or**
         c. **Treat the contract as discharged** and the repudiation as an **offer to rescind, or**
         d. **Urge performance** under the contract and sue later if efforts are futile.
      2. Non-breaching party must try to **mitigate the damage.**

3. **Repudiating party can retract** the repudiation, except where the other party:
   a. **Sues for breach,**
   b. **Changes position in reliance** on the repudiation, or
   c. **States the repudiation is** considered **final.**
4. **Right to demand adequate assurances:** Where the conduct of a party is not unequivocal enough to rise to the level of an anticipatory repudiation, but does cause **reasonable grounds for insecurity** about their forthcoming performance, the insecure party can **demand adequate assurances** of due performance. This must be done in **writing.** The insecure party may **suspend their own performance** until receiving adequate assurances.
   a. **Failure to timely respond**: A **repudiation** of the contract occurs when a party who received a **justified written demand** for adequate assurances fails to respond within a reasonable time, not to exceed **30 days.**

Issue spotting tip: Several issues tend to cluster with **anticipatory repudiation.** Look for **PER** and/or **contract modification** and/or the **right to demand adequate assurances.**

B. **Material breach under common law:** A contract breach is material where there was **not substantial performance** on the contract. A material breach will excuse the performance of the non-breaching party. The following are factors to consider in the analysis:
   1. Party **did not receive substantial benefit of the bargain.**
   2. **Extent of any part or full performance.**
   3. **Willfulness of breach:** The more intentional it is, the more likely it's a material breach.
   4. **Time is *not* of the essence** in a contract **unless specifically agreed to**, and thus a delay will not amount to a material breach.
   5. **Divisible contract:** A divisible contract is one where the parties have divided up their performance into **agreed equivalents**, which means that each corresponding part performance is roughly equal to the corresponding part of compensation. (E.g.: *A* and *B* agree that *B* will paint 15 identical cars of *A* for $500 each.) These are similar to installment contracts under the UCC.
      a. **Breach of a divisible contract:** For purposes of breach, each agreed equivalent **operates as a separate contract.**
C. **Material breach under UCC:** The rules for breach are different under the UCC.
   1. **Perfect tender:** The "perfect tender" rule applies to contracts for a **single delivery** and provides that if the goods tendered **fail to conform** to the contract **in any respect**, the buyer has three choices:
      a. **Reject the whole** within a reasonable time, **or**
      b. **Accept the whole, or**
      c. **Accept any commercial unit** (i.e., a "whole" part—a set of 12 mugs if sold in packs of 12; or one machine if sold individually) **and reject the rest.**
   2. **Exception—installment contracts:** The "perfect tender" rule does not apply to installment contracts where the parties have contracted for more than one delivery (here the right to reject is determined by **"substantial conformity"** and whether the nonperfect tender **substantially affects the contract**; buyer cannot reject if seller can cure).

Exam tip: One way an offer can be accepted is by the shipment of nonconforming goods. When this happens, it is both an acceptance of the offer and a simultaneous breach of the same contract because the goods tendered fail under the "perfect tender" rule, so look for these issues to go together.

---

3. **Seller's right to cure:** The buyer's right to reject nonconforming goods is subject to the seller's right to cure the defect. A seller may cure the defect any time before performance is due, with the following provisions:
   a. **Notice:** The seller must give notice to the buyer; **and**
   b. **New tender:** The seller must make a new tender within the time for performance. The seller may even make a new tender *after* the time for performance if the seller has a **reasonable belief** this would be acceptable to the buyer.
D. **Minor breach:** If a breach is not material, it is a minor breach and the nonbreaching party **may recover damages but must still perform**.

> **Exam tip:** Always analyze if a breach is material or minor. There is rarely a clear answer, so use all the facts and argue both ways where appropriate.

E. **Warranties:** There are several contract warranties that may be violated.
   1. **Express:** An express warranty is made explicitly.
   2. **Implied warranty of merchantability** warrants that goods will be **fit for the ordinary purpose** for which such goods are used. (Warranty can be disclaimed—i.e., goods sold "as is.")
   3. **Warranty of fitness for a particular purpose** only applies where the **buyer relies** on the **seller's judgment to select appropriate goods** for a stated purpose. (Warranty can be disclaimed but only if in writing and conspicuous).
   4. **Implied covenant of good faith and fair dealing** is inherent in every contract.
F. **Accord and satisfaction**
   1. **Accord:** An accord is an agreement where one party promises to **render substitute performance** and the other promises to **accept that substitute** in discharge of the existing duty. It does not discharge the obligation under the original agreement until the substitute performance has been completed (a satisfaction). **Consideration is required**.
   2. **Satisfaction:** A satisfaction is the **performance of the accord,** which then discharges both the original agreement and the accord. If the accord is breached the other party can sue on the original contract or the accord.

VI. **DEFENSES TO CONTRACT ENFORCEMENT:** These defenses can arise at any time in the contract life cycle and **discharge the duty to perform** under the contract.
   A. **Contract defenses:** Though not "defenses" in the traditional sense, **any failure of the underlying contract can operate as a defense to enforcement**, such as:
      1. **No mutual assent or mistake.**
      2. **Lack of consideration.**
      3. **No writing, where a writing is required by the SOF.**
      4. **Misrepresentation, fraud, or duress** at the time of contracting.
         a. **Misrepresentation/fraud.**
         b. **Undue influence/duress:** Extreme pressure, coercion, or threat that leads to invalidation of the contract (for undue influence look at susceptibility to pressure due to the relationship).
      5. **Unconscionability:** Unfairness at the time of contracting.
      6. **Lack of capacity** to contract because of **minority** or **mental incapacity** (not being of sound mind or intoxicated).
      7. **Illegality of contract.**
      8. **Condition precedent not met:** When one party must satisfy a condition before the other party's performance is due, and the condition has not been satisfied, it serves as a defense to the nonperformance of the second party.
   B. **Impossibility** occurs when a supervening, unforeseeable event makes performance **impossible** and thus discharges performance. The event must be one that **neither party assumed the risk** of, and performance must be literally impossible. Examples include destruction of the contract subject matter, illegality, death, or incapacity—modernly impracticability is the best argument).

C. **Impracticability** occurs when the occurrence of an event the parties assumed would not occur makes performance **extremely and unreasonably difficult.** The event must concern a **basic assumption** of the contract and the parties must not have **allocated the risk** of that event to the party seeking to use this defense (financial losses are usually insufficient for impracticability).

D. **Frustration of purpose** occurs when a party's purpose for entering the contract is destroyed by supervening events. Both parties **must know the purpose** of the contract, the event must **not be reasonably foreseeable**, and **frustration must be total**.

> **Exam tip:** Think very broadly for defenses/excuses to a contract. All potential problems with the underlying contract can serve as a defense to the contract. Impossibility, impracticability, and frustration of purpose are an issues cluster. Impossibility is rarely an excuse, but impracticability might be.

VII. **CONTRACT REMEDIES:** information about contract remedies is also contained in the remedies chapter.

A. **Measure of damages**

1. **Potential damage limitation issues:** The concepts below have the potential to limit a damages award. These limitations apply to expectation, consequential and incidental damages.

   a. **Foreseeable:** Damages must be foreseeable by a **reasonable person at the time of contracting,** or if the damages are unusual, the defendant needs actual notice of their possibility.

   b. **Unavoidable: There is a duty to mitigate losses.** This comes up most frequently in consequential damages for a sales contract where the buyer does not try to "cover" by obtaining goods from an alternate supplier.

   c. **Certainty:** Damages must be able to be calculated with certainty, and **not too speculative** (e.g., lost profits for a new business). If too uncertain, think of reliance damages as an option.

   d. **Causation:** Damages must be caused by the breach.

2. **Common law: Expectation damages** compensate a plaintiff for the **value of the benefit of the bargain the plaintiff expected to receive** from the contract. Expectation damages put the plaintiff in the position they would have been in if the contract was performed. (Also called *compensatory damages*.)

   a. **Real property:** This would be the difference between the **contract price and market price**.

      1. **Abatement:** Where the property measures less than the contract indicates, the court can abate the price commensurate with the actual property size.

   b. **Services:** This would be calculated by the **cost of substitute performance.**

3. **UCC expectation damages formulas**

   a. **Buyer's UCC damages—seller has goods and seller in breach**

      1. Damages are the difference between the **contract price and the cover price** (if buyer covered) OR the **contract price and market price** at the time the buyer learned of the breach.

      2. **In addition,** with either method the buyer can also recover **consequential damages** and **incidental damages** (all compensatory damages).

   b. **Buyer's UCC damages—buyer has goods and seller in breach:** Typically the seller has tendered defective goods and the buyer has kept them. Damages are the **difference between perfect goods and the value as tendered.**

   c. **Seller's UCC damages—seller has goods and buyer in breach**

      1. **If the seller resold the goods:** Damages are the difference between the **contract price and the resale price**.

      2. **If the seller did not resell the goods:** Damages are the difference between the **contract price and the market price** (as of the time delivery was to occur).

3. **Lost volume seller:** A "lost volume" seller is one who has a virtually unlimited supply of good to sell. A lost volume seller can recover **lost profits** if the seller:
    a. Has a big enough **supply to make both** the contracted sale and the resale,
    b. Would have **likely made both** sales, and
    c. Would have made a **profit on both** sales.
4. **In addition,** the seller may also recover for **incidental damages,** but *not* consequential **damages**.
    d. **Seller's UCC damages—buyer has goods and buyer in breach:** The measure of damages is the **full contract price**.
4. **Consequential damages** compensate for damages that are a **direct and foreseeable consequence** of the contract nonperformance and are unique to each plaintiff (e.g., lost profits). Consequential damages can be recovered **in addition** to expectation damages. These damages must be **foreseeable at the time of contracting**.
5. **Incidental damages** are damages for **expenses reasonably incurred** by the buyer or seller as a direct result of the breach. This includes costs such as those incurred while storing the goods, shipping the goods, inspecting them, reselling them, finding an alternative supplier, etc. (Also called *compensatory damages*.)
6. **Reliance damages** put the plaintiff in the position they would have been in had the **contract never been made**. They are used primarily where there is a contract but the expectation damages are too uncertain to calculate, so reliance damages will compensate for expenses reasonably incurred in reliance on the contract. (Also called *compensatory damages*.)
7. **Liquidated damages** are damages in an amount stipulated to in the contract. They are allowable when actual damages are **difficult to calculate,** and the amount agreed to is a **reasonable approximation** of the anticipated loss from a breach. The clause can't appear punitive and, if proper, provides the **only measure of damages recoverable** for breach.
8. **Nominal damages** are awarded where the plaintiff's rights have been violated but no financial loss has been sustained.
9. **Punitive damages** are *not* **awarded** for a standard breach of contract.

> **Exam tip:** The most frequently tested damages are expectation, consequential, and the potential limitations on damages (foreseeable, unavoidable, certainty, and causation).

B. **Legal restitutionary remedies**
1. **Quasi-contract (also referred to as restitution or quantum meruit)** is not actually a "contract" at all; rather, it is a contract implied in law to prevent injustice where there is **no enforceable contract but some relief is fair** because the **defendant has derived a benefit** and it would be unfair to allow the defendant to keep that benefit without paying money to the plaintiff in restitution. **The measure of relief is often the value of the benefit conferred.** Typical situations are:
    a. **No attempt to contract,** but defendant derived a benefit.
    b. **Unenforceable contract.**
    c. **Plaintiff in material breach** but defendant received a benefit.

> **Quasi-contract fact triggers:**
> - D allows construction (e.g., fence, garage) and says nothing
> - Contract fails (e.g., firm offer expires) but advertising in reliance
> - Contract fails (e.g., condition precedent not met) but partial performance (e.g., software program)
> - Contract fails (e.g., indefinite terms) but full performance

2. **Replevin** applies when the plaintiff wants their **personal property** returned.
3. **Ejectment** applies when the plaintiff wants their **real property** returned.

C. **Equitable restitutionary remedies**
   1. **Reformation** permits the contract to be **rewritten** to accurately reflect the agreement of the parties where the parties have a **meeting of the minds**, but the **writing is in error,** such as a scrivener's error.
   2. **Rescission** permits a party to **undo a bargain** where there is *no* **meeting of the minds.**
   3. **Grounds for rescission or reformation:** Allowed where a contract has resulted from fraud, misrepresentation, duress, or mistake.
   4. **Defenses**: The equitable defenses of **laches** and **unclean hands** apply.

D. **Temporary restraining orders** and **preliminary injunctions** can apply in contract. See the Remedies chapter for rules.

E. **Specific performance** applies where a party is **ordered by the court to render the promised performance** under the contract (permanent injunction in contract).
   1. **Valid Contract** is required with **definite and certain terms**.
   2. **Conditions** imposed on the plaintiff must be satisfied (plaintiff in good faith did their part under the contract).
   3. **Inadequate legal remedy:** Money damages can be inadequate because:
      a. **Certainty:** The monetary value of the damages can't be calculated with certainty.
         1. **Too speculative** and uncertain to calculate.
         2. **Defendant insolvent** so a damages award is worthless.
         3. **Multiplicity of lawsuits:** Because the breach gives rise to an ongoing problem or multiplicity of lawsuits.
      b. **Property in question is unique**
         1. **Real property:** Real property is always unique.
         2. **Special personal property:** Where the item is rare or has special personal significance, such as a family bible.
   4. **Mutuality of performance:** Both parties must be eligible to have their performance under the contract ordered by the court.
   5. **Feasibility of enforcement:** The order must be feasible for the court to enforce.
      a. **Jurisdiction issues:** Present a problem where the actions to be supervised are out of the court's jurisdiction and contempt power.
      b. **Court supervision issues**
         1. **Multiple series of events** poses greater potential problems.
         2. **Act requiring skill, taste, or judgment.**
         3. **Personal services** (involuntary servitude concerns). Consider an injunction on the other party if services are involved (enjoin them from performing elsewhere).
   6. **No applicable Defenses**
      a. **Traditional equitable remedy defenses**
         1. **Laches** is an **unreasonable delay** that is **prejudicial** to the defendant.
         2. **Unclean hands:** The plaintiff is engaging in **unfair dealing** in the **same disputed transaction.**
      b. **Other contract defenses:** Any failure of the contract operates as a defense that will prevent specific performance including mistake, misrepresentation, failed consideration, lack of capacity, SOF, and sale to a "bona fide purchaser" (one who took for value without notice of the situation that gives rise to the dispute).

> **Memorization tip:** Memorize the specific performance elements with the sentence "**c**hocolate **c**heesecake **i**s **m**y **f**avorite **d**essert." (**C**ontract, **C**onditions, **I**nadequate legal remedy, **M**utuality of performance, **F**easibility of enforcement, and **D**efenses are not applicable.) Each element should be established, but you should provide more expansive analysis on the elements that have more facts available to use in the analysis.

CONTRACTS ISSUES TESTED MATRIX

	Crossover	UCC	Offer	Accept	Consideration/ Promissory Estoppel	K Terms/PER	Conditions/Waiver	K Modification	Anticipatory Repudiation	SOF/Other Defenses	Discharge/ Excuse of Perf.	Performance/Breach or Warranty	Third-Party Issues	Dmgs./Quasi-K	Specific Perf.
February '24 Q5 Brian purchases maple topping from Sam		X	X	X	X					X		X		X	
July '22 Q1 Bath buys candles from Scents and boxes have water damage, covers with Hot and lightning melts candles		X	X	X	X					X	X	X		X	
July '19 Q5 Sam sells his 1965 classic Edris car to Bob and Charlie, then dies		X	X	X	X					X		X		X	X
February '20 Q3 Barn Exports hires Sam to paint a ceiling border for the lobby	Remedies		X	X	X	X				X		X		X	X
July '18 Q1 Farmer Stan sells tomatoes to Best Sauce, but rain delays the crop		X						X	X	X				X	
February '18 Q1 Austin sold Beverly a warehouse with a leaky roof	Prof. Resp.									X				X	
July '16 Q3 Dirt replaced gas-powered equipment and Builder	Remedies					X			X		X	X		X	
February '16 Q6 Bing Surfboards and Super Chemicals epoxy	Remedies	X	X	X	X	X						X		X	
February '15 Q1 Marta and Don have Bait Mate cooler contract	Remedies	X							X			X		X	
July '14 Q1 Percy and Daria landscaping contract	Remedies		X	X	X	X	X	X	X			X		X	X
July '13 Q4 Ben and Carl construction contract with Sun solar panels	Remedies		X	X	X			X			X	X		X	X
July '12 Q4 Dentist Della and Peter dental hygienist	Remedies		X	X	X	X		X	X	X		X		X	X

Continued>

	Crossover	UCC	Offer	Accept	Consideration/ Promissory Estoppel	K Terms/PER	Conditions/Waiver	K Modification	Anticipatory Repudiation	SOF/Other Defenses	Discharge/ Excuse of Perf.	Performance/Breach or Warranty	Third-Party Issues	Dmgs./Quasi-K	Specific Perf.
July '11 Q3 — Al gives Dr. Betty his office building			X	X	X					X					
February '10 Q4 — Lou, partner of firm, and Chris, the paralegal	Remedies		X	X	X		X			X				X	X
February '10 Q1 — Pat & Danco k for 4 computer programs					X	X	X	X	X					X	
February '09 Q5 — Developer & Highlands parcel			X	X		X	X				X	X		X	
July '08 Q4 — Barry & rare phaeton car	Remedies	X							X					X	X
July '08 Q3 — Owner & Builder; redwood fence			X	X									X	X	
July '07 Q5 — Paula, art acquisition & Monay painting	Remedies	X			X					X				X	X
July '06 Q3 — Resi-Clean & cleaning services			X	X	X	X	X				X	X		X	
February '06 Q5 — Marla, Larry & widget buyer	Prof. Resp.		X	X	X					X					
July '05 Q5 — Stan & Barb contract for 100 acres	Remedies		X	X	X	X	X		X	X				X	X
July '05 Q2 — Developer, ASI, MPI	Real Property					X							X		
February '05 Q2 — PC & Mart; Model X computers		X	X	X	X		X			X		X		X	
July '02 Q4 — Travelco & golf vacation to Scotland					X					X	X				
February '02 Q2 — Berelli & special Tabor tomatoes	Remedies	X			X									X	X
February '01 Q6 — Owens/Carter & new garage			X	X							X	X		X	
February '00 Q5 — Seller & Buyer; 10,000 tires		X			X							X			

Continued>

CONTRACTS PRACTICE ESSAYS, ANSWER GRIDS, AND SAMPLE ANSWERS

Contracts Question 1
February 2020, Question 3

Barn Exports hired Sam, an up-and-coming artist whose work was recently covered in Modern Buildings Magazine, to paint a one-of-a-kind artistic design along the border of the ceiling in its newly renovated lobby. After discussing the work, Ed, the president of Barn, and Sam signed a mutually drafted handwritten contract, which states in its entirety:

> Sam shall paint a unique design along the entire ceiling border of all public areas of the first-floor lobby. Barn shall pay $75,000 upon completion of the work.

When Sam began work, he was surprised that the new plaster ceiling in the lobby had not been sanded and sealed. Sam complained, but was told by Ed that preparation was part of his responsibilities. Although Sam disagreed, he spent four days sanding and sealing the ceiling. When Sam finished painting, he submitted a bill for $78,000, having added $3,000 for labor and supplies used in preparing the ceiling. In response, Barn sent a letter to Sam stating that, because he had not painted the borders in the two public restrooms in the lobby, no payment was yet due. Barn's letter also stated that it had recently spoken to several artists who perform similar work and learned that "surface preparation" was typically the responsibility of the artist.

According to Sam, before the contract was signed, he told Ed that the restrooms could not be included because his paints were not suitable for the high humidity in those locations.

Sam sued Barn for breach of contract in the amount of $78,000.

Barn countersued for specific performance to have the borders in the bathrooms painted.

1. Is Sam likely to prevail in his breach of contract lawsuit against Barn and if so, what damages will he likely recover? Discuss.

2. Is Barn likely to prevail in its lawsuit seeking specific performance against Sam? Discuss.

Contracts Question 1 Assessment
February 2020, Question 3

This is a typical example of a common law-based contracts essay question. This contract is for the provision of services—painting—and thus the common law rules apply. Recently the examiners have been testing more on UCC, but this question represents a recent common law question and includes a call on remedies.

Contracts questions are approximately evenly split between testing the common law or the UCC. The questions will either focus primarily on contract formation with a series of communication that must be analyzed to determine if, and when, a contract is formed, or the contract formation will be easy to establish, and the issues will primarily relate to defenses to formation, breach, and/or remedies. While all contracts questions typically include at least some discussion of remedies, like this question, about half of the contracts questions cover remedies to such an extent we would consider them to be crossover questions.

This question covers the commonly tested topics of breach and damages, but it also covers the much less commonly tested area of contract interpretation and the parol evidence rule. Since interpreting contract terms is infrequently tested, you may have a moment of uncertainty while you pondered how best to handle the issue. In the end, the "plain meaning" rule is so simple it could be overlooked. If you are ever uncertain or stuck, think of the question as a roleplay and brainstorm. If you represented Sam, what argument would you make to argue that "painting" does not include surface preparation? And if you represented Barn, what argument would you make to argue that it does? Think of the rules you can tie into those arguments, use headings to guide your reader, and write your argument in IRAC format. There are a variety of terms an applicant could have used to make these arguments. It is especially important to use headings when the issues are less obvious, like the contract interpretation issue here. Headings will help the grader find your analysis, which is what they are looking for in your answer.

When a question tells you the parties formed a contract, or the parties "agreed," or "signed a . . . contract," like in this question, do not waste time on contract formation issues. That is your tip that there are few points, if any, associated with discussing those issues. We recommend very quickly establishing the terms of the contract like shown here and moving on to discuss the major issues.

As a general rule on essays, whenever you can split your analysis into sections, you should do so. Your analysis will be more thorough and typically gain more points. Here, there are two terms in the completion of the contract (fact sets) that the parties disagreed over: 1.) the prep work, and 2.) the lobby bathrooms. The analysis of the two fact sets will be factually distinct, so it is best to think of them separately. As you can see by our organization, we organize by issue/rule first, then split the analysis out by the two factual issues using sub-headings for each fact set for clarity. This approach works well anytime there is more than one fact set that you are using to analyze a rule. It is a common pattern in essay questions because the bar examiners like to see that you can analyze the same rule using different facts, and frequently you will reach different conclusions because of the factual differences.

Make note of the areas highlighted in **bold** on the corresponding grid. The bold areas highlight the issues, analysis, and conclusions that are likely **required** to receive a passing score on this question.

Issue	Rule	Fact Application	Conclusion
Governing Law	• UCC applies to the sale of goods (tangible moveable items) • Common Law applies to all other agreements, including services	Here, the parties have contracted for Sam to paint a one-of-a-kind artistic design along the border of the ceiling in Barn's new lobby. Sam will be providing a service of his artistic talent, so the common law will govern.	Common law applies
Is Sam likely to prevail in a breach of contract lawsuit against Barn and if so, what damages will he likely recover?			
Contract Formation	Contract requires an offer with clear and definite terms, acceptance, and consideration.	• Here the parties entered into a "mutually drafted" handwritten contract that states, **"Sam shall paint a unique design along the entire ceiling border of all public areas of the first-floor lobby. Barn shall pay $75,000 upon completion of the work."** • This is sufficient to show mutual assent of offer and acceptance. • The consideration is the exchange of Sam's artistic ability for Barn's $75,000.	Contract is properly formed
Mistake	A contract is voidable for mutual mistake if: • The mistake was to a basic assumption at the time K formed; • Material effect on K; and • Adversely party didn't assume the risk	• Barn may argue there was a mutual mistake as to what "all public areas of the first-floor lobby" entailed, since Barn claims it includes the restrooms, and Sam claims it does not. The discrepancy on what was to be painted would have an effect on Sam's performance, thus the contract could be voided. • However, the discrepancy about the area to be painted is minor compared to the contract as a whole, so it more likely did not have a material effect on the contract.	Unlikely there is a mutual mistake
Contract Interpretation Vague Terms	Contract terms are given their plain meaning. For vague terms, courts will look to the following for guidance: • Course of performance • Course of dealing • Custom and usage	• **There are two terms to the contract that must be interpreted to determine if there has been a breach, and the rights of the parties.** Surface Preparation • **Here, the contract itself states Sam will "paint" the ceiling, but it does not mention which party is responsible for surface preparation, so this term is unaddressed in the contract.** • **Sam asserts this means Barn was responsible for surface preparation and he had to perform the task at a cost of $3,000, while Barn argues it was Sam's responsibility.** • **There's no evidence of prior dealings between Sam and Barn to provide guidance, but Barn asserts that artists performing similar work indicate the trade custom is for the artist to provide surface preparation.** • Unless Sam can provide evidence to rebut this, it is unlikely the contract will be interpreted to require Barn to provide the surface preparation. <u>Lobby Bathrooms</u> • Barn will argue the public spaces of the lobby should include the public bathrooms. • Sam will argue that bathrooms are not included in the definition, but unless Sam has more evidence (see PER discussion below), it is more likely Barn will prevail by relying on the plain meaning of the words "public area" since the bathrooms are open to the public.	Likely the surface preparation was included in the term "painting"

Continued>

Issue	Rule	Fact Application	Conclusion
Parol Evidence Rule (PER)	• The PER limits the extent to which evidence of discussions prior to or contemporaneous with contract can be admitted. • A total integration means the document is intended to include all terms and no extrinsic evidence is allowed. • A partial integration is intended to be the final expression of the agreement but does not include all terms. Extrinsic evidence can be introduced to supplement the agreement, but not to contradict.	**Lobby Bathrooms** • **Barn asserts that "all public areas of the lobby" includes the two public restrooms, while Sam disagrees. Sam wants to bring in parol evidence to prove his point.** • Here, it is likely the contract is a partially integrated contract since it is short, consisting of only two handwritten lines. Thus, Sam can introduce supplemental evidence. • **Sam would testify that before the contract was signed, he told Ed of Barn that the restrooms could not be included because his paints were not suitable for high humidity environments. Consequently, Sam will argue that the contract was not intended to cover the public bathrooms.** • Barn would argue the extrinsic evidence contradicts the terms included in the contract, which includes "all" public areas. • **It is most likely Sam can testify to clarify what the parties meant by "all public areas" of the lobby.**	**PER will be allowed regarding the bathroom humidity**
Breach	• **Major** — non-breaching party does not receive substantial benefit of bargain. Discharges non-breaching party's duty to perform. • **Minor** — non-breaching party receives substantial benefit of bargain. Non-breaching party must still perform but can recover damages for any loss.	• It is most likely that Sam was obligated to paint the lobby ceiling border, but was not required to paint the bathroom ceilings, and Sam has fully performed. • **Even if Sam were found obligated to paint the ceiling border of the lobby bathrooms and did not, he would have substantially performed under the contract** since logically the lobby space would be substantially larger than the square footage allotted the bathrooms and painting the lobby ceiling conferred a substantial benefit to Barn. • **Sam's breach is minor and would not excuse Barn from performing** under the contract, though they could recover damages for any loss incurred by Sam's failure to fully perform. • **Barn has refused to pay anything, so they are in major breach** since Sam performed at least $75,000 of work and received no payment in return, so Sam has not received the substantial benefit of the bargain.	**Sam's breach, if any, is minor Barn's breach is major**
Damages — Expectation	Put non-breaching party in position had K been performed	• Had Barn performed, Barn would have paid Sam the $75,000 owed for performance under the contract, so **Sam can collect $75,000, though he is unlikely to get the additional $3,000 for the prep work.**	**Sam likely collects $75,000**

Continued>

Issue	Rule	Fact Application	Conclusion
Damages—Consequential	A direct and foreseeable consequence of the contract nonperformance	• Sam can recover consequential damages, though no facts establish here.	Consequential damages are recoverable
Damages—Incidental	Ordinary expenses incurred in responding to the contract breach	• Sam can recover incidental damages, though no facts establish here.	Incidental damages are recoverable

Is Barn likely to prevail in its lawsuit seeking specific performance against Sam?

Issue	Rule	Fact Application	Conclusion
Specific Performance	• **Valid K (certain terms)** • **Conditions Met** • **Inadequate legal remedy** • **Mutuality of performance** • **Feasibility** • **No Defenses (laches, or unclean hands)**	• There is a valid contract as discussed above. Though some terms are ambiguous, it would likely not prevent a court from ordering specific performance. • Barn would have to pay the $75,000 owed under the contract, but there is no indication Barn can't do so, so the condition precedent of payment can be satisfied. • Typically, damages are the preferred remedy for breach of contract. Barn will argue there is an **inadequate legal remedy and that only Sam can paint the ceiling since Sam is an "up and coming" artist and he created a unique design**, and they would want the bathrooms to match the lobby. • **Sam will argue that this is a services contract and ordering him to personally paint the ceiling would amount to indentured servitude, which the courts are loathe to order, so the court would not order Sam to perform.** • In addition, it is not feasible for the court to enforce such an order because painting is a task requiring skill and judgment, making it difficult for a court to determine if it were done satisfactorily. • There is no evidence here of undue delay or unclean hands by Barn. • **Given that this is a personal services contract, the court would not order Sam to specifically perform.** Should the court find the bathrooms were included and Sam did not substantially perform, the court would order damages to compensate Barn.	**The court will not order specific performance**

Contracts Question 1 Sample Answer
February 2020, Question 3

Governing Law

The UCC applies to the sale of goods, which are tangible moveable items. The common law applies to all other agreements, including contracts for the provision of services.

Here, the parties have contracted for Sam to paint a one-of-a-kind artistic design along the border of the ceiling in Barn's new lobby. Sam will be providing a service of his artistic talent, so the common law will govern.

1. Is Sam likely to prevail in a breach of contract lawsuit against Barn and if so, what damages will he likely recover?

Contract Formation

Contract formation requires an offer with clear and definite terms, an acceptance, and consideration.

Here the parties entered into a "mutually drafted" handwritten contract that states, "Sam shall paint a unique design along the entire ceiling border of all public areas of the first-floor lobby. Barn shall pay $75,000 upon completion of the work." This is sufficient to show mutual assent of offer and acceptance. The consideration is the exchange of Sam's artistic ability for Barn's $75,000. The contract is properly formed.

Mistake

A contract is voidable for mutual mistake if the mistake was to a basic assumption at the time contract was formed, the mistake has a material effect on the contracts, and the adversely impacted party did not assume the risk of the mistake.

Barn may argue there was a mutual mistake as to which rooms "all public areas of the first-floor lobby" included, since Barn claims it included the restrooms, but Sam claims it does not. The discrepancy on what rooms were to be painted would have an effect on Sam's performance, thus the contract could be voided. However, the discrepancy about the area to be painted is minor compared to the contract as a whole, so it more likely did not have a material effect on the contract so it is unlikely to be voided for a mutual mistake.

Contract Interpretation/Vague Terms

Contract terms are given their plain meaning when a court is interpreting their meaning. To interpret vague or ambiguous terms, the court will consider the parties course of performance, course of dealing, and the custom in the industry for guidance.

There are two terms to the contract that are in dispute and must be interpreted to determine if there has been a breach, and the rights of the parties. They are the surface preparation, and lobby bathrooms.

Surface Preparation

Here, the contract itself states Sam will "paint" the ceiling, but it does not mention which party is responsible for surface preparation before painting, so this term is unaddressed in the contract. Sam asserts this means Barn was responsible for surface preparation, but since they didn't prepare the surface, Sam had to do the task before he could paint at a cost of $3,000. Barn argues it was Sam's responsibility. There is no evidence of prior dealings between Sam and Barn to provide guidance, but Barn asserts that artists performing similar work indicate the trade custom is for the artist to provide surface preparation. Unless Sam can provide evidence to rebut this, it is unlikely the contract will be interpreted to require Barn to provide the surface preparation and Sam will not be able to recover the additional $3,000 he billed Barn.

Lobby Bathrooms

Barn argues the public spaces of the lobby should include the public bathrooms. While Sam argues the bathrooms are not included, unless Sam has more evidence (see PER discussion below), it is more likely

Barn will prevail by relying on the plain meaning of the words "public area," since the bathrooms are open to the public.

Parol Evidence Rule (PER)

The PER limits the extent to which evidence of discussions prior to or contemporaneous with the making of the contract can be admitted to interpret the contract. Whether the evidence can be admitted depends on if the document is a total or partial integration. A total integration means the document is intended to include all terms and no extrinsic evidence is allowed. A partial integration is intended to be the final expression of the agreement but does not include all terms, so extrinsic evidence can be introduced to supplement the agreement, but not to contradict.

Lobby Bathrooms

Barn asserts that "all public areas of the lobby" includes the two public restrooms, while Sam disagrees. Sam wants to bring in parol evidence to prove his point. Barn would argue extrinsic evidence contradicts the terms included in the contract, which includes "all" public areas. Here, it is likely the contract is a partially integrated contract since it is short, consisting of only two handwritten lines. Thus, Sam can introduce supplemental extrinsic evidence. Therefore, Sam would testify that before the contract was signed, he told Ed of Barn that the restrooms could not be included because his paints were not suitable for painting high humidity environments. Consequently, Sam will argue that the contract was not intended to cover the public bathrooms.

It is most likely Sam would be allowed to testify about the earlier statement about the bathroom humidity and a court would find the contract did not include the bathrooms.

Breach

A major breach occurs when the non-breaching party does not receive the substantial benefit of the bargain. A major breach discharges the non-breaching party's duty to perform. A minor breach occurs when the non-breaching party still receives the substantial benefit of bargain. A minor breach does not excuse the non-breaching party's performance, but they can recover damages for any loss.

Here, it is most likely that Sam was obligated to paint the lobby ceiling border, but was not required to paint the bathroom ceilings, and Sam has fully performed. Even if Sam were found obligated to paint the ceiling border of the lobby bathrooms and did not, he would have substantially performed under the contract since logically the square footage of the lobby space would be substantially larger than the square footage allotted to the bathrooms, and painting the lobby ceiling conferred a substantial benefit to Barn. Thus, Sam's breach, if any, is minor and would not excuse Barn from performing under the contract, though they could recover damages for any loss incurred by Sam's failure to fully perform.

Barn has refused to pay anything, so they are in major breach since Sam performed at least $75,000 of work and received no payment in return, so Sam has not received the substantial benefit of the bargain.

Sam's breach, if any, is minor while Barn's breach is major.

Damages — Expectation

Expectation damages are intended to put the non-breaching party in the position they would be in had the contract been fully performed.

Here, had Barn performed, Barn would have paid Sam the $75,000 owed for performance under the contract, so Sam can collect $75,000, though he is unlikely to get the additional $3,000 for the prep work.

Damages — Consequential and Incidental

Consequential damages are a direct and foreseeable consequence of the contract nonperformance. Incidental damages are ordinary expenses incurred in responding to the breach. Sam can also recover consequential and incidental damages, though no facts establish them here.

2. Is Barn likely to prevail in its lawsuit seeking specific performance against Sam?

Specific Performance

Specific performance is an equitable remedy where the court orders a party to perform under the contract. It requires a valid contract with certain terms, any conditions imposed on a party are satisfied, there is an inadequate legal remedy, both parties can be ordered to perform, it is feasible for a court to enforce, and there are no defenses.

Here, there is a valid contract as discussed above. Though some terms are ambiguous, it would likely not prevent a court from ordering specific performance. If specific performance were ordered, Barn would have to pay the $75,000 owed under the contract, but there is no indication Barn can't do so, thus the condition precedent of payment can be satisfied.

Typically, damages are the preferred remedy for breach of contract. However, Barn will argue there is an inadequate legal remedy and that only Sam can paint the ceiling since Sam is an "up and coming" artist and he created a unique design. Further, they would want the bathrooms to match the lobby and be painted by the same artist. In response, Sam will argue that this is a services contract and ordering him to personally paint the ceiling would amount to indentured servitude, which the courts are loathe to order, so the court would not order Sam to personally perform.

In addition, it is not feasible for the court to enforce such an order because painting is a task requiring skill and judgment, making it difficult for a court to determine if it were done satisfactorily. Here, there is no evidence of undue delay or unclean hands by Barn.

Given that this is a personal services contract, the court would not order Sam to specifically perform. Should the court find the bathrooms were included and Sam did not substantially perform, the court would order damages to compensate Barn.

Contracts Question 2
February 2024, Question 5

Brian, owner of a commercial bakery, and Sam, owner of a bakery supply business, met for the first time and discussed Brian's inability to find a reliable source of maple topping. When Sam told Brian he could supply the maple topping, they orally agreed that Sam would immediately ship 500 gallons of topping at $20 per gallon. Sam then added that he did not want to ship without something in writing, and Brian replied: "I will send written confirmation tomorrow."

For the next three weeks, Brian was busy negotiating a conference center catering contract and forgot to send Sam the confirmation. The catering contract obligated Brian to provide large quantities of pastries with maple topping. Brian then recalled his promise to Sam and sent him a purchase order on his standard form for 5,000 gallons of maple topping at $20 per gallon, to be delivered to Brian's place of business in two weeks.

Sam received Brian's purchase order but did not notice the change in gallonage. He saw the delivery date, but in light of Brian's delay in sending the confirmation, he did not believe it was firm. That same day, Sam sent a signed acknowledgment restating Brian's purchase order items and then left on a four-week vacation to a remote locale.

Upon his return, Sam shipped 500 gallons of maple topping to Brian. By that time, Brian was in default of the catering contract due to lack of maple topping. Brian had tried but had been unable to reach Sam while he was on vacation. Because Brian had been unsuccessful in obtaining an alternate source of maple topping, the conference center canceled its contract, resulting in $100,000 in lost profits.

Brian refused delivery of the 500 gallons of maple topping and sued for breach of contract, seeking the $100,000 in lost profits.

1. Is there an enforceable contract between Brian and Sam? If so, what are the terms? Discuss.

2. Is Brian likely to prevail on his claim against Sam? If so, what damages is he likely to recover? Discuss.

Contracts Question 2 Assessment
February 2024, Question 5

We included this question because it provides some issue spotting challenges. Most of the issues raised are not difficult to identify, but there is at least one where it is much less clear which rules you would analyze to solve the problem posed. Under the stress imposed by the tight one-hour time limit on the exam, applicants can feel uncertain about how to best handle some of the issues raised in this question and so they panic. Once you panic, you can't think clearly, so the first thing to do if that happens is stay calm. Remember, if the issue spotting is difficult for you, it is difficult for all test takers and using an issue spotting checklist is a good way to feel in control when facing some uncertainty in the exam, and you will feel uncertain at some point in the exam.

This UCC-based contracts essay question is typical in that there are a series of communications between the parties, and you must analyze the legal import of each communication. It might be helpful to jot down on the top of your answer who is who (Brian = buyer, Sam = seller). It seems obvious, but during the stress of an exam, it is easy to get confused on who the parties are. If you look at the sample answer you can see how we inserted the terms (buyer) and (seller) into the first call of the question so that information was easy to reference as we built the answer.

Analyze each communication sequentially to determine if a contract has formed. Here, the first communication stated the parties "agreed" so the contract formation analysis can be truncated. The written confirmation is the first issue that is more challenging to work with. A good technique to use to issue spot is to pretend the plaintiff Brian is telling you this story and you need to explain to him the legal import of each event that occurred. When you think about the question in a more real-world way like that, it can help to identify the rules you can use to solve the problem. For example, Brian said the parties agreed, but also that he would send a written confirmation but didn't. In real life, you would explain to him that the oral agreement formed a contract, but the statute of frauds requires certain contracts to be in writing, etc. Then, Brian sent a purchase order three weeks later for a much larger quantity then what the parties originally discussed. You would want to problem solve by trying to identify any rules that could be implicated by that action. Could it be the necessary writing required under the statute of frauds? If not, what could it be? This is an example where facts can be used to make multiple arguments because you are using the same fact of Brian's purchase order to analyze several rules. But if you picture yourself problem solving and advising Brian, it is exactly what you would do. Since you didn't find an enforceable contract yet, you would go back to your issues checklist and start all over, asking if this new communication can implicate a new contract, which will allow Brian to recover.

When you use the technique of issue spotting by pretending one of the parties is a client, be sure to change sides and issue spot the situation as if you are representing the other party. This will ensure you see both sides of the situation and don't miss any issues or competing arguments on an issue.

When writing your answer, be sure to keep your eye on where the points are and spend your time accordingly. The points are always going to be in areas with two-sided analysis, and in areas of ambiguity, like the purchase order here. Don't shy away from analyzing the areas of ambiguity because you are unsure of yourself. Instead, you should lean into those areas in your analysis, while identifying the ambiguity because that is what the higher scoring answers will do.

Make note of the areas highlighted in **bold** on the corresponding grid. The bold areas highlight the issues, analysis, and conclusions that are likely **required** to receive a passing score on this question.

Issue	Rule	Fact Application	Conclusion
Is there an enforceable contract between Brian and Sam? If so, what are the terms?			
Governing Law	UCC applies to the sale of goods Common Law applies to all other agreements	• Maple topping is a good, so the UCC rules govern the agreement.	UCC applies
Merchants	Merchants—those who regularly deal in goods of the kind	• Brian owns a commercial bakery and is a merchant buying topping. • Sam owns a bakery supply business and is a merchant selling topping.	Both parties are merchants.
Contract Formation	Contract requires an offer, acceptance, and consideration. • Offer is the intent to enter into an agreement, with definite and certain terms, communicated to the offeree. • Acceptance is manifestation of assent to the offer. • Consideration is the bargained for exchange.	• Here, Sam and Brian "orally agreed" to a deal. • Sam would supply and "immediately" ship to Brian 500 gallons of topping at $20 per gallon, so the quantity, time for performance, parties, price, and subject matter are specified. • The consideration is that Sam would supply topping in exchange for money paid by Brian. • Therefore, the parties came to an agreement, which will be binding, unless a defense applies.	Oral contract formed
Statute of Frauds Merchant's Confirming Memo	Contracts for the sale of goods over $500 require writing. The writing must include all material terms and be signed by the party to be charged. A merchant's confirming memo can be enforced against both parties between two merchants.	• The contract is for goods over $500 so the statute of frauds applies. **Written Confirmation Request** • Here, after the parties agreed, Sam said that "he did not want to ship without something in writing," and Brian promised to send a written confirmation the following day. Had Brian sent the confirmation as promised, the SOF would be satisfied. However, since he didn't, it was not, thus **the contract was not enforceable.** [The unsatisfied written confirmation request needed to be **analyzed**, but could have also been analyzed as a contract modification, or a condition precedent.]	SOF is not satisfied

Continued>

Issue	Rule	Fact Application	Conclusion
Merchant's Confirming Memo (continued)		**Brian's Purchase Order (PO)** • Brian may argue the **PO was a merchant's confirming memo which satisfies the statute of frauds.** • Here, the confirmation was not sent immediately but was **sent three weeks later, which was not reasonable.** Further, the **terms were materially different since they agreed to 500 gallons of topping and the purchase order was for 5,000 gallons of topping.** Another difference in terms is that **instead of delivery occurring immediately, the topping was to be delivered in two additional weeks,** which is five weeks after the original agreement. • **The purchase order is not a merchant's confirming memo of the original agreement.**	
Battle of Forms	• An acceptance which varies from the offer is allowed under the UCC. • Conflicting terms are knocked out, and additional terms will enter the contract. • Any confirmation will act as an acceptance even if the terms are different so long as they don't materially alter the agreement. [One of these rules should have been used to analyze the PO]	• Brian may argue the original conversation was an offer, and his purchase order was an acceptance, but the offer would have terminated for lapse of time by then. • Here, **the PO quantity term is substantially different and 10X larger than the original agreement, which is a material change of the quantity term.** • The PO is not an acceptance. [You should have analyzed the material term change facts using one of these rules, but this discussion could have been folded into the SOF analysis above.]	Purchase order is not an acceptance
Offer	Offer is the intent to enter into an agreement, with definite and certain terms, communicated to the offeree.	• **The PO shows Brian's intent to be bound, includes all essential terms (5,000 gallons at $20 per gallon and the delivery date) and is communicated in writing to Sam.**	Brian's PO is a new offer
Acceptance	Acceptance is manifestation of assent to the offer.	• **Sam sent a signed acknowledgement of Brian's PO which manifests assent, and since it was in writing, it also satisfies the SOF and a contract formed.** • Though Sam did not subjectively think the date was a firm date or notice the quantity term, his subjective knowledge is irrelevant and **Sam's objective manifestation of agreement to the delivery date and quantity controls.**	Sam accepted

Continued>

Issue	Rule	Fact Application	Conclusion
Defense: Mistake	A contract can be reformed for mutual mistake if: • A mistake on a basic assumption of the contract • Material effect on K • Adverse party didn't assume the risk Unilateral mistake • The other party knew or should have known of the mistake	• Brian was not mistaken here since he intended to order 5,000 gallons, so there is no mutual mistake. • Sam will argue he made a unilateral mistake when he did not notice that Brian's purchase order was for 5,000 gallons, instead of the original agreed to amount of 500, and Brian did not sufficiently call attention to the big difference in quantity term. Sam will argue the numbers look similar and the difference is only one zero, so this was a reasonable mistake. • While a 10X increase in quantity has a material effect on the contract, it was Sam's responsibility to read the PO. • It is unlikely the court will allow Sam to rescind the contract because of his own failure to read the PO.	A mistake defense will not be successful
Contract Terms		• Sam must supply 5,000 gallons of maple topping for $20/gallon, delivered in two weeks from the date of the purchase order.	
Is Brian likely to prevail on his claim against Sam? If so, what damages is he likely to recover?			
Breach	• UCC perfect tender of goods.	• Here, **Sam delivered 500 instead of 5,000 gallons of topping** so there was not perfect tender, and Sam cannot cure his mistake since the **delivery was two weeks late.** Brian even tried unsuccessfully to reach Sam. • **Brian can reject the imperfect delivery and sue for breach.**	Sam is in breach
Damages—Expectation	• Put non-breaching party in position it would be in had K been performed • UCC the difference between the cover price and contract price • Damages must be able to be calculated with certainty caused by the breach, foreseeable, and unavoidable	• **Brian was unable to cover because he could not find an alternative supplier,** making expectation damages difficult to calculate. • This breach caused Brian to breach on his own conference center catering contract, **causing lost profits,** which is the better measure of damages.	Recoverable

Continued>

Issue	Rule	Fact Application	Conclusion
Damages — Consequential	• **Direct and foreseeable consequence of the breach** • **Damages must be able to be calculated with certainty caused by the breach, foreseeable, and unavoidable**	• **Brian lost the certain amount of $100,000 in profit because he could not fulfill his contract to supply pastries to the conference center.** • **Damages must be foreseeable at the time of the contracting** either because the parties discussed it or as a natural and probable consequence. Brian told Sam he needed a reliable source of topping **so it is foreseeable Brian would lose business if Sam breached. However, Sam had no knowledge of Brian's large conference center contract** since it was negotiated after they entered into the original oral agreement. Sam thought the topping was for a much smaller business that only required 500 gallons of maple topping, not 5,000 gallons. For this reason, lost profits may be recoverable, but a **full $100,000 loss was unforeseeable at the time of contracting. The loss was unavoidable because Brian tried to find another supplier unsuccessfully.**	Likely some lost profit may be recoverable, but not the whole $100k
Damages — Incidental	Ordinary expenses incurred in responding to the contract breach	• Brian can recover incidental damages if established.	Recoverable

Contracts Question 2 Sample Answer
February 2024, Question 5

1. Is there an enforceable contract between Brian (buyer) and Sam (seller)? If so, what are the terms?

Governing Law

The UCC applies to contracts for the sale of goods, and the common law applies to all other agreements.

Here, the parties are contracting for maple topping, which is a good, so the UCC rules will govern the agreement.

Merchants

Special rules can apply under the UCC for contracts with merchants. A merchant is one who regularly deals in goods of the kind in the contract.

Here, since Brian owns a commercial bakery and is a merchant buying topping and Sam owns a bakery supply business and is a merchant selling topping, both parties are merchants.

Contract Formation

Contract formation requires an offer, acceptance, and consideration. An offer must have the intent to enter into an agreement, with definite and certain terms, which is communicated to the offeree. An acceptance is manifestation of assent to the terms of the offer. Consideration is the bargained for exchange.

Here, Sam and Brian "orally agreed" to a deal for maple topping. Sam agreed to supply and "immediately" ship to Brian 500 gallons of topping at $20 per gallon, so the terms of quantity, time for performance, parties, price, and subject matter are sufficiently specified. The consideration is that Sam would supply topping in exchange for money paid by Brian.

Therefore, the parties came to an oral agreement, which will be binding, unless a defense applies.

Statute of Frauds (SOF)

Certain contracts must be in writing to be enforceable, including contracts for the sale of goods over $500. The writing must include all material terms and be signed by the party to be charged. However, when both parties are merchants, a merchant's confirming memo sent by one party can be enforced against both parties.

Here, the contract is for goods of maple topping over $500 (500 gallons at $20/gallon) so the SOF applies, and a writing is required to memorialize the oral agreement.

Written Confirmation Request

Here, after the parties agreed, Sam said that "he did not want to ship without something in writing," and Brian promised to send a written confirmation the following day. Had Brian sent the confirmation as promised, which would be a merchant's confirming memo, the SOF would be satisfied. However, since Brian didn't follow through, the SOF was not satisfied, and the contract was not enforceable.

Brian's Purchase Order (PO)

As an alternative, Brian may argue the PO was a merchant's confirming memo which satisfies the statute of frauds. A merchant's confirming memo should be sent timely.

Here, the confirmation was not sent immediately as promised, but was sent three weeks later, which was an unreasonable delay. Further, the terms in the confirmation were materially different since they orally agreed to 500 gallons of topping, but the purchase order was for 5,000 gallons of topping. Another material difference in terms is that instead of delivery occurring "immediately" as originally agreed (which was already three weeks late), the topping was to be delivered in two additional weeks, which is five weeks after the original agreement.

For these reasons, the purchase order is not a merchant's confirming memo of the original agreement, and the SOF is not satisfied.

Battle of Forms

Any confirmation of an agreement will act as an acceptance even with additional terms so long as they don't materially alter the agreement. Between merchants, different terms will be knocked out and gap fillers will supply the missing terms where reasonable.

Here, Brian may argue the original conversation was an offer, and his purchase order was the acceptance, but the oral offer would have terminated for lapse of time by the time Brian sent the PO three weeks later. Since the PO quantity term is substantially different and 10X larger than the original agreement, there is a material change of the quantity term, so the purchase order cannot function as an acceptance.

Offer

An offer is the intent to enter into an agreement, with definite and certain terms, communicated to the offeree.

Here, the PO shows Brian's intent to be bound since it is an order, includes all essential terms (5,000 gallons at $20 per gallon and the delivery date), and is communicated in writing to Sam. Therefore, Brian's PO was a new offer.

Acceptance

An acceptance is a manifestation of assent to the terms of the offer.

Here, Sam sent a signed acknowledgement of Brian's PO which objectively manifests Sam's assent to the terms on the PO, and since it was in writing, which also satisfies the SOF, a contract formed.

Though Sam did not subjectively "believe" the delivery date was firm or notice the increased quantity term, Sam's subjective knowledge is irrelevant since his objective manifestation of agreement to the terms of the PO controls, which includes the delivery date and quantity specified in the PO.

Therefore, Sam accepted the offer outlined in Brian's PO.

Defense: Mistake

A contract can be reformed for mutual mistake when a mistake is made on a basic assumption of the contract, it has a material effect on the contract, and the adverse party didn't assume the risk of the mistake. The contract can be reformed for a unilateral mistake if the other party knew or should have known of the mistake.

Sam will attempt to get the contract reformed for mistake. Here, Brian was not mistaken since he intended to order 5,000 gallons of topping, so there is no mutual mistake. However, Sam will argue he made a unilateral mistake when he did not notice that Brian's purchase order was for 5,000 gallons, instead of the original agreed-to amount of 500 gallons, and Brian did not sufficiently call attention to the big difference in quantity term. Sam will argue the numbers look similar since the difference is only one zero, so this was a reasonable mistake to make. While a 10X increase in quantity has a material effect on the contract, it was Sam's responsibility to read the PO, so it is unlikely the court will allow Sam to rescind the contract because of his own failure to read the PO.

Consequently, a mistake defense is unlikely to be successful for Sam.

Contract Terms

The parties have a contract and Sam must supply 5,000 gallons of maple topping for $20/gallon, delivered within two weeks from the date of the purchase order.

2. Is Brian likely to prevail on his claim against Sam? If so, what damages is he likely to recover?

Breach

The UCC requires the perfect tender of goods, and if the goods tendered fail in any way the buyer can reject the delivery. However, the seller is given a reasonable opportunity to cure the defect.

Here, Sam delivered 500 gallons of topping instead of 5,000 gallons of topping so there was not perfect tender under the contract, and Sam cannot cure his mistake since the delivery was already two weeks late. Brian even tried unsuccessfully to reach Sam while Sam was unreachable on vacation. Brian can reject the imperfect delivery and sue Sam for breach.

Damages — Expectation

Expectation damages compensate the plaintiff for the value of the bargain they expected and should put the non-breaching party in the position it would be in had the contract been performed properly. In a UCC contract, expectation damages are measured as the difference between the cover price and contract price. All damages must be able to be calculated with certainty, caused by the breach, foreseeable, and unavoidable.

Here, Brian tried to cover with another supplier but was unable to find an alternate source of maple topping, so the damages were unavoidable. Since Brian could not cover, expectation damages are difficult to calculate with certainty. However, Sam's breach caused Brian to breach his own conference center catering contract, resulting in lost profits, which is the better measure of damages.

Damages — Consequential

Consequential damages compensate for damages that are a direct and foreseeable consequence of the breach. They are unique to the plaintiff, such as lost profits, but must be foreseeable at the time of contracting.

Here, Brian lost the certain amount of $100,000 in profit because he could not fulfill his contract to supply pastries to the conference center. The loss was caused by the breach and unavoidable because Brian tried to find another supplier unsuccessfully. Damages must be foreseeable at the time of the contracting either because the parties discussed the situation or as a natural and probable consequence of the contract. Brian told Sam he needed a reliable source of topping for his commercial bakery, so it is foreseeable Brian would lose business if Sam breached. However, Sam had no knowledge of Brian's large conference center contract since it was negotiated three weeks after Sam and Brian entered into their original oral agreement. While Sam could foresee Brian's losses, Sam thought the topping was for a much smaller business that only required 500 gallons of maple topping, not 5,000 gallons.

For these reasons, Brian's lost profits may be recoverable, but likely not in the full amount of $100,000 since the magnitude of the loss was unforeseeable to Sam at the time of contracting.

Damages — Incidental

Incidental damages are the ordinary expenses incurred in responding to the contract breach.

Here, Brian can recover for any incidental damages incurred in trying to respond to Sam's breach.

Contracts Question 3
July 2016, Question 3

Dirt, a large excavating company, recently replaced all of its gas-powered equipment with more efficient diesel-powered equipment. It placed the old gas-powered equipment in storage until it could sell it.

On May 1, Builder, a general contractor for a large office development, and Dirt signed a valid written contract under which Dirt agreed to perform all the site preparation work for a fee of $1,500,000. Dirt estimated its total cost for the job at $1,300,000. The contract states: "Dirt hereby agrees to commence site work on or before June 1 and to complete all site work on or before September 1." Because no other work could begin until completion of the site preparation, Builder was anxious to avoid delays. To ensure that Dirt would give the job top priority, the contract also states: "Dirt agrees to have all of its equipment available as needed to perform this contract and shall refrain from undertaking all other jobs for the duration of the contract."

On May 29, an unusual high pressure weather system settled over the state.

As a result, on May 30, in an effort to reduce air pollution, the state banned use of all diesel-powered equipment.

On June 2, Dirt told Builder about the ban and stated that it had no way of knowing when it would be lifted. Builder told Dirt to switch to its gas-powered equipment. Dirt replied that using its old gas-powered equipment would add $500,000 to its costs and asked Builder to pay the increased expense. Builder refused.

On June 4, seeing that no site work had begun, Builder emailed Dirt stating that their contract was "terminated."

On June 8, Builder hired another excavating company, which performed the work for $1,800,000.

Dirt has sued Builder for terminating the contract. Builder has countersued Dirt for the $300,000 difference between the original contract price and what it paid the new contractor.

1. Is Dirt likely to prevail in its suit? Discuss.

2. Is Builder likely to prevail in its countersuit? Discuss.

Contracts Question 3 Assessment
July 2016, Question 3

This is a typical example of a common law-based contracts essay question. This contract is for the provision of services — site preparation work — and thus the common law rules apply.

Mutual assent is frequently tested on the bar exam with a detailed fact scenario requiring analysis of multiple communications between the parties. This question is an example of an essay question where mutual assent is not at issue since the fact pattern states the parties "signed a valid written contract." Do not waste time establishing the existence of the contract; simply identify the applicable law, parties, and pertinent contract terms and move on to the issues the facts raise in the question.

This is also a good example of a fact pattern where events occur after the contract is entered into. As always, chronology and timing is very important in contracts questions. If an event occurs that prohibits a party from performing when they are set to perform (here, Dirt was to start on or before June 1), consider issues related to discharge as well as anticipatory repudiation and breach issues. These issues tend to cluster together where there is a subsequent event that interferes with one or both parties' abilities to perform.

It is essential that you know and understand the nuances of the contracts rules, especially how the various issues often arise together and which issues trigger other issues. For example, when anticipatory repudiation is at issue, breach is almost always an issue since that is one of the remedies available under anticipatory repudiation. Also, if anticipatory repudiation is at issue, then look for the reasons the party might not have been able to perform and go through your discharge issues such as impossibility, impracticability, and frustration of purpose (all of which should have been raised here). It is worth noting that the defenses of impossibility, impracticability, and frustration of purpose are often all raised when one is at issue. These defenses are usually an issue cluster, and where you spot one, typically all three should be analyzed under the facts in order to demonstrate your understanding of the differences between the three doctrines.

Finally, it is important to note that questions like this often have strong arguments on both sides. As is the case here, your conclusion did not matter. What does matter is that you see both sides. In fact, the state-released answers came to opposite conclusions on this question.

Make note of the areas highlighted in **bold** on the corresponding grid. The bold areas highlight the issues, analysis, and conclusions that are likely **required** to receive a passing score on this question.

Issue	Rule	Fact Application	Conclusion
Applicable Law	• **UCC applies to goods** • **CL applies to other contracts**	**Here, k to prepare site for an excavation (provide a service) so common law governs.**	**Common law governs**
Formation of contract	Offer, acceptance, consideration	Here, Builder and Dirt "signed a valid written contract," so all formation requirements met.	Valid contract
Call # 1: D's Suit			
Anticipatory Repudiation	• **Unequivocal** expression • Before time for performance due • That they will not perform • **Nonrepudiating** party can: sue immediately, suspend performance, treat K as discharged, or urge performance	Here, B emailed D that "their contract was terminated" on June 4, which was months before the completion deadline of Sept. 1. On June 8, B also hired another excavating company to perform the work indicating that B would not perform their end of the K with D and this was all clear and unequivocal and before time for performance. D can thus sue immediately as they have done.	B anticipatorily repudiated the contract.

Breach	• **Material breach — not substantial performance; consider factors:**
	  • **Party did not receive substantial benefit of the bargain**
	  • Extent of performance/cost
	  • Willfulness
	  • Time of essence in K or not
		B breached by not allowing D to complete the contract and perform prior to the due date so D did not get to have any of the benefit (the lost profits of $200,000).
		
		D will assert that time was not of the essence since the start and end date were in the contract, but the end date was more critical than the start date as D could have still finished on time.
		
		B will counter that time was of the essence since dates were set; since K did not specify time of the essence is not a strong argument.
			B breached and **time not of the essence so breach is minor**

Continued>

Issue	Rule	Fact Application	Conclusion
Promise v. Condition	• **Promise** — must complete and does not affect other party's promise (noncompletion is breach) • **Condition** — event that must occur before performance of other party is due • Courts favor promises over conditions	**Start date term** • B will defend their anticipatory **repudiation by claiming D starting on or before June 1st was a condition to payment; but it is likely that D's late start was a minor breach (see above) and thus would not discharge the entire K.** • Court would most likely find the start date a promise and not a condition and thus it would not affect B's duties under the K. Use of all equipment available B will also defend their anticipatory repudiation by claiming D did not use "all" of their equipment available, but D will argue that they still had months to complete the K and did not need to use "all" equipment within 3 days of the start due to the increase in cost with the gas-powered equipment; B could argue that D could have started on time if they used "all" of their equipment such as the gas-powered; but since they still had months left to complete it the start date was likely a minor breach and not "all" equipment had to be used as of that date.	Start date is a promise and late start not a material breach. Could have concluded either way on use of all equipment.
Expectation Damages	**Put the party in the position they would have been in had the K been performed.** Damages limitations include: • Foreseeable • Unavoidable • Certain • Causation	Here D expected to make a profit of $200,000. These damages were foreseeable at the time the K was formed since that was D's anticipated profit and the damages were unavoidable; D could not mitigate damages since the K prevented D from entering into other Ks so they could give priority to this K; profit certain as price set up front and caused by B giving K to another excavator.	Could conclude either way — based on promise/breach to use "all" equipment, but most likely D entitled to lost profits of $200,000.

Continued>

Issue	Rule	Fact Application	Conclusion
Call # 2: B's countersuit			
Anticipatory Repudiation/Breach	See rules above.	• **B will argue that D anticipatorily repudiated the contract when D told B about the ban and asked for D to pay the additional cost to use the gas-powered equipment. However, this is not an unequivocal expression that D won't perform.** Also, not starting on time is not an unequivocal expression that D won't perform by Sept. 1, the time when performance is due. • As discussed above, D did breach the start time promise in the K but it was minor since time was not of the essence.	D minor breach possible (could have concluded either way) but could be discharged if excuses valid below.
Duty to Perform—Discharge by Unforeseen Events	• Impossibility—supervening, unforeseeable event (objective std.) makes performance literally impossible. • Impracticability—occurrence of an event the parties assumed would not occur makes performance extremely and unreasonably difficult. • Frustration of purpose—purpose for entering the contract is destroyed by supervening events.	• **D will argue that it was impossible to perform since the unusual weather forced a ban on all diesel equipment but since D could have still used gas-powered equipment and finished by the time the K set it was not impossible.** • **Might be extremely and unreasonably difficult since weather unusual and thus not foreseeable but usually monetary damages are not sufficient to make a K impracticable** and since D could have spent $500,000 more to use gas it might not be too unreasonable. But this would make D's profit turn into a deficit of $300,000—but it is unlikely to rise to extremely difficult still and D arguably assumed the risk by including "all" equipment in the language of the contract. • **Purpose of contract not frustrated as purpose was still to prepare the site regardless of what equipment was used to do so.**	D won't likely be excused from performance if in fact D did breach.

Continued>

Issue	Rule	Fact Application	Conclusion
Mistake	A contract is voidable for mutual mistake if: • **The mistake was to a basic assumption at the time K formed;** • **Material effect on K; and** • **Adverse party didn't assume the risk** Unilateral also requires that the other party knew or should have known of the mistake.	D will argue that both parties had a mutual mistake as to what was meant by "all" equipment available. D will argue that since they recently replaced all of their gas-powered equipment with diesel and put the gas-powered in storage until they could sell it, that equipment wasn't included in "all" equipment. Also, D would not have made the K price as they did if they knew they might have to use gas-powered since they would lose $300,000 on the K; B will argue "all" meant "all" including gas-powered equipment; this is a basic assumption at the time of K and would materially affect the K in terms of costs. **Most likely that since D could have clarified what "all" meant they assumed the risk and the mistake would not be mutual.** If it was a unilateral mistake then there could be no reason B would have known of it; B knew D had gas-powered equipment and expected them to use it, and D never told B that the cost was only considered using diesel.	Mistake not a good defense for D.
Expectation Damages	See above rule.	B is asking for the $300,000 difference between what they were supposed to pay D ($1,500,000) and what they actually paid after D didn't start on time ($1,800,000). Damages foreseeable that B would need to cover if D could not perform and B did mitigate damages by hiring the other company; price certain but damages not likely caused by D since D didn't have an opportunity to complete the K before B hired other company.	Could conclude either way but most likely B will not recover $300,000 since D was not able to complete the K because B repudiated it by terminating it.

Contracts Question 3 Sample Answer
July 2016, Question 3

Applicable Law

The UCC applies to contracts involving goods and the common law governs all other contracts. Here, the contract requires Dirt (D), a large excavating company, to do site preparation work for Builder (B), a large excavating company. Since the site preparation involves construction, a service, the common law will govern this contract.

Contract Formation

A valid contract requires offer, acceptance, and consideration. Here, Builder and Dirt "signed a valid written contract," so all formation requirements were met and there is a valid written contract.

1: D's Suit

Anticipatory Repudiation

Anticipatory repudiation occurs when there is an unequivocal expression by one party before time for performance is due that they will not perform under the contract. When this occurs, the nonrepudiating party can sue immediately, suspend performance, treat the contract as discharged, or urge performance.

Here, B emailed D that "their contract was terminated" on June 4th, which was months before the completion deadline of Sept. 1. On June 8th, B also hired another excavating company to perform the work, indicating that B would not perform their end of the contract with D, and this was all clear and unequivocal and before time for performance, which was job completion by Sept. 1. Thus, D can sue immediately as they have done here due to B anticipatorily repudiating their contract.

Breach

A breach is material when one party has not substantially performed. The court will consider factors such as whether the party received the substantial benefit of the bargain, the extent of performance, the cost to remedy the breach, and the willfulness of the breach. In addition, time being of the essence will not amount to a material breach unless the contract specifies that time is of the essence. Dates alone do not amount to a time-is-of-the-essence clause.

Here, B breached by not allowing D to complete the contract and perform prior to the due date, so D did not receive any of the benefit, which would be their lost profits of $200,000.

Further, D will assert that time was not of the essence since the start and end dates were both in the contract, but the end date was more critical than the start date as D could have still finished on time had they been given the opportunity to do so.

B will argue that time was of the essence since the dates were clearly set and because B could not begin other work until this work was complete. Further, B needed D to make this job a priority and thus the contract prohibited D from undertaking all other jobs and to have all equipment available to perform. However, since the contract did not specifically state that the start date was of the essence and it isn't clear if D knew that B was anxious to avoid delays and knew that other work could not be done until D's work was done, the start date will not be considered to meet the time-is-of-the-essence requirements for a material breach. Thus, D's failure to start on the start date was a minor breach and B's failure to allow D to complete or start performance would be a material breach.

Promise v. Condition

A promise is a term that one party must complete and does not affect the other party's promises. If one party fails to fulfill a promise, that party is in breach and this does not affect the other party's duty to fulfill its promises. A condition is an event that must occur before performance of the other party is due. Courts favor promises over conditions.

Start date term

B will defend their anticipatory repudiation by claiming that the term that D must start on or before June 1st was a condition to their payment, but it is more likely that D's late start was a minor breach (see above) and thus would not discharge the entire contract nor would it affect B's duties and promises under the contract. Further, a court would most likely find the start date a promise and not a condition since payment wasn't conditioned on D starting on a particular date, but rather performance by Sept. 1. Thus, D's failure to start on time would not affect B's duties under the contract.

Use of all equipment available

B will also defend their anticipatory repudiation by claiming D did not use "all" of its equipment available, but D will argue that they still had months to complete the contract and did not need to use "all" equipment within three days of the start due to the increase in cost with the gas-powered equipment. However, D could have started on time if they used "all" of their equipment such as the gas-powered equipment, but since they still had months left to complete the site preparation, the start date delay was a minor breach and not "all" equipment had to be used as of that date for the contract to remain in effect. Thus, the failure on D's part to use all equipment, including gas-powered equipment, to start on time would be a minor breach and not permit B to terminate the contract entirely. Thus, B is still in breach for terminating the contract regardless of D's promises and D's minor breach.

Expectation Damages

Expectation damages are designed to place the party in the position they would have been in had the contract been performed. Damages will be awarded only if they were foreseeable at the time the contract was formed, the non-breaching party mitigates its damages, the damages can be calculated with certainty, and the damages are caused by the breach.

Here, D expected to make a profit of $200,000 since the contract price was $1,500,000 and their estimated cost for the job was $1,300,000.

These damages were foreseeable at the time the contract was formed since that was D's anticipated profit and they knew how much it would cost to complete the job. Further, damages were unavoidable because D could not mitigate damages since the contract prevented them from entering into other contracts so they could give priority to this contract. In addition, the amount would be certain as the contract price was set up front as well as the estimated cost to complete the job. Finally, the damages were caused by B terminating the contract and giving it to another excavating company.

Even though D may have breached their promise to use "all" equipment, B did not have the right to terminate the contract early. Thus, D would most likely be entitled to lost profits of $200,000.

2: B's Countersuit

Anticipatory Repudiation

See rules above. Here, B will argue that D anticipatorily repudiated the contract when D told B about the ban and asked for B to pay the additional cost to use the gas-powered equipment. However, this is not an unequivocal expression that D won't perform as they still had months left to complete the contract and it is possible the ban would have been lifted soon or that D could have still used the gas-powered equipment later to complete the contract on time. Also, not starting on time is not an unequivocal expression that D won't perform by Sept. 1 since it is possible they could have started three days late or more and still performed on time.

Breach

As discussed above, D did breach the start time promise in the contract, but it was minor since time was not of the essence. Further, if D has a valid excuse, their late start could be excused (as discussed below).

Impossibility

Impossibility discharges performance when there is a supervening, unforeseeable event based on an objective standard that makes performance literally impossible when neither party assumed the risk. Here, while there was unusual weather that forced a ban on the use of all diesel equipment, it was still possible for D to complete performance and start it on time as D could have used their gas-powered equipment since D still had access to it as it was in storage until they could sell it. Further, the fact that another company was able to perform the contract (albeit for a higher price) shows that D also could have completed the contract. Thus, impossibility will not discharge D's duty to perform.

Impracticability

Impracticability is the occurrence of an event the parties assumed would not occur that makes performance extremely and unreasonably difficult. The event must concern a basic assumption of the contract for which neither party assumed the risk.

Here, the use of gas-powered equipment rather than diesel equipment as D planned might be extremely and unreasonably difficult since D would have to lose $300,000 on the contract rather than profit $200,000. Further, arguably the risk was not assumed by either party since the weather was "unusual" and thus not foreseeable along with the recent ban on diesel equipment. But usually, monetary losses alone are not sufficient to make a contract impracticable and since D could have spent $500,000 more to use gas it might not be too unreasonable. Further, it is possible that D assumed the risk by including "all" equipment in the language of the contract rather than just diesel equipment. It is most likely that a court will not excuse D's performance based on impracticability.

Frustration of Purpose

Frustration of purpose discharges performance when the purpose for entering the contract is destroyed by supervening events. Here, the purpose of the contract was not frustrated as the purpose was still to prepare the site regardless of what equipment was used to do so. Thus, D will not be excused from performance based on frustration of purpose.

Mistake

A contract is voidable for mutual mistake if the mistake was to a basic assumption at the time the contract was formed, the mistake had a material effect on the contract, and the adversely affected party didn't assume the risk. Unilateral mistake also requires that the other party knew or should have known of the mistake.

D will argue that there was a mutual mistake as to what was meant by the term "all" equipment available. D will argue that since they recently replaced all of their gas-powered equipment with diesel and put the gas-powered equipment in storage until they could sell it, that this equipment wasn't included in "all" equipment. Also, D would not have set the contract price as they did if they knew they might have to use gas-powered and lose $300,000 on the contract. On the other hand, B will argue "all" meant "all" including gas-powered equipment and that if D didn't want to use "all" available equipment they should have clarified this in the contract. This term is also a basic assumption at the time of contract and would materially affect the contract in terms of costs.

Since D could have clarified what "all" meant they most likely assumed the risk and the mistake would not be considered mutual.

As to unilateral mistake there is no reason B would have known of the mistake because B knew D had gas-powered and expected them to use it as B told D to use it when D first informed B of the ban. Further, D never told B that the cost for the contract was only considered using diesel as the only possible equipment. Thus, mistake would not be a good defense for D.

Expectation Damages

See rule above. Here, B is asking for the $300,000 difference between what they were supposed to pay with D ($1,500,000) and what they actually paid after D didn't start on time ($1,800,000).

Damages are foreseeable in that B would need to cover if D could not perform and B did mitigate damages by hiring the other company. The price is certain as well, but the damages are not likely caused by D since D didn't have an opportunity to complete the contract before B hired the other company. Most likely B will not recover the $300,000 since D was not able to complete the contract because B repudiated it by terminating it early.

Contracts Question 4
July 2018, Question 1

In January, Stan, a farmer, agreed in a valid written contract to sell to Best Sauce-Maker Company (Best), 5,000 bushels of tomatoes on July 1, at $100 per bushel, payable upon delivery. On May 15, Stan sent Best the following e-mail:

"Heavy rains in March-May slowed tomato ripening. Delivery will be two weeks late."

Best replied:

"Okay."

On May 22, an employee of Delta Bank (Delta), where Best and Stan banked, told Best that rains had damaged Stan's tomato crops and that Stan would be unable to fulfill all his contracts. Best called Stan and asked about the Banker's comment. Stan said:

"Won't know until June 10 whether I'll have enough tomatoes for all my contracts."

Best replied:

"We need a firm commitment by May 27, or we'll buy the tomatoes elsewhere."

Stan did not contact Best by May 27. On June 3, Best contracted to buy the 5,000 bushels it needed from Agro-Farm for $110 per bushel.

On June 6, Stan told Best:

"Worry was for nothing. I'll be able to deliver all 5,000 bushels."

Best replied:

"Too late. We made other arrangements. You owe us $50,000."

Concerned about quickly finding another buyer, Stan sold the 5,000 bushels to a vegetable wholesaler for $95 per bushel.

Stan sued Best for breach of contract. Best countersued Stan for breach of contract.

Has Stan and/or Best breached the contract? If so, what damages might be recovered, if any, by each of them? Discuss.

Contracts Question 4 Assessment
July 2018, Question 1

This question is one that presents with a lot of factual and legal ambiguity. After the original contract formation there is a series of communications between the parties. Using an issue spotting checklist will help, but the issue spotting isn't clear-cut here since it is not always certain how a particular issue will conclude, which impacts the issues you discuss subsequently. The mistake some students make is they feel strongly about their conclusion on a particular issue, so they fail to analyze other issues that would be raised based on the other arguable conclusion, even when there are facts available to do so. Let the facts guide you to the issues the bar examiners expect you to analyze. There are no red herring facts (a red herring is something included to fool you and point you in the wrong direction) in the essay questions, so you should always use all the available facts to issue spot.

This is a good example of a question where a passing answer required you to fully analyze opposite alternative outcomes. When the conclusion on an issue could go either way, and that impacts the issues that follow, you need to issue spot the remaining issues based on both conclusions. For example, in this question, the request for adequate assurances needed to be in writing and wasn't, so it was likely improper for Best to consider Stan's failure to respond by 5/27 a repudiation. You could think that is game over since it is a clear rule and Best did not satisfy the writing requirement. We thought the same thing at first. However, if you didn't allow for the possibility that a judge might decide otherwise, you would have missed most of the rest of the issues raised by the facts in this question. Let the facts guide you. If you get attached to the rightness of your conclusion about the adequate assurances request, you would have missed discussing the subsequent issues about Stan's potential revocation of the repudiation, Stan's defense of impracticability, and Best's damages. When in doubt, let the facts that are available to use guide your issue spotting. If the facts are included in the question, you can bet they are on the grading rubric, too. If the bar examiners provided information you can use to calculate damages for Best, they expect you to analyze those damages, even if you think that is an unlikely result. In this situation, you can always signal to the reader that you think Best is unlikely to recover based on your earlier analysis, but if they do, here is the damages calculations given the appropriate rules and facts.

Make note of the areas highlighted in **bold** on the corresponding grid. The bold areas highlight the issues, analysis, and conclusions that are likely **required** to receive a passing score on this question.

Issue	Rule	Fact Application	Conclusion
Governing Law	• UCC applies to the sale of goods. • Common Law applies to all other agreements.	This contract is for tomatoes, which are movable tangible goods, so the UCC governs the contract.	**UCC applies**
Merchants	• Merchants are those who regularly deal with goods of a particular kind.	Stan is a tomato farmer and Best makes sauce, so both are merchants in a contract for tomatoes.	Merchants
Contract Formation	Contract requires an offer with clear and definite terms, acceptance, and consideration.	• Stan and Best have a valid written contract with the specified terms that Stan sell 5,000 bushels of tomatoes on July 1st to Best at $100 per bushel, payable upon delivery. • The consideration is the exchange of tomatoes for money.	Contract established
Anticipatory Repudiation	• Unequivocal expression by a party that they will not perform.	• On May 15 Stan sent an email stating, "Heavy rains in March-May slowed tomato ripening. Delivery will be two weeks late." This is the clear and unequivocal expression by Stan that he will not perform on July 1st, when performance is due, so Stan likely anticipatorily repudiated. • Best could treat the repudiation as a breach, but it is unclear what they meant when they responded, "okay."	5/15 e-mail could be an anticipatory repudiation
Contract Modification	**Under the UCC a contract can be modified with mutual assent and good faith, and consideration is not required.**	• In the alternative, **the 5/15 e-mail could be a request by Stan to modify the contract,** pushing the delivery date out by 2 weeks. **Stan has a good faith reason for the request since there were heavy rains, and it is more likely Best responded with mutual assent when they replied, "okay."** • **It is more likely the "okay" was an agreement to modify the delivery date of the contract.**	5/15 e-mail was likely a contract modification

Continued>

Issue	Rule	Fact Application	Conclusion
Demand for Adequate Assurances	**If reasonable grounds for insecurity about forthcoming performance, the insecure party can demand adequate assurances of due performance.** • **Demand must be done in writing.** • **Party can suspend their own performance until receiving adequate assurances.** **A repudiation occurs** when a party who received a justified written demand for adequate assurances fails to respond within a reasonable time, not to exceed 30 days.	• On 5/22 a bank employee told Best that the rains ruined Stan's crops and Stan wouldn't be able to fulfill his contracts. Since the bank employee knew both Best and Stan and presumably their business, this was a reasonable ground for Best to have insecurity about Stan's ability to fulfill the contract, especially since Stan already alerted Best about the heavy rains. • Best will assert they made a request for adequate assurances from Stan on 5/22. • However, Best should have demanded adequate assurances in writing, but instead they phoned Stan, so this was not a proper demand for adequate assurances. • Once a request for adequate assurances is made, the responding party has a reasonable time to respond, which is typically 30 days. Stan said he would know two weeks later, on 6/10, which seems a reasonable amount of time and is less than 30 days. Best said that they needed a firm commitment by 5/27, or they would buy tomatoes elsewhere. Here, Best only gave Stan 5 days to respond, which was not reasonable since the delivery date was still over a month out. • Best will argue this was a reasonable amount of time given that they needed time to find another supplier. • This was not a proper request for adequate assurances since it was verbal and more likely did not give Stan a reasonable amount of time to respond, so Stan did not breach by failing to give adequate assurances by 5/27.	Likely not a proper request for adequate assurances because verbal and likely untimely
Anticipatory Repudiation	• **An unequivocal expression by a party that they will not perform.** • Non-repudiating party may sue immediately, wait for performance and then sue, treat K as discharged, or urge performance.	• **Best will argue that when Stan did not respond to their request for a firm commitment by 5/27, this was an unequivocal expression Stan would not perform and an anticipatory repudiation.** • Best improperly treated the contract as repudiated when they proceeded to buy the 5,000 bushels of tomatoes they needed from another supplier, Agro-Farm.	Best will argue Stan anticipatorily repudiated

Continued>

Issue	Rule	Fact Application	Conclusion
Revocation of Repudiation	A repudiation can be retracted, except where the other party: • Sues for breach, • **Changes position in reliance on the repudiation,** or • States the repudiation is considered final.	• If Stan's failure to respond by 5/27 is seen as a failure to provide adequate assurances and a repudiation, that repudiation could be revoked. • On 6/6, Stan told Best, "I'll be able to deliver all 5,000 bushels," which would serve to revoke the earlier repudiation, and the revocation was within the time to perform under the original agreement, so it was timely made. • **However, Best will argue it came too late since they had already changed their position in reliance on the repudiation based on hearing no response from Stan on 5/27, so they contracted with Agro-Farm to supply the tomatoes they needed.**	**If Stan anticipatorily repudiated, the revocation was untimely**
Duty to Perform Discharged by Unforeseen Events	• Impossibility is a supervening, unforeseeable event (objective std.) and it makes performance literally impossible. • **Impracticability is the occurrence of an event the parties assumed would not occur makes performance extremely and unreasonably difficult.**	• As an alternative, Stan may argue that the heavy rain was unforeseen and made it impractical for him to perform under the contract. • However, rain is a normal occurrence, and even heavier than typical rain would be foreseeable by a farmer, so this would not provide Stan with an effective defense. • Stan could have obtained the tomatoes elsewhere to fulfill the contract.	**There is no impracticability of impossibility defense**
B's Expectation Damages	• Puts non-breaching party in position it would be in had K been performed (for UCC cover price or market price less the contract price). • Must mitigate damages.	• If Stan is in breach, Best can recover compensatory damages, which is the difference between the contract price and the cover price. • Best paid Agro-Farm $110/per bushel for the 5,000 bushels, so Stan would owe Best the difference between the $110/bushel price and the original $100/bushel price for 5,000 bushels, which is $50,000. • B could also recover for any consequential or incidental damages if established.	B receives $50,000
S's Expectation Damages	• Put non-breaching party in position it would be in had K been performed (for UCC cover price or market price less the contract price).	• If Best is in breach, Stan can recover the difference between his cover price and the contract price. • Stan sold the tomatoes to a vegetable wholesaler for $95/per bushel, so Best would owe the difference between the contract price of $100/per bushel and the cover price of $95/per bushel, for a total of $25,000. • Stan could also recover for any consequential and incidental damages if established.	S receives $25,000

Continued>

Contracts Question 5
February 2015, Question 1

Marta operated a successful fishing shop. She needed a new bait cooler, which had to be in place by May 1 for the first day of fishing season.

On February 1, Marta entered into a valid written contract with Don to purchase a Bait Mate cooler for $5,500 to be delivered no later than April 15.

On February 15, Don called Marta and told her that he was having trouble procuring a Bait Mate cooler. Marta reminded Don that meeting the April 15 deadline was imperative. "I'll see what's possible," Don responded in a somewhat doubtful tone. Concerned that Don might be unable to perform under the contract, Marta immediately sent him the following fax: "I am worried that you will not deliver a Bait Mate cooler by April 15. Please provide your supplier's guarantee that the unit will be available by our contract deadline. I want to have plenty of time to set it up." Believing that Marta's worries were overblown and not wanting to reveal his supplier's identity, Don did not respond to her fax.

When Don attempted to deliver a Bait Mate cooler on April 16, Marta refused delivery. Marta had purchased a Bait Mate cooler from another seller on April 14, paying $7,500, which included a $2,000 premium for one-day delivery by April 15.

Have Marta and/or Don breached the contract? If so, what damages might be recovered, if any, by each of them? Discuss.

Contracts Question 5 Assessment
February 2015, Question 1

This question is a typical UCC question that focuses on what events occur after contract formation. As seen with Question 3 above, where formation was not an issue under the common law, this question is an example of a UCC question where formation is not an issue. As seen above, this is determined because the facts state that the parties "entered into a valid written contract." Thus, any time spent on formation was not necessary.

This question is testing UCC principles regarding breach and performance issues. Whenever you have an essay that doesn't discuss formation, it is best to determine whether the UCC or common law principles apply and then have a post-formation checklist of all possible issues that might arise under either the UCC (which is the case here) or common law. Thus, here go back to your issues checklist that you wrote out (on your virtual scratch paper or whiteboard) initially when you organized this essay and make sure that you have issues like the right to demand adequate assurances and the response for it, as well as breach, cover, and damages under the UCC. If you are missing any of the tested issues here you need to make sure that your issues checklists are working properly for you and if not, be sure to add any issues you are missing each time you organize or write out an essay. Your issues checklist should be personal to you and might not be exactly like the one in this book. You need to make them such that they are useful to you, so you don't miss issues on exams. And you should have a UCC one as well as a common law one to ensure that you see the different issues that arise under each.

As with most contracts questions, this question has issues arise in chronological order. As such, your issues checklists should likely mirror the order here. Another helpful reminder that comes from this essay is the skill of seeing both sides and being objective. Here you should pay close attention to the timing of when Marta ordered the new cooler and see both sides as to how she possibly waited too long, which could arguably limit her remedies (conclusion either way would be fine but seeing both sides is critical). Another good reminder in this essay is that you need to use all relevant facts such as the fact that Marta included a desire to know the supplier, which could be construed as not "justified" for purposes of adequate assurances. This fact leads to a two-sided argument as well as logical inferences, both of which improve your analysis.

Make note of the areas highlighted in **bold** on the corresponding grid. The bold areas highlight the issues, analysis, and conclusions that are likely **required** to receive a passing score on this question. In general, the essay grids are provided to assist you in analyzing the essays and are much more detailed than what a student should create during the exam to organize their response to a question.

Issue	Rule	Fact Application	Conclusion
Applicable Law	• UCC applies to goods. • CL applies to other contracts. • Goods are moveable tangible objects. • Merchants are those who regularly deal with goods of a particular kind or have special knowledge about the goods.	Bait coolers are moveable tangible goods and thus the UCC will apply. As a fishing shop owner, M regularly deals with bait coolers; D also regularly deals with bait coolers since he sells them to businesses, so both are merchants.	UCC governs.
Formation of Contract	Offer, acceptance, consideration	Here, the parties "entered into a valid written contract" for D to provide M a Bait Mate cooler for $5,500 to be delivered by April 15. Since the contract is valid there are no applicable defenses to discuss (SOF would be at issue because goods over $500 but the contract is written which would satisfy the SOF).	Valid contract.
Anticipatory Repudiation	• Unequivocal expression • Before time for performance due • That they will not perform • Nonrepudiating party can: sue immediately, suspend performance, treat K as discharged, or urge performance.	D expressed to M that he might not be able to deliver the cooler to her by April 15 because he was having trouble procuring a Bait Mate cooler; he would see what's possible after M reminded him that the April 15 deadline was imperative; not an unequivocal expression that he could not perform because he wasn't sure if he could perform and used a doubtful tone indicating he might be able to perform.	No anticipatory repudiation.
Right to Demand Adequate Assurances	• If reasonable grounds for insecurity about forthcoming performance, the insecure party can demand adequate assurances of due performance. • Demand must be done in writing. • Party can suspend their own performance until receiving adequate assurances.	D's response did cause reasonable grounds for insecurity about his performance. A reasonable person would be concerned if they were told that a performance might not occur and that the other party would see what was "possible," especially when told so in a doubtful tone indicating it is more likely they won't be able to perform. Also, a fax is sufficient as a demand in writing.	M was permitted to demand adequate assurances.

Continued>

Issue	Rule	Fact Application	Conclusion
Response to Adequate Assurances	A repudiation of the contract occurs when a party who received a justified written demand for adequate assurances fails to respond within a reasonable time not to exceed 30 days.	• Arguably her request that he provide the supplier's guarantee was not justified since she should have only requested assurances that D would perform, not his supplier, since the contract was between her and D. • M sent her response immediately after their Feb. 15 conversation and thus, **D should have responded within 30 days but as of March 15 D had not yet responded, which resulted in a repudiation of the contract.** • **Although D didn't want to reveal his supplier's identity and believed that M's worries were overblown, he was required to respond to her demand within a reasonable time not to exceed 30 days because her concern was justified as discussed above.**	**D did not respond as required.**
Breach/Cover	When a seller fails to deliver or repudiates a contract, the buyer may cancel the contract and cover by seeking the reasonable purchase of other goods in good faith without unreasonable delay.	• Here, after D's repudiation, M covered by purchasing another cooler on April 14; **she paid $7,500 which was $2,000 more than the contract price which may be a reasonable amount given she had to pay for one-day delivery.** • However, it is possible that waiting almost a month after D's repudiation to cover the day before she needed it was not reasonable and might amount to an unreasonable delay to cover.	Unreasonable delay may be the cause of the additional $2,000 expense she incurred.
Perfect Tender Rule	UCC also requires perfect tender such that all goods must be delivered per the contract specifications or the buyer can reject the goods.	**Even if he didn't repudiate he still didn't perform as he was a day late, which would not amount to a perfect tender as the deadline was imperative.**	**D in breach and M could reject goods.**
Expectation Damages	Put the party in the position they would have been in had the contract been performed. Under the UCC—difference between the contract price and the cover price.	• **M will seek damages in the amount of $2,000 since that amount would put her in the position she would have been in had D delivered the cooler on time since this is the difference in cover and contract.** • D will seek damages for the $5,500 arguing M waited unreasonably to cover and actually covered one day prior to performance being due; however, he will likely be unsuccessful in his argument because M was entitled to cover since he repudiated the contract; further, he did not deliver at the time performance was due as he delivered it one day late which is not perfect tender and M was entitled to reject delivery.	M can get $2,000 in expectation damages provided no limitations barring recovery.

Continued>

Issue	Rule	Fact Application	Conclusion
Limitations on Damages	**Damages limitations include:** • Foreseeable • **Unavoidable** • Certain • Causation	• Damages foreseeable at the time of K formation because D knew deadline April 15; although it is unclear whether he knew at that time that it was imperative for her first day of fishing season in her fishing shop • **Arguably M did not mitigate her damages as she waited one month past the deadline when D needed to respond to her adequate assurances demand; delay could have been avoided possibly if other seller would have been able to supply it in advance of that date; but it is possible she waited until the day before since she was still waiting for D to respond; even if she could have waited one more day for the date performance was due, D would have still breached as he did not deliver it on time as required and she would have ordered the cooler anyway for a one-day premium delivery fee at that time.** • $2,000 amount would be certain as she likely has the receipt from the other seller with proof of payment. • $2,000 additional expense was caused by D's repudiation as M would not have purchased another cooler the day before performance was due if D would have responded to her request.	D breached the contract but conclusion could go either way based on whether M mitigated her damages and/or had an unreasonable delay in covering—key was to argue both ways and then conclude as to the one most likely and why.
Consequential Damages	**Those that are a direct and foreseeable consequence of the contract nonperformance.**	None apply beyond the amount already covered by expectation damages above.	No consequential damages.
Incidental Damages	**Ordinary expenses incurred in responding to the contract breach.**	None apply beyond the amount already covered by expectation damages above.	No incidental damages.

Contracts Question 6
February 2006, Question 5

Marla is a manufacturer of widgets. Larry is a lawyer who regularly represents Marla in legal matters relating to her manufacturing business. Larry is also the sole owner and operator of a business called Supply Source ("SS"), in which he acts as an independent broker of surplus goods. SS is operated independently from Larry's law practice and from a separate office.

At a time when the market for widgets was suffering from over-supply, Marla called Larry at his SS office. During their telephone conversation, Marla told Larry that, if he could find a buyer for her excess inventory of 100,000 widgets, Larry could keep anything he obtained over $1.00 per widget. Although Marla thought it unlikely that Larry would be able to sell them for more than $1.25 per widget, she said, ". . . and, if you get more than $1.25 each, we'll talk about how to split the excess." Larry replied, "Okay," and undertook to market the widgets.

During a brief period when market demand for widgets increased, Larry found a buyer, Ben. In a written agreement with Larry, Ben agreed to purchase all 100,000 widgets for $2.50 each. Ben paid Larry $250,000. Larry then sent Marla a check for $100,000 with a cover letter stating, "I have sold all of the 100,000 widgets to Ben. Here is your $100,000 as we agreed."

When Marla learned that Ben had paid $2.50 per widget, she called Larry and said, "You lied to me about what you got for the widgets. I don't think the deal we made over the telephone is enforceable. I want you to send me the other $150,000 you received from Ben, and then we'll talk about a reasonable commission for you. But right now, we don't have a deal." Larry refused to remit any part of the $150,000 to Marla.

1. To what extent, if any, is the agreement between Larry and Marla enforceable? Discuss.

2. In his conduct toward Marla, what ethical violations, if any, has Larry committed? Discuss.

Contracts Question 6 Assessment
February 2006, Question 5

Sometimes a bar exam essay question will come along that has a "deal-breaker" issue contained in it. Deal-breaker issues are usually tricky to spot and require more thought than usual. Where there is a deal-breaker issue, a panicked reading of the facts and frantic essay writing will almost certainly lead to failure.

This contracts question is an older question, but it is an excellent example of a question with a tricky deal-breaker issue in it. There is no easy way to know if there is a deal-breaker issue in a question. As always, let the facts guide you. Slow down and carefully read the facts. If there is a fact that seems odd or unusual, take a moment to think it through and figure out why that fact is in the question. Essay questions are very carefully drafted. Consequently, there are usually never any "red-herring" type facts. Each fact is contained in the question for a reason, and you need to figure out what that reason is.

We always recommend that students read the question through once without making any notes to get a feel for the story. Doing so also prevents jumping to conclusions and heading down the wrong path. This question provides an excellent example of how reading too fast and jumping to conclusions can lead to a failing essay. The first sentence of the question states that Marla manufactures widgets. A student may read that sentence and jump to the conclusion that widgets are goods and, therefore, the UCC governs the contract, jotting down "UCC" on the virtual scratch paper/ dry erase board and proceeding to the next sentence. But that is incorrect. Further reading of the question reveals that while Marla manufactures widgets, she is contracting with Larry to provide the broker service of finding a buyer for her surplus widgets. Thus, Larry is providing a service (finding a buyer) not purchasing widgets (goods), so the common law governs the contract. During the extreme time pressure of the exam, it is easy to miss such a subtle distinction. But a reading of paragraph two should cause a student to stop and question what the contract is about because the deal outlined is unusual or atypical. Usually, a contract is for one party to sell something and the other to buy it. However, this deal is more complicated than that, so it should cause you to slow down and figure out what is really going on. Don't become distracted by focusing on the details provided regarding the contract terms. Always be clear about what the basis of the bargain is and affirmatively decide which law governs the contract. Once you figure out that the common law applies, the rest of the question is pretty easy. It is worth noting that it is important to identify the Statute of Frauds as a potential issue, even though the conclusion is that it's inapplicable. Remember: Use the facts to prove, or disprove, an issue.

Though the contracts issues are much more heavily weighted, this question is actually a crossover question because one of the calls of the question pertains to professional responsibility (PR). Even if you haven't started reviewing the PR rules at this point in your studies, you should have enough knowledge of the rules to muddle through this question since the PR issues here aren't particularly difficult. It is certain that PR will be tested on every California bar exam, so a mini-review of PR here is helpful.

Make note of the areas highlighted in **bold** on the corresponding grid. The bold areas highlight the issues, analysis, and conclusions that are likely **required** to receive a passing score on this question.

Issue	Rule	Fact Application	Conclusion
Call #1 (Enforceable Agreement)			
Applicable Law	• UCC applies to goods • CL to other contracts	Here, goods are involved because M manufactures widgets, *but* the contract is for L's services as broker to perform the service of finding M a buyer for her surplus widgets. M is not selling goods to L, so CL applies. [*Note:* One state-released answer discussed this concept within a SOF discussion, but still discussed the ultimate issue that CL, not UCC, applies.]	CL governs.
Offer	• **Present intent to be bound** • **Definite and certain terms** • **Identified offeree**	• M showed intent to be bound by calling L at SS office. M wanted to get rid of excess widgets she could not sell herself; offers L a share of profit to find buyer. • **Definite and certain terms:** quantity of 100,000 widgets, L keeps amount between $1 and $1.25 per widget; they will discuss later amounts over $1.25, if any. Possibly uncertain terms due to this later discussion, but more likely, since they agreed to later discuss, that they could later determine a fair amount to split excess of $1.25, and a court could use analogy of UCC (even though not UCC) to find a "reasonable" price here for excess in the event they could not agree.** • Identifiable offeree is L as she called him at his SS office.	Yes, offer.
Acceptance	Unilateral k requires performance to accept.	Here, unilateral contract because M seeking L to perform by finding her a buyer. L did perform by finding Ben to buy all widgets for $2.50 per widget.	Yes, acceptance.
Consideration	Bargained-for exchange.	M agreed to share part of the profit on the widget sale with L; L agreed to perform the service of finding a buyer for the widgets.	Yes, consideration.
Defenses: SOF	Sale of goods over $500 needs a writing.	Here, goods themselves not being sold between M and L—their contract not for sale of goods, but rather for L to find buyer for M—so contract between M and L not for sale of goods.	SOF not applicable.

Continued>

Issue	Rule	Fact Application	Conclusion
Quasi-contract	Court can award value of benefit conferred to one party to avoid unjust enrichment.	Here, even if offer not valid above (due to indefinite terms) and no valid contract, court would still award L fair market value or reasonable share of profits to avoid M's unjust enrichment. Same principle applies to M for excess over $1.25 that L kept; M should get a fair share of that.	Quasi-k would apply if k not valid.
Call #2 (Ethical Violations)			
Duty of Loyalty/ Conflict **(Business Transaction with Client)**	**L must not enter a business transaction with a client unless** • **Terms are fair and reasonable to the client** • **Terms fully disclosed in writing to client** • **Client advised in writing to seek independent counsel** • **Client gives informed consent in writing**	Here, L, a lawyer, entered into an agreement with a client, M, as he regularly represents her manufacturing business. • Terms were likely fair and reasonable to client as M made the terms herself. • Terms not in writing as this was an oral contract over the phone. Also, not all terms fully disclosed because of ambiguity of share if price exceeds $1.25. • **Client not advised to seek independent counsel.** • **Client didn't give informed consent in writing.**	**L breached ethical duty.**
Duties of honesty/ communication	L owes a duty to communicate with client and be honest with client and public at large.	**Here, L did not disclose the excess he made over $1.25 and refused to give M any part of this when they agreed to discuss how to split the excess at a later time.**	**L breached ethical duties.**

PART 6 *CRIMES*

CRIMINAL LAW TABLE OF CONTENTS

CRIMINAL PROCEDURE TABLE OF CONTENTS

INTRODUCTION TO CRIMES

This chapter covers both criminal law and criminal procedure. Although you likely took these as two distinct courses in law school, we have combined them here because that is the way they are primarily tested on the California bar exam. Criminal procedure is frequently the subject of a crossover question and often crosses with criminal law, evidence or constitutional law.

The key to both criminal law and criminal procedure is in the approach to the most heavily tested topics, including murder—even though it took a nap for a few years (but it recently made a comeback)—which they often like to test in conjunction with other felonies or conspiracy and accomplice liability; the search and seizure provisions of the Fourth Amendment; and some Fifth and Sixth Amendment issues. It is imperative to approach each specific issue in the appropriate order when you organize and write out your essays to ensure that you don't inadvertently omit any key elements or steps that are crucial and can affect the entire conclusion, so pay close attention to the order in which each particular element or step is addressed in the outline.

While issues checklists and fact triggers are extremely useful for many subjects, they are not as helpful for these subjects. However, one cluster that tends to stand out is conspiracy, accomplice liability, and murder with an underlying felony, as they like to ask about murder for a defendant who didn't actually commit the murder but was involved somehow with another crime such as conspiracy to rob a store, and then someone died, triggering a murder call. Generally, the calls of the questions are specific and typically direct you to discuss murder and any lesser included offenses, or specifically indicate that the defendant is alleging a violation of their Fourth, Fifth, or Sixth Amendment rights. Thus, it is important to not only know the rules and their elements, but also to know specifically what rights are covered by each of the applicable amendments. For example, you must know that *Miranda* rights are invoked under the Fifth Amendment. Likewise, you must know that the lesser-included offenses for murder include voluntary and involuntary manslaughter. While the calls tend to be comparatively more specific in crimes essay questions, you are required to know how the issues interrelate in order to properly spot all of the issues.

Similarly, while fact triggers can be extremely useful for many other subjects, in criminal law it is a bit more simplified. For instance, if there is a dead person, you probably need to address murder. Issue spotting is generally straightforward on crimes essays because the facts are obvious, and the calls tend to be specific. Nonetheless, it is still a good idea to memorize the issues checklist and pay attention to the fact triggers available to ensure success in the rare event that you receive an open-ended question call. We have also included specific issue spotting checklists for certain topics.

What is critical to success on a crimes essay, in addition to knowing how to approach each specific issue, is having a full understanding of how the rules apply. This is one subject where rote memorization—without a clear understanding of how and why the rules apply, and the subtle distinctions between the rules—can lead to trouble. For example, the bar examiners can create a fact pattern that raises both conspiracy and accomplice liability as issues. However, if you don't understand the difference between the two issues, you may either inadvertently omit one issue from your response or analyze both issues in the same way, even though the rules have slightly different requirements. The subtle differences in the rules often result in different outcomes between the two crimes.

ISSUES CHECKLIST

CRIMINAL LAW

Crimes Against the Person
Assault
Battery
Mayhem
Kidnapping
Rape
Homicide

Theft Crimes
Larceny
Embezzlement
False pretenses
Robbery
Extortion
Theft
Burglary
Receipt of stolen property
Arson

Incomplete Crimes
Solicitation
Attempt
Conspiracy
Merger

Accomplice Liability
Defenses
Self-defense
Defense of others
Defense of property
Insanity
Intoxication
Necessity
Mistake
Entrapment

CRIMINAL PROCEDURE

Fourth Amendment
Arrest
Routine stops
Search and seizure
    Exceptions
        SILA
        Plain view
        Automobile
        Consent
        Exigent circumstances
        Stop and frisk

Fifth Amendment
Miranda warnings
Right to counsel
Right against self-incrimination
Double jeopardy
Due process

Sixth Amendment
Right to counsel
Right to confront witnesses
Right to jury
Right to speedy trial

Exclusionary Rule
Good Faith Warrant Exception
Confessions/Identification
Voluntariness
Due process
Pleas

Eighth Amendment
Bail
Sentencing

MEMORIZATION ATTACK SHEET

CRIMES AGAINST PERSONS

◆ **Assault**
  - Attempt to commit battery, or
  - Intent to place another in fear of imminent injury
  - Aggravated if deadly weapon used

◆ **Battery**
  - Intentional or reckless
  - Causing
  - Injury or offensive touching
  - Aggravated if deadly weapon used

◆ **Mayhem**
  - Permanent dismemberment or disablement of body
  - Modernly treated as aggravated battery

◆ **Kidnapping**
  - Unlawful confinement
  - Move or conceal in secret place
  - Aggravated if ransom/crime/child
  - False imprisonment = lesser-included offense

◆ **Rape**
  - Unlawful sexual intercourse
  - Not spouse (not modernly)
  - No consent
  - Modern gender neutral

◆ **Murder**
  - Unlawful killing
  - With malice (4 ways)
    ◆ Intent to kill
      - Presumed if deadly weapon
    ◆ Intent to commit grievous bodily injury
    ◆ Reckless indifference
    ◆ Felony murder rule
      - Natural and probable consequence
      - During commission
      - Felony independent of killing
      - Not liable if co-felon killed by nonfelon (maj.)
      - Jx split if bystander killed
        - Agency (D not liable)
        - Proximate cause (D liable)
  - Actual and proximate cause
  - Intent can transfer
  - Fleeing felon — deadly force ok if escape, threat, warning, objective

◆ **Voluntary manslaughter**
  - Reasonable provocation
  - D in fact provoked
  - No time to cool off, and
  - D did not cool off
  - OR imperfect self-defense

◆ **Involuntary manslaughter**
  - Gross negligence
    ◆ D disregards substantial danger of serious harm/death
  - OR misdemeanor manslaughter

◆ **Degrees of murder**
  - 1st degree
    ◆ Premeditation, and
    ◆ Deliberation
    ◆ OR felony murder rule (FMR) — dangerous felonies
  - 2nd degree
    ◆ All murders that are not 1st degree or manslaughter

◆ **Defenses** — see below

THEFT CRIMES

◆ **Larceny**
  - Trespassory taking and carrying away
  - Of personal property
  - Of another
  - With intent to permanently deprive

◆ **Embezzlement**
  - Fraudulent conversion
  - Of personal property
  - Of another
  - By one in lawful possession

◆ **False pretenses**
  - D knowingly makes
  - False representation
  - Past or present material fact
  - Causes another to
  - Convey title

◆ **Robbery**
  - Larceny elements, and
  - Property taken from person or their presence
  - Through force or fear

◆ **Extortion**
  - Threat of future harm
  - Deprive owner of property

- ◆ **Theft**
  - Illegal taking
  - Of another's property
- ◆ **Burglary**
  - Breaking and entering
  - Of dwelling house
  - Nighttime
  - Intent to commit felony
  - Modern any structure and time
- ◆ **Receipt of stolen property**
  - Knowingly
  - Receive, conceal, or dispose of
  - Stolen property
  - Intent to deprive owner
- ◆ **Arson**
  - Malicious burning
  - Dwelling house
  - Of another
  - Modern most structures and explosives

INCHOATE CRIMES

- ◆ **Solicitation**
  - Request or encourage
  - Another to commit a crime
  - Intent that they do so
  - Merges into actual crime
- ◆ **Conspiracy**
  - Agreement
  - Two or more people
    - ◆ Modern unilateral ok
  - Intent to commit unlawful act
  - Majority require overt act
  - Co-conspirator liable if
    - ◆ Foreseeable
    - ◆ In furtherance of objective
  - Does not merge
  - Withdrawal defense
- ◆ **Attempt**
  - Intent to commit crime
  - Substantial step (beyond mere preparation)
  - Merges into actual crime

ACCOMPLICE LIABILITY

- ◆ **Principal 1st—commits crime**
- ◆ **Accomplice (principal 2nd)**
  - Aids, abets, encourages
  - Carrying out of a crime
  - Doesn't commit actual crime
  - Liable for additional crimes of accomplices if:
    - ◆ Foreseeable
- ◆ **Accessory before the fact (not present)**
- ◆ **Accessory after the fact**
- ◆ **Modern distinctions**
- ◆ **Withdrawal**

DEFENSES

- ◆ **Self-defense**
  - Reasonable belief
  - Reasonable force
- ◆ **Defense of others**
  - Reasonable belief
  - Reasonable force
  - Min.: stands in shoes
- ◆ **Defense of property**
  - Reasonable force
  - No deadly force
- ◆ **Insanity**
  - *M'Naghten* test
    - ◆ D has mental disease
    - ◆ D can't understand, or
    - ◆ D doesn't know wrong
  - Irresistible impulse
    - ◆ D has mental disease
    - ◆ D unable to control conduct/conform
  - *Durham* test
    - ◆ Conduct product of mental illness (but for test)
  - Model Penal Code
    - ◆ D lacks capacity
    - ◆ D cannot appreciate criminality or conform
- ◆ **Intoxication**
  - Voluntary
    - ◆ Negates specific intent
  - Involuntary
    - ◆ Possible defense to all
- ◆ **Necessity**
  - Reasonable belief
  - Necessary to avoid
  - Imminent and greater injury to society
- ◆ **Mistake**
  - Of fact
    - ◆ Negates specific intent
    - ◆ Negates general intent if mistake reasonable
  - Of law
    - ◆ No defense
- ◆ **Impossibility**
  - Factual
    - ◆ D makes mistake about an issue of fact
    - ◆ No defense
  - Legal
    - ◆ D thinks act is criminal but it isn't
    - ◆ Valid defense
- ◆ **Entrapment**
  - Law enforcement
  - Induces D to commit crime
  - D wasn't predisposed to commit crime

FOURTH AMENDMENT

- ◆ **Arrest**
  - Need warrant if in home
  - Warrant based on probable cause
  - Probable cause is reasonable belief a law is violated
- ◆ **Routine stops okay**
  - Automobile stop
    - ◆ Reasonable suspicion
    - ◆ Objective standard
  - Fixed checkpoints for compliance with laws
  - Stop and frisk (see below)
- ◆ **Search and seizure**
  - Govt. action required
  - Expectation of privacy
    - ◆ Open Fields
    - ◆ Sensory Enhancing Technology
    - ◆ Dog sniffing
    - ◆ Location tracking
  - Warrant based on
    - ◆ Probable cause
      - Connected
      - Found in place
      - Informant (totality of circ.)
    - ◆ Neutral magistrate
    - ◆ Description
    - ◆ Knock and announce
  - No warrant needs exception
    - ◆ SILA
      - Lawful arrest
      - Area within access/immediate control
      - Protective sweep ok
    - ◆ Plain View
      - Legitimately on premises
    - ◆ Automobile
      - Probable cause
      - Impound (can search)
    - ◆ Consent
      - Voluntarily
    - ◆ Exigent circumstances
      - Destruction of evidence
      - Injury to persons
      - Hot pursuit
    - ◆ Stop and Frisk
      - Reasonable suspicion
      - Articulable facts
      - Pat down for weapons okay

FIFTH AMENDMENT

- ◆ *Miranda* **warnings**
  - Right to remain silent
  - Anything they say can be used against them
  - Right to attorney
    - ◆ Custodial
    - ◆ Interrogation by police
      - Likely to elicit incriminating response
      - Suspect must know police are questioning
    - ◆ Exception: public safety
    - ◆ Cannot re-*Mirandize* until 14 days later
- ◆ **Waiver of** *Miranda*
  - Voluntarily
  - Knowingly, intelligently
- ◆ **Right to Counsel (***Miranda***)**
  - Unambiguous request by accused to invoke
  - Police must cease all questioning
- ◆ **Right against self-incrimination**
  - Only to testimony, or
  - Communicative evidence
  - Could expose them to criminal liability
- ◆ **Double jeopardy**
  - Cannot be tried for same offense twice
  - Applicable if jury or 1st witness sworn in
- ◆ **Due process**
  - Voluntary confessions
  - No unnecessarily suggestive ID

SIXTH AMENDMENT

- ◆ **Right to counsel**
  - Critical stage (post-charge)
  - Line-up, show-up, or sentencing
  - Not for photo id, handwriting, fingerprints, physical evidence
  - Ineffective assistance
    - ◆ Counsel performance deficient
    - ◆ Based on reasonably competent attorney
    - ◆ Different result if not deficient
  - Substitute attorney if justice requires
  - D can waive right
- ◆ **Right to confront witnesses**
  - Adverse/hostile witness
  - Compel testimony or cross-examine
  - Only for testimonial statements
    - ◆ Nontestimonial if ongoing emergency
  - Co-defendants
    - ◆ Redact statement, or
    - ◆ Other D takes stand

- ◆ **Right to jury trial**
  - For serious offenses
  - With potential for > 6 months in jail
  - D can waive right
  - At least 6 jurors to start
  - Federal and state crime: unanimous
  - Need impartial jury
  - Jury not fair cross-section if D can prove
    - ◆ Group excluded is distinctive
    - ◆ # in representative group not reasonable compared to # in community
    - ◆ Systematic exclusion
- ◆ **Right to speedy trial**
  - Case-by-case decision
  - Court balances:
    - ◆ Length of delay
    - ◆ Reason for delay
    - ◆ Prejudice to D
    - ◆ Time and manner in which D asserted right
- ◆ **Right to preliminary hearing**
  - Need probable cause if not established
  - D can waive right

EXCLUSIONARY RULE

- ◆ **Judge-made doctrine**
  - Can't use evidence if found in violation D's 4th, 5th, or 6th Amend. rights
  - D needs standing—his own rights violated only
- ◆ **Fruit of the poisonous tree**
  - Other evidence stemming from violation inadmissible too
  - Exceptions
    - ◆ Independent source
    - ◆ Inevitable discovery
    - ◆ Purged taint
    - ◆ Violation of knock and announce
- ◆ **Can still use evidence**
  - To impeach

- In civil, parole, or grand jury hearings
- ◆ **Good faith warrant exception**
  - Improper warrant results in 4th Amend. violation
    - ◆ Evidence not barred if officers act in good faith
    - ◆ Except lie/no probable cause/defective on face

CONFESSION/ID/MISC.

- ◆ **Voluntary confessions**
  - No police coercion
  - Totality of circumstances
  - Mental illness irrelevant
- ◆ **Due process: identification**
  - No unnecessarily suggestive ID of the defendant
  - Totality of circumstances
  - ID unfair to D
- ◆ **Plea bargain**
  - Voluntary, intelligent
  - No obligation to plea
  - Judge doesn't have to accept

EIGHTH AMENDMENT

- ◆ **Bail**
  - Not excessive/unduly high
  - Court considers:
    - ◆ Seriousness of offense
    - ◆ Weight of evidence against D
    - ◆ D's financial abilities
    - ◆ D's character
- ◆ **Cruel/unusual punishment**
  - Penalty cannot be grossly disproportionate to crime
  - No death if mentally retarded or (mandatory) minor
  - Victim statements allowed during penalty phase
  - Jury considers mitigating circumstances against death

CRIMINAL LAW RULE OUTLINE

I. CRIMES AGAINST THE PERSON

A. **Assault** is either an attempt to commit a battery or the intent to place another in reasonable apprehension of imminent injury. Aggravated assault if deadly weapon used.

B. **Battery** is the intentional or reckless causing of a bodily injury or an offensive touching to another. Aggravated battery if deadly weapon used.

C. **Mayhem** is the permanent dismemberment or disablement of a bodily part. Modernly it is treated as aggravated battery.

D. **Kidnapping** is the unlawful confinement of another, involving movement or concealment in a secret place. Aggravated if for ransom, to commit another crime, or if children are taken.
   1. **False Imprisonment** is a lesser-included offense to kidnapping. False imprisonment is the unlawful confinement of a person without their consent.

E. **Rape** is the unlawful sexual intercourse of a female, not one's wife, without her consent. Modernly rape is gender-neutral and marriage is irrelevant.

F. **Homicide** is the unlawful taking of the life of another. The two types of homicide are murder and manslaughter.
   1. **Murder** is the **unlawful killing** of another person with **malice aforethought**.
      a. **Malice** is the requisite mental state for murder and can be established by:
         1. An **intent to kill** (desire to kill or knowledge to a substantial certainty death will occur);
            a. Use of a **deadly weapon** or instrument creates the inference of an intent to kill.
         2. An **intent to commit grievous bodily injury**;
         3. A **reckless indifference** to an unjustifiably high risk to human life (also known as "depraved heart" murder); or
         4. An **intent to commit a dangerous felony,** known as the **felony murder rule**.
            a. The intent to commit certain dangerous felonies supplies the malice requirement for murder where death is a **natural and probable consequence** (foreseeable) of the defendant's conduct and occurs **during the commission** of the felony, even if the death is accidental.
            b. The **underlying felony must be independent** of the killing (i.e., felony cannot be aggravated battery).
               i. **Death of co-felon:** The majority of courts hold that a defendant is **not liable** for the death of a co-felon when a **non-felon kills the co-felon** during commission of the felony (e.g., a co-felon is killed by a police officer or victim). (Also called the *Redline* view).
               ii. **Death of bystander:** Jurisdictions are **split** as to whether a defendant is liable for murder when the **non-felon victim, or a police officer, kills a bystander** during the commission of the felony. In **agency theory** jurisdictions the defendant is **not liable** (majority rule); In **proximate cause theory** jurisdictions the defendant is **liable** (minority rule).
            c. **Inherently dangerous felonies:** The felony murder rule typically applies to the following inherently dangerous felonies:
               i. Burglary
               ii. Arson
               iii. Rape
               iv. Robbery
               v. Kidnapping
               vi. Traditionally, mayhem and sodomy were also included. Modernly, more felonies are considered dangerous and could be included depending on the jurisdiction.
      b. **Causation:** The defendant's conduct must also be the **cause in fact** (but for test) and the **proximate cause** (foreseeable) of the death.

> **Exam tip:** Generally, in homicide essays, causation is a minor issue that can be addressed in one or two sentences. However, when the defendant did not do the actual killing, always argue both sides of the causation issue. For example, where the victim kills themself, a third-party kills the victim, or the killing was not contemplated or was far removed from events, causation should be addressed.

   c. **Intent can transfer** for murder (just as in torts) but not for attempted murder.

   d. **"Fleeing felon":** Under the "fleeing felon standard," a law enforcement officer **can use deadly force** against a fleeing felon if:

     1. The use of deadly force is **necessary to prevent the felon's escape;**

     2. The fleeing felon has **threatened the officer with a weapon** or the officer has probable cause to believe that the felon has **committed a crime** involving the infliction or threatened infliction of serious physical harm; and

     3. The officer gives the felon some **warning** of the imminent use of deadly force, if feasible.

     4. The officer's intent will be judged **objectively** from the perspective of a reasonable officer at the scene.

2. **Manslaughter:** In most states there are two types of manslaughter, voluntary and involuntary.

   a. **Voluntary manslaughter:** There are two types of voluntary manslaughter—heat of passion and imperfect self-defense.

     1. **Heat of passion:** Murder can be reduced to **voluntary manslaughter** if the defendant killed in the heat of passion and the following requirements are met:

       a. **Reasonable provocation:** Defendant acted in response to a provocation that would cause a reasonable person to lose self-control,

       b. **Acted in heat of passion:** Defendant **was in fact provoked** at the time they acted,

       c. **No cooling off time:** There was **insufficient time for a reasonable person to cool off** between the provocation and the killing, and

       d. **Defendant did not cool off:** The defendant **did not in fact cool off** by the time they killed.

     2. **Imperfect self-defense:** Murder may also be reduced to **voluntary manslaughter** if the defendant kills under an **unreasonable mistake** about the need for deadly self-defense or the **defendant started the altercation.**

> **Exam tip:** Even if a call asks specifically about murder, always remember that murder can be mitigated to manslaughter if there is reasonable provocation. So, if the facts give rise to manslaughter, always consider addressing this issue as it might negate a murder conviction or charge.

   b. **Involuntary manslaughter** can arise two ways.

     1. **Gross (criminal) negligence:** Involuntary manslaughter arises when a person's behavior is grossly negligent and the conduct results in the death of another. Gross negligence is the **disregard of a very substantial danger of serious bodily harm or death.**

     2. **Misdemeanor-manslaughter:** Involuntary manslaughter also arises when the defendant commits a **misdemeanor** and a **death occurs accidentally during its commission** or for **felonies that don't rise to the level** of murder under the FMR.

3. **First-degree murder** (statutory murder) can arise two ways.

   a. **Premeditation and deliberation:** First-degree murder applies when the killing was the result of premeditation (defendant **had time to reflect** upon the idea of killing, even if only for a moment) and deliberation (defendant acted in a **cool and dispassionate** manner).

   b. **Enumerated inherently dangerous felony** under an application of the **felony murder rule,** such as the felonies of **M**ayhem, **R**obbery, **S**odomy, **B**urglary, **A**rson, **R**ape, or **K**idnapping. Think **MRS. BARK**. Other felonies might also be included depending on the jurisdiction.

4. **Second-degree murder (also statutory murder):** If the murder does **not rise to the level of first-degree** murder and is **not reduced to manslaughter**, the defendant will be guilty of second-degree murder.

> **Issue spotting tip:** If the defendant did not actually kill the victim themself, always consider their possible liability for murder as an accomplice, as a co-conspirator, or through application of the felony murder rule.

5. **Defenses** may apply to murder (see section V. below for defenses).

> **Exam tip:** Use our "bullet proof murder approach" to accurately analyze any fact pattern with a killing. First, consider whether the preliminary issues of accomplice liability and/or inchoate offenses are present. Then, define murder. Next, list all four types of malice and analyze those that are applicable to the facts. Next, analyze any voluntary or involuntary manslaughter issues present, which will serve to reduce the murder charge. Next, if manslaughter does not clearly apply, analyze whether the murder will be first or second degree. Lastly, consider if any defenses are at issue under the facts. If the call is specific and asks about first-degree murder or manslaughter, etc., you can go directly to those types of murder/manslaughter in accordance with the call.

BULLET PROOF MURDER APPROACH

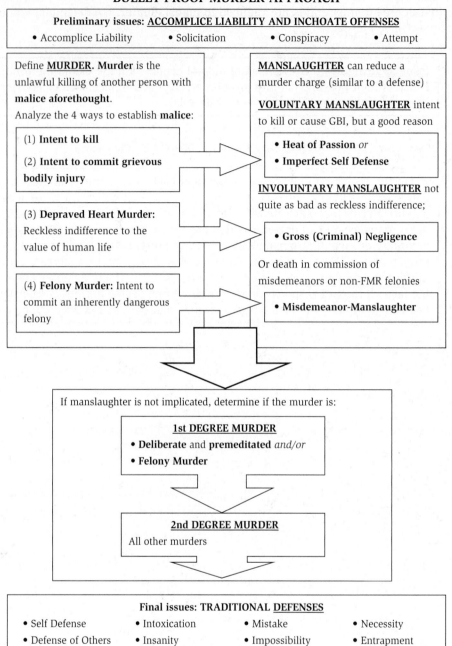

Preliminary issues: ACCOMPLICE LIABILITY AND INCHOATE OFFENSES

- Accomplice Liability
- Solicitation
- Conspiracy
- Attempt

Define **MURDER**. **Murder** is the unlawful killing of another person with **malice aforethought**.

Analyze the 4 ways to establish **malice**:

(1) **Intent to kill**

(2) **Intent to commit grievous bodily injury**

(3) **Depraved Heart Murder:** Reckless indifference to the value of human life

(4) **Felony Murder:** Intent to commit an inherently dangerous felony

MANSLAUGHTER can reduce a murder charge (similar to a defense)

VOLUNTARY MANSLAUGHTER intent to kill or cause GBI, but a good reason

- **Heat of Passion** *or*
- **Imperfect Self Defense**

INVOLUNTARY MANSLAUGHTER not quite as bad as reckless indifference;

- **Gross (Criminal) Negligence**

Or death in commission of misdemeanors or non-FMR felonies

- **Misdemeanor-Manslaughter**

If manslaughter is not implicated, determine if the murder is:

1st DEGREE MURDER
- **Deliberate** and **premeditated** *and/or*
- **Felony Murder**

2nd DEGREE MURDER
All other murders

Final issues: TRADITIONAL DEFENSES

- Self Defense
- Defense of Others
- Intoxication
- Insanity
- Mistake
- Impossibility
- Necessity
- Entrapment

II. THEFT CRIMES

A. **Larceny** is the trespassory taking and carrying away of personal property of another with the intent to permanently deprive the owner of the property (steal). Intent occurs at the time of the taking. **Larceny by trick** occurs when the defendant tricks the other party and obtains possession through fraud or deceit.

B. **Embezzlement** is the fraudulent conversion of personal property of another by one who is already in lawful possession of that property. Some states include real property as well.

> **Exam tip:** For embezzlement, the embezzler always has lawful possession; whereas for larceny, the person taking the property does not have lawful possession.

C. **False pretenses** occurs when the defendant knowingly makes a false representation of a past or present material fact, which causes the person to whom it was made to convey title to the misrepresenter who intends to defraud.

> **Exam tip:** If the victim is tricked into giving up possession, it could be larceny (by trick) as opposed to false pretenses because no title has passed, so look to see if title passes.

D. **Robbery** is a larceny and, in addition, the property has been taken from the person or presence of the owner through force, or by placing the owner in fear.

E. **Extortion** is a threat of future harm to deprive an owner of his property.

F. **Theft** is the illegal taking of another person's property. Some jurisdictions use theft as a catch-all crime for property crimes.

G. **Burglary** is a breaking and entering of the dwelling house of another at nighttime with intent to commit a felony therein. Modernly, most jurisdictions include any type of structure and any time of day.

H. **Receipt of stolen property** is a crime when one knowingly receives, conceals, or disposes of stolen property with the intent to permanently deprive the owner of their property.

I. **Arson** is the malicious (malice includes reckless disregard) burning of the dwelling house of another. Modernly most jurisdictions include most structures and burning includes damages caused by explosives too (not just fire).

> **Exam tip:** Theft crimes are frequently tested on the MCQs and have been appearing more on essays in the most recent years. However, when tested on the essay, they are usually tested in conjunction with FMR or conspiracy or accomplice liability, so look for all of those issues when theft crimes are tested. Larceny, robbery, and burglary are the felonies most commonly tested in a conspiracy turned murder type essay.

III. SOLICITATION, CONSPIRACY, AND ATTEMPT (INCHOATE CRIMES)

A. **Solicitation** occurs when one requests or encourages another to commit a crime with the intent that the person solicited does commit the crime, regardless of whether they agree to do so.

B. **Conspiracy** is an **agreement** between **two or more persons** who **intend to commit** an **unlawful act** or a lawful act by unlawful means.

1. The **agreement can be implied or inferred** and does not require that all persons commit the actual act.

2. **Mere knowledge is insufficient** to establish the intent necessary to commit the unlawful act.

3. **At common law**, the conspiracy occurred the moment the agreement was made, but the **majority of jurisdictions now require an overt act**, which can be as little as preparation, to form the conspiracy.

4. A **unilateral conspiracy** is allowed **modernly**, such that the party who agrees to commit the unlawful act can be convicted of conspiracy even if only one party has genuine criminal intent, such as when the agreement is with an undercover police officer. **Common law** requires the conspiracy be **bilateral,** with two guilty minds.

5. **Liability for crimes of co-conspirators:** Conspirators are liable for the crimes of co-conspirators if the crimes were committed **in furtherance of the objective** and were **reasonably foreseeable.**

6. **Common Defenses**
   a. **Withdrawal:** Once the agreement is made and the conspiracy is formed, one **cannot withdraw** from the conspiracy liability, but they **can withdraw for purposes of future crimes** of co-conspirators if they **communicate their withdrawal** to all co-conspirators (some jurisdictions allow communications to authorities to serve as withdrawal if timely made) and **take an affirmative action** to withdraw (i.e., neutralize assistance already rendered).
   b. **Factual impossibility** is not an effective defense (see section V.H below).

C. **Attempt** is an **act done with intent to commit a crime** and an affirmative act, or **substantial step**, in furtherance of the intent to commit the crime, beyond mere preparation.

D. **Merger**
   1. **Solicitation and attempt merge** into the actual crime so defendant cannot be charged in addition to the actual crime.
   2. **Conspiracy does not merge** into the actual crime and can be charged in addition to the actual crime.

> **Inchoate crimes fact triggers:**
> - More than one person in fact pattern
> - Hiring another person for any reason
> - Multiple parties taking part in an activity, even if not all parties are aware of the details
> - One person helping out another

E. **Defenses**
   1. **Factual impossibility** is **not** a defense (see section V below).
   2. **Legal impossibility** is a defense (see section V below).

> **Issue spotting tip:** When the facts raise the issue of conspiracy, always consider accomplice liability as well since they often arise together. And if the defendant is not guilty of a future crime committed by a co-conspirator because the crime was not in furtherance of the objective, then consider accomplice liability as an alternative.

IV. **ACCOMPLICE LIABILITY**
   A. **Principal in the first degree:** One who commits the actual crime.
   B. **Accomplice (also called principal in the second degree):** An accomplice is one who **aids, abets, assists, or encourages** the carrying out of a crime and is present physically or constructively.
      1. The **accomplice is liable** for **the crime** they assisted or encouraged if the principal carried out the crime.
      2. **Mere knowledge is insufficient** to establish the intent to aid or encourage in the crime.

3. **Additional crimes:** Accomplices are **liable for additional crimes** committed by the principal in the course of committing the intended crime, so long as the crimes were a **natural and probable consequence** (foreseeable).

C. **Accessory before the fact** is an accomplice who **aids, abets, or encourages** the principal but **is not present** at the crime.

D. **Accessory after the fact** is an accomplice who knowingly gives assistance to a felon, for the purpose of **helping them avoid apprehension** following commission of a crime.

E. **Modern rules:** Modernly **principals, accomplices, and accessories before the fact** are **all guilty of the criminal offense** and are all considered parties to the crime. Modernly, an **accessory after the fact** is charged with **obstruction of justice.**

F. **Defenses**

1. **Withdrawal:** An accomplice **can withdraw** before the crime is committed, but if they already assisted they must render their prior assistance ineffective.

Exam tip: Know the difference between accomplice liability and conspirator liability. Often on exams, differing outcomes may result in terms of the defendant's liability when analyzing these two issues based on the actions of other accomplices or co-conspirators. For example, if two defendants conspire to kidnap a victim to get ransom and one of them later rapes the victim (and that D had prior sexual assault crimes), then the other D (non-rapist) might not be liable for the rape under co-conspirator liability because rape wasn't in furtherance of the kidnapping objective, but they could be liable under accomplice liability since the rape was foreseeable given the other D's past sexual crimes.

V. **DEFENSES**

A. **Self-defense:** A person has a **right to self-defense** against unlawful force but must use **reasonable force** in response; a person may use **deadly force** in defense only if they hold a **reasonable belief that they face deadly force** against them. The majority of jurisdictions indicate there is no **duty to retreat** (even in minority jurisdictions there is no duty to retreat in one's home).

1. **Imperfect self-defense:** Where a person kills in self-defense as a result of an **unreasonable belief that they faced deadly force** against them, murder charges can be reduced to charges of **voluntary manslaughter.**

B. **Defense of others:** It is permissible to use **reasonable force to defend another** when one **reasonably believes** that the other person would be justified in using such force and the amount of force used is reasonable (majority rule).

1. **Minority rule: "Stands in shoes":** A person may use force to defend another only if the **person being defended** was themself **justified** in using force for self-defense.

C. **Defense of property** allows an individual to use a **reasonable amount of force** — though never deadly force — to protect their real or personal property.

D. **Defense of insanity:** Depending on the jurisdiction, there are various tests for insanity.

1. *M'Naghten* **test:** The defendant must show that they suffered from a **mental disease** causing a **defect in their reasoning powers** that resulted in them not understanding the **nature and quality of their act** or that they **did not know that their act was wrong.**

2. **Irresistible impulse test:** The defendant must show that they were **unable to control their conduct and conform** their conduct to the law due to a **mental illness.**

3. *Durham* **test:** The defendant must show that their **conduct** was the **product of a mental illness** (but for test). (This standard is broader than the other two tests above.)

4. **Model Penal Code:** The defendant must show that they **lacked substantial capacity to appreciate the criminality** of their conduct or **conform their conduct to the requirements of the law.** (This is a blend of the other tests.)

> **Exam tip:** Whenever insanity or the defendant's mental stability is at issue, be sure to go through all four types of insanity. Use headings and IRAC each one separately.

E. **Intoxication**
   1. **Voluntary, self-induced intoxication** is only a defense to specific intent crimes (first-degree murder, assault, incomplete crimes, theft crimes) such that the intoxication may have prevented the defendant from formulating the requisite specific intent.
   2. **Involuntary intoxication** is treated as an illness and may be a defense to all crimes, as it negates the intent to commit the crime when an intoxicating substance is ingested unknowingly or under duress.

F. **Necessity** may be a defense if the defendant reasonably believed that commission of the crime was necessary to avoid an imminent and greater injury to society than that involved in the crime (objective standard used).
   1. Common law required necessity to be caused by **forces of nature**.
   2. Some jurisdictions don't allow a defendant to claim necessity if they **created the danger**.

G. **Mistake**
   1. A **mistake of fact** may negate a specific intent crime (first degree murder, incomplete crimes, assault, theft crimes) as well as malice, and may negate a general intent crime if the mistake was reasonable (e.g., you take a jacket that you think is yours when it is not; no intent to steal property so no larceny).
   2. A **mistake (ignorance) of law** is generally not a defense (e.g., you didn't know the speed limit was 65 so you drove 75 — you're still violating the law).

H. **Impossibility**
   1. **Factual impossibility** arises when the defendant makes a mistake such that it would be factually impossible to complete the crime. This is not usually a valid defense (e.g., you intend to shoot someone, but the gun isn't loaded; you're still guilty of attempt).
   2. **Legal impossibility** arises when the defendant incorrectly believes that what they are doing is criminal when it is not. This is a valid defense. (e.g., you intended to import foreign goods which you thought was illegal, but it wasn't illegal, so no criminal act was committed).

I. **Entrapment** exists where a law enforcement official, or someone cooperating with them, **induces** a person to commit a crime that they **weren't otherwise predisposed to commit**. The majority of states look at the subjective intent of the defendant.

CRIMINAL PROCEDURE RULE OUTLINE

I. THE **FOURTH AMENDMENT** PROTECTS INDIVIDUALS AGAINST UNREASONABLE SEARCHES AND SEIZURES OF PROPERTY AND AGAINST UNLAWFUL ARRESTS.
   A. **Arrest**
      1. **Warrant:** An arrest warrant is generally not required for an arrest unless a person is arrested in their home.
         a. **Probable cause required:** An arrest warrant must be issued based on probable cause, which is a **reasonable belief that the person violated the law**.
   B. A **routine stop** by the government is typically permitted.
      1. **Automobile stop:** The police may randomly stop automobiles if there is a **reasonable suspicion** of wrongdoing based on **articulable facts** (i.e., swerving in traffic). All occupants may also be asked to exit the vehicle for any reason.
      2. **Checkpoints/roadblocks:** The police may set up fixed checkpoints to test for compliance with laws relating to driving or if special law enforcement needs are involved, such as immigration. The stops must be based on some neutral, articulable standard.
      3. **Stop (*Terry* stop) and frisk:** Police may also stop and frisk individuals without arresting them if they believe the individual is armed and dangerous (see section I.C.4.f below).
   C. **Search and seizure of property:** A **search warrant is required** for a **government search** and seizure of property that is located where one has a **reasonable expectation of privacy**.
      1. **Government action required:** The Fourth Amendment search and seizure protections apply only against actions by the government. Government action includes individuals acting under the direction of the government.
      2. **Reasonable expectation of privacy:** The defendant must have a reasonable expectation of privacy in the property or place being searched or seized. This is based on a **totality of the circumstances** (e.g., one has a reasonable expectation of privacy in their **home and its curtilage**, such as a garage).
         a. **Open fields/fly overs:** Areas outside the home that are held out to the public **do not have a reasonable expectation of privacy** (e.g., some distant barns, yards visible by plane, discarded trash, odors emanating from your car, property, etc.). Courts will consider:
            1. The **proximity** of the area to the house,
            2. Whether the **area is enclosed** by a structure, such as a fence or wall,
            3. The **nature of the use** of the structure or area in question, and
            4. The **steps taken** by the individual to protect privacy in the area.
         b. **Sensory enhancing technology** will violate a reasonable expectation of privacy (e.g., heat/thermal imagers not allowed), but **technology available to the public may be permitted** (e.g., binoculars, telescopes). Electronic eavesdropping is not acceptable (fine to listen through walls though).
         c. **Dog sniffing:** Dogs are permitted to sniff luggage at airports and cars during a legitimate traffic stop but **the stop cannot be extended beyond the time reasonably required** to complete the stop's mission **unless there is reasonable suspicion of a violation** other than a traffic infraction. Police **cannot use dogs to sniff homes without a warrant** or warrant exception (the dog cannot create the probable cause).
         d. **Location tracking:** Placing tracking devices on cars and people is not allowed, unless the car came with a pre-installed tracking device that the individual allowed to remain on the car. An individual also has an expectation of privacy in their cell phone company cell-site locations that are tracked.
      3. **Warrant is required:** Where a person has a reasonable expectation of privacy, the police need a search warrant based on **probable cause** to search and seize property. A warrant must be:
         a. **Based on probable cause:** Probable cause is established where it is reasonable that the items to be searched:
            1. Are **connected with criminal activities,** and
            2. **Will be found in the place** to be searched.
            3. If based on **informant information,** sufficiency is determined by the **totality of circumstances**.

b. **Issued by a neutral magistrate:** The search warrant is issued based on facts presented to a neutral and detached magistrate.

c. **Description:** The search warrant must **describe with particularity** the **premises to be searched** and the **items to be seized**.

d. **Knock and announce before execution:** To execute the search warrant, the police must knock and announce themselves before entering the premises, unless exigent circumstances exist. If there is no response, the police can enter and seize the items described but **may not exceed the scope** of the warrant.

Search and seizure fact triggers:
- Police search a home/car
- Police stop a car at a checkpoint
- Police search clothing on a person
- Police search a person's belongings
- Police arrest a person anywhere with or without a warrant
- Police stop a person in a car or on foot for violating a law
- Police use a dog to sniff out drugs/other contraband

---

4. **Exceptions to the warrant requirement:** If the police conduct a search or seizure without a valid search warrant, there may be an applicable exception.

   a. **Search incident to a lawful arrest (SILA):** When the police are making a lawful arrest, they may search the **area within the arrestee's immediate control** (their wingspan).

      1. **Protective sweep:** Under SILA, police may also conduct a protective sweep of all or part of the premises where an arrest takes place if they have a **reasonable belief** based on specific and articulable facts that other **dangerous individuals may be present.**

      2. **Vehicle:** Under SILA, the police may search a car and its compartments if it is reasonable to believe that the **arrestee might access the vehicle** at the time of the search or the **vehicle contains evidence** of the offense causing the arrest.

   b. **Plain view:** The police may make a warrantless search if they see an object or **contraband in plain view**, so long as they are legitimately on the premises or have a **right to be in the position to obtain the view**.

   c. **Automobile:** If police have **probable cause** to believe that a vehicle contains contraband or evidence of a crime, they may search the **whole automobile** and any **container** therein that **might contain the objects** for which they are searching.

      1. If the driver is arrested, the police may legally **impound the car**, transport it to the station house, and search it there without a warrant.

Issue spotting tip: Although the police may not search a suspect's vehicle compartments under SILA if the suspect does not have access to the car (such as if the suspect is held in a police car), the police can still get around a Fourth Amendment violation under the automobile exception if they have probable cause. So, consider both of these exceptions when an automobile is involved, and remember that without an arrest, SILA will not be applicable.

---

   d. **Consent:** The police may make a warrantless search if the person whose premises, items, or person will be searched voluntarily consents, based on the totality of the circumstances.

   e. **Exigent circumstances:** The police may conduct a search or seizure without a warrant if they have probable cause and it is necessary to:

      1. Prevent imminent **destruction of evidence,**

      2. Prevent imminent **injury to persons,** or

      3. Search for a felony suspect of whom the police are in **hot pursuit** and reasonably believe has entered particular premises.

f. **Stop (*Terry* stop) and frisk:** A police officer may **stop and frisk** a person if the police have a **reasonable suspicion** (based on the totality of circumstances) of **criminal activity** or involvement that is supported by **articulable facts**.

1. The brief detention may include a **pat-down** search of outer clothing for weapons if the suspect **appears dangerous** and under the **plain feel doctrine**, they may **seize contraband** discovered if its identity is immediately apparent.

Memorization tip: Use the mnemonic **SPACES** to remember the exceptions for the warrant requirement (**S**earch incident to a lawful arrest, **P**lain view, **A**utomobile, **C**onsent, **E**xigent circumstances, and **S**top and frisk). On most exams, the police will search a home or car without a warrant, thus requiring analysis of the applicable exceptions. Make sure you first analyze the government conduct and REOP before jumping right into the exceptions. Also, as discussed in section IV below, if there is a defective warrant, consider the good faith exception.

BULLET PROOF 4TH AMENDMENT APPROACH

Preliminary issues:
- Government action
- Standing/REOP: violation of <u>own</u> rights

4th Am. protects against **unreasonable searches and seizures** of property and **unlawful arrests**.

Search or Seizure

Routine stop is permissible if objective standard

All other searches/seizures require:

(1) **Government action**, and

(2) **Reasonable expectation of privacy**
- Open fields/flyovers (not allowed if not open to public generally)
- Sensory enhancing technology (not allowed unlessreadily available)
- Dog sniffing (not allowed at house)
- Location tracking (no GPS, cell-site)

Was there a **warrant**?

NO → Does **exception** apply?
- o **SILA**
- o **Plain View**
- o **Automobile**
- o **Consent**
- o **Exigent circumstances**
- o **Stop and frisk**

YES → Was the warrant valid?
- o Based on **probable cause**
- o Issued by **neutral magistrate**
- o **Describes** item/place
- o **Knock and announce**

NO → **Good Faith Warrant Exception?**

NO → NO

Arrest

Was there a warrant?

NO → Was it at D's house?

NO → OK if probable cause

YES

YES → Warrant based on **probable cause** (**reasonable belief** law violated)?

NO

4th Am Violation

Evidence suppressed - **Exclusionary Rule**

II. FIFTH AMENDMENT

A. **Miranda:** When a suspect is taken into custody by the police and is under interrogation, their confession will be admissible against them only if they have received the requisite *Miranda* warnings, informing them that they have the **right to remain silent**, that **anything they say can be used against them**, that they have the **right to have an attorney** present, and if they cannot afford an attorney, **one will be appointed** for them.

1. *Miranda* **warnings apply to custodial interrogations.**

a. **Custodial:** A suspect is "in custody" when a **reasonable person would believe that they are not free to leave** based on the totality of the circumstances.

b. **Interrogation** includes words or actions by the police that they should know are **reasonably likely to elicit an incriminating response** from the suspect.

1. **Suspect must be aware:** A custodial interrogation does not occur when a suspect speaks to an undercover agent or government informant and the suspect does not know that they are speaking to a law enforcement officer, even if the suspect is in jail.

2. **Public safety exception:** *Miranda* warnings **do not apply** to questioning that is reasonably prompted by a concern for public safety.

3. **Re-*Miranda*ize:** Once the suspect has **unambiguously** invoked their rights under *Miranda*, the **police cannot re-*Miranda*ize the suspect** in an attempt to get the suspect to speak, unless there has been a sufficient break in custody (14 days are deemed sufficient).

Miranda **fact triggers:**

- Police place an informant with the suspect (whether they work for the government or not)
- Police give *Miranda* rights or re-*Miranda*ize a suspect
- Police question a suspect at any time
- Suspect confesses
- Suspect placed in a line-up
- Suspect admits a crime at a car stop

Exam tip: Remember that just because a set of facts triggers the issue of *Miranda* doesn't mean that *Miranda* has been violated. Rather, it is just an indicator that you need to discuss the issue and explain why the suspect's *Miranda* rights were or were not violated. Also, on an essay you don't need to state what exactly the police say during the warning, just analyze the main rule (custodial interrogation).

---

4. **Waiver of *Miranda*:** A suspect may waive their *Miranda* rights, expressly or implicitly, but such a waiver is admissible only if it is **voluntarily, knowingly,** and **intelligently** made. Mere silence is insufficient to demonstrate a waiver.

B. **Fifth Amendment right to counsel under *Miranda*:** When the accused unambiguously indicates that they wish to speak to counsel, the police are required to **cease all questioning** until the suspect has consulted a lawyer, and the **lawyer must be present** while any **further questioning** occurs.

Exam tip: Remember that even if a suspect's confession was obtained in violation of *Miranda*, it only limits the confession from being introduced in the prosecution's case-in-chief, but it is still admissible to impeach the suspect defendant. Compare and contrast this with confessions that are not voluntary and are the result of police coercion, which cannot be used to impeach the defendant.

C. **Fifth Amendment right against self-incrimination:** This right protects a criminal defendant from compulsion to give testimony or communicative evidence that could expose them to criminal liability.

> **Exam tip:** Remember to focus on whether the statement or evidence is testimonial or communicative and not physical evidence. Physical evidence such as fingerprinting, line-ups, blood samples, photographs, and other identification procedures are not protected by the Fifth Amendment right against self-incrimination.

D. **Fifth Amendment double jeopardy:** This protects an individual from being tried for the same offense twice or a lesser-included offense after jeopardy attaches. Jeopardy attaches when the jury has been empaneled and sworn in for a jury trial, or when the first witness has been sworn in for a bench trial (doesn't apply to preliminary hearings or grand juries).

E. **Fifth Amendment due process**, which is applicable to the states through the **Fourteenth Amendment**, requires that:
   1. **Confessions be made voluntarily (based on the totality of the circumstances)**, and
   2. **Identifications** are not **unnecessarily suggestive** and so conducive to mistaken identification that it is unfair to the defendant. (See section V below.)

III. **SIXTH AMENDMENT**
   A. **Right to effective counsel:** A suspect against whom formal criminal proceedings have been commenced has a right to effective counsel at any **critical stage (i.e., post-charge line-up or show-up, preliminary hearings to prosecute, sentencing, etc.).** This right does not apply to photo identifications, or when police take physical evidence from a suspect such as handwriting samples or fingerprints. This right is offense specific (defendant must invoke their right to counsel for each offense charged).
   1. **Standard of effectiveness:** To establish ineffective assistance of counsel, the defendant must prove that counsel's performance was deficient in that counsel **did not act as a reasonably competent attorney** would have acted, and that this deficiency was prejudicial such that, but for the deficiency, the **result would have been different.**
   2. **Attorney substitution:** A court will **allow** the defendant to substitute their attorney **if the interests of justice so require**, taking into account any conflicts, the interests of the defendant and the court, and the timeliness of the request.
   3. **Self-representation:** The defendant is permitted to knowingly and intelligently **waive their right to counsel** and represent themself.
   B. **Right to confront adverse witnesses:** The Sixth Amendment allows a defendant in a criminal prosecution the right to confront adverse witnesses.
   1. **Compel testimony:** The right to confront includes issuing subpoenas to compel testimony of an adverse or hostile witness, as well as to **cross-examine** hostile witnesses.
   2. **Testimonial statements:** The prosecution may not admit testimonial statements by a third person against the defendant unless the **declarant is available for cross-examination either** at the time the statement was made or during trial.
      a. **Statements are nontestimonial when** made in the course of police interrogation under circumstances objectively indicating that the primary purpose of the interrogation is to enable police assistance to meet an ongoing emergency, such as a 911 call.
      b. **Statements are testimonial when** the circumstances indicate that there is no on-going emergency, and that the primary purpose of the interrogation is to establish or prove past events potentially relevant to later criminal prosecution.
   3. **Joint co-defendants** can raise "right to confront" issues.
      a. **Confession of one co-defendant:** Where two defendants are jointly tried and one of them confesses, the right to confront adverse witnesses **prohibits use of that statement** against

the other defendant unless the **statement can be redacted** or the co-defendant who made the statement **takes the stand** and subjects themselves to cross-examination.

    b. **Severance of joint trial:** Where co-defendants are charged for the same crime, courts prefer joint trials for judicial economy, but will sever the co-defendants if a joint trial would **result in substantial prejudice** to one of the defendants.

> **"Right to confront" fact triggers:**
> - Co-defendants
> - Witness does not take the stand
> - Witness dies
> - Witness cannot be found

  C. **Right to a jury trial:** Criminal defendants have the right to a jury trial for serious offenses that have a potential imprisonment of greater than six months.

    1. **Waiver permitted:** The defendant may **voluntarily, knowingly,** and **intelligently** waive their right to a jury trial.

    2. **Number of jurors required:** Juries must consist of **at least 6 persons** to start and can consist of 12 persons.

    3. **Unanimous verdicts:** Federal and state criminal trials require **unanimous verdicts.**

    4. **Impartial jurors:** A jury must be impartial, consisting of a fair cross-section of a community.

      a. A **jury does not consist of a fair cross-section of a community if** the defendant can prove that:

        1. The group alleged to be excluded is a **distinctive group** in the community,

        2. The representation of this group in the jury pool is **not fair** and reasonable **in relation to the number of such persons in the community,** and

        3. This underrepresentation is due to **systematic exclusion** of the group in the jury-selection process.

    5. **Voir dire:** During voir dire each side (not party) has **unlimited strikes for cause** (bias, prejudice, related to a party, etc.) and **limited peremptory strikes** (the number varies by jurisdiction—CA allows 20 if death/life sentence or 10 otherwise in criminal trial) that may be used for any reason, so long as the reason is gender and race neutral (some courts have expanded this to include sexual orientation neutral, religious affiliation, etc.).

    6. **Discrimination not permitted:** The equal protection clause of the Fourteenth Amendment prevents the state or any state actor, including the court, from intentionally discriminating against a distinctive group in selection of the jury pool.

  D. **The right to a speedy trial:** The Sixth Amendment right to a speedy trial is viewed on a case-by-case basis with the court balancing the following factors:

    1. The **length** of the delay,

    2. The **reason** for the delay,

    3. The **prejudice** to the defendant as a result of the delay, and

    4. The **time and manner** in which the defendant asserted their right.

  E. **Right to a preliminary hearing:** A defendant who pleads not guilty has a right to a preliminary hearing if probable cause has not been established unless they waive such right. (The rules for preliminary hearings vary among jurisdictions.)

IV. THE EXCLUSIONARY RULE AND GOOD FAITH WARRANT EXCEPTION

  A. **The exclusionary rule** is a judge-made rule that **prohibits the prosecution from introducing evidence** obtained in violation of a defendant's Fourth, Fifth, or Sixth Amendment rights.

    1. **Standing required:** The defendant must have standing to assert the exclusionary rule, such that the evidence wrongfully obtained must have been in violation of the **defendant's own constitutional rights** and not any third person's.

2. **"Fruit of the poisonous tree":** Evidence wrongfully obtained is **inadmissible** as the "fruit of the poisonous tree"—in other words, evidence that is found as a result of the original wrongfully obtained evidence is inadmissible—subject to the following **exceptions:**
    a. **Independent source:** The evidence obtained could have been obtained from an independent source separate from the illegal source; or
    b. **Inevitable discovery:** The evidence obtained would inevitably have been discovered by other police techniques, had it not first been obtained through illegal discovery; or
    c. **Purged taint:** There are a sufficient number of **additional factors that intervened between the original illegality and the final discovery** that the link is too tenuous, such that the intervening factors have purged the taint of the illegal discovery; or
    d. **Violations of the knock and announce rule.**
3. **Allowed for impeachment:** Illegally obtained evidence **may still be used to impeach** the defendant but not any witnesses.
4. **The exclusionary rule does not apply to** civil proceedings, grand juries, and parole proceedings.

> **Exam tip:** Whenever there is a possible Fourth, Fifth, or Sixth Amendment violation, consider the potential application of the exclusionary rule and briefly mention it. Be certain that the defendant has "standing" and is the one whose rights were violated and not a third person. Analyze any exceptions that might allow the evidence to come in, despite a violation. Lastly, mention that the evidence can still be used to impeach the defendant.

B. **The good faith warrant exception:** Where an officer acts in **reasonable reliance** on a facially valid search warrant issued by a proper magistrate and the warrant is **ultimately found to be unsupported by probable cause**, the exclusionary rule will not apply, and the evidence will not be barred.
   1. **Exceptions:** The good faith warrant exception does not apply (and thus the evidence will be excluded under the exclusionary rule) where:
       a. **The affiant knew the information they were providing in the affidavit was false,** or they would have known except for their reckless disregard of the truth, or
       b. **There was a lack of probable cause** such that the magistrate's reliance on the affidavit was unreasonable, or
       c. The warrant was **defective on its face.**

V. **ADDITIONAL CONFESSION, IDENTIFICATION, AND MISCELLANEOUS ISSUES**
   A. **Due Process—Confessions must be voluntary:** Under the Fourteenth Amendment, confessions must be made voluntarily **without police coercion,** in light of the **totality of the circumstances,** with the court considering the susceptibility of the suspect and the environment and methods used.
      1. **Nongovernmental coercion:** A confession obtained by nongovernmental coercion is admissible.
      2. **Confession by person who is mentally ill:** A confession made by a person suffering from mental illness is admissible.
      3. **Police coercion:** Where a confession is the result of police coercion, the prosecution **cannot use it during its case-in-chief *or* to impeach the defendant.** This rule is in contrast to a confession obtained in violation of *Miranda*, which is still admissible for impeachment purposes.
   B. **Due process in identification:** A defendant's due process rights are violated if an identification of the defendant based on the totality of the circumstances is **unnecessarily suggestive** and so conducive to mistaken identification that it is **unfair** to the defendant.

> **<u>Due process fact triggers:</u>**
> - Defendant is identified on the way to any court hearing or show-up
> - Defendant is identified alone or not in a line-up or at a courthouse
> - Defendant and the witness are at the same location at the same time
> - Defendant is distinct in some way from others in a line-up
> - Defendant admits that they did something when speaking to police

C. **Plea bargains:** A defendant can settle by plea bargain to receive a less serious charge or a lighter sentence if they are competent, understand the charge, and understand the consequences of the plea.
   1. **Voluntary and intelligently:** Plea bargains must be made voluntarily and intelligently; in open court and on record.
   2. The prosecutor has **no obligation to agree to a plea** and the **judge can refuse** to accept the guilty plea if they think the defendant didn't commit the crime.

> **<u>Issue spotting tip:</u>** This outline is organized by Amendment since most essays ask whether the defendant's Fourth, Fifth, or Sixth Amendment rights have been violated. Thus, you should memorize all issues that stem from each Amendment. However, memorize the following mini-issues checklist for issues that arise in conjunction with one another when a defendant confesses.
>
> - Voluntariness
> - Due process
> - *Miranda*
> - Waiver of *Miranda*
> - Fifth Amendment right to counsel

VI. **EIGHTH AMENDMENT**
   A. **Bail:** The Eighth Amendment requires that **bail shall not be excessive or unduly high** based on several factors, including the following:
      1. The **seriousness** of the offense,
      2. The **weight of the evidence** against the defendant,
      3. The defendant's **financial abilities**, and
      4. The defendant's **character**.
   B. **Cruel and unusual punishment:** The Eighth Amendment prohibits cruel and unusual punishment by preventing the penalty imposed on the defendant from being **grossly disproportionate** to the seriousness of the crime.
      1. **A defendant cannot be sentenced to death** if:
         a. At least one juror finds the defendant is **mentally retarded**, or
         b. The defendant was a **minor** at the time of the crime.
      2. A **minor cannot be sentenced** to a **mandatory** life without parole sentence.
      3. **Victim impact statements** during the penalty phase do not violate a defendant's Eighth Amendment right against cruel and unusual punishment.
      4. **Mitigating circumstances:** When considering the death penalty, the jury must consider mitigating circumstances, such as the defendant's age, capacity, previous criminal liability, duress, other defendants' involvement, and any other factors that mitigate against imposition of a death sentence.

CRIMES ISSUES TESTED MATRIX

	Crossover Subject	Murder/ Manslaughter	Other Crimes	Conspiracy/Accomplice Liability	Attempt/Solicitation	4th Amend. Arrest/Search & Seizure	5th Amend. Miranda Counsel Self-incrimination	6th Amend. Right to Counsel Right to Confront Speedy Trial	6th Amend. Right to Jury Juror Issues	Exclusionary Rule	Voluntary Confessions Pleas	Due Process Or Pre-trial issues	8th Amend. Penalty, Sentencing	Defenses
February '24 Q4 — Acme bank was robbed by a man Tessa ID'd as Dan	CA Evidence							X				X		
July '23 Q4 — Homeless Deborah starts a fire to stay warm and kills Stuart		X	Larceny, Burglary, Arson				X	X			X			X
February '22 Q1 — Jim and Fred rob Salma at a store and shot Chris		X	Assault, Larceny, Robbery	X	X	X				X				
July '21 Q4 — Detective Anna questions David over heroin sales						X	X	X		X				
October '20 Q4 — Tall Don and Short Al broke into Vic's house			Larceny, Robbery, Burglary	X								X		X
July '19 Q3 — Delia uses toy gun to rob Oscar of his Roman coins			Robbery			X	X			X				
February '18 Q4 — Officer Ava looks for missing 4-yr.-old Claire at Don's house					X	X				X				
February '17 Q6 — Informant Alan tells Alan about Debbie's plan to kill husband						X								X
July '15 Q3 — Owen had a hunch Dora sells meth; drove to house						X				X				
July '14 Q4 — Officer Prowl stops Dan and car radio falls out						X	X	X		X	X			

Continued>

	Crossover Subject	Murder/Manslaughter	Other Crimes	Conspiracy/Accomplice Liability	Attempt/Solicitation	4th Amend. Arrest/Search & Seizure	5th Amend. Miranda Counsel Self-incrimination	6th Amend. Right to Counsel Right to Confront Speedy Trial	6th Amend. Right to Jury Juror Issues	Exclusionary Rule	Voluntary Confessions Pleas	Due Process Or Pre-trial Issues	8th Amend. Penalty Sentencing	Defenses
February '13 Q1 Max sells stolen paintings; sons A, B, C help with business			Receipt of stolen prop.	X	X									
July '12 Q6 Dan works at a church and steals donated gun			Theft crimes			X	X			X				
July '11 Q1 Vicky sells computers; Dan tries to steal them with Eric's pickup			Several	X	X									
July '10 Q5 Harriet on porch, Don walks up with gun & she thinks it's a toy			Kidnapping		X	X				X	X			X
July '09 Q6 Polly, uniformed police officer, stops speeding car with cocaine						X	X	X						
February '08 Q3 Dan's neighborhood overrun by gangs, but Dan refuses to join		X					X	X		X				X
July '07 Q4 Dan stood on the capitol steps, lights a fire & kills a pedestrian	Con. Law	X			X									X
February '07 Q3 Dan, mental patient, kills V in grocery store after he was insulted		X												X

Continued>

	Crossover Subject	Murder/Manslaughter	Other Crimes	Conspiracy/Accomplice Liability	Attempt/Solicitation	4th Amend. Arrest/Search & Seizure	5th Amend. Miranda Counsel Self-incrimination	6th Amend. Right to Counsel Right to Confront Speedy Trial	6th Amend. Right to Jury Juror Issues	Exclusionary Rule	Voluntary Confessions Pleas	Due Process Or Pre-trial Issues	8th Amend. Penalty Sentencing	Defenses
February '06 Q6 Deft saw officer Oscar attempt to arrest Friend, who was resisting arrest						X	X	X		X		X		X
July '04 Q1 Dan, Art & Bert rob Vince's Store; Vince kills Art		X	Extortion/ Stolen Prop.	X				X						
February '04 Q1 Bank robbed at 1:00 pm by man with a shotgun and an accent						X	X			X				
February '03 Q3 Don is a passenger in V's car; takes a drug and kills V	Evidence	X					X	X				X		X
February '01 Q3 Duce & Cody arrested for armed robbery and both confess						X	X	X						
July '00 Q4 Ruth the reporter observes illegal dog fight	Con. Law						X							
February '00 Q6 Picasso sketch taken from museum and purchased in Switzerland	Evidence					X	X	X						

CRIMES PRACTICE ESSAYS, ANSWER GRIDS, AND SAMPLE ANSWERS

Crimes Question 1
July 2023, Question 4

Deborah was homeless and without money. One night, the temperature was below freezing and continuing to drop. Deborah realized she might die if she did not find shelter. She found a run-down house with an attached garage that had a door connecting it to the house. Deborah thought the house was unoccupied. She went around to the side of the garage, looked through a window, and saw a stack of wood. Deborah decided to go into the garage, take some of the wood, and build a fire outside the garage to keep herself warm. She broke the window to get into the garage. Because of the extreme cold, Deborah decided to stay in the garage. She gathered wood scraps and paper, started a small fire to keep herself warm, and fell asleep. A spark from the fire ignited some oil on the floor. Deborah awoke to flames and smoke. She then escaped through the window she had broken. The fire quickly engulfed the house where it killed Stuart as he was sleeping in his bed.

Officer Oliver, who was patrolling the area, saw Deborah walking on the sidewalk three blocks from the fire. When Officer Oliver asked her what she was doing outside on such a cold night, Deborah said, "I started the fire."

Deborah is charged in criminal court and moves to suppress her statement "I started the fire."

1. With what crime or crimes can Deborah reasonably be charged; what defense or defenses can she reasonably raise; and what is the likely outcome? Discuss.

2. Should the court grant Deborah's motion to suppress her statement? Discuss.

Crimes Question 1 Assessment
July 2023, Question 4

This is a time-consuming crimes question to organize because it requires you to run through a list of all crimes since the first call is not specific. It also makes it clear that you need to analyze defenses. And always make sure you answer the call as to the likely outcome. Further, there are many crimes tested in this essay, so you have to be organized and concise to address all issues within the time constraints. Possible crimes that you should have spotted from your checklist include larceny, burglary, arson, murder, and manslaughter. That is quite the long list of crimes, not including the applicable defenses and the entire second call. The second call then asks about Deborah's motion to suppress her statement, so you know you are dealing with Criminal Procedure and likely a confession. Thus, have your mini-checklist for confessions ready to go.

As to the crimes you should have spotted in the first call, larceny, burglary, and arson are all very straightforward and easy if you know your rules. Since they are heavily tested on the multiple-choice portion of the bar exam, you should have these rules memorized. Then on essays, just quickly go through each element and it is a fairly simple IRAC for each crime.

As to the crime of murder, it is important to start out with your common law murder rules and the four types of malice. After analyzing those, move onto manslaughter and statutory murder. The intent to kill and cause bodily harm types of malice can easily be dismissed but quickly mention that there was no intent to kill or harm anyone since the facts tell you that she just wanted to stay warm and thought the house was unoccupied. As to the reckless disregard/depraved heart, you could have seen both sides here but both state-released answers found there was no reckless disregard, and more facts lean toward that outcome since she thought the house was unoccupied and started a small fire just to stay warm and didn't seem to see the oil. Thus, if timing were an issue you could just address that side and call it good enough. As to FMR, you needed to see that the underlying felony was arson and that FMR was possible since all elements are met there. You should have also seen how the FMR triggers first-degree murder (although one state-released answer missed this connection). Similarly, only one state-released answer addressed causation, which you should have analyzed because the defendant didn't kill the victim herself. These last two issues where only one state-released answer addressed an issue is proof that your answer doesn't have to be perfect to pass. Rather, holistically and overall, both answers showed the grader they understood most of the issues and how the rules apply, even if both answers did leave some points on the table, which is understandable with so many issues to analyze.

Then for manslaughter, the obvious choice was involuntary manslaughter through gross negligence. It is important to see that here you should have found that her actions could rise to involuntary manslaughter, even if they didn't rise to reckless disregard murder. This shows the line between murder and manslaughter, and this is a great example to show the graders you understand the difference between the two.

As to the defenses, there were a few ways to approach these. One way is addressing a defense (or even a counterargument such as there was no malice) after each crime. The other way would be to address all crimes and then do all defenses. Either way would be sufficient so long as you addressed some defenses, with necessity being a key defense.

As to call two, this was likely worth far less than call one. You should have allocated ¾ of your time on call one and ¼ on call two. Call two was very simple in that you needed to note how her confession was voluntary and that *Miranda* rights were not needed as she wasn't under custodial interrogation. Overall, this essay was doable if you knew your rules well and organized your essay first to ensure adequate timing on all issues.

Finally, make note of the areas highlighted in **bold** on the corresponding grid. The bold areas highlight the issues, analysis, and conclusions that are likely **required** to receive a passing score on this question. In general, the essay grids are provided to assist you in analyzing the essays and are much more detailed than what a student should create during the exam to organize their response to a question.

Issue	Rule	Fact Application	Conclusion
1. Crimes Deborah can be charged with and defenses available			
Larceny	• Trespassory taking and carrying away • Personal property of another • Intent to permanently deprive owner of property	• Here, Deborah trespassed onto what she thought was an unoccupied house w/o permission and went into the garage and took wood from the stack as well as wood scraps and paper and burned it; arguably she didn't carry it away since she decided to stay in the garage, but she still moved the wood which is sufficient for a carrying away. • **The wood and paper belonged to the owner, not her, so it was not her personal property.** • **She intended to permanently deprive the owner of the wood b/c she burned it and can't unburn it and was homeless, so she had no way of paying for it.**	D could be charged w/ larceny
Burglary	• **Breaking and entering** • **Dwelling house of another** • **At nighttime** • **Intent to commit a felony therein** • **Modernly most structures ok and any time of day**	• **Deborah broke through the window of the garage and entered the garage.** • Of another's house (presumably Stuart's) and the garage is considered part of the dwelling house but modernly any structure would be ok. • **She intended to take the wood to start a fire to stay warm (so larceny) but may not be a felony — if not a felony, then no burglary.**	D could be charged w/ burglary if larceny is a felony
Arson	• **Malicious burning (malice can include reckless disregard)** • **Dwelling house of another** • **Modernly most structures and explosives ok**	• Deborah acted with reckless disregard to the lives of others and the risk that the structure could start on fire by starting a fire indoors and then falling asleep especially since most homes are built of wood, there was wood already in the garage, and flammable oil; she might argue she wasn't aware of the oil but it is still reckless to start a fire indoors and then fall asleep and not monitor it. [State answers both gave some reason *why* it would be reckless but used different facts.] • **Garage was a dwelling house of another as discussed above.**	D could be charged w/ arson

Continued>

Issue	Rule	Fact Application	Conclusion
Common Law Murder	**Unlawful killing of another person with malice aforethought.** Malice can be proven by • **Intent to kill** (desire or knowledge to a substantial certainty), • **Intent to commit grievous bodily injury,** • **Reckless indifference to the value of human life,** or • **Intent to commit a dangerous felony (FMR).** **Under the FMR, malice is implied if death was a natural and probable consequence of D's conduct, the death occurred during the commission of the felony,** even if death was accidental, and the underlying felony **must be independent of the killing.** D's conduct must also be the cause in fact (but for) and proximate cause (foreseeable) of the death.	• No intent to kill or harm anyone as Deborah thought the house was unoccupied, only started the fire to stay warm, and it accidentally spread. • Arguably no reckless indifference to human life since it was inside a garage, the fire was small, and there is no indication she knew of the oil nearby and she did not think anyone was in the house. • However, one should know that fires spread especially if indoors and people can be sleeping anywhere including in what appears to be an unoccupied home (as she was) so one should know that fires are dangerous and can spread killing others if not properly maintained. • **Here felonies of arson and burglary possible both of which are inherently dangerous felonies.** • **Death is a natural and probable cause of arson as people die from fires in homes all the time** which is why the fire quickly engulfed the house making it harder for people, especially at night, to escape a fire. • **Death occurred during the felony as the house was engulfed in flames at the time Stuart died.** • Death was independent of the arson even though an accident. But for Deborah starting the fire or burglarizing Stuart's home, the house would not have started on fire and Stuart wouldn't have been killed in his bed. Arguably it was not foreseeable that someone was there in bed since the house seemed to be unoccupied, but it is foreseeable that a fire inside a garage could spread and start a bigger fire killing someone especially since it was the middle of the night when people are sleeping; and many people might live in houses that seem unoccupied especially people like Deborah who are homeless and trying to stay warm.	**D could be charged w/ common law murder for** reckless disregard or **FMR.**

Continued>

Issue	Rule	Fact Application	Conclusion
Involuntary Manslaughter	**Gross (criminal negligence):** Involuntary manslaughter arises when a **person's behavior is grossly negligent and the conduct results in the death of another.** Gross negligence is the **disregard of a very substantial danger of serious bodily harm or death.**	**Might not be a disregard of a high substantial danger of serious bodily harm or death since it was inside a garage,** the fire was small, and there is no indication she knew of the oil nearby and she did not think anyone was in the house. **However, one should know that fires spread especially if indoors with other wood nearby and people can be sleeping anywhere including in what appears to be an unoccupied home** (as she was) so one should know that fires are dangerous and can spread killing others if not properly maintained.	**D's murder charge can be reduced to involuntary manslaughter.**
1st v. 2nd Degree	**1st degree is premeditated (time to reflect) and deliberate (cool and dispassionate),** or via FMR if an enumerated inherently dangerous felony. **All other murder: 2nd degree**	Here Deborah didn't intend to kill anyone so no premeditation or deliberation to murder anyone, but arson and burglary **trigger the FMR** for first degree murder.	1st degree murder possible if they don't charge her with involuntary manslaughter.
Defense: Necessity	**Necessity may be a defense if D reasonably believed that commission of the crime was necessary to avoid an imminent and greater injury to society** than that involved in the crime (objective standard used). Common law required the necessity to be caused by forces of nature. Many jurisdictions don't allow D to claim necessity for a danger they created.	For larceny/burglary: Here, the temperature was below freezing and continuing to drop so Deborah thought she would die if she didn't find some shelter which might make it reasonable to break into a garage that she thought was unoccupied to stay alive, but not necessarily start a fire if perhaps the garage enclosure alone could have kept her alive, but with the temperatures a fire might have been necessary. For arson: For reasons above, maybe a fire was necessary but not to be reckless and start it inside a garage with other wood and sleep while it was burning so the burning wasn't necessary as it was done. For murder: Typically, necessity won't be a defense to a murder charge.	**Necessity might be a defense to the theft crimes but not murder.**

Continued>

Issue	Rule	Fact Application	Conclusion
Defense: Mistake	A mistake of fact may negate a specific intent crime (such as first-degree murder and theft crimes) as well as malice, and may negate a general intent crime if the mistake was reasonable.	Arguably Deborah mistakenly thought the house was unoccupied when it was actually occupied by Stuart which was a mistake of fact. This could negate a first-degree murder charge but not necessarily involuntary manslaughter as she should have checked the home before starting a fire and falling asleep; as to larceny and burglary, her mistake wasn't reasonable b/c if the house was unoccupied the garage likely wouldn't be locked with firewood in there (but could argue other way if maybe abandoned).	Mistake likely won't be a valid defense

2. Deborah's motion to suppress her statement

Issue	Rule	Fact Application	Conclusion
Voluntariness/Due Process	**Confessions must be voluntary without police coercion,** in light of totality of the circumstances, considering the susceptibility of the suspect and environment and methods used.	**Here, Deborah freely told officer Oliver that she started the fire** when Oliver didn't even ask her about the fire, so he wasn't trying to coerce her into any particular response other than **ask her what she was doing walking around in below freezing temperatures in the middle of the night.**	**D's statement was voluntary**
5th Amend.: *Miranda*	To receive *Miranda* warnings, D must be in custodial interrogation. • **Custody**—not free to leave • **Interrogation**—words or actions by the police that they should know are reasonably likely to elicit an incriminating response	**Here, Deborah was not given *Miranda* warnings, but the Officer only asked her what she was doing outside on such a cold night as she was on the sidewalk so she wasn't in custody.** Arguably he could have been interrogating her if he knew about the fire three blocks away and wanted to see if she knew about it, but there was no reason for the Officer to think she had anything to do with the fire or that he knew about it as he was patrolling the area and might not have seen the fire yet.	**No *Miranda* violation**
5th Amend.: right against self-incrimination	Protects a criminal D from compulsion to give testimony or communicative evidence that could expose them to criminal liability.	Deborah wasn't forced to give testimony here as she voluntarily said she started the fire while standing on the sidewalk.	No 5th Am. violation
6th Amend.: right to counsel	**D has a right to counsel for all critical stages include post-charge questioning.**	**Deborah hadn't been arrested or charged yet so no right to counsel.**	No 6th Am. violation

Conclusion: The court should deny Deborah's motion to suppress her statement.

Crimes Question 1 Sample Answer
July 2023, Question 4

1. Crimes Deborah can be charged with and defenses available

Larceny

Larceny is the trespassory taking and carrying away of the personal property of another with the intent to permanently deprive them of their property.

Here, Deborah trespassed onto what she thought was an unoccupied house without permission and went into the garage and took wood from the stack as well as wood scraps and paper. Arguably she didn't carry it away since she decided to stay in the garage, but she still moved the wood which is sufficient for a carrying away. Further, the wood, wood scraps, and paper belonged to the owner, not her, so it was not her personal property. And given that she burned the materials, she intended to permanently deprive the owner of them because she cannot bring back items that are burned and used, and given that she was homeless, she had no way of paying for or replacing the materials. Thus, Deborah could reasonably be charged with larceny.

Burglary

Burglary is the breaking and entering of a dwelling house of another, at nighttime, with the intent to commit a felony therein. Modernly, most jurisdictions expand dwelling to any structure and any time of day is considered.

Here, Deborah broke through the window of the garage and entered the garage so there was a breaking and entering. The dwelling was the garage to Stuart's house so it was not Deborah's, and the garage is likely considered part of the dwelling house because it is usually part of the house, but modernly any structure would be included. Further, she intended to take the wood to start a fire to stay warm, so she intended to commit larceny therein. It is not clear if larceny would be a felony, but if it is a felony, then Deborah could be charged with burglary.

Deborah could likely be charged with burglary if larceny is a felony.

Arson

Arson is the malicious burning of the dwelling house of another. Malice includes the reckless disregard, and modernly dwelling house is expanded to include all structures.

Here, Deborah acted with reckless disregard to the lives of others and the risk that the structure could start on fire by starting a fire indoors and then falling asleep, especially since most homes are built of wood, there was wood already in the garage, and flammable oil. She might argue she wasn't aware of the oil but it is still reckless to start a fire indoors and then fall asleep and not monitor it. Further, the garage was likely a dwelling house of another as discussed above. Thus, Deborah could be charged with arson.

Common Law Murder

Murder is the unlawful killing of another person with malice aforethought. Malice can be proven by an intent to kill, an intent to commit grievous bodily injury, a reckless indifference to the value of human life, or through an intent to commit a dangerous felony (FMR).

Intent to kill/grievous bodily injury

Here, there was no intent to kill or harm anyone as Deborah thought the house was unoccupied, only started the fire to stay warm, and it accidentally spread quickly causing the entire house to become engulfed.

Reckless disregard (depraved heart)

Arguably one should know that fires spread quickly, especially if indoors, and people can be sleeping anywhere including in what appears to be an unoccupied home, as Deborah herself did, so one should know that fires are dangerous and can spread killing others if not properly maintained. However, Deborah did not act with reckless indifference to human life since it was inside a garage, the fire was small, and there is no indication she knew of the oil nearby and she did not think anyone was in the house. Overall, she likely did not act with reckless disregard for another human life.

FMR

Under the FMR, malice is implied if the death was a natural and probable consequence of defendant's conduct, the death occurred during the commission of the felony, even if it was accidental, and the underlying felony must be independent of the killing.

Here there are felonies of arson and burglary possible, both of which are inherently dangerous felonies. The death was a natural and probable cause of arson as people die from fires in homes all the time which is why the fire quickly engulfed the house making it harder for people, especially at night, to escape a fire. Further, the death occurred during the felony as the house was engulfed in flames due to the arson, at the time Stuart died. Finally, the death was independent of the arson, and it was an accident.

Thus, Deborah could be charged with felony murder.

Causation

Defendant's conduct must also be the cause in fact (but for) and proximate cause (foreseeable) of the death.

Here, but for Deborah starting the fire or burglarizing Stuart's home, the house would not have started on fire and Stuart wouldn't have been killed in his bed. Arguably it was not foreseeable that someone was there in bed since the house seemed to be unoccupied, but it is foreseeable that a fire inside a garage could spread and start a bigger fire, killing someone, especially since it was the middle of the night when people are sleeping. Further, it is always possible that people live in houses that seem unoccupied, especially people like Deborah who are homeless and trying to stay warm.

Therefore, causation is likely sufficient to prove murder.

Overall, Deborah could be charged with common law murder for reckless disregard or under the felony murder rule.

Involuntary Manslaughter

Involuntary manslaughter arises when a person's behavior is grossly negligent and the conduct results in the death of another. Gross negligence is the disregard of a very substantial danger of serious bodily harm or death.

Here, Deborah starting a fire in a garage to stay warm might not rise to the level of a high substantial danger of serious bodily harm or death since it was inside a garage, the fire was small, and there is no indication she knew of the oil nearby and she did not think anyone was in the house. However, one should know that fires spread quickly, especially if indoors with other wood nearby, and people can be sleeping anywhere including in what appears to be an unoccupied home, just as she did, so one should know that fires are dangerous and can spread killing others if not properly maintained.

Thus, it is possible that Deborah's murder charge can be reduced to involuntary manslaughter.

First and Second-Degree Murder

First-degree murder can be charged if the murder was premeditated, meaning the defendant had time to reflect on the killing, and deliberate, meaning the defendant acted in a cool and dispassionate manner. First-degree murder can also be established through the felony murder rule if defendant committed an enumerated inherently dangerous felony.

All other murders that are not reduced to manslaughter are second-degree murders.

Here Deborah didn't intend to kill anyone so there was no premeditation or deliberation to murder anyone, but arson and burglary trigger the FMR for first-degree murder. Thus, first-degree murder is possible if her murder charge isn't reduced to involuntary manslaughter.

Defense — Necessity

Necessity may be a defense if the defendant reasonably believed that commission of the crime was necessary to avoid an imminent and greater injury to society than that involved in the crime, using an objective standard.

Larceny/burglary charge

Here, the temperature was below freezing and continuing to drop so Deborah thought she would die if she didn't find some shelter, which might make it reasonable to break into a garage that she thought was unoccupied, to stay alive. However, it might not have been necessary to start a fire if perhaps the garage enclosure alone could have kept her alive, but with the temperatures below freezing a fire might have been necessary to survive. Thus, necessity could possibly be an excuse to the larceny and burglary charges.

Arson charge

For reasons above, maybe a fire was necessary, but not to be reckless and start it inside a garage with other wood and sleep while it was burning, so the burning wasn't necessary in the manner in which it was done. Thus, necessity probably wouldn't be a valid defense for arson.

Murder charge

Typically, necessity won't be a defense to a murder charge so this will not work.

Defense — Mistake

A mistake of fact may negate a specific intent crime, such as first-degree murder and theft crimes, as well as malice, and may negate a general intent crime if the mistake was reasonable.

Arguably Deborah mistakenly thought the house was unoccupied when it was actually occupied by Stuart which was a mistake of fact. This could negate a first-degree murder charge but not necessarily involuntary manslaughter as she should have checked the home before starting a fire and falling asleep. As to larceny and burglary, her mistake wasn't reasonable because if the house was unoccupied, then the garage likely wouldn't be locked with firewood in there. While one might argue that the owner could have abandoned the house with firewood and left it locked, it seems unreasonable that supplies would be there under those circumstances. Thus, mistake most likely would not be a valid defense.

2. Deborah's motion to suppress her statement

Voluntariness/Due Process

Confessions must be made voluntarily without police coercion, in light of totality of the circumstances, considering the susceptibility of the suspect and environment and methods used.

Here, Deborah freely told the officer that she started the fire when he didn't even ask her about the fire, so he wasn't trying to coerce her into any particular response other than ask her what she was doing walking around in below freezing temperatures in the middle of the night. Thus, Deborah's statement that she started the fire was voluntary.

5th Amendment *Miranda* Rights

Police must issue *Miranda* warnings to suspects in custodial interrogation. One is in custody when they are not reasonably free to leave. Interrogation occurs when there are words or actions by the police that they should know are reasonably likely to elicit an incriminating response.

Here, Deborah was not given *Miranda* warnings, but the officer only asked her what she was doing outside on such a cold night as she was on the sidewalk in the middle of the night in freezing temperatures. So, she wasn't in custody.

Arguably the officer could have been interrogating her if he knew about the fire three blocks away and wanted to see if she knew about it, but there was no reason for the officer to think she had anything to do with the fire or that he even knew about it as he was patrolling the area and might not have seen the fire yet. Thus, there was no *Miranda* violation.

5th Amendment Right Against Self-incrimination

This right protects a criminal defendant from compulsion to give testimony or communicate evidence that could expose them to criminal liability. Here, Deborah wasn't forced to give testimony as she voluntarily said she started the fire while on the sidewalk. Thus, there was no 5th Am. violation.

6th Amendment Right to Counsel

Defendant has a right to counsel for all critical stages including post-charge questioning. Here, Deborah hadn't been arrested or charged yet so her right to counsel didn't attach yet. Thus, there is no 6th Amendment violation.

Overall, the court should deny Deborah's motion to suppress her statement.

Crimes Question 2
July 2015, Question 3

Owen, a police officer, had a hunch that Dora might be selling methamphetamine from her house in the country. To learn more, Owen drove to Dora's house with a drug-detection dog and waited until she left.

Owen first walked the drug-detection dog around Dora's house. At his direction, the dog jumped up on the porch, sniffed the front door, and indicated the presence of methamphetamine.

Owen then propped a ladder on the back of the house, climbed to the top, and peered into a second-story bedroom window. He saw a small box on a bedside table, but could not read the label. He used binoculars to read the label, and saw that it listed ingredients that could be used to make methamphetamine.

Owen went back to his car, saw Dora return home, and then walked back to the house and crouched under an open window. He soon overheard Dora telling a telephone caller, "I can sell you several ounces of methamphetamine."

Dora was arrested and charged with attempting to sell methamphetamine. Dora has moved to suppress evidence of (1) the drug-detection dog's reaction, (2) the small box, and (3) the overheard conversation, under the Fourth Amendment to the United States Constitution.

How should the court rule on each point? Discuss.

Crimes Question 2 Assessment
July 2015, Question 3

While the Fourth Amendment has been tested since the beginning of the bar exam, the specific rules relating to drug-detecting dogs and the use of sensory-enhancing technology had not been tested prior to this question. This is a relatively new area of law as emerging technology has heavily affected our current times and the use of dogs for work-related ventures has also increased, thus giving rise to new case law that has addressed whether these uses constitute a search based on a person's reasonable expectation of privacy.

This is a good time to discuss what you might do on a question like this if you didn't know the law. The best approach would be to use the facts and try to think about what makes logical sense (basically use your common sense) as to what would be fair and reasonable in this situation. And always be sure to see both sides if you aren't sure of the answer (which will be most of the time).

Here, for example, if you did know the rules then you would know that this situation is not a clear-cut case. It requires you to objectively view both sides. For that reason, the state-released answers come to opposite conclusions on the last call regarding the phone conversation. This is because case law has developed such that we know that overhearing phone calls is not a violation of one's privacy. But use of wiretapping or electronic means to overhear a call is a violation of privacy. Then there was the case of listening to calls through walls at an apartment complex. That, too, was deemed acceptable. This fact pattern gives you a hypothetical not yet decided by the courts—eavesdropping under an open window at a house in the country when the officer was only there due to an improper use of a drug-detecting dog. Thus, there is no exact case law on point, which means you need to use the current rules you have (or common sense if you don't know them) and use ALL facts to see both sides to the argument.

Using all of the facts on this exam is critical to your analysis and being objective. This question was not an issue spotting question as the call was very specific as to what items were at issue as well as the Fourth Amendment. The points come from your ability to use the facts effectively. Make sure you highlight or underline all facts as you use them to ensure you do use all facts to bolster your analysis. Facts that were easily omitted on this exam include that O "had a hunch," D's house was "in the country," the dog sniffed "at his direction," "second-story" was observed, "O crouched" under the window but it was "open," and so forth. Look at your answer now and see if you used all of these facts. If not, those are points left on the table. To remedy this next time, highlight or underline facts as you use them.

To see which issues are of greater weight on this essay, make note of the areas highlighted in **bold** on the corresponding grid. The bold areas highlight the issues, analysis, and conclusions that are likely **required** to receive a passing score on this question. In general, the essay grids are provided to assist you in analyzing the essays and are much more detailed than what a student should create during the exam to organize their response to a question.

Issue	Rule	Fact Application	Conclusion
4th Amend.	4th Amend. protects against unreasonable search and seizure where there is government action, and property or place searched or seized is one in which D has reasonable expectation of privacy (REOP). A warrant is required for all searches unless an exception applies.	Here, the drug-detecting dog's actions, the viewing of the small box, and the overheard conversation will all be analyzed to see if D's 4th Amendment rights were violated. **Here, Owen is a police officer and thus there is government action for all items below.** REOP will be addressed with each item below. **There was no search warrant for any of the below items so an exception will need to apply if there was a reasonable expectation of privacy.**	4th Am. applicable Gov. action present No warrant
Exclusionary Rule	Exclusionary rule is a judge-made rule that prohibits prosecution from introducing evidence obtained in violation of a defendant's 4th, 5th, or 6th Amend. rights.	**Here, if any of the above actions violate the 4th Amendment then the evidence obtained will be excluded.**	
Fruit of the Poisonous Tree	Evidence that is found as a result of the original wrongfully obtained evidence is also inadmissible unless: • The evidence obtained could have been obtained from an independent source; or • The evidence obtained would inevitably have been discovered; or • Additional factors intervened between the original illegality and the final discovery that the link is too tenuous.	**All actions will be analyzed with these doctrines in mind.**	

Continued>

Issue	Rule	Fact Application	Conclusion
(1) Drug-detection dog's reaction			
REOP (Open Fields/Dogs)	**Areas outside the home that are held out to the public do not have a reasonable expectation of privacy** Courts will consider: • The proximity to the house, • If the area is enclosed by a fence/wall, • The nature of the use of the structure in question, and • The steps taken by the individual to protect privacy. Dogs are permitted to sniff luggage at airports and cars during a legitimate traffic stop but **cannot be used to sniff homes without a warrant or warrant exception** (the dog cannot create the probable cause).	Here, O used the dog to sniff D's front door. Arguably, the door was open to the public as anyone can access the front door making it possible open fields, but the home was "in the country" making it seem unlikely that a police dog would be going by her front door. And the dog didn't naturally smell anything but rather was guided to the porch and directed to jump up on the porch followed by O's "hunch." Thus, the nature of the use is questionable as is the use of the dog to sniff the home deliberately without a warrant. Use of the dog was essentially a trespass when it was directed by O to jump on the porch and sniff for drugs.	REOP violated so warrant needed or exception needed and none here Evidence suppressed
(2) Small box			
REOP (Open Fields/Technology)	**See rules above for open fields rules.** **Sensory-enhancing technology will violate a reasonable expectation of privacy (e.g., heat/thermal imagers not allowed), but technology available to the public may be permitted.**	Here, the backyard may be open to the public in the "open fields" as you could perhaps see it from a plane and it isn't clear if it is fenced in, especially since D lives in the country. However, D would expect the inside of her house to be private and O had to use a ladder and was peering into a second-story bedroom, not a family room visible from the first floor street view; a reasonable person expects their bedroom on a second floor to be private especially since the only way to view it is with a ladder. Binoculars are likely acceptable to use since they are widely available to the public unlike heat-sensing technology. The problem is that O was only able to use them once he improperly used a ladder and peered into an upstairs window.	**REOP violated** No warrant so evidence suppressed unless valid exception

Continued>

Issue	Rule	Fact Application	Conclusion
Plain View	Police may make a warrantless search if they see an object or contraband when they are legitimately on premises or have a right to be in the position to have the view.	Here while the box was in plain view with binoculars (allowed per above), the view was only from atop a ladder in a backyard and thus not truly in plain view from a place that O had a legitimate right to be present.	No plain view Evidence suppressed
Fruit of the Poisonous Tree	Rules above	Also under the fruit of the poisonous tree, O only likely went to look in the house after the dog indicated the presence of methamphetamines; thus, his initial illegal search lead to the discovery of the small box so it would also be excluded under the fruit of the poisonous tree even if the box discovery itself was acceptable (which is likely isn't). None of the exceptions to the rule apply either as it would not have been discovered independently, the box would not have inevitably been discovered, and there were no intervening factors making the link too tenuous so as to purge the taint.	Evidence of small box suppressed
(3) Overheard conversation			
REOP	Electronic eavesdropping is not acceptable (fine to overhear conversations or to listen through walls though).	Here, arguably O did overhear the conversation, which is usually acceptable, especially since the window was open and he wasn't using electronic devices to overhear the conversation. But, he was listening "crouched" under an open window in the "back" of D's house that was out "in the country." Thus, a reasonable person would not expect anyone to overhear their conversations while in their house out in the country. Since the area was so remote and he was not likely entitled to be at the back of the house anyway, D would likely have a REOP to that call.	Could conclude either way here (key was to see both sides) Most likely evidence suppressed
Fruit of the Poisonous Tree	Rules above	Same analysis as above	Evidence of conversation suppressed

Crimes Question 2 Sample Answer
July 2015, Question 3

Fourth Amendment

The Fourth Amendment protects against unreasonable searches and seizures where there is government action and the property or place searched or seized is one in which D has reasonable expectation of privacy.

Here, the drug-detecting dog's actions, the viewing of the small box, and the overheard conversation will all be analyzed to see if D's Fourth Amendment rights were violated.

Government Action

Here, Owen is a police officer and thus there is government action for all items below.

Reasonable Expectation of Privacy

Reasonable expectation of privacy will be addressed with each item below.

Warrant Requirement

A warrant is required for all searches and seizures unless an exception applies.

Here there was no warrant so an exception will be needed if the Fourth Amendment is applicable to these searches and seizures (which will depend on whether there was a reasonable expectation of privacy in the places and items searched as discussed below).

Exclusionary Rule

The exclusionary rule is a judge-made rule that prohibits the prosecution from introducing evidence obtained in violation of a defendant's Fourth, Fifth, or Sixth Amendment rights. Here, if any of the actions violate the Fourth Amendment, then the evidence obtained will be excluded.

Fruit of the Poisonous Tree

Evidence that is found as a result of the original wrongfully obtained evidence is also inadmissible unless: (1) the evidence obtained could have been obtained from an independent source; (2) the evidence obtained would inevitably have been discovered; or (3) additional factors intervened between the original illegality and the final discovery so that the link is too tenuous. All actions will be analyzed with these doctrines in mind.

1. Drug-detection dog's reaction

Privacy — Open Fields

Areas outside the home that are held out to the public do not have a reasonable expectation of privacy. To determine whether areas are public, courts will consider factors including the proximity to the house of the area searched, if the area is enclosed by a fence/wall, the nature of the use of the structure in question, and the steps taken by the individual to protect privacy.

Here, arguably a person's front porch area and front door are open to the public as anyone can access the front door, making it possibly viewed as "open fields."

However, here the home was "in the country" making it seem unlikely that a police officer and his police drug-sniffing dog would be in the area wandering by her front door. The reason O was present was due to his "hunch" that D was selling methamphetamines and not based on any particular probable cause (which if he did have he could have received a warrant prior to going to her house). Thus, his presence at her home in the country, due to his hunch, would not be expected by a reasonable person. If he alone was simply present and just on the front porch, it would likely not be a violation of her privacy, but he used a dog to sniff her property, which is where the violation likely occurred as discussed below.

Privacy — Dogs

Dogs are permitted to sniff luggage at airports and cars during a legitimate traffic stop but police cannot use dogs to sniff homes without a warrant or warrant exception and the dog cannot create the probable cause to obtain the warrant.

Here, O used the dog to sniff D's front door. And the dog didn't naturally smell anything but rather was guided to the porch and "directed" to jump up on the porch followed by O's "hunch." Thus, the nature of the use is questionable, as is the use of the dog to sniff the home deliberately without a warrant. The use of the dog was essentially a trespass when it was directed by O to jump on the porch and sniff for drugs since there was no reason for O or the dog to be present.

As a result, D had a reasonable expectation of privacy in her front porch against the dog sniffing for drugs. Since O did not have a warrant to use the dog to search the porch and no warrantless exceptions apply, the evidence will be suppressed.

2. Small box

Privacy — Open Fields

See above for open fields rules.

Here, the backyard may be open to the public in the "open fields" as you could perhaps see it from a plane and it isn't clear if it is fenced in, especially since D lives in the country. If there is no fence and the area is wide open as is often the case in the country, then there may be less privacy to the open space including a backyard.

However, D would expect the inside of her house to be private and O had to use a ladder and was peering into a second-story bedroom, not a family room visible from the first floor street view. A reasonable person expects her bedroom on a second floor to be private especially since the only way to view it is with a ladder regardless of whether wandering around to the backyard itself was acceptable. Thus, using a ladder in one's backyard to view into a window would not be in the "open" as you could only see that area by using a ladder and peering in which otherwise would not be possible on foot.

Privacy — Use of Technology

Sensory enhancing technology will violate a reasonable expectation of privacy. For example, use of heat and thermal imagers are not allowed. But technology available to the public is permitted.

Binoculars are likely acceptable to use to see fine print such as ingredients not otherwise visible to the naked eye because they are widely available to the public and commonly used, unlike heat sensing technology. The problem is that O was only able to use them once he improperly used a ladder and peered into an upstairs window. Thus, D did have a reasonable expectation of privacy as to the contents, including the small box, in her second-story bedroom. Since there was no warrant for this search, the evidence should be suppressed barring any valid exceptions.

Plain View

Police may make a warrantless search if they see an object or contraband when they are legitimately on the premises or have a right to be in the position to have the view.

Here, while the box was in plain view with binoculars (allowed per above), the view was only from atop a ladder in a backyard and thus not truly in plain view from a place that O had a legitimate right to be present. Thus, the evidence of the small box ingredients will be suppressed.

Fruit of the Poisonous Tree

See rules above.

Also under the fruit of the poisonous tree, O only went to look in the house after the dog indicated the presence of methamphetamines and thus his initial illegal search lead to the discovery of the small box so it would also be excluded under the fruit of the poisonous tree even if the box discovery itself was acceptable (which is likely isn't). None of the exceptions to the fruit of the poisonous tree rule apply either as the box would not have been discovered independently, the box would not have inevitably been discovered, and there were no intervening factors making the link too tenuous so as to purge the taint. Thus, the evidence would also be suppressed under this theory too.

3. Overheard conversation

Electronic eavesdropping requires a warrant, as one has a reasonable expectation of privacy in private calls. However, one does not have a reasonable expectation of privacy in conversations that are overheard, even if they are overhead by listening through walls.

Here arguably O did overhear the conversation, especially since the window was open and he wasn't using electronic devices to overhear the conversation and thus, O could argue that D did not have a reasonable expectation of privacy in her conversation. If she wanted a private conversation she could have closed the window or spoken away from the windows such that her conversation could not be overheard.

However, O was listening "crouched" under an open window in the "back" of D's house that was out "in the country," which indicates it wasn't a conversation that one would expect could be overheard. Thus, a reasonable person would not expect anyone to overhear her conversations while in her house out in the country. Since the house was in the country and O was not likely entitled to be at the house anyway, D would likely have a reasonable expectation of privacy in this conversation. Since there was no warrant and no warrantless exceptions, the call conversation evidence would likely be suppressed.

Fruit of the Poisonous Tree

Rules above. For the same reasons expressed above in call 2, the evidence could also be excluded under this theory as well.

Crimes Question 3
July 2009, Question 6

Polly, a uniformed police officer, observed a speeding car weaving in and out of traffic in violation of the Vehicle Code. Polly pursued the car in her marked patrol vehicle and activated its flashing lights. The car pulled over. Polly asked Dave, the driver, for his driver's license and the car's registration certificate, both of which he handed to her. Although the documents appeared to be in order, Polly instructed Dave and his passenger, Ted: "Stay here. I'll be back in a second." Polly then walked to her patrol vehicle to check for any outstanding arrest warrants against Dave.

As she was walking, Polly looked back and saw that Ted appeared to be slipping something under his seat. Polly returned to Dave's car, opened the passenger side door, looked under the seat, and saw a paper lunch bag. Polly pulled the bag out, opened it, and found five small bundles of what she recognized as cocaine.

Polly arrested Dave and Ted, took them to the police station, and gave them *Miranda* warnings. Dave refused to answer any questions. Ted, however, waived his *Miranda* rights, and stated: "I did not know what was inside the bag or how the bag got into the car. I did not see the bag before Dave and I got out of the car for lunch. We left the windows of the car open because of the heat. I did not see the bag until you stopped us. It was just lying there on the floor mat, so I put it under the seat to clear the mat for my feet."

Dave and Ted have been charged jointly with possession of cocaine. Dave and Ted have each retained an attorney. A week before trial, Dave has become dissatisfied with his attorney and wants to discharge him in favor of a new attorney he hopes to select soon.

What arguments might Dave raise under the United States Constitution in sup- port of each of the following motions, and how are they likely to fare:

1. A motion to suppress the cocaine? Discuss.

2. A motion to suppress Ted's statement or, in the alternative, for a separate trial? Discuss.

3. A motion to discharge his present attorney and to substitute a new attorney in his place? Discuss.

Crimes Question 3 Assessment
July 2009, Question 6

This criminal procedure question is typical and covers Fourth Amendment search and seizure issues, which is a heavily tested area within criminal procedure. Be methodical and follow all steps when organizing a response that incorporates the Fourth Amendment since analysis of the issue(s) at each step is required to receive the maximum points on the essay. Otherwise, it is easy to forget obvious issues, such as the requirement that you need government action for the Fourth Amendment to apply. Although the state action requirement is obviously met (since Polly is a police officer), you must still address it in your answer, and the failure to do so will result in missing easy points.

Also, if mnemonics work well for you, remember the mnemonic SPACES for the exceptions to a warrantless search. On most exams that test the Fourth Amendment, the facts will include a warrantless search. On the rare occasion when the fact pattern includes a search warrant, it will probably be improperly executed, thus raising the issue of the good faith exception. Just be sure that you don't use the good faith exception to an improperly executed warrant as one of the exceptions applicable to a warrantless search. It is crucial that you understand which exceptions apply to each factual situation. Pay especially close attention to whether there was a warrant for the arrest or search and, if there was, whether it was properly executed since this is the determinative issue from which all of the other issues flow.

It is important to fully understand the distinction between the search incident to a lawful arrest (SILA) exception and the automobile exception. Students often don't fully comprehend the differences between the two exceptions. Remember that for SILA to apply, there must be a lawful arrest, whereas lawful arrest is not required for the automobile exception to apply. Similarly, under SILA the police cannot search the compartments within a car if the suspect does not have access to them, such as when the suspect is in the back of the police car or handcuffed. However, under the automobile exception, the police can search the car compartments if there is probable cause to believe that they contain contraband. Keep these distinctions in mind because when one of them is inapplicable, the other one may apply.

Finally, remember that although you only need one exception to admit the evidence under a warrantless search, the bar examiners expect an IRAC of every possible exception where there are corresponding facts. Thus, even if SILA is met, don't stop there. Go through all possible remaining exceptions that might be applicable or that have facts that correspond to them. This will ensure that you receive maximum points by using all facts and spotting all issues.

To see which issues are of greater weight on this essay, make note of the areas highlighted in **bold** on the corresponding grid. The bold areas highlight the issues, analysis, and conclusions that are likely **required** to receive a passing score on this question. In general, the essay grids are provided to assist you in analyzing the essays and are much more detailed than what a student should create during the exam to organize their response to a question.

Call #1: Motion to Suppress Cocaine

Issue	Rule	Fact Application	Conclusion
4th Amend.	4th Amend. protects individuals against unreasonable searches and seizures of property and against unlawful arrests.	Here, there was a search of Dave's car and thus a 4th Amend. analysis is warranted.	
Govt. Action	There must be government action (as opposed to private) for the 4th Amend. search and seizure protections to apply.	Here, Polly, a uniformed police officer, who works for the government, searched Dave's car, found the cocaine, and arrested Dave and Ted.	Yes, govt. action
Reasonable Expectation of Privacy	D must have a reasonable expectation of privacy in the property or place being searched or seized.	Here, Dave has a reasonable expectation of privacy in his car since most individuals do not allow random people to access their car, especially compartments and storage not in plain view.	Dave has standing
Search Warrant	Generally, police need a search warrant based on probable cause, in which it is reasonable that places to be searched are connected with criminal activities and items will be found in places to be searched.	Here, Polly did not have a search warrant at the time she searched Dave's car and found the cocaine. Thus, Dave will argue that the search was invalid and violated his 4th Amend. rights.	No warrant
Routine Auto Stop	The police may randomly stop automobiles if there is a reasonable suspicion of wrongdoing based on an objective standard.	Here, Polly stopped Dave's car because it was speeding and weaving in and out of traffic in violation of the Vehicle Code, thus giving her a reasonable suspicion that he was violating the traffic laws.	Routine stop permissible
Exception to Warrantless Search	If police conduct a search or seizure without a valid search warrant, there must be an applicable exception.	Since Polly did not have a search warrant to search Dave's car, Dave can argue that evidence of the cocaine should be suppressed.	Need warrant exception
SILA	When police are making a lawful arrest, they may search the area within the arrestee's immediate control.	Here, the police made a lawful arrest, but not until after Polly searched Dave's car and found the cocaine. Thus, this exception will not be applicable.	No SILA exception
Plain View	Police may make a warrantless search if they see an object or contraband when they are legitimately on the premises or have a right to be in position to have that view.	Here, the bag was not in plain view because it was under the passenger seat. In fact, Polly didn't even know what Ted slipped under the seat and had to open his door to access it, proving that it was not in plain view. Further, the cocaine was inside the paper bag and not visible even under the seat.	No plain view exception

Continued >

Continued>

Issue	Rule	Fact Application	Conclusion
Automobile	**If police have probable cause to believe that a vehicle contains contraband, they may search the whole automobile and any container therein.** If the driver is arrested, police may impound the car, transport it to the station house, and search it there without a warrant.	Here, Dave will argue that the car contained contraband because he was speeding and weaving in and out of traffic, which is a routine traffic violation that is not typically associated with cocaine or contraband. However, Polly can argue that when drivers speed and weave in and out of traffic, they could be drunk or under the influence of drugs, and, coupled with the fact that she saw Ted appear to slip something under the seat, it gave her probable cause or reasonable belief that there was contraband under the seat, if anything, as he could have reached down to tie his shoes and not actually slip anything under the seat, which could have been the reason for the unsafe driving. **Since Polly had no idea what Ted was placing under the seat and Ted was not the one who was driving, it is unlikely that her belief that there was contraband was reasonable.** Further, she then saw a paper lunch bag, which would not likely be associated with alcohol or contraband as it relates to Dave violating the traffic laws.	**No automobile exception**
Consent	Police may make a warrantless search if the person whose premises, items, or person will be searched voluntarily consented considering the totality of the circumstances.	Here, Dave did not consent to his car being searched. Instead, Polly just opened the passenger door where Ted was seated, looked under the seat, saw the bag, pulled it out, and opened it without permission from either Dave or Ted.	No consent exception
Exigent Circumstances	The police may conduct a search or seizure without a warrant if they have probable cause and it is necessary to • Prevent imminent destruction of evidence, • Prevent imminent injury to persons, or • Search for a felony suspect in hot pursuit that the police reasonably believe has entered particular premises.	Here, Polly would not have probable cause to believe that Dave or Ted would destroy the evidence because she didn't even know it existed until after she searched. Nor would she reasonably suspect, from a routine traffic stop, that it existed to begin with. Further, there is no danger to persons or a hot pursuit in progress.	No exigent circumstances exception

Issue	Rule	Fact Application	Conclusion
Stop and Frisk	Police officers may stop and frisk a person if they have reasonable suspicion of criminal activity or involvement that is supported by articulable facts. Brief detention may include pat-down search for weapons if the suspect appears dangerous and armed.	Here, although the stop may be reasonable due to the speeding, the search was not reasonable as there was no reasonable suspicion of criminal activity other than traffic violations. Also, the detention gave Polly no reason to assume Dave and Ted were armed or dangerous as they did not act inappropriately, but rather provided her with the documents she requested, such as Dave's license and registration.	No stop and frisk exception
Exclusionary Rule	Exclusionary rule is a judge-made rule that prohibits the prosecution from introducing evidence obtained in violation of a D's 4th, 5th, or 6th Amend. rights. D must have standing to assert the exclusionary rule, such that evidence obtained must have been in violation of D's own constitutional rights and not any third person's.	Here, since the cocaine was obtained in violation of Dave's 4th Amend. rights, it will be excluded. Also, Dave has standing as it was his car that was searched and the evidence is now being used against him.	Cocaine suppressed
Call #2: Suppress Ted's Statement/Separate Trial			
6th Amend.: Right to Confront	Prosecution may not admit testimonial statements by a third person against D unless the declarant is available for cross-examination either at the time the statement was made or during trial. Statements are testimonial when circumstances indicate no ongoing emergency, and that the primary purpose of interrogation is to establish or prove past events potentially relevant to later criminal prosecution. **Where two Ds are jointly tried and one of them confesses, right to confront adverse witnesses prohibits use of that statement unless the statement can be redacted or the co-D who made the statement takes the stand and subjects themself to cross-examination.**	Here, Ted's statement that he didn't know what was in the bag or how it got into the car and that it just appeared there after lunch when they left the windows down due to the heat is testimonial because it was made in response to questions by the police at the police station, which can prove events relevant to the charge of cocaine, which was found in the bag. **The problem here is that if Ted doesn't take the stand to testify, which he may not since he is a co-defendant, Dave has the right to cross-examine him about the statement, which is not possible if Ted doesn't testify.** However, arguably, the statement is not adverse to Dave since it doesn't implicate Dave. Rather, it indicates that neither Dave nor Ted had anything to do with the cocaine and that it was likely placed in the car when they were at lunch since there was easy access and the windows were rolled down. On the other hand, it can be inferred that if Ted had nothing to do with the paper bag in Dave's car, then the jury may find that it must have been Dave. Since this interpretation is possible, the court might suppress Ted's statement.	Court is likely to suppress Ted's statement

Continued>

Issue	Rule	Fact Application	Conclusion
Severance	Where co-Ds are charged for the same crime, courts prefer joint trials for judicial economy, but will **sever the co-Ds** if a joint trial would result in substantial prejudice to one of the Ds.	As discussed above, Ted's statement doesn't directly implicate Dave and in fact, it tends to indicate that someone else is to blame for the bag being put in the car, which would not result in any prejudice to Dave, especially not substantial prejudice. If Ted and Dave implicate each other, then a new trial would be necessary as the testimony from each would violate the 6th Amend. rights of the other, and each would have the right to cross-examine the other.	Court will not likely sever the co-defendants based on Ted's statement
Call #3: Motion to Discharge/Substitute Attorney			
Right to Effective Counsel	Suspect against whom formal criminal proceedings have been commenced has the **right to effective counsel** at any post-charge line-up or show-up.	Here, Dave retained an attorney, rather than having one appointed to him, but this does not mean that he cannot replace this attorney with another attorney. The problem here is that he has become dissatisfied with his attorney the week before trial for unknown reasons. Although he has the right to an attorney of his choice, the court will need to consider whether it is fair to substitute new counsel at this stage of the proceedings.	**Yes, right to effective counsel**
Right to Substitute Attorney	A court will allow D to **substitute a new attorney if the interests of justice** so require, taking into account any conflicts, the interests of D and the court, and the timeliness of the request.	Here, it is unclear why Dave has become dissatisfied with his attorney so it is difficult to determine whether the court would grant his motion. However, since trial is scheduled to begin in one week and there doesn't appear to be any major conflict or concern from the facts, it is unlikely that the court would substitute the attorney as this would affect and delay Ted as well as Dave and would not be efficient for the courts since the court already scheduled the trial for those dates.	**Unlikely court will grant motion for new attorney**

Crimes Question 3 Sample Answer
July 2009, Question 6

1. Motion to Suppress Cocaine

Fourth Amendment

The Fourth (4th) Amendment protects individuals against unreasonable searches and seizures of property and arrest. Here, there was a search of Dave's car and thus a 4th Amendment analysis is warranted.

Government Action

There must be government action in order for the 4th Amendment search and seizure protections to apply. Here, Polly, a uniformed police officer who works for the government, searched Dave's car, found the cocaine, and arrested Dave and Ted. Therefore, there is government action.

Reasonable Expectation of Privacy

The defendant must have a reasonable expectation of privacy in the property or place being searched or seized.

Here, Dave has a reasonable expectation of privacy in his car since most individuals do not allow random people to access their car, especially compartments and storage areas not in plain view. Therefore, Dave has standing to asset a violation under the 4th Amendment.

Search Warrant

Generally, the police need a search warrant based on probable cause, in which it is reasonable that the items to be searched are connected with criminal activities and the items will be found in the place to be searched.

Here, Polly did not have a search warrant at the time she searched Dave's car and found the cocaine. Thus, Dave will argue that the search was invalid and violated his Fourth Amendment rights.

Routine Automobile Stop

The police may randomly stop automobiles if there is a reasonable suspicion or wrongdoing based on an objective standard.

Here, Polly stopped Dave's car because it was speeding and weaving in and out of traffic in violation of the Vehicle Code, thus giving her a reasonable suspicion that Dave was violating the traffic laws. Thus, the initial automobile stop was permissible.

Exceptions to a Warrantless Search

If the police conduct a search or seizure without a valid search warrant, there must be an applicable exception. Since Polly did not have a search warrant to search Dave's car, Dave can argue that evidence of the cocaine should be suppressed, barring any valid exceptions.

SILA

When the police are making a lawful arrest, they may search the area within the arrestee's immediate control. Here, the police made a lawful arrest, but not until after Polly searched Dave's car and found the cocaine. Thus, this exception will not be applicable.

Plain View

The police may make a warrantless search if they see an object or contraband when they are legitimately on the premises or have a right to be in the position to have the view.

Here, the bag was not in plain view because it was under the passenger seat. In fact, Polly didn't even know what Ted slipped under the seat, if anything, since it only appeared that he was slipping something under the seat, and she had to open his door to access it, proving that it was not in plain view. Further, the cocaine was inside the paper lunch bag and not visible even under the seat. Therefore, this exception will not apply.

Automobile

If the police have probable cause to believe that a vehicle contains contraband, they may search the whole automobile and any container therein. Further, if the driver is arrested, the police may impound the car, transport it to the station house, and search it there without a warrant.

Here, Dave will argue that Polly did not have probable cause to believe that the car contained contraband because he was speeding and weaving in and out of traffic, which is a routine traffic violation that is not typically associated with cocaine or contraband.

However, Polly can argue that when drivers speed and weave in and out of traffic, they could be drunk or under the influence of drugs. This possibility, coupled with the fact that she saw Ted appear to slip something under the seat, gave her probable cause or a reasonable belief that there was contraband under the seat, which could have been the reason for the unsafe driving.

Overall, since Polly had no idea what Ted was placing under the seat, if anything, since it only appeared that he was slipping something under the seat, and Ted was not the one who was driving, it is unlikely that her belief that there was contraband was reasonable. Further, she then saw a paper lunch bag, which would not likely be associated with alcohol or contraband as it relates to Dave violating the traffic laws. Therefore, this exception will not be applicable.

Consent

The police may make a warrantless search if the person whose premises, items, or person will be searched voluntarily consented considering the totality of the circumstances. Here, Dave did not consent to his car being searched. Instead, Polly just opened the passenger door where Ted was seated, looked under the seat, saw the bag, pulled it out, and opened it without permission from either Dave or Ted. Thus, there was no consent.

Exigent Circumstances

The police may conduct a search or seizure without a warrant if they have probable cause and the search is necessary to prevent imminent destruction of evidence, imminent injury to persons, or if they are pursuing a felony suspect and reasonably believe the suspect in hot pursuit has entered particular premises.

Here, Polly would not have probable cause to believe that Dave or Ted would destroy the evidence because she didn't even know it existed until after she searched under the seat. Nor would she reasonably suspect that it existed to begin with from a routine traffic stop since they were not being chased for drugs, but rather for typical traffic violations. Further, there is no danger to persons or a hot pursuit in progress. Thus, there are no exigent circumstances that would allow a warrantless search.

Stop and Frisk

A police officer may stop and frisk a person if the police have a reasonable suspicion of criminal activity or involvement that is supported by articulable facts. The brief detention may include a pat-down search for weapons if the suspect appears dangerous and armed.

Here, although the stop may be reasonable due to the speeding and weaving in and out of traffic, the search was not reasonable as there was no reasonable suspicion of criminal activity other than typical traffic violations.

Also, the detention gave Polly no reason to assume Dave and Ted were armed or dangerous since they did not act inappropriately, but rather provided her with the documents she requested, such as Dave's license and registration. Thus, the stop and frisk exception is inapplicable.

Exclusionary Rule

The exclusionary rule is a judge-made rule that prohibits the prosecution from introducing evidence obtained in violation of a defendant's 4th, 5th, or 6th Amendment rights. The defendant must have standing to assert the exclusionary rule such that the evidence obtained must have been in violation of the defendant's own constitutional rights and not any third persons.

Here, since the cocaine was obtained in violation of Dave's 4th Amendment rights, it will be excluded. Also, Dave has standing since it was his car that was searched and the evidence is now being used against him.

Overall, Dave will be successful in his motion and the cocaine will be suppressed as it was seized in violation of his 4th Amendment rights.

2. Suppress Ted's Statement or Separate Trial

Sixth Amendment Right to Confront Adverse Witnesses

The prosecution may not admit testimonial statements by a third person against the defendant unless the declarant is available for cross-examination either at the time the statement was made or during trial. Statements are testimonial when the circumstances indicate that there is no ongoing emergency, and that the primary purpose of the interrogation is to establish or prove past events potentially relevant to later criminal prosecution.

Here, Ted's statement that he didn't know what was in the bag or how it got into the car and that it just appeared there after lunch when they left the windows down due to the heat is testimonial because it was made in response to questions by the police at the police station which can prove events relevant to the charge of cocaine, which was found in the bag.

Thus, Ted's statement invokes the Sixth (6th) Amendment.

Co-defendants

Where two defendants are jointly tried and one of them confesses, the right to confront adverse witnesses prohibits use of that statement unless the statement can be redacted or the co-defendant who made the statement takes the stand and subjects themself to cross-examination.

The problem here is that if Ted doesn't take the stand to testify, which is his right as a co-defendant, Dave will not be able to cross-examine him regarding his statement.

However, arguably, the statement is not adverse to Dave since it doesn't implicate Dave. Rather, it indicates that neither Dave nor Ted had anything to do with the cocaine and that it was likely placed in the car when they were at lunch since there was easy access and the windows were rolled down.

Although Dave will likely argue that a reasonable juror could infer from Ted's statement that if Ted had nothing to do with the paper bag in Dave's car, then it must have been Dave's cocaine since the jurors may not believe that some random person placed the bag under the seat when the windows were rolled down. Since this interpretation is possible and Dave would not have a chance to cross-examine Ted, the court will likely suppress Ted's statement.

Severance

Where co-defendants are charged for the same crime, courts prefer joint trials for judicial economy but will sever the co-defendants if a joint trial would result in substantial prejudice to one of the defendants.

As discussed above, Ted's statement doesn't directly implicate Dave and in fact, it tends to indicate that someone else is to blame for the bag being put in the car, which would not result in any prejudice to Dave, especially not substantial prejudice.

However, if Ted and Dave implicate each other, separate trials could be necessary as the testimony from each would violate their 6th Amendment rights to confront each other.

Overall, the court will not likely sever the co-defendants based on Ted's statement, but rather just suppress it.

3. Motion to Discharge/Substitute Attorney

Right to Effective Counsel

A suspect against whom formal criminal proceedings have been commenced has a right to effective counsel at any post-charge line-up or show-up.

Here, Dave retained an attorney, rather than have one appointed to him, but this does not mean that he cannot replace this attorney with another attorney. The problem here is that he has become dissatisfied with his attorney the week before trial for unknown reasons.

Although he has the right to an attorney of his choice, the court will need to consider whether it is fair to substitute new counsel at this stage of the proceedings.

Right to Substitute Attorney

A court will allow the defendant to substitute their attorney if the interests of justice so require, taking into account any conflicts, the interests of the defendant and the court, and the timeliness of the request.

Here, it is unclear why Dave has become dissatisfied with his attorney, so it is difficult to determine if the court would grant his motion. However, since trial is scheduled to begin in one week and there doesn't appear to be any major conflict or concern from the facts, it is unlikely that the court would substitute the attorney as this would affect and delay Ted as well as Dave and would not be efficient for the courts since the court already scheduled the trial for those dates.

Thus, given the timing of the request, it is unlikely that the court will grant Dave's motion for a new attorney, barring any serious conflict or problem.

Crimes Question 4
February 2022, Question 1

Jim and Fred armed themselves with handguns and drove to a store on Avon Street. They both went into the store, drew their guns, and demanded that Salma, an employee, give them the store's money. After Salma handed Jim the money, he nervously dropped his gun. The gun discharged when it hit the floor, and the bullet hit and killed Chris, a store customer. Salma then got a shotgun from under the counter and shot Fred, killing him. Jim picked up his gun, ran out of the store, and drove back to his apartment.

Later that evening, Jim saw Salma while walking down Park Street. Thinking that he could eliminate her as a witness, Jim shot at Salma with his gun, but the bullet missed her. Jim then drove away in his car.

A few minutes later, Police Officer Bakari saw Jim driving down the street. Officer Bakari, who had no knowledge of the events at the store or on Park Street, pulled Jim over because Jim looked nervous. When Jim got out of his car, Officer Bakari noticed a bulge under his shirt. Officer Bakari then patted Jim down and found Jim's gun. Officer Bakari arrested Jim for possession of a concealed firearm and seized the gun.

1. With what crime(s) could Jim reasonably be charged regarding the events at the store? Discuss.

2. With what crime(s) could Jim reasonably be charged regarding the incident on Park Street? Discuss.

3. Under the Fourth Amendment to the United States Constitution, can Jim successfully move to suppress Jim's gun from being introduced into evidence at trial? Discuss.

Crimes Question 4 Assessment
February 2022, Question 1

This was a rough start for question 1 right out of the gate on anyone's bar exam. While crimes questions are usually ones that we like to see, this one was a doozy. The state bar decided to rest testing murder for about a decade and then in recent years it has made a comeback with a vengeance because the questions have been very complex with the murder being tied to felonies, or in this question conspiracy and accomplice liability with multiple parties and multiple crimes involved. To that end, let's talk about how you need to approach these types of questions to maintain your sanity.

First, you should read the calls of the question. You can see that both call one and two are broad and ask about what crimes in general Jim can be charged with so think of (or jot on scratch paper) a quick issues checklist of possible crimes. Note also that each call focuses you in on a different location/set of events. So don't assume that he couldn't be charged with the same crime for different victims or locations. Use that checklist for both calls. Then, call three is our classic criminal procedure call, focusing on suppressing a gun as evidence, so that has the 4th Amendment written all over it.

As to the first call, there were a variety of crimes you could have discussed. And these crimes were spread out among three possible victims—Salma, Chris, and Fred. The crimes that were likely point-worthy included conspiracy, assault, larceny, robbery, burglary, common law murder (for two victims), manslaughter (for two victims), and statutory murder (for two victims). Since there are so many issues here you did not need to address all of them to pass. You must have addressed conspiracy, robbery, and the murder for both of the deceased victims. However, one state-released answer went into assault and larceny and burglary, all of which were possible charges, yet they did not go into how there could be involuntary manslaughter. Meanwhile, the other state-released answer went into involuntary manslaughter but didn't go into assault, larceny (but did as part of robbery obviously), or burglary. When there are so many issues, you can miss some of the minor ones and still pass so long as you do well on the big main issues as both answers did here.

Call two was much simpler, with the attempted murder being the main issue with a possible dash of assault on the side. The key was knowing all of these rules. Although the theft crimes have been heavily tested on the multiple-choice portion of the bar exam, you need to know the rules cold for essays like these. If you know the rules, you can easily and quickly run through the elements and analyze them fairly quickly and accurately. You also need to know the nuanced rules within felony murder as they like to test those. And while this essay didn't test murder as it relates to co-conspirator liability or accomplice liability, you should always consider that as a possible path to being charged with murder too. It's been a while since they've tested murder like that, but it can rear its ugly head one day again, so be on the alert and make sure you understand how these concepts relate to one another.

The last call was a simple Fourth Amendment call which started out with the initial stop being unreasonable. There were no applicable exceptions, and you needed to discuss how the fruit of the poisonous tree barred the evidence derived from that illegal stop. This was an easy one, but after call one, you likely didn't have much time left for calls two and three. But again, managing your time is a key part to your success. Here, you should have spent most of your time on call one with less than half of your time on calls two and three combined. This is why organizing your essays before you begin to write them out is crucial.

Finally, make note of the areas highlighted in **bold** on the corresponding grid. The bold areas highlight the issues, analysis, and conclusions that are likely **required** to receive a passing score on this question. In general, the essay grids are provided to assist you in analyzing the essays and are much more detailed than what a student should create during the exam to organize their response to a question.

1. Jim's crimes at the store

Issue	Rule	Fact Application	Conclusion
Conspiracy	**Conspiracy requires** • **An agreement** • **Between two or more persons** • **Intent to commit an unlawful act** **The majority of jurisdictions require an overt act.**	**Given that Jim and Fred both armed themselves, drove to a store with their guns drawn, and demanded money, it seems as though they both agreed to rob the store, which is unlawful. And there are two of them.** **They actually robbed the store so there is an overt act.**	**Jim can be charged with conspiracy to commit a robbery.**
Assault	An attempt to commit a battery or the intent to place another in reasonable apprehension of imminent injury. Aggravated assault if deadly weapon used.	Jim might not have intended to actually harm or batter Salma but he did draw a gun on her and demanded the money so a reasonable person would be in apprehension of being shot, which is an imminent injury, when they were being robbed at gunpoint. And since a gun is a deadly weapon, it would be aggravated assault.	Jim can be charged with aggravated assault.
Larceny	• Trespassory taking and carrying away • Personal property of another • Intent to permanently deprive owner of property	• Jim trespassed onto the store property by demanding money without permission and took away the money once Salma gave it to him; she gave him money due to the threat, not voluntarily. • The money was the store's personal property, not Jim's. • Jim intended to keep the money with Fred and not return it.	Jim can be charged with larceny.
Robbery	**Larceny, plus the property has been taken from the person or presence of the owner through force,** or by placing the owner in fear.	**Jim used force and threat of fear by drawing a gun on Salma so she would think he would shoot her if she didn't give him the money.**	**Jim can be charged with Robbery** (instead of Larceny since that would be a lesser-included offense).
Burglary	• Breaking and entering • Dwelling house of another • At nighttime • Intent to commit a felony therein Modernly most structures ok and any time of day	Although Jim went to the store (modernly a structure) and during day is o.k. modernly, with the intent to commit a felony of robbery, he did not break and enter the store b/c it was normal business hours and the doors were open.	Jim is not likely to be charged with burglary.

Continued>

Issue	Rule	Fact Application	Conclusion
Murder (Chris)	**Murder is the unlawful killing of another person with malice aforethought. Malice can be proven by** • **An intent to kill (desire or knowledge to a substantial certainty),** • **An intent to commit grievous bodily injury,** • **A reckless indifference to the value of human life, or** • **An intent to commit a dangerous felony (FMR).** **Under the FMR, malice is implied if death was a natural and probable consequence of D's conduct, the death occurred during the commission of the felony, even if death was accidental, and the death was independent from the felony.** The D's conduct must also be the cause in fact and the proximate cause of the death.	• **Jim did not have the intent to kill or seriously injure Chris b/c he nervously dropped the gun and didn't aim it at Chris on purpose but rather it discharged when it hit the floor.** • **Maybe no reckless disregard b/c nervously dropped gun, and it discharged accidentally when it hit the floor,** but anytime a gun is used in a robbery there is a chance that things can go wrong and someone can die, especially to a customer in the store at the time of the robbery. • **FMR b/c committing robbery.** • Death by a gunshot from someone robbing a store at gunpoint is a natural and probable consequence as accidents with guns occur during robberies, robbery was ongoing during the accidental shooting, and the shooting was independent of the robbery. But for D not robbing the store, he wouldn't have had a gun to drop and shoot anyone, including Chris. While it might not be foreseeable that one would get nervous and drop a gun and it would discharge just right to shoot and kill a customer, it is foreseeable that things go wrong during robberies and innocent people can be killed.	Jim is likely to be charged with Chris' murder.
Manslaughter (Chris)	Voluntary manslaughter occurs during the heat of passion or imperfect self-defense Involuntary manslaughter occurs through gross negligence (disregard of a very substantial danger of serious bodily harm or death) or misdemeanor manslaughter.	Jim was not provoked to shoot Chris and didn't shoot him; also not defending himself so no voluntary manslaughter. It is possible that Jim robbing a store at gunpoint indicated a disregard of a substantial danger of death because anything can happen when loaded guns are involved and used to threaten others, including them accidentally discharging for any reason.	Jim's murder charge can be reduced to involuntary manslaughter.
1st v. 2nd Degree (Chris)	**1st degree is premeditated (time to reflect) and deliberate (cool and dispassionate), or via FMR if an enumerated inherently dangerous felony.** **All other murder: 2nd degree.**	**Jim did not premeditate or kill Chris in a deliberate manner as he nervously dropped the gun and it accidentally discharged, but FMR for robbery can be 1st degree.**	**1st degree murder possible.**

Continued>

Issue	Rule	Fact Application	Conclusion
Murder (Fred)	**Same rules as above and:** **Maj.: D is not liable for the death of a co-felon when a non-felon kills the co-felon during commission of the felony.** (*Redline view*) Min.: D is liable for co-felon death.	• **Jim didn't have the intent to kill or injure Fred as he was his co-conspirator and Jim didn't shoot him or ask Salma to shoot him.** • Similar to above for reckless disregard, **possible Jim did nothing to disregard Fred's life as he didn't purposefully drop the gun or shoot Fred himself**, but anytime robberies occur with loaded guns, anything is possible as victims or others can have guns and shoot people. • **FMR — same as above and in maj. jx, Jim would not be liable as Salma, the victim, killed Fred, not Jim;** but in the min. of jx, Jim would be liable. But for Jim not robbing the store and dropping his gun nervously, Salma wouldn't have pulled out a gun and shot Fred; it is foreseeable that victims or anyone else could be armed and fight back against armed robbers.	**Jim could be charged with Fred's murder but only in a minority of jx**
Manslaughter (Fred)	Same rules as above.	Jim didn't shoot Fred so wasn't provoked; no self-defense but could argue disregard for death as discussed above with Chris when robbing stores at gunpoint.	Jim could be charged with involuntary manslaughter
1st v. 2nd Degree (Fred)	**Same rules as above.**	**Jim did not premeditate or kill Fred in a deliberate manner as he didn't shoot Fred, and no FMR in maj. jx under** *Redline* **view.**	1st degree murder not likely for Fred in maj. jx

2. Jim's crimes at Park Street

Issue	Rule	Fact Application	Conclusion
Attempted Murder	**Attempt is an act done with intent to commit a crime and an affirmative act, or substantial step, in furtherance of the intent to commit the crime, beyond mere preparation.**	**Jim attempted to murder Salma b/c he shot his gun at her with intent to eliminate her as a witness, so kill her. He took a substantial step b/c he actually fired the shot at her but missed.**	**Jim can be charged with attempted murder.**
Assault	See rules above.	Jim did attempt to commit a battery by shooting at Salma but missed, but it is not clear that she saw the shot fired or suffered any apprehension. It would be aggravated battery b/c deadly weapon used.	Jim might be able to be charged with aggravated assault.

Continued>

3. Suppressing the gun

Issue	Rule	Fact Application	Conclusion
Routine Automobile Stop	The police may randomly stop automobiles if there is a reasonable suspicion of wrongdoing based on articulable facts.	Here, Officer Bakari stopped Jim b/c he looked nervous which is not likely sufficient for a reasonable suspicion of wrongdoing since the officer had no knowledge of the events at the store and there were no articulable facts to base the suspicion on.	Officer had no reason to pull over Jim.
4th Amendment	Protects against unreasonable searches and seizures. Need: • Gov. action • REOP Generally, a warrant is needed to search a person unless an exception applies.	• Jim was pulled over by the police officer Bakari so there is gov. action. • Jim has a REOP to items in his private car and on his person. There was no warrant, so an exception is needed.	No warrant so need an exception.
Exception—Automobile Stop	If police have probable cause to believe that a vehicle contains contraband or evidence of a crime, they may search the whole automobile and any container therein that might contain the objects for which they are searching.	Here, there was no probable cause to believe the automobile contained evidence of a crime since the officer didn't even know about the crime or any crime.	Not a valid exception.
Exception—*Terry* stop and frisk	A police officer may stop and frisk a person if the police have a reasonable suspicion (based on the totality of circumstances) of criminal activity or involvement that is supported by articulable facts. The brief detention may include a pat-down search of outer clothing for weapons if the suspect appears dangerous, and under the plain feel doctrine, they may seize contraband discovered if its identity is immediately apparent.	As discussed above with the original stop, there was no reasonable suspicion of criminal activity b/c the officer wasn't aware of the events at the store and only thought Jim looked nervous, which alone is not articulable facts giving rise to criminal activity. If the stop was permissible, the officer could ask Jim to get out of the car and pat him down if he appeared dangerous which could be possible since the officer noticed a bulge and under the plain feel doctrine, he could seize the gun he felt in the bulge.	Likely not a valid exception, but if it was then the pat down and seizure would be permissible.
Exclusionary Rule/Fruit of the Poisonous Tree	Judge-made rule that prohibits the prosecution from introducing evidence obtained in violation of a defendant's Fourth, Fifth, or Sixth Amendment rights. D must have standing for their own rights violated. Evidence wrongfully obtained is inadmissible as the "fruit of the poisonous tree" barring a few exceptions.	As discussed above, the initial stop was likely in violation of Jim's 4th Am. rights so the evidence obtained from that stop, including the gun at issue, is likely also inadmissible as no exceptions apply.	Jim can likely suppress the gun from being introduced as evidence at trial.

Continued>

Crimes Question 5
July 2021, Question 4

Detective Anna was about to subject David, who was lawfully in custody, to interrogation because she had received a tip from an anonymous informant that David was involved in transporting heroin. Detective Anna advised David of his Miranda rights and asked him if he knew anything about heroin shipments. David replied, "I am not sure if I need a lawyer or not." Detective Anna next asked David how he was transporting the heroin. David responded, "If I had anything to do with it, I would use my car." Detective Anna released David from custody when he refused to answer any more questions. Detective Anna then sent a message to all police officers, describing David's car, stating that it was believed to be involved in transporting heroin.

Later that day, Officer Baker, who had heard Detective Anna's message, saw the car described in the message. Officer Baker decided to follow the car to see if the driver would do anything that could justify stopping the car. When the car ran a red light, Officer Baker stopped the car and ordered the driver, who was in fact David, out of the car. Officer Baker then did a pat-down search of David and found a cell phone in his pocket. Officer Baker turned on the cell phone, saw a text message icon, clicked on the icon, and found a message to David stating, "The heroin is in the trunk; deliver it to the warehouse." Officer Baker then searched the trunk of the car, where he found 30 pounds of heroin. He arrested David and arranged for the car to be taken to the police impound lot for processing.

David is charged with transportation of heroin. David moves to suppress:

1. His statement, "If I had anything to do with it, I would use my car";

2. The text message that stated, "The heroin is in the trunk; deliver it to the warehouse"; and

3. The heroin found in the trunk of the car.

How should the court rule on each of the motions to suppress? Discuss.

Crimes Question 5 Assessment
July 2021, Question 4

This is a straight-up criminal procedure question. The call asks only about suppressing evidence. The first piece of evidence is a statement, so you should be considering admissions and issues that correspond to incriminating statements, usually triggering Fifth and Sixth Amendment issues. The second piece of evidence is a text message, so that will likely involve some discussion involving the Fourth Amendment and a search and any relevant exceptions. The third piece of evidence involves heroin found in the truck which seems to be derived from the text message in call two, so there you will likely be thinking about the exclusionary rule and fruit of the poisonous tree.

At this point, you have already started to engage your mind in your criminal procedure rules so that when you read the facts next, you have an idea of what you will be looking for. Then, after reading the facts, you can come back to the calls, and review what issues you spotted with your issues checklist in mind. The tricky part about the first call is that you need to know the rules for *Miranda* and confessions well and the difference between a defendant's right to counsel under the Fifth Amendment from the right to counsel under the Sixth Amendment. Here, David had no right to counsel under the Sixth Amendment and didn't properly invoke his right to one under the Fifth Amendment. For those reasons, his statement would likely come in.

As to the text message search, you needed to follow the yellow brick road, so to speak. First, look to see what happened. The first thing was the stop, so it is easiest to discuss that first. That was fairly straightforward since David ran a red light. Next was the ordering David out of the car, which is permissible. This is when things go sideways because the officer can do a pat-down search, but you have to know your rules well to know what they can search for — contraband, not just anything to their heart's desire. So, when the officer found the cell phone, he needed to stop there. He could not open it, look at it, click on messages, etc. At this point you have a search violation, so you need to look for an exception. When there aren't any available, you need to tie it back to the exclusionary rule. The issues aren't that complicated if you have an approach for how you want to walk through search and seizure questions. We have created a Fourth Amendment Bullet Proof Approach to help guide you through some of these types of questions.

The last call was really testing the fruit of the poisonous tree, but you should have also addressed the overarching rule by referencing your Fourth Amendment rules above and making sure no exceptions apply. Then, go into the fruit of the poisonous tree rules.

Another point worth noting is that recently the examiners have released sample answers that like to show how smart they are by naming every case they can think of. While this might make them seem smarter, it is not necessary to pass the essays. It has not been something they've ever required and until recently, most essays in most subjects did not name drop numerous cases, so don't feel like you have to name cases to pass the essays. Just know the rules and be able to accurately recall the rules and properly analyze them. That is all you need to pass.

Finally, make note of the areas highlighted in **bold** on the corresponding grid. The bold areas highlight the issues, analysis, and conclusions that are likely **required** to receive a passing score on this question. In general, the essay grids are provided to assist you in analyzing the essays and are much more detailed than what a student should create during the exam to organize their response to a question.

1. Statement "If I had anything to do with it, I would use my car."

Issue	Rule	Fact Application	Conclusion
5th Amendment *Miranda*	**To receive *Miranda* warnings, D must be in custodial interrogation.** • **Custody — not free to leave** • **Interrogation — words or actions by the police that they should know are reasonably likely to elicit an incriminating response**	• David was lawfully in custody so he was not likely free to leave. • David was arguably being interrogated b/c Detective Anna was trying to get info from David since she received an anonymous tip he was transporting heroin. But the facts indicate that the Detective did advise David of his *Miranda* rights and then asked him questions about the shipments.	David was given adequate *Miranda* warnings.
5th Amendment right to counsel under *Miranda*	**When the accused unambiguously indicates that they wish to speak to counsel, the police are required to cease all questioning** until the suspect has consulted a lawyer, and the lawyer must be present while any further questioning occurs.	**Although David responded to Detective Anna's question about the heroin shipments with him "not sure" about needing a lawyer, his uncertainty was not an unambiguous request for counsel, so Anna could keep questioning him.** He needed to say something like "I need to speak to a lawyer first."	David's right to counsel under *Miranda* was not invoked.
Voluntariness/Due Process	**Confessions must be voluntarily without police coercion**, in light of totality of the circumstances, considering the susceptibility of the suspect and environment and methods used.	Since David was given *Miranda* warnings and did not invoke his right to counsel under them, **he voluntarily responded to Anna's question about how he was transporting the heroin** since he could have refused to answer her questions, as he did later.	David voluntarily told Anna he would have used his car.
5th Amendment right against self-incrimination	Protects a criminal D from compulsion to give testimony or communicative evidence that could expose them to criminal liability.	David was not forced to give testimony or evidence as he voluntarily answered questions when he could have invoked his right to counsel but didn't.	No 5th Am. violation
6th Amendment right to counsel	**D has a right to counsel for all critical stages including post-charge questioning.**	**David was not formally charged and had not even been arrested yet for his Sixth Am. right to counsel to attach.**	No 6th Am. Violation

Continued>

Issue	Rule	Fact Application	Conclusion
The court should deny David's motion to suppress his statement about his car.			
2. Text message "The heroin is in the trunk; deliver it to the warehouse."			
Routine Automobile Stop	The police may randomly stop automobiles if there is a reasonable suspicion of wrongdoing based on articulable facts. Officers can also order all occupants out of the car.	Here, Officer Baker stopped David b/c he ran a red light, which is a violation of the law, so there were articulable facts that prove his wrongdoing. Although the officer heard Detective Anna's message describing David's car, he did not pull David over until he had a valid reason to do so, and following a car on a public road is not a violation of their rights. Once stopped, Officer Baker was able to order David out of the car.	Officer had a valid reason to pull David over.
4th Amendment	4th Amend. protects against unreasonable search and seizure where there is government action, and property or place searched or seized is one in which D has reasonable expectation of privacy. A warrant is required for all searches unless an exception applies.	Once David was out of the car, Officer searched David and found his cell phone, turned it on, saw a text message, and clicked on the icon to read it. There was gov. action since Officer was a police officer. And David has a REOP in his private cell phone, especially in a message not opened. Officer did not have a warrant to search David's phone so an exception must be met.	4th Am. applicable Gov. action present REOP present No warrant
Terry stop and frisk	A police officer may stop and frisk a person if the police have a reasonable suspicion (based on the totality of circumstances) of criminal activity or involvement that is supported by articulable facts. The brief detention may include a pat-down search of outer clothing for weapons if the suspect appears dangerous, and under the plain feel doctrine, they may seize contraband discovered if its identity is immediately apparent.	Officer had a reasonable suspicion of criminal activity because of Detective Anna's message about David believed to be involved in transporting heroin, and he had the car description, and David was the one she sent the message about and he was able to pull him over as discussed above. The pat-down might have been fine if the officer thought David was armed or dangerous, which isn't clear b/c Anna's message didn't indicate any danger, but criminals involved in drug sales are often armed and dangerous, so it is possible. Another problem with the pat-down might be that a phone is not necessarily contraband to be seized as most people have cell phones.	Stop and frisk likely fine but not likely seizure of the cell phone.

Continued>

Issue	Rule	Fact Application	Conclusion
Search incident to a lawful arrest	When the police are making a lawful arrest, they may search the area within the arrestee's immediate control (their wingspan). And they may search a car and its compartments if it is reasonable to believe that the arrestee might access the vehicle at the time of the search or the vehicle contains evidence of the offense causing the arrest.	Here, David was not arrested at the time of the cell phone search b/c he was only pulled over for running a red light, which doesn't result in being arrested, so this would not work. And even if he did find the cell phone, he can't open up messages and read them.	SILA not a valid exception.
Exclusionary rule	**A judge-made rule that prohibits the prosecution from introducing evidence obtained in violation of a defendant's Fourth, Fifth, or Sixth Amendment rights.** **D must have standing for their own right violated.**	**Since the search of the phone violated David's Fourth Amendment rights, the evidence should be excluded.**	Exclusionary rule bars evidence of cell phone search.
The court should grant David's motion to suppress evidence of the text message.			
3. The heroin found in the trunk of the car.			
4th Amendment	See above for rules.	**Regarding the search of the trunk:** **There was gov. action since Officer was a police officer and David has a REOP in his private car, especially the trunk that is not visible to the public.** **Officer did not have a warrant to search David's trunk so an exception must be met.**	4th Am. applicable Gov. action present REOP present No warrant
Exception — Automobile	**If police have probable cause to believe that a vehicle contains contraband or evidence of a crime, they may search the whole automobile and any container therein that might contain the objects for which they are searching.**	Here arguably there was no probable cause to believe the automobile contained evidence of a crime, since David only ran a red light and the officer didn't have consent to look at David's phone so he didn't know anything about the trunk until he read the phone text message. However, Anna's message did state that it was believed that David's car was involved in transporting heroin so perhaps that was sufficient probable cause to believe his car contained contraband even without the phone message. The problem is that the officer didn't check the trunk until after reading the phone message.	Could make an argument either way.

Continued>

Issue	Rule	Fact Application	Conclusion
Search incident to a lawful arrest	Same as above and with cars the officers can search the car and its compartments if the arrestee can access it.	Here, David was not arrested at the time of the trunk search either b/c he was arrested after the officer found the 30 pounds of heroin.	SILA not a valid exception.
Fruit of the Poisonous Tree	Evidence wrongfully obtained is inadmissible as "fruit of the poisonous tree" unless: • **The evidence obtained could have been obtained from an independent source; or** • **The evidence obtained would inevitably have been discovered; or** • **Additional factors intervened between the original illegality and the final discovery that the link is too tenuous.**	**The heroin was obtained based on the wrongfully searched cell phone, but it is possible that:** • The evidence could have been obtained anyway based on Anna's description or by impounding the car and searching it as there might have been probable cause to impound it based on Anna's description and report, **but not likely since not impounded until after the arrest based on the phone search and trunk search.** • **The heroin would have inevitably been discovered too if they impounded the car, but there is no reason to impound a car for someone who runs a red light.**	Could conclude either way but evidence likely will be suppressed as fruit of the poisonous tree.

Could conclude either way here but most likely the evidence will be suppressed b/c of the fruit of the poisonous tree.

Crimes Question 6
February 2013, Question 1

Max imports paintings. For years, he has knowingly bought and resold paintings stolen from small museums in Europe. He operates a gallery in State X in partnership with his three sons, Allen, Burt, and Carl, but he has never told them about his criminal activities. Each of his sons, however, has suspected that many of the paintings were stolen.

One day, Max and his sons picked up a painting sent from London. Max had arranged to buy a painting recently stolen by Ted, one of his criminal sources, from a small British museum.

Max believed the painting that they picked up was the stolen one, but he did not share his belief with the others.

Having read an article about the theft, Allen also believed the painting was the stolen one but also did not share his belief.

Burt knew about the theft of the painting. Without Max's knowledge, however, he had arranged for Ted to send Max a copy of the stolen painting and to retain the stolen painting itself for sale later.

Carl regularly sold information about Max's transactions to law enforcement agencies and continued to participate in the business for the sole purpose of continuing to deal with them.

Are Max, Allen, Burt, and/or Carl guilty of:

    (a) conspiracy to receive stolen property,

    (b) receipt of stolen property with respect to the copy of the stolen painting, and/or,

    (c) attempt to receive stolen property with respect to the copy of the stolen painting?

Discuss.

Crimes Question 6 Assessment
February 2013, Question 1

This question is a rather straightforward criminal law question that does not require any issue spotting since the issues are all set out for you in each of the calls. Recent bar exam questions are becoming more specific and not testing issue spotting as much as whether you can properly analyze the issues. Thus, it is imperative that you understand the rules and pay close attention to facts that change the outcome. Often the facts will seem minor but will impact the essay substantially. For example, here the fact that Burt arranged for the painting to be a copy and not the actual stolen one changes the result for him as to guilt (in his case, not guilty) for attempt. While the others may be guilty, he will not be since he knew it wasn't actually stolen. Similarly, Burt's side deal makes him guilty of conspiracy with Ted, unlike Allen and Carl. So subtle factual differences change the outcome substantially for each party.

Also, the question does not specifically tell you to discuss defenses or which defenses are applicable, but discussing defenses is essential to properly analyzing the facts and answering the questions posed. Thus, you should write out a mini-checklist of all defenses applicable to crimes questions to ensure you do not overlook any. If you tend to forget to discuss defenses, you should always write them out as part of the checklist with every question. Also, remember that the bar examiners expect you to address defenses regardless of whether they specifically ask about them. The reason for this is because you cannot be convicted of a crime if there is a valid defense. Thus, to answer the calls of the question posed here, you must consider defenses (here either mistake or impossibility were the defenses you should have raised).

A final point on questions like these: Make sure you organize your answer thoroughly before writing it out. How you choose to approach this question in your answer might change once you have organized it. For example, one state-released answer organized each call by party and separated out the four parties. However, the other state-released answer did not organize by party but rather pointed out where various parties differed from others leading them to different results. Either way was acceptable, but one method might work better for you in terms of timing. Usually it is wise to separate out parties, but here two of the parties had the same facts for conspiracy so they could have been combined. Similarly, all of the parties had the same analysis for receipt of stolen goods so they could all be analyzed together (which would save time). Thus, sometimes organizing by parties with similar analysis is acceptable and saves time. But where the actions of the parties are different it is often best to separate the parties to ensure you properly address each one as required.

Finally, be sure to make note of the areas highlighted in **bold** on the corresponding grid. The bold areas highlight the issues, analysis, and conclusions that are likely **required** to receive a passing score on this question. In general, the essay grids are provided to assist you in analyzing the essays and are much more detailed than what a student should create during the exam to organize their response to a question.

Issue	Rule	Fact Application	Conclusion
Call (a): Conspiracy			
Conspiracy	**Conspiracy is an agreement between two or more persons who intend to commit an unlawful act or** a lawful act by unlawful means. The agreement can be implied or inferred and does not require that all persons commit the actual act. **At common law, conspiracy occurred the moment the agreement was made, but the majority of jurisdictions now require an overt act,** which can be as little as preparation, to form the conspiracy. A minority of jurisdictions allows for a unilateral conspiracy where only one party agrees.	<u>Max</u> **Here, M did agree with T to receive stolen property as he has knowingly bought and resold stolen paintings from museums in Europe and recently agreed with T to buy the stolen painting as T was one of his criminal sources. Thus M and T agreed to buy/sell a stolen painting.** Arguably, T did not agree since T had a side deal with M's son, B, that he would not give M the actual painting but a copy. However, it appears that M and T initially agreed to the stolen painting and then B who knew about it talked to T so M and T agreed first and the agreement occurred. Also, in a unilateral jx this could be sufficient even if T knew the painting wasn't stolen to begin with and planned on only giving him a copy. **The overt act could be when they all picked up the painting sent from London.** <u>Allen</u> A did not agree with anyone to receive any stolen property. While it appears A believed it was stolen after reading an article about theft, he did not communicate with anyone or share his belief with anyone. <u>Burt</u> B agreed with T to receive the stolen property at a later date since he arranged for T to send a copy and keep the original to sell later so he agreed with T to commit an unlawful act by selling the painting later. Same overt act as M above. <u>Carl</u> C did not agree with anyone to receive stolen property. Rather he was working with law enforcement agencies and selling them information and this is the only reason he continued to participate in the business so he was agreeing to work with police but not with intent to commit an unlawful act. For all of them the existence of a partnership alone to operate a gallery does not mean that they all agreed to commit an unlawful act as operating a gallery alone is not unlawful.	**M and B are guilty of conspiracy, barring any defenses** **A and C are not guilty of conspiracy**

Continued>

Issue	Rule	Fact Application	Conclusion
Call (b): Receipt of Stolen Property			
Receipt of Stolen Property	A crime when one knowingly receives, conceals, or disposes of stolen property with the intent to permanently deprive the owner of his property.	**Max** While M did intend to deprive the owner of the painting, the painting he received was not stolen as it was only a copy. **Allen** A also believed the painting was stolen after reading the article but didn't know for certain. And, as with M, it wasn't a stolen painting. **Burt** B did know about the theft of the painting and in fact arranged with T to send the copy so he too could not be guilty of receipt of the stolen property since they only received the copy, but when he does receive the actual painting to sell it later he will be guilty. **Carl** Like the above parties, the painting was a copy and not stolen and C was working with the police so he would not be intending to permanently deprive the owner of it anyway.	**None of them are guilty of receipt of stolen property**
Call (c): Attempt			
Attempt	Attempt is an act done with intent to commit a crime and an affirmative act, or substantial step, in furtherance of intent to commit the crime (beyond mere preparation).	**Max** M had the specific intent to receive stolen property since he had been doing it for years and used T as a criminal source; he did not know that B arranged for a copy to be given instead so he intended to receive the stolen property. And he took a substantial step in furtherance of the crime by picking up the painting. **Allen** A also believed the painting was stolen and picked it up without saying anything so he intended to receive stolen property too. **Burt** Since B arranged for a copy and knew it wasn't the original stolen painting he did not have the intent to steal with respect to the copy of the stolen painting. It is possible he could still be liable for the actual copy since he did intent to steal that and took a step by having T hold onto it and make a copy but he would not be guilty for the copy itself for attempt.	**M, A, and C are guilty of attempt** **B is not guilty of attempt** C most likely is not guilty of attempt (state released answers came to opposite conclusions for C)

Continued>

417

Issue	Rule	Fact Application	Conclusion
		Carl	
		As C was working with the police he did not intend to receive stolen property because his intent was to report it to law enforcement. On the other hand, C did go along with everything and actually did attempt to receive the stolen painting (but it is likely law enforcement would grant him immunity for providing information).	
Impossibility*	**Factual impossibility** arises when D makes a mistake concerning an issue of fact; not a valid defense. **Legal impossibility** arises when D incorrectly believes that what he is doing is criminal when it is not; a valid defense.	Here since the copy was not the actual painting this factual impossibility does make it such that they are not guilty for receipt of stolen property but it does not work for attempt since they still intended to steal the actual copy (except B).	Not a valid defense for attempt but works for actual crime of receipt of stolen property
Mistake of Fact*	Mistake of fact negates any specific intent crime, as well as malice and general intent crimes if the mistake was reasonable.	Here M, A, and C were mistaken as to the fact that the painting was a copy but they still intended to steal the actual copy so the fact that it was a copy doesn't negate their intent to attempt to steal the actual copy.	Not a defense to attempt

*You needed to address at least one of the above defenses, but not both.

PART 7 _EVIDENCE_

EVIDENCE TABLE OF CONTENTS

INTRODUCTION TO EVIDENCE

Evidence essay questions feel different than questions in other subjects. Evidence questions are almost always "racehorse style" with a great many issues tested (sometimes as many as 25 or more) but with comparatively thin factual analysis. Besides knowledge of evidence rules, the two main skills being tested with an evidence question are 1) issue spotting, and 2) time management.

First, in order to pass evidence essay questions, it is imperative that you spot all of the issues, and there will be a great many. Evidence requires a more detailed issues checklist than other subjects to successfully issue spot the question. There are two reasons for this: 1) There are more legal issues in evidence compared to other subjects, and 2) the issues don't necessarily jump out at you; you have to go looking for them. For this reason, it is best to have a detailed checklist and "run" each piece of evidence through the checklist looking for pertinent issues while organizing your answer. Obviously, this approach takes time and you won't be fast at it the first few times you do it. Like any skill you are trying to develop, the more you practice, the better you get. It is essential to practice answering evidence essay questions under timed conditions to get the hang of it.

The other important skill being tested with an evidence essay question is time management. One hour goes by quickly when faced with an essay containing 25 to 30 legal issues. Even though there is a lot to write, and it is tempting to start right away, 10-15 minutes of the one-hour allotted time should be spent organizing the essay in order to properly spot all of the issues. Though some rules will have more elements than others, the depth of analysis (meaning the amount of factual analysis and factual inferences available to use in the analysis of any one issue) is likely to be similar from issue to issue. This makes pacing yourself somewhat easier because you don't need to worry about going from deep analysis to shallow analysis as you move from issue to issue. Typically, evidence is uniformly composed of comparatively shallow analysis. Therefore, the goal is to write at a sufficient pace to cover all of the issues in the allotted time. Again, practicing a truncated analysis is essential because you will not know the level of detail you can use to cover 25 to 30 issues in an hour until you try to do it. The worst thing you can do is not finish your answer (which will cause you to fail the question) so you must practice successfully completing an evidence essay in one hour.

Evidence essays can look different than other essays. They will often arise in one of two ways: 1) as a series of paragraphs discussing some items of evidence and then several specific calls about the admissibility of certain items of evidence, or 2) as a transcript of "Questions and Answers," each of which represents various evidentiary issues. Evidence questions are rarely crossover questions, but when they are, evidence generally crosses with Criminal Procedure, but has crossed over with professional responsibility and other subjects too.

In evidence, both the federal rules and California rules are eligible for testing. At the end of an essay the question will indicate which rules to use to answer the question. Lately, they have asked more questions using the California rules, but the bar examiners don't seem overly concerned about applicants mistakenly using the federal name for a concept on a California essay. The evidence rules in this outline are based on the Federal Rules of Evidence (FRE). Where the law in California (California Evidence Code, or CEC) differs from the federal rules, it will be noted. If it is not so noted, assume the California rules and federal rules are the same. Pay special attention to the areas of law where the California rule is different than the federal rule because those are favorite testing areas.

ISSUES CHECKLIST

RELEVANCE

Logical
Legal (balancing test)
Prop. 8 (and exemptions)

PUBLIC POLICY EXCLUSIONS

Subsequent remedial measures
Liability insurance
Offers to: pay medical bills/settle/plead guilty

WITNESS ON THE STAND

Personal knowledge
Form of the question
    Objections (NUCALF)
Present recollection refreshed
Opinion (lay or expert)

PRIVILEGES

Attorney-client
Dr.-Patient
Marital—Spousal immunity and marital
    communications

CHARACTER

Character "at issue"
Civil or criminal
Other purpose for character
evidence (I PIK A MOP)

IMPEACHMENT

HEARSAY

Nonhearsay purpose

HEARSAY EXCEPTIONS

Admissions
Party admission
Adoptive admission
Vicarious admission
Co-conspirator admission
Witness statements
Medical diagnosis and treatment
Then-existing state of mind
PSI
Excited utterance
Prior statement of available witness
PIS
PCS
PID
Documents
Past recollection recorded
Business records
Public records
Learned treatise
Declarant unavailable
Former testimony
Dying declaration
Statement against interest
Forfeiture by wrongdoing
Catchall exception

DOCUMENTS ADMITTED INTO EVIDENCE

Relevance
Authentication
Best evidence rule
Hearsay exceptions

JUDICIAL NOTICE

MEMORIZATION ATTACK SHEET

RELEVANCE

- **Logical**
  - FRE: fact more or less probable
  - CEC: disputed fact
- **Legal**
  - Probative v. prejudice balancing test
- **Prop. 8 (Cal. Crim. Court)**
  - Opens door to character
  - Rape shield laws
  - Media member
  - Court may exclude (§352)
  - Secondary Evidence Rule
  - Hearsay
  - Exclusionary rules of U.S. Constitution
  - Exclusionary rules of Cal. post-1982
  - Privileges

PUBLIC POLICY EXCEPTIONS

- **Subsequent remedial measures**
  - Except
    - Ownership & control
    - Precautions infeasible rebut
    - Other party destroyed evidence
- **Liability insurance**
  - Except
    - Ownership & control
    - Impeachment
    - Admission
- **Offers medical expenses**
  - FRE exception: admission
  - CEC exception: none
- **Settlement offer**
  - Disputed claim only
  - CEC: applies to mediation also
- **Offers to plead**
  - Cal. exception: Prop. 8 may allow
- **Cal. expression of sympathy**
  - Except: admission of fault

WITNESS EXAMINATION

- **Personal knowledge required**
- **Objection: form of the question**
  - Narrative
  - Unresponsive
  - Compound
  - Argumentative
  - Leading
  - Assumes Facts not in evidence

- **Present recollection refreshed**
  - W shown item to refresh
  - W then testifies from memory
- **Lay opinion**
  - FRE: not scientific or specialized knowledge
- **Expert opinion**
  - Assists trier of fact
  - W qualifies as expert
  - Opinion based on sufficient facts
  - Reliable principles used
    - FRE: *Daubert* standard
    - CEC: *Kelly/Frye* standard
  - Applied principles reliably

PRIVILEGES

- **Attorney-client**
  - Client: person or corporation
  - Confidential communications (intended as confidential)
  - Professional services is purpose of communication
  - Holder: client
  - Lasts until
    - FRE: after death
    - CEC: estate settled
  - Exceptions
    - Further crime or fraud
    - Dispute w/lawyer
    - Two or more consult
    - CEC: prevent death or SBH
- **Doctor-patient**
  - FRE: no Dr.-patient privilege
  - CEC: communication made for diagnosis & treatment only
- **Psychotherapist-patient**
  - Fed. & Cal. both have
- **Self-incrimination**
- **Marital adverse testimony (spousal immunity)**
  - During marriage
  - Holder: witness spouse
  - Fed.: criminal only
  - Except: cases between spouses
- **Marital confidential communication**
  - During & after marriage
  - Holder: both spouses
  - Except: cases between spouses
- **CEC-only privileges**
  - Counselor-victim
  - Clergy-penitent
  - News reporters

CHARACTER EVIDENCE

- ◆ **3 types of character evidence**
  - Reputation
  - Opinion
  - Specific acts
- ◆ **Civil Court rules**
  - Not for conduct in conformity
  - Except: character "at issue"
  - FRE exception: sexual assault/child molestation
  - Rape shield: rape/sex assault
    - ◆ FRE: if probative value substantially outweighs prejudice; reputation only if P puts reputation in issue
    - ◆ CEC: only to prove P's sexual conduct w/ the D
- ◆ **Criminal Court rules: D's character**
  - D must "open door"
  - Pertinent character trait only
  - If D on stand: truthfulness at issue
  - Except: P can open door in sexual assault/child molestation
  - FRE exception: if D offers on V character, prosecution can match for D
  - CEC exception: if D offers on V's *violent* character, Prosecution can match for D
  - CEC exception: domestic violence/elder abuse
- ◆ **Criminal Court rules: V's character**
  - D must "open door"
  - Pertinent character trait only
  - Except: rape shield rules apply
  - FRE exception: D offers that V 1st aggressor, Prosecution can rebut that V peaceful
- ◆ **D's character: form of evidence**
  - Direct exam: no specific acts
  - Cross (to rebut)
    - ◆ FRE: all 3 forms, but no extrinsic evidence allowed
    - ◆ CEC: no specific acts
- ◆ **V's character: form of evidence**
  - Direct exam
    - ◆ FRE: no specific acts
    - ◆ CEC: all 3 forms allowed
  - Cross: all 3 forms allowed
  - FRE exception: D offers that V 1st aggressor, Prosecution can rebut that V peaceful
  - Rape shield
    - ◆ No reputation/opinion
    - ◆ Specific acts only for
      - 3rd-party source of semen/injury
      - Prior consent w/ D
    - ◆ CEC: reasonable belief of consent

- ◆ **Other purpose character**
  - Intent
  - Preparation
  - Identity of perpetrator, M.O.
  - Knowledge of fact or event
  - Absence of mistake/accident
  - Motive
  - Opportunity
  - Plan or scheme
- ◆ **Habit or custom**
- ◆ **Similar happenings**

IMPEACHMENT

- ◆ **Character for truthfulness**
  - Reputation & opinion okay
  - Specific acts
    - ◆ FRE: okay, but no extrinsic evid. allowed
    - ◆ CEC
      - Civil: not allowed
      - Criminal: allowed
  - Criminal conviction
    - ◆ Crimen falsi: ok unless 10 years old
    - ◆ Felony
      - Criminal D: okay if probative value outweighs prejudicial effect
      - Others: okay unless prejudicial effect substantially outweighs probative value
    - ◆ Misdemeanor
      - FRE: not allowed
      - CEC:
        - Civil: not allowed
        - Criminal: if moral turpitude
- ◆ **Prior inconsistent statement**
  - Extrinsic evidence allowed if explain or deny
- ◆ **Bias**
  - Extrinsic evidence allowed if explain or deny
- ◆ **Sensory or mental defect**
- ◆ **Contradiction by another W**
- ◆ **Rehab impeached witness**
  - Meet the attack
  - Good character if attacked
  - Prior consistent statement
- ◆ **Bolstering the witness**
  - FRE: not allowed
  - CEC: allowed

HEARSAY & EXCEPTIONS

- ◆ **Hearsay: Out-of-court statement; offered for truth of matter asserted**

- ◆ **Nonhearsay purpose**
  - Effect on listener/reader
  - Declarant's state of mind
  - Independent legal significance
- ◆ **Admissions: any statement**
  - **Party admissions**
  - **Adoptive:** manifest belief in truth of statement
  - **Vicarious:** employee or agent statement in course of relationship
    - ◆ CEC: employee negligence only
  - **Co-conspirator:** during & in furtherance of the conspiracy
- ◆ **Witness statements: other hearsay exceptions**
  - **Medical purpose diagnosis & treatment**
    - ◆ Cause okay, but not fault
    - ◆ CEC: child abuse victim only
  - **State of mind:** then-existing mental, emotional, physical state (not memory/belief)
  - **Present sense impression**
    - ◆ Describe event/condition
    - ◆ While perceiving
    - ◆ CEC: describing declarant's own conduct only
  - **Excited utterance**
    - ◆ Startling event
    - ◆ Statement made while under stress of event
    - ◆ CEC: Spontaneous statement
- ◆ **Prior statement of available W's**
  - **Prior inconsistent statement**
  - **Prior consistent statement**
  - **Prior identification**
- ◆ **Document exceptions**
  - **Past recollection recorded**
    - ◆ Firsthand knowledge
    - ◆ Fresh @ time of recording
    - ◆ W recollection impaired now
    - ◆ Record accurate @ time made
  - **Business record**
    - ◆ Business activity
    - ◆ Regular practice to keep
    - ◆ Firsthand knowledge
    - ◆ Business duty to report
    - ◆ Timely @ time made

- • **Public record**
  - ◆ Agency record of own acts
  - ◆ Matters observed w/duty to report
  - ◆ Investigative reports
  - ◆ FRE: not against criminal D
- • **Learned treatise**
- ◆ **Declarant unavailable exceptions**
  - **Unavailabilty is established by**
    - ◆ Privileged
    - ◆ Death or illness
    - ◆ Can't procure W reasonably
    - ◆ Witness refuses to testify
    - ◆ Witness can't remember
  - **Former testimony**
    - ◆ Civil case only
      - • FRE: predecessor in interest only
      - • CEC: similar interest in prior proceeding & deposition in same proceeding allowed
  - **Dying declaration**
    - ◆ Re: circumstances of death
    - ◆ While believing death imminent
    - ◆ FRE: civil & criminal homicide only & death not required
    - ◆ CEC: death required & allows "OJ" exception for physical abuse
  - **Statement against interest**
    - ◆ Financial or penal interest
    - ◆ CEC: social interest, too
  - **Forfeiture by wrongdoing**
- ◆ **Residual "catch-all" exception**

DOCUMENTS

- ◆ **Establish relevance**
- ◆ **Authentication**
  - Real evidence: distinct characteristic or chain of title
  - Demonstrative: fair representation
  - Writings/recordings
  - Self-authenticating documents
- ◆ **Best evidence rule (Cal.: SER)**
  - Original or copy
- ◆ **Summaries of voluminous writings**

JUDICIAL NOTICE

- ◆ **Judicial notice allowed if**
  - Not subject to reasonable dispute
  - Generally known in jurisdiction
  - Capable of accurate & ready determination

EVIDENCE RULE OUTLINE

> The rules in the California Evidence Code (CEC) are similar to the Federal Rules of
> Evidence (FRE). Assume the rules are the same, unless otherwise noted.

I. **PRELIMINARY EVIDENCE CONCEPTS**
  A. **Direct or circumstantial:** Evidence can be direct or circumstantial.
    1. **Direct evidence** can automatically resolve an issue.
    2. **Circumstantial evidence** only resolves an issue if additional reasoning is used.
  B. **Type of evidence:** Evidence can come in **several forms.**
    1. **Testimonial evidence** is when a witness makes an assertion in court.
    2. **Real evidence** is the actual physical thing involved in the case (e.g., gun).
    3. **Demonstrative evidence** is a tangible item that illustrates a concept (e.g., map of accident
       scene).

II. **RELEVANCE:** Only relevant evidence may be admitted.
  A. **Logical relevance definition: All evidence must be logically relevant.**
    1. **FRE:** Evidence is relevant if it has **any tendency to make a fact more or less probable** than it
       would be without the evidence and the fact is of consequence in determining the action.
    2. **CEC:** Evidence is relevant if it tends to be **material** to a **disputed fact.** (While the language
       used is different, as applied the FRE and CEC yield the same result.)
  B. **Legal relevance exclusion:** A **balancing test** is used to determine legal relevance. Otherwise
     relevant evidence may be excluded if its **probative value is substantially outweighed by the
     danger of unfair prejudice, confusion of issues, misleading the jury, or wasting time. (FRE 403;
     CEC 352)**

> **Issue spotting tip:** On an essay, for each piece of evidence always first determine if
> the evidence is **logically relevant**. But only analyze if the evidence is **legally relevant**
> using the balancing test where there is the potential for the evidence to have an unfairly
> prejudicial effect. (E.g.: Where there is an exception to a public policy exclusion, or
> when hearsay is being admitted for a nonhearsay purpose, or where character evidence
> is allowed for a purpose other than to show conduct in conformity—such as to show
> motive or identity, or where the meaning of the evidence is ambiguous or could be
> unfairly seen in a negative light, etc.)

  C. **California Proposition 8** is the "Victim's Bill of Rights," which provides that in **criminal** trials in
     California state courts, **all relevant evidence is admissible,** even if objectionable under the CEC,
     subject to a few special exemptions. (Cal. Const. Amend., 1982, "Victims' Bill of Rights.") The
     result is evidence that would otherwise be inadmissible becomes admissible under Prop. 8.
    1. **Exemptions to Proposition 8**
      a. **Defendant** still must **"open the door"** to bring in evidence of **their own character** before
         the prosecution can do so.
      b. **Rape shield laws** still limit evidence of a **victim's character.**
      c. **Members of media** still can't be held in contempt for refusing to reveal a **confidential news
         source,** etc.
      d. **Court** still has the **power to exclude** evidence using the legal relevance balancing test if the
         probative value is substantially outweighed by the danger of unfair prejudice, confusion
         of issues, misleading the jury, or wasting time. (CEC 352 still applies.)
      e. **Secondary evidence rule** still applies.

f. **Hearsay** may still not be admitted, unless subject to an exception.

g. **Exclusionary rules** based on the **U.S. Constitution** still apply (e.g., *Miranda*, Confrontation Clause, etc.).

h. **Exclusionary rules** that were adopted by the **California legislature** with a 2/3 vote after 1982 still apply. (1982 is the year Prop. 8 passed.)

i. **Privileges** that already existed in 1982 still apply (e.g., attorney-client, professional, and both marital privileges).

Memorization tip: Use the mnemonic **DR M**ammal **C**ounts **SHEEP** to remember the nine Prop. 8 exemptions.

Exam tip: If the essay concerns a **criminal case** in **California state court,** first, in your essay introduction, provide the general Prop. 8 rule that all relevant evidence is admissible, subject to exemptions. Then, for each piece of evidence: 1) Apply the ordinary rules of evidence (general CEC rules of evidence and objections); 2) explain that despite the ordinary rules, Prop. 8 permits the admission of all relevant evidence unless one of the exemptions applies; and 3) if no Prop. 8 exemption applies, the evidence will be admitted. (But, always consider if the court will exclude for legal relevance due to unfair prejudice under CEC 352.)

III. **PUBLIC POLICY EXCLUSIONS:** Otherwise-relevant evidence can be **excluded for public policy reasons**. This is because we want to encourage certain types of behaviors for the greater good of society.

A. **Subsequent remedial measures:** The purpose for this policy exclusion is that we want to encourage people to repair dangerous conditions without fear that doing so is an admission of fault.

1. **General rule:** Evidence of safety measures, or **repairs performed after** an accident, are **not admissible to prove culpable conduct**.

a. **FRE only:** In addition, in a **products liability** action, evidence of safety measures are **not admissible** to show **defective product design**.

2. **Exception:** Evidence of subsequent remedial measures **is admissible to establish:**

a. **Ownership or control:** Showing ownership or control of an instrumentality is allowed (e.g., the slippery steps were repaired by the defendant, so the defendant is the owner of the steps); or

b. **Precaution not feasible:** To **rebut** a claim that the precaution was not feasible; or

c. **Destruction of evidence:** That the **other party** destroyed evidence.

B. **Liability insurance:** The purpose for this policy exclusion is that we want to encourage people to have insurance without fear that doing so suggests they have deep pockets or carry insurance because they are generally negligent.

1. **General rule:** Evidence of liability insurance is **not admissible to prove culpable conduct** (such as negligence or defendant's ability to pay a judgment).

2. **Exception:** Evidence of liability insurance **is admissible to establish:**

a. **Ownership or control:** Showing ownership or control of an instrumentality is allowed (e.g., the liability policy is held by the car owner); or

b. **Impeachment**; or

c. **Admission of fault made in conjunction** with a statement regarding the possession of liability insurance is **admissible.** For example, the statement "I have plenty of insurance" said after an injury-producing accident may be admitted as evidence that the declarant felt they were at fault for the injury.

C. **Offers to pay medical expenses:** The purpose for this policy exclusion is that we want to encourage people to offer to pay medical expenses without fear it is the equivalent of an admission of fault.

1. **General rule: Offers to pay medical**, hospital, or similar expenses occasioned by an injury are **not admissible to prove liability** for that injury.
2. **FRE only exception: Collateral admissions of fact** made during an offer to pay medical expenses **are admissible.** (But, not under the CEC.)

D. **Settlement offers:** The purpose for this policy exclusion is that we want to encourage people to attempt to settle their disputes.
1. **General rule:** An offer to settle a claim and related statements are **not admissible to prove the claim's validity, liability, or amount**.
   a. **Disputed claim only:** This rule only applies to a claim that is **disputed as to validity or amount**. It does not apply if a claim has not yet been made.

   > **Issue spotting tip:** Look for a declarant to blurt out a settlement offer at the scene of an accident before it is clear there is a disputed claim. If so, this exclusion will not apply to exclude the evidence.

2. **CEC: Mediation proceeding** discussions are also **not admissible.**

E. **Offer to plead guilty:** The purpose for this policy exclusion is that we want to encourage people to plea bargain since it aids judicial economy.
1. **General Rule:** An **offer to plead** guilty to a crime, and **all related statements** made during plea negotiations, are **not admissible to prove** that a **criminal defendant** is **guilty, or a consciousness of guilt.**
2. **California only exception:** Such statements may come in under **Prop. 8.**

F. **Expressions of sympathy**
1. **CEC only rule:** Evidence of expressions of sympathy are **not admissible in civil actions** that are related to the **death or suffering** of an accident victim, but **statements of fault** made in connection with the sympathy **are admissible.**

G. **Immigration status**
1. **CEC only rule:** Immigration status is **not admissible** or discoverable in a **personal injury** or wrongful death case.

> **Exam tip:** The purpose behind the public policy exclusions have been included since this may help you craft analysis, for example if the evidence would be admitted as an exception to an exclusion and you need to do a FRE 403 balancing test (since the evidence could still be prejudicial.) In the interest of time, you would likely not want to include this information as part of your rule statement.

IV. **WITNFSS EXAMINATION** (Witness on the Stand)
A. **Flow of testimony**
1. **Direct examination: Leading questions are not permitted** unless the witness is "hostile." A leading question is one that is framed to suggest the desired answer.
2. **Cross examination: Leading questions are usually permitted**, and cross examination is limited to the subject matter of the direct examination.
3. **Re-direct examination** is limited to the subject matter of the cross examination.
4. **Re-cross examination** is limited to the subject matter of the re-direct examination.
B. **Competence to testify:** Whenever a witness is testifying from the stand, their competence to testify is potentially at issue.
1. **Personal knowledge:** A witness must have **personal knowledge** of the matter about which they are testifying.
2. **Truthful testimony**: A witness must declare that they will **testify truthfully**.
C. **Role of the judge**
1. The trial judge may **call witnesses** and may **ask questions** of any witness.

2. **CEC:** A judge presiding at a trial is **incompetent to testify** at that trial, provided a party objects (same for a juror).

D. **Objections to the form of the question** (or answer)
   1. **Narrative:** Questions calling for a narrative are too broad (e.g., "So, what happened?").
   2. **Unresponsive:** The witness's answer is unresponsive to the question.
     a. **CEC:** A motion to strike can be made by either party, not just the examining party.
   3. **Compound question:** Two questions are contained in one question (e.g., "Did you beat your wife and steal your neighbor's money?").
   4. **Argumentative:** The question is unnecessarily combative (e.g., "Do you really expect the jury to believe this nonsense?").
   5. **Leading question** (on direct): The question itself is phrased to suggest the answer the questioner desires (e.g., "Isn't it true that Ace's has been fixing prices?").
   6. **Facts:** Assumes facts not in evidence (e.g., "When did you make your will?" when there is no evidence the witness ever made a will).

> **Memorization tip:** Use the mnemonic **NUCALF** to remember the form of the question objections.

> **Issue spotting tip:** Whenever an essay is presented in transcript format, be sure to look for issues pertaining to the witness's competence to testify (**personal knowledge**) and potential **objections to the form of the question** or **nonresponsive answer**.

E. **Present recollection refreshed** is a technique that allows any **item** (photo, document, etc.) to be used to **refresh a witness's memory** where the witness's recollection is currently uncertain. Once shown the item, the witness must then **testify from their refreshed memory**.
   1. **Not evidence:** The item used to refresh is not considered evidence and may be otherwise inadmissible evidence.
   2. **Right to inspect:** The adversary has a right to inspect the item, cross examine, and introduce pertinent portions into evidence.
   3. **CEC:** Whether the refreshing is done before or during trial by means of a document, the **writing must be produced** or testimony is stricken unless the document is unavailable.

> **Issue spotting tip: Present recollection refreshed** is often confused with past recollection recorded. With present recollection refreshed the item shown to the witness is a memory stimulus, which then allows the witness to *testify entirely from memory*. **Past recollection recorded** (see section X.D.1) is a hearsay exception and applies when the document consulted *does not actually refresh* the witness's memory, so the document is then read into the record.

F. **Opinion testimony**
   1. **Lay opinion** is admissible if rationally based on the **witness's perceptions** and is **helpful to the trier of fact.** These are not legal conclusions, but opinions (e.g., estimating driving speed, identity of a person, value of property, familiarity of handwriting, physical condition, etc.).
     a. **FRE only:** Lay opinion may **not** be based on scientific or **specialized knowledge**.
   2. **Expert opinion is admissible if all of the following pertain:**
     a. **Specialized knowledge** will **assist the trier of fact** in understanding the evidence or determining a fact.
     b. The witness **is qualified as an expert** by knowledge, skill, experience, training, or education.
     c. The testimony **is based on sufficient facts** or data. The expert's opinion may be based on:

    1. **Firsthand knowledge;**

    2. **Observation of prior witnesses**; or

    3. A **hypothetical question** posed by counsel.

  d. The testimony is the product of **reliable principles** and methods.

    1. **FRE:** The *Daubert/Kumho* standard of reliability requires the substance of the expert's testimony to be:

      a. **Peer reviewed and published** in scientific journals,

      b. **Tested** and subject to retesting,

      c. **Known for a low error rate**, and

      d. Subject to a **reasonable level of acceptance**.

      e. Based on the existence and maintenance of **standards and controls used**.

    2. **CEC:** The *Kelly/Frye* standard of reliability requires that:

      a. The proponent must prove that the **underlying scientific theory** and the instruments it uses, and

      b. It has been **generally accepted as valid** and reliable in the relevant scientific field.

        i. **CEC exception:** The standard **does not apply** to **medical and nonscientific** testimony.

  e. The witness **has applied the principles reliably** to the facts of the case.

V. PRIVILEGES

  A. A **privilege** provides testimonial protection for certain relationships, allowing one claiming the privilege to refuse to disclose, or prohibit others from disclosing, specified confidential information.

    1. **Federal privilege rules** apply in federal court for criminal, federal question, or federal law cases. The **federal common law applies** since there is no FRE regarding privileges.

    2. **State privilege rules** apply in federal court diversity jurisdiction, or in state court.

  B. **Types of privileges**

    1. **Attorney-client:** A **client has a right** not to disclose any **confidential communication** between the attorney and the client relating to the **professional relationship**.

      a. **Client:** A client can be an **individual**, as well as a **corporation.**

        1. **Federal common law:** Applies to **employees/agents if authorized** by the corporation to make the communication to the lawyer.

        2. **CEC:** Applies to **employees/agents** if the **natural person to speak** to the lawyer on behalf of the corporation, or the employee did something for which the corporation may be held liable and the corporation instructed the employee to tell its lawyer what happened. (While the language is different, as applied, both FRE and CEC rules yield the same result.)

      b. **Confidential communications:** The privilege **applies only to communications** that are **intended** to be confidential.

        1. The presence of a **third party** may serve to waive the privilege where it defeats the confidentiality requirement, unless where necessary (e.g., a translator).

        2. **Does not apply to physical evidence** turned over to the lawyer, only to communications, so the presentation of physical evidence (e.g., a gun) is not privileged.

        3. **CEC only: Allows the privilege holder to stop eavesdroppers** and other wrongful interceptors from revealing information.

      c. **Professional services:** The communication must be made for the **purpose of facilitating legal services**, though a fee need not be paid.

      d. **Holder of the privilege:** Only the **client holds the privilege** and the lawyer may assert it on the client's behalf.

      e. **Privilege lasts until:**

        1. **Federal common law: After death,** with the exception of a will contest.

        2. **CEC:** Privilege evaporates when the dead client's **estate has been fully distributed** and their personal representative has been discharged.

      f. **Exceptions:** The privilege does not apply if:

        1. **Crime or fraud:** The communication was used in *furtherance* of something the client should have known was a **crime *or* fraud**; or

    2. **Dispute with lawyer:** The communication relates to a dispute between the lawyer and client; or

    3. **Two or more parties consult** on a matter of common interest and the communication is **offered by one against another**; or

    4. **CEC only:** Lawyer reasonably believes the disclosure is **necessary to *prevent* a criminal act** that is likely to result in **death** or **substantial bodily harm**. This exception is to "prevent" the crime, so this exception does not apply to a crime already committed.

  g. **Note: Attorney work product** is material prepared in **anticipation of litigation**, and it is generally not discoverable (protected) absent a showing of **substantial need**. (See Civ. Pro. chapter Sec. II.D.3.c.)

2. **Doctor-patient privilege**

  a. **Federal common law:** There is **no federal doctor-patient privilege**, except for the special case of psychotherapists (see section V.B.3 below).

  b. **CEC:** The doctor-patient privilege applies only to communications made to medical personnel for the **purpose of medical diagnosis and treatment**.

    1. **CEC exceptions:** The privilege does not apply if:

      a. **Patient puts their physical condition in issue.**

      b. Doctor's assistance was **sought to aid wrongdoing.**

      c. **Dispute** between **doctor and patient.**

      d. Information the **doctor is required to report.**

      e. **Commitment, competency, or license revocation** proceedings.

3. **Psychotherapist-patient and social worker-client privilege**

  a. **Federal common law:** There is a federal **psychotherapist-patient privilege** for confidential communications.

  b. **CEC:** There is a licensed **psychotherapist-patient or social worker-client privilege** for confidential communications.

    1. **CEC exceptions:** The privilege does not apply if:

      a. **Patient puts their mental condition in issue.**

      b. Services were **sought to aid wrongdoing.**

      c. **Dispute** between **psychotherapist/social worker and patient.**

      d. Patient is a **danger to self and others.**

      e. **Therapist is court appointed.**

      f. Patient is a **minor and possible crime victim.**

4. **Self-incrimination:** The **Fifth Amendment** provides that no person shall be compelled to be a witness against themself.

5. **Marital privileges:** There are two types of marital privileges.

  a. **Adverse testimony privilege (spousal immunity):** One spouse **cannot be compelled** to testify against the other spouse.

    1. **Duration:** It can only be **claimed during the marriage** but covers information **learned before or during** the marriage.

    2. **Holder: Only the witness spouse** holds the privilege, so the witness spouse may testify if they want.

    3. **Federal common law:** Applies to **criminal** cases only.

    4. **CEC:** Applies to **criminal and civil cases** and the **spouse is privileged from being called to the witness stand.**

    5. **Exception:** Does not apply in **actions between the spouses** or in cases involving **crimes against the testifying spouse** or either spouse's children.

    6. **Effect:** Invoking the privilege makes the spouse **unavailable for hearsay purposes.**

  b. **Marital confidential communications privilege:** One spouse **may not disclose** the **confidential communications** of the other **made during the marriage**.

    1. **Duration:** The **privilege survives the marriage**, but only covers **statements** (not acts) made during marriage.

    2. **Holder: Both spouses** may assert the privilege not to disclose and one spouse **may prevent the other spouse** from disclosing.

3. **Exception:** Does not apply in actions **between the spouses** or in cases involving **crimes against the testifying spouse** or either spouse's children.

4. **Effect:** Invoking the privilege makes the spouse **unavailable for hearsay purposes**.

6. **CEC-only privileges**
    a. **Counselor-victim** privilege for confidential communications between a counselor and a victim of **sexual assault or domestic violence**.
    b. **Clergy-penitent** privilege for penitential communications.
    c. **News reporters** are immune from contempt of court for refusal to **disclose sources**.

> **Exam tip:** For an essay exam where a privilege is at issue, establish the following: (1) the relationship, (2) that the communication is confidential, (3) which party holds the privilege, and (4) if any exceptions apply.

VI. CHARACTER EVIDENCE

A. **Form of character evidence:** There are three methods used for proving a person's character. They are **reputation, opinion**, and **specific acts**. The purpose for the character evidence, and whether the case is civil or criminal determines which type of character evidence, if any, can be admitted.
   1. **Reputation:** Testimony regarding one's reputation in the community.
   2. **Opinion:** Testimony regarding the witness's opinion of the person.
   3. **Specific acts** engaged in by the person in question, which the witness testifies to in court.

B. **Civil court character evidence**
   1. **Rules**
       a. **General rule:** Character evidence is generally **not admissible to prove conduct in conformity** with that character trait on a particular occasion.
       b. **Character "at issue" exception:** Character evidence is admissible where character is **"at issue" and is an essential element** of the case.

> **Character "at issue" fact triggers:**
>
> • Wrongful death (because a person's value is dependent on their character)
> • Negligent entrustment
> • Defamation (because a person's character matters when assessing reputational damage)

   c. **FRE exception:** Character can be admitted in cases based on **sexual assault or child molestation**. (**CEC has no such exception**.)
   d. **Rape shield provisions in civil court:** Rape and sexual assault cases have special rules, known as "rape shield" provisions, which generally disallow evidence of a rape or sexual assault **victim's past sexual conduct**.
       1. **FRE:** Plaintiff **must put their reputation in issue** for reputation evidence to be admitted. Reputation, opinion, and specific acts evidence are only admissible if the **probative value substantially outweighs the danger of unfair prejudice**. (A higher standard than typical balancing test.)
       2. **CEC:** Defendant cannot offer evidence of plaintiff's prior sexual conduct unless to prove **prior sexual conduct with the defendant**.
   2. **Form of evidence:** Where character evidence will be admitted, all three forms of evidence (reputation, opinion, and specific acts) are generally allowed.

C. **Criminal court character evidence** (generally not admissible to prove conduct in conformity)
   1. **Rules:** Where character evidence is allowable, the character trait must always be **pertinent** to the case, but the rules for admission differ depending on whose character it is.
       a. **Defendant's character**

1. **General rule: Only the defendant can "open the door"** to evidence of a **pertinent** character trait, but once the door is opened, the prosecution can rebut as to that character trait.

2. **Exceptions** to general rule
   a. **FRE and CEC: Prosecution can be the first to offer** character **"propensity"** evidence in **sexual assault or child molestation** cases.
   b. **FRE only:** Where the **defendant offers** evidence of the **victim's character,** prosecution can offer evidence that the **defendant has the same character** trait. For example, if the defendant claims the victim has a violent character, the prosecution can offer evidence about the defendant's violent character.
   c. **CEC only:** Where the **defendant offers** evidence of the **victim's violent character,** prosecution can offer evidence that the defendant has violent character. (Note: CEC rule applies only to the character trait of violence and is narrower than FRE counterpart.)
   d. **CEC only:** In prosecution for **domestic violence or elder abuse,** prosecution may offer evidence that the defendant committed other acts of domestic violence or elder abuse.

3. **Credibility: A defendant testifying on the stand** always puts their **credibility and character for truthfulness** at issue, but not necessarily their general character.

   b. **Victim's character**
   1. **General rule: Only the defendant can "open the door"** to evidence of a **victim's pertinent character trait**, but once opened, the prosecution can rebut as to that character trait.
   2. **FRE-only exception:** If **defendant claims** or offers evidence that the **victim** was the **first aggressor**, the prosecution may offer evidence of the **victim's character for peacefulness**.
   3. **Rape and sexual assault case special rules:** "Rape shield" provisions **generally disallow** evidence of a rape or sexual assault victim's past sexual conduct, subject to the specific form of evidence rules that follow.

2. **Form of evidence** allowed depends on whose character trait it is and if it is raised during direct or cross examination.
   a. **Defendant's character**
   1. **Direct examination:** Only **reputation and opinion** evidence are allowed to show character; **no specific acts** evidence is allowed.
   2. **Cross examination** (to rebut defendant's character evidence)
      a. **FRE: All three** forms of evidence are allowed in cross-examination (**reputation, opinion**, and **specific acts**). But, while specific acts may be asked about, **no extrinsic evidence regarding the specific act is allowed**, so the prosecutor is stuck with the witness's answer.
      b. **CEC:** Only **reputation and opinion** evidence are allowed to rebut; **no specific acts** evidence is allowed. (subject to Prop. 8).

   b. **Victim's character**
   1. **Direct examination**
      a. **FRE:** Only **reputation and opinion** evidence are allowed to show character; **no specific acts** evidence is allowed.
      b. **CEC: All three** forms of evidence are allowed to show character (**reputation, opinion**, and **specific acts**).
   2. **Cross examination** (to rebut victim's character evidence): **All three** forms of evidence (**reputation, opinion**, and **specific acts**) are allowed to show character (FRE and CEC).
   3. **FRE-only exception:** If the **defendant claims** or offers evidence that the **victim was the first aggressor**, the prosecution may offer evidence of the victim's character for **peacefulness** only by **reputation and opinion** evidence, **no specific acts** evidence is allowed.

    4. **Rape and sexual assault case special rules in criminal court:** "Rape shield" provisions **generally disallow evidence of a rape or sexual assault victim's past sexual conduct.**

        a. **Reputation and opinion** evidence are **always inadmissible.**

        b. **Specific acts** are **only admissible** to prove the limited issues of:

            i. **Third party is the source** of semen or injury to the victim; or

            ii. **Prior acts** of consensual intercourse **with the defendant**; or

            iii. **Constitutionally** required.

        c. **CEC only: Defendant can offer** victim's prior sexual conduct to show they **reasonably believed the victim consented**, but not to show that the victim did consent.

D. **"Other purpose" for character evidence allowed (civil and criminal):** While character evidence of other crimes, wrongs, or specific bad acts **are not generally admissible to show conduct in conformity with the character trait**, such **specific acts** evidence **may be admissible for some other purpose,** such as to show:

    1. **Intent** to commit the act. Where intent is a part of a crime, such as forgery, evidence that the defendant committed similar prior wrongful acts could be admitted to negate a claim of good faith.

    2. **Preparation** to commit the act. Evidence of preparatory steps taken to commit the act can be admissible.

    3. **Identity of the perpetrator,** including M.O. (modus operandi). Prior acts can be used to establish that the defendant engaged in a specific pattern of behavior that leads to revealing their identity.

    4. **Knowledge** of some fact or event.

    5. **Absence of mistake or accident.** Evidence that the defendant engaged in similar misconduct in the past would negate any possibility of a mistake or accident.

    6. **Motive** to commit the crime. The defendant's alleged commission of a prior crime that in some way facilitates the commission of the crime of which they are presently accused points to a motive to engage in the later crime (e.g., the theft of special ink is probative that the defendant engaged in counterfeiting).

    7. **Opportunity** to commit the act.

    8. **Plan** or scheme. Evidence of a common plan or scheme can be shown by specific acts undertaken to further the plan or scheme.

> **Memorization tip:** Use the mnemonic **I PIK A MOP** to remember the "other purposes" that specific acts character evidence may be admitted to prove.

> **Issue spotting tip:** When character is at issue, always consider if the evidence can be admitted for some "other purpose." When character evidence is allowable for "other purposes," always do the **legal relevance balancing test** from section II.B. above to determine if the evidence should be excluded because it is too prejudicial.

> **Exam tip:** Character evidence can be challenging to analyze, so always consider and discuss the following issues:
>
> 1. Determine if the case is civil or criminal. If criminal, is the evidence regarding the defendant or the victim? Apply the rules.
> 2. Identify the form of the evidence presented (reputation, opinion, specific acts) and if it is admissible in that form.
> 3. Determine if there is an "other purpose" for admitting the evidence. If so, identify it and do the legal relevance balancing test.

> **Character evidence fact triggers:**
>
> - Prior conviction of any kind
> - Evidence someone is a liar (e.g., lied on tax return, perjury case)
> - Evidence someone is a bad person (e.g., violent, shady bookkeeping practices, abusive to family/friends, sells drugs, sexual misconduct, prior malpractice cases)
> - Wrongful death or defamation where character is in issue.

VII. OTHER CIRCUMSTANTIAL EVIDENCE

A. **Habit and custom** is a **regular response to a repeated situation** and is admissible to show conduct in conformity with that regular response on a particular occasion.

1. **Applies to persons and businesses.**

   a. **Person:** Evidence of a person's habit is admissible to show the person **acted in accordance** with the habit on a particular occasion (e.g., driver who always fastens their seatbelt before driving).

   b. **Business practices:** The routine practice of an organization is admissible to show the **practice was followed** by the business on a particular occasion (e.g., outgoing mail placed in the outbox is collected and mailed every day at 3 p.m.).

2. **Three factors** are considered to determine if a behavior is habit or custom evidence:

   a. The more **specific** the behavior, the more likely it's habit.

   b. The more **regular** the behavior, the more likely it's habit.

   c. The more **unreflective or semi-automatic,** the more likely it's habit.

B. **Similar happenings:** Evidence that similar happenings occurred in the past (or failed to occur) are allowed if the events are **substantially similar**. Typically, this evidence is used to show a prior accident or injury, or the absence of a past accident or injury.

VIII. IMPEACHMENT

A. **Impeachment:** A witness's credibility may be impeached by **cross-examination** (or on direct, if witness is "hostile"), or with the proper foundation, by **extrinsic evidence** (e.g., other witnesses). Either party may impeach a witness.

1. **Five main ways to impeach a witness:**

   a. **Character for truthfulness:** This can be shown by **reputation** and **opinion**, past crimes, and/or past **specific bad acts**. (See section VIII.A.2 below.)

   b. **Prior inconsistent statement (PIS):** A witness may be impeached by a prior inconsistent statement.

      1. **Extrinsic evidence** may be used to prove the PIS only if:

         a. The witness who made the PIS is given an opportunity to **explain or deny the PIS,** and

         b. The proponent of the PIS is given an opportunity to **interrogate** the **impeaching witness**.

      2. **FRE limitation:** If the PIS is **not given under oath**, the PIS can only be used for **impeachment** purposes, so it will not be admitted for its truth. (CEC does not have this limitation.)

   c. **Bias:** A witness may be impeached by a showing of bias, self-interest, or motive.

      1. **Extrinsic evidence** is allowed if the witness is given an opportunity to **explain or deny**.

   d. **Sensory or mental defect:** A witness may be impeached by showing that their capacity to observe or remember is impaired.

   e. **Contradiction of a witness's testimony by another witness.** A witness may contradict the testimony of a prior witness, but this rule is limited because the contradiction can't concern a collateral matter. A collateral matter would be when the contradiction is on a fact not material to the case, so it only contradicts the witness.

2. **Impeaching witness's *character for truthfulness*.** (From VIII.A.1.a above. Note that this is accomplished through character evidence regarding truthfulness, so be mindful of the character evidence rules discussed above.)
   a. **Reputation and opinion regarding truthfulness are allowed**, but **no specific acts** may be inquired into that led to the witness's opinion or the person's reputation.
   b. **Specific bad acts that are probative of truthfulness may be raised in certain circumstances:**
      1. **FRE: Specific bad acts** that are probative of *truthfulness* may be inquired into on **cross-examination** but are always subject to the legal relevance balancing test (See section II.B. above).
         a. The question must be made in **good faith**.
         b. **Extrinsic evidence is not allowed** to prove the bad act, so the questioner is stuck with the answer received from the witness.
      2. **CEC: The rules differ depending on whether the case is civil or criminal.**
         a. **Civil court: Prohibits** the extrinsic evidence and the initial cross examination.
         b. **Criminal court:** Prop. 8 **permits** both the initial cross examination and the extrinsic evidence (subject to the legal relevance balancing test in section II.B. above).
   c. **Impeaching with criminal conviction**
      1. **Crimen falsi (FRE):** All crimen falsi convictions (felonies and misdemeanors) for **crimes involving** a **false statement are admissible** and the **judge may not exclude** under the legal relevance balancing test, unless the conviction (e.g., forgery, perjury, embezzlement, etc.) is more than ten years old.
      2. **Felony conviction**
         a. **FRE:** A **balancing test** is used to determine admissibility, depending on witness status.
            i. **Witness is criminal defendant:** The conviction is admissible only if the probative value outweighs its prejudicial effect.
            ii. **Other witness:** The conviction is admissible unless the prejudicial effect *substantially* outweighs the probative value. (Higher standard than used for the criminal defendant.)
         b. **CEC: Felony convictions** are admissible if:
            i. It has **not been expunged**, pardoned, etc., and
            ii. The felony involves **moral turpitude**, and
            iii. Subject to **legal relevance balancing test** (See section II.B. above).
      3. **Misdemeanor conviction**
         a. **FRE:** Misdemeanors that are not crimen falsi are **not admissible to impeach**.
         b. **CEC**
            i. **Civil court: Misdemeanors cannot be used** to impeach a witness.
            ii. **Criminal court:** Misdemeanors can only be used if the crime involves **moral turpitude**.
      4. **Old convictions**
         a. **FRE:** May not be used if **more than ten years** have elapsed from both the conviction and the prison term, unless specific facts make the probative value of the conviction substantially outweigh the prejudicial effect.
         b. **CEC: No time limit imposed** for remoteness, but an older conviction is a factor to consider in the CEC 352 balancing test.

Impeachment evidence fact triggers:

- Witness on the stand
- Character evidence at issue
- Prior conviction of any kind
- Prior bad behavior (e.g., sell drugs, accused of sexual misconduct, bad driving, accused of excessive force)

---

3. **Rehabilitating impeached witnesses**
   a. **Must meet the attack:** The rehabilitating evidence must support the witness's credibility in the same respect as the attack.
   b. **Good character:** Can show witness's good character where evidence of their **character for untruthfulness** has been shown.
   c. A **prior consistent statement (PCS)** can be used to rebut an express or implied charge of recent fabrication, or that witness's testimony was the product of improper motive.

B. **Bolstering the witness's credibility**
   1. **FRE: Bolstering is not allowed.** A lawyer may not offer evidence supporting a witness's credibility until after it has been attacked.
   2. **CEC: Bolstering is allowed in criminal cases**. Either side may offer evidence supporting a witness's credibility before it has been attacked.

IX. **HEARSAY IS INADMISSIBLE UNLESS AN EXCEPTION APPLIES.**
   A. **Hearsay** is an **out-of-court statement** offered for the **truth of the matter** asserted. Hearsay is **inadmissible** unless an **exception** applies.
      1. **"Out of court"** means that the declarant made the statement at some time and place other than while testifying at the current trial or hearing.
         a. This includes a declarant repeating their own prior out-of-court statement.
      2. The **statement** can be oral or written, or even nonverbal conduct if it is intended as a communicative assertion (e.g., a shake of the head).
      3. **Truth of the matter:** Offered to prove the truth of the matter asserted in the statement.
   B. **Nonhearsay purpose: An out-of-court statement may be nonhearsay by definition when it is not being offered for the truth** of the matter asserted, but for some other reason, such as in the following situations where evidence is offered to show:
      1. **Effect on listener or reader**, such that the listener or reader was put on notice of some information, obtained certain knowledge, had a certain emotion, or behaved reasonably or unreasonably.
      2. **Declarant's state of mind**
         a. **Knowledge** of facts, or
         b. **Mental state** (e.g., declarant stating "I'm Abraham Lincoln" is offered not to prove its truth, but that the declarant is delusional).
      3. **Independent legal significance:** A statement that itself has legal significance (e.g., solicitation, words of defamation, words establishing a contract).

<u>**Nonhearsay purpose fact triggers:**</u>

- Effect on listener where put on notice (e.g., listener told brakes are bad, or drill bit is defective).
- Knowledge/mental state where information provides **motive** for subsequent act. (E.g., *A* is told his girlfriend is cheating with *X* and *A* subsequently beats up *X*. The information is the motive for the attack; it need not be a true statement.)

<u>**Issue spotting tip:**</u> Where statements that would otherwise be hearsay are being admitted <u>because</u> the statement is not being offered for its truth, but rather for the purpose of establishing one of the exceptions above, always do the **legal relevance prejudicial balancing test** because there is always a danger of unfair prejudice when evidence is admissible for one purpose but not another.

C. **Multiple hearsay** occurs where an out-of-court statement quotes or paraphrases another out-of-court statement. **Each level of hearsay must fall within an exception** to be admissible.

> **Multiple hearsay fact triggers:**
>
> - Police report including bystander or witness statement
> - Work order containing mechanic's observations
> - Surgical report containing observation of medical personnel
> - Witness testifying about what another person told him a third party said

D. **Hearsay Policy:** The following policies behind the hearsay rule and hearsay exceptions can provide key points of analysis in an essay question.
   1. **Hearsay rule purpose:** The purpose of the hearsay rule is that some communications are suspect because of the **danger of misinterpretation** without the speaker present to clarify. The hearsay dangers are ambiguity, insincerity, incorrect memory, and inaccurate perception.
   2. **Hearsay exception purpose:** The purpose of the hearsay exceptions is that where circumstances provide an **aura of authenticity** to a statement, it should be admissible.

X. **HEARSAY EXCEPTIONS, EXEMPTIONS AND EXCLUSIONS**
   A. **Admissions** are excluded from the hearsay rule and will be admitted.
      1. **Party admission:** A party admission is **any statement** made by a party, and it may be offered against them. The statement need not be against declarant's interest.
         a. **CEC** calls this a hearsay "exception" not "exemption."
      2. **Adoptive admission:** An adoptive admission is a statement made by another where the party **knows of its content** and voluntarily **manifests belief in the truth** of the statement by words or action.
         a. **Silent adoptive admission:** Adoptive admission can be made by silence if a **reasonable person would have spoken up**, but always subject to the Fifth Amendment right to remain silent. For example, if at an accident scene one party says, "it's all your fault," this may be an adoptive admission by silence because a reasonable person would have refuted the statement if they were not at fault.
      3. **Vicarious admission:** A vicarious or representative admission can arise two ways.
         a. **Explicit authorization:** A statement made by an authorized spokesperson of party.
         b. **Employee or agent:** A statement made by an agent/employee of the party concerning a transaction within the **scope of the agent/employee relationship** and made **during the existence** of the relationship.
            1. **CEC is narrower:** A statement by an employee of a party is a party admission of that employer only where **negligent conduct of that employee** is the basis for employer's liability in a case of respondeat superior.
      4. **Co-conspirator admissions** are statements made **during the course** of the conspiracy and **in furtherance** of the conspiracy.
         a. **Confrontation Clause:** However, a co-conspirator admission is subject to the confrontation clause requirement that a defendant is allowed to confront their accusers, so if the co-conspirator refuses to testify, the co-conspirator admission will not be admitted.
   B. **Spontaneous, excited, or contemporaneous statement hearsay exceptions**
      1. **Medical diagnosis or treatment statements:** A statement made for the **purpose** of medical diagnosis or treatment is admissible.
         a. Statement may be made by a **third person** if made to help obtain treatment.
         b. Statement may include the **cause** of the condition, but **not statements of fault**.
         c. **CEC:** Statement of **past or present physical condition** is only admissible if made to obtain medical diagnosis and treatment by a **child abuse victim**.
      2. **Statement of then-existing mental, emotional, or physical condition** is admissible to show the condition or state of mind.
         a. **Does not apply to a statement of memory or belief.**
      3. **Present sense impression (PSI):** A statement is admissible if describing or **explaining an event** or condition and **made while declarant was perceiving** the event or condition or immediately thereafter.

a. **CEC contemporaneous statement:** Applies to a statement explaining **the declarant's own conduct** and made **while the declarant engaged in that conduct** (narrower than FRE).
4. **Excited utterance:** A statement is admissible if relating to a **startling event** or condition and **made while the declarant was still under the stress** of excitement caused by the event or condition.
   a. **CEC** calls this a **spontaneous statement.**

> **Excited utterance/Spontaneous statement fact triggers:**
>
> - Any statement followed by an exclamation mark!
> - Witness to a car accident
> - Descriptions that someone is angry or shouting

C. **Prior statements of *available* witnesses**
1. **Prior inconsistent statement (PIS):** A PIS is **substantively admissible**, and not merely admissible for impeachment purposes, if:
   a. **Oath:** The PIS was made under oath as part of a formal proceeding.
   b. **Cross examination:** The declarant is subject to cross examination concerning the PIS.
   c. **CEC:** PIS need not be made under oath to be admissible.
2. **Prior consistent statement (PCS):** A PCS is only admissible **substantively** if offered to **rebut a charge** of recent fabrication, or improper motive. It need not be made under oath.
3. **Prior identification (PID)** of a person, made after perceiving the person, is **substantively admissible** if the **declarant testifies** at trial.
D. **Document hearsay exceptions**
1. **Past recollection recorded:** If a witness **cannot testify from memory**, a party may **introduce** a **written record** of an event.
   a. **Requirements** must be satisfied by witness:
      1. **Firsthand knowledge** of the sponsoring witness.
      2. Events were **fresh in the memory** when record was made.
      3. Witness now has **impaired recollection.**
      4. Record was **accurate when written**.
   b. **Document will be read to jury:** The writing itself is not admissible evidence, unless an adverse party requests it, but its contents may be read to the jury.

> **Issue spotting tip: Past recollection recorded** applies when the document consulted to refresh memory *does not actually refresh* the witness's memory, so if it otherwise qualifies, the document is then read into the record. **In contrast, present recollection refreshed** allows an item to be shown to the witness as a memory stimulus, which then allows the witness to testify entirely from memory.

2. **Business record** is admissible where a **sponsoring witness** establishes the record was kept in the course of **regularly conducted business activity.**
   a. **Business activity** includes events, conditions, opinion, or diagnosis.
      1. **CEC:** Does not allow opinions or diagnoses.
   b. **Regular practice** to keep such a record.
   c. **Personal knowledge:** The record is made by a person with personal knowledge of the information contained in the record. Requires:
      1. **Firsthand knowledge** by original supplier of information.
      2. **Business duty to report:** The record must be made by one with a business duty to report.

> **Exam tip:** Look for information contained in reports that is provided by those without a business duty to report, such as an accident witness.

    d. **Timeliness:** Made at or near the time of matters referenced.
3. **Public records and reports**
    a. **FRE:** They are admissible if within one of the following categories:
       1. **Agency's record of its own activities.**
       2. **Matters observed in the line of duty** and under a **duty to report**.
       3. **Investigative reports** with factual findings resulting from investigations made.
       4. **Criminal case limitation—FRE only: Criminal prosecution** cannot use matters **observed by police officers** or police investigations against a criminal defendant. (CEC does not have the limitation.)
    b. **CEC:** They are admissible if:
       1. Making the record was in the **scope of duty**,
       2. The record was made **near the time of matters described**, and
       3. The **sources** of information and **time** of preparation indicate **trustworthiness**.

> **Issue spotting tip:** Multiple hearsay problems are often found in business records or public records. The first level of hearsay is the record itself; the second level of hearsay can occur where the record contains information provided by another person. Remember, each level of hearsay must have a hearsay exception for the evidence to be admitted.

    4. **Learned treatise and commercial publications**
      a. **FRE:** Admissible if called to the attention of an **expert witness** and established as **reliable authority**.
      b. **CEC:** Admissible only for facts of **general notoriety and interest**.
  E. **Declarant *unavailable* hearsay exceptions:**
    1. **Witness is unavailable:** To utilize the following hearsay exceptions, the witness must be deemed unavailable. The witness's unavailability can be established in one of the following ways:
      a. **Privileged** from testifying.
      b. **Death or illness** prevents witness from testifying.
      c. **Reasonable means** can't procure the witness.
      d. **Witness refuses to testify** despite a court order.
        1. **CEC** requires refusal to be made out of fear.
      e. **Witness unable to remember.**
        1. **CEC** requires total memory loss.
    2. **Four hearsay exceptions requiring witness unavailability:**
      a. **Former testimony:** Former testimony is admissible where the party against whom the testimony is now offered had, during the earlier hearing or deposition, an opportunity to examine that person and a **similar motive to develop the testimony**.
        1. **Civil cases only**
          a. **FRE only:** Allows **predecessor in interest** to have been present in earlier proceeding to develop testimony.
          b. **CEC only:** Allows if **anyone with a similar interest** was present in earlier proceeding, or it is being offered against the person who offered it on their own behalf in the earlier proceeding, or against a successor in interest of such person.
          c. **CEC only: Deposition** testimony given in the **same civil action** is admissible for all purposes if deponent is unavailable at trial or lives more than 150 miles from the courthouse.
      b. **Dying declaration:** A dying declaration is admissible where a statement is made by a declarant, while **believing their death was imminent**, and is concerning the cause or **circumstances of their impending death**.
        1. **FRE:** Only allowed in **civil** and **criminal** *homicide* cases. Declarant **need not be dead, but only be unavailable** (pursuant to the reasons established above in section X.E.1.)

2. **CEC:** Applies to **all civil and criminal cases** and declarant must **actually be dead**.
3. **CEC "OJ" exception — statement describing physical abuse:** Applies to allow a statement made at or near the time of injury or threat, describing infliction or threat of physical abuse, in writing, recorded, or made to police or medical professional, under trustworthy circumstances.

  c. **Statement against interest:** A statement against interest is admissible if, **at the time** it was made, it was against the **declarant's financial or penal interest**.
1. **FRE:** If offered to **exculpate** the accused, there must be **corroborating evidence**.
2. **CEC:** Called a **declaration against interest** and includes a statement against one's **social interest**.
3. Note: The Confrontation Clause may keep the statement out of evidence.

  d. **Forfeiture by wrongdoing:** A hearsay exception will apply where a party has engaged in **witness tampering** intended to make the witness unavailable.

F. **Residual "catch-all" hearsay exception (FRE):** An otherwise hearsay statement may be admissible if **trustworthy**, is regarding a **material fact**, is **more probative** on the point than other evidence, and **notice** is given to the opposing side. (CEC does not have, but judges have discretion.)

Memorization tip: Hearsay exceptions are the second-most frequently tested evidence principle (after relevance). To aid memorization of the hearsay exceptions, group them into categories:

- Four **admissions** (party, adoptive, vicarious, co-conspirator) **C**aptain **A**merica **V**alues **P**eter-Parker (**C**o-conspirator, **A**doptive, **V**icarious, **P**arty);
- Four **witness statements** (medical, then-existing state, PSI, excited utterance) **M**ulan and **P**ocahontas **S**ave **E**eyore and **S**titch (**M**edical, **P**resent **S**ense impression, **E**xcited utterance, then-existing **S**tate);
- Three **prior statements** of available witnesses (PIS, PCS, Prior Identification) **P**epper **C**an **I**nfluence **I**ronman (**P**rior — **C**onsistent, **I**nconsistent, **I**dentification);
- Four **documents** (PRR, business, public, learned writing) **P**ixar keeps **R**aising **R**evenue with **B**uzz **L**ightyear **P**opularity (**P**rior **R**ecollection **R**ecorded, **B**usiness record, **L**earned writing, **P**ublic record);
- Four **declarant unavailable** (former testimony, dying declaration, declaration against interest, forfeiture by wrongdoing). **U**nstoppable **S**uperhero **A**vengers **I**ncluding **F**alcon and **T**hor **F**ind **W**onderwoman and **D**are Devil (**U**navailable — **S**tatement **A**gainst **I**nterest, **F**ormer **T**estimony, **F**orfeiture by **W**rongdoing, **D**ying **D**eclaration).

Exam tip: To properly analyze a piece of evidence, always include each hearsay exception that potentially applies under the facts. If the question is a real racehorse and many exceptions could apply, analyze the exception that is the best fit to the facts, and one more that also works, then move on.

XI. **DOCUMENTS, REAL EVIDENCE, AND DEMONSTRATIVE EVIDENCE**
  A. **Relevance:** All **documentary evidence must be relevant** to be admissible.
  B. **Authentication:** All evidence, other than testimony, **must be authenticated** as genuine to be admitted. Authentication is proof that the item **is what the proponent claims** it is.
    1. **Methods of authentication**
      a. **Real evidence:** Physical evidence can be authenticated by **distinctive characteristics** or **chain of custody**.
      b. **Demonstrative evidence** must be a **fair representation**.
      c. **Writings and recordings** can be authenticated by admissions, eyewitness testimony, voice identification, handwriting verifications (expert or nonexpert with personal knowledge, or trier of fact with sample comparisons), circumstantial evidence (e.g., postmark, address), etc.

1. **Ancient documents** can be authenticated by evidence that the document is in a condition to be free from suspicion of inauthenticity, was found in a place such a writing would be kept, and it is at least:

    a. FRE: 20 years old

    b. CEC: 30 years old

d. **Self-authenticating documents:** Certain documents are self-authenticating, such as **certified copies** of public records (e.g., deeds), official publications, newspapers, and periodicals.

    1. **FRE only: Business records** and **trade** inscriptions.

    2. **CEC only:** Signature of **notary** or domestic public employee.

Authentication fact triggers:

- Phone call, especially if voice disguised or muffled
- Signed greeting card found by a third party
- Signature on letter
- Report of any kind

C. **Best evidence rule (FRE) and secondary evidence rule (CEC):** To prove the **contents** of a writing (including photos, X-rays, recordings), the original writing must be produced. **Machine duplicates are also allowed** unless the authenticity of the original is disputed.

  1. If **original or photocopy is unavailable:** Oral testimony is admissible, and the CEC even allows handwritten duplicates.

  2. **Best evidence rule (BER) does not apply** when the fact to be proved exists independently of the writing (e.g., witness can testify from personal knowledge), where writing is collateral (minor), voluminous records, or public records.

D. **Summaries of voluminous writings:** If original documents are so voluminous that they can't be conveniently introduced into evidence, a summary may be introduced through a sponsoring witness.

Exam tip: Whenever a **document** is being introduced into evidence always analyze the following five issues: 1) relevance, 2) authentication, 3) BER, 4) hearsay, and 5) any applicable hearsay exceptions. Also, look for double hearsay when there is a statement contained in a document.

XII. PROCEDURAL ISSUES

A. **Burdens of proof:** There are two different burdens of proof.

  1. **Burden of production:** Where a party has the burden of production, that party must come forward and **produce evidence to establish that fact** or issue.

  2. **Burden of persuasion:** The produced **evidence must be sufficient** to establish the fact or issue.

    a. **Civil case:** The burden typically rests with the **plaintiff** and usually must be established to a **preponderance of the evidence** standard.

    b. **Criminal case:** The burden of persuasion rests with the **prosecution** and must be proven **beyond a reasonable doubt.**

B. **Presumptions** are inferences that the jury must draw from a set of facts.

  1. A **civil case presumption** operates to shift the burden of **producing evidence** (not persuasion) to the opposing party.

    a. Examples of rebuttable presumptions: mail delivery, legitimacy, sanity, that a death is not suicide, death from seven years' absence, etc.

  2. **There is no criminal case presumption.** The burden of production and persuasion is always on the prosecution to prove every element of a crime beyond a reasonable doubt.

C. **Judge and jury allocations**

1. The **judge** decides issues of **law.**
2. The **jury** decides issues of **fact.**

XIII. JUDICIAL NOTICE

A. **Judicial notice** is the process of establishing facts without presenting evidence. The court can take judicial notice of facts **not subject to reasonable dispute** because they are either:
    1. **Generally known** within the jurisdiction, or
    2. Capable of **accurate and ready determination** by a source whose accuracy cannot be reasonably questioned.
B. **Instructions and judicial discretion**
    1. **FRE:** A party **must request judicial notice** to **compel** judicial notice. If not requested, the court has discretion to take judicial notice. Judicial notice can occur at any time, even on appeal.
        a. **Civil case:** The jury *must* **accept** the judicially noticed fact.
        b. **Criminal case:** The jury *may* **accept** the judicially noticed fact.
    2. **CEC:** Whether requested or not, the court **must take judicial notice of matters generally known** within jurisdiction. CEC does not distinguish between civil and criminal.

EVIDENCE ISSUES TESTED MATRIX

		Crossover	Cal or Fed	Relevance	Prop. 8	Policy Exclusions	Personal Knowledge	Form of Questions	Lay Opinion	Expert Opinion	Privileges	Character & Habit	Impeachment	Hearsay & Exceptions	Authentication	BER / SER	Judicial Notice
F '23 Q5	Pedro sues Gallery about value of painting		Fed	X			X		X	X				X	X	X	
F '22 Q4	Atty Anita represented Dan for murder and is called to testify	Prof resp	Cal	X			X				X			X	X		
F '21 Q1	Paul sues Dell's Dept. store for PI from a fall		Cal	X		X	X	X				X	X	X			
F '20 Q4	Des is charged with cocaine distribution		Cal	X	X		X				X	X	X	X	X		
F '19 Q4	Dave in Cal; Petra in NV; water tank leak dispute	Civ Pro	Fed	X		X	X		X					X	X		
J '18 Q2	Deb is charged with spousal battery		Cal	X	X		X					X		X	X	X	
F '17 Q3	Pete hit by Donna's Pizza delivery driver		Fed	X		X								X	X	X	
F '16 Q5	Pam fired from Ace Mfg Co, sues D for defamation		Cal	X			X					X		X	X		
J '14 Q2	ABC airliner crashes due to neg. maintenance		Fed	X						X			X	X	X	X	
J '12 Q3	Dean charged with murder of Vicky		Cal	X	X		X		X		X		X	X			
F '12 Q3	David & Paul car accident, kills V, Molly testifies		Fed	X		X	X		X			X		X	X	X	
July '11 Q2	Doctor performs Perry's back surgery	Civ Pro	Fed	X							X						
February '11 Q6	Green's Grocery & lottery ticket w/ wrong #s	Remedy	Fed	X										X			
July '10 Q3	David & Vic fight; Vic has heart attack		Cal	X	X		X					X	X	X	X		

Continued>

Date	Scenario	Crossover	Cal or Fed	Relevance	Prop. 8	Policy Exclusions	Personal Knowledge	Form of Questions	Lay Opinion	Expert Opinion	Privileges	Character & Habit	Impeachment	Hearsay & Exceptions	Authentication	BER/SER	Judicial Notice
July '09 Q3	Paula & Dan in a car accident		Cal	X	X	X	X		X	X				X	X	X	
February '09 Q3	Dustin commits robbery; ex-wife Wendy on stand		Cal	X	X		X	X	X		X			X		X	
July '07 Q3	Dave, Mechanic, bad brakes & car accident		Fed	X			X		X					X		X	
February '07 Q6	Officer Will, Calvin's cocaine, & Donna's car		Fed	X			X			X		X		X	X	X	
July '05 Q4	Dan charged with arson of failing business		Fed	X			X					X		X	X	X	
July '04 Q4	Victor on fire from gasoline; Dan charged		Fed	X			X	X				X		X		X	X
July '03 Q3	Dan assaults off-duty policeman in bar fight		Fed	X		X	X	X		X		X	X	X		X	
February '02 Q6	Phil v. Dirk, the barber, for hair loss		Fed	X			X	X	X					X	X	X	X
July '01 Q3	Walker v. TruckCo for car accident		Fed	X			X	X				X	X	X		X	
July '00 Q1	Dan sells heroin @ Guy's Bar		Fed	X								X	X	X	X	X	
February '00 Q6	Picasso sketch taken from museum	Crimes	Fed											X			

EVIDENCE PRACTICE ESSAYS, ANSWER GRIDS, AND SAMPLE ANSWERS

Evidence Question 1
February 2020, Question 4

Des is on trial in a California superior court for possession with intent to distribute hundreds of pounds of cocaine from January through October in 2019.

At trial the prosecution called Carol, a severed co-defendant, who had pleaded guilty to reduced charges in exchange for testifying against Des. Carol testified that through 2019, she had acted as a "distributor" for a ring of cocaine dealers. In that role, Carol had sold hundreds of pounds of cocaine to many people, including Des, during the period of the charged crime. Carol further testified that all her customers agreed to sell cocaine. The prosecutor asked Carol to identify a notebook, which Carol testified was hers, and which she used to keep track of income and expenses related to the cocaine sales as each occurred. Carol testified that on pages 1–2 of the notebook were notations of sales of cocaine from January through April of 2019 by Carol to various people other than Des. She further testified that on pages 3–4 were notations of sales from May through October in 2019 to various people, including Des. The court admitted pages 1–4 into evidence.

On cross-examination, Des's attorney asked Carol if the prosecutor, Pete, had offered her a reduced sentence in exchange for her testimony. Carol answered, "No." Des's attorney then called Carol's attorney, Abe, to the stand and asked him the same question. Pete asserted attorney-client privilege. The court denied the assertion of privilege, and Abe testified that the reduction of charges against Carol had been in exchange for Carol agreeing to testify against Des.

Des took the stand and denied the charge. On cross-examination, Pete asked Des if it was true that eleven years earlier he had been convicted of forgery, a felony. Des answered, "Yes."

1. Assuming all credible objections were timely made, did the court properly admit:

   a. Pages 1–4 of the notes? Discuss.

   b. Evidence of Des's conviction for forgery? Discuss.

2. Did the court properly deny the assertion of attorney-client privilege? Discuss.

Answer according to California law.

Evidence Question 1 Assessment
February 2020, Question 4

When you realize you have an evidence question on the bar exam, take a deep breath because you need to be on your "A" game and be a fast typist since it is difficult to write a passing evidence essay in under 1500 words. Evidence questions are notoriously racehorse style. Typically, they are all about issue spotting (as many as twenty+ issues is common) and working quickly, but the analysis is straightforward. This particular question seems comparatively more manageable than most evidence questions since there are "only" approximately ten important issues, but that should raise your suspicions. When an evidence question seems comparatively easy, like here, be wary because usually that means the analysis is a bit more complicated.

With an evidence question, the first thing you need to do is get your bearings regarding the law that applies. The first fact you should note is if you are in California court and applying the California Evidence Code (CEC), or if you are in federal court applying the Federal Rules of Evidence (FRE). This is typically noted in the last line of every question. The second thing you want to identify is if you are in criminal court or civil court. This brief assessment will help to narrow down the rules eligible for testing on the question so it is a bit easier to issue spot. Though applicants are expected to use the correct body of law on the question, the bar examiners do not seem to be sticklers about using the exact correct terminology and accidently applying the wrong rule is not fatal to a passing score. The bar examiners seem appropriately more focused on the factual analysis.

This question specifically asks the applicant to answer according to California law, which is significant because the question concerns a criminal defendant in a California court, making Prop. 8 applicable. When an essay concerns a criminal case in California do the following: First, start with the Prop. 8 rule (all relevant evidence is admissible, subject to exemptions) in your essay introduction. Then, for each piece of evidence do the following: 1) Apply the ordinary CEC rules of evidence; 2) Explain that despite the ordinary rules, Prop. 8 permits the admission of all relevant evidence unless one of the nine exemptions apply; and 3) Determine if one of the nine Prop. 8 exemptions will exclude the evidence.

Evidence questions are usually mostly focused on issue spotting, but this question required a bit more thought to properly spot some of the issues. In particular, the analysis of the attorney-client privilege issue required the applicant to take a step back and think through the scenario of what must have happened (a reasonable factual inference) for Carol to get a deal from the prosecutor. A knee jerk reaction that since they are questioning Carol's attorney, the information from her attorney must be privileged is incorrect here. It is also worth noting that this analysis is more sophisticated, and it is contained in the last call of the question. If an applicant had misjudged their time and short-changed their answer on the last call, it would be hard to achieve a passing score on this question.

Always pay special attention to the details in the introductory paragraphs, which will identify the type of case and procedural posture to provide context for your issue spotting and analysis. In this case, Des has been charged with possession with intent to distribute hundreds of pounds of cocaine from January through October in 2019. The dates become important because in analyzing the evidence, the applicant needed to identify that some of the evidence the prosecutor sought to admit did not implicate Des during some of the time period in question. This is a good example of facts that make the legal relevance balancing test important to discuss.

Evidence questions typically involve some role playing and feel a bit like a real court situation. This question asks you to take the role of the judge and analyze if the judge properly admitted various pieces of evidence. It makes a nice presentation to phrase your answer as responsive to the question, such as identifying if each piece of evidence was, or was not, properly admitted.

Make note of the areas highlighted in **bold** on the corresponding grid. The bold areas highlight the issues, analysis, and conclusions that are likely **required** to receive a passing score on this question.

Issue	Rule	Fact Application	Conclusion
Prop 8	Prop. 8 is known as the "Victim's Bill of Rights" and provides all relevant evidence is admissible in criminal trials, subject to several exemptions including rules of evidence relating to the U.S. Constitution, hearsay, character, privileges existing in 1982, exclusions after 1982 ratified by 2/3 vote of legislature, and CEC 352.	Des is charged with possession with intent to distribute hundreds of pounds of cocaine.	Prop. 8 applies
Assuming all credible objections were timely made, did the court properly admit: Pages 1–4 of the notes?			
Relevance	All evidence must be relevant. Evidence is relevant if it tends to be material to a disputed fact.	• The disputed fact is Des' involvement in the cocaine business. • Carol's notebook is relevant since it shows Carol's knowledge and tracking of the ring of dealers in the local cocaine business, which involved Des.	Logically relevant
Authentication	Proof that the document is what the proponent claims it to be.	• The pages of the notebook must be authenticated to be admitted as evidence. Here, Carol testified that the notebook the prosecutor showed her was her notebook, which she used to track her cocaine business. • Carol has authenticated the notebook.	Authenticated
Hearsay	• An out-of-court statement offered for the truth of the matter asserted. • Hearsay is inadmissible unless an exception applies. ○ Hearsay rules apply under Prop 8.	• The notebook is an out-of-court statement since it is a notebook already in existence before the trial. • It is being offered for the truth of the notations in the notebook about who Carol sold cocaine to. • The notebook is hearsay and will be excluded unless an exception applies.	Hearsay
Co-conspirator Statement	Hearsay exception. A co-conspirator admission is a statement made by a co-conspirator of a party, during the course of the conspiracy, and in furtherance of the conspiracy.	• Des is accused of possessing cocaine with an intent to distribute from Jan. through Oct. 2019. In the notebook, Carol notes she sold to Des from May to Oct. 2019. • Here, Carol and Des conspired to buy and sell cocaine. Carol's notations were made contemporaneously during the course of the conspiracy from January–October 2019.	Admissible as the admission of a co-conspirator

Continued>

Issue	Rule	Fact Application	Conclusion
Co-conspirator Statement (continued)		• **The notations were also made in furtherance of the conspiracy to track her business of buying and selling cocaine, an illegal substance.** • However, since Carol's notes do not reflect the conspiracy with Des from Jan. to April on pages 1-2, those pages should arguably not be admitted. • **Pages 3-4 of the notebook can come in as a co-conspirator admission as an exception to hearsay.**	
Business Record Hearsay Exception	Hearsay exception, admissible if it: • **Records a business activity event** • **Regular practice to keep record** • **Made by a person with knowledge (business duty to report)** • **At or near time of matters indicated**	• **Here, Carol dutifully recorded her cocaine business income and expenses in her notebook as each sale occurred.** • **It seems it was Carol's regular practice to track such records, had knowledge of the events as they transpired,** and it was her business, so she had a **business duty** to herself **to report** the business. • Likely notations were made at or near the time of the events. • However, Des can argue it may not qualify as a business record since it is recording an illegal enterprise and there was no motivation to keep accurate records.	Likely will qualify as a business record
Confrontation Clause	A defendant has a right to confront their accusers.	• Des has the opportunity to confront Carol since she has taken the stand here, so the Confrontation Clause will not provide a bar to the admission of the notes.	Not a bar
Balancing Test (CEC 352)	**The court has discretion to exclude evidence if its probative value is substantially outweighed by the danger of unfair prejudice, confusion of issues, misleading the jury, or wasting time.**	• **Pages 3-4 of the notebook are highly probative of Des' involvement as a cocaine distributor, and are not unfairly prejudicial since they characterize Des' involvement in the cocaine business.** • **However, pages 1-2 of the notebook are not highly probative of** Des's involvement since there are no notations of him transacting over cocaine during that time. Since Des has been charged going back to January, this may be **unfairly prejudicial** since it implies Des was involved in distributing with Carol from January-April, even though his involvement is not reflected in her notebook.	The court correctly admitted pages 3-4, but erred in admitting pages 1-2
Evidence of Des's conviction for forgery?			
Relevance	**Evidence is relevant if material to a disputed fact.**	• Des was convicted of forgery, which reflects on his truthfulness since it is a crime of dishonesty or moral turpitude. Here, while Des is charged with cocaine distribution and it is unrelated to forgery, Des has testified in his own defense, so his trustworthiness is relevant.	Logically relevant

Continued>

Issue	Rule	Fact Application	Conclusion
Character–Prior Conviction	Character evidence is generally not admissible to prove conduct in conformity with that character trait on a particular occasion.	• Des has not opened the door to other traits of his character, besides his honesty, so character evidence may not be admitted to establish Des's bad character, and he acted in conformity with his bad character.	Character evidence
Impeachment	**A witness may be impeached with convictions for crimes involving dishonesty or false statements.**	• **Here, Des has testified, so he is putting his character for truthfulness at issue since the honesty of a witness is always in issue. Des took the stand and denied the charge, so his character for honesty is at issue.** • **One can be impeached by a prior criminal conviction. Here, Des was convicted of felony forgery 11 years ago. Forgery is a crime involving dishonesty** as an element of the crime itself, which has much bearing on Des's truthfulness. • **Under the federal rules, a conviction may not be admitted if the conviction is over 10 years old, but California does not impose a time limit for remoteness.**	**Prior conviction admissible**
Balancing Test (CEC 352)	**Relevant evidence can still be excluded if its probative value is substantially outweighed by its prejudicial value.** Prop 8 allows the balancing test.	• **Age of conviction, 11 years old weighs against admission since it is remote in time and potentially less probative of Des' current trustworthiness. However, a fraud conviction, even an older one, is very probative of Des' truthfulness.** • The risk of unfair prejudice is that the jury would brand Des a criminal and thus he must be guilty of this crime, too, rather than just weigh the conviction as evidence of his truthfulness. • On balance, unfair prejudice does not substantially outweigh the probative value of the conviction.	**The court did not err in admitting the forgery conviction**
Did the court properly deny the assertion of attorney-client privilege?			
Attorney-Client Privilege	**A client has a right not to allow disclosure of confidential communications between attorney and client relating to their professional relationship.** Prop 8 allows attorney-client privilege.	• Here, Carol was asked if she was offered a reduced sentence in exchange for her testimony, and she said "no." • The court denied Abe's claim of attorney-client privilege, and Abe testified Carol was offered a reduction in charges in exchange for testifying. • **Here, Pete the prosecutor offered Carol a deal, which she took. Any conversations with Pete are not confidential since he is a 3rd party. Abe is not being asked about any confidential communication between him and Carol, rather he is being asked about the fact that Carol accepted a reduction in charges in exchange for her testimony.** • Had Abe been asked about his private conversations with Carol regarding the deal, it would have fallen within the privilege, but that is not what was asked here. • **The court did not err in allowing Abe's testimony.**	**The court did not err in allowing Abe's testimony**

Evidence Question 1 Sample Answer
February 2020, Question 4

Prop 8

Prop. 8 is known as the "Victim's Bill of Rights" in California and provides that all relevant evidence is admissible in criminal trials, subject to several exemptions including rules of evidence relating to the U.S. Constitution, hearsay, character, privileges existing in 1982, exclusions after 1982 ratified by 2/3 vote of legislature, and CEC 352.

Here, Des is charged with possession with intent to distribute hundreds of pounds of cocaine and Prop. 8 applies.

Assuming all credible objections were timely made, did the court properly admit: Pages 1-4 of the notes?

Relevance

All evidence must be relevant. Evidence is relevant if it tends to be material to a disputed fact.

Here, the disputed fact is Des' involvement in the cocaine business. Carol's notebook is logically relevant since it shows Carol's knowledge and tracking of the ring of dealers in the local cocaine business, in which Des was a distributor.

Authentication

Documents must be authenticated to be admissible, which is proof that the document is what the proponent claims it to be.

The pages of Carol's notebook must be authenticated to be admitted as evidence. Here, Carol testified that the notebook the prosecutor showed her was her notebook, which she used to track her cocaine business. Carol has authenticated the notebook.

Hearsay

Hearsay is an out of court statement offered for the truth of the matter asserted. Hearsay is inadmissible unless an exception applies. Hearsay rules apply under Prop 8.

Here, the notebook is an out of court statement since it is a notebook already in existence before the trial. It is being offered for the truth of the notations made in the notebook about who Carol sold cocaine to. The notebook is hearsay and will be excluded unless an exception applies.

Co-conspirator Statement

A co-conspirator admission is a hearsay exception. It is a statement made by a co-conspirator of a party, made during the course of the conspiracy, and in furtherance of the conspiracy.

Here, Des is accused of possessing cocaine with an intent to distribute from Jan. through Oct. 2019. In her notebook, Carol notes that she sold cocaine to Des from May to Oct. 2019. Carol and Des conspired to buy and sell cocaine and the details are noted in Carol's notebook. Carol's notations were made contemporaneously during the course of the conspiracy from January-October 2019. The notations were also made in furtherance of the conspiracy to track her cocaine ring business of buying and selling cocaine, an illegal substance. However, since Carol's notes do not reflect the conspiracy with Des from Jan. to April on pages 1-2, those pages should arguably not be admitted. Pages 3-4 of the notebook should come in as a co-conspirator admission as an exception to hearsay.

Carol's notebook pages 3-4 are admissible as the admission of a co-conspirator.

Business Record

A business record can be a hearsay exception and admissible if it records a business activity event, was a regular practice to keep a record, made by a person with knowledge, and made at or near time of matters indicated.

Here, Carol dutifully recorded her cocaine business income and expenses in her notebook as each sale occurred. It seems it was Carol's regular practice to track such records, had knowledge of the events as they transpired, and since it was her business, she had a business duty to herself to report on the business. Likely the notations were made at or near the time of the events.

However, Des can argue the notebook may not qualify as a business record since it is recording an illegal enterprise and there was no motivation to keep accurate records, which defeats the purpose of the business records hearsay exception.

Nonetheless, likely the notebook will qualify as a business record and be admissible.

Confrontation Clause

A defendant has a right to confront their accusers.

Here, this right is not implicated since Des had the opportunity to confront Carol. She has taken the stand here, so the Confrontation Clause will not provide a bar to the admission of the notes.

Balancing Test (CEC 352)

The court has discretion to exclude evidence if its probative value is substantially outweighed by the danger of unfair prejudice, confusion of issues, misleading the jury, or wasting time. Prop 8 allows the balancing test.

Here, pages 3-4 of the notebook are highly probative of Des' involvement as a cocaine distributor, and while prejudicial since they implicate Des, they are not unfairly so since if accurate, they characterize the facts of Des' involvement in the cocaine business.

However, pages 1-2 of the notebook are not highly probative of Des's involvement since there are no notations of him transacting with Carol for cocaine during that time. Since Des has been charged with distribution going back to January, it may be unfairly prejudicial to include pages 1-2 since it implies that Des was involved in distributing with Carol from January-April, as charged, even though his involvement during that time is not reflected in her notebook.

The court correctly admitted pages 3-4, but erred in admitting pages 1-2 of the notebook.

Evidence of Des's conviction for forgery?

Relevance

Evidence is relevant if material to a disputed fact.

Des was convicted of forgery, which reflects on his truthfulness since it is a crime of dishonesty or moral turpitude. Here, while Des is charged with cocaine distribution and it is unrelated to forgery, Des has testified in his own defense, so his trustworthiness is logically relevant.

Character — Prior Conviction

Character evidence is generally not admissible to prove conduct in conformity with that character trait on a particular occasion.

Here, Des has not opened the door to other traits of his character, besides his honesty by testifying, so character evidence may not be admitted to establish that Des has bad character, and that he acted in conformity with his bad character.

Impeachment

A witness may be impeached with convictions for crimes involving dishonesty or false statements.

Here, Des has testified, so he has put his character for truthfulness at issue since the honesty of a witness is always in issue. Des took the stand and denied the charges against him, so his character for honesty is at issue. A witness can be impeached by a prior criminal conviction. Here, Des was convicted of felony forgery 11 years ago. Forgery is a crime involving dishonesty as an element of the crime itself, which has much bearing on Des's truthfulness since he has been adjudicated a liar by a court.

Under the federal rules, a conviction may not be admitted if the conviction is over 10 years old, subject to a balancing test, but California does not impose a time limitation which excludes consideration of a conviction for remoteness.

The prior forgery conviction is admissible.

Balancing Test (CEC 352)

Relevant evidence can still be excluded if its probative value is substantially outweighed by its prejudicial value.

Here, the age of the conviction, at 11 years old, weighs against admission since it is remote in time and potentially less probative of Des' current level of trustworthiness. However, a fraud conviction, even an older one, is highly probative of Des' truthfulness.

The risk of unfair prejudice is high in that the jury would brand Des a criminal and thus he must be guilty of this crime of cocaine distribution, too, rather than just weigh the previous conviction as evidence regarding the truthfulness of his testimony.

On balance, the risk of unfair prejudice does not substantially outweigh the high probative value of the conviction. The court did not err in admitting the forgery conviction.

Did the court properly deny the assertion of attorney-client privilege?

Attorney-client Privilege

A client has a right not to allow disclosure of confidential communications between the attorney and client relating to their professional relationship. Prop 8 allows attorney-client privilege.

Here, Carol was asked if she was offered a reduced sentence in exchange for her testimony, and she said "no." The prosecutor called Abe, Carol's attorney, and then denied Abe's claim of attorney-client privilege. Subsequently, Abe testified that Carol was offered a reduction in charges in exchange for testifying. Pete, the prosecutor, offered Carol a deal, which she accepted. Any conversations between Carol and Abe and Pete are not confidential since he is a 3rd party. Abe is not being asked about any confidential communication between him and Carol, rather he is being asked about the fact that Carol accepted a reduction in charges in exchange for her testimony. Had Abe been asked about his private conversations with Carol regarding the deal, it would have fallen within the privilege, but that is not what was asked here, so it does not.

The court did not err in allowing Abe's testimony.

Evidence Question 2
February 2023, Question 5

Pedro brought a fraud and breach of contract action against Gallery in federal court.

At a jury trial, Pedro testified that he purchased a painting from Gallery for $200,000 after seeing an advertisement bearing Gallery's logo stating that the painting was the only painting by a noted 17th century artist available for sale in the world. On Pedro's motion, a photocopy of the advertisement was admitted into evidence. Pedro also testified that the painting was worth only $10,000 because it was a reproduction of the original and that he based his valuation on the average of three appraisals of the painting by art dealers.

Pedro called Rex, a chemistry professor, who had been retained by four art galleries to determine the age of paintings. Rex testified that the painting had been painted within the past 50 years and was a painted reproduction of the original painting. He testified that he had used the XYZ technique on Pedro's painting to arrive at his conclusion. Rex testified that he had tested the XYZ technique on paintings of known ages and that the results corresponded with their known age. He testified that the XYZ technique was reliable and used by most experts to determine the age of paintings. After cross-examination, Rex was excused and left the courtroom.

Gallery called Marie, and both parties stipulated that she is an expert in dating works of art. She testified that a publication entitled "The Science of Dating Works of Art" is generally recognized as a reliable authority. She then quoted an excerpt from that publication that asserted the XYZ technique is not reliable for determining the age of works of art. Gallery moved, and the court received, the excerpt into evidence as an exhibit.

Gallery then offered into evidence a journal article authored by Rex that included a statement that the XYZ technique is not reliable for determining the age of works of art.

Assuming all proper objections and motions to strike were timely made, should the court have admitted:

1. The photocopy of the advertisement? Discuss.

2. Pedro's testimony about the value of the painting? Discuss.

3. Rex's testimony about the age of the painting? Discuss.

4. The excerpt from "The Science of Dating Works of Art"? Discuss.

5. Rex's journal article? Discuss.

Answer according to the Federal Rules of Evidence.

Evidence Question 2 Assessment
February 2023, Question 5

This is a typical evidence question, but this one asks the applicant to answer using the Federal Rules of Evidence. There are just under twenty issues to discuss covering five different pieces of evidence, so it is a racehorse as expected where a large quantity of issues must be covered. In addition to testing the rules for evidence, they also put your issue spotting ability and time management skills to the test on all evidence questions.

One thing that is very typical about this question is that you are analyzing the same rules over and over in relation to different pieces of evidence. For example, logical relevance is at issue for each of the five items of evidence. Hearsay is at issue for three of the items of evidence, with a variety of different hearsay exceptions present. Since timing is often a problem in an evidence essay, we recommend practicing writing a truncated IRAC and have provided a sample of what that looks like in this sample answer for the issues of relevance, witness competence, and hearsay. After you have introduced a rule once, like logical relevance in the first call, thereafter instead of writing out the full rule for relevance in IRAC form when it comes up in call two, make a heading for relevance (the "I" for your IRAC), but then skip straight to the analysis. Use the key terms from the logical relevance rule (more or less probable and fact) and explain specifically how the evidence in question has a tendency to make a fact more or less probable than it would be without the evidence (the "R" and "A" for your IRAC). For example, in call two, there is not a stand-alone rule for relevance. Instead, after the relevance header the analysis says in full, "Pedro brought an action for fraud asserting the painting he bought from Gallery was not a rare original by a 17th century artist as advertised, so the advertisement has a tendency to to show that it is *more probable than not* that the gallery made the representations about the painting and is relevant." This one sentence identifies the *key terms from the rule*, explains how the facts from the question prove up the rule, and concludes. The one sentence efficiently combines the "RAC" from the IRAC all in one sentence.

Writing a truncated IRAC is an important skill to have available in your arsenal to use in bar essays, and evidence questions are the perfect place to practice them because you can likely use them in every practice question. You do need to be strategic about where you use a truncated IRAC since it is only appropriate to use them on "slam dunk" type issues. However, those types of minor issues are never worth very many points, but they still need to be included to fully analyze and answer a question. So, how do you know when to use a truncated IRAC? There are two times: 1.) If virtually every applicant will say the same thing in answer on an issue because the fact is not in dispute and easy to establish, that issue is a minor issue. Minor issues are not the place where a grader looks carefully. If you can quickly answer the minor issues using a truncated IRAC, then you bought yourself some time to spend on the major issues where there are more facts to use, or lots of factual ambiguity, or two-sided analysis since those areas are where the big points are. You want to do a great job on the major issues, and strategic use of a truncated IRAC can buy you the time to do just that. 2.) If you are running out of time to answer a question. If you have misjudged your time and know you can't get to everything, take the last five minutes and write a quick truncated IRAC on all remaining issues. It is much better to include an issue, even if you didn't do a great job on it, than to leave an issue off your answer. For each issue, write a heading (so it is easy for the grader to see you included it) and then jump right to the point in a quick analytical sentence that combines the key rule elements with the facts that prove that rule/element. You will at least get partial credit, and if all the other applicants ran out of time, too, your answer will be better than most. Remember, the essays are graded on a curve, so you just need to write a better answer than the other guy.

Make note of the areas highlighted in bold on the corresponding grid. The **bold** areas highlight the issues, analysis, and conclusions that are likely **required** to receive a passing score on this question.

Issue	Rule	Fact Application	Conclusion
The photocopy of the advertisement?			
Relevance	**Evidence is relevant if it has any tendency to** make a fact **more or less probable** than it would be without it and the fact is **of consequence** in determining the action.	• Pedro brought an action for fraud asserting the painting he bought from Gallery was not an original as advertised, so the advertisement has a tendency to make it more probable than not that the representations by the gallery weren't accurate.	Logically relevant
Authentication	**Proof that the document is what the** proponent claims it to be.	• Pedro provided testimony of the advertisement with the Gallery logo, which is sufficient to authenticate it.	Authenticated
Best Evidence Rule	**To prove contents of a writing the original must be introduced (copy ok).**	• A photocopy, like Pedro is introducing here, is acceptable to prove the contents of a writing, here the advertisement, unless there is some dispute as to its accuracy. • The advertisement satisfies the best evidence rule.	Satisfied
Hearsay	**An out of court statement offered for the truth of the matter asserted.**	• The advertisement is a communication from out of court, and it is being offered to assert the truth of the contents of the advertisement. • It will be excluded as hearsay, unless an exception allows it in.	Hearsay
Independent Legal Significance	**A statement that itself has legal significance is not hearsay.**	• However, there is an exception if the statement is being admitted for a non-hearsay purpose, such as here where the advertisement itself has legal significance as the false statement, which is an element of the underlying fraud case. • The advertisement is admissible.	Satisfied
Admission of Party Opponent	**Any statement by a party opponent is admissible.**	• The advertisement can also be admitted as the statement of a party opponent since it is Gallery's advertisement.	Satisfied
Pedro's testimony about the value of the painting?			
Relevance	**Evidence is relevant if it has any tendency to** make a fact **more or less probable** than it would be without it and the fact is **of consequence** in determining the action.	• The true value of the painting has a tendency to make it more probable than not that Gallery engaged in a fraudulent misrepresentation about the painting's rare origins as a 17th century original worth $200,000.	Logically relevant
Competence — Personal Knowledge	**A witness must have personal knowledge of facts to which they are attesting.**	• Pedro's estimation of the value is based on information he obtained from three others and is not based on his own personal knowledge.	Not established

Continued>

Issue	Rule	Fact Application	Conclusion
Lay Opinion	Lay opinion is admissible only if it is rationally based on the witness's perceptions and **helpful to the trier of the fact** and not based on specialized knowledge.	• **Pedro also testified that the painting was worth only $10,000 because it was a reproduction of the original and that he based his valuation on the average of three appraisals of the painting made by art dealers.** • While a valuation of the painting would be helpful to the trier of fact, **this opinion is not based on Pedro's perceptions**, but rather is specialized knowledge he based on **information he learned from other appraisers and averaged together.**	Improper lay opinion
Hearsay	An out-of-court statement offered for the truth of the matter asserted.	• The appraisals are out of court statements being offered for their truth, the valuations of the painting, and they are hearsay and inadmissible. • If the appraisals were in writing, the documents themselves should be admitted, not testimony about their contents.	Hearsay with no exception
Rex's testimony about the age of the painting?			
Relevance	Evidence is relevant if it has any tendency to make a fact more or less probable than it would be without it and the fact is of consequence in determining the action.	• **Information about the age of the painting has a tendency to make it more probable than not that the Gallery made misrepresentations about the painting's rare origins.**	Logically relevant
Competence	A witness must have personal knowledge of facts to which they are attesting.	• Rex is a chemistry professor who is an expert in dating paintings, so he is testifying about facts within his personal knowledge.	Established
Expert Opinion	Expert opinion is admissible if: • **Assists trier of fact,** • **Witness is qualified,** • **Based on sufficient facts,** • **Used reliable principle and methods, and** • **Applied principles reliably to facts of case.**	• **Information about the age of the painting will assist the trier of fact in determining if a fraud has occurred since the age was** allegedly misrepresented. • **As a chemistry professor who had been retained by four art galleries to determine the age of paintings, Rex is qualified as an expert.** • Rex based his opinion on the sufficient facts of evaluating the painting and using XYZ technique. • **Rex used the XYZ technique to determine the age of the painting and testified that the XYZ technique was reliable and used by most experts to determine the age of paintings.** • Rex testified that he had tested the XYZ technique on paintings of known ages and that the results corresponded with their known age, so presumably he applied the same principles reliably to this painting. • However, while it was apparently not raised while Rex was on the stand, the reliability of XYZ is in dispute since the publication, "The Science of Dating Works of Art," states XYZ is not reliable. Further, Rex himself authored a journal article saying XYZ was not reliable for determining the age of art. (see below)	**Expert opinion likely allowed**

(Continued>)

Issue	Rule	Fact Application	Conclusion
The excerpt from "The Science of Dating Works of Art"?			
Relevance	Evidence is relevant if it has any tendency to make a fact more or less probable than it would be without it and the fact is **of consequence** in determining the action	• The excerpt can be used to make it more probable than not that the XYZ technique is not reliable and impeach Rex, so it is relevant.	Logically relevant
Authentication	Proof that the document is what the proponent claims it to be.	• Marie, as an expert in dating works of art, testified that a publication entitled, "The Science of Dating Works of Art" is generally recognized as a reliable authority.	Authenticated
Hearsay	An out-of-court statement offered for the truth of the matter asserted.	• The contents of the publication are out of court statements, which are being offered for their truth that XYZ is unreliable. It is inadmissible hearsay unless an exception applies.	**Hearsay**
Learned Treatise Hearsay Exception	Scientific texts and treatises may be admitted for substantive truth if reliable authority.	• Here, Marie is a reliable expert, and the contents of the publication can be admitted. The excerpts that the XYZ technique is not reliable for determining the age of works of art can be admitted and should be read to the jury, rather than admitted as evidence.	**Learned Treatise**
Rex's journal article?			
Relevance	Evidence is relevant if it has any tendency to make a fact more or less probable than it would be without it and the fact is **of consequence** in determining the action.	• The article has a tendency to make it more probable than not that the XYZ technique is not good practice, and that **Rex is a liar and is relevant.**	Logically relevant
Best Evidence Rule Authentication	To prove contents of a writing the original must be introduced.	• A journal article can be self-authenticating.	**Authenticated**
Hearsay	An out-of-court statement offered for the truth of the matter asserted.	• The statements in the article were made out of court and are being offered to prove XYZ is unreliable, so it is hearsay and excluded unless an exception applies.	**Hearsay**
Learned Treatise Hearsay Exception	Scientific texts and treatises may be admitted for substantive truth if reliable authority.	• It is unclear if the journal article, authored by Rex, is considered reliable authority. If so, the contents may be read to the jury.	Admissible
Prior Inconsistent Statement Hearsay Exception Impeachment	• A prior inconsistent statement is **substantively admissible if made under oath** in a formal proceeding and subject to cross examination. • A prior inconsistent statement can be admitted to impeach if the witness is given an opportunity to explain or deny the statement.	• Here, **Rex's statement in the journal** that the XYZ technique is not reliable for determining the age of works of art is **inconsistent with his testimony on the stand.** • However, since it was not made under oath, the contents of the article **cannot be admitted substantively** as a prior inconsistent statement. • Had Rex been asked about this on the stand, it could have been admitted to impeach Rex by his own prior inconsistent statement.	Not admissible

Evidence Question 2 Sample Answer
February 2023, Question 5

The photocopy of the advertisement?

Relevance

Evidence must be relevant to be admissible. Evidence is relevant if it has any tendency to make a fact more or less probable and is of consequence to the action.

Pedro brought an action for fraud asserting the painting he bought from Gallery was not a rare original by a 17th century artist as advertised, so the advertisement has a tendency to to show that it is more probable than not that the gallery made the representations about the painting and is relevant.

Authentication

Authentication must be done to prove that the document is what the proponent claims it to be. Pedro provided testimony about the advertisement with the Gallery logo, which is sufficient to authenticate it.

Best Evidence Rule

To prove contents of a writing the original must be introduced, but a photocopy is acceptable unless the accuracy is disputed.

A photocopy of the advertisement, like Pedro is introducing here, is acceptable to prove the contents of the writing, unless there is some dispute as to its accuracy. Therefore, the advertisement satisfies the best evidence rule.

Hearsay

Hearsay is an out of court statement offered for the truth of the matter asserted. It is inadmissible unless there is an exception.

The advertisement is a communication which occurred out of court, and it is being offered to assert the truth of the contents of the advertisement. Thus, it is hearsay and will be excluded, unless an exception applies.

Independent Legal Significance

A statement that itself has independent legal significance is not considered hearsay.

Pedro has accused Gallery of fraud. The misrepresentation about the origins of the painting were contained in the advertisement. When the statement is being admitted for a non-hearsay purpose, such as here where the advertisement itself has independent legal significance as the false misrepresentation, which is an element and the basis for of the underlying fraud case, it is admissible.

Admission of Party Opponent

Any statement by a party opponent is admissible.

Here, the advertisement can also be admitted as the statement of a party opponent since it is Gallery's advertisement.

The photocopy of the advertisement should have been admitted.

Pedro's testimony about the value of the painting?

Relevance

The true value of the painting has a tendency to make it more probable than not that Gallery engaged in a fraudulent misrepresentation about the painting's rare origins as a 17th century original worth $200,000, so it is relevant.

Competence-Personal knowledge

A witness must have personal knowledge of the facts to which they are attesting.

Here, Pedro's estimation of the value of the painting is based on information he obtained from three art dealers, so it is not based on his own personal knowledge.

Lay Opinion

Lay opinion is admissible only if it is rationally based on the witness' perceptions, helpful to the trier of the fact, and not based on specialized knowledge.

Pedro also testified that the painting was worth only $10,000 because it was a reproduction of the original and that he based his valuation by averaging the value of three appraisals made of the painting by art dealers. While a valuation of the painting would be helpful to the trier of fact since this dispute is about the value of the painting, this opinion is not based on Pedro's perceptions at all. Rather, Pedro's opinion is based on information he learned from three other appraisers, who have specialized knowledge, which he then averaged together. As such, it is improper lay opinion and should not have been admitted.

Hearsay

The appraisals are out of court statements, and they are being offered for their truth, which is the valuations of the paintings, thus they are hearsay and inadmissible. If the appraisals were made in writing, the documents themselves should be admitted, not testimony about their contents. Information about the appraisals is hearsay with no exception and should not be admitted.

Pedro's testimony about the value of the painting should not have been admitted.

Rex's testimony about the age of the painting?

Relevance

Information about the age of the painting has a tendency to make it more probable than not that the Gallery made misrepresentations about the painting's rare origins and is relevant.

Competence

A witness must have personal knowledge of facts to which they are attesting. Here, Rex is a chemistry professor who is an expert in dating paintings, so he is testifying about facts within his personal knowledge.

Expert Opinion

An expert opinion is admissible if it assists the trier of fact, the witness is qualified as an expert, is based on sufficient facts, the expert used reliable principles and methods, and those methods were applied reliably to facts of case.

Here, information about the age of the painting will assist the trier of fact in determining if a fraud has occurred since the age of the painting was allegedly misrepresented. As a chemistry professor who had been retained by four art galleries to determine the age of paintings, Rex is qualified as an expert in dating paintings. Rex based his opinion on the sufficient facts by evaluating the painting using XYZ technique. Rex used the XYZ technique to determine the age of the painting and also testified as an expert that the XYZ technique was reliable and used by most experts to determine the age of paintings. Rex testified here that he had tested the XYZ technique on paintings of known ages and that the results corresponded with their known age, so presumably he applied the same principles reliably to this painting.

However, while the issue was apparently not raised while Rex was on the stand, the reliability of the XYZ technique is in dispute since the publication, "The Science of Dating Works of Art," states XYZ is not reliable, and Rex himself authored a journal article saying XYZ was not reliable for determining the age of art. (see below)

It is likely the expert opinion of Rex is allowed.

Rex's testimony about the age of the painting should have been admitted.

The excerpt from "The Science of Dating Works of Art"?

Relevance

The excerpt from the publication can be used to prove that it is more probable than not that the XYZ technique is not reliable and to impeach Rex, so it is relevant.

Authentication

Marie, as an expert in dating works of art testified that a publication entitled "The Science of Dating Works of Art" is generally recognized as a reliable authority, so it is authenticated.

Hearsay

The contents of the publication are out of court statements, which are being offered here for their truth that XYZ is unreliable. Therefore, it is inadmissible hearsay unless an exception applies.

Learned Treatise

Scientific texts and treatises may be admitted for their substantive truth if they are reliable authority.

Here, Marie is a reliable expert and the contents of the publication can be admitted for their substantive truth. The excerpts that the XYZ technique is not reliable for determining the age of works of art can be admitted and should be read to the jury, rather than admitted as evidence.

The publication should have been admitted.

Rex's journal article?

Relevance

Rex's article has a tendency to show that it is more probable than not that the XYZ technique is not good practice, and that Rex is a liar, which is relevant since he is a testifying witness and stated that the XYZ technique is good practice for dating art.

Best Evidence Rule
Authentication

To prove contents of a writing the original must be introduced. A journal article is a publication that can be self-authenticating.

Hearsay

The statements in the article are made out of court and are being offered to prove that the XYZ technique is unreliable, so the article is hearsay and should be excluded unless an exception applies.

Learned Treatise Hearsay Exception

It is unclear if the journal article, authored by Rex, is considered a reliable authority. If so, the contents may be read to the jury as a hearsay exception for a learned treatise.

Prior Inconsistent Statement Hearsay Exception

A prior inconsistent statement is substantively admissible if it was made under oath in a formal proceeding and subject to cross examination.

Here, Rex's statement in the journal article that the XYZ technique is not reliable for determining the age of works of art is inconsistent with his testimony on the stand. However, since the statement in the article was not made under oath, the contents of the article cannot be admitted substantively as a prior inconsistent statement.

Impeachment

A prior inconsistent statement can be admitted to impeach a witness, but the witness must be given an opportunity to explain or deny the statement.

Had Rex been asked about this on the stand, the article could have been admitted to impeach Rex by his own prior inconsistent statement.

The journal article should have been admitted if it is considered a reliable authority.

Evidence Question 3
July 2009, Question 3

While driving their cars, Paula and Dan collided and each suffered personal injuries and property damage. Paula sued Dan for negligence in a California state court and Dan filed a cross-complaint for negligence against Paula. At the ensuing jury trial, Paula testified that she was driving to meet her husband, Hank, and that Dan drove his car into hers. Paula also testified that, as she and Dan were waiting for an ambulance immediately following the accident, Dan said, "I have plenty of insurance to cover your injuries." Paula further testified that, three hours after the accident, when a physician at the hospital to which she was taken asked her how she was feeling, she said, "My right leg hurts the most, all because that idiot Dan failed to yield the right-of-way."

Officer, who was the investigating police officer who responded to the accident, was unavailable at the trial. The court granted a motion by Paula to admit Officer's accident report into evidence. Officer's accident report states: "When I arrived at the scene three minutes after the accident occurred, an unnamed bystander immediately came up to me and stated that Dan pulled right out into the path of Paula's car. Based on this information, my interviews with Paula and Dan, and the skid marks, I conclude that Dan caused the accident." Officer prepared his accident report shortly after the accident.

In his case-in-chief, Dan called a paramedic who had treated Paula at the scene of the accident. Dan showed the paramedic a greeting card, and the paramedic testified that he had found the card in Paula's pocket as he was treating her. The court granted a motion by Dan to admit the card into evidence. The card states: "Dearest Paula, Hurry home from work as fast as you can today. We need to get an early start on our weekend trip to the mountains! Love, Hank."

Dan testified that, as he and Paula were waiting for the ambulance immediately following the accident, Wilma handed him a note. Wilma had been identified as a witness during discovery, but had died before she could be deposed. The court granted a motion by Dan to admit the note into evidence. The note says: "I saw the whole thing. Paula was speeding. She was definitely negligent."

Assuming all appropriate objections were timely made, should the court have admitted:

1. Dan's statement to Paula about insurance? Discuss.

2. Paula's statement to the physician? Discuss.

3. Officer's accident report relating to:

   a. The unnamed bystander's statement? Discuss.

   b. Officer's conclusion and its basis? Discuss.

4. Hank's greeting card? Discuss.

5. Wilma's note? Discuss.

Answer according to California law.

Evidence Question 3 Assessment
July 2009, Question 3

This question is one of the most difficult evidence questions, but it is still a good practice question. This is a super racehorse question since there are more than 30 issues to analyze. It is even more challenging when you realize it was the last question of the morning session (when students received all three morning questions at once) and if a student had mismanaged their time earlier in the day, it would be almost impossible to finish this question. While there were many issues, not all the potential analysis was critical to succeeding on this question. Once again, successful issue spotting is the key to a passing score, as you can see by noting the bold areas in the attached grid.

One of the first things to do is determine which rules to use to answer the question. Here, at the end of the question you are instructed to use California law.

Though we typically recommend using a traditional IRAC format for essay answers on the other subjects, evidence essays do not lend themselves to using a perfect IRAC format for all issues — there simply isn't a sufficient amount of time. Practice weaving together the rules, factual analysis, and conclusion in one or two sentences (depending on the complexity) and doing a truncated analysis.

When organizing the essay, make note of the areas where there actually is some substance to the factual analysis. This will typically be in those areas where there are a lot of facts to use, or something pivotal is happening. If you aren't sure, asking yourself what the point of each paragraph is should help to sharpen your focus. For example, in this question the key analytical focus should be on a few big issues: the prejudicial impact of the statement regarding liability insurance in call 1; the possible ways of getting the statement made to the doctor into evidence in call 2; the double hearsay, the spontaneous bystander statement (because there were so many facts to use right on point), and the officer's lack of foundation as an expert in call 3; the nonhearsay purpose for entering the card in call 4; and the improper lay opinion regarding an ultimate issue in call 5. When writing, pay a bit more attention to the analysis in these areas. For all other issues the analysis should be truncated. Where there is a multi-part rule but only facts pertaining to one of the elements are available, it is advisable on this type of racehorse question to jump straight to the point and element at issue. Minor issues can be properly dispatched with one well-written sentence.

Make note of the areas highlighted in bold on the corresponding grid. The bold areas highlight the issues, analysis, and conclusions that are likely required to receive a passing score on this question.

Issue	Rule	Fact Application	Conclusion
Prop. 8	**In a Cal. criminal case, all relevant evidence is admissible unless exempt.**	**Here, it is not a criminal case, but civil, so Prop. 8 is not applicable.**	Prop. 8 not applicable
Call #1 (D Stmt. to P)			
Logical Relevance	**Relevant if material to a disputed fact.**	**Shows that D is likely at fault (disputed fact) if he thought his insurance would need to pay.**	Logically relevant
Legal Relevance	**Probative value v. unfair prejudice**	**It was probative to prove D was possibly at fault, but could prejudice a jury because insurance means ability to pay.** [Note: One state-released answer argued this under admission analysis.]	Legally relevant because doesn't rise to unfair prejudice level
Public Policy Exclusion: Liability Insurance	**Inadmissible to prove culpable conduct.** (Admissible to prove ownership, control, or as part of an admission.)	**Statement is not admissible to prove D was negligent or at fault,** but can admit if it shows D's admission of fault (since he expected his insurance to pay).	Not admissible for culpable conduct, but okay if admission
Public Policy Exclusion: Offer to Pay Medical	**Offers to pay medical bills and any admissions made with the offer are inadmissible.**	It was likely not an offer to pay medical bills, but rather just an acknowledgment that P has insurance.	Not an offer to pay medical, so not excluded
Personal Knowledge	Must have personal knowledge of facts.	P was there and D made statement to P.	P has personal knowledge
Hearsay	**Out-of-court statement offered to prove the truth of the matter asserted is inadmissible.**	Here, D's statement was made out of court, but was not likely offered to prove the truth that he had insurance; rather, offered to show that he was likely at fault and believed his insurance would pay due to his fault.	Likely not hearsay
Spontaneous Statement	Made at or near time of startling event.	Car accident is a startling event and statement was made immediately after.	Hearsay exception
Hearsay Exception: Admission	**Party admission:** any statement by a party offered by a party opponent.	**Here, statement was made by P, a party, by D, a party opponent, so it is an admission.**	Even if hearsay, admissible as it is admission
Answer Call of Q		Could have concluded either way depending on above issues	Either way is okay

Continued>

Issue	Rule	Fact Application	Conclusion
Call #2 (P Stmt. to Dr.)			
Logical Relevance	See above	**Shows P's injuries and that D was at fault (disputed fact) because he failed to yield the right of way.**	Logically relevant
Legal Relevance	See above	First part of statement (leg hurt) was probative to show P damages and not prejudicial as that was her injury. Second part of statement (D not yielding) could be prejudicial as it implicates he is at fault and not very probative in that it needs to be verified and need his side of story.	Prejudicial, so likely would not come in [one answer came to opposite conclusion]
Personal Knowledge	See above	P made statement so she is aware of it.	Personal knowledge
Hearsay	See above	• **Statement to physician made out of court** at the hospital, and • Statement 1: P's leg injury offered to prove damage for negligence, • Statement 2: D didn't yield the right of way offered to prove truth, so • **Both statements offered to prove truth**, so inadmissible hearsay.	Both statements inadmissible hearsay unless exception applies
Hearsay Exception: Spontaneous Statement	**Hearsay statement relating to a startling event or condition is admissible when made while declarant was still under the stress of excitement caused by the event or condition.**	• Here, since P was injured and at hospital, P could still be under the stress of excitement caused by accident. • While car accident is a startling event, **P's statement to Dr. was 3 hours after the accident, so possibly not still under the stress of the accident**; likely would have calmed down by then.	Could conclude either way, but likely not still under excitement of accident
Hearsay Exception: State of Mind or Physical Cond. Medical Treatment	• **Hearsay statement of declarant's then-existing physical condition is admissible to show the physical cond.** • **CEC narrow if made for diagnosis or treatment—declarant must be a minor describing child abuse/ neglect.**	• Statement 1 (leg hurts): Made at hospital in response to physician question—likely so physician could treat her; thus, in Cal., **response would not come in as P was not a minor describing child abuse/neglect.** • Statement 2 (D not yielding right of way): Not about physical condition or medical treatment, so not applicable.	Possible exception for 1st part of statement; not for 2nd part
Hearsay Exception: Contemp. Statement	Explaining conduct of declarant made while the declarant was engaged in the conduct.	Statement was made 3 hours after accident, not during conduct, but, perhaps during conduct of receiving medical treatment and describing feelings.	Could go either way

Continued>

Issue	Rule	Fact Application	Conclusion
Answer Call of Q		Court likely improperly admitted the statement.	No
Call #3 (O's Accident Rpt.): a. Bystander Stmt.			
Logical Relevance	See above	Shows D at fault (disputed fact).	Relevant
Legal Relevance	See above	**Probative to show D more likely at fault,** but could be prejudicial as D cannot cross-examine O as to investigation methods and report since O is unavailable at trial.	Prejudicial [one answer came to opposite conclusion]
Personal Knowledge	Witness must have personal knowledge of facts.	Bystander was at scene of accident and witnessed it, so personal knowledge.	Personal knowledge
Hearsay (Double)	See above — need exceptions for both levels	Statement was out of court at scene of accident and offered to prove truth that D was at fault (two statements — bystander and report itself).	Hearsay — inadmissible unless exception
Hearsay Exception: Public Records	Hearsay record of a public office is **admissible if** (i) record describes activities of the office, (ii) **record describes matters observed pursuant to duty imposed by law,** or (iii) factual findings from investigation	Here, record made by O, who had a duty to report details of accident, but the bystander was not under a duty to report any details, so statement by bystander would not come in through report.	No public record exception
Hearsay Exception: Business Record	Hearsay admissible if it is (1) records a business activity event, (2) regular practice to keep record, (3) made by a person with knowledge, (4) at or near time of matters indicated.	Here, police report record of accident kept in course of business, but usually police reports are not admissible under business records as CEC doesn't allow opinions or diagnosis, and report contains police officer opinion of what occurred.	No business record exception
Spontaneous Statement	See above	**Bystander immediately came to O, and O arrived at scene only 3 minutes after accident, so bystander likely still under excitement of accident.**	Hearsay exception, so admissible
Contemporaneous Statement	See above	Here, accident did not involve bystander conduct, so statement not made while bystander was involved in any conduct.	No exception

Continued>

Issue	Rule	Fact Application	Conclusion
Call #3 (O's Accident Rpt.): b. O's Conclusion			
Relevance	See above	Proves D is at fault; see above for prejudicial statement.	See above
Lay Opinion	**Admissible only if rationally based on the witness's perceptions and helpful to the trier of the fact.**	Here, O's opinion is rationally based on perception of interviewing witnesses, skid marks, and accident scene evidence; also helps jury understand where the cars skidded and what others witnessed.	Admissible as lay opinion
Expert Opinion	**Expert opinion is admissible if (1) assists trier of fact, (2) witness is qualified, (3) based on sufficient facts, (4) used reliable principle and methods, and (5) applied principles reliably to facts of case.**	Here, (1) assists jury as indicated above in lay opinion; (2) police office may be qualified to determine skid marks as investigating officer, but **no indication he properly analyzed the skid marks or was qualified expert**; (3) not clear whether O report was based on sufficient facts but had skid marks and witness statements; (4) unclear if O used reliable principle; (5) not clear if applied principles reliably.	**Not expert opinion**
Hearsay	See above	Statement was made out of court shortly after accident and offered to prove truth that O thought D was at fault.	Hearsay inadmissible unless exception
Public Record Exception	See above	O under duty to report his conclusions and based on factual findings (interviews, skid marks, etc.), so they likely could come in.	
Answer Call of Q		Hearsay exception, but may be too prejudicial so court improperly admitted report.	Likely too prejudicial to admit
Call #4 (H Greeting Card)			
Relevance	See above	**Show P may have been at fault, not D (disputed fact).**	Relevant
Hearsay/Nonhearsay	See above	**Statement was made on card out of court, but not to show P and H were going to get an early start on weekend, but to show effect on reader since P may have been speeding to get home.**	Not hearsay
Authentication	**Proof that the document is what the proponent claims it to be.**	Paramedic found note but can't verify that it is in fact a note from H; he can only verify that he found it in P's pocket and its contents, but can't verify H wrote it or that its contents were true.	Likely not authenticated

Continued>

Issue	Rule	Fact Application	Conclusion
Secondary Evidence Rule	Original writing must be produced.	Actual card admitted.	SER okay
Answer Call of Q		Court improperly admitted card.	Shouldn't have admitted
Call #5 (W's Note)			
Logical Relevance	See above	Show that P may have been at fault due to speeding (disputed fact).	Relevant
Legal Relevance	See above	It was probative to show that P may have been at fault, but prejudicial for the same reason. Note was conclusory and P has no opportunity to cross-examine W, as W is dead.	Prejudicial [one answer came to opposite conclusion]
Personal Knowledge	See above	D cannot verify that W wrote the note or observed the accident, only that he received it from her.	No personal knowledge
Hearsay	See above	**W's statement was made out of court at accident scene, and offered to prove P was speeding and at fault (truth of matter).**	Hearsay
Spontaneous Stmt.	See above	Unclear if made at accident during time of event.	Hearsay exception
Lay Opinion	See above	Statement 1: W observed whole thing, so based on her perception; it's likely one can tell if a car is speeding based on other cars or their own speed, but unsure how W knew or observed P speeding, but would be helpful to jury to know if P seemed to be going faster than a normal car should have been going. **Statement 2: W can't make judgment if P was negligent because that is for a jury to decide, not based on W's perception.**	1st statement likely ok as lay opinion2nd statement not ok
Authentication	**See above**	**W personally handed note to D, who can testify as to such,** but cannot verify that W wrote note.	Likely not authenticated
Secondary Evid. Rule	See above	Here, actual note admitted.	SER okay
Answer Call of Q		Court improperly admitted note.	Shouldn't have admitted

Evidence Question 3 Sample Answer
July 2009, Question 3

Prop. 8

All relevant evidence is admissible in a Cal. criminal case, but this is a civil case so Prop. 8 doesn't apply.

Question 1

Logical Relevance

Evidence is relevant if it is material to a disputed fact, and the insurance comment is material to the disputed fact of fault so it's relevant.

Legal Relevance

Relevant evidence may be excluded if its probative value is outweighed by the danger of unfair prejudice. Insurance availability could be probative of fault and, while prejudicial because one could think defendant has deep pockets to pay since insured, it is not unfairly so.

Liability Insurance

Evidence of liability insurance is not admissible to show fault but is allowed to show ownership or control or as part of an admission. For public policy reasons, Dan's statement regarding insurance is not admissible to show culpability, but the court can admit the admission of fault aspect of the statement, which can be inferred from Dan's expectation of paying for damages with his insurance.

Offers to Pay Medicals

Evidence of an offer to pay medical bills and any corresponding admissions are inadmissible for public policy reasons. It is unlikely Dan's statement was an offer to pay medical bills here, but more likely that it was an acknowledgement that he has insurance available to pay.

Personal Knowledge

Paula was present at the scene and has personal knowledge of Dan's statement so she can testify.

Hearsay

Hearsay is an out-of-court statement offered for the truth of the matter asserted and is inadmissible unless subject to an exception. Dan's statement was made out of court at the accident scene but is likely being offered not to prove Dan actually has insurance, but that Dan felt responsible for the accident, so the statement is likely not hearsay.

Spontaneous Statement

A spontaneous statement is a hearsay exception where it is made at or near the time of a startling event and while still under the stress from the event. Dan's statement was made at the startling event of the accident scene, and if the statement is hearsay this exception will apply.

Admission

Any statement made by a party opponent may be admitted. Dan is the party opponent to Paula so his statement at the scene is an admission and admissible.

Dan's statement regarding the insurance should be admitted.

Question 2

Logical Relevance

P's statement to the doctor tends to show the disputed facts of the extent of her injuries and that Dan is at fault for failure to yield.

Legal Relevance

While somewhat probative, the statement about Dan being at fault is also somewhat prejudicial since it establishes the ultimate issue in the case, but it will likely still be admitted. The statement about the leg injury is not prejudicial and allowable.

Personal Knowledge

P's statement is made from her own experience and observation, so she has personal knowledge.

Hearsay

P's statement was made out of court at the hospital. The part about the leg injury is offered for its truth about the extent of her injury. The part about D's failure to yield is also offered for its truth that D was at fault in the accident. Both statements are hearsay and inadmissible unless an exception applies.

Spontaneous Statement

Since P was injured in the accident and her statement was made when she was transported to the hospital by ambulance, she may have still been under the stress of the startling event of the car accident. However, the statement occurred three hours after the accident, so it is likely she had sufficient time to calm down and was not still under the excitement so this hearsay exception will not apply.

State of Mind

This provides a hearsay exception for statements of declarant's then-existing state of mind/bodily condition. In California, the exception is narrowed to statements made for purpose of diagnosis and treatment or it must be a minor child describing child abuse, which is inapplicable here.

Contemporaneous Statement

There is a hearsay exception for one explaining her conduct, if the statement is made at the time declarant is engaged in the conduct. Since P's statement was made three hours after the accident, it was not made at the time P was engaged in the conduct, so this exception will not apply.

There is no applicable hearsay exception, so the court likely improperly admitted P's statement.

Question 3

a. Bystander Statement

Logical Relevance

The bystander statement is relevant to help establish the disputed fact of accident fault.

Legal Relevance

The bystander statement is probative to show D is more likely at fault; however, it is somewhat prejudicial since D can't cross examine O as to the contents of the report since O is unavailable. Nonetheless, the statement is relevant.

Personal Knowledge

The bystander has personal knowledge since she was an eyewitness to the accident.

Hearsay — Double

There are two levels of hearsay: 1) Bystander statement contained in 2) O's report. Both were made out of court at the scene of the accident and offered for their truth of D's fault for the accident. Each hearsay level must have an exception, or the statement/report won't be admissible as hearsay.

Public Records

Record of a public office is admissible if it describes the office activities, describes matters observed pursuant to a duty, or reports investigative findings. Here, O had a duty to prepare his investigation report, but the bystander was under no such duty to report on the accident, so the bystander statement won't qualify under the public records hearsay exception.

Business Records

A business record can also be an exception to the hearsay rule. While the police report records a normal business event, which is a regular practice, made by one with knowledge, and made timely, under the California rule, the record does not qualify if it contains opinions or diagnosis. Since O's report contains opinions, it is inadmissible under this exception also.

Spontaneous Statement

The bystander was on the scene, and when O arrived three minutes after the accident, the bystander immediately gave her statement and was likely still under the excitement of the startling accident that had just occurred. Therefore, the bystander's statement is admissible as a spontaneous statement.

Contemporaneous Statement

Since the accident did not involve any conduct of the bystander, her statement cannot come in as a contemporaneous statement describing her own conduct.

b. O's Conclusion

Relevance

O's conclusions help prove the disputed fact of fault for the accident. Legal relevance is supra.

Lay Opinion

Lay opinion is admissible only if rationally based on witness's perception and is helpful to the trier of fact. O's opinion is based on his perception of interviewing witnesses, observing the scene, skid marks and other accident scene evidence, and would help the jury understand where the cars skidded, and what others witnessed. It is admissible lay opinion.

Expert Opinion

An expert opinion is permissible if it assists the trier of fact, the witness is qualified, the opinion is based on sufficient facts, reliable principles were used, and they were applied reliably to the case facts. A police officer is likely qualified to render an opinion of skid marks, but there is no evidence here he was qualified as an expert or properly analyzed the skid marks. It is unclear if O's report was based on sufficient facts, used reliable principles, or applied them reliably to the facts of the case, but it did contain witness statements and skid mark analysis. Without more details, O's opinion is insufficient as expert testimony.

Hearsay

The report was made out of court and offered for its truth of O's observations regarding accident fault, which were contained in the report, so it is inadmissible unless an exception applies.

Public Record

O was under a business duty to prepare the report and include his findings and observations, so the report should be admissible under the public record exception.

Question 4

Relevance

The greeting card is relevant to establish the disputed fact of fault for the accident because it may show that P was at fault, not D.

Hearsay

The statement is made as an inscription on a greeting card, which is out of court. However, it is not being offered for its truth, that P and H were going to get an early start on the weekend, but rather is being offered to show that P may have been speeding in a rush to get home to start the weekend.

Authentication

In order to be admitted, all documents must be authenticated that they are what they purport to be. The paramedic found the card in P's pocket, but other than that can't verify that H wrote it or that the contents were true, so it will not be admitted since it can't be authenticated.

Secondary Evidence Rule

An original writing must be produced, which can be done here as the actual card was admitted. However, the court should not have admitted the card since it was not properly authenticated.

Question 5

Logical Relevance

W's note is relevant to establish the disputed fact of fault for the accident.

Legal Relevance

W's note is probative of fault but is unduly prejudicial because it is conclusory as to fault and there is no opportunity to question W since she is dead and unavailable to testify.

Personal Knowledge

The note appears to be based on W's observations at the scene.

Hearsay

W's note was made out of court and is being offered for the truth that P was at fault for causing the accident by speeding. The note is inadmissible hearsay unless an exception applies.

Spontaneous Statement

It is unclear if the note was made while under the stress of the startling car accident, so it can't come in as a spontaneous statement.

Lay Opinion

W's statement that she observed the accident and P was speeding is based on her perception, and lay people can typically estimate car speed, though it's unclear the method she used to do so. It is helpful for the jury to know P's car was going fast, so this opinion is acceptable as evidence. W's statement that P was negligent should not be admitted because it is an improper lay opinion since it goes to the ultimate issue the jury is to decide.

Authentication

W personally handed the note to D, and D can so testify. However, D has no way to verify that W actually wrote the note, so it can likely not be properly authenticated.

Secondary Evidence Rule

The original was admitted, so the secondary evidence rule is satisfied. However, the court improperly admitted the note since it couldn't be properly authenticated and was unduly prejudicial.

Evidence Question 4
February 2021, Question 1

On January 15, Paul fell down the stairwell of Dell's Department Store ("Dell"). Paul sued Dell for personal injuries, alleging he fell because one of the steps was broken. The following occurred at a jury trial in the California Superior Court while Dell's manager, Mark, was being examined by Dell's attorney:

QUESTION: Where were you when Paul fell down the stairs?

ANSWER: I was standing nearby with my back to the stairs talking to Carol, a store customer, when I heard the noise of the fall.

(1) QUESTION: Has Paul sued Dell before?

ANSWER: Yes, five times that I personally know about.

(2) QUESTION: No one saw the accident. Right?

ANSWER: That's right. A thorough investigation was unable to find anyone who saw Paul fall on the stairs.

Mark was then cross-examined by Paul's attorney as follows:

(3) QUESTION: Isn't it true that you used to be employed by Paul as a cashier in his grocery store and that he fired you for stealing money from the cash register?

ANSWER: That is what he claimed.

(4) QUESTION: The stairs were repaired the day after Paul fell. Weren't they?

ANSWER: Yes.

(5) QUESTION: Didn't Carol, the store customer, exclaim at the time of the accident: "Oh no! A man just fell on that broken step"?

ANSWER: So, what?

QUESTION: Is this the report that Dell's insurance company prepared following an investigation of the accident?

ANSWER: Yes. That is the report the insurance company gave me. They always prepare a report in case we get sued.

Paul's attorney then moved to enter into evidence the insurance company's report. The report states: "Steps on the stairs at the store are in very poor condition."

   A. What objections could Paul's attorney and Dell's attorney reasonably make to the questions or answers to Mark's testimony numbered (1) to (5) above, and how should the court rule on each objection? Discuss.
   B. What objections could Dell's attorney reasonably make to the motion to enter the insurance company's report into evidence and how should the court rule? Discuss.

Answer according to California law.

Evidence Question 4 Assessment
February 2021, Question 1

This was the first essay question of the day, it is long, and there were predictably a lot of issues to discuss. At a glance you should note you are in a California civil court before you begin issue spotting. It has been a recent trend for the evidence questions to run long, and even exceed one page of text. At the time this question was asked, the exam was administered in person and the bar examiners provided an applicant with all three questions for the morning at the beginning of the three-hour testing block. It would have been challenging not to exceed the one hour per question allotted on this first question, which would have a negative impact on the other morning questions.

In a remote testing situation, applicants answer one question at a time, so there is no chance of going over on time on one question, which then subsequently short-changes the time available for the other questions in the three-hour block. However, it is still imperative to budget your time properly within the one hour per question to ensure you are able to fully answer the question posed in one hour, especially on an evidence question. This means that you should plan to make strategic choices at the outset about how to best spend your time to garner points. In this question, there are six specific calls. While call four is straightforward, all the others have multiple issues to discuss and some issues, like relevance, can be discussed in every call. Budgeting your time properly is crucial to obtaining a passing score.

It is common for an important issue with more sophisticated analysis to be contained in the last call of the question, and that occurs in this question. The last call is about the admissibility of the insurance company report. Both of the state-released answers (which are high scoring passing answers) discussed hearsay and the business records exception. Aside from that they analyzed completely different issues. One answer included the issues of protected attorney work product, and the policy exclusion regarding insurance. The other answer analyzed relevance, authentication, and a vicarious admission. It is unusual to have such divergence in issues between the two released answers, which shows how many issues logically could have been included in a thorough discussion of the last call. We suspect every person who took this question likely felt like they failed it because everyone would have seen some issues that they simply did not have time to analyze. We share this with you to reinforce that these essays are graded on a curve, there is room for a variety of appropriate answers, and it is impossible to know how well you did on any question because it does depend on the answers of the other applicants.

Evidence questions typically involve some role playing to replicate a real court situation. This question is an example of a typical transcript-style evidence question, which consists of a series of questions posed to a witness and the witness's answers to those questions. Here, you are asked to analyze five points in the transcript and the admissibility of the insurance company report. Issues regarding the "form of the question" and "witness competence" are typically present in a transcript style question, so be sure to look for them. Impeachment is also typically at issue, as it is here. Aside from those issues, this question covers other typical evidence issues of relevance, character, hearsay, and various hearsay exceptions.

Pay special note of the bolded areas on the grid since those were the important issues and it would have been impossible to write on all the issues on the grid within the time allotted. A typical student can write approximately 1500 words in a one-hour essay (which is what our sample answers in this book model), but this grid alone contains over 1650 words and the concepts aren't yet written in complete sentences as one must do to write an answer. The grid here provides some guidance and inspiration, but do not be discouraged if you could not write this much in one hour. Few bar takers can.

Make note of the areas highlighted in **bold** on the corresponding grid. The bold areas highlight the issues, analysis, and conclusions that are likely **required** to receive a passing score on this question.

Issue	Rule	Fact Application	Conclusion
Objections to (1) Has Paul sued Dell before?			
Relevance	Evidence is relevant if material to a disputed fact.	• **Paul's prior suit is material to the disputed fact that Paul has some other motive for suing Dell and this suit has no merit.**	Relevant
Character	• **Character evidence is generally not admissible to prove conduct in conformity with that character trait on a particular occasion.** • Character evidence is allowed to show some other purpose, such as motive, intent, and plan or scheme.	• **Here, the question appears to attempt to establish that Paul has prior suits against Dell's that were likely frivolous, which would show Paul has bad character to embellish or lie about an injury claim, which would generally be inadmissible.** • However, there are several other purposes to admit the evidence. The prior suits could show some nefarious intent on Paul's part, such as that his motive for suing is part of a money-making scheme, with this suit being one in a series of frivolous suits.	**Inadmissible character** except the question is allowable to show intent, motive or common scheme.
Balancing Test (CEC 352)	The court has discretion to exclude evidence if its probative value is substantially outweighed by the danger of unfair prejudice, confusion of issues, misleading the jury, or wasting time.	• This evidence is prejudicial to Paul and makes him look bad, but since he sued Dell's five times before it is highly probative as to Paul's motivation for this suit and his veracity.	Legally relevant
Objections to (2) No one saw the accident, right?			
Relevance	Evidence is relevant if material to a disputed fact	• **Whether anyone witnessed the accident is relevant to the material fact of the disputed fact of if Paul is telling the truth about the fall.**	Relevant
Form of Q: Leading	A leading question suggests the question answer.	• Paul's attorney can object to the form of the question as leading since it is phrased in such a way as to suggest to Mark the correct answer to the question. • **The form of the question is improperly leading.**	Leading
Personal Knowledge	A witness must have personal knowledge of facts to which they are attesting.	• Paul's attorney can object that Mark does not have personal knowledge about what he is being asked about, that "no one" saw the accident. However, it may be fair for Mark to testify about the results of the investigation or the basis for his knowledge.	**Lack of personal knowledge**

Continued>

Issue	Rule	Fact Application	Conclusion
Objections to (3) "Isn't it true. . . he fired you. . ."			
Relevance	Evidence is relevant if material to a disputed fact.	• Evidence of Mark being fired by Paul at a previous job is material to the disputed fact of Mark's truthfulness as a witness. Having been fired before by Paul may give Mark a motive to lie.	Relevant
Character	Character evidence is generally not admissible to prove conduct in conformity with that character trait on a particular occasion.	• Paul's attorney is asking Mark about a "prior bad act" of stealing money from the cash register at a previous job to suggest Mark may be angry at Paul and be motivated to lie.	**The question is improper character evidence**
Impeachment Bias Prior Bad Acts	A witness may be impeached for bias. **Can impeach with character evidence** (prior bad acts regarding truthfulness, but not with extrinsic evidence).	• The attorney may try to impeach Mark as being biased against Paul because of the previous firing. • Since Mark testified, he can be impeached. Paul's attorney can ask about Mark's prior bad acts, so long as there is a good faith belief in the basis of the question. However, the attorney may not bring in extrinsic evidence to prove up the prior bad act, so Paul's attorney will be stuck with Mark's answer, which here is, "That is what he claimed." [A passing answer needed some analysis of impeachment.]	**The question can be used to impeach Mark**
Form of Q: Leading	An answer that is non-responsive to the question is not permitted.	• Since Mark is on cross examination, a leading question is proper. • Compound questions, like this one, are improper.	**Leading question allowed**
Hearsay	Hearsay is an out-of-court statement offered for the truth of the matter asserted. Inadmissible unless there is an exception.	• Mark's answer to the question refers to an out-of-court statement (by "they") for the truth of the matter asserted, which is that they claimed Paul fired Mark from his grocery store for stealing from the cash register. • His answer is hearsay, and will be excluded, unless there is an exception.	Hearsay
Objections to (4) The stairs were repaired. . .			
Relevance	Evidence is relevant if material to a disputed fact.	• The evidence of a repair of the stairs is material to the disputed claim that the stairs were in disrepair and responsible for Paul's fall.	Relevant

Continued>

Issue	Rule	Fact Application	Conclusion
Subsequent Remedial Measures	**Evidence of subsequent repairs are inadmissible to prove culpable conduct.**	• **Evidence of repairing the stairs after Paul's fall is inadmissible because it is a subsequent remedial measure, which is disallowed for public policy reasons.**	Subsequent remedial measure
Objections to (5) "Oh no! A man just fell…"			
Relevance	Evidence is relevant if material to a disputed fact.	• The statement is material to the disputed fact that Paul did fall on the stairs.	Relevant
Non-responsive	An answer that is non-responsive to the question is not permitted.	• Mark's response of, "So what?" should have been stricken as non-responsive to the question.	Non-responsive
Hearsay	An out-of-court statement offered for the truth of the matter asserted.	• **Carol's statement was said out of court while at the grocery and is being offered for the truth that Paul fell on the broken step and fell down the stairs.** • Dell's attorney should object to the question as hearsay, which is inadmissible unless an exception applies.	Hearsay
Excited Utterance Hearsay Exception	**A statement relating to a startling event made while declarant was still under the stress of excitement caused by the event.**	• **Carol's exclamation "Oh no!" was made while she was startled by seeing Paul fall down the stairs. Seeing someone take a fall is a startling event and it appears she made the statement contemporaneously.** • **It can be admitted as an excited utterance hearsay exception.**	**Excited utterance**
Contemporaneous Statement Hearsay Exception	**A statement explaining** the declarant's own **conduct** made while declarant is engaged in the conduct.	• The statement does not qualify as a contemporaneous statement hearsay exception because in Cal. one must be describing their own actions, and here Carol was describing watching Paul.	Not a contemporaneous statement
Lay opinion	Lay opinion is admissible only if it is rationally based on the witness's perceptions and helpful to the trier of the fact.	• Carol can observe that the stairs were broken and needs no special training to make such an observation, so it is a permissible lay opinion as to the cause of the fall.	Lay opinion
Insurance Company Report			
Relevance	Evidence is relevant if material to a disputed fact.	• The insurance report is material to the disputed fact of what happened when Paul fell.	Relevant
Authentication	Proof that the document is what the proponent claims it to be.	• Mark was able to authenticate the report.	Authentic

Continued>

Issue	Rule	Fact Application	Conclusion
Attorney Work Product	Documents made in anticipation of litigation are protected attorney work product except in case of necessity.	• Here, the insurance company "always prepares a report in case we get sued," after the investigation of an accident, so the work product doctrine will likely exclude the report. Paul's attorney may argue they have a substantial "need" since Dell's repaired the stairs, and Paul's side is unable to do an inspection themselves.	Protected (not discoverable)
Hearsay	An out-of-court statement offered for the truth of the matter asserted.	• **The report is an out-of-court statement which is being offered for the truth asserted, that "steps on the stairs at the store are in very poor condition."**	Hearsay
Business Record Hearsay Exception	Business record is admissible if: • **records a business activity** • **regular practice to keep record** • **made by a person with knowledge** • **at or near time of matters indicated**	• **It is possible the report would qualify as a business record and be admitted as a hearsay exception.** • The store always prepares a report after an accident, which is a regular practice, but it may be prepared in anticipation of litigation, which is not a regular business activity. • **The report is made with the investigator who has knowledge** of the stair condition. • **The report was made at a time shortly after the investigation.** • However, Mark is probably not the appropriate sponsoring witness since he did not prepare the report.	Likely not a business record
Public Policy — Liability Insurance	• Evidence of liability insurance is not admissible to prove culpable conduct • Except: Admission of fault in conjunction is admissible	• While the insurance report would not be admissible to show that Dell can afford to pay the judgment because they have insurance, it may be admitted for the admission that is contained in the report, that "steps on the stairs at the store are in very poor condition."	Likely admissible for the admission
Balancing Test (CEC 352)	The court has discretion to exclude evidence if its probative value is substantially outweighed by the danger of unfair prejudice, confusion of issues, misleading the jury, or wasting time.	• While the information about liability insurance is somewhat prejudicial to Dell, it is not unfairly so since it captures the truth, and the information about the disrepair of the stairs is highly probative, so it will be admitted.	Likely legally relevant

<u>Note:</u> There was more variety than typical in the issues discussed regarding the insurance report in the two state released answers. The only issues they both discussed were hearsay and the business records exception. We have included a variety of the other issues, but they were not required to pass this question.

Evidence Question 5
February 2016, Question 5

Mike, Sue, Pam, David, and Ed worked at Ace Manufacturing Company. Mike had been the president and Sue supervised Pam, David, and Ed.

Pam was fired. A week later, David circulated the following email to all the other employees:

> I just thought you should know that Pam was fired because she is a thief. Sue caught her stealing money from the petty cash drawer after Pam's affair with Mike ended.

A month later, Mike died.

Pam sued David for defamation.

At trial, Pam testified that, although it is true she was fired, the remaining contents of the email were false. Pam called Ed, who testified that he had received the email at work, that he had printed it, and that he had received hundreds of other unrelated emails from David. Pam introduced a copy of the email through Ed.

In defense, David called Sue, who testified that she had caught Pam stealing $300 from the petty cash drawer, and that, when Sue confronted Pam and accused her of taking the money, Pam simply walked away. David himself testified that the contents of the email were true. He also testified that he had overheard Pam and Mike yelling at each other in Mike's office a few weeks before Pam left; that he recognized both of their voices; and that he heard Pam cry, "Please don't leave me!," and Mike, in a measured tone, reply, "Our affair is over—you need to get on with your life."

Assume all appropriate objections were timely made.

Should the court have admitted:

1. The email? Discuss.

2. Sue's testimony? Discuss.

3. David's testimony about

    a. what Pam said to Mike? Discuss.

    b. what Mike said to Pam? Discuss.

Answer according to the California Evidence Code.

Evidence Question 5 Assessment
February 2016, Question 5

This type of evidence question lists a series of events in chronological order. You are told to use the California Evidence Code and assume that all appropriate objections were made. Thus, your focus when spotting issues should be centered on the reasons why the court should or should not admit the evidence. It is important to remember that you often must analyze the "objections" to see if the court should admit the evidence. For example, even if the proper objection to hearsay was made, which you are told to assume it was, you still need to analyze the possible exceptions to see if the court should admit the evidence despite the hearsay objection. Don't mistakenly believe that because the objections have been made, you need not discuss hearsay, relevance, and so on. If you avoided analysis of all issues for which an objection can be made, you wouldn't discuss any issues.

There are four specific pieces of evidence to analyze, and you need to identify all issues that could reasonably be raised for each. Like most evidence questions there are a lot of issues to discuss, in this question approximately 25 issues spread over the 4 calls, so your analysis has got to be quick and to the point. There is no need to rewrite full rule statements once you've written them out once. Rather, you should weave the key rule elements into your analysis. On the simple issues, it is acceptable to be cursory in an evidence question and don't be afraid to do so as a time management strategy. However, be strategic about where you can get away with cursory analysis and where you can't. And, on every evidence question, always remember to discuss the logical relevance of each piece of purported evidence, even if briefly.

This is an interesting question because the civil case is for defamation. Since the basis of defamation is a false and derogatory statement, look for the character evidence exception since character evidence should be admitted, but not to prove conduct in conformity. You should also look for statements that would be hearsay in another context, but in a defamation case, the statements would not be hearsay because they would not being coming in for their truth, but for some other reason, such as a fact of independent legal significance (to prove the elements of defamation) or the effect on the hearer. All evidence questions have similarities, but they are all slightly different, such as this one testing in the defamation context. You should do as many practice questions as you can to see all of the different ways the issues can be raised, and which facts naturally trigger which issues.

Finally, answer the call of the question by stating whether the court should have admitted the evidence. Make note of the areas highlighted in bold on the corresponding grid. The **bold** areas highlight the issues, analysis, and conclusions that are likely **required** to receive a passing score on this question.

Issue	Rule	Fact Application	Conclusion
Cal. Prop. 8	Criminal trials in Cal. — all relevant evidence is admissible, subject to several exemptions.	This is a defamation case in civil court so Prop. 8 does not apply.	No Prop 8
1. Should the court have admitted the email?			
Relevance	**Evidence is relevant if it tends to be material to a disputed fact.**	Pam's cause of action is against David for defamation and David's email contains the statements, which are the basis of the defamation claim, **thus the email is material to the disputed fact of if the defamatory statements were made and published.**	Relevant
Legal Relevance	**Evidence can be excluded if its probative value is substantially outweighed by its prejudicial value.**	The email is highly probative of the alleged defamatory statement and while it could be prejudicial to Pam because it accuses her of theft, it is **not unfairly prejudicial** since it is Pam who is trying to prove the defamatory statements were made.	Legally relevant
Authentication	All documentary evidence must be authenticated as genuine in order to be admitted.	**Ed testified that he has personal knowledge of the email because he received it from David and it was one of many hundred he had received from David at work.**	Authenticated
Secondary Evidence	To prove the contents of a writing, the original must be produced, though machine duplicates are allowed unless the original's authenticity is in dispute.	Pam introduced a printed copy of the email, which is sufficient to authenticate and introducing the copy is proper.	Satisfied
Hearsay	**Hearsay is an out-of-court statement offered to prove the truth of the matter asserted, and is inadmissible unless an exception applies.**	The email is an **out-of-court statement made by David** at work. However, it is **not being offered to prove the truth of the matter in the statement** — that Pam was thief — but rather it is being offered because **Pam is claiming the statements are false,** which is the heart of her defamation claim.	Not hearsay
Fact of Independent Legal Significance	A statement that itself has legal significance is not hearsay.	**The fact the statement was made at all has legal significance because it is the basis of the defamation claim.**	Fact of ind. legal significance
Party Admission	A party admission is a statement made by a party and offered against them. Admissions are exceptions from hearsay and are admissible.	David **made this statement, which is being offered against him,** and he is the defendant in this case, so the statement should come in as a party admission.	Party admission

Continued>

Issue	Rule	Fact Application	Conclusion
Conclusion	The email was properly admitted.		
2. Should the court have admitted Sue's testimony?			
Relevance	**Evidence is relevant if it tends to be material to a disputed fact.**	**Sue's testimony is relevant to the issue of whether the contents of the email were true, which is a disputed fact.**	Relevant
Legal Relevance	Evidence can be excluded if its probative value is substantially outweighed by its prejudicial value.	Sue's testimony is probative of David's defense of truth. While the evidence is prejudicial to Pam and accuses her of theft, it is **not unfairly prejudicial** since it is Pam who has raised the issue of the defamatory statements with her suit.	**Legally relevant**
Personal Knowledge	**To be competent, a witness must have personal knowledge of facts to which they are attesting.**	Sue is testifying based on her own personal knowledge of her interaction and that she observed Pam stealing.	**Witness is competent**
Character Evidence	**Character evidence is generally not admissible** to prove conduct in conformity with that character trait on a particular occasion, **however it is admissible when character is "at issue"** and an essential element of the case.	**Pam is claiming the accusations of theft in David's email are false so she has put her character in** issue. Consequently, **Sue's testimony that she saw Pam stealing $300 from the cash drawer will be admitted.Sue's testimony can also be admitted to** impeach **Pam** since Pam testified that the statement in the email (that she stole) were false.	**"At issue" character evidence admissible**
Hearsay	**Hearsay is an out-of-court statement offered to prove the truth of the matter asserted, and is inadmissible unless an exception applies.**	**Sue's conversation with Pam took place at work, which is out of court.** Though Pam did not speak, her action of walking away can be considered assertive conduct. However the statement here may be offered for a reason other than for its truth.	Hearsay
Effect on Listener	**An out-of-court statement may be non-hearsay if it is not offered for its truth, but for the effect on the listener.**	Pam's walking away in response to Sue's theft accusation could be admitted to show the **effect of the accusation on the listener, Pam.**	Likely not an effect on listener

Continued>

Issue	Rule	Fact Application	Conclusion
Party Admission Adoptive by Silence	An adoptive admission is a statement made by another where the party knows and **voluntarily manifests a belief in the truth of the statement** by words or actions. An admission can be made by silence if a reasonable person would have spoken or responded.	**When Sue accused Pam of stealing, you would expect a reasonable person to deny the accusation and defend herself. By saying nothing and walking away, it is likely Pam has manifested a belief in the truth of the accusation.** [The factual analysis was important though the issue could have been raised as a party admission, an adoptive admission, or silence as an adoptive admission.]	Party admission
Conclusion	The court was correct to admit the testimony.		
3a. Should the court have admitted David's testimony about what Pam said to Mike?			
Relevance	Evidence is relevant if it tends to be material to a disputed fact.	**The testimony is material to the disputed fact of whether Pam had an affair with Mike and the truth of the email, a key subject in the defamation action.**	Relevant
Legal Relevance	Evidence can be excluded if its probative value is substantially outweighed by its prejudicial value.	While the evidence is prejudicial to Pam and accuses her of infidelity, it is **not unfairly prejudicial** since it is Pam who has raised the issue of the defamatory statements with her suit.	Legally relevant
Authentication	All evidence must be authenticated as genuine.	**David testified that he recognized Pam's and Mike's voices and since he worked with them, he could testify to their voices without seeing them.**	Authenticated
Hearsay	**Hearsay is an out-of-court statement offered to prove the truth of the matter asserted, and is inadmissible unless an exception applies.**	This is an **out-of-court statement** since Pam said it in Mike's office. If it is being admitted for its truth, that Pam asked Mike not to leave her, it will be inadmissible unless an exception applies.	Hearsay
Party Admission	**A party admission is a statement made by a party and offered against them. Admissions are exceptions from hearsay and are admissible.**	**Since Pam is a party to the action, the statement can come in as a party admission.**	Party admission
Excited Utterance	A statement is admissible if relating to a startling event and made while the declarant was still under the stress caused by the event. [Could also include prior inconsistent statement]	Pam and Mike were in a fight and yelling and **Pam cried out in an excited voice**, "Please don't leave me!" which may have been a startling event since it sounds like Pam was upset.	Excited utterance
Conclusion	The court was correct to admit the testimony.		

Continued>

Issue	Rule	Fact Application	Conclusion
3b. Should the court have admitted David's testimony about what Mike said to Pam?			
Relevance	**Evidence is relevant if it tends to be material to a disputed fact.**	**Mike's statement tends to prove the disputed fact that Pam's affair with Mike ended.**	**Relevant**
Legal Relevance	Evidence can be excluded if its probative value is substantially outweighed by its prejudicial value.	While the evidence is prejudicial to Pam and accuses her of infidelity, it is not unfairly prejudicial since it is Pam who has raised the issue of the defamatory statements with her suit.	Legally relevant
Authentication	**All evidence must be authenticated as genuine.**	**David testified that he recognized Pam's and Mike's voices and since he worked with them, he could testify to their voices without seeing them.**	**Authenticated**
Hearsay	**Hearsay is an out-of-court statement offered to prove the truth of the matter asserted, and is inadmissible unless an exception applies.**	This is an **out-of-court statement** since Mike said it in his office. If it is being admitted for its truth, that Mike told Pam the affair was over, it will be inadmissible unless an exception applies.	**Hearsay**
Excited Utterance	A statement is admissible if relating to a startling event and made while the declarant was still under the stress caused by the event.	**Mike's** reply was not made under the stress of a startling event since he **spoke in a measured tone.**	**Not an excited utterance**
Dying Declaration	**A statement made by declarant, while believing death was imminent, concerning the cause or circumstances of his impending death and is a hearsay exception in all Cal.** civil and criminal cases and **declarant must be dead.**	**While Mike died** a month after the statement was made, **which is required for the dying declaration exception in California,** his statement was not made **in the belief his death was imminent, nor was** it regarding the circumstances of his impending death.	**Not a dying declaration**
Statement Against Interest	A statement against interest is one made by unavailable declarant & against her financial or penal interest when made. In California, it can be against one's social interest. **The declarant must be unavailable.** [Other exceptions that could have been discussed, but were not required, were present mental of physical condition, effect on listener, present state of mind]	Mike is unavailable to testify since he died a month after making the statement. **The statement is against Mike's interest** since admitting his infidelity could hold him up to adverse social **judgments and stigma.** He could have also exposed himself to financial liability as Pam's boss.	**Statement against interest**
Conclusion	The court was correct to admit the testimony.		

Evidence Question 6
February 2002, Question 6

Phil sued Dirk, a barber, seeking damages for personal injuries resulting from a hair treatment Dirk performed on Phil. The complaint alleged that most of Phil's hair fell out as a result of the treatment. At a jury trial, the following occurred:

A. Phil's attorney called Wit to testify that the type of hair loss suffered by Phil was abnormal. Before Wit could testify, the judge stated that he had been a trained barber prior to going to law school. He took judicial notice that this type of hair loss was not normal and instructed the jury accordingly.

B. Phil testified that, right after he discovered his hair loss, he called Dirk and told Dirk what had happened. Phil testified that Dirk then said: (1) "I knew I put too many chemicals in the solution I used on you, so won't you take $1,000 in settlement?" (2) "I fixed the solution and now have it corrected." (3) "Don't worry because Insco, my insurance company, told me that it will take care of everything."

C. Phil produced a letter at trial addressed to him bearing the signature "Dirk." The letter states that Dirk used an improper solution containing too many chemicals on Phil for his hair treatment. Phil testified that he received this letter through the mail about a week after the incident at the barbershop. The court admitted the letter into evidence.

D. In his defense, Dirk called Chemist, who testified as an expert witness that he applied to his own hair the same solution that had been used on Phil and that he suffered no loss of hair.

Assume that, in each instance, all appropriate objections were made. Did the court err in:

1. Taking judicial notice and instructing the jury on hair loss? Discuss.

2. Admitting Phil's testimony regarding Dirk's statements? Discuss.

3. Admitting the letter produced by Phil? Discuss.

4. Admitting Chemist's testimony? Discuss.

Evidence Question 6 Assessment

February 2002, Question 6

This evidence essay question is older, but is a great practice question because it poses some challenges. The question covers a less common topic — judicial notice — and covers several of the public policy exceptions to relevance. Many bar questions are formatted like this one in that they cover a particular area of law in depth by slightly altering the facts so your answer can demonstrate your facility with the rules and their nuances by applying the rule to a variety of facts.

The first challenge is an organizational one. Paragraph B contains three numbered statements that Dirk said to Phil during their phone conversation. Call two of the question asks if the court erred in admitting Dirk's statements. Whenever the facts are broken down into paragraphs, or into numbered statements like this one, it is always easiest to work with the material by analyzing each piece of information separately. The danger in doing otherwise is that it is easy to miss spotting all the issues when working with the statements as a group. Once the three statements from paragraph B are separated and analyzed it is very easy to see that they share some issues (relevance, hearsay, party admission) but, while each statement raises the issue of public policy exclusions, each statement raises a different exclusion (settlement offers, subsequent remedial repairs, liability insurance). Once the statements have been separated and organized on your virtual scratch paper, you can easily see where you can make an efficient use of "supra" to streamline your analysis. Another approach would be to use headings to indicate where the three statements are being analyzed together (relevance, hearsay, party admission), and where they are being analyzed separately (the three public policy exclusions).

The second challenge posed by this question is time management. When this question was originally administered, it was the last essay question of the exam (day three, question six) and the last question call (number four) covers the lengthy rule for expert witnesses. Not only does the rule have multiple elements, but also the analysis is more sophisticated. The proposed expert was an expert in chemistry, but his testimony was regarding hair loss. Further, the methodology used to form his opinion was to test the chemical solution on his own head and report his findings. You don't have to know a lot about the scientific method to realize that method can't be reliable! It isn't a particularly difficult issue to spot, even for a student fuzzy on the rule or suffering from fatigue. The challenge is in managing your time throughout the question, so there is enough time to properly answer call four. This question also provides a great example of why organizing your answer before you start writing is so important. If you organize before you start writing, you will unravel the problem posed by call two (three statements in one question) before you start writing, and you will realize that call four is going to take some time to write. You can then apportion your time and pace yourself accordingly.

This question dates from 2002 and thus before California evidence was tested, which is why it does not specify which law to use. However, the attached answer grid has been altered to include the California rules along with the federal rules so you can test yourself on how to answer the question with either the federal rules or the California rules.

Make note of the areas highlighted in **bold** on the corresponding grid. The bold areas highlight the issues, analysis, and conclusions that are likely **required** to receive a passing score on this question.

Issue	Rule	Fact Application	Conclusion
Call #1			
Judicial Notice	**The court can take judicial notice of facts not subject to reasonable dispute,** either generally known or capable of accurate and ready determination.	It is not easily verifiable or universally known that this type of hair loss is not normal and so an inappropriate topic for judicial notice. The Judge's personal experience as a barber is not a proper use of judicial notice.	Court erred
Call #2: Stmt. 1 — Settle			
Logical Relevance	**Evidence is relevant if it has any tendency to make a fact more or less probable and is of consequence to the action.** CEC: fact must be in dispute.	Dirk's negligence is at issue, so an offer to settle the claim has a **tendency to make it more probable than not that Dirk was responsibility for Phil's injuries.**	Relevant
Legal Relevance	Relevant evidence can still be excluded if its probative value is substantially outweighed by its prejudicial value.	The probative value is not outweighed by any prejudicial effect here because the public policy exclusion applies.	Relevant
Public Policy Exclusion: Settlement Offer	**Not allowed to show liability, but must have a disputed "claim" first** (liability or amount).	**Assuming there is a disputed claim here,** since Dirk's statement regarding settlement for $1,000 was made in response to Phil's phone call notifying Dirk of the hair loss trouble, **this statement is inadmissible to show liability.**	**Excluded, court erred in admitting**
Hearsay	**Hearsay statement offered for the truth of the matter asserted.**	This statement was made out of court on the telephone and is offered for its truth — that Dirk made a settlement offer and implicitly admitted liability — so it is inadmissible unless an exception applies.	**Hearsay, unless exception**
Party Admission	**Any statement by a party opponent is admissible.** FRE: nonhearsay; CEC: exception	Dirk admitted that he put too many chemicals in the solution used on Phil. **The statement is admissible as a party admission.**	Allowed as an admission, but see above
Call #2: Stmt. 2 — Solution Fix			
Logical Relevance	See above	Dirk's negligence is at issue and testimony that the solution had to be fixed implies something was wrong with it and **makes Dirk's negligence more probable than not.**	Relevant

Continued>

Issue	Rule	Fact Application	Conclusion
Public Policy Exclusion: Subsequent Remedial Measures	**Evidence of subsequent safety measures, or repairs performed after an accident, are inadmissible to prove culpable conduct**, but are allowed to show ownership or control, or (FRE) to show defective product design.	**Public policy excludes** testimony of subsequent remedial measures because of the chilling effect on people fixing defective products or conditions. **The only purpose of the testimony is to show Dirk's liability. Therefore, the statement that the solution needed to be fixed is inadmissible.** If Dirk claims the solution wasn't his or that fixing it was impossible, the statement is admissible.	**Excluded, court erred in admitting**
Hearsay	See above	Statement is made out of court on the telephone and offered to prove that solution needing fixing, **so it is inadmissible unless an exception applies.**	**Hearsay, unless exception**
Party Admission	See above	Dirk admitted the solution was now fixed and the **statement is admissible as a party admission.**	Allowed, so court didn't err, but see above
Call #2: Stmt. 3 — Insurance			
Logical Relevance	See above	Dirk implied he was responsible, which **makes the fact more probable of his fault for the injury to Phil.**	**Relevant**
Public Policy Exclusion: Liability Insurance	**Not allowed to show liability**, but an admission made is allowed.	**Public policy excludes evidence of insurance** because of the danger it will imply the defendant has deep pockets to pay or has insurance because he's careless, so **Dirk's statement regarding his insurance is inadmissible.**	**Excluded, court erred in admitting**
Hearsay (Double)	See above. Need exceptions for each level to be admissible.	Dirk's statement is made out of court on the telephone and offered for the truth that he is at fault for Phil's injuries. There are two levels of hearsay: 1) Insurance Co.'s statement to Dirk; 2) Dirk's repeating of their statement to Phil.	**Hearsay, not allowed**
Party Admission	See above	As analyzed supra, **Dirk's statement can come in as a party admission.**	Allowed, so court didn't err
Call #3			
Logical Relevance	See above	The letter makes it **more probable than not that Dirk is liable** since he admitted using an improper solution.	Relevant

Continued>

Issue	Rule	Fact Application	Conclusion
Authentication	**Proof that the document is what the proponent claims it to be.**	**Dirk's signature would have to be authenticated.**	Must be authenticated
Best Evidence Rule	Original writing must be produced. CEC: secondary evidence rule	The letter is being admitted so this rule is complied with.	Allowed
Hearsay	See above	The letter was written out of court and is offered for the truth that Dirk used too many chemicals in the solution, causing Phil's hair loss.	**Hearsay**
Party Admission	See above	**Dirk's statement** that the solution was improperly prepared **is a party admission** and is admissible as such.	Allowed, so court didn't erro
Call #4			
Logical Relevance	See above	Has a tendency to show the solution Dirk used was responsible for Phil's hair loss.	Relevant
Expert Opinion	**Expert opinion is admissible if:** 1) **assists trier of fact,** 2) **witness is qualified,** 3) **based on sufficient facts,** 4) **used reliable principles and methods, and** 5) **applied principles reliably to facts of case.**	1) Expert testimony would assist trier of fact because hair chemicals are outside common knowledge. 2) **Witness has no specialized knowledge of hair loss, and is only an expert in chemistry.** 3) **Personal observation and use of the product on oneself is not an appropriate scientific method.** 4) **Opinion was inappropriately based on personal experience, not scientific method.** 5) Not applied reliably to the case.	Court erred in admitting

PART 8 *PROFESSIONAL RESPONSIBILITY*

PROFESSIONAL RESPONSIBILITY TABLE OF CONTENTS

INTRODUCTION TO PROFESSIONAL RESPONSIBILITY

Professional responsibility is one subject that (except Feb. 2015) is tested as an essay on every single bar exam. Often, it comprises an entire essay question; sometimes it is covered both on its own and as a crossover question on the same exam. It is often crossed over with business associations, but can cross over with nearly every subject eligible for testing. To fully prepare, write out or organize several essays covering all of the possible tested issues since it will show up on your bar exam in one format or another.

A unique trait to professional responsibility essays is that the conclusion *does* matter. Unlike other subjects where the conclusion is rarely important, professional responsibility generally requires you to reach the correct conclusion in order to receive full credit on an issue. Another difference from the other subjects is that the bar examiners are looking for a more thorough academic and explanatory type discussion in professional responsibility.

You will notice that the rules are stated in the outline in a more general way, with some sub-rules. However, when using the rules in an essay, you can customize or tweak the rule so that it applies more directly to the factual situation. You do not need to list the entire rule but only the part(s) of the rule raised by the facts. Since professional responsibility tests both the ABA and California rules, you must know both and be able to distinguish them. This is extremely important since you must follow the directions in the call of the question, which usually asks you to answer according to both bodies of law. Thus, where there is a distinction between the two rules, you must identify the distinction and specifically refer to the rule as being either ABA or California, so it is clear to the examiners which source of law you are analyzing. Although you don't need to identify the source of the rule with particularity, the examiners test your knowledge of the California Rules of Professional Conduct, relevant sections of the California Business and Professions Code, and leading federal and state case law on the subject, in addition to the ABA Model Rules of Professional Conduct and ABA Model Code of Professional Responsibility. Since 2006, all professional responsibility essays have specifically asked the examinees to answer according to California and ABA authorities, so earlier state-released answers might not analyze both rules but always practice answering according to both. The rules contained in the following outline only apply to the ABA if the rule is labeled "ABA" and only apply to California if labeled "Cal." All other rules are substantially the same for both the ABA and California. When there is no difference between the ABA and California rule, you do not need to label them as ABA or Cal., but rather just state the rule. Also note that California essays use the terms "lawyer" and "attorney" interchangeably and vary on each essay administration.

On professional responsibility essays, the calls are often very broad, asking you to identify any ethical violations. Thus, using the issues checklist is crucial to success on this subject. It is often necessary to issue spot by reviewing each "action" the attorney takes as if it was its own mini essay. For example, you may need to spot all issues that arise when the attorney begins to represent two clients who do not share the same interest. This single "action" can lead to multiple issues, such as conflict of interest, duty of confidentiality, withdrawal, etc. Then, the attorney might help one party do something, which could give rise to a whole different set of issues, some of them being duplicative with those raised in the prior fact paragraph. Therefore, unlike other subjects, in professional responsibility looking at each "action" individually, rather than looking at the entire fact pattern collectively, generally spots the issues. As a result, you often have answers that break down the essay by the attorney "action" (with headings for each action), followed by issue headings for the potential ethical violations corresponding to that action. As a result, you often have the same issues tested multiple times in one essay for each different "action."

Lastly, it is important to note that professional responsibility rules are continually changing. California made major changes in 2018 and then continued to make changes five more times through 2024. It is possible that they will continue to change the rules, so check the State Bar Website for recent changes at https://www.calbar.ca.gov/attorneys/conduct-discipline/rules/rules-of-professional-conduct.

ISSUES CHECKLIST

LAWYER-CLIENT RELATIONSHIP

Creation of attorney-client relationship
Duty of loyalty
   Conflicts of interest
     General rule/exceptions
     Specific conflicts between clients
       Insurance
       Corp./organizational
       No aggregate settlements
       Former clients
       Government employees
       Imputed firm disqualification
       L leaves firm
   Compensation by 3rd parties
   Client & lawyer's personal interest
     Personal beliefs/relationships
     Sexual relationship
     Business transactions
     Gifts
     Proprietary interest
     Literary/media rights
     Financial assistance to clients
     Limiting malpractice
     Settlement of claims
Duty to communicate
Scope of representation
Duty of confidentiality

Attorney-client privilege
Duty to avoid fee misunderstandings
   Regular
   Contingent
   Fee splitting/sharing
   Referral fees/gifts
   Flat fees/retainers/advances
Duty of competence
Duty of diligence
Duty to safekeep property
Withdrawal

PROFESSIONAL INTEGRITY

Advertising/solicitation
Unauthorized practice of law
Liability for other lawyer's misconduct
Duty of fairness
   To represented/unrepresented parties
   To court
   To opposing counsel
   Duty of decorum to tribunal
   Trial publicity rules
   Special prosecutor duties
   Lawyer as witness
Reporting ethical violations
Duty to report ethical violations
Duty to public/profession

MEMORIZATION ATTACK SHEET

CREATION OF L-C RELATIONSHIP

- ◆ L owes duty of conf.
- ◆ Based on C's perception

DUTY OF LOYALTY

- ◆ **Conflicts of interest**
- ◆ **Current and future conflicts**
- ◆ **Current clients**
  - Not okay if C's interest directly adverse to another
- ◆ **Current client and client, 3P, or personal interest**
  - Significant risk that
  - Representation materially limited by
  - L's responsibility to clients, 3P, self
- ◆ **Exception to conflicts**
  - L's reasonable belief
  - Not prohibited by law
  - Claims not against each other
  - Informed written consent
- ◆ **No risk limitation (Cal.)**
  - Even if no sig. risk
  - Written disclosure needed if:
    - ◆ Relationship w/ party/witness
    - ◆ Related/lives w/ party/witness
    - ◆ Intimate relationship w/ party/witness
- ◆ **Types of conflicts**
  - Two or more clients (Cs)
  - C and third party
  - C and L's personal interest
- ◆ **Cal. okay if L represents insured and insurer**
- ◆ **Corp./organization**
  - L acts best interest of organization only
  - If L knows associated person engaged in wrongdoing
  - Likely to result in substantial injury to organization
  - L refers up to internal higher authority
  - ABA only: if needed, refer out
  - Cal. only: if needed, resign/withdraw; no outside referral unless death/sub. bodily harm
- ◆ **No aggregate settlements/pleas**
- ◆ **Former client**
  - May not represent another
  - If case same or substantially related
  - Unless informed written consent
- ◆ **Former/current govt. employee**
  - May not represent privately/in gov.
  - If L participated personally & substantially
  - Unless informed written consent

- ◆ **Imputed firm disqualification**
  - Conflict for L applies to entire firm, unless:
    - ◆ Based on L's personal interest, or
    - ◆ Former C and firm
    - ◆ Timely screened
    - ◆ Not same or substantially related or
    - ◆ Written notice to former client/certify compliance
  - C can waive—informed written consent
- ◆ **L leaves firm**
  - Firm okay to represent C with interest adverse
  - To previous client of L
  - Unless matter substantially the same, and
  - Any remaining firm L has confidential information
  - C can waive—informed written consent
- ◆ **Compensation by 3rd party**
  - Informed consent
  - No interference with L & client
  - Information remains confidential
- ◆ **L relationships/beliefs**
  - Use general COI rules
- ◆ **Sexual relations with client**
  - Okay if preexisting, consensual
- ◆ **Business transactions okay if:**
  - Terms fair/reasonable
  - Terms fully disclosed in writing to client
  - Advised to seek independent counsel
  - Informed written consent
  - Cal.: L's role also disclosed in writing
- ◆ **Gifts**
  - L can't solicit substantial gifts
  - Prepare an instrument that gives gifts
  - Unless relative
  - Must be fair & no undue influence
  - Okay if independent L
- ◆ **Proprietary interest**
  - L cannot acquire
  - Unless lien for fees or contingency in civil case
- ◆ **Literary/media rights**
  - Can't obtain during rep.
- ◆ **Financial assistance (ABA)**
  - Only to advance in contingent
  - Court costs/litigation expenses
  - Or indigent clients/pro bono/clinic
- ◆ **Financial assistance (Cal.)**
  - After employment
  - Okay to loan if written IOU

◆ **Limiting malpractice (ABA)**
  • Okay if advise independent counsel
◆ **Limiting malpractice (Cal.)**
  • Never okay
◆ **Settlement claims**
  • Okay if advised in writing to seek outside L

DUTY TO COMMUNICATE

◆ **Promptly inform client**
◆ **Status of case**
◆ **Promptly respond to client**
  • Okay to delay if client will harm another

SCOPE OF REPRESENTATION

◆ **L decides legal strategy**
◆ **Client decides substantive issues: pleas, offers, settlements, jury trial issue**

DUTY OF CONFIDENTIALITY

◆ **ABA—L cannot reveal, unless:**
  • Informed consent
  • Impliedly authorized
  • L reasonably believes necessary to:
    ◆ Prevent death or SBH
    ◆ Prevent, mitigate, rectify crime/fraud of financial injury
  • Comply with law/ct. order
  • Secure legal advice
  • Establish claim or defense for L
  • Resolve COI
◆ **Cal.—L cannot reveal, unless:**
  • Necessary to prevent death or SBH
    ◆ Disclosure optional
    ◆ Try to dissuade first
    ◆ Inform client of planned reveal
  • Establish claim or defense for L
  • Compelled by law/State Bar Act

ATTORNEY-CLIENT PRIVILEGE

◆ **Attorney-client**
  • Confidential communication is intended
  • Professional service is purpose
  • Holder: client
  • Person or corporation
  • Lasts until:
    ◆ FRE: after death
    ◆ CEC: estate settled
  • Exceptions:
    ◆ L's services to further crime or fraud
    ◆ Dispute w/ lawyer
    ◆ CEC: prevent crime w/ death/SBH

FEE MISUNDERSTANDINGS

◆ **ABA: reasonable fees**
◆ **Cal.: not unconscionable fees**
  • Time limitations
  • Experience, reputation, ability
  • Nature and length of relationship
  • Time, labor, novelty, difficulty
  • Fee customarily charged
  • Likelihood to preclude other employment
  • Amount involved/results obtained
  • Whether fixed or contingent fee (Think TENT FLAW)
  • Cal.: L fraud or overreaching
  • Cal.: L not disclose mat. facts
  • Cal.: Sophistication of L/client
  • Cal.: Amount of fee/proportion
  • Cal.: Informed consent
◆ **Fee agreements**
  • How fee calculated
  • Nature of services
  • Responsibilities of L & client
◆ **Fee agreements > $1,000 Cal.**
  • In writing, unless:
    ◆ Corporate client
    ◆ Emergency
    ◆ Client waives writing in writing
    ◆ Previous client & similar service
◆ **Fee disputes: Arbitration**
  • Cal. requires/ABA only mandated if law
◆ **Contingency fee agreement**
  • In writing
  • Signed by client (and L in Cal.)
  • Method for fee and %
  • Expenses to deduct & when
  • Not for domestic/criminal cases
  • Cal.: negotiable unless health care (set % then)
◆ **Fee splitting/sharing**
  • Prohibited with non-L
  • With Ls, okay if:
    ◆ Client consents in writing
    ◆ ABA: total fee reasonable
    ◆ ABA: proportionate
    ◆ Cal.: Ls enter written agreement
    ◆ Cal.: total fee not increased b/c of division
    ◆ Cal.: full written discl. terms before consent
◆ **Gifts/referral fees**
  • Don't give value, unless
    ◆ Reas. advertising costs
    ◆ Qualified referral service
    ◆ Approved by authority
  • Nominal ok/no promise for future referrals
  • Reciprocal okay if not exclusive and client informed

◆ **Cal. Retainer Fee**
  • Non-refundable okay
  • If disclosure & C agrees in writing
  • To ensure L availability
◆ **Cal. Flat Fee**
  • Okay as completed payment
  • If > $1000 need writing
  • $ okay in L operating acct.
◆ **Other Advance Fees**
  • In client trust account
  • Withdraw as earned

DUTY OF COMPETENCE

◆ **ABA: Knowledge, skill, thoroughness**
◆ **Cal.: No intent., repeatedly, reckless., gross neg. fail to act competent**
◆ **Cal.: Includes learning and skill and mental, physical, emotional ability**
◆ **Okay to associate with competent attorney or become one or refer out**

DUTY OF DILIGENCE

◆ **ABA: Reas. diligence and promptness**
◆ **Cal.: No intent., repeatedly, reckless., gross neg. fail to act diligently**
◆ **Cal.: Diligence = commitment, dedication, no neglect, unduly delay**

SAFEKEEPING PROPERTY

◆ **Money—trust account separate**
  • Accounting kept for 5 yrs.
◆ **Prompt payment**
  • Disputed $ L can hold
  • Cal.: need IOLTA
◆ **Physical property—keep separate/label/ journal**

WITHDRAWAL

◆ **Mandatory—Shall if:**
  • Violation of rules
  • Mental/physical condition
  • Discharged
  • Cal.: knows client's action to harass
◆ **Permissive—May if:**
  • Fraud/crime using L (reas. belief)
  • Used L for crime/fraud
  • Repres. unreasonably difficult
  • Client fails to fulfill obligation
  • Good cause
  • ABA: no materially adverse effect on client
  • ABA: unreasonable financial burden on L
  • ABA: Client's action repugnant to L
  • Cal.: Client assents
  • Cal.: L's mental/physical condition make it difficult
  • Cal.: Continue likely to violate PR rules
  • Cal.: Client has no good faith; L can't work with co-counsel
◆ **Duty to client on withdrawal**
  • Reasonable notice
  • Surrender papers and property
  • Refund fees not earned

ADVERTISING/SOLICITATION

◆ **No false/misleading communication**
  • Truthful
  • Name/address required
◆ **No direct soliciting/exceptions**
◆ **Cal. presumes violation if:**
  • Express guaranty or warranty
  • Testimonial without disclaimer
  • No fee without recovery label unless client cost disclosed
◆ **Specialist if approved**

UNAUTHORIZED PRACTICE

- ◆ No partnering with non-L
- ◆ Cal.: Report to state bar if hire disbarred L

LIABILITY FOR OTHER L

- ◆ Liable for other L prof. resp. if ratify or supervise and could mitigate
- ◆ Subordinate L ok to follow L if reas.

FAIRNESS

- ◆ Represented parties need L
- ◆ Unrep. parties L can't imply disinterested
- ◆ Corp. consent to speak
- ◆ To court
- ◆ To opposing counsel
  - • No falsity, tamper evidence, etc.
  - • Return inadvertent sent materials
  - • Cal.: no suppress evidence, pay witness, secret witness
- ◆ No influence jurors, judge
- ◆ Trial publicity — no extrajudicial statement if material prejudice
- ◆ Prosecutors must give D exculpatory evidence/remedy wrongful conv.
- ◆ L can't be witness in own trial unless uncontested issue or value of services

REPORTING ETHICAL VIOLATIONS

- ◆ Must report another L violation
- ◆ Cal.: must report self

DUTY TO PUBLIC/PROFESSION

- ◆ No lies, fraud, crime, frivolous claims
- ◆ Cal.: no harass, threaten

PROFESSIONAL RESPONSIBILITY RULE OUTLINE

I. **LAWYER-CLIENT RELATIONSHIP**
  A. **Creation of Attorney-Client Relationship**
    1. **Prospective Client:** A person who consults with a lawyer for the purpose of retaining the lawyer or securing legal service or advice is a prospective client and the lawyer **owes this person a duty of confidentiality** and the **duty to avoid conflicts of interest**.
    2. **Actual Client:** Creation of the lawyer-client relationship considers what a **client's reasonable perception** is as to whether a relationship has been formed even if a formal agreement has not been created.

> **Issue spotting tip:** It is key to remember that lawyers owe duties to prospective clients. This is often tested when a corporate employee seeks legal advice from a company's attorney and reveals information that is harmful to the company. This triggers several issues such as the duty of confidentiality and duty of loyalty, which turn on whether the employee is now viewed as a prospective client or a current client. The key to understanding professional responsibility is seeing how the issues all relate to each other.

  B. **Duty of loyalty:** A lawyer has a duty of loyalty to their client that requires the lawyer to put the **interest of their client above all other interests** and to avoid any actual (current) or potential (future) conflicts of interest.
    1. **Concurrent conflict of interest general rule:** A lawyer **may not represent a client** where there is a **conflict of interest**. A concurrent conflict of interest can arise several ways.
      a. **Between current clients:** A concurrent conflict of interest exists if the representation of **one client is directly adverse to another client**.
      b. **Between a current client and another:** A concurrent conflict of interest exists if there is a **significant risk** that the representation of one or more clients will be **materially limited** by the lawyer's **responsibilities** to **another client**, a **former client**, a **third person,** or by a **personal interest** of the lawyer.
      c. **Exception to concurrent conflicts of interest: A lawyer may still represent the client** despite a concurrent conflict **if:**
        1. The lawyer **reasonably believes** that the lawyer will be able to provide **competent and diligent representation** to each affected client, and
        2. The representation is **not prohibited by law**, and
        3. The clients are **not asserting a claim against each other** in the same litigation (not directly adverse), and
        4. Each client gives **informed consent, confirmed in writing (Cal. requires informed written consent)**.
          a. **ABA informed consent, confirmed in writing** means the informed consent (which can be oral) must later be transmitted to a writing (unlike the Cal. rule that also requires the "informed" part—the disclosures—to be in writing).
          b. **Cal. informed written consent** means that *both* the disclosures and the consent must be in writing.
      d. **Cal. no risk limitation:** Even if the **significant risk** that lawyer's representation of the client will be **materially limited is NOT present**, a lawyer must still provide **written disclosure** of the relationship to the client and **meet the above exceptions** if:
        1. The **lawyer** has or knows that another **lawyer in lawyer's firm** has any kind of **relationship to a party or witness,** or
        2. The lawyer knows or reasonably should know that **another party's lawyer** is **related** to lawyer, **lives with** lawyer, is a **client** of lawyer or their firm, or is in an **intimate relationship** with lawyer.

2. **Specific rules for conflicts** (*between clients*):
    a. **Insurance (Cal. only):** Lawyers are permitted to represent both **insurers and insureds** whereby the insurer has the contractual right to unilaterally select counsel for the insured, resulting in **no conflict** of interest.
    b. **Corporate/organizational client:** A lawyer employed by an organization or corporation represents the organization/corporation and must act in the **best interest of the organization/corporation.**
        1. **Representation of organization's individuals:** A lawyer **may** also **represent the organization's officers**, directors, employees, shareholders, or other constituents **if the requirements for the exception to represent those with concurrent conflicts** are met (see I.B.1.c. and d above).
            a. When a lawyer represents a corporation/organization, they must **explain the identity of their client to constituents** (i.e., officers, directors, employees, etc.) when the lawyer knows or should know that the **organization's interests are adverse** to the interests of the constituents.
        2. **Reporting misconduct to a higher authority:** If the lawyer **knows** that an **officer, employee, or other person** associated with the organization is engaged in (or intends to engage in) **action that** (Cal. — lawyer knows or reasonably should know) is a violation of a legal obligation or a law reasonably imputable to the organization and is **likely to result in substantial injury to the organization**, the lawyer *shall* **report up**, and **refer the matter to a higher authority** in the organization, *unless* the lawyer **reasonably believes** that it is **not in the best interest** of the organization to do so (**Cal. requires that the duty of confidentiality be maintained** *unless* death or substantial bodily injury is likely — see I.E.2 below).
            a. **Failure to act by higher authority:** If the **highest authority fails to take action** and the lawyer **reasonably believes the violation will result in substantial injury** to the organization:
                i. **ABA only:** The lawyer *may* **report out and reveal information**, even if confidential, if such disclosure is **necessary to prevent the injury.**
                ii. **Cal. only:** The lawyer *may not* **report out and disclose information outside** the organization if it will violate the duty of **confidentiality**; rather the lawyer should **urge reconsideration** of the matter to the higher authorities within the organization, **resign** from representation, **or withdraw** from representation, *unless* death or substantial bodily injury is likely — see I.E.2 below.
    c. **No aggregate settlements or guilty pleas:** A lawyer who represents **two or more clients** shall not participate in making an aggregate settlement of the claims of or against the clients or, in a criminal case, an aggregate agreement as to guilt or pleas, unless each client gives **informed written consent.** Cal. states this does not apply to class actions.
    d. **Former client:** A lawyer who **formerly represented a client** in a matter **shall not** thereafter **represent another** person in the **same or substantially related manner** in which that person's interests are **materially adverse** to the former client *unless* the former client gives informed consent, confirmed in writing (**Cal. informed written consent**).
    e. **Former government employee:** A lawyer who has **formerly** served as a government employee **shall not represent** a client in connection with a matter in which the lawyer participated **personally and substantially** as a government employee unless the governmental agency gives **informed consent, confirmed in writing (Cal. informed written consent).**
        1. The same standard applies to lawyers who served as judges, adjudicative officers, law clerks, arbitrators, mediators, or other third-party neutral persons, but **all parties must** give informed **consent**, confirmed in writing (Cal. informed written consent).
    f. **Current government employee:** A lawyer **currently** serving as a government employee **shall not participate** in a matter in which the lawyer **participated personally and substantially** while **in private practice** unless the government agency gives its **informed consent, confirmed in writing** (Cal. **informed written consent**).

> **Issue spotting tip:** The imputed disqualification and screening rules also apply to former and current government employees. (See section I.B.g. immediately below.)

> **Memorization tip:** The rules for former client, former gov. employee, and current gov. employee all have similar standards to analyze that focus on their involvement in the prior cases, so focus on that if you can't recall the specific rule.

   g. **Imputed firm disqualification: A conflict for one** attorney in a firm is **imputed to all other attorneys in the firm,** resulting in their disqualification, *unless:*
      1. The conflict is based on a **personal interest** of the disqualified (Cal. states prohibited) lawyer and does not present a **significant risk** of **materially limiting** the representation by the other firm attorneys, or
      2. The conflict is based on a **former client** at a **prior firm,** the conflicted lawyer is **timely screened** behind an ethical wall from any participation in the matter, the former client is provided **written notice** and a description of the screening procedures, and
         a. **ABA only:** The client is given **certifications of compliance** with the ethics rules and screening procedures upon request, and
         b. **Cal. only**: The prohibited lawyer **did not substantially participate** in the **same or a substantially related** matter.
      3. A **client can waive** any imputed disqualification with **informed consent, confirmed in writing (Cal. informed written consent).**
   h. **Lawyer leaves firm:** When a lawyer has terminated an association with a firm, the firm **may thereafter represent** a person with **interests materially adverse** to those of a former client represented by the formerly associated lawyer **unless:**
      1. The matter is the **same or substantially related**, and
      2. Any remaining lawyer has **confidential information** that is material to the matter.
      3. This conflict can be **waived** if **each affected client** gives **informed consent, confirmed in writing (Cal. informed written consent).**

> **Fact triggers for conflicts *between clients*:**
> - Lawyer represents a company for an issue that lawyer previously worked on as a board member/lawyer with another organization
> - Representation of organizations with constituents that come to the lawyer for advice
> - Joint business partners (i.e., book author and editor)
> - Co-defendants represented by the same lawyer

  3. **Specific rules for conflicts between *client and a third party*:** A lawyer **shall not** accept **compensation from third parties** to represent the client **unless:**
   a. The client gives **informed consent: Cal. requires informed *written* consent** at or before the time of the agreement or as soon as reasonably practicable, unless court ordered, authorized by law, or the lawyer is working for a public agency/non-profit org., and
   b. There is **no interference** with the lawyer's **independent professional judgment** or with the lawyer-client relationship, and
   c. Information relating to the representation remains **confidential**.
  4. **Specific rules for conflicts between a *client and the lawyer's personal interest***
   a. **Lawyer's personal relationships and beliefs:** When a lawyer is **related to opposing counsel,** has a **past or current relationship with opposing counsel,** or has a **personal belief** that may interfere with their current representation, **apply the general rule and its exceptions** above (see I.B.1.).
   b. **Sexual relations with clients**

    1. **ABA:** A lawyer **shall not** have sexual relations with a client *unless* **a consensual sexual relationship existed** *before* the lawyer-client relationship commenced.

    2. **California follows the ABA rule and** clarifies that the above rule **does not apply to** sexual relations with the **lawyer's spouse or registered domestic partner.**

        a. **California defines sexual relations** as including sexual intercourse or the touching of an intimate part of another person for the purpose of sexual arousal, gratification, or abuse.

  c. **Business transactions with clients:** A lawyer **shall not enter into a business transaction** with a client or knowingly acquire an **ownership, pecuniary,** or similar **interest adverse** to the client **unless:**

    1. The **terms are fair** and reasonable to the client, and

    2. The **terms are fully disclosed in writing** to the client in an understandable manner (**Cal.** also requires that the lawyer's role in the **transaction be fully disclosed** in writing), and

    3. The client is advised **in writing** to **seek independent counsel** (or in Cal. that the client is actually represented by an independent lawyer of the client's choice), and

    4. The **client gives informed written consent** to the **essential terms** and the lawyer's role (and per the ABA whether the lawyer is representing the client in the transaction).

    5. **Exception:** A lawyer can acquire a **lien to secure the lawyer's fees** or contract with a client for a reasonable **contingency fee** in a civil case.

  d. **Solicitation of gifts:** A lawyer **shall not** *solicit* **any substantial gift** from a client **or prepare an instrument** that gives the lawyer, or a person related to the lawyer, a gift unless the lawyer/person is **related** to the client.

    1. If allowed, the gift must be **fair** and made **without undue influence.**

    2. **Cal. additional exception:** A lawyer may accept a gift if the client has been **advised by an independent lawyer** who has provided a certificate of independent review.

  e. **Proprietary interest (ABA):** A lawyer **shall not acquire a proprietary interest** in the cause of action or subject matter of **litigation unless to:**

    1. Acquire a **lien to secure the lawyer's fees,** or

    2. Contract with a client for a **reasonable contingency fee** in a civil case.

> **Issue spotting tip:** Cal. doesn't have this proprietary interest rule, but does allow liens to secure fees and contingency fees. Most essays involve lawyers taking stock or a percent of a business **unrelated** to the representation itself (property the client owned separately that is not in dispute) which invokes the **business transaction rule.** The ABA **proprietary interest rule** would be only addressed if the interest was **related to the representation** (i.e., a percentage of stocks, property, etc. that the lawyer was helping the client get **in the current litigation**), but the regular business transaction rule would still be analyzed for Cal. in that situation.

  f. **Literary/media rights (ABA):** Prior to the conclusion of representation, a lawyer **shall not make** or negotiate an **agreement giving the lawyer literary or media rights** to a **portrayal** or account based on information **relating to the representation.**

    1. Cal. allows such a contract only for **criminal indigent clients** with informed written consent (otherwise Cal. uses the business transaction rule for this scenario).

  g. **Financial assistance/advances to clients**

    1. **ABA only:** A lawyer **shall not provide financial assistance** to a client in connection with litigation, **with the exception of:**

        a. **Contingency cases:** A lawyer may advance **court costs and expenses of litigation** in contingency cases, the repayment of which is dependent on the case outcome, **or**

        b. **Indigent clients:** A lawyer can advance **court costs and expenses of litigation** on behalf of indigent clients. If the lawyer is representing the client through law school clinics or pro bono, they can also provide modest gifts for food, rent, transportation, and medicine.

    2. **Cal. only:** A lawyer may **lend** money to the client **after employment**, for **any purpose,** if the client promises in **writing to repay** the loan.

h. **Limiting malpractice liability**

    1. **ABA only:** A lawyer **may not agree to limit** their malpractice liability to the client **unless the client is represented by independent counsel.** Agreements to arbitrate claims are allowed if the client is informed.

    2. **Cal. only:** California does **not allow a lawyer** to contract with a client to **limit their malpractice liability.**

i. **Settlement of claims**: A lawyer shall **not settle a claim or potential claim** for such liability with an **unrepresented** client or former client **unless that person is advised in writing** to **seek independent counsel** and is given a reasonable opportunity to do so (**or** if they are **represented** by independent counsel).

Fact triggers for conflicts between a *client and lawyer's personal interests:*

- L is friends with C or is related to C
- L has or had a relationship with C, or opposing counsel
- L has an interest in the subject matter in which they are assisting C or their beliefs are opposite the C's
- L's payment depends on the outcome of the case and how much money is spent in litigation
- L is offered a job by opposing counsel
- L has an interest in a company being sold or acts on inside information

---

Exam tip: Conflicts of interest (COI) are the most heavily tested issues on professional responsibility essays. Be sure to first start by looking at what type of conflict exists; then, determine whether it is a **potential (future) or actual (current) conflict** (it can start out as potential and turn into actual). Next, **identify the corresponding ABA and Cal. rules.** Most essays require you to analyze the general conflicts rule and its exceptions first. Then, you narrow in on a specific rule if applicable. Often the facts give rise to multiple conflicts. There is a "conflicts of interests testing chart" at the end of the chapter. You should make sure you understand how all these conflicts are tested in those essays and the various levels of depth required in the analysis for each one (which varies depending on other issues being tested). Also note how the same facts give rise to numerous conflicts and different rules. Don't assume since you addressed one COI, you are done. Spot them all to earn maximum points.

C. **Duty to communicate:** The lawyer shall **promptly inform the client** of any decision that affects the client's informed consent as well as reasonably consult with the client and keep them informed of the **status of the case,** including any settlement and plea offers, and **promptly respond** to client communications and reasonable requests for information.

    1. A lawyer may **delay transmission** of information to a client if the **lawyer reasonably believes** that the client would be likely to react in a way that may **cause imminent harm** to the client or others.

    2. **Cal.:** Lawyer must **notify the client of funds** or other property the lawyer received on behalf of the client **within 14 days.**

D. **Scope of representation:** The lawyer must abide by the **client's substantive decisions** (e.g., settle, plea, or waive jury trial, expenses, testify, appeal) after the lawyer has consulted with the client. The **lawyer** is responsible for employing the appropriate **legal strategy** (e.g., motions, discovery, witness or evidence use, etc.).

> **Issue spotting tip:** Often when the lawyer fails to inform the client about a possible settlement, offer, or plea, it invokes both the issues of the scope of the representation and the lawyer's duty to communicate. As a result, if scope is involved, always address the duty to communicate as well.

E. **Duty of confidentiality**
1. **Duty of confidentiality (ABA):** A lawyer **shall not reveal** information relating to the representation of a client, **except the lawyer *may* in the following situations:**
   a. The client gives **informed <u>C</u>onsent,**
   b. The disclosure is **impliedly <u>A</u>uthorized** to represent the client,
   c. The lawyer **reasonably believes the disclosure is necessary** to prevent reasonably certain **<u>D</u>eath or substantial bodily harm,**
   d. To *prevent* the client from committing a **<u>C</u>rime or fraud** or to *mitigate* or *rectify* a crime or fraud committed by the client that has resulted or is reasonably certain to result in **substantial injury to the financial interests** or property of another **and** the client is or has **used the lawyer's services** to do so,
   e. To **<u>C</u>omply with a court order** or other law,
   f. To **secure legal <u>A</u>dvice** about the lawyer's compliance with ethics rules,
   g. **To establish a claim or <u>D</u>efense** on behalf of the lawyer in a **controversy between the lawyer and the client**, or in defense of the conduct the client was involved in with the lawyer's services (e.g., defend malpractice, or collect fees), or
   h. To detect or **resolve <u>C</u>onflicts of interest** arising from a change in employment or reorganization (cannot compromise the attorney-client privilege).

> **Memorization tip:** <u>C</u>ats <u>A</u>nd <u>D</u>ogs <u>C</u>an <u>C</u>uddle <u>A</u>nd <u>D</u>ream <u>C</u>onstantly

2. **Duty of confidentiality (Cal.):** A lawyer **shall not reveal** information relating to the representation of a client **without the informed consent of the client, except the lawyer *may* in the following situations:**
   a. When the lawyer **reasonably believes** it is **necessary** to **prevent a criminal act** that the lawyer **reasonably believes** is likely to result in **death or substantial bodily harm, however** the lawyer **must:**
      1. First make a **good faith effort** to **persuade the client** not to commit the act, and
      2. **Inform** the client of the lawyer's ability to reveal the information, and
      3. **Only reveal as much information as necessary** to prevent the act.
   b. When **authorized by the State Bar Act or other law.**
   c. **To establish a claim or defense** on behalf of the lawyer in a **controversy between the lawyer and the client**, or in defense of the conduct the client was involved in with the lawyer's services. (E.g., defend malpractice, or collect fees.)
3. **Difference between Cal. and ABA rule: Cal. is much stricter** and provides fewer grounds permitting revealing confidential information.

> **Exam tip:** Remember that Cal. is extremely strict with regard to confidentiality, much more so than the ABA. Also, whenever there is a conflict of interest between clients or an organization and one of its constituents, always raise the duty of confidentiality since it is always a possible violation since the lawyer can accidentally disclose information from one client to the other in these situations. Many exams often raise the issue even if the lawyer has yet to disclose any information. Thus, even if the call asks what violations the lawyer has committed, it is best to raise the issue to let the grader know there is a likelihood of disclosure and the lawyer could easily violate the duty of confidentiality in that situation.

F. **Attorney-client privilege** is an *evidentiary privilege* that allows a client to keep **confidential all communications** with their attorney, **intended to be confidential,** made for the **purpose of facilitating legal services.** The client can **refuse to testify** and **prevent their attorney from testifying.** (Also see evidence chapter Sec. V.B.1.)

1. **Client:** A client can be an **individual,** as well as a **corporation.**
   a. **Federal common law:** Applies to **employees/agents if authorized** by the corporation to make the communication to the lawyer.
   b. **CEC:** Applies to **employees/agents** if the **natural person to speak** to the lawyer on behalf of the corporation, or the employee did something for which the corporation may be held liable and the corporation instructed the employee to tell its lawyer what happened. (While the language is different, as applied, both FRE and CEC rules yield the same result.)

2. **Confidential communications:** The communication must be **intended to be confidential.**
   a. The presence of a **third party** may serve to **waive** the privilege, unless where necessary (e.g., translator).
   b. **Does not apply to physical evidence** turned over to the lawyer, only to communications, so the presentation of physical evidence (e.g., a gun) is not privileged.
   c. **CEC only:** Allows the priviledge holder to stop **eavesdroppers** and other wrongful inceptors from revealing confidential information.

3. **Professional services:** The communication must be made for the **purpose of facilitating legal services**, though a fee need not be paid.

4. **Holder of the privilege:** Only the **client holds the privilege,** and the lawyer may assert it on the client's behalf.

5. **Privilege lasts until:**
   a. **Federal law**: **After death**, with the exception of a will contest.
   b. **CEC:** Privilege evaporates when the dead client's **estate has been fully distributed,** and their personal representative has been discharged.

6. **Exceptions:** The attorney client privilege **does not apply** if:
   a. **Crime or fraud:** The communication was used in *furtherance* of something the client should have known was a *crime or* fraud; or
   b. **Dispute with lawyer:** The communication relates to a dispute between the lawyer and client; or
   c. **Two or more parties** consult on a matter of common interest and the communication is offered **by one against another;** or
   d. **CEC only:** Lawyer **reasonably** believes the disclosure is **necessary to** *prevent a criminal act* that lawyer **reasonably believes** is likely to result in **death or substantial bodily harm.**

7. **Note: Attorney work product is material prepared in anticipation of litigation, and it is generally not discoverable (protected)** absent a showing of substantial need (see Civ. Pro. chapter **Sec.** II.D.3.c.).

> **Exam tip:** The duty of confidentiality is an **ethical duty** and applies to **any disclosure of a communication**, regardless of whether the client requests it; whereas the attorney-client privilege is an **evidentiary privilege** and is much narrower and only applies when the lawyer or client will be **testifying in a judicial proceeding** about confidential **communications pertaining to the legal services.**

G. **Duty to avoid fee misunderstandings**
1. **Regular fee agreements**
   a. **ABA:** All fees must be **reasonable** considering the following factors:
      1. **Time limitations** imposed by the client or circumstances,
      2. **Experience, reputation,** and **ability** of the lawyer;
      3. **Nature** and **length of the relationship** with the client;
      4. **Time and labor, novelty** and **difficulty,** and skill required;
      5. **Fee customarily charged** in the locality for similar services;
      6. **Likelihood** that the acceptance will **preclude other employment;**
      7. **Amount involved** and results obtained; and
      8. **Whether** the fee is **fixed or contingent.**

    b. **California:** Fees may **not be illegal or unconscionable** based on the same ABA factors above as well as these additional factors:
        1. Whether the lawyer engaged in **Fraud** or overreaching in setting the fee,
        2. Whether the lawyer failed to **Disclose** material facts,
        3. **Sophistication** of both the lawyer and the client,
        4. The **Amount** of the fee in proportion to the value of the services performed,
        5. Whether the client gave informed **Consent** to the fee.

> **Memorization tip:** Since there are so many factors, think of **TENT FLAW** to remember the ABA reasonable/Cal. unconscionable factors. Think of yourself camping and having a tent mishap. . . picture it now. For the Cal. additional factors think of **F**urry **D**ogs **S**atisfy **A**nxious **C**lients. On an essay, you will usually not have time to go through all factors so pick 4-5 that the facts give rise to and analyze those.

    c. **Fee agreements should state:**
        1. How the fee is **calculated,**
        2. The general **nature of the legal services,** and
        3. The **responsibilities** of the lawyer and the client.
    d. **Writing requirement:**
        1. **ABA** *prefers* **a writing** but **does not require one for** regular fee agreements as long as the scope and fees are **communicated** to the client within a **reasonable time** after commencing representation.
        2. **California** requires all fee agreements **over $1,000 to be in writing** *unless:*
            a. The client is a **corporation,**
            b. The agreement was made during an **emergency,**
            c. The client **waives** the writing **requirement in writing,** or
            d. The services are for a **previous client with similar services** in which the fee can be implied.
    e. **Fee dispute arbitration: Cal. requires** a lawyer to **notify a client** of their right to **mandatory fee dispute arbitration** prior to suing the client for fees, whereas the **ABA only requires arbitration if** such a procedure has been established as **mandatory by a state bar or law.**

2. **Contingency fee agreements**
    a. A **contingency fee agreement** is one in which the fee is **dependent on the outcome** of the matter and must:
        1. Be in **writing,**
        2. Be **signed by the client** (**Cal.** requires the agreement to be **signed by both** the lawyer and client with each having a copy),
        3. State the **method by which the fee is to be determined,** including **percentages** in the event of a settlement, trial, or appeal,
        4. State the **litigation and other expenses to be deducted** from the recovery, and
        5. State whether such **expenses will be deducted before or after the contingent fee is calculated** (**Cal.** looks at how disbursements and costs will affect the contingency fee and client's recovery and if the client will have to pay any related matters not covered by the agreement).
    b. **Cal.** further requires that the agreement state that the **fee is negotiable** (*unless* the claim is for **negligence against a health care provider**).
    c. **Domestic or criminal cases:** A lawyer **may not** enter into a **contingent fee agreement** in a **domestic relations** matter (i.e., dissolution of marriage, spousal or child support, but recovery of post-judgment balances due are allowed) or a **criminal case.**

> **Issue spotting tip:** When there is a contingency fee agreement, look for potential conflict of interest issues since the lawyer has a stake in the case outcome.

3. **Fee splitting**
   a. **ABA: Division of fees between lawyers** who are **not in the same firm** may be made only if:
      1. The **division is proportionate** to the services performed by each lawyer, or each lawyer assumes joint responsibility for the representation,
      2. Client **agrees** to the arrangement and **the agreement is confirmed in writing**, and
      3. The total fee is **reasonable**.
   b. **Cal.: Division of fees between lawyers** who are **not in the same firm** may be made only if:
      1. The **lawyers enter** into a **written agreement** to divide the fee,
      2. The client **consents in writing** after **full written disclosure** that the fees will be divided along with the **identity** of the lawyers and the **terms** of the division, and
      3. The total fee is **not increased** simply because of the division of fees.
4. **Fee sharing with non-lawyers:** A lawyer **may not share** legal fees with a non-lawyer.
5. **Referral Fees/Gifts for Recommendations:** A lawyer **shall not give** (**Cal.** says compensate or promise) **anything of value to a person** for recommending the lawyer's services *unless:*
   a. It is for **reasonable advertisement costs,** or
   b. It is for a **qualified referral service, or**
   c. It is a **nominal gift as an expression of appreciation** not intended as compensation for the recommendation or future recommendations, or
   d. They are referring clients to another **lawyer or nonlawyer professional** pursuant to a **reciprocal referral agreement** (Cal. says arrangement) if it is **not exclusive** and the client is **informed** of the agreement.
6. **Cal. Retainer Fees:** A lawyer may agree to or collect a fee that that is "earned on receipt" or **"non-refundable,"** or in similar terms if **the client agrees in writing** after **disclosure that they cannot get a refund**.
   a. **Purpose:** A true retainer is to **ensure the lawyer's availability** to the client during a specified period or for a specified matter.
7. **Cal. Flat Fees:** A lawyer may charge a flat fee **for specified legal services** that constitutes **complete payment** for the performance regardless of the amount of work done (i.e., $5,000 to draft a will and trust). Fees **over $1,000 must be in writing** and **signed** by the client.
   a. **Deposit of funds:** Funds may be deposited into the **law firm's operating account** until earned, but the firm **must disclose to the client in writing** that they have a right to have the funds deposited into a **client trust account** until earned and the client can get a **refund in the event of termination,** or services not completed.
8. **Cal. Non-Flat Fee Advance Fees and all ABA Advance Fees:** A lawyer shall deposit into a **client trust account** legal fees and expenses paid in advance, to be **withdrawn only as earned** or expenses incurred.

H. **Duty of competence**
   1. **ABA:** A lawyer shall competently represent the client with the legal **knowledge, skill, thoroughness,** and **preparation** reasonably necessary for the representation.
   2. **Cal.:** A lawyer must not **intentionally, recklessly, with gross negligence, or repeatedly** fail to perform legal services with competence.
      a. A lawyer's duty to act competently includes **mental, physical**, and **emotional** ability, as well as staying informed of new law and technology.
   3. **ABA and Cal.:** A lawyer can associate or **consult with another competent lawyer, acquire the necessary skills** to become competent *before* performance is required, or **refer the matter** to another competent lawyer.

I. **Duty of diligence**
   1. **ABA:** A lawyer shall act with **reasonable diligence** and **promptness** in representing a client.
   2. **Cal.:** A lawyer shall not **intentionally, repeatedly, recklessly, or with gross negligence** fail to act with reasonable diligence in representing a client.
      a. **Reasonable diligence means** timeliness and that a lawyer acts with **commitment and dedication** to the interests of the client and does **not neglect or disregard**, or **unduly delay** a legal matter entrusted to the lawyer.

> **Issue spotting tip:** The duty of competence is likely at issue any time the fact pattern indicates that the lawyer is newly admitted, is being asked to practice in an area of law with which they are unfamiliar, or when the lawyer misjudges a case (i.e., missed that the other side had strong defenses). The duty of diligence is often an issue when the lawyer does something wrong with timing (i.e., spends very little time on a case, delays a case, etc.).

J. **Duty to safekeep client's property:** A lawyer shall hold property of clients, or third persons connected with a representation, **separate from the lawyer's own property**.
   1. **Client trust account:** Funds must be kept in a **client trust account** in the state the lawyer is located (outside jurisdictions allowed with client's written consent) and lawyer must **keep accounting records** for **five years**.
      a. **Exception:** A lawyer may deposit their **own funds** into a client trust account to pay **bank service charges**.
      b. **Cal. exception: Flat fees** can be placed in a firm's **operating account** (see section I.G.7. above).
      c. **Cal.** requires all **trust accounts be registered with the State Bar** and that **lawyers open an IOLTA** (Interest on Lawyer's Trusts Account) account.
   2. **Prompt payment:** Lawyer must **promptly** (Cal. presumes prompt is within 45 days) **pay the client any funds due** (e.g., settlement proceeds) along with a **full accounting**. But if there is a contingency agreement, lawyer may hold back the funds they reasonably believe they are due.
   3. **Fee dispute with client:** Lawyer must **send any money not in dispute** and leave disputed portion in trust account pending dispute resolution. **Cal.** allows clients to have mandatory fee **arbitration** for fee disputes and the **ABA** only requires it when required by a state bar or law.
   4. **Safekeep client's physical property:** A lawyer shall **hold a client's or third party's physical property** that is connected with the lawyer's representation **separate** from the lawyer's own property. The **separate client property** must also:
      a. Be **identified and labeled**,
      b. Be stored in a **safe place** (i.e., safe deposit box) and safeguarded, and
      c. Be **tracked in a written journal** (and kept for at least 5 years after distribution).
K. **Withdrawal:** Withdrawal is a possible issue whenever ethical rules are violated or will be violated.
   1. **Mandatory withdrawal:** A lawyer **shall withdraw** from representation when:
      a. The representation will result in a **violation of the rules** of **professional** conduct.
         1. **ABA:** Also includes violation of **other law**.
         2. **Cal.:** Also includes violation of the State Bar Act (which includes the CA Business and Professions Code).
      b. The lawyer's **mental or physical condition** materially impairs (Cal. says renders representation unreasonably difficult) the lawyer's ability to represent the client; or
      c. The lawyer is **discharged** by the client.
      d. **Cal. only:** The lawyer **knows or should know** that the client is bringing an action **without probable cause** or to **harass or maliciously injure** a person.
      e. **ABA only:** Client seeks to **use lawyer's services to commit or further a crime** or fraud.
   2. **Permissive withdrawal**
      a. **ABA and Cal.:** A lawyer **may withdraw** from representation when:
         1. The client insists on action involving the lawyer's services that (per ABA **lawyer reasonably believes**) **is fraudulent or criminal**, or
         2. The client has used the lawyer's services to **perpetrate a crime or fraud** (**Cal.** says lawyer **reasonably believed** it was a crime or fraud), or
         3. The representation has been rendered **unreasonably difficult** by the client, or
         4. The **client fails substantially to fulfill an obligation** (Cal. includes breach of a material term) to the lawyer regarding the lawyer's services and has been given **reasonable warning** that the lawyer will withdraw unless the obligation is fulfilled, or
         5. Other **good cause** exists.

    b. **ABA only:** In addition to the rule above, ABA also permits withdrawal when:
1. The client has used the lawyer's services to perpetrate a crime or fraud, or
2. The client insists upon taking **action that the lawyer considers repugnant** or with which the lawyer has a **fundamental disagreement**, or
3. The lawyer can do so **without material adverse effect** on the interests of the client, or
4. The representation will result in an **unreasonable financial burden** on the lawyer.

    c. **Cal. only:** In addition to the common rules above, Cal. also permits withdrawal when:
1. The client **insists** on presenting claims or defenses that **cannot be supported by good faith or good law**, or
2. The client knowingly and freely **assents** to the termination, or
3. **Lawyer's mental and physical condition** renders it difficult to continue, or
4. A continuation is likely to result in **violation of the California Rules** of Professional Conduct or the State Bar Act, or
5. The lawyer is **unable to work with co-counsel**.

3. **Duty to client upon withdrawal:** When the court grants permission for withdrawal, the lawyer shall protect the client's interests, and:
    a. Provide the client with **reasonable notice** to allow time to seek other counsel,
    b. **Surrender papers and property** (the lawyer may retain a copy at their own expense), and
    c. **Refund any advanced fees** not yet earned.

> **Exam tip:** Anytime the lawyer has violated a rule of professional responsibility or engaged in any of the activities that support withdrawal, you should mention withdrawal briefly and explain why the attorney may want to withdraw and whether it would be permissive or mandatory. You do not need to state the entire rule. Only select portions of the rule that are applicable to the facts and analyze those.

II. PROFESSIONAL INTEGRITY
A. Advertising/solicitation
1. **Advertising allowed: Advertising must not be false or misleading.** A lawyer **may advertise** services through written, recorded or electronic communication, including public media, *unless* the prospective client has made it known to the lawyer of their desire to not be solicited. All advertisements must:
    a. **Be truthful.** A lawyer **shall not make false or misleading communications** about the lawyer or the lawyer's services.
    b. Contain the **name and address** (ABA says contact information which can include a telephone number) of at least one lawyer responsible for its content.

2. **No direct solicitation:** A lawyer **may not conduct in-person,** live telephone, or real-time electronic contact for **pecuniary gain, subject to the following exceptions:**
    a. **Free legal services** (not motivated by pecuniary gain),
    b. **Family members** or those with a **close personal relationship** to lawyer,
    c. **Prior professional relationships** or other lawyers, or
    d. **Prepaid or group legal service plans** operated by an organization, not owned or directed by the lawyer that sells plans/subscriptions to **people who are not known** to have a specific legal problem.

3. **Cal. only label:** Those **known to be in need of legal services in a particular matter** can be contacted by written, recorded, or electronic communication if the advertisement includes the word **"Advertisement"** or similar words on the outside of the envelope and at the beginning and end of any recorded or electronic communication, **unless** it is **apparent that it is an advertisement.**

> **Rule understanding tip:** "Live" communication does not likely include chat rooms or text messages (i.e., forums that recipients can easily disregard — unless they are being harassed) in Cal. (the ABA specifically says those are not included). And lawyers **cannot use runners or cappers** (others) to avoid liability for improper solicitations.

4. **Cal. presumes** the following communications to be in **violation of the rules:**
   a. Express **guarantees** or warranties.
   b. **Testimonials** or endorsements **without a disclaimer** that it is not a guarantee, warranty, or prediction of results.
   c. **"No fee without recovery"** communications, unless it expressly discloses whether the **client will be liable for costs.**
   d. **Solicitations in prisons and hospitals** and similar institutions.
   e. **Impersonations or dramatizations** unless there are disclosures indicating they are such.
5. **Specialists:** A lawyer shall not imply or state that they are **certified as a specialist** in a particular field of law, unless:
   a. The lawyer has been **certified as a specialist** by the ABA or a state-approved organization, and
      1. **Cal.** requires it to be an organization certified by the Board of Legal Specialization or other entity **accredited by the Cal. State Bar.**
   b. The **name of the certifying organization is clearly identified** in the communication.
   c. A lawyer is **allowed to communicate** that they **"practice"** in a particular field of law or that their firm **"specializes in"** a particular field of law, but such communications are subject to the false and misleading standards.

B. **Unauthorized practice of law**
   1. **No practice with a non-lawyer:** A lawyer **shall not practice** with or form a partnership or association with a non-lawyer **to provide legal service.**
      a. A lawyer **shall not share legal fees** with a non-lawyer.
      b. A **non-lawyer shall not direct or control** the lawyer's professional judgment.
      c. **Disbarred lawyers:** A lawyer cannot hire a disbarred lawyer to **perform legal services,** but they **can perform non-legal tasks** such as research or clerical work.
         1. **Notification:** The CA State Bar and the client **must both be informed in writing** of the employment of the disbarred attorney.

C. **Liability for others lawyer's conduct**
   1. **Responsible for another lawyer's ethical violation:** A lawyer shall be **responsible for another lawyer's violation** of the Rules of Professional Conduct if the lawyer knowingly **ratifies the conduct,** or is a **partner,** or has **direct supervisory authority** over the other lawyer and could have **mitigated** the consequences.
      a. **Subordinate lawyer:** A lawyer **does not violate these rules** if they act in accordance with a **supervisory lawyer's reasonable resolution** of an **arguable question** of professional duty.

D. **Duty of fairness:** A lawyer has a **general duty of fairness to third parties, opposing counsel,** and the **court.**
   1. **Duty of fairness to represented parties:**
      a. **Represented persons:** A lawyer **shall not communicate with people known to be represented** by another lawyer in that matter **unless** the other lawyer has **consented,** or the communication is **authorized** by law or court order.
      b. **Represented Corporation/Organization:** A lawyer must **obtain consent** of **organization's lawyer** before speaking with:
         1. One who supervises or **regularly consults with organization's lawyer,** or
         2. One who has the **authority to obligate** the organization regarding the matter at issue, or
         3. One whose **conduct in the matter may be imputed** to the organization.

2. **Duty of fairness to unrepresented parties:** When a lawyer communicates with an unrepresented person in a matter, the lawyer shall **not state or imply that they are disinterested** and must make **reasonable efforts to correct any misunderstandings** (i.e., identify who they represent). The lawyer also shall **not give legal advice** to that person, other than advise them to seek independent counsel.

3. **Duty of fairness to the court:** A lawyer shall not knowingly:
   a. **Make a false statement** of fact or law to a tribunal or fail to correct a false statement of material fact or law previously made,
   b. **Fail to disclose adverse legal authority**, or
   c. **Offer evidence that the lawyer knows to be false (perjury).**
      1. If a lawyer **knows that their client or a witness** will offer material **evidence that is false**, the lawyer shall **take remedial measures** including trying to **persuade the client or witness** not to offer the evidence and if necessary, **disclosure to the tribunal** (Cal. says subject to lawyer's duty of confidentiality).
      2. If a lawyer has tried to persuade a client or witness not to offer false evidence and they refuse, the lawyer **must refuse to offer false evidence**.
         a. **Exception:** A lawyer must allow a **criminal defendant** to testify even if they know it is false by allowing them to testify in **narrative form**.
   d. A lawyer who knows the **client intends to engage in fraudulent or criminal activity** shall take reasonable **remedial measures**, including, if necessary and permissible, disclosure to the tribunal (Cal. says subject to lawyer's duty of confidentiality).

4. **Duty of fairness to opposing counsel:** As to the opposing counsel and their party, a lawyer **shall not:**
   a. **Unlawfully obstruct** another party's access to **evidence**, or destroy or conceal (**Cal. includes suppress**) documents or other material;
   b. **Falsify evidence** or induce others to do so;
   c. **Fail to promptly notify** the sender of the inadvertent disclosure of attorney work product or privileged material.
      1. Inadvertent disclosure does not waive the attorney/client privilege if the holder took reasonable steps to prevent disclosure and rectify the error.
      2. An attorney receiving inadvertently disclosed documents must stop examining the content promptly, notify the sender, and not use the document to their advantage.
   d. **Knowingly disobey the court rules;**
   e. **Allude to any matter** the lawyer does not reasonably believe is relevant or will **not be supported by admissible evidence** during trial (Cal. says to not assert personal knowledge of facts);
   f. **ABA: Make a frivolous discovery request** or fail to reasonably comply with discovery requests;
   g. **ABA: Request others to refrain from giving relevant information** unless a relative or agent of client;
   h. **Cal.: Pay a witness to testify** unless for reasonable expert fees, compensation for loss of time for witness to testify, or reasonable expenses incurred (ABA allows witness expenses to paid as permitted by law);
   i. **Cal.: Advise a person to secrete themself** or leave the jurisdiction to avoid being available to testify.

5. **Duty of decorum to the tribunal** (judges, jurors, employees, etc.): A lawyer **shall not:**
   a. **Seek to influence jurors, judges**, or other officials,
   b. **Communicate ex parte** with such persons during proceedings,
   c. **Engage in conduct intended to disrupt proceedings**, or
   d. **Communicate with jurors** after they are discharged if they don't want to communicate.

6. **Trial publicity:** A lawyer who is participating in an investigation or litigation or a matter **shall not make** an extrajudicial statement that the lawyer knows or reasonably should know will be **publicly disseminated** and have a **substantial likelihood of materially prejudicing** the proceeding.
   a. The **lawyer may state** the **claim, offense**, or **defense** involved; the information in the **public records**; that an **investigation is in progress**; **requests for information**; **warnings** of danger; and the **status of the accused** in a criminal case.

    b. The following are more **likely than not prejudicial**, and should not be publicly stated:
      1. **Character, credibility, reputation,** or criminal record of a suspect or witness;
      2. Possibility of a **guilty plea** or **contents of a confession** or any **test results;**
      3. **Opinion as to guilt or innocence** of criminal defendant; or
      4. Information the lawyer reasonably knows is **likely to be inadmissible.**
  7. **Special duties of public prosecutors: Public prosecutors shall**
    a. **Refrain from prosecuting** charges that are **not supported by probable cause;**
    b. Make **reasonable efforts** to ensure the accused is advised of the **right to counsel;**
    c. **Not seek** to obtain **waivers** of rights from an **unrepresented accused;**
    d. Make **timely disclosure** to the defense of all **exculpatory evidence;**
    e. **Refrain from making extrajudicial statements** that have a **substantial likelihood** of heightening **public condemnation** of the accused (Cal. says use reasonable care); and
    f. Disclose to the court and investigate **new evidence** that shows **defendant might not have committed** a crime;
    g. **Seek to remedy known wrongful convictions.**
  8. **Lawyer as witness:** A lawyer shall **not act as an advocate in a trial** in which the **lawyer is likely to be a witness** unless the lawyer's testimony relates to an **uncontested issue,** or the nature and **value of legal services** rendered.

> **Exam tip:** Anytime a lawyer takes any action that may disadvantage another party, opposing counsel, or alter evidence, consider the duty of fairness. If there is an action occurring in the facts that is not specified in the rules above but seems questionable, mention the duty of fairness. Use common sense to determine what you think the lawyer should do and what you would do as an ethical lawyer. Label the discussion "Duty of Fairness" and analyze why the actions are or are not fair and/or ethical to others.

E. Duty to report ethical violations
  1. **ABA:** A **lawyer who knows that another lawyer** has committed a **violation** of the Model Rules that **raises a substantial question as to that lawyer's honesty,** trustworthiness, or fitness as a lawyer **shall** inform the appropriate professional authority.
  2. **Cal.:** A lawyer must inform the State Bar when they know of credible evidence that **another lawyer** has committed a **criminal act or engaged in dishonesty or misrepresentations** or misappropriated funds that raise **a substantial question as to that lawyer's honesty,** trustworthiness, or fitness as a lawyer.
  3. **Cal. self-reporting:** A lawyer must **report themselves** within 30 days when they have been:
    a. Sued for **malpractice** 3 times in 12 months.
    b. Found **civilly liable for fraud,** breach of fiduciary duty, etc.
    c. **Sanctioned** more than $1,000.
    d. **Charged with a felony.**
    e. **Convicted** of a **serious crime.**
    f. **Disciplined** in Cal. or another jurisdiction.
F. Duty to the public/profession
  1. **Be truthful:** A lawyer **shall not** make a **false statement** of material fact or law to others, or **fail to disclose** material facts not protected under the duty of confidentiality, **or engage in conduct involving dishonesty, fraud, or deceit.**
  2. **No frivolous claims:** A lawyer **shall not bring or defend** a proceeding unless there is a **good faith basis in law and fact** for doing so.
  3. **No criminal conduct:** A lawyer **shall not** counsel a client to engage, or assist a client, in **criminal or fraudulent conduct,** but may counsel the client to discuss the legal consequences and assist them in making a good faith effort to understand the law. A **lawyer shall not commit a criminal act** that reflects adversely on their own **honesty, trustworthiness,** or fitness as a lawyer.
  4. **No harassment/discrimination:** Cal. prohibits a lawyer from seeking, accepting, or continuing employment to conduct a defense or case **without probable cause** or for the purpose of

harassing or maliciously injuring any person. The ABA also prohibits harassment and discrimination as determined by federal and state law.

5. **No threats: Cal. prohibits a lawyer from threatening** to present criminal, administrative, or disciplinary charges **to obtain an unfair advantage** in a **civil dispute.**

> **Exam tip:** Similar to the broad scope of the duty of fairness, anytime a lawyer acts inappropriately in a fact pattern, you should also address the lawyer's duty to the public/profession. Use common sense to determine what you think the lawyer should do and what you would do as an ethical lawyer. Label the discussion "Duty to the Public/Profession" and analyze why the actions are or are not fair and/or ethical to others.

TESTING FREQUENCY OF CONFLICTS OF INTEREST (2014 TO 2024)

General Rule Triggered	
Conflicts between clients (current, former, or prospective)	
July 2024	Potential conflict when attorney Rita agreed to jointly represent Paul against Dani and Rita already knew Dani (facts unclear how they knew each other or the status of their relationship).
July 2023	Potential conflict when corp. employee asks corp. L for advice and discloses confidential info that is damaging to company; actual conflict when employee asks L to keep info from CEO at company
February 2023	Potential conflict with L's prior pro bono work (former client) against chemical use and current client who is being sued for its chemicals AND actual conflict when L disclosed info about the current client's lawsuit to the prior pro bono org. client (note state answers did a very cursory analysis here due to other issues and timing — good example of spotting an issue and doing a truncated IRAC)
February 2020	Potential conflict when L agrees to represent non-profit org. but a board member asks L to hide her salary info from other board members; actual when L can't protect the board member's confidences without harming the non-profit org.
July 2018	Potential conflict when L represents his niece and her friend as co-defendants in a robbery since both could turn on each other
July 2016	Actual conflict when L represents ABC to challenge a statute and P, the President of ABC, tells L that P filed false documents with the EPA
Conflicts between client and lawyer (lawyer's personal interest)	
February 2024	Actual conflict when L asked client for season tickets if she succeeded in his assault case so she lied in court so he could win (then she would get tickets)
February 2023	Potential conflict with L's prior pro bono work against chemical use and current client who is being sued for its chemicals (L personally disagrees with use of the chemicals); Actual conflict when L disclosed info about the current client's lawsuit to his prior pro bono organization members (note state answers did a very cursory analysis here due to other issues and timing — good example of spotting an issue and doing a truncated IRAC)
July 2022	Potential and actual conflict when L possibly settled too quickly for her own benefit since based on contingency (note state answers did a very cursory analysis here due to other issues and timing — good example of spotting an issue and doing a truncated IRAC)
February 2022	Actual conflict when L put her own interest and opinions first and didn't believe C so she turned over evidence and emails between her and C to the prosecutor (note only one state answer briefly mentioned L's loyalty to C but these facts do give rise to L putting her own beliefs above C's interest but it was a minor issue)
July 2021	Actual conflict when L1 shares an office with L2 and L1's son is the receptionist for both; the son left out a document for L2 that involved L1's client but L1 didn't disclose lies she uncovered that were helpful to her client because she wanted to protect her son's mistake
February 2021	Actual conflict when L gets distracted by relationship with client and almost misses deadlines
October 2020	Potential conflict when L represents client and opposing counsel is L's prior romantic partner
July 2019	Potential conflict when L receives job offer from opposing counsel law firm
July 2018	Potential conflict when L represents his niece and her friend as co-defendants in a robbery since L could favor his niece's interests

General Rule Triggered	
Conflicts between client and lawyer (lawyer's personal interest) (continued)	
February 2017	Potential conflict when L had a prior relationship with opposing counsel 2 years ago
July 2016	Potential conflict when L represents ABC to challenge a statute that was enacted due to the help of an org. L was a member of; L disagrees with ABC's objective
February 2016	Potential conflict when L represents boyfriend Contractor; Actual conflict when the relationship status affects her representation
February 2015	Potential and actual conflicts when L represents Online, Inc. and sells it to a company his wife owns stock in, then enters joint venture with another company that L owns making L a lot of money
July 2014	Actual conflict when AB Law represents Sid Co., and Lawyer A buys stock in a company that Sid planned to buy
Special Conflict Rule Triggered	
Organization as a Client	
July 2023	Entry level employee of a mortgage company comes to L with proof of fraudulent lending practices when L represents the company
February 2023	L represents company being sued for personal injury; L previously did pro bono work for an org. with interests adverse to company
February 2020	Board member asks L to represent its non-profit organization and to hide salary info about board member to the rest of the org.
July 2016	L represents ABC Corp. to challenge a statute that was enacted due to the help of an org. L was a member of and helped
February 2015	L represents Online, Inc. and sells it to LargeCo. where wife is a SH
Limiting Malpractice	
July 2022	L agreed to give client more money from a personal injury settlement if client agreed not to sue her
February 2016	L represents boyfriend Contractor and he agrees not to sue for malpractice
Sexual Relations with Client	
February 2021	L initiates sexual relationship with client
February 2016	L represents boyfriend Contractor and has sexual relations
Financial assistance/Advancing Fees	
July 2022	L agreed to pay client's costs upfront since client had no money
July 2018	L represents co-defendants in a robbery and agrees to advance all costs
Business Transaction with Client	
February 2015	L represents Online, Inc. and sells it to LargeCo., where wife is a major SH; LargeCo. enters joint venture with TechCo. which L owns
Solicitation of Gifts	
February 2024	L asks for season tickets to represent an athlete
Imputation of Conflicts	
July 2019	L receives job offer from opposing counsel law firm

PROFESSIONAL RESPONSIBILITY ISSUES TESTED MATRIX

	Crossover	Duty of Loyalty/Conflicts	Duty to Communicate/Scope of Representation	Duty of Confidentiality	Attorney-Client Privilege/Work Product	Fees & Splitting/Gifts/Loans	Duties of Competence/Diligence	Attorney-Client Relationship/Sexual Relations	Withdraw/File Return	Solicitation/Advertising	Fairness to Parties/Counsel/Court	Unauthorized Practice Law/Report Ethics Violation	Duties to Public/Profession
July '24 Q3 Attorney August represents Paul against real estate broker Dani		X	X	X		X	X				X	X	X
February '24 Q3 Criminal defense atty Allison represents athlete Davos		X	X	X		X	X				X		X
July '23 Q3 Employee Eric at MoreHome tells GC Laura about falsified docs		X	X	X			X	X	X				
February '23 Q4 Atty Andy represents LawnCare for weed killer suit		X	X	X		X	X	X	X		X		
July '22 Q3 Clint hired lawyer Linda to represent him v. Dan for injuries		X	X			X	X						
February '22 Q4 Atty Anita represented Dan for murder and is called to testify	Evidence	X	X	X	X		X		X		X		
July '21 Q2 Lawyers Laura (family law) & Alex (tax law) share a suite		X	X	X			X		X		X		X
February '21 Q4 Linda Lawyer gives Chiro gifts for clients he sends to her		X	X			X	X	X	X	X	X	X	X
October '20 Q1 Lawyer Mary represents Peg in a sexual harassment suit v. Doug		X	X	X			X	X	X		X		X
February '20 Q2 Ellen hired lawyer Linda to develop an employment agreement for her & Nonprofit		X	X	X	X		X	X					
July '19 Q4 Larry is at ABC Firm & represents Jones who is sued by XYZ		X		X			X		X		X	X	X
February '19 Q5 Atty Ann shared law practice w/ Kelly, who was disbarred			X			X	X					X	X
July '18 Q3 Betty & Sheila charged w/ armed robbery hire Betty's uncle Lou		X		X		X	X						X

Continued>

	Fact Pattern	Crossover	Duty of Loyalty/Conflicts	Duty to Communicate/Scope of Representation	Duty of Confidentiality	Attorney-Client Privilege/Work Product	Fees & Splitting/Gifts/Loans	Duties of Competence/Diligence	Attorney-Client Relationship/Sexual Relations	Withdraw/File Return	Solicitation/Advertising	Fairness to Parties/Counsel/Court	Unauthorized Practice Law/Report Ethics Violation	Duties to Public/Profession
February '18 Q1	Beverly hired lawyer Lou over roof problem & expert lied	Contracts						X				X		X
July '17 Q2	Don defrauds Claire, then dies & Don's lawyer is asked to testify	Evidence	X		X	X		X		X		X		X
February '17 Q5	Len represents Claire, who sues Hotel, but is a vexatious litigant		X	X				X		X				X
July '16 Q6	ABC hired Len, member of Equal, to challenge statute		X		X			X						X
February '16 Q3	Lawyer and Client Contractor have a sexual relationship		X				X	X	X					
July '15 Q5	Henry is GC of Online Inc. and self-deals with LargeCo./TechCo	Bus. Assoc.	X	X				X		X				
July '14 Q3	AB Law represents computer manufacturer Sid v. Renco	Bus. Assoc.	X	X	X	X		X						X
February '14 Q1	Prosecutor Patty proceeds without disclosures to defense							X				X		X
July '13 Q1	Patty hires Tom, who refers case to Alan				X		X	X			X			X
February '13 Q2	Carol hires Abel to sue landlord			X	X			X				X		
July '12 Q2	ABC Legal LLP leases office to David	Community Property	X				X	X						
February '12 Q5	Lawyer for Peter injured by chemicals		X		X		X	X			X	X		
July '11 Q4	Austin, physician, becomes lawyer		X	X	X		X	X				X	X	
February '11 Q5	Bob owns 51% of Corp; Cate owns 30%	Bus. Assoc.	X		X		X	X						
July '10 Q2	Hazardous waste, tax attorney Anne		X	X	X	X		X						
February '10 Q2	ABC LLP leased offices to attorneys	Bus. Assoc.	X		X	X								
July '09 Q5	Diane builds dam for children's camp	Civ. Pro./Remedies			X	X								

Continued>

Exam	Fact Pattern	Crossover	Duty of Loyalty/Conflicts	Duty to Communicate/Scope of Representation	Duty of Confidentiality	Attorney-Client Privilege/Work Product	Fees & Splitting/Gifts/Loans	Duties of Competence/Diligence	Attorney-Client Relationship/Sexual Relations	Withdraw/File Return	Solicitation/Advertising	Fairness to Parties/Counsel/Court	Unauthorized Practice Law/Report Ethics Violation	Duties to Public/Profession
July '09 Q2	Attorney Alex & Dusty, movie actor		X									X		X
February '09 Q1	Betty, ABC, Lucy Lawyer, XYZ		X		X		X	X						
July '08 Q1	Alex, solo law practice, Booker		X		X		X	X					X	
February '08 Q6	Attorney Albert and Barry form Lawco	Bus. Assoc.					X						X	
February '08 Q2	Acme Paint, Lawyer June, lead in paint		X		X					X				
February '07 Q2	Rita and Fred form Rita's Kitchen	Bus. Assoc.	X		X			X						
July '06 Q5	Client hit by truck driven by Driver		X	X			X	X	X					X
February '06 Q5	Larry represents Marla; widgets	Contracts	X	X			X	X				X		X
July '05 Q6	Lawyer Lou dates Client Sally		X	X					X		X	X		
July '05 Q3	Lawyer works for SI and helps Carole	Bus. Assoc.	X	X	X			X						
February '05 Q4	Ann, Officer Patty, employment discr.	Evidence				X					X	X		X
July '04 Q5	L, 10 yrs. as Deputy District Attorney						X	X				X		X
February '04 Q3	L represents Sis in divorce, Dad's estate		X		X		X	X				X		
July '03 Q5	L employed by ChemCorp.		X		X					X				X
July '03 Q1	D contacts L for tax advice; L buys stock	Bus. Assoc.	X									X		X
February '03 Q4	L hired by City, later works for W & Z		X		X		X							
July '02 Q3	Betty, son Todd, Attorney Alice		X	X			X	X				X		
February '02 Q4	Richard, trust; wife Alicia is attorney	Wills and Trusts	X	X	X			X				X		X
July '01 Q5	Attorney Ann represents Harry	Torts					X					X		X
February '01 Q5	Jones & Smith ads and fees										X			

Professional Responsibility Question 1
July 2022, Question 3

Clint hired Linda, a lawyer, to represent him in a personal injury lawsuit against Dan, the driver of the car that collided with Clint's car, thereby causing him serious bodily injury. Clint could not afford to pay Linda, so Linda told Clint not to worry about paying anything until there is a recovery in the case. Linda told Clint that if a recovery is obtained, Linda would take 50% as her attorney fee and Clint will get the other half, less any costs Linda incurred. Clint orally agreed to this fee arrangement.

Dan's insurance company, Acme Insurance (Acme), emailed Linda before Linda completed any substantive work on the case, and offered to settle the matter for $100,000. Linda was thrilled and replied to the email that she accepted the settlement offer. Linda then told Clint about the settlement. Clint was relieved that the case settled so quickly.

Acme delivered a check for $100,000 payable to Linda, who deposited it into her law firm's business account. Linda then wrote a check from that account to Clint for $50,000, minus her costs, and mailed it to him. Upon receipt of the check, Clint complained about Linda's fee and threatened to sue Linda for malpractice and report her to the State Bar. Linda offered to return $10,000 of the fee in exchange for an agreement releasing Linda from all liability associated with the representation. Clint accepted and executed the release.

What ethical violations, if any, has Linda committed? Discuss.

Answer according to California and ABA authorities.

Professional Responsibility Question 1 Assessment
July 2022, Question 3

Professional responsibility (PR) is the most frequently tested subject on the California bar exam, so make sure you organize far more PR essays than we have in this chapter. Often the call of the question on PR essays is broad just as you find in this essay. However, in recent years, the examiners have been asking some very specific questions that give rise to some of the more nuanced rules, which is why it is wise to be well prepared and know the PR rules cold. We have provided both types of questions for you to practice.

Since the essays require you to answer according to both ABA and California rules, you must have a good command of the areas where the laws are different between these sources. We have included differences where they apply in both the outline and essay answer grids/answers. Make sure you make a note of every rule you missed or didn't correctly analyze. Also, note how PR essays are best to organize by event/factual occurrence. Usually, each factual event results in several issues and then sometimes the same issues are tested again later in the essay under a new factual event.

This question explores some typical and frequently tested topics, including the duty to loyalty, duty to communicate, duty of competence, and fees. However, it also tests some less frequently tested topics, including limiting malpractice and fee disputes.

The first factual event is the formation of the lawyer-client relationship, under which you could discuss attorney-client relationship formation and the issues surrounding the fee agreement—for this we recommend using a mini-issues checklist for fees so that you ensure you don't miss any issues pertinent to the fee arrangement here. These issues were rather straightforward if you knew the rules, but many students make the mistake of not spotting all fee related issues.

The next factual event involves the lawyer's communication with the insurance company, which raises several other issues such as the duty of loyalty (conflict of interest), duty to communicate, scope of the representation, and duty of competence and diligence. These were also straightforward issues, and the key was ensuring you properly spotted all issues. Pay close attention to the duty of loyalty conflict of interest as that is one of the most heavily tested issues and you want to be able to quickly and easily spot all conflicts of interest as those are usually worth a decent amount of points. Here, you should also have a mini-issues checklist for all possible conflicts of interest. From there you can easily see that here the personal interest of the lawyer (getting money fast and spending as little time as possible) could influence her decision and put her own interest ahead of her client's.

The last event involved the lawyer collecting the money and her dispute with the client over the amount of money. This gave rise to depositing and distributing client money, a new conflict of interest (different from the one you addressed above) as this one involves limiting malpractice, which is not as heavily tested, what a lawyer should do with disputed fees, and the duty of competence (but this issue can often be addressed as a lawyer who is violating the rules and doing things incorrectly usually isn't that competent).

Since PR essays tend to give to numerous issues, some of which are repetitive with each new factual event, it is wise to properly allocate your time before writing out your answer. This way you know how much depth you can go into on both rules and analysis to ensure you fully answer all issues, even if some involve a more truncated IRAC.

Note the areas highlighted in **bold** on the corresponding grid. The bold areas highlight the issues, analysis, and conclusions that are likely **required** to receive a passing score on this question. In general, the essay grids are provided to assist you in analyzing the essays and are much more detailed than what a student should create during the exam to organize their response to a question.

Issue	Rule	Fact Application	Conclusion
Initial Lawyer-Client Conversation			
Formation of Relationship	Lawyer-client relationship is formed when C reasonably perceives that L is representing them or by an actual agreement.	Here, C asked L to represent him but couldn't afford to pay. Since L agreed to represent him if C allowed her to keep 50% and C agreed, a relationship was formed.	**L-C relationship formed**
Contingency Fee Agreement	**Contingency fee agreements are those in which the fee is dependent on the outcome and must include:** • **A writing** • **Signed by C** (Cal. requires signed by both C & L w/ each provided a copy) • **State** the method to determine the fee and % • **Litigation & other expenses to deduct** and when deducted (Cal. looks at other fees not covered by the agreement that affect C)	**Here, L's fee of 50% depends on if C wins his case so it is a contingency fee agreement.** • **There is no writing as it was made orally** • **Not signed by C or L** • L did say (orally) that she would keep 50% and C would get the other half, less any costs, but she did not say when those costs would be deducted.	**L violated duty to enter a valid contingency fee agreement**
Reasonable/ Unconscionable Fees	**ABA:** Fees must be **reasonable**, considering factors including time limitations imposed by C; the **experience and ability of L**; nature and length of relationship; the time, labor, **novelty, difficulty, and skill involved; fee customarily involved; likelihood of precluding other employment**; amount involved and results obtained; and whether the fee is fixed or contingent. **Cal:** Fees must not be illegal or **unconscionable** and looks at same factors as ABA as well as whether L engaged in fraud or overreaching, L failed to disclose material facts, **amount in proportion to services provided**, and whether C gave informed consent. [Just list 4-5 factors at issue, not all]	Here, this seems to be a straightforward **personal injury case** as car accidents are common, no limitations imposed by C, L didn't give up other employment, the outcome was quick for C b/c the insurance co. emailed her before she did any substantive work, amount recovered ($100,000) seemed fine as C was happy and relieved but not a really high amount for a serious bodily injury, and **fee was contingent but higher (50%) than most PI contingency fees (around 30%)**. In Cal. the fee of $60K L took **seems disproportionate to the amount of work L had to do** which was simply to accept the settlement offer and C did not give informed consent b/c C didn't understand how the fee would be calculated with the expenses coming out based on C's response.	**Fee unreasonable and unconscionable**
Advancing Fees	**ABA: L may not provide financial assistance to C unless it is for a contingency case, or the C is indigent.** Cal.: L may advance money to C for any purpose if C promises to pay it back in writing.	**Here, L promised to pay for the representation upfront b/c C didn't have any money so L promised C he would only pay if he recovered money in the case, so it was a contingency case, but there was no writing of their agreement.**	**Advancing fees was acceptable but need a writing**

Continued>

Issue	Rule	Fact Application	Conclusion
Acme's Settlement Offer			
Duty to Communicate	L shall promptly inform C of decisions that affect their case, reasonably consult with C, and keep C informed of the status of the case, such as settlement offers.	Here, L did not properly communicate with C about the fees upfront and amount of expenses to be deducted. L also did not promptly (or at all) inform C of the settlement offer prior to accepting it as required.	L violated the duty to communicate
Scope of Representation	C makes the substantive decisions (such as whether to take a settlement offer) and L makes the strategic decisions.	Here, L accepted the settlement offer when it was C's decision to make as to whether to accept the offer, even if it was a good offer.	L violated the scope of representation
Duty of Competence	ABA: L shall competently represent C with the legal knowledge, skill, thoroughness, and preparation reasonably necessary for the representation. Cal.: L must not intentionally, recklessly, with gross negligence, or repeatedly fail to perform legal services with competence.	Here, L did not act with legal knowledge or thoroughness or properly prepare since she quickly accepted Acme's settlement offer without doing any substantive work on the matter. She could not determine whether that amount was fair without doing some amount of investigation into the matter. **For the same reasons, her actions were reckless with regard to properly investigating the case. She also acted reckless and without knowledge when she violated the rules and accepted the settlement offer as she should know that C is the one who needs to decide those issues.**	L violated her duty of competence
Duty of Diligence	ABA: L shall act with reasonable diligence and promptness in representing a C. Cal.: L shall not intentionally, repeatedly, recklessly, or w/ gross negligence fail to act with reasonable diligence in representing C.	Here, L did not act diligently b/c she did no substantive work on the matter and just accepted a settlement offer.	L violated her duty of diligence
Duty of Loyalty	L owes a duty of loyalty to act in the best interest of C and avoid all conflicts of interest. A conflict of interest exists if there is a significant risk that the representation of C will be materially limited by L's personal interest. L may still represent C despite the conflict if L reasonably believes they can provide competent and diligent representation to C, representation is not prohibited by law, Cs are not directly adverse if between two Cs, and C gives informed consent, confirmed in writing (Cal. informed written consent).	Here, L owes a duty of loyalty to C. When L accepted the settlement offer, she may have been putting her own interests before C's since she could easily earn $50,000 without doing any substantive work on an issue. However, C might have been able to recover more had she done a more thorough investigation into his case. Since she actually accepted the settlement offer and was thrilled with it before discussing it with C, her representation was materially limited by her own personal interest to settle the case quickly.	L violated her duty of loyalty

Continued>

Issue	Rule	Fact Application	Conclusion
Duty of Loyalty (continued)		She could have not reasonably believed she could provide competent representation since she didn't even investigate his case or perform any substantive work on it and C was never even told about the risks of taking such a quick settlement to understand the conflict, so he could not have consented to it and there was no writing anyway.	
Accepting the Settlement Check			
Client Trust Account/ Commingling Funds	**L shall hold C's money separate from L's money. C's money must be kept in a client trust account** (Cal.: trust account must be registered with Cal. State Bar).	Here, L deposited C's $100,000 settlement check into her firm's business account instead of C's trust account which is now allowed.	**L violated her duty to hold C's funds in a separate account**
Fee Disbursements	L must promptly (Cal. says within 45 days) pay C any funds due along with an accounting, but L may hold back money they believe is owed to them.	L seemed to promptly pay C but did not provide an accounting to him as required.	L violated her duty to promptly pay and account to C
Fee Disputes	**Any disputed funds must remain in C's trust account.** Cal. allows mandatory fee arbitration for fee disputes.	**L could keep the disputed amount of $10,000 in C's trust account but not in the business account.**	**L violated her duty involving disputed funds**
Limiting/ Settling Malpractice Liability	ABA: L may not limit their liability to C w/o advising C to seek independent counsel. Cal.: L may not limit their liability to C. **L may not settle a claim/potential claim w/ an unrepresented C unless they are advised in writing to seek independent counsel.**	C was not independently represented nor was he **advised to seek independent counsel** so L violated all rules. Also, even if L could settle a claim with C provided he was advised to seek independent counsel, in Cal., she could not limit her liability but could only settle a claim, **but C was not told to seek independent counsel in writing either way.**	**L violated her duty on limiting and settling liability**

Professional Responsibility Question 1 Sample Answer
July 2022, Question 3

Initial Lawyer-Client Conversation

Formation of Relationship

A lawyer-client relationship is formed when the client reasonably perceives that the lawyer is representing them or by an actual agreement. Here, Clint, the client, asked the Linda, the lawyer, to represent him but couldn't afford to pay. Since Linda agreed to represent him if Clint allowed her to keep 50% and Clint agreed, a relationship was formed.

Contingency Fee Agreement

Contingency fee agreements are those in which the fee is dependent on the outcome and must include a writing, be signed by the client, and in Cal. by both the lawyer and the client with each retaining a copy, state the method to determine the fee and the percentage, state the litigation and other expenses to deduct and whether they should be deducted before or after the contingency fee is calculated, and Cal. looks at any other fees not covered by the agreement that might affect the client.

Here, Linda's fee of 50% depends on whether Clint wins his case, so it is a contingency fee agreement. However, there is no writing as it was made orally. As such there is no agreement signed by Clint or Linda. Although Linda did say that her fee would be 50% and Clint would get the other half, less any costs, she did not say when those costs would be deducted and what those costs would include. Thus, Linda violated her duty to enter a valid contingency fee agreement.

Reasonable/Unconscionable Fees

Under the ABA, fees must be reasonable, considering factors including time limitations imposed by the client; the experience and ability of the lawyer; the nature and length of their relationship; the time, labor, novelty, difficulty, and skill involved; the fee customarily involved; the likelihood of precluding other employment; the amount involved and results obtained; and whether the fee is fixed or contingent. In Cal., the fee must not be illegal or unconscionable and Cal. considers the same ABA factors as well as whether the lawyer engaged in fraud or overreaching when setting the fee, whether the lawyer failed to disclose material facts, the amount in proportion to the services provided, and whether the client gave informed consent.

Here, this seems to be a straightforward personal injury case as car accidents are common; there are no limitations imposed by Clint; Linda didn't give up other employment; the outcome was quick for Clint and Linda because Acme, the insurance company, emailed Linda before she did any substantive work on the matter; the amount recovered, $100,000, seemed fine as Clint was happy and relieved and Linda was thrilled, but it may not be a really high amount for a serious bodily injury; and the fee was contingent, not fixed, but the percentage retained by Linda seemed higher than most contingency agreements as most are around 30-33% and her percentage was 50% as well as costs in addition to that amount.

In Cal. the fee she earned, which totaled $60,000 out of the $100,000, seems disproportionate to the amount of work Linda had to do, which was simply to accept the settlement offer because she accepted it before doing any substantive work on the matter. Further, Clint did not give informed consent because he didn't understand how the fee would be calculated with the expenses coming out as evidence by his response to Linda and threat to sue her.

Thus, overall it seems that the fee was likely unreasonable and unconscionable.

Advancing Fees

Under the ABA, a lawyer may not provide financial assistance to the client unless it is for a contingency case, or the client is indigent. In Cal., the lawyer may advance money to the client for any purpose if the client promises to pay it back in writing.

Here, Linda promised to pay for the representation upfront because Clint didn't have any money so it seems he may have been indigent. As a result, Linda promised Clint that he would only have to pay if a recovery was obtained, so it was a contingency case, but there was no writing of their agreement. Thus, the advancement of any fees was acceptable, but the agreement needs to be in writing. Thus, Linda violated the rules.

Acme's Settlement Offer

Duty to Communicate

A lawyer shall promptly inform the client of any decision that affects their case, reasonably consult with the client, and keep the client informed of the status of the case, such as settlement offers.

Here, Linda did not properly communicate with Clint about the fees upfront and amount of expenses to be deducted as she should have. Linda also did not promptly inform Clint of the settlement offer prior to accepting it as required because she accepted it on his behalf before telling him about it. Thus, Linda violated the duty to communicate.

Scope of Representation

The client makes the substantive decisions, such as whether to take a settlement offer, and the lawyer makes the legal strategic decisions. Here, Linda accepted the settlement offer when it was Clint's decision to make as to whether to accept the offer, even if it was a good offer. Thus, Linda violated the scope of her representation.

Duty of Competence

Under the ABA, a lawyer shall competently represent a client with the legal knowledge, skill, thoroughness, and preparation reasonably necessary for the representation. In Cal., a lawyer must not intentionally, recklessly, with gross negligence, or repeatedly fail to perform legal services with competence.

Here, Linda did not act with legal knowledge or thoroughness or properly prepare since she quickly accepted Acme's settlement offer without doing any substantive work on the matter. She could not properly and competently determine whether that amount was fair without doing some amount of investigation into the matter.

For the same reasons, her actions were reckless with regard to properly investigating the case. She also acted reckless and without knowledge when she violated the rules and accepted the settlement offer as she should know that Clint is the one who needs to decide those issues. Thus, Linda violated her duty of competence.

Duty of Diligence

Under the ABA, a lawyer shall act with reasonable diligence and promptness in representing a client. In Cal., a lawyer shall not intentionally, repeatedly, recklessly, or with gross negligence fail to act with reasonable diligence in representing a client. Here, Linda did not act diligently because she performed no substantive work on the matter and just accepted a settlement offer. Thus, Linda violated her duty of diligence.

Duty of Loyalty

A lawyer owes a duty of loyalty to act in the best interest of their client and avoid all conflicts of interest. A conflict of interest exists if there is a significant risk that the representation of the client will be materially limited by lawyer's personal interest.

A lawyer may still represent the client despite the conflict if they reasonably believe they can provide competent and diligent representation to the client, representation is not prohibited by law, clients are not directly adverse if between two clients, and the client gives informed consent, confirmed in writing (Cal. requires informed written consent).

Here, Linda owes a duty of loyalty to Clint. When Linda accepted the settlement offer, she may have been putting her own interests before Clint's since she could easily earn $50,000 without doing any substantive work on an issue. However, Clint might have been able to recover more had she done a more thorough investigation into his case. Since she actually accepted the settlement offer and was thrilled with it before discussing it with Clint, her representation was materially limited by her own personal interest to settle the case quickly.

Further, she could have not reasonably believed she could provide competent representation since she didn't even investigate his case or perform any substantive work on it and she never even told Clint about the risks of taking such a quick settlement for him to understand the conflict, so he could not have consented to it and there was no writing anyway. Thus, Linda violated her duty of loyalty.

Accepting the Settlement Check

Client Trust Account/ Commingling Funds

A lawyer shall hold a client's money separate from lawyer's money. A client's money must be kept in a client trust account. Cal. requires the trust account to be registered with the Cal. State Bar. Here, Linda deposited Clint's $100,000 settlement check into her firm's business account instead of Clint's trust account which is not allowed. Thus, Linda violated her duty to hold Clint's funds in a separate client trust account.

Fee Disbursements

A lawyer must promptly (Cal. says within 45 days) pay a client any funds due along with an accounting, but they may hold back money they believe is due to them. Here, Linda seemed to promptly pay Clint but did not provide an accounting to him as required. Thus, Linda violated her duty to promptly pay and account to C.

Fee Disputes

Any disputed funds must remain in the client's trust account. Cal. allows mandatory fee arbitration for fee disputes. Here, Linda could keep the disputed amount of $10,000 in Clint's trust account but not in the business account. Thus, Linda violated her duty to keep the disputed funds in Clint's trust account.

Limiting/Settling Malpractice Liability

Under the ABA, a lawyer may not limit their liability to a client without advising the client to seek independent counsel. In Cal., a lawyer may not limit their liability to a client. Under both the ABA and Cal. rules, a lawyer may not settle a claim or potential claim with an unrepresented client unless they are advised in writing to seek independent counsel and given a reasonable time to do so.

Here, Clint was not independently represented nor was he advised to seek independent counsel, so Linda violated all rules. Also, even if Linda could settle a claim with Clint, provided he was advised to seek independent counsel, in Cal., she could not limit her liability but could only settle a claim, but Clint was not told to seek independent counsel in writing either way. Thus, Linda violated her duty on limiting and settling liability.

Professional Responsibility Question 2
July 2023, Question 3

Laura is general counsel for MoreHome Mortgage Company (MoreHome), a California corporation. Eric is an entry-level mortgage advisor at MoreHome.

Eric approached Laura and gave Laura a package of documents that he obtained through his position at MoreHome. The documents demonstrate that MoreHome employees are falsifying the financial history of many mortgage applicants so they can qualify for mortgages they could not otherwise obtain. The documents also show that it is MoreHome's policy to push risky mortgages onto unsuspecting customers.

Eric confided in Laura that he was troubled to have learned of these practices himself and wanted Laura's legal advice on what do to. Eric said that he has never engaged in these practices himself and does not want Mianne, MoreHome's Chief Executive Officer (CEO), to learn of their discussion. Laura told Eric she would think about it and get back to him. Eric left all of the documents with Laura as she requested.

Laura knows that the practices shown in the documents and described by Eric constitute a crime under state law. Laura also knows that the State Attorney General is aggressively investigating similar practices by mortgage companies in the state, although Laura is not aware of whether MoreHome has been identified as a target for investigation.

Immediately after Eric left Laura's office, Laura called Mianne and informed her of Eric's visit and about Eric's concerns. Mianne instructed Laura not to do anything with the documents and to give them to Mianne. Laura consulted with outside counsel regarding what to do with the documents and based on that advice, and against Mianne's instructions, Laura provided copies of the documents to the State Attorney General.

What ethical violations, if any, has Laura committed? Discuss.

Answer according to California and ABA authorities.

Professional Responsibility Question 2 Assessment
July 2023, Question 3

This professional responsibility essay tests one of the most heavily tested topics — duty of loyalty with a corporation as the client. A common issue cluster that arises when the lawyer is representing an organizational client is the duty of loyalty, duty of confidentiality, and withdrawal. Often these essays involve an employee approaching the general counsel with information that is damaging to the company. The employee usually thinks that the lawyer represents them and will keep their confidences private when in fact the lawyer represents the corporation. However, if the lawyer gives the employee the impression that they have created a lawyer-client relationship, then the lawyer may need to maintain the employee's confidences, which puts the lawyer in a conflict-of-interest scenario since often the employee's interest is adverse to the organization's interest and the lawyer is now in a bind. Hence, the issues of confidentiality and withdrawal are companion issues.

Since conflicts of interest are heavily tested, and as evidenced by the conflicts of interest testing frequency chart, you should practice enough essays testing this topic so you thoroughly understand the rules involving organizational clients, including when the lawyer may or must report up and out as that issue is often triggered in these essays.

This essay in particular finds the lawyer in a peculiar situation when the employee shares information with her about fraudulent activity occurring in the company she represents. Adding to the problems counsel now faces, the employee has asked her to not to inform the CEO of the company of the issues the employee discovered which puts the lawyer in a bind raising the conflict of interest and the duty of confidentiality issues. And when she does report the information up against the employee's wishes and shares the information with the CEO anyway, you should determine whether she owed a duty of confidentiality to the employee now and thus violated that by her disclosure. Since the lawyer is now aware of a crime being committed, she must disclose the problem but then she would violate the employee's confidences. Her best approach would be to try to withdraw from the representation as a result.

It is important to note that neither state-released answer did a great job on these issues. This is likely due to the sheer volume of issues and rules being tested in a one-hour essay. As a result, students had to figure out how to manage their time and address the various issues, which is quite the challenge on many bar exam essays, especially in professional responsibility. For this reason, they gave somewhat truncated rules and did not go into too much depth on the issues but were at least in the right ballpark. You don't need to hit a home run, but you at least need to hit the ball, which is what they did. Other graded actual essays that did a more thorough analysis of the duty of loyalty issue scored 75/80 scores, but those answers missed some of the other issues like communication, etc.

Time allocation is crucial to success on bar exam essays. And the best way to improve that is to organize as many essays as you can on a particular topic so that approaching these questions is habitual and not a "Find Waldo" mission. Also note how this is essay three and you may already be feeling fatigued (and often professional responsibility and Evidence are essay three). So, managing your time is an important factor in your success and this essay provides a great opportunity to practice that skill. It also shows you that you don't need to be perfect to pass and in fact some of your rules can even be incomplete and/or inaccurate and you can still pass.

Note the areas highlighted in **bold** on the corresponding grid. The bold areas highlight the issues, analysis, and conclusions that are likely **required** to receive a passing score on this question. In general, the essay grids are provided to assist you in analyzing the essays and are much more detailed than what a student should create during the exam to organize their response to a question.

Continued>

Issue	Rule	Fact Application	Conclusion
Eric Approaches Laura			
Lawyer-Client Relationship Formation [One state answer addressed this but both should have and other essays that scored 75/80 scores did address it]	Lawyer-client relationship is formed when C reasonably perceives that L is representing them or by an actual agreement. When this occurs, L owes a duty of confidentiality to the prospective C.	Here, Eric approached Laura for legal advice so he must have understood that she was the GC for MoreHome, but he also asked her to keep his disclosures confidential, indicating he likely thought that he had a legal relationship with Laura now too b/c he thought his request would be honored even if it was not good for MoreHome. And she even told him that she would get back to him, making him likely think she was helping him. As a result, Laura now arguably owed Eric a duty of confidentiality.	L formed a L-C relationship with E
Duty of Loyalty—Corporate Conflicts of Interest [Neither state-released answer did a good job here likely due to timing issues with so many issues being tested in one essay — but note some essays that scored 75/80 scores did address this issue in more detail]	**L owes a duty of loyalty to their C and must avoid conflicts of interest.** **L employed by a corp. represents the corp. and must act in the best interest of the corp.** L may also represent the corp.'s officers, directors, employees, etc. if there is no conflict in doing so. A conflict of interest exists if there is a significant risk that the representation of one or more clients will be materially limited by L's responsibilities to another client, even a prospective one. Where there is a conflict, L may represent the clients only if L reasonably believes there will not be an adverse effect, the clients are not directly adverse, it is not against the law, and the client gives informed consent, confirmed in writing (Cal. informed written consent).	**Laura owes a duty of loyalty to her client MoreHome b/c she is the GC for the corp., so she must act in their best interest and not Eric's, one of MoreHome's lower-level employees.** Thus, her reporting the info and trying to help MoreHome against Eric's wishes or Mianne's was likely in MoreHome's best interest. If Eric's interests aligned with MoreHome's then she could represent him as well as MoreHome, but since he requested her not to disclose the information to the CEO, it is unlikely that their interests are aligned and there is a potential conflict of interest. There is a significant risk that the representation of Eric will be materially limited by Laura's responsibilities to MoreHome b/c she needs to disclose the info Eric told her to help protect MoreHome and prevent further legal violations since the actions disclosed are already a crime under state law. Laura cannot reasonably believe that she can represent both Eric and MoreHome b/c keeping the info private is not in the best interest of MoreHome b/c she needs to disclose the info to the higher ups as discussed above and possibly out to rectify the crime being done. And there is no indication that MoreHome gave informed written consent.	A potential conflict of interest exists for Laura between Eric and MoreHome

531

Issue	Rule	Fact Application	Conclusion
Corporate employee disclosure	When L represents a corp., they must explain the identity of their client to employees when L knows or should know that the corp.'s interests are adverse to those of the employee.	Here, Laura did not inform Eric that MoreHome was her client or explain to him that she represented them and not him.	L violated her duty to inform E
Laura's Actions			
Reporting Corporate Misconduct Up	If L knows that an officer, employee, or other person associated with the corp. is engaged in action that is a violation of a law reasonably imputable to the corp. and is likely to result in substantial injury to the corp., L shall report up, and refer the matter to a higher authority in the corp., unless L reasonably believes that it is not in the best interest of the corp. to do so. Cal. requires that the duty of confidentiality be maintained unless death or substantial bodily injury is likely.	Laura knows, based on the documents Eric provided her, that MoreHome employees are falsifying the financial history of many mortgage applicants so they can qualify for mortgages they otherwise could not obtain and the policy of MoreHome is to push risky mortgages onto unsuspecting customers. Laura also knows that these practices constitute a crime under state law and that the State Attorney General is aggressively investigating similar practices by mortgage companies in the state. Since the corp. is currently committing a crime it is likely to result in substantial injury to MoreHome and L shall report up to a higher authority, which would include the CEO, Mianne. But Laura might have allowed Mianne reasonable time to respond or report it to other higher up officials too. In Cal., Laura could be in trouble by violating her duty of confidentiality to Eric if she formed a L-C relationship with him and now owed him a duty (which is why she may need to withdraw as discussed below).	**L can report up under the ABA but may have issues with Cal.**
Reporting Corporate Misconduct Out	If the highest authority fails to take action and L reasonably believes the violation will result in substantial injury to the corp.: ABA: L may report out and reveal info, even if confidential, if such disclosure is necessary to prevent the injury.	Here, the CEO, Mianne, failed to act as she told Laura not to do anything with the documents and to give them to her. Laura could reasonably believe that the violation is already a crime that is being aggressively investigated by the state AG and will result in substantial injury to the corp.	**L can report out under the ABA rules but not Cal.**

Continued>

Issue	Rule	Fact Application	Conclusion
	Cal.: L may not report out and disclose info outside the corp. if it will violate the duty of confidentiality but L should urge reconsideration of the matter to the higher authorities within the corp., resign or withdraw from representation **unless death or substantial bodily injury is likely.**	Under the ABA **she may report out and reveal the info to the State AG b/c it is necessary to prevent injury to the corp. as their stock prices or revenue could be harmed.** **In Cal. she could not reveal the info to the State AG b/c** there is no risk of death or substantial injury, so she needed to urge Mianne to reconsider and **perhaps go to another higher up board member** or seek withdrawal. **Seeking outside advice from another lawyer would be fine** as that would be confidential and have its own duty of confidentiality attached to that legal advice.	
Duty of Confidentiality	**L shall not reveal information relating to the representation of a C.** **ABA Exceptions:** C gives informed consent, disclosure is impliedly authorized, **to prevent C from committing a crime or fraud** or to mitigate or rectify a crime or fraud committed by C that will result in substantial injury to another and C has used L's services to do so. **Cal. Exception: To prevent a criminal act that will result in death or substantial bodily harm** but first must persuade C to not commit the act, inform C of the ability to reveal the info, and only reveal as much as necessary.	**To MoreHome:** **Laura is able to report out and disclose private info as discussed above under the ABA and not Cal. for the same reasons** IF they used L's services to do the crime or fraud which doesn't seem to be the case. **To Eric:** Laura was able to reveal the info Eric shared with her under the ABA for the same reasons she was with MoreHome IF her services were used in the crime or fraud, but not under Cal. for the same reasons as with MoreHome.	**L may not have violated her duty under the ABA but did under Cal.**
Mandatory Withdrawal	**L shall withdraw if the representation will result in a violation of the PR rules,** or under the ABA in other law; ABA also if **C uses L's services to commit or continue to commit a crime.** [only list means possibly at issue]	If Laura has a conflict between Eric and MoreHome then she will need to withdraw and since she may have violated other rules here by reporting out for Cal. when not allowed, she may need to withdraw. Also, under the ABA, **the current situation with MoreHome involves a violation of the law as the acts are crimes so she must withdraw under that as well.**	**L must withdraw**

Continued>

Issue	Rule	Fact Application	Conclusion
Permissive Withdrawal	**L may withdraw if C insists on action involving L's services that are fraudulent or criminal,** C has used L's services to perpetrate a crime or fraud, or other good cause. ABA: **If L finds acts of C so repugnant.** [only list means possibly at issue]	Since Mianne is failing to rectify the crime and now Laura is involved, it is likely that Laura's continued representation will involve actions that are criminal if the acts are not stopped.	**L can likely withdraw**
Duty of Competence	**ABA: L shall competently represent C** with the legal knowledge, skill, thoroughness, and preparation reasonably **necessary for the representation.** **Cal.: L must not intentionally, recklessly, with gross negligence, or repeatedly fail to perform legal services with competence.**	**Here, Laura immediately acted when she realized the corp. was violating the law and she even consulted with outside counsel to ensure she was properly following the laws and rules.** But she likely should have done her own research and investigation as well to help mitigate the risk. And she may need to seek withdrawal, or her continued representation could amount to a violation of her duty of competence.	Could conclude either way
Duty of Diligence	**ABA: L shall act with reasonable diligence and promptness** in representing a C. **Cal.: L shall not intentionally, repeatedly, recklessly, or w/ gross negligence fail to act with reasonable diligence** in representing C.	**Here, Laura acted promptly as she immediately informed the CEO, Mianne, of the issues Eric brought to her attention.** But she could have acted with more diligence in investigating the matter before reporting it out so she may have failed to act with reasonable diligence there.	Could conclude either way
Duty to Communicate	**L shall promptly inform C of decisions that affect their case,** reasonably consult with C, **and keep C informed of the status of the case,** such as settlement offers.	**Here, Laura did communicate the information about the fraudulent mortgage practices to the CEO immediately,** but she should have also reported to her that she reported out the information as well.	Could conclude either way
Duty to the Public and Profession [One state answer addressed this issue]	L shall not counsel a C to engage, or assist a C, in criminal or fraudulent conduct, but may counsel the C to discuss the legal consequences and assist them in making a good faith effort to understand the law. L shall not engage in conduct involving dishonesty, fraud, or deceit.	Here, L did not engage in or assist any criminal conduct as she immediately reported the activity both within the corp. and outside of it so she did not engage in the fraud or encourage it.	L did not violate her duty to the public or profession

Professional Responsibility Question 2 Sample Answer
July 2023, Question 3

Eric Approaches Laura

Lawyer-Client Relationship Formation

A lawyer-client relationship is formed when the client reasonably perceives that the lawyer is representing them or by an actual agreement. When this occurs, the lawyer owes a duty of confidentiality to the prospective client.

Here, Eric approached Laura for legal advice so he must have understood that she was the General Counsel for MoreHome, but he also asked her to keep his disclosures confidential, indicating he likely thought that he had a legal relationship with Laura now too because he thought his request would be honored even if it was not good for MoreHome. And she even told him that she would get back to him, making him likely think she was helping him. As a result, Laura now arguably owed Eric a duty of confidentiality and formed a lawyer-client relationship with Eric.

Duty of Loyalty — Corporate Conflicts of Interest

A lawyer owes a duty of loyalty to their client and must avoid potential and actual conflicts of interest. A lawyer employed by a corporation represents the corporation and must act in the best interest of the corporation. A corporate lawyer may also represent the corporation's officers, directors, employees, and other constituents if there is no conflict in doing so.

A conflict of interest exists if there is a significant risk that the representation of one or more clients will be materially limited by the lawyer's responsibilities to another client or a prospective client. Where there is a conflict, a lawyer may represent the clients only if the lawyer reasonably believes there will not be an adverse effect, the clients are not directly adverse, the representation is not against the law, and the client gives informed consent, confirmed in writing under the ABA or informed written consent in Cal.

Here, Laura owes a duty of loyalty to her client MoreHome because she is the General Counsel for the corporation so she must act in their best interest and not Eric's, one of MoreHome's lower-level employees. Thus, her reporting the information that Eric shared with her by trying to help MoreHome against Eric's wishes, and even against Mianne's desires when she reported out, was likely in MoreHome's best interest since she was working on rectifying fraudulent activities going on at MoreHome by other employees.

If Eric's interests aligned with MoreHome's then she could represent him as well as MoreHome but since he requested that she not disclose the information he shared with her to the CEO, it is unlikely that their interests are aligned and there is a potential conflict of interest.

Here, there is a significant risk that the representation of Eric will be materially limited by Laura's responsibilities to MoreHome because she needs to disclose the information Eric told her to help protect MoreHome and prevent further legal violations since the actions disclosed are already a crime under state law.

Further, Laura cannot reasonably believe that she can represent both Eric and MoreHome because keeping the information private, per Eric's request, is not in the best interest of MoreHome because she needs to disclose the information to the higher ups as discussed above and possibly out to rectify the crime being done. And there is no indication that MoreHome gave informed written consent.

Thus, a conflict of interest exists for Laura between Eric and MoreHome and no exceptions apply.

Corporate Employee Disclosure

When a lawyer represents a corporation, they must explain the identity of their client to employees when the lawyer knows or should know that the corporation's interests are adverse to those of the employee. Here, Laura did not inform Eric that MoreHome was her client or explain to him that she represented them and not him. Thus, Laura violated her duty to properly inform Eric.

Laura's Actions

Reporting Corporate Misconduct Up

If a lawyer knows that an officer, employee, or other person associated with the corporation is engaged in action that is a violation of a law reasonably imputable to the corporation and is likely to result in substantial injury to the corporation, the lawyer shall report up, and refer the matter to a higher authority in the corporation, unless the lawyer reasonably believes that it is not in the best interest of the corporation to do so. Cal. requires that the duty of confidentiality be maintained unless death or substantial bodily injury is likely.

Here, Laura knows, based on the documents Eric provided her, that MoreHome employees are falsifying the financial history of many mortgage applicants so they can qualify for mortgages they otherwise could not obtain and the policy of MoreHome is to push risky mortgages onto unsuspecting customers. Laura also knows that these practices constitute a crime under state law and that the State Attorney General is aggressively investigating similar practices by mortgage companies in the state. Since the corporation is currently committing a crime, it is likely to result in substantial injury to MoreHome because they can lose their corporate status, shareholders can be affected, or their stock prices can drop. As a result, Laura shall report up to a higher authority, which would include the CEO, Mianne.

But Laura might have allowed Mianne reasonable time to respond or report it to other higher up officials too. Further, in Cal., Laura could be violating her duty of confidentiality since she likely formed a lawyer-client relationship with Eric and now owes him a duty to maintain his confidences unless an exception is met (as discussed below). Overall, Laura can report up under the ABA but may have issues with Cal.

Reporting Corporate Misconduct Out

If the highest authority fails to take action and the lawyer reasonably believes the violation will result in substantial injury to the corporation, then under the ABA, the lawyer may report out and reveal confidential information if such disclosure is necessary to prevent the injury. In Cal., the lawyer may not report out and disclose information outside the corporation if it will violate the duty of confidentiality, but the lawyer should urge reconsideration of the matter to the higher authorities within the corporation, and resign or withdraw from representation, unless death or substantial bodily injury is likely at which point they can report out.

Here, the CEO, Mianne, failed to act as she told Laura not to do anything with the documents and to give them to her. Further, Laura could reasonably believe that the violation is a crime that is being aggressively investigated by the State Attorney General and as such, it will result in substantial injury to the corporation as discussed above.

Thus, under the ABA she may report out and reveal the information to the State Attorney General because it is necessary to prevent injury to the corporation as their stock prices or revenue could be harmed. However, in Cal. she could not reveal the information to the State Attorney General because there is no risk of death or substantial injury, so she needed to urge Mianne to reconsider and perhaps go to another higher up board member or seek withdrawal.

Seeking outside advice from another lawyer would be fine as that would be confidential and have its own duty of confidentiality attached to that legal advice. Thus, Laura can report out under the ABA rules but not Cal.

Duty of Confidentiality

A lawyer shall not reveal information relating to the representation of a client unless under the ABA, the client gives informed consent, disclosure is impliedly authorized, or to prevent the client from committing a crime or fraud or to mitigate or rectify a crime or fraud committed by the client that will result in substantial injury to another and the client has used the lawyer's services to do so. Cal. allows revealing confidential information to prevent a criminal act that will result in death or substantial bodily harm, but the lawyer must first persuade the client to not commit the act, inform the client of the lawyer's ability to reveal the information, and only reveal as much as necessary.

In regard to MoreHome as a client, Laura is able to report out and disclose private information related to the falsifying financial documents for the same reasons discussed above under the reporting up and out, but only if the client used Laura's services to do the crime or fraud which doesn't seem to be the case. As to Eric, Laura was able to reveal the information Eric shared with her under the ABA for the same reasons she was with MoreHome but again only if her services were used in the crime or fraud. But Cal. would prohibit revealing any information for both clients since no death or bodily injury is likely to occur.

Thus, Laura may not have violated her duty under the ABA but did under Cal.

Mandatory Withdrawal

A lawyer shall withdraw if the representation will result in a violation of the rules of professional responsibility, or under the ABA it would violate any other law, or the client used the lawyer's services to commit or continue to commit a crime.

Here, if Laura has a conflict between Eric and MoreHome then she will need to withdraw as that would violate the rules of professional responsibility to continue to represent both of them. And since she may have violated other rules here by reporting out for Cal. when it was not allowed, she may need to withdraw. Also, under the ABA, the current situation with MoreHome involves a violation of the law as the falsifying the documents actions are crimes so she must withdraw under that as well. Thus, Laura must withdraw under both ABA and Cal. rules.

Permissive Withdrawal

A lawyer may withdraw if the client insists on action involving the lawyer's services that are fraudulent or criminal, the client has used the lawyer's services to perpetrate a crime or fraud, or other good cause exists. The ABA also allows withdrawal if the lawyer finds the actions of the client to be so repugnant that they cannot continue to represent them.

Since Mianne is failing to rectify the crime and now Laura is involved, it is likely that Laura's continued representation will involve actions that are criminal if the acts are not stopped. Thus, Laura can likely withdraw.

Duty of Competence

Under the ABA, a lawyer shall competently represent the client with the legal knowledge, skill, thoroughness, and preparation reasonably necessary for the representation. In Cal., the lawyer must not intentionally, recklessly, with gross negligence, or repeatedly fail to perform legal services with competence.

Here, Laura immediately acted when she realized the corporation was violating the law and she even consulted with outside counsel to ensure she was properly following the laws and rules. But she likely should have done her own research and investigation as well to help mitigate the risk. And she may need to seek withdrawal, or her continued representation could amount to a violation of her duty of competence. Thus, Laura may have violated her duty of competence.

Duty of Diligence

Under the ABA a lawyer shall act with reasonable diligence and promptness in representing a client. In Cal., a lawyer shall not intentionally, repeatedly, recklessly, or with gross negligence fail to act with reasonable diligence in representing a client.

Here, Laura acted promptly as she immediately informed the CEO, Mianne, of the issues Eric brought to her attention. But she could have acted with more diligence in investigating the matter before reporting it out so she may have failed to act with reasonable diligence there. Thus, it is possible that Laura did not act diligently.

Duty to Communicate

A lawyer shall promptly inform the client of decisions that affect their case, reasonably consult with the client, and keep the client informed of the status of the case.

Here, Laura did communicate the information about the fraudulent mortgage practices to the CEO immediately, but she should have also reported to her that she reported out the information as well. Thus, she might not have sufficiently communicated to the client.

Duty to the Public and Profession

A lawyer shall not counsel a client to engage, or assist a client, in criminal or fraudulent conduct, but may counsel the client to discuss the legal consequences and assist them in making a good faith effort to understand the law. Further a lawyer shall not engage in conduct involving dishonesty, fraud, or deceit.

Here, Laura did not engage in or assist any criminal conduct as she immediately reported the activity both within the corporation and outside of it, so she did not engage in the fraud or encourage it. Thus, Laura did not violate her duty to the public or profession.

Professional Responsibility Question 3
July 2013, Question 1

Patty was hit by a car, whose driver did not notice her because he was texting. Joe, a journalist, wrote a story about Patty's "texting" accident. Patty contacted Tom, a real estate attorney, and asked him to represent her in a claim against the driver. Tom agreed, and entered into a valid and proper contingency fee agreement. Tom later told Patty that he had referred her case to Alan, an experienced personal injury attorney, and she did not object. Unknown to Patty, Alan agreed to give one-third of his contingency fee to Tom.

Thereafter, Alan sent a $200 gift certificate to Joe with a note stating: "In your future coverage of the 'texting' case, you might mention that I represent Patty."

Patty met with Alan and told him that Walter, a homeless man, had seen the driver texting just before the accident. Alan then met with Walter, who was living in a homeless shelter, and said to him: "Look, if you will testify truthfully about what you saw, I'll put you up in a hotel until you can get back on your feet."

1. What ethical violation(s), if any, has Tom committed? Discuss.

2. What ethical violation(s), if any, has Alan committed? Discuss.

Answer according to both California and ABA authorities.

Professional Responsibility Question 3 Assessment
July 2013, Question 1

This question provides a nice opportunity to engage in some role playing and display to the bar graders that you understand how the ethics rules work in a real-life situation. In this question a client asks a lawyer to represent her in a case in which the attorney has no experience. This is a very typical situation in which a new lawyer may find themselves, so it is important that you can display that you understand the ethical obligations of a novice lawyer in that situation.

This question also has the inexperienced lawyer referring the case to another lawyer who is experienced in the type of case presented. Again, this is a typical situation in which new lawyers regularly find themselves. Of course, the lawyer in the fact pattern has bungled the fee agreement and the referral, which provides you with much opportunity to explain how the referral should have been properly handled.

Sometimes in a professional responsibility question, the facts don't clearly lead to the discussion of any particular rule and several rules could be violated by the behavior in question. For example, here the referral attorney engages in some questionable behavior with a reporter and a case witness. There could be a lot of rules a bar exam taker could use to anchor the discussion on either of these points, but what is really important is the factual discussion of the unethical behavior. If you are ever not sure which rule to use in your analysis, you can always use a general rule, such as the duty of fairness (to the profession, to opposing counsel, etc.) and then be sure to include robust analysis of the facts. Don't let your uncertainty about which rule or precise issue heading to use deter you from jumping into a full factual discussion. That is usually where most of the points are. As you can see from the bolding on the corresponding grid, sometimes the heading and rule to use is unclear and many rules would work equally well, but the possibly unethical behavior itself is what requires your full analysis and is fairly easy to analyze. Don't agonize over it; pick a rule that works given the facts and dive into the factual analysis. You'll get most, if not all, of the points for that issue.

It is important to note that some rules have changed since this essay administration so the rules in the state-released answers may be slightly different than the ones you used and those in the grid as the grid contains updated rules and bolded parts of the rules that the original essays addressed but didn't have the current rule.

Note the areas highlighted in **bold** on the corresponding grid. The bold areas highlight the issues, analysis, and conclusions that are likely **required** to receive a passing score on this question. In general, the essay grids are provided to assist you in analyzing the essays and are much more detailed than what a student should create during the exam to organize their response to a question.

Issue	Rule	Fact Application	Conclusion
1. What ethical violations has Tom committed?			
Agreement to represent Patty			
Duty of Competence	ABA: **L shall represent C with the legal knowledge, skill, thoroughness, and preparation reasonably necessary.**	Patty's claim is in tort for a car accident and Tom is a real estate attorney, which is not related to personal injury law. Tom should not have agreed to take a case in an area he had no knowledge of, though he could have acquired skill in this area, or associated with an attorney experienced in personal injury.	Tom likely breached the duty of competence
	Cal.: L must not intentionally, recklessly, with gross negligence, or repeatedly fail to perform legal services with competence.		
	Both ABA and Cal.: L may acquire the necessary skills, consult with another competent L, or refer the matter to another competent L.	**Tom could have associated with Alan, an experienced personal injury attorney**, but instead, Tom referred the entire case to Alan after accepting it, which is likely impermissible since he should have referred the case before agreeing to take it on.	
Referring Patty's case to Alan			
Referral Agreements and Fees	A reciprocal referral agreement between lawyers is permissible if it is **not exclusive and the client is informed** of the agreement.	There is no indication here of an exclusive reciprocal agreement between Tom and Alan.	**The referral to Alan was improper**
	L may not give anything of value to a person for recommending L's services unless it is for a qualified referral service or a nominal gift as an expression of appreciation not intended as compensation for the recommendation or future recommendations.	**Tom did not get Patty's informed consent for his referral to Alan** because he told her about the referral after the fact.	
		Since Alan is giving 1/3 of his contingency fee to Tom, it is more accurately classified as fee splitting than as a referral fee. However, if it is a referral fee it is only allowed if it was a nominal gift, not intended as compensation for the recommendation, which here it was; and 1/3 of the contingency fee would not be nominal as that is the typical fee a L would charge overall in a personal injury case.	
Fee Splitting Among Lawyers	Division of fees between Ls who are **not in the same firm** may be made:ABA: **Only if the division is proportionate, C agrees to the arrangement, the agreement is confirmed in writing, and the total fee is reasonable.**	**Alan agreed to give Tom 1/3 of his contingency fee,** which amounts to fee splitting among lawyers not in the same firm. Tom did not get Patty's consent in writing, informed or otherwise, for the fee splitting since Patty knew nothing about the fee splitting arrangement, in violation of both the ABA and Cal rules.	**The fee splitting agreement was improper**

Continued>

Issue	Rule	Fact Application	Conclusion
Fee Splitting Among Lawyers (continued)	**Cal.: If there is a written agreement between Ls to divide the fee, C consents in writing after full written disclosure that fees will be divided along with identity of the Ls and division terms, and total fee is not increased by the division.**	**Further, under the ABA the fee division is not proportionate to their work since Tom did nothing other than secure the client in exchange for 1/3 of the total recovery.**	
		It is unclear if the total fee is reasonable since the total contingency fee % is unknown, but it appears that the total amount was not increased to accommodate Tom's 1/3 share.	
Duty of Communication	**L shall promptly inform C of decisions that affect their informed consent,** reasonably consult with C, **and keep C informed of the status of the case.**	**Tom did not consult with Patty before referring the case to Alan or inform Patty that he had no experience in personal injury.** Patty's agreement after the fact does not excuse the violation.	**Tom breached the duty of communication**
Duty of Confidentiality	L may not reveal confidential information. One exception is if C gives their informed consent.	In referring the case to Alan, Tom likely had to disclose confidential information and did so without Patty's consent.	Tom breached the duty of confidentiality
Contingency Fee Agreement	A contingency fee agreement **must be in writing, be signed by C** (Cal. requires signed by C and L w/ each provided a copy), **state the method by which the fee is determined including percentages, and state the expenses to be deducted from recovery and when they will be deducted.** Cal. requires that the agreement state that the fee is negotiable unless the claim is for negligence against a healthcare provider.	**Tom and Patty entered into a "valid and proper contingency fee agreement."**	Contingency fee agreement was proper
2. What ethical violations has Alan committed?			
Fee agreement regarding representing Patty			
Referral Fees and Agreements	Rule supra	For the same reasons discussed above with Tom, Alan has violated the rules.	**Accepting the referral was improper**
Fee Splitting	Rule supra	For the same reasons discussed above with Tom, Alan has violated the rules.	**The fee splitting agreement was improper**

(Continued>)

Issue	Rule	Fact Application	Conclusion
Contingency Fee Agreement	Rule supra	Alan should have Patty sign a new contingency agreement with him to avoid any dispute.Cal. also requires Alan to sign the new agreement and both be given a copy.	Alan needed a new contingency fee agreement
$200 gift from Alan to Joe			
Duty of Fairness/ Trial Publicity	L who is participating in an investigation or litigation or a matter shall not make an extrajudicial statement that L knows or should reasonably know will be publicly disseminated and have a substantial likelihood of materially prejudicing the proceeding. One exception is information in the public records.	**Here, Alan made an extrajudicial statement by requesting that Joe, in exchange for a $200 gift card, mention that Alan was Patty's attorney when Joe released news of the story since he was a journalist.** But since this information was public knowledge since the attorney is listed on the case, it would not be violating the rules and is not dishonest. **While it might seem that the $200 gift to a journalist suggests that Alan is trying to influence coverage of case,** which seems more like a bribe and is unethical because it is not the type of conduct that promotes public confidence in the profession, it is permitted by the rules since the information was public knowledge. [Any discussion of the $200 gift would be acceptable here.]	Alan's payment of $200 was likely permissible
Advertising	**Advertising must not be false or misleading.** L may advertise services through public media so long as they are truthful and contain the name and address of L.	Arguably, Alan is asking for free advertising, which could be misleading to the public since future coverage of the texting case may not be unbiased because of Alan's payment. **However, Alan only asked that Joe mention that Alan was the attorney on record, which he was.** But Alan should have included his address for Joe to include as well.	Conclude either way
Solicitation	L may not conduct in-person, live telephone, or real-time electronic contact.	No violation here because newspaper coverage and ads do not constitute direct solicitation.	No violation of solicitation rules

Continued>

Issue	Rule	Fact Application	Conclusion
Alan's meeting with Walter			
Duty of Fairness **Improper Influence on Witness**	L shall not unlawfully obstruct evidence. ABA: L may not request others to refrain from giving relevant information unless a relative or agent of client. **Cal.: L may not pay a witness to testify unless for** reasonable expert fees, compensation for loss of time for witness to testify, or reasonable expenses incurred.	**It would be unfair to pay Walter money in exchange for favorable testimony. By offering to pay for a hotel until Walter, who is homeless, "gets back on his feet," Alan is essentially paying for more than just his testimony since this expense goes far beyond paying for reasonable witness expenses.** Further, Walter may be so influenced that he is disinclined to talk to driver's lawyer because of the financial incentive or he may be harder to locate since he would move from the homeless shelter, which is unfair to the opposing party. **However, Alan has asked for Walter's "truthful testimony,"** so he does not appear to be soliciting perjury, **but it appears that his offer of shelter is dependent on Walter's testimony, so it appears improper nonetheless.** [Many headings would be acceptable so long as there was a sufficient factual discussion of Alan's improper attempt to influence Walter's testimony.]	**Alan has breached his ethical duties by offering to put Walter in a hotel**

Professional Responsibility Question 3 Sample Answer
July 2013, Question 1

1. What ethical violations has Tom committed?

Agreement to Represent Patty

Duty of Competence

Under the ABA, a lawyer shall represent their client with the legal knowledge, skill, thoroughness, and preparation reasonably necessary. In Cal., a lawyer must not intentionally, recklessly, with gross negligence, or repeatedly fail to perform legal services with competence. Under both bodies of law, a lawyer may acquire the necessary skills, consult with another competent lawyer, or refer the matter to another competent lawyer.

Here, Patty's claim is in tort for a car accident and Tom is a real estate attorney, which is not related to personal injury law. Tom should not have agreed to take a case in an area he had no knowledge of, though he could have acquired skill in this area, or associated with an attorney experienced in personal injury, such as Alan who was an experienced personal injury attorney. Tom also could have referred Patty to another experienced lawyer such as Alan at the time she sought his assistance. However, Tom referred the entire case to Alan after accepting it, which is likely impermissible since he should have referred the case before agreeing to take it on.

Thus, Tom likely breached the duty of competence.

Referring Patty's Case to Alan

Referral Agreements and Fees

A reciprocal referral agreement between lawyers is permissible if it is not exclusive and the client is informed of the agreement. However, a lawyer may not give anything of value to a person for recommending the lawyer's services unless it is for a qualified referral service or a nominal gift as an expression of appreciation not intended as compensation for the recommendation or future recommendations.

Here, there is no indication of an exclusive reciprocal agreement between Tom and Alan, but Tom did not get Patty's informed consent for his referral to Alan because he told her about the referral after the fact. Further, since Alan is giving 1/3 of his contingency fee to Tom, it is more accurately classified as fee splitting than as a referral fee. Even if it was a referral fee, 1/3 of the contingency fee would not be a nominal gift as that is the typical fee a lawyer would charge overall in a personal injury case.

Therefore, the referral to Alan was improper.

Fee Splitting Among Lawyers

Division of fees between lawyers who are not in the same firm may be made under the ABA only if the division is proportionate, the client agrees to the arrangement and the agreement is confirmed in writing, and the total fee is reasonable. They are only allowed in Cal. if there is a written agreement between the lawyers to divide the fee, the client consents in writing after full written disclosure that fees will be divided along with identity of the lawyers and division terms, and the total fee is not increased by the division.

Here, Alan agreed to give Tom 1/3 of his contingency fee, which amounts to fee splitting among lawyers not in the same firm. Tom did not get Patty's consent in writing, informed or otherwise, for the fee splitting since Patty knew nothing about the fee splitting arrangement, which is in violation of both the ABA and Cal rules. Further, under the ABA the fee division is not proportionate to their work since Tom did nothing other than secure the client in exchange for 1/3 of the total recovery. It is unclear if the total fee is reasonable since the total contingency fee % is unknown, but it appears that the total amount was not increased to accommodate Tom's 1/3 share.

Overall, the fee splitting agreement was improper.

Duty of Communication

A lawyer shall promptly inform the client of decisions that affect their informed consent, reasonably consult with the client, and keep the client informed of the status of the case. Here, Tom did not consult with Patty before referring the case to Alan or inform Patty that he had no experience in personal injury. Patty's agreement after the fact does not excuse the violation. Thus, Tom breached the duty of communication.

Duty of Confidentiality

A lawyer may not reveal confidential information. One exception is if the client gives their informed consent. Here, when Tom referred the case to Alan, he likely had to disclose confidential information and did so without Patty's consent. Thus, Tom breached the duty of confidentiality.

Contingency Fee Agreement

A contingency fee agreement must be in writing, be signed by the client (Cal. requires it to be signed by both the client and the lawyer with each retaining a copy), state the method by which the fee is determined including percentages, and state the expenses to be deducted from recovery and when they will be deducted. Cal. requires that the agreement state that the fee is negotiable unless the claim is for negligence against a health care provider. Here, Tom and Patty entered into a "valid and proper contingency fee agreement." Thus, the contingency fee agreement was proper.

2. What ethical violations has Alan committed?

Fee Agreement Regarding Representing Patty

Referral Fees and Agreements

See above for rule. For the same reasons discussed above with Tom, Alan has violated the rules. Thus, accepting the referral was improper.

Fee Splitting

See above for rule. For the same reasons discussed above with Tom, Alan has violated the rules. Thus, the fee splitting agreement was improper.

Contingency Fee Agreement

See above for rule. Here, Alan should have Patty sign a new contingency agreement with him to avoid any dispute.

Cal. also requires Alan to sign the new agreement and both Alan and Patty be given a copy. Thus, Alan needed to execute a new contingency fee agreement.

$200 Gift from Alan to Joe

Duty of Fairness/Trial publicity

A lawyer who is participating in an investigation or litigation or a matter shall not make an extrajudicial statement that the lawyer knows or should reasonably know will be publicly disseminated and have a substantial likelihood of materially prejudicing the proceeding. One exception is information already available in the public records.

Here, Alan made an extrajudicial statement by requesting that Joe, in exchange for a $200 gift card, mention that Alan was Patty's attorney when Joe released news of the story since he was a journalist. But since this information was public knowledge since the attorney is listed on the case, it would not be violating the rules and is not dishonest.

While it might seem that the $200 gift to a journalist suggests that Alan is trying to influence coverage of case, which seems more like a bribe and would be unethical because it is not the type of conduct that promotes public confidence in the profession, it is permitted by the rules since the information was public knowledge and he simply asked that his name be listed as the attorney, which is true and unrelated to the facts of the case.

Therefore, Alan's $200 gift card to Joe was likely permissible.

Advertising

Advertising must not be false or misleading. A lawyer may advertise services through public media so long as they are truthful and contain the name and address of the lawyer.

Arguably, Alan is asking for free advertising, which could be misleading to the public since future coverage of the texting case may not be unbiased because of Alan's payment. However, Alan only asked that Joe mention that Alan was the attorney on record, which he was. But Alan should have included his address for Joe to include as well if it is considered an actual advertisement, which it likely isn't since it isn't even clear that Joe would write an article about the case as Alan just assumed there would be future coverage of the case. Most likely there was no advertisement, so Alan likely didn't violate the rules.

Solicitation

A lawyer may not conduct in-person, live telephone, or real-time electronic contact. There was no violation here because newspaper coverage and ads do not constitute direct solicitation.

Alan's Meeting with Walter

Duty of Fairness/Improper Influence on Witness

A lawyer shall not unlawfully obstruct evidence. Under the ABA, a lawyer may not request others to refrain from giving relevant information unless a relative or agent of client. In Cal., a lawyer may not pay a witness to testify unless it is for reasonable expert fees, compensation for loss of time for a witness to testify, or reasonable expenses incurred.

Here, it would be unfair to pay Walter money in exchange for presumably favorable testimony since Walter saw the driver texting just before the accident. By offering to pay for a hotel until Walter, who is homeless, "gets back on his feet," Alan is essentially paying for more than just his truthful testimony since this expense goes far beyond paying for reasonable witness expenses. Further, Walter may be so influenced that he is disinclined to talk to driver's lawyer because of the financial incentive offered by Alan or he may be harder to locate since he would move from the homeless shelter to a hotel selected by Alan, which is unfair to the opposing party.

However, Alan has asked for Walter's "truthful testimony," so he does not appear to be soliciting perjury, but it appears that his offer of shelter is dependent on Walter's testimony, so it appears improper, nonetheless. Thus, Alan has attempted to improperly influence a witness by offering to put Walter in a hotel.

Professional Responsibility Question 4
February 2016, Question 3

Contractor and Lawyer had been in a consensual sexual relationship for months. Contractor could not afford to hire an experienced lawyer to defend him against Plaintiff's complex construction defect case and to bring a cross-complaint. Contractor told Lawyer, who had never handled such matters, that he wouldn't sue her for malpractice if she would defend him for half her regular rate. Lawyer felt pressured because of their relationship.

Lawyer told Contractor she would defend him for half-price, but she would only bring his cross-complaint on contingency at her regular rate of 30 percent of any recovery. Contractor agreed. Although they continued to have sexual relations, their personal relationship deteriorated. Lawyer forgot to make a scheduled court appearance in the case.

At trial Plaintiff lost, and Contractor won $100,000 on his cross-complaint. Lawyer deposited the $100,000 in her Client Trust Account. She told Contractor she would send him $70,000. Contractor said Lawyer must send an additional $15,000 because she agreed to represent him for half-price on everything, including the contingency fee.

1. Did Lawyer commit any ethical violation by agreeing to represent Contractor? Discuss.

2. Did Lawyer commit any ethical violation by failing to make the court appearance? Discuss.

3. What should Lawyer do with the money in the Client Trust Account? Discuss.

Answer according to California and ABA authorities.

Professional Responsibility Question 4 Assessment
February 2016, Question 3

This is a comparatively easy professional responsibility question, which was a gift since it was the last question in the morning session. And as explained in the above question assessments, it is not uncommon for the bar examiners to throw a professional responsibility (or Evidence) essay as the last question so you are not your sharpest self. Unlike the broad call that just asks about all ethical violations the lawyer committed in general, this essay shows the other style of professional responsibility testing where they ask very specific question calls, but of course you are still asked to answer according to both ABA and California law. It is worth noting that both released passing answers were a scant four pages each. The key takeaway is that they properly spotted all necessary issues and showed the graders that they understood how the rules would apply (and how lawyers essentially get into trouble). Speaking of trouble, if you ever actually follow the State Bar news you would probably be amazed at the number of attorneys that they publicly post about getting disbarred (with years of loan debt still to pay), or disciplined, or publicly censored, etc. Check it out and make sure you never become one of those statistics by knowing these rules! These rules are crucial to both the bar exam and in real practice.

Professional responsibility can be a subject that lends itself to a robust factual discussion. Typically, it is perfectly acceptable to discuss the gist of the rule in more general terms compared to the specificity needed for other subjects, especially when so many issues are capable of being tested, the rules have numerous subparts, and there are two bodies of law to know. However, what is important is a full discussion of the lawyer's conduct and why it is or is not a violation of the professional responsibility rules and standards applying both the ABA and California rules. This question raises the issue of Lawyer's sexual relationship with her client. While that relationship is not a violation of the rules, it is important to use that relationship as the basis for a good factual discussion of how it impacts her duties of competence, loyalty, and diligence to her client. And this is the type of a real-life scenario that you might find yourself in one day since often family, friends, or significant others ask those they know that are lawyers for legal advice (just like people ask their doctor friends for medical advice). Be very careful when blurring the lines of personal and professional as you could end up in a bar essay fact pattern. In this essay, there is also a lot of opportunity to analyze the many deficiencies in the fee agreement. Notice that all calls of the questions are not created equal. The first call has many more issues to discuss than the second and third calls.

In recent years the bar examiners have seemed to focus their questions on the particular areas of law where the rules differ between the ABA Model Rules and/or the ABA Code and the California rules, and this question is no exception. This type of a question necessarily requires a full recitation of each rule, including the identification of whether the rule is ABA or California, and a full discussion of the facts as applied to each of the differing rules. Where the rules are substantially similar, it is not necessary to identify the separate rules in the answer. However, it is key to make the distinction where the rules differ.

Finally, make note of the areas highlighted in **bold** on the corresponding grid. The bold areas highlight the issues, analysis, and conclusions that are likely **required** to receive a passing score on this question. In general, the essay grids are provided to assist you in analyzing the essays and are much more detailed than what a student should create during the exam to organize their response to a question.

Issue	Rule	Fact Application	Conclusion
1. Lawyer representing Contractor			
Sexual Relationships with Clients	L **shall not** have sexual relations with a C **unless a consensual sexual relationship existed before** the lawyer-client relationship commenced.	**Lawyer and Contractor had a pre-existing sexual relationship** for months prior to Lawyer agreeing to represent Contractor, so the **relationship does not automatically violate the rules.** However, the sexual relationship may impact other professional responsibility duties as described below.	**The sexual relationship itself is permissible,** unless it caused L to perform incompetently.
Duty of Loyalty Conflict of Interest	L has the duty of loyalty to **put the interest of the C above all other interests and avoid conflicts of interest.** A conflict of interest exists when there is a **significant risk** that the representation of the C will be **materially limited by L's personal interest.** L may still represent C if L reasonably believes they can provide competent and diligent representation, it is not against the law, clients are not directly adverse if two clients, and C gives informed consent, confirmed in writing (Cal. informed written consent).	**Lawyer's own interest in her sexual relationship with Contractor could materially limit her competent representation of Contractor** since it is difficult to separate the personal relationship from the professional. **Lawyer felt pressured to take on Contractor's case because of their relationship, despite her inexperience in complex construction defect cases,** which shows that there is a significant risk that the representation will be materially limited since she doesn't know that area of law well and only agreed to do it b/c of their relationship. While Lawyer may have reasonably believed she could provide competent and diligent representation by learning that area of law, Lawyer needed to notify Contractor about the potential conflict of interest inherent in their sexual relationship and obtain his informed written consent.	**L has likely violated her duty of loyalty.**
Duty of Competence	ABA: L shall represent C with the **legal knowledge, skill, thoroughness, and preparation** reasonably necessary. Cal.: L must not intentionally, recklessly, with gross negligence, or repeatedly fail to perform legal services with competence. **Both: L may associate or consult with another competent L or acquire the necessary skills to become competent.**	**Lawyer agreed to represent Contractor in a complex construction defect case, despite not having any experience with this type of case.** **There is no indication Lawyer has taken any measures to educate herself in the construction defect field or associate herself with a more competent attorney. Accordingly, Lawyer is not competent to handle this type of case.**	**L has violated the duty of competence.**

Continued>

Issue	Rule	Fact Application	Conclusion
Limiting Malpractice Liability	**ABA:** L **may not** agree to limit their malpractice liability to C **unless C is represented by independent counsel.** **Cal.:** L **may not prospectively limit their malpractice liability.**	**There is no indication that Contractor was represented by independent counsel, so Lawyer has violated the ABA rule. Lawyer also violated the Cal. rule,** b/c it disallows limits on liability.	**L has violated the rules limiting malpractice liability.**
Fee Agreement	**ABA:** Fees must be **reasonable**, considering factors including the **experience and ability of L**; the time, labor, novelty, **difficulty**, and skill required; and whether the fee is fixed or contingent.. **Cal.:** Fees must not be **illegal or unconscionable,** looking at the same factors and the ABA and others such as the sophistication of L and C and whether the C gave informed consent. **Cal.:** Fee agreements over **$1,000 must be in writing, except** if C is a corporation, C waives the writing requirement in writing, the legal services are for a **previous C with similar services,** or there is an emergency.	Lawyer agreed to accept half her regular rate to defend Contractor against a complex construction defect case, which **seems reasonable, and not unconscionable because the case was difficult but she had little experience so charging less was fair.** However, given that she was completely inexperienced in construction defect, it may not have been reasonable if it would take her too long to become competent in the area or she was unable to competently defend him due to the complexity of the case. **The agreement regarding the defense of the construction defect suit was not reduced to a writing,** which is acceptable under the ABA rule. However, since **Contractor is not likely a corporation,** Lawyer has not performed similar services for him since this is the first time she's represented him, and the amount of fees **was likely over $1,000, the agreement needed to be in writing to satisfy the Cal. rule.**	**The fee agreement needed to be in writing to satisfy the Cal. rule.**
Contingency Fee Agreement	**A contingency fee agreement must be in writing; signed by C** (Cal. requires it to be signed by C and L w/ each provided a copy), state the **method** by which the fee is determined, including percentages; state **expenses** to be **deducted** from recovery and whether they are to be deducted **before or after** the contingent fee is calculated. **Cal. requires that the agreement state that the fee is negotiable** unless it is negligence against a healthcare provider.	A 30% contingency fee agreement seems reasonable, but it may not have been if it was the result of duress or undue influence. **The contingency fee agreement on the cross complaint needed to be in writing and signed by the client,** but there is no indication of a writing here. Further, Lawyer failed to clarify the expenses to be deducted from recovery and whether they would be **deducted before or after the fee calculation.** **The Cal. rule also requires the lawyer to sign the agreement** and that the client be notified the fee is negotiable, neither of which happened here.	**The contingency fee agreement violates the ABA and Cal. rules.**

Continued>

Issue	Rule	Fact Application	Conclusion
2. Failure to make court appearance			
Duty of Competence	L shall represent C with the **legal knowledge, skill, thoroughness, and preparation** reasonably necessary. **Cal.: L must not intentionally, recklessly, with gross negligence, or repeatedly fail to perform** legal services with competence.	It appears that Lawyer missed the court appearance because of the deterioration of her sexual relationship with Contractor. **Failure to attend a scheduled court appearance would be a lack of preparation and thoroughness needed to represent the client, but may not rise to the level of intentionally for Cal. b/c it** seems she forgot to attend and it wasn't on purpose, **but this still could be considered reckless as it substantially affects clients when their lawyers don't attend court appearances.**	**L likely breached the duty of competence.**
Duty of Diligence	ABA: L shall act with **reasonable diligence and promptness** in representing C. Cal.: L shall not **intentionally**, repeatedly, **recklessly**, or with gross negligence fail to act with reasonable **diligence** in representing C. Cal. says diligence means that L does not neglect or disregard a legal matter entrusted to L.	A reasonably diligent lawyer would attend all court appearances. **Failure to make the court appearance shows a lack of diligence and promptness, and that L acted recklessly.** Also, in Cal., L neglected a legal matter entrusted her by not appearing in court which meets the definition of diligence in Cal.	**L likely breached the duty of diligence.**
3. Client trust account			
Fee Dispute	When there is a fee **dispute with a C, the L must send any undisputed portion to C promptly** and **keep the disputed portion in C's trust account** until the dispute is resolved.	Since there was **no dispute as to $70,000** of the $100,000 Contractor won on his cross-complaint with a 30% contingency fee, **Lawyer must promptly send the undisputed portion to Contractor.** Contractor claims the contingency fee is ½ price, which is 15%, so Lawyer may pay herself $15,000, which is undisputedly owed to her as a fee for her services. **The remaining $15,000 must remain in Contractor's trust account, pending resolution of the dispute.**	L should **pay C $70K**, pay herself $15K and **leave $15K in C's trust account.**

551

Professional Responsibility Question 5
February 2024, Question 3

Allison, a criminal defense attorney, represented Davos, a professional athlete, through a valid written retainer agreement. Davos was charged with assaulting Caren at a restaurant. Allison asked Davos to gift her season tickets to Davos' games if she prevailed in the criminal case. At trial, the prosecution presented the restaurant's surveillance videotape as evidence which showed the assault, along with a video surveillance expert, who identified Davos in the video.

Allison presented the testimony of two witnesses: (1) Wilfred, who was waiting tables at the restaurant, and saw an argument between Davos and Caren but did not see an altercation; and (2) Eileen, an experienced video technician, who testified that, in her opinion, there was no assault based on the poor quality of the video. When Allison and Eileen had previously watched the video together, they both agreed that the video showed strong evidence of the assault.

Allison agreed to pay Wilfred an hourly fee, roughly equal to his hourly wages and tips at the restaurant, for his time in testifying *and* for an entire day of preparation, but only if Wilfred refused to meet with the prosecution before trial.

Once Eileen agreed to change her opinion and testify that there was no assault based on the quality of the video, Allison agreed to pay Eileen $500 per hour for testifying at the trial. In her closing argument, Allison argued that the video showed that there was no assault, and that in her own opinion, after considering the evidence, Davos was not guilty.

What ethical violations, if any, has Allison committed with respect to:

   A. Request for season tickets to Davos' games? Discuss.

   B. Payments to Wilfred? Discuss.

   C. Payment to Eileen? Discuss.

   D. Presentation of Eileen's expert opinion? Discuss.

   E. Allison's statements in closing argument? Discuss.

Answer according to California and ABA authorities.

Professional Responsibility Question 5 Assessment
February 2024, Question 3

This is an example of one of the most specific professional responsibility essays they have tested with several very specific calls. At first it might seem overwhelming, but in reality, they are doing part of the breakdown for you by doing this. As we suggest, you usually need to organize these essays by event and then issue spot within each event. By giving you specific calls, they kindly break down the events for you. So now you just need to issue spot within each of these calls (events). Keep in mind as you issue spot each call that some issues can be tested in more than one call. So don't dismiss an issue just because you've already analyzed it in another call.

Another thing that is atypical with this question is the issues it tests because it tests a criminal defense attorney and witness involvement triggering some more nuanced rules involving fairness and decorum to the tribunal and opposing counsel. It also tests one of the very specific types of conflicts of interest involving gifts, which requires you to analyze the special rule for gifts as well as the general rule since now the outcome might affect the lawyer's own personal interest. This is an example of how conflicts of interest can raise different rules requiring factual analysis of all applicable rules. It is a good idea to look at the conflicts of interest chart to see which essays trigger the general rule as well as some other specialized rule. You need to train your brain to spot all possible rules that are triggered and not just narrow in on the most obvious one. It is also a good idea to see how in-depth the analysis goes or doesn't go in regard to each of the types of conflicts. When a special rule is being tested, such as here with gifts, spend most of your time on that special rule and quickly address the general rule if timing is an issue. Here, one of the state released answers didn't even go into the general rule but they addressed other issues such as competence that the other state-released answer didn't address. This is why there are two state-released answers—you will see that they can both be different but yield the same result, a passing score. What is common is that both answers noted that the key issues in each call while each answer focused on different minor issues or went into more depth on one issue compared to the other answer. You need to look at the answers holistically and see what the key parts were that you needed to pass.

The part that may be more difficult for you is addressing the witness issues, including the lawyer being a witness, because those are less frequently tested issues and give rise to paying witnesses and possibly encouraging them to commit perjury on the stand (big, big trouble then!). But keep in mind that even if you cannot recall the specific rules, you know that overall, there is a big issue called "fairness" that encompasses so many little nuanced rules. So, use the facts and common sense to craft your analysis about what might possibly be wrong with a lawyer paying a witness to not talk to the opposing party and to lie at trial. You don't need to have a specific rule memorized to know that this behavior is unbecoming of a lawyer. Use your common sense and analyze the facts as you think they should be analyzed. Pretend you are the opposing counsel and found out about these actions of your opposing counsel. That might help guide your analysis to some extent if you find yourself stuck.

While the fairness issues are not always tested, it is a good idea if you found yourself struggling on this essay to at least memorize a list of ways in which a lawyer can violate their ethical duties here (i.e., no false statements, no lying, no obstructing evidence, no paying a witness unreasonable fees, etc.). One thing we recommend is creating your own mini-issues checklists for some of these trickier areas based on issues you've spotted as you organize more essays. Keep a running tab of all fairness/decorum issues you come across in essays and then memorize that list. You can even add a few facts to create a corresponding fact trigger list to guide you on these essays. Then, on the real bar exam, you will have likely exposed yourself to many of these issues and won't feel as overwhelmed if they appear on your bar exam. You will simply jot down your list and know you've got this!

Note the areas highlighted in **bold** on the corresponding grid. The bold areas highlight the issues, analysis, and conclusions that are likely **required** to receive a passing score on this question. In general, the essay grids are provided to assist you in analyzing the essays and are much more detailed than what a student should create during the exam to organize their response to a question.

Issue	Rule	Fact Application	Conclusion
1. Request for Season Tickets to Davos' Game			
Duty of Loyalty— Conflict of Interest for Solicitation of Gifts [one answer did not go through this rule but it was still likely worth points because it was an issue and one answer did go through it but you wouldn't fail by omitting it]	**L shall not solicit any substantial gift from C** unless L is related to C, or in Cal., C is advised by an independent L who has provided a certificate of independent review. If allowed, the gift must be fair and made w/o undue influence.	Here, the lawyer, **Allison, asked the client, Davos, to gift her season tickets to Davos' games if she prevailed which was likely a substantial gift b/c Davos was a professional athlete and professional games are usually expensive**, especially season tickets. There is no indication that Davos is related to Allison and there is no indication that Davos was advised by an independent lawyer. And there may have been undue influence if he felt compelled to agree so that Davos would represent him since she is the one who suggested it.	**Allison violated the duty of loyalty for soliciting gifts**
Duty of Loyalty— Conflict of Interest with L's Personal Interests	L owes a duty of loyalty to act in the best interest of C and avoid all conflicts of interest. A conflict of interest exists if there is a significant risk that the representation of C will be materially limited by L's personal interest. L may still represent C despite the conflict if L reasonably believes they can provide competent and diligent representation to C, representation is not prohibited by law, Cs are not directly adverse if between two Cs, and C gives informed consent, confirmed in writing (Cal. informed written consent).	Here, Allison owes a duty of loyalty to Davos to avoid conflicts of interest. There may be a significant risk of material limitation by Allison's personal interests since now she has a vested interest in the outcome of the trial b/c she will get season tickets if she prevails. However, this likely will motivate her to help Davos even more because she benefits if he is acquitted so it likely won't materially limit her representation. She could reasonably believe she could competently represent him still b/c she is a criminal defense attorney, but she still should have obtained his written informed consent since there is a possible conflict.	Allison might have a conflict of interest so she should obtain Davos' informed written consent
Retainer Fees	L may collect a retainer fee if **C agrees in writing** after disclosure they cannot get a refund.	Here, **Allison and Davos entered into a "valid written retainer agreement"** so it is presumed all requirements are met.	**Retainer Agreement Valid**

Continued>

Issue	Rule	Fact Application	Conclusion
Contingency Fees	**A contingency fee agreement must be in writing,** signed by C (Cal. requires signed by L and C w/ each provided a copy), state the method by which the fee is determined, including percentages, state what expenses will be deducted and when. Cal. also requires the agreement to state the fee is negotiable unless for negligence against a healthcare provider. **They are not allowed in criminal or domestic cases.**	Here, it isn't clear that the gift for season tickets was part of their valid written fee agreement as it seems as though that request came after the agreement, but it **appears as a contingency agreement since Allison receiving the season tickets is dependent on prevailing in the criminal case.** Even if it is in writing, **contingency fees are not allowed in criminal cases and Allison is a criminal defense attorney representing Davos for criminal assault so a contingency fee agreement would not be allowed.**	**Allison violated the rules for contingency agreements**
Duty of Competence	ABA: L shall competently represent C with the legal knowledge, skill, thoroughness, and preparation reasonably necessary for the representation. Cal.: **L must not intentionally, recklessly, with gross negligence, or repeatedly fail to perform legal services with competence.**	While Allison is a criminal defense attorney and can likely competently defend Davos in an assault charge, she did not act with the necessary legal knowledge and was reckless by requesting a substantial gift from the client which can appear as though she was exerting undue influence on the client.	Allison violated her duty of competence
2. Payments to Wilfred			
Duty of Fairness/ Paying a Witness	ABA: Allows witnesses to be paid as permitted by law. **Cal.: L may not pay a witness to testify unless for reasonable expert fees, compensation for loss of time for witness to testify, or reasonable expenses incurred.**	Here, **Wilfred is a lay witness** b/c he waited tables at a restaurant and **saw an argument, but not an altercation,** between Davos and Caren, who Davos is charged with assaulting. **Allison offered to pay him an hourly fee, roughly equal to his salary and tips at the restaurant, for his time in testifying which seems like reasonable compensation for time he would miss at work.** **But paying Wilfred for an entire day of preparation might be excessive since he shouldn't need to prepare** as he is only testifying as to what he witnessed, and **Allison can't pay him to testify** but only for reasonable expenses incurred or loss of time and **it likely won't take him a full day of time.**	**Allison violated her duty of fairness**

Continued>

Issue	Rule	Fact Application	Conclusion
Duty of Fairness to Opposing Counsel	L shall not obstruct another party's access to evidence and L shall not engage in conduct involving dishonesty. ABA: L may not request others to refrain from giving relevant information unless a relative or agent of client.	**Allison may have been obstructing the prosecution from access to evidence when she tried to prevent a witness from talking to the prosecution by paying them witness fees which is improper.** She also possibly engaged in dishonesty since she knows that Wilfred was likely to testify that he saw the argument but not altercation but thought there was an assault when he saw the full video, which shows he didn't actually see anything to testify about. **When Allison offered to pay Wilfred but only if he refused to meet with the prosecution before trial, she was improperly attempting to have Wilfred refrain from giving relevant information to the other side** and Wilfred was not a relative or agent of the client as he was just a witness.	**Allison violated her duty of fairness**
Duty of Competence	See rule above.	Allison did not act with skill and knowledge and was reckless and possibly even acted intentionally when she tried to prevent Wilfred from talking to the prosecution by what could be perceived as bribing him by paying him for time she wasn't ethically allowed to pay for.	Allison violated her duty of competence
3. Payment to Eileen			
Duty of Fairness/ Paying a Witness	**ABA: Allows witnesses to be paid as permitted by law.** Cal.: L may not pay a witness to testify unless for reasonable expert fees, compensation for loss of time for witness to testify, or reasonable expenses incurred.	**Allison improperly agreed to pay Eileen $500 per hour** b/c that is an excessive fee and not reasonable for her time unless Eileen as an experienced video technician makes $500 an hour such that her time is worth that amount. **But the fact that she only agreed to pay that amount once she agreed to change her testimony shows the expense was more of a bribe and not for her actual time.**	**Allison violated her duty of fairness**

Continued>

Issue	Rule	Fact Application	Conclusion
Duty of Fairness to Opposing Counsel	**L shall not engage in conduct involving dishonesty, fraud, or deceit.** **L shall not falsify evidence or induce others to do so.** ABA: **L may not request others to refrain from giving relevant information** unless a relative or agent of client.	**Allison was dishonest when she agreed to pay $500 to Eileen once she agreed to lie and change her opinion from agreeing the video showed an assault to no assault based on the quality of the video.** Allison also induced Eileen to falsify evidence by paying her $500/hr. which seems excessive. Allison was also preventing Eileen from giving relevant info. since she knew she was lying and did so likely b/c of her $500/hr. bribe.	**Allison violated her duty of fairness**
Duty of Competence	See rule above.	Allison intentionally violated the rules and put her client at risk of having a mistrial which was reckless.	Allison violated her duty of competence
4. Presentation of Eileen's Expert Opinion			
Duty of Candor to the Tribunal/ Fairness to Opposing Party	**L shall not falsify evidence or induce others to do so or offer evidence L knows to be false (perjury).** **If L knows a witness will offer material that is false, L should take remedial measures to avoid it such as persuading the client or disclosing it to the tribunal,** and if the witness refuses, L must refuse to offer the evidence.	**This $500 induced Eileen to falsify evidence by changing her story since she originally believed the video,** as an expert experienced video technician, **showed an assault, and then testified that it showed no assault due to the quality of the video is perjury** since she is testifying in court. **The problem is that Allison is the one who encouraged the perjury rather than refuse to allow Eileen to falsely testify or stop her from doing so.**	**Allison violated her duty of decorum to the court and opposing party**
5. Alison's Statements in Closing Argument			
Duty of Candor to the Tribunal/Use of False Evidence	L shall not falsify evidence or induce others to do so. It can be prejudicial for L to publicly give an opinion as to the guilt or innocence of a criminal defendant.	Allison argued the video showed no assault and used witnesses she paid to lie to agree with that which is essentially offering false evidence.	Allison violated her duty of candor to the tribunal
Lawyer as Witness	**L shall not act as an advocate in a trial in which L is likely to be a witness** unless L's testimony relates to an uncontested issue, or the nature and value of legal services rendered.	**Allison acted like a witness in Davos' trial when she stated that in her own opinion, after considering the evidence, Davos was not guilty, which is acting like a witness** and was not allowed b/c his guilt was not an uncontested issue and did not relate to the value of her services.	**Allison violated her duty not to act as a witness**

Professional Responsibility Question 6
February 2021, Question 4

Linda Lawyer is just starting out in practice. She arranges with Chiro, a chiropractor, to give Linda's name to his patients who have been in car accidents or falls. When Linda recovers money in contingent-fee lawsuits for Chiro's patients, she gives Chiro a gift, which they have agreed will be 5% of Linda's fee. If Linda recovers nothing, Chiro receives no gift. They also form a partnership, in which Chiro's services are described as "marketing."

Pete is one of Chiro's chiropractic partners. Chiro sends Pete to Linda because Pete is seeking a divorce from his wife Alice.

Pete tells Linda he can never forgive Alice because she was unfaithful. Pete tells Linda that he's having money problems and asks that she take the case on a contingency basis. Linda tells him she'll consider it if he'll have drinks with her. Pete feels he has little choice, and goes out with her. Linda initiates a sexual relationship with Pete, and agrees to take the case. Linda is increasingly distracted from Pete's case by her desire to spend time with him, sometimes filing papers hurriedly and narrowly avoiding deadlines.

Tom, Alice's divorce lawyer, calls Linda one day and says, "I know you're having sex with Pete. Either you settle this case cheaply, or I'll report you to the Bar." Linda decides to beat Tom at his own game and, without telling him, calls the Bar herself and reports his threat.

1. What ethical violations, if any, has Linda committed with respect to her:

   a. Financial arrangement with Chiro? Discuss.

   b. Partnership with Chiro? Discuss.

   c. Relationship with Pete? Discuss.

   d. Accepting Pete's case on a contingency basis? Discuss.

2. What ethical violations, if any, has Tom committed? Discuss.

Answer according to California and ABA authorities.

Professional Responsibility Question 6 Assessment
February 2021, Question 4

This is somewhat of a hybrid style of testing where the first call is filled with specific calls and the second call is broad asking about ethical violations in general. Note also that they are asking about two lawyers here as opposed to the typical one lawyer. The good news is you know that with four specific calls directed toward Linda's ethical violations, there won't be as many issues to discuss for Tom like you would ordinarily see in a single open-ended broad call type question with one lawyer. You can also see by the calls that at least two of the four calls for Linda involve fee agreements. One call asks about a partnership, which often involves some form of unauthorized practice of law. The other call asks about a relationship, which usually involves some conflict of interest. So just from the specific calls in the first question you know what issues are likely to arise, but it's still a good idea to jot down your issues checklist to make sure you don't miss any issues, especially since you need it for call two anyway.

When going through the first call, the issues or referral fees and fee sharing should be the more obvious ones, but solicitations might not have been so obvious. This is why using a checklist is helpful. There are facts that give rise to this issue because you could argue that Linda is using Chiro to solicit clients in person. This is against the rules and tests a more nuanced rule of using cappers or others to solicit clients on lawyer's behalf.

The partnership call was fairly straightforward and just required you to understand the unauthorized practice of law rules. The relationship call was also a bit tricky because the sexual relations conflict of issue was obvious, but sometimes you might forget to also address the general conflicts of interest rule as it relates to lawyer not competently representing client because of their new personal conflict. This rule allows you to discuss the nearly missed deadlines and hurried paper filings that shows how their representation is affected by their personal interest in spending more time with the client, which is a separate issue from the special rule involving sexual relations with a client. It is a good idea to look at the conflicts of interest testing chart to see how facts give rise to more than one conflict requiring you to analyze a special rule as well as the general rule.

The contingency basis call was also fairly straightforward. It is important to note how both state-released answers discussed the duty of competence but under different calls. The reality is this issue could have been raised under every call since lawyer's actions and violations in every call indicate a lack of competence, but the key was making sure you at least addressed the issue somewhere and in some capacity, even if you didn't see all facts giving rise to the issue. It is also important to note that some of you might have spotted withdraw as an issue, which is fine, but remember you don't have time to get into details and the facts don't indicate that the lawyer tried to withdraw so be quick and mention that once lawyer violates the rules they should likely withdraw—but don't focus too much time there if you did address it, because the calls were specific and didn't ask about withdraw and withdraw alone isn't an ethical violation, but rather something lawyer should do in response to their ethical violations. As such, that was not a required issue and why you don't see it in either state-released answer. So, if you did address, you should have been very brief.

Finally, call two was broad but there were only two issues that needed to be addressed, and both were obvious with Tom's threat and reporting to the State Bar. If you couldn't remember the specific rules here, just use your common sense and think about whether you think it is appropriate to threaten someone to get what you want—hopefully not! Also, make sure you are allocating sufficient time for each call and trying to time yourself as you go through each call, so you don't run out of time. This will improve with more practice so keep up the good work!

Note the areas highlighted in **bold** on the corresponding grid. The bold areas highlight the issues, analysis, and conclusions that are likely **required** to receive a passing score on this question. In general, the essay grids are provided to assist you in analyzing the essays and are much more detailed than what a student should create during the exam to organize their response to a question.

Issue	Rule	Fact Application	Conclusion
1(a). Financial Arrangement with Chiro			
Referral Fees/ Gifts	**L shall not give (Cal. says compensate or promise) anything of value to a person for recommending L's services unless:** • It is for reasonable advertisement costs, • It is for a **qualified referral service,** • It is a **nominal gift as an expression of appreciation not intended as compensation for the recommendation** or future recommendations, or • They are referring Cs to another L or nonlawyer professional pursuant to a **reciprocal referral agreement (Cal. says arrangement) if it is not exclusive and C is informed** of the agreement.	**Here, Linda made an arrangement with Chiro, a non-lawyer who is a chiropractor, in which Chiro would give Linda names of his patients who were in car accidents.** And if Linda recovered money in their cases, she would **give Chiro 5% of her fee, so it was reciprocal,** and Linda was giving value to another person for recommending her services. **This was not acceptable b/c Chiro's referrals of patients to Linda were not from a qualified referral service nor were they made pursuant to a proper reciprocal referral agreement** b/c there is no indication that clients were informed of the agreement or that a formal agreement was even formed. This also was not a nominal gift either b/c 5% may be a lot depending on the recovery and it **seems as though the arrangement was to give that amount in return for the continued referrals and not just a gift of appreciation,** which is not allowed.	**L violated her duty regarding referral fees**
Fee Sharing with Non-Lawyers	**L may not share legal fees with a non-lawyer.**	**Here Linda is sharing 5% of her legal fees with a non-lawyer b/c Chiro is a chiropractor which is not allowed.** She may try to argue that she already earned the money so it is not sharing fees but since the fee is coming from her services and it is a set %, it would be sharing fees.	**L violated her duty on fee sharing**
Solicitations	**L may not conduct in-person,** live telephone, or real-time electronic contact for **pecuniary gain,** except for: • Free legal services, • Family members, close personal, or prior professional relationship to L, • Prepaid or group legal service plans operated by an organization. Cal. presumes solicitations in hospitals or similar institutions to be improper. **L cannot use runners or cappers to avoid liability for solicitations.**	Here, Linda didn't reach out to any potential clients in person, but she **arguably used Chiro to act as a capper or agent for her by having him refer clients to her when they came in person** to his chiropractor office. These referrals were for Linda to represent them **for pecuniary gain since her arrangement with Chiro was to pay him 5% of her fees** she earned from the clients. Even though they labeled their agreement as "marketing," it is in-person solicitation since Chiro gives the patients her name in person when they come in. The clients were not related to Linda or have any prior relationship, so no exception applies. Cal. might consider a chiropractor office to be a presumed violation since it could be like a hospital where accident victims go for rehabilitation.	**L violated her duty not to solicit clients**

Continued>

Issue	Rule	Fact Application	Conclusion
1(b). Partnership with Chiro			
Unauthorized Practice of Law	L shall **not** practice with or form a partnership or association with a non-lawyer to provide legal service.	Here, Linda, a lawyer, formed a **partnership with a non-lawyer b/c Chiro is a chiropractor**. While they indicated the partnership was for "marketing," it appears that Linda was giving legal services to Chiro's patients and then sharing 5% of the recovered fee with Chiro, which is both sharing fees with a non-lawyer and providing legal services.	**L violated her duty for unauthorized practice of law**
Fee Sharing with Non-Lawyers	L may **not** share legal fees with a non-lawyer.	Same analysis covered above.	**L violated her duty on fee sharing**
1(c). Relationship with Pete			
Sexual Relations with Client (Conflicts of interest)	L shall **not** have sexual relations with C *unless* a consensual sexual relationship existed *before* the lawyer-client relationship commenced.	Here, Linda did not start having a sexual relationship with Pete until after their lawyer-client relationship commenced b/c Pete came to her seeking a divorce from Chiro's referral and Linda asked him to have drinks with her after that point. While she initiated a sexual relationship with Pete and agreed to take the case, Pete felt he had little choice but to go out with her so it is likely that he thought she represented him or would before their sexual relationship began.	**L violated her duty of loyalty to not have sexual relations with a client**
Conflict of Interest—L's personal interest	A conflict of interest exists if there is a **significant risk that the representation of C will be materially limited by the personal interest of L.** **Exception: L may still represent C if:** • **L reasonably believes that they will be able to provide competent and diligent representation**, and • The representation is not prohibited by law, and • Cs are not asserting a claim against each other in the same litigation if between Cs, and • **C gives informed consent**, confirmed **in writing (Cal. says informed written consent)**.	Here, there is a significant risk that Linda's representation of Pete will be materially limited by her personal interest b/c she initiated a sexual relationship with him which has **distracted her** and caused her to make mistakes such as filing papers hurriedly and narrowly avoiding deadlines. While she might think she can competently represent him despite her feelings, her belief would not be reasonable b/c she's already made mistakes as discussed and is distracted. Further, **there is no indication that Pete provided written informed consent.**	**L violated her duty to avoid conflicts of interest**

Continued>

Issue	Rule	Fact Application	Conclusion
Duty of Competence [one answer discussed this under another call]	ABA: **L shall competently represent C with the legal knowledge, skill, thoroughness, and preparation reasonably necessary** for the representation. Cal.: L must not intentionally, recklessly, with gross negligence, or repeatedly fail to perform legal services with competence.	Here, Linda was **distracted by her new relationship** with Pete b/c she wanted to spend more time with him, so she did not prepare or act reasonable or without negligence since she filed **papers hurriedly and narrowly avoided missing deadlines.** **She also shouldn't have taken the case in the first place since it seems she was seeking to take personal injury cases and took a divorce case so it's not clear if she knows family law and she did not consult with another lawyer at all.**	**L violated her duty of competence**
Duty of Diligence	**ABA:** L shall act with **reasonable diligence** and **promptness** in representing C. Cal.: L shall not intentionally, repeatedly, recklessly, or with gross negligence fail to act with reasonable diligence in representing C.	Here, Linda did not act with diligence and promptness b/c she hurriedly filed papers and narrowly avoided missing deadlines which shows she was acting reckless or negligently due to her distractions with her relationship with Pete.	L violated her duty of diligence
1(d). Accepting Pete's case on a contingency basis			
Contingency Fee Agreement	A **contingency fee agreement** is one in which the fee is **dependent on the outcome** of the matter and must: • Be in **writing,** • Be signed by the client (Cal. requires the agreement to be signed by both the lawyer and client with each provided a copy), • State the method by which the fee is to be determined, including percentages, • State the litigation and other expenses to be deducted from the recovery and when they will be deducted. **They are prohibited in criminal and domestic relations cases.**	Here, **Linda entered into a contingency fee agreement with Pete** b/c he was having money problems and asked her to take the case on a contingency basis. There is no indication the agreement was in writing or any of the requirements were met, and **b/c it was for a divorce, Linda could not agree to represent him on a contingency basis.**	**L violated the rules for contingency fees**

Continued>

Issue	Rule	Fact Application	Conclusion
2. Tom's ethical violations			
Reporting Ethical Violations	**L who knows that another L** has committed **a violation** of the Model Rules that raises a substantial question as to that L's honesty, trustworthiness, or **fitness as a L shall inform the appropriate professional authority.** Cal.: L must inform the State Bar when they know of credible evidence that another L has committed a criminal act or engaged in dishonesty or misrepresentations or misappropriated funds that raise a substantial question as to that L's honesty, trustworthiness, or fitness as a L. [Note the CA rule wasn't in effect at the time of this essay but today this rule would likely be required to pass]	Here, **Tom knows that Linda is violating the ethical rules by having sexual relations with a client and that this was not a pre-representation relationship** since Pete was married to Alice before and did not know Linda. **Thus, Tom should report Linda's violations to the State Bar.**	**Tom violated his duty to report ethical violations**
Duty of Fairness— Threats	**Cal. prohibits L from threatening** to present criminal, **administrative,** or disciplinary **charges to obtain an unfair advantage** in a civil dispute.	Here, Tom threatened that he would report Linda to the Bar about her sexual relations with Pete, the client, if she didn't settle the case cheaply, which shows the threat was in order to gain an advantage in the divorce which is not permitted.	**Tom violated the duty of fairness**

PART 9 *REAL PROPERTY*

REAL PROPERTY TABLE OF CONTENTS

INTRODUCTION TO REAL PROPERTY

Real property questions are often dependent on the sequence of events, similar to a contracts question. It can be helpful to sketch a brief timeline of the important events and dates in the fact pattern to keep the events straight. Sometimes it is also helpful to visualize the facts. This is particularly true with easements.

Many students feel that real property is a struggle, and the average scores on real property questions on the bar exam tend to bear this out. This is unfortunate because the questions that logically can be posed on the bar exam regarding real property are actually straightforward, the issues are fairly easy to spot, and the analysis is usually not particularly complex. So, why do students struggle with real property? Mostly, because the language is difficult to work with, which makes the concepts more difficult to understand and remember. The language is archaic and the words don't often sound as though they mean what they actually do mean. For example, look at the similar concepts of *easements, real covenants,* and *equitable servitudes*. The concepts are similar because they all pertain to the use of land, but the concepts are distinct. Many, but not all, of the elements are the same, however there is nothing about the words themselves to give away the differences between the concepts. To make the situation worse, equitable servitudes are interchangeably called *restrictive covenants*; though a restrictive covenant is not exactly the same thing as a real covenant, which is also called just a *covenant*. The only thing that can be done to tame the tangle is to actually memorize the concepts. A general understanding of the principles will absolutely not foster success on a real property essay because it is much too easy to get the concepts confused and merged together when they aren't properly memorized and understood with specificity.

Estates in land is another area that causes a lot of confusion or anxiety for bar examinees. The good news is that estates in land are infrequently tested on the essay portion of the bar exam, and when they are tested it is usually in a brief way. This makes sense because estates in land do not actually lend themselves to the sort of robust factual analysis that the bar examiners are looking to assess in the essay portion of the exam. You do need to have an understanding of the different estates in land for the essay portion of the exam, and you must understand the details of estates in land for the multiple choice portion of the exam.

For the real property portion of the essay exam, focus on the frequently tested topics of land acquisition, joint property ownership, landlord-tenant issues, and limitations on land use. The vast majority of real property questions cover issues in those categories in some combination. Issue spotting a real property exam is easy if you focus on the three main areas of inquiry:

(1) Has property been acquired, and are there any issues related to that acquisition? This query covers the issues of adverse possession, land sale contracts, mortgages, deeds, wills, and recording acts.

(2) Who has an interest in the property in question? This query covers the issue of estates in land, joint ownership issues, and landlord-tenant issues.

(3) Are there any limits on the way the property can be used? This query covers the issues of easements, covenants, equitable servitudes, and zoning.

ISSUES CHECKLIST

HAS PROPERTY BEEN ACQUIRED?

Adverse possession
Land sales contracts
Mortgages
Deeds
Wills
Recording acts/notice

WHO HAS AN INTEREST IN THE PROPERTY?

Estates in land
Freehold estates
Future interests
Joint ownership (concurrent estates)
Joint tenants
Tenants in common
Tenancy by the entirety
Landlord/tenant
Types of tenancies
Rent disputes
Condition of premises
Waste
Fixtures
Assignment and sublease

ARE THERE LIMITS ON LAND USE?

Easements
Real covenants
Equitable servitudes
Zoning

MEMORIZATION ATTACK SHEET

LAND ACQUISITION ISSUES

- ◆ **Adverse possession**
  - Actual possession
  - Open and notorious
  - Hostile (no consent)
  - Continuous
  - Statutory period
- ◆ **Land sale contract**
  - Contract law reqmt.: SOF
    - ◆ Writing
    - ◆ Parties identified
    - ◆ Signed by one to be bound
    - ◆ Describes land
    - ◆ States consideration
    - ◆ SOF part perform. except:
      - Possession
      - Improvements
      - Payment
  - Marketable title
  - Equitable conversion
  - Remedy for breach
    - ◆ Damages
    - ◆ Specific performance
      - Contract is valid
      - Conditions satisfied
      - Inadequate legal remedy
      - Mutuality of perform
      - Feasibility of enforce
      - No defenses
- ◆ **Mortgage**
  - Writing required
  - Foreclosure
    - ◆ Judicial foreclosure
    - ◆ Priority of loans
      - Purchase money mortgage
      - Order—fees, sr., jr., unsecured
    - ◆ Deficiency
  - Redemption
- ◆ **Deeds**
  - Requires
    - ◆ Parties
    - ◆ In writing and signed by grantor
    - ◆ Describe land
    - ◆ Words of intent
    - ◆ No consideration required

- ◆ **Three types of deeds**
  - Quitclaim
  - Warranty—general
    - ◆ Seisin
    - ◆ Right to convey
    - ◆ Encumbrances
    - ◆ Title
    - ◆ Quiet enjoyment
    - ◆ Further assurances
  - Statutory special
- ◆ **Deed delivery**
  - Intent to make present transfer
  - Acceptance
- ◆ **Merger—contract merges into deed & deed controls**
- ◆ **Damages—purchase price or difference in value**
- ◆ **Defenses—laches, unclean hands, waiver**
- ◆ **Will**
  - Ademption
  - Exoneration
  - Lapse & antilapse
- ◆ **Recording acts**
  - **Three types of acts**
    - ◆ Pure race
    - ◆ Pure notice
    - ◆ Race-notice
  - **Protect bona fide purchasers**
    - ◆ Take for value
    - ◆ No notice
  - **Three types of notice**
    - ◆ Actual
    - ◆ Inquiry
    - ◆ Record (constructive)
- ◆ **Chain of title issues**
  - Estoppel by deed
  - Shelter doctrine

ESTATES IN LAND

- ◆ **Freehold estates**
  - Fee simple absolute
  - Fee tail
  - Fee simple defeasible
    - ◆ FS determinable
    - ◆ FS subject to condition subsequent
    - ◆ FS subject to executory interest
  - Life estate

- **Future interests**
  - Possibility of reverter
  - Right of reentry
  - Reversion
  - Remainder
    - Vested
    - Contingent
    - Alternative contingent
  - Executory interest
    - Shifting
    - Springing
- **Technical rules**
  - No absolute restraints on alienation
  - Destructibility of contingent remainders
  - RAP—Rule Against Perpetuities: interest must vest not later than 21 years after life in being at creation of the interest. Applies to:
    - Contingent remainders
    - Executory interests
    - Options in gross
    - Class gifts
    - Powers of appointment

JOINT OWNERSHIP

- **Joint tenancy**
  - Automatic right of survivorship
  - Equal right to occupy whole
  - Equal shares
  - Creation of joint tenancy
    - Time
    - Title
    - Interest
    - Possession
    - Express right of survivorship
  - **Severance of joint tenancy**
    - Conveyance
    - Not severed by will, any attempt is void
    - Mortgage
      - Lien theory: does not sever
      - Title theory: does sever to that JT's share
    - Lease: jurisdictions are split
- **Tenancy in common**
  - Equal right to occupy
  - Nonequal shares okay
  - Can sell, will, or gift
  - No right of survivorship
- **Tenancy by entirety**
  - Spouses only (some jx same-sex partners)
  - Right to survivorship
  - Severed by death, divorce, or agreement
- **Co-tenancy rules**
  - Right to possession
  - Accounting

- Tax/mortgage: proportionate share & may seek reimbursement
- Improvements: no right to reimbursement
- Necessary Repairs: right to contribution
  - Partition action

LANDLORD-TENANT

- **Types of tenancies**
  - Term for years
  - Periodic tenancy
  - Tenancy at will
  - Tenancy at sufferance
- **LL-T issues**
  - Duty to pay rent
  - Possession of premises
    - Holdover tenant
    - Eviction
    - Abandonment
  - Condition of premises
    - Covenant of Quiet Enjoyment
      - Interfere w/ T's use & enjoyment
    - Constructive eviction
      - Virtually uninhabitable
      - Substantial interference with use
      - Notice
      - LL doesn't respond
      - T timely moves out
    - Partial actual eviction
      - Can't occupy some portion
      - Can withhold entire rent
    - Warranty of habitability
      - Terminate & move; or
      - Repair & deduct; or
      - Pay reduced rent & sue
    - No retaliatory eviction
    - Tort liability—LL must
      - Maintain common areas
      - Fix latent defects
      - Repair nonnegligently
      - Duty to inspect areas open to public
- **Waste** (life tenant & LLT tenants)
  - Voluntary (decreases value)
  - Permissive (neglect)
  - Ameliorative (alterations)
- **Fixtures (MARIA)**
  - Method of attachment: imbedded/perm.
  - Adapted to fit real estate
  - Removal would destroy chattel/cause damage
  - Intention of party who installed chattel
  - Agreement
- **Assignment and sublease**
  - Assignment: entire interest
  - Sublease: less than entire interest

LAND USE

- ◆ **Easements—right to use land**
  - Affirmative or negative
  - Appurtenant (adjoining land)
    - ◆ Dominant—receives benefit
    - ◆ Servient—burdened to give benefit
  - In gross (to a person)
  - **Creation of easement**
    - ◆ **Express (written)**
    - ◆ **By implication**
      - Originally one parcel
      - Severed
      - Use existed prior to severance
      - Reasonably necessary
    - ◆ **By necessity**
      - Common ownership
      - Strictly necessary
      - No prior use required
    - ◆ **By prescription**
      - Actual use
      - Open and notorious
      - Hostile (no consent)
      - Continuous
      - Statutory period
    - ◆ **Estoppel (reliance)**
  - **Scope of easement**
  - **Maintain/repair easements**
  - **Transfer of easement**
  - **Termination of easement**
    - ◆ Estoppel (reliance)
    - ◆ Necessity ends
    - ◆ Destruction
    - ◆ Condemnation of property
    - ◆ Release
    - ◆ Abandonment with action
    - ◆ Merger of parcels
    - ◆ Prescription (in reverse)
- ◆ **Real Covenants (promises)**
  - **Burden runs with land**
    - ◆ Writing
    - ◆ Intent
      - ◆ Touches & concerns land
      - ◆ Horizontal & vertical privity
      - ◆ Notice
  - **Benefit runs with land**
    - ◆ Writing
    - ◆ Intent
    - ◆ Touches & concerns land
    - ◆ Vertical privity only
    - ◆ No notice required
- ◆ **Equitable servitudes (restrictions on land use)**
  - **Runs with land if:**
    - ◆ Writing
    - ◆ Intent
    - ◆ Touches & concerns land
    - ◆ No privity required
    - ◆ Notice required
  - **Servitude implied from common scheme**
    - ◆ Common plan or scheme
    - ◆ Notice
    - ◆ Writing not required
- ◆ **Termination of covenants & equitable servitudes**
  - Most same as easements and
  - Changed conditions (DREAM CC for all)
- ◆ **Profit (take from land)**
- ◆ **License (permission to use land)**
- ◆ **Water rights**
  - Drain surface water
  - Riparian rights
  - Ground water
- ◆ **Lateral & subjacent support**
  - Natural state affected SL
  - Improvement can be SL or neg.
- ◆ **Zoning**
  - For public health and safety
  - Must be reasonable
  - Cum. hierarchy; Noncum. only zoned use
  - Variance if undue hardship
  - Nonconforming use allowed or amortization

REAL PROPERTY RULE OUTLINE

I. **LAND ACQUISITION ISSUES:** Many issues in real property center around the acquisition of real property or an interest in real property. Typically property is acquired by adverse possession or by an inter vivos transfer, such as through a land sale contract or by granting a deed, or by a devise in a will.

A. **Adverse possession** allows one who has **wrongfully entered a property to obtain possession** of that property when there has been **actual possession, which is open and notorious, and the possession is hostile continuously for the statutory period.**

1. **Requirements:**

    a. **Actual possession:** The claimant must actually have exclusive use of the property, which means they must **physically occupy** the premises.

        1. **Exclusive use:** The **true owner must be excluded** from (not sharing) the premises and the property may not be open to the public.

        2. **Partial possession:** A reasonable **percentage of the property must be actually used.** A claimant may only claim possession of the portion of the property actually used. (E.g., If a claimant occupies 1 acre of 200-acre parcel, they may only claim adverse possession of the 1 acre.)

        3. **Tenant possession:** The claimant **may lease the premises to a tenant** to satisfy the actual possession element.

    b. **Open and notorious and visible possession:** The claimant must possess and use the property in a way that a **typical owner** of similar property would use the property. The use must be sufficiently open to **put the true owner on notice** of the trespass by the adverse possessor. (E.g., If a typical owner would only use the land in the summer months, the adverse possessor may only use the land seasonally also.)

    c. **Hostile possession:** Possession of the land must be **without the owner's consent.**

        1. **Hostile possession is simply not permissive**; it does not mean that the possession must be done in a hostile manner.

        2. **Boundary disputes:** Where one property owner occupies land, mistakenly thinking it is their own but it actually belongs to the adjacent property owner, this possession can be deemed hostile (most courts will fix to agreed line if there was uncertainty and the agreed line was used for a long time).

        3. **Ouster of a co-tenant** is required to find a hostile possession with concurrent property owners since all co-tenants have equal right to possession of the property.

            a. **Ouster** occurs when **a co-tenant claims an exclusive right** to possession and refuses occupancy to their co-tenant.

    d. **Continuous use** for the given **statutory period**

        1. **Statutory period:** At common law it is 20 years; it varies among the states but is typically 10 to 15 years (with some states as few as 5 years, like Cal.).

        2. **Continuous possession** means that the **owner may not reenter** to regain possession during the statutory time. If they do, the adverse possessor's statutory time period for possession starts over.

        3. **Seasonal use** of a property may still satisfy the continuous possession element if this is the way a **typical owner of similar property would use the land**. The intermittent activities must be of the sort only done by true owners. (E.g., Erecting a small cabin to use during hunting season may be typical seasonal use, but simply using the property to hunt would not be since nonowners would do the same.)

        4. **Tacking: One adverse possessor may tack their time with the time of another adverse possessor** to meet the required statutory period for adverse possession if the two adverse possessors are in **privity** (e.g., adverse possessor leases the premises to another and acts as landlord).

2. **Effect of adverse possession:** Adverse possession **does not convey marketable title.** However, the title can be perfected and made marketable by means of a **judicial action to quiet title.**

> **Adverse possession fact triggers:**
>
> - Attempted transfer of property that is ineffective and the purported new owner acts like an owner (contract fails to meet SOF, deed not properly delivered, etc.)
> - Fact pattern includes events occurring 15 to 20 years in the past
> - Seasonal use of a property, such as a vacation home or hunting cabin
> - Building is placed over the property line and onto neighbor's land

B. **Land sale contract:** The **contract** for a conveyance of an interest in real estate typically **governs the agreement until the time of closing**, at which time the **deed** becomes the operative document governing the land transfer under the **merger doctrine**.
   1. **Contract law governs** a contract for the sale of an interest in land.
      a. **Statute of Frauds (SOF) applies.**
         1. **SOF requirements:**
            a. The contract must be **in writing,**
            b. Name the **parties,**
            c. **Signed by the party to be bound,**
            d. Sufficiently **describe the land,** and
            e. State some **consideration** (e.g., purchase price and manner of payment).
         2. **Part performance exceptions to the SOF:**
            a. **Possession** of the land by the purchaser.
            b. **Substantial improvements** are made to the premises.
            c. **Payment** for part or all **of the purchase price**.

> **Exam tip:** Think **PIP** to remember the exceptions (**P**ossession, **I**mprovements, **P**ayment). And know that most courts require 2 out of the 3 for the exception to apply.

   2. **Marketable title:** There is an implied promise in every land sale contract that the seller covenants to transfer marketable title at the time of closing. **Marketable title is title free from reasonable doubt** about the seller's ability to convey what they purport to convey.

> **Marketable title fact triggers:**
>
> - **Encumbrances,** such as an outstanding mortgage or lien (but the seller has until escrow closes to pay it off)
> - **Record chain of title** indicating the seller does not have a full interest in the property to convey
> - An undisclosed **easement** that reduces "full enjoyment" of the premises
> - **Use restrictions,** such as real covenants

   3. The **doctrine of equitable conversion** provides that upon **signing the contract**, the **buyer is deemed the owner** of real property, even though the escrow closing has not yet occurred. If the property is destroyed (through no fault of either party) prior to closing, the risk of that loss is imposed on the buyer of the property. Some states have statutes that provide for the opposite result.
   4. **Remedy for breach of land sale contract:** The nonbreaching party to a land sale contract can sue for **damages** or **specific performance**. Specific performance is usually the preferred remedy because land is unique.
      a. **Damages:** Typically, damages are calculated as the **difference between the market price and the contract price**.
      b. **Specific performance** is a permanent injunction in contract where the court orders the defendant to perform on the contract as promised. (See Remedies chapter for more details.) The following requirements must be met:

1. **Contract is valid.**
2. **Contract conditions** imposed on the plaintiff are satisfied.
3. **Inadequate legal remedy:** Damages can be inadequate because they are too speculative to calculate with certainty, the defendant is insolvent, there is potential for a multiplicity of suits, or because **property is unique,** so money damages are inadequate to compensate for the loss of that property. (**Real property is always unique.**)
4. **Mutuality of performance:** Both parties to the contract must be eligible to have their performance under the contract ordered by the court.
5. **Feasibility of enforcement:** The injunction cannot be too difficult for the court to enforce (the court looks at supervision and jurisdictional issues).
6. **No defenses,** such as laches, unclean hands, or any defenses to the underlying contract (e.g., lack of consideration, SOF, sale to a bona fide purchaser, etc.).

> **Exam tip:** Use the mnemonic **Chocolate Cheesecake Is My Favorite Dessert** to memorize the six essential elements of specific performance: valid **C**ontract, contract **C**onditions satisfied, **I**nadequate legal remedy, **M**utuality of performance, **F**easibility of enforcement, and no **D**efenses.

C. **Security interests in land:** Real property is often encumbered by a mortgage or other security interest.
  1. **Mortgage:** A mortgage is a financing arrangement that **conveys a security interest in land** where the parties intend the land to be **collateral** for the repayment of a monetary obligation. The buyer and/or borrower is the **mortgagor.** The lender is the **mortgagee.**
     a. **Writing required**
        1. **Statute of Frauds:** A mortgage must typically be in writing and satisfy the SOF.
        2. **Exception to SOF:** An **equitable mortgage** can occur. (E.g., A buyer delivers a deed to the mortgagee rather than signing a note or mortgage deed. Parol evidence is allowable to show intent of the parties.)
     b. **Rights of the parties:** Until a foreclosure occurs, if ever, the **buyer-mortgagor** has **right to possession of the property and title**; the **creditor-mortgagee** has a **lien,** which grants the right to look to the land and foreclose in the event of default. Mortgages are transferable.
     c. **Foreclosure** is a process by which the **mortgagee may reach the land** in satisfaction of the debt if the mortgagor is in default on the loan.
        1. **Judicial foreclosure:** A mortgagee must foreclose by proper judicial proceeding.
        2. **Priority of loans:** After the land is sold, the proceeds will be used to satisfy the debt(s) secured by the property. Any **secured debts** (those where the property is pledged as collateral for repayment) are **paid first** in descending **order of priority** (usually chronologically). Each mortgagee/lien holder is entitled to **payment in full** before a lower-ranking creditor receives any payment.
           a. **Purchase money mortgage (PMM)** is a mortgage given to secure a loan that enables the debtor to **originally purchase the property.** A PMM **receives priority** over non-PMM mortgages, but in some jurisdictions a **PMM may not also get a deficiency judgment** against the debtor.
           b. **Order of payment from foreclosure proceeds:** (1) Fees from attorneys/trustees (2) PMM or secured senior interests (3) Secured junior interests (4) Unsecured interests. The foreclosure of junior interests will not affect senior interests but the foreclosure of senior interests will destroy all junior interests.
        3. **Anti-deficiency statutes** limit a lender to receiving **no more than the value of the loan.** Any excess remaining is returned to the buyer from the proceeds of a foreclosure sale after paying off all debts.
        4. **Deficiency judgment** occurs when the **property is worth less than the amount owed** on the outstanding loan(s). A lender can sue the debtor **personally** for the deficiency difference only if:

          a. There was a **judicial foreclosure**; and

          b. In some jurisdictions, if the loan was **not a "purchase money mortgage."**

    d. **Redemption:** When a mortgage is **paid off**, the property is "redeemed" from the mortgage (this equitable redemption is allowed before foreclosure sale). Some states have **statutory redemption** allowing the mortgagor a fixed period of time *after* foreclosure to redeem (pay off) the mortgage.

2. **Deed of trust** is similar to a mortgage, except the debtor is the trustor and the deed of trust is given to a third-party trustee.

3. **Installment contract:** A buyer makes a down payment and pays off the balance in installments. The difference between this and a mortgage is that the buyer does not receive a deed until the land is paid off, and the vendor gets forfeiture rather than foreclosure. Typically, if the buyer is in default, the seller gets back the property and gets to keep the installment payments.

D. **Conveyance by deed:** A deed is a document that **serves to pass legal title** from the grantor to the grantee when it is **lawfully executed** and **properly delivered**.

1. **Deed requirements:** Much like a land sale contract, a deed must meet the following formalities to be lawfully executed (with the big difference being that consideration is not required for a deed):

    a. **Identification of the parties.**

    b. **In writing and signed by the grantor**, which is witnessed or notarized.

    c. Adequate **description of the property.**

    d. **Words of intent** (word **"grant"** is sufficient).

    e. **No consideration is required** (it may be an inter vivos gift).

2. **Three types of deeds**

    a. **Quitclaim deed:** A quitclaim deed conveys **whatever interest the grantor actually has** in the property but contains **no covenants of title** (promises about what that interest is).

    b. **General warranty deed:** Warrants against all defects in title and contains **six covenants for title.** Three of the covenants are present and three are future covenants.

        1. **Present covenants** are **breached at the time of the sale** (when deed is delivered), if breached at all.

            a. **Seisin:** Grantor warrants they **own what they purport to own.**

            b. **Right to convey:** Grantor warrants they have the **power to make the conveyance** (title alone is sufficient).

            c. **Against encumbrances:** Grantor warrants there are **no undisclosed mortgages, liens, easements, or use restrictions** on the land. The majority rule finds this covenant would be considered breached even if the purchaser had notice of the encumbrance.

        2. **Future covenants** run with the land, are continuous, and are **breached**, if ever, **at the time the grantee is disturbed in possession.**

            a. **Warranty of title:** Grantor promises to **defend** should there be any **lawful claims of title** asserted by others.

            b. **Quiet enjoyment:** Grantor promises grantee will not be disturbed in **possession** by any third parties' **lawful claims of title.**

            c. **Further assurances:** Grantor will do whatever **future acts are reasonably necessary** to perfect title.

> **Issue spotting tip:** Look for a warranty deed issue where there is an undisclosed easement.

    c. **Statutory special warranty deed:** Some states enforce promises by statute where the grantor promises (on behalf of themselves only) that they haven't conveyed the property to others and that the estate is free from encumbrances.

3. **Delivery of deed:** A deed must be **properly delivered** and **accepted** to have effect.

    a. **Delivery requirements**

        1. **Intent of present transfer:** Words or conduct indicating the grantor's **intent to make a present transfer** of the deed. (Parol evidence is allowed to prove intent). The following create a strong presumption of present intent to transfer:

        a. **Recording** the deed.

        b. Grantor **physically delivering the deed** to the grantee.

    2. **Acceptance of the deed** by the grantee must also occur. Rejection of the deed by the grantee defeats delivery, but acceptance is usually presumed.

  b. **Title passes immediately** to the grantee upon **proper delivery**, thus it is **not revocable.**

> **Deed delivery fact triggers:**
> - Handing the deed to a third party with instructions
> - Placing the deed somewhere, such as a locked box

  4. **Merger doctrine:** Once the property closes, the **deed**, rather than the underlying land sale contract, becomes the **operative document governing the transaction**. Any obligation imposed in the contract is deemed discharged at closing unless the obligation is repeated in the deed.

  5. **Damages if covenant(s) breached**: If there are title issues, then damages awarded are the lesser of the purchase price or the cost to defend or perfect the title; if there are encumbrances, then damages awarded are the lesser of the difference between the amount paid and the value of land with the encumbrance, or the cost of removing the encumbrance.

  6. **Defenses** to breaches of covenants can include **unclean hands, laches,** and **waiver** (similar to land sales contract defenses).

E. **Devise by will:** Property may be conveyed by will. (See Wills chapter for more details.) Several issues can arise.

  1. **Ademption** occurs where a testator has devised a **specific property to a specific party** under their will, but that specific property is **no longer a part of the estate** at the time of testator's death. The general rule is that the gift is "adeemed," in other words **fails**, and the legatee gets nothing.

  2. **Exoneration** provides that when a person receives a bequest of specific property, and that **property is subject to a lien** or mortgage, the **encumbrance will be paid off** from the estate's personal property, and the recipient receives the property "free and clear" of the mortgage, unless the testator indicated a contrary intent.

  3. **Lapse and anti-lapse:** The common law doctrine of **lapse** provides that if a beneficiary named in a will **predeceases the testator, the bequest fails**. Most states have **anti-lapse** statutes that allow the predeceased beneficiary's **heirs to take**, especially if they are kin to the testator.

> **Issue spotting tip:** The intersection of wills and real property can provide the basis for a crossover question. Similar to wills, property may also be conveyed by a private or charitable trust (and crossover with a trusts question).

F. **Recording acts** function to provide a purchaser of land with a mechanism to determine whether there is an earlier transaction regarding the property that is inconsistent with their own transaction. The recording acts provide a buyer with a way to **ensure they are getting good title.**

  1. **Common law rule:** Without a recording act in place, the **common law rule of "first in time, first in right"** applies.

  2. **Three types of recording acts**

    a. **Pure race statutes:** The first to record wins. This statute rewards the winner of the race to the recorder's office. (Not commonly used either on the bar exam or in real life.)

    b. **Pure notice statutes:** A subsequent bona fide purchaser (BFP) prevails over a grantee that didn't record.

      1. Language example: "No conveyance or mortgage of real property shall be good against subsequent purchasers **for value** and **without notice** thereof, unless the same be recorded according to law."

    c. **Race-notice statutes:** A subsequent BFP that records first prevails over a grantee that didn't record first.

  1. Language example: "No conveyance or mortgage of real property shall be good against subsequent purchasers **for value** and **without notice**, who shall **first record**."

 3. **Recording acts protect bona fide purchasers (BFPs)**, including **mortgagees**.

  a. **Bona fide purchaser (BFP)**: A BFP is one who **takes for value** *and* **is without notice** of the prior interest.

   1. **Recording acts don't protect donees, heirs, and devisees** because they don't take "for value." However, the court won't look into the adequacy of the consideration so long as it is more than nominal.

   2. **Notice can be provided three ways:** Notice can occur by **actual**, **inquiry**, or **record** (constructive) notice. (See I.F.5 below.)

  b. **The recording acts only protect subsequent grantees**, never the first grantee. This is because the common law rule of "first in time, first in right" will apply, unless a recording act functions to allow the second grantee to take over the first grantee.

 4. **Recording acts apply to** every instrument by which an **interest in land** can be created or modified or can be recorded, including conveyances, mortgages, life estates, restrictive covenants, easements, etc.

> **Exam tip:** The examiners may not tell you which type of recording act statute governs. Rather, they may provide statute language and expect you to determine which type of statute it is. Analyze the language and look for key words: "records first" likely means a race statute; "good faith" and "for value" alone likely means a notice statute; and if both "records first" and "good faith" and/or "for value" are included in the statute, then it is likely a race-notice statute.

 5. There are **three types of notice.**

  a. **Actual notice** occurs when, prior to the time of closing, the buyer has **actual subjective knowledge** of a prior, unrecorded interest.

  b. **Inquiry notice** occurs where the purchaser of a property is in possession of facts, or could make an inspection of the property, which would lead a **reasonable person to make further inquiry** (e.g., possession of the premises by one who is not the record owner, or visible evidence of the existence of an easement such as a well-worn path). Notice is imputed whether the purchaser makes the inquiry or not.

  c. **Record (constructive) notice** occurs when the prior interest was **properly recorded within the chain of title**. Where the prior interest is properly recorded in the grantor-grantee indexes, such that one searching the indexes would find it, notice is imputed.

   1. **Exception — "wild deeds":** A wild deed is one that is recorded, but not in such a way that a reasonable search of the grantor-grantee index would disclose it (i.e., not within the chain of title). Wild deeds do not provide constructive notice.

> **Memorization tip:** Remember **AIR** for the types of notice: **A**ctual, **I**nquiry and **R**ecord.

> **Issue spotting tip:** The issue of "notice" can arise in several ways:
> - Recording acts
> - Sale to a BFP as a defense to an easement (especially inquiry notice)
> - Equitable servitudes (including implied reciprocal servitudes)
> - Real covenants (for burden to run with the land)

 6. **Chain of title issues**

  a. **Estoppel by deed:** If one purports to convey an interest in realty that one **does not own**, but they **subsequently obtain an interest** in that realty, they cannot deny the validity of that conveyance and the estate will **automatically transfer to the grantee**. Estoppel by deed does not apply to a transfer by quitclaim deed.

    b. **Shelter doctrine:** One who takes from a BFP will **"stand in the shoes" of the BFP** and can prevail against any entity against which the transferor-BFP would have prevailed in their own action (even if transferee had notice).

II. ESTATES IN LAND

A. **Freehold estates** offer a present possessory interest in the estate.

    1. **Fee simple absolute** conveys absolute ownership of potentially infinite duration. It is the most unrestricted and longest estate.

    2. **Fee tail** allows an owner of land to ensure that the property remains within the family. It lasts only as long as there are lineal blood descendants of the grantee. Modernly, it is virtually abolished.

    3. **Fee simple defeasible** allows a property to be held or conveyed to another; however, the property is subject to a stated limitation. There are three types:

        a. **Fee simple determinable** *automatically* terminates at the occurrence of a specified event. If the specified event occurs, the property automatically reverts back to *grantor.*

            1. **Possibility of reverter** is the future interest the grantor retains.

            2. **Created by words of duration** such as "so long as," "during," "while," "until," or "unless."

        b. **Fee simple subject to condition subsequent** has the potential to terminate an estate at the occurrence of a stated event, but the termination is *not automatic.*

            1. **Right of reentry** is the future interest the grantor retains, but it is not automatic and must be exercised to have effect.

            2. **Created by words that carve out a right of reentry** in the grantor and includes conditional language such as "but if," "provided that," or "upon condition that" to identify the conditional event.

        c. **Fee simple subject to an executory interest** *automatically* terminates a preceding estate at the occurrence of a stated event, but the estate then *passes to a third person* rather than reverting to the grantor.

            1. **Executory interest** is the future interest the third party holds (it is subject to the Rule Against Perpetuities).

    4. **Life estate** is an interest that lasts for the lifetime of a person.

        a. A **life estate pur autre vie** is similar to a life estate but lasts for the lifetime of an identified third party (not the life tenant).

        b. **Defeasible:** A life estate may be defeasible like a fee simple such that the life estate ends before the life tenant dies if the limiting event occurs.

        c. **Conveyable:** A life estate holder may convey their interest, but not an estate greater than what is held, so for no longer than their own lifetime or the pur autre vie lifetime.

        d. **Waste:** A life tenant has a duty not to commit waste on the property. (See IV.C below.)

B. **Future interests** offer the potential for a future interest in an estate.

    1. **Possibility of reverter** follows a fee simple determinable.

    2. **Right of reentry** follows a fee simple subject to a condition subsequent.

    3. **Reversion** is created when the holder of an estate transfers to another something less than the entire estate (it is vested and not subject to RAP).

    4. **Remainder** is a future interest that can only become possessory upon the expiration of a prior possessory estate created by the same instrument. A remainder never follows a defeasible fee.

        a. **Vested remainder** is one created in an ascertained person and that is not subject to a condition precedent.

        b. **Contingent remainder** is one created in an unascertained person (i.e., unborn), or one that is subject to a condition precedent, or both.

        c. **Alternative contingent remainder** occurs where both contingent parties have the capacity to take over and it pivots on the same condition (e.g., to *A* for life, then to *B* and their heirs if *B* marries *C*, otherwise to *D*).

5. **Executory interest** is an interest in favor of a future grantee and follows a fee simple subject to an executory limitation. There are two types:
   a. **Shifting executory interest** always follows a defeasible fee and cuts short the prior interest. (It shifts from one interest holder to another interest holder.)
   b. **Springing executory interest** becomes possessory at some point in the future, without cutting short a prior interest. (It springs from owner's interest to become possessory in another interest holder.)

Estate	Language	Future Interest
Fee simple absolute	"To A" "To A and his heirs"	None
Fee tail	"To A and the heirs of his body"	Reversion in grantor, or remainder in third party
Fee simple determinable	"To A so long as…" "To A during…" "To A while…"	Possibility of reverter (automatic forfeiture)
Fee simple subject to a condition subsequent	"To A upon condition that…" "To A provided that…" "To A, but if…" **Plus right to reentry language must be included	Right of reentry (not automatic, must exercise or it's waived)
Fee simple subject to an executory interest	"To A, but if X occurs, to B"	Executory interest (shifting)
Life estate; life estate pur autre vie	"To A for life" "To A for the life of B"	Reversion in grantor, or remainder in third party

C. **Technical rules**
   1. **Absolute restraints on alienation are void,** such as a condition that a property may never be sold. However, reasonable restraints on alienation will be upheld, such as a condition that a property only be used for a certain purpose.
   2. **Rule of destructibility of contingent remainders**
      a. **At common law,** a contingent remainder was destroyed if it was still contingent at the time the preceding estate ended.
      b. **Modernly,** the rule is mostly abolished, so the remainderman's interest would be converted to a springing executory interest.
   3. **Rule Against Perpetuities (RAP)** provides that no interest is good unless it must vest, if at all, not later than 21 years after some life in being at the creation of the interest. RAP is easier to work with once the interests to which it can be applied are identified.
      a. **RAP only applies to**
         1. Contingent remainders
         2. Executory interests
         3. Options "in gross" or right of first refusal to purchase land
         4. Class gifts
         5. Powers of appointment
      b. **RAP does not apply to** certain types of interests because it is not possible for them to violate RAP.
         1. Vested remainders (vests at creation)
         2. Reversion (vests at creation)
         3. Possibility of reverter (vests at creation)
         4. Right of reentry (vests at creation)

   c. **Five-step technique to assess RAP issues**
     1. Classify the future interests to determine if RAP applies
     2. Identify the measuring life in being
     3. Identify the triggering event (when an interest must vest or fail)
     4. Analyze the possibilities of what could possibly happen (postpone the triggering event 21 years after the lives in being are dead and assess)
     5. Strike the clause that violate RAP and reclassify the interest
   d. A **"wait and see" approach** is used as an alternative to RAP in some jurisdictions where the interest will be found valid if it actually vests within 90 years of creation.

> **Exam tip:** Estates in land are very infrequently tested on the essay portion of the bar exam, though they are tested on the MCQs. We have included a brief overview of estates in land issues because they are eligible for testing (even if rarely essay tested), and it would seem remiss to eliminate estates in land rules entirely. Though the review here is brief, it is likely much more than what is necessary to properly prepare for the essay exam. Most essays that test future estates test life estates.

III. JOINT OWNERSHIP (CONCURRENT ESTATES)

  A. **There are three types of joint property ownership:**
    1. **Joint tenancy**
    2. **Tenancy in common**
    3. **Tenancy by the entirety**
  B. **Joint tenancy** is when **two or more people** hold a **single, unified interest** in a property with a **right of survivorship.**
    1. Attributes
      a. **Automatic right to survivorship:** At the death of one joint tenant, the remaining joint tenant *automatically* becomes the owner of the deceased joint tenant's interest.
      b. **Equal right to occupy:** Each joint tenant has an equal right to occupy the entire premises.
      c. **Equal shares:** Each joint tenant must own the property in equal shares with the other joint tenants (e.g., two parties each with 1/2 interest, or three parties each with 1/3 interest).
      d. At common law, a joint tenancy was presumed, but today a tenancy in common is presumed unless the right of survivorship is clearly expressed.
    2. **Creation of a joint tenancy:** A joint tenancy requires the **four unities** and an **express right of survivorship.**
      a. **Time:** Interest created at the same time.
      b. **Title:** Parties take in the same title.
      c. **Interest:** Identical equal interests.
      d. **Possession:** Same right to possession of the premises.
    3. **Severance of a joint tenancy:** Unilateral action by one joint tenant may sever the joint tenancy (creating a tenancy in common).
      a. **Conveyance:** A conveyance (sale or inter vivos transfer) made by one joint tenant will sever a joint tenancy.
        1. **Severance with two joint tenants:** The remaining joint tenant will hold the property with the new owner as tenants in common.
        2. **Severance with three or more joint tenants:** The new owner will take their portion as a tenant in common to the remaining joint tenants, but the remaining joint tenants will continue to have a joint tenancy with each other only. (E.g., Three joint tenants—*A*, *B*, and *C*—each have a 1/3 interest. *A* sells their interest to *D*. *D* holds a 1/3 interest as a tenant in common to *B* and *C*. *B* and *C* continue to have a joint tenancy with each other.)
      b. **Will:** A joint tenancy **cannot be devised by will.** Any attempt is void because the decedent's interest is extinguished at death since their interest automatically transfers to the surviving joint tenant.

    c. **Mortgage:** One joint tenant may not encumber the interest of the other joint tenant. The effect of one joint tenant obtaining a mortgage is dependent on whether the jurisdiction adopts the lien theory or title theory approach.

       1. **Lien theory** (majority rule): The execution of a mortgage by one joint tenant does not sever the joint tenancy.

       2. **Title theory** (minority rule): The execution of a mortgage by one joint tenant on their share will sever the joint tenancy as to their share only.

       3. **For both theories:** The joint tenancy is severed if the mortgage is actually foreclosed and the property is sold.

    d. **Lease:** The courts are split as to whether issuing a lease severs a joint tenancy.

C. **Tenancy in common** is a concurrent estate where two or more own a property with no right of survivorship.

    1. **No right of survivorship.**

    2. **Equal right to occupy:** Each co-tenant has a joint right to possession of the whole property and owns an interest in the property jointly with another.

    3. **Nonequal shares acceptable:** Co-tenants may hold different proportionate interests. (E.g., *A* owns 1/3 interest and *B* owns 2/3 interest.)

    4. Co-tenant **may sell, will, or gift their interest.** The new grantee will step in the shoes of the grantor.

    5. At common law, a joint tenancy was presumed, but **modernly a tenancy in common is presumed** where there are multiple owners.

D. **Tenancy by the entirety** is similar to a joint tenancy, but only between **spouses** and in some jurisdictions same-sex partners.

    1. Recognized in 25 states and Washington D.C., but **not recognized in community property states**.

    2. **Neither tenant can unilaterally convey** their share or encumber the entire property or break the right of survivorship.

    3. **Severance:** May only be **severed by divorce, death, mutual agreement**, or execution by a joint creditor of both parties.

E. **Co-tenancy general rules**

    1. **Possession and use of the property by one co-tenant**

       a. **Each co-tenant has the right to possess the whole** property, but no co-tenant has the right to exclusively possess any part of the property.

       b. **No duty to account for profits and losses:** A co-tenant in possession has no duty to account to another co-tenant for

          1. **The fair rental value of their own occupancy** of the premises, or

          2. Any **profits** retained from their own use of the land.

             a. **Except,** any net profits received from **exploitations** of the land that reduce the value of the land, such as mining, and any **rents** collected from third parties must be **shared**. (See section III.E.2.b below.)

          3. A co-tenant is **solely responsible for their own losses** from their use of the property and may not seek contribution.

       c. **Ouster:** If a co-tenant has refused occupancy to their co-tenant and claims an exclusive right to possession, this constitutes an ouster.

          1. The co-tenant must account to their ousted co-tenant for the **fair rental value** of the premises.

          2. An ousted co-tenant may also bring an action to regain possession.

    2. **Accounting** of payments made and received on behalf of the jointly owned property

       a. **Payments made — general rule**

          1. **Taxes and mortgage interest:** Co-tenants are responsible for their **proportionate share** of carrying costs, such as taxes and mortgage interest payments.

          2. **Payments in excess of share:** Where a co-tenant has made payments on behalf of the property for taxes, repairs, or mortgage payments that are in excess of their pro rata share, they **may seek contribution,** but there is no automatic right to collect the pro rata

share from the co-tenant. The co-tenant may deduct these payments from rents received, or seek reimbursement "off the top" if the property is sold.

3. **Improvements/Repairs:** Co-tenants have no right to reimbursement for improvements but can seek contribution for **necessary** repairs.
    b. **Payments received—general rule:** Co-tenants must share net rents received from third parties, or net profits received from the exploitation of the land itself (e.g., mining).
    c. General **duty of fair dealing** between all co-tenants.
3. **Partition:** This occurs when, through voluntary agreement or judicial action if in the best interest of all parties, the **property is divided**, or ordered sold and the proceeds distributed.
    a. **Accounting:** Each party has a right to have an accounting and be reimbursed for taxes or repairs paid in excess of their proportionate share.
    b. Partition is not available to a tenancy by the entirety, only joint tenant or tenants in common.
4. **Encumbrance:** A co-tenant **may encumber their own share** of the property with a loan or judgment lien but may not encumber the share of their co-tenant.

> **Exam tip:** Typical joint ownership issues may include possible severance, such as an inter vivos conveyance of one co-tenant's interest, and/or accounting issues among the co-tenants. Essays often start with a joint tenancy that is severed resulting in a tenancy in common.

IV. **LANDLORD AND TENANT:** A tenancy is created when an owner of land conveys to another a lesser interest in a property. In addition to the life estate (covered in section II) there are several types of tenancies.

A. **Types of tenancies**
1. **Tenancy for years** refers to a lease for a fixed period of time. It refers to any fixed time period such as one day, two months, one year, five years, etc.
    a. **SOF writing required** for terms greater than one year.
    b. **Automatic termination:** No notice is required to terminate because a term of years automatically terminates on the end date of the time period.
2. **Periodic tenancy:** Automatically continues from one period to the next, unless one of the parties terminates the lease by giving notice of termination (e.g., leases running month-to-month, year-to-year, etc.).
    a. Can be **created by implication** if the lease includes a start date, but there is no stated end date.
    b. **Written notice is required to terminate** a periodic tenancy since the tenancy is automatically renewed in the absence of notice of termination. At common law, notice must be in accordance with the length of the time period and at the end of a natural lease period, except that if the lease is one year or longer, only six months' notice is required.
    c. A **holdover tenant** is one whose lease has terminated, but who remains in the premises and tenders rent, which the landlord accepts. A holdover tenant is considered to have a periodic tenancy with the time period for the tenancy being the time period of the previously expired lease.
3. **Tenancy at will** is a tenancy for no fixed period of time, which can be terminated at any time.
    a. Created by **express** agreement or by **implication** where the tenant takes possession with permission, but there is no specified start date or time period identified for paying rent.
    b. Can be **terminated at any time** by either party.
4. **Tenancy at sufferance** is created when a tenant wrongfully holds over past the expiration of a valid lease.
    a. **Landlord election:** When a tenant holds over, the landlord has the option to evict the tenant or hold them over to another term as a tenant with a periodic tenancy.

B. **Common areas of dispute in landlord and tenant**
   1. **Duty to pay rent:** The tenant has the duty to pay rent in the amount agreed to. A tenant may have the following **defenses** available for the nonpayment of rent:
      a. **Failure to deliver possession** of the premises.
      b. Breach of the **covenant of quiet enjoyment.** (See section IV.B.3 below.)
      c. **Constructive eviction.** (See section IV.B.3 below.)
      d. **Destruction of the premises** through no fault of the landlord, or the tenant. At common law the tenant had to continue paying rent, but modernly many states allow the tenant to terminate the lease.
      e. **Potential contract defenses,** such as frustration of purpose.
      f. **Surrender of the premises** by the tenant, which the landlord accepts.
      g. **Re-letting of the property after an abandonment** done on behalf of the tenant. If the new tenant's rent is less, the old tenant will owe the difference, so long as they were properly notified.
   2. **Possession of the premises**
      a. **Holdover tenant**
         1. At common law, a landlord could use reasonable force to remove a holdover tenant and reclaim the property.
         2. Modernly, a **landlord must not engage in self-help,** such as manually removing the tenant.
      b. **Eviction:** A landlord may typically terminate a lease for a material breach. A landlord must evict through the courts or continue the rental relationship, give notice, and sue for damages.
      c. **Abandonment:** If a tenant abandons the premises, the landlord may:
         1. **Accept the surrender** and terminate the lease; or
         2. **Re-let** on behalf of the tenant (tenant must be **notified**); or
         3. **Leave the premises vacant and sue for rent** as it becomes due.
            a. **Traditionally,** there was **no duty to mitigate.**
            b. Modernly, most courts impose a **duty to mitigate** on the landlord.
   3. **Condition of rental premises**
      a. **Common law:** Tenant takes premises **"as is"** and landlord has no duty to repair or duty to make the premises fit or habitable.
      b. **Modern view:** The landlord must **maintain all common areas, fix latent defects** of which the landlord has knowledge, and, if the landlord chooses to make repairs, they must **make repairs nonnegligently.**
      c. **Implied covenant of quiet enjoyment:** Implied in every lease. The landlord warrants that they, or anyone acting on their behalf or with superior title, will **not interfere with tenant's use and enjoyment** of the premises. (Does not include the acts of strangers.) Can be breached by:
         1. **Constructive eviction** is when the premises are in such disrepair they are virtually uninhabitable. It is treated as an eviction.
            a. Applies to **residential and commercial** leases.
            b. **Requires** that
               i. **The premises are virtually uninhabitable** for their intended use because of a **substantial interference** with the property use and enjoyment caused by the landlord or persons acting on their behalf;
               ii. **Notice** is given to the landlord by the tenant;
               iii. The landlord **fails to meaningfully respond**; and this
               iv. Causes the tenant to **actually move out** within a **reasonable time.**
         2. **Actual eviction:** Tenant excluded from entire premises due to a holdover tenant or paramount title holder.
         3. **Partial actual eviction**
            a. Landlord makes it physically impossible for the tenant to occupy **all or some portion** of the premises.
            b. Tenant may **withhold the entire rent** and does not have to move out.

d. **Implied warranty of habitability** applies to **residential leases only** and requires that the premises must be fit for **human habitation**. Where the premises are not habitable, the tenant has the option to:
1. **Terminate the lease and move out**; or
2. **Make repairs and deduct** the cost from the rent; or
3. **Pay reduced rent**, remain on the premises, and sue for damages.
e. **Retaliatory eviction is barred.** A tenant may not be evicted, have a periodic lease terminated, or have a tenancy for years not renewed because the tenant has asserted that the premises are not habitable.

> **Issue spotting tip:** Look for the issues cluster of the condition of the rental premises, implied warranty of habitability, implied covenant of quiet enjoyment, constructive eviction, and possibly retaliatory eviction. Often, if one issue is present, they all will be.

f. **Tort liability of landlord and tenant**
1. **Landlord** must
a. **Maintain all common areas**,
b. **Fix any latent defects** of which the landlord has knowledge, and
c. Any **repairs assumed must be made nonnegligently.**
d. There is a **duty to inspect** for defects if the premises are held **open to the public**.
2. **Tenant** is treated like an owner for purposes of tort liability to third parties who come on the property.
C. **Doctrine of waste:** A tenant (applies to a life tenant under a life estate or a regular rental tenant) must prevent waste and cannot damage leased premises without effecting repair. There are three types of waste:
1. **Voluntary waste** occurs when a tenant engages in conduct, intentionally or negligently, that causes a **decrease in the value** of the premises.
2. **Permissive waste** occurs when the tenant **neglects** the property and it falls into disrepair or does not make ordinary repairs.
3. **Ameliorative waste** occurs when a tenant makes **substantial alterations to the property even if they increase the value** of the premises. The tenant must restore the premises to the original condition.
D. **Fixtures**
1. **Fixtures are items that were once moveable chattel** but that have become **so attached to the premises they are deemed fixtures** and considered part of the real estate. The following factors are considered to determine if an item is a fixture:
a. **Method of attachment:** The item is **firmly imbedded in or permanently attached** to the real estate.
b. **Adaptability:** The item is **peculiarly adapted** or fitted to the real estate.
c. **Removal:** Removing the item would **destroy the chattel or cause damage to the real estate**.
d. **Intention:** For **owners who add chattel to their own property**, courts look at their objective intention at the time (usually the problem arises when they want to sell the house and take the item with them). But courts will also look at intentions of tenants or landlords who add chattel as well.
e. **Agreement:** For **landlord/tenants** who add chattels, courts look at whether there was an agreement in their lease; for owners courts look at agreements in the purchase contract with the buyer and owner-seller.

> **Memorization tip:** Think MARIA. First, distinguish whether the dispute is between the owner/seller and a buyer or a landlord and tenant. Then, go through the factors above, keeping in mind that intent is usually the most important factor in most jurisdictions.

2. **Trade fixtures are those affixed to the real estate by a commercial tenant** for use in business. There is a **strong presumption** that trade fixtures are **removable**. The tenant is responsible for repairing any damage resulting from its removal.

> **Issue spotting tip:** Look for the issues cluster of waste and fixtures since they are usually both present if one is. Note that the issue of waste can also arise in relation to the conduct of a life tenant.

E. **Assignments and subleases**
1. **General rule:** An **interest in a lease is transferable** unless the parties agree otherwise. Prohibitions against assignment and/or subleasing are enforceable.
2. **Assignment is the transfer of the entire interest** remaining on the lease term.
   a. **New tenant is personally liable** to landlord for the rent because there is privity of estate.
   b. **Old tenant is also liable** to the landlord for the rent, unless the landlord specifically releases the old tenant by a novation, because there is privity of contract.
3. **Sublease is the transfer of anything less than the entire interest** remaining on the lease term.
   a. **New tenant is not personally liable** to the landlord for the rent because a sublease does not provide privity of estate.
   b. **Old tenant is liable** to the landlord for the rent because there is privity of contract.

V. **LAND USE ISSUES**
A. **Easements:** An easement is the **right to use the land of another.** Easements are nonpossessory property interests.
1. **Easements can be affirmative or negative.**
   a. **Affirmative** easements entitle the holder to do something on another's land (e.g., use a driveway).
   b. **Negative** easements prevent the landowner from doing something on their own land. These are not common. (E.g., Owner cannot develop land in a way that blocks the neighbor's view.)
2. **Two types of easements**
   a. **Appurtenant easement** is an easement that benefits a particular parcel of land and only occurs when the easement benefit is tied to a particular piece of land. There are **two estates** created by an appurtenant easement:
      1. **Dominant estate** is **the benefited parcel**—in other words the holder of the easement. Possessor must be benefited in their *physical use and enjoyment* of the tract of land (it can't just make the land more profitable).
      2. **Servient estate is the burdened parcel**—in other words the parcel providing the benefit to the dominant estate.
   b. **Easement in gross** is an easement whose benefit is provided to an *individual* (or company) and is not tied to a particular piece of land (e.g., Neighbor can fish in my pond).
3. **Creation of easements:** There are five ways to create an easement.
   a. **Express creation** in writing in a deed or will.
      1. The **SOF writing requirements apply.**
      2. **Reservation in grantor** is a type of express easement where the grantor passes title to the land but reserves for themself the right to continue to use the land for some purpose. Typically, this is included in the grant or deed and only gives the grantor the right to use the land.
   b. **Creation by implication from prior use** has the following requirements:
      1. Land was **originally one parcel** with **common ownership**.
      2. The **land is severed** into more than one parcel.
      3. The **use of the property existed *prior* to the severance**.
      4. The easement is **reasonably necessary** to the dominant land's use and enjoyment of the property.

    c. **Easement by necessity** has the following requirements:
1. Land was **originally one parcel** with **common ownership** by one party just prior to when the need for easement by necessity arose.
2. The **land is severed** into more than one parcel, and that severance deprives one lot of important access (e.g., access to the road or utilities).
3. **Easement is strictly necessary.** The necessity must exist **at the time of the conveyance** (e.g., landlocked parcel).
4. **Prior use is not required.**

    d. **Easement by prescription** is obtained using the same principles as adverse possession. Requirements:
1. **Actual use:** The claimant must have actual use of the property that is adverse to the servient parcel. Unlike adverse possession, it need not be exclusive use.
2. **Open, notorious, and visible use** of the property.
3. **Hostile use,** which is without the owner's consent.
4. **Continuous use** for the given **statutory period.** Tacking is allowed to satisfy the statutory period.

    e. **Easement by estoppel** can occur where the servient parcel allows use of the property such that it is reasonable that the user will substantially change their position in reliance on the belief that the permission will not be revoked.

4. **Scope of easements**
   a. **Present and future needs:** Courts assume the easement intends to meet both present and future needs of the dominant parcel due to **normal, foreseeable development** of the dominant estate. (E.g., An easement may be widened to accommodate wider cars.)
   b. **Excessive use:** Increased use that unreasonably interferes with the use of the servient estate is not permitted.
   c. **Remedy** for excessive use or misuse is an **injunction** and/or **damages**, but the easement will not be terminated.

5. **Maintenance and repair of easements**
   a. The **servient owner is not required** to repair and maintain the easement.
   b. The **dominant owner has an implied right to repair** and maintain the easement unless both estates make use of the easement, then the court will apportion the repair costs between them based on their use.

6. **Transfer of easements**
   a. **Servient (burdened) estate transfer: An easement runs (passes) with the land** and transfers to the new owner of a servient estate **except** if the purchaser of the servient estate is a BFP who took for value with no notice. (Note: Inquiry notice may be present with a visible easement.)
   b. **Dominant (benefited) estate transfer:** Whether the benefit runs with the land depends on whether the easement is appurtenant or in gross.
      1. **Appurtenant easements** normally run (pass) automatically with the transfer of the dominant (benefited) estate.
      2. **In gross easements**
         a. **Common law** rule is that easements in gross are **not transferable**.
         b. **Modernly, commercial** easements in gross are **transferable.**

7. **Termination of easements:** Easements may terminate in several ways.
   a. **Estoppel:** The servient owner materially changes position in reasonable reliance on the easement holder's assurances that the easement will no longer be enforced.
   b. **Necessity:** Easement by necessity ends when the **necessity ends.**
   c. **Destruction** of servient land, so long as it is not willful destruction by the owner.
   d. **Condemnation** of servient estate by eminent domain.
   e. **Release** in **writing** by easement holder to the servient owner.
   f. **Abandonment action:** The easement holder **demonstrates by physical action the intent** to never use the easement again. Words alone or mere nonuse will not be sufficient to constitute abandonment.

g. **Merger doctrine:** The easement is extinguished when title to both the dominant and servient parcels become vested in same person.

h. **Prescription:** An easement can be terminated by employing the principals of prescription where there is an adverse, continuous *interruption* of the easement for the statutory period.

Memorization tip: Use the mnemonic **END CRAMP** to remember the eight ways an easement can terminate.

Easement essay approach: Use the following approach for easements to ensure getting all available points: 1) Identify the type of easement (affirmative or negative), (appurtenant or in gross), and if appurtenant, identify the parcels (dominant and servient); 2) Identify how the easement was created; 3) Then, discuss any of the following issues *if* they are raised by the facts: scope, maintenance/repair, transfer and/or termination.

Easement fact triggers:

- Right to use of an adjacent parking lot for a business
- Right to use specified parking spaces
- Right to use a driveway, road, or pathway

Issue spotting tip: Other issues that commonly arise as a cluster with easements are notice (since sale to a BFP would cause an easement not to transfer), particularly inquiry notice (since easements are often visible upon inspection), deed delivery, recording acts, and warranty deeds (since an undisclosed easement would violate many of the warranties).

B. **Real covenants** (also called restrictive covenants) are **written promises** between two parties about how land is to be used that meet certain technical requirements, such that the **promises "run with the land,"** meaning they are binding on future purchasers/holders of the land. The requirements are different depending on whether the benefit or burden of the covenant is running with the land. **The remedy for breach of a covenant is money damages.**

1. **Burden to "run with the land"** requirements:
   a. **Writing** required between *original* parties/owners (often in the deed).
   b. **Intent** that the promise applies to successors to the property.
   c. Must **"touch and concern"** the land. For the *servient* parcel, this means the promise **restricts the use of the servient parcel** in some way, thus decreasing the use or enjoyment, or requires the servient parcel to do something.
   d. **Horizontal and vertical privity is required** for the burden to run.
      1. **Horizontal privity** refers to the privity between the **original promising parties**. They must have shared some interest in the land *aside from* the covenant itself (e.g., developer/purchaser, landlord/tenant).
      2. **Vertical** (downstream) **privity** requires that the **successor**, such as a buyer, now is the **holder of the entire interest** that the party making the covenant had (e.g., grantor/grantee, landlord/tenant, buyer/seller, mortgagor/mortgagee, assignor/assignee of lease).

Exam tip: When tested on bar exam essays, both vertical and horizontal privity have been present and easy to establish.

---

e. **Notice is required** (can be actual, inquiry, or record (constructive) notice).

f. **Modernly**, the Restatement 3rd of Property **does not require the elements of touch and concern or privity**. All real covenants are presumed valid unless they are illegal, violate public policy, or are unconstitutional.

> **Exam tip:** Modernly, the Restatement 3rd has discarded the touch and concern and privity requirements and instead looks to affirmative covenants as running to the successor to the estate of the same duration and negative covenants are treated like easements. You can mention this on an exam; however, the bar examiners still seem to want a full analysis of all elements for the benefit to run or the burden to run (see Q1).

> **Memorization tip:** Use the mnemonic **WITCH VaN** to remember the requirements for a real covenant **burden** to run.
>
> - **W**riting
> - **I**ntent
> - **T**ouch and **C**oncern
> - **H**orizontal and **V**ertical privity
> - **N**otice
>
> (Picture that the van can carry the burden.)

2. **Benefit to "run with the land"** requirements:
   a. **Writing** required between *original* parties/owners.
   b. **Intent** that the promise applies to successors to the property.
   c. Must **"touch and concern"** the land. For the *dominant* parcel, this means the promise **benefits the dominant parcel by increasing the use or enjoyment** of the property.
   d. **Vertical privity** is required, meaning the **successor** now is the **holder of the entire interest** that the party making the covenant had (e.g., grantor/grantee, landlord/tenant, or mortgagor/mortgagee).
   e. **No horizontal privity or notice is required.**
   f. **Modernly**, the Restatement 3rd of Property **does not require the elements of touch and concern or privity.** All real covenants are presumed valid unless they are illegal, violate public policy, or are unconstitutional.

> **Memorization tip:** Use the mnemonic What Is The Common Value to remember the requirements for a real covenant **benefit** to run with the land (identifies the requirements in common with the burden running requirements).
>
> - **W**riting
> - **I**ntent
> - **T**ouch and **C**oncern
> - **V**ertical privity

3. **Termination or modification** of covenants is **allowed in the following circumstances:**
   a. **Destruction, Release, Estoppel, Abandonment, Merger, Condemnation** (as described in easements above), and
   b. **Changed conditions:** Neighborhood conditions have changed so significantly that it would be inequitable to enforce the restriction in the covenant.

> **Memorization tip:** Think DREAM CC (or DREAM Cotton Candy)

C. **Equitable servitudes** (also called covenants) **are restrictions on how land may be used.** Equitable servitudes are similar to real covenants but have no privity requirements. (E.g., Property may be used for residential purposes only or painted a particular shade of beige.) **The remedy for breach of an equitable servitude is an injunction in equity.** There are two types:
   1. **Equitable servitudes will "run with the land"** and bind successors if
      a. **Writing** is typically required unless implied as discussed below.
      b. **Intent** that the promise applies to successors to the property.
      c. Must **"touch and concern"** the land.
         1. **Dominant parcel:** The promise **benefits the dominant parcel by increasing the use or enjoyment** of the property.
         2. **Servient parcel:** The promise **restricts the use of the servient parcel** in some way, thus decreasing the use or enjoyment, or requires the servient parcel to do something.
      d. **Notice is required** (can be actual, inquiry, or constructive (record) notice).
      e. **No horizontal or vertical privity is required.**

   > **Memorization tip:** Use the mnemonic **W**hen **I**njunction is **T**he **C**ertain **N**eed to remember the requirements for an equitable servitude to run with the land.
   > - **W**riting
   > - **I**ntent
   > - **T**ouch and **C**oncern
   > - **N**otice

   > **Equitable servitude fact triggers:**
   > - Prohibition against opening a store or restaurant or competing business within a specified area, such as within five miles
   > - Prohibition against allowing another similar store to lease space in the same shopping center
   > - CCR's of a condo prohibiting certain conduct, such as an artist loft community only allowing on-premises sale of art made "in house"
   > - Covenant in an apartment lease, such as not to disturb other tenants
   > - Subdivision owners must pay annual fee to one security company

   2. **Servitude implied from a common scheme** (also called an implied reciprocal servitude, reciprocal negative servitude, or common scheme doctrine): Court can imply a reciprocal equitable servitude if the **original owner intended a "common plan or scheme" and the purchaser has notice** of the scheme. The **remedy for a breach is an injunction** in equity.
      a. The **common plan or scheme** is typically evidenced by the **developer's building plans** in a **recorded plat**, or a general pattern of restrictions, or an oral representation to early buyers (e.g., a new housing development where a contract with a company regarding the provision of security services has been recorded, or where all homes are only one story).
      b. **Notice is required** and can be actual, inquiry, or record (constructive) notice. **Inquiry notice can be provided by a visual inspection** of the neighborhood that gives the appearance of conforming to certain standards. Record notice exists if the restriction is recorded in the plat.
      c. **No SOF writing is required.**
   3. **Termination and modification** of equitable servitudes is the same as for covenants (see above).

   > **Exam tip:** Real covenants and equitable servitudes are very similar. In an exam it is typically acceptable to analyze one or the other since the elements are mostly similar if the facts don't state which remedy is sought. However, it's best to note the differences, too, such as the remedy allowed under each.

D. **Profit** (profit a prendre) entitles its holder to the right to enter the servient estate land and **remove soil or a product of the land** itself. A profit is similar to an easement (e.g., mining minerals, drilling for oil, removing timber, hunting, or fishing). It may be appurtenant or in gross and is created and terminated like an easement.

E. **License is the mere right to use the licensor's land** for some specific purpose, and it is revocable at the will of the licensor.
   1. **Difference from easement: A license may be freely revoked** (unless consideration provided) and is merely a privilege and not an interest in the land.
   2. **Oral agreements** produce a **license,** not an easement. However, it is possible the oral license created an easement by estoppel with detrimental reliance.

F. **Water rights**
   1. **Drainage of surface waters**
      a. **Using surface water:** An owner may use all they want.
      b. **Getting rid of surface water** has three different approaches:
         1. **Common enemy:** Owner may cast water onto neighbor's land.
         2. **Natural flow theory:** Owner has strict liability for interfering with natural flow.
         3. **Reasonable use doctrine** allows owner to act reasonably.
   2. **Riparian rights** (waterfront streams and lakes that abut property)
      a. **Reasonable use theory:** Each riparian owner may use as much water as they reasonably need (courts consider the purpose and extent of the use).
      b. **Prior appropriation doctrine:** Used by some states, including California. An owner (need not be riparian) must obtain a permit to use the water, and priority of use is determined by permit date.
   3. **Ground water:** An owner may make reasonable use of ground water drawn from their property.

G. **Right to lateral and subjacent support:** Every landowner has a right to receive necessary physical support from **adjacent soil (lateral support)** and **underlying soil (subjacent support).**
   1. **Lateral support:** The right to lateral support (adjacent property) is absolute.
      a. **Natural state:** A landowner is *strictly liable* if their excavation causes adjacent land to subside while in its natural state.
      b. **Improvements:** If land has been improved (e.g., buildings), an adjoining landowner is *strictly liable* for its excavation only if it is shown that the **land would have collapsed in its natural state**; if it would not have collapsed in its natural state, then the landowner **may be liable through** *negligence*.
   2. **Subjacent support** arises when something is removed from below the surface of the land. The owner of the surface land has a right to not have the surface subside, which includes the buildings as well as the natural state.

> **Exam tip:** Profits, licenses, water rights, and the right to lateral and subjacent support are infrequently tested. If an essay does raise the issue of land support it might be necessary to go through a negligence analysis too if land collapses that may not have collapsed in its natural state.

H. **Zoning**
   1. **Purpose:** The Tenth Amendment allows states to regulate the use and development of land through zoning for the protection of the health, safety, comfort, morals, and **general welfare of its citizens**.
   2. **Standards:** Zoning regulations must be **reasonable, not arbitrary**, and have a **substantial relation** to the public benefits above.
   3. **Types of zoning ordinances:**
      a. **Cumulative:** Creates a **hierarchy of uses of land**; land zoned for a particular use may be used for the **stated purpose or for any higher use** (e.g., a house could be built in an industrial zone, but a factory could not be built in a residential zone).
      b. **Noncumulative:** Land may only be used for the purpose for which it is zoned.

4. **Variance:** A property owner can seek a variance (waiver) from a zoning regulation if they can show **unnecessary hardship** due to the unique features of the property or practical difficulty. The harm to the neighboring areas will also be considered.
   a. **Nonconforming use:** Use of property that was allowed under zoning regulations at the time the use was established but is no longer permitted under the new zoning laws. Some statutes allow these nonconforming uses to continue and some statutes provide for termination of these uses by reasonable **amortization** provisions (provide a time frame for the owners to comply with the new zoning regulations).
      1. **Improvements and rebuilding:** The majority of jurisdictions find that any change or improvement must comply with the new zoning regulation and that if the structure is destroyed, the rebuilt building must comply with the new zoning regulations.

   > **Exam tip:** Facts giving rise to zoning may also raise a takings issue as these issues often arise together in real life. See more on takings in the Constitutional Law outline.

REAL PROPERTY ISSUES TESTED MATRIX

Date	Fact Pattern	Crossover Subject	Adverse Possession	Inter Vivos Transfer or Warranty Deed	Mortgage Foreclosure	Recording Acts Notice	Future Interests	Joint Ownership Concurrent Estates	LLT Types Rent & Premises Condition	LLT Waste Fixtures	LLT Assignment or Sublease	Easements	Real Covenants &/or Equitable Servitudes	Water or Land Support Rights
July '24 Q2	Olivia conveys lots A and B on Greenacre						X					X		
February '23 Q3	Tuan rents a warehouse								X	X				
February '21 Q5	Ed conveys an easement to Fran, buys organic produce from Gloria											X	X	
October '20 Q3	Andrew conveys ½ of Havenwood to his brother Elmo, but his son develops it		X					X						
Feb '19 Q3	Lois rents to Tammy, a loud band and the shower has only cold water								X	X				
February '18 Q3	Len has a wandering dog and a backyard smokehouse	Torts Con Law										X		
July '16 Q2	Al deeds easement to Ben for road and deeds farm to Carol			X		X						X		
July '15 Q6	City rezoned commercial to residential within 3 months	Con Law (takings)												
July '15 Q2	Oscar conveys Greenacre to Martha and Lenny						X	X						
February '15 Q2	Amy and Bob sell Blackacre to David and he leases to Ellen					X		X			X		X	
February '14 Q4	Ira buys machine shop from Jane and it collapses	Not c/o but also zoning/variance			X									X
February '12 Q6	Donna leased 2nd story from Perry and broke lease due to cheese smell								X		X			
July '11 Q5	Andy deeds Blackacre to Beth & Chris jointly		X			X	X	X						
February '11 Q3	Leo has 3 consecutive lots & lot 3 has Grill restaurant										X	X	X	
July '08 Q5	Ann, Betty & Celia own a condo as joint tenants			X			X	X						

Continued>

Date	Fact Pattern	Crossover Subject	Adverse Possession	Inter Vivos Transfer or Warranty Deed	Mortgage Foreclosure	Recording Acts Notice	Future Interests	Joint Ownership Concurrent Estates	LLT Types Rent & Premises Condition	LLT Waste Fixtures	LLT Assignment or Sublease	Easements	Real Covenants &/or Equitable Servitudes	Water or Land Support Rights
July '07 Q1	Larry leases 4-room office suite to Tanya	Contracts							X					
February '07 Q1	Builder sells shopping mall, but reserves parking	Torts							X		X	X		
February '06 Q3	Mike has 30-year office lease from Olive	Con Law								X	X			
July '05 Q2	Developer subdivides home sites & security contract w/ ASI/MPI	Contracts				X							X	
February '05 Q5	Cousins Alice & Bill buy a house as joint tenants							X	X					
February '04 Q4	Lori owns shopping center; leases to Tony, who transfers to Ann								X		X		X	
February '03 Q2	Olga wants to give Blackacre to niece Nan	Wills		X			X							
July '02 Q2	Able owns Whiteacre, and Baker owns Blackacre			X	X	X						X		
July '01 Q2	Artist leased condo to Weaver who transfers it to Sculptor								X		X		X	
July '00 Q2	Sam sells Paul a lakefront parcel, once owned by Owen	Contracts Wills	X	X	X									

REAL PROPERTY PRACTICE ESSAYS, ANSWER GRIDS, AND SAMPLE ANSWERS

Real Property Question 1
February 2021, Question 5

Ed owned a parcel of land on the north side of a rural highway. A lane connected the highway to the small country inn Ed operated on the land. Ten years ago, Ed entered into a signed written agreement conveying a right-of-way easement over the lane to Fran, his neighbor north of his parcel. Fran operated a commercial farm with a small bunkhouse for farm workers on her land. She often used Ed's lane to access the farm and bunkhouse from the highway.

Recently, Fran announced that she was converting her farm into a 50-lot residential subdivision and the bunkhouse to a computer server center. She informed Ed that she wanted to run new electric lines and a fiber optic cable along the lane.

Fifteen years ago, Ed and Gloria, his then-neighbor on the south side of the highway, had entered into a signed written agreement in which Gloria covenanted that she and her successors in interest would use her property only as a commercial organic garden and, in exchange, Ed would purchase produce from Gloria for use in his country inn. Soon thereafter, Gloria sold her land to Henry. Ed continued to buy produce from Henry.

Recently, Henry informed Ed that the more intense development Fran had planned for her parcel and the increased traffic along the highway justified the conversion of Henry's garden into a combination truck stop and diner.

Ed objected to Fran's and Henry's intended changes and decided to sue both of them to enforce his rights.

1. What rights and interests do Ed and Fran each have in the lane, and may Fran, over Ed's objection, carry out her plans for the lane? Discuss.

2. What rights and interests do Ed and Henry each have in the garden property, and may Henry, over Ed's objection, carry out his plans for that property? Discuss.

Real Property Question 1 Assessment
February 2021, Question 5

Real property essay questions are usually manageable. They typically have a comparatively modest number of issues to cover, like the five in this question, the analysis has more depth, and timing is not as challenging as it can be for other subjects. This question is a very typical real property essay question. It covers the major land use issues of easements, real covenants, and equitable servitudes. It is not a difficult question if you remember the rules.

The facts here focus on the scope and use of the easement, rather than the formation of the easement. There are two key arguments to make: The planned development of the property and the desire to use the easement for a use other than that specifically permitted in the written agreement. You need to make some reasonable factual inferences to make these arguments. For example, all you know is that this farm is farmland on a rural highway. From those facts, you need to make reasonable inferences to create arguments in the analysis of the easement and real covenant sections.

The real covenant discussion should include an accurate recitation of the rule and an application of all pertinent facts. The issue is if the covenant runs with the land to a new owner. Since it is the burdened parcel that has a new owner, the analysis should focus on if the burden runs with the land. The facts for each element must be analyzed separately. The weightier discussion is regarding notice. The facts are vague on what type of notice, if any, the new buyer had about the covenant. When the facts are vague, like here, you want to make some reasonable factual inferences, but be sure to identify them as inferences, with an argument on both sides, and a full discussion of the three types of notice. There were no facts to indicate that Henry had actual notice of the covenant, but since he continued to sell the organic produce to Ed, it can be inferred that he may have had actual notice. It is also reasonable to infer that nothing would have provided inquiry notice and that since the covenant wasn't identified as having been recorded, it is fair to assume it wasn't recorded so there is no constructive notice.

The equitable servitude discussion should note the difference between an equitable servitude and a real covenant, which is that equitable servitudes do not require privity, and the remedy is injunctive relief. Here, since the real covenant would fail for privity, it is important to note Ed could enforce the equitable servitude, assuming Henry had notice.

While this question is not difficult if you remember the rules, this question provides a good lesson in what you can do if you can't remember the rules, or all the elements of a particular rule. If you are in a jam in the moment and you can't remember all the elements necessary for a real covenant burden to run with the land (WITCH VaN), remember what you can, and then use some educated guesses to make up the rest. For example, one of the overarching themes in real property is that we don't hold a new property owner (BFP) responsible when they did not have notice. You can almost always use that rule. Here, including that rule and analysis alone would have garnered many points on this essay. The statute of frauds applies to land, so there is probably a writing requirement, and so on. You can also let the facts guide you to what is a likely rule given the facts they've included. For example, Fran wants to turn rural farmland into a big development. Even if you didn't remember the exact rule that the scope of an easement can be expanded for "normal foreseeable development," you can use common sense to argue that this use would exceed what Ed expected. Don't be afraid to be wrong. No points are deducted for included incorrect or imperfect rules and if you are off topic, the graders will just ignore that discussion. Provide a heading, use the rule you came up with, answer in IRAC format, and focus your energy on the analysis. You got this!

Note the areas highlighted in **bold** on the corresponding grid. The bold areas highlight the issues, analysis, and conclusions that are likely **required** to receive a passing score on this question. The grid is provided to assist you in assessing your own performance. In general, the essay grids are provided to assist you in analyzing the essays and are much more detailed than what a student should create during the exam to organize their response to a question.

Issue	Rule	Fact Application	Conclusion
What rights and interests do Ed and Henry each have in the lane, and may Fran, over Ed's objection, carry out her plans for the lane?			
Easement	An easement is a non-possessory property interest **giving one the right to use the land of another.** Easements can be: • Affirmative or negative • **Appurtenant or in gross** An express easement is created in writing.	• **The easement is express and was created in a signed written agreement, satisfying the statute of frauds.** • This is an affirmative easement since it gives Fran the right to do something on Ed's land. • It is an appurtenant easement because Fran owns an adjacent parcel of land north of Ed's parcel. **Ed's land is the servient/burdened estate** because Fran is allowed to use the land on Ed's parcel. **Fran's land is the dominant/ benefitted estate** since it benefits by having access to the highway by Ed's lane. • Here, for 10 years Fran has had a **right of way easement over the lane.**	Fran has an express appurtenant easement in Ed's lane
Use of Easement	**Scope of easement:** it is intended to meet both present and future needs of the dominant parcel due **to normal, foreseeable development.** Easement holder has a right to maintain the easement.	• **In addition to using the easement as she has been, Fran can use the road as needed for normal, foreseeable development.** • Fran has used the lane for access to **her commercial farm and small bunkhouse for her farm workers. Fran wants to convert her farm and bunkhouse into a 50-lot residential subdivision and a computer service center. In addition, she wants to run new electric and fiber optic cable.** • It is not foreseeable that Fran would seek to develop her farm, which is located on a rural highway near Ed's small country inn, into a 50-lot residential subdivision and commercial computer service center. This would be an unreasonable and excessive increase in traffic over the land since the inhabitants of 50 units and a commercial business are significantly more than the traffic Ed is used to over the past 10 years from Fran's farm and small bunkhouse of farm workers. Such a large amount of traffic would unreasonably interfere with Ed's use of his own property. • Further, **Fran seeks to increase the scope of the easement to allow her to lay cable and electrical lines for her new development. This will not be permitted** because it exceeds the scope of her easement since Fran only has a "right of way" easement, which permits travel over the road to access Fran's parcel. • Ed can get an injunction to stop Fran.	Fran may not use the lane for her development or to lay electrical or cable lines

Continued>

Continued>

Issue	Rule	Fact Application	Conclusion
What rights and interests do Ed and Henry each have in the garden property, and may Henry, over Ed's objection, carry out his plans for that property?			

Real Covenant	Promises between parties about how land is to be used. To bind successors there must be:
	
	• **Writing (of promise between original parties/ owners)**
	• **Intent (to bind future successors)**
	• **Touch and concern the land** (benefit dominant estate by increased use or enjoyment; restrict servient estate by decreased use or enjoyment)
	• **Horizontal Privity** (between originally promising parties)
	• **Vertical Privity**
	• **Notice**
	  ○ **Actual (subjective)**
	  ○ **Inquiry (facts put on notice to look into further)**
	  ○ **Record (properly in chain of title)**
		• 15 years ago, neighbors Ed and Gloria entered a signed written agreement about how Gloria could use her land. Gloria has since sold, and Ed seeks to enforce the agreement against the new owner.
		• The agreement itself states that Gloria "she and her successors in interest" which indicates the original contracting parties clearly intended to bind future successors of the property.
		• **The agreement touches and concerns the land since Gloria promised she would use her land only as a commercial organic garden, while Ed promised in exchange to purchase produce from Gloria for use at his country inn.** Gloria's servient estate is restricted in how it can be used, and she has a buyer for her produce, while Ed's dominant estate gets the benefit of ready access to organic produce for his inn which he has **agreed to buy.**
		• Horizontal privity requires the original contracting parties have some shared interest in the land apart from the covenant itself. Here, Ed and Gloria are neighbors and share no other interest, so **horizontal privity is not established.**
		• **Vertical privity exists because Gloria sold her entire interest in the property to Henry.**
		• **The burden will run to a new owner only if they have notice.**
		• Henry may have had actual notice of the agreement since he continued to sell produce to Ed.
		• **While the property was currently being used as an organic garden and Henry continued to do so and continued to sell produce to Ed,** there is nothing inherent in this use that would put Henry on inquiry notice that it was the only way the property could be used.
		• There is no indication the covenant was recorded such that it would provide Henry with constructive notice.
		• **Even if Henry did have notice, Ed will not be able to recover damages because there was no horizontal privity.**
			Ed cannot get damages

Issue	Rule	Fact Application	Conclusion
Equitable Servitude	**The rule is the same as it is for real covenants except equitable servitudes are** • **No privity requirement** • **Enforced in equity**	• An equitable servitude would allow Ed to get an injunction to stop Henry from building the truck stop. • **There is no privity requirement to enforce an equitable servitude, and all other elements were established above.** • **If Henry did have notice, Ed would be able to get an injunction stopping Henry from changing his use of the land from a commercial garden.**	**Ed can likely get an injunction**
Changed Neighborhood Conditions	**Neighborhood conditions have changed so significantly, it would be inequitable to enforce the restriction in the covenant.**	• If the servitude were found to bind successors, **Henry could argue that neighborhood conditions had changed so substantially that it would be inequitable to enforce the restriction in the covenant.** • Ed will assert the neighborhood has not yet changed and that Fran may not be able to build her subdivision since she may not be able to get utilities without using his easement. Further, the existence of a better commercial opportunity is not a good reason to extinguish the covenant. • However, assuming Fran can go through with her plans, Henry will argue that neighbor Fran's plan to convert her farm into a 50-lot residential subdivision with a commercial computer service center is a significant neighborhood change from the existing commercial farm with small bunkhouse for workers. The neighborhood will change from rural farming to bustling residential and commercial. [One of the arguments above was necessary to pass.]	Henry can likely prove changed conditions

Real Property Question 1 Sample Answer
February 2021, Question 5

1. What rights and interests do Ed and Henry each have in the lane, and may Fran, over Ed's objection, carry out her plans for the lane?

Easement

An easement is a non-possessory property interest giving the holder the right to use the land of another. It can be affirmative or negative, and appurtenant or in gross. An express easement is created in writing.

Here, Fran has a right to use the lane on Ed's land, which gives her the right to use the land of another. The easement is express and was created in a signed written agreement, satisfying the statute of frauds. This is an affirmative easement since it gives Fran the right to do something on Ed's land. Fran's easement is appurtenant because Fran owns an adjacent parcel of land north of Ed's parcel. Ed's land is the servient/burdened estate because Fran is allowed to use the land on Ed's parcel. Fran's land is the dominant/benefitted estate since her estate benefits by having access to the highway by using the lane on Ed's property.

Here, for 10 years Fran has had an express right of way easement in Ed's lane.

Use of Easement

The scope of an easement is intended to meet both present and future needs of the dominant parcel due to normal, foreseeable development. The easement holder also has a right to maintain the easement.

Here, in addition to using the easement as she has been to access her farm, Fran can use the road as needed for the farm's normal, foreseeable development. Fran has used the lane for access to her commercial farm and small bunkhouse for her farm workers. Fran now wants to convert her farm and bunkhouse into a 50-lot residential subdivision and turn the bunkhouse into a computer service center. In addition, she wants to run new electric and fiber optic cable to her property along the lane.

Ed will assert it is not foreseeable that Fran would seek to develop her farm, which is located on a rural highway near Ed's small country inn, into a 50-lot residential subdivision and commercial computer service center. This would be an unreasonable and excessive increase in traffic over the lane since the inhabitants of 50 residential units and a commercial business are significantly more than the traffic Ed is used to having over the past 10 years from Fran's farm and small bunkhouse of farm workers. Such a large amount of traffic would unreasonably interfere with Ed's use of his own property.

Further, Fran seeks to increase the scope of the easement to allow her to lay cable and electrical lines for her new development. This will not be permitted because it exceeds the scope of her easement since here Fran only has a "right of way" easement, which permits travel over the road to access Fran's parcel. A "right of way" easement would not include the permanent installation of cables.

Fran may not use the lane for her development or to lay electrical or cable lines and Ed can get an injunction to stop Fran.

2. What rights and interests do Ed and Henry each have in the garden property, and may Henry, over Ed's objection, carry out his plans for that property?

Real Covenant

A real covenant is an enforceable promise between parties about how land is to be used. To bind successors in interest to a real covenant it must be in writing there must be intent to bind future successors, it must touch and concern the land, there must be horizontal privity, vertical privity, and notice to the successor.

Writing

The original parties to the agreement are Ed and Gloria, who were neighbors. 15 years ago, they entered a signed written agreement about how Gloria could use her land. Gloria has since sold, and Ed seeks to enforce the agreement against the new owner, Henry.

Intent

The agreement itself states that Gloria "and her successors in interest," which indicates the original contracting parties clearly intended to bind future successors of Gloria's property.

Touch and Concern

The covenant must touch and concern the land which means it benefits the dominant estate by increased use or enjoyment and restricts the servient estate by decreased use or enjoyment of that land. Here, the agreement touches and concerns the land since Gloria promised she would use her land only as a commercial organic garden, while Ed promised in exchange to purchase produce from Gloria for use at his country inn. Gloria's servient estate is restricted in how it can be used and in exchange she has a buyer for her produce, while Ed's dominant estate gets the benefit of ready access to organic produce for his inn which he has agreed to buy.

Horizontal Privity

To bind a successor, there must be horizontal privity between the original promising parties, which means the original contracting parties have some shared interest in the land apart from the covenant itself. Here, Ed and Gloria are neighbors, but they share no other interest in the land, such as grantor/grantee or landlord/tenant, so horizontal privity is not established.

Vertical Privity

There must also be vertical privity between the original promising party and the successor, which means the successor holds the entire durational interest the covenantor had. Here, vertical privity is established because Henry bought Gloria's entire interest in the property.

Notice

The burden of a covenant will run to a new owner only if they have notice. Notice can be established by actual notice, record notice, or inquiry notice.

Henry may have had actual subjective notice of the agreement since he continued to sell produce to Ed. The facts do not state he had notice, but it is probably that Gloria told Henry of the agreement, which is why he continued to sell the produce to Ed.

One can have constructive notice when the covenant is recorded properly in chain of title. However, there is no indication here that the covenant was recorded such that it would provide Henry with constructive notice.

A successor can also have inquiry notice, which is when visible facts put one on notice that they should look further into the situation. At the time of purchase, the property was being used as an organic garden, and after the sale Henry continued to do so and continued to sell produce to Ed. However, there is nothing inherent in this use of organic farming and selling the produce to a local business that would put Henry on notice that it was the only way the property could be used. Likely, Henry did not have inquiry notice.

It is not clear that Henry had notice of the covenant, but even if Henry did have notice, Ed will not be able to recover damages for the breach of the covenant because there was no horizontal privity.

Equitable Servitude

Ed would likely prefer to enforce the agreement than recover for damages anyways. An equitable servitude is essentially the same as a real covenant, except there is no privity requirement and are enforced in equity.

An equitable servitude would allow Ed to get an injunction to stop Henry from building the truck stop. There is no privity requirement to enforce an equitable servitude, which was a problem with the real covenant, and all other elements were established above.

If Henry did have notice as discussed above, Ed would be able to get an injunction stopping Henry from changing his use of the land from a commercial organic garden.

Changed Neighborhood Conditions

A real covenant or equitable servitude will not be enforced when neighborhood conditions have changed so significantly, it would be inequitable to enforce the restriction in the covenant.

If the servitude were found to bind successors, Henry could argue that neighborhood conditions had changed so substantially that it would be inequitable to enforce the restriction in the covenant. Ed will assert the neighborhood has not yet changed and that Fran may not be able to build her subdivision since she may not be able to get utilities to it without using his easement. Further, the existence of a better commercial opportunity is not a good reason to extinguish the covenant.

However, assuming Fran can go through with her plans, Henry will argue that neighbor Fran's plan to convert her farm into a 50-lot residential subdivision with a commercial computer service center is a significant neighborhood change from the existing commercial farm with small bunkhouse for workers located in a rural neighborhood. Fran's development would change the neighborhood from rural farming to a bustling residential and commercial zone with much traffic.

Henry can likely prove changed conditions in the neighborhood as a way to prevent enforcement of the covenant/servitude.

Real Property Question 2
July 2016, Question 2

Al owned a farm.

In 1990, Al deeded an easement for a road along the north side of the farm to his neighbor Ben. Ben immediately graded and paved a road on the easement, but did not record the deed at that time. Al and Ben both used the road on a daily basis. The easement decreased the fair market value of the farm by $5,000.

In 2009, Al deeded the farm to his daughter Carol and she recorded the deed.

In 2011, Ben recorded his deed to the easement.

In 2012, Carol executed a written contract to sell the farm to Polly for $100,000. The contract stated in part: "Seller shall covenant against encumbrances with no exceptions." During an inspection of the farm, Polly had observed Ben traveling on the road along the north side of the farm, but said nothing.

In 2013, Carol deeded an easement for water lines along the south side of the farm to Water Co., the local municipal water company. The water lines provided water service to local properties, including the farm. Water Co. then recorded the deed. The easement increased the fair market value of the farm by $10,000.

In 2014, after long delay, Carol executed and delivered to Polly a warranty deed for the farm and Polly paid Carol $100,000. The deed contains a covenant against all encumbrances except for the easement to Water Co. and no other title covenants. Polly recorded the deed.

In 2015, Polly blocked Ben's use of the road and objected to Water Co.'s construction of the water lines.

Ben has commenced an action against Polly seeking declaratory relief that the farm is burdened by his easement. Polly in turn has commenced an action against Carol seeking damages for breach of contract and breach of the covenant under the warranty deed.

1. What is the likely outcome of Ben's action? Discuss.

2. What is the likely outcome of Polly's:

    a. Claim of breach of contract? Discuss.

    and

    b. Claim of breach of the covenant under the warranty deed? Discuss.

Real Property Question 2 Assessment
July 2016, Question 2

This property question covers some frequently tested real property issues, such as easements, notice, and the recording acts. This question also covers some more obscure essay issues, such as land sales contracts and breach of contract, the covenants in a general warranty deed, and the merger doctrine. The challenge for this question is that the facts are vague in areas. The facts indicate that a deed had been recorded, but do not identify the applicable recording act in the jurisdiction. This makes the analysis a bit trickier because it is unclear what the conclusion should be. The best thing to do in this situation is identify for the reader that "if this happens, then this is the result" for each of the possibilities.

The other challenge posed by this question is that if a student does not know the rules regarding land sales contracts and deeds and merger, then it is difficult to answer both prongs of Question 2. While not heavily tested, you cannot answer the entire question unless you know these rules in detail. Further, property questions can be similar to contracts questions in that the sequence of events is very important. It is often helpful to note the timeline of the significant events to keep the events, parties, and dates straight. It may also be helpful to picture a diagram of the property involved, especially on a question such as this where an easement is being described. Imagining the easement on the property gives a clearer picture of the events that have transpired. For example:

Al's farm	Ben's land
------------------Road (1990)------------------ XXXXXX Water lines (2013) XXXXXX	

- 1990 Al deeds easement for road to Ben
- Ben immediately graded and paved road; used daily
- 2009 Al deeds farm to Carol
- 2011 Ben records deed
- 2012 Carol contracts to sell farm to Polly
- Polly observes Ben using road
- 2013 Carol deeds easement for water lines
- 2014 Carol gives warranty deed to Polly
- 2015 Polly blocks Ben and water company

Picturing the facts and timeline this way makes it easier to see how notice might apply and when events occurred and people may have been on notice. You can jot notes on the virtual scratch paper, or white board, or put them at the top of your answer, just be sure to delete.

Note the areas highlighted in **bold** on the corresponding grid. The bold areas highlight the issues, analysis, and conclusions that are likely **required** to receive a passing score on this question.

Issue	Rule	Fact Application	Conclusion
1. Ben's Action			
Easement	**An easement is the right to use the land of another.** Easements are nonpossessory property interests.	**Al deeded Ben an easement for a road along the north side of the farm. This is an express easement as it was in writing in the deed.**	**Ben has an express easement**
	An express easement is created in writing. Appurtenant easements benefit a particular parcel of land and require two estates—one dominant (benefited estate) and one servient (burdened estate).	**It is appurtenant since it involves Al's farm, which is burdened by the road and Ben's estate as the neighbor since he is benefited with the ability to use the road.**	
	Scope of easement: It is intended to meet both present and future needs of the dominant parcel due to normal, foreseeable development.	The **scope of an easement** is not likely exceeded as Ben used the road as a road and while he graded it and paved it that is likely reasonable for long term use as he and Al used it daily.	
Termination	Easements can be terminated in a variety of ways such as estoppel, destruction, release, abandonment, and merger.	Here, Ben did not change in position for estoppel, the road was not destroyed, no release was provided, Ben did not abandon it, and the two parcels are not owned by one person.	Easement not terminated
Transferability of Easements	An appurtenant easement burden passes automatically with servient land, **unless the new owner is BFP** (took for value, no notice).	Here it must be determined whether Carol or Polly were BFPs.	Easement can transfer unless Polly is a BFP as discussed below
		As to Carol, she would likely not be a BFP because it doesn't appear that she paid value as her father, Al, deeded her the land. Thus she paid no value.	
		As to Polly, she did pay value as she paid Carol $100,000 for the land. If Polly didn't have notice of the easement, then she would be a BFP.	
Notice	**Notice** can be provided three ways: • **Actual** (subjective) • **Inquiry** (facts put on notice to look into further) • **Record** (properly in chain of title)	Polly did not have actual notice in the deed as the road easement was not mentioned in the deed.	Since Polly had notice she would not be a BFP
		Polly had inquiry notice as she saw Ben using the road and a reasonable inspection would reveal a graded and paved road that was used daily by Ben.	(One state-released answer incorrectly concluded here as they left out notice needed for a BFP)
		Polly would also be on record notice since Ben recorded his easement in 2011 and Polly didn't record her deed until 2014 so she could have seen Ben's easement in the chain of title had she searched.	
		Thus, Polly had notice.	

Continued>

607

Issue	Rule	Fact Application	Conclusion
Shelter Doctrine	One who takes from a BFP will "stand in the shoes" of the BFP and prevail against any entity against which the transferor-BFP would have prevailed in their own action (even if transferee had notice).	Here, if Carol was a BFP then Polly could stand in Carol's shoes and prevail against Ben even though Polly had notice. However, Carol was not a BFP as discussed above because she did not pay value.	**Shelter doctrine inapplicable**
Recording Acts	Recording acts protect BFPs but do not protect donees, heirs, or devisees. **Common law: first in time, first in right** **Other jurisdictions: notice, race-notice, or race statutes** Recording acts provide a mechanism to protect a subsequent purchaser from a prior inconsistent transaction. [Note: Both state-released answers went into detail about the 3 types, but if you established upfront that neither Carol nor Polly are BFPs then a detailed analysis of the recording statutes would not be necessary as they only protect BFPs. Thus, you could have passed this answer without discussing these recording acts at all. The bolded parts were both discussed in the state-released answers but not necessary to write an accurate answer.]	Since neither Carol nor Polly are BFPs the recording statutes would not serve to protect either of them. However, if for some reason Carol did pay value or is deemed a BFP then the rules would apply. **If the common law rule applies, Ben keeps the easement since his easement was first in time.** **A notice or race notice statute would not protect either Carol or Polly as they both had notice as indicated above via inquiry notice at a minimum and for Polly she would have record notice too since she recorded in 2014 and Ben recorded in 2011. However, Carol would not have record notice since she recorded in 2009 before Ben recorded in 2011.** However, since Carol included the easement in her deed to Polly she seems to have had actual notice of the easement. **In a pure race jurisdiction, Carol would prevail because she recorded first but Polly would not unless she was protected by the Shelter Doctrine (which is unlikely as discussed above).**	**Ben would prevail in any jurisdiction since neither Carol nor Polly are BFPs**

2.a. Polly's Breach of Contract Claim

Issue	Rule	Fact Application	Conclusion
Land Sales Contract	The contract for a conveyance of an interest in real estate typically governs the agreement until the time of closing, at which time the deed becomes the operative document governing the land transfer.	Here, Carol executed a written contract in 2012 to sell Polly the farm for $100,000. The contract covenanted against encumbrances and did not mention any easements.	**Land sales contract in 2012**
Marketable Title	**Marketable title is implied in every land sale contract and is title free from reasonable doubt.**	An easement reduces the value of a property; therefore an easement would make title unmarketable.	**Title was unmarketable**

Continued>

Issue	Rule	Fact Application	Conclusion
Merger Doctrine	In a contract for the sale of land, once the deal has closed, the contract merges with the deed and the deed controls.	The deed will control, so Polly will need to look at the deed for breach.	**Deed controls and Polly does not have a breach of contract claim**

2.b. Polly's Breach of Covenant Under the Warranty Deed

Issue	Rule	Fact Application	Conclusion
Warranty Deed	**A warranty deed warrants against all defects in title** and contains 6 covenants. Present covenants: • Seisen • Right to convey • **Against encumbrances**: grantor warrants there are no mortgages, liens, **easements**, or use restrictions on the land. Maj. rule — can be breached even if purchaser had notice. Future covenants: • Warranty of title • Quiet enjoyment • Further assurances Damages would include the difference in value between the purchase price and the value with the encumbrance, or the cost to remove the encumbrance. Defenses: unclean hands, laches, or waiver.	In 2014, Carol executed and delivered a warranty deed to Polly for the farm and Carol paid Polly $100,000. Here, the covenant at issue is the covenant against encumbrances in the deed itself since there are two easements associated with the land. **Road Easement** Here, this easement was excluded from the deed and the deed stated that only the water company easement was included. As this is a present covenant it was breached at the time of the sale. In a majority jx the fact that Polly had notice as discussed above would be irrelevant. **Water Company Easement** Polly might argue that this easement was not in the land sales contract in 2012 and that Carol waited and only delivered the deed after a long delay thus trying to commit some type of fraud or misrepresentation on Polly amounting to unclean hands or laches. **However, this easement was in the deed and thus Polly was aware of it and could have disputed it at the time it was delivered and not pay rather than wait a year in 2015 to block it.**	Carol is in breach of the covenant against encumbrances for Ben's easement only and Polly should recover $5,000 from Carol (if in a majority jx); if in a minority jx then she would recover nothing as she was on notice of Ben's easement

Real Property Question 2 Sample Answer
July 2016, Question 2

1. Ben's Action

Easement

An easement is the right to use the land of another. Easements are nonpossessory property interests.

Express Appurtenant Easement

An express easement is created in writing. Appurtenant easements benefit a particular parcel of land and require two estates. One estate is the dominant or benefited estate and the other estate is the servient or burdened estate.

Here, there was an express easement as Al deeded Ben an easement for a road along the north side of the farm. This is an express easement as it was in writing in the deed. It is appurtenant since it involves Al's farm, which is burdened by the road, and Ben's estate, since he is the neighbor and being benefited with the ability to use the road.

Scope of Easement

The scope of an easement is intended to meet both present and future needs of the dominant parcel due to normal, foreseeable development. The dominant estate has a duty to repair and maintain the easement. Here, Ben is within the scope of the easement as he uses the road daily as he was granted permission to do. Further, it is not likely that Ben exceeded the scope when he graded and paved the road as that is likely reasonable for long-term use since he and Al use it daily.

Termination

Easements can be terminated in a variety of ways including estoppel, destruction, release, abandonment, and merger. Here, Ben did not change his position for estoppel, the road was not destroyed, no release was provided, Ben did not abandon the easement, and the two parcels are not owned by one person. Thus, the easement has not been terminated.

Transferability of Easements

An appurtenant easement burden passes automatically with servient land, unless the new owner is a bona fide purchaser (BFP). A BFP is one who takes for value and without notice.

To determine if Carol or Polly are BFPs and can prevent Ben's easement from passing when the land is transferred, it must be determined whether Carol or Polly paid value and took without notice.

As to Carol, she would likely not be a BFP because it doesn't appear that she paid value as her father, Al, deeded her the land. Thus, she paid no value.

As to Polly, she did pay value as she paid Carol $100,000 for the land. If Polly didn't have notice of the easement then she would be a BFP. Thus, the easement will transfer unless Polly is a BFP, depending on her notice as discussed below.

Notice

Notice can be provided three ways. The first is actual notice in which the purchaser is actually informed of the easement, such as it being included in the deed or purchaser told about it. The second type of notice is record notice in which the easement can be discovered upon a search of the property in a grantor-grantee index. The third type of notice is inquiry notice when a reasonable inspection of the property would reveal the easement.

Here, Polly did not have actual notice in the deed as the road easement was not mentioned in the deed, nor does it appear that Carol specifically told her about it. However, Polly would be on record notice since

Ben recorded his easement in 2011 and Polly didn't record her deed until 2014 so she could have seen Ben's easement in the chain of title had she searched.

Polly also had inquiry notice as she saw Ben using the road and a reasonable inspection would reveal a graded and paved road that was used daily by Ben. Thus, Polly had notice.

Since Polly had notice she would not be a BFP and the easement would transfer with the servient estate.

Shelter Doctrine

One who takes from a BFP will "stand in the shoes" of the BFP and prevail against any entity against which the transferor-BFP would have prevailed in his own action even if transferee had notice.

Here, if Carol was a BFP then Polly could stand in Carol's shoes and prevail against Ben even though Polly had notice. However, Carol was not a BFP as discussed above because she did not pay value. Thus, the Shelter Doctrine is inapplicable.

Recording Acts

Recording acts protect BFPs but do not protect donees, heirs, or devisees. Under the common law it was first in time, first in right. Modernly, courts use three tests depending on the jurisdiction. There are notice statutes that find that a BFP prevails over a grantee who didn't record. Race notice statutes find that a BFP who records first prevails over a grantee who didn't record first. And race statutes find that the first to record prevails.

Since neither Carol nor Polly are BFPs, the recording statutes would not serve to protect either of them. However, if for some reason Carol did pay value or is deemed a BFP then the rules would apply.

If the common law rule applies, Ben keeps the easement since his easement was first in time. A notice or race notice statute would not protect either Carol or Polly as they both had notice as discussed above via inquiry notice at a minimum as they both had the opportunity to inspect the land and see Ben using the road. Polly would have record notice too since she recorded in 2014 and Ben recorded in 2011. However, Carol would not have record notice since she recorded in 2009 before Ben recorded in 2011. However, since Carol included the easement in her deed to Polly she seems to have had actual notice of the easement.

In a pure race jurisdiction, Carol would prevail because she recorded first, but Polly would not unless she was protected by the Shelter Doctrine since she recorded after Ben. Overall, Ben would most likely prevail in any jurisdiction since neither Carol nor Polly are BFPs.

2.a. Polly's Breach of Contract Claim

Land Sales Contract

The contract for a conveyance of an interest in real estate typically governs the agreement until the time of closing, at which time the deed becomes the operative document governing the land transfer.

Here, Carol executed a written contract in 2012 to sell Polly the farm for $100,000. The contract covenanted against encumbrances and did not mention any easements.

Marketable Title

Marketable title is implied in every land sale contract and is title free from reasonable doubt. An easement reduces the value of a property; therefore, an easement would make title unmarketable.

Merger Doctrine

In a contract for the sale of land, once the deal has closed, the contract merges with the deed and the deed controls. Here, since the deed was delivered in 2014, the deed will control, so Polly will need to look at the deed for breach of covenants in the deed.

Thus, Polly does not have a breach of contract claim.

2.b. Polly's Breach of Covenant Under the Warranty Deed

Warranty Deed

A warranty deed warrants against all defects in title and contains six covenants. There are three present covenants, including seisen, the right to convey, and right against encumbrances. The future covenants include warranty of title, quiet enjoyment, and further assurances.

Here, the covenant contained in the deed and at issue is the covenant against encumbrances. In 2014, Carol executed and delivered a warranty deed to Polly for the farm and Carol paid Polly $100,000. The deed contained a covenant against all encumbrances except for the easement to Water Co. and no other title covenants.

Covenant Against Encumbrances

In this covenant, the grantor warrants there are no mortgages, liens, easements, or use restrictions on the land. The majority of courts find that this covenant can be breached even if the purchaser had notice.

Here, there are two encumbrances on the land as there are two easements attached to the land, the use of the road by Ben and the Water Company water lines.

Road Easement

Here, this easement was excluded from the deed and the deed stated that only the water company easement was included. As this is a present covenant, it was breached at the time of the sale. In a majority of jurisdictions the fact that Polly had notice as discussed above would be irrelevant. Thus, the road easement is a breach of the covenant against encumbrances.

Water Company Easement

Defenses of unclean hands, laches, or waiver are applicable to covenants. Here, Polly might argue that this easement was not in the land sales contract in 2012 and that Carol waited and delivered the deed only after a long delay, thus trying to commit some type of fraud or misrepresentation on Polly amounting to unclean hands or laches. However, this easement was in the deed and thus Polly was aware of it and could have disputed it at the time the deed was delivered and not pay rather than wait a year in 2015 to try to block it. Thus, this easement does not breach the covenant of encumbrances.

Remedy

Damages would include the difference in value between the purchase price and the value with the encumbrance, or the cost to remove the encumbrance. Here, the difference in the value of the land with the easement and without it is $5,000. Thus, since Carol is in breach of the covenant against encumbrances for Ben's easement only, Polly should recover $5,000 from Carol in a majority of jurisdictions. If in a minority jurisdiction, then she would recover nothing as she was on notice of Ben's easement. As to the water company easement she will not recover anything as there was no breach and even if there was a breach, the easement increased the value of the property by $10,000, so she benefits from the easement.

Real Property Question 3
February 2012, Question 6

Donna was looking for a place to live. Perry owned a two-story home, with the second story available to lease.

Donna and Perry signed a two-year lease that provided, in part: "Lessee may assign the leased premises only with the prior written consent of Lessor."

Upon moving in, Donna discovered that the water in her shower became very hot if Perry ran water downstairs. When Donna complained to Perry about the shower and asked him to make repairs, Perry refused, saying, "I'll just make sure not to run the water when you are in the shower."

Perry soon adopted a new diet featuring strong-smelling cheese. Donna told Perry that the smell of the cheese annoyed and nauseated her. Perry replied: "Too bad; that's my diet now."

After constantly smelling the cheese for three weeks, Donna decided to move out and to assign the lease to a friend who was a wealthy historian.

Donna sought Perry's consent to assign the lease to her friend. Perry refused to consent, saying, "I've had bad experiences with historians, especially wealthy ones." Thereafter, every time Donna took a shower, Perry deliberately ran the water downstairs.

After two weeks of worrying about taking a shower for fear of being scalded and with the odor of cheese still pervasive, Donna stopped paying rent, returned the key, and moved out. At that time, there were twenty-two months remaining on the lease.

Perry has sued Donna for breach of the lease, seeking damages for past due rent and for prospective rent through the end of the lease term.

What defenses may Donna reasonably raise and how are they likely to fare? Discuss.

Real Property Question 3 Assessment
February 2012, Question 6

This question is another example that real property questions are comparatively manageable. Landlord-tenant is a popular testing area in real property and any questions in this topic area will look a lot like this essay question. This real property question is typical in that it only has five main issues to discuss, though two of the issues had to be analyzed twice since there were two distinct fact sets to analyze.

This fact pattern centers on a residential real estate lease, rather than a commercial lease. This question covers several landlord-tenant rules, but the issue spotting is not difficult, and successfully passing this question hinges on detailed and meaningful factual analysis of the issues presented. There are many facts to work with and include in the discussion and analysis of the various potential bases for a constructive eviction. While the issue spotting was simple, the organization of an answer was more challenging in this question.

In this essay, there are two distinct problems with the lease, the hot water and the stinky cheese. This provides a good opportunity to be thoughtful with your organization. Whenever you have two different facts sets but are going to be applying the same rule to them, always use subheadings and then analyze them separately. For example, within the implied warranty of habitability analysis and the constructive eviction analysis, there are subheadings for the hot water, with a full analysis of the rule following, and then the stinky cheese, with a full analysis of the rule following. The facts are distinct for each fact set, so you want to be sure to analyze each element of your rule to each fact set separately. Using this approach ensures that you do not merge the facts and miss key analysis. Organizing by fact set within each rule makes for a much cleaner presentation than if you were to analyze each set of facts under each rule element. In general, this is how you want to handle organization in any situation in which there is more than one fact set that needs to be applied to a rule.

The issue of Donna's attempt to assign the lease to her friend could have been handled as an assignment discussion near the beginning of the answer, or at the end in the duty to mitigate discussion, or in both places. Providing clear headings ensures the grader can find the discussion. This is especially important when there is more than one way an essay can be logically organized or more than one place an issue can be discussed.

Make note of the areas highlighted in **bold** on the corresponding grid. The bold areas highlight the issues, analysis, and conclusions that are likely **required** to receive a passing score on this question.

Issue	Rule	Fact Application	Conclusion
What defenses may Donna reasonably raise and how are they likely to fare?			
Tenancy for years	• A lease for a fixed period of time is a tenancy for years. • Statute of frauds (SOF) requires a writing if the lease term is longer than one year.	• **Perry and Donna agreed to a 2-year lease for the 2nd floor, which is a term of years, for a 2-year term.** • They "signed" a lease, so the SOF is satisfied. • Perry has a duty to give Donna possession of the premises and Donna has a duty to pay rent. **Donna must pay rent for the 2 years of the lease,** unless she has a defense.	The SOF will not provide a defense
Duty to Repair	Landlord must maintain all common areas and fix latent defects.	• **Donna discovered she would get scalded by hot water when showering if Perry was using the water downstairs.** • Since Donna rented the 2nd floor of Perry's home and the plumbing seems connected, she can argue the plumbing system is a common area with a defect which Perry should have repaired. • When Donna notified Perry of the problem, he refused to fix it. • Perry breached his duty to maintain the common areas and repair latent defects.	Modernly, Donna can defend because Perry breached his duty to repair
Implied Warranty of Habitability	Residential premises must be fit for human habitation If not habitable, the tenant may: • **Terminate the lease and move out,** • **Make repairs and deduct the cost from the rent, or** • **Pay reduced rent, remain on premises, and sue for damages.**	<u>Hot Shower</u> • **The water in Donna's shower became very hot if Perry ran water downstairs.** • Donna will assert a shower is an essential part of a rental and it should not be dangerous to use, so the rental was not fit for human habitation. • **Donna notified Perry** of the water problem, and his proposed solution was to "make sure not to run the water when you are in the shower," which is not a failsafe solution to the problem. • **The scalding water is a safety hazard which made the premises uninhabitable, and Donna was within her rights to terminate the lease, return the keys, and move out,** especially since she gave Perry the opportunity to make repairs. • Donna has a defense to paying the remaining 22 months of rent. <u>Stinky Cheese</u> • Perry adopted a new diet featuring a strong-smelling cheese which annoyed and nauseated Donna. • **Donna will assert the strong smell of the cheese made the rental uninhabitable.**	Donna could defend on the implied warranty of habitability for the hot shower water

Continued>

Issue	Rule	Fact Application	Conclusion
Implied Warranty of Habitability (continued)		• **However, Perry will argue that a food smell is more preference based, and even an unpleasant smell would not make nearby premises uninhabitable.** Further, the smell would only be present several times a day at mealtimes and Donna could always close her windows at that time. • Perry's cheese likely did not make the premises uninhabitable. [Anytime you need to apply a rule to two separate fact sets, like the hot shower and stinky cheese here, separate the analysis out into separate sections. This will make your analysis much more clear, prevents you from skipping key analysis, and makes it easier for the grader to follow.]	
Implied Covenant of Quiet Enjoyment Constructive Eviction	A landlord warrants that they will not interfere with the tenant's quiet use and enjoyment of the property. Constructive eviction occurs when: • **A substantial interference makes premises virtually uninhabitable (disrepair)** • **Tenant notifies the landlord** • Landlord fails to meaningfully respond • **Causing tenant to move out within a reasonable time.**	**Hot Shower** • **The plumbing became scalding in Donna's shower when Perry was using his water. Perry began deliberately running the water on purpose to annoy Donna,** which is a substantial interference with Donna's use and enjoyment of the property since she was unable to shower. • **Donna notified Perry** and in response he did it deliberately. • Perry's "fix" of refraining from running the water while Donna showered was not a meaningful response since the problem persisted. After Donna tried to assign the lease and mentioned her dislike of the cheese smell, Perry began deliberately running his water when Donna showered to scald her in retaliation. Donna was unable to shower in peace for 2 weeks. • In response, Donna stopped paying rent and moved out within 2 weeks, which is a reasonable amount of time to give Perry to fix the problem. **Stinky Cheese** • Perry ate foul smelling cheese which nauseated Donna and he refused to stop, saying "that's too bad." • While Donna will assert this is also a substantial interference since the smell from Perry's cheese was so bad it made her nauseated, Perry will argue it is likely not so substantial for the same reasons above about the habitability of the premises.	Donna can defend on the constructive eviction for the hot shower

Continued>

616

Issue	Rule	Fact Application	Conclusion
Private Nuisance	Substantial, unreasonable interference w/ another's use/ enjoyment of land.	• Donna could attempt to prove the stinky cheese was bad enough to rise to the level of a substantial interference using a nuisance theory. Depending how bad the smell was, it is possible the cheese could be found to be a substantial interference.	It is unlikely the cheese is a private nuisance
Duty to Mitigate Assignment	• A landlord has a duty to mitigate damages. • An interest in a rental property is assignable, unless the parties agree otherwise. • An assignment is a transfer of the entire rental period to another.	• Assuming Donna was found liable for the lease and wrongfully vacated, she can argue that Perry is not mitigating his damages. • **Here, the lease terms require Perry's prior written consent to assign the lease, which Donna sought.** • **Donna tried to mitigate the loss of rental income to Perry by trying to assign the lease to a new tenant, her friend the wealthy historian.** • **Perry refused to accept the assignment because he had "bad experiences" with wealthy historians.** Though Perry was within his rights to refuse the assignment under a normal circumstance as permitted by the lease so long as he is not discriminatory, **his refusal is not reasonable** given that his reason is idiosyncratic. It is not based on a trait that would make the historian a bad tenant, such as a lack of credit worthiness. • Perry has a duty to use reasonable efforts to mitigate his damages by reletting the 2nd floor, **so he would not be entitled to the full 22 months of rent from Donna. If Perry does receive damages, it will be reduced for his failure to mitigate.** [The assignment could have logically been discussed in this section, or in the beginning.]	**Perry must mitigate any damages**

Real Property Question 3 Sample Answer
February 2012, Question 6

What defenses may Donna reasonably raise and how are they likely to fare?

Tenancy for years

A lease for a fixed period of time is a tenancy for years. The statute of frauds (SOF) requires a lease for a term longer than one year to be in writing.

Perry and Donna agreed to a 2-year lease for the rental of the 2nd floor of Perry's home, which is a term of years, for a 2-year term. They "signed" a lease, so the SOF is satisfied. Consequently, Perry has a duty to give Donna possession of the premises and Donna has a duty to pay rent. There was a valid "no assignment" provision, which is discussed below.

Donna must pay rent for the 2 years of the lease, unless she has another defense since the SOF will not provide a defense to the lease.

Duty to Repair

Modernly, a landlord must maintain all common areas of the premises and fix latent defects. At common law, there was no such duty, and a tenant took the premises "as is."

Upon moving in, Donna discovered she would get scalded by hot water when showering if Perry was also using the water downstairs in his unit. Since Donna rented the 2nd floor of Perry's home and the plumbing seems connected, she can argue the plumbing system is a common area which Perry should repair. The plumbing problem is also a latent defect Perry must repair since it was not visible upon inspection. When Donna notified Perry of the problem, he refused to fix it.

Perry breached his duty to maintain the common areas and repair latent defects. Modernly, this provides a defense for Donna because Perry breached his duty to repair.

Implied Warranty of Habitability

Residential premises must be fit for human habitation. If the rental premises are not habitable, the tenant may terminate the lease and move out, or make repairs and deduct the cost from the rent, or pay reduced rent, remain on premises, and sue the landlord for damages.

There are two potential issues with habitation, the too-hot shower and Perry's bad smelling cheese.

Hot Shower

The water in Donna's shower became very hot if Perry ran water downstairs. Donna will assert a shower is an essential part of a rental and it should not be dangerous to use, so the rental was not fit for human habitation. Donna notified Perry of the too-hot water problem, and his proposed solution was to "make sure not to run the water when you are in the shower," which is certainly not a failsafe solution to the problem since it leaves much room for human error. The scalding water made the premises uninhabitable, because Donna would be burned when showering, which is a safety hazard, or she was unable to bathe at all, which is unsanitary. Donna was within her rights to terminate the lease, return the keys, and move out, especially since she gave Perry every opportunity to make repairs.

Donna has a good defense to paying the remaining 22 months of rent.

Stinky Cheese

Perry adopted a new diet featuring a strong-smelling cheese which annoyed and nauseated Donna. Donna will assert the strong smell of the cheese made the rental uninhabitable. However, Perry will argue that a food smell problem is more preference based, and even an unpleasant smell would not make nearby premises uninhabitable. Further, the smell would only be present several times a day at mealtimes and Donna could always close her windows at that time. Consequently, Perry's cheese likely did not make the premises uninhabitable.

Donna could defend on the remaining rent owed on the implied warranty of habitability basis for the hot shower water.

Implied Covenant of Quiet Enjoyment/Constructive Eviction

A landlord warrants that they will not interfere with the tenant's quiet use and enjoyment of the property. A constructive eviction occurs when a substantial interference makes the premises virtually uninhabitable because they are in a state of disrepair, the tenant notifies the landlord, the Landlord fails to meaningfully respond, and this causes the tenant to move out within a reasonable time.

There are two potential issues causing a substantial interference, the too-hot shower and Perry's bad smelling cheese.

Hot Shower

The plumbing became scalding in Donna's shower when Perry was using his water downstairs. Once Perry learned Donna was unhappy, Perry began deliberately running the water on purpose to annoy Donna, which is a substantial interference with Donna's use and enjoyment of the property since she was unable to shower at a reasonable and safe temperature. Donna promptly notified Perry of the too-hot water problem and in response he began running his water deliberately, rather than fix the problem. Perry originally promised to "fix" the problem by refraining from running the water while Donna showered. This solution was not a meaningful response since the problem persisted. After Donna tried to assign the lease to a friend and mentioned her dislike of the strong cheese smell, Perry began deliberately running his water when Donna showered to scald her in retaliation. As a result, Donna was unable to shower in peace and safety for 2 weeks. In response, Donna stopped paying rent and moved out within 2 weeks, which is a reasonable amount of time given to Perry to fix the problem.

Stinky Cheese

Perry ate foul smelling cheese which nauseated Donna. When Donna complained, Perry refused to stop, saying "that's too bad." Donna will assert this is also a substantial interference with her use and enjoyment of the property since the smell from Perry's cheese was so bad it not only annoyed her, but also made her nauseated. However, Perry will argue a bad smell from food is likely not so substantial an interference with her use and enjoyment, for the same reasons above about the habitability of the premises.

Donna can defend on the remaining rent owed on the basis of a constructive eviction for the overly hot shower water.

Private Nuisance

A private nuisance is the substantial, unreasonable interference with another's use and enjoyment of their land.

Donna could attempt to prove the stinky cheese was bad enough to rise to the level of a substantial interference using a nuisance theory. Depending how bad the smell was, it is possible the cheese could be found to be a substantial interference, but that is unlikely.

Duty to Mitigate/Assignment

If a tenant wrongfully abandons the property, modernly a landlord has a duty to mitigate their damages.

An interest in a rental property is assignable, unless the parties agree otherwise. An assignment is a transfer of the entire rental period to another.

Assuming Donna is found liable for the lease because she wrongfully abandoned the property, she can argue that Perry did not properly mitigate his damages.

Here, the lease terms require Perry's prior written consent to assign the lease, which Donna sought. Donna tried to mitigate the loss of rental income to Perry by trying to assign the lease to a new tenant, her friend the wealthy historian. However, Perry refused to accept the assignment because he had "bad experiences" with wealthy historians. Though Perry was within his rights to refuse the assignment under a normal circumstance as permitted by the lease so long as he is not violating discrimination laws, Donna will assert that his refusal is not objectively reasonable given that his reason is idiosyncratic. His refusal to approve the assignment is not based on a trait that would make the historian a bad tenant, such as a lack of cleanliness or credit worthiness. Rather, Perry has an inherent dislike of wealthy historians because of his past experiences. If Perry does not want to rent to Donna's friend, he could still mitigate his damages by reletting the premises to another tenant. There are no facts to suggest Perry has tried to rent the 2nd floor to another.

Perry has a duty to use reasonable efforts to mitigate his damages by reletting the 2nd floor, so he would not be entitled to the full 22 months of rent from Donna if it was found that she wrongfully abandoned the property. If Perry does receive damages from Donna, which is unlikely since she has several good defenses to her failure to pay rent, any damages will be reduced for his own failure to mitigate his losses.

Real Property Question 4
October 2020, Question 3

Andrew, a widower with three adult children (Bobby, Carol, and Dylan), owned a forty-acre parcel of wooded land called Havenwood. In 1988, Andrew by written deed validly conveyed the north half of Havenwood to his brother Elmo.

In 1989, Andrew died, leaving a valid will that gave "all my real estate to Bobby, Carol, and Dylan as joint tenants with right of survivorship." Carol and Dylan lived out of state. Bobby lived near Havenwood.

In 1990, without permission from anyone, Bobby cut down some trees and prepared a number of campsites on both the north and south halves of Havenwood. He sometimes used one campsite himself and rented out the other sites during the spring and summer each year. Bobby paid taxes on the entire property using the rental fees he collected, keeping the remaining profits.

In 2017, Dylan asked Bobby about the land and Bobby told Dylan that it was none of his business. Bobby said, "I've improved the land and, anyway, I'm the youngest and it will be mine in the end." Dylan then by written deed validly conveyed his interest in Havenwood to Fred, his friend, as a gift. Dylan told Carol what had happened, and she had a written deed drawn up validly conveying her interest in Havenwood "from Carol as a joint tenant to Carol as a tenant in common."

In 2018, Bobby died leaving a valid will that gave his entire estate to Sam, his son. Sam continued renting the campsites and paying taxes, keeping the remaining profits, and occasionally using one campsite himself, just as his father had done.

1. What right, title or interest in Havenwood, if any, are currently held by Elmo, Fred, Carol and Sam? Discuss.

2. Are any claims available to or against Sam for payment of taxes or recovery of rental fees? Discuss.

Real Property Question 4 Assessment
October 2020, Question 3

This real property question includes testing on some less frequently tested topics, including a variety of issues that arise with joint ownership of property, and adverse possession. It has a few more issues than a typical real property question, but they aren't challenging. If you knew the rules, you should not have had trouble analyzing this question, but you may have again found the organization more challenging.

While there are two calls of the question, we found this question more manageable by first figuring out what was going on by analyzing all the events sequentially since the order of events impacted the analysis. From an organizational standpoint, it might have been challenging to determine when it was best to address the adverse possession issue. You could have done it early on when the facts first raise it, but we opted to put it near the end because that way all the embedded sub-issues, including tacking, could best be discussed in one tidy section.

There was a lot going on here factually since the property ownership kept changing hands. This is the type of question that makes us long for the old days where applicants had scratch paper. Today, it is unclear if you will be allowed real scratch paper to work with, or you may have the option to use virtual scratch paper (which won't be as helpful here) or a 8.5 x 11 or 9 x 12 white board (dry erase). We recommend you use your white board for these types of essays to draw out the parcels and plot out the owners and timeline. If you choose to use your virtual scratch paper instead be sure to delete your notes to yourself before submitting your final essay. We also recommend that you practice your essays in this format during bar prep to mimic the real bar-exam like experience.

Make note of the areas highlighted in **bold** on the corresponding grid. The bold areas highlight the issues, analysis, and conclusions that are likely **required** to receive a passing score on this question.

Issue	Rule	Fact Application	Conclusion
What right, title or interest in Havenwood, if any, are currently held by Elmo, Fred, Carol and Sam?			
Transfer by deed	A deed passes legal title from grantor to grantee if lawfully executed and properly delivered.	• In 1988 Andrew validly conveyed the north half of Havenwood to his brother Elmo by written valid deed. At this point, Andrew owned the south half, and Elmo owned the north half.	Elmo owns N. Havenwood in fee simple
Transfer by will	Property may be devised through a properly executed will, which takes effect upon the testator's death.	• In 1989, when Andrew died his valid will devised "all of my real estate" to his adult children, **Bobby, Carol, and Dylan, as joint tenants with a right of survivorship.**	Bobby, Carol, and Dylan take S. Havenwood by will
Joint tenancy	**Two or more hold a single unified interest in a property. Created with the four unities and an express right of survivorship:** • **Interest created at the same time** • **Parties take the same title** • **Equal interest** • **Equal right to possession**	• Here, through his will which took effect upon his death, Andrew conveyed all of his real estate to Bobby, Carol, and Dylan as "joint tenants with a right of survivorship." • **The interest in S. Havenwood was created at the same time,** which was upon Andrew's death through his will. • **Bobby, Carol, and Dylan took with the same "joint tenant" title,** and they took in three equal shares. • **All three also have an equal right to possession of S. Havenwood.** Though only Bobby took possession of the property since only he lived locally, Carol and Dylan could have if they wanted. • **The four unities of joint tenancy are satisfied.**	**Bobby, Carol, and Dylan own South Havenwood as joint tenants in fee simple**
Ouster	When one joint tenant claims an exclusive right to possession and refuses occupancy to their co-tenants.	• Dylan may argue that Bobby "ousted" him from S. Havenwood when in 2017 he asked Bobby about the land, and Bobby told Dylan it was "none of his business." However, one rude statement will be insufficient to demonstrate Dylan was refused occupancy and ousted from the property. • **There is no evidence here that Bobby ever claimed the exclusive right to possession or prevented his co-tenants from using the property.**	No ouster
Severance of joint tenancy — Fred	• **A joint tenancy can be severed by conveyance of their share.** • A tenant in common has an equal right to possession, but no automatic right of survivorship. • The new owner takes their share as tenant in common, while the remaining JT are JT to each other.	• In 2017, Dylan conveyed his 1/3 interest in S. Havenwood to his friend Fred, as a gift. • This conveyance destroys the four unities and severs the joint tenancy. Consequently, Fred would take his 1/3 interest in S. Havenwood as a tenant in common to Bobby and Carol. However, Bobby and Carol remain joint tenants to each other.	**Bobby and Carol remain joint tenants to each other, but Fred holds his 1/3 as a tenant in common**

Continued>

Issue	Rule	Fact Application	Conclusion
Severance of joint tenancy—Carol	Rule above	• In 2017 **Carol reconveyed her interest in S. Havenwood to herself as a tenant in common.** This effectively severed the joint tenancy she continued to hold with Bobby.	Bobby, Carol, and Fred hold as tenants in common
Transfer by will	Rule above	• In 2018 **when Bobby died, he left a valid will leaving his entire estate to his son, Sam.** Sam will take Bobby's 1/3 tenant in common share of S. Havenwood.	Sam, Carol, and Fred hold as tenants in common
Adverse possession	One who has wrongfully entered property can obtain possession if • Actual exclusive possession • Open, notorious and visible • Hostile • Continuous use for the • Statutory period (tacking allowed)	**North Havenwood** • The issue is if Sam has obtained adverse possession of a part of N. Havenwood. • In 1990 Bobby cut trees and created campsites on both South and North Havenwood. The campsites have been rented ever since during the spring and summer months. **Bobby took actual possession of the portion of land holding the campsites on Elmo's property and it was not open to the public and Elmo did not also use the property.** It is not clear if the campsites covered the entire 20 acres, but if the possession was on only part of the land, a partial possession is sufficient to establish the possession of that land. • **Bobby's use of the land was open, notorious, and visible since** he cut down trees from wooded land and prepared campsites, which were regularly rented to others and would be noticeable upon any inspection of the property. • **Bobby's use of the property was hostile since it was done "without permission from anyone," including the true owner, Elmo.** • The use of the property must be continuous, but seasonal use is satisfactory if that is how a true owner would use the property. **Here, the campsites were only used in the spring and summer months.** Since Bobby used his own lot in exactly the same way, it can be presumed that the seasonal use in the warmer months is consistent with how a true owner would use the property. As such, continuous use is established. • **The property was used for 28 + years in this manner, which likely satisfies the statutory period.** If needed, tacking can be used to establish the statutory requirement. **Since Sam used the property in the same way as his father Bobby, their periods of ownership could be added together to meet the statute.** **South Havenwood** • **Bobby cannot establish adverse possession to all of S. Havenwood against his siblings since there was no ouster.**	Bobby/Sam acquired N. Havenwood by adverse possession

Continued>

Issue	Rule	Fact Application	Conclusion
Are any claims available to or against Sam for payment of taxes or recovery of rental fees?			
Duty to account	**Co-tenants have no duty to account to their co-tenants for profits and losses from their own use of the land** • **Co-tenants are responsible for their own proportionate share of carrying costs (taxes).** • **A co-tenant who pays in excess of their share can seek reimbursement from their co-tenants.** • **Co-tenants must share profits received from third parties.**	**Rental income—S. Havenwood** • All three joint tenants had equal right to possess S. Havenwood. Here, Bobby, and then Sam, were the only ones to use the property. Bobby cut down trees and created campsites, which he rented to others and occasionally used himself. Bobby/Sam paid taxes on the whole property out of their profits from the campsite operation and kept the balance. • Bobby/Sam owes nothing to their co-tenants for their own use of the campsites. • **Bobby should have shared the net profits from the campsites with his co-tenants. Carol and Dylan/Fred can seek contribution from Bobby for their share of the net profits for the campground operation** that occurred on S. Havenwood. **Taxes** • All joint tenants are responsible for paying 1/3 of the taxes, but the campground operation provided enough to cover the bill, and the taxes were be paid out of the land profits, which covered Carol and Dylan/Fred's shares. • Sam cannot get reimbursement from the joint tenants for the taxes paid since he paid them out of the campsite profits. **Rental income—N. Havenwood** As discussed above, Sam acquired N. Havenwood through adverse possession and does not owe anyone for the rental fees he/Bobby collected nor can he seek contribution for the taxes paid.	**Carol and Dylan/Fred can seek contribution for the net profits** Bobby/Sam cannot get reimbursement for the taxes

Real Property Question 5
July 2008, Question 5

Ann, Betty, and Celia purchased a 3-bedroom condominium unit in which they resided. Each paid one-third of the purchase price. They took title as "joint tenants, with right of survivorship."

After a dispute, Betty moved out. Ann and Celia then each executed a separate deed by which each conveyed her respective interest in the condominium unit to Ed. Each deed recited that the conveyance was "in fee, reserving a life estate to the grantor." Ann recorded her deed and delivered the original deed to Ed. Celia also recorded her deed and left the original deed with Ann in a sealed envelope with written instructions: "This envelope contains papers that are to be delivered to me on demand or in the event of my death then to be delivered to Ed." Celia recorded the deed solely to protect her life estate interest. Ann, without Celia's knowledge or authorization, mailed a copy of Celia's deed to Ed.

Subsequently, Ann and Celia were killed in a car accident. Betty then moved back into the condominium unit. She rented out one bedroom to a tenant and used the other bedroom to run a computer business. Betty paid all costs of necessary repairs to maintain the unit.

Ed commenced an action against Betty, demanding a share of the rent she has collected. He also demanded that she pay rent for her use of the premises.

Betty cross-complained against Ed, demanding that he contribute for his share of the costs of necessary repairs to maintain the unit.

1. What are the property interests of Betty and Ed, if any, in the condominium unit? Discuss.

2. What relief, if any, may Ed obtain on his claims against Betty for past due rent for her use of the condominium unit and for a share of the rent paid by the tenant? Discuss.

3. What relief, if any, may Betty obtain on her claim against Ed for contribution for the costs of maintaining the condominium unit? Discuss.

Real Property Question 5 Assessment

July 2008, Question 5

This real property question covers some areas that are less commonly essay tested, including the joint ownership of property and the rights and responsibilities among the joint owners to each other, conveyance by deed, and a minor future interest issue.

The possibility of having future interests tested on the essay exam strikes fear into the heart of most students. However, this question provides a good example of how future interests may be raised on an essay question without cause for concern. The content of the future interest rules simply don't lend themselves to extensive essay testing. Bar examiners are looking to assess a bar applicant's analytical skills, and future interests don't create much analytical opportunity. It is more likely that future interests will come up as they are raised in this question: The future interest in question is a life estate, which is a very easy issue to spot and identify. The identification of the life estate provides the setup for the major issue, which is the proper delivery of the deed purporting to grant the life estate. As is typical in essay questions, there are two slightly different fact scenarios pertaining to the deed delivery so that you can demonstrate to the bar graders your nuanced understanding of the delivery rules.

Another typical aspect of this essay question is the ambiguity in the facts pertaining to Celia's delivery of her deed. The facts are purposely ambiguous regarding whether or not Celia intended a present delivery of the deed. Whenever facts are obviously ambiguous, such as they are here, it is a clue to you that you must analyze both sides of the issue. On bar essays, major points are always allocated for (1) the full analysis of a pivotal issue, (2) the analysis of an issue where there is an abundance of facts available to use in the analysis, and (3) the analysis of any issue where there are facts available to argue both sides of the issue. This doesn't mean that you should create contrary arguments when they really aren't there. But, when the facts are obviously ambiguous, as they are here, you can be certain that identifying both sides of the issue and presenting the competing arguments is essential to receiving a passing score on that essay. The conclusion you reach on an issue where the conclusion could go either way isn't important. However, it is always wise to be mindful that the conclusion you reach may have an effect on other issues. Be careful not to be so firm in the adoption of your conclusion that you fail to spot issues that may be raised if you had reached the opposite conclusion and write yourself out of the question.

Note the areas highlighted in **bold** on the corresponding grid. The bold areas highlight the issues, analysis, and conclusions that are likely **required** to receive a passing score on this question.

Issue	Rule	Fact Application	Conclusion
Call #1: Property Interests of B & E			
Joint Tenancy	2 or more own a single unified interest with the right of survivorship.	There are 3 of them, which is an acceptable number since it is more than 2, and the right of survivorship is expressly stated since A, B, and C all purchased the condo and took title as "joint tenants, with right of survivorship."	**Yes, JT created**
	Need 4 unities: same time, same title, same interest, and right to possess the whole, and grantor clearly expresses right of survivorship.	**They appear to have taken the same title, at the same time, and each have equal interests and in fact even paid in equal amounts (though this is not required), and they each have the right to possess the whole and in fact appeared to initially all live in the condo.**	
Severance of JT	JT is not destroyed by one party moving out since a JT simply needs to have the right to possess the whole; one needn't do so.	B moving out of the condo does not sever the JT because she still had the right to possess the whole, but chose not to do so.	**JT became TIC (if conveyances valid; see below)**
	An inter vivos transfer will sever the JT and create a tenancy in common with the parties whose interests have been transferred.	**When A and C transferred their interests to E by executing a separate deed, which gave him a fee simple as a remainderman and A & C each a life estate, they severed the JT, making it a tenancy in common between E and B assuming their conveyances were valid. (See below.)**	
	Tenants in common have no right of survivorship and own an individual part with the right to possess the whole.		
Conveyance by Deed	Need lawful execution and delivery/acceptance.	Here, both A and C's deeds appear to be in writing since they are executed deeds, identify A & C & E, and it is likely that both A and C signed the deed and described the land.	**A's deed to E is valid—severing JT as to A**
	Lawful execution: in writing, identifies parties, signed by grantor, and adequate property description.		
Delivery of Deed	For delivery to be valid, the grantor must demonstrate a present intent to transfer the interest; physical transfer to grantee is not necessary.	**A delivered her deed to E and recorded it, indicating that she presently intended for E to have her fee simple remainder interest, and it appears that E did not reject that delivery, so he accepted it and the deed is properly delivered as to A's interest.**	C's deed valid to E—could have concluded either way [each state-released answer concluded differently but both argued both sides]
	The delivery must also be accepted.	**C also recorded her deed, but did so only to protect her life estate interest, indicating her intent may have only been for herself and not for E; however, she knew she was recording E's interest as well as her own since it was in the deed and she chose to record; also, C would have no reason to protect her life estate if she didn't intend for E to take as a fee simple as a remainder.**	If conveyance valid, E takes C's 1/3 interest; if not valid, then JT not severed and B still JT with C while tenant in common with A
	A JT must devise their interest during their life and cannot devise it through a will or after death.		

Continued>

Issue	Rule	Fact Application	Conclusion
Delivery of Deed (continued)		**Arguably, C may have intended to transfer her interest after her death and not presently since she left the deed with A in a sealed envelope instructing A to deliver it back to C upon her request or to E at C's death, which would not sever the** JT or make a present conveyance to E if it wasn't intended to be delivered until after C died — also, there appears to be the ability for C to revoke since she can ask for it back. **However, C still executed the deed, giving E the fee simple and recorded it knowing this. Further she still intended E to take as a remainder, she simply wanted to ensure her own interest in a life estate. A's delivery of the deed to E against C's wishes would not suffice for delivery if C didn't intend to transfer because it is C's intent that controls.**	
Death of A and C	At the death of a life estate holder, the remainder takes the property.	**Here, since A's transfer and delivery were clearly valid, E would take 1/3 of A's share in the condo, making him a tenant in common with B.**	Answer depends on above
	In the event of joint tenants, the remaining JT takes the deceased JT portion.	As to C, if JT severed, then E will take C's 1/3 interest, giving E a total of 2/3 interest in the condo as a tenant in common, with B having a 1/3 interest. If JT not severed, then B will take C's 1/3 interest as the surviving JT, giving B 2/3 interest and E 1/3 interest as tenants in common.	E and B are TIC with either E having 2/3 and B 1/3 or vice versa
Call #2: Ed v. Betty			
Tenants in Common	2 or more own with no right of survivorship; each owns an individual part and each has a right to possess the whole.	As indicated above, E and B are now tenants in common, indicating they can both possess the whole and must comply with rules among co-tenants.	Co-tenant rules apply
		Due to both being able to possess the whole, B would not have to pay rent for herself to occupy the land and use it as she desires.	**B doesn't owe E rent for her use of the premises**

Continued>

Issue	Rule	Fact Application	Conclusion
Co-tenant Rights	Co-tenants in possession have the right to retain profits from their own use of the property. Co-tenants must share net rents from 3rd parties.	As a co-tenant, B is able to use the property for her own use and retain the profits, as she did here by running her own computer business—so all profits from this business would belong to her only. As to the rent from the 3rd-party tenant, B would have to share the profits from that rental with E in proportion to their ownership interests (either 1/3 or 2/3, depending on above).	E gets nothing for B's business profits, but will get a portion of rent from the 3rd-party tenant
Call #3: Betty v. Ed			
Co-tenant Rights	Co-tenants must share costs for necessary repairs, but there is no right to reimbursement for improvements.	Since the repairs appear to be necessary to maintain the unit, E would have to contribute to the repairs in proportion to his ownership.	E owes B for his share of the repairs

Real Property Question 6
February 2014, Question 4

Jane owned a machine shop. It had one slightly buckled wall. It had been built years prior to Town's adoption of a zoning ordinance that permits office buildings and retail stores, but not manufacturing facilities.

Ira purchased the machine shop from Jane for $500,000. He gave her $50,000 in cash and a promissory note for an additional $50,000 secured by a deed of trust. He borrowed the other $400,000 from Acme Bank (Acme), which recorded a mortgage. Acme was aware of Jane's promissory note and deed of trust prior to the close of escrow.

Donna owns a parcel adjoining Ira's machine shop. She recently began excavation for construction of an office building. Ira complained to Donna that the excavation was causing the shop's wall to buckle further, but she did nothing in response.

Shortly thereafter, Ira's machine shop collapsed. Ira applied to Town for a building permit to rebuild the shop, but Town refused. He then defaulted on his obligations to Jane and Acme.

Ira has sued Donna seeking damages, and he has sued Town seeking issuance of a building permit. Acme has filed a foreclosure suit against Ira, and Jane has demanded a proportionate share of the proceeds from any foreclosure sale.

1. How is the court likely to rule on Ira's claim for damages against Donna? Discuss.

2. How is the court likely to rule on Ira's request that Town issue a building permit? Discuss.

3. How is the court likely to rule on Jane's claim for a proportionate share of the proceeds from any foreclosure sale? Discuss.

Real Property Question 6 Assessment
February 2014, Question 4

This real property question is more difficult for most students than the average property question because the issues raised are issues that are infrequently tested and some of them are tested for the first time in this essay. Thus far, the state bar has tested takings only a few times. This question is one of first impression with zoning and variances. Further, it tests mortgages, which are not heavily tested on the essays either.

When you get a question of first impression like this on the exam, it can be nerve-racking because you are not certain how to best approach answering the question. It may be reassuring to know that everyone else taking the exam probably feels exactly the same way you do. There is usually at least one question out of the five essay questions administered on each bar exam that leaves everyone stumped. Do your best, and then move on and don't think about it again. And although the land support and zoning issues might have thrown you off, you should have studied mortgages for the multiple choice portion of the exam. Further, you have common sense and were able to successfully navigate through three or four years of law school exams, so believe in yourself and don't let your nerves get the best of you.

As to the first call about Donna's excavation, even if you didn't know the rules for lateral land support, common sense would dictate that there must be some fairness or consideration for the property of others. Thus, common sense would force you to discuss something about whether it was fair and right. While you might not go into strict liability, negligence might always be a cause of action you can resort to when one party does some act that causes damage to another person. This is why understanding how issues are tested and how subjects relate to one another is critical. The more you can see how different areas of law collide, the more likely you will be able to articulate some argument for a question for which you don't quite know the official rules. Similarly, with zoning think about why towns should be able to zone. Common sense indicates that public benefit/safety might be an issue without knowing a rule. Here you needed to use logical inferences too since they don't tell you why they implemented the zoning rule.

Finally, pay close attention to the calls of the question, as they are very specific. Thus, when Call 1 asks for damages, you can write out a checklist of every possible issue that you can think of that would award a plaintiff damages (negligence would, of course, be one). Then, look at that list and determine which issue(s) are most likely to be worth points. Also, use the facts and highlight them as you use them to ensure you are analyzing all of them. One of the most important factors the bar examiners look for is whether you can use the facts to articulate and pose arguments. If you can make a strong argument using the facts, even if your rule isn't perfect, you will earn some points.

Note the areas highlighted in **bold** on the corresponding grid. The bold areas highlight the issues, analysis, and conclusions that are likely **required** to receive a passing score on this question.

Issue	Rule	Fact Application	Conclusion
1. Ira v. Donna			
Lateral Land Support	**A landowner is strictly liable if their excavation causes adjacent land to subside while in its natural state.** **If it subsides due to improvements such as buildings on it and would not have subsided without the additional structures, then the landowner may still be liable for negligence for their excavation.**	Ira owned a machine shop adjacent to Donna's parcel and Donna began excavation on her parcel to construct an office building. This construction caused Ira's wall to collapse, but since it was already slightly buckled before the excavation began it is not clear it would have collapsed in its natural state. Thus, Donna will not be strictly liable but may be liable if negligent.	Donna not strictly liable for Ira's collapsed wall
Negligence	Negligence requires duty, breach, actual and proximate cause, damages, and no valid defenses.	Donna had a duty to excavate as a reasonably prudent person would. While it isn't clear she did anything wrong, she did continue excavating after Ira told her that his wall was buckling further. A reasonable person might stop and have someone look at it or make some effort to avoid the wall completely buckling but Donna likely did not act reasonably by doing nothing. But for the excavation the wall would not have collapsed. It is foreseeable that the wall would collapse since it was already slightly buckled and Ira told Donna about it. Damages in that wall collapsed and can't rebuild due to new zoning. Defenses could be comparative negligence since Ira did nothing to further support the wall and he knew it was buckling further.	Ira might be able to succeed due to Donna's negligence but his damages would be offset by his own negligence

Continued>

Issue	Rule	Fact Application	Conclusion
2. Ira's request for building permit			
Zoning	**Cities are permitted to regulate the use and development of land through zoning** for the protection of the health, safety, comfort, morals, and general welfare of its citizens. Zoning laws must be reasonable and not arbitrary and have a substantial relation to the public benefit. Zoning can be cumulative, such that land can be used for the stated purpose or any higher use or noncumulative and only used for the stated purpose.	Town's zoning ordinance that only permitted office buildings and retail stores and not manufacturing facilities like Ira's machine shop is likely beneficial to the public in that it is safer for people to walk around in retail stores and office buildings without manufacturing shops that often have dangerous moving parts and machines; also retail stores and office buildings don't tend to emit as much noise, pollution, debris, etc., as manufacturing facilities. Thus, the zoning ordinance appears to be reasonable. This zoning appears limited and noncumulative in that it allows only retail and office buildings, but even if it was cumulative, a manufacturing building would not be a higher use than retail/office. [Note: One answer went into takings laws too. It wasn't necessary to go into takings but a brief discussion would have been fine. You needed to see the zoning issues at least and have a brief discussion of why Town is allowed to zone like this.]	**Zoning regulation permitted**
Variance	**A property owner can seek a variance (waiver) from a zoning regulation if they can show unnecessary hardship** due to the unique features of the property or practical difficulty. **The harm to the neighboring areas will also be considered.**	**Although Ira requested a building permit from Town to rebuild the machine shop, Town refused because zoning prohibits manufacturing buildings.** However, Ira can show that he will suffer an undue hardship as he just gave Jane $50,000 in cash for the shop, a promissory note that he will pay her $50,000 more and he borrowed $400,000 from Acme to finish paying off the $500,000 purchase price. If he cannot operate the shop, then he will lose his livelihood arguably along with $500,000. But it isn't clear if he can move the shop elsewhere either. Since the machine shop has been there long before the zoning regulation, it does not seem as though it harms the neighborhood although manufacturing facilities do likely produce more pollution and noise than retail and office buildings and thus it could harm the area.	Could conclude either way (state-released answers came to opposite conclusions here)

Continued>

Issue	Rule	Fact Application	Conclusion
Nonconforming Use	**Use of property that was allowed under zoning regulations at the time the use was established but is no longer permitted under the new zoning laws:** Some statutes allow these uses to continue and some statutes provide for termination of these uses by reasonable amortization provisions (provide a time frame for the owners to comply with the new zoning regulations). The majority of jurisdictions find that if the structure is destroyed, the new building must comply with the new zoning regulations.	**Since the machine shop existed years prior to the zoning ordinance it would be a nonconforming use and should be grandfathered in.** But since the wall collapsed and now the building needs to be rebuilt, most jurisdictions will require it to conform to the new zoning ordinance. Thus, in most jurisdictions Ira could not rebuild, as it would not fit within the new zoning regulations.	Ira cannot rebuild in a majority of jurisdictions

3. Jane's claim for a proportionate share of the foreclosure proceeds

Issue	Rule	Fact Application	Conclusion
Deed of Trust	Deed of trust is similar to a mortgage, except the debtor is the trustor and the deed of trust is given to a third-party trustee.	Here, Ira was the trustor of a $50,000 promissory note to pay Jane who was the intended beneficiary of this deed of trust. Since Jane is still owed this $50,000, she wants a proportional share of the foreclosure sale by Acme. Whether she can get a share depends on the priority of distribution with the mortgage.	Jane has an interest in getting paid her $50,000.
Mortgage	**A mortgage is a financing arrangement that conveys a security interest in land where the parties intend the land to be collateral for the repayment of a monetary obligation.** The buyer and/or borrower is the mortgagor. The lender is the mortgagee.	**Ira obtained a mortgage from Acme that allowed him to pay Jane $400,000.** Ira is the mortgagor and Acme is the mortgagee.	Ira has a mortgage from Acme
Foreclosure	**Foreclosure is a process by which the mortgagee may reach the land in satisfaction of the debt if the mortgagor is in default.**	**Since Ira defaulted on his obligations to Acme, Acme as the mortgagee was within its rights to foreclose on the property.**	**Acme permitted to foreclose**

Continued>

Issue	Rule	Fact Application	Conclusion
Priority	Debts secured by the property are paid in descending order of priority (usually chronologically). Each mortgagee/lien holder is entitled to payment in full before a lower-ranking creditor receives any payment. Purchase money mortgage (PMM) is a mortgage given to secure a loan that enables the debtor to originally purchase the property. A PMM receives priority over non-PMM mortgagee. Order of payment from foreclosure proceeds: (1) Fees from attorneys/trustees; (2) PMM or secured senior interests; (3) secured junior interests; (4) unsecured interests. The foreclosure of junior interests will not affect senior interests, but the foreclosure of senior interests will destroy all junior interests.	Here, Jane's promissory note was prior to Acme's mortgage and thus chronologically it would be paid first if timing considered. However, it isn't clear if Jane recorded her deed of trust and Acme recorded their interest so depending on the jurisdiction Acme might be able to have priority if a BFP. Further, both Jane and Acme's interests are secured and PMM type interests as both helped Ira to secure the property. Thus it is necessary to determine how the outcome and priority could be affected in various recording jurisdictions. **Jane was a senior interest and thus her note would not be extinguished by Acme's foreclosure.**	Based on timing, Jane would have priority and her note would not be extinguished by Acme's foreclosure **Jane should be paid first**
Recording Acts	In race jx — first to record wins In notice — subsequent BFP prevails over a grantee who didn't record In race-notice — a subsequent BFP that records first prevails over a grantee that didn't record first Notice can be actual, inquiry, or record	If race jx, then Acme would prevail as it recorded first. If notice or race notice, Acme had notice because it was aware of Jane's promissory note and thus Acme would not be a BFP.	Under notice and race notice Jane would be paid first, but if pure race, then Acme might be paid first

PART 10 _REMEDIES_

REMEDIES TABLE OF CONTENTS

INTRODUCTION TO REMEDIES

Remedies is the second most frequently tested essay subject. A remedies essay question will always arise within the context of a fact pattern involving another substantive area of law. For this reason, remedies questions are usually, but not always, crossover questions. A crossover question is one that tests two or more substantive areas of law within one essay fact pattern. Remedies questions typically cross over with contracts, torts, or real property, though any subject on the California bar exam is eligible and they've recently crossed over Remedies with Constitutional Law and Business Associations so any subject is fair game.

As for the substance of remedies, though they are not identical, there are many overlapping concepts between the remedies available in tort, contract, and property. Consequently, remedies can be organized in a variety of ways for the purposes of memorization and recall. Remedies is organized here by the underlying subject (torts, contracts, property), but it is equally valid to organize the material by listing all legal remedies and then all equitable remedies, or by the underlying cause of action, or some other way. The best way to organize the material is the way that makes the most sense to you. It is not important how the material is organized, just that it is done in a way that it is easy to recall and is memorable so that issues aren't missed and rules are recalled accurately.

When faced with a remedies essay question, the first step is to identify the underlying substantive area of law and that the defendant in question is responsible. A plaintiff can't obtain a remedy against a random person who didn't do anything actionable to the plaintiff, such as commit a tort or breach a contract or violate some law. Further, there can't be a discussion of remedies without first identifying if there is an underlying cause of action giving rise to the remedy. If there isn't an underlying cause of action that would support a remedy, identify the remedy the plaintiff would seek (if there were an underlying cause of action) and conclude that the relief sought won't be granted.

Pay careful attention to the call of the question and only answer the question asked. The call can ask about remedies directly or use other phrases such as "relief" or "liabilities" or ask about a particular type of remedy. The calls often can ask about "rights and remedies" or "rights and liabilities." These types of calls are directing you to analyze the underlying substantive issue (the right) as well as the remedy. The depth of discussion on the underlying cause of action depends entirely on the call of the question. If the question is asking for a discussion of the underlying cause of action be sure to go through your checklist for that subject, in addition to your remedies checklist, to issue spot the exam. As always, carefully read each sentence of the fact pattern to determine if the facts contained therein give rise to a legal issue or can be used to bolster the factual analysis of a rule.

Unless directed otherwise by the call of the question, legal remedies should be discussed first, then equitable remedies. First discuss the legal remedy of all available types of money damages, how they are measured, and use the facts and factual inferences available to make calculations. Next, discuss any appropriate legal restitutionary remedies, including money restitution, replevin, or ejectment. Next, discuss any appropriate equitable restitutionary remedies, including constructive trust or equitable lien in tort, and/or rescission or reformation in contract. Lastly, address the equitable remedy of the various types of injunction.

To help with issue spotting, we have included a chart at the end of the chapter that aligns the most commonly tested remedies with their corresponding underlying substantive causes of action.

ISSUES CHECKLIST

TORTS REMEDIES

Damages
Compensatory
  Causal
  Foreseeable
  Certain
  Unavoidable
Nominal
Punitive

Legal restitution
Money
Replevin (chattel)
Ejectment (real property)

Equitable restitution
Constructive trust
Equitable lien

Injunction (equity)
TRO
Preliminary injunction
Permanent injunction

Defenses
Laches
Unclean hands
Free speech/religion
Ineffective defenses

PROPERTY REMEDIES

Encroachments
Waste

CONTRACTS REMEDIES

Damages
Expectation
  Causal
  Foreseeable
  Certain
  Unavoidable
Consequential
  Causal
  Foreseeable
  Certain
  Unavoidable
Incidental
Reliance
Liquidated
Nominal
No punitives

Legal restitution
Money (quasi-contract)
Replevin (chattel)
Ejectment (real property)

Equitable remedies
Rescission
Reformation

Injunction (equity)
TRO
Preliminary injunction
Specific performance

Defenses (equitable)
Laches
Unclean hands
Contract defenses

MEMORIZATION ATTACK SHEET

LEGAL DAMAGES — TORT

◆ **Compensatory**
  • General (all P's)
  • Special (this P)
  • Past and future

◆ **Compensatory limitation**
  • Causation
  • Foreseeable
  • Certainty
  • Unavoidable

◆ **Nominal**
◆ **Punitive**

LEGAL RESTITUTION — TORT

◆ **Money restitution**
  • Benefit to D
◆ **Replevin** (chattel)
◆ **Ejectment** (real property)

EQUITABLE RESTITUTION — TORT

◆ **Constructive trust**
  • Wrongful act
  • Legal title to convey
  • Inadequate legal remedy
    ♦ Damages too speculative
    ♦ Insolvent D
    ♦ Replevin not available
    ♦ Property is unique
  • Property can be traced
    ♦ P gets benefit of value increase
    ♦ Property must be solely traceable
    ♦ Lowest intermediate balance rule
  • Third-party priority
    ♦ BFP over P
    ♦ P over unsecured creditors
  • No deficiency judgment

◆ **Equitable lien**
  • Wrongful act
  • Legal title for security interest
  • Inadequate legal remedy
    ♦ Damages too speculative
    ♦ Insolvent D
    ♦ Replevin not available
    ♦ Property is unique
  • Property can be traced
    ♦ Okay if not solely traceable
    ♦ Lowest intermediate balance rule
  • Third-party priority
    ♦ BFP over P
    ♦ P over unsecured creditors
  • Deficiency jgmt. allowed

INJUNCTION — TORT (EQUITY)

◆ **TROs**
  • Irreparable harm
  • Likelihood success on merits
  • Inadequate legal remedy
    ♦ Damages too speculative
    ♦ Inadequate because health/safety issue
    ♦ Insolvent D
    ♦ Replevin, ejectment unavailable
    ♦ Multiplicity of suits
    ♦ Prospective tort
    ♦ Property is unique
  • Balancing of hardships/public int.
  • No defenses
    ♦ Laches
    ♦ Unclean hands
    ♦ Free speech/religion

◆ **Preliminary injunction**
- Irreparable harm
- Likelihood of success on merits
- Inadequate legal remedy
  - ◆ Damages too speculative
  - ◆ Inadequate because health/safety issue
  - ◆ Insolvent D
  - ◆ Replevin, ejectment unavailable
  - ◆ Multiplicity of suits
  - ◆ Prospective tort
  - ◆ Property is unique
- Balancing of hardships
- No defenses
  - ◆ Laches
  - ◆ Unclean hands
  - ◆ Free speech/religion

◆ **Permanent injunction**
- Inadequate legal remedy
  - ◆ Damages too speculative
  - ◆ Inadequate because health/safety issue
  - ◆ Insolvent D
  - ◆ Replevin, ejectment unavailable
  - ◆ Multiplicity of suits
  - ◆ Prospective tort
  - ◆ Property is unique
- Property/protectable interest
- Feasibility of enforcing
- Balancing of hardships/public int.
- No defenses
  - ◆ Laches
  - ◆ Unclean hands
  - ◆ Free speech/religion

LEGAL DAMAGES—CONTRACT

◆ **Types of legal damages**
- Expectation
  - ◆ **Damage limitations**
    - Causation
    - Foreseeable
    - Certainty
    - Unavoidable
    - Liquidated clause controls
  - ◆ Consequential
    - Causation
    - Foreseeable
    - Certainty
    - Unavoidable
  - ◆ Incidental
  - ◆ Reliance
  - ◆ Liquidated damages
    - Difficult to calculate
    - Reasonable relationship
  - ◆ Nominal damages
  - ◆ No punitives in contract

LEGAL RESTITUTION—CONTRACT

◆ **Quasi-contract** (money restitution)
- Benefit to D
◆ **Replevin** (chattel)
◆ **Ejectment** (real property)

EQUIT. REMEDIES—CONTRACT

◆ **Rescission** (invalidate K)
◆ **Reformation** (rewrite the K)
◆ **Equitable defenses**
- Laches
- Unclean hands

INJUNCTION—CONTRACT (EQUITY)

◆ **TROs** (see tort injunction)
◆ **Preliminary injunction** (see tort injunction)
◆ **Specific performance**
- Contract is valid
- Contract conditions satisfied
- Inadequate legal remedy
  - ◆ Damages too speculative
  - ◆ Inadequate because health/safety issue
  - ◆ Insolvent D
  - ◆ Replevin or ejectment unavailable
  - ◆ Multiplicity of suits
  - ◆ Property is unique
- Mutuality of performance
- Feasibility of enforcement
- No defenses
  - ◆ Laches
  - ◆ Unclean hands
  - ◆ Defense to contract

REMEDIES RULE OUTLINE

I. FUNDAMENTAL CONCEPTS

    A. **Remedy at law** (legal remedy) is **money damages** to compensate a plaintiff for a loss and it is the remedy preferred by the courts.

    B. Restitution remedies **prevent the unjust enrichment** of the defendant. Restitutionary remedies can be legal (money or return of property) or equitable.

    C. **Remedy in equity** is not the preferred remedy. One must establish that the **remedy at law is inadequate** to receive an equitable remedy (these can be provisional or permanent).

    D. **Election of remedy:** Plaintiff may choose one of several available recoveries in satisfaction of a *single loss*. This doctrine prevents double recovery, but does not limit complementary remedies (i.e., plaintiff in a nuisance claim can be awarded both an injunction against future harm and damages for losses that have already occurred as those are not a "single" loss).

> **Exam tip:** It is important to understand the difference between "legal" and "equitable" remedies and have a mini-issues checklist in mind for both categories because the call of the question might only ask about one or the other and you need to know which remedies fall into each category to properly answer the call. Similarly, you need to understand which remedies are "provisional" and which remedies are "permanent," because sometimes the calls ask about those and you need to distinguish them to properly answer the call.

II. TORTS REMEDIES

    A. **Legal damages:** Damages are a legal remedy **awarded to make a plaintiff whole**. There are various measures of damages available as a remedy for tort.

        1. **Compensatory damages** are awarded to compensate the plaintiff for injury or loss. They are measured by the monetary value of the plaintiff's harm.

            a. **Potential issues that can limit compensatory damages:**

                1. **Causation:** Damages must be caused by the tortious act. This is actual **"but-for" causation** analysis.

                2. **Foreseeable:** Damages must be foreseeable by a reasonable person **at the time of the tortious act**. This is standard proximate cause foreseeability analysis.

                3. **Certainty:** Damages must be capable of being **calculated with certainty** and not be overly speculative.

> **Exam tip:** Certainty is usually an issue when the damages are for future losses that are difficult to ascertain, such as damages due to an ongoing nuisance.

                4. **Unavoidable:** A plaintiff has a duty to take **reasonable steps to mitigate their losses.** The avoidable consequences doctrine limits damages to those that could not reasonably have been avoided.

> **Exam tip:** The list above is a mini-checklist of issues to consider when analyzing tort damages. These concepts have the **potential to limit an award of damages,** and if any facts in an essay question raise any of these topics as an issue, they should be thoroughly analyzed. However, if no facts are available that raise the issues, they need not be discussed. The limitations on damages are heavily tested and analysis of those issues are often where your points are earned.

b. **Types of damages:** There are two different types of compensatory damages in tort.
   1. **General damages** are noneconomic losses directly attributable to the tort that **all plaintiffs** would have because they **flow as a natural result** of the tort (e.g., pain and suffering, disfigurement, etc.).
   2. **Special damages** are economic losses directly attributable to the tort that some plaintiffs may have and are **unique to each specific plaintiff** (e.g., medical bills, lost wages, etc.).
c. **Past and future damages**. When calculating general and special damages, one must account for both past and future damages, subject to the rules limiting damages noted above.
   1. **Past losses:** A plaintiff can recover for past losses.
   2. **Future losses:** A plaintiff can recover for anticipated future losses, so long as they can be **calculated with reasonable certainty**.
d. **Measure of damages in tort** for compensatory damages varies depending on the tort but attempt to compensate for the value of the plaintiff's harm.
   1. The measure of damages is determined **at the time of the loss**.
   2. The measure of damages depends on the tort and type of damages.
      a. **Conversion:** The **fair market value** which can be determined by the market rate or the amount another person is willing to pay for the item.
      b. **Trespass to chattels/land:** The **cost to repair** if economically feasible (for partially destroyed items/land) or the **rental value of an item** for the time of deprivation.
      c. **Other torts (i.e., battery, negligence, nuisance, fraud etc.):** Amount of medical expenses, amount of lost income or earning capacity, pain and suffering (amounts often limited by jurisdiction), future medical expenses (difficult to ascertain but rely on expected life expectancy and care needed), diminution in value to land, and for fraud compensatory damages can be measured by out of pocket losses or benefit of the bargain.
      d. **Loss of consortium/wrongful death:** Amount other spouse contributed/living spouse would have received (household contributions, wages, etc.).
2. **Pure economic loss** is not recoverable for most torts, absent a showing of property loss or personal injury.
   a. **Exception:** The tort of **intentional interference with business relations** does allow for pure economic loss recovery.
3. **Nominal damages** are awarded where the plaintiff's rights have been violated but the plaintiff sustained no loss. They serve to vindicate plaintiff's rights.
4. **Punitive damages** are awarded where the defendant has displayed willful, wanton, or malicious tortious conduct. They are measured by an appropriate punishment for defendant's misconduct. Punitive damages are only awarded if:
   a. **Actual damages are awarded** (compensatory damages, nominal damages, or restitutionary damages); and
   b. **Culpability** of defendant is greater than "negligence"; and
   c. **They are relatively proportionate** to actual damages. (Typically, a single-digit multiplier of actual damages — e.g., a maximum of nine times actual damages.)

> **Exam tip:** When issue spotting the exam, be sure to look for facts that may raise the **four potential limitations** on compensatory damages: causation, foreseeability, certainty, and duty to mitigate. Often only one will really be at issue while the others will be fairly straightforward. In addition, there are **different measures of damages** that can be suffered by a plaintiff, so consider whether the plaintiff is entitled to compensatory damages — either general or special — nominal damages, or punitive damages. Lastly, use the facts available to **make damages calculations,** if possible.

B. **Legal restitution** is appropriate where the **defendant has derived a benefit**, or been *unjustly* enriched, and it would be **unfair to allow the defendant to keep that benefit** without compensating the plaintiff, or where the plaintiff wants their property back. The goal of restitution is to **prevent *unjust* enrichment**. It is measured by the benefit received by the defendant.

1. **Money restitution** is a legal remedy where the plaintiff is awarded the **monetary value of the benefit received** by the defendant. It is measured by the reasonable value or profits from the defendant's gain.

   a. **Election of remedies:** A plaintiff can elect to recover compensatory damages or money restitution, but not both.

   > **Exam tip:** A fact pattern indicating the **defendant has benefited from plaintiff's loss** will often trigger a discussion of restitution. A plaintiff can recover either compensatory damages or money restitution, but not both. However, on an essay answer both should be discussed, if appropriate, to demonstrate the difference between the two concepts since the rules and calculations will be different as one focuses on plaintiff's loss and the other focuses on defendant's gain.

2. Replevin allows the **recovery**, before trial, of a specific **chattel** (personal property) **wrongfully taken** from plaintiff, who has the **right to possession**.

   a. The property is ordered returned and the plaintiff can receive damages for the time they were deprived of their chattel.

3. **Ejectment** is used to **recover** specific **real property** from which a plaintiff who has the **right to possession** was **wrongfully excluded**.

   b. The property is ordered returned and the plaintiff can receive damages for the time they were deprived of their real property.

C. **Equitable restitution** is only available when the **remedy at law** (i.e., money damages) is **inadequate**. The goal of any equitable remedy is to **prevent unjust enrichment**.

1. **Constructive trust** is a legal fiction created by a court to **compel the defendant to convey *title*** to **unjustly retained specific property to the plaintiff** and restores the property to the plaintiff that has been wrongfully acquired by the defendant. A constructive trust requires:

   a. A **wrongful act** has led to the retention of property from its rightful owner (e.g., embezzlement, fraud, theft, conversion, etc.—note even an innocent mistake or breach of fiduciary duties can be a wrongful act).

   b. **Defendant has legal title to *convey*:** Since the court will order the defendant to **reconvey title** to the plaintiff, the defendant must have wrongfully obtained legal title to the property; mere possession is not enough.

      1. **Caveat: A thief** is deemed to have **legal title to wrongfully obtained cash** in their possession, but **not legal title** to wrongfully obtained **property**.

   > **Issue spotting tip:** If defendant does not have legal title (i.e., they stole a painting), then consider replevin as a remedy.

   c. **Inadequate legal remedy:** The remedy at law, typically money damages, must be inadequate. There are several reasons the legal remedy can be inadequate:

      1. **Money damages are too speculative** to calculate with certainty.
      2. **Insolvent defendant** such that any damages award is worthless.
      3. **Replevin is unavailable** because the property has been sold and thus can't be ordered returned to plaintiff.
      4. **Property is unique** so money damages are inadequate to compensate for the loss of that property.
         a. **Real property is always unique** since no two properties are exactly the same.
         b. **Personal property is not unique, except** if it is one-of-a-kind or very rare, or if the item has special personal significance to the plaintiff.

> **Exam tip:** Inadequate legal remedy is an element in many remedies issues. In an essay, always discuss all of the reasons the legal remedy is inadequate under the fact pattern given.

d. **Property can be traced:** A constructive trust can apply to specific property acquired by a wrongdoer that is traceable to the wrongful behavior. If the improperly retained property has changed form because it was sold or exchanged for new property, the rightful owner can "trace" and obtain a constructive trust for the new property (e.g., embezzled funds could be traced to a bank account or to real property purchased with them).

   1. **Plaintiff receives the benefit of any increase in property value** accrued by the passage of time or the change in property form because it would be unfair to allow the wrongdoer to receive the benefit of any gain.

   2. **Property must be *solely* traceable to current form** and not commingled with other property because title to the new property will be given to the plaintiff (e.g., embezzled funds used to remodel an existing home aren't solely traceable so a constructive trust won't be imposed).

   3. **Exception: Lowest intermediate balance rule applies to commingled funds.** When the wrongdoer commingles wrongfully obtained funds with their own funds in a single account, use the following rules to determine if the wrongfully obtained funds can be traced to the money remaining in the account to support a constructive trust.

      a. **First in, first out** approach presumes the first money put into the account would be presumed the first money withdrawn.

      b. **Investor/spender fiction** presumes a defendant **invests/spends their own money first**, so any investments/expenditures are deemed to come from the wrongdoer's own funds first, and any balance is subject to the constructive trust.

      c. **Modernly,** many courts allow plaintiff the ability to **elect tracing** of withdrawn funds to either the wrongdoer or wrongfully obtained property where they may yield the **most advantageous** result.

      d. **Once traced proceeds are withdrawn, they are gone.** If the wrongfully obtained funds can't be traced to a new piece of property, the funds are gone and the plaintiff cannot get a constructive trust.

e. **Priority of plaintiff over third parties** with an interest

   1. **Bona fide purchaser (BFP) with legal title prevails over plaintiff.** (A BFP is one who **took for value without notice** of the facts giving rise to the potential constructive trust.)

      a. **Secured creditors** (i.e., mortgage and car lenders) **are BFPs.**

   2. **Plaintiff prevails over unsecured creditors** (i.e., credit card issuers) since plaintiff is regaining their own property, which is a higher priority.

f. **No deficiency judgment** will be awarded for any shortfall. The plaintiff will receive title to the property and be precluded from obtaining a deficiency judgment for any shortfall.

2. **Equitable lien** creates a *security interest* in property held by the defendant. This is a legal fiction implied by the court where the **property acts as collateral for the money owed to the plaintiff.** An equitable lien is similar to a constructive trust, except property can be traced to commingled funds with an equitable lien and a deficiency judgment is permitted. An equitable lien requires:

   a. A **wrongful act** has led to the retention of property from its rightful owner (e.g., embezzlement, fraud, theft, conversion, etc. — note even an innocent mistake or breach of fiduciary duties can be a wrongful act).

   b. **Legal title:** Since the court will order a **security interest** in the property itself, the defendant must have wrongfully obtained legal title to the property; mere possession is not enough.

      1. **Caveat: A thief** is deemed to have **legal title** to wrongfully obtained **cash** in their possession, but **not legal title** to wrongfully obtained **property.**

c. **Inadequate legal remedy:** The remedy at law, typically money damages, must be inadequate. There are several reasons the legal remedy can be inadequate:
   1. **Money damages are too speculative** to calculate with certainty.
   2. **Insolvent defendant,** such that any damages award is worthless.
   3. **Replevin is unavailable** because the property has been sold and thus can't be ordered returned to plaintiff.
   4. **Property is unique** so money damages are inadequate to compensate for the loss of that property.
      a. **Real property is always unique** since no two properties are exactly the same.
      b. **Personal property is not unique, except** if it is one-of-a-kind or very rare, or if the item has special personal significance to the plaintiff.
d. **Property can be traced:** An equitable lien can apply to specific property acquired by a wrongdoer that is traceable to the wrongful behavior. If the improperly retained property has changed form because it was sold or exchanged for new property, the rightful owner can "trace" and obtain an equitable lien on the new property (e.g., funds used to remodel existing real property could be traced to embezzled funds).
   1. **Property *need not be solely traceable* to current form:** *Unlike a constructive trust,* with an equitable lien it is acceptable to trace the plaintiff's property to a different piece of property even if the two are commingled and the plaintiff's property (or money traced from that property) was used to improve another piece of property properly owned by the defendant. The plaintiff can obtain an equitable lien on the commingled property in the amount of the debt.
   2. **Lowest intermediate balance rule applies to commingled funds.** When the wrongdoer commingles wrongfully obtained funds with their own funds in a single account, use the following rules to determine if the wrongfully obtained funds can be traced to the money remaining in the account to support an equitable lien.
      a. **First in, first out** approach presumes the first money put into the account would be presumed the first money withdrawn.
      b. **Investor/spender fiction** presumes a defendant **invests/spends their own money first**, so any investments/expenditures are deemed to come from the wrongdoer's own funds first, and any balance is subject to the equitable lien.
      c. **Modernly,** many courts allow plaintiff the ability to **elect tracing** of withdrawn funds to either the wrongdoer or wrongfully obtained property where they may yield the **most advantageous** result.
      d. **Once traced proceeds are withdrawn, they are gone.** If the wrongfully obtained funds can't be traced to a new piece of property, the funds are gone and the plaintiff cannot get an equitable lien.
e. **Priority of the plaintiff over third parties** with an interest
   1. **Bona fide purchaser (BFP) with legal title prevails over plaintiff.** (A BFP is one who took for **value** and **without notice** of the facts giving rise to the potential equitable lien.)
      a. **Secured creditors** (i.e., mortgage and car lenders) **are BFPs.**
   2. **Plaintiff prevails over unsecured creditors** (i.e., credit card issuers) since plaintiff is regaining their own property, which is a higher priority.
f. **Deficiency judgments are allowed.** *Unlike a constructive trust,* an equitable lienholder can also obtain a deficiency judgment for any shortfall. Thus, an equitable lien is the preferred remedy when the property has **decreased in value** because of the passage of time, or a change in property form.

> **Exam tip:** Unless instructed otherwise, usually on an essay you must **analyze both** constructive trust and an equitable lien and use the facts to explain which of the two is the better remedy to use under the circumstances and why. **Constructive trust is better when the value of the wrongfully acquired property goes up** (because plaintiff will receive the benefit of the increase in value to prevent defendant's unjust enrichment). **Equitable lien is better when the value of the wrongfully acquired property goes down** (because plaintiff can still get a deficiency judgment for the difference), or when **property can't be solely traced** to its current form.

D. Injunction is an **equitable remedy** where the court **orders one to perform an act** (affirmative or mandatory injunction) **or stop performing an act** (negative injunction). There are three types, with many similar requirements:

1. **Temporary restraining orders (TROs)** are designed to **preserve the status quo** for a **short time** pending further litigation regarding a preliminary injunction. TROs are granted for only a short time, typically ten days (fourteen under federal rules but some states permit longer TROs). **Notice** is required, but a TRO **can be obtained ex parte** in exceptional circumstances, such as an emergency or when notice would result in the very harm one is trying to avoid. A TRO in most jurisdictions requires:

   a. **Irreparable harm** during **waiting time** if not granted (this is the time waiting for the preliminary injunction hearing). The harm must be actual and imminent.

   b. **Likelihood of success on the merits** of the underlying claim.

   > **Exam tip:** Often you are required to analyze the underlying claim (i.e., nuisance, etc.), which makes remedies most frequently tested in a crossover essay.

   c. **Inadequate legal remedy:**
      1. **Money damages are too speculative** to calculate with certainty.
      2. **Money damages may be inadequate** to compensate for the potential loss. This is especially true where there is a health or safety concern.
      3. **Insolvent defendant,** such that any damages award is worthless.
      4. **Replevin or ejectment is unavailable.**
      5. **Multiplicity of suits:** An ongoing wrong — for example, an ongoing nuisance for toxic waste dumping or continuing trespass — would lead to a multiplicity of suits by the same litigants over the same issue if not resolved by an injunction.
      6. **Prospective tort** where the tort has not occurred yet but is expected to occur (e.g., imminent pollution).
      7. **Property is unique,** so money damages are inadequate to compensate for the loss of that property.
         a. **Real property is always unique** since no two properties are exactly the same.
         b. **Personal property is not unique, except** if it is one-of-a-kind or very rare, or if the item has special personal significance to the plaintiff.

   d. **Balancing of hardships** must favor plaintiff. The court will weigh the **hardship to the plaintiff if the TRO is denied** against the **hardship to the defendant if the TRO is granted**. The court will also consider the following factors:
      1. A **large disparity in hardships** weighs in favor of the more severely impacted party.
      2. **Willful misconduct** weighs very heavily against the wrongdoer.
      3. **Public interest:** The hardship to the public and/or any public benefit should be factored into the analysis. For example, where a toxic polluter is also the region's biggest employer, the public would have an interest in both sides.

> **Exam tip:** There is a lot of factual analysis (and points to earn) when **balancing the hardships.** It is important to use **all of the facts** and factual inferences, present **both sides,** consider the public interest, come to a conclusion, and **explain why** the hardships balance in the favor of the party you conclude should prevail. There are times when the hardships are not balanced in a TRO but you can easily discuss these in a TRO and then supra them in your preliminary injunction analysis. Note that some jurisdictions separate out the public interest as its own element and some jurisdictions combine the irreparable harm/inadequate legal remedy since they are really two sides of the same coin (i.e., if money can't fix the problem resulting in an inadequate legal remedy, then often there is also irreparable harm if the harm isn't stopped). The key is discussing all "pieces" of this puzzle to earn maximum points.

   e. **No defenses** are available. Laches and unclean hands are equitable defenses.
      1. **Laches** provides a defense when the plaintiff has **unreasonably delayed,** resulting in **prejudice to the defendant**.
      2. **Unclean hands** provides a defense when a plaintiff has conducted themself **unfairly in the transaction in dispute**.
      3. **Free speech or freedom of religion** could be a possible defense to an injunction for protestors or others and they will likely try to argue that any injunction is a prior restraint. (This is how the examiners cross over constitutional law with remedies).
      4. **Ineffective defenses** that may be raised if the facts give rise to them:
         a. **Coming to the nuisance:** Modernly, this is one of several elements used to determine if there is a nuisance at all and does not provide an effective defense to a nuisance action.
         b. **Sale to a bona fide purchaser** is not an effective defense to the tort of conversion (where one is trying to get their personal property returned by a permanent injunction). However, sale to a BFP is a valid defense in a contract action.

> **Exam tip: Injunction defenses** are frequently tested. Analyze laches whenever a time delay is stated in the facts. Analyze unclean hands whenever one party expressed any idea/wish/desire to the other party that was later ignored. Often, after analyzing, the conclusion is that the defense is ineffective.

> **Memorization tip:** For TROs use the mnemonic **I**rish **L**ads **I**nhale **B**eef **P**ies in **D**ublin. Irish for **I**rreparable harm; Lads for **L**ikelihood of success on the merits; Inhale for **I**nadequate legal remedy; Beef Pies for **B**alancing hardships (and **P**ublic interest reminder); Dublin for no **D**efenses.

2. **Preliminary injunctions** are designed to **preserve the status quo pending a full trial** on the merits. A preliminary injunction is harder to obtain than a TRO, but it is easier to obtain than a permanent injunction. The elements for a preliminary injunction are the same as those required for the TRO, but a preliminary injunction can never be ex parte (so notice is always required) and plaintiff must post a bond. The main difference is the timing and purpose.

> **Memorization tip:** Use the same memorization tip as with TROs since the elements are the same: **I**rish **L**ads **I**nhale **B**eef **P**ies in **D**ublin. If you did not analyze the hardships in the TRO, make sure you do so here.

> **Exam tip:** To help guide your organization and focus your analysis, first identify what the party wants to obtain from the TRO or preliminary injunction (e.g., to prevent a car from being shipped to another, to stop a building from being built, etc.). Once you determine what the party wants it is easier to decide which remedy would be best to accomplish their goal. When you aren't certain whether the plaintiff should seek a TRO or a preliminary injunction mention both since the elements are the same. Fully analyze all elements once. Then, identify the difference between the two remedies and when each one will likely be sought and why (or perhaps both should be sought).

> **Issue spotting tip:** You may see TROs and Preliminary injunctions also called interlocutory orders or provisional remedies in the essay question calls.

3. **Permanent injunction** is where a court orders one to **perform an act or stop performing an act** after holding a full trial on the merits. A permanent injunction requires the following:
   a. **Inadequate legal remedy:**
      1. **Money damages are too speculative** to calculate with certainty.
      2. **Money damages may be inadequate** to compensate for the potential loss. This is especially true where there is a health or safety concern.
      3. **Insolvent defendant,** such that any damages award is worthless.
      4. **Replevin or ejectment is unavailable.**
      5. **Multiplicity of suits:** An ongoing wrong—for example, an ongoing nuisance for toxic waste dumping or continuing trespass—would lead to a multiplicity of suits by the same litigants over the same issue if not resolved by an injunction.
      6. **Prospective tort** where the tort has not occurred yet but is expected to occur (e.g., imminent pollution).
      7. **Property is unique,** so money damages are inadequate to compensate for the loss of that property.
         a. **Real property is always unique** since no two properties are exactly the same.
         b. **Personal property is not unique, except** if it is one-of-a-kind or very rare, or if the item has special personal significance to the plaintiff.
   b. **Property/protectable interest:** The requirement of a protectable property interest is a historical one and not an element analyzed in all jurisdictions. California does not require a property right, and **modernly, invasions of personal rights** can support an injunction. Modernly, in jurisdictions that require this, they look at whether the plaintiff had a right violated (similar to likelihood of success on the merits for a preliminary injunction but now it has been determined that they did succeed on the merits and thus it is equivalent to an irreparable injury if not remedied).
   c. **Feasibility of enforcement:** The injunction cannot be too difficult for the court to enforce. (Note this is not an element considered in federal courts, but it is good to discuss it otherwise.)
      1. **Negative injunctions** are **easier to enforce** because of the court's power to order contempt for noncompliance.
      2. **Affirmative injunctions** are **more difficult to enforce.**
         a. **Series of acts** over a period of time can be **more difficult to enforce** than one required act.
         b. **Act requiring taste, judgment, or skill** is **difficult to enforce** because of the difficulty in determining if the act has been properly performed.
      3. **Jurisdictional issues** cause enforcement problems where the court would have to supervise events **out of their jurisdiction** or assert **control over nonparties** to the litigation (i.e., injunction sought over a project in the middle of the ocean).

d. **Balancing of hardships** must favor plaintiff. The court will weigh the **hardship to plaintiff if the injunction is denied** against the **hardship to defendant if the injunction is granted**. The court will also consider the following factors:
1. A **large disparity in hardships** weighs in favor of the more severely impacted party.
2. **Willful misconduct** weighs very heavily against the wrongdoer.
3. **Public interest:** The hardship to the public and/or any public benefit should be factored into the analysis. (Note in federal courts, this is a separate element.)

e. **No defenses.** Laches and unclean hands are equitable defenses.
1. **Laches** provides a defense when the plaintiff has **unreasonably delayed**, resulting in **prejudice to the defendant**.
2. **Unclean hands** provides a defense when a plaintiff has conducted themself **unfairly in the transaction in dispute**.
3. **Free speech or freedom of religion** could be a possible defense to an injunction for protestors or others and they will likely try to argue that any injunction is a prior restraint. (This is how the examiners cross over constitutional law with remedies.)
4. **Ineffective defenses** that may be raised:
   a. **Coming to the nuisance:** Modernly, this is one of several elements used to determine if there is a nuisance at all and **does not provide an effective defense** to a nuisance action.
   b. **Sale to a bona fide purchaser** is not an effective defense to the tort of conversion (where one is trying to get their personal property returned by a permanent injunction) because a converter does not obtain lawful title. However, sale to a BFP is a valid defense in a contract action.

> **Memorization tip:** Use the mnemonic **I Pray For Big Desserts** to memorize the five essential elements of a permanent injunction: **I**nadequate legal remedy, **P**roperty/protectable interest, **F**easibility of enforcement, **B**alancing of hardships, and no **D**efenses.

> **TRO/Injunction Fact Triggers:**
>
> - P seeks to prevent a car from shipping out of the country
> - P seeks to prevent a person from selling an item (e.g., car, rare tomatoes, lakefront property) to another person
> - P seeks to prevent a company from selling a product to someone else
> - P seeks to prevent construction of buildings or structures (e.g., water dam)
> - P seeks to prevent an alleged nuisance
> - P seeks to prevent a competitor business from operating
> - P seeks to prevent a rehab center from opening in their neighborhood
> - P seeks to prevent the sale of land to another
> - P seeks to stop someone from cutting down 100-year-old trees

III. **CONTRACTS REMEDIES**
   A. **Legal damages** are applicable where the parties have a contract, the defendant is in breach, and the plaintiff has been injured by the breach and wants money to compensate for the loss.
   1. **Types of damages**
      a. **Expectation damages** (compensatory damages) in contract compensate plaintiff for the **value of the benefit plaintiff expected to receive** from the contract. They are measured by the plaintiff's injury stemming from the contract nonperformance (the goal is to put the plaintiff in the position they would have been in had the contract been performed).

> *1.* **Potential limitations on contract expectation** (and consequential) **damages**
>> *a.* **Causation:** Damages must be caused by the contract breach.
>> *b.* **Foreseeable:** Damages must be foreseeable to a **reasonable person** at the time of **contract formation**.
>> *c.* **Certainty:** Damages must be capable of being **calculated with certainty** and not be overly speculative. (Past losses are often easier to calculate than future losses. It is often difficult to calculate with certainty future losses, particularly for a new business.)
>> *d.* **Unavoidable:** A plaintiff has a **duty to take reasonable steps to mitigate their losses;** in a contract this usually involves **"cover."** The avoidable consequences doctrine limits damages to those that could not reasonably have been avoided.
>> *e.* A **liquidated damages** clause that is valid will control and be the **only measure of damages allowed** for breach of the underlying contract.

Exam tip: Consider the limitations as a mini-checklist of issues to consider when analyzing contract **expectation (compensatory) and consequential damages.** These concepts have the **potential to** reduce or eliminate **an award of damages,** and if any facts in an essay question raise any of these topics as an issue, they should be thoroughly analyzed before calculating damages.

> *2.* Formulas for UCC expectation damages are located in the Contracts chapter, section VII.A.3.
> *b.* **Consequential damages** seek to compensate for damages that are a **direct and foreseeable consequence** of the contract not being performed and are found *in addition* to expectation **damages.**
>> *1.* **Foreseeable at time of contracting:** There must be communication of information such that the consequential damages are foreseeable to the defendant at the time of contracting.
>> *2.* **The potential limitations on contract damages** (causation, foreseeable, certainty, and unavoidable) noted immediately above in section (a) also **apply to consequential damages.**
>> *3.* Examples include loss of rental income, lost sales, expenses to look for another job, etc.
> *c.* **Incidental damages** include those *costs* **reasonably incurred** when the other party is in breach, such as damages incurred by a seller in reselling goods resulting from a buyer's breach (e.g., storage, transportation costs).
> *d.* **Reliance damages** seek to put the **plaintiff in the same position** they would have been in had the contract never been made. Reliance damages are measured by the losses incurred as a result of reasonable reliance on the contract. These can be awarded **in place of expectation damages** when damages are difficult to calculate, such as lost profits for a new business.

Exam tip: Reliance damages contemplate reliant actions by plaintiff *before the breach* and after the contract was formed whereas **consequential** damages contemplate damages caused *by the breach*.

> *e.* **Liquidated damages** are stipulated to in a clause in the contract. A valid liquidated damages clause **controls** a damages award and will be the measure of damages when:
>> *1.* Damages are **difficult to calculate**; and
>> *2.* The stipulated amount in the liquidated damages clause bears a **reasonable relationship to the anticipated loss and is not a penalty.**

f. **Nominal damages** serve as a declaration that the contract has been breached, but plaintiff has sustained **no loss**. They serve to vindicate the plaintiff's rights.

g. **Punitive damages are *not* awarded in contract**, unless the misconduct rises to the level of an independent tort, such as fraud.

> **Exam tip:** When calculating contract damages take the **plaintiff's point of view** and determine the value of the contract to the plaintiff had the contract been properly performed. Consider any applicable limitation on damages. If the fact pattern provides numbers, use them to **calculate the damages**. If the fact pattern does not provide numbers, use descriptors, such as "lost wages" to explain the potential damages available. **Include all possible damages** in your calculations.

B. **Legal restitution** is appropriate where the **defendant has derived a benefit**, or been *unjustly* enriched, and it would be **unfair** to allow the defendant to keep that benefit without compensating the plaintiff, or where the plaintiff wants their property back. The **goal of restitution is to prevent *unjust* enrichment**. It is measured by the benefit received by the defendant.

1. **Quasi-contract** (money restitution) applies where there is no legally binding contract, but the **defendant has derived a benefit** and **fairness requires payment** to the plaintiff. It is measured by the **value of the benefit unjustly retained**. Quasi-contract can arise three ways:

   a. **No attempt to contract:** The plaintiff can recover the value of the benefit unjustly retained by defendant (e.g., emergency services).

   b. **Unenforceable contract:** The plaintiff can recover the value of the benefit unjustly retained by defendant (e.g., contract is illegal, SOF failure, etc.).

   c. **Breached contract**, but recovery depends on status of plaintiff.

      1. **Plaintiff is nonbreacher:** Plaintiff can recover the **value of the benefit conferred**, or the plaintiff can get their property back.

         a. The **majority rule** allows for recovery in **excess of the contract price** if that is the benefit conferred. The **minority rule** limits recovery to the **contract price** even if defendant's benefit was higher.

      2. **Plaintiff is in breach:** The traditional majority rule provides for no recovery. The modern trend allows for recovery with limits not to exceed the contract price less damages caused by plaintiff's breach.

2. **Replevin** allows the **recovery**, before trial, of a specific **chattel** (personal property) **wrongfully taken** from the plaintiff, who has the **right to possession**.

   a. The property is ordered returned and the plaintiff can receive damages for the time they were deprived of their chattel.

   b. Most jurisdictions require plaintiff to post a **replevin bond** in case the court rules in favor of defendant, in which case plaintiff will also be required to pay defendant's legal fees and costs.

3. **Ejectment** is used to **recover** specific **real property** from which the plaintiff, who has the **right to possession**, was **wrongfully excluded**.

   a. The property is ordered returned and the plaintiff can receive damages for the time they were deprived of their real property.

> **Exam tip:** Unlike equitable restitution, legal restitution does not depend on the inadequacy of alternative remedies and plaintiff can request a jury trial with legal restitution.

C. **Equitable remedies** are only available when the **remedy at law** (i.e., money damages) is **inadequate**. The goal of any equitable remedy is to **prevent unjust enrichment.** Two common equitable remedies that are specific to contracts include rescission and reformation.

1. **Rescission** permits a party to **invalidate a contract** and restores the parties to the position each would have been in if the bargain had not been entered into.

a. **No meeting of the minds:** There must be a contract formation problem resulting from fraud, duress, mistake, material misrepresentation, lack of consideration, etc. (see Contracts and Torts chapters for underlying substantive issues) such that there was no meeting of the minds.

b. Typically, only **available to the wronged party**.

c. **Equitable defenses** of **laches** and **unclean hands** are applicable.

> **Issue spotting tip:** Unless the call is specific, make sure that quasi-contract or replevin (both adequate legal remedies) aren't available before considering rescission. However, if the facts give rise to a fraud, mistake, etc. that warrants raising the rescission issue, then quickly analyze it but ultimately point out it will not be a viable remedy because of the adequate legal remedies.

2. **Reformation permits a contract to be rewritten by the court to reflect the parties' true agreement when:**
   a. **Meeting of the minds:** The parties had a meeting of the minds, and
   b. **Contract as written doesn't reflect the parties' agreement** because of an error.
      1. **Proper grounds** for reformation include fraud, material misrepresentation, mistake (e.g., scrivener's error), etc. (see Contracts and Torts chapters for underlying substantive issues).
   c. Typically, only **available to the wronged party**.
   d. **Equitable defenses** of **laches** and **unclean hands** are applicable.

D. **Injunction** is an **equitable remedy** where the court **orders one to perform an act** (affirmative or mandatory injunction) **or stop performing an act** (negative injunction). There are three types, with many similar requirements:
   1. **TROs** are the same as in tort. (See II.D.1 above.)
   2. **Preliminary injunctions** are the same as in tort. (See II.D.2 above.)
   3. **Specific performance** is a permanent injunction in contract where the **court orders the defendant to perform on the contract** as promised. The following requirements must be met:
      a. **Contract is valid:** The contract must be valid and the terms sufficiently **definite and certain** so that it can be enforced.
      b. **Contract conditions** imposed on the plaintiff are satisfied.
      c. **Inadequate legal remedy** (some courts look at irreparable harm here too):
         1. **Money damages are too speculative** to calculate with certainty.
         2. **Money damages may be inadequate** to compensate for the potential loss. This is especially true where there is a health or safety concern.
         3. **Insolvent defendant,** such that any damages award is worthless.
         4. **Replevin or ejectment is unavailable**.
         5. **Multiplicity of suits:** An ongoing wrong would lead to a multiplicity of suits by the same litigants over the same issue if not resolved by an injunction.
         6. **Property is unique,** so money damages are inadequate to compensate for the loss of that property.
            a. **Real property is always unique** since no two properties are exactly the same.
            b. **Personal property is not unique, except** if it is one-of-a-kind or very rare, or if the item has special personal significance to the plaintiff.
      d. **Mutuality of performance:** Both parties to the contract must be **eligible** to have their performance under the contract **ordered by the court**. This is only at issue where one party could not be ordered to perform (e.g., contract for the sale of illegal goods, the contracting party is a minor, they already sold the item, etc.).
      e. **Feasibility of enforcement:** Specific performance cannot be too difficult for the court to enforce.
         1. **Negative injunctions** are **easier to enforce** because of the court's power to order contempt for noncompliance.

2. **Affirmative injunctions** are **more difficult to enforce**. Specific performance is an affirmative injunction.

    a. **Series of acts** over a period of time can be **more difficult to enforce** than one required act.

    b. **Act requiring taste, judgment, or skill** is **difficult to enforce** because of the difficulty in determining if the act has been properly performed.

    c. **Personal services contract** will likely not be ordered because the court will not order a person to personally perform work for another.

3. **Jurisdictional issues** cause enforcement problems where the court would have to supervise events **out of their jurisdiction** or assert **control over nonparties** to the litigation.

f. **No defenses.** Laches and unclean hands are equitable defenses.

    1. **Laches** provides a defense when the plaintiff has **unreasonably delayed**, resulting in **prejudice to the defendant**.

    2. **Unclean hands** provides a defense when a plaintiff has conducted themself **unfairly in the transaction in dispute**.

    3. **Defenses to the underlying contract:** Any failure of the underlying contract can operate as a defense since a valid contract is a requirement for an injunction (e.g., lack of consideration, SOF, sale to a bona fide purchaser, unconscionability, etc.).

Exam tip: When dealing with a land sales contract in real property, a court may order specific performance with an abatement in price if there is a defect in title or the land isn't as promised. This arises in real property crossover questions. Also, since this is an equitable remedy, the court has a lot of discretion and can consider the balance of hardships and public interest (some courts do while others do not).

Memorization tip: Use the mnemonic **"Chocolate Cheesecake Is My Favorite Dessert"** to memorize the six essential elements of specific performance: valid **C**ontract, contract **C**onditions satisfied, **I**nadequate legal remedy, **M**utuality of performance, **F**easibility of enforcement, and no **D**efenses.

Issue spotting tip: If the call of the question is not specific, the facts will guide you as to which equitable remedy to analyze. For example, P will want a TRO/preliminary injunction when the act P is trying to prevent is imminent and cannot be undone (i.e., stop P from shipping a rare car out of the country). P may also seek specific performance as a more permanent solution to enforce the seller to perform under the contract and give P the car. This concept operates the same whether in tort or contract.

IV. **REAL PROPERTY REMEDIES ISSUES:** Remedies issues can arise in a real property context. The typical remedies are damages, an ejectment, or an injunction, and they operate the same in a property context as they do in a contract or tort context.

A. **Encroachments** are trespasses where a defendant's structure invades the plaintiff's property. This could also be seen as an adverse possession action. With an encroachment, a plaintiff is entitled to damages, ejectment, and injunction.

B. **Waste** occurs where there is an "injury" to real property by one with a present interest against a future interest holder.

1. **Voluntary waste** is a deliberate, destructive act. The remedy is damages for the diminution of value or the cost of repair, and/or an injunction.

2. **Permissive waste** occurs when the property is poorly maintained. The remedy is damages for the cost of repair. Injunction is not usually available because supervision problems make enforcement infeasible.

3. **Ameliorative waste** is where a present interest holder makes impermissible improvements to the property that actually enhance the property's value. Though a present interest holder is not permitted to do this, there are no damages because there is no loss in value. However, an injunction may be granted.

Cause of action	Common remedies
Torts	
Nuisance	Damages Injunctive relief
Trespass to Chattels	Damages Replevin Quasi-contract (possible as an alternative to tort) Injunctive relief
Conversion	Damages Restitution Constructive Trust/Equitable Lien
Trespass to Land	Damages Restitution Quasi-contract (possible as an alternative to tort) Injunctive relief Ejectment (if wrongfully excluded)
Personal injuries (assault, battery, negligence, etc.)	Damages Injunction (if harm ongoing)
Survival statutes/wrongful death	Damages
Defamation	Damages Injunction (usually doesn't work because of 1st Am. right to speech)
Invasion of Privacy	Damages Injunctive relief
Fraud	Damages Restitution Replevin Constructive Trust/Equitable Lien
Contracts	
Breach of contract	Damages Restitution/Quasi-contract Replevin Rescission/Reformation Injunctive relief
Real Property	
Encroachment	Damages Ejectment Injunctive relief
Easements	Damages Injunctive relief
Waste	Damages Injunctive relief

REMEDIES ISSUES TESTED MATRIX

	Crossover Subject (Other Substantive Issues)	Tort/Bus. Assoc. Damages	Restitution in Tort $	Injunction Tort/Con. Law/Other	Replevin/Ejectment	Constructive Trust/Equitable Lien	Contract Damages	Quasi-contract/Restitution	Rescission	Reformation	TRO, Preliminary/Injunction Contract	Specific Performance	Defenses: Unclean Hands/Laches/etc.
July '24 Q5 — Denise helps her uncle Perry sell autographed baseballs but lies to him and buys a car w/ $ she made		X	X			X			X				X
July '23 Q5 — Barbara bought Steve's land with embezzled $ and didn't include Steve's mineral rights in land sale documents		X				X			X	X	X	X	X
February '22 Q3 — Arnold and Betty started Durable Paint, Inc. and leased a bldg.; financial issues arose [state bar labeled as crossover but mainly Bus. Assoc.]	Bus. Assoc. (partnership formation and liability, authority, promoters, contract adoption, pierce corp. veil, etc.)	X											
February '22 Q3 — Diane built a large open-air theater and the noise and vibration bothers neighbor Pedro	Torts (nuisance, trespass to land)	X		X									
February '21 Q2 — Bright purchased a tractor motor from SM which malfunctioned several times	Contracts (breach of contract, warranties)						X		X				
October '20 Q5 — Pam agrees to buy Daniel's house with 2 paintings but contract omitted one of them								X		X	X	X	X
July '19 Q2 — A church in Clear City burned down so new ordinance against candles; churches fighting it	Con. Law (standing, ripe, moot, free speech, religion)			X									
July '17 Q3 — Rick agrees to purchase rare chess queen piece from Sam but doesn't disclose true value to Sam											X	X	X
February '17 Q2 — Betty buys condo from Steve and later finds out parking unavailable and someone murdered there	Torts (fraud)	X							X				X

Continued>

Exam	(Fact pattern)	Crossover Subject (Other Substantive Issues)	Tort/Bus. Assoc. Damages	Restitution in Tort $	Injunction Tort/Con. Law/Other	Replevin/Ejectment	Constructive Trust/Equitable Lien	Contract Damages	Quasi-contract/Restitution	Rescission	Reformation	TRO, Preliminary Injunction Contract	Specific Performance	Defenses: Unclean Hands/Laches/etc.
February '16 Q4	Pop buys insurance from Insurco; multicar collision; Insurco won't pay	Contracts/torts (fraud; misrepresentation; mutual mistake; parol evidence)								X	X			X
February '15 Q4	Steve to sell land w/ Top Rd easement, but breaches to sell to Tim							X	X		X	X	X	
July '14 Q1	Daria hires Percy to landscape and repudiates	Contracts (breach, anticipatory repudiation)						X	X	X			X	
February '14 Q6	Angela hires Mark to buy house with bats from Carol		X	X			X	X						
July '13 Q6	Doug dumps trees on Paul's lot causing flood	Torts (trespass to land, trespass to chattel, conversion)	X	X	X	X								
February '13 Q3	Mary and Frank buy storefront with embezzled funds	Contracts (SOF)	X	X			X							X
July '12 Q4	Della (dentist) hires Peter as a hygienist	Contracts (formation, SOF, part performance, equitable estoppel)						X	X				X	
February '11 Q6	Green's Grocery & lottery ticket w/ wrong numbers	Evidence (hearsay, hearsay exceptions, parol evidence)							X	X	X			
February '10 Q4	Pat, partner of law firm & Chris the paralegal	Contracts (formation, defenses, gift, condition, waiver)						X	X				X	X
July '09 Q5	Diane builds dam for camp for disadvantaged kids	Civ. Pro. (res judicata); Prof. Resp. (confidentiality)			X									X
July '08 Q4	Barry & Sally; rare Phaeton car	Contracts (anticipatory repudiation)				X		X				X	X	
July '07 Q5	Paula the art dealer & Monay painting	Contracts (SOF, mistake, misrepresentation)											X	X

Continued>

	Crossover Subject (Other Substantive Issues)	Tort/Bus. Assoc. Damages	Restitution in Tort $	Injunction Tort/Con. Law/Other	Replevin/Ejectment	Constructive Trust/Equitable Lien	Contract Damages	Quasi-contract/Restitution	Rescission	Reformation	TRO, Preliminary/Injunction Contract	Specific Performance	Defenses: Unclean Hands/Laches/etc.
July '06 Q3	Resi-Clean housecleaning advertises with coupons						X						
February '06 Q5	Marla, Larry & widget buyer							X					
July '05 Q5	Stan & Barb; land sale/water rights						X					X	X
July '04 Q6	Jack's "Star" uncut diamond & Chip the master diamond cutter	X					X						
July '03 Q2	Polly & Donald buy a house, but Donald uses embezzled funds					X							X
February '02 Q2	Berelli & the specialty Tabor tomatoes				X		X				X	X	X
February '01 Q4	Diane's office bldg & Peter's restaurant and garden	X	X	X									X
February '00 Q2	Chemco processing plant discharges waste into river	X		X									X
July '00 Q6	Don makes pottery & causes an electrical surge	X											

Contracts (formation, defenses, modification, breach, performance)

Contracts (formation, defenses); Prof. Resp. (conflict, honesty)

Contracts (PER, condition, price abatement, anticipatory repudiation)

Torts (negligence, wrongful death, legal malpractice)

Wills & Trusts (purchase money resulting trust)

Contracts (formation, anticipatory repudiation)

Torts (trespass to land, conversion, ejectment)

Torts (nuisance, trespass to land)

Torts (strict liability, nuisance, negligence)

REMEDIES PRACTICE ESSAYS, ANSWER GRIDS, AND SAMPLE ANSWERS

Remedies Question 1
July 2023, Question 5

Steve owned property in the state of Columbia that Barbara offered to buy for $500,000. Steve agreed to sell, provided that he retained the mineral rights and had access to the land. Barbara later accepted Steve's conditions and said that she would tell her attorney to prepare the necessary papers. When Steve met with Barbara to sign the papers, he asked if the documents included his conditions and she assured him that they did. In fact, Barbara had not told her attorney of Steve's conditions and they were not in the papers that he and Barbara signed.

Shortly after the sale, Steve decided to investigate whether his former property had any mineral deposits. Barbara refused to let Steve and his geologist on the property and erected barricades to prevent their access. It was then that Steve realized that the documents he signed omitted his conditions.

Barbara had purchased Steve's property in cash, which included $250,000 of funds that she had embezzled from her employer, Acme Company (Acme). Barbara later embezzled another $20,000 from Acme, which she deposited in her checking account containing $5,000 at the time. The following month, she paid off $25,000 of her outstanding debts, bringing her checking account balance to zero. Subsequently, Barbara deposited $10,000 of her own money into the checking account. Shortly thereafter, Acme fired Barbara after discovering her embezzlement.

Both Steve and Acme have brought suit against Barbara.

1. What equitable remedies does Steve have against Barbara? Discuss.

2. What equitable remedies does Acme have against Barbara? Discuss.

3. What amount of money, if any, can Acme recover as part of an equitable remedy from Barbara's checking account? Discuss.

Remedies Question 1 Assessment
July 2023, Question 5

This may be labeled by the state bar as a straight remedies essay and after a quick read of the calls, they do specifically ask about equitable remedies in the first two calls and the "amount of money" Acme can recover from a bank account (which has the lowest intermediate balance rule in a constructive trust/equitable lien written all over it). However, you will see that there are underlying substantive areas that must be adequately addressed to properly analyze some of the remedies. This is a common testing pattern in remedies essays where you must know the rules to the underlying substantive issues to do well on the remedies issues.

In accordance with the calls, the first thing you need to do is have a list of all possible equitable remedies as a checklist from which you can issue spot. Note that call one focuses on Steve and call two focuses on Acme. Both calls have Barbara as the defendant. Then call three further focuses in on Acme's remedy in regard to the amount of money it can also recover from Barbara's checking account. Be sure to keep your parties straight and answer the calls accordingly.

As to call one, it is best to organize the issues as they would arise in real life with a TRO coming before a preliminary injunction, and then later specific performance. That being said, you will see the state-released answers address the issues in no particular order, and in fact bounce around a bit, making it difficult to follow. This just shows you that it is most important to actually spot all the issues and include them some-where, although a more coherently organized essay will be easier for the graders to follow.

As to the first call, there are several issues that needed to be addressed. This was definitely a racehorse style remedies essay. While you needed to analyze TRO, Preliminary Injunction, Specific Performance, Rescission, and Reformation, the underlying issues of fraud/misrepresentation and mistake were common to several of those issues and needed a thorough analysis too. The good thing is that many of these issues have over-lapping elements. Thus, using supra was your greatest asset on this exam. Don't waste your time repeating rules or analyzing elements/issues you already addressed. Analyze them once and then refer to them in other issues as you go through the issues.

Call two focused on constructive trust and equitable lien, but note how call three specifically asked about the amount in the checking account. This tells you that call three focuses on the checking account, so it is likely that call two focuses on the property itself in terms of seeking a constructive trust or equitable lien. If you analyzed all assets that Barbara owns in call two then you could reference that analysis in call three as it pertains to the checking account, but it is better to specifically follow the calls and answer each call as they asked.

You should also note how the analysis in calls two and three became quite truncated in terms of the bolding in the grid. This is likely due to timing issues. What is important is that you spotted and addressed all issues. If timing is closing in on you, then cut to the chase on the remaining issues so the graders can see that you understand the rules and are able to adequately explain why a remedy is or is not possible. Part of learning how to write passing essay answers is managing your time and knowing when to go through each element in detail and when to quickly address the ones at issue to save time. The more practice essays you organize, the better you will get at perfecting this skill.

Finally, make note of the areas highlighted in **bold** on the corresponding grid. The bold areas highlight the issues, analysis, and conclusions that are likely **required** to receive a passing score on this question. In general, the essay grids are provided to assist you in analyzing the essays and are much more detailed than what a student should create during the exam to organize their response to a question.

Issue	Rule	Fact Application	Conclusion
1. Equitable remedies for Steve v. Barbara			
Temporary Restraining Order (TRO) [Irish Lads Inhale Beef Pies in Dublin]	To prevent injustice before preliminary injunction hearing • Irreparable harm • Likelihood of success • Inadequate legal remedy • Balance of hardships/public int. • No Defenses — laches/unclean hands **Can be issued ex parte (w/o notice) and lasts 10-14 days** [Note defenses could have been analyzed separately after all equitable remedies — either approach was fine]	**Steve may want to seek a TRO to ensure Barbara doesn't remove any minerals** as well as ask that she remove the barricades that are preventing him from accessing the property. • **Property is unique so if he cannot access the land and access his mineral rights then he will suffer irreparable harm as he can't get access to those particular minerals on this land in any other way.** • **It is likely Barbara acted fraudulently by failing to include Steve's mining rights in the contract as they agreed and Steve should be able to reform or rescind the K as discussed below.** • Since land is unique, money won't fix the problem with him accessing his mineral rights. • **Steve's hardship is great b/c he might lose all mineral rights if Barbara destroys or depletes the minerals, whereas Barbara's hardship is minor b/c she can replace the barricades later if she wins and it doesn't appear she is using the minerals so she wouldn't be harmed there and she might not want to share access to her land with someone else but that is what she orally agreed to; balances favor Steve.** • **Laches — Barbara might argue that Steve should have read the K and not waited until he tried to access the land to seek relief, but he did file suit as soon as he realized the signed K didn't contain the conditions he agreed to.** • Steve did not act in bad faith so no unclean hands.	Steve can likely obtain a TRO

Continued>

Issue	Rule	Fact Application	Conclusion
Preliminary Injunction	Same elements as TRO above, plus To maintain the "status quo" until full trial on the merits & notice required	Same analysis as above	**Steve can likely obtain a preliminary injunction**
Specific Performance [Chocolate Cheesecake Is My Favorite Dessert]	Equitable remedy: orders a party to perform under the contract if • **Contract valid** • Conditions of P satisfied • **Inadequate legal remedy** • Mutuality of performance • Feasibility • No Defenses	• **Contract between Steve and Barbara would be valid as it was in writing as is required for real property, contains all terms, the land description, and parties; and as reformed (discussed below) it would also contain the mineral rights terms.** • P fulfilled his conditions by selling the land. • **Inadequate legal remedy — see above.** • Steve has performed and sold the land, and Barbara can perform by allowing Steve to access the land. • Court can supervise the issue by requiring Barbara to amend the K and allow Steve access to the land as they agreed; may be difficult for them to ensure that she gives Steve access but they could force her to either remove the barricades or add access for him. • **See above for defenses.**	Steve can likely obtain specific performance [state-released answers both analyzed feasibility differently resulting in them reaching different conclusions — key is they both discussed the element]
Reformation	Remedy where the court rewrites the contract if there is: • **Meeting of minds**, and • **Contract as written doesn't reflect agreement** because of an error (fraud/misrepresentation, mistake, etc.)	Here, there is an agreement for Steve to sell Barbara his land provided he retain mineral rights and access to the land. However, the latter part of the agreement didn't end up in the final K due to Barbara's misrepresentation/fraud. • As discussed below, there was fraud/misrepresentation by Barbara to reform the K.	Steve can reform the K
Fraud/Misrepresentation	• Misrepresentation of material fact • Scienter (knowledge/reckless of falsity) • Intent to induce plaintiff's reliance • Justifiable reliance • Damage	• Barbara misrepresented to Steve that the documents contained his condition that he maintain mineral rights and access which is a material fact as that was what they agreed to. • She knew this was false b/c she didn't even tell her attorney about these terms and knew it wasn't in the K. • She intended to induce reliance on Steve b/c she assured him the terms were in there so he would sign the K when she knew they weren't. • He did rely on her assurance the terms were in there which is why he signed the K and later tried to access the property to assess the minerals. • He suffered damage as she won't allow him access to the land to assess the minerals.	Barbara is liable for fraud/misrepresentation so K can be reformed

(Continued>)

Issue	Rule	Fact Application	Conclusion
Mistake	Mutual mistake — made by both parties to the contract • Mistake as to basic assumption of the K • Mistake has material effect • Risk of mistake not imposed on party seeking to avoid the K Unilateral mistake — made where one party to the deal makes a mistake. • Must establish elements of mutual mistake, and • **Other party knows or should have known about that mistake**	No mutual mistake b/c Barbara not mistaken as to the contents of the K b/c she didn't tell her attorney to include the mineral rights in the K as they agreed. Here, the mistake was as to a basic assumption of the K since Steve only sold the land if he retained mineral rights and access and it was a material effect since now he can't access the land; **also Barbara knew of the mistake b/c she deliberately didn't tell her attorney to include it and then lied to Steve about it being in the K.**	**Mistake can allow reformation of the K**
Rescission	**Remedy where the court invalidates a contract because there has been no meeting of the minds in contract formation.** **Grounds for rescission can include: mistake; fraud/misrepresentation.** **See above for rules on fraud/ misrepresentation and mistake.**	Similar to reformation above, the court can rescind the K since Barbara acted fraudulently and there was a mistake in the K. Then, Steve would get his property back and he would need to give Barbara her $500,000 back.	**The court can rescind the K**
2. Equitable Remedies for Acme v. Barbara			
Constructive Trust	Compels D to convey title to property where: • Wrongful act by D • **D has legal title** • Inadequate legal remedy • **Property can be traced** (detailed rules in call 3) • P has priority over 3rd parties (not for BFPs) • No deficiency judgment allowed **Best to use when value of property increases because P gets the increase in value.** [Note the state-released answers both addressed unjust enrichment — this is the main driving force for all equitable remedies so arguably this could be raised for any equitable remedy]	• **Barbara acted wrongfully by embezzling money from Acme.** • **Barbara has legal title to cash and then she used the cash to purchase the property from Steve and she now has title to that property** as well as title over her bank account. • Since Barbara only has $10K in her bank account, there is an inadequate legal remedy b/c she doesn't have enough cash to pay Acme back the original $250K as well as the additional $20K. • **Acme can trace $250K to the property**, but the property is now commingled with the other $250K she had to use to pay the full $500K but the full $250K is traceable to the property so Acme can get the increase in value of the property arguably. • Acme has priority over P as she owns the land and her bank account. • If value of land goes down, no deficiency judgment is allowed.	**Acme could seek a CT over the property**

Continued>

Issue	Rule	Fact Application	Conclusion
Equitable Lien	**Same elements as constructive trust above, except:** • **Conveys a security interest not title** • **Tracing can be made to property not solely traceable to current form** • Deficiency judgments are allowed **Best to use when the property value decreases** because P can get a deficiency judgment.	**Same as above but now the tracing allows Acme to put a lien on the property for the amount of $250K owed** from her embezzled funds she used on the house; and they can trace the other $20K back to her bank account.	**Acme could seek an EL over the property,** but a CT would be better as the value is worth more than the amount embezzled
3. Amount of money Acme can recover			
Constructive trust/equitable lien Tracing/ commingled funds for monetary recovery	**Same elements as above for CT/EL.** Various approaches are allowed for tracing money in a CT/EL when applying the **lowest intermediate balance rule to commingled funds:** • First in, first out presumes the first money put into the account would be presumed the first money withdrawn. • **Investor/spender fiction presumes D invests/spends their own money first so the remaining funds are subject to the CT/EL.** **Once the funds are gone they are gone.**	**The elements are the same as above for CT/EL but the focus here is on the tracing in the bank account.** Under the first in, first out rule, **Barbara's own money was the first in** with her account containing $5,000, after which she added $20,000 of embezzled funds and then paid off $25,000 in outstanding debts resulting in a $0 balance. So all of the funds were gone. She later deposited $10,000 of her own money which would remain her own money because all of the embezzled funds were spent and once they are exhausted and gone they are gone. Same with the investor/fiction as all funds were depleted so the new $10,000 of her personal funds would not be traceable to the embezzled funds.	**Acme cannot recover the amount in the bank account through an equitable remedy**

Remedies Question 1 Sample Answer
July 2023, Question 5

1. Equitable remedies for Steve v. Barbara

Temporary Restraining Order (TRO)

A TRO is designed to prevent injustice before a preliminary injunction hearing. It can be issued ex parte without notice and generally lasts 10-14 days. A TRO requires irreparable harm, a likelihood of success, inadequate legal remedy, balancing of the hardships in plaintiff's favor including a focus on the public interest, and no valid defenses such a laches or unclean hands.

Here, Steve may want to seek a TRO to ensure Barbara doesn't remove any minerals as well as ask that she remove the barricades that are preventing him from accessing the property. Here, the property is unique so if Steve cannot access the land and access his mineral rights then he will suffer irreparable harm as he can't get access to those particular minerals on this land in any other way. Further, it is likely Barbara acted fraudulently by failing to include Steve's mineral rights in the contract as they agreed, and Steve should be able to reform or rescind the K as discussed below, so there is a likelihood of success on the merits. Next, since land is unique, money won't fix the problem with him being unable to access the land and assess his mineral rights.

As to Steve's hardship, it is great because he might lose all mineral rights if Barbara destroys or depletes the minerals, whereas Barbara's hardship is minor because she can replace the barricades later if she wins and it doesn't appear she is using the minerals and if she was, she was not supposed to under their agreement, so she wouldn't be harmed. Although she might not want to share access to her land with someone else, that is what she orally agreed to, which is the only reason Steve agreed to sell her the land. Thus, the balances favor Steve.

As to defenses, Barbara might argue that Steve should be barred by laches for unduly delaying his suit because he didn't read the terms before he signed the contract. However, he did file suit as soon as he realized the signed contract didn't contain the conditions he agreed to and he relied on her word that the terms were in there when he signed it. Further, Steve did not act in bad faith so unclean hands would not be a valid defense either. Therefore, Steve can likely obtain a TRO.

Preliminary Injunction

A preliminary injunction requires the same elements as a TRO, but it is used to maintain the "status quo" until a full trial on the merits and notice is required. The same analysis would apply as above so Steve can likely obtain a preliminary injunction.

Specific Performance

Specific performance is an equitable remedy where a court orders a party to perform under the contract if they had a valid contract, all conditions required by the plaintiff were fulfilled, there is an inadequate legal remedy, both parties can perform as required by the contract, it is feasible for the court to enforce, and there are no valid defenses.

Here, the contract between Steve and Barbara would be valid since it was in writing as is required for real property, contains all terms (subject to the omitted term regarding Steve's access and mineral rights that can be later added in under reformation as discussed below), the land description, and parties. Steve fulfilled his conditions by selling the land. There is an inadequate legal remedy as discussed above. Steve has performed by selling his land, and Barbara can perform by allowing Steve to access the land and the minerals. Further, the court can supervise the issue by requiring Barbara to amend the contract and allow Steve access to the land as they agreed. Although it may be difficult for the court to ensure that she gives Steve access, they could force her to either remove the barricades or add access for him and hold her in contempt if she refuses to do so. As to defenses, the same analysis applies as above. Thus, Steve can likely obtain specific performance.

Reformation

Reformation is an equitable remedy where the court rewrites the contract if there is a meeting of minds, and the contract as written doesn't reflect that agreement because of an error due to fraud, misrepresentation, or mistake.

Here, there is an agreement for Steve to sell Barbara his land provided he retain mineral rights and access to the land. However, the latter part of the agreement didn't end up in the final contract due to Barbara's misrepresentation/fraud and unilateral mistake.

Fraud/Misrepresentation

Fraud or misrepresentation occurs when there is a misrepresentation of material fact, knowledge of the falsity, intent to induce plaintiff's reliance, justifiable reliance, and damage to plaintiff.

Here, Barbara misrepresented to Steve that the document contained his condition that he maintain mineral rights and access, which is a material fact as that was what they agreed to. She knew this was false because she didn't tell her attorney about these terms and knew it wasn't in the contract. She further intended to induce reliance on Steve because she assured him the terms were in there so he would sign the contract when she knew they weren't. Further, he did rely on her assurance the terms were in there which is why he signed the contract only after asking her if the terms were in there, and later he tried to access the property to assess the minerals but was unable to do so. Finally, he suffered damages as she won't allow him access to the land to assess the minerals. Thus, Barbara is liable for fraud/misrepresentation so the contract can be reformed on this ground.

Mistake

A mistake can be mutual or unilateral. A mutual mistake is one made by both parties to the contract in which the mistake pertains to a basic assumption of the contract, the mistake has a material effect, and the risk of mistake is not imposed on party seeking to avoid the contract. A unilateral mistake is one made where one party to the deal makes a mistake and requires the same elements as mutual mistake, and the other party knows or should have known about that mistake.

Here, there is no mutual mistake because Barbara was not mistaken as to the contents of the contract because she didn't tell her attorney to include the mineral rights in the contract as they agreed. However, there was a mistake as to a basic assumption of the contract since Steve only sold the land if he retained mineral rights and access and it was a material effect because now he can't access the land. Also, Barbara knew of the mistake because she deliberately didn't tell her attorney to include it and then lied to Steve about it being in the contract. Thus, there was a unilateral mistake which is a ground under which the court can reform the contract.

Overall, the court can reform the contract on the grounds of Barbara's fraud or unilateral mistake.

Rescission

Rescission is an equitable remedy where the court invalidates a contract because there has been no meeting of the minds in contract formation. Similar to reformation, grounds for rescission can include mistake and fraud or misrepresentation.

Similar to reformation above, the court can rescind the contract since Barbara acted fraudulently and there was a mistake in the contract. If the court were to rescind the contract, then Steve would get his property back and he would need to give Barbara her $500,000 back.

Overall, the court can order the contract to be rescinded.

2. Equitable remedies for Acme v. Barbara

Constructive Trust

A constructive trust is an equitable remedy where the court compels the defendant to convey title to property where the defendant committed a wrongful act, defendant has legal title to the property, there is an inadequate legal remedy, the property can be traced to the wrongfully obtained funds, plaintiff has priority over third parties at issue, and there are no deficiency judgments allowed. A court will often impose a constructive trust when the value of the property increases because plaintiff obtains the increase in value.

Here, Barbara acted wrongfully by embezzling money from Acme. Barbara has legal title to the cash she embezzled as well as the property she purchased with the cash and her bank account. Since Barbara only has $10K in her bank account, there is an inadequate legal remedy because she doesn't have enough cash to pay Acme back the original $250K as well as the additional $20K she later embezzled. Further, Acme can trace the $250K to the property but the property is now commingled with the other $250K she had to use to pay the full $500K but the full $250K is traceable to the property so Acme can get the increase in value of the property arguably. The bank account tracing will be discussed below. Acme has priority over Barbara as she owns the land and her bank account and there are no other parties involved.

Overall, Acme could seek a constructive trust over the property and get the full value of the property.

Equitable Lien

An equitable lien is an equitable remedy similar to a constructive trust, but it only conveys a security interest in the property for the amount wrongfully taken. Further, tracing can be made to property not solely traceable to its current form and deficiency judgments are allowed. An equitable lien is best to use when the property value decreases because plaintiff can obtain a deficiency judgment.

The same analysis applies as above in the constructive trust, but now the tracing allows Acme to put a lien on the property for the amount of $250K owed from her embezzled funds she used to purchase the house. And Acme can trace the other $20K back to her bank account (see below for that analysis).

Overall, Acme could seek an equitable lien over the property but a constructive trust would be better as the value is worth more than the amount embezzled since she purchased it for $500,000.

3. Amount of money Acme can recover

Constructive Trust/Equitable Lien

See above for rules. For tracing, there are various approaches courts use when applying the lowest intermediate balance rule to commingled funds. One approach is the first in, first out approach which presumes the first money put into the account would be presumed the first money withdrawn. Another approach is the investor/spender fiction which presumes defendant invests/spends their own money first, so the remaining funds are subject to the constructive trust or equitable lien. Under all theories, once the funds are exhausted and spent, they are gone.

The analysis on all elements other than the tracing are the same as above. As the tracing, under the first in, first out rule, Barbara's own money was the first in with her account containing $5,000, after which she added $20,000 of embezzled funds and then she paid off $25,000 in outstanding debts, resulting in a $0 balance. So, all of the funds were gone.

She later deposited $10,000 of her own money which would remain her own money because all of the embezzled funds were spent and once they are exhausted and spent they are gone.

The same result would apply with the investor/fiction approach as all funds were depleted so the new $10,000 of her personal funds would not be traceable to the embezzled funds. Therefore, Acme cannot recover the amount in the bank account through an equitable remedy.

Remedies Question 2
July 2008, Question 4

Barry is the publisher of Auto Designer's Digest, a magazine that appeals to classic car enthusiasts. For years, Barry has been trying to win a first place award in the annual Columbia Concours d'Elegance ("Concours"), one of the most prestigious auto shows in the country. He was sure that winning such an award would vastly increase the circulation of his magazine and attract lucrative advertising revenues. This year's Concours was scheduled to begin on June 1, with applications for entry to be submitted by May 1.

Sally owned a 1932 Phaeton, one of only two surviving cars of that make and model. The car was in such pristine condition that it stood a very good chance of winning the first place prize.

On April 1, Barry and Sally entered into a valid written contract by which Barry agreed to buy, and Sally agreed to sell, the Phaeton for $200,000 for delivery on May 25. In anticipation of acquiring the Phaeton, Barry completed the application and paid the nonrefundable $5,000 entry fee for the Concours.

On May 10, Sally told Barry that she had just accepted $300,000 in cash for the Phaeton from a wealthy Italian car collector, stating "That's what it's really worth," and added that she would deliver the car to a shipping company for transport to Italy within a week.

1. Can Barry sue Sally before May 25? Discuss.

2. What provisional remedies might Barry seek to prevent Sally from delivering the Phaeton to the shipping company pending resolution of his dispute with Sally, and would the court be likely to grant them? Discuss.

3. Can Barry obtain the Phaeton by specific performance or replevin? Discuss.

4. If Barry decides instead to seek damages for breach of contract, can he recover damages for: (a) the nondelivery of the Phaeton; (b) the loss of the expected increase in circulation and advertising revenues; and (c) the loss of the $5,000 nonrefundable entry fee? Discuss.

Remedies Question 2 Assessment
July 2008, Question 4

Most remedies essay questions are crossover questions testing both the underlying substantive area of law giving rise to the need for a remedy and the potential remedies, and this question is no exception. For this question, the underlying claim is for breach of contract on the sale of a rare car, though it primarily tests remedies. There is one call of the question devoted to the contracts issue and three calls addressing various specific remedies. This is a good example of what current essay questions look like, with very specific calls of the question. The good thing about this type of a question is that the issue spotting is easier since the specificity of the question limits the possible issues. The bad thing about this type of a question is that if you can't recall the specific rule that corresponds to the call of the question, there is nowhere to hide and it's hard not to panic and mess up the whole question. This is why it is essential to memorize all of the rules in order to succeed on the essay portion of the exam.

Below is a review of the essential points contained in the state-released passing student answers:

1. Can Barry sue Sally before May 25? A full discussion of the anticipatory repudiation issue and the result is necessary. Since the question itself states that the contract was written and valid, analysis of the underlying contract is unnecessary and a waste of valuable time.

2. Are any provisional remedies available, and would the court grant them? This section is challenging to organize and may be done in several ways. The order of presentation is not as important as making it easy for the grader to find the key analysis by using issue headings for each legal concept. That way, even if you've chosen to organize in an atypical way, issue headings allow the grader to easily find the issues and key analyses. While TROs and preliminary injunctions have several elements, a passing answer could focus analysis only on the elements at issue in this fact pattern—here, a full analysis of the inadequate legal remedy and balancing of hardships elements is required. Because the call of the question specifically asks about provisional remedies, a full discussion of a temporary restraining order and preliminary injunction is necessary. The provisional remedies of TRO and preliminary injunction are being tested with increasing frequency.

3. Can B obtain the Phaeton (car) by specific performance or replevin? Analysis of this call is a very straightforward application of facts to the rules, but you must know your rules.

4. Can B recover breach of contract damages for the nondelivery of the car, the loss of anticipated revenues, and the $5,000 entry fee? The damages analysis on the nondelivery of the car is straightforward but be sure to analyze separately each category of damages asked about. Damages relating from the loss of magazine revenues and the loss of entry fee should focus on analysis of the uncertainty and unforeseeability of damages of this type.

Note the areas highlighted in **bold** on the corresponding grid. The bold areas highlight the issues, analysis, and conclusions that are likely **required** to receive a passing score on this question. In general, the essay grids are provided to assist you in analyzing the essays and are much more detailed than what a student should create during the exam to organize their response to a question.

Issue	Rule	Fact Application	Conclusion
1. Can Barry sue before 5/25?			
Contract	K requires mutual assent: offer, acceptance, consid. K defenses?	• Valid written contract per the facts. Sally sells rare Phaeton car to Barry for $200k, delivery on May 25. • S may claim hardship/unconscionability (as to price) or unilateral mistake, but none will work here since it appears to be a bargained-for exchange.	**Valid contract**
Anticipatory Repudiation	• **Promisor indicates they won't perform prior to the time performance is due.** • **Buyer may treat as immediate breach and sue.**	• On April 1, S and B have a **valid written k** w/ delivery of car on May 25. On May 10, **S told B she sold the same car** to a wealthy Italian car collector for $300k, delivery w/in 1 week, which is **a clear indication S does not intend to perform.** • Since S has indicated she sold car to another, **B may treat the repudiation as final and sue for breach immediately.**	**There is an anticipatory repudiation** and **B may sue immediately for breach of k**
2. Provisional remedies?			
Temporary Restraining Order (TRO) [Irish Lads Inhale Beef Pies in Dublin]	To prevent injustice before preliminary injunction hearing • Irreparable harm • **Likelihood of success** • Inadequate legal remedy • Balance of hardships/public int. • No defenses	• 10 days only & okay ex parte to prevent car from being shipping immediately. • **Irreparable harm b/c car gone in 1 week out of country w/out TRO.** • **S willfully breached valid k, so B likely to win and succeed on underlying claim.** • **Cars not usually "unique,"** but here only 2 in world so **$ can't compensate b/c very rare/irreplaceable,** unable to replace in time for Concours auto show so legal remedy inadequate. • Great hardship on **B b/c may be deprived of only opportunity to buy a Phaeton. Hardship to S is slight** b/c even though lost opportunity to sell for $300k ($100k more) she still has car and can sell later if she wins. • No defenses.	**B should receive a TRO** to prevent S from delivering the car to the shipper

Continued>

Issue	Rule	Fact Application	Conclusion
Preliminary Injunction	Same elements as **TRO** above, plus • To maintain the "status quo" until full trial on the merits & notice required	Put in place awaiting trial on merits, requires the above and: • Car will ship to another buyer w/out injunction so need car to remain available pending trial outcome	**B should also receive a preliminary injunction**
3. Can B obtain the Phaeton?			
Specific Performance [Chocolate Cheesecake Is My Favorite Dessert]	Equitable remedy: orders a party to perform under k if • **Contract valid** • **Condition of P satisfied** • **Inadequate legal remedy** • **Mutuality** • **Feasibility** • **No Defenses**	• **K is valid** ($200k for Phaeton) • P can perform by paying the $200k (can put in escrow) • Discussion **supra** • **Both can perform here** b/c she still has car and he can pay • **No supervision problems w/ court order that S tender car and B pay $200k** (supra) • None (supra)	**B should be granted specific performance**
Replevin	Allows P to recover specific property before trial w/ hearing.	**Car is specifically identified** and sheriff could seize the Phaeton, but it may be hard to find so this is not a superior remedy to specific performance.	**Allowed**, but not the best remedy
4.a. Recover damages — Nondelivery of car?			
Expectation (Compensatory) **Damages**	In K, puts P in same position as if D performed on K Damages must be causal, foreseeable, unavoidable, and certain.	B would get benefit of the bargain, market price less k price. **S would have to pay $100k difference b/t k price** ($200k) **and market price** ($300k), which is causal, foreseeable, certain, and unavoidable. **If B can cover** by buying the other Phaeton, B can recover **the difference in price plus incidental costs.**	B will likely get **$100k in damages**

Continued>

Issue	Rule	Fact Application	Conclusion
4.b. Recover damages — Loss of revenues?			
Consequential **Damages**	Damages for any losses resulting from breach, which are **foreseeable** at time k entered into; damages must be causal, foreseeable, unavoidable, and certain.	B wants to recover for his loss of anticipated revenues from magazine circulation increases and advertising revenues from his expected first-place win at the Concours auto show. However, **a win is uncertain** (he's tried for years) and **future increases in revenues are speculative.** Further, **if S did not know B's purpose** of the car purchase, these damages are **not foreseeable at the time k was entered into.**	**B will not recover**
4.c. Recover damages — Loss of $5k entry fee?			
Consequential **Damages** or Reliance Damages	See rule above for consequential damages Reliance damages put the plaintiff in the position they would have been in had the contract never been made. [Note: you could have analyzed these as consequential or reliance damages.]	**If S did not know B's purpose** of the car purchase, and that he entered the auto show contest, these damages are **not foreseeable at the time k was entered into.** Reliance damages can be awarded instead of expectation/consequential which would return the $5K to B as if the contract had never been entered.	B will not recover

Remedies Question 2 Sample Answer
July 2008, Question 4

1. Barry — Sue Before May 25

Contract

A binding contract requires mutual assent, which includes an offer and acceptance, and consideration. There is a valid written contract here. Sally is selling a rare Phaeton car to Barry for $200,000 with delivery on May 25. Sally may try to ineffectively argue some defenses to enforcement of the contract, such as unconscionability as to price or unilateral mistake, but there does appear to be a bargained-for exchange and a valid contract.

Anticipatory Repudiation

An anticipatory repudiation happens when a promisor indicates they will not perform under the contract prior to the time performance is due. Sally and Barry entered into a valid contract on April 1 with a delivery date of May 25. On May 10, prior to the time Sally was due to perform, Sally informed Barry she had sold the car to a wealthy Italian car collector for $300,000 instead, and was going to deliver the car to the new buyer in one week. Selling the rare car to another buyer is a clear and unequivocal indication that Sally does not intend to perform under her contract with Barry since the subject matter of the contract will be sold to another. Barry may treat this repudiation as a final and immediate breach and sue immediately to enforce the contract even though the time for performance is not yet due.

2. Provisional Remedies

Temporary Restraining Order

Barry will first seek a temporary restraining order to prevent Sally from delivering the car to the Italian buyer in one week until the court can hold the preliminary injunction hearing. Barry will seek two types of injunctions: a negative injunction to prevent Sally from delivering the car to the Italian, and a mandatory injunction requiring Sally to deliver the car to Barry.

A TRO is available for a short period (usually no more than 10-14 days) pending a preliminary injunction hearing where irreparable harm will occur in its absence, the plaintiff has a likelihood of success on the merits, the remedy at law is inadequate, the hardships on both sides are balanced, and there are no valid defenses.

Here, Barry will suffer irreparable harm without the TRO because the car will be shipped out of the country in one week. Barry will likely succeed on the merits of the underlying breach of contract claim because Sally is willfully breaching because she made a more lucrative deal to sell the car to another buyer. While cars are usually not unique and therefore the remedy at law could be adequate, the Phaeton car here is very unique since there are only two in the world. Money will not adequately compensate for the loss of buying this particular rare car, especially since Barry plans to enter it in the prestigious Concours auto show. The hardship to Sally would simply be preventing her from shipping the car at this moment and selling the car to another until the trial occurs, but not necessarily forever, and at most would be a monetary loss only for her. For Barry the hardship is great because once the car is shipped overseas he cannot get it back and it is irreplaceable. Finally, there are no valid defenses. Thus, Barry should obtain a TRO.

Preliminary Injunction

Barry may also attempt to obtain a preliminary injunction. These are put in place pending a trial on the merits and require a showing of the same elements as a TRO (supra), and that the injunction is necessary to maintain the status quo until a full trial on the merits can be heard. The preliminary injunction is necessary to maintain the status quo since if one is not granted, the Phaeton will be shipped to the Italian buyer and unavailable. Here, as discussed above, the hardships balance in Barry's favor because there is a great hardship on Barry since he will be deprived of his only opportunity to buy the rare Phaeton, and the hardship on Sally is slight since though she may have lost the opportunity to make this $300,000 deal, she can still sell the car at a later time if she wins. Since there are no applicable defenses and all elements are met as discussed above, Barry should receive a preliminary injunction.

3. Barry — Get the Phaeton Itself

Specific Performance

Specific performance is an equitable remedy where the court orders a party to perform under a contract. To obtain specific performance, a party must establish a valid contract, all conditions imposed are satisfied, there must be an inadequate legal remedy, there is mutuality of performance, the order is feasible to enforce, and no defenses apply. As discussed supra there is a valid contract. Barry can perform by tendering the $200,000 owing on the contract, so conditions imposed on him are satisfied. The remedy at law is inadequate (discussed supra). Modernly, courts only require the mutuality of performance, which is satisfied here since both parties can perform under the contract since Sally still has the car to deliver and Barry can pay for it. There are no court supervision problems since the court can order Sally to tender the car and Barry to tender the $200,000, so the order is feasible to enforce. There are no valid defenses, so Barry can get specific performance, and this is his best remedy since it gives him the car itself.

Replevin

Replevin is a legal restitutionary remedy, which allows a party to recover specific personal property before a trial that was wrongfully taken from plaintiff who has the right to possession. Since the Phaeton car is specifically identified, the sheriff could seize it for replevin, but it may be difficult to find, so specific performance is a superior remedy.

4. Damages

Nondelivery of Car

Expectation Damages

Expectation damages for breach of contract put a plaintiff in the same position they would have been in had the contract been fully performed. Damages must be proven with certainty, caused by the breach, foreseeable, and plaintiff must have mitigated their losses. Here, Barry can receive the benefit of the bargain, so Sally would have to pay the market price ($300,000) less contract price ($200,000). If Barry could cover by buying the other Phaeton, he can recover the difference in price plus any incidental costs incurred. The amount would be certain ($100,000), caused by Sally breaching the contract, foreseeable as there are only two of these rare cars and Barry wanted this car, and unavoidable as Barry can't replace it as there are only two. Thus, Barry can recover $100,000 in expectation damages for nondelivery of the car.

Loss of Revenue

Consequential Damages

Consequential damages compensate for any losses resulting from the breach that are foreseeable at the time the contract is entered into. The same limitations discussed above apply. Barry wants to recover for his loss of anticipated revenues from increased magazine circulation and advertising revenues based on his expected first-place finish at the Concours auto show. However, a win at the auto show is uncertain since he's tried unsuccessfully for years. Further, future revenue increases from circulation and advertising are speculative and are not certain to occur. Lastly, if Sally did not know of Barry's purpose in purchasing the Phaeton, these damages would also not have been foreseeable at the time of contracting. Barry will not be able to recover his anticipated loss revenue.

Loss of Entry Fee

Consequential Damages

See above for rules.

The loss of the Concours auto show entry fee could also be consequential damages. Again, if Sally did not know Barry's purpose for buying the car was to enter the auto show, the entry fee would not have been foreseeable at the time of contracting and thus would not be recoverable by Barry.

Reliance Damages

Reliance damages seek to put the plaintiff in the position they would have been in had the contract never been entered into. These are awarded instead of expectation or consequential damages.

Here, Barry could try to seek the return of the $5,000 entry fee as reliance damages but that would act as if the contract was never entered so he wouldn't be able to obtain expectation damages. Thus, this would not be his best remedy.

Remedies Question 3
February 2015, Question 2

Steve owned two adjoining improved tracts of land, Parcels 1 and 2, near a lake. Parcel 1 bordered the lake; Parcel 2 bordered Parcel 1 and was adjacent to an access road. Steve decided to sell Parcel 1 to Belle. Belle admired five 100-year-old oak trees on Parcel 1 as well as its lakefront location.

On February 1, Steve and Belle executed a contract for the sale of Parcel 1 at a price of $400,000. The contract specified that the conveyance included the five 100-year-old oak trees. In addition, the contract stated that Belle was to have an easement across Parcel 2 so that she could come and go on the access road. Although the access road was named Lake Drive, Steve and Belle mistakenly believed that it was named Top Road, which happened to be the name of another road nearby. The contract referred to the access easement as extending across Parcel 2 to Top Road, which would not have been of any use to Belle. The contract specified a conveyance date of April 1.

Later in February, Steve was approached by Tim, who offered Steve $550,000 for Parcel 1. Steve decided to breach his contract with Belle and agreed to convey Parcel 1 to Tim. Despite Belle's insistence that Steve honor his contract, he told her that he was going ahead with the conveyance to Tim in mid-April, and added, "Besides, our contract is no good because the wrong road was named."

In March, Belle learned that, in April, Steve was going to cut down the five 100-year-old oak trees on Parcel 1 to better the view of the lake from Parcel 2.

1. What equitable remedies can Belle reasonably seek to obtain Parcel 1? Discuss.

2. What legal remedies can Belle reasonably seek if she cannot obtain Parcel 1? Discuss.

Remedies Question 3 Assessment
February 2015, Question 2

This question is a good example of a pure remedies question with very narrow calls, which informs you that the bar examiners are not looking for a discussion of the underlying contract issues, except as they pertain to the analysis of the remedies' issues. The calls also require you to know the difference between equitable and legal remedies, which is why it is important to know which remedies fall into each category. The fact pattern is not overly complicated, and the question should feel manageable within the one-hour time limit. The three forms of injunctive relief continue to be popular testing areas. This question also tests reformation, which, along with rescission, is a more complicated issue to address.

Since call one specifically asks about equitable remedies, it is a good idea to include all potential equitable remedies, which includes the three types of injunctions and reformation. When analyzing TRO and preliminary injunctions, the elements are essentially identical so it is important to identify the few differences between the two, such as that a TRO can be obtained ex-parte. Another distinction is that for the element of irreparable harm it is important to keep the case timeline in mind. With a TRO, you are measuring the irreparable harm to plaintiff while awaiting the preliminary injunction hearing. With the preliminary injunction, you are measuring the irreparable harm to plaintiff while awaiting a full trial on the merits for the specific performance hearing (or the permanent injunction if this were a tort case.) The focus on the different timelines could make for different analysis. In this particular case, the analysis is exactly the same, so "supra" can be used since the potential harm is the same for both the short 10-day time period of the TRO and the longer period while awaiting the full trial for specific performance. Nonetheless, this is worth noting since the analysis could be different depending on the facts, and if so, the distinctions would be important.

A small complication in the facts here is that there are two distinct potential irreparable harms contemplated by these facts. Here, these potential irreparable harms include the cutting down of the trees, and the proposed sale of Parcel 1 to Tim. It is always a good idea to separate out factually different arguments whenever possible for a clearer presentation, and to ensure you don't miss any key analysis by merging factual situations. You can either use headings such as "trees" and "sale to Tim" to separate the concepts, or at a minimum, analyze the facts in different paragraphs to provide guidance to the bar grader as demonstrated in the sample answer.

The second call focuses on legal remedies which usually focuses on damages so be sure to have a mini-checklist handy for all legal remedies to make sure you don't miss any key issues. Luckily here the only legal issue you needed to address was damages, so this call was easy and worth a lot less than call one.

Finally, make note of the areas highlighted in **bold** on the corresponding grid. The bold areas highlight the issues, analysis, and conclusions that are likely **required** to receive a passing score on this question. In general, the essay grids are provided to assist you in analyzing the essays and are much more detailed than what a student should create during the exam to organize their response to a question.

Issue	Rule	Fact Application	Conclusion
1. Equitable Remedies			
Temporary Restraining Order [Irish Lads Inhale Beef Pies in Dublin]	**Equitable remedy to prevent injustice; short duration (10-14 days); can be ex-parte for good cause,** can be negative or mandatory • **Irreparable harm if not granted** • **Likelihood of success** • **Inadequate legal remedy** • **Balancing hardships** • No defenses	• Belle will request a TRO ordering Steve not to cut 100-year-old oak trees or sell the lake front property to Tim. • Irreparable harm—Trees: The 100-year-old oak trees Belle admired and were important to her decision to buy property **can't be easily replaced** since once cut it will take 100 years to regrow. • Irreparable harm—Sale to Tim: **If Tim is a bona fide purchaser, Belle can't get specific performance for Parcel 1 once the sale goes through. Further, though the TRO is only 10-14 days and the proposed sale to Tim will close mid-April, a TRO is needed** because Steve could accelerate the sale. • **Steve will argue the contract has a mistake and is invalid,** but the **contract here is valid** since it can be reformed to reflect the parties' true agreement (as analyzed below) **so Belle should prevail and succeed on the merits.** • **Parcel 1 is a unique lakefront property with 100-year-old trees,** so it's unique and a legal remedy of money is inadequate. • **Harm to Belle is great** because if Steve is permitted to sell to Tim, Belle will potentially forever **be deprived of owning Parcel 1. Further,** the trees are irreplaceable since if **Steve cuts the trees down, it will take 100 years to replant and grow trees of that size.** • **Harm to Steve is comparatively slight since he is only deprived of his improved view of lake for a few months** while the case gets resolved, and he will still ultimately be able to sell the **property to someone,** it's just unclear who at this time. • No defenses apply.	TRO will be granted

Continued>

Issue	Rule	Fact Application	Conclusion
Preliminary Injunction	Maintains status quo until trial **Same elements as above**	Same analysis as above in TRO.	Preliminary injunction will be granted
Specific Performance [Chocolate Cheesecake Is My Favorite Dessert]	Equitable remedy orders a party to perform on contract: • **Contract is valid** • **Conditions on P met** • **Inadequate legal remedy** • **Mutuality of performance** • **Feasibility of enforcement** • **No defenses**	• **Contract for land with price $400,000, parties (Belle and Steve) and adequate property description** (Parcel 1). Steve will argue the contract is invalid because the terms are not sufficiently definite and certain since the road Lake Drive was mistakenly identified as Top Road. However, as indicated below, the contract can be reformed to reflect the parties' true agreement so it is valid. • **Belle can pay** the $400,000 as promised. • **Land is unique** and here lakefront with five 100-year-old oak trees so money cannot compensate adequately. • **Both parties can perform** under the contract (Belle pay $400,000 and Steve convey Parcel 1). • **Feasible to enforce** one land transaction since court can order Steve to complete the transaction, and no jurisdiction problems. • No facts to indicate laches or unclean hands or any other defense.	Order for specific performance will be granted
Reformation	Contract rewritten by court if • **Meeting of minds** • **Contract as written doesn't reflect agreement** because of mutual mistake	• Both parties **agreed for Belle to have an easement** over Lot 2 to the access road. • **Both mistakenly believed the access road was named "Top Road"** but the road was actually named "**Lake Drive**" so they made a **mutual mistake** and the contract did not accurately reflect their bargain so the court can reform the contract.	The contract will be reformed to substitute "Lake Drive" for "Top Road"
2. Legal Remedies			
Expectation Damages	**Benefit non-breaching party expects from the contract** **Difference between contract price and fair market value** Damages must be certain, causation met, foreseeable, and unavoidable	• Belle can get the difference between the **contract price ($400,000)** and the **fair market value, which is presumably the $550,000** Tim agreed to pay for the property, thus Belle will get **damages of $150,000**, and incidental/consequential damages, if any. • Damages certain at $150,000 as indicated above, caused by Steve's breach if he won't sell to Belle and sells to Tim, foreseeable Belle will want damages if she can't obtain the actual parcel, and nothing she can do to mitigate damages since no other parcel is the same.	Belle will be awarded damages of $150,000

Remedies Question 3 Sample Answer
February 2015, Question 4

1. Equitable Remedies

Temporary Restraining Order (TRO)

A TRO is an equitable remedy in which the court orders a defendant to take an action, or refrain from taking an action, as a means to preserve the status quo for a short time, typically 10-14 days, until there can be a preliminary injunction hearing. A TRO will be granted where the plaintiff can establish: 1) they will suffer irreparable harm in the absence of the order, 2) they are likely to succeed on the merits of their claim, 3) the remedy at law is inadequate, 4) the balancing of the hardships to each party favors granting the TRO, and 5) there are no valid defenses. In special circumstances a TRO can be issued ex-parte without notice to the defendant where the plaintiff can establish a good faith attempt at notice, or there is good cause to not provide notice.

Here, Belle would seek a TRO ordering Steve to not cut down the trees or sell Parcel 1 to another buyer, both of which are negative injunctions ordering Steve to refrain from doing something he would otherwise be able to do.

Irreparable Harm

Belle must establish that she will suffer irreparable harm in the absence of the TRO. Here, Belle contracted with Steve to purchase Parcel 1 because of the lakefront location and her admiration for the 100-year-old oak trees on the property. The trees were so important to Belle that they were included in the contract terms, but now Steve wants to sell Parcel 1 to Tim and cut down the trees to improve his own lake view from Parcel 2. If the TRO is denied and Tim is allowed to cut the trees down, Belle will suffer irreparable harm because the trees are 100 years old and not easy to replace since it would take 100 years for newly planted trees to grow this large.

Belle would also suffer irreparable harm if Tim were permitted to sell Parcel 1 to Tim. If Tim does not know of the earlier contract with Belle and pays the $550,000 in value, Tim would be a bona fide purchaser of the land and thus the sale to him would be final and Belle would not be able to recover the property through specific performance. Though the conveyance to Tim is not scheduled to happen until mid-April, which would be after the short 10-14-day TRO window, Belle would be able to successfully argue that in the absence of the TRO, nothing would prevent Steve from accelerating the close of the sale to Tim, leaving her irreparably harmed.

Likelihood of Success on the Merits

Belle should be able to establish she is likely to succeed on the merits of her claim since she and Steve have a valid written contract. While Steve may argue that the contract is invalid because of a mutual mistake and thus Belle won't succeed on the merits, his argument will not succeed, as described below in reformation.

Inadequate Legal Remedy

Parcel 1 is a unique piece of lakefront property with 100-year-old oak trees, which Belle wants to own, thus the remedy at law of money damages would be inadequate because no two properties are the same and money cannot adequately replace the property and trees.

Balancing of Hardships

The hardship to Belle if the TRO is denied is great because Steve would be permitted to cut down the trees and sell Parcel 1 to Tim, forever denying Belle the right to own the property as contracted. While Steve may assert there is hardship in not being permitted to improve his own view and that the TRO could negatively impact his deal with Tim, the hardship to Steve if the TRO is granted is comparatively slight. The TRO would merely prevent him from cutting down trees that have been in the same location for 100 years for a few more months, and though he would like an enhanced view, it is no more than a minor inconvenience. Further, Steve's hardship is comparatively slight because whether Belle ultimately prevails or not, Steve will still be permitted to sell Parcel 1. The only issue is if he will have to honor the contract with Belle or be allowed to sell it to Tim or a different buyer. Thus, the equities balance in Belle's favor.

Finally, there are No Valid Defenses

Belle should succeed in her efforts to get a TRO ordering Steve not to cut down the trees or sell Parcel 1.

Preliminary Injunction

A preliminary injunction is similar to a TRO in that it is designed to preserve the status quo, but it will remain in place pending a full trial on the merits and notice is required. The test for a preliminary injunction is the same as that for a TRO as discussed above.

Here, Belle would seek a preliminary injunction ordering Steve to not cut down the trees or sell Parcel 1 until the full trial on the merits. For the same reasons noted above, the court would grant Belle a preliminary injunction pending trial.

Specific Performance

Specific performance is an equitable remedy that requires the defendant to actually perform under the contract, rather than pay legal damages for breach. Specific performance is available as a remedy where there is 1) a valid contract, 2) all conditions imposed on the plaintiff can be satisfied, 3) the remedy at law is inadequate, 4) there is mutuality of performance, 5) the order is feasible for the court to enforce, and 6) there are no defenses.

Here, Belle would seek the court to order Steve to perform on their contract and convey Parcel 1.

Valid Contract

For the sale of land, a contract must specify the parties, the price, and adequately describe the property. On February 1, Belle and Steve executed a contract that included an adequate description of Parcel 1 and the price of $400,000, so there was a valid contract.

Conditions on Plaintiff Satisfied

Though Belle has not yet paid the $400,000, she would be able to do so.

Inadequate Legal Remedy

Belle seeks enforcement of a contract for the purchase of land. Land is unique and no two parcels would ever be the same, especially here where the land is lakefront and includes five 100-year-old oak trees. Money cannot adequately compensate Belle for the loss of Parcel 1.

Mutuality of Performance

Both parties to the contract are eligible to have their performance under the contract ordered by the court since Steve can be ordered to convey Parcel 1 to Belle, and Belle could be ordered to pay Steve the $400,000.

Feasibility of Enforcement

The enforcement of a specific performance order is feasible because it only requires the court to supervise the single transaction of requiring Steve to convey Parcel 1 to Belle and there are no jurisdictional issues.

No Defenses

The equitable defenses of laches (unreasonable delay) or unclean hands (bad faith) can prevent a specific performance order. Here, there is no indication that laches applies and that Belle has delayed in bringing the action, or that there was any prejudice to Steve. Nor are there any facts here to indicate Belle has unclean hands and has engaged in unfair dealing of any kind. Thus, there are no applicable defenses.

Reformation

Reformation permits the court to rewrite the contract when it does not reflect the true agreement of the parties. It requires that there was a meeting of the minds, but that the contract does not reflect that agreement due to fraud or mistake.

Here, Steve and Belle had a meeting of the minds about their deal, where they both agreed that Belle would have an easement across Parcel 2 that went to the access road. However, while they both mistakenly believed that the access road was named "Top Road" and that is what was reflected in the written contract, the access road was actually named "Lake Drive." Belle will request the contract be reformed to reflect the agreement of the parties and provide an easement over Parcel 2 to Lake Drive since both she and Steve believed that is what they agreed to.

The reformation will be granted.

2. Legal Remedies

Should Belle not be able to obtain equitable relief, she would be entitled to expectation damages.

Expectation Damages

Expectation damages compensate the plaintiff for the value of the benefit the plaintiff expected to receive from performance of the contract. The goal is to put the plaintiff in the position they would have been in if the contract were fully performed. In a land sale contract, the measure of damages would be the difference between the contract price and the fair market value of the land at the time of the sale. All damages must be capable of being calculated with certainty, caused by the breach, foreseeable, and unavoidable by the plaintiff.

While Belle had a contract to purchase Parcel 1 for $400,000, shortly thereafter Steve contracted with Tim to purchase the same piece of land for $550,000. Since Tim agreed to pay the higher price of $550,000, it is likely that $550,000 represents the fair market value of Parcel 1. Thus, in the absence of equitable relief, Belle would be entitled to a damages award of $150,000, which is the difference between the contract price and the fair market value as reflected in Tim's purchase price.

The damages amount is certain as indicated above, the damages would be caused by Steve's breach and sale to Tim if it went through, the damages are foreseeable since Steve knows that Belle wanted this particular land and there is no other land like it, and damages are unavoidable since Belle cannot purchase another property like it. Thus, Belle can recover expectation damages.

In addition, though there are no facts to indicate this here, if Belle had incurred any reasonably foreseeable consequential or incidental damages, she would be able to recover for those damages as well.

Remedies Question 4
February 2016, Question 4

Pop obtained a liability insurance policy from Insurco, covering his daughter Sally and any other driver of either of his cars, a Turbo and a Voka. The policy limit was $100,000.

On the application for the policy, Pop stated that his cars were driven in Hometown, a rural community, which resulted in a lower rate than if they were driven in a city. However, Sally kept and also drove the Voka in Industry City while attending college there.

Subsequently, Pop asked Insurco to increase his coverage to $500,000; Insurco agreed if he paid a premium increase of $150; and he did so. Days later, as he was leaving for Sally's graduation, Pop received an amended policy. He failed to notice that the coverage had been increased to $250,000, not $500,000.

Unfortunately, while driving the Turbo in Industry City, Pop caused a multi-vehicle collision. At first, Insurco stated it would pay claims, but only up to $250,000. Six months later, Insurco informed Pop that it would not pay any claim at all, because of his statement on the application for the policy that both the Turbo and the Voka were located in Hometown.

Insurco filed a complaint against Pop for rescission of the policy. Pop filed a cross-complaint to reform the policy to increase coverage to $500,000.

1. What is the likelihood of success of Insurco's complaint, and what defenses can Pop reasonably raise? Discuss.

2. What is the likelihood of success of Pop's cross-complaint, and what defenses can Insurco reasonably raise? Discuss.

Remedies Question 4 Assessment
February 2016, Question 4

As with the great majority of remedies questions, this question is a crossover question, but it is atypical because the specific calls appear to focus only on remedies, with the first call on rescission and defenses, and the second call on reformation and defenses. However, there are concepts from other subjects embedded in some of the remedies rules, and this question shines a light on those topics. The underlying basis for obtaining rescission or reformation derives from torts (fraud/misrepresentation) and contracts (mutual and unilateral mistake). Thus, the torts and contracts issues must be analyzed as a foundation to properly analyze the rescission and reformation issues.

Rescission and reformation are difficult testing areas in remedies, because they naturally offer the opportunity for a crossover question and require students to understand more nuanced areas of law in torts and contracts to adequately analyze the remedies. This is why it is important to organize as many different essays as you can and expose yourself to every possible issue they have tested. We try to select a variety of essays in this book so you are exposed to different topics such as reformation and rescission, but we recommend you utilize the issues tested matrix to organize even more essays on each topic. Ideally you want to organize 3-5 essays on each topic to see all the ways they can possibly test an issue. Crossover questions are also a great way to test more subjects since one of the five essays will be professional responsibility, leaving only four essays to test all other remaining subjects.

The question calls here also ask specifically about the defenses each party might raise. The fact pattern clearly raises the equitable defenses, but it is always a good idea to consider the equitable defenses of laches and unclean hands every time you are analyzing any equitable remedies, even if it is just to state why they are inapplicable under the facts. Because defenses were specifically asked about, you must address some defenses to pass this essay.

There are many ways to approach memorizing remedies that will work. Some students find it useful to memorize all remedies as a separate subject divided into substantive categories, which is how this book is organized. Other students find it useful to group remedies with the particular subject to which they correspond. For this reason, we included a chart of commonly tested issues for each substantive issue. You need to determine which method works best for you by writing out a few crossover substantive rights/remedies questions to see which method enables you to spot all relevant remedies.

Finally, make note of the areas highlighted in **bold** on the corresponding grid. The bold areas highlight the issues, analysis, and conclusions that are likely **required** to receive a passing score on this question. In general, the essay grids are provided to assist you in analyzing the essays and are much more detailed than what a student should create during the exam to organize their response to a question.

Issue	Rule	Fact Application	Conclusion
Rescission	**Rescission is an equitable remedy, where the court invalidates a contract because there has been no meeting of the minds in contract formation.** • Grounds for rescission can include: mutual mistake; unilateral mistake; fraud/ misrepresentation; misrepresentation of a material fact (even if not fraudulent).	• Because rescission is an equitable remedy, a court has discretion. • Insurco will assert there was no meeting of the minds in the contract formation process and seek rescission on the grounds of fraud/misrepresentation, mutual mistake, and unilateral mistake.	Insurco will seek rescission
Fraud	**Misrepresentation of material fact** • **Scienter (knowledge/ reckless of falsity)** • **Intent to induce plaintiff's reliance** • **Justifiable reliance** • **Damage**	• **When applying for the liability insurance policy, Pop made the misstatement of fact indicating that his cars were "driven in Hometown," a rural community,** which is cheaper to insure because there would be less traffic and risk of accident in a rural area. • **Pop was likely aware of the falsity of the statement since he knew the Voka was mostly driven in Industry City by Sally while she attended college there.** • Insurco would argue it was made with intent to induce reliance since **most consumers know their rate will increase in a more urban area,** so Pop lied to save money. Pop could argue that the Voka was only located in Industry City when college was in session, and Hometown was the Voka's permanent home base. • **Insurco can establish justifiable reliance on Pop's false statement because the rates were tied to the location of the cars.** • **Insurco would not have entered into the contract at that lower rate, had it been aware that the car was driven in Industry City.** [Needed analysis of fraud, but conclude either way]	Rescission likely permitted on the basis of fraud
Mutual Mistake	**Mutual mistake is made by both parties to the contract** • **Mistake as to basic assumption of the k** • Mistake has material effect • Risk of mistake not imposed on party seeking to avoid the k	• Where the cars are driven is a basic assumption of the contract because the location determines the rate because of the **likelihood of loss.** • **Insurco was mistaken as to this fact because it provided Pop a lower rate on his car insurance, believing that his two cars were driven in Hometown, not City,** and this would have a material effect since the car location dictated the rates. • However, it is unlikely Pop was mistaken since Sally is his daughter and used the Voka in Industry City while attending college.	No rescission for mutual mistake

Continued>

Issue	Rule	Fact Application	Conclusion
Unilateral Mistake	**Unilateral mistake is where one party to the deal makes a mistake.** • Must establish elements of mutual mistake, and • **Other party knows or should have known about that mistake**	• Insurco was mistaken about where the cars were driven, which is a material fact underlying the contract • Mutual mistake elements analyzed above • Pop was aware of Insurco's mistake since he supplied the erroneous information. [Needed some analysis of unilateral mistake, but you could have blended the two mistake analyses together]	Recission for unilateral mistake likely met.
Laches	Unreasonable delay in bringing suit, resulting in prejudice to defendant	• **Insurco's delay in bringing a rescission suit six months after the accident may be unreasonable because** at first, Insurco agreed to pay $250,000. • **Insurco should have had all the information it needed to make a decision about paying the claim and if Insurco intended not to pay, it should have made that clear right after the accident.** • Insurco could argue that they were unable to ascertain the Voka's location in Industry City until they conducted an investigation because **Pop lied that the Voka was only driven in Hometown. As such, the delay was not unreasonable, and Pop should not be allowed to benefit from his own inequitable conduct.** • **No facts indicate Pop was actually prejudiced from Insurco's 6-month delay in seeking rescission.**	Laches defense is unlikely to succeed
Overall Conclusion	The court will likely permit rescission of the contract based on fraud/misrepresentation.		
Pop's cross-complaint and Insurco's defenses			
Reformation	Reformation is an equitable remedy where the court rewrites the contract if there is: • **Meeting of minds** • **Contract as written doesn't reflect agreement because of mutual mistake**	• Reformation is typically available only to the wronged party. • **Because reformation is an equitable remedy, a court has broad discretion in deciding whether it should be awarded, taking into account all of the equities.** • Pop will argue coverage was increased from $100K to $250K rather than $500K, and the court should reform the contract.	Pop will seek reformation

Continued>

Issue	Rule	Fact Application	Conclusion
Mutual Mistake	Mutual mistake is made by both parties to the contract <ul><li>Mistake as to basic assumption of the k</li><li>Mistake has material effect</li><li>Risk of mistake not imposed on party seeking to avoid the k</li></ul>	<ul><li>Pop and Insurco made a valid contract modification and **agreed that the coverage would be increased to $500K.**</li><li>**Insurco mistakenly increased coverage only to $250K** likely due to scrivener's error or some other error, since **both parties clearly intended the amended contract increase coverage to $500K, not $250K.** Pop further complied with his end of the bargain by paying the $150.</li><li>**Issuing the policy for $250K appears to have been a mutual mistake** since the written agreement did not reflect the parties' agreement and it appears a clerical error was made. **The mistake regards a basic assumption of the contract, since the liability limit is a key element of an insurance contract.**</li></ul>	Reformation likely permitted on the basis of mutual mistake
Parol Evidence Rule	<ul><li>**For integrated contracts (intended by the parties to be a final agreement),** no evidence is permitted of prior or contemporaneous agreements inconsistent with the contract's terms.</li><li>**Parol evidence rule is inapplicable to evidence of contract formation defect.**</li></ul>	<ul><li>Insurco would argue that the amended policy was a final integration and parol evidence bars contemporaneous statements.</li><li>However, **Pop is alleging facts that entitle him to reformation based on a defect in contract formation, thus the parol evidence rule does not apply.**</li></ul>	**PER does not apply**
Unclean Hands	**Plaintiff has conducted themself unfairly in the transaction in dispute.**	<ul><li>Here, Insurco has strong arguments for application of this defense, given that it can **likely show that Pop fraudulently induced the contract by intentionally misleading Insurco** into believing the two cars were located in Hometown, when in reality the Voka was located in Industry City. Pop's unfair conduct in inducing the contract at more favorable terms will likely serve as a defense to any claim for reformation.</li></ul>	Unclean hands will provide a defense for Insurco
Overall Conclusion	Pop will be unable to have the contract reformed because Insurco can successfully defend with unclean hands.		

Remedies Question 5
February 2022, Question 3

Thirty years ago, Diana built a large open-air theater to provide an outdoor multi-use entertainment venue. On weekdays, Diana rents the venue to the local dance companies. On weekend evenings, Diana hosts rock concerts at the theater. Revenue from the rock concerts funds most of the operating costs of the venue. The theater employs about 200 people and has been a focus of the city's cultural scene. When built, its location was near the edge of the city. As time went by, city development expanded to include housing in the vicinity of the theater.

Pedro recently purchased a house in a subdivision located adjacent to the theater. Although Pedro knew about the theater when he bought his house, he thought that the new house was a perfect place to raise a family.

As soon as Pedro moved into his new house, he was horrified by the noise and vibration coming from the theater during rock concerts. He could feel the floor shake and could not have a normal conversation because of the loud noise. Pedro later learned that his neighbors complained to Diana about the noise and vibration, that they were unsuccessful in obtaining relief, and that they decided to live with it in the end.

Pedro approached Diana. She explained that she had already taken steps to mitigate the negative impact by requiring that all concerts end by 11:00 p.m. and setting a maximum noise level. Diana explained that the facility could not survive economically without rock concerts and that rock concerts were, by their nature, loud.

A few days later, in an effort to find out if she might be able to relieve Pedro of some of his discomfort, Diana went to his house to determine whether sound-deadening materials might be added. She forgot to tell Pedro that she was coming. Diana let herself into Pedro's backyard, took some measurements, and left without disturbing anything.

Pedro intends to sue Diana.

1. What claims may Pedro reasonably assert against Diana? Discuss.

2. What remedies may Pedro reasonably seek? Discuss.

Remedies Question 5 Assessment
February 2022, Question 3

This is the main way in which the examiners test a permanent injunction. They almost always cross it over with a nuisance in torts. Thus, this is a torts/remedies crossover question. While we do have a crossover section at the end of the book, it is important to have this type of crossover question here in the remedies section as this is the main way to expose you to the remedy of a permanent injunction (not that we assumed you wouldn't be responsible and do all crossover essays too . . . but just in case, here it is!).

The reason you know that you have to discuss the nuisance in detail here as well as the injunction is because call one specifically asks about "claims" Pedro may assert, which means the underlying substantive issues. Call two focuses specifically on the "remedies" Pedro may seek. After reading the call, you won't know which claims and remedies are at issue, but after a quick read of the facts (remember to read the facts once without annotating to quickly get the big picture), the fact pattern has nuisance written all over it with "loud noise" and "vibration." You also have facts as to a trespass to land when Diana goes into the backyard without permission.

This essay is similar to the February 2000 essay (although that one was more difficult with numerous types of injunctions at issue—that essay was in our prior book editions), which is why exposing yourself to as many essays as you can helps with your future issue spotting and organization. Some students express concern over an essay being "old," but there are only so many ways they can test the issues. If you review old and new essays you will see many similarities among testing patterns. For this reason, we recommend you organize as many essays as you can, both new and old, to improve your fact pattern recognition and essay approaches.

Call one tests both public and private nuisance with the results being different as there might be facts that give rise to a possible private nuisance but because Pedro's harms are the same as everyone else's there is no public nuisance. This is a great way for the examiners to test your understanding of the differences between the two types of nuisance. As to the trespass to land, that is an easy straightforward minor issue.

Call two tests damages but those are fairly straightforward. The injunction issue is where the examiners can determine how well you can analyze the facts, particularly focusing on the balancing of hardships element. That is a fact-rich element that requires you to fully use all relevant facts and consider the public interest as well. Make sure you highlight or underline the facts as you use them to ensure you are using all facts and not omitting any arguments and leaving points on the table. There are a lot of facts that go to both Pedro's harms as well the value of the theater to the community. Be sure to use all of these facts to earn maximum points.

It is also worth noting that one state-released answer addressed preclusion, but it isn't clear whether the neighbors actually filed a suit against Diana or just complained to her and gave up. Without specific facts these issues couldn't be fully analyzed, so if you did address this, be brief and move on as there weren't facts to establish the basic elements here. Also note that TRO and preliminary injunctions were not what they were looking for as the harm was already ongoing and Pedro would want to stop it permanently and there is no reason a court would issue an emergency TRO for concerts that had already been going on for 30 years. So, focus your time on the permanent injunction here.

Finally, make note of the areas highlighted in **bold** on the corresponding grid. The bold areas highlight the issues, analysis, and conclusions that are likely **required** to receive a passing score on this question. In general, the essay grids are provided to assist you in analyzing the essays and are much more detailed than what a student should create during the exam to organize their response to a question.

Issue	Rule	Fact Application	Conclusion
1. Claims Pedro may assert			
Private Nuisance	**Substantial and unreasonable interference with another private individual's use or enjoyment of their land.** • Substantial is annoying to the **average person.** • Unreasonable interference occurs when the harm to P outweighs the utility of D's conduct or the harm caused to P is greater than P should be required to bear without consideration. • Courts consider the nature, extent, and frequency of the harm, the neighborhood, land value, and alternatives for D. **Defense—coming to the nuisance is only effective if P came to the nuisance for the purpose of bringing a lawsuit.** [Note this could be discussed here or later]	Here, **Pedro was horrified by the noise and vibration coming from the rock concerts which interfered with his enjoyment of his home because the floors would shake, and he could not have a normal conversation due to the loud noise.** The interference was substantial b/c other neighbors previously complained about the noise and vibration to Diana indicating it was annoying to the average person. The interference may be unreasonable b/c Pedro's harm of being unable to have a conversation in his home and have the floors vibrate might outweigh Diana's conduct of having rock concerts. **However, it might not be unreasonable as there is value to the community as the theater employs 200 people and all concerts end by 11 pm and have a maximum allowed noise level and** only holds concerts on weekends, so it is possible Pedro's harm is not greater than Diana's conduct, and **she did go to his house to see if she could try to install sound-deadening materials.** **Diana could argue that Pedro came to the nuisance since the theater has been around for 30 years and it wasn't until later that the city developed houses there, but this defense usually does not work.**	**P might have a viable private nuisance claim** (but other neighbors were not successful in their earlier attempts to obtain relief but it isn't clear that they sued for a nuisance)
Public Nuisance	**Substantial and unreasonable interference with the community's health, morals, welfare, safety, or property rights.** Courts consider factors such as the location of the nuisance, the frequency and duration, the degree of damage, and the social value of the activity. **Recovery by a private party is only available if the private party suffered damaged that is different in kind and not merely in degree from that suffered by the public.**	Here, arguably the health and safety of the public is being interfered with due to the loud noise and vibrations for similar reasons discussed above. However, Pedro does not suffer damages that are different in kind than others as they **can all hear the noise and other neighbors have already tried to seek relief before for the same problems.** Also, the degree of damage is limited to certain hours and there is a maximum noise level, and the theater employs 200 people so it helps the community. Also, the theater has been there for 30 years and offers local dance companies the ability to use the facilities during the week and the **theater has been a focus of the city's cultural scene.** Also, the theater was built near the edge of the city and the city developed housing near the theater, which was already there.	**Pedro cannot succeed in a public nuisance claim**

Continued>

Issue	Rule	Fact Application	Conclusion
Trespass to Land	**Intentional, physical invasion of the land of another.** Harm to the land is not required.	**Here, Diana went to Pedro's house to determine if she could install sound-deadening materials and let herself into his backyard w/o permission, so she intentionally and physically invaded his property.** The fact that she didn't do any damage does not matter.	Pedro has a valid claim for TTL.
Claim and issue preclusion [Only one state released answer addressed this so it was not necessary to pass]	Claim preclusion bars re-litigation of subsequent claims when there is a final valid judgment on the merits, the same parties are involved, and the same claims. Issue preclusion bars re-litigation of subsequent issues.	Here, it isn't clear whether the same "claims" were actually litigated b/c the facts indicate that neighbors previously "complained to Diana" and were unsuccessful in obtaining relief, but it isn't clear that they ever filed a suit or if they just simply complained to her and gave up. And Pedro wasn't a party to the prior cases if there were cases. For the same reasons, it isn't clear any particular issues were decided either.	No claim or issue preclusion likely.

2. Remedies Pedro may assert

Issue	Rule	Fact Application	Conclusion
Compensatory Damages	**Awarded to P to compensate for loss or injury; measured by the monetary value of P's harm. Damages can be economic or non-economic.** Limitations: • Causation • Certainty • Foreseeable • Unavoidable Past and future damages available **P can recover the costs to repair land for TTL or nuisance and/or for the diminution of value.**	**Pedro didn't incur any costs associated with the nuisance or TTL so the only damages he might seek are for his discomfort and interference with the enjoyment of his land.** The damages aren't certain as there is not a set amount by which to determine but they are caused by Diana's theater and the noise and vibrations. Arguably it is foreseeable that residents will be affected by loud rock concerts nearby, but these concerts and the theater have been there for 30 years and at the edge of the city so it was not foreseeable to Diana that years later people would build houses nearby. **Diana might argue that Pedro didn't mitigate his damages since he moved to the area with the existing theater that is known to host rock concerts on weekends. However, a court might award him the diminution in value of his land, if any.** However, the concerts were there before he purchased the property so it is likely that the value he paid already reflected this possible nuisance since the neighbors had previously complained about it and he just recently bought the house.	Pedro might be able to recover damages for the diminution in value to his property, if any.
Nominal Damages	**P can obtain nominal damages when their rights have been violated but there is no actual harm.**	If P cannot obtain compensatory damages, he might be able to obtain nominal damages, at least for the TTL claim.	P can recover nominal damages.

Continued>

Issue	Rule	Fact Application	Conclusion
Punitive Damages	**Punitive damages are awarded to punish D for intentional conduct** when P is awarded actual damages, D's culpability is greater than negligence, and the damages are proportional (single-digit multiplier).	D did not intentionally try to interfere w/ P's enjoyment of his home or harm his land b/c she operated the theater years before he moved there and only entered his land to try to reduce the noise.	P cannot recover punitive damages
Permanent Injunction [I Pray For Big Desserts]	**A negative injunction will enjoin the D from performing an act. It requires:** **Inadequate legal remedy** • Money damages too speculative • Money damages are inadequate • Multiplicity of suits/**ongoing harm** • Property unique Property/protectable right (hist. reqmt. — modernly success on the merits) **Feasible to enforce** **Balancing of hardships** • **Balance the hardship to P if denied to hardship to D if granted** • Large disparity in hardships • Willful misconduct • **Public interest** **No defenses** • **Coming to the nuisance** • Laches	Here, Pedro would seek to have the court order Diana to stop hosting rock concerts at the theater. • **Since the harm is ongoing due to a continued nuisance,** damages would not remedy the problem b/c the noise and vibrations would continue; and since Diana has already limited the noise level and time, she cannot adequately solve the problem with money. • There is a property interest as Pedro owns his home. • **Since this is a negative injunction and the court can just order Diana to cease the concerts, they can hold her in contempt if she refuses to comply** so supervision should not be an issue and there are no jurisdictional issues. • Pedro will argue that his hardship is severe as he has to endure loud noise and vibrations and can't have a conversation in his own home. **And neighbors have also complained about the noise issues.** • However, his interference is limited to weekends only and to certain hours not after 11 pm and Diana has already limited the noise maximum level. • Further, the theater has been there for 30 years and was there before the houses, it was built near the edge of the city and the City later developed housing near the theater, it rents out the facility to local dance studios during the week and depends on the weekend rock concerts for revenue, and it employs 200 employees and is the focus of the city's cultural scene, so there is a value to the public in having the theater both in terms of money and activities. • **See above for coming to the nuisance** and no laches b/c Pedro just recently moved in.	Pedro likely will not succeed in a permanent injunction

Remedies Question 6
October 2020, Question 5

Daniel's house is for sale. In his living room are two valuable original paintings by Artist, one of the California coastline and the other of a field of Golden State wildflowers. Daniel recently refused an offer from Museum to purchase the paintings for $10,000 each.

Pam went to Daniel's house hoping to buy it before she left on a business trip. As Pam, Daniel and his real estate broker, Bill, inspected the house, Pam noticed the paintings in the living room, commenting that they were beautiful and seemed designed to fit in the house. Pam then offered $400,000 for the house and another $50,000 if the sale included the two paintings. Daniel agreed and asked Bill to draft a contract for the sale of the house and the two paintings for $450,000. Bill promised to have the contract ready before Pam left town the next day.

Bill drafted a written contract, which Daniel signed even though he noticed that Bill had mistakenly omitted from the sale the painting of the California coastline.

Daniel met Pam at the train station, as her train was about to depart. Daniel gave the contract to Pam, telling her, "This is what we agreed to and I've already signed it." Pam's train started to move, so she quickly signed the contract without reading it and jumped on board the train.

When Pam returned from her trip, she was horrified to find that the California coastline painting was not in the house. She immediately telephoned Daniel to ask about the painting, but he told her, "That's what the contract we signed provides," and hung up.

Six months after Pam moved into the house, she noticed in a local newspaper advertisement that Daniel was offering to sell the Artist painting of the California coastline to the highest bidder at an auction two weeks later.

1. What remedy or remedies can Pam reasonably obtain against Daniel? Discuss.

2. What defense or defenses can Daniel reasonably raise? Discuss.

Remedies Question 6 Assessment
October 2020, Question 5

This is a very common remedies question where one call asks about remedies and the other call asks about defenses. This is also common in that the bar examiners label this question as a pure remedies question but some of the remedies you need to address require you to also analyze the underlying issues, such as whether the contract was valid for specific performance, or whether there was fraud or a mistake for rescission or reformation.

This is another example of a racehorse style essay. While it is often recommended that you address remedies starting with legal remedies, then restitution, then equitable remedies, if you started this essay with equitable remedies first due to timing and quickly added in the legal damages at the end (or even within your specific performance or other issues when analyzing whether there was an inadequate legal remedy) that was fine on this particular essay because the equitable and restitutionary remedies were worth more points and the legal remedies were minor. However, one benefit to analyzing the legal remedy of damages first is you can supra that analysis when analyzing the inadequate legal remedy element in your later equitable remedies.

Note that since call two specifically asks about defenses, you should make a concerted effort to discuss some defenses there and not all of them in call one to show the grader you are following directions. However, some of the possible defenses that you discuss here are needed to establish grounds for particular remedies. For example, you need to show some ground to reform or rescind a contract. Here, fraud/misrepresentation and mistake are possible grounds to argue the remedies of reformation and rescission, so naturally those possible defenses will be addressed in call one and then you can reference them in call two. Similarly, some contract defenses might be discussed in call one when analyzing whether there is a valid contract for specific performance. But you could also analyze those in call two and refer below to the defenses when analyzing that element of specific performance. Remember also that when remedies questions ask about defenses and the fact pattern involves a contract, always consider all contract defenses as possible defenses to address.

Remember when thinking about defenses to think broadly. Here both state-released answers raised the parol evidence rule as a possible defense because the facts gave rise to it (whenever there is a discussion of terms before the contract is signed and those terms do not appear in the written contract it is advisable to raise the PER). Another defense that the facts gave rise to in this essay was laches because Pam waited six months after moving into the house and didn't seek relief. The key was to raise some defenses, but not all answers will raise the same defenses and that is fine.

The key to success is practice, practice, practice, and more practice. Practice will improve your issue spotting, your rule understanding and rule recall, your timing, and your overall confidence when approaching the real bar exam because you will have seen most (if not all) of what they throw your way. Keep practicing and do more problems in our crossover section!

Finally, make note of the areas highlighted in **bold** on the corresponding grid. The bold areas highlight the issues, analysis, and conclusions that are likely **required** to receive a passing score on this question. In general, the essay grids are provided to assist you in analyzing the essays and are much more detailed than what a student should create during the exam to organize their response to a question.

Issue	Rule	Fact Application	Conclusion
1. Remedies Pam can obtain			
Expectation (Compensatory) **Damages**	In k, puts P in same position as if D performed on k. For goods, the difference is the contract price and the market value of the item. Damages must be causal, foreseeable, unavoidable, and certain.	Here, if Daniel gave Pam the painting she would have a painting arguably valued at $25K if she agreed to pay $50K for two paintings assuming both were of equal value. Both were original paintings by Artist and both were of nature — the CA coastline and the Golden State wildflowers — so arguably both were similar in price. Arguably the value of each was only $10K since Museum offered $10K each to Daniel for the paintings but since P offered $25K each then perhaps that is the market value. They can also wait to see how much he gets at the auction to see the market value there. Price certain b/c can find values in what Pam offered or the auction or Museum, caused by Daniel not ensuring the k had the terms they agreed to and lying to Pam about it, foreseeable she wanted the paintings since she paid extra for them and told him she wanted them, and unavoidable b/c they are originals so they can't be found elsewhere.	**Pam could get damages**
Replevin	Allows recovery of a specific chattel before trial that was wrongfully taken from P who has the right to possession.	Here, Pam will have the right to possess the painting once the k has been reformed in which she can seek replevin for Daniel to turn over the painting before trial. If it is too difficult to find or have the sheriff seize it, then she will need to go to trial for specific performance.	Pam can seek replevin
Reformation	**Remedy where the court rewrites the contract if there is:** • **Meeting of minds, and** • **Contract as written doesn't reflect agreement** because of an error (fraud/misrepresentation, **mistake,** etc.)	Here there was a meeting of the minds as they both agreed that **Daniel would sell her the house and two paintings for $400K and $50K respectively.** **The k as written doesn't state that b/c the attorney forgot to include one of the paintings** and Daniel noticed that but didn't say anything to Pam about the terms all being in the k as agreed (**hence the fraud/misrepresentation and mistake as discussed below**).	**Pam can have the k reformed to reflect their original agreement as to both paintings**

Continued>

Issue	Rule	Fact Application	Conclusion

Fraud/ Misrepresentation	• Misrepresentation of material fact
	• **Scienter** (knowledge/reckless of falsity)
	• Intent to induce plaintiff's reliance
	  ○ Justifiable reliance
	• Damage
		• Daniel misrepresented that both paintings were in the k when he knew one was not in there and he told Pam they were both in there & the painting was material to the k as she agreed to pay an extra $50K for the two paintings
		• He knew it was false as he noticed the one painting wasn't in the k
		• He intended to induce her reliance by lying to her and having her sign it as she was in a hurry boarding the train
		  ○ Her reliance was justified as she believed him and had to quickly board a train and thought he was telling the truth
		• Damage b/c she doesn't have one painting that she paid for and he wants to sell it at an auction
			Fraud/ misrepresentation can be grounds to reform the k

Mistake	Mutual mistake — made by both parties to the contract • Mistake as to basic assumption of the k • Mistake has material effect • Risk of mistake not imposed on party seeking to avoid the k Unilateral mistake — made where one party to the deal makes a mistake • Must establish elements of mutual mistake, and • Other party knows or should have known about that mistake	No mutual mistake b/c Daniel not mistaken as to the contents of the k b/c he noticed it wasn't in there; but could argue he did instruct the attorney Bill to include both paintings so maybe b/c the attorney made a mistake in the drafting it was a mutual mistake. • Painting was a basic assumption of the k for the extra $50K for the two paintings • Material effect as she paid for a painting she didn't get and was horrified it wasn't in the house when she returned; could argue risk of mistake on her for not reading the k but in a hurry to board a train and Daniel assured her everything they agreed to was in the k • Could be a unilateral mistake since Daniel noticed the missing term and only Pam didn't but arguably she should have known about the mistake since she could have read the k herself and not relied on what he told her but Daniel knew about the mistake and lied to her w/o fixing it first	Mistake can allow reformation of the k

Continued>

Issue	Rule	Fact Application	Conclusion
Rescission	Remedy where the court invalidates a contract because there has been no meeting of the minds in contract formation. Grounds for rescission can include: mistake; fraud/misrepresentation. See above for rules on fraud/misrepresentation and mistake.	As discussed above Pam has valid arguments for fraud/misrepresentation and mistake, so she could also seek to rescind the contract since there was no meeting of the minds as she thought it included both paintings and now Daniel is claiming it did not. If the k were rescinded then she would return the property and the one painting and Daniel would refund her the $450K she paid.	Pam could seek rescission but not the best remedy b/c she won't get what she really wants which is the house & both paintings
Temporary Restraining Order (TRO) [Irish Lads Inhale Beef Pies in Dublin]	**To prevent injustice before preliminary injunction hearing** • **Irreparable harm** • **Likelihood of success** • **Inadequate legal remedy** • **Balance of hardships** • **Willful misconduct/public int.** • No Defenses — laches/unclean hands **Can be issued ex parte (w/o notice) and lasts 10-14 days.**	**Pam might seek a TRO to prevent Daniel from selling the painting at the auction in two weeks** since timing is crucial b/c once it is sold to a BFP, Pam might not be able to get it back. • **Irreparable harm b/c Daniel plans to sell it at an auction to the highest bidder in two weeks and even if Pam tries to get it, she might not be the highest bidder and a BFP would then have it and it's an original so she couldn't get another one like it.** • **Pam likely to succeed in having k reformed so that Daniel would be in breach (see below under reformation).** • Remedy inadequate for same reasons if no other original and money can't replace it unless she can guarantee she is the highest bidder. • **Hardship for Pam is great b/c painting is an original and she can't obtain another one; but for Daniel his hardship is just money and he is the wrongdoer by lying to her about the k after they agreed and he realized the attorney made a mistake.** • Pam did not act in bad faith but arguably her delay might be viewed as unreasonable (see below).	Pam can likely obtain a TRO
Preliminary Injunction	**Same elements as TRO** above, plus **To maintain the "status quo" until full trial on the merits & notice required; bond required**	**Same as above but now Pam can prevent Daniel from selling the painting until after a full trial on the merits but she will need to post a bond and give Daniel notice.**	Pam can obtain a preliminary injunction

Continued>

Issue	Rule	Fact Application	Conclusion
Specific Performance [Chocolate Cheesecake Is My Favorite Dessert]	• **Contract valid; needs offer w/ definite & certain terms, acceptance, consideration, no defenses** • **Conditions of P satisfied** • **Inadequate legal remedy** • Mutuality of performance • **Feasibility** • **No Defenses** [Note the contract formation could be discussed above too on its own]	• k for the sale of a house but comes with paintings so house would be common law & paintings are goods so UCC governs those (could argue primary purpose is house so all CL should govern but courts can split them) • **Pam offered to pay $400K for the house & $50K for the 2 paintings** • **Daniel agreed and asked attorney Bill to draft a written contract** • **Terms omitted one painting but both parties signed the written contract** • **Consideration $ for house/paintings** • **P presumably paid the full price for house ($400K) & paintings ($50K)** since she's living there so **all conditions on her part are met** • Arguably $ could fix the problem b/c she could receive the difference in value for the paintings (as discussed above), but **these are original valuable paintings so she could not get another original of the one painting so it is unique & money won't adequately fix the problem** unless she could buy it at the auction and then get the damages for the difference in price which is possible • Since the painting isn't sold yet at the auction, Daniel could still perform and give Pam the painting and she already performed by paying him for it • **Court can order that painting be turned over to Pam** and hold Daniel in contempt if he doesn't do so; no jx issues • **See below in call two for defenses**	Pam can likely obtain specific performance
Election of remedies	P may choose one of several available recoveries in satisfaction of a single loss.	Since P wants the house and both paintings as they originally agreed she will be better off seeking the TRO & preliminary injunction so he can't sell the painting and then specific performance so he has to give her the painting (if replevin won't work).	Pam will need to elect a remedy

Continued>

Issue	Rule	Fact Application	Conclusion
2. Defenses Daniel can raise			
Defense SOF	**Sale of goods over $500 requires writing & sale of real property requires a writing.**	**SOF requires a writing because painting was over $500 (at $25k if each worth the same amount). Writing must be signed by Daniel, the party to be charged, but the writing doesn't include the painting so need to reform the k to include it.**	k not enforceable because of SOF, unless exception
SOF Exception: Promissory Estoppel [could also try to argue goods paid for or real property—possession, payment]	Rely to detriment, and reliance reasonable and foreseeable.	Pam relied on Daniel's promise that both paintings would be included in the k and she paid $50K for both; and thought it was in the k b/c Daniel told her before she signed quickly at the train station that everything they agreed to was in there when he knew that the one painting was not in there; she signed the k in reliance on what he told her and it is foreseeable she will suffer damages if she pays for a painting she doesn't get.	Promissory estoppel can **overcome SOF here even if term not in writing**
Parol Evidence Rule	**Bars introduction of evidence of prior or contemporaneous agreements that contradict a written contract if the contract is intended as a final and complete expression of the parties.** **Exception for fraud in the contract formation.**	**Daniel will argue that the PER bars any evidence that they agreed to the painting before the written contract since the written contract doesn't contain that term. However, here the court might allow the evidence to show the fraud in the formation or defects in formation.**	**PER likely won't bar the evidence of their earlier discussions**
Laches	**P unreasonably delays causing prejudice to D.**	Here, when Pam returned from her trip and was horrified that the CA coastline painting was not in the house she called Daniel immediately, but when he told her that was what the k they signed said and hung up, she did nothing for 6 months until after she saw the local newspaper advertisement about the painting, which could be an unreasonable delay since she paid $25K for it based on their agreement. **But even with the delay, she arguably did not cause prejudice to Daniel b/c he can wait a bit longer to sell the painting and a court will likely find he was the wrongdoer and she gets the painting anyway and he already got paid for it.**	**Laches won't likely bar Pam's claims**
Fraud/misrepresentation	See above.	See above.	See above
Mistake	See above.	See above.	See above
Unavoidable (for limit on damages)	See above.	See above.	See above

PART 11 TORTS

TORTS TABLE OF CONTENTS

INTRODUCTION TO TORTS

Torts essay questions typically involve fewer issues compared to some of the other subjects; however, the factual analysis of each issue often has greater depth, and many issues can be argued both ways. Consequently, torts essays are fact-intensive and not only require the use of all applicable facts in the analysis, but also application of logical factual inferences to fully and successfully analyze some of the issues and rule elements. To do this, it is best to approach a torts essay (once you have determined that the subject is torts after reading the call or facts if the subject isn't clear from the call) by quickly writing out your issues checklist for torts (on virtual scratch paper or the dry erase board), including all applicable defenses. Since torts questions are often limited in scope to subtopics, such as when a question exclusively focuses on products liability, defamation and privacy torts, or intentional torts, you may wish to develop a mini-checklist to use for the subtopics to save time. Next, you should read the facts carefully once to get the general idea of what torts issues the fact pattern raises. Then, re-read the fact pattern and cross-reference your issues checklist to spot the issues as you read each sentence. Organize your answer by the call of the question (if there is more than one) and then note the issues chronologically as they arise under each call. If there is only one call of the question, organize the issues sequentially as they arise in the facts.

After you have spotted all the issues, you should write out the rule elements for each issue and match the applicable facts or factual inferences that correspond to each element. As you use the facts, you can highlight them in the fact pattern. This ensures you have used all the question facts when you are finished organizing or writing (depending on whether you organized in short-hand form on your white board or virtual scratch paper or wrote your answer as you organized in your actual answer). Should you find some "homeless facts" (some facts that are unused), you should review those facts with your issues checklist to ensure that you haven't missed any issues. Remember: There are rarely "red herrings" in a bar essay question, so all the facts should be used. Often, the "homeless" facts will correspond to either a missed issue or a missed rule element within an issue, resulting in missed analysis. Given that the analysis portion of torts essays is the most heavily weighted part of your essay, you want to take every precaution to avoid missing these points.

Torts essays lend themselves to making logical factual inferences to properly analyze the elements of many issues. For example, when discussing duty and breach within a negligence issue, the facts will not tell you what a reasonable manufacturer would do. Rather, you will need to make a logical inference. To illustrate, in an essay involving a manufacturer failing to include the side effects of a drug, the facts will not tell you that it is common for manufacturers to include such warnings. However, you can logically infer in your negligence analysis (one of the five theories for products liability) that the manufacturer breached its duty to act as a reasonable, prudent manufacturer under the circumstances because a reasonable manufacturer would not only list all side effects on the drugs but would also likely advertise these side effects and require doctors to review them with patients prior to prescribing the drug. These types of logical, factual inferences are common in torts essays and are often required to receive maximum points in your analysis.

Finally, because torts is such a fact-intensive subject, pay special attention to the various fact patterns that commonly trigger an issue to help you with issue spotting. These fact triggers are included in the torts outline.

ISSUES CHECKLIST

INTENTIONAL TORTS/DEFENSES

Battery
Assault
IIED
False imprisonment
Trespass to land
Trespass to chattels
Conversion
Defenses

NEGLIGENCE

STRICT LIABILITY

Animals
Ultrahazardous activities

PRODUCTS LIABILITY

Strict liability
Negligence
Warranty
Misrepresentation
Intent
Defenses

OTHER TORTS

Defamation
Privacy torts
Misrepresentation
Misuse of process
Interfere w/business relations
Nuisance

THIRD-PARTY ISSUES

MEMORIZATION ATTACK SHEET

INTENTIONAL TORTS

- **Battery**
  - Intentional
  - Harmful/offensive contact
- **Assault**
  - Intentional
  - Causing apprehension of
  - Imminent
  - Harmful/offensive contact
- **IIED**
  - Intentional/reckless by
  - Extreme & outrageous conduct causing
  - Severe emotional distress
  - Bystander IIED
- **False imprisonment**
  - Intentional
  - Confinement/restraint
  - Bounded area
  - No reasonable means of escape
  - P aware or harmed
- **Trespass to land**
  - Intentional
  - Physical invasion of
  - Real property of another
- **Trespass to chattels**
  - Intentional
  - Interference with
  - P's use or possession
  - Chattel
- **Conversion**
  - Trespass to chattels with
  - Substantial interference
  - D pays full value

INTENTIONAL TORT DEFENSES

- **Consent**
  - Express
  - Implied
- **Self-defense**
  - Reasonable force
- **Defense of others**
  - Reasonable belief other person could defend
  - Reasonable force
- **Defense of property**
  - Reasonable force to
  - Prevent property tort

- **Recapture chattels**
  - Fresh pursuit
  - Reasonable force
- **Shopkeeper's privilege**
  - Temporarily detain
  - Reasonable belief stolen
- **Arrest under legal authority**
- **Necessity**
  - Reasonably necessary
  - To prevent great harm
  - Public: no damages
  - Private: pay for damage

NEGLIGENCE

- **Duty of care**
  - Duty owed to
    - Foreseeable Ps only (Cardozo)
    - Everyone (Andrews)
  - "Reasonable person" standard
  - Special duty rules
    - No affirmative duty unless
      - Special relationship
      - Caused danger
      - Volunteer rescuer
    - Firefighter
    - Children
    - Bailment
    - Landowners
      - Natural/artificial conditions outside
      - Trespasser
      - Attractive nuisance
      - Invitee: business purpose
      - Licensee: social guest
      - Landlord-tenant
    - Negligence per se
      - Class persons
      - Type of harm
- **Breach**
  - Fail to meet standard of care
  - BPL balancing test
  - Res ipsa loquitur
- **Actual cause**
  - But-for test
  - Alternative causes
  - Joint tortfeasors (substantial factor)
- **Proximate cause**
  - Reasonable foreseeability
  - Eggshell-skull P
  - Intervening causes

◆ **Damages**
  • Causal
  • Foreseeable
  • Certain
  • Unavoidable
◆ **NIED**
  • Zone of danger
  • Bystander
  • Special cases
◆ **Defenses**
  • Contributory negligence
  • Comparative negligence
  • Assumption of risk

STRICT LIABILITY

◆ **Animals**
  • Trespass/Wild
  • Domestic if known propensity
◆ **Ultrahazardous Activity**
  • Significant risk of serious harm
  • Can't eliminate risk with reasonable care
  • Not common in community
◆ **For both, also analyze causation and damages**

PRODUCTS LIABILITY — 5 THEORIES

◆ **Strict liability**
  • Commercial supplier
  • Places product in stream of commerce
  • Product is defective
    ◆ Manufacturing
    ◆ Design
      • Consumer expect. test
      • Risk-utility
    ◆ Warning
  • Actual cause
  • Proximate cause
  • Damages
◆ **Negligence** (see above)
◆ **Warranties**
  • Express
  • Implied
    ◆ Merchantability
    ◆ Fitness for a particular purpose
◆ **Misrepresentation** (see below)
◆ **Intentional**
  • Substantial certainty
◆ **Defenses for all theories**

FRAUD/MISREPRESENTATION

◆ **Fraud/Intentional misrepresentation**
  • Misrepresentation of fact
  • Knowing/recklessly
  • Intent to induce P reliance
  • Causation-actual reliance
  • Justifiable reliance
  • Pecuniary damages
◆ **Negligent misrepresentation**
  • Same as above
  • Business/professional
  • No reasonable grounds to think true

NUISANCE

◆ **Private nuisance**
  • Substantial, unreasonable interference
  • Use/enjoyment of property
◆ **Public nuisance**
  • Substantial, unreasonable interference
  • Health, safety, property rights of community
  • Private party can recover w/ different damage only
◆ **Defenses**
  • Legislation (persuasive)
  • Assumption of risk/comparative negligence
  • Coming to nuisance = no

DEFAMATION

◆ **Common law**
  • Defamatory statement
  • Of or concerning P
  • Publication to 3rd party who understands
  • Intentional or negligently
  • Causation
  • Damages
    ◆ Libel: presumed
    ◆ Slander: prove special unless slander per se
◆ **Constitutional law (addl.)**
  • Public concern
  • Fault in publication by D
    ◆ Public figure — malice
    ◆ Private person — negligence
◆ **Defenses**
  • Consent
  • Truth
  • Privilege — absolute/qualified

PRIVACY RIGHTS

◆ **Appropriation**
  • P's name or picture
  • Unauthorized use for
  • D's commercial advantage
◆ **Intrusion upon seclusion**
  • Intrusion of private aspect
  • In private place
  • Highly offensive to a reasonable person
◆ **False light**
  • Publicly
  • Attribute views to P
  • In false light
  • Highly objectionable to reasonable person
◆ **Public disclosure of private facts**
  • Public disclosure
  • Private facts
  • Highly offensive to reasonable person

MISUSE OF LEGAL PROCESSES

◆ **Malicious prosecution**
  • Legal proceedings
  • End in P's favor
  • No probable cause
  • Improper purpose
  • Damages
◆ **Abuse of process**
  • Wrongful use of process
  • Ulterior purpose
  • Damage P

INTERFERENCE

◆ **Interference with business relations**
  • Contract or business expectancy
  • D's knowledge of same
  • Intentional interference
  • Damages
◆ **Defense: Privilege**
  • Fair competition
◆ **Interference with family relations**
  • Consortium and services for spouse or child

THIRD-PARTY ISSUES

◆ **Vicarious liability**
  • Scope of employment
  • Employee vs. independent contractor
◆ **Multiple Ds**
  • Joint & several liability
  • Contribution
  • Indemnity

OTHER RULES

◆ **Survival rights**
  • COA survives death
◆ **Wrongful death**
  • Next of kin can recover
◆ **Tort immunity**
  • Governmental
  • Intrafamily

TORTS RULES OUTLINE

I. INTENTIONAL TORTS

A. Prima facie case: All intentional torts require an **act** by the defendant, the defendant's **intent** to bring about some physical or mental **effect** upon another person, and the effect must be legally **caused** by defendant's act or something the defendant set in motion.

1. **Intent** occurs either directly, such as when the defendant takes volitional action with the **purpose** to bring about the effect, or indirectly when the defendant **knows with substantial certainty** that a particular effect will occur.

2. **Transferred intent** will provide the requisite intent when the defendant held the necessary intent with respect to one person but instead **commits a different tort against** that **person or any other person**, or the **intended tort against a different person. Except,** transferred intent cannot be invoked with the intentional torts of conversion or intentional infliction of emotional distress (IIED).

> **Exam tip:** When analyzing intentional torts on an exam, pay attention to the possibility of **transferred intent** when the person harmed is not the one to whom the harm was directed or when the harm is of a different type of tort than that intended.

3. **Causation** is the effect legally caused by the defendant's act or some action that is set in motion by defendant. Causation can also be satisfied if the defendant's act was a **substantial factor** in bringing about the effect. [Note: Causation is typically not analyzed for intentional torts.]

B. Battery is the **intentional** infliction of a **harmful or offensive** bodily **contact**.

1. **Intent:** Intent to contact can be satisfied either through establishing defendant's **purpose** or **knowledge with substantial certainty**.

2. **Harmful or offensive:**
   a. **Harmful** contact causes **pain or bodily damage**; or
   b. **Offensive** contact offends a **reasonable person's sense of dignity**.

3. **Contact:** The bodily contact can be **direct** or **indirect**; and includes contact with an object closely identified with plaintiff's body.

C. Assault is the **intentional** causing of an **apprehension** of an **imminent harmful** or **offensive contact.**

1. **Intent:** Intent to cause apprehension or contact can be satisfied either through establishing defendant's **purpose** or **knowledge with substantial certainty**. For an assault, the plaintiff can intend to cause apprehension of an imminent touching, or intend to make contact.

2. **Causing apprehension of:** The plaintiff must be put in immediate apprehension of an imminent harmful or offensive touching. Thus, the **plaintiff must be aware** of the threat.

3. **Imminent:** The defendant must have the **apparent present ability** to carry out the threat.

4. **Harmful or offensive contact**
   a. **Harmful** contact causes **pain or bodily damage**; or
   b. **Offensive** contact offends a **reasonable person's sense of dignity**.

D. Intentional infliction of emotional distress (IIED) is the **intentional or reckless** infliction of **severe emotional or mental distress** caused by defendant's **extreme and outrageous** conduct.

1. **Intent** to cause emotional distress can be satisfied three ways: 1) By the **purpose** to cause emotional distress; or 2) with **knowledge with substantial certainty** that emotional distress will result; or 3) with **reckless disregard** of the high probability emotional distress will occur. Transferred intent cannot be used to satisfy the intent element.

2. **Severe emotional distress:** The emotional distress suffered by the plaintiff must be severe, though bodily harm/physical symptoms are *not* required.

3. **Extreme and outrageous** conduct is that **beyond all possible bounds of decency**.

4. **Bystander IIED** (third-person liability) occurs where the defendant intentionally or recklessly directs extreme and outrageous conduct at someone other than the plaintiff (third person*).* The plaintiff (bystander) can recover for IIED if:
   a. Plaintiff was physically **present,** and
   b. **Known** by the defendant to be present, and is either
   c. A **close relative** of the third person, or
   d. **Suffers bodily harm** as a result of the severe emotional distress (e.g., heart attack).

E. **False imprisonment** occurs where the defendant **intentionally** causes the plaintiff to be **confined,** restrained, or detained to a **bounded area** with **no reasonable means of escape**, of which the plaintiff is either **aware or harmed**.
   1. **Intent:** Intent to confine can be satisfied either through establishing defendant's **purpose** or **knowledge with substantial certainty**.
   2. **Confined,** restrained, or detained.
   3. **Bounded area:** Confinement must be within a bounded area.
   4. **No reasonable means of escape**.
   5. **Awareness:** Plaintiff must be **aware** of the confinement or **suffer harm** from the confinement.

F. **Trespass to land** is the **intentional physical invasion** of the **land of another**.
   1. **Intent:** Intent to enter land is satisfied by the **purpose** to voluntarily invade the land of another. However, the defendant only needs to intend to invade the land they invade, and need not intend to invade the *land of another,* so any mistake as to land ownership will *not* provide a defense.
   2. **Physical invasion** of the land does not require that the land be harmed, and includes:
      a. The entry onto another's land without permission;
      b. Remaining upon the land without the right to be there; or
      c. Placing or projecting an object upon land without permission.
   3. **Real property** of another.

G. **Trespass to chattels** is an **intentional interference** with a person's **use or possession** of a **chattel**.
   1. **Intent:** Intent to interfere with chattels is satisfied by the **purpose** to interfere with the chattel of another. However, the defendant only needs to intend to interfere with the chattel, so a mistake as to chattel ownership will *not* provide a defense.
   2. **Interference with use or possession** which precludes the chattel owner from using or possessing their chattel. Typically, this will be for a temporary time period.
   3. **Chattel** is personal property.
   4. **Damages:** The measure of damages is the chattel's loss of value caused by the loss of use.

H. **Conversion** is an **intentional interference** with the plaintiff's **possession** or ownership of **property** that is **so substantial** that it warrants requiring the defendant to pay the property's **full value**.
   1. **Intent:** Intent to interfere with chattel is satisfied by the **purpose** to interfere with the chattel of another. However, the defendant only needs to intend to interfere with the chattel, so a mistake as to chattel ownership will not provide a defense. Transferred intent cannot be used to satisfy the intent element.
   2. **Substantial interference with use or possession:** The interference with the chattel must be so substantial that it warrants the defendant pay the chattel's full value. For example, interference is substantial where one takes possession of a chattel, transfers possession of a chattel to a third person, refuses to return a chattel, or destroys a chattel.
   3. **Chattel** is personal property.
   4. **Damages:** The measure of damages is the chattel's market value at the time of the conversion.

II. DEFENSES TO INTENTIONAL TORTS

A. **Consent:** Plaintiff consents to defendant's conduct. Consent can be express or implied.
   1. **Scope:** Conduct may not go beyond the scope of the consent given.
   2. **Consent to crimes:** Courts are split as to when the defendant's act against plaintiff is a criminal act. The majority of courts hold that plaintiff's consent is ineffective in this situation.

B. **Self-defense:** A person is entitled to use **reasonable force** to prevent any threatened harmful or offensive bodily contact, and any threatened confinement or imprisonment.
   1. **Deadly force:** Use of deadly force is only allowed if the defendant is in danger of death or serious bodily harm.

2. **Degree of force:** Defendant may only use the degree of force **reasonably necessary** to prevent the threatened harm.

C. **Defense of others:** A person may use **reasonable force** to defend another person when they **reasonably believe** that the other person could have used force to defend themself. The same rules regarding use of force apply as in self-defense.

D. **Defense of property:** A person may use **reasonable force** to defend their real or personal property.

    1. **Warning required:** Defendant must first make a verbal demand that the intruder stop, unless it reasonably appears that it would be futile or dangerous.

    2. **Deadly force:** Defendant may only use deadly force **if non-deadly force will not suffice,** and the defendant reasonably believes that without deadly force, **death or serious bodily harm** will result.

        a. **Mechanical devices:** A property owner may only use a mechanical device to protect their property if they would have been privileged to use the same degree of force if present at the time.

E. **Recapture of chattels**: A property owner has the general right to use **reasonable force** to regain possession of chattels wrongfully taken by another.

    1. **Fresh pursuit:** The property owner must be in fresh pursuit of the taken chattel.

    2. **Deadly force is not allowed** to recapture of chattels.

F. **Shopkeeper's privilege:** Shopkeepers have a privilege to **temporarily detain** individuals whom they **reasonably believe** to be in possession of **shoplifted goods**.

    1. **Temporarily detain:** Temporary detention is allowed for a **reasonable time** to investigate if shoplifting has occurred, which is typically for 10 to 15 minutes. The police must be called to make an arrest.

G. **Arrest under a legal authority** is allowed as a defense when the defendant was exercising their legal rights and duties by restraining the plaintiff.

H. **Necessity:** A person may interfere with the real or personal property of another when it is reasonably and apparently **necessary to prevent great harm** to third persons or the defendant themself.

    1. **Public necessity** applies when the threatened harm was to the **community at large** or to many people. Should property be damaged by the public necessity, **no compensation is owed**.

    2. **Private necessity** applies when a person acts to prevent injury to **themself or their property**, or another's person or property. Should damage to property result from the private necessity, the defendant **must pay for any damage**.

Exam tip: Although intentional torts are not heavily tested on the essays, when they are tested, it is useful to write out a quick **issues checklist** of all intentional torts and their defenses. In addition, it is common for more than one intentional tort to apply to a given fact pattern, so consider all possible intentional torts. Lastly, always look at the potential **applicable defenses,** as these are always issues that should be raised and analyzed even if you ultimately find that they do not apply.

III. **NEGLIGENCE**

A. **Prima facie case:** Defendant's conduct imposes an unreasonable risk upon another, which results in injury to that other person. Plaintiff must prove the following elements: **duty, breach, actual cause, proximate cause, and damages**.

B. **Duty of care:** A person has a duty to act as a **reasonable person**. There are two duty considerations to assess: to whom the duty is owed and the applicable standard of care.

    1. **To whom duty of care is owed**

        a. **Foreseeable plaintiffs:** The **majority** of courts hold that a duty is only owed to **foreseeable plaintiffs in the zone of danger** (Cardozo view).

        b. **Everyone:** A **minority** of courts hold that a duty is owed to **everyone** including unforeseeable plaintiffs (Andrews view).

2. **Standard of care**
   a. **General:** A person has a duty to act as a **reasonable person under the circumstances**, unless a special duty standard of care applies (see III.B.2.b below for the special duties of care).
      1. The circumstances considered in determining what is reasonable generally include the physical characteristics of defendant but does not include the mental characteristics of defendant.
   b. **Special duty rules:**
      1. **Affirmative duties to act:** Defendant generally has **no duty to take affirmative action** to help plaintiff, **except:**
         a. **Special relationship:** A defendant has an affirmative duty to act where there is a special relationship, such as a business or landowner holding premises open to the public, or landlords and tenants, or other special relationships;
         b. **Causing the danger:** A defendant has an affirmative duty to act when their **conduct placed plaintiff in danger**; or
         c. **Volunteer rescuer "Good Samaritan":** Where a defendant voluntarily begins to render assistance to plaintiff, they **must proceed with reasonable care**.
      2. **Professionals** and tradespersons are required to possess the **knowledge and skill** of a member of their profession or occupation in good standing.
         a. **Firefighter's rule.** Firefighters, police officers, and other professional risk takers who are injured in the **line of duty** are **prohibited from suing for negligence** for injuries sustained **stemming from the inherent risks** they assume with their profession.
      3. **Children** have a duty to conform to the conduct of a child of like age, intelligence, and experience.
         a. **Exception — child engaged in adult activity:** Children engaged in a **potentially dangerous activity** normally pursued only by adults are held to an adult standard of care.
      4. **Bailment duties** (Where bailee holds possession of bailor's goods/property.)
         a. **Bailor duties:** For a **gratuitous** bailment, the bailor must inform of known, dangerous defects in the chattel. For a bailment for **hire**, the bailor must inform of chattel defects of which they are or should be aware.
         b. **Bailee duties:** Standard of care depends on who benefits from the bailment. Where the sole benefit is for the bailor, the standard of care is low for the bailee. Where the sole benefit is for the bailee, a higher standard of care is imposed. Where the bailment is mutually beneficial, an ordinary standard of care is imposed.
      5. **Landowners and occupiers:** The standard of care depends on whether the damage occurs outside the premises or on the premises.
         a. **Damage** occurs **outside the premises:**
            i. **Natural conditions: No duty** exists to protect one **outside** the premises from damage caused by hazardous **natural conditions** on the premises.
            ii. **Artificial conditions:** A duty exists to prevent one **outside** the premises from damage caused by an **unreasonable risk of harm** for unreasonably dangerous **artificial conditions**.
         b. **Damage** occurs **on the premises:** When damage occurs on the premises, the **status of the plaintiff** as a trespasser, invitee, licensee, and/or status as landlord or tenant **determines the standard of care**.
            i. **Trespassers:** A landowner generally owes **no duty to make the land safe or warn of dangerous conditions** to undiscovered trespassers or invitees/licensees that go beyond the scope of their invitation.
               (A) **Exceptions** to general trespasser rule
                  (1) **Known or frequent trespassers:** There is a duty to warn known or frequent trespassers of **known dangers and artificial conditions** that pose a risk of **death or serious bodily harm**.

    (2) **Attractive nuisance doctrine:** A landowner must exercise **ordinary care** to avoid **foreseeable injury to children** if
        (I) The owner **knew or should have known** that the area is one where **children trespass**;
        (II) The condition poses an **unreasonable risk** of **serious injury or death**;
        (III) The children **do not discover the risk** or realize the danger **due to their youth**;
        (IV) The **benefit to the owner** and **expense to remedy the condition is slight compared to the risk**; and
        (V) The owner **fails to use reasonable care** to eliminate the danger.

Issue spotting tip: When there are **children** involved in a tort fact pattern, always consider the **attractive nuisance doctrine** as a possible issue when evaluating negligence. Also, the children do not have to be "attracted" to the area or object at issue since that is not part of the rule.

---

    ii. **Invitee** enters the land in response to an invitation by owner to do **business** or as a public invitee for land **open to the public** at large. The owner has a **duty to make a reasonable *inspection* to find hidden dangers** and take affirmative action to remedy a dangerous condition (make necessary repairs).
    iii. **Licensee** enters the land with the **owner's consent** for their own purpose (e.g., social guests). An owner has a **duty to *warn* of all known dangerous conditions** that create an unreasonable risk of harm that the **licensee is unlikely to discover** and to **use reasonable care** in conducting its active operations on the property. However, there is no duty to repair or inspect the premises.
  c. **Landlord-tenant standards of care:** There are special standards of care imposed on landlords and tenants.
    i. **Lessee of realty:** Lessee (tenant) has a general **duty to maintain the premises** and has the **same duties owed by landowners** noted above.
    ii. **Lessor of realty:** In addition to the duties generally owed by landowners noted above, the lessor (landlord) must:
        (A) **Warn tenant of existing dangers** they **know or should know** that the tenant/lessee is not likely to discover.
        (B) **Repair not negligently:** If the lessor **promises to repair,** they must not do so negligently.
        (C) **Maintain common areas:** Lessor must use **reasonable care** to maintain the common areas.

Memorization tip: Since there are so many different standards, a mnemonic to help memorize the different duty categories is **A**ll **P**ets **C**an **B**ring **L**ove (for the main standard of care categories – **A**ffirmative, **P**rofessional, **C**hildren, **B**ailment, and **L**and). If you want to memorize the individual categories within these, you can also remember **S**ome **C**uddle **V**ery **N**icely **A**nd **T**ake **I**n **L**ots of **L**ove **T**oo – the first three go to Affirmative and the rest go to landowner duties; other broad categories don't have sub-categories (**S**pecial relationship, **C**ausing the danger, **V**olunteer rescuer, **N**atural conditions, **A**rtificial conditions, **T**respasser, **I**nvitee, **L**icensee, **L**andlord/ **T**enant).

---

6. **Negligence per se**—A **violation of a statute** can establish the duty and breach elements of negligence.
   a. **Negligence per se:** Defendant is negligent per se if they:
      i. **Violate a statute** without excuse; and
      ii. **Plaintiff** is within **the class of persons** the statute is designed to protect; and
      iii. **Injury** stems from the **type of harm** the statute is designed to guard against.
   b. **Violation of statute may be excused:** Defendant's violation may be excused if
      i. Compliance would create a **greater risk** of harm; or
      ii. The defendant was **incapacitated**; or
      iii. The defendant was **unaware** of the **factual circumstances** that made the statute applicable.
   c. **Establishes duty and breach:** Negligence per se analysis establishes the elements of duty and breach in negligence, but plaintiff must still prove **causation and damage**.
   d. **Compliance** with a statute does not itself establish that defendant was not negligent.

> **Exam tip:** When addressing duty in negligence, analyze the general negligence duty first. It may be a slam-dunk, but if the plaintiff is unforeseeable, do a full Cardozo/Andrews analysis. Next, identify the general standard of care, and then analyze any other special duties that potentially apply. For example, if there is a statute in the fact pattern, analyze negligence under both the general duty standard as well as the negligence per se standard. Lastly, do not forget to analyze the remaining elements of negligence.

C. **Breach of duty**
   1. **Breach:**
      a. Generally, breach occurs when the defendant's conduct **fails to conform to the applicable standard of care.**
      b. **BPL balancing test** determines if the **risk** is outweighed by its **utility**. Breach occurs when the **probability of loss** and **gravity of loss** is greater than the **burden** of taking precautions (PL > B).
   2. **Res ipsa loquitur** means **"the thing speaks for itself"** and can be used to establish breach of duty in situations where the event transpiring creates an inference that the defendant was probably negligent because:
      a. The accident is a type that **ordinarily does not occur in the absence of negligence**; and
      b. **Other causes**, including the conduct of the plaintiff and third persons, are sufficiently **eliminated** by the evidence (such as when the defendant had exclusive control).
D. **Actual Cause (causation in fact)**
   1. **But-for test:** Generally, **but for** the defendant's act, the injury to plaintiff would not have resulted.
   2. **Multiple faults causing harm**
      a. **Alternative causes where only one act at fault:** When there are two acts, but **only one** of which could have **caused the injury**, but it is unknown which act caused the injury, the **burden of proof shifts to each defendant** to show that the other caused the harm.
      b. **Joint tortfeasors use substantial factor test:** Where two or more defendants are at fault and their **conduct combines** to cause the harm to the plaintiff, they will all be **jointly and severally liable**, since their actions were each a substantial factor in causing the injury.
E. **Proximate cause**
   1. **Reasonable foreseeability test:** Generally, a defendant is liable for all harmful results that were **reasonably foreseeable**.
      a. **Eggshell-skull plaintiff:** The defendant is also liable for any additional and **unforeseen physical consequences** caused by plaintiff's weakness or susceptibility because the defendant **takes the plaintiff as they are.**

2. **Intervening causes**
    a. **Foreseeable:** Defendant is **liable** for all **foreseeable intervening causes** (such as subsequent medical malpractice and negligence by rescuers).
    b. **Unforeseeable:** Defendant is generally **not liable** for **superseding intervening causes** that are not a normal response or are **not a reasonably foreseeable reaction** to the situation created by defendant's conduct; superseding intervening causes often result from an interruption in the chain of causation.

> **Exam tip:** When analyzing negligence issues, the majority of the points and analysis are in analysis of the breach and proximate cause elements since those elements tend to be the most fact-intensive. Further, since there are no "homeless" facts in the essays, use all the facts available to analyze these two elements. Finally, it is often necessary to use logical inferences when analyzing these elements. The facts will not tell you what a reasonable person ordinarily does to determine whether the defendant owed a duty and breached a duty, so to properly analyze these elements, you will need to make a logical inference as to what a reasonable person would have done in the given situation. For example, a reasonably prudent driver stops at red lights.

F. **Damages**
    1. **Actual injury required:** Damages require an actual injury to the plaintiff and nominal damages are not available for negligence.
    2. **Types of damages:** Plaintiff may recover damages for direct loss, out-of-pocket economic losses stemming from the injury, pain and suffering, and hedonistic damages (loss of ability to enjoy life).
    3. **Establishing damages:** In addition to establishing that the damages/harms are **caused** by the defendant's conduct, that the damages were **foreseeable**, can be calculated with **certainty**, and were **unavoidable** (e.g., seek treatment to mitigate damages).
    4. **Punitive damages** are available only if the defendant's conduct was wanton and willful.

> **Exam tip:** Generally, damages are clear since someone is injured. Usually, this element can be established with one line of analysis. Likewise, actual causation can similarly often be analyzed in one sentence using the "but for" rule. So, remember to **wisely allocate your time** when analyzing the elements of negligence since each element is not equally weighted in points.

> **Negligence fact triggers:**
>
> - Actions or omissions by people
> - Manufacturers, workers, or employees doing a job or task (often incorrectly)
> - Mistakes (failure to file claims timely, secure chemicals, supervise children, leave car running, etc.)
> - Manufacturers or companies using cheaper products that are less safe when alternative products are available

G. **Negligent infliction of emotional distress (NIED):** Defendant is liable for NIED when the defendant engages in **negligent conduct** that causes the plaintiff to suffer **serious emotional distress**.

1. **Zone of danger and in fear for own safety:** Plaintiff suffers a threat of a physical impact that **directly causes serious emotional distress**. Most jurisdictions require physical symptoms (e.g., miscarriage, heart attack).
2. **Bystander in fear for others' safety:** Plaintiff suffers serious emotional distress from contemporaneously perceiving (see, hear, etc.) bodily injury to a close family member, without threat of personal threat impact. Most jurisdictions do not require physical symptoms.
3. **Special cases:** A person has a special relationship with the tortfeasor and suffers serious emotional distress (e.g., mishandling a dead body, misreporting a death, incorrect terminal diagnosis). Most jurisdictions do not require physical symptoms.

IV. **DEFENSES TO NEGLIGENCE**
   A. **Contributory negligence** is where the plaintiff's own negligence contributes proximately to their injuries, and is a complete bar to recovery. This system is abolished in most jurisdictions.
   B. **Comparative negligence** applies when the plaintiff's own negligence has also contributed to their injuries, but it does not completely bar recovery. The liability is divided between the plaintiff and defendant **in proportion to their relative degrees of fault.**
      1. **Pure comparative negligence** allows recovery in proportion of fault regardless of how negligent the plaintiff was, but plaintiff's recovery will be reduced by their proportionate negligence. Plaintiff's share is deducted "off the top."
      2. **Partial comparative negligence** bars the plaintiff's recovery if their negligence was more serious than the defendant's (in some states, at least as serious). This typically means that the plaintiff's **recovery is barred** where their own negligence was **more than 50%.**
   C. **Assumption of the risk:** Plaintiff may be denied recovery if they assumed the risk of any damage caused by defendant's act where they **knew of the risk** and **voluntarily consented** despite the risk.

> **Exam tip:** Always discuss defenses with negligence. It is best to address all three defenses quickly, each with its own heading. Rarely is a full negligence discussion necessary to establish plaintiff's contributory negligence, but the issue should still be raised as a possibility.

V. **STRICT LIABILITY, which is liability without fault, applies to the following activities:**
   A. **Animals:** An owner is strictly liable for:
      1. **Trespass: Reasonably foreseeable damage** done by a trespass of their **animals**;
      2. **Wild animals:** Non-trespass injuries caused by wild animals that result from a **dangerous propensity that is typical of the species**; and
      3. **Domestic animals known to be dangerous:** Injuries caused by domestic animals only if the owner **knew or had reason to know** of that particular animal's **dangerous propensities**.
   B. **Ultrahazardous/abnormally dangerous activities:** An activity is abnormally dangerous if it is:
      1. An activity that creates a **significant risk of serious harm**;
      2. The **risk cannot be eliminated** by the exercise of reasonable care;
      3. The activity is not **common in the community**.
   C. **Products liability** (see section VI below)
   D. **Defenses**
      1. **Assumption of the risk** (above) is a defense to strict liability.
      2. **Comparative negligence** (above) may provide a defense in most jurisdictions.
      3. **Contributory fault** (above) is **not** a defense to strict liability.

> **Exam tip:** Remember strict liability establishes the duty and breach elements, but you still need to prove causation and damages.

VI. PRODUCTS LIABILITY

A. **Five theories are available to establish products liability for a commercial seller:** Strict tort liability, negligence, warranty, misrepresentation, and intent.

B. **Strict liability:** A seller of a product has strict liability (liablity without fault) for personal injuries caused by a defective product. Plaintiff must prove the following elements: **commercial supplier, defective product, actual cause, proximate cause, and damages**.

   1. **Commercial supplier:** A commercial supplier is one who places a product in the **stream of commerce** without substantial alteration. A commercial supplier includes retailers and other nonmanufacturers (e.g., wholesalers, component manufacturers, etc.), and the product manufacturer.

   2. **Product is defective:** There are three ways a product can be defective: manufacturing defect, design defect, and warning defect.

      a. **Manufacturing defect** exists when the product is different and more dangerous than all the others because it **deviated from its intended design**. In other words, the product was **not manufactured as intended**.

      b. **Design defect** exists when all products of a line are the same and they all bear a feature whose **design itself is defective** and unreasonably dangerous; courts use the following two tests to establish a design defect:

         1. **Consumer expectation test:** A product's performance must meet the **minimum safety expectations** of its ordinary users **when used in a reasonably foreseeable** manner.

         2. **Risk-utility test:** A product is defective if the **risk of danger inherent in the design outweighs the benefits** of such design and the danger could have been reduced or avoided by the adoption of a **reasonable, cost-effective alternative design.** The court will consider the **cost and utility** of an alternative design compared to the cost and utility of the current design.

      c. **Warning defect** exists when the maker **fails to give adequate warnings** as to a **known (or should have been known) danger** in the product or in a particular use of the product that is nonobvious. Some courts use **risk-utility analysis** when the risk could have been reduced or avoided by reasonable instructions or warnings.

      d. **Compliance with industry standards** does not establish that a product is *not* defective; but lack of compliance can establish that a product *is* defective.

> **Exam tip:** In products liability questions, there is often more than one defect, so consider all three product defect possibilities and analyze each separately. Most of the analysis in products liability questions will involve establishing the defective product since most facts are applicable to that element.

   3. **Actual cause:** Plaintiff must show that **but for** the defect, they would not have been injured and that the **defect existed at the time it left defendant's control**.

   4. **Proximate cause:** Same analysis as in negligence cases (foreseeability).

   5. **Damages:** Physical injury or property damage must be shown. There is no recovery for purely economic loss.

   6. **Defenses**

      a. **Assumption of the risk** is a defense.

      b. **Contributory negligence** is **not** a defense.

      c. **Comparative negligence** for product misuse may be a defense, depending on the jurisdiction, but not if the plaintiff's negligence or product misuse was **foreseeable**.

      d. **Disclaimers of liability** are **not effective**.

      e. **Compliance with industry standards** does not establish that a product is not defective, so this will **not provide an effective defense**.

C. **Negligence:** See Section III above. However, note that **retailers and wholesalers** are rarely liable under a negligence theory for products liability since they only have a duty to inspect or warn of *known* dangers. A manufacturer likely will be liable under a negligence theory.

D. **Warranty**

1. **Express warranty:** An express warranty is any statement of fact or promise concerning goods. The plaintiff need only show that the product did not live up to its warranty to establish breach of express warranty.

2. **Implied warranty of merchantability:** A warranty of merchantability is implied in every sale of goods, warranting that they are **fit for the ordinary purpose** for which the goods are used.

3. **Fitness for a particular purpose:** A warranty of fitness for a particular purpose is implicated in every sale of goods when the **seller knows** or has reason to know that the buyer wants the goods for a **particular purpose** and the **buyer relies on the seller's judgment** to recommend a suitable product.

4. **Defenses**
   a. **Assumption of the risk** is a defense.
   b. **Comparative negligence** for product misuse (unless plaintiff's negligence/misuse was foreseeable) is a defense.
   c. **Failure to give notice** of breach within a reasonable time under the UCC.

E. **Misrepresentation of fact:** Seller will be liable for misrepresentations of fact concerning a product when the statement was a **material fact concerning quality or uses of goods** and the seller **intended to induce reliance** by the buyer and **did in fact rely**. Plaintiff must still prove actual cause, proximate cause, and damages. Comparative negligence can operate as a defense, unless defendant's misrepresentation was intentional.

F. **Intent:** Defendant is liable if defendant **intended the consequences** or knew they were **substantially certain** to occur. (Defenses are the same as for intentional torts; punitive damages allowed here.)

Products liability fact triggers:

- Manufacturers of products
- Retail sellers
- Products
- Injury due to use of product
- Instructions for product use or lack of instructions
- Company decides to use cheaper or less safe technology when other options available

VII. MISREPRESENTATION
A. **Fraud: Intentional misrepresentation** is common law fraud or deceit. One must prove:
1. **Misrepresentation** (by actions or intentional concealment) of a **material fact,**
2. Made with **knowledge of statement's falsity** or **reckless indifference** of the truth (scienter),
3. **Intent to induce plaintiff's reliance** on the misrepresentation,
4. **Causation** (actual reliance by plaintiff),
5. **Justifiable reliance** by plaintiff, and
6. **Pecuniary damages** to plaintiff.
B. **Negligent misrepresentation** requires establishing:
1. **Misrepresentation** by defendant in a **business or professional capacity,**
2. **Negligence standard:** Defendant acted with **no reasonable grounds for believing the misrepresentation to be true,**
3. **Intent to induce plaintiff's reliance** on the misrepresentation,
4. **Causation** (actual reliance by plaintiff),
5. **Justifiable reliance by plaintiff,** and
6. **Pecuniary damages** to plaintiff.

VIII. NUISANCE
A. **Private nuisance** is a **substantial, unreasonable interference** with another private individual's **use or enjoyment of their land** or land in which they have an interest.
1. **Substantial interference** is interference that is offensive, inconvenient, or **annoying to the average person** in the community.
2. **Unreasonable interference:** The interference is unreasonable if either
   a. The **harm to plaintiff outweighs the utility** of defendant's conduct; or
   b. The **harm caused to plaintiff** is greater than plaintiff should be required to bear **without consideration.**
   c. **Test for both:** Consider the nature, extent, and frequency of the harm, and the neighborhood, land value, and alternatives available for defendant.
B. **Public nuisance** is a **substantial, unreasonable interference** with the **community's** health, morals, welfare, safety, or property **rights.**
1. **Interference:** Courts consider factors establishing harm to the community including the **location of the nuisance,** the **frequency and duration,** the **degree of damage,** and the **social value** of the activity.
2. **Recovery by a private party** is only available if the private party suffered damage that is **different in kind** and not merely in degree from that suffered by the public.
C. **Remedies for nuisance** include damages and injunctive relief.
D. **Defenses for nuisance**
1. **Legislative authority** is persuasive but not an absolute defense (e.g., zoning ordinance that permits the conduct in the location).
2. **Assumption of the risk** and **comparative negligence** are defenses if the plaintiff's case rests on a negligence theory.
3. **Coming to the nuisance** is a bar only if plaintiff came to the nuisance for the sole purpose of bringing a harassing lawsuit. Otherwise, coming to the nuisance is not a valid defense.

> **Exam tip:** Many nuisance issues arise where the call of the question asks whether the court should grant an injunction to a plaintiff. To analyze whether the court should grant the injunction, you must analyze the "likelihood of success on the merits" element, which necessitates analysis of the underlying nuisance claim. Go through private and/or public nuisance (as appropriate) and always consider applicable defenses.

> **Nuisance fact triggers:**
>
> - Toxic chemicals/pollution
> - Power interruptions
> - Odors
> - Obstruction of views

IX. DEFAMATION

A. **Common law defamation** occurs when a false and **defamatory statement** of or **concerning plaintiff** is **published to a person** other than the plaintiff causing **damage to the plaintiff's reputation.**

1. **Defamatory statement** is a **false** statement that holds the plaintiff up to **contempt or public ridicule. Pure opinions** or **true statements** are not defamatory statements. "Statement" is construed broadly to include visual images, satire, etc.

2. **Of or concerning plaintiff**: The plaintiff must be identifiable.

3. **Publication to a third party:** The publication must be made to a third party who **understands** the statement to effectuate publication.

   a. **Repeaters** are also publishers.

4. **Standard of fault in publication**: The publication can be made **intentionally** (knowledge of falsity) **or negligently** (insufficient reasonable care as to falsity). It is the intent to publish the statement, not the intent to defame that satisfies this element.

   a. **Matters of public concern:** The **constitutional law defamation standard** of fault applies when the defamation is regarding a matter of public concern. (See rules at IX.B. below.)

4. **Causation:** The statement **need not have actually harmed** the plaintiff's reputation, but the plaintiff must show that it would have had it been believed.

5. **Damages** depend on the **type of defamation.**

   a. **Libel** is written or **printed publication** of a defamatory statement. This includes any communication embodied in physical or permanent form, including records, or radio or TV broadcasts.

      1. For libel, the plaintiff does not need to prove special damages and **general damages are presumed.**

   b. **Slander** is **spoken** or verbal defamation.

      1. For slander, the plaintiff must **prove special damages**, which means the plaintiff has suffered some **pecuniary loss** as a result of the slander, except damages are presumed for slander per se.

      2. For **slander per se**, damages are presumed. Slander per se identifies the plaintiff as having:

         a. **Business or professional** unfitness,

         b. A **loathsome disease** (historically a sexually transmitted disease or leprosy),

         c. Committed a **crime** of moral turpitude (most crimes), or

         d. Serious **sexual misconduct**, which historically was an unchaste woman.

> **Memorization tip:** Use <u>BaD</u> <u>CaSe</u> to remember slander per se. <u>B</u>usiness; <u>D</u>isease; <u>C</u>rime; <u>S</u>exual misconduct.

B. **Constitutional law defamation requirements** must be analyzed if the defamation is a matter of **public concern.** Constitutional defamation requires that the plaintiff prove the **elements of common law defamation** (as noted above) and establish **fault** in the publication on the part of the defendant. The test to determine fault depends on the **status of the plaintiff** as a public figure or private person.

1. **Public figure:** A public figure has achieved **pervasive fame** or notoriety or **voluntarily assumed a role** in a public controversy.
    a. **Actual malice standard:** When the plaintiff is a public figure, actual malice must be proven. Actual malice exists when the defendant made the statement with either (1) **knowledge that it was false,** or (2) **reckless disregard** as to whether it was true or false.
    b. **Damages are presumed** if actual malice is shown.
2. **Private person:** A private person is any person not considered a public figure and is afforded more protection since they have less opportunity to set the record straight.
    a. **Negligence standard:** When the plaintiff is a private person the publisher need only be negligent regarding the falsity of the statement if the statement involves a matter of public concern.
    b. **Only actual injury damages** are recoverable (not necessarily pecuniary). But, if malice exists, damages are presumed and punitive damages are allowed.
C. **Defenses to defamation**
    1. **Consent**
    2. **Truth**
    3. **Absolute privilege** extends to remarks made during **judicial or legislative proceedings**, by federal government and most state **government officials**, and between **spouses**. This privilege exists even if defendant acted with malice.
    4. **Qualified privilege** extends to statements made to **protect the publisher's interests** if the defamation relates directly to those interests, or for the protection of the recipient or a third party, or to act in the **public interest** or report on public proceedings. This **privilege can be lost** if the defendant abuses it by acting with actual malice or publishing the statement excessively when it is not reasonably necessary.

Exam tip: For defamation questions, always start by asking whether the issue is a matter of public or private concern. If you can argue both ways as to whether the matter is public or private (as is often the case), analyze common law defamation and include analysis of the constitutional elements and any applicable defenses. Likewise, if you can argue both ways that the plaintiff is a public and private figure, analyze both rules, since this will affect the damages element. Recently, defamation questions have included very specific calls asking about each element of defamation. Analyze each element as requested to answer the specific calls.

Defamation fact triggers:

- Reporters
- Newspaper articles
- Radio station broadcasts
- Any publication or writing

X. PRIVACY TORTS

A. **Appropriation (of plaintiff's picture or name)** is the **unauthorized use** of the **plaintiff's picture or name** for the defendant's **commercial purpose.** Also called the right to publicity.
B. **Intrusion upon seclusion** is the intrusion into a **private aspect** of the plaintiff's life in a **private place** that is **highly offensive to a reasonable person.** Also called intrusion into private affairs or solitude.
C. Placing plaintiff **in false light** occurs where (1) one **attributes to plaintiff views** they do not hold or actions they do not take; (2) the false light is **objectionable to a reasonable person** under the circumstances; and (3) the publication is **public.**

1. **Public interest:** If the matter is of public interest, **malice** must be proved (First Amendment limitation).
2. **Public figures:** Plaintiff must prove **actual malice** on the part of the defendant.
D. **Public disclosure of private facts** is the **public disclosure of true private facts** that are not a matter of legitimate public concern, the release of which is **highly offensive to a reasonable person,** and **not a legitimate concern of the public.** Also called publicity of private life or invasion of privacy.

Issue spotting tip: Privacy issues often arise in combination with defamation questions. So, when you recognize a defamation issue and/or a privacy issue, always write out a brief issues checklist of all possible defamation and privacy issues and defenses.

Memorization tip: Use **A FLIP** to remember the privacy torts. **A**ppropriation; **F**alse **L**ight; **I**ntrusion upon seclusion; **P**ublic disclosure of private facts.

Privacy fact triggers:

- Disclosure of information
- Offensive statements or comments
- Secret recordings
- False pretenses to obtain information
- Facts that give rise to defamation

XI. **OTHER TORTS**
   A. **Misuse of legal processes**
      1. **Malicious prosecution** occurs when there is an:
         a. **Institution of criminal proceedings** (and civil proceedings in most jurisdictions) against plaintiff;
            1. Prosecutors are immune from liability.
            2. The defendant can be any person actively involved in bringing about the proceedings.
         b. **Termination of proceedings in plaintiff's favor;**
         c. **Absence of probable cause** for the institution of the proceedings;
         c. **Improper purpose** of the accuser in bringing suit; and
         d. **Damages** suffered by the accused.
      2. **Abuse of process** occurs when the defendant **intentionally misuses legal process** (e.g., depositions, discovery tools, etc.) for an **ulterior purpose** and the defendant committed a willful act in a wrongful manner that caused **damage** to the plaintiff.
   B. Tortious interference with business relations
      1. **Prima facie case** requires establishing:
         a. **Contractual relationship** or **valid business expectancy** between two parties,
         b. A third party **knew or should have known of the relationship** or expectancy,
         c. **Intentional interference** by the third party inducing breach or termination of the relationship or expectancy, and
         d. **Damages**.
      2 **Defense-Privilege:** Defendant's conduct may be privileged where it is **fair competition** in a proper **attempt to obtain business** for itself or protect its interests, particularly if the defendant uses **fair methods.**

C. **Tortious interference with family relationships:** A spouse may bring an action for interference with consortium and services caused by defendant's intentional or negligent actions against the other spouse. A parent can also recover for the loss of a child's services and consortium.

XII. THIRD-PARTY ISSUES

A. **Vicarious liability occurs when one person commits a tortious act** against a third party, and **another person is liable** to the third party for the tortious act. Vicarious liability is **imposed based on a special relationship** between the tortfeasor and the person found vicariously liable. One who is vicariously liable may seek contribution or indemnification for damages paid to the plaintiff from the tortfeasor more directly responsible for the harm.

1. **Respondeat superior:** When an **employee** commits a tort during the **scope of employment**, the employer will be vicariously liable. Similarly, when an **agent** commits a tort during the scope of the agency, the principal has vicarious liability.

   a. **Employee:** An employee is one who works **subject to the close control** of the person who hired them.

   b. **Scope of employment:** The tort is within the scope of employment if the tortfeasor was acting with the **intent to further the employer's business purpose**, even if the act itself was forbidden.

2. **Independent contractor:** One who hires an independent contractor is generally not vicariously liable for the torts of that person, **except if:**

   a. The employer is **negligent in hiring** that person, or

   b. The **duty is nondelegable** because work occurs in a **public place** or the work involves **inherently dangerous activities,** such that there is a peculiar risk of physical harm to others.

B. **Multiple defendants**

1. **Joint and several liability** exists where **two or more negligent acts combine** to proximately cause an **indivisible harm**, making each defendant liable for the entire harm. Plaintiff can recover the entire loss from any defendant, regardless of that defendant's share of the total responsibility.

2. Contribution allows a defendant jointly and severally liable and who **pays more than their pro rata** share, to **obtain reimbursement** from another defendant for any amount paid over the pro-rata share.

3. **Indemnity** occurs when the responsibility for the **entire loss** is shifted from one tortfeasor to another. Indemnity is appropriate where one tortfeasor is only derivatively liable for the other tortfeasors conduct, such as an employer vicariously liable, or a wholesaler liable for strict products liability may seek indemnity from the manufacturer responsible for the product defect.

XIII. OTHER TORT RULES

A. **Survival and wrongful death**

1. **Survival actions** allow one's cause of action to survive the death of one or more of the parties.

   a. **Exception:** These actions do not include defamation, right to privacy, or malicious prosecution.

2. **Wrongful death** acts grant recovery for **pecuniary injury** resulting to the spouse and next of kin for a wrongful death and allows recovery for **loss of support and consortium**. The decedent's creditors have no interest in the amount recovered under a wrongful death claim.

B. **Tort immunity from liability**

1. **Governmental (sovereign) immunity:** Modernly, most states and the federal government waive immunity from suit for ministerial acts (those performed operationally), and thus can be sued for most torts. However, most governmental entities retain sovereign immunity for acts taken at the decision-making level.

2. **Intrafamily immunity:** Most jurisdictions now allow family members to sue each other for tortious injury to person or property, except parents retain broad discretion for supervision.

TORTS ISSUES TESTED MATRIX

		Crossover Questions	Intentional Torts	Negligence or NIED	Strict Liability (Abnormally Dangerous Activity or Animals)	Products Liability (Any of the 5 theories)	Fraud/ Misrepre-sentation	Nuisance	Defamation	Privacy	Malicious Prosecution/ Abuse of Process	Interference with Business Relations	3rd-Party Liability Issues
July '23 Q1	Sam leases office from ABC law firm Amy causes a car accident	Bus. Assoc.		X									
July '23 Q2	DishWay's dish soap causes illness			X		X							
February '22 Q3	Pedro complains about loud open-air theatre	Remedies	TTL					X					
July '21 Q3	Allergic reaction to sabotaged mashed potatoes			X									Vicarious
February '20 Q1	Law prof accuses Paul in class of cheating		IIED						X				
February '19 Q2	Bob & Carol see puppies & chimp				X								
February '18 Q3	Len has a wandering dog and a backyard smokehouse	Real Prop Con Law	TTL	X				X					
July '17 Q5	Doug hits an electric pole, Harry's house burns			X	X								Joint & Several
February '17 Q2	Steve sells Betty a condo where previous owner was murdered	Remedies					X						

Continued>

	Question	Crossover Questions	Intentional Torts	Negligence or NIED	Strict Liability (Abnormally Dangerous Activity or Animals)	Products Liability (Any of the 5 theories)	Fraud/Misrepre-sentation	Nuisance	Defamation	Privacy	Malicious Prosecution/Abuse of Process	Interference with Business Relations	3rd-Party Liability Issues
February '16 Q2	Jack thinks neighbor Nancy is an alien		Assault, IIED, TTC, Battery, Conv., Defense of Others										
July '14 Q6	Caterer undercooks chicken wings			X									Vicarious
July '13 Q6	Doug hauls trees across Paul's country lot	Remedies	TTL, TTC, Conversion										
February '13 Q4	Darla sells highly toxic fumigation gas			X	X	X							
February '11 Q4	Gayle, 16, leaves high school and hits officer Paula			X									Vicarious
July '10 Q1	Homeowner kept a handgun; Burglar stole it		Battery, Assault, TTC/Conversion, IIED	X									
July '09 Q1	Patty transports human organs and David blocks bridge	Civil Proc.			X						X		
February '09 Q4	ConsumerPro lists Paul as ambulance-chaser attorney								X				
February '08 Q1	Peter, pet pigeon, injured on high-voltage wire fence			X	X								
July '07 Q2	Consumer burned by soup using Cold Drink Blender			X		X							Indemnify
February '07 Q1	Builder sold mall to Owner & reserved parking spaces	Real Prop.						X					

Continued>

Date	Fact Pattern	Crossover Questions	Intentional Torts	Negligence or NIED	Strict Liability (Abnormally Dangerous Activity or Animals)	Products Liability (Any of the 5 theories)	Fraud/Misrepresentation	Nuisance	Defamation	Privacy	Malicious Prosecution/Abuse of Process	Interference with Business Relations	3rd-Party Liability Issues
July '06 Q1	Paul & Clerk, Delta Gas; candy & carbon monoxide poisoning		False Imprison.	X									Vicarious
February '06 Q1	Oscar v. Autos, Inc. Roadster for injury to child			X		X							
July '04 Q6	Jack's "Star" uncut diamond & Chip the master diamond cutter	Remedies		X									Survival/ Wrongful Death
July '03 Q4	Paula v. KXYZ Radio for broadcasting eavesdropped conversation								X	X			
July '02 Q5	Sally v. Manufacturer of allergy pills for eyesight side effect			X		X							
July '01 Q5	Attorney Ann advises Harry on ugly divorce from Wilma	Prof. Resp.							X		X		
February '01 Q4	Diane's office bldg & Peter's restaurant and garden	Remedies	TTL/ Conversion					X	X				
July '00 Q6	Don makes pottery & causes an electrical surge	Remedies	TTL/TTC/ Conversion	X	X							X	
February '00 Q3	Lee comments about Judge Bright's unfairness after trial	Prof. Resp.							X				
February '00 Q2	Chemco processing plant discharges waste into river	Remedies	TTL					X					

TORTS PRACTICE ESSAYS, ANSWER GRIDS, AND SAMPLE ANSWERS

Torts Question 1
July 2023, Question 2

DishWay developed a new dishwasher powder that it named UltraKlean. The company advertised widely that UltraKlean was "a revolutionary, safe product with the most powerful cleaning agent ever." This advertisement accurately represented that UltraKlean contained a new cleaning agent that made the product more effective than other dishwasher powders.

DishWay knew the cleaning agent could cause severe stomach pain if ingested, but this is true of all detergent products. What DishWay did not know was that a potentially dangerous amount of UltraKlean residue tended to remain on aluminum cookware after a wash cycle. It is not unusual for dishwasher powders to leave a harmless amount of residue on different surfaces. During product development, DishWay tested UltraKlean on some surfaces but not on aluminum because there was no indication that it would work differently on aluminum than on other surfaces. The residue was not detectable to the eye, and there was no flaw in DishWay's manufacturing process. DishWay's instructions on the product only stated that the product should not be ingested.

Paul purchased a box of UltraKlean from DishWay. The first time he used it was to wash some aluminum pots. The next day, Paul used several of those pots to prepare a meal. Shortly after finishing the meal, Paul experienced severe stomach pain, which required him to be hospitalized. Laboratory test results revealed the cleaning agent in UltraKlean caused Paul's stomach pain.

What products liability claims may Paul bring against DishWay? Discuss.

Torts Question 1 Assessment
July 2023, Question 2

This question is an excellent example of a typical products liability question, which is a favorite testing area in torts. You may notice the call asked you, "What product liability *claims* may Paul bring . . ." which is a hint that they don't want you to only discuss strict products liability. On the essay, the bar examiners like to ensure you are competent in assessing all the ways in which a case can be brought for a product that causes injury.

As you can see after organizing your answer, while the majority of the analysis is in the strict products liability issue, they do want you to include analysis of at least three additional ways a plaintiff could bring suit for injury caused by a product. Students can often confuse and combine the issues under strict products liability and negligence for products liability. To avoid any confusion or loss of points, we recommend that you start with the strict products liability issue first, and then do the negligence for products liability analysis second. This approach requires that you first go through the necessary rules and elements for strict products liability, such as commercial supplier, placing the product into commerce, the three types of defects, and so forth. As you can see, a great bulk of the analysis is in proving up the defective product, which is typical in a products liability question. Once you have completed the strict products liability analysis, move on to negligence with a full discussion of duty and breach (which are different than in strict products liability), and "supra" causation and damages (because the analysis there will be the same). Be sure to separate out each component of each cause of action and analyze them separately. You will notice you are using some of the same facts repeatedly, but you should be using them to prove up different elements as you go.

Always consider all five theories of products liability when it is at issue since students often forget about warranty, misrepresentation, and intent. This question has facts that raise the issues of express warranty, implied warranty of merchantability, and misrepresentation. You did not need to discuss the intent theory to pass this question since there are no facts that raise intentional misconduct by the manufacturer, but sometimes it's hard to decide if you should include an issue or not. If you are not sure, it is better to err on the side of inclusion. However, if it is not clear that an issue is a major issue, then it is likely a minor issue, so be brief and concise when analyzing it. For example, a discussion of intent wasn't necessary to pass this question, but we briefly mentioned it and explained why it will not provide the basis for a cause of action here. That's the best way to handle issues when you aren't sure if you should include them or not.

If you missed any of the key facts or arguments, make a resolution now to highlight the facts on your next essay and use all of the facts. This will improve your analysis and your ability to pass this question.

A sample answer is included for this question. The sample answer is not a model or perfect answer, but rather is of passing quality that realistically could be written in one hour.

Make note of the areas highlighted in **bold** on the corresponding grid. The bold areas highlight the issues, analysis, and conclusions that are likely **required** to receive a passing score on this question.

Torts Question 1

Issue	Rule	Fact Application	Conclusion
What products liability claims may Paul bring against DishWay?			
Products Liability	There are five theories under which one can establish products liability: **strict products liability, negligent products liability, warranty, misrepresentation** of facts, and intent.		
Strict Products Liability	**A seller of a product is liable without fault for personal injuries caused by a defective product if a commercial supplier put the product into the stream of commerce.**		
	<u>Commercial Supplier (Strict Duty)</u> A commercial supplier has a strict duty to ensure products are free from defect. **A commercial supplier is one who places a product in the stream of commerce** without substantial alteration. A commercial supplier includes retailers and other non-manufacturers, as well as the product manufacturer.	Here, **DishWay is the developer of UltraKlean and they put it in the stream of commerce** without alteration by advertising it widely and **making it available for purchase by consumers, such as Paul who purchased a box.**	**DishWay is a commercial supplier**
	<u>Defective Product</u> There are three ways to prove a product was defective: manufacturing defect, design defect, and warning defect.		
	Manufacturing Defect The product is different and more dangerous because it was **not manufactured as intended.**	DishWay developed UltraKlean with the most powerful cleaning agent ever. They knew the cleaning agent could cause pain if ingested, but **the box Paul bought and used was the same as all the boxes and manufactured as intended.**	**No manufacturing defect**

Continued>

Issue	Rule	Fact Application	Conclusion
Strict Products Liability (continued)	**Design Defect** **All products of a line are the same and all have a feature whose design itself is defective and unreasonably dangerous.** Two tests are used to establish design defect: **Consumer Expectation Test** **A product's performance must meet the minimum safety expectations of its ordinary users when used in a reasonably foreseeable manner.** **Risk-Utility Test** **A product is defective if the risk of danger inherent in the design outweighs the benefits** of such design and the danger could have been reduced or avoided by the adoption of a reasonable, cost-effective alternative design.	Here, **Paul used UltraKlean soap to wash aluminum pots in his dishwasher** and then used the pots to cook a meal. Subsequently, he got severe stomach pain and was hospitalized. Since UltraKlean is a cleaning agent and designed to clean dishes and cookware in dishwashers, Paul's use was a normal expected use by an ordinary consumer. Aluminum pots are not unusual. **An ordinary consumer would not expect to get sick** from residue left on their cookware after using a dishwashing soap. Here, **the risk is that using UltraKlean on aluminum pots will cause illness** when they are used to cook after washing. The risk of illness outweighs the **benefit** of having a product with "the most **powerful cleaning agent ever.**" Further, the danger could have been reduced or avoided by running tests during product development on all types of cookware since DishWay knew the cleaning agent could cause severe stomach pain if ingested. Though it is nice to have a superior cleaning agent, it is not worth the risk of getting sick.	**Design defect under both the consumer expectation test and risk utility test**
	Warning Defect **The product maker fails to give adequate warning as to a known (or should have been known) danger in the product** or in a particular use of the product that is nonobvious.	Here, **DishWay** knew that all detergents can cause stomach pain and **provided instructions warning against ingesting.** Paul will argue the **warning is incomplete and ineffective.** DishWay did not know that a dangerous amount of residue was left on aluminum cookware after washing, rather than a harmless amount of residue, and failed to warn consumers of this risk. However, they should have known because had they tested the product on various cookware surfaces, they would have discovered this risk and could have either changed the product or provided a proper warning. DishWay did neither.	**Warning defect**
	Actual Cause But for the defect, the plaintiff would not have been injured.	**But for Paul using UltraKlean to wash his aluminum pots he would not have been injured** and hospitalized with stomach pain.	**Actual cause established**

Continued>

Issue	Rule	Fact Application	Conclusion
Strict Products Liability (continued)	<u>Proximate Cause</u> **A defendant is liable for all harmful results that are reasonably foreseeable.**	All detergent products can cause severe stomach pain if ingested, so it is **reasonably foreseeable that Paul would suffer harm after using a cleaning product that left a dangerous amount of residue** on aluminum cookware.	**Proximate cause established**
	<u>Damages</u> **Physical injury to the plaintiff** or property damage must be shown. There is no recovery for purely economic loss.	Here, Paul suffered **severe stomach pain necessitating hospitalization**, and likely resulting pain and suffering.	**Paul can recover damages**
Defenses—Assumption of Risk	Where plaintiff knows of the risk and voluntarily consents despite the risk.	While DishWay may argue all detergent products can cause stomach pain, the residue was undetectable to the human eye, so Paul could not have known of the risk and voluntarily consented.	Paul did not assume the risk
Conclusion Products Liability	DishWay is strictly liability for Paul's injury.		
Negligence	**Defendant had a duty to the plaintiff, breached the duty, the breach was the actual and proximate cause of the harm suffered, and there were damages to the plaintiff.**		
	<u>Duty</u> **A commercial supplier has a duty to act as a reasonable commercial supplier.** Under the majority Cardozo view, a duty is owed to all foreseeable plaintiffs. Under the minority Andrews view, a duty is owed to everyone, including unforeseeable plaintiffs.	Here, a duty is owed to Paul. Under the majority rule or the minority rule, **a duty is owed to a product user or purchaser.**	**Duty**

Continued>

Issue	Rule	Fact Application	Conclusion
Negligence (continued)	**Breach** **A breach exists when the commercial supplier's conduct falls below the appropriate standard of care.**	**A product developer has a duty to act as a prudent developer.** While DishWay did not know of the dangerous residue left on aluminum cookware, **a prudent product developer would have tested the product on all types of cookware**, especially since cleaning agents are known to cause stomach pain if ingested. Paul will argue they failed to properly develop and test UltraKlean since they only tested the residue on some cookware surfaces and **not aluminum because they erroneously assumed it would not work differently than the other cookware.**	Breach
	• Actual Cause • Proximate Cause • Damages • Defenses — Assumption of the Risk	**See supra** in product's liability discussion.	
Conclusion Negligence	**DishWay is negligent.**		
Express Warranty	A statement of **fact or promise concerning goods** and **the product fails to conform** to those standards.	Here, UltraKlean was **advertised** as "a revolutionary, safe product with the most powerful cleaning agent ever." However, since it made Paul sick, **it was not a "safe product."**	**Express warranty breached**
Implied Warranty of Merchantability	**Implied** in a sale of goods, it ensures they are **fit for the ordinary purposes** for which the goods are used.	Here, DishWay warranted the soap was "safe" and effective for use in a dishwasher. However, **the warranty was breached since using the soap in an ordinary manner caused serious illness** to Paul.	**Implied warranty breached**
Misrepresentation of Fact	A seller makes a **statement of material fact** concerning quality or uses of goods, and **intends to induce reliance** by the **buyer, who did** in fact **rely**. Plaintiff must still prove actual cause, proximate cause, and damages.	Here, DishWay **represented that UltraKlean was "safe"** when it was not. This was done to **induce sales, and Paul likely relied** on this advertisement, as intended, when he purchased the UltraKlean.	**Misrepresentation if Paul relied**
Intent	A defendant is liable to anyone injured by an unsafe product if the defendant intended the consequences or knew they were substantially certain to occur.	Here, DishWay did not know of the danger of their product, so they did not intend for anyone to get injured.	No liability for an intent cause of action

Question 1 Sample Answer

What products liability claims may Paul bring against DishWay?

Products Liability

There are five theories under which one can establish products liability: strict products liability, negligent products liability, warranty, misrepresentation of facts, and intentional.

Strict Products Liability

A seller of a product is liable without fault for personal injuries caused by a defective product if a commercial supplier put the product into the stream of commerce.

Commercial Supplier

A commercial supplier has a strict duty to ensure products are free from defect. A commercial supplier is one who places a product in the stream of commerce without substantial alteration, which includes retailers and other non-manufacturers, as well as the product manufacturer.

Here, DishWay is a commercial supplier since they are the developer of UltraKlean dishwashing soap. They put it in the stream of commerce without alteration by advertising the product widely and making it available for purchase by consumers, such as Paul who purchased a box.

Defective Product

There are three ways to prove a product is defective: manufacturing defect, design defect, and warning defect.

Manufacturing Defect

A manufacturing defect exists when a product is different and more dangerous because it was not manufactured as intended.

Here, DishWay developed UltraKlean with the most powerful cleaning agent ever. They knew the cleaning agent could cause pain if ingested, as all detergent could, but the box Paul bought and used was the same as all the boxes and manufactured as intended, so there is no manufacturing defect.

Design Defect

A design defect exists when all products of a line are made the same and they all have a feature whose design itself is defective and unreasonably dangerous. Two tests are used to establish design defect: the consumer expectation test and the risk-utility test. Paul will argue there is a design defect under both tests.

Consumer Expectation Test

Under the consumer expectation test, a product's performance must meet the minimum safety expectations of its ordinary users when used in a reasonably foreseeable manner.

Here, Paul used the UltraKlean soap to wash aluminum pots in his dishwasher and then afterwards he used them to cook a meal. Subsequently, he got severe stomach pain necessitating hospitalization. Since UltraKlean is a cleaning agent and is designed to clean dishes and cookware in dishwashers, Paul used the product in the way we would expect from a normal ordinary consumer. Aluminum pots are not unusual in a kitchen so there was nothing unforeseeable in Paul's usage of the soap. An ordinary consumer would not expect to get sick from residue that was left on their cookware after using a dishwashing soap, especially when it was undetectable.

There is a design defect under the consumer expectation test.

Risk-Utility Test

Under the risk-utility test, a product is defective if the risk of danger inherent in the design of the product outweighs the benefits of such design and where the danger could have been reduced or avoided by the adoption of a reasonable, cost-effective alternative design.

Here, the risk is that using UltraKlean on aluminum pots will subsequently cause illness when they are used to cook. The risk of illness outweighs any benefit of having a dishwashing product with "the most powerful cleaning agent ever" because reasonable people would tolerate a less clean dish if it meant not getting sick. Further, the danger here could have been reduced or avoided by running tests during product development on all types of cookware and dish materials, especially since DishWay already knew the cleaning agent could cause severe stomach pain if ingested. Though it is nice to have a superior cleaning agent, it is not worth the risk of consumers getting sick.

There is a design defect under the risk-utility test.

Warning Defect

A warning defect exists when the maker of a product fails to give adequate warning as to a known (or should have been known) danger in the product or in a particular use of the product that is nonobvious.

Here, DishWay knew that all detergents can cause stomach pain and provided instructions to purchasers warning against ingesting the soap. However, Paul will argue the warning is incomplete and ineffective.

DishWay did not know that a dangerous amount of residue was left on aluminum cookware after washing, rather than a harmless amount of residue, and failed to warn consumers of this risk. However, DishWay should have known of the more serious risk because had they tested the product on various cookware surfaces, they would have discovered this risk. They then could have either redesigned the product or provided a proper warning of the actual risk of using the soap on aluminum, but DishWay did neither, so there is a warning defect.

Actual Cause

Plaintiff must show that but for the defect, they would not have been injured, and that the defect existed at the time it left the defendant's control.

Here, but for Paul using UltraKlean to wash his aluminum pots, he would not have been injured with severe stomach pain.

Proximate Cause

A defendant is generally liable for all harmful results that are reasonably foreseeable.

All detergent products can cause severe stomach pain if ingested, therefore it is reasonably foreseeable that Paul would suffer harm after using a cleaning product that left a dangerous amount of residue on his aluminum cookware.

Damages

A plaintiff must establish that they have suffered physical injury or property damage. There is no recovery for purely economic loss.

Here, Paul suffered severe stomach pain necessitating hospitalization. He can recover for any pain and suffering, medical bills, loss of work, etc.

Defenses — Assumption of Risk

Plaintiff may be barred from recovery where plaintiff knows of the risk and voluntarily consents despite the risk.

While DishWay may argue that all detergent products can cause stomach pain if ingested, the residue on the pots was undetectable to the human eye, so Paul could not have known of the risk and voluntarily consented. Therefore, Paul did not assume the risk.

Negligence

A party is liable for personal injuries caused by a product if the defendant had a duty to the plaintiff, breached the duty, the breach was the actual and proximate cause of the harm suffered, and there were damages to the plaintiff.

Duty

A commercial supplier has a duty to act as a reasonable commercial supplier. Under the majority Cardozo view, a duty is owed to all foreseeable plaintiffs. Under the minority Andrews view, a duty is owed to everyone, including unforeseeable plaintiffs.

Under the majority rule or the minority rule, a duty is owed to a product user or purchaser by the commercial supplier of the product. Therefore, DishWay had a duty to Paul.

Breach

A breach exists when the commercial supplier's conduct falls below the appropriate standard of care.

A product developer has a duty to act as a reasonable prudent developer. While DishWay did not know of the dangerous residue left on aluminum cookware, a prudent product developer would have tested the product on all types of cookware, especially since cleaning agents are known to cause stomach pain if ingested. Paul will argue DishWay failed to properly develop and test UltraKlean since they only tested the residue on some cookware surfaces and not aluminum because they erroneously assumed it would not work differently than the other cookware. Therefore, DishWay is in breach.

The elements of actual cause, proximate cause, damages, and defenses are discussed supra.

Paul will likely succeed in a negligence claim against DishWay.

Express Warranty

A breach of an express warranty is when a statement of fact or promise is made concerning goods, and the product fails to conform to those standards.

Here, UltraKlean was advertised as "a revolutionary, safe product with the most powerful cleaning agent ever." However, since it made Paul sick, it was not a "safe product" and failed to conform to the promise, breaching the express warranty.

Implied Warranty of Merchantability

An implied warranty of merchantability is implied in every sale of goods, ensuring that they are fit for the ordinary purposes for which the goods are used.

Here, DishWay warranted the soap was "safe" and effective and it is implied it can be used to wash cookware in a dishwasher. However, the warranty was breached since using the soap in an ordinary manner caused serious illness to Paul.

Misrepresentation of Fact

A misrepresentation is where a seller makes a statement of material fact concerning quality or uses of goods, and intends to induce reliance by the buyer, who did in fact rely. Plaintiff must still prove actual cause, proximate cause, and damages.

Here, DishWay represented that UltraKlean was "safe" when it was not. This was done in advertising to induce sales, and Paul likely relied on this advertisement, as intended, when he purchased the UltraKlean. If Paul did rely on the misrepresentation, Paul can bring a misrepresentation claim as well.

Intent

A defendant is liable to anyone injured by an unsafe product if the defendant intended the consequences or knew they were substantially certain to occur.

Here, DishWay did not know of the danger of their product, so they did not intend for anyone to get injured. Therefore, Paul cannot bring an intent cause of action.

Torts Question 2

February 2008, Question 1

Peter, a twelve-year old, was playing with his pet pigeon in a field near his home, which is adjacent to a high voltage electricity power substation. The substation is surrounded by a six-foot tall chain link fence topped with barbed wire. Attached to the fence are twelve 10 inch by 14 inch warning signs, which read "Danger High Voltage."

Peter's pigeon flew into the substation and landed on a piece of equipment. In an attempt to retrieve his pet, Peter climbed the surrounding fence, then scaled a steel support to a height of approximately ten feet from where the bird was stranded. When Peter grasped the bird, it fluttered from his hand, struck Peter in the face, causing Peter to come into contact with a high voltage wire, which caused him severe burns.

Peter's father is contemplating filing a lawsuit on Peter's behalf against the owner and operator of the substation, Power and Light Company (PLC), to recover damages arising from the accident.

What causes of action might Peter's father reasonably assert against PLC, what defenses can PLC reasonably raise, and what is the likely outcome on each? Discuss.

Torts Question 2 Assessment
February 2008, Question 1

Among torts questions, this is a "racehorse" question. It only tests two major issues, but there are many sub-elements to analyze and an abundance of facts to use and factual inferences to make given the limited time. It tests strict liability for abnormally dangerous activities, negligence, including attractive nuisance and many defenses, all of which must be fully analyzed in one hour. It is a challenging question to organize and write within an hour.

This essay question tests the very commonly tested tort of negligence, but also includes the less commonly tested areas of attractive nuisance and non-products strict liability for conducting abnormally dangerous activities.

The name of the game in a torts essay is using all available facts and making reasonable factual inferences. Often, the conclusions aren't important so long as the facts are well utilized. In this question, there were some great facts to use, such as the description of the "Danger High Voltage" signs, including their dimensions (10 inch by 14 inch) and that the chain link fence was 6 foot tall and topped with barbed wire. A passing answer should use those type of facts with specificity to analyze the issues, rather than ignore the facts or summarize them in a general way.

Another important point to notice with this question is that the facts are somewhat ambiguous. It is reasonable to make inferences from the facts that lead your answer in a different direction from another student's answer. One student could argue that 12 signs were numerous, while another student could argue 12 were a scant amount given what must have been the large size of the substation. Both are legitimate arguments given the ambiguity of the facts, so don't be afraid to make some assumptions when conducting analysis, just be sure you characterize them as such. For this reason, students could have ended up using the facts well and still come to completely different conclusions and that is perfectly fine so long as your analysis makes sense. In fact, both state-released passing answers came to opposite conclusions on the strict liability issue.

If you miss any of the issues or rules below, you should rewrite your answer or at least those missed issues. Further, you should rewrite any issues where you find that you omit key facts and/or arguments. Writing out essays properly is the best practice you can do to pass the essay portion of the bar exam. For more questions that test these particular issues, or other issues, review the Torts Issues Tested Matrix at the end the torts chapter.

Finally, make note of the areas highlighted in **bold** on the corresponding grid. The bold areas highlight the issues, analysis, and conclusions that are likely **required** to receive a passing score on this question. In general, the essay grids are provided to assist you in analyzing the essays and are much more detailed than what a student should create during the exam to organize their response to a question.

Issue	Rule	Fact Application	Conclusion
Peter v. PLC			
Strict Liability — Abnormally Dangerous Activity	There is strict liability for abnormally dangerous activities. An activity is abnormally dangerous if: • The activity that creates a **significant degree of risk of serious harm;** • The **risk cannot be eliminated** by the exercise of reasonable care; and • The activity is not **common in the community.**	• A high voltage electricity substation poses a high degree of risk of serious harm because a **high voltage electrocution could cause serious injury or death to a person.** • PLC would assert that providing electricity to the community is essential and that there is a reduced risk of serious harm since a 6-foot tall fence topped with barbed wire surrounded the substation, and there was signage warning of the dangers. • Since high voltage electricity **is inherently dangerous, it is likely impossible to eliminate the risk of injury** despite the exercise of reasonable care, such as seen here with the warnings and fencing. • Assuming it is necessary to have high voltage electric substations in more densely populated areas, the **high social utility in providing electricity to the population is not outweighed by the danger posed by having such a substation, especially since that risk cannot be minimized by taking appropriate precautions.** • A high voltage electric substation is not uncommon since **electricity is necessary** for a modern society and it is common for electricity to be provided to the community. • Peter would assert that it is not appropriate to locate a high voltage power substation in what is likely a residential area since the substation was adjacent to a field near Peter's home. • However, it is possible that the only way to provide electricity in the local area is to have a high voltage substation nearby, even if that means one is located in a more densely populated area.	PLC will be strictly liable [Could have concluded either way]
Defense Assumption of Risk	Plaintiff may be denied recovery if they assumed the risk of any damage caused by defendant's act where they **knew of the risk** and **voluntarily consented** despite the risk.	If Peter were to establish that the substation is an abnormally dangerous activity, PLC would assert Peter assumed the risk when he entered the property knowing it was dangerous. A **12-year-old child would have been able to read the prominent warning signs and been able to appreciate the danger** of climbing a barbed wire topped 6-foot fence to gain access to the location.	If PLC was strictly liable, Peter assumed the risk

⟨Continued⟩

Issue	Rule	Fact Application	Conclusion
Negligence	**Duty** A person or business has a duty to use **reasonable care**. Under the majority view the duty is owed to all **foreseeable plaintiffs**. **Attractive Nuisance** A landowner must exercise ordinary care to prevent foreseeable injury to children if: • The owner knew, or should have known, the area is one where children trespass • The condition poses an unreasonable risk of serious injury or death. • The **children do not discover the risk or realize the danger due to their youth** • The **benefit to owner and expense to remedy the condition is slight compared to the risk** • The owner fails to use reasonable care to eliminate the danger **Breach** A breach occurs when the defendant's conduct falls short of the applicable standard of care. **Actual Cause** **But for** the defendant's act, the injury to plaintiff would not have resulted.	PLC had a duty to act as a reasonable provider of high voltage electricity. It is foreseeable a person exposed to high voltage could be injured. **A child playing in an adjacent field from the substation is a foreseeable plaintiff.** A landowner with an attractive nuisance has a greater duty. • Because of the measures taken with signage and fencing to keep trespassers out, it is likely PLC did not think children would trespass on the substation. • However, **the substation was near homes so children trespassers are foreseeable** since local children would play in an open field. • High voltage electricity poses an unreasonable risk of serious injury and death. • **A child of 12 would be able to appreciate the danger** of high voltage electricity by reading the 12 large warning signs (10 x 14) and seeing the barbed wire fence to keep people out, but younger children may not appreciate the danger. • There is no way to completely remedy the condition since it is **not possible to make high voltage electricity entirely safe.** • However, the risk would be greatly diminished if the **fence were higher, or were made of something more difficult to climb than chain link.** • PLC could have taken **additional steps to diminish the risk of danger** by making the substation more difficult to access with better fencing. • PLC would assert they were reasonable since they built a 6-**foot tall fence, topped with barbed wire and had 12 large warning signs** to keep people out of the danger posed by the substation.	Peter should prevail in his negligence claim

Continued>

Issue	Rule	Fact Application	Conclusion
Negligence (continued)	**Proximate Cause** Defendant is liable for all: • **Reasonably foreseeable** harmful results; and foreseeable intervening causes **Damages** Plaintiff can recover for actual injury.	• However, **PLC's conduct may have fallen short** of the appropriate standard of care since they could have built a better, taller, and harder-to-climb fence. Perhaps they could have used bigger and more warning signs. • **But for PLC's failure to build a better fence, Peter would not have been able to enter the substation and been injured.** • Peter's severe burn injuries were a foreseeable harmful result from contact with a high voltage wire. • While the **pet pigeon struck Peter in the face**, it's foreseeable to chase a pet bird in a neighborhood, so this is not so unusual that it is considered an unforeseeable **intervening force.** • Peter suffered a severe **burn injury** and will be able to recover for damages resulting from the injury.	
Defense Assumption of Risk	Plaintiff may be denied recovery if they assumed the risk of damage where they knew of the risk and voluntarily consented despite the risk.	It is possible Peter's recovery will be denied if he assumed the risk by climbing the fence after appreciating the danger and likely seeing the warning signs, as discussed above.	Peter's recovery may be denied because he assumed the risk
Defense Comparative Negligence	Plaintiff's own negligence may limit recovery if it contributed to their injuries. Liability is divided in proportion to fault.	In jurisdictions that follow the comparative negligence theory, **Peter's recovery can be reduced by the proportionate amount attributed to his own negligence.**	Peter's recovery may be reduced because he was also negligent

Torts Question 2 Sample Answer
February 2008, Question 1

Peter v. PLC

Strict Liability

There is strict liability for abnormally dangerous activities. An activity is abnormally dangerous if the activity creates a high degree of risk of serious harm, the risk cannot be eliminated by the exercise of reasonable care, and the activity is not common in the community.

A high voltage electricity substation poses a high degree of risk of serious harm because a high voltage electrocution could cause serious injury or death to a person. PLC would assert that the provision of electricity to the community is an essential service and that they have appropriately reduced the risk of serious harm since they have surrounded the substation with a 6-foot-tall fence topped with barbed wire, and there was conspicuous signage around the property stating, "Danger High Voltage."

Assuming it is necessary to have high voltage electric substations located in more densely populated areas, the high social utility in providing electricity to the population is not outweighed by the danger posed by having such a substation, especially since that risk cannot be minimized to an acceptable level by taking appropriate precautions.

Since high voltage electricity is inherently dangerous, it is likely impossible to completely eliminate the risk of injury despite the exercise of reasonable care, such as seen here with the warnings and fencing.

A high voltage electric substation is not uncommon since electricity is necessary for a modern society and it is common for electricity to be provided to the community. However, Peter would assert that it is not common or appropriate to locate a high voltage power substation in what is likely a residential area since the substation was adjacent to a field near Peter's home. Peter would argue that the substation should be relocated to a less populated area. However, it is possible that the only way to provide electricity in the local area is to have a high voltage substation located nearby, even if that means one must be located in a more densely populated area.

PLC will be strictly liable.

Defenses—Assumption of Risk

Plaintiff may be denied recovery if they assumed the risk of any damage caused by the defendant's act where they knew of the risk and voluntarily consented despite the risk.

If Peter were able to establish that the substation is an abnormally dangerous activity, PLC would assert that Peter assumed the risk when he entered the property knowing it was dangerous. A 12-year-old child would have been able to read the prominent warning signs and been able to appreciate the danger implied from his need to climb a barbed-wire-topped, 6-foot fence in order to gain access to the substation.

If PLC were found strictly liable, it is likely Peter assumed the risk.

Negligence

A party is liable under a negligence theory if the plaintiff can show that the defendant had a duty to the plaintiff, breached the duty, the breach was the actual and proximate cause of the harm suffered, and there were damages to the plaintiff.

Duty

A person or business has a duty to use reasonable care. Under the majority view (Cardozo), such a duty is owed to all foreseeable plaintiffs. The minority view (Andrews) is that a duty is owed to everyone.

PLC had a duty to act as a reasonable provider of high voltage electricity and use reasonable care. It is foreseeable that a person exposed to high voltage electricity could be injured. A child playing in an adjacent field from the substation is in the zone of danger and is a foreseeable plaintiff.

Attractive Nuisance

A landowner must exercise ordinary care to prevent foreseeable injury to children if the landowner knew, or should have known, that the area is one where children trespass; the condition poses an unreasonable risk of serious injury or death; the children do not discover the risk or realize the danger due to their youth; the benefit to owner and expense to remedy the condition is slight compared to the risk; and the owner fails to use reasonable care to eliminate the danger.

A landowner with an attractive nuisance has a greater duty of care. Because of the measures taken with warning signs and fencing to keep trespassers out, it is likely PLC did not think children would trespass on the substation. However, the substation was located near homes, so children trespassers would be foreseeable, since local children would likely play in the open field that was adjacent to the substation.

High voltage electricity poses an unreasonable risk of serious injury and death. A child of age 12 would be able to appreciate the danger of high voltage electricity by reading the 12 large signs (10x14) that said, "Danger High Voltage." Further, a 12-year old would understand that a fence is topped with barbed wire in order to keep trespassers out and would be capable of inferring that the location was dangerous. However, younger children may not appreciate the danger.

There is no way to completely remedy the condition since it is not possible to make high voltage electricity entirely safe. However, the risk of injury would be greatly diminished if the fence were higher than 6 feet, or were constructed with something more difficult to climb than chain link. The expense of building a better fence is slight in comparison to the very dangerousness of the condition on the premises.

PLC could have taken additional steps to diminish the risk of danger by making the substation more difficult to access with better fencing. The substation was likely an attractive nuisance.

Breach

A breach occurs when the defendant's conduct falls short of the applicable standard of care.

PLC would assert that they were behaving reasonably since they built a 6-foot-tall fence topped with barbed wire to keep people out of the substation and had 12 large warning signs posted warning of the danger posed by the substation.

However, PLC 's conduct may have fallen short of the appropriate standard of care since they could have built a better, taller, and harder-to-climb fence to surround the substation. In addition, perhaps they could have used bigger and more warning signs. It is likely PLC is in breach.

Actual Cause

Plaintiff must show that but for the defendant's act, the injury to plaintiff would not have resulted.

But for PLC's failure to build a better fence around the substation, Peter would not have been able to enter the substation and be injured.

Proximate Cause

A defendant is liable for all harmful results that are reasonably foreseeable, and for any intervening causes that are foreseeable.

Peter's severe burn injuries were a foreseeable harmful result that came from his contact with a high voltage wire at PLC since electricity causes burn injuries.

While the mechanism of injury was odd since Peter's pet pigeon struck Peter in the face when he tried to grasp it, it is foreseeable that a person would chase a pet bird in a neighborhood. This is not such an unusual occurrence that it would be considered an unforeseeable intervening force and thus, it will not break the chain of causation and absolve PLC of responsibility.

Damages

Physical injury to the plaintiff or property damage must be shown.

Peter suffered a severe burn injury and will be able to recover for all damages that resulted from the injury.

Defenses — Assumption of the Risk

A plaintiff may be denied recovery if they assumed the risk of damage where they knew of the risk and voluntarily consented despite the risk.

As discussed above, it is possible Peter's recovery will be denied if he assumed the risk by climbing the fence after appreciating the danger and likely seeing the warning signs. Peter's recovery may be denied because he assumed the risk.

Defenses — Comparative Negligence

In jurisdictions that follow the comparative negligence theory, the plaintiff's own negligence may limit recovery if his own negligence contributed to his injuries. Liability is divided between plaintiff and defendant in proportion to fault.

Assuming Peter is found to be negligent also as discussed above, Peter's recovery can be reduced by the proportionate amount attributed to his own negligence.

Torts Question 3
February 2020, Question 1

Paul, an actor, had small but memorable roles in two recent Hollywood blockbusters. Paul was also a first-year law student. He began having difficulty keeping up with his studies and became increasingly anxious about failing. He told his Legal Research and Writing professor, Dan, about his anxiety and doubts about his ability to timely complete a research paper Dan had assigned. Dan noticed that Paul appeared unusually anxious and suggested he go see the school counselor.

Paul returned to the apartment that he shared with Jack, who was also enrolled in Dan's Legal Research and Writing class.

The day before the research paper was due, Jack looked for his paper in his room but could not find it. Later, after Jack returned home from school, he found the paper on his desk where he thought he had originally placed it. After submitting the paper, Jack became suspicious that Paul might have copied parts of Jack's paper on the day that it seemed to be missing. Jack went to Dan's office and told him about his suspicions. Dan pulled from a stack of submitted papers what he thought was Paul's paper. When Jack saw the paper, he recognized the footnotes and said that Paul had "copied all of the footnotes from my paper."

The next day, Dan told Jack and Paul's class that "I hope no other student has copied his footnotes from another student's paper like that two-bit actor Paul." Paul was in class and heard the statement. Deeply humiliated, Paul suffered a severe panic attack, but did not seek medical treatment.

Dan later discovered that he had inadvertently shown Jack his own paper and not Paul's paper and that Paul had not copied Jack's or any other person's materials.

Paul has sued Dan based on his statement to the class.

What claim(s) may Paul reasonably raise against Dan; what defenses may Dan reasonably assert; what damages, if any, may Paul recover; and what is the likely outcome? Discuss.

Torts Question 3 Assessment
February 2020, Question 1

This tort question tests on the less commonly tested issue of defamation. Many students do not learn about defamation in first year torts class, and have just learned it for the bar exam, so they are less familiar with it conceptually. The call here breaks the question into the claims Paul may raise, potential defenses, damages, and the likely outcome. Even though this might not be the most logical way to organize your answer, we recommend formatting your response in accordance with the call of the question. Since the question first asks what claim(s) Paul may reasonably raise, an issues checklist will help you to spot beyond the obvious defamation cause of action.

To successfully and completely analyze this call, you need to have a full understanding of defamation, which illustrates why you need to understand your rules well and have fact triggers that help you understand which facts give rise to the various issues, rather than just memorize the rules alone. Rote memorization will enable you to write out a rule statement, but it will not help you to analyze the specific details of that rule as is required here. A good illustration of this is that many students will memorize the rules for defamation, such as, "defamation is a defamatory statement, of and concerning the plaintiff. . . ." However, if you don't fully understand what exactly a defamatory statement is because you simply memorized the rules alone, then you might find yourself in trouble on exams such as this one. A person who truly understands the rules, and doesn't simply memorize them, knows that a defamatory statement is one that is not mere opinion, but rather a statement that is based on specific facts and adversely affects one's reputation. With this knowledge and a full understanding of the rule, you would be able to properly analyze the difference between the two potentially defamatory statements.

The best way to fully understand the rules and how they apply is to see the relation between the rules and the fact triggers and to do as many practice essays as you can for each type of issue, especially focusing on those issues where you struggle or perhaps covering subjects you did not cover during law school. The Issues Tested Matrix at the end of the torts chapter provides further guidance as to which questions cover the various tested issues. Some of the particular torts issues that are not found in this section can be found in the crossover section. Further, for additional practice, the California state bar website has available all questions from the past several years, including two high-passing student answers. With the rules here, the fact triggers, the practice questions, assessment aids, and other information, you can practice writing out essays until you fully comprehend each issue and are able to articulate and understand how to apply every rule in an essay.

Make note of the areas highlighted in **bold** on the corresponding grid. The bold areas highlight the issues, analysis, and conclusions that are likely **required** to receive a passing score on this question.

Issue	Rule	Fact Application	Conclusion
What claims may Paul reasonably raise against Dan?			

Defamation	To prove defamation, P must prove:
	
	• **Defamatory statement** (false and holds P up to contempt or public ridicule; doesn't include opinions unless based on specific facts)
	
	• **Of or concerning P**
	
	• **Published to a 3rd party**
	• **Fault in publication** (this could have been analyzed after common law defamation as con law defamation)
	  • **Public figure**—one who has achieved **fame or notoriety**, or voluntarily assumed a role in public controversy. **P must prove malice** (knowledge that the statement was false or **a reckless disregard as to whether it was false**)
	  • **Private person**—the publisher need only be negligent in publication
	
	• **Causation** (harmed reputation)
	• Damages (see below—since call separated out damages)
		There are two potential defamatory statements. **D accused P of copying footnotes from another student's paper and also called him a "two-bit actor."**
		
		The statement about the footnotes is **false** because the D made an error and **P did not cheat** on the paper. A cheating accusation would **hold P up to contempt and public ridicule** since P is a law student and this conduct implicates the serious ethical violation of **cheating, which would damage P's reputation.**
		
		P may argue the "two-bit" **actor** comment is also defamatory since it **disparages P's acting skills.** However, D will argue the comment is a mere opinion, and thus does not qualify as a false and defamatory statement.
		
		Since D made the statements about "that two-bit actor Paul" and **identified P by name** in front of the legal writing class, **the class knew both statements were of or concerning P.**
		
		D published the statement to the entire legal writing class where P was present, so it was published to many third parties.
		
		Since P is an actor with small but memorable **roles in two recent blockbuster films,** he has achieved fame or notoriety, so he is likely a **public figure,** making this a matter of **public concern.**
		
		If P is a public figure, the statement must have been made with malice. Here, P will argue D showed **reckless disregard for the truth** by not ensuring he was correct before accusing P of cheating. After hearing Jack's suspicions, Dan pulled out what he thought was P's paper and upon seeing the footnotes, Jack said P copied Jack's footnotes. **It was reckless for D not to take the simple step of verifying the paper in question was P's before making a serious accusation about cheating.**
		
		However, **D will argue he was not reckless,** but rather reasonably believed that P cheated based on Jack's word. D also knew **P was having trouble in class and was anxious** about finishing his paper timely which made the cheating accusation reasonable. This argument will not be compelling since it would have been easy to take steps to verify the accusation.
		
		While less likely, if P is considered a private person since this occurred in a law school context and he only had small roles in films, D will likely be found negligent in his publication of the defamatory statement since he took no steps to verify the accuracy of the cheating accusation.
		
		Here, it is unclear if the statement actually caused damage to P's reputation, but that is not necessary. P need only show the statement would have caused damage to his reputation, if believed. **An accusation of cheating by his professor would damage the reputation of a law student** and future lawyer since upholding high ethical standards is critical in the profession. For analysis on damages—see below (separate per call).
		
		[Note: the various elements of defamation could have been organized several ways, but use headings to make it easy on the graders to find the components.]
			D is likely liable for defamation

(Continued>)

Issue	Rule	Fact Application	Conclusion
IIED	• **Intentional** or reckless infliction of • **Severe emotional distress** • Caused by D's **extreme and outrageous conduct**	D intentionally **disparaged P to the class** and did so knowing P had the particular sensitivity of anxiety, since D even suggested P see the school counselor. P was deeply humiliated and had a **severe panic attack** in response. While D will argue it was not extreme and outrageous, D's behavior of **accusing a student with known anxiety of falsely cheating is extreme and outrageous** and beyond the bounds of human decency of academic privacy and professionalism. A professor should know better.	D is likely liable for IIED
NIED	• **Negligent conduct causes** • **Serious emotional distress**	While D's conduct in falsely accusing P of cheating in front of his class is at least negligent, and **P suffered a severe panic attack**, **most jurisdictions require a physical impact, injury, or harm.** This is missing here since P sought no treatment for his severe panic attack and there is **no indication of a physical harm**, but some jx might find the panic attack itself as sufficient harm.	**D is unlikely to recover for NIED**
What defenses may Dan reasonably assert?			
Truth	The truth is a complete defense to defamation.	Since P did not cheat on his paper, the statement about copying the footnotes was false, so the truth will not work as a defense. It is unclear if P really is a "two-bit actor," but since that statement is more opinion than fact, it is not actionable.	The truth will not provide a defense
No Actual Malice		D's best defense is to argue that P is a public figure, so the actual malice standard applies, and then argue his conduct does not rise to the level of actual malice, as described above. However, he will not likely be successful.	D likely did have actual malice
What damages, if any, may Paul recover?			
Damages for defamation	**For slander (spoken defamation), P must prove special damages (pecuniary loss) unless slander per se applies** where P is identified as having **professional unfitness**, and damages are presumed.	Here, D made the defamatory statement in class, so it is **slander.** If regular slander is found, P would need to prove special pecuniary damages. Here, P had a severe panic attack and felt deeply humiliated, but he had no ascertainable financial damages, so he would not recover anything. However, P will argue **slander per se applies when one is accused of having professional unfitness**, and **being accused of plagiarism and cheating would indicate a law student was unfit to be a lawyer, where high ethical standards must be maintained. For slander per se, special damages are presumed**, so P would be able to recover. D may argue that since P is not yet a lawyer, the statement is not about his professional fitness, but since P is in professional school and the statement implicates P's ethics, it will be considered slander per se.	**P can recover for presumed damages under slander per se**
Damages for IIED	Compensatory damages	**P did not seek treatment for the severe panic attack, but that need not be shown to recover for IIED.** P's testimony about his emotional distress would be sufficient to establish damages. Though, D may argue that P failed to mitigate his damages since he didn't seek treatment. If this is true, P's damages may be reduced.	**P can recover for IIED**

Question 3 Sample Answer
February 2020, Question 1

What claims may Paul reasonably raise against Dan?

Defamation

To prove defamation, a plaintiff must prove the defendant made a defamatory statement, of or concerning the plaintiff, the fault in publication standard is satisfied, and that it caused harm to plaintiff's reputation.

Defamatory Statement

A defamatory statement is one which is false and holds the plaintiff up to contempt or public ridicule. Statements of opinion do not qualify unless the opinion is based on specific identifiable facts.

Here, Dan made two potential defamatory statements. Dan, a professor, 1.) accused his student Paul of copying footnotes from another student's paper, and 2.) called him a "two-bit actor" in front of Paul's legal writing class. The statement about the footnotes is false because Paul did not cheat on his paper. Rather, Dan made an error when he showed what he thought was Paul's paper to Paul's roommate Jack. However, Dan accidently showed Jack his own paper, so Jack was mistaken when he subsequently accused Paul of copying his footnotes in the paper. A cheating accusation would hold Paul up to contempt and public ridicule since Paul is a law student and cheating implicates a serious ethical violation, which would significantly damage Paul's reputation among his fellow law students.

Paul may argue the "two-bit" actor comment is also defamatory since it disparages Paul's acting skills. However, Dan will successfully argue the comment is a mere opinion, and thus does not qualify as a false and defamatory statement.

Of or Concerning Plaintiff

It must be clear to others the statement was made about Paul. Since Dan made the statements about cheating and "that two-bit actor Paul," which identified Paul by name in front of his legal writing class, the classmates knew both statements were concerning Paul.

Published to a Third Party

Dan published the false statement to Paul's entire legal writing class where Paul was present, so it was published to many third parties.

Fault in Publication

To determine the standard of fault required by the defendant in the publication of the statement, it depends on if the statement is one of public concern, and it also depends on the status of the plaintiff as a private or public person.

A public figure is one who has achieved fame or notoriety, or voluntarily assumed a role in a public controversy. For public figures, the plaintiff must prove malice, which is knowledge that the statement was false or a reckless disregard as to whether it was false.

Since Paul is an actor with small but memorable roles in two recent blockbuster films, Paul has likely achieved fame or notoriety and is a public figure, thus making this is a matter of public concern. Here, Paul will argue Dan showed reckless disregard for the truth by not ensuring he was correct before accusing Paul of cheating. After hearing Jack's suspicions about Paul, Dan pulled out what he thought was Paul's paper and upon seeing the footnotes, Jack said Paul copied Jack's footnotes. It was reckless for Dan not to take the simple step of verifying Paul's authorship of the paper in question before making a serious accusation about cheating. It would have been simple for Dan to look at the name on the paper, or cross reference an exam number, and it was reckless not to do so.

However, Dan will argue he was not reckless, but given the circumstances, he reasonably believed that Paul cheated based on Jack's word. Dan also knew that Paul was having trouble in class and was anxious about finishing his paper timely, which made the cheating accusation reasonable. This argument will not be compelling since it would have been easy to take steps to verify the authorship of the paper.

If Paul is considered a private person, the publisher need only be negligent in publication.

While less likely, Paul may be considered a private person since this statement occurred in a law school context and Paul only had small roles in films, so he was not a major celebrity. Even so, Dan will likely still be found negligent in his publication of the defamatory statement since he took no steps to verify the accuracy of the cheating accusation.

Causation

The defamatory statement must cause harm the plaintiff's reputation.

Here, it is unclear if the statement actually caused damage to Paul's reputation, but that is not necessary. Paul need only show the statement would have caused damage to his reputation, if believed. An accusation of cheating by his professor would damage the reputation of a law student (and future lawyer) since upholding high ethical standards is critical in the legal profession.

IIED

Intentional or reckless infliction of severe emotional distress caused by the defendant's extreme and outrageous conduct.

Here, Dan intentionally disparaged Paul to the class and did so knowing that Paul had a sensitivity of anxiety, since Dan even suggested Paul see the school counselor. Paul was deeply humiliated by the accusation and had a severe panic attack in response. While Dan will argue his statement was not extreme and outrageous, Dan's behavior of falsely accusing a student with known anxiety of cheating is extreme and outrageous and beyond the bounds of human decency, especially in the context of academic privacy and professionalism. A professor should know better, and Paul can likely recover damages for IIED.

NIED

Negligent conduct that causes serious emotional distress.

While Dan's conduct in falsely accusing Paul of cheating in front of his class is at least negligent, and Paul suffered a severe panic attack in response, most jurisdictions require a physical impact, injury or harm to recover for NIED. This harm is missing here since Paul sought no treatment for his severe panic attack and there is no indication of him suffering physical harm, so Dan is unlikely to recover for NIED.

What defenses may Dan reasonably assert?

Truth

Truth is an absolute defense to defamation.

However, since Paul did not cheat on his paper, the statement about him copying footnotes was false, so the truth will not work as a defense. It is unclear if Paul really is a "two-bit actor," but since that statement is more opinion than fact, it is not actionable. The truth will not provide a defense.

No Actual Malice

Dan's best defense is to argue that Paul is a public figure, so the actual malice standard applies, and then try to argue that his conduct of accusing Paul of cheating does not rise to the high actual malice standard. However, as described above Dan will still not likely be successful since Dan probably did act with reckless disregard of the truth.

What damages, if any, may Paul recover?

Damages for Defamation

For slander, which is spoken defamation, a plaintiff must prove special damages (pecuniary loss) unless it was slander per se, because damages are presumed where the plaintiff is identified as having professional unfitness.

Here, Dan made the defamatory statement in class, so it is slander. If regular slander is found, Paul would need to prove special pecuniary damages. Here, Paul had a severe panic attack and felt deeply humiliated, but he seems to have had no ascertainable financial damages, so he would not recover anything.

However, Paul will argue slander per se applies when one is accused of having professional unfitness, and being accused of plagiarism and cheating in law school would indicate a law student was unfit to be a lawyer, where high ethical standards must be maintained. For slander per se, special damages are presumed, so Paul would be able to recover damages.

Dan may argue that since Paul is not yet a lawyer, the statement was not about his professional fitness, but since Paul is in professional school and the statement implicates Paul's professional ethics, it will likely be considered slander per se. Damages will try to compensate Paul for the long-term effect of the reputational damage to him professionally.

Damages for IIED

Compensatory damages can compensate for direct economic losses, as well as pain and suffering.

Paul did not seek treatment for his severe panic attack, but that need not be shown to recover under IIED. Paul's testimony about his emotional distress would be sufficient to establish damages. Dan may argue that Paul failed to mitigate his damages since he didn't seek treatment for his panic attack, but it is unlikely Paul would have his damages reduced, though this is probably unlikely since a plaintiff is not required to seek medical treatment.

Torts Question 4
July 2010, Question 1

Homeowner kept a handgun on his bedside table in order to protect himself against intruders. A statute provides that "all firearms must be stored in a secure container that is fully enclosed and locked." Burglar broke into Homeowner's house while Homeowner was out and stole the handgun.

Burglar subsequently used the handgun in an attack on Patron in a parking lot belonging to Cinema. Patron had just exited Cinema around midnight after viewing a late movie. During the attack, Burglar approached Patron and demanded that she hand over her purse. Patron refused. Burglar drew the handgun, pointed it at Patron, and stated, "You made me mad, so now I'm going to shoot you."

Patron fainted out of shock and suffered a concussion. Burglar took her purse and fled, but was later apprehended by the police. Cinema had been aware of several previous attacks on its customers in the parking lot at night during the past several years, but provided no lighting or security guard.

Under what theory or theories, if any, might Patron bring an action for damages against Homeowner, Burglar, or Cinema? Discuss.

Torts Question 4 Assessment
July 2010, Question 1

This torts question is good for practice because there are several causes of actions, several defendants, and an abundance of two-sided analyses throughout. It covers the heavily tested issue of negligence, and some intentional torts against multiple defendants.

Generally, intentional torts are straightforward and easy to approach when you know the rules. They are more heavily tested on the multiple-choice questions but do occasionally arise on the essays. Since they aren't frequently tested on the essay, intentional torts are not included on the regular torts issues checklist. Therefore, when intentional torts are at issue on an essay, you should write out, on your white board or virtual scratch paper, a quick mini-issues checklist for all seven intentional torts and their defenses. This is crucial to help you avoid missing any issues and/or defenses since they can overlap. Students will often see either assault or battery, but not both, when one more clearly stands out. Without a checklist approach, students tend to focus on the obvious one to the exclusion of the other(s).

Negligence analysis is often time-consuming and worth many points in an essay. Further, it is heavily tested and has been for years. Many times, as in this question, negligence will arise several times in one essay from the actions of various parties. Here, the negligence analysis is complicated since there are many facts (and factual inferences) to analyze regarding the elements of duty, breach, and causation for both defendants. The bar examiners expect you to analyze both sides where the facts are ambiguous or where key facts can be argued both ways, which comes up several times in this question. It is helpful to pretend the fact pattern is a story a client is telling you and you issue spot to problem solve, but then imagine yourself shifting sides to issue spot it from their opponent's point of view.

Using all of the facts in the analysis is necessary to pass this question. If there are any facts you haven't used to issue spot or in analysis, then you are leaving out arguments and losing points. Further, always keep in mind that one fact can correspond to multiple issues. Just because you have used a fact once does not mean that it cannot go with another issue as well.

Another unique trait about this particular essay was how they tested the issues. Many students analyzed Crimes on this essay, and thus failed this essay. Although the examiners used words such as "Burglar" and "attack" and it involved actions which could be criminal, the call of the question told you to address theories for "an action at damages," which tells you that you are in the land of torts and not crimes. This is why it is crucial to always carefully read the call of the question first before reading the facts.

With accurate mini-issues checklists and full use of the facts, this type of torts question is one in which you can easily write a passing answer. Make note of the areas highlighted in **bold** on the corresponding grid. The bold areas highlight the issues, analysis, and conclusions that are likely **required** to receive a passing score on this question.

Issue	Rule	Fact Application	Conclusion
Q1: Patron (P) *v.* **Homeowner (H)**			
Negligence	• **Duty (reasonable person under the circumstances)** • **Cardozo (foreseeable Ps)** • **Andrews (everyone)**	• Homeowner's duty was of a reasonable gun owner. • Under **Cardozo**, duty is owed to a foreseeable plaintiff in the zone of danger. Under Andrews view, a duty is owed to everyone, which **includes P.** • **H will argue** zone of danger is only in their home where they kept the gun, so **P at the Cinema was not a foreseeable plaintiff in the zone of danger.** • However, P will argue the zone of danger **extends to the Cinema** because **guns can be carried to other locations.** • Likely, H had a duty to P.	Negligence
	• **Negligence *per se*** establishes duty and breach • **Violation of statute** • **Class of persons**	• **A statute required all guns to be kept in a locked container**, and here, the gun was on a bedside table and not in a locked container, so it was violated. • **P will argue** the statute is designed to protect all victims of unsecured guns, and she is in the class of persons since she **was injured by an unsecured gun.** • However, **H will argue the class of persons likely intended to be protected by the statute is children** or people in the home.	
	• **Type of harm**	• **P will argue the statute intends to protect from injuries caused by a gun and she was injured by a gun.** • However, H will argue the statute intends to protect from gunshots, which does not apply here since P fainted upon seeing the gun. • Negligence *per se* is likely established, but if not, P can still prove up breach of duty.	
	• **Breach (falls below standard of care)**	• At a minimum, a reasonable gun owner who keeps a gun for self-defense foresees possible intruders and breaches their duty by keeping a gun in plain sight while out of the home.	
	• **Actual Cause (but for test)**	• **But for H** leaving the gun unsecured in plain sight, **B likely would not have stolen gun** and used H's gun to threaten shooting P, causing injury.	
	• **Proximate Cause (foreseeability test)**	• H will argue the **gun theft and the criminal acts of B were unforeseeable superseding causes that break the chain of causation.** • However, the criminal acts must be unforeseeable. **Since H kept gun for protection** from intruders, **criminal intruders were foreseeable**, and that they might **steal the gun and use it** in another crime is also foreseeable.	
	• **Damages**	• Since **P suffered shock and a concussion** and her purse was taken by B, she suffered both a physical injury and a loss of property, which are damages.	

(Continued>

Issue	Rule	Fact Application	Conclusion
Q2: Patron (P) v. Burglar (B)			
Assault	• **Intentional** • **Causing apprehension of** • **Imminent** • **Harmful or offensive contact**	• B likely **desired** to cause apprehension **by pointing the gun and threatening "I'm going to shoot you,"** to **scare P into giving up her purse** out of fear of being shot. • P was **in fear** from B's threat because she **fainted from shock** upon seeing the gun. • A **gunshot** would be harmful since it can cause serious injury or death, and the harm was imminent since **B pulled a gun, placing P in immediate danger.**	Assault
Battery	• **Intentional** • **Harmful or offensive** • **Contact**	• B took P's purse after she fainted, which would be harmful or offensive. • However, it is **not clear that B touched P**. If P's purse was on her person when B took purse, it could be considered "closely associated" with her body to satisfy the touching element. But, if the purse was not, then P was not "touched" by B.	**Likely, no battery**
IIED	• **Intentional** or reckless infliction of • **Severe emotional distress** • Caused by D's **extreme and outrageous conduct**	• B at least recklessly caused severe emotional distress by pointing a gun and threatening P. • **Fainting from shock** is sufficient to establish that the emotional distress was severe. • **Robbing a person at gunpoint and threatening to shoot** is outside the bounds of decency and extreme and outrageous since the victim would think they could die.	IIED
Trespass to Chattel/ Conversion	• **Intentional** • **Interference with** • **Chattel** • **Damages:** (TTC = loss of value; Conversion = full value)	• B **desired** to interfere with P's purse because **B took the purse, P's property.** • If **P gets her purse back,** then she can recover for **loss of use under trespass to chattels.** • **If P does not get her purse back,** then she can recover for the full value of her property under **conversion.**	**Trespass to chattel and/or conversion**

Continued>

Issue	Rule	Fact Application	Conclusion
Q3: Patron (P) v. Cinema (C)			

Negligence	• **Duty (reasonable person under the circumstances)**
	   • Cardozo (foreseeable Ps)
	   • Andrews (everyone)
	 • **Duty — invitee — a business** owner owes a duty to make **reasonable inspections** to find hidden dangers and take affirmative action to remedy dangerous conditions
	 • **Breach (falls below standard of care)**
	 • **Actual Cause (but for test)**
	 • **Proximate Cause (foreseeability test)**
	 • **Damages**
		• Since C is a landowner and P is a paying customer of C, C owes P a **duty under the business invitee standard (to inspect, make safe, warn of dangerous conditions)**. The duty is owed to C as a patron under either view.
		 • **C knew of prior attacks in its parking lot but took no actions to make this dangerous condition safe by hiring extra security or providing** lighting or warnings, which a reasonable owner would, so they **breached their duty.**
		 • **But for C not providing better safety and security for its parking lot, B would not have robbed P, causing her injury.**
		 • C will argue, as above, that third party criminality is an unforeseeable superseding cause of P's injury that breaks the causal chain. However, **C knew of "several" prior attacks on its customers in the parking lot at night, but did nothing to remediate, so this attack was also foreseeable.**
		 • Since P suffered a concussion and her purse was taken by B, she suffered both physical injury and a loss of purse, which are damages for which she can recover.
			Negligence

Torts Question 5
February 2016, Question 2

Jack believed that extraterrestrial aliens had come to earth, were living undercover as humans, and were planning a full-scale invasion in the future. Jack believed that his next-door neighbor, Nancy, was one of these aliens.

One day, Nancy called Jack on the phone to complain that Jack's children were playing in her yard. Jack yelled that his children could play wherever they wanted to. He also said that he was going to kill her.

The next day, Nancy approached Jack, who was playing in his yard with his children. She reminded him to keep his children out of her yard. Jack picked up a chainsaw and said, "When the invasion comes, I am going to use this baby to cut off your head!"

From the other side of the street, Ben saw Jack angrily raise the chainsaw at Nancy. Ben ran across the street and knocked Jack to the ground and injured him.

Later that week, Jack decided that he could wait no longer. He saw Nancy's car, which he believed to be an alien spaceship, parked on the street. He snuck over to her car and cut the brake lines, hoping Nancy would have a minor accident and be taught a lesson.

Unaware that her car had been tampered with, Nancy lent it to Paul. When the brakes failed to work, Paul drove off a mountain road and was severely injured.

1. What tort causes of action, if any, may Nancy bring against Jack, and how is each likely to fare? Discuss.

2. What tort causes of action, if any, may Jack bring against Ben, and how is each likely to fare? Discuss.

3. What tort causes of action, if any, may Paul bring against Jack, and how is each likely to fare? Discuss.

Torts Question 5 Assessment
February 2016, Question 2

This torts question raises the less commonly essay-tested area of intentional torts. Generally, intentional torts are straightforward and easy to approach when you know the rules. They are more heavily tested on the multiple-choice questions but do tend to occasionally arise on the essays. Since they aren't frequently tested on the essay, intentional torts are not included on our regular torts issues checklist. Therefore, when intentional torts are at issue on an essay, you should write out, on your white board or virtual scratch paper, a quick mini-issues checklist for all seven intentional torts and their defenses. This is crucial to help you avoid missing any issues and/or defenses. Students will often see either assault or battery, but not both, because one of them will clearly stand out. Without a checklist approach, students tend to focus on the obvious one to the exclusion of the other(s). Further, defenses are often overlooked, resulting in missed points. Using a mini-issues checklist with all defenses will help avoid this shortfall. By utilizing an accurate mini-issues checklist to issue spot, this type of torts question is one in which you can easily write a passing answer.

Always think of an essay fact pattern as an exercise in role playing since writing a passing answer to an essay question requires that a student role play to solve the problem posed in the call of the question. The student should pretend that the client is sitting across from them, and the story depicted in the fact pattern is the client's story. First, this approach allows a student to better see both sides to the issues since they will need to anticipate their opponent's arguments. This strategy also encourages a problem-solving approach and will naturally enable a student to focus on which issues are "slam-dunks" and which issues pose a problem because the answer is not so clear-cut. Those murkier areas are always the issues that are worth the most points, and it is important to then allocate your time properly in accordance.

Some facts may raise ambiguities that are difficult to handle. For example, in this question, Jack is clearly mentally ill, and a student would need to address this fact, even though there isn't an obvious way to best handle it. The worst thing a student could do is ignore Jack's obvious mental illness, because the student wasn't sure what to do. It is much better to acknowledge ambiguous or confusing facts and address them, just like a capable lawyer would. For this question, Jack's mental state would not protect him from liability for his conduct since there is no insanity or mental capacity defense for *intentional* torts, and that was the point. In some obvious way, the student needs to make that clear in their response in order to get a passing score on this essay.

Make note of the areas highlighted in **bold** on the corresponding grid. The bold areas highlight the issues, analysis, and conclusions that are likely **required** to receive a passing score on this question.

Issue	Rule	Fact Application	Conclusion
Nancy v. Jack			
Jack's Mental State	Jack's mental state needed to be addressed somewhere in the analysis of this essay. A student could have handled it in several ways, such as addressing it in the beginning as part of the analysis of Jack's ability to form intent, or at the end where Jack would ineffectively try to claim the defense of insanity.		**Jack's mental state will not relieve him of liability for his torts**
Assault: Phone Call	• Intentional • Causing apprehension • Imminent	• **Jack acted with intent** because he had the purpose to cause Nancy apprehension of an imminent harmful contact when he **threatened to kill her.** Though it appears Jack is delusional, his impaired mental condition does not prevent him from forming intent, as he has done here. • Nancy must have been aware of the threat to feel apprehension, which she was here since **she heard Jack's threat** on their phone call, but this will **not be sufficient to satisfy the apprehension element because words alone are not sufficient to cause apprehension in the absence of other actions.** • The threatened contact is **harmful** since Jack threatened to kill Nancy, but the threat must also be imminent. **Since the threat was made over the phone, Jack did not have a present immediate ability to carry out his threat to kill Nancy, thus he did not cause Nancy to have apprehension of an imminent harmful touching.**	Not an assault
	• Harmful/offensive contact	[Since there are two separate incidents of assault, be sure to analyze them separately.]	
Assault: Chainsaw Incident	• Intentional • Causing apprehension • Imminent	• Jack acted volitionally by **picking up the chainsaw** in a threatening manner while saying " . . . I'm going to use this baby to **cut off your head.**" Jack acted **with intent** when his actions demonstrated his stated purpose to cut off Nancy's head. • In addition to threatening to cut off Nancy's head, Jack **picked up a dangerous chainsaw to emphasize his threat,** so since Jack's **behavior was more than making a mere verbal threat, he caused Nancy apprehension.** • An imminent threat must be immediate, and **not a threat of future harm.**	Not an assault [Could have concluded either way based on your analysis]

Continued>

Issue	Rule	Fact Application	Conclusion
Assault: Chainsaw Incident (continued)		**Jack will assert that his threat was not immediate since he threatened to cut off Nancy's head "When the invasion comes. . ."** which would be at some time in the future. Though it is unclear when in the future that might be. **Nancy will claim that Jack's threat was sufficiently imminent since she had no way of knowing when the "invasion" might come.** Further, **Jack's delusional state,** coupled with his nonsensical claim that he would wait for the invasion to cut off Nancy's head, would do nothing to lessen Nancy's apprehension of an imminent attack, especially since Jack was holding a chainsaw while threatening to cut off her head with that same chainsaw. Given, Jack's peculiar behavior, **Nancy would have felt the threat was imminent.** [The conclusion didn't matter, but it was important to argue both sides on the element of imminence.]	
	• **Harmful/offensive contact**	• Jack's threat to cut off Nancy's head with a chainsaw would be a harmful contact.	
IIED	• Intentional/reckless infliction by • **Extreme and outrageous conduct** causing • Severe emotional distress	• Jack may not have had the purpose to cause emotional distress, but at a minimum he was reckless with respect to it being caused. • Jack's conduct of **threatening to cut off Nancy's head** while wielding a **chainsaw is beyond all bounds of human decency and is extreme and outrageous conduct.** • While Nancy was likely disturbed by Jack's behavior, she will be able to recover only if she suffered severe emotional distress and no facts establish that here. [Note: Students may have additionally discussed IIED in relation to the telephone death threat and the cutting of Nancy's brake lines. This was appropriate, but likely not necessary to pass the question.]	If Nancy can show she suffered severe emotional distress she can recover
Trespass to Chattel	• **Intentional** • **Interference with** • **P's use or possession** • **In a chattel** • Damages for loss of use	• In his belief that Nancy's car was an alien spaceship, **Jack's conduct was intentional when he acted with the purpose to tamper with Nancy's brake lines** so she would have a minor car accident. • Nancy's car was interfered with because **Jack cut the brake lines.** • **Nancy had the right to the use and possession of her car, a chattel.** • Jack would be responsible to pay **damages to repair the car and for Nancy's loss of use of the chattel while it is repaired.**	Trespass to chattel

Continued>

Issue	Rule	Fact Application	Conclusion
Conversion	Trespass to chattel elements, and • Substantial interference with the chattel • **Damages are market value**	The interference with the car was substantial since the cut brake lines led to the car being driven off a mountain road. It is likely the car is totaled. **Since the car was likely destroyed, damages will be assessed as the market value of the car.**	Conversion
Jack v. Ben			
Battery	• **Intentional infliction** • **Harmful or offensive** • **Contact**	• **Ben was in fear for Nancy's safety** and acted with the purpose to **knock Jack to the ground when he ran across the street** and did so, establishing intent. • Jack experienced a **harmful contact** since being knocked to the **ground** was likely painful.	Battery
Defense of Others	Reasonable belief another is threatened with unlawful force and could use self defense Uses reasonable force proportionate to the threat	• Ben was on the other side of the street when he saw **Jack angrily raise the chainsaw at Nancy** and may have even heard Jack's threat to cut off her head. **It would be reasonable to think Nancy was being threatened with unlawful force and was in a position to use self-defense, so even if Ben was mistaken, his belief was reasonable in the circumstances.** • While Jack's force was deadly, **Ben's response was measured and non-deadly since he only knocked Jack to the ground** to prevent an attack. **Ben's force was proportionate and reasonable in light of the apparent threat and his defense of others would provide a valid defense to Jack's battery action.**	**Valid defense**
Paul v. Jack			
Battery	• Intentional infliction • **Transferred intent** • **Harmful or offensive** • **Contact**	• Jack had the purpose that Nancy to be injured in a car accident when her brakes failed. • **The intent to cause an intentional tort to one person can be transferred to another person.** Jack's intent to cause the intentional tort of battery to Nancy can be transferred to Paul, who was the person actually harmed when he borrowed Nancy's car and the cut brake lines caused an accident. • Paul was severely injured in the accident when Nancy's car drove off the mountain road, so there was a harmful touching of Paul.	Battery

Torts Question 6
July 2004, Question 6

Jack owned the world's largest uncut diamond, the "Star," worth $1 million uncut, but $3 million if cut into finished gems. Of the 20 master diamond cutters in the world, 19 declined to undertake the task because of the degree of difficulty. One mistake would shatter the Star into worthless fragments.

One master diamond cutter, Chip, studied the Star and agreed with Jack in writing to cut the Star for $100,000, payable upon successful completion. As Chip was crossing the street to enter Jack's premises to cut the Star, Chip was knocked down by a slow moving car driven by Wilbur. Wilbur had driven through a red light and did not see Chip, who was crossing with the light. Chip suffered a gash on his leg, which bled profusely. Though an ordinary person would have recovered easily, Chip was a hemophiliac (uncontrollable bleeder) and died as a result of the injury. Chip left a widow, Melinda.

Jack, who still has the uncut Star, engaged Lawyer to sue Wilbur in negligence for the $2 million difference between the value of the diamond as cut and as uncut. Lawyer allowed the applicable statute of limitations to expire without filing suit.

1. What claims, if any, may Melinda assert against Wilbur, and what damages, if any, may she recover? Discuss.

2. What claims, if any, may Jack assert against Lawyer, and what damages, if any, may he recover? Discuss.

Torts Question 6 Assessment
July 2004, Question 6

This is a great question to practice with because it is a more challenging tort question to issue spot. You should utilize your issues checklist after reading the call of the question to decide which issues the facts raise, but this question requires a bar applicant to demonstrate their deeper understanding of how the more conceptually simple torts concepts fit together and interrelate. It is no accident that this was question 6, the last question at the end of the third day of the exam before the exam changed to the two-day format. It is also no accident that the most complicated issue is contained in the last call of the question. It is a favorite bar examiner tactic to end the testing session with a complicated call.

The first challenge is that Chip, the person who is the recipient of the tortious conduct, is deceased. Before addressing any tort actions, it is imperative that students explain to the reader/grader that Chip's tort action can survive his death since an action can be brought on his behalf in a survival action. Further, his widow can bring her own wrongful death claim for the loss of her husband. It's a quick and simple issue to raise, but without this simple set up, it gives the appearance the student does not have sufficient mastery of the concepts and believes Chip can sue from beyond the grave.

The negligence action against Wilbur is simple, with most of the points allocated to the eggshell plaintiff issue and a thorough discussion of damages, given the many facts available to use given the uncertainty of Chip's ultimate success in cutting the diamond. The second call is the one that is more challenging to organize and conceptualize and there are many ways a student could have presented their answer. Jack is suing Lawyer for malpractice because Lawyer missed a statute of limitations deadline in Jack's underlying suit against Wilbur for negligence. Legal malpractice is nothing more than a negligence action. While establishing duty and breach is easy, the trickier issues are causation and damages. Jack can only prevail and receive damages from Lawyer if he would have been successful in his underlying suit against Wilbur. Essentially, this requires the analysis of a case (negligence against Wilbur) within a case (negligence against Lawyer.) Though Lawyer has breached his duty, the problem with recovering against him revolves around the same difficulty with proving damages with certainty as was discussed in Melinda's action, as well as that Wilbur would not have had a duty to Jack in the underlying case.

If you miss any of the issues or rules below, you should rewrite your answer or at least those missed issues. Further, you should rewrite any issues where you find that you omit key facts and/or arguments. Writing out essays properly is the best practice you can do to pass the essay portion of the bar exam. For more questions that test these particular issues, or other issues, review the Torts Issues Tested Matrix at the end the torts chapter.

Finally, make note of the areas highlighted in **bold** on the corresponding grid. The bold areas highlight the issues, analysis, and conclusions that are likely **required** to receive a passing score on this question. In general, the essay grids are provided to assist you in analyzing the essays and are much more detailed than what a student should create during the exam to organize their response to a question.

Issue	Rule	Fact Application	Conclusion
1. Melinda v. Wilbur			
Standing: Survival or Wrongful Death	A survival or wrongful death action allows a surviving spouse to assert a claim on behalf of the deceased spouse and in their own right for loss of consortium.	**Melinda has standing as Chip's widow to bring suit** under a survival or wrongful death cause of action asserting a claim on Chip's behalf. As a widow, Melinda may also have her own claim for loss of consortium. Melinda will need to establish the underlying tort claim.	**Melinda has standing**
Negligence			
	Duty: A person owes a duty to others to act as a reasonable person would under the circumstances.	**A driver owes a duty of reasonable care to all foreseeable plaintiffs,** which includes other drivers and pedestrians. Chip was a pedestrian crossing the street when Wilbur ran a red light, hitting Chip.	**Wilbur owed a duty of care to Chip.**
	Breach: A person breaches the duty of care when they fail to act as a reasonably prudent person would in similar circumstances.	**Wilbur ran a red light and hit Chip,** a pedestrian who was crossing with the light. **A reasonably prudent driver would not run a red light. Even though Wilbur was driving slowly, and failed to see Chip,** it is never reasonable for a driver to run a red light. Therefore, Wilbur breached his duty.	**Wilbur breached his duty**
	Negligence per se: A violation of an applicable statute satisfies the element of duty and breach when the statute is intended to protect this class of person from this type of harm.	Under a negligence per se analysis, Wilbur may also be found to be in breach since there is likely a criminal statute related to running red lights. Since such a statute's purpose would likely be to protect pedestrians from injury, its violation would establish Wilbur's negligence per se.	Wilbur may be negligent per se
	Actual cause is established by the "but for" test.	**But for Wilbur's conduct of running the red light and hitting Chip, Chip would not have died.**	Actual cause is established
	Proximate cause: A person is liable for all foreseeable harmful results directly resulting from their negligent conduct. Eggshell plaintiff: **A defendant is still liable for damages if the plaintiff has a condition that makes them more susceptible to injury.**	It is foreseeable that a pedestrian crossing the street with the light **could be harmed when Wilbur ran the red light.** Wilbur will argue that Chip's death is unforeseeable because Chip suffered from the unusual medical condition of hemophilia, which causes uncontrolled bleeding. **While a typical person perhaps wouldn't die from receiving a gash on his leg, a defendant "takes his plaintiff as he finds him."** As a hemophiliac, Chip was more susceptible to injury and died from uncontrolled bleeding caused by the gash on his leg suffered in the accident. **Here, the type of injury suffered by Chip is exactly the type of injury that is the foreseeable result of negligent driving.** The unforeseeable nature of Chip's medical condition will not insulate Wilbur from liability and Wilbur will be the proximate cause of Chip's death.	**Proximate cause is established**

Continued>

Issue	Rule	Fact Application	Conclusion
	Damages: Compensatory damages are awarded where they are foreseeable, certain, unavoidable, and caused by the negligent conduct.	**Damages will be awarded for Chip's medical bills, lost wages, funeral expenses, and pain and suffering.** Melinda will also be able to recover for loss of consortium. Wilbur will argue that the **$100,000 contract** to cut the star diamond should not be recoverable because the damages are too uncertain. **Chip would have been paid only upon successful completion of the contract to cut the "star" diamond, and 19 of 20 master diamond cutters declined the job because it was too difficult and one mistake** would shatter the $1 million diamond. **It is unlikely Melinda will be able to recover the $100,000.**	Damages are recoverable, but not likely the $100,000
2. Jack v. Lawyer			
Legal Malpractice	Legal malpractice is a **negligence** claim requiring **duty, breach, causation,** and **damages.** **Jack v. Wilbur:** Negligence — duty breach, causation, and damages	A lawyer has a duty to file claims in a timely fashion. Here, **Lawyer did not file Jack's claim against Wilbur within the statute of limitations,** which is a **clear breach of the duty to act as a reasonably competent lawyer.** **However, Jack can recover damages against Lawyer only if Jack can establish that he would have prevailed in the underlying suit against Wilbur** that was not timely filed. **Wilbur did not have a duty to Jack** because Jack, as a contracting party with Chip, **was not a foreseeable plaintiff to the car accident.** Jack was not at the scene of the accident and it **would not be foreseeable to Wilbur that hitting Chip would cause an injury to Jack** because of the unusual situation that Chip was the only diamond cutter in the world willing to try to cut the star diamond. Further, as noted above it is **not certain that Chip would have been successful** at cutting the star diamond, increasing its value, since 19 of 20 master diamond cutters refused the job.	**Jack will not prevail against Lawyer because he can't establish prevailing in the underlying suit against Wilbur**

PART 12 *WILLS AND TRUSTS*

WILLS TABLE OF CONTENTS

TRUSTS TABLE OF CONTENTS

INTRODUCTION TO WILLS AND TRUSTS

Wills and trusts are two distinct subjects, but they are combined here since they are related and often cross over with each other. Recently, the bar examiners have been crossing over wills with community property.

Wills are commonly tested by a fact pattern in which a testator has a will detailing provisions for distributing the testator's assets. Unless the facts indicate that a valid will exists, it is first necessary to address the will's validity. Then, organize the question by each asset, and analyze all issues pertaining to each asset in the testator's estate. Another way the subject of wills is commonly tested is with a fact pattern concerning the issues pertaining to the execution of the will itself, rather than what the testator intends to distribute in their will.

Trusts questions often arise in fact patterns concerning the trustee's conduct and the resulting effect on the beneficiaries, which requires analysis of the trustee's duties and liabilities. Trust questions may also involve particular trust types, such as a charitable trust, and then require analysis of the cy pres doctrine and other potential trusts, such as a resulting trust if the trust fails. A testamentary trust is one way the examiners will test both wills and trusts in the same question.

The details are important in wills and trusts questions. Pay careful attention to all the parties because often there are more parties identified in the facts than will benefit from the trust or take under the will. You are expected to discuss how the will or trust will affect all the parties included in the facts, not just those named in the will or trust. Also, pay close attention to the call of the question and/or parties claiming a share of the estate so that you don't inadvertently omit any parties. Lastly, always consider if there is a two-sided argument. Often, there are competing arguments that result in different possible distributions, all of which must be identified.

Remember that on an essay exam the key is to use the facts to both prove and disprove the rules. This comes up frequently in wills and trusts questions where an element is clearly not met, but there are facts that raise the issue so it must be discussed. For example, the examiners often test the issue of "incorporation by reference," but typically the document referenced was not in existence at the time of the execution of the will and thus is not incorporated. Many students think about the issue and quickly dismiss it in their head, because the incorporation fails; as a result, they do not include the issue in their essay and miss easy points. Generally, if an issue crosses your mind, it is worthy of inclusion, even if it is a minor issue or one that is clearly not met. Address it quickly and move on to maximize your points.

Finally, wills and trusts questions can be difficult to organize because there are so many parties and assets at issue. It may be helpful to make a quick timeline identifying the dates and events, and/or a diagram of the people and how they relate, on your white board or virtual scratch paper. This helps put the facts into perspective. Then, organize your essay by the call of the question, whether it is by person, asset, duties breached, or any other pertinent issue.

ISSUES CHECKLIST

WILLS

Validity
Execution
Capacity/intent
Conflict of laws

Components of a Will
Integrated
Incorporation by reference
Acts of indep. legal
    significance
Codicil
Pour-over will

Revocation
Physical act
Subsequent will
Operation of law
DRR

Revival

Distribution
Classification of gifts
Ademption
Abatement
Exoneration
Lapse/anti-lapse
Survivor rights
Bars to succession

Intestate Distribution

Contracts Relating to Wills

TRUSTS

Creation/Validity
Limitations
Types of Trusts
Express
Testamentary
Pour-over
Secret
Semi-secret
Spendthrift
Support
Discretionary
Charitable
Honorary
Totten
Resulting
Constructive

Administration
Powers of trustee
Duties of trustee
    Account and inform
    Not to delegate
    Impartiality
    Due care
        Invest
        Diversify
    Segregate
    Loyalty
    Invest
    Defend
    Enforce
Liabilities of trustee
Liabilities of third parties
Allocation

Modification/Revocation
Termination
Remedies

MEMORIZATION ATTACK SHEET

WILL VALIDITY/CREATION

- ◆ **Execution**
  - Writing
  - Signed by T, or in their presence & at their direction
  - Signed by 2 witnesses
  - Witnesses know T's will
  - Witnesses see T sign or acknowledge T signature at same time
  - Except: C&C evidence of T's intent
- ◆ **Holographic will**
  - T's signature
  - Material provisions in T's handwriting
  - Invalid if no date and unclear which will is new
- ◆ **Capacity/intent**
  - 18 years old
  - Sound mind/competent
  - Fraud in the execution (forgery)
  - Fraud in the inducement (misrepresentations)
  - Fraud preventing execution or revocation
  - Common law undue influence
    - ◆ T **S**usceptible to influence
    - ◆ **O**pportunity to influence
    - ◆ **U**nnatural disposition
    - ◆ Beneficiary active in **P**rocuring disposition
  - Cal statutory undue influence
    - ◆ Excessive **P**ersuasion
    - ◆ **C**auses another to **A**ct or **R**efrain
    - ◆ **O**vercomes their **F**ree will
    - ◆ Results in **I**nequity
    - ◆ Can use circumstantial evidence
      - **V**ulnerability
      - Influencer's **A**uthority
      - **A**ctions of **I**nfluencer
  - Presume fraud/undue influence if devise is to
    - ◆ Drafter
    - ◆ One in fiduciary relationship with T/transcribed
    - ◆ Care custodian w/in 90 days
    - ◆ Employee or cohabitant of any of the above
    - ◆ Partner, SH, or employee of a law firm involved
    - ◆ Exceptions:
      - Blood relative
      - Less than $5k
      - Attorney consult
- ◆ **Conflicts of laws**
  - Valid if complies w/ laws of state of:
    - ◆ Execution
    - ◆ Place of death
    - ◆ Domicile

WILL COMPONENTS

- ◆ **Integration**
  - Present at time of will
  - T's intent
  - Extrinsic evidence ok
- ◆ **Incorporation by reference**
  - Existed at time of will
  - Will shows T's intent
  - Sufficiently described
- ◆ **Acts of independent legal significance**
  - Separate from effect in will
- ◆ **Codicil**
  - Amendment to will
  - Republishes will as of date of codicil
  - Same formalities of will, or holographic will
- ◆ **Pour-over will**
  - Identifies trust in will
  - Terms set forth in document other than will
  - Trust executed before, at same time, or w/in 60 days as will

WILL REVOCATION

- ◆ **By physical act**
  - Presumed destroyed if will last with T and now gone
- ◆ **By subsequent will**
  - Express or implied
- ◆ **By operation of law**
  - Omitted child/spouse/partner
  - Exceptions:
    - ◆ Intent on face of will
    - ◆ Transfer outside will
    - ◆ Spouse waived
    - ◆ Child's other parent takes most
- ◆ **DRR**
  - T revokes 1st will
  - Mistakenly believes 2nd will valid when it isn't
  - If T knew 2nd will not valid, would not have revoked 1st will
  - 1st will probated anyway

WILL REVIVAL

- ◆ 1st will revoked
- ◆ 2nd will revoked
- ◆ 1st will revived if T intended to revive it
- ◆ Extrinsic evidence okay

WILL DISTRIBUTION

- ◆ **Classification of gifts**
  - Specific gift
    - ◆ Identifiable property
    - ◆ Stock splits/dividends to beneficiary
  - General gift
  - Demonstrative gift
    - ◆ General, but specifies property or fund to take from
  - Residuary — remainder
- ◆ **Ademption**
  - By extinction
    - ◆ Gift no longer there
    - ◆ Look at T's intent
  - By satisfaction
    - ◆ Given to beneficiary during life
- ◆ **Abatement**
  - Gifts reduced to pay all debts
  - Reduced in order:
    - ◆ Property not in will
    - ◆ Residuary gifts
    - ◆ General — nonrelative
    - ◆ General — relative
    - ◆ Specific — nonrelative
    - ◆ Specific — relative
- ◆ **Exoneration**
  - Property doesn't abate to exonerate mortgage, lien, deed of trust, etc.
- ◆ **Lapse/anti-lapse**
  - Predeceased beneficiary gift lapses to residue
  - If beneficiary kindred, anti-lapse, so gift to issue
  - Simultaneous death — apply lapse or anti-lapse
- ◆ **Survivor's rights**
  - Widow elects under will or statutory share
  - Spouse can set aside transfer of CP or QCP
  - Omitted heirs take intestate share unless the exceptions above in will revocation are met

- ◆ **Bars to succession**
  - No-contest — can bring if probable cause
  - Killers treated as predeceased

INTESTATE DISTRIBUTION

- ◆ **Intestate succession**
  - All CP and QCP to surviving spouse
  - All SP to spouse if no child; 1/2 if 1 child; 1/3 if 1 + children
  - If no spouse/partner, then to
    - ◆ Issue
    - ◆ Parents
    - ◆ Issue of parents
    - ◆ Grandparents
    - ◆ Issue of grandparents
    - ◆ Issue of predeceased spouse
    - ◆ Next of kin
    - ◆ Parents of predeceased spouse
    - ◆ Issue of parents of predeceased spouse
    - ◆ Escheat to state
  - Heir must survive decedent by 120 hours
- ◆ **Per capita — generation**
  - 1st generation with living
  - Each living gets one share
  - Shares of all deceased split equally between next generation living
- ◆ **Per capita — representation**
  - 1st generation with living
  - Each living gets one share
  - Share of deceased goes to their issue equally
  - If deceased has no issue, goes back to all at that level
- ◆ **Strict per stirpes**
  - 1st generation with living or deceased with issue
  - Each living or deceased issue gets one share
- ◆ **Children**
  - Adopted treated as natural
  - Step or foster take only if
    - ◆ Relationship during child's minority
    - ◆ Continued through life
    - ◆ Legal barrier prevented adoption

WILL CONTRACT ISSUES

- **K to make a will, not make a will, revoke a will established by**
  - Material provisions of K in will
  - Reference in will to K and extrinsic evidence
  - Writing signed by decedent
  - Clear and convincing evidence
- Joint or mutual wills do not create presumption of K
- Remedy for breach of contract is constructive trust

TRUST CREATION/VALIDITY

- **Trust created by**
  - Declaration by owner
  - Transfer of property during owner's life to trustee
  - Transfer by owner in will
  - Power of appointment
  - Enforceable promise
- **Validity requires**
  - Settlor's intention
  - Trust property
  - Legal purpose
  - Ascertainable beneficiary
  - Court can appoint trustee

TRUST LIMITATIONS

- Real property needs writing
- Personal property may be oral
- Invalidation — see Wills (fraud, undue influence, capacity)

TYPES OF TRUSTS

- Express — all above validity requirements met
- Testamentary — in will
- Pour over — see pour-over will above (in Will Components)
- Secret — no intent on face but beneficiary named in will
- Semi-secret — no beneficiary named, but intent there
- Spendthrift — beneficiary cannot alienate his interest
- Support — for beneficiary's health, education, maintenance
- Discretionary — trustee can distribute/ withhold from beneficiary

- Charitable — benefits society
  - Cy pres — if can't be done, court tries to substitute
- Honorary — no charitable or private beneficiary
- Totten — beneficiary takes money left over in bank acct.
- Resulting — implied in fact; goes back to settlor's estate
  - Arises from
    - Purpose of trust ends
    - Trust fails
    - Illegal trust
    - Excess corpus
    - Purchase money resulting trust
    - Semi-secret
- Constructive — applied to prevent unjust enrichment for fraud, self-dealing, etc.

TRUST ADMINISTRATION

- **Powers of trustee**
  - Enumerated and implied
- **Duties of trustee**
  - **A**ccount and inform
  - **N**ot to **D**elegate unless uses skill and due care
  - **I**mpartiality (treat all beneficiaries fairly)
  - **D**ue care
    - **I**nvestigate
    - **D**iversify
  - **S**egregate and earmark
  - **L**oyalty — no self-dealing or conflicts of interest
  - Prudently **I**nvest
    - Statutory lists
    - UPIA — look at portfolio as a whole; reasonable
  - **D**efend actions and **E**nforce claims
  - Mnemonic: **"AND I DID SLIDE"**
- **Liabilities of trustee**
  - Personally liable for violating trustee duties
  - Liable for torts and contracts if within scope
- **Duties of 3rd parties**
  - Transfer to BFP cuts off beneficiary's interest
  - Transfer to non-BFP can be set aside by beneficiary
  - 3rd party can hold property as constructive trustee

◆ **Allocation**
  • Income to beneficiary
  • Principal to remainderman
  • Trustee uses best judgment in allocating

MODIFICATION/REVOCATION

◆ Majority: Settlor can modify or revoke only if right reserved
◆ Minority: Settlor can modify or revoke even if right not reserved
◆ Court can modify to meet settlor's intent or for cy pres

TRUST TERMINATION

◆ Trustee cannot terminate
◆ Beneficiaries can terminate if all competent, all consent & doesn't frustrate trust purpose
◆ Court can terminate if trust purpose frustrated/impossible
◆ Lapse and anti-lapse apply

BREACH OF TRUST REMEDIES

◆ Trustee cannot offset losses
◆ Damages, constructive trust, tracing, equitable lien, remove trustee, surcharge for resulting loss

WILLS RULE OUTLINE

I. **VALIDITY OF A WILL**

  A. **Execution**

    1. **A valid will must meet the formalities of being in writing, signed, and witnessed.**

      a. **Writing:** The will must be in writing.

      b. **Signed:** The will must be:

        1. **Signed by the testator**, or

        2. **Acknowledgment of signature:** Signed by someone in the testator's presence and at their direction as proxy.

      c. **Two witnesses:** The will requires the **signature** of two witnesses who:

        1. **Know the document is a will;** and

        2. **Both are present at the same time to witness** the testator's signing of the will or acknowledgment of testator's signature. However, it is not necessary for the two witnesses to sign attesting to that fact at the same time, but they must sign the will in the testator's lifetime.

> **Exam tip:** The two witnesses must witness the testator signature (or acknowledgement of signature) at the same time, but do not necessarily need to sign themselves to attest to that fact at the same time or in each other's presence.

    2. **Witness issues**

      a. **Not properly witnessed:** If witness requirements are not satisfied, the will can still be treated as properly executed if the proponent of the will establishes by **clear and convincing evidence that the testator intended** the document to be testator's will at the time it was signed.

      b. **Interested witnesses:** Witnesses **should not be "interested witnesses."** An interested witness creates a **rebuttable presumption** that the witness procured the devise by duress, menace, fraud, or undue influence, **unless there are two other uninterested witnesses,** or the devise is made solely in a fiduciary capacity.

    3. **Holographic will:** A will that does not comply with the formalities required for a valid will can qualify as a valid holographic will if the **signature and material provisions are all in the testator's handwriting.**

      a. **Undated:** If the holographic will does not have a date and there is doubt as to whether it or another will controls, the holographic will is invalid to the extent of any inconsistencies.

> **Witness fact triggers:**
>
> **Invalid:** Neighbors to act as witnesses—cannot go from one house to the other to sign if they aren't both present at the same time to see testator sign or acknowledge their signature.
>
> **Invalid:** Witness doesn't realize it is testator's will.
>
> **Valid:** Two witnesses that see testator sign with each present, but each sign separately themselves or take will around corner or to another room to sign as a witness.
>
> **Valid:** Witness is a friend and given a gift in the will, but testator later executes a valid holographic will/codicil, which republishes original will eliminating interested witness problems in first will.

B. **Capacity and intent** are measured at the time of will execution.

   1. **"Of legal age and sound mind":** An individual must be at least **18 years old** and of **sound mind** to make a valid will.

      a. **Mental capacity:** An individual is not mentally competent to make a will if, at the time the will is made, they are unable to:

         1. Understand the **nature of the testamentary act,**
         2. Understand the nature and **situation of their property,** and
         3. Remember and understand their **relations with family** members that are affected by the will.

      b. **Mental disorder:** An individual is not mentally competent to make a will if they suffer from a mental disorder that results in **hallucinations or delusions** that cause them to devise property in a way that they would not have done but for the disorder.

      c. Courts can also **appoint conservators** to make wills on behalf of people if the court thinks the testator lacks capacity or is being taken advantage of through undue influence.

   2. **No duress, menace, fraud, or undue influence:** The execution or revocation of a will or part of a will is ineffective to the extent that it was procured by duress, menace, fraud, or undue influence.

   3. **Fraud** is the **misrepresentation,** deceit, or concealment of a **material fact, known to be false** by the wrongdoer, with the **intent to deprive a person of property or legal rights** or cause injury, and **does in fact deprive** that person.

   4. **Fraud can occur at three points in the process.**

      a. **Fraud in the execution** occurs when a testator is **unaware they are signing a will** or the will is **forged** by another, resulting in the **entire will** being **invalid.**

      b. **Fraud in the inducement** occurs when a wrongdoer influences the testator through **misrepresentations** to include provisions in a will, resulting in only those particular **fraudulent provisions** being **invalid.**

      c. **Fraud preventing will execution or revocation** occurs when fraud is implemented to prevent a will execution or revocation; **courts are split** when a will was not executed as some courts apply **intestate succession** and others create a **constructive trust;** but a court will still probate the will if already executed and the **wrongdoer will take under a constructive trust.** (See Remedies chapter.)

   5. **Undue influence at common law** is found when:

      a. The testator was **<u>S</u>usceptible to the influence,**
      b. The beneficiaries had **<u>O</u>pportunity to influence** this disposition,
      c. The testator left an **<u>U</u>nnatural disposition** of their property, and
      d. The beneficiaries were **active in <u>P</u>rocuring this disposition.**

> <u>**Memorization tip:**</u> **SOUP** is common to remember common law undue influence.

---

   6. **California Statutory Undue influence**

      a. Requirements:

         1. **<u>E</u>xcessive <u>P</u>ersuasion**
         2. That **<u>C</u>auses** another person to **<u>A</u>ct or <u>R</u>efrain** from acting
         3. By **<u>O</u>vercoming** that person's **<u>F</u>ree will,** and
         4. Results in **<u>I</u>nequity.**

      b. **Proof:** Cal. statutory undue influence may be proven by **circumstantial evidence.** The court will consider factors such as the **<u>V</u>ulnerability** (e.g., illness, capacity, age) of the victim, the **<u>I</u>nfluencer's <u>A</u>uthority** (e.g., relationship), and **<u>A</u>ctions of <u>I</u>nfluencer** (i.e., coercion).

> **Memorization tip:** Every **P**owerful **CAR** **O**perates **F**rom **I**nside. To then remember the circumstantial evidence factors you can add **VIA** **A**n **I**gnition to the end of that sentence.

7. **Fraud or undue influence is presumed** in an instrument making a donative transfer to:
   a. The **person who drafted** the instrument,
   b. A person in a **fiduciary relationship with the transferor who transcribed the instrument** or caused it to be transcribed,
   c. A **care custodian** of the transferor adult during the period services were provided, or within 90 days of provision of services,
   d. A **cohabitant or employee** of any of the above people (in a-c).
   e. A **partner, shareholder, or employee** of a law firm in which a person in (a or b above) has an ownership interest.
   f. **Exceptions to the presumption** include when:
      1. The beneficiary is a **blood relative or cohabitant** of the transferor, or
      2. The property transferred is **valued at $5,000 or less**, or
      3. An **independent attorney reviews** the instrument and counsels the transferor without the beneficiary being present.
   g. The **presumption can be rebutted** by **clear and convincing** evidence.

> **Issue spotting tip:** Whenever a witness takes under the will, even if it is a relative, always think about the undue influence issue. In addition, always consider undue influence when the devise seems unusual, such as the testator giving away part of the estate to his fortune-teller.

> **Fraud fact triggers:**
> - Concealing a letter that one knows would change the testator's will
> - Lying to the testator about the existence or survival of a child or family member
> - Informing testator that they must do something in their will while knowing that it is not true

C. **Conflict of laws:** A written will is validly executed if its execution complies with the law of the place where the **testator is domiciled at the time of execution** of the will, or **domiciled at the time of death,** or complies with the law of the place where the **will was executed**.

II. COMPONENTS OF A WILL
A. **External documents**
   1. **Integration:** Papers are integrated into the will if they were **present at the time** of the execution of the will and the **testator intended them to be part of their will**, such as several writings connected by a sequence of thought, folded together, stapled, or physically forming one document. **Extrinsic evidence is permitted** to show intent and the presence of papers.

> **Issue spotting tip:** Integration is at issue anytime there are papers or a reference to papers or notes outside of the will, whether they are found with the will or referenced in the will.

2. **Incorporation by reference:** A writing outside the will may be incorporated by reference into the will if the writing **existed at the time the will was executed** and the will manifests the **intent to incorporate** it and sufficiently **describes the writing** so that it is identifiable.
    a. **Validity not required:** The document referenced need not be valid.
    b. **Special rule for limited tangible personal property:** A **writing**, even if it cannot be incorporated by reference, **may be admitted into probate when it disposes of limited tangible personal property** if the writing:
        1. **Was referred to** in the will,
        2. Is **dated** and either in the **testator's handwriting or signed** by them,
        3. Describes the **items** and **beneficiaries** with reasonable certainty, and
        4. Each item identified may **not exceed $5,000** and the total value of the identified property cannot exceed **$25,000**.
            a. **Tangible personal property does not include** real property, bank accounts, documents of title, securities, money that is common coin or currency (normal U.S. money, not collectibles), and property used in a trade or business.

Issue spotting tip: Anytime you issue spot integration, you should also consider incorporation by reference. These two issues often arise together as a cluster and should both be addressed, even if only one of them is met, anytime a document outside the will is referenced in the will.

Incorporation by reference fact triggers:

- A will that leaves any property to a person named in a document outside the will
- Any pieces of paper found near the will when the will mentions outside documents (even if it isn't clear that those are the papers incorporated by reference, it still raises the issue)
- A holographic will or codicil that addresses another will or mentions the other will (attempts to incorporate provisions of one will into the other)

---

3. **Acts of independent legal significance:** A will may dispose of property by **reference to acts and events** that have independent legal significance apart from their effect in the will. For example, a gift to each employee working for testator at the time of their death.

Exam tip: Always consider if an act of independent legal significance will effectively dispose of property that otherwise cannot be disposed of because of the failure to properly integrate or incorporate. **Examples** of references to acts of independent significance include providing income to one for life through a trust (non-testamentary purpose); paying employees based on performance, not just through the will; a reference to newspaper clippings (which provide news and are not just testamentary); collections of articles to devise, etc.

B. **Codicil: A codicil is an amendment to an existing will** made by the testator to change, explain, or republish their will. It **must meet the same formalities** as a will or holographic will.
    1. **Revocation of a codicil** leaves the remaining **will valid**, but **revocation of a will revokes** both the **will and the codicil.**
    2. **Republication: A validly executed codicil** operates as a **republication of the will** as of the date on the codicil. This new date can remedy any interested witness issues as well since the will is now republished without witnesses this time (this assumes the codicil

is holographic and doesn't need witnesses but if the codicil is typed like a regular will then new uninterested witnesses will be required if the previous will witnesses were interested).

C. **Pour-over will:** A pour-over will is a will that identifies a trust created by the testator into which they can **"pour over" their probate assets** and thus avoid going through probate if the assets are less than $184,500 (as of 2025).

    1. A **pour-over will is valid** if:

        a. The **trust is identified** in the will,

        b. The **terms are set forth in an instrument other than the will**, and

        c. The **trust was executed concurrently with, before, or within 60 days after** the will execution.

III. REVOCATION OF A WILL

A. **Revocation by physical act:** A will or part of a will can be revoked by a **physical act** of the testator or another person in the testator's presence and at the testator's direction. The physical act can include the will being **burned, torn, canceled, destroyed, or obliterated** with the **intent to revoke it.**

    1. **Presumed revoked:** It is **presumed that the testator destroyed the will** with the intent to revoke it if the testator's will was last in the testator's possession and the testator was competent until death.

    2. **Duplicate revoked**: A will executed in duplicate is revoked if one of the duplicates is destroyed, torn, burned, cancelled, or obliterated with the intent to revoke it.

    3. **Cross out one of two beneficiaries:** Where there is a devise to *A* and *B* and *B* has been crossed out, *B*'s portion **goes to the will residue**, not to *A*. Sometimes, the entire devise is revoked (look at testator's intent) but crossing out a gift cannot increase the remaining beneficiary's gift.

B. **Revocation by subsequent will:** A will or part of a will is revoked by a subsequent will, which either **expressly revokes** the previous will or part of it, or **impliedly revokes** the previous will or part of it **through inconsistencies**.

C. **Revocation by operation of law:** A devise is partially revoked by operation of law to accommodate an unintentionally **omitted spouse or child or subsequent domestic partner,** or to **remove all devises to a previous spouse/domestic partner** after dissolution or annulment.

    1. **Omitted spouse** or domestic partner: will receive **an intestate share** if they were married after the will was made, **unless they were**:

        a. **Intentionally omitted** as indicated on the face of will, or

        b. **Otherwise provided for outside the will** with an **intent** to do so in lieu of the will, or

        c. **Waived** their right to their share in a **valid agreement**.

    2. **Omitted children** will also receive their intestate share **if born or adopted *after*** the will (or codicil) was made unless:

        a. **Intentionally omitted** as indicated on the face of will, or

        b. **Otherwise provided for outside the will** with an **intent** to do so in lieu of the will, or

        c. The decedent had other children and devised substantially all the estate to the **other parent of the omitted child.**

Issue spotting tip: Whenever a child or spouse, even if it is an ex-spouse, claims part of the testator's estate, bring up the issue of omitted heir even if you quickly dismiss it because the spouse is an ex-spouse or because an exception applies, such as when the testator left all the estate to the other parent when there were already other children in existence. Raise the issue and use the facts to establish that the requirements are not met. Also look to see if a codicil was created as it republishes the will as of that date and thus the spouse or child would no longer be omitted if they existed before the codicil was executed. Be sure to point this out on an essay.

> **Omitted child or spouse fact triggers:**
> - Parent mistakenly believes child or spouse is dead
> - Child born or adopted after will was executed
> - Parent unaware of child's existence at time will was executed
> - Parent doubts child is theirs at time will was executed

D. **Dependent relative revocation (DRR):** Courts will apply the doctrine of dependent relative revocation where the testator **revokes their first will** (or part of it) on the **mistaken belief** that a **substantially similar second will or codicil would be effective, but it is not effective** at death (often because the subsequent will or codicil was also revoked), and but for the mistake the testator would not have revoked their first will. The court will **disregard the revocation made by the subsequent will** and allow the **first will to take effect**.

> **DRR fact triggers:**
> - Testator made new will because they mistakenly thought the beneficiary in their old will was dead
> - Testator changes will because they reconcile with persons not in will, but new will is not valid
> - New will is not a valid holographic will, but testator crossed out part of old will thinking the new will was valid

   1. **Invalid second will:** If the second will is invalid due to fraud, duress, menace, undue influence, or ineffective execution, then the revocation of the first will was never valid so **DRR is not applicable**.

   2. **DRR only revives the most recently revoked instrument,** such that if a second will revoked a first will and then a third will revoked the second will, the first will would be still be revoked **unless** it is clear from the third will that the testator intended for the first will to take effect.

> **Exam tip:** About half of the time the issue of DRR arises it applies, and half of the time it does not. Even if DRR doesn't apply — perhaps due to failed witness requirements, or the other will was not actually being revoked as it appeared — still spot the issue, briefly explain why DRR doesn't apply, and move on.

IV. REVIVAL OF A WILL

A. **Revival:** When a will is revoked by a physical act or a subsequent will, and then the subsequent will is revoked as well, **the first will is revived if the testator intends for it to be revived.** Extrinsic evidence is permitted when revocation is performed by a physical act.

V. WILL DISTRIBUTION ISSUES

A. **Classification of testamentary gifts**
   1. **Specific gift:** A specific gift is a gift of **specific, identifiable property.** (E.g., my diamond earrings, my beach cottage in Malibu, my 2018 Cadillac, my ABC stock portfolio, etc.)
      a. **Stock splits and dividends** generally both result in the additional shares being distributed to the beneficiary (courts used to prevent stock dividends from going to the beneficiary under the common law but most courts allow it modernly). Courts look at testator's intent.
   2. **General gift:** A general gift is a gift from the **general assets** of the estate and does not include specific property.

3. **Demonstrative gift:** A demonstrative gift is a general gift that **specifies** the **property** or a **particular fund** from which the gift should be made.
4. **Residuary gift:** A residuary gift is **what remains** of the estate after all other gifts have been satisfied and debts and taxes are paid.

> **Exam tip:** Whenever a gift is devised that consists of a house, car, stocks, etc., but does not contain a specific address or model, argue the facts both ways—that it can be a specific gift or a general gift—and always discuss the testator's intent, even if you must make inferences to do so.

B. **Ademption** applies where a **specific gift** devised has **changed form** from that identified in the will or no longer exists.
   1. **A specific gift adeems by extinction** if the specific item identified in the will is not part of the estate at the time of the testator's death—in other words, the specific gift is **void** and that purported devisee takes nothing.
      a. Courts will look at the **testator's intent** in determining whether the gift adeems, such that the beneficiary takes nothing.
      b. The beneficiary is **entitled to a general pecuniary gift** of equal value where the specific gift involved securities that **changed form**, a conservator that sold the property, or eminent domain.
   2. **A gift adeems by satisfaction** if the testator's will provides for deduction of the **lifetime gift**, the testator or the beneficiary declare in writing that the gift is satisfied, or the same property is given to the beneficiary during their lifetime.

> **Ademption fact triggers:**
> - Testator leaves condo or house to beneficiary but later sells it
> - Testator leaves car to beneficiary but doesn't still own it at time of death
> - Testator leaves specific stocks or shares to beneficiary but sells or transfers them prior to death

C. **Abatement** occurs when **gifts are reduced** to enable the estate to pay all debts and legacies that it otherwise would be unable to pay.
   1. **Order of gift abatement**
      a. Property not disposed of by the will
      b. Residuary gifts
      c. General gifts to nonrelatives
      d. General gifts to relatives
      e. Specific gifts to nonrelatives
      f. Specific gifts to relatives
D. **Exoneration** applies when a gift of property is made that is **subject to an encumbrance**, such as a loan, and the will requires the encumbrance to be paid off so that the devisee **takes the property free and clear** of the mortgage.
   1. The general rules of **abatement** apply to enable exoneration.
   2. Where a will requires that a gift of specific property be exonerated from a mortgage (deed of trust, or lien), a **specific gift of other property cannot be abated** for the purpose of exonerating the encumbered property.
E. **Lapse and anti-lapse rules** apply when the persons taking under a will are **no longer alive** at the time of the testator's death.

1. **Lapse:** Traditionally and in some jurisdictions, when a beneficiary predeceased the testator, the gift to the beneficiary **lapsed and fell into the residue,** or was distributed via intestate succession if there was no residue.

2. **Anti-lapse: Modernly** and in **California,** when a beneficiary predeceases the testator, the **issue of the beneficiary** will take in their place, thus **avoiding the lapse** of the gift, **unless a contrary intention** appears in the will.

   a. **Kindred only:** Anti-lapse only applies if the predeceased beneficiary is the testator's kindred (blood relative or adopted person) or kindred of a surviving, deceased, or former spouse.

   b. **Issue will take per capita** if they are the same degree of relation, or per capita with representation if of a more remote degree.

   c. **Class/residuary gifts:** Anti-lapse also applies to **class gifts. It does not apply to residuary gifts when other beneficiaries remain** (the remaining residuary devisees will take the gift of the deceased beneficiary).

   d. **Issue includes** all **lineal descendants,** not just children.

3. **Simultaneous death:** If both the testator and the beneficiary die simultaneously and it cannot be determined by clear and convincing evidence that the beneficiary died first, then the **beneficiary is determined to have predeceased** the testator and the devise lapses, unless anti-lapse applies.

F. **Survivor rights**

1. **Widow's election:** A widow's election allows a widow, widower or a surviving domestic partner to elect to keep their share **devised** under the decedent spouse's will **or** to take their **statutory share,** which is their **half** of the community property (CP) and the quasi-community property (QCP), if the decedent spouse attempted to dispose of more than half of the CP or QCP and there are no children (one-third if there are children).

2. **Property transfers:** A surviving spouse or domestic partner can **set aside transfers** of property or interests of CP and QCP made by the decedent spouse during marriage, to the extent of half if the transferee has retained the property, or, if the transferee has not retained the property, the surviving spouse can **obtain half of the proceeds** or value at the time of transfer.

3. **Omitted spouses/partners/children** (see section III.C. above).

G. **Bars to succession**

1. **No-contest clause:** A no contest clause in a will **penalizes a beneficiary if they contest** the instrument and will be enforced only if it is a direct contest brought without probable cause on the grounds of forgery, lack of due execution, lack of capacity, menace, duress, fraud, undue influence, revocation, or disqualification of a beneficiary in a fiduciary relationship to the testator, or if specifically mentioned in the no-contest clause.

2. **Killers:** Intentional and felonious killers **do not take** under the will or by intestacy, and are treated as having predeceased the testator, and anti-lapse provisions do not apply.

VI. **INTESTATE DISTRIBUTION:** When the decedent dies without a will, intestate succession distribution rules are used.

A. **Surviving spouse:** When decedent leaves a surviving spouse:

1. **Community property (CP):** For all CP and quasi-community property (QCP), the **surviving spouse** or domestic partner **takes all** of the CP and QCP.

2. **Separate property (SP):** For the decedent's SP, the surviving spouse **takes all** of it **only if the decedent did not leave any surviving issue, parent, siblings, or issue of siblings.**

   a. Where **decedent dies leaving surviving spouse or domestic partner and**

      1. **One child, or parents, or their issue:** The surviving spouse takes **one-half of the SP.**

      2. **More than one child, or their issue:** The surviving spouse takes **one-third of the SP.**

B. **Intestate succession order:** Applies 1.) when decedent dies **without leaving a surviving spouse** or domestic partner, or 2.) **for the portion of the estate remaining after the surviving spouse receives their share,** as noted above. The shares of each will depend on the distribution scheme in effect (see sec. VI.E. below).

1. To issue (children and their descendants)
2. To parents, if no issue
3. Issue of parents, if none of the above (siblings and their descendants)
4. Grandparents, if none of the above
5. Issue of grandparents, if none of the above (aunts and uncles)
6. Issue of predeceased spouse/partner, if none of the above (stepchildren)
7. Next of kin, if none of the above
8. Parents of predeceased spouse/partner, if none of the above (parents-in-law)
9. Issue of parents of predeceased spouse/partner, if none of the above (sisters- and brothers-in-law)
10. Escheat to state, if none of the above

C. **120-hour rule:** For intestate succession to apply, the **heir must survive the decedent by 120 hours,** or they will be deemed to have predeceased the decedent, unless the application of the 120-hour rule would result in an escheat to the state.

D. **Advancement:** If a person dies **intestate, property that the decedent gave to an heir during lifetime** is treated as an advancement against that heir's share of the intestate estate **only if the decedent declared and the heir acknowledged such in a writing**.

E. **Per capita — representation distribution**

1. **Per capita:** When intestate succession applies per capita at each generation (Probate Code § 247), the first generation with living takers is allocated a share in which all living persons at that generational level take an equal share; next, the shares of all deceased persons at that generational level are combined and then divided equally among the takers at the next generational level in the same way, resulting in persons of the same degree of kinship to the decedent always taking equal shares.

2. *Per capita example: X* has three children, *A, B,* and *C. A* has two children, *A1* and *A2; B* has no children; *C* has one child, *C1. A* and *C* are deceased. At *X*'s death, *X*'s estate is divided among three shares at the first generational level with living heirs because there are three children at that level, *A, B,* and *C.* Each are attributed one-third of the estate. *B* will take his one-third share since he is alive. The remaining two-thirds of the estate will be equally distributed among the next level of heirs alive, which includes *A1, A2,* and *C1.* They will each take two-ninths of the estate (each takes equal shares of the remaining two-thirds).

3. **Modern per stirpes, or per capita with representation** (Probate Code § 240) makes an equal distribution at the first level of living heirs. If any of those heirs are deceased and leave issue still living, their share will be distributed equally between their issue. If any deceased heirs don't leave issue, then their share will be added back to the original distribution and divided among the remaining closest heirs.

4. *Modern per stirpes, or per capita with representation, example:* Assume the same family as above. *B* will take one-third as above, but now *A*'s two children will split *A*'s one-third, such that *A1* and *A2* will each take one-sixth, and *C*'s child, *C1*, will take *C*'s entire one-third. Note that if *A, B,* and *C* were all deceased, the first level of distribution would begin at the level of *A1, A2,* and *C1.* So, all three of them would each take one-third.

5. **Strict per stirpes** (Probate Code § 246) makes an equal distribution at the first level in which there are surviving heirs or deceased heirs who left issue; the issue of the deceased heirs share their parents' share equally.

6. *Strict per stirpes example:* Strict per stirpes operates the same as the modern per stirpes example for the first part, but note that if *A, B,* and *C* were all dead, their one-third share would be distributed among their heirs if they left issue. So, since *B* left no issue, *B*'s one-third would be distributed equally between *A* and *C*, such that *A*'s issue would take one-half and *C*'s issue would take one-half, resulting in *A1* and *A2* receiving one-fourth and *C1* receiving one-half.

> **Exam tip:** Whenever distribution is at issue and there are multiple generational levels, draw diagrams for each level and cross out the heirs who are dead or put circles around those who are alive and boxes around those who are dead so you can clearly see which issue go with which parents, and so forth, to determine the proper fractions that each issue will take depending on the type of representation applied. Typically, you need not do the math in your answer; identifying the fraction is satisfactory.

F. **Children**
1. **Parent-child relationship exists** between parents and natural as well as adopted children.
2. **Adoption severs** the relationship of a natural parent and an adopted child unless the spouse of the natural parent adopts the child, and the adopted child and natural parent lived together at any time as parent and child.
3. **Step and foster children:** For the purposes of intestate succession, a relationship exists between a parent and step or foster children **only if** the relationship began during **child's minority,** continued **throughout the lifetime** of parties, and a **legal barrier prevented adoption.**

VII. **CONTRACTS RELATING TO WILLS:** These typically arise when two or more testators are coordinating their testamentary efforts.
A. **Proving the contents of a contract to make a will,** to revoke a will or to not revoke it, or to die intestate may be established by **one** of the following:
1. A provision in the will that states the **material provisions of the contract;**
2. An **express reference in a will,** or other instrument to a contract, and extrinsic evidence that proves the terms of the contract;
3. A **writing signed by the decedent** evidencing the contract; or
4. **Clear and convincing evidence** of an agreement that is enforceable in equity.
B. The existence of **joint or mutual wills** does not create a presumption of a contract to make or revoke a will.
C. The **remedy for breach of contract** relating to wills is a constructive trust (see Remedies outline).

TRUSTS RULE OUTLINE

I. TRUST CREATION AND VALIDITY

    A. **Trust definition:** A trust is a relationship in which a **trustor** gives a **trustee** the right to **hold legal title** to property under a **fiduciary duty to manage**, invest and safeguard the **trust assets** for the **benefit** of the designated **beneficiary.**

    B. **Methods for creating a trust:** A valid trust may be created by one of the following methods:

        1. A **declaration** by a property owner that they hold the property as trustee.

        2. A **transfer of property during the owner's lifetime** to another as trustee.

        3. A **transfer of property by means of a will** taking effect upon the owner's death (testamentary trust).

        4. An exercise of a **power of appointment** to another person as trustee.

        5. An **enforceable promise** to create a trust.

    C. **Requirements for a valid trust:** In addition to the method of creation above, a valid trust requires that the following be established:

        1. **Intent:** The settlor must manifest an **intent to create the trust.**

            a. **Precatory (or wishful) language,** such as "I wish" or "I hope," **is inadequate** to establish intent.

        2. **Property (res):** Trust must have **identifiable property.** The property cannot be an expectancy under a will or illusory.

        3. **Purpose:** The trust must have a **purpose** that is not illegal or against public policy.

        4. **Beneficiary:** There must be an ascertainable **beneficiary,** unless it is a charitable trust, or the selection of the beneficiary is left to the discretion of the trustee.

> **Exam tip:** Sometimes there is an argument on both sides regarding the settlor's intent to create a trust or if the language is too precatory. After arguing both sides, explain why one side has the better argument.

    D. **Trustee need not be named:** The court will appoint a trustee if one is not named in the trust but if it is a trust by deed then it might fail for lack of delivery per deed requirements.

II. LIMITATIONS ON TRUSTS

    A. **Real property:** A trust for real property must be in **writing and signed** by either the trustee or the settlor or their authorized agent.

    B. **Personal Property:** The existence of an **oral** trust of **personal property** may be established by **clear and convincing evidence.**

    C. **Invalidation:** The **execution or revocation** of a trust is ineffective to the extent that it was procured by **duress, menace, fraud, or undue influence.** See Wills Rule Outline section I.B since the rules are the same for wills and trusts.

III. TYPES OF TRUSTS: There are many types of trusts.

    A. **Express:** An express trust is where property is transferred from **one owner to another** and meets the above requirements, such that a **trustee holds legal title** for the **benefit of a beneficiary,** with the settlor having a present manifestation of **intent** to create the trust for a legal purpose.

        1. **Inter vivos trust:** An inter vivos trust occurs when the settlor creates a trust which exists during their lifetime for the benefit of the settlor and/or any other beneficiaries. In most jurisdictions, a **trust is presumed revocable** unless otherwise specified.

            a. **Revocable trust:** Typically, the settlor retains a right to modify or revoke the trust. However, upon settlor's death, an inter vivos trust becomes irrevocable.

b. **Creditors** can reach the trust assets during the settlor's life since the settlor retains the power to transfer and control the trust property.

B. **Testamentary:** A testamentary trust is one **created by a will,** and the will contains the material provisions of the trust, and the **trust arises upon the death** of the testator.
   1. In contrast, an inter vivos trust exists during the life of the settlor, and if revocable, it becomes irrevocable upon the settlor's death.

C. **Pour over:** A pour-over trust is one that is structured to **receive and dispose of assets at the settlor's death**. A pour-over trust is often established through the settlor's will.

D. **Secret:** A secret trust occurs when the settlor leaves a **gift to the beneficiary** on the face of their will without indicating an intent to create a trust in the will but does so **in reliance on a promise that the beneficiary will hold the property in trust for another**.

E. **Semi-secret:** A semi-secret trust occurs when the settlor leaves a gift in their will to a **person in trust** but **does not identify the beneficiary** of the trust.
   1. **Majority rule:** The majority of jurisdictions declare semi-secret trusts **invalid and apply a resulting trust** (see III.L below).
   2. **Minority rule:** A minority of jurisdictions allow **extrinsic evidence** to prove the trust.

F. **Spendthrift:** A spendthrift trust occurs when the **beneficiary cannot voluntarily (or involuntarily) alienate their interest,** such that their interests are **protected from creditors** unless for necessaries, alimony and child support, or government creditors. In other words, the beneficiary is protected from their own fiscal irresponsibility and can't transfer their interest in the trust and most creditors cannot reach the trust to satisfy claims.

G. **Support:** A support trust directs the trustee to make **limited distributions to pay for the beneficiary's support**, health, maintenance, or education, and is **not accessible by creditors** to the extent it would interfere with the support.

H. **Discretionary:** A discretionary trust gives the **trustee discretion** to distribute or withhold payments, principal, or income to the beneficiary.

I. **Charitable:** A charitable trust is one that is for **charitable purposes and benefits society** (indefinite number of beneficiaries).
   1. **Cy pres doctrine:** When a charitable objective becomes impossible or impracticable to fulfill, courts often apply the cy pres doctrine and **substitute another similar charitable object** that is as near as possible to the settlor's intent.
      a. **Under UTA** (Uniform trust code): Settlor's general charitable intent is presumed and application of cy pres doctrine is mandatory.
   2. **Resulting:** If the cy pres doctrine will not fulfill the settlor's intent, the courts will apply a resulting trust (see III.L below).

Issue spotting tip: Trusts established to care for one's animals do not qualify as charitable trusts. Rather, a charitable trust must benefit society, such as a trust to create a library or a public park. Always consider the cy pres doctrine as a possible issue when charitable trusts are at issue.

Charitable trust fact triggers:
- Donor dies before gifting stocks, bonds, etc., to build a library, park, etc.
- Trust for a home for the elderly, children, sick, etc., and the company implementing the trust goes out of business
- Trust for group of people that do most activities with the settlor (raises issue because it does benefit some members of society, but note that it won't qualify as charitable because it doesn't benefit society in a more general way)

J. **Honorary:** An honorary trust is one in which there is neither a private beneficiary nor a charitable purpose. Generally, these trusts are **invalid, except** to care for **pets** or maintain **cemetery plots**. However, once the pet dies, a resulting trust is applied.

K. **Totten:** A Totten trust is one where the settlor places money in a **bank account** with instructions that the named **beneficiary takes any amount left at the death** of the settlor.

L. **Resulting:** A resulting trust is an implied-in-fact trust based upon the **presumed intent** of the parties and will **transfer the property back to the settlor or their estate** when:

1. The **purpose of the trust is satisfied** or ends,
2. An **express trust fails,**
3. A **charitable trust ends** and the cy pres doctrine is inapplicable,
4. The trust is **illegal,**
5. There is **excess corpus** in the trust,
6. A **purchase money resulting trust** results where one party (beneficiary) pays consideration for property but allows title to the property to be taken in the name of another (trustee), or
7. There is a **semi-secret trust.**

Resulting trust fact triggers:

- Trust to care for someone for life but they predecease the settlor
- Trust to give to someone that engages in a certain activity with the settlor, such as fishing, but then settlor becomes unable to do the activity themself
- Trust to help a business, group, or society that ceases to exist
- Trust that fails due to being invalid

M. **Constructive:** A constructive trust (see Remedies chapter) is applied as a **remedy to prevent unjust enrichment** when:

1. There is **self-dealing or breach of fiduciary duties,**
2. There is **fraud** in the inducement or **undue influence,**
3. **Secret trusts** are involved, or
4. **Oral real estate trusts** are created.

IV. TRUST ADMINISTRATION

A. **Powers of the trustee:** Trustees have all **enumerated powers** expressed in the trust itself and pursuant to the law. Trustees have the **implied powers** necessary and appropriate to carry out the terms of the trust, such as to sell or lease trust property, incur reasonable expenses, borrow money, or operate a business.

B. **Duties of the trustee:** A trustee has a duty to:

1. **Account** to and inform the beneficiaries with a statement of income and expenses of the trust on a regular basis, even if not requested.
2. **Not Delegate their trustee duties** to others (traditional rule). **Modernly, delegation is allowed** if the trustee exercises due care and skill when selecting agents.
3. **Be Impartial** when dealing with the **income beneficiaries** and the **remainderman** beneficiaries.
4. **Use Due care** and act as a **reasonable prudent person** dealing with trust affairs, which includes the duty to **Investigate** any investment and a duty to **Diversify** investments.
5. **Segregate** and earmark trust funds and **not commingle** the trust funds with the trustee's own funds, such that all trust funds are clearly labeled as such.
6. **Duty of Loyalty** is owed, and the trustee may **not participate in self-dealing,** must **avoid conflicts of interest**, and must **treat all beneficiaries equitably.**

> **<u>Duty of loyalty fact triggers:</u>**
> - Trustee sells shares/trust property for less than fair market value to benefit themself or their company
> - Trustee deals with corporation that they work for in relation to their trustee duties
> - Trustee gives money unequally to beneficiaries

7. **Prudently <u>I</u>nvest** the trust property to make it productive for the beneficiaries under one of the following methods depending on the jurisdiction:
   a. **Common law utilizes various statutory lists** of good investments, which include federal government bonds, federally insured certificates of deposit, first deeds of trust in real estate, and stock of publicly traded corporations.
   b. **Uniform Prudent Investor Act (UPIA)**, adopted in a majority of jurisdictions, provides that a prudent investor's performance is measured in the **context of the entire trust portfolio** as a whole and as part of an overall investment strategy having risk and return objectives reasonably suited to the trust.

> **<u>Issue spotting tip:</u>** This issue arises when the trustee invests in risky or unknown endeavors, or in a new corporation and ends up losing the trust money.

8. **<u>D</u>efend** actions that may result in a loss to the trust and **<u>E</u>nforce** claims that are part of the trust property.

> **<u>Memorization tip:</u>** Remember the trustee duties with the mnemonic **AND I DID SLIDE** (**<u>A</u>**ccount/**<u>N</u>**ot **<u>D</u>**elegate/**<u>I</u>**mpartial/**<u>D</u>**ue care/**<u>I</u>**nvestigate/**<u>D</u>**iversify/**<u>S</u>**egregate/**<u>L</u>**oyalty/**<u>I</u>**nvest/**<u>D</u>**efend/**<u>E</u>**nforce).

C. **Liabilities of the trustee:** A trustee is **personally liable** for
   1. **Violating their trustee duties**.
   2. **Torts** committed by themself, and their agents if they were committed within the scope of supervision, against third parties.
   3. **Contracts** made within the **scope of their trust supervision**, unless the contract itself provides otherwise.
D. **Duties and liabilities of third parties**
   1. **Transfer of property to a bona fide purchaser** (pay for value, took without notice) cuts off a beneficiary's interest, but if the transfer is not to a bona fide purchaser, then the beneficiary can set aside the transaction.
   2. **A third party who knowingly receives trust property** will hold that property as a **constructive trustee** and will be liable for any losses to the trust. (See Remedies chapter.)
E. **Allocation of trust:** Unless the trust itself states otherwise, trust assets are allocated as follows:
   1. **Beneficiaries** of a trust are entitled to **income** from interest income, cash dividends, and net business income, **but must pay interest** on any **loan debt, taxes, or minor repairs**.
   a. **Creditors:** A beneficiary's creditors can reach their interest in the trust to satisfy claims but may not reach the trust property.

2. **Remaindermen** of a trust are entitled to **principal from the net proceeds** on the sale of an asset, stock dividends, and profits from sale of stock, but must **pay the principal part of the loan debt and for major repairs**.

3. **Subject to the trustee's best judgment:** The trustee can utilize their best judgment in carrying out the terms of the trust to follow the settlor's intent even if this requires them to disregard the above rules and provide for a different allocation.

V. MODIFICATION OR REVOCATION OF THE TRUST

A. **Majority rule:** A settlor can **modify or revoke** the trust **only if** the power is **expressly reserved** in the trust.

B. **Minority rule, including California: Trusts are revocable** unless stated otherwise.

C. **Modification:** The **court can modify the trust**, such as for cy pres purposes or changed circumstances due to unforeseen circumstances and necessity, to meet the settlor's intent.

VI. TERMINATION

A. **Trustee:** A trustee has **no power to terminate** the trust except as provided in the trust.

B. **Beneficiary:** Beneficiaries **may compel termination** of the trust if they are all competent, all consent, and termination does not frustrate the purpose of the trust.

C. **Settlor:** A settlor **can terminate** the trust if they **reserved the power** to do so.

D. **Court:** A court **can terminate** the trust if the purpose becomes frustrated or impossible or illegal, or if there are changed circumstances.

E. **Lapse/anti-lapse rules** also apply to trusts. (See Wills Rules Outline, section V.E.)

VII. REMEDIES

A. **Breach of trust** remedy options include **damages**, a **constructive trust**, tracing and an **equitable lien** on the property (see Remedies chapter), **ratification** of the transaction and **waiver** of the breach, **suit for resulting loss** (surcharge), or **removal** of the trustee.

B. **The trustee cannot offset the losses** where one breach results in a gain and another results in a loss.

C. **Laches:** The trustee can argue laches if the beneficiary waited an **unreasonably long time** to bring a claim that, as a result, **caused prejudice** to the trustee or other beneficiaries.

WILLS AND TRUSTS ISSUES TESTED MATRIX

	Crossover	Will Validity	Will Composition	Will Revocation and/or Revival	Will Gift Classification Ademption Abatement	Will Lapse & Anti-lapse	Will Survivor Rights	Will Intestate Succession	Trust Creation & Validity	Type of Trust		Trustee Duties and/or Liabilities	Trust Termination Modification Revocation
July '22 Q5 Hari & Wanda live 15 years out of state, then 5 in Cal. H dies leaving a will and preprinted form.	Comm Prop	X		X			X						
July '21 Q5 Hank makes will in State X while single, then marries, has child and moves to Cal.	Comm Prop	X					X						
February '19 Q1 Hank and Wendy live in non-CP state, retire in Cal. and have Cal. condo, house, and debts.	Comm Prop	X					X					X	
February '18 Q5 Ted has company START, marries, has will, adopts Bob, signs codicil, marries Nell, has Carol, and dies.			X			X	X	X					
February '17 Q1 Mary leaves to kids A and B in will and then marries B and changes will		X	X	X	X		X	X					

Continued >

		Crossover	Will Validity	Will Composition	Will Revocation and/or Revival	Will Gift Classification Ademption Abatement	Will Lapse & Anti-lapse	Will Survivor Rights	Will Intestate Succession	Trust Creation & Validity	Type of Trust	Trustee Duties and/or Liabilities	Trust Termination Modification Revocation
February '16 Q1	Wendy creates trust for her, Dot, and Sis and then revokes in a will		X							X	Express/ Testamentary	X	X
February '15 Q6	Tess's will leaves trust for Greg and Susie and then to Zoo		X		X					X	Testamentary/ Charitable		
July '14 Q5	Henry and Wynn married; Wynn set up trust with Sis as trustee; buys XYZ stock	Comm. Prop.								X	Express/ Charitable	X	
July '13 Q5	Ted creates will while married to Wilma who dies; Ted remarries Bertha		X	X									
July '12 Q5	Mae executes will leaving out Dot and giving to Sam and church		X	X	X		X	X	X				
February '12 Q1	Sam creates trust for children A, B, C; D claims omitted heir				X		X	X			Express Intervivos Revocable	X	
February '11 Q1	Tess, a widow, left estate to children per stirpes		X		X	X	X	X					
February '10 Q3	Hank & Wendy had two children, Aaron & Beth							X	X		Express	X	

Continued >

	Crossover	Will Validity	Will Composition	Will Revocation and/or Revival	Will Gift Classification Ademption Abatement	Will Lapse & Anti-lapse	Will Survivor Rights	Will Intestate Succession	Trust Creation & Validity	Type of Trust	Trustee Duties and/or Liabilities	Trust Termination Modification Revocation
July '08 Q6 — Hal & Wilma lived in NY; W's will for XYZ; Carl, Sis	Comm. Prop.		X		X							
February '08 Q4 — Wilma, $1 million trust with church as beneficiary		X					X		X	Express/ Charitable	X	X
February '07 Q4 — Tom, from CA, executed a will and was married to W	Comm. Prop.		X	X			X	X				
July '06 Q6 — Tom, a patient at Happy Home, executes a will		X		X			X	X	X	Testamentary/ Charitable/ Result		
February '06 Q2 — Tim & Anna divorce, try to reconcile but fail to do so	Comm. Prop.						X	X				
February '05 Q6 — Sam executed a valid trust naming Tom as trustee									X	Testamentary/ Spendthrift	X	X
July '04 Q3 — Hank, avid skier, daughter Ann, married W later	Comm. Prop.	X	X				X	X	X	Resulting/ Express		
July '03 Q6 — Tom's will left to Al, Beth, Carl, & State University				X	X	X		X				

Continued >

		Crossover	Will Validity	Will Composition	Will Revocation and/or Revival	Will Gift Classification Ademption Abatement	Will Lapse & Anti-lapse	Will Survivor Rights	Will Intestate Succession	Trust Creation & Validity	Type of Trust	Trustee Duties and/or Liabilities	Trust Termination Modification Revocation
July '03 Q2	Polly & Donald bought a house in D's name alone	Remedies	X							X	Constructive/ Purchase $ Result		
February '03 Q2	Olga, a widow, owned Blackacre; 70th birthday	Real Prop.			X								
July '02 Q1	Theresa and Henry, child Craig, second child Molly	Comm. Prop.		X	X				X				
February '02 Q4	Richard creates trust at the urging of wife	Prof. Resp.						X		X	Express	X	
July '01 Q6	Ted, a widower, had a child Deb, and three brothers		X				X	X		X	Testamentary		
July '00 Q3	Hal & Wanda create a trust with Hal's separate property		X	X	X		X	X		X	Express/ Resulting		
February '00 Q4	Tom, a childless bachelor, executed a typed will		X	X	X	X	X						

WILLS AND TRUSTS PRACTICE ESSAYS, ANSWER GRIDS, AND SAMPLE ANSWERS

Wills and Trusts Question 1
February 2018, Question 5

In 2001, Ted, who was married to Wendy, signed a valid will bequeathing all of his property as follows: "$10,000 of my separate property to my daughter Ann; then $2,000 of my separate property to each person who is an employee of my company, START, at the time of my death; and all the rest of my separate property, plus all of my share of our community property to my beloved wife of 20 years, if she survives me." No other gifts were specified in the will.

In 2003, Wendy died.

In 2005, Ted adopted a child, Bob.

In 2006, Ted signed a valid codicil to his 2001 will stating that, "I hereby bequeath $10,000 of my separate property to my beloved son, Bob. All the rest of my 2001 will remains the same."

In 2011, Ted married Nell.

In 2012, Ted and Nell had a child, Carol.

In 2016, Ted died, leaving his 2001 will and his 2006 codicil as his only testamentary instruments. After all debts, taxes, and expenses had been paid, Ted's separate property was worth $90,000, and his share of the community property was worth $100,000. At death, Ted still owned START, which by then had ten employees, none of whom had been an employee of START in 2001.

What rights, if any, do Nell, Ann, Bob, Carol and the START employees have in Ted's estate? Discuss. Answer according to California law.

Wills and Trusts Question 1 Assessment
February 2018, Question 5

This is a straightforward wills question, and it is not particularly difficult. This question covers wills only, though as you will see by the other questions in this chapter, wills and trusts are often both included in a question. Wills and trusts also crosses over easily with community property. In fact, the three most recent wills and trusts questions have been full community property crossover questions, so that is something applicants should be prepared to tackle on the exam. You can see a sample of wills and trusts question crossed over with community property issues in question four of our crossover chapter at the end of this book. In this chapter, we attempted to highlight the questions that are solely focused on the wills and trusts issues. While this question is not considered a crossover question, as with many wills and trusts questions, it still requires you to have a basic understanding of community property rules, since they are necessary to determining the intestate shares of different parties.

This question covers some commonly tested areas, including will validity and modification through a codicil, lapse and anti-lapse, and omitted spouses and children. The one issue that is less commonly tested is the acts of independent significance. That concept can be more difficult for some students to understand, but the will here is a good example of how that rule can be used to analyze the facts here. Ted wanted to provide $2,000 to each person who was employed by his company at the time of his death. At the time he wrote the will, it would be impossible to determine who those beneficiaries would be since they could only be determined in the future. However, the doctrine of acts of independent legal significance works perfectly to help identify the names of those beneficiaries by referencing documents kept by the START company to fill the gaps in the will. The records aren't kept by the START company for any testamentary purpose, since they are used internally to run the business, so they fit the definition of acts of legal significance. This doctrine is sometimes referred to as "facts" of independent legal significance, so it might help you to think of it that way since here it is the "fact" of who is an employee of START at the time of Ted's death that has independent legal significance.

The only challenge a student might have with this question is determining the best way to organize their answer. The call of the question asks about the rights various people have in Ted's estate, which is a common question call for wills and trusts, and you definitely need to answer the question they asked. However, to make that determination, it is important to first analyze the events in chronological order. We opted to analyze the issues in chronological order, but once we were able to make determinations about the potential beneficiaries mentioned in the call, we identified them by including their names in our headers to guide the grader. Another option would have been to analyze all the legal issues in the fact pattern, and then have a small section at the end with a header for each person and a summary of what each of the named potential beneficiaries would take, referring to the earlier analysis in your answer. The question also did not specifically ask about the rights of Wendy, Ted's predeceased spouse, but that issue must be addressed since she is referenced in his first will. You could have had a header for Wendy, or we opted to simply address her in the lapse/anti-lapse section.

Make note of the areas highlighted in **bold** on the corresponding grid. The bold areas highlight the issues, analysis, and conclusions that are likely **required** to receive a passing score on this question.

Issue	Rule	Fact Application	Conclusion
What rights, if any, do Nell, Ann, Bob, Carol, and START employees have in Ted's estate?			
Cal. Community Property Rules	• **All property acquired during marriage is CP.** • **All property acquired before or after marriage or by gift, inheritance, bequest or devise is SP.**	• Ted and Wendy are in California, so California community property rules apply to the analysis.	**Cal. CP rules apply**
2001 Will	• Testator must have capacity and comply with the formalities for a valid will. • **Each spouse may devise all SP and ½ of their CP.**	• **Facts indicate that the 2001 will was valid.** • Ted was married at the time he drafted the will. Here, Ted did not exceed his testamentary power since he did not attempt to leave more than his own SP and his half of the CP. • The 2001 will left from his SP: $10,000 to daughter Ann, $2,000 to each of his START employees at the time of his death, with the residue of his property to his "beloved wife of 20 years, if she survives me."	2001 will is valid
Lapse Anti-lapse	• **Lapse: When a beneficiary dies prior to receiving their interest, the gift to the beneficiary lapses.** • **Anti-lapse: In Cal, the issue of a predeceased beneficiary will take in their place if the beneficiary is testator's kindred.** • <u>Except</u>: **If a contrary intent is expressed in the will itself.**	• **California has an anti-lapse statute which may preserve a gift even if the beneficiary predeceases the testator, but it would not apply here, because Wendy is not the kindred of Ted.** • **Further, Ted's will expressed a contrary intention that his wife must survive him to take under the will so the anti-lapse statute will not apply. Wendy died in 2003, so her share will lapse and fall into the residue.**	**Anti-lapse will not apply**
2006 Codicil	A codicil is an amendment to an existing will made by the testator to change, explain, or republish the will. It must meet the same formalities as a will or holographic will.	• **Here the facts specify that Ted's 2006 codicil is valid.** • **The 2006 codicil republishes the will as of the date of the codicil.** • **The only change in the codicil is that Ted left $10,000 to his recently adopted son Bob. An adopted child is treated the same as a naturally born child.** Bob would have been entitled to be treated as an omitted child had Ted not amended his 2001 will with the codicil.	2006 codicil is valid

Continued >

Issue	Rule	Fact Application	Conclusion
Nell—Omitted Spouse Intestate Share	**Omitted spouse** will receive an **intestate share** if they were married after the will was made, **unless they were:** • **Intentionally omitted** as indicated on the face of will, or • **Otherwise provided for outside the will** with an **intent** to do so in lieu of the will, or • **Waived** their right to their share in a **valid agreement.** Intestate share is all CP, and 1/3 SP if decedent leaves more than one issue.	• Nell may claim that she's entitled to the residue of Ted's estate and Ted's half of the community property based on the residuary clause in the 2001 will. Although the will did not mention Wendy by name, Ted's residuary clause referred to "my beloved wife of 20 years." This reference was clearly to Wendy, not to Nell, because she married Ted only 5 years prior to his death. Nell's claim will fail. • Ted had no spouse in 2006 when he executed the codicil. • **There is no indication here that Nell was intentionally omitted, or provided for outside the will, or waived her right to a share of Ted's estate.** • **An omitted spouse is entitled to take their intestate share of the decedent's property. Thus, the omitted surviving spouse would receive all of the decedent's CP ($100,000) and 1/3 of the decedent's SP ($30,000) since he left three children, which is more than one surviving issue.** • An omitted spouse's share is first taken from the property not passing through the testator's will. Here, Ted died with $90,000 in SP. He made gifts of $10,000 each to two children, Ann and Bob, for a total of $20,000. He also left $2,000 to START employees and there were 10 at the time of his death. This would total $20,000. This would leave $50,000 remaining. Nell would be entitled to $30,000 and this would be satisfied out of the $50,000 in SP not passing through T's will.	Nell receives an intestate share of all the CP and $30,000 of Ted's SP
Ann and Bob	Adopted children are treated the same as natural children for distribution.	• Ann and Bob were provided for in the will and codicil. • Ann will receive the $10,000 SP she was left in the 2001 will. • **After Bob was adopted, Ted executed a codicil, which provided for Bob, so he will receive the $10,000 SP he was left in the codicil.**	Ann and Bob take $10,000 SP each

Continued >

Issue	Rule	Fact Application	Conclusion
Carol — Omitted Child Intestate Share	A child born after a will is executed is entitled to an intestate share unless: • Omission is intentional, • Child is provided for outside the will, or • Testator left all or substantially all of their estate to the other parent of the child.	• Carol was not provided for in the will. The omission was not intentional since she was born after. Nothing in the will indicates that it was Ted's intention to not provide for after-born children, or that Carol was provided for outside of the will. Finally, Ted's will did not leave all or substantially all of his property to the other parent of the child. In fact, Carol's mother Nell was also omitted from the will. • **Thus, Carol is entitled to her intestate share.** As noted earlier, under the laws of intestacy, when a decedent dies with a surviving spouse and surviving children, all of the decedent's CP passes to the surviving spouse and 1/3 of the decedent's SP also goes to the surviving spouse. **The other two thirds of the SP is divided equally between the surviving children. Carol would be entitled to 1/3 of that amount, $20,000.** • T died with $90,000 of SP. Nell would be entitled to 1/3 or $30,000. Carol would be entitled to 1/3 of the remaining $60,000 for a total of $20,000. • Carol's share can be satisfied out of Ted's SP not passing through his will. Thus, there would be no need to abate the other gifts.	Carol takes an intestate share of $20,000 SP
START Employees Acts of Independent Legal Significance	Acts of independent significance permit a court to fill in certain blanks in a testator's will by referring to documents effectuated during the testator's lifetime for primarily non-testamentary motives.	• Although the individual employees who are to receive $2,000 are not named in the will, a court could use acts of independent significance to identify the beneficiaries. START's employment records are maintained for reasons apart from Ted's testamentary purposes, such as payroll, and can be used to identify the beneficiaries. • The START employees employed at the time of Ted's death will each receive $2,000.	The START employees take $2,000 SP each

Wills and Trusts Question 1 Sample Answer
February 2018, Question 5

What rights, if any, do Nell, Ann, Bob, Carol, and START employees have in Ted's estate?

Cal. Community Property Rules

California is a community property state, and all property acquired by the labor of each spouse during marriage is community property (CP). All property acquired before or after marriage or by gift, inheritance, bequest or devise is separate property (SP).

Ted resided in California, so California community property rules apply to the analysis of Ted's estate.

2001 Will

A testator must have capacity to make a will and comply with all formalities to create a valid will. Each spouse is permitted to devise all of their SP and ½ of their CP.

The facts indicate that the 2001 will was valid. Ted was married to Wendy at the time he drafted the 2001 will. Here, Ted did not exceed his testamentary power since he did not attempt to leave more than his own SP and his half of the CP. The 2001 will left $10,000 from his SP to daughter Ann, $2,000 from his SP to each of his START employees at the time of his death, with the residue of his property to his "beloved wife of 20 years, if she survives me."

Lapse/Anti-lapse

When a beneficiary dies prior to receiving their interest under a will, the gift to that beneficiary lapses. However, many jurisdictions, including California, have an anti-lapse statute, which provides the issue of a predeceased beneficiary will take in their place if the beneficiary is testator's kindred, unless a contrary intent is expressed in the will itself.

California's anti-lapse statute may preserve a gift even if the beneficiary predeceases the testator, but it would not apply here, because Wendy is not the kindred of Ted. Further, Ted's will expressed a contrary intention that his beloved wife must survive him to take under his will, so the anti-lapse statute will not apply to preserve Wendy's gift under the will. Since Wendy died in 2003, her share will lapse and fall into the residue of Ted's estate.

2006 Codicil

A codicil is an amendment to an existing will made by the testator to change, explain, or republish the will. It must meet the same formalities as a will or holographic will.

Here, the facts specify that Ted's 2006 codicil is valid, which also serves to republish his will as of the date of the codicil. The only change in the codicil is that Ted left $10,000 to his recently adopted son, Bob. An adopted child is treated the same as a naturally born child, so even if Ted had not amended his 2001 will with the codicil, Bob would have been entitled to be treated as an omitted child for purposes of Ted's estate.

Nell — Omitted Spouse/Intestate Share

An omitted spouse will receive an intestate share if they were married after the will was made, unless they were intentionally omitted as indicated on the face of will, or otherwise provided for outside the will with an intent to do so in lieu of the will, or they waived their right to their share in a valid agreement. The spousal intestate share is all CP, and 1/3 of SP when decedent leaves more than one issue.

First, Nell may claim that as Ted's wife she's entitled to the residue of Ted's estate and Ted's half of the community property based on the residuary clause in the 2001 will that provided for Ted's "wife." Although the will did not mention Wendy by name, Ted's residuary clause referred to "my beloved wife of 20 years." This reference was clearly to Wendy and not to Nell because Nell married Ted only five years prior to his death, so Nell's claim to take under the will as Ted's wife will fail.

Ted had no spouse in 2006 when he executed the codicil and he married Nell five years later, never issuing another will. There is no indication here that Nell was intentionally omitted, or provided for outside the will, or waived her right to a share of Ted's estate. Nell, as an omitted spouse, is entitled to take her intestate share of Ted's property. Here, Nell, as the omitted surviving spouse, would receive all of the Ted's CP ($100,000) and 1/3 of the decedent's SP (1/3 of $90,000 = $30,000) since Ted left three children, which is more than one surviving issue.

An omitted spouse's share is first taken from the property not passing through the testator's will. Here, Ted died with $90,000 in SP. He made gifts of $10,000 each to two children, Ann and Bob, for a total of $20,000. He also left $2,000 to START employees and there were ten at the time of his death. This would total another $20,000. This would leave $50,000 remaining in SP. Nell would be entitled to $30,000 and this would be satisfied out of the $50,000 remaining in SP that had not passed through Ted's will.

As an omitted spouse, Nell will receive an intestate share of all the CP and $30,000 of Ted's SP.

Ann and Bob

Adopted children are treated the same as natural children for distribution.

Ted's children Ann and Bob were provided for in the will and codicil. Ann will receive the $10,000 from SP she was left in Ted's 2001 will. After Bob was adopted in 2005, Ted executed a codicil in 2006, which provided for Bob, so Bob will receive the $10,000 from SP he was left in the 2006 codicil.

Consequently, Ann and Bob are provided for in the will and take $10,000 from SP each.

Carol — Omitted Child/Intestate Share

A child born after a will is executed is entitled to an intestate share unless the omission is intentional, the child is provided for outside the will, or the testator left substantially all of their estate to the other parent of the child.

Here, Carol is an omitted child. She was born after the execution of the codicil in 2006, so the omission of Carol was not intentional. The will itself does not indicate that it was Ted's intention to not provide for any after-born children, or that he provided for Carol outside of the will. Finally, Ted's will did not leave all or substantially all of his property to the other parent of the omitted child, Carol. In fact, Carol's mother Nell was also omitted and received nothing from the will.

Therefore, Carol is entitled to her intestate share. As noted earlier, under the laws of intestacy, when a decedent dies with a surviving spouse and more than one surviving children, all of the decedent's CP passes to the surviving spouse and 1/3 of the decedent's SP also goes to the surviving spouse. The other 2/3 of the SP is divided equally between the surviving children. Since Ted has three children, Carol would be entitled to 1/3 of that amount. Here, Ted died with $90,000 of SP. Nell would be entitled to 1/3 or $30,000. Then, Carol would be entitled to 1/3 of the remaining $60,000, for a total of $20,000 going to Carol. There is sufficient SP to satisfy Carol's share, so there would be no need to abate the other gifts.

Carol takes an intestate share of $20,000 from Ted's SP.

Acts of Independent Legal Significance — START Employees

Acts of independent legal significance is a doctrine that permits a court to fill in certain blanks in a testator's will by referring to documents effectuated during the testator's lifetime for primarily non-testamentary motives.

Here, Ted's will provides for $2,000 to go to each of the START employees employed at the time of his death. Although the individual employees who are to receive $2,000 are not named in the will, a court could use acts of independent significance to fill that gap and identify the beneficiaries. START's employment records are maintained for reasons apart from Ted's testamentary purposes, such as for interior record keeping and paying payroll, but they can also be used here to identify the names of the beneficiaries. Here, at the time of Ted's death, there were ten START employees that could be identified through reference to the independent legal significance of the START records.

The ten START employees employed at the time of Ted's death will each receive $2,000 from Ted's SP.

Wills and Trusts Question 2
February 2016, Question 1

Wendy, a widow, owned a house in the city and a ranch in the country. She created a valid inter vivos trust, naming herself and her daughter, Dot, as co-trustees, and providing that she had the power to revoke or amend the trust at any time in writing, by a document signed by her and delivered to her and Dot as co-trustees. At Wendy's death, Dot was to become the sole trustee, and was directed to hold the assets in trust for the benefit of Wendy's sister, Sis, until Sis's death. At Sis's death, the trust was to terminate and all assets be distributed to Dot. The sole asset in the trust was Wendy's ranch.

Years later, Wendy prepared a valid will in which she stated, "I hereby revoke the trust I previously established, and leave my house and my ranch to my son, Sam, as trustee, to be held in trust for the benefit of my brother, Bob. Five years after my death the trust shall terminate, and all assets then remaining in the trust shall be distributed outright to Sam."

Wendy died. Following her death, both Dot and Sam were surprised to find her will.

Dot has refused to serve as trustee under the inter vivos trust, and claims that, as a result, the trust fails and that the ranch should immediately be given to her.

Sam has agreed to serve as trustee under the testamentary trust, and claims that the ranch is part of the trust. Sam then sells the house, at fair market price, to himself in his individual capacity, and invests all the assets of the trust into his new business, Sam's Solar. Bob objects to sale of the house and to Sam's investment.

1. What interests, if any, do Dot, Sam, and/or Bob have in the house and the ranch? Discuss.

2. What duties, if any, has Sam violated as trustee of the testamentary trust, and what remedies, if any, does Bob have against him? Discuss.

Wills and Trusts Question 2 Assessment
February 2016, Question 1

Question one is exclusively a wills question, and this question is exclusively a trusts question. Question five in this chapter provides a good example of what to expect in a question where wills and trusts are both tested in one question. This question tested some commonly tested trusts issues.

The first call of the question asks about the interests that various people have in a house and ranch. Upon reading the fact pattern, you can quickly determine the house and ranch are the property (res) belonging to the testator, Wendy. Wendy first created a trust for the ranch, and then attempted to revoke it with her subsequent will. Interestingly, there was no need to analyze her will to answer this question, because the will here only served to attempt to revoke her prior inter vivos trust, and then created a new testamentary trust. There was no other information about the will that needed to be analyzed. If you included a section about the will, it was fine to do so, but it was likely not worth any points since it was not necessary to solve the problem. One issue that might have puzzled you for a moment was what to do about the information that Wendy identified the method to properly revoke the trust in her first trust, but then those guidelines weren't followed when she tried to revoke the trust through her will. She would have been fine to do that, except she herself outlined the proper method to revoke her first trust, and then didn't follow her own rule. You might have had a moment of thinking, "...what am I supposed to do with that?" It is an uncommonly tested issue, but this provides a great opportunity for you to think like a lawyer and use what you know to solve a problem. This fact raises a rule that is so basic you might not even think of it, which is that the testator can create their own guidelines in writing that must be followed, and then they need to be followed. It is similar to contracts where the parties can agree to the terms they want for their contract. Since Wendy didn't follow her own rule she created, the revocation is invalid, so the trust for the ranch remains in effect.

While the first call here focused on the trust formation issues, the second call focused on the commonly tested area of trustee duties. Use the AND I DID SLIDE mnemonic to remember the duties for issue spotting. The duty violations were not hard to issue spot on these facts, but the call also asked about the remedies for Bob. Remedies for breach of trustee duties is not commonly asked, so many students were unsure about what remedies they needed to discuss. The only clear remedy everyone should have included was the removal of the trustee. Aside from that, different students discussed damages, or equitable remedies, and that seemed fine with the bar examiners. However, the equitable remedies constructive trust discussion was more on point under these facts because of the tracing issue. Asking the court to set aside the sale is another creative option that works well with these facts. When you aren't sure what to do because the examiners ask a less typical question like this, be sure not to ignore it. Be bold. Think like a problem-solving lawyer. Use the rules you do know, write in an IRAC format, and use your common sense.

Make note of the areas highlighted in **bold** on the corresponding grid. The bold areas highlight the issues, analysis, and conclusions that are likely **required** to receive a passing score on this question.

1. What interests, if any, do Dot, Sam, and/or Bob have in the house and the ranch?

Issue	Rule	Fact Application	Conclusion
Trust	A valid trust requires: • Intent to create a trust • Property (res) • Lawful purpose • Beneficiary • Trustee	• Wendy, the trust settlor, has intent to establish a trust with a document described as a **valid inter vivos trust.** • **The trust res is Wendy's ranch.** • The lawful purpose is to hold property in trust. • **Beneficiary upon Wendy's death is her sister Sis,** and at Sis's death, to Wendy's daughter, Dot. • **Trustee is Wendy and Dot as co-trustees** and at Wendy's death, Dot was to be sole trustee. Settlor can be the trustee.	Valid inter vivos trust
Revocation of Trust	A trust is presumed revocable even if the settlor did not reserve the power to revoke.	• Here, the trust is revocable since **Wendy reserved the right to revoke or amend at any time in writing, by a document signed by her and delivered to her and Dot as co-trustees.** • Wendy subsequently prepared a valid will and stated, "I hereby revoke the trust I previously established." • **By this statement, Wendy satisfied the writing requirement of revocation.** • **However, the will was never delivered to Dot,** since she was surprised to discover it following Wendy's death. • Since the will was not delivered to Dot, the requirements in the trust for revocation were not met.	The inter vivos trust for the ranch was not properly revoked
Trustee	The court can appoint a trustee.	• Dot refused to serve as trustee for the inter vivos trust and claims this makes the trust fail. • **However, a validly created trust does not fail when a trustee or successor trustee refuses to serve. The court will appoint a trustee to carry out the instructions of the settlor,** which is to benefit Sis during her lifetime. • **Here, Sis will be the beneficiary of the trust assets (ranch) for her life, and upon Sis's death the trust terminates, and all assets are distributed to Dot.** Dot has a future vested remainder interest in the trust. [Though future interests are implicated, it was not necessary to identify them by name to pass this question.]	**The ranch trust remains valid, Dot has a remainder interest**

Continued >

Issue	Rule	Fact Application	Conclusion
Testamentary Trust	A valid trust requires: • **Intent to create a trust** • **Property (res)** • **Lawful purpose** • **Beneficiary** • **Trustee**	• **Through her valid will, Wendy created a testamentary trust.** • As settlor, **Wendy's will specified her intent that property was left to Sam as a trustee.** • **The trust res is Wendy's house. However, the ranch is not part of testamentary trust because the inter vivos trust was not properly terminated.** • The lawful purpose is to hold the property in trust. • **The beneficiaries are Bob and Sam.** • **The trustee is Sam.** A person can be both a trustee and a beneficiary. • **Here, upon Wendy's death, Sam is the trustee of the house and Bob is the beneficiary. However, five years after Wendy's death, the trust terminates, and Bob's interest terminates, and all trust assets go to Sam.** Sam holds the future interest of a fee simple subject to an executory interest.	The house trust is valid, Bob is the beneficiary for 5 years, Sam has a vested remainder interest

2. What duties, if any, has Sam violated as trustee of the testamentary trust and what remedies does Bob have against him?

Issue	Rule	Fact Application	Conclusion
Duty of Loyalty	A trustee has a fiduciary duty of loyalty to the trust and may not engage in self-dealing.	• **Here, Sam engaged in self-dealing by selling the trust house to himself in an individual capacity. Even though the sale was at fair market price, it breaches** the duty of loyalty. Courts use "no further inquiry" approach when analyzing self-dealing. • **Sam further breached the duty of loyalty by investing all trust assets in his own new business.**	Sam breached the duty of loyalty
Duty of Impartially	A trustee has a duty of impartiality when considering the income beneficiaries and remaindermen.	• Sam is both trustee and the remainderman beneficiary since he will receive all trust assets after 5 years, while Bob is the income beneficiary for the first 5 years. • As trustee, Sam must act in the best interest of both Bob and himself. • Though it is unclear what income is being distributed to Bob, if any, **Sam likely violated his duty of impartiality when he sold the house and invested all proceeds in his own business.** • Sam knew he was going to receive all the trust property in 5 years, and he was **partial to his own interests** as the remainderman beneficiary and ignored the interests of Bob as the current income beneficiary.	Sam breached his duty of impartiality
Duty to Invest Prudently Diversify	A trustee has a duty to invest prudently, and investigate and diversify investments.	• Prudent investor should diversify trust assets by spreading the asset over a variety of investments to reduce risk. • Sam sold the house, which was the only trust asset and **invested all proceeds in his new business,** Sam's Solar, **rather than diversifying** by investing in several investments. Even if the business were not owned by Sam, it is extremely risky to invest all the assts in a new business since many new businesses fail.	Sam breached his duty to diversify

Continued >

Issue	Rule	Fact Application	Conclusion
Trustee Removal	**A trustee who breaches their duty may be removed.**	• Bob can petition the court to remove Sam as trustee since Sam has breached several fiduciary duties he owed as the trustee. **The court can appoint a new trustee.**	**Sam should be removed as trustee**
Damages	A beneficiary can seek monetary damages from a trustee who breached their duties.	• A trustee is personally liable for breaching trustee duties, so Bob can seek damages from Sam. • Assuming the trust lost money because of Sam's investment in his own business, Bob can recover. Bob can likely get at least the rental value of the house for the five years he was the income beneficiary. Bob may also recover the amount by which Sam was unjustly enriched by his breach.	Bob can receive damages
Equitable Remedies	• A constructive trust can be imposed on one improperly holding trust property • Tracing can be used to trace an asset to its current form • Petition to set aside sale	• Since the home proceeds were used to invest in Sam's Solar, Bob can attempt to trace the home proceeds to Sam's Solar and have a constructive trust imposed on Sam's business. • Another alternative would be for Bob to petition the court to set aside the home sale since Sam sold the house to himself, he is not a bona fide purchaser.	Bob can get a variety of other equitable remedies

Wills and Trusts Question 2 Sample Answer
February 2016, Question 1

1. What interests, if any, do Dot, Sam, and/or Bob have in the house and the ranch?

Inter vivos Trust

Creation of a valid trust requires the settlor's intent to create a trust, designation of trust property (res), a lawful trust purpose, a designated beneficiary, and a trustee. It can be inter vivos or testamentary.

Here, Wendy is the trust settlor, and she showed intent to establish a trust with a document described as a valid inter vivos trust. The sole trust res is Wendy's ranch. The lawful purpose of the trust is to hold property in trust. The beneficiary upon Wendy's death is her sister Sis, and at Sis's death, the trust terminates with all assets going to Wendy's daughter, Dot. Wendy and Dot are co-trustees, but at Wendy's death, Dot was to be the sole trustee. The trust settlor can also be the trustee, so this is allowed.

Wendy intended the trust to exist during her lifetime, so she created a valid inter vivos trust.

Revocation of Trust

In California, a trust is presumed revocable absent a contrary intent specified, even if the settlor did not reserve the power to revoke.

Here, while the trust would be presumed revocable, the trust is clearly revocable since Wendy specifically reserved the right to revoke or amend at any time in writing, by a document signed by her and delivered to her and Dot as co-trustees. Since Wendy specified a method to revoke her trust, her wishes control. Wendy attempted to revoke her trust by a statement in her subsequently executed will. The statement in the will, "I hereby revoke the trust I previously established," serves to satisfy the revocation writing requirement of revocation. However, the writing also needed to be delivered to Wendy and Dot, as co-trustees. While Wendy received delivery since she had a copy of the will which was found after her death, the will was never delivered to Dot, since Dot was surprised to discover it following Wendy's death. Since the will was not delivered to Dot, the requirements delineated in the trust for revocation were not met.

The inter vivos trust for the ranch was not properly revoked. Therefore, the trust remains with Dot as sole trustee, holding the ranch in trust for Sis, until her death, at which point the trust terminates and Dot receives all assets.

Trustee

While a trust typically appoints the trustee, the court can appoint a trustee when needed, such as when an appointed trustee is unwilling to fill the role.

Here, Dot is refusing to serve as trustee for the inter vivos trust and claims this makes the trust fail. However, a validly created trust does not fail when a trustee or successor trustee refuses to serve. The court will simply appoint a trustee to carry out the instructions of the settlor, which here is to benefit Sis during her lifetime.

Sis will be the beneficiary of the trust assets (ranch) for her life, and upon Sis's death the trust will terminate, and all assets will be distributed to Dot. Therefore, Dot has a future vested remainder interest in the trust.

The ranch trust remains valid, and Dot has a remainder interest.

Testamentary Trust

Creation of a valid trust requires the settlor's intent to create a trust, designation of trust property (res), a lawful trust purpose, a designated beneficiary, and a trustee. It can be inter vivos or testamentary.

Through her valid will, Wendy subsequently created a testamentary trust which becomes effective upon her death. As the settlor, Wendy's will specified her intent that property was left to Sam as a trustee. The trust res for the testamentary trust is Wendy's house. Though Wendy's will specified the testamentary trust should include both the house and ranch, the ranch is not part of testamentary trust because the inter vivos trust was not properly terminated as discussed earlier. The lawful purpose is to hold the property in trust.

The beneficiaries for the house are Bob and Sam. While Sam is a beneficiary, he is also the trustee, which is fine because a person can be both a trustee and a beneficiary.

Here, upon Wendy's death, Sam is the trustee of the house and Bob is the beneficiary. However, five years after Wendy's death, the trust terminates, and Bob's interest terminates, and all trust assets go to Sam outright. Therefore, Sam holds the future interest of a fee simple subject to an executory interest.

The house trust is valid with Bob as the beneficiary for 5 years, and Sam holding a vested remainder interest.

2. What duties, if any, has Sam violated as trustee of the testamentary trust and what remedies does Bob have against him?

Duty of Loyalty

A trustee has a fiduciary duty of loyalty to the trust and may not engage in self-dealing. A trustee has a duty to act as a reasonable trustee and in the best interest of the beneficiaries.

Here, Sam engaged in self-dealing by selling the sole trust asset, the house, to himself in his individual capacity. Even though the sale was at fair market price, selling trust property to oneself is self-dealing that is a clear breach of the duty of loyalty. Self-dealing is a serious violation of the duty of loyalty, and courts use the "no further inquiry" approach when analyzing self-dealing.

Sam further breached the duty of loyalty by investing all trust assets from the sale of the house into his own new business, Sam's Solar. Again, a reasonable trustee would not invest all trust assets in a new business, nor would they engage in self-dealing.

Sam breached his duty of loyalty.

Duty of Impartially

A trustee has a duty of impartiality when investing to consider the interests of the income beneficiaries and the remaindermen.

Sam is both a trustee of Wendy's trust and the remainderman beneficiary since he will receive all trust assets after 5 years, while Bob is the income beneficiary for the first 5 years. As the trustee, Sam must act as a reasonable trustee and in the best interest of both Bob and him. Though it is unclear what income is being distributed to Bob, if any, Sam still likely violated his duty of impartiality when he sold house and invested all proceeds into his own business. Sam knew he was going to receive all the trust property in 5 years, and he was partial to his own interests as the remainderman beneficiary by selling the home and using those assets for his business. This action gave no consideration to Bob's interest as the current income beneficiary of the trust.

Sam breached his duty of impartiality by favoring the needs of the remainderman beneficiary.

Duty to Invest Prudently and Diversify

A trustee has a duty to invest prudently, and investigate investment opportunities, and diversity investments. Many jurisdictions provide lists of appropriate investments.

A prudent investor should diversify trust assets by spreading the assets over a variety of productive investments to reduce risk. Here, Sam sold the house, which was the only trust asset, and invested all proceeds in his new business, Sam's Solar, rather than diversifying by investing in several productive investments to spread the risk. Even if the business were not solely owned by Sam, it is extremely risky to invest all the trust assets in a new business since many new businesses fail. It prudent to use the lists of appropriate investments.

Sam breached his duty to diversify and prudently invest.

Trustee Removal

A trustee who breaches their duty may be removed.

Bob can petition the court to remove Sam as trustee since Sam has breached several fiduciary duties he owed as the trustee. The court can appoint a new trustee.

Sam should be removed as trustee.

Damages

A beneficiary can seek monetary damages from a trustee who breached their duties.

A trustee is personally liable for the breach of trustee duties, so Bob can seek damages from Sam. Assuming the trust lost money because of Sam's investment in his own business, Bob can recover damages for the loss. At a minimum, Bob can recover at least the rental value of the house for the five years he was the trust income beneficiary. Bob may also recover the amount by which Sam was unjustly enriched by his breach.

Bob can receive damages.

Equitable Remedies

There are a variety of equitable remedies Bob may seek.

A constructive trust can be imposed on one improperly holding trust property and tracing can be used to trace an asset to its current form. Since the home proceeds were used to invest in Sam's Solar, Bob can attempt to trace the home proceeds to Sam's Solar and have a constructive trust imposed on Sam's business for his benefit.

Another alternative would be for Bob to petition the court to set aside the home sale. Here, Sam sold the trust house to himself, so he is not a bona fide purchaser, and a court may put the sale aside to ensure Bob receives the benefits as intended under Wendy's trust.

Wills and Trusts Question 3
July 2013, Question 5

In 2000, Ted was married to Wilma, with whom he had a child, Cindy. Wilma had a young son, Sam, from a prior marriage. Ted typed a document entitled "Will of Ted," then dated and signed it. Ted's will provided as follows: "I give $10,000 to my stepson. I give $10,000 to my friend, Dot. I leave my share of all my community property to my wife. I leave the residue consisting of my separate property to my daughter, Cindy. I hereby appoint Jane as executor of this will."

Ted showed his signature on the document to Jane and Dot, and said, "This is my signature on my will. Would you both be witnesses?" Jane signed her name. Dot was about to sign when her cell phone rang, alerting her to an emergency, and she left immediately. The next day, Ted saw Dot. He had his will with him and asked Dot to sign. She did.

In 2010, Wilma died, leaving her entire estate to Ted.

In 2011, Ted married Bertha.

In 2012, Ted wrote in his own hand, "I am married to Bertha and all references to 'my wife' in my will are to Bertha." He dated and signed the document.

Recently, Ted died with an estate of $600,000, consisting of his one-half community property share of $300,000 in the $600,000 home he owned with Bertha plus $300,000 in a separate property bank account.

What rights, if any, do Bertha, Sam, Dot, and Cindy have in Ted's estate? Discuss.

Answer according to California law.

Wills and Trusts Question 3 Assessment
July 2013, Question 5

This is an average wills essay in that it requires you to address a variety of issues and requires you to fully understand the rules. As with all exams it is crucial that you not only memorize the black letter law but that you understand what it means. For example, on this essay you need to know the formalities required for a testator to create a valid will. If you just memorized that you need two witnesses to sign and see the testator sign the will, then you might not get full credit for explaining why it is sufficient that Dot signed the next day. The key is to understand and point out that both witnesses were present to acknowledge Ted's signature, which is required, but both do not need to sign the will itself at the same time, so the fact that Dot signed the next day is perfectly fine. But you can see that you need to understand when the witnesses need to be there together and when they need to sign and witness the testator's signature.

Notice also how this question addresses issues in a natural chronological order, which is why it is helpful to have your issues checklist in an order that will most likely mirror the order you will need to address issues on an exam. For example, a codicil is always an issue that arises after you have addressed a will as this is usually a document that the testator creates later or updates their will in handwriting leading to this issue as well as a holographic will being discussed. Thus, the order of your issues checklist should always act as an approach to exams also.

When analyzing the wills provisions to distribute the estate you will find the same result, in that one issue leads to the next. For example, when you first start with the $10,000 to the stepson you see that this issue first requires analysis of the validity of the will itself. Once you determine it is valid, this provision is fine. Then, you look to Dot, which makes you analyze the interested witness issue to determine if she can take. Then, you look to wife and see that you need to address the new document updating T's wife to Bertha. This updated document serves to help both Dot and Bertha because it takes care of Dot's interested witness issue due to its republication date and includes Bertha as the new wife. It also requires you to analyze other issues such as incorporation by reference, integration, and acts of independent legal significance. Then, you move onto the residue for Cindy, which results in all the remaining property going to Cindy. Thus, going through each party provided for in the will also results in the same issue spotting and linear order of issues as your checklist.

To succeed on wills and trusts questions, you must see how one issue relates to another and how the result from one issue can lead to different issues being discussed, depending on the conclusion you reach. Be sure to have a firm understanding of how the principles are interrelated in wills and trusts before trying to write out an essay. When you do try to write out essays, read the facts in a very linear way and start at the top of your issues checklist and look for one issue to lead you to the next.

To see which issues were of greater weight on this essay, make note of the areas highlighted in **bold** on the corresponding grid. The bold areas highlight the issues, analysis, and conclusions that are likely **required** to receive a passing score on this question.

Issue	Rule	Fact Application	Conclusion
Creation of a Valid Will	A valid will requires the testator to have capacity, intent, and meet all will formalities.		
Capacity	Must be 18 years old.Must have mental capacity: • Understand the nature of the act, • Understand situation of their property, and • Understand relations with family members Cannot be suffering from an insane delusion	As Ted was married with a child it appears he was older than 18 years old. T understands he is creating a will by calling it "Will of Ted" and knows his property and what is community and separate as he distinguishes them; and he recognizes family including his stepson and natural child and current wife.	T has capacity
Intent	T must intend to create a will. Courts will often look to T's intent in determining whether a will is valid.	T created "Will of Ted" on his own volition in the event of his death so it is likely he intended to create a will.	T intended to create a will
Will Formalities	Need: • A writing • Signed by T • 2 witnesses to see T sign or acknowledge T's signature at the same time • 2 witnesses sign the will (don't need to sign at the same time) and understand what they are signing	• Will in writing as T typed a document titled "Will of Ted" • T dated and signed the document • T showed his signature to Jane and Dot at the same time and asked them to be his witnesses • Jane signed it then and Dot signed it the next day as an emergency call prevented her from signing then but this is fine as she acknowledged T's signature at the same time as Jane and they don't both need to sign it at the same time so long as they both sign it in T's lifetime and both knew it was his will as he told them	2000 Will of Ted is valid
Interested Witness	A person who takes under a will and is a witness creates a rebuttable presumption of undue influence that can be rebutted by clear and convincing evidence. Undue influence under the common law occurs when T is susceptible to influence, beneficiary has opportunity to influence, there is an unnatural result, and beneficiary helped actively procure result. In Cal., need excessive persuasion that causes T to act or refrain from acting overcoming their free will that results in inequity.	Since Dot is both a witness and a beneficiary under T's will there is a presumption of undue influence. There are no facts to show D unduly influenced T here and as discussed below the will is republished from a codicil. Under the common law, T was not susceptible to influence, and D did not influence him or help procure the result as T created the will without her input; and it isn't uncommon to leave gifts to friends when you have taken care of all family members, which T did. Under Cal. rule, D did not persuade T at all and his freewill was not overcome and the distribution is equitable.	Dot will still take under the will

Continued >

Issue	Rule	Fact Application	Conclusion
Codicil	**A codicil is an amendment to an existing will made by the testator to change, explain, or republish their will. It must meet the same formalities as a will or holographic will.**	**In 2012 when T wrote in his own handwriting that he is married to Bertha and all references to "my wife" in his will are to Bertha, there were no witnesses and thus it cannot be a valid attested will.**	2012 codicil not a valid attested will
Holographic Will/Codicil	A will that does not comply with the formalities required for a valid will can qualify as a valid holographic will if the **signature and material provisions are all in the testator's handwriting.**	**The 2012 document had T's signature.** It isn't clear if the material provisions are in T's handwriting as he only refers to replacing Wilma with Bertha and references his other will but does not have all other distributions in his handwriting. But it could be a valid holographic codicil as it amends the other will and all additions and changes are in T's handwriting. **Since the court will consider extrinsic evidence to follow T's intent it is likely that T intended for Bertha to replace Wilma.**	Holographic will/codicil valid
Republication	**A validly executed codicil operates as a republication of the will as of the date on the codicil.**	**The 2012 holographic codicil/will republishes the original will from 2000 and thus the interested witness issue with Dot will no longer be an issue.**	**Will republished to 2012**
Integration	Papers present at the time of the execution of a will that T intended to be part of their will are integrated into the will.	The new document that T signed for Bertha to be his wife in his will would not be integrated with the original will since it was not in existence at the time of the original will. However, the original will may be able to be integrated into the new document since it was in existence and T did describe it.	Integration possible
Incorporation by Reference	**A document is incorporated by reference when a will refers to a document outside the will if the document is already in existence, the will refers to and shows intent to incorporate, and the document is sufficiently described in the will.**	**Here the will from 2000 was already in existence at the time T created the holographic codicil/will and the new document refers to the old will and there was only one prior will so it is sufficiently described.**	**Original will could be incorporated by reference to new holographic codicil/will**
Acts of Independent Legal Significance	A will may dispose of property by reference to acts and events that have independent legal significance apart from their effect in the will.	Here, marriage is an act of independent significance as people get married for purposes outside of a will and thus T's disposing of his CP to B by reference to calling B his wife may constitute an act of independent legal significance.	Naming B as wife could be an act of independent legal significance

Continued >

Issue	Rule	Fact Application	Conclusion
Distribution	Specific gifts are first distributed followed by general gifts and then the remainder to the residue.		
$10,000 to Stepson	General gifts are those not from a particular source.	**Arguably Sam is the "stepson" since Sam was T's stepson from W's prior marriage when he first drafted his will; this can also be proven by extrinsic evidence.**	**Sam will receive $10,000 from the $300,000 SP funds bank account**
$10,000 to Dot	Also a general gift, as above.	**Since D is no longer an interested witness, she will take her gift too.**	**Dot will receive $10,000 from the $300,000 SP funds bank account**
Share of CP to wife	A person can will away their half of the community property as they desire.	**Since B is T's wife and the codicil is valid, he can give her his half of the CP**	**B will receive $300,000 of T's ½ of the community property in their home**
Residue/SP to Cindy	The residue is the remaining amount after all gifts have been distributed.	**Here Cindy will take the remaining funds in T's separate property bank account after the two general gifts to Sam and Dot are paid.**	**C will take $280,000 remaining in the SP bank account**

Wills and Trusts Question 3 Sample Answer

July 2013, Question 5

Creation of a valid will

A valid will requires the testator to have capacity, intent, and meet all will formalities.

Capacity

A testator must be 18 years old and have mental capacity such that they understand the nature of the testamentary act, understand the nature and situation of their property, and remember and understand the relations with family members who take under their will. Further, the testator cannot be suffering from an insane delusion.

Here, Ted (T) was married with a child and appears to have been older than 18 years old. Further, T understood he was creating a will by calling it "Will of Ted" and he seems to have known his property and even that he owned both community and separate property as he distinguishes them in his devises. Finally, he seems to recognize and remember family including his stepson and natural child and wife. Thus, T had capacity.

Intent

T must intend to create a will. Courts will often look to testator's intent in determining whether a will is valid. T created "Will of Ted" on his own volition in the event of his death, so it is likely he intended to create a will.

Will Formalities

To be valid, an attested will must be in writing, signed by testator, have two witnesses to see testator sign or acknowledge their signature at the same time, and be signed by two witnesses who understand what they are signing, even though the two witnesses need not sign at the same time or in the presence of each other.

Here, the will was in writing as T typed a document titled "Will of Ted." He also dated and signed the document. Further, T showed his signature to Jane and Dot at the same time and asked them to be his witnesses. Thus, they both acknowledged his signature, even though they did not see him sign it and it was at the same time. As to the witnesses signing it, Jane signed it immediately. Dot signed it the next day as an emergency call prevented her from signing then, but this is permissible as both witnesses don't need to sign it at the same time so long as they both sign it in T's lifetime, which they did. Thus, T's 2000 will is valid.

Interested Witness

A person who takes under a will and is a witness creates a rebuttable presumption of undue influence, which can be rebutted by clear and convincing evidence. Undue influence under the common law occurs when a testator is susceptible to influence, the beneficiary has opportunity to influence, the resulting will is unnatural, and the beneficiary helped actively procure the result. And California statutory law finds undue influence when there is excessive persuasion that causes a testator to act or refrain from acting that overcomes their free will and results in inequity.

Since D is both a witness and a beneficiary under T's will, there is a presumption of undue influence. There are no facts to show D unduly influenced T here, since T created his own will without any influence by D. Further, as discussed below, the will is republished from a codicil which eliminates the concern over D being an interested witness.

Under the common law, T was not susceptible to influence, and D did not influence him or help procure the result as T created the will without her input. And it isn't uncommon to leave gifts to friends when you have taken care of all family members, which T did.

Under the California rule, D did not persuade T at all and his freewill was not overcome and the distribution is equitable. Thus, Dot will still take under the will.

Codicil

A codicil is an amendment to an existing will made by the testator to change, explain, or republish their will. It must meet the same formalities as a will or holographic will.

In 2012, when T wrote in his own handwriting that he is married to Bertha and all references to "my wife" in his will are to Bertha, there were no witnesses and thus it cannot be a valid attested will.

Holographic Will/Codicil

A will that does not comply with the formalities required for a valid will can qualify as a valid holographic will if the signature and material provisions are all in the testator's handwriting.

Here, the 2012 document had T's signature. It isn't clear if the material provisions are in T's handwriting as he only refers to replacing Wilma with Bertha and references his other will, but does not have all other distributions in his handwriting and they are outlined in the other typed will. However, the reference to his other will may be sufficient if it incorporates the other will or is a valid holographic codicil. It could be a valid holographic codicil as it amends the other will and all additions and changes are in T's handwriting.

Further, since the court will consider extrinsic evidence to follow T's intent it is likely that T intended for Bertha to replace Wilma. Thus, the holographic will/codicil will be valid.

Republication

A validly executed codicil operates as a republication of the will as of the date on the codicil. The 2012 holographic codicil/will republishes the original will from 2000 and thus the interested witness issue with Dot will no longer be pertinent.

Integration

Papers present at the time of the execution of a will that the testator intended to be part of their will are integrated into the will.

Here, the new document that T signed for Bertha (B) to be his wife in his will would not be integrated into the original will since it was not in existence at the time of the original will. However, the original will may be able to be integrated into the new document since it was in existence and T did describe it and only had one will. Thus, it is possible that the old will is integrated into the new one.

Incorporation by Reference

A document is incorporated by reference when a will refers to a document outside the will if the document is already in existence, the will refers to and shows intent to incorporate, and the document is sufficiently described in the will.

Here the will from 2000 was already in existence at the time T created the holographic codicil/will, the new document refers to the old will, and there was only one prior will, so it is sufficiently described. Thus, the original will could be incorporated by reference to new holographic codicil/will.

Acts of Independent Legal Significance

A will may dispose of property by reference to acts and events that have independent legal significance apart from their effect in the will.

Here, marriage is an act of independent legal significance as people get married for purposes outside of a will and thus T's disposing of his CP to B by reference to calling B his wife may constitute an act of independent legal significance.

Distribution

Specific gifts are first distributed followed by general gifts and then the remainder to the residue.

$10,000 to Stepson

General gifts are those not from a particular source. Arguably Sam is the "stepson" since Sam was T's stepson from W's prior marriage when he first drafted his will. Even if there was an ambiguity as to who T's stepson was, the courts will try to follow T's intent and thus this can also be proven by extrinsic evidence as well. Overall, Sam will receive $10,000 from the $300,000 SP funds bank account.

$10,000 to Dot

As with Sam, Dot's devise is also a general gift. Since Dot is no longer an interested witness, she will take her gift too. Thus, Dot will receive $10,000 from the $300,000 SP funds bank account.

Share of CP to Wife

A person can will away their half of the community property as they desire. Since B is T's wife and the codicil is valid, he can give her his half of the CP. Thus, B will receive $300,000 of T's ½ of the community property in their home.

Residue/SP to Cindy

The residue is the remaining amount after all gifts have been distributed. Here, Cindy will take the remaining funds in T's separate property bank account after the two general gifts to Sam and Dot are paid. C will take the $280,000 remaining in the SP bank account.

Wills and Trusts Question 4

February 2017, Question 1

Mary was a widow with two adult children, Amy and Bob.

In 2010, Mary bought Gamma and Delta stock. She then sat at her computer and typed the following:

> This is my will. I leave the house to Amy and my stock to Bob. The rest, they can split.

Mary printed two copies of the document. She signed and dated both copies in the presence of her best friend, Carol, and her neighbor, Ned.

Carol had been fully advised of the contents and signed both copies. Although Ned had no idea as to the bequests, he declared that he was honored to be a witness and signed his name under Mary's and Carol's signatures on both copies. Mary placed one copy in her safe deposit box.

In 2014, Mary married John. She soon decided to prepare a new will. She deleted the old document from her computer and tore up one copy. She forgot, however, about the other copy in her safe deposit box.

On her corporate stationery with her business logo emblazoned on it, Mary wrote:

> I leave John my Gamma stock. My Delta stock, I leave to Bob. Amy is to get the house.

Mary signed the document. She neither dated the document nor designated a recipient for her remaining property.

In 2015, Mary sold her Delta stock and used the proceeds to buy Tango stock. In 2016, Mary died, survived by John, Amy, and Bob.

Mary's estate consists of Gamma stock, Tango stock, her house, and $200,000 in cash in separate property funds.

What rights, if any, do Amy, Bob, and John have in the assets in Mary's estate? Discuss.

Answer according to California law.

Wills and Trusts Question 4 Assessment
February 2017, Question 1

This is a straight wills question that focuses on the creation and revocation of a will and then creating a new will. The question also tests a few requirements of creation of valid wills in detail, such as knowing that a witness must know it is the testator's will but the facts might confuse you because they specifically include that Ned had no idea as to the bequests, but he did agree to be a witness. This fact is there to test your understanding of the rule that a witness must know they are signing testator's will. It does not require for the witness to understand every bequest or to have even read the contents of the will. Rather, if the witness understands it is testator's will that is sufficient. This fact is there for a reason so don't ignore it. As discussed in the introduction of the book there should be no homeless facts on the bar exam essay questions. Thus, if you see a fact that you have not used, be sure to go back through your issues checklist to ensure you aren't missing any issues to which it could apply. Next go through all rules for issues you spotted to ensure it doesn't go to an element that you may be missing. Finally, if you have all issues and rules correct, see which element it goes to and add that fact into your analysis to bolster your analysis or see an argument or side that you didn't previously see.

Similarly, the question tested the rules for revocation, and you needed to know more than just the basic revocation rules because you needed to know what happened when only one document was revoked and another duplicate copy remained. The duplicate is also revoked if one of the duplicates is destroyed and that was the testator's intent. Remember with wills questions that if you are ever unsure about something always refer back to the testator's intent, because courts always want to follow the testator's intent, and the court can hear extrinsic evidence to prove the testator's intent. On an exam, if in doubt, you can always go back to this general rule/policy.

The examiners also like to test wills in both the attested form as well as the holographic form. Sometimes one will be valid and the other will not. Sometimes they will all be valid. Often the facts chronologically follow the various wills issues, such as here with formation of an attested will, then revocation of that will, then formation of a holographic will. Your issues checklist will mirror the order of issues most of the time. Finally, it is important to answer the call of the question and specifically state what each identified party will receive. It is recommended that you summarize the overall distribution at the end, after going through each party individually.

To determine whether you spotted and analyzed the major issues and properly allocated your time to the various issues, make note of the areas highlighted in **bold** on the corresponding grid. The bold areas highlight the issues, analysis, and conclusions that are likely **required** to receive a passing score on this question.

Issue	Rule	Fact Application	Conclusion
Valid Will (2010 Will)	A valid will requires the testator to have capacity, intent, and meet all will formalities.		
Capacity	Must be 18 years old.\n\n**Must have mental capacity:**\n\n• Understand the nature of the act,\n• Understand situation of their property, and\n• Understand relations with family members\n\nCannot be suffering from an insane delusion	M appears to be over 18 as she is already a widow with two adult children.\n\nShe also understands the nature of her act as she has prepared a will and had two others witness it, implying she understands the law/requirements; she knows which property she owns and wants to leave to her various family members; she knows which family members are hers, such as her children.	M has capacity
Formalities	Need:\n\n• A writing\n• Signed by T\n• 2 witnesses to see T sign or acknowledge their signature at the same time\n• 2 witnesses sign the will (don't need to sign at the same time) and understand what they are signing	• M's 2010 will is written as she typed it on her computer.\n• M signed the will and dated it.\n• M had her best friend Carol and her neighbor Ned there when she signed it so it was in the presence of two witnesses at the same time.\n• Both Carol and Ned signed the will too.\n• Carol had been fully advised of the contents and knew it was M's will but Ned had no idea as to the bequests but he still declared that he was honored to be a witness and thus he still knew he was signing her will and the fact that he didn't know the contents is irrelevant.	M's will is valid
Revocation by Physical Act (2010 Will)	A will or part of a will can be revoked by a physical act. The physical act can include the will being burned, torn, canceled, destroyed, or obliterated with the intent to revoke it.\n\nIt is presumed that the testator destroyed the will with the intent to revoke it if the testator's will was last in the testator's possession and testator was competent until death.\n\nA will executed in duplicate is revoked if one of the duplicates is destroyed, torn, burned, cancelled, or obliterated with the intent to revoke it.	Here, M had two copies of the will and both were exactly the same but one was in the safe deposit box and the other with her. The one with her she destroyed by tearing it up. She also deleted the copy on her computer. She did this after marrying John in 2014 as it was likely her intent to destroy the old will and make her new one as she did to include her new husband.\n\nThe fact that she forgot about the safe deposit box copy doesn't matter since she intended for her original will to be destroyed and revoked and the court can hear extrinsic evidence to prove this intent.	M's first will is revoked

Continued >

Issue	Rule	Fact Application	Conclusion
Revocation by Subsequent Will (2014 Will)	A will or part of a will is revoked by a subsequent will, which either expressly revokes the previous will or part of it, or impliedly revokes the previous will or part of it through inconsistencies.	When M executed a holographic will in 2014 if this will is valid then it will also act to revoke the prior will because it includes her new husband and thus is inconsistent with her old will.	If valid, the new will revoke her prior will
Holographic Will (2014 Will)	**A will that does not comply with the formalities required for a valid will can qualify as a valid holographic will if the signature and material provisions are all in the testator's handwriting. T still needs capacity as well.**	**Here the new will M executed in 2014 was handwritten entirely in her handwriting as it was on her corporate stationery with her business logo on it and she signed it and the material provisions were all in her handwriting devising her assets to her children and husband. T's capacity is the same as above.**	2014 will valid
Distribution	For married couples, one spouse can will away their half of the community property and all of their separate property. Community property consists of property acquired during marriage. Separate property is property acquired before or after marriage or through inheritance.		
Amy's Rights			
Type of Gift	A specific gift is a gift of specifically identifiable property. A general gift comes out of general funds and is not directed to come from a particular source.	The will devises "the house" to Amy, which infers it is not a specific gift as it doesn't say "my" house and it isn't clear if there is more than one and there is no address. **But since it seems as though her estate only consists of her house then it can be inferred that there is only one house.** Also since M left the house to Amy before she married John it can be inferred that the house would have been her separate property enabling her to dispose of it as she sees fit.	Likely a general gift; **house goes to Amy**

Continued >

Issue	Rule	Fact Application	Conclusion
Bob's Rights			
Specific Gift	See rule above for specific gift.		
Ademption	A specific gift adeems by extinction if it is not part of the estate at the time of the testator's death. For stocks, courts have allowed the stock to follow to the new stock as that is often the testator's intent.	Here M left Bob a specific gift as she left him "my Delta stock." But in 2015 she sold her Delta stock and used the proceeds to buy Tango stock. The courts would likely follow M's intent and trace the Delta stock to the Tango stock and give Bob the Tango stock. The Delta stock was purchased in 2010 prior to M's marriage to John and thus it would be separate property and M is free to devise it to Bob.	Bob would get the Tango stock
John's Rights	See above for specific gift.	The Gamma stock is still there and a specific gift since she gave "my Gamma stock" to John.	John gets the Gamma stock
$200,000 in Cash in Separate Property Funds	When property is not distributed under a will, it will be distributed through intestate succession. Under intestate succession, when a spouse leaves one child, the living spouse will get ½ of the remaining property and the child the other ½. When there is more than one child, the other spouse gets 1/3 of the property and the other children split the other 2/3.	Here the remaining $200,000 of M's separate property is not disposed of in the will and thus will pass through intestate succession. Since M has two children, John, her spouse, will take 1/3 of the $200,000 and her two grown kids, Amy and Bob will each get 1/3 as well.	John, Amy, and Bob will each get 1/3 of the $200,000

Wills and Trusts Question 5
February 2015, Question 6

In 2011, Tess, age 85, executed a valid will, leaving all her property in trust for her grandchildren, Greg and Susie. Income from the trust was to be distributed to the grandchild or grandchildren then living each year. At the death of the last grandchild, any remaining assets were to go to Zoo for the care of its elephants.

In 2012, the court appointed Greg as conservator for Tess, because of Tess's failing mental abilities.

In 2013, the court authorized Greg to make a new will for Tess. Greg made a new will for Tess leaving Tess's entire estate to Susie and himself outright. Greg, without consulting Tess, then signed the will, in the presence of two disinterested witnesses, who also signed the will.

In 2014, Tess found a copy of the will drafted by Greg, and became furious. She immediately called her lawyer, described her assets in detail, and instructed him to draft a new will leaving her estate in trust to Susie alone and excluding Greg. Income from the trust was to be distributed to Susie each year. At Susie's death, any remaining assets were to go to Zoo for the care of its elephants. The new will was properly executed and witnessed.

In 2015, Tess died. That same year, Zoo's only remaining elephant died.

Zoo has petitioned the court to modify the trust to provide for the care of its animals generally.

1. Is Zoo's petition likely to be granted? Discuss.

2. What rights, if any, do Greg, Susie, and Zoo have in Tess's estate? Discuss. Answer according to California law.

Wills and Trusts Question 5 Assessment
February 2015, Question 6

Approximately one third of the time wills and trusts will crossover in the same question, one third of the questions are wills only, and one third of the questions are trusts only, though any combination may crossover with community property. This is a typical wills and trusts crossover question. Typically, it occurs as it does here, where one party writes a will which includes a testamentary trust. Tess executed a will, which included a testamentary trust; thus, both wills and trusts issues will need to be discussed. It is useful to note that this question specified to only answer *call 2* according to California law. The examiners are specific about this because the California bar exam tests specific provisions from the California probate code for wills, as well as case law that further interprets the code provisions. However, trusts is tested based on general common law rules for trusts, so your knowledge of trusts doesn't have to be California-specific. The rule outlines provided in this book reflect this.

The first call asks about Zoo's petition, which is to modify the trust. However, you can't answer that question until you analyze the entire sequence of events that transpired, starting with will and trust validity. This pattern is common for wills and trusts questions. This might be the first question we've seen where a conservator was assigned for a testator, so those rules are not commonly tested. However, using some basic rules and common sense can get you through that analysis.

A major issue on this question was the undue influence analysis regarding Greg. The presumption applied directly, and there was not much Greg could do to overcome the presumption here given the facts. Then, the validity of Tess's new will is also a major issue. Since Tess had been awarded a conservator previously, she would have a steep hill to climb to overcome the impression that she did not have the capacity to enact a new will. However, under these facts, Tess can demonstrate her capacity, so the new will is valid.

All of the preceding issues needed to be analyzed before you are able to answer the call of the question regarding the Zoo's petition to modify the trust. This then raises the major issues of charitable trusts and the cy pres doctrine. However, once you have gotten to the end of that analysis, it is simple to answer the second call of the question because all of the supporting analysis is already complete. Make a heading for each person and in that section briefly explain their rights in Tess's estate by referring to the preceding analysis.

Make note of the areas highlighted in **bold** on the corresponding grid. The bold areas highlight the issues, analysis, and conclusions that are likely **required** to receive a passing score on this question.

Issue	Rule	Fact Application	Conclusion
1. Is Zoo's petition likely to be granted?			
2011 Will Validity	**A will is valid if all formalities are met, and the testator has capacity.**	• In **2011 Tess executed a valid will**, so it is assumed all requirements are satisfied.	**2011 will is valid**
Valid Trust	A testamentary trust transfers property by means of a will upon the owner's death. A valid trust requires: • **Intent of testator** • **Trust property** • **Legal purpose** • **Beneficiary** • Trustee	• In her will, Tess left all her property in trust for her grandchildren upon her death, which is a **testamentary trust.** • Tess intended to create a trust. • **The trust res is all of Tess's property.** • **The purpose is to distribute the income to her grandchildren**, Greg and Susie, then living each year they are alive, and then provide elephant care, which is a lawful purpose. • **The beneficiaries are Tess's two grandchildren**, with the **Zoo receiving the remaining assets for elephant care upon the death of Greg and Susie.** • A trustee is not named, but that won't defeat the trust as the court can appoint one. • **Tess created a valid testamentary trust.**	**2011 trust is valid**
2013 New Will Validity	**A will is valid if all formalities are met, and the testator has capacity** • Writing • Witnessed properly	• **Greg was appointed Tess's conservator because of her failing mental abilities.** In his role as conservator, Greg created a new will. The will was in writing, properly witnessed by two disinterested witnesses, and **signed by Greg in his role as conservator.** • Greg will argue the will is valid because the formalities are satisfied.	The 2013 will was properly executed
Conservator/Fiduciary	• **A conservator can make a will on behalf of a conservatee.** • **A conservator owes a fiduciary duty of care and loyalty.**	• A conservator has the authority to make legal decisions, such as drafting a new will. Here, in 2013 the court authorized Greg to make a new will for Tess. • Here, **Greg created a new will for Tess, leaving her entire estate to himself and Susie outright, without consulting Tess,** which is a breach of his fiduciary duty of care. • **Greg failed to consult with Tess** and disregarded what he knew were Tess's wishes to benefit the elephants at the zoo. Instead, he violated his duty of loyalty by **benefitting himself when the new will left himself half of the entire estate, rather than just the income produced.**	**Greg violated his fiduciary duty as a conservator**

Continued >

Issue	Rule	Fact Application	Conclusion
Undue Influence	• Undue influence is presumed in an instrument making a donative transfer to the person who drafted it or a person in a fiduciary relationship with the transferor who transcribed the instrument. • An exception applies when the beneficiary is a blood relative of the transferor.	• Here, Greg did not try to directly influence Tess. Rather he took his position of authority as her conservator and abused it **by substituting his own judgment to draft a new will**, rather than doing what Tess wanted or what was best for Tess. • California law creates a **presumption of undue influence where a fiduciary causes a will to be transcribed to their benefit, which is what Greg did here.** • While Greg may argue he is Tess's blood relative as her grandson, and the exception applies, he will not be successful since Tess was angry he changed her will.	The 2013 will is likely invalid for undue influence
Revocation of 2011 Will	A will may be revoked by a subsequent instrument.	• In the unlikely event the new 2013 will is found valid, it would have the effect of revoking Tess's earlier 2011 will.	If valid, the 2013 will revokes the 2011 will
2014 Will Validity Testamentary Capacity	A testator under conservatorship can still execute a will if they can establish their capacity. Must be 18 years old. Must have mental capacity: • Understand the nature of the act, • Understand situation of their property, and • Understand relations with family members.	• Here, **the court had appointed a conservator for Tess because of her failing mental capacity. However, if Tess has testamentary capacity, she can still execute a will.** At 88, she is over 18 years old. • **Here, upon finding the 2013 will, Tess was furious, which shows she understood what was happening.** • Tess demonstrated her ability to understand the nature of her act since she called her lawyer to write a new will. • **She was able to describe her assets in detail, so she knew her property.** • She also knew her relations with family members since she **purposely excluded Greg from the will because she was angry that he had changed her will to his own benefit, yet she still provided for Susie, her other grandchild.** She also demonstrated her understanding by reinstating the provision that Zoo provides care for the elephants. • Tess can demonstrate her mental capacity and the properly executed 2014 will is valid.	**Tess can demonstrate mental capacity and the 2014 will is likely valid**
Revocation by Subsequent Will	A will may be revoked by a subsequent instrument.	• **Tess's 2014 will implicitly revoked all prior wills** since the dispositions are inconsistent with the earlier wills.	**The 2014 will is valid**

Continued >

Issue	Rule	Fact Application	Conclusion
Charitable Trust Cy Pres	• A charitable trust is one that is for charitable purposes and benefits society. • When the charitable objective cannot be fulfilled, under the cy pres doctrine the court may substitute another similar charitable object that is as near as possible to the settlor's intent.	• Here, **the gift to the Zoo is a charitable trust** because it benefits society as a whole by providing elephant care through the Zoo, where the public goes to enjoy animals. • Unfortunately, the last Zoo elephant died in 2015, the same year Tess died. **Tess's charitable purpose to care for the Zoo elephants is impossible to fulfill because the Zoo has no elephants.** • Assuming they do not obtain any more elephants, **the cy pres doctrine can be used to substitute a similar charitable purpose,** as the Zoo suggests here to **care for the other Zoo animals.** As an alternative, the court could give the gift to a different zoo with elephants. • Since Susie is still alive, the Zoo's petition is premature. However, if they have no elephants when Susie dies, their petition would likely be granted.	**Zoo has a charitable trust and the cy pres doctrine could be used** in the future

2. What rights, if any, do Greg, Susie, and Zoo have in Tess's estate?

Issue	Rule	Fact Application	Conclusion
Greg		• **Tess intentionally omitted Greg from her will and trust because she was angry at him** for abusing his role as conservator and changing her will to his benefit without her knowledge.	**Greg has no rights to Tess's estate.**
Susie		• Assuming the 2014 will is found valid, **Susie will receive the income from Tess's trust for life.**	**Susie receives the trust income for her life.**
Zoo		• **Zoo is the remainder beneficiary of the trust** and has a future interest in the trust property. **They will receive any remaining trust assets** for the care of its elephants, or if there are none, all the animals upon Susie's death.	**Zoo has a future interest in the trust.**

Wills and Trusts Question 6
February 2010, Question 3

Hank and Wendy married, had two children, Aaron and Beth, and subsequently had their marriage dissolved.

One year after dissolution of the marriage, Hank placed all his assets in a valid revocable trust and appointed Trustee. Under the trust, Trustee was to pay all income from the trust to Hank during Hank's life. Upon Hank's death, the trust was to terminate and Trustee was to distribute the remaining assets as follows: one-half to Hank's mother, Mom, if she was then living, and the remainder to Aaron and Beth, in equal shares.

Trustee invested all assets of the trust in commercial real estate, which yielded very high income, but suffered rapidly decreasing market value.

Hank, who had never remarried, died three years after establishing the trust. At the time of his death, the trust was valued at $300,000. Subsequently, it was proved by DNA testing that Hank had another child, Carl, who had been conceived during Hank's marriage to Wendy, but was born following dissolution of the marriage. Wendy, Carl's mother, had never told Hank about Carl.

Wendy, Mom, Aaron, Beth, and Carl all claim that they are entitled to a portion of the trust assets.

1. At Hank's death, what claims, if any, do the trust beneficiaries have against Trustee? Discuss.

2. How should the trust assets be distributed? Discuss.

Answer this question according to California law.

Wills and Trusts Question 6 Assessment
February 2010, Question 3

This is a pure trusts question that gives rise to the heavily tested area of trustee duties. Whenever going through trustee duties, be sure to use the mnemonic "AND I DID SLIDE" to recall all trustee duties. Your checklist may just include the general category of "trustee duties" on it. That is fine so long as you expand on this and write out all the potential trustee duties using the mnemonic once you realize that trustee duties are at issue. Also pay attention to which trustee duties trigger other duties. For example, almost all violations of duties (e.g., loyalty or diversifying assets) also trigger the duty of care because if one engages in conflicts or doesn't diversify and so forth then they are often not exercising due care. Pay attention to various issue clusters that often arise together when analyzing trustee duties.

Make sure that when you are going through the facts and highlighting or underlining the facts you have used, always consider using the same facts again and again for the various trustee duties. As indicated above, the same facts that give rise to one trustee duty will also give rise to other trustee duties. So, be sure to consider all facts with each type of trustee duty to ensure you don't miss any duties and/or omit analysis by failing to use the pertinent facts.

Regarding call 2, you should approach this call as you would other wills and trusts questions by going through the parties in the order in which they are listed in the question. Then, issue spot and identify each issue that is applicable to each of them. In addition, always sum up the distribution at the end, and identify what each party will receive.

This question also shows you how the issues related to omitted heirs, gifts, and abatement apply and operate the same in a trust as they do in a will. If you have a difficult time remembering the issues that apply to both wills and trusts, then you may want to modify your issues checklist accordingly. Otherwise, you risk missing these issues on trusts questions. Take a moment to review which issues apply to both and keep a mental note and/or adjust your issues checklist accordingly.

Finally, be sure to make note of the areas highlighted in **bold** on the corresponding grid. The bold areas highlight the issues, analysis, and conclusions that are likely **required** to receive a passing score on this question.

Issue	Rule	Fact Application	Conclusion
Call #1: Beneficiaries v. Trustee			
Duty of Care	Trustee must act as a reasonable, prudent person dealing with their own affairs; this includes the duty to investigate.	**Here, investing all assets of the trust in commercial real estate is not reasonable because there is the risk of losing all assets when they are all in one investment; rather, a reasonable investor would diversify his investments.**	Trustee breached duty of care
Duty to Invest/ Diversify	Split in authority: • Statutory lists: Good investments include first deeds of trust in real estate, federally insured certificates of deposit, federal govt. bonds, stock of publicly traded corps. • Uniform Prudent Investor Act (UPIA): Adopted by most states, uses prudent investor test (performance measured in context of entire trust portfolio).	**T should not have invested all assets in commercial real estate.** Under the statutory list authorities, real estate is likely acceptable, but not all assets in commercial real estate. As for the UPIA, the fact that the entire trust portfolio was in one investment is likely not prudent, resulting in low performance for some of the beneficiaries; **T should have diversified the assets among a variety of investments.**	Trustee breached duty to invest/diversify
Duty of Loyalty/ Fairness	**Duty to treat all beneficiaries equally without favoring any one beneficiary over the others.**	Here, T favored H as a beneficiary by investing in real estate since the investment yielded high income, which under the trust went to H during his life, but the investments suffered from rapidly decreasing market value. This leaves little value to the other beneficiaries — Mom, Aaron, and Beth — when H dies since they would all take the remaining assets, which wouldn't be worth much due to the decrease in market.	Trustee breached duty of loyalty/fairness to all beneficiaries
Call #2: Trust Assets			
Wendy	A spouse is entitled to their half of the community property at divorce. Omitted spouse is entitled to intestate share of trust or estate if omitted when trust was made before marriage.	Here, it appears that **H and W were already divorced at the time that H set up the valid revocable trust** so the trust assets would be coming from H's SP; also, since divorced, W is not an omitted spouse.	W gets nothing
Mom, Aaron, Beth	A beneficiary will take under the trust, barring any abatement.	**M is entitled to 1/2 of the $300k, and A and B will split the other 1/2,** so M will get $150k, and A and B each get $75k, barring any abatement for C (see below).	**M, A, and B will take subject to C's interest (below)**

Continued >

Issue	Rule	Fact Application	Conclusion
Carl	Omitted child is entitled to intestate share of trust; other beneficiaries abate to allow this; if child born but settlor unaware of child's existence, child still receives intestate share. Intestate share: If no spouse, then the issue take all, in equal shares.	C is H's son, as established by DNA evidence, and he was conceived while married to W but born after dissolution, indicating he may be an accidentally omitted child. Here, H set up the trust 1 year after his divorce to W, indicating that C was born prior to the trust being established; however, H did not know of C since W never told H about C, so there is no way H could have included C in his trust at that time, and since he included his other children, he likely would have included C, too. C's intestate share would be 1/3 of the trust, since he would be splitting it with his siblings, A and B, so C's intestate share would be $100k, which is 1/3 of the trust's worth.	C is treated as an omitted child and is entitled to take his intestate share under the trust, which is $100k
Abatement	Gifts will be reduced to satisfy the share of an omitted child by taking pro rata from other beneficiaries.	Since C will get an intestate share of $100k taking pro rata, 1/2 ($50k) of his intestate share will come from M, since she is entitled to 1/2 of the remaining trust, and the other 1/2 ($50k) will come from A and B equally, who are taking the remaining 1/2 of the trust.	Mom will take $100k Carl will take $100k Aaron will take $50k Beth will take $50k Wendy will take $0

PART 13 *CROSSOVER QUESTIONS*

INTRODUCTION TO CROSSOVER QUESTIONS

A crossover question is an essay question that tests legal issues from more than one substantive area of law. The bar exam is unpredictable, and while there have been administrations of the California bar exam with no crossover questions, there are other administrations that have three or four crossover questions. A typical crossover question will cover two substantive subjects, and sometimes a question will cover three subjects. Any subject is eligible to be included in a crossover question, and any subject can cross over with any other subject. However, some subjects lend themselves to being crossed over better than other subjects. Further, some subjects naturally cross over together, so there is some predictability to the types of crossover questions you may encounter. Usually, the calls on crossover questions are very specific so they do make issue spotting easier.

The issues tested matrices at the end of each subject indicate which questions are crossover questions and with which subjects they cross over. However, the most heavily tested crossover subjects are those that are already crossed over in the chapters within this book such as criminal law and criminal procedure (even though these were two distinct courses in law school) and wills and trusts. Remedies is also frequently crossed over with the underlying substantive law of torts, contracts, or property (with contracts being the clear winner). Finally, the most heavily tested crossover subject is professional responsibility. Another subject that they have crossed over almost exclusively in the most recent years is wills and trusts. They have crossed it over with community property all but once between 2018 and 2024. Other questions are labeled as crossovers by the bar examiners but are really equivalent to only one subject, such as takings questions that the bar examiners label as real property *and* constitutional law but only test one issue of constitutional law but in a real property context, and thus there lies the nexus. Even some recent business associations questions have been labeled as crossovers with remedies but are really just full-blown business association essays. Naturally all of the testable subjects can cross over both on the bar exam and in real life.

Answering crossover questions is a new skill that you will need to practice since most students have never taken a law school exam that covered more than one substantive area of law on the same question. The questions included for practice here are typical of the range of crossover questions you may encounter on an actual bar exam. However, we recommend you look at the issues tested matrices and expose yourself to as many crossover questions as possible.

CROSSOVER QUESTION PRACTICE ESSAYS, ANSWER GRIDS, AND SAMPLE ANSWERS

Crossover Question 1
February 2024, Question 4

Acme Bank (Bank) was robbed in December 2022. On January 15, 2023, Dan was charged with robbing Bank. In April 2023, Officer Pat showed Tessa, the teller who was robbed, photographs of six men, each of whom were the same race, approximate age, and had blond hair and a mustache like Dan. Tessa immediately selected the photograph of Dan, saying he was the robber, and signed her name on it.

Before trial in the Superior Court, Dan moved to suppress the photograph under the Sixth Amendment to the United States Constitution, claiming that it should be suppressed because his attorney was not present when Tessa was shown the photographs. The motion was denied.

At trial, the parties stipulated that the photograph Tessa had selected was neither a business record nor an official record. The prosecutor called Tessa, who in court identified Dan as the robber. On cross-examination, defense counsel asked Tessa whether she had made a statement to the defense investigator in February 2023, that the robber had black hair and no mustache. Tessa admitted to having made the statement, but testified that it was incorrect because the robber did have blond hair and a mustache. On redirect, Tessa again identified the photograph of Dan as the robber. This was the same photograph Tessa had signed previously. The photograph was admitted into evidence.

In the defense case, Dan testified that he was not the robber and that he had been visiting his mother in Alaska for three weeks, including one week before and two weeks after the robbery.

In rebuttal, the prosecutor called Chet, the custodian of records from Credco, a credit union. Chet identified records from a Credco automated teller machine (ATM) located down the street from Bank. Chet testified that the ATM records were created as part of Credco's regular course of business. Chet further testified that the records reflect a withdrawal was made from Dan's account the day before the robbery, using a personal identification number (PIN) assigned to Dan's account.

1. Did the court properly deny Dan's motion to suppress the photograph? Discuss.

2. Assuming all reasonable objections were timely made, did the court properly admit under the California Evidence Code:

   a) Tessa's testimony about her statement to the defense investigator? Discuss.

   b) The photograph with Tessa's signature? Discuss.

   c) The ATM records? Discuss.

Crossover Question 1 Assessment
February 2024, Question 4

This essay is a common crossover of criminal procedure and evidence. It leans heavier on the evidence side and tests California evidence, which isn't as common. But it is good to see how some crossovers are not weighted equally in terms of each subject, such as this essay. It is also good to see how with many crossovers, the calls are more specific and issue spotting is less of a problem.

In the first call, Dan is moving to suppress the photograph. A quick read of the facts shows you he argued his Sixth Amendment Right to Counsel was violated. This is a quick get-in, get-out issue. You know your rule, and of course they are testing a small exception to the rule in that it doesn't apply to photo identifications, even though formal proceedings had already commenced. Given this issue is also heavily tested on the multiple-choice, you should have known this rule and been able to address it quite quickly. It is important to note that both state-released answers quickly mentioned the possibly suggestive identification under the Due Process Clause and 5th Amendment. However, that wasn't necessary because Dan specifically filed a motion under the 6th Amendment, not the 5th Amendment. Read the facts carefully to avoid wasting time on non-issues.

The second call asks about whether three items were properly admitted and tells you to analyze them using California's Evidence Code. You can see that the facts are laid out in chronological order to not only align with the calls but also each item asked about. The first paragraph of the facts informs you about the robbery and that formal proceedings had commenced. The second paragraph speaks to the photograph identification. Both of those paragraphs go to the first call. The third paragraph then speaks about the Tessa's statement at trial on cross examination, which goes to (a) in call two. Then, in the same paragraph, Tessa is shown the photograph she signed and it was admitted into evidence, which goes to (b) in call two. The fourth paragraph then speaks to Dan's alibi and the last paragraph discusses his use of an ATM, which rebuts his alibi testimony. These facts go to (c) in call two. So as you can see, the facts follow the calls fairly easily, making it easy for you to organize this essay if you just follow the yellow brick road.

While there was no issue spotting involved in the first call, the second call did require you to issue spot within each item asked, as is common in evidence questions. So, you should have your evidence issues checklist ready to go and keep the California distinctions in mind as you are asked to follow California law. Another trick to answering evidence questions is that when there are numerous issues, as is often the case, there is a strategy to earning points. For example, when hearsay is tested, there could be numerous exceptions or exemptions that can be raised. For timing purposes, address the most obvious and on point exception/exemption and then address one more. Then, later if you have time, come back and add in others. Similarly, for the first piece of evidence go through relevance and thereafter just give a quick one-liner for each item unless the relevance of the item is truly at issue (such as when there is a conviction that may be too prejudicial). This helps you get through all the issues while still earning a sufficient number of points to pass.

Also, since the same issues are tested numerous times when addressing each item of evidence, you should not repeat the rules but rather use "see above" rather than waste time retyping or cutting and pasting the rules all over again. Spend more time on new issues you haven't already addressed, like a new hearsay exception on later items of evidence.

Note the areas highlighted in **bold** on the corresponding grid. The bold areas highlight the issues, analysis, and conclusions that are likely **required** to receive a passing score on this question. In general, the essay grids are provided to assist you in analyzing the essays, and are much more detailed than what a student should create during the exam to organize their own response to a question.

Continued>

Issue	Rule	Fact Application	Conclusion
1. Dan's Motion to Suppress			
6th Am. Right To Counsel	**A suspect against whom formal proceedings have been commenced has a right to effective counsel at any critical stage.** **Does not apply to photo identifications.**	Here, D's 6th Am. right to counsel attached when he was charged with robbing the bank on Jan. 15, 2023. The photo identification took place in April after formal proceedings commenced. However, this was not an in-person identification but rather a photo identification, so the 6th Am. did not apply as that is not considered a critical stage, so there was no 6th Am. violation.	The court properly denied D's motion
2a. Tessa's testimony about her statement			
Prop 8	Prop. 8 is known as the "Victim's Bill of Rights" and provides all relevant evidence is admissible in criminal trials, subject to several exemptions including rules of evidence relating to the U.S. Constitution, hearsay, character, privileges existing in 1982, exclusions after 1982 ratified by 2/3 vote of legislature, and CEC 352.	Dan is charged with robbing Bank, a crime, in California Superior Court, so prop 8 applies.	Prop. 8 applies
Logical Relevance	**All evidence must be relevant. Evidence is relevant if it tends to be material to a disputed fact.**	• The disputed fact is whether D had black or blond hair and a mustache or not. • **This is material b/c it proves whether D was the one who robbed the bank.** • It is also relevant b/c it calls into question T's credibility which is important since she was the teller and one who identified D.	**Logically relevant**
Legal Relevance	**Otherwise relevant evidence may be excluded if its probative value is substantially outweighed by the danger of unfair prejudice, confusion of issues, misleading the jury, or wasting time.**	• **The probative value is high b/c the evidence tends to prove that D did not commit the crime and impeaches T's testimony.** • **Would not confuse the jury or mislead them as T was the teller who changed her description of D.** • No unfair prejudice b/c T is on the stand and can be questioned and it simply relates to D's identity which is at issue.	**Legally relevant**

Issue	Rule	Fact Application	Conclusion
Hearsay	• An out of court statement offered for the truth of the matter asserted. • Hearsay is inadmissible unless an exception applies. • Hearsay rules apply under Prop 8.	• T's statement to the defense investigator was made **out of the courtroom and before the trial even started.** • P might try to argue it was offered for the truth to show that T made a statement to the investigator in Feb. 2023 that the robber had black hair and no mustache. • **However, it was not offered for the truth but rather D used it on cross-examination to impeach T's credibility with a prior inconsistent statement.**	Not Hearsay
Prior Inconsistent Statement (PIS)	• **PIS is substantively admissible and not merely for impeachment purposes** if the declarant is subject to cross examination. • CEC does not require that the statement be made under oath.	• Here, the statement T made to the investigator in Feb. 2023 was that **D had black hair and no mustache.** • **This prior statement is inconsistent with her current statement on the stand that D had blond hair and a mustache.** She is on the stand, so she is subject to cross examination.	PIS so prior statement admissible
Impeachment	A witness may be impeached by cross examination for a prior inconsistent statement.	As discussed above, T's statement about D having blond hair and a mustache was inconsistent with her prior statement, so she can be impeached.	**Prior statement admissible to impeach**
2b. The photograph with Tessa's signature			
Logical Relevance	See above.	The evidence tends to prove that it was D who robbed the bank, which is in dispute since D claims he didn't rob the bank.	Logically relevant
Legal Relevance	See above.	• **The probative value is high b/c it tends to prove D robbed the bank.** • **The prejudicial value doesn't outweigh the probative value** b/c the jury can choose to believe the photo or what she said to the investigator as they've heard both of her statements and she was given photographs of 6 men all of the same race, approximate age, and had blond hair so it wasn't prejudicial to use this particular photo that she selected fairly.	Legally relevant
Authentication	Proof that the document is what the proponent claims it to be.	T identified the photograph in court that she previously signed so it was authenticated.	Authenticated

Continued>

Issue	Rule	Fact Application	Conclusion
Secondary Evidence Rule	Original document must be used to prove the contents unless an exception applies. Duplicates are admissible if it is an exact copy.	It seems the original photo was produced and copies are fine in Cal. anyway.	SER met
Hearsay	See above.	• **The photo itself is not a statement, but T's signature is and it was made out of court in April 2023.** • **It was presumably offered for the truth that T signed the photo and identified D as the robber with blond hair and a mustache.**	Hearsay
Prior Identification (PID)	**PID of a person** made after perceiving the person is substantively **admissible** if the declarant testifies at trial.	Here, previously identified D in the photo and again in court and she is testifying at trial, so the PID is admissible.	**Photo admissible as a PID**
Prior Consistent Statement (PCS)	A PCS is only admissible substantively if offered to rebut a charge of recent fabrication, or improper motive. It need not be made under oath.	Here, arguably T made a prior consistent statement since what she identified in the photo and her signature was a statement and it is consistent with her statement during the trial that it was D with blond hair and a mustache and that her statement to the investigator was incorrect. **Because T told the investigator that the suspect had black hair and no mustache, D could argue that she had a motive to fabricate at the time** she made the ID to the officer in the photo.	**Photo also admissible as a PCS**
Confrontation Clause	**The 6th Am provides Ds with the right to confront adverse witnesses such as to cross-examine the declarant.**	Here, T testified in court for D to cross-examine so there was no violation.	No 6th Am. violation
2c. The ATM Records			
Logical Relevance	See above.	The evidence tends to prove that D was near the Bank at the time of the robbery which is in dispute b/c D said he was in Alaska visiting his mother at the time.	**Logically relevant**

Continued>

Issue	Rule	Fact Application	Conclusion
Legal Relevance	See above.	• **The probative value is high b/c it tends to prove D was in town the day before and near the bank when it was robbed** when he claimed he was in Alaska for 3 weeks. • **The prejudicial value doesn't outweigh the probative value** b/c the jury can choose to believe D that he was in Alaska or they can choose to believe that the ATM records show he was in town. But it could be prejudicial b/c anyone can borrow someone's debit card and their pin number.	Legally relevant
Authentication	See above.	C had personal knowledge of the ATM records b/c he was the Credco custodian of records and testified they were created during the regular course of business. **And he testified the ATM was properly working** since the records reflected a withdrawal from D's account.	Authenticated
Hearsay/Non-HS Purpose	See above.	• **The ATM record was a statement of withdrawals and made out of court on the day before the robbery by a machine, not a declarant.** • **Arguably it was offered for the truth of the matter that D's card was used on the date it indicated.** • However, it is possible that it was offered to show that D was in town and not for the fact he took money out.	Not Hearsay so admissible
Business Record	Business records are admissible where a sponsoring witness establishes the record was kept in the course of regularly conducted business activity.	• Here, the business record of the ATM records were created in the regular course of business as C testified and C would be the sponsoring witness who testified to these facts.	Business Record so admissible

Crossover Question 1 Sample Answer
February 2024, Question 4

1. Dan's Motion to Suppress

6th Am. Right To Counsel

A suspect against whom formal proceedings have been commenced has a right to effective counsel at any critical stage. This right does not apply to photo identifications.

Here, Dan (D's) 6th Am. right to counsel attached when he was charged with robbing the bank on Jan. 15, 2023. The photo identification took place in April after formal proceedings commenced. However, this was not an in-person identification but rather a photo identification, so the 6th Am. did not apply as that is not considered a critical stage of the proceedings, so there was no 6th Am. violation.

Thus, the court properly denied D's motion.

2a. Tessa's Testimony about her statement

Prop 8

Prop. 8 is known as the "Victim's Bill of Rights" and provides all relevant evidence is admissible in criminal trials, subject to several exemptions including rules of evidence relating to the U.S. Constitution, hearsay, character, privileges existing in 1982, exclusions after 1982 ratified by 2/3 vote of legislature, and CEC 352. Dan is charged with robbing Bank, a crime, in California Superior Court, thus Prop 8 applies.

Logical Relevance

All evidence must be relevant. Evidence is relevant if it tends to be material to a disputed fact.

Here, the disputed fact is whether D had black or blond hair and a mustache or not. This is material because it proves whether D was the one who robbed the bank. It is also material because it calls into question Tessa (T's) credibility which is important since she was the teller and the one who identified D. Thus, the evidence is logically relevant.

Legal Relevance

Otherwise relevant evidence may be excluded if its probative value is substantially outweighed by the danger of unfair prejudice, confusion of issues, misleading the jury, or wasting time.

Here, the probative value is high because the evidence of D's physical description tends to prove that D did not commit the crime and impeaches T's testimony. Further, the evidence would not confuse the jury or mislead them as T was the teller who changed her description of D. And there is no unfair prejudice because T is on the stand and can be questioned and it simply relates to D's identity which is at issue. Thus, it is legally relevant.

Hearsay

Hearsay is an out-of-court statement offered for the truth of the matter asserted. Hearsay is inadmissible unless an exception or exemption applies. Hearsay rules apply under Prop 8.

Here, T's statement to the defense investigator was made out of the courtroom and before the trial even started. P might try to argue it was offered for the truth to show that T made a statement to the investigator in Feb. 2023 that the robber had black hair and no mustache. However, it was not offered for the truth but rather D used it on cross examination to impeach T's credibility with a prior inconsistent statement. Thus, the statement is not hearsay.

Prior Inconsistent Statement (PIS)

PIS is substantively admissible and not merely for impeachment purposes if the declarant is subject to cross examination. The CEC does not require that the statement be made under oath. Here, the statement T made to the investigator in Feb. 2023 was that D had black hair and no mustache. This prior statement is inconsistent with her current statement on the stand that D had blond hair and a mustache. Also, she is on the stand, so she is subject to cross examination. Therefore, the statement is a prior statement, so it is admissible.

Impeachment

A witness may be impeached by cross examination for a prior inconsistent statement. As discussed above, T's statement about D having blond hair and a mustache was inconsistent with her prior statement, so she can be impeached. Thus, the prior statement is also admissible to impeach T. So the court properly admitted it.

2b. The photograph with Tessa's signature

Logical Relevance

See above for rule. The evidence tends to prove that it was D who robbed the bank which is in dispute since D claims he didn't rob the bank. Thus, the evidence is logically relevant.

Legal Relevance

See above for rule. The probative value is high because it tends to prove D robbed the bank. The prejudicial value doesn't outweigh the probative value because the jury can choose to believe T's statement about the photo or what she said to the investigator as they've heard both of her statements. Further, T was given photographs of 6 men all of the same race, approximate age, and had blond hair so it wasn't prejudicial to use this particular photo that she selected fairly from the photo line up. Most likely it is legally relevant.

Authentication

Proof that the document is what the proponent claims it to be. T identified the photograph in court that she previously signed so it was authenticated.

Secondary Evidence Rule (SER)

Under the SER, the original document must be used to prove the contents unless an exception applies. Duplicates are admissible if it is an exact copy. It seems the original photo was produced and copies are fine in Cal. anyway, so the secondary evidence rule is met.

Hearsay

See rule above. The photo itself is not a statement, but T's signature is and it was made out of court in April 2023. It was presumably offered for the truth that T signed the photo and identified D as the robber with blond hair and a mustache. Thus it was hearsay.

Prior Identification (PID)

A PID of a person is made after perceiving the person and is substantively admissible if the declarant testifies at trial. Here, T previously identified D in the photo and again in court and she is testifying at trial, so the PID is admissible. Thus, the photo is admissible as a PID.

Prior Consistent Statement (PCS)

A PCS is only admissible substantively if offered to rebut a charge of recent fabrication or improper motive. It need not be made under oath.

Here, arguably T made a prior consistent statement since she identified D previously in the photo line up and signed the photo of D, which is consistent with her statement at trial that D (and the robber) had blonde hair and a mustache. Because T told D's investigator that the suspect had black hair and no mustache, which is different description of the robber, D could argue that she had a motive to fabricate at the time she made the ID to the officer in the photo line up. Thus, in response to the charge of recent fabrication, the photo is also admissible as a PCS. So the court properly admitted it.

Confrontation Clause

The 6th Am. provides a defendant with the right to confront adverse witnesses, such as to cross-examine the declarant. Here, T testified in court for D to cross-examine so there was no 6th Am. violation.

2c. The ATM Records

Logical Relevance

See above for rule. The evidence tends to prove that D was near the Bank at the time of the robbery which is in dispute because D said he was in Alaska visiting his mother at the time. Thus, it is logically relevant.

Legal Relevance

See above for rule. The probative value is high because it tends to prove D was in town the day before and near the bank when it was robbed when he claimed he was in Alaska for 3 weeks. It could be prejudicial because anyone can borrow someone's debit card and their pin number. However, the prejudicial value doesn't outweigh the probative value because the jury can choose to believe D that he was in Alaska or they can choose to believe that the ATM records show he was in town. Thus, it is legally relevant.

Authentication

See above for rule. C had personal knowledge of the ATM records because he was the Credco custodian of records and testified they were created during the regular course of business. And he testified the ATM was properly working since the records reflected a withdrawal from D's account. Thus, the ATM record was authenticated.

Hearsay/Non-HS Purpose

See rule above. The ATM record was a statement of withdrawals and made out of court on the day before the robbery by a machine, not a declarant. Arguably it was offered for the truth of the matter that D's card was used on the date it indicated. However, it is possible that it was offered to show that D was in town and not for the fact he took money out. Thus, the record is not hearsay and admissible.

Business Record

Business records are admissible where a sponsoring witness establishes the record was kept in the course of regularly conducted business activity. Here, the business record of the ATM records were created in the regular course of business as C testified and C would be the sponsoring witness who testified to these facts. Thus, the ATM record is a business record, so it is admissible and properly admitted by the court.

Crossover Question 2
July 2009, Question 5

Diane owns a large country estate to which she plans to invite economically disadvantaged children for free summer day camp. In order to provide the children with the opportunity to engage in water sports, Diane started construction to dam a stream on the property to create a pond. Neighbors downstream, who rely on the stream to irrigate their crops and to fill their wells, immediately demanded that Diane stop construction. Diane refused. Six months into the construction, when the dam was almost complete, the neighbors filed an application in state court for a permanent injunction ordering Diane to stop construction and to remove the dam. They asserted causes of action for nuisance and for a taking under the United States Constitution.

After a hearing, the state court denied the application on the merits. The neighbors di d not appeal the ruling.

Thereafter, Paul, one of the neighbors and a plaintiff in the state court case, separately retained Lawyer and filed an application for a permanent injunction against Diane in federal court asserting the same causes of action and requesting the same relief as in the state court case. Personal jurisdiction, subject matter jurisdiction, and venue were proper. The federal court granted Diane's motion to dismiss Paul's federal court application on the basis of preclusion.

Infuriated with the ruling, Paul told Lawyer, "If the court can't give me the relief I am looking for, I will take care of Diane in my own way and that dam, too." Unable to dissuade Paul and after telling him she would report his threatening comments to criminal authorities, Lawyer called 911 and, without identifying herself, told a dispatcher that "someone is on his way to hurt Diane."

1. Was the state court's denial of Diane's neighbors' application for a permanent injunction correct? Discuss. Do not address substantive property or riparian rights.

2. Was the federal court's denial of Paul's application for a permanent injunction correct? Discuss. Do not address substantive property or riparian rights.

3. Did Lawyer commit any ethical violation when she called 911? Discuss. Answer according to both California and ABA authorities.

Crossover Question 2 Assessment
July 2009, Question 5

This crossover question covers three substantive areas of law: remedies, civil procedure, and professional responsibility. These three subjects do not logically go together, nor is it common for them to be tested together, but expect the unexpected when it comes to crossover questions. The nice feature of this question is that there are three distinct question calls and each call covers a different substantive area.

There is also not much mystery involved in which issues are being tested. The first call of the question specifically asks about a permanent injunction. The third call of the question specifically asks about any ethical violations Lawyer may have committed.

The second call of the question is worth looking at in more detail. The question asks if the court was correct in denying Paul's application for a permanent injunction. A close look at the second paragraph reveals that Paul's federal court application (for a permanent injunction) was denied on the basis of "preclusion." This should have tipped you off that you were dealing with claim preclusion, also known as res judicata. Thus, the second call of the question calls for analysis of res judicata.

Aside from discerning the issue in the second call, the question is very straightforward. The rules being tested are clear, and there are many facts and factual inferences available to use in the analysis. There is much opportunity to analyze both sides on many of the issues and/or elements on this question. In fact, failure to do so will result in not receiving a passing score. Where there are facts to use on both sides of an issue you are expected to argue both sides, such as here on the injunction (particularly on the balancing and laches defense elements) and whether Lawyer's conduct was reasonable in light of the duty of confidentiality.

Note the areas highlighted in **bold** on the corresponding grid. The bold areas highlight the issues, analysis, and conclusions that are likely **required** to receive a passing score on this question. In general, the essay grids are provided to assist you in analyzing the essays, and are much more detailed than what a student should create during the exam to organize their own response to a question.

Issue	Rule	Fact Application	Conclusion
Call #1			

Permanent injunction (I Pray For Big Desserts)	**Inadequate legal remedy**
	• **Money damages are inadequate**
	  • Multiplicity of suit
	  • Difficult to calculate w/ certainty
	  • Land is unique
	Property right
	• **Protectable interest required**
	  • Traditional rule: real prop. only
	  • **Modernly: any prop. interest**
	Feasibility: not too difficult for court to enforce
	  • Negative: easier to enforce
	  • **Mandatory/ affirmative: harder**
	Balancing of hardships to Plaintiff if denied vs. to defendant if granted & consider willful misconduct and any public interest
	Defense: Laches
	Plaintiff's unreasonable delay prejudices defendant
		Money damages are too inadequate because the damage caused by **crop damage and empty wells** is uncertain, and **money does not solve the problem** since an alternative water source is unclear. The harm is ongoing, which could lead to a multiplicity of suits, and **land is unique and irreparably harmed if without access to water.**
		
		Diane may argue that crop loss and loss of well water could be adequately compensated with money for crop loss and the cost of an alternative water source or the diminished land value, but since water is essential, it is likely the **remedy at law is inadequate.**
		
		Downstream neighbors have a protectable property interest in the water since the stream runs through their properties and they used the water before Diane built the dam. **There is a property interest.**
		
		The "stop building the dam" part of the injunction is a negative injunction and easily enforceable through the court's contempt power.
		
		The "remove the dam" part of the injunction is affirmative and requires more court supervision, but probably is feasible to enforce because it is in the court's jurisdiction, no special skills are required, nor is a prolonged time period necessary to achieve the result.
		
		Neighbors: If the injunction is denied, the neighbors lose access to water for their crops and wells, which is a great harm.
		
		Diane: If the injunction is granted, Diane is restricted in the use of her own property and can't build the dam for the disadvantaged kids and she loses the money expended. **[Note: It was necessary to make some argument for Diane.]**
		
		Public: The public has an interest since there is a community benefit from Diane's free camp for disadvantaged kids, but the crops will also help the public since presumably they are a food source for the general public. The interest of the public favors neither side.
		
		On balance, there is a larger hardship to the plaintiffs who would have to go without water. Further, Diane may be able to provide water sports in another manner, such as a pool, and water sports are not essential like drinking water is. Balancing favors granting the injunction.
		
		The neighbors waited 6 months until the dam was almost complete before filing suit, which may have been unreasonable and Diane was prejudiced since she **wasted time and money** spent building the dam during this time period.
			The court's denial of the injunction was improper
			
			The court's denial of the injunction was improper
			
			[Note: Could conclude either way for the defense of laches here.]

Continued>

Issue	Rule	Fact Application	Conclusion
Permanent injunction (continued)		However, the neighbors did immediately ask Diane to stop, putting her on notice. Also, they likely didn't know the extent of the negative effect until the dam was partially constructed. Further, 6 months is not too long of delay, so laches will not provide a defense.	
Call #2			
Res judicata	**Claim preclusion** **Valid final judgment on the merits** Federal: final when rendered Cal.: final at conclusion of appeals **Same plaintiff/same defendant in the same order** **Same claim in prior and subsequent case**	**Judgment was rendered by state court in the prior action** after a hearing "on the merits" and the court denied the neighbors' application for an injunction against Diane. The claim for a permanent injunction was based on the nuisance claim and taking grounds. The plaintiffs did not appeal and it is a final judgment. **Paul was one of the plaintiffs in the prior state court case and both suits are brought against the same defendant, Diane,** so this element is satisfied. **Paul is asserting the same nuisance and taking claims in the 2nd case** that he asserted in the 1st case, and is requesting the same relief, so the 2nd case involves the same claim as the 1st. The primary rights theory, which is allowed in Cal., allows for a different cause of action for each primary right invaded, but since both cases involve the same rights, the primary rights theory is inapplicable.	**The court was correct to dismiss Paul's application since res judicata precludes Paul's claim**
Call #3			
Duty of confidentiality	**General rule (ABA & Cal.):** Lawyer can't reveal confidential client information without client consent. **ABA exception:** Permissive, but not required. **Permits to extent reasonably believes necessary to prevent reasonably certain death or serious bodily injury.** **Cal. Rule exception:** Permissive but not required. Permits to prevent criminal act likely to lead to death or serious bodily injury **and requires an attempt to dissuade and inform client of planned disclosure.**	Paul has not given Lawyer consent to reveal any information here. **ABA exception:** Paul has threatened to "take care of Diane in my own way and that dam, too," which is vague about the type of harm Paul intends to inflict on Diane, and thus it may not have been reasonable for Lawyer to believe death or serious bodily injury was imminent.** Paul also made the statement at the time when he was upset from losing so it may have been an idle threat. But Paul was "infuriated" with the ruling** and was unable to calm down even after **Lawyer attempted to dissuade Paul.** In addition, Lawyer seemed to believe harm was imminent since she told the dispatcher that Paul was "on his way" to hurt Diane. It was probably reasonable that Lawyer believed Paul could kill or cause serious bodily harm to Diane and thus the disclosure was permissive. [Note: Could conclude either way here.] **Cal. exception: Lawyer did attempt to dissuade Paul and talk him out of confronting Diane and informed Paul she would report his threatening comments to the criminal authorities,** so Lawyer was likely permitted to disclose the confidential information and is not subject to discipline.	Could conclude either way

Crossover Question 2 Sample Answer
July 2009, Question 5

1. State Court's Denial of Diane's Neighbors' Claim for Permanent Injunction

Permanent Injunction

A permanent injunction occurs when a court orders one to perform an act or stop performing an act. The following requirements must be met for the court to order a permanent injunction: (1) The remedy at law must be inadequate, (2) there must be a property interest to protect, (3) the hardships must balance in favor of the party seeking the injunction, (4) the decree must be feasible for the court to enforce, and (5) there must be no viable defenses.

Inadequate Legal Remedy

The remedy at law, which is typically money damages, must be inadequate to obtain the remedy of a permanent injunction. Money damages can be inadequate because of concerns over a multiplicity of suits, or damages may be too speculative and difficult to calculate with certainty. Where real property is involved money damages are often inadequate because land is unique. Diane has dammed a stream and her downstream neighbors will suffer losses to their land and crops because of a resulting lack of water. These losses are difficult to calculate with certainty since crop yields fluctuate. Further, the downstream neighbors' loss of their source of water for their wells can't be adequately compensated with money since water is required to maintain life, and no amount of money will suffice for the lack of water since the availability of a dependable alternative source of water is unclear. Lastly, the harm to the neighbors is ongoing and a multiplicity of suits will follow if this is not resolved by an injunction. Diane may argue that the crop loss can be compensated with money, as can the cost of an alternative source of water or the resulting diminished land value. However, since water is a necessity of life and this damage is ongoing until the dam is removed, money damages are an inadequate remedy.

Property Right

California does not require a plaintiff to have a property right to obtain an injunction. While at one time a property interest was required to obtain an injunction, modernly, they can be obtained for invasions of personal rights as well. The downstream neighbors have a property interest here since the stream that has been damned by Diane runs through their lands and they had used the water prior to Diane's construction of the dam.

Feasibility

Feasibility of enforcement requires that the injunction sought cannot be too difficult for the court to enforce. Ordering Diane to stop construction on the dam is a negative injunction and is easily enforceable by the court through the court's power of contempt. The neighbors have also asked the court to order Diane to remove the dam, which is an affirmative injunction since it requires Diane to take an action and thus necessitates more court supervision. Though this part of the injunction would require some supervision by the court, it is still feasible to enforce since the land is within the court's jurisdiction, no special skills are required, nor is a prolonged time period necessary to achieve the result. Further, it could easily be verified if Diane complied with the order.

Balancing of Hardships

The court will balance the hardships to determine if the hardships weigh in favor of the plaintiff and injunctive relief is appropriate. The court will weigh the hardship to plaintiff if the injunction is denied against the hardship to defendant if the injunction is granted. Any willful misconduct or hardship to the public and/or any public benefit can also be factored into the analysis. If the injunction is denied, it poses a great hardship on the neighbors because they will be deprived of the stream water they use to irrigate their crops and fill their wells, and this could potentially negatively impact the larger community if the public relies on these crops as a food source. If the injunction is granted, Diane will suffer the hardship of being deprived the ability to use her own property as she wishes and the public will be deprived of a free camp with water sports for disadvantaged children. Further, Diane may be able to provide water sports in another manner, such as a pool, and water sports are not essential like drinking water is. The public interest favors neither party. Since water is essential to maintaining life and providing water sports for disadvantaged children is merely a fun recreational pursuit, the hardships balance in favor of the neighbors and the injunction should be granted.

No Defenses

Courts will not order an injunction where there is a valid defense.

Laches

Laches is an equitable defense that applies when the plaintiff has unreasonably delayed, resulting in prejudice to the defendant. The neighbors waited six months before filing suit, which had the prejudicial effect of allowing Diane to expend additional time and money on the dam's construction since by then construction was almost complete. However, the neighbors did promptly ask Diane to stop construction, putting her on notice of a potential problem. Further, since it is unlikely the neighbors could have understood the full negative impact of the dam prior to its full construction, it was not unreasonable to delay and laches will not apply.

Conclusion

The court's denial of the injunction was improper.

2. Federal Court's Denial of Paul's Application for Permanent Injunction

Res Judicata (Claim Preclusion)

Res judicata prevents a subsequent suit on the same cause of action where there has been a valid final judgment on the merits in a suit between the same parties over the same claim.

Valid Final Judgment on the Merits

The neighbors, including Paul, first filed an action in state court asking for a permanent injunction ordering Diane to stop construction and remove the dam. After the hearing, the court denied the application "on the merits" of the case so there was a valid final judgment on the merits. The neighbors chose not to appeal the verdict and the ruling is final and the judgment is valid.

Same Parties

Res judicata only bars a subsequent suit where the subsequent cause of action is brought by the same plaintiff and against the same defendant. Paul and the other neighbors were the plaintiffs in the first suit and Diane was the defendant. In the subsequent suit over the same claim Paul was a plaintiff and Diane was the defendant, therefore the subsequent case involves the same parties and this requirement is satisfied.

Same Claim

The subsequent cause of action must involve the same claim for res judicata to preclude the subsequent suit. However, in California, the "primary rights" doctrine allows separate suits relating to the same transaction so long as they assert different primary rights (i.e., personal injury vs. property damage). In the first suit the plaintiffs asserted a cause of action for nuisance and a taking under the U.S. Constitution. Paul's subsequent suit asserted the exact same causes of action of nuisance and taking and requested the same relief as the first suit, so the primary rights doctrine is inapplicable. Consequently, since the suits involve the same claim, this requirement is satisfied.

Conclusion

The court's denial of Paul's application for a permanent injunction was correct.

3. Lawyer's Ethical Violations

Duty of Confidentiality

The general rule under the ABA prohibits a lawyer from revealing information relating to the representation of a client without the client's informed consent. Similarly, California law requires a lawyer to maintain inviolate client confidences. However, this rule is subject to an exception that applies in this situation. Paul's lawyer disclosed Paul's confidences when she called 911 anonymously warning, "someone is on his way to hurt Diane." Even though Lawyer did not identify herself or Paul, she is in violation of the general rule since she disclosed Paul's confidential communications by relating that "someone is on his way to hurt Diane" to the 911 dispatcher, unless an exception applies.

ABA Duty of Confidentiality Exception

A lawyer is permitted, but is not required, to reveal confidential information relating to the representation of a client to the extent the lawyer reasonably believes necessary to prevent reasonably certain death or substantial bodily harm. The question here is if Lawyer reasonably believed the disclosure of Paul's confidential statements were necessary to prevent Diane's certain death or substantial bodily harm. Lawyer may not have been reasonable in believing confidential disclosure was necessary to prevent death or substantial bodily injury to Diane since Paul's threat to "take care of Diane in my own way and that dam, too" was vague and not specific about the harm he would inflict on Diane. Further, Paul was upset from losing his case at the time and may have just been making idle threats in anger. However, Paul was "infuriated" at the time he made the threat and did not calm down even after Lawyer attempted to dissuade him and talk him out of his threatened retaliation. In addition, Lawyer seemed to believe harm was imminent since she told the dispatcher that Paul was "on his way" to hurt Diane. On balance, it was probably reasonable for Lawyer to fear Paul would cause death or substantial bodily injury to Diane. Thus, the disclosure of confidential information is permissible and Lawyer will not be subject to discipline.

California Duty of Confidentiality Exception

As analyzed above, a lawyer may, but is not required, to reveal confidential information to the extent the lawyer believes reasonably necessary to prevent a criminal act that the lawyer reasonably believes is likely to result in death of, or substantial bodily harm to, an individual. The California exception also requires that before revealing confidential information, the lawyer shall, if reasonable, make a good faith effort to persuade the client not to commit the criminal act, and inform the client of the lawyer's decision to reveal the confidences. Though she was unsuccessful in her efforts, Lawyer did attempt to dissuade Paul from his plan to "take care of" Diane and informed Paul that she would report his threats to the criminal authorities before doing so. Consequently, Lawyer is not subject to discipline for her disclosure.

Crossover Question 3
February 2018, Question 3

Len, an excellent chef, installed a smokehouse in his backyard three years ago to supply smoked meats to his friends. Len's neighbor, Michelle, enjoyed the mild climate and spent most of her time outdoors. She found the smoke and smells from Len's property very annoying and stopped having parties outdoors after receiving complaints from some of her guests. She asked Len multiple times to stop using the smokehouse, but he rebuffed her requests.

Len has frequently invaded Michelle's patio to retrieve his dog when it wandered from home. Michelle put up a "no trespassing" sign and a wire fence between their parcels. After the dog dug a hole under the fence, Len cut some of the wires and entered Michelle's property anyway, telling her that he had been fetching his wandering dog from her patio for at least ten years and wouldn't stop now.

Last week, the Town filed suit to condemn Michelle's land for a public park. It tendered to the court as compensation a sum substantially exceeding the prices of comparable parcels recently sold in the neighborhood. Michelle argues that the amount is insufficient because it is substantially less than a sum she turned down for her parcel a few years ago and it does not include compensation for relocation costs.

1. If Michelle sues Len regarding his continued use of the smokehouse, what claims, if any, may she reasonably raise, what defenses, if any, may he reasonably assert, and what is the likely outcome? Discuss.

2. If Michelle sues Len regarding fetching his dog, what claims, if any, may she reasonably raise, what defenses, if any, may he reasonably assert, and what is the likely outcome? Discuss.

3. Is Michelle likely to prevail in her argument for additional compensation from Town? Discuss.

Crossover Question 3 Assessment
February 2018, Question 3

While the State Bar didn't label this essay as a crossover question, it clearly is. It covers issues involving real property, torts, and constitutional law. Real property and torts crossovers like this are common since a nuisance (which is a tort) often impacts real property such that one's right to use their property as they desire is affected. That is essentially what occurred here. Michelle wasn't able to use her outdoor area to host parties as she liked because of Len's possible nuisance with his backyard smokehouse that emitted smoke and smells. In real life, these torts and real property rights often arise together.

This question also nicely ties in a little trespass issue (also a tort) with Len's dog wandering onto Michelle's property and of course her "no trespassing" sign which relates to her real property. Then, of course they end the story with a nice takings issue (which clearly stems from both real property and constitutional law). Overall, this is a nice essay to see how various subjects intersect.

Since the issues are more obvious in a crossover essay, issue spotting is less of a concern. However, be sure to follow the call and when it asks about defenses too, you need to make sure you address defenses separately for both call one and two. Then, after going through all substantive issues and all applicable defenses, be sure to state the likely outcome to show the graders you are following the directions and answering the calls as asked.

As to the first call, clearly nuisance was the issue being tested, which should have been obvious as anytime there are smells or noise or light that is affecting another's use of land, you should think of nuisance. The key was seeing that M might have a valid private nuisance claim but not a public nuisance as there are no facts as to the public being affected. Also, be sure to address defenses, even if you find that none would be valid — the key is using facts to trigger defenses that could be raised, even if not met. It didn't really matter which defenses you addressed but you needed at least some possible defenses. Some options could be laches, coming to the nuisance, or statute of limitations. State answers varied on which defenses they included.

The second call was simple intentional torts, and they were obvious as well. You needed to see the TTL, but one state-released answer didn't see the TTC/Conversion argument, which tells you it was a minor issue that wouldn't sink your ship. Again, you needed to discuss defenses. This is where it gets a little tricky. While an easement is not a traditional defense, it is an argument that L would likely use to defend his position. So, when thinking of defenses always think beyond traditional defenses. Here the fact that he has been going on her land for 10 years should have triggered your easement by prescription issue. Other defenses could vary such as necessity and consent, but everyone should have discussed the easement (and probably necessity).

The last call was a rather simple takings question. It was an outright takings with permanent deprivation, so you didn't need to go through the more nuanced rules of temporary or regulatory takings. Those types of questions would have the takings be the entire essay due to the depth of analysis needed on those specific rules. Here, it was very obvious that a public park was a public use and the key was understanding your rules so you know when the fair market value is determined. There wasn't much to analyze here; it just tested whether you knew your rules. Overall, this was a very doable essay so long as you knew your rules.

Note the areas highlighted in **bold** on the corresponding grid. The bold areas highlight the issues, analysis, and conclusions that are likely **required** to receive a passing score on this question. In general, the essay grids are provided to assist you in analyzing the essays, and are much more detailed than what a student should create during the exam to organize her own response to a question.

Issue	Rule	Fact Application	Conclusion
1. Michelle v. Len for use of smokehouse			
Private Nuisance	**Substantial and unreasonable interference with another private individual's use or enjoyment of their land.** • **Substantial is annoying to the average person.** • **Unreasonable interference occurs when the harm to P outweighs the utility of D's conduct** or the harm caused to P is greater than P should be required to bear without consideration. • Courts consider the nature, extent, and frequency of the harm, the neighborhood, land value, and alternatives for D.	• It is possible that the smoke and smell might be annoying to the average person such as M depending on how much smoke and smell are emitted; however, some people find the smell of good BBQ pleasant and no other neighbors seem to be complaining. • M will assert the smokehouse is unreasonable b/c it prevents her from enjoying the outdoors which she has done for years and prevents her from having her parties, during which even guests complained about the smell and smoke. • L will argue that he is an excellent chef and his friends enjoy his barbequing skills and that he is just BBQing for his friends and not as a business. • The interference w/ M's land would be b/c she has to endure the smoke and smell and can't use her outdoor space as she wants to host her parties. • M's use and enjoyment is affected b/c she can't host her outdoor parties.	M might have a viable private nuisance claim
Public Nuisance	**Substantial and unreasonable interference with the community's health**, morals, welfare, safety, or property rights. **Recovery by a private party is only available if the private party suffered damaged that is different in kind and not merely in degree from that suffered by the public.**	While M might claim that only she suffers from smoke and smell as she is L's neighbor, it is unlikely that other neighbors or the community at large can't also see the smoke and smell the smell. M's damage would not be different in kind to the public at large.	M cannot succeed in a public nuisance claim
Defense — Statute of Limitations	**Most torts claims have a statute of limitations that bar legal action if not brought within a certain time.**	Here, M waited 3 years to bring the claim so it might be barred under the SOL.	SOL could bar M's claim
Defense — Laches	P's claims are barred if they unreasonably delay in bringing suit and it caused prejudice to D.	Here, M waited 3 years to bring the suit which could be an unreasonable delay, but she did ask him to stop and he rebuffed her requests and it isn't clear that her delay caused any prejudice to L since he simply BBQs for friends.	No laches defense

Continued>

Issue	Rule	Fact Application	Conclusion
Defense — Coming to the nuisance	Coming to the nuisance is when one moves to a place when the alleged nuisance already existed, and it is typically not a valid defense.	L has been BBQing for the last 3 years, and it is not clear when M moved there, but it seems she lived there before he started to BBQ since she used to host outdoor parties without having the smoke and smell interfere.	Coming to the nuisance won't be a valid defense
2. Michelle v. Len for fetching dog			
Trespass to Land	**Intentional, physical invasion of the land of another.** **Harm to the land is not required.**	Here, L entered M's property past a fence with a no trespassing sign which was a physical invasion. And it was intentional b/c L wanted to get his dog back and even had to cut wire M put up to access the yard. While no harm is required, L did damage M's land by cutting her wire fence between their properties.	**M has a valid claim for TTL**
Defense — Necessity	A person may interfere with the real and personal property of another when it is reasonably and apparently necessary to prevent greater harm to third persons or the defendant themselves. **D must pay for any damages caused from the private necessity.**	L trespassed to retrieve his dog who dug a hole to get to M's land and since there was a wire fence, **L needed to cut the fence to get to his dog**, which was reasonably and apparently necessary so the dog wouldn't be harmed without supervision or possibly harm someone else. **L must pay for the damages he caused including the cost to repair the hole and the wire in the fence.**	**L might have a valid defense for necessity**
Consent	P consents to D's conduct. Can be express or implied.	Since L has been fetching his dog for 10 years, it is possible that M has consented over the years, but since she put up a no trespassing sign and built a wire fence, it seems she did not consent and if she did previously she revoked it.	No consent
Defense — L had an easement	**An easement is the right to use the land of another.** • They can be negative or affirmative. • Affirmative easements entitle the holder of the easement to do something on another's land. • **An easement can be created by prescription** (actual use, open and notorious and visible use, hostile use, and continuous use for the statutory period).	L will argue that M has allowed him to use his land to retrieve his dog since he has frequently invaded her patio to retrieve his dog for the last 10 years, and thus he has an easement by prescription which is similar to adverse possession. • L actually used the land b/c he went onto the property and cut her wires to retrieve his dog. • **The use was open and notorious and visible since L** frequently went on the land and even cut wires so it was obvious he went; **and since M enjoyed spending time outdoors she likely knew L was continually retrieving his dog over a 10 year period;** in fact she likely put up the wire fence to stop the dog from coming over, which would infer she knew L was coming over to get the dog back if it was on her patio.	**L might have had an easement**

Continued>

Issue	Rule	Fact Application	Conclusion
Defense — L had an easement (continued)		• **It was without M's permission since she** had a no trespassing sign up and put up wire fencing. • **It is unclear what the statutory period is but if 10 years then L meets that.**	
Trespass to Chattels (TTC) / Conversion	TTC is the intentional interference with a person's use or possession of a chattel; if the interference is so substantial that it warrants paying full value it is a conversion.	Here, L interfered with M's fence when he cut the wires and also with her land when his dog dug a hole. If the fence can be repaired he needs to pay for the repairs but if it is destroyed he needs to pay for a new fence.	L liable for TTC and possibly conversion
Necessity & Consent	See above.	See above. Same arguments apply.	Likely a necessity, but no consent
3. Michelle v. Town for additional compensation			
Takings	The Takings Clause of the 5th Am. provides that private property may not be taken for public use without just compensation. • Public use is construed liberally and satisfied if the state's use of the property is rationally related to a conceivable public purpose. • Just compensation is measured by the market value of the property at the time of the taking.	**Town is taking M's land since it filed a suit to condemn her land for a public park.** • A public park would be public use and use of the property is rationally related to a public park purpose that can be used by everyone to do various activities. • Since the sum it offered her exceeds the prices of comparable parcels recently sold in the neighborhood, it is likely above market value. The fact that she had offers that were higher a few years ago is irrelevant since the market price is measured at the time of the taking, not a few years ago. Also, they do not need to include relocation costs.	**M will not prevail in her argument for additional compensation**

Crossover Question 3 Sample Answer
February 2018, Question 3

1. Michelle v. Len for use of smokehouse

Private Nuisance

A private nuisance occurs when there is a substantial and unreasonable interference with another private individual's use or enjoyment of their land.

Substantial interference

A substantial interference is one that is annoying to the average person.

Here, it is possible that the smoke and smell might be annoying to the average person such as M depending on how much smoke and smell are emitted. However, some people find the smell of good BBQ pleasant, and no other neighbors seem to be complaining.

Unreasonable interference

An unreasonable interference occurs when the harm to plaintiff outweighs the utility of defendant's conduct, or the harm caused to plaintiff is greater than plaintiff should be required to bear without consideration. Courts consider the nature, extent, and frequency of the harm, the neighborhood, land value, and alternatives for D.

M will assert the smokehouse is unreasonable because it prevents her from enjoying the outdoors which she has done for years and prevents her from having her parties, during which even guests complained about the smell and smoke making it seem it was unreasonable. L will argue that he is an excellent chef, and his friends enjoy his barbequing skills and that he is just barbequing for his friends and not as a business or anything.

With another's private use or enjoyment of their land

M's use and enjoyment of her land is affected because she has to endure the smoke and smell and can't use her outdoor space as she wants to do to host her outdoor parties.

Overall, M might have a viable private nuisance claim.

Public Nuisance

A public nuisance is a substantial and unreasonable interference with the community's health, morals, welfare, safety, or property rights. Recovery by a private party is only available if the private party suffered damage that is different in kind and not merely in degree from that suffered by the public.

While M might claim that only she suffers from smoke and smell as she is L's neighbor, it is unlikely that other neighbors or the community at large can't also see the smoke and smell the smell. Since M's damages are not different in kind to those suffered by the public, M cannot succeed in a public nuisance claim.

Defense — Statute of Limitations (SOL)

Most torts claims have a statute of limitations that bar legal action if not brought within a certain time. Here, M waited 3 years to bring the claim so it might be barred under the SOL. Thus, a SOL less than 3 years could bar M's claim.

Defense — Laches

Laches bars a plaintiff's claim if they unreasonably delay in bringing suit and it caused prejudice to defendant. Here, M waited 3 years to bring the suit, which could be an unreasonable delay, but she did ask L to stop and he rebuffed her requests and it isn't clear that her delay caused any prejudice to L since he simply barbeques for friends. Thus, laches will not likely be a valid defense.

Defense — Coming to the nuisance

Coming to the nuisance is when one moves to a place when the alleged nuisance already existed, and it is typically not a valid defense. Here, L has been barbequing for the last 3 years and it is not clear when M moved there but it seems she lived there before he started to barbeque since she used to host outdoor parties without having the smoke and smell interfere. Thus, coming to the nuisance won't be a valid defense.

2. Michelle v. Len for fetching dog

Trespass to Land (TTL)

Trespass to land occurs when there is an intentional, physical invasion of the land of another. Harm to the land is not required. Here, L entered M's property past a fence with a "no trespassing" sign which was a physical invasion. And it was intentional because he wanted to get his dog back and even had to cut wire that she put up to access the yard. While no harm is required, L did damage her land by cutting her wire fence between their properties. Thus, M has a valid claim for TTL.

Defense — Necessity

A person may interfere with the real and personal property of another when it is reasonably and apparently necessary to prevent greater harm to third persons or the defendant themselves. Defendant must pay for any damages caused from the private necessity.

L trespassed to retrieve his dog who dug a hole to get to M's land and since there was a wire fence, L needed to cut the fence to get to his dog, which was reasonably and apparently necessary so the dog wouldn't be harmed without supervision or possibly harm someone else. L must pay for the damages he caused including the cost to repair the hole and the wire in the fence. Overall, L might have a valid defense for necessity.

Consent

Plaintiff has a valid defense if defendant consented to defendant's conduct. Consent can be express or implied. Since L has been fetching his dog for 10 years, it is possible that M has consented over the years, but since she put up a "no trespassing" sign and built a wire fence, it seems she did not consent and if she did previously consent, her recent actions with the sign and fence likely revoked any prior consent. Thus, there is no consent.

Defense — L had an easement

An easement is the right to use the land of another. They can be negative or affirmative. Affirmative easements entitle the holder of the easement to do something on another's land. An easement can be created by prescription if there is actual use; open, notorious and visible use; hostile use; and continuous use for the statutory period.

Here, L will argue that M has allowed him to use his land to retrieve his dog since he has frequently invaded her patio to retrieve his dog for the last 10 years, and thus he has an easement by prescription which is similar to adverse possession.

L actually used the land because he went onto the property and cut her fence wires to retrieve his dog. The use was open and notorious and visible since L frequently went on the land and even cut wires, so it was obvious he went on the land. And since M enjoyed spending time outdoors, she likely knew L was continually retrieving his dog over a 10-year period. In fact, she likely put up the wire fence to stop the dog from coming over, which would infer she knew L was coming over to get the dog back if it was on her patio.

Further, the use was without M's permission since she had a no trespassing sign up and put up wire fencing. It is unclear what the statutory period is but if 10 years then L meets that.

It is possible that L has a valid easement.

Trespass to Chattels (TTC)/Conversion

TTC is the intentional interference with a person's use or possession of a chattel; if the interference is so substantial that it warrants paying full value it is a conversion. Here, L interfered with M's fence when he cut the wires and also with her land when his dog dug a hole. If the fence can be repaired, he needs to pay for the repairs, but if it is destroyed, he needs to pay for a new fence. Thus, L is liable for TTC and possibly conversion.

Necessity

See rule above. The same arguments apply here. The TTL and conversion could be defended as a necessity.

Consent

See rule above. The same arguments apply here. There was likely no consent.

3. Michelle v. Town for additional compensation

Takings

The Takings Clause of the 5th Amendment provides that private property may not be taken for public use without just compensation. Public use is construed liberally and satisfied if the state's use of the property is rationally related to a conceivable public purpose. Just compensation is measured by the market value of the property at the time of the taking.

Here, Town is taking M's land since it filed a suit to condemn her land for a public park. A public park would be public use and use of the property is rationally related to a public park purpose that can be used by everyone to do various activities.

Since the sum Town offered her exceeds the prices of comparable parcels recently sold in the neighborhood, it is likely above market value. The fact that she had offers that were higher a few years ago is irrelevant since the market price is measured at the time of the taking, not a few years ago. Also, they do not need to include relocation costs.

Thus, M will not prevail in her argument for additional compensation.

Crossover Question 4
July 2014, Question 5

Henry and Wynn married in 2000. During the first ten years of their marriage, Henry and Wynn lived in a non-community property state. Henry worked on writing a novel. Wynn worked as a history professor. Wynn kept all her earnings in a separate account.

Eventually, Henry gave up on the novel, and he and Wynn moved to California. Wynn then set up an irrevocable trust with the $100,000 she had saved from her earnings during the marriage. She named Sis as trustee and Henry as co-trustee. She directed that one-half the trust income was to be paid to her for life, and that the other one-half was to be paid to Charity, to be spent only for disaster relief, and that, at her death, all remaining assets were to go to Charity.

Wynn invested all assets in XYZ stock, which paid substantial dividends, but decreased in value by 10%. Charity spent all the income it received from the trust for administrative expenses, not disaster relief.

Later, Sis sold all the XYZ stock and invested the proceeds in a new house, in which she lived rent-free. The house increased in value by 20%.

Henry has sued Sis for breach of trust, and has sued Charity for return of the income it spent on administrative costs.

1. What is the likely result of Henry's suit against Sis? Discuss.

2. What is the likely result of Henry's suit against Charity? Discuss.

3. What rights, if any, does Henry have in the trust assets? Discuss. Answer according to California law.

Crossover Question 4 Assessment
July 2014, Question 5

This is a very typical wills and trusts and community property crossover question. Sometimes the examiners cross over wills with community property and sometimes trusts. The questions are very similar either way. There is often a couple that marries either in California or out of state and thus has various assets that need to be classified as separate, community, or quasi-community property. Then one of the spouses executes a will or trust and thus wills and trusts issues need to be addressed. These two subjects cross over regularly on the bar exam and in real life.

As is often the case with crossover questions, it is easier to spot the issues because the calls are more specific. Here, Call 1 directs you to answer about Henry's suit. As he has filed for breach of trust, you need to quickly establish that a trust was created and then look at the trustee duties. For the duties you can simply write out all possible trustee duties on a checklist and quickly go through it to determine which ones are at issue. The second call asks about Henry's suit against Charity so you need to look at your rules for charitable trusts. The last call then asks about community property as it asks about what Henry's rights are in the trust assets. A clue that this last call is about community property is that it tells you to answer according to California law unlike Calls 1 and 2, and thus it cannot be asking about trusts. Further, it asks about the particular assets in the trust. Finally, the way the essay is drafted lends itself to a community property essay since there is a W and H married in a non-community property state. They would not give you these types of facts if they didn't want you to address community property laws at some point.

As with all questions, highlight the facts you have used so you know which facts still need a home. If you have homeless facts, then you have missed an issue, rule, or argument in the analysis. Thus, you have left points on the table. So be sure to use all facts, especially in crossover questions since it is easy to skip over rules or arguments when you are juggling multiple subjects at once even though the calls are generally more specific.

Finally, note the areas highlighted in **bold** on the corresponding grid. The bold areas highlight the issues, analysis, and conclusions that are likely **required** to receive a passing score on this question. In general, the essay grids are provided to assist you in analyzing the essays, and are much more detailed than what a student should create during the exam to organize her own response to a question.

Issue	Rule	Fact Application	Conclusion
Trust creation	To create a trust, the settlor must have the intent to create a trust, there must be property (res), a valid purpose, and an ascertainable beneficiary. If a trustee is not named, a court will appoint one.	Here, Wynn is the settlor as she created the trust with the intent to benefit her and Charity. The property (res) is the $100,000 she saved from her separate account. And there is a valid purpose to provide herself ½ of the funds as a beneficiary during her lifetime as well as ½ to Charity, which will benefit during her lifetime and receive all remaining trust funds at her death for disaster relief. Thus both beneficiaries are ascertainable too. And she named two co-trustees, Sis and Henry. Thus, all elements are met to create a valid trust.	**Trust valid**
Types of trust	An express trust is created where property is transferred from one owner to another and meets the above requirements, such that a trustee holds legal title for the benefit of a beneficiary, with the settlor having a present manifestation of intent to create the trust for a legal purpose. A charitable trust is one that is for charitable purposes and benefits society.	Wynn created an express trust for herself and Charity since she is an ascertainable beneficiary. A charitable trust does not have a particular beneficiary but rather benefits society. Thus part of her trust acts as a charitable trust since it benefits society by aiding in disaster relief and then at her death it would be a charitable trust as all of the remaining funds would be for Charity. But for now, it is an express trust. She also indicated that the trust was irrevocable.	Express and charitable
Trustee powers	Trustees have all enumerated powers expressed in the trust itself and pursuant to the law. Trustees have the implied powers necessary and appropriate to carry out the terms of the trust, such as to sell or lease trust property, incur reasonable expenses, borrow money, or operate a business.	Wynn gave Sis and Henry the enumerated power to distribute ½ of the funds to her during her life and ½ to Charity for disaster relief and then the remainder to Charity at her death for disaster relief.	Trustees have power to distribute funds
1. Henry v. Sis			
Trustee Liability	A trustee is liable for breaching any of their trustee duties.	Here, if Sis has breached any of her trustee duties, then she would be liable personally. As a co-trustee, Henry has a duty to ensure that what she does is in the best interest of the trust so if she has acted outside the scope of her duties then he should bring suit to prevent her from causing more damage to the trust beneficiaries.	Henry can file suit to prevent Sis from violating the trustee duties or for remedies if she did already violate them

Continued>

Issue	Rule	Fact Application	Conclusion
Trustee Duty of Loyalty/No Self-Dealing	**Duty of Loyalty is owed and the trustee may not participate in self-dealing, must avoid conflicts of interest, and must treat all beneficiaries equally.**	**Wynn invested all of her assets in XYZ stock, which decreased 10%, but as she was also the beneficiary she could use the funds as she wanted. But Sis later sold all of the XYZ stock and purchased a house in which she is living rent free. Thus, Sis is personally benefiting from the trust and self-dealing, which is not in the best interested of the trust.** However, the house has increased 20% in value so she could argue that it is in the best interest of the trust since the stock had decreased in value by 10%, but since she is still living rent-free she is self-dealing and the trust beneficiaries would benefit if she was paying rent and not using the trust property for her own benefit.	Sis breached her duty of loyalty
Trustee Duty of Impartiality	Trustees must be impartial when dealing with the income beneficiaries and the remainderman beneficiaries.	Here Sis has a duty to be impartial to both Wynn and Charity since they are both income beneficiaries and Charity is the remainderman beneficiary as well if there are still funds remaining. Since the trust is not producing income (because of Sis's self-dealing described above), the investment seems to favor the remainder beneficiary over the income beneficiaries.	Sis breached her duty to be impartial
Trustee Duty to Prudently Invest and Diversify	**A trustee has a duty to prudently invest funds.** A trustee has a duty to diversify investments. Common law utilizes various statutory lists of good investments, which include federal government bonds, federally insured certificates of deposit, first deeds of trust in real estate, and stock of publicly traded corporations. Uniform Prudent Investor Act (UPIA), adopted in a majority of jurisdictions, provides that a prudent investor's performance is measured in the context of the entire trust portfolio as a whole and as part of an overall investment strategy having risk and return objectives reasonably suited to the trust. [Several rules could have been appropriately referenced here]	**Sis invested all of Wynn's assets on one investment by purchasing the house, which arguably could be a good investment** under common law as it is a deed in real **estate and its value is up 20%, but real estate is known to fluctuate. Also the sale of stock itself might have been a good investment since the stock was down by 10%, though it had provided good dividend income.** Under the UPIA, looking at the investment as a whole, purchasing a house does not involve a lot of risk but the return is arguably not reasonably suited for Wynn since she isn't using the house and isn't benefiting at all during her life as the funds aren't available unless the house is sold; and it isn't being rented since Sis is staying there rent-free. And since **she didn't diversify the trust at all this too could result in the overall portfolio not being a good investment** since all of it is dependent on the housing market.	**Sis likely breached her duty to prudently invest and diversify trust funds**

(Continued)

Issue	Rule	Fact Application	Conclusion
Trustee Duty of Care	**Trustees must use due care and act as a reasonably prudent person** dealing with their own affairs, which includes their duty to **investigate** any investment and a duty to **diversify** investments	**Sis did not act as a reasonably prudent person would by investing all of the stock sale funds in one property** that she could use personally to live in rent-free since this does not benefit the beneficiaries at all until they sell the property. The trust intended for the beneficiaries to use trust income during their life to spend. Since Sis did not pay rent, the beneficiaries are not earning any money as intended; it also isn't clear that she acted reasonably in purchasing the house as it isn't clear she investigated the various options for the trust funds but rather used them to buy the house to benefit herself personally.	Sis breached her duty of care
Breach of trust remedies	**Breach of trust remedy options include damages, a constructive trust,** tracing and an equitable lien on the property (see Remedies chapter). Or the injured party could ratify the transaction and waive breach, sue for resulting loss (surcharge), or **remove the trustee.**	Henry can seek damages for any losses incurred by Sis investing in the house on behalf of the beneficiaries. **He can request damages for rent money that she should have been paying for staying in the property.** He could also ask the court to set aside the property sale unless it was to a BFP, then it cannot do so, but since the house is up 20% it might be best to sell it. **He can also ask the court to remove Sis as a trustee such that he is the only trustee since she breached her trustee duties.**	**Court will likely remove Sis as trustee, make her pay rent money for time living in house,** and review house investment to see if Henry should sell it, set it aside, or keep it
2. Henry v. Charity			
Trust Remedies	A resulting trust is an implied-in-fact trust based upon the presumed intent of the parties and will transfer the property back to the settlor or his estate when an express trust fails. A constructive trust is applied to avoid unjust enrichment.	**Here since Charity did not use the funds for disaster relief as directed they are not following the trust purpose.** As such, the court could require them to repay the funds they have wrongfully used by imposing a resulting trust. Charity may argue that using the funds for administrative purposes is acceptable, but the trust terms are explicit here. A court could also impose a constructive trust over the funds to avoid Charity using them improperly until they can pay them back.	Charity will have to pay back the funds it improperly used

Continued>

Issue	Rule	Fact Application	Conclusion
3. Henry's interest in the house			
Community property and separate property presumptions	CP — All property acquired during marriage while domiciled in California is presumed to be community property. SP — All property acquired before or after marriage or by gift, devise, descent, or bequest is presumed to be separate property. QCP — All property acquired by either spouse while domiciled in a non-community property state which would have been classified as community property had the parties been domiciled in California at the time of acquisition is considered quasi-community property.	Here the house that Sis purchased was purchased with XYZ stock, which was acquired during marriage while Wynn and Henry lived outside California. Had they lived in California the XYZ stock would be presumed to be CP since it was purchased from her earnings as a history professor unless the presumption can be rebutted. Thus the XYZ stock was QCP, as was the house purchased with the stock sale proceeds.	House is QCP
QCP treatment	During marriage, QCP is treated as SP for each spouse, but at death or divorce, it is treated as CP.	The home was purchased with QCP proceeds and it will be treated as SP since Henry and Wynn aren't divorced and Wynn isn't dead. Upon her death or their divorce it would be treated as CP and Henry would be entitled to a ½ share. Since Sis sold the stock to buy the house, Henry could trace the QCP funds to the house and still get ½ of the house value. **Since it isn't clear that Wynn is dead or they are divorced, Henry would not have any right in the house at this time.**	Henry doesn't have an interest in the house at this time

Crossover Question 5
July 2015, Question 5

Online, Inc. was duly incorporated as an Internet service provider. Its articles of incorporation authorized issuance of 1,000 shares of stock at $1,000 par value.

Online initially issued only 550 shares to its shareholders as follows: Dick and Sam each received 200 shares and Jane received 150 shares. Online's Board of Directors (composed of Jane, Sam, and Harry) named Jane as the Chief Executive Officer and named Harry as General Counsel.

Online's business grew substantially in the following months. Still, Online was short on cash; as a result, instead of paying Jane $10,000 of her salary in cash, it issued her 50 additional shares with the approval of its Board of Directors.

Looking to expand its operations, Online sought to enter a strategic partnership with LargeCo, Inc. Jane had learned about LargeCo through Harry's wife, who she knew was the majority shareholder of LargeCo. Jane directed Harry to negotiate the terms of the transaction with LargeCo. In the course of Harry's negotiations with LargeCo, LargeCo offered to acquire the assets of Online in exchange for a cash buy-out of $1,000,000. Harry telephoned Jane and Sam; Jane and Sam agreed with Harry that the offer was a good idea; and Harry accepted LargeCo's offer.

Two days after completion of the transaction, LargeCo announced a joint venture with TechCo, which was solely owned by Harry. The joint venture was valued at $10,000,000. In its press release, TechCo described the joint venture as a "remarkable synergy of LargeCo's new technology with TechCo's large consumer base."

The following week, Dick learned of LargeCo's acquisition of Online's assets. An expert in technology matters, he was furious about the price and terms of the acquisition, believing that the value of Online had been seriously underestimated.

1. What are Dick's rights and remedies, if any, against Jane, Sam and/or Harry? Discuss.

2. What ethical violations, if any, has Harry committed? Discuss. Answer according to California and ABA authorities.

Crossover Question 5 Assessment
July 2015, Question 5

This is quite the complex crossover essay. While the subjects often and easily crossover, these are both diffi-cult subjects. And usually, most crossover questions make issue spotting easier as the calls are usually more specific. Well, that isn't the case with this question. In fact, both questions are broad. And you can't even tell what subject is being tested in the first call until you read the facts. Asking about "rights and remedies" could be torts or contracts or any subject really. However, when you read the first sentence and see "incorporated" followed by "articles of incorporation" you can guess pretty quickly that you are in hell . . . or we mean the land of business associations. Then call two is clearly professional responsibility as it asks about ethical viola-tions and asks you to answer according to California and ABA authorities. So, after you've read the facts to get an idea about what is going on, we recommend you write out your issues checklists for both subjects (broadly) so you can adequately issue spot. And you can expand on areas later after you've spotted the big issues/areas.

When issue spotting the first call, you can see that one shareholder is affected by the decisions of three direc-tors. Two of the directors are also officers of the corporation — one is the GC and one is the CEO. You have to figure out what issues are raised by looking at each event as you go through the facts. The first event is when Online issues J shares of stock because they don't have cash to pay her salary. This was a really tricky issue if you don't know the nuanced rules of what par value means for stock. This means that the stock has to sell for at least that value. So, here when the par value is $1,000 that means each share must sell for at least $1,000. So, selling J 50 shares is equal to $50,000, not the $10,000 they need to pay her in her salary. The term (though not needed to pass) for when stock is a lower value is called "watered" stock because its value has essentially been watered down. So, what should be worth $50,000 here is worth $10,000. You didn't need to label the stock "watered" but you did need to understand that the value they gave her far exceeded her salary. This goes to their duty of loyalty and care.

The other issues are more obvious and have easier rules to analyze because they are more heavily tested rules and common facts. So, you next needed to see how J told H to negotiate with LargeCo when she knew that H's wife was the majority SH. So, this gives rise to both duty of loyalty and care. Then, the manner in which H finalized the deal was wrong and all of the directors should have known that they can't institute a fundamental corporate change without a formal meeting or a shareholder vote. So once again, we have duty of loyalty and care issues.

Finally, we see that the value the company sold for seems to have been significantly lower than it should have been. Hence, more loyalty and care issues.

Call two is fairly straightforward in that H as a lawyer breached his duty of loyalty and care as a lawyer (in addition to as a director and officer). The key here was seeing that there were two possible conflicts — one as a personal interest conflict which triggers your main conflicts rule, and another with a business transaction which has its own rule. Make sure anytime conflicts arise, you go through all possible conflicts as often more than one is at issue. This is why having mini-checklists for conflicts come in handy.

While this essay was difficult and overwhelming, the best way to prepare is to expose yourself to as many difficult and crazy questions as you can. This not only helps you see more fact patterns since there are only so many ways they can test things, but it also boosts your confidence and comfort level with the subjects.

Note the areas highlighted in **bold** on the corresponding grid. The bold areas highlight the issues, analysis, and conclusions that are likely **required** to receive a passing score on this question. In general, the essay grids are provided to assist you in analyzing the essays, and are much more detailed than what a student should create during the exam to organize their own response to a question.

Issue	Rule	Fact Application	Conclusion
Dick's Rights and Remedies against Jane, Sam, and Harry			
Direct Suit	A SH may bring a suit for breach of fiduciary duty owed to the SH (not the corp. itself). Any recovery goes directly to the SH.	Dick (D) is a SH since he received 200 shares from Online. As a SH, D could sue Jane, Sam, and Harry as they are all directors of Online, if they breached their fiduciary duties.	D can pursue a direct action against J, S, and H
Shareholder derivative suit	A SH may bring a derivative suit on behalf of the corp. for harm done to the corp. **The SH bringing the suit must own stock, adequately represent the corp., and first make a demand of the directors** to redress the injury (and wait 90 days for response); used to be excused if demand would be futile (no longer excused under modern law); and post a bond if required. **Recovery goes back to the corporation, not the SH directly.**	**D is a SH who owns 200 shares of stock in Online, so he adequately represents the corporation since he has just as much stock as anyone else in the company and is the only non-Director SH, and he should make a demand on the Board if possible.** **But it seems the transaction was already completed, so a demand might be futile and the board were the ones who voted for the transaction also making the demand futile.**	**D can likely pursue a SH derivative action (but may need to make a demand on the board if possible)**
Duty of Loyalty	A director and officer owe a duty of loyalty to the corp. to put the interests of the corp. above their own interests. **Conflict of interest (self-dealing): A director has a COI when they** (or a corp. they own or have a relationship with, **or their family member) enter into a contract with the corp. or have a beneficial financial interest in a contract.** • Self-dealing contracts are presumed unfair and voidable. • **Conflict can be cured if:** • **Authorized by disinterested board members after material disclosure; or** • **Approved by majority of disinterested SHs after material disclosure; and**	*Jane* Self-dealing (shares of stock): Here, J was the CEO and both an officer and director and may have had a COI in self-dealing when she voted to award herself an additional 50 shares of stock b/c this could be a beneficial financial interest. • However, it was cured when the other two board members, S and H, who were disinterested, authorized and voted for it, and it was fair b/c it was to replace the $10,000 salary that they couldn't pay her b/c it was short on cash. However, the shares were valued at $1000 par value so times 50 shares would be $50,000 which is 5x more than the $10,000 owed to her (which means the stock was issued below par and is called watered stock). So, there might not have been a cure of the conflict.	Jane might have breached her duty of loyalty **Harry violated his duty of loyalty for self-dealing, usurping corporate opportunity, and unfair competition**

Continued>

Continued>

Issue	Rule	Fact Application	Conclusion
Duty of Loyalty (continued)	• **The transaction is fair to the corporation.** **Usurping a corporate opportunity:** A director may not personally act on a business opportunity without first **offering it to the corporation** where the corporation would expect to be presented the opportunity. • Director may take the opportunity only after good faith rejection of the opportunity by the corporation if there was full disclosure of all material facts to a disinterested board majority. • **Remedy — Director disgorges profits**/ constructive trust Unfair competition: A director may not unfairly compete with the corporation.	<u>Harry</u> **Self-dealing:** H was the GC, so he was both a director and officer and may have had a COI with self-dealing b/c his wife was a major SH of LargeCo, the company he was working with to buy Online. He also entered into an agreement with LargeCo with his own Techco Company, which happened 2 days after the initial purchase of Online but likely he was discussing the joint venture with them before since large ventures aren't figured out in two days. So H knew he was likely going to get a financial benefit as well if LargeCo purchased Online. • It appears that the other directors J and S did authorize the acquisition since they said it was a "good idea," **but it is unclear if that over the phone constituted an approval or that J and S were given material disclosures.** Also, D wasn't on the phone to approve it and he was a SH. • Also, it doesn't seem the transaction was fair to Online based on D's assessment as an expert in technology matters as he thinks the value of Online was seriously underestimated. **Since Online sold its assets for only $1,000,000 and then LargeCo and TechCo entered a joint venture worth $10,000,000 it seems the increase in LargeCo's value was too high for the sale to be fair.** • **So, H's COI for self-dealing was not cured.** **Usurp Corp. Opp.:** H also possibly usurped a corporate opportunity if he could have had TechCo enter a joint venture with Online since Online sold to LargeCo and it wasn't until after LargeCo acquired Online that TechCo entered this joint venture. Unfair Competition: H also possibly unfairly competed with Online by owning TechCo, which had a large consumer base and entered a joint venture with the company that purchased Online.	

Issue	Rule	Fact Application	Conclusion
Duty of care/BJR	An officer owes the corporation a duty of care to act as a reasonably prudent person would act under similar circumstances. The business judgment rule protects officers who manage the corporation in good faith and in the best interests of the corp. and its SHs.	**Issuance of Stock to J** As explained above, Online issued J stock worth $50,000 when she was only short $10,000 of her salary so the stock was not at the $1,000 par value it was supposed to be so they did not act reasonably. Arguably it was in the best interest of the corp. and in good faith since they were short on cash and couldn't pay J, but the amount of shares offered was likely unreasonable still b/c it was 5x the value owed to her. **LargeCo acquiring Online** J knew that H's wife was the majority SH of LargeCo, yet she directed him to negotiate terms with them which was not reasonable b/c she knew of the conflict and relationships. Also, both J and S just agreed on the phone it was a good idea without inquiring as to more details which was not reasonable when selling an entire company's assets. Also, when H entered a joint venture with his TechCo company 2 days after LargeCo acquired Online, it seems that the deal was not in good faith or reasonable b/c it was worth $10,000,000 when he agreed to sell Online for only $1,000,000. None of their actions seem to be made in good faith or in the best interests of the corp. since the corp. sold its assets for under market value so the BJR won't protect their decisions. **Fundamental Change— No SH Vote** J, S, and H did not act with reasonable care when they sold all assets which is a fundamental change b/c they didn't follow proper procedures by having a special meeting and notifying SH and allowing all SH to vote since D didn't know about it until after the deal.	J, S, and H all breached their duty of care in several instances

Conclusion: D can seek to have J, S, and H disgorge any profits or rescind the transaction if possible and get any other damages incurred.

Continued>

Issue	Rule	Fact Application	Conclusion
Harry's ethical violations			
Conflict of interest — H's personal interest	**L has a duty of loyalty to their C that requires L to put the interest of the C above all other interests.** A COI exists if there is a significant risk that the representation of one or more Cs will be materially limited by L's personal interest. **Exception: L reasonably believes they can still provide competent and diligent representation to C**, representation is not prohibited by law, clients not directly adverse, **and C gives informed consent, confirmed in writing (CA — informed written consent).**	Here, there is a significant risk that H's representation of Online will be materially limited by his own personal interest since **his wife is the majority SH of the company he is negotiating with to purchase Online.** **Also, H owns TechCo and appears to have been working on a joint venture with LargeCo when they purchased Online since that deal was announced 2 days after the deal.** H could not reasonably believe he could provide competent representation (and here didn't) since he put his own company and interest ahead of Online. **Also, he did not receive informed written consent from Online** since the other directors just orally agreed to it over the phone.	**H violated his duty of loyalty**
Conflict of interest — Business transaction with C	**L shall not enter into a business transaction with a C unless the terms are fair and reasonable, terms are fully disclosed in writing to C, C is advised in writing to seek independent counsel, and C gives informed written consent.**	Here, arguably H entered into a business transaction with Online b/c his wife was the majority SH of LargeCo, the company that purchased all of Online's assets. And H entered a joint venture (and likely planned it sooner) with **LargeCo 2 days after they purchased Online.** **The terms weren't fair since Online only made $1,000,000 and the new venture was worth $10,000,000 and there were no disclosures in writing and no written consent.**	**H violated his duty of loyalty**
Duty of Competence	ABA: L shall competently represent C with legal knowledge, skill, thoroughness, and preparation. Cal. — L must not intentionally, recklessly, with gross negligence, or repeatedly fail to competently perform legal services.	H, as the GC for Online, breached several duties including loyalty and care by selling stock for below par value, entering a transaction where his wife was a majority SH, and accepting LargeCo's offer without proper board approval and SH approval. Overall, he did not act with knowledge or skill and did perform negligently if not intentionally to harm Online.	L violated his duty of competence

Crossover Question 6
July 2008, Question 2

To protect the nation against terrorism, the President proposed the enactment of legislation that would authorize the Secretary of Homeland Security ("the Secretary") to issue "National Security Requests," which would require businesses to produce the personal and financial records of their customers to the Federal Bureau of Investigation ("the FBI") without a warrant. Congress rejected the proposal.

Thereafter, in response, the President issued Executive Order 999 ("the Order"). The Order authorizes the Secretary to issue "National Security Requests," which require businesses to produce the personal and financial records of their customers to the FBI without a warrant. The Order further authorizes the Secretary to require state and local law enforcement agencies to assist the FBI in obtaining the records.

Concerned about acts of terrorism that had recently occurred in State X, the State X Legislature passed the "Terrorism Prevention Act" ("the Act"), requiring businesses in State X served with National Security Requests pursuant to the Order to produce a copy of the records to the State X Department of Justice.

1. Is the Order within the President's authority under the United States Constitution? Discuss.

2. Assuming the Order is within the President's authority, does the Order preempt the Act? Discuss.

3. Assuming the Order is within the President's authority and does not preempt the Act, do the Order and the Act violate the Fourth Amendment to the United States Constitution on their face? Discuss.

Crossover Question 6 Assessment
July 2008, Question 2

This crossover question covers constitutional law and criminal procedure, which is a fairly common subject combination. However, it is an unusual question because the constitutional law issues tested are issues pertaining to an executive order, including the power of the president to act against the will of Congress, the war power of a president, and the president's duty to ensure that laws are faithfully executed. This is the only time these rules have been tested on the essay portion of the California bar exam, so it caused a lot of panic in many bar takers. You have to expect that at least one question will be a doozy!

The fact pattern concerns legislation proposed by the president, but rejected by Congress, that was designed to protect the nation against terrorism and that included a provision that the Secretary of Homeland Security could issue "National Security Requests," which require businesses to produce certain business records to the FBI without a warrant. Since Congress rejected the president's proposed legislation, the president issued the same proposed legislation as an executive order. A state then passed an act that was potentially preempted by the executive order. The final call of the question asks if any of this will pass constitutional muster under the Fourth Amendment.

The first call tends to give students the most trouble since it covers issues that had never before been tested on the essay portion of the bar exam. As you will notice by reviewing the following grid, students can approach the first call in a variety of ways that are acceptable. The common analysis that the bar graders were looking for in a passing answer is bolded in the grid, and you can see that the rules and analysis that are necessary to pass the first call are not particularly difficult. The second and third calls are much more straightforward and should not be difficult, assuming a student wisely budgets their time and doesn't spend an inordinate amount of time on the first call.

Note the areas highlighted in **bold** on the corresponding grid. The bold areas highlight the issues, analysis, and conclusions that are likely **required** to receive a passing score on this question. In general, the essay grids are provided to assist you in analyzing the essays, and are much more detailed than what a student should create during the exam to organize her own response to a question.

Issue	Rule	Fact Application	Conclusion
Call #1: President's Authority			
Presidential action against the will of Congress	If the president acts contrary to Congress, they must do so within the president's constitutional powers alone.	Here, the president acted contrary to Congress because the president issued the executive order after Congress rejected the very same proposal, indicating that the president must have their own executive constitutional power to enact the executive order. Any possible powers allowing this will be discussed below. [Note: Both state-released passing answers discussed this issue differently. The key is that both pointed out that **the president acted contrary to Congress.**]	**President acted contrary to Congress**
Vesting Clause	Executive power invested in president.	See above	See above
Foreign affairs	President has power over many foreign affairs.	Although terrorism can involve foreign affairs, the order here has to do more with domestic information, not foreign information. Even if foreign information is sought, too, the presidential power will not extend if it is not the type of information pertaining to foreign policies that the president is typically involved with, such as signing treaties and dealing with foreign presidents and other heads of foreign countries.	Likely no presidential power here
War powers/War Powers Resolution	**The president is the commander in chief.** The president has the constitutional power not only to retaliate against any person, organization, or state suspected of involvement in terrorist attacks on the United States, but also against foreign states suspected of harboring or supporting such organizations.	**Here, the president has the power to act as commander in chief,** which generally comes into play when there is a war ensuing, not in regard to turning over customer, personal, and financial records from businesses. **However, arguably, if there is a war on terror and the information sought would help stop this war on terror, it is possible that it is within the president's power to request such information, but this typically involves military use and deployment of troops, not customer records,** nor is clear as to how this information will help the president combat terrorism.	**Likely no presidential power here**
Take care/execute laws clause	**The president is to make sure the laws are faithfully executed.**	Here, the president's best argument to enforce the order is under the power to make sure the laws are faithfully executed. The law against committing terrorist acts could arguably be one in which the president is trying to ensure faithful execution of the laws and keep the nation safe.	**Possibly valid presidential power here**

Continued>

Issue	Rule	Fact Application	Conclusion
10th Amend. commandeering	Prevents Congress from commandeering the states; powers not delegated to Congress are reserved to the states.	Here, Congress cannot require state and local law enforcement agencies to assist the FBI in obtaining the records because Congress does not have the power to commandeer the states.	No presidential authority to make Congress act here
Call #2: Preemption			
Preemption	Express or implied; state law is invalid if it conflicts with federal law.	Here, the state statute does not directly conflict with the Order as it does not have the state acting contrary to the Order; further, there does not appear to be any interference with the state statute and the Order as they both request the same information, and the state statute may in fact help to execute and comply with the Order and further help combat terrorism and protect the nation, in particular State X.	No preemption
Contracts Clause	Cannot interfere with existing contracts.	The state statute could affect existing contracts of confidentiality but that would not affect preemption.	
Call #3: 4th Amend.			
Search and seizure	4th Amend. protects against unreasonable searches and seizures.

Need govt. action and a reasonable expectation of privacy.

Warrant needed unless search incident to a lawful arrest, automobile exception, plain view exception, consent, hot pursuit, or stop and frisk. | Here, the govt. is acting by issuing the Order and requiring the Secretary of State and states to assist the FBI in obtaining these financial records of customers.

Arguably, customers do not have a reasonable expectation of privacy when they hand their information, such as bank records, over to businesses or third parties.

However, here, the request appears to go beyond bank records and the like in that all of customers' personal and financial records would be available with no limitations apparent in the Order.

Here, the Order requires production of this financial and customer information without a warrant and no warrant exceptions are applicable here since there is no arrest, automobile, hot pursuit, stop and frisk, or consent involved. | Conclude either way depending on whether you found expectation of privacy in the information sought |